Infants and Children
Prenatal Through Middle Childhood

NINTH EDITION

Laura E. Berk

Illinois State University

 Pearson

Executive Portfolio Manager: Ed Parsons
Manager, Content Strategy: Pamela Chirls
Managing Editor: Tom Pauken
Senior Producer: Katharine Glynn
Assistant Editor: Rachel Trapp-Gardner
Development Editors: David Chodoff, Judy Ashkenaz
Editorial Assistant: Kaylee Navarra
Full-Service Project Management:
   Pearson CSC, Monica Moosang
Digital Producer: Elissa Senra-Sargent
Director, Product Marketing: Brad Parkins
Photo Researcher: Sarah Evertson—ImageQuest
Interior Designer: Carol Somberg

Cover Designer: Joel Gendron, Lumina Datamatics
Full-Service Vendor: Pearson CSC
Composition Specialist: Jeff Miller
Copyeditor and References Editor: Josephine Cepeda
Proofreader: Karen Jones
Indexer: Linda Herr Hallinger
Printer/Binder: LSC Communications, Inc.
Cover Printer: Phoenix Color, Hagerstown
Cover Art: "We Are in the Forest," Soumita Banerjee,
   8 years, India. Reprinted with permission from
   the International Museum of Children's Art,
   Oslo, Norway.

Library of Congress Control Number: 2019919487

1 2020

Rental Edition
ISBN 10: 0-13-663671-3
ISBN 13: 978-0-13-663671-7

Instructor's Review Edition
ISBN 10: 0-13-549697-7
ISBN 13: 978-0-13-549697-8

Revel Access Card
ISBN 10: 0-13-549691-8
ISBN 13: 978-0-13-549691-6

About the Author

Laura E. Berk is a distinguished professor of psychology at Illinois State University, where she has taught child, adolescent, and lifespan development for more than three decades. She received her bachelor's degree in psychology from the University of California, Berkeley, and her master's and doctoral degrees in child development and educational psychology from the University of Chicago. She has been a visiting scholar at Cornell University, UCLA, Stanford University, and the University of South Australia.

Berk has published widely on the effects of school environments on children's development, the development of private speech, and the role of make-believe play in development. Her empirical studies have attracted the attention of the general public, leading to contributions to *Psychology Today* and *Scientific American*. She has also been featured on National Public Radio's *Morning Edition* and in *Parents Magazine, Wondertime,* and *Reader's Digest.*

Berk has served as a research editor of *Young Children,* a consulting editor for *Early Childhood Research Quarterly,* and an associate editor of the *Journal of Cognitive Education and Psychology.* She is a frequent contributor to edited volumes, having written the article on social development in *The Child: An Encyclopedic Companion* and the article on Vygotsky in *The Encyclopedia of Cognitive Science.* She is coauthor of the chapter on make-believe play and self-regulation in the *Sage Handbook of Play in Early Childhood* and the chapter on psychologists writing textbooks in *Career Paths in Psychology: Where Your Degree Can Take You,* published by the American Psychological Association.

Berk's books include *Private Speech: From Social Interaction to Self-Regulation; Scaffolding Children's Learning: Vygotsky and Early Childhood Education; A Mandate for Playful Learning in Preschool: Presenting the Evidence;* and *Awakening Children's Minds: How Parents and Teachers Can Make a Difference.* In addition to *Infants and Children,* she is author of the best-selling texts *Exploring Child and Adolescent Development, Child Development, Development Through the Lifespan,* and *Exploring Lifespan Development,* published by Pearson.

Berk is active in work for children's causes. She serves on the governing boards of the Illinois Network of Child Care Resource and Referral Agencies and of Artolution, an organization devoted to engaging children, youths, and families in community-based public art projects around the world as a means of promoting trauma relief and resilience. She is also founding donor of Illinois Art Station, an initiative that provides educative and self-expressive experiences in the visual arts to children, adolescents, and their families in her community, with a special focus on reaching underserved and at-risk young people, while enriching student and faculty opportunities across disciplines. Berk has been designated a YWCA Woman of Distinction for her service in education. She is a fellow of the American Psychological Association, Division 7: Developmental Psychology.

Features at a Glance

Contents

chapter 4
Birth and the Newborn Baby   116

PART III

INFANCY AND TODDLERHOOD: THE FIRST TWO YEARS

chapter 5
Physical Development in Infancy and Toddlerhood   152

chapter 6

Cognitive Development in Infancy and Toddlerhood   196

chapter 7

Emotional and Social Development in Infancy and Toddlerhood   240

PART IV

EARLY CHILDHOOD: TWO TO SIX YEARS

chapter 8

Physical Development in Early Childhood   280

A Personal Note to Students

My more than 30 years of teaching child development have brought me in contact with thousands of students like you—students with diverse college majors, future goals, interests, and needs. Some are affiliated with my own field of psychology, but many come from other related fields—education, sociology, anthropology, biology, family studies, social service, and health sciences, to name just a few. Each semester, my students' aspirations have proved to be as varied as their fields of study. Many look toward careers in applied work—teaching, caregiving, nursing, counseling, social work, school psychology, and program administration. Most hope someday to become parents, whereas others are already parents who come with a desire to better understand and rear their children. And almost all arrive with a deep curiosity about how they themselves developed from tiny infants into the complex human beings they are today.

My goal in preparing this ninth edition of *Infants and Children* is to provide a textbook that meets the instructional goals of your course as well as your personal interests and needs. To achieve these objectives, I have grounded this book in a carefully selected body of classic and current theory and research brought to life with stories and vignettes about children and families, most of whom I have known personally. In addition, the text highlights the joint contributions of biology and environment to the developing child, explains how the research process helps solve real-world problems, illustrates commonalities and differences among ethnic groups and cultures, and pays special attention to policy issues that are crucial for safeguarding children's well-being in today's world. Woven throughout the text is a unique pedagogical program that will assist you in mastering information, integrating the various aspects of development, critically examining controversial issues, applying what you have learned, and relating the information to real life.

I hope that learning about child development will be as rewarding for you as I have found it over the years. I would like to know what you think about both the field of child development and this book. I welcome your comments; please contact me at infantschildrenadolescents9e@gmail.com.

Laura E. Berk

Preface for Instructors

In preparing this ninth edition of *Infants, Children, and Adolescents,* I drew inspiration from the hundreds of students of child development with whom I have worked in more than three decades of college teaching. As in previous editions, I aimed for a text that is intellectually stimulating, provides depth as well as breadth of coverage, portrays the complexities of child development with clarity and excitement, and is relevant and useful in building a bridge from theory and research to children's everyday lives.

The nearly three decades since *Infants, Children, and Adolescents* first appeared have been a period of unprecedented expansion and change in theory and research. This ninth edition represents these rapidly transforming aspects of the field, with a wealth of new content and enhanced teaching tools:

■ *Diverse pathways of change are highlighted.* Investigators have reached broad consensus that variations in biological makeup, everyday tasks, and the people who support children in mastery of those tasks lead to wide individual differences in children's paths of change and resulting competencies. This edition pays more attention to variability in development and to major theoretical perspectives—including neurobiological, ecological, sociocultural, dynamic systems, and epigenesis—that attempt to explain it. Multicultural and cross-cultural findings, along with international comparisons, are enhanced throughout the text and in revised and expanded Cultural Influences boxes.

■ *The complex, bidirectional relationship between biology and environment is given greater attention.* Accumulating evidence on development of the brain, motor skills, cognitive and language competencies, temperament and personality, emotional and social understanding, and developmental problems underscores the way biological factors emerge in, are modified by, and share power with experience. The interconnection between biology and environment is revisited throughout the text narrative and in Biology and Environment boxes with new and updated topics.

■ *Inclusion of interdisciplinary research is expanded.* The move toward viewing thoughts, feelings, and behavior as an integrated whole, affected by a wide array of influences in biology, social context, and culture, has motivated developmental researchers to strengthen their ties with other areas of psychology and with other disciplines. Topics and findings included in this edition increasingly reflect the contributions of educational psychology, social psychology, health psychology, clinical psychology, neurobiology, pediatrics, sociology, anthropology, social service, and other fields.

■ *The links among theory, research, and applications—a theme of this book since its inception—are strengthened.* As researchers intensify their efforts to generate findings that can be applied to real-life situations, I have placed greater weight on social policy issues and sound theory- and evidence-based interventions and practices. Further applications are provided in the Applying What We Know tables, which give students concrete ways of building bridges between their learning and the real world.

■ *The educational context of development becomes a stronger focus.* The home, school, and community are featured as vital educational contexts in which the child develops. Research on effective teaching practices appears in all chapters and in new and revised Social Issues: Education boxes.

■ *The role of active student learning is made more explicit.* Ask Yourself questions at the end of each major section have been revised to promote three approaches to engaging actively with the subject matter: *Connect, Apply,* and *Reflect.* This feature assists students in thinking about what they have read from multiple vantage points. The *Look and Listen* feature presents students with opportunities to observe what real children say and do and attend to influences on children in their everyday environments.

Text Philosophy

The basic approach of this book has been shaped by my own professional and personal history as a teacher, researcher, and parent. It consists of seven philosophical ingredients that I regard as essential for students to emerge from a course with a thorough understanding of child development:

1. An understanding of major theories and the strengths and shortcomings of each. The first chapter begins by emphasizing that only knowledge of multiple theories can do justice to the richness of child development. As I take up each age period and domain of development, I present a variety of theoretical perspectives, indicate how each highlights previously overlooked aspects of development, and discuss research that evaluates it. Consideration of contrasting theories also serves as the context for an even-handed analysis of many controversial issues.

2. An appreciation of research strategies for investigating child development. To evaluate theories, students must have a firm grounding in research methods and designs. In addition to a special section in Chapter 1 covering research strategies and a section in Chapter 5 devoted to neurobiological methods, numerous studies are discussed in sufficient detail throughout the text for students to use what they have learned to critically assess the findings, conclusions, and implications of research.

3. Knowledge of both the sequence of child development and the processes that underlie it. Students are provided with a discussion of the organized sequence of development along with processes of change. An understanding of *process*—how complex combinations of biological, psychological, and environmental events produce development—has been the focus of most recent research. Accordingly, the text reflects this emphasis. But new information about the timetable of change has also emerged. Current evidence on the sequence and timing of development, along with its implications for process, is presented throughout the text.

4. An appreciation of the impact of context and culture on child development. A wealth of research indicates that children live in rich physical and social contexts that affect all domains of development. Throughout the text, students travel to distant parts of the world as I review a growing body of cross-cultural evidence. The text narrative also discusses many findings on socioeconomically and ethnically diverse children within the United States and on children with varying abilities and challenges. Besides highlighting the role of immediate settings, such as family, neighborhood, and school, I make a concerted effort to underscore the influence of larger social structures—societal values, laws, and government programs—on children's well-being.

5. An understanding of the joint contributions of biology and environment to development. The field recognizes more than ever before the joint roles of hereditary/constitutional and environmental factors—that these contributions to development combine in complex ways and cannot be separated in a simple manner. Numerous examples of how biological dispositions can be maintained as well as transformed by social contexts are presented throughout the text.

6. A sense of the interdependency of all domains of development— physical, cognitive, emotional, and social. Every chapter takes an integrated approach to understanding children, illustrating how physical, cognitive, emotional, and social development are interwoven. Within the text narrative and in the Ask Yourself questions at the end of major sections, students are referred to other sections of the text to deepen their grasp of relationships among various aspects of change.

7. An appreciation of the interrelatedness of theory, research, and applications. Throughout, I emphasize that theories of child development and the research stimulated by them provide the foundation for sound, effective practices with children. The links among theory, research, and applications are reinforced by an organizational format in which theory and research are presented first, followed by practical implications. In addition, a current focus in the field—harnessing child development knowledge to shape social policies that support children's needs—is reflected in every chapter. The text addresses the current condition of children in the United States and around the world and shows how theory and research have combined with public interest to spark successful interventions.

Text Organization

The chronological organization of this text assists students in thoroughly understanding each age period. It also eases the task of integrating the various domains of development because each is discussed in close proximity. At the same time, a chronologically organized text requires that theories covering several age periods be presented piecemeal. This creates a challenge for students, who

must link the various parts together. To assist with this task, I frequently remind students of important earlier achievements before discussing new developments, referring back to related sections with page references. Also, chapters devoted to the same topic (for example, cognitive development) are similarly organized, making it easier for students to draw connections across age periods and construct an overall view of developmental change.

New Coverage in the Ninth Edition

Child development is a fascinating and ever-changing field, with constantly emerging new discoveries and refinements in existing knowledge. The ninth edition represents this burgeoning contemporary literature with more than 1,500 new citations. Cutting-edge topics throughout the text underscore the text's major themes. Here is a sampling of updated and new content:

CHAPTER 1   Introduction to the developmental systems perspective • The current, intense interest among information-processing researchers in "executive" processes, enabling children to manage their thoughts, emotions, and actions • Biology and Environment box on resilience • Social Issues: Health box on how family chaos undermines children's well-being • Cultural Influences box on immigrant youths • Enhanced discussion and examples of research strategies, including the implications of confounding variables for the accuracy of findings in experimental research

CHAPTER 2   Genetic sex as a spectrum rather than a dichotomy • Social and cultural influences on the male-to-female birth sex ratio, with special attention to prenatal sex-selective abortion in China • Older paternal age and increased risk of DNA mutations contributing to psychological disorders, including autism and schizophrenia • Fetal medicine and gene therapy, including the recent breakthrough in treating beta thalassemia • Adoption and developmental outcomes, including the importance of openness in communication with children • Impact of poverty on development • Social Issues: Education box on the impact of worldwide education of girls, reporting findings from a four-country study in Mexico, Nepal, Venezuela, and Zambia • Cultural Influences box on familism and development of Hispanic children and youths • Public policies and development, including current statistics on the condition of children and families in the United States compared with other Western nations • Epigenesis, including the role of methylation as an epigenetic mechanism • Biology and Environment box on epigenetic transmission of maternal stress to children

CHAPTER 3   Prenatal brain growth and sensory and behavioral capacities • Teratogens, including tobacco, marijuana, alcohol, the Zika virus, and environmental pollution • Epigenetic changes induced by prenatal teratogens that contribute to long-term developmental consequences • Biology and Environment box on self-regulation therapy for children with fetal alcohol spectrum disorder (FASD) • Consequences of severe emotional stress during pregnancy • Social Issues: Health box on the Nurse–Family Partnership—reducing maternal stress and enhancing child development through social support • Cultural Influences box on culturally sensitive prenatal health care and implications for birth outcomes

CHAPTER 4 Generational transmission of low birth weight • Interventions for preterm and low-birth-weight infants, including exposure to recordings of the mother's voice and heartbeat and to kangaroo care • Birth-related hormonal changes in mothers and fathers and implications for infant caregiving • Adaptiveness of newborn reflexes • Cultural variations in soothing infant crying • Long-term persistence of newborn odor and taste preferences • Transition to parenthood, including interventions that foster parental adjustment • Parental depression and child development

CHAPTER 5 Early brain development, including adaptive functions of programmed cell death and synaptic pruning • Lateralization of the cerebral cortex, including early development of handedness • Infants placed in depleted orphanages, with emphasis on results from the Bucharest Early Intervention Project and implications for infancy as a sensitive period for healthy brain growth • Infant sleep, including contributions of parental feeding practices and bedtime routines • Implications of restful sleep for learning and memory in the first two years • Cultural Influences box addressing parent–infant cosleeping and bedsharing • Social Issues: Health box on low-level lead exposure and children's development • Long-term consequences of malnutrition in infancy and toddlerhood, with special attention to the role of malnutrition-induced epigenetic changes • Infant statistical learning as a built-in broadly applied learning capacity • The controversy over newborns' capacity to imitate adult facial expressions, head movements, and hand gestures • Influence of caregiving practices and physical surroundings on motor development • Infant speech perception, including bilingual infants • Newborns perception of object unity

CHAPTER 6 Tool use and problem solving in infants and toddlers • Toddlers' grasp of pictures and video as symbols, including experiences that enhance their symbolic understanding • Introduction to the concept of executive function • Gains in control of attention and emergence of working memory in the first year • Influence of adult verbal labeling on toddlers' categorization and flexibility of problem solving • Evaluation of Early Head Start • Biology and Environment box on thiamine (vitamin B1) deficiency in the first year and later language impairment, with implications for a sensitive period for language development • Infants' use of parental feedback to master native-language sounds • Infants' grasp of the shared nature of word meanings and the communicative function of language • Importance of one-on-one communication with a responsive adult for early language development, in both real-life and video contexts

CHAPTER 7 Development of basic emotions in infancy, including smiling, laughter, anger, fear, and sadness, along with cultural variations • Cultural variations in early development of emotional self-regulation • Ethnic differences in development of temperament • Temperament and individual differences in susceptibility to the effects of good and poor parenting • Cultural variations in infants' expressions of attachment security • Early rearing of infants in institutions followed by placement in adoptive homes, with consequences for brain development and emotional and social adjustment • Cultural differences in views of sensitive caregiving, including proximal care in non-Western cultures • Joint contributions of infant genotype, temperament, and parenting to disorganized/disoriented attachment • Contributions of fathers' involvement in caregiving to attachment security and later development • Grandparents as primary caregivers and attachment figures in skipped-generation families • Roles of temperament and parenting in early sibling relationships • Early peer sociability, including toddlers' sensitivity to playmates' needs as reflected in helping and sharing • Development of self-recognition in the second year, including body self-recognition • Implications of toddlers' expanding self-awareness for positive social behaviors

CHAPTER 8 Advances in brain development in early childhood, with enhanced attention to the prefrontal cortex and executive function • Health status of U.S. young children, including tooth decay and childhood immunizations • Biology and Environment box on childhood poverty and brain development • Young children's screen media use and sleep disturbances • Influence of parenting practices on young children's healthy eating • Parental influences on unintentional injuries in early childhood • Importance of supporting preschoolers' and kindergartners' efforts to draw and print

CHAPTER 9 Evidence bearing on the controversy over the contribution of make-believe play to development • Factors contributing to children's grasp of conservation • Social Issues: Education box on how children's gestures during problem solving facilitate cognitive change • Development of executive function in early childhood, including the roles of parental scaffolding and SES • Development of memory in early childhood, with attention to the distinction between episodic and semantic memory • Cognitive attainments and social experiences that contribute to mastery of false belief in early childhood • Development of mathematical reasoning in early childhood, with attention to the importance of understanding cardinality • Academic benefits of Montessori preschool education • Social Issues: Education box on teaching through guided play • Strengthening preschool intervention for economically disadvantaged children through Head Start REDI • Educational screen media • Preschoolers' strategies for word learning, including cultural variations • Importance of conversational give-and-take with adults for language progress in early childhood

CHAPTER 10 Gains in emotional understanding and emotional self-regulation in early childhood • Preschoolers' recognition of self-conscious emotions in themselves and others • Contributions of sociodramatic and rough-and-tumble play to emotional and social development • Cultural variations in attitudes toward children's solitary play • Implications of early childhood friendships for children's psychological adjustment and social competence • The controversy over whether an innate moral sense exists, serving as the springboard for moral development • Negative impact of material rewards on children's prosocial behavior • Prevalence of corporal punishment in the United States and developmental consequences • Contributions of language, theory of mind, parenting, and peer and sibling experiences to development of moral understanding in early childhood • Development of young children's aggression, including the role of parental gender-role attitudes, exposure to media violence, and gender differences • Effects of prenatal androgen exposure on gender typing • Gender typing in young children's everyday environments, with implications for gender-stereotyped beliefs and behaviors • Biology and Environment box on transgender children • Consequences of child abuse and neglect, including increased risk of other forms of victimization • Early intervention to prevent child maltreatment, with special attention to Healthy Families America home visiting program

CHAPTER 11   Global rise in overweight and obesity, with cross-national comparisons of child and adolescent rates • Genetic and environmental contributions to childhood obesity, including metabolism, child temperament, insufficient sleep, parenting practices, family stress, screen media use, and the broader food environment • Cross-national variations in childhood myopia rates, related to time spend reading, writing, and doing other close work • Child temperament and risk of nocturnal enuresis • School-age children's unrealistic optimism about their risk of unintentional injuries • Contributions of children's physical fitness to cognitive development and academic achievement • Influence of parents and coaches on children's participation in organized sports and gains in athletic skills • Contributions of fathers' rough-and-tumble play to children's emotional and social adjustment and self-regulation

CHAPTER 12   Gains in executive function in middle childhood, including related changes in the brain, implications for academic learning, and interventions that enhance executive function • Biology and Environment box on children with attention-deficit hyperactivity disorder • Strategies for promoting cognitive self-regulation, including opportunities for children to teach academic content to others • Cultural Influences box on the Flynn Effect, addressing dramatic gains in IQ from one generation to the next • Contributions of spelling to reading progress • Importance of school-age children's expanding grasp of numerical magnitudes for mathematical understanding • Cultural variation in views of intelligent behavior, with implications for minority children's intellectual strengths • Role of poverty in accounting for ethnic variations in IQ • Diverse cognitive benefits of bilingualism • Bilingual education, including the rapid growth of two-way language immersion programs in U.S. public schools • Benefits of cooperative learning and the community of learners approach, in which collaboration becomes a schoolwide value • Social Issues: Education box on effectiveness of magnet schools in enhancing academic achievement, especially among ethnic minority students • Academic learning through interactive screen media, including video game play • Features of school programs that support learning and development of gifted children • U.S. academic achievement in international perspective

CHAPTER 13   Ethnic variations in development of self-esteem • Negative impact of inflated praise on children's self-esteem • Differential impact of growth and fixed mindsets about ability on children's academic motivation and performance • Influence of parent and teacher communication on children's mindsets about ability • Contributions of recursive thought and high-quality friendships to advances in moral understanding • Racial/ethnic and socioeconomic prejudices in school-age children, and effective ways to reduce prejudice • Strategies for helping peer-rejected children • Biology and Environment box on bullies and their victims • School-age children's gender-stereotyped beliefs about achievement • Role of sex-segregated peer associations in school-age children's gender typing • Never-married parent families, with special attention to African-American men's involvement with their children • Parent training for custodial parents in divorced families • Effects of maternal and dual-earner employment on child development • Cultural Influences box on the impact of ethnic and political violence on children, with special attention to children separated from their parents and other adult relatives at the U.S. southern border

Pedagogical Features

Maintaining a highly accessible writing style—one that is lucid and engaging without being simplistic—continues to be one of my major goals. I frequently converse with students, encouraging them to relate what they read to their own lives. In doing so, I aim to make the study of child development involving and pleasurable.

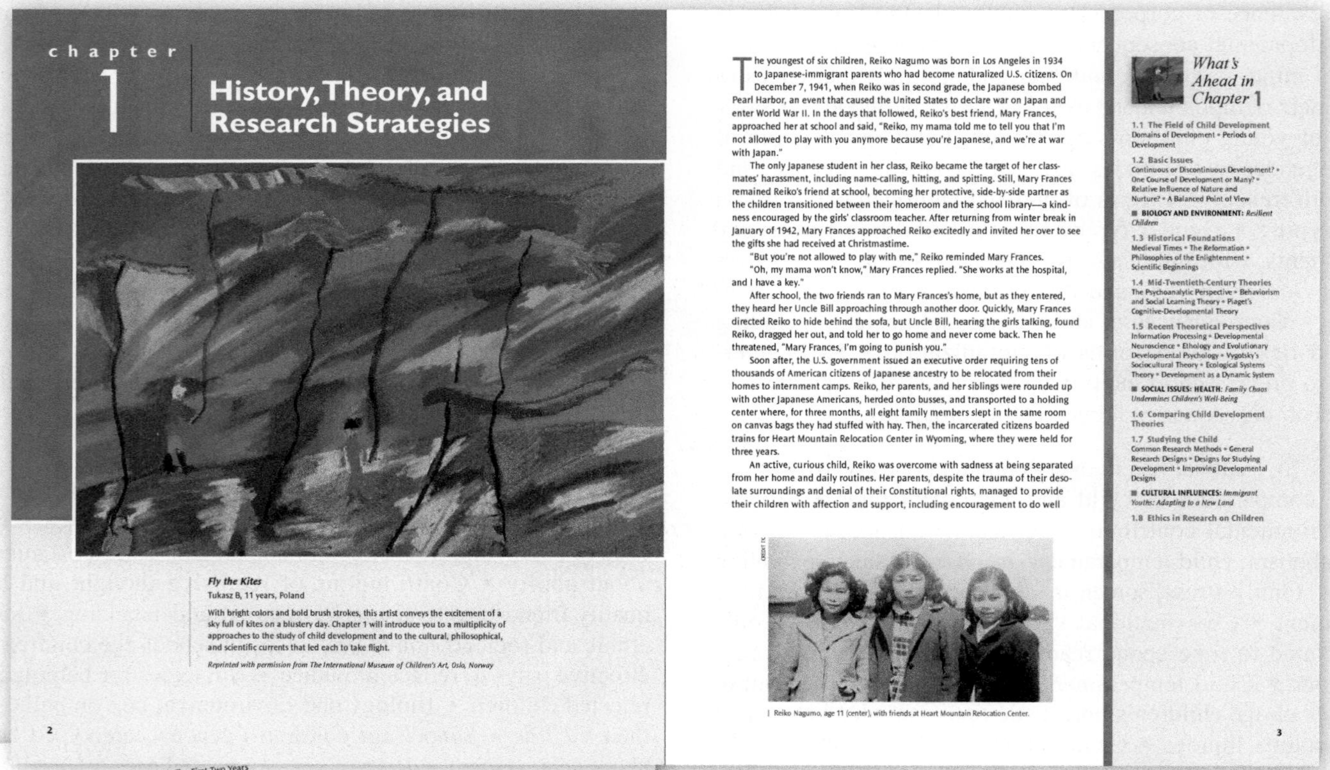

chapter 1

History, Theory, and Research Strategies

Fly the Kites

Tukasz B, 11 years, Poland

With bright colors and bold brush strokes, this artist conveys the excitement of a sky full of kites on a blustery day. Chapter 1 will introduce you to a multiplicity of approaches to the study of child development and to the cultural, philosophical, and scientific currents that led each to take flight.

Reprinted with permission from The International Museum of Children's Art, Oslo, Norway

2

The youngest of six children, Reiko Nagumo was born in Los Angeles in 1934 to Japanese-immigrant parents who had become naturalized U.S. citizens. On December 7, 1941, when Reiko was in second grade, the Japanese bombed Pearl Harbor, an event that caused the United States to declare war on Japan and enter World War II. In the days that followed, Reiko's best friend, Mary Frances, approached her at school and said, "Reiko, my mama told me to tell you that I'm not allowed to play with you anymore because you're Japanese, and we're at war with Japan."

The only Japanese student in her class, Reiko became the target of her classmates' harassment, including name-calling, hitting, and spitting. Still, Mary Frances remained Reiko's friend at school, becoming her protective, side-by-side partner as the children transitioned between their homeroom and the school library—a kindness encouraged by the girls' classroom teacher. After returning from winter break in January of 1942, Mary Frances approached Reiko excitedly and invited her over to see the gifts she had received at Christmastime.

"But you're not allowed to play with me," Reiko reminded Mary Frances.

"Oh, my mama won't know," Mary Frances replied. "She works at the hospital, and I have a key."

After school, the two friends ran to Mary Frances's home, but as they entered, they heard her Uncle Bill approaching through another door. Quickly, Mary Frances directed Reiko to hide behind the sofa, but Uncle Bill, hearing the girls talking, found Reiko, dragged her out, and told her to go home and never come back. Then he threatened, "Mary Frances, I'm going to punish you."

Soon after, the U.S. government issued an executive order requiring tens of thousands of American citizens of Japanese ancestry to be relocated from their homes to internment camps. Reiko, her parents, and her siblings were rounded up with other Japanese Americans, herded onto busses, and transported to a holding center where, for three months, all eight family members slept in the same room on canvas bags they had stuffed with hay. Then, the incarcerated citizens boarded trains for Heart Mountain Relocation Center in Wyoming, where they were held for three years.

An active, curious child, Reiko was overcome with sadness at being separated from her home and daily routines. Her parents, despite the trauma of their desolate surroundings and denial of their Constitutional rights, managed to provide their children with affection and support, including encouragement to do well

CREDIT TK

Reiko Nagumo, age 11 (center), with friends at Heart Mountain Relocation Center.

What's Ahead in Chapter 1

1.1 The Field of Child Development
Domains of Development • Periods of Development

1.2 Basic Issues
Continuous or Discontinuous Development? • One Course of Development or Many? • Relative Influence of Nature and Nurture? • A Balanced Point of View

■ BIOLOGY AND ENVIRONMENT: *Resilient Children*

1.3 Historical Foundations
Medieval Times • The Reformation • Philosophies of the Enlightenment • Scientific Beginnings

1.4 Mid-Twentieth-Century Theories
The Psychoanalytic Perspective • Behaviorism and Social Learning Theory • Piaget's Cognitive-Developmental Theory

1.5 Recent Theoretical Perspectives
Information Processing • Developmental Neuroscience • Ethology and Evolutionary Developmental Psychology • Vygotsky's Sociocultural Theory • Ecological Systems Theory • Development as a Dynamic System

■ SOCIAL ISSUES: HEALTH: *Family Chaos Undermines Children's Well-Being*

1.6 Comparing Child Development Theories

1.7 Studying the Child
Common Research Methods • General Research Designs • Designs for Studying Development • Improving Developmental Designs

■ CULTURAL INFLUENCES: *Immigrant Youths: Adapting to a New Land*

1.8 Ethics in Research on Children

3

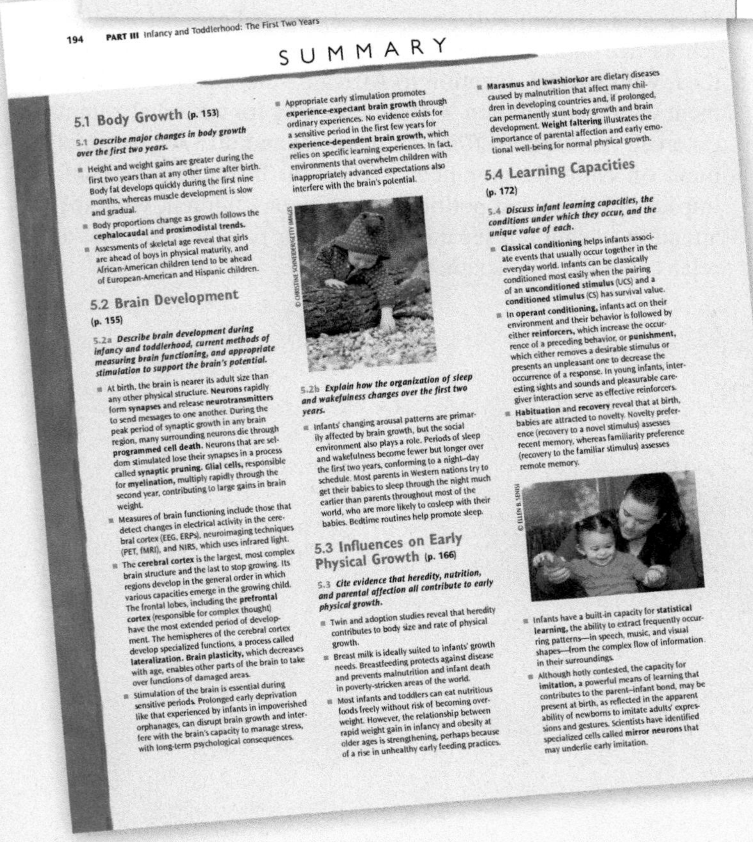

194 PART III Infancy and Toddlerhood: The First Two Years

SUMMARY

5.1 Body Growth (p. 153)

5.1 ***Describe major changes in body growth over the first two years.***

- Height and weight gains are greater during the first two years than at any other time after birth. Body fat develops quickly during the first nine months, whereas muscle development is slow and gradual.
- Body proportions change as growth follows the **cephalocaudal** and **proximodistal trends.**
- Assessments of skeletal age reveal that girls are ahead of boys in physical maturity, and African-American children tend to be ahead of European-American and Hispanic children.

5.2 Brain Development (p. 155)

5.2a ***Describe brain development during infancy and toddlerhood, current methods of measuring brain functioning, and appropriate stimulation to support the brain's potential.***

- At birth, the brain is nearer its adult size than any other physical structure. **Neurons** rapidly form **synapses** and release **neurotransmitters** to send messages to one another. During the peak period of synaptic growth in any brain region, many surrounding neurons die through **programmed cell death.** Neurons that are seldom stimulated lose their synapses in a process called **synaptic pruning. Glial cells,** responsible for **myelination,** multiply rapidly through the second year, contributing to large gains in brain weight.
- Measures of brain functioning include those that detect changes in electrical activity in the cerebral cortex (EEG, ERPs), neuroimaging techniques (PET, fMRI), and NIRS, which uses infrared light.
- The **cerebral cortex** is the largest, most complex brain structure and the last to stop growing. Its regions develop in the general order in which various capacities emerge in the growing child. The frontal lobes, including the **prefrontal cortex** (responsible for complex thought) have the most extended period of development. The hemispheres of the cerebral cortex develop specialized functions, a process called **lateralization. Brain plasticity,** which decreases with age, enables other parts of the brain to take over functions of damaged areas.
- Stimulation of the brain is essential during sensitive periods. Prolonged early deprivation like that experienced by infants in impoverished orphanages, can disrupt brain growth and interfere with the brain's capacity to manage stress, with long-term psychological consequences.
- Appropriate early stimulation promotes **experience-expectant brain growth** through ordinary experiences. No evidence exists for a sensitive period in the first few years for **experience-dependent brain growth,** which relies on specific learning experiences. In fact, environments that overwhelm children with inappropriately advanced expectations also interfere with the brain's potential.

© CHRISTINE SCHNEIDER/GETTY IMAGES

5.2b ***Explain how the organization of sleep and wakefulness changes over the first two years.***

- Infants' changing arousal patterns are primarily affected by brain growth, but the social environment also plays a role. Periods of sleep and wakefulness become fewer but longer over the first two years, conforming to a night–day schedule. Most parents in Western nations try to get their babies to sleep through the night much earlier than parents throughout most of the world, who are more likely to cosleep with their babies. Bedtime routines help promote sleep.

5.3 Influences on Early Physical Growth (p. 166)

5.3 ***Cite evidence that heredity, nutrition, and parental affection all contribute to early physical growth.***

- Twin and adoption studies reveal that heredity contributes to body size and rate of physical growth.
- Breast milk is ideally suited to infants' growth needs. Breastfeeding protects against disease and prevents malnutrition and infant death in poverty-stricken areas of the world.
- Most infants and toddlers can eat nutritious foods freely without risk of becoming overweight. However, the relationship between rapid weight gain in infancy and obesity at older ages is strengthening, perhaps because of a rise in unhealthy early feeding practices.
- **Marasmus** and **kwashiorkor** are dietary diseases caused by malnutrition that affect many children in developing countries and, if prolonged, can permanently stunt body growth and brain development. **Weight faltering** illustrates the importance of parental affection and early emotional well-being for normal physical growth.

5.4 Learning Capacities (p. 172)

5.4 ***Discuss infant learning capacities, the conditions under which they occur, and the unique value of each.***

- **Classical conditioning** helps infants associate events that usually occur together in the everyday world. Infants can be classically conditioned most easily when the pairing of an **unconditioned stimulus** (UCS) and a **conditioned stimulus** (CS) has survival value.
- In **operant conditioning,** infants act on their environment and their behavior is followed by either **reinforcers,** which increase the occurrence of a preceding behavior, or **punishment,** which either removes a desirable stimulus or presents an unpleasant one to decrease the occurrence of a response. In young infants, interesting sights and sounds and pleasurable caregiver interaction serve as effective reinforcers.
- **Habituation** and **recovery** reveal that at birth, babies are attracted to novelty. Novelty preference (recovery to a novel stimulus) assesses recent memory, whereas familiarity preference (recovery to the familiar stimulus) assesses remote memory.

© ELLEN B. SENISI

- Infants have a built-in capacity for **statistical learning,** the ability to extract frequently occurring patterns—in speech, music, and visual shapes—from the complex flow of information in their surroundings.
- Although hotly contested, the capacity for **imitation,** a powerful means of learning that contributes to the parent–infant bond, may be present at birth, as reflected in the apparent ability of newborns to imitate adults' expressions and gestures. Scientists have identified specialized cells called **mirror neurons** that may underlie early imitation.

Chapter Introductions and Vignettes About Children

To provide a helpful preview of chapter content, I include an outline and overview in each chapter introduction. To help students construct a clear image of development and to enliven the text narrative, each chronological age division is unified by case examples woven throughout that set of chapters. For example, within the infancy and toddlerhood section, we look in on three children, observe dramatic changes and striking individual differences, and address the impact of family background, child-rearing practices, parents' and children's life experiences, and child-care quality on development. Besides a set of main characters who bring unity to each age period, many additional vignettes offer vivid examples of development and diversity.

End-of-Chapter Summaries

Comprehensive end-of-chapter summaries, organized according to the major divisions of each chapter and highlighting important terms, remind students of key points in the text discussion. Learning objectives are included in the summary to encourage focused review.

Look and Listen

This active-learning feature presents students with opportunities to observe what real children say and do; speak with them or with professionals invested in their well-being; and inquire into community programs and practices that influence development. Look and Listen experiences are tied to relevant text sections, with the goal of making the study of development more authentic and meaningful.

Ask Yourself Questions

Active engagement with the subject matter is supported by revised and expanded study questions at the end of each major section. Three types of questions prompt students to think about child development in diverse ways: **Connect** questions help students build an image of the whole child by integrating what they have learned across age periods and domains of development. **Apply** questions encourage application of knowledge to controversial issues and problems faced by children, parents, and professionals who work with them. **Reflect** questions make the study of child development personally meaningful by asking students to reflect on their own development and life experiences.

Learning Objectives

In the text margins next to each main head, learning objectives guide students' reading and study.

Enhanced Art and Photo Program

The art and page-layout style present concepts and research findings with clarity and attractiveness, thereby aiding student understanding and retention. Each photo has been carefully selected to complement the text discussion and to represent the diversity of children around the world.

LOOK and LISTEN

In your community, what after-school programs are available, and how plentiful are they in low-income neighborhoods? If possible, visit a program, observing for supportive adult involvement, academic assistance, and enrichment activities.

13.7a Cite common fears and anxieties in middle childhood, and discuss their impact on children's adjustment.

13.7b Discuss factors related to child sexual abuse, its consequences for children's development, and its prevention and treatment.

13.7c Cite factors that foster resilience in middle childhood.

Mai at 6 years   Mai at 8 years   Mai at 10 years

Henry at 6 years   Henry at 8 years   Henry at 10 years

FIGURE 11.1   Body growth during middle childhood. Mai and Henry display a continuing slow, regular pattern of growth that began in early childhood. Around age 9, girls begin to grow at a faster rate than boys as the adolescent growth spurt draws near.

Three Types of Thematic Boxes

Thematic boxes accentuate the philosophical themes of this text:

Social Issues boxes discuss the impact of social conditions on children and emphasize the need for sensitive social policies to ensure their well-being. They are divided into two types:

Social Issues: Education boxes focus on home, school, and community influences on children's learning—for example, *Worldwide Education of Girls: Transforming Current and Future Generations, Children's Gestures Facilitate Cognitive Change,* and *School Recess—A Time to Play, a Time to Learn.*

Social Issues: Health boxes address values and practices relevant to children's physical and mental health. Examples include *Family Chaos Undermines Children's Well-Being, The Pros and Cons of Reproductive Technologies,* and *Family Stressors and Childhood Obesity.*

Biology and Environment boxes highlight growing attention to the complex, bidirectional relationship between biology and environment. Examples include *Thiamine Deficiency in the First Year and Later Language Impairment, Childhood Poverty and Brain Development,* and *Transgender Children.*

Cultural Influences boxes deepen the attention to culture threaded throughout the text. They highlight both cross-cultural and multicultural variations in child development—for example, *Familism Promotes Competence in Hispanic Children and Youths, Culturally Sensitive Prenatal Health Care: Perspectives of Expectant Mothers,* and *Impact of Ethnic and Political Violence on Children.*

Sample Page Excerpts

APPLYING WHAT WE KNOW

Signs of Developmentally Appropriate Infant and Toddler Child Care

PROGRAM CHARACTERISTIC	SIGNS OF QUALITY
Physical setting	Indoor environment is clean, in good repair, well-lighted, and well-ventilated. Fenced outdoor play space is available. Setting does not appear overcrowded when children are present.
Toys and equipment	Play materials are appropriate for infants and toddlers and are stored on low shelves within easy reach. Cribs, highchairs, infant seats, and child-sized tables and chairs are available. Outdoor equipment includes small riding toys, swings, slide, and sandbox.
Caregiver–child ratio	In child-care centers, caregiver–child ratio is no greater than 1 to 3 for infants and 1 to 6 for toddlers. Group size (number of children in one room) is no greater than 6 infants with two caregivers and 12 toddlers with two caregivers. In family child-care homes, caregiver is responsible for no more than 6 children; within this group, no more than 2 are infants or toddlers. Staffing is consistent, so infants and toddlers can form relationships with particular caregivers.
Daily activities	Daily schedule includes times for active play, quiet play, naps, snacks, and meals. It is flexible rather than rigid, to meet the needs of individual children. Atmosphere is warm and supportive, and children are never left unsupervised.
Interactions among adults and children	Caregivers respond promptly to infants' and toddlers' distress; hold, talk to, sing, and read to them; and interact with them in a manner that respects the individual child's interests and tolerance for stimulation.
Caregiver qualifications	Caregiver has some training in child development, first aid, and safety.
Relationships with parents	Parents are welcome anytime. Caregivers talk frequently with parents about children's behavior and development.
Licensing and accreditation	Child-care setting, whether a center or a home, is licensed by the state. In the United States, voluntary accreditation by the National Association for the Education of Young Children, *www.naeyc.org/accreditation*, or the National Association for Family Child Care, *www.nafcc.org*, is evidence of an especially high-quality program.

Source: Copple & Bredekamp, 2009.

Applying What We Know Tables

In this feature, I summarize research-based applications on many issues, speaking directly to students as parents or future parents and to those pursuing different careers or areas of study, such as teaching, health care, counseling, or social work. The tables include *Do's and Don'ts for a Healthy Pregnancy, Signs of Developmentally Appropriate Infant and Toddler Child Care, Regulating Screen Media Use,* and *Fostering a Growth Mindset About Ability and a Mastery-Oriented Approach to Learning.*

MILESTONES

Development in Early Childhood

2 YEARS

Physical
- Throughout early childhood, height and weight increase more slowly than in toddlerhood. (281)
- Balance improves; walking becomes smooth and rhythmic; running emerges. (296–297)
- Jumps, hops, throws, and catches with rigid upper body. (297)
- Puts on and removes simple items of clothing. (297–298)
- Uses spoon effectively. (297)
- First drawings are gestural scribbles. (298)

Language
- Vocabulary increases rapidly. (345)
- Uses a coalition of cues—perceptual and, increasingly, social and linguistic—to figure out word meanings. (347)
- Speaks in simple sentences that follow basic word order of native language. (347)
- Adds grammatical markers. (348)
- Displays effective conversational skills. (349)

Emotional/Social
- Understands causes, consequences, and behavioral signs of basic emotions. (358)
- Begins to develop self-concept and self-esteem. (356–358)

3–4 YEARS

Physical
- May no longer need a daytime nap. (287)
- Running, jumping, hopping, throwing, and catching become more refined, with flexible upper body. (296–297)
- Galloping and one-foot skipping appear. (297)
- Pedals and steers tricycle. (297)
- Uses scissors. (297)
- Uses fork effectively. (297)
- Draws first picture of a person, using tadpole image. (299)
- Distinguishes writing from nonwriting. (302)

Cognitive
- ...symbolic function of drawings... of real-world spaces. (290, 310)
- ...tion, reasons about transforma-...
- ...stands cause-and-effect rela-...
- ...plified, familiar situations. (314)
- ...day knowledge into hierarchi-... categories. (314–316)
- ...resentation. (310–311, 317)
- ...ech to guide behavior during... ks. (319)
- ...ve function, including inhibi-... ting of attention, and working... ty. (323–324)
- ...call routine events. (326)
- ...at beliefs can determine...
- ...g of numbers up to ten, counts... rasps cardinality. (334)

Milestones Tables

A Milestones table appears at the end of each age division of the text. The tables summarize major physical, cognitive, language, emotional, and social attainments, providing a convenient aid for reviewing the chronology of child development.

- Reproductive technologies, such as donor insemination, in vitro fertilization, and surrogate motherhood, enable individuals to conceive children who otherwise would not. However, the technologies raise legal and ethical concerns.
- Many adults who cannot conceive or who are likely to transmit a genetic disorder choose adoption. Although adopted children tend to have more learning and emotional problems than children in general, most fare well in the long run. Warm, supportive parenting that includes open communication about adoption contributes to favorable development.

2.3 Environmental Contexts for Development (p. 65)

2.3 Discuss aspects of children's multi-layered environment that influence their development and well-being.

- In the family—the first and most enduring context for development—the behaviors of each member affect those of the others in a dynamic, ever-changing system of direct and indirect influences. Warm, gratifying family ties, which foster effective *coparenting*, help ensure children's psychological health.
- Socioeconomic status (SES) profoundly affects family functioning and children's development. Higher-SES parents tend to have smaller families, to value independence, and to engage in warm, verbally stimulating interaction with children. Lower-SES parents tend to value obedience and to use more commands, criticism, and physical punishment.
- In affluent families, parental physical and emotional unavailability may impair youths' adjustment. Poverty and homelessness undermine effective parenting and pose serious threats to children's development.

- Children benefit from supportive ties between the family and community, including stable, socially cohesive neighborhoods that provide constructive leisure and enrichment activities. High-quality schooling and parent involvement in children's education enhance academic achievement, educational attainment, and life chances.
- The values and practices of cultures and subcultures affect all aspects of children's daily life. Extended families, common among many ethnic minorities, help protect family members from the negative effects of poverty and other stressful life conditions. The Hispanic cultural value of *familism*, which elevates family needs above individual concerns, is associated with multiple positive developmental outcomes.
- Cross-national differences in *collectivism–individualism* powerfully affect **public policies** aimed at addressing social problems. Largely because of its strongly individualistic values, the United States lags behind other developed nations in policies safeguarding children and youths.

2.4 Understanding the Relationship Between Heredity and Environment (p. 78)

2.4 Explain the various ways heredity and environment may combine to influence complex traits.

- **Behavioral genetics** examines the contributions of nature and nurture to diversity in human traits and abilities. **Heritability estimates**, derived from **kinship studies**, attempt to quantify the influence of genetic factors on such complex traits as intelligence and personality. However, the accuracy of this approach has been challenged.
- In **gene–environment interaction**, heredity influences each individual's responsiveness to qualities of the environment. In **gene–environment correlation**, children's genes affect the environments to which they are exposed, at first passively and evocatively. At older ages, children actively choose environments that complement their heredity, a process called *niche-picking*.
- **Epigenesis** reminds us that development is best understood as a series of complex, bidirectional exchanges between heredity and all levels of the environment. Epigenetic research is uncovering biochemical processes—such as **methylation**—through which the environment can modify gene expression.

IMPORTANT TERMS AND CONCEPTS

allele (p. 54)
autosomes (p. 53)
behavioral genetics (p. 78)
carrier (p. 55)
chromosomes (p. 51)
coparenting (p. 66)
deoxyribonucleic acid (DNA) (p. 51)
dominant–recessive inheritance (p. 55)
epigenesis (p. 82)
familism (p. 75)
fraternal, or dizygotic, twins (p. 53)
gametes (p. 53)
gene (p. 52)

gene–environment correlation (p. 80)
gene–environment interaction (p. 80)
genetic counseling (p. 60)
genomic imprinting (p. 57)
genotype (p. 51)
heritability estimate (p. 78)
heterozygous (p. 54)
homozygous (p. 54)
identical, or monozygotic, twins (p. 54)
incomplete dominance (p. 55)
kinship studies (p. 78)
meiosis (p. 53)
methylation (p. 82)

mutation (p. 57)
niche-picking (p. 81)
phenotype (p. 51)
polygenic inheritance (p. 58)
prenatal diagnostic methods (p. 62)
protein-coding genes (p. 52)
public policies (p. 76)
regulator genes (p. 52)
sex chromosomes (p. 53)
socioeconomic status (SES) (p. 67)
subculture (p. 74)
X-linked inheritance (p. 56)
zygote (p. 53)

In-Text Key Terms with Definitions, End-of-Chapter Term List, and End-of-Book Glossary

In-text highlighting of key terms and definitions encourages students to review the central vocabulary of the field in greater depth by rereading related information. Key terms also appear in an end-of-chapter page-referenced term list and an end-of-book glossary.

Acknowledgments

The dedicated contributions of a great many individuals helped make this text a reality and contributed to refinements and improvements in this ninth edition.

Reviewers

An impressive cast of reviewers provided many helpful suggestions and constructive criticisms, as well as encouragement and enthusiasm, for the organization and content of the text. I am grateful to each one of them.

For the First Through Eighth Editions

Scott Adler, York University
Mark B. Alcorn, University of Northern Colorado
Joseph Allen, University of Virginia
William Aquilino, University of Wisconsin, Madison
Armin W. Arndt, Eastern Washington University
Martha Arterberry, Colby College
Shannon Audley-Piotrowski, Smith College
Lamia Barakat, Drexel University
Cecelia Benelli, Western Illinois University
Kathleen Bey, Palm Beach Community College
Janet J. Boseovski, University of North Carolina, Greensboro
Heather Bouchey, University of Vermont
Donald Bowers, Community College of Philadelphia
Michele Y. Breault, Truman State University
Jerry Bruce, Sam Houston State College
Kristy Burkholder, University of Wisconsin, Madison
Melissa Burnham, University of Nevada, Reno
Lanthan D. Camblin, University of Cincinnati
Nicole Campione-Barr, University of Missouri, Columbia
Joseph J. Campos, University of California, Berkeley
Linda A. Camras, DePaul University
Gustavo Carlo, University of Nebraska—Lincoln
Lynn Caruso, Seneca College
Nancy Taylor Coghill, University of Southwest Louisiana
Raymond Collings, SUNY Cortland
Diane Brothers Cook, Gainesville College
Jennifer Cook, Kent State University
Roswell Cox, Berea College
Ronald Craig, Edinboro University of Pennsylvania
Zoe Ann Davidson, Alabama A&M University
Sheridan DeWolf, Grossmont College
Matthew DiCintio, Delaware County Community College
Constance DiMaria-Kross, Union County College
Jacquelynne Eccles, University of Michigan
Jeff Farrar, University of Florida
Bronwyn Fees, Kansas State University
F. Richard Ferraro, University of North Dakota
Kathleen Fite, Southwest Texas State University
Peter Flynn, Northern Essex Community College
Kate Fogarty, University of Florida
Trisha Folds-Bennett, College of Charleston
Nancy Freeman, University of South Carolina
William Friedman, Oberlin College

Jayne Gackenbach, MacEwan University
Eugene Geist, Ohio University
Sabine Gerhardt, University of Akron
Abi Gewirtz, University of Minnesota
Dominic Gullo, Drexel University
Kristine Hansen, University of Winnipeg
Vivian Harper, San Joaquin Delta College
Algea Harrison, Oakland University
Janice Hartgrove-Freile, North Harris Community College
Shanta Hattikudur, Temple University
Vernon Haynes, Youngstown State University
Bert Hayslip, Jr., University of North Texas
Sandra Hellyer, Butler University
Joan Herwig, Iowa State University
Paula Hillmann, University of Wisconsin, Waukesha
Robert Hiltonsmith, Radford University
Hiu-Chin Hsu, University of Georgia
Shayla Holub, University of Texas, Dallas
Christie Honeycutt, Stanly Community College
Malia Huchendorf, Normandale Community College
Lisa Huffman, Ball State University
Clementine Hansley Hurt, Radford University
Jennifer Jipson, California Polytechnic State University
Scott Johnson, New York University
Joline Jones, Worcester State University
Zsuzsa Kaldy, University of Massachusetts Boston
Kate Kenney, Howard Community College
Shirin Khosropour, Austin Community College
Elisa Klein, University of Maryland
John S. Klein, Castleton State College
Sarah Kollat, Pennsylvania State University
Claire Kopp, Claremont Graduate School
Murray Krantz, Florida State University
Eugene Krebs, California State University, Fresno
Carole Kremer, Hudson Valley Community College
Gary W. Ladd, University of Illinois, Urbana–Champaign
Deborah Laible, Lehigh University
Linda Lavine, State University of New York at Cortland
Sara Lawrence, California State University, Northridge
Gail Lee, Jersey City State College
Judith R. Levine, State University of New York at Farmingdale
Miriam Linver, Montclair State University
David Lockwood, Humber College
Frank Manis, University of Southern California
Stuart Marcovitch, University of North Carolina Greensboro
Martin Marino, Atlantic Cape Community College
Trent Maurer, Georgia Southern University
Mary Ann McLaughlin, Clarion University of Pennsylvania
Megan McLelland, Oregon State University
Annie McManus, Parkland College
Cloe Merrill, Weber State University
Daniel Messinger, University of Miami
Rich Metzger, University of Tennessee at Chattanooga
Amy H. Mezulis, Seattle Pacific University
Karla Miley, Black Hawk College
Amanda Morris, Oklahoma State University—Tulsa
Winnie Mucherah, Ball State University
Joyce Munsch, California State University, Northridge
Dara Musher-Eisenman, Bowling Green State University
Jennifer Trapp Myers, University of Michigan
Virginia Navarro, University of Missouri, St. Louis

Larry Nelson, Brigham Young University
Angela Nievar, University of North Texas
Peggy Norwood, Red Rocks Community College
Peter V. Oliver, University of Hartford
Behnaz Pakizegi, William Patterson University
Virginia Parsons, Carroll College
Karen Peterson, University of Washington, Vancouver
Julie Poehlmann, University of Wisconsin—Madison
Tom Power, Washington State University
Kavita Prakash, Heritage College
Joe M. Price, San Diego State University
Cathy Proctor-Castillo, Long Beach Community College
Verna Raab, Mount Royal College
Raghu Rao, University of Minnesota
Mary Kay Reed, York College of Pennsylvania
Maggie Renken, Georgia State University
Michael Rodman, Middlesex Community College
Alan Russell, Flinders University
Pamela Schulze, University of Akron
Tizrah Schutzengel, Bergen Community College
Johnna Shapiro, Illinois Wesleyan University
Elizabeth Short, Case Western Reserve University
Dorothy Sluss, James Madison University
Delores Smith, University of Tennessee
Gregory Smith, Dickinson College
Laura Sosinsky, Fordham University
Thomas Spencer, San Francisco State University
Carolyn Spies, Bloomfield College
Kathy Stansbury, University of New Mexico
Connie Steele, University of Tennessee, Knoxville
Janet Strayer, Simon Fraser University
Marcia Summers, Ball State University
Daniel Swingley, University of Pennsylvania
Christy Teranishi, Texas A&M International University
Joan E. Test, Missouri State University
Dennis Thompson, Georgia State University
Tracy Thorndike-Christ, Western Washington University
Virginia Tompkins, Ohio State University
Connie K. Varnhagen, University of Alberta
Athena Vouloumanos, McGill University
Judith Ward, Central Connecticut State University
Shawn Ward, Le Moyne College
Alida Westman, Eastern Michigan University
Jayne White, Drury University
Colin William, Columbus State Community College
Belinda Wholeben, Rockford College
Sue Williams, Southwest Texas State University
Deborah Winters, New Mexico State University
Ilona Yim, University of California, Irvine
Nicole Zarrett, University of South Carolina, Columbia

For the Ninth Edition

Jennifer Bruzek, Jacksonville State University
Elizabeth Sherwood Burns-Nader, University of Alabama
Lucas Butler, University of Maryland, College Park
Namisi Chilungu, Georgia State University
Katie Dorman, University of Florida
Kate Forgarty, University of Florida
Frederick Foster-Clark, Millersville University

Kristin Homan, Grove City College
Lisa Jackson, Schoolcraft College
Zsuzsu Kaldy, University of Massachusetts, Boston
Mike Mensink, University of Wisconsin, Stout
Winnie Mucherah, Ball State University
Angela Nievar, University of North Texas
Maggie Renken, Georgia State University
Amy Resch, Citrus College
James Rodgers, Hawkeye Community College
David Rudek, Aurora University
Tracey Ryan, University of Bridgeport
Brandi Stupica, Alma College
Joan E. Test, Missouri State University
Voltaire Villanueva, Foothill College
Jennifer Weaver, Boise State University

Editorial and Production Team

I have been fortunate to collaborate with a highly capable editorial team at Pearson Education. It has been a great pleasure to work once again with Tom Pauken, Managing Editor, who oversaw the preparation of the fourth and eighth editions of *Infants and Children* and who returned to edit this ninth edition as well as its supplements package. It is difficult to capture in words all of Tom's contributions: His perceptive recommendations for text revisions and new videos, keen organizational skills, responsive day-to-day communication, insightful problem solving, interest in the subject matter, patience, thoughtfulness, and sense of humor (at just the right moments) greatly enhanced the quality of the text. I am deeply appreciative of the many years Tom has invested his wide-ranging talents in my titles, and I look forward with pleasure to working with him on future projects.

Monica Moosang, Project Manager, coordinated the complex production tasks for the ninth edition, transforming my manuscript into an exquisitely beautiful text. I am grateful for Monica's attention to detail, flexibility, efficiency, and commitment. Josephine Cepeda provided outstanding copyediting and Karen Jones, impeccable proofreading.

Rachel Trapp-Gardner, Editorial Assistant, has been nothing short of amazing. In addition to spending countless hours expertly gathering and organizing scholarly literature, she assisted in vital ways with supplement planning and writing and editing of assessments. Two development editors contributed in invaluable ways. David Chodoff reviewed each chapter as I completed it, offering excellent suggestions that helped ensure that each thought and concept was precisely expressed and well developed. Judy Ashkenaz analyzed reviewers' recommendations in preparation for text revision, prepared diverse components of the Instructor's Resource Manual, and assumed many other editorial tasks. My appreciation to Judy for her work on more editions of *Infants, Children, and Adolescents* than any other member of the publishing team.

Phil Vandiver of Contemporary Visuals in Bloomington, IL, has been an invaluable partner for many years in creating high-quality instructional videos to complement my texts. For this edition, he produced an inspiring set of 10 new video segments covering diverse topics in child development.

My sincere gratitude to Brad Parkins, Director of Product Marketing, for yet another first-rate effort to ensure that up-to-date information about the text and its teaching and learning resources reaches Pearson's sales force. Many thanks, as well, to two other Pearson leaders: Ed Parsons, Senior Publisher of Arts and Sciences, took responsibility for the overall management of my texts. His grasp of the unique needs of authors of multiple titles and effective problem solving made possible this ninth edition. Since Ed's departure, Pamela Chirls, Manager of Content Strategies, has assumed these responsibilities. It has been a pleasure to get to know Pam; her knowledge and commitment to high-quality texts and supplements was evident in our first conversation.

Friends and Family

Throughout my many months of writing, my long-time friend Jana Edge ensured that a five- to six-mile early morning walk preceded my sitting down at my desk. For extraordinary counsel, I am immensely grateful to Devereux Chatillon.

Last but not least, I thank my family for being there for me during three decades of work on my suite of Pearson titles. My sons, David and Peter, grew up with my texts, passing from childhood to adolescence and then to adulthood as successive editions were written. David has a special connection with the books' subject matter as an elementary school teacher. Peter is now an experienced attorney, and his vivacious and talented wife Melissa is part of a new generation of university faculty engaged in innovative teaching and research. All three continue to enrich my understanding through reflections on events and progress in their own lives. My husband, Ken, willingly put on hold much in our life together to accommodate the challenges and pace of this revision.

Laura E. Berk

REVEL

Revel is an immersive learning experience designed for the way today's students read, think, and learn. Designed in consultation with educators and students nationwide, REVEL is Pearson's newest, fully digital method of delivering course content.

REVEL for *Infants and Children* further enlivens the text with a wealth of author-overseen and author-produced interactive media and assessments—all integrated within the narrative to provide opportunities for students to engage deeply with course content while reading. Greater student engagement leads to more thorough understanding of concepts and improved performance throughout the course.

To learn more about REVEL, visit www.pearsonhighered.com/REVEL.

Instructor Resources

An array of high-quality instructor materials accompanies the ninth edition of *Infants, Children, and Adolescents*.

Instructor's Resource Manual (IRM) This thoroughly revised IRM can be used by first-time or experienced instructors to enrich classroom experiences. Each chapter includes a chapter summary and outline, learning activities, and new lecture enhancements presenting cutting-edge topics, with article citations and suggestions for expanding on chapter content in class.

Test Bank The Test Bank contains over 1,500 multiple-choice and essay questions, all page-referenced to chapter content.

Pearson MyTest This secure online environment allows instructors to easily create exams, study guide questions, and quizzes from any computer with an Internet connection.

PowerPoint Presentation The PowerPoint presentation provides outlines and illustrations of key topics for each chapter of the text.

"Explorations in Child Development" DVD and Guide This revised DVD with 10 new segments is over six hours in length and contains more than 50 narrated videos, designed for classroom use, that illustrate the many theories, concepts, and milestones of child development. The DVD and Guide are available only to instructors who are confirmed adopters of the text.

About the Cover and Chapter Opening Art

I would like to extend grateful acknowledgments to the International Museum of Children's Art, Oslo, Norway; the International Child Art Foundation, Washington, DC; and Children's Museum of the Arts, New York, NY, for the exceptional cover image and chapter opening art, which depict the talents, concerns, and viewpoints of young artists from around the world. The awe-inspiring collection of children's art gracing this text expresses family, school, and community themes; good times and personal triumphs; profound appreciation for beauty; and great depth of emotion. I am pleased to share with readers this window into children's creativity, insightfulness, sensitivity, and compassion.

1

History, Theory, and Research Strategies

Fly the Kites

Tukasz B., 11 years, Poland

With bright colors and bold brush strokes, this artist conveys the excitement of a sky full of kites on a blustery day. Chapter 1 will introduce you to a multiplicity of approaches to the study of child development and to the cultural, philosophical, and scientific currents that led each to take flight.

Reprinted with permission from The International Museum of Children's Art, Oslo, Norway

The youngest of six children, Reiko Nagumo was born in Los Angeles in 1934 to Japanese-immigrant parents who had become naturalized U.S. citizens. On December 7, 1941, when Reiko was in second grade, the Japanese bombed Pearl Harbor, an event that caused the United States to declare war on Japan and enter World War II. In the days that followed, Reiko's best friend, Mary Frances, approached her at school and said, "Reiko, my mama told me to tell you that I'm not allowed to play with you anymore because you're Japanese, and we're at war with Japan."

The only Japanese student in her class, Reiko became the target of her class-mates' harassment, including name-calling, hitting, and spitting. Still, Mary Frances remained Reiko's friend at school, becoming her protective, side-by-side partner as the children transitioned between their homeroom and the school library—a kind-ness encouraged by the girls' classroom teacher. After returning from winter break in January of 1942, Mary Frances approached Reiko excitedly and invited her over to see the gifts she had received at Christmastime.

"But you're not allowed to play with me," Reiko reminded Mary Frances.

"Oh, my mama won't know," Mary Frances replied. "She works at the hospital, and I have a key."

After school, the two friends ran to Mary Frances's home, but as they entered, they heard her Uncle Bill approaching through another door. Quickly, Mary Frances directed Reiko to hide behind the sofa, but Uncle Bill, hearing the girls talking, found Reiko, dragged her out, and told her to go home and never come back. Then he threatened, "Mary Frances, I'm going to punish you."

Soon after, the U.S. government issued an executive order requiring tens of thousands of American citizens of Japanese ancestry to be relocated from their homes to internment camps. Reiko, her parents, and her siblings were rounded up with other Japanese Americans, herded onto busses, and transported to a holding center where, for three months, all eight family members slept in the same room on canvas bags they had stuffed with hay. Then, the incarcerated citizens boarded trains for Heart Mountain Relocation Center in Wyoming, where they were held for three years.

An active, curious child, Reiko was overcome with sadness at being separated from her home and daily routines. Her parents, despite the trauma of their deso-late surroundings and denial of their Constitutional rights, managed to provide their children with affection and support, including encouragement to do well

What's Ahead in Chapter 1

© UNIVERSITY LIBRARY, CALIFORNIA STATE UNIVERSITY, SACRAMENTO

| Reiko Nagumo, age 11 (center), with friends at Heart Mountain Relocation Center.

academically in the camp's makeshift school using barracks as classrooms. Soon, Reiko's buoyancy returned: She passed time playing "school" and "library" with other camp children and made playing cards, checkerboards, and other games out of cardboard. Charitable organizations sent in teachers with whom Reiko forged close relationships.

When the war ended in 1945, Reiko and her family moved back to their former neighborhood. Memories of peer mistreatment caused Reiko to fear returning to school, but as she set foot in the play yard, a teacher welcomed her and made her feel safe. Reiko soon found Mary Frances—the only child who reached out and took her hand in friendship.

In the years that followed, Reiko and Mary Frances lost contact. Reiko went on to earn bachelor's and master's degrees in nursing and pursued an adventurous international opportunity as a public health nurse before returning to California to work in a hospital neonatal intensive care unit. Now retired, she regularly gives talks to schoolchildren about her wartime experiences of internment and what we can learn from history. Reiko never forgot Mary Frances, who befriended her during a time of intense prejudice against anyone Japanese. As she grew old, Reiko began to search for her. Seventy years after the two friends had last seen each other, they were reunited (Elk Grove Unified School District, 2018; PBS, 2018).

• • •

Reiko's story raises a wealth of fascinating issues about child development:

- What determines the physical, mental, and behavioral attributes that Reiko and Mary Frances share with their agemates and those that make each child unique?
- How did Reiko manage to sustain an active, curious disposition despite the trauma of internment? What enabled Mary Frances to remain Reiko's steadfast friend in the face of adult and peer condemnation?
- In what ways are children's home, school, and neighborhood experiences the same today as they were in Reiko and Mary Frances's generation, and in what ways are they different?
- How do historical events—for Reiko, wartime persecution and dislocation—affect children's development and well-being?

These are central questions addressed by **child development,** a field of study devoted to understanding constancy and change from conception through adolescence. Child development is part of a larger, interdisciplinary field known as **developmental science,** which includes all changes we experience throughout the lifespan (Lerner et al., 2014; Overton & Molenaar, 2015). The interests and concerns of the thousands of investigators who study child development are enormously diverse. But all have a common goal: to describe and identify those factors that influence the consistencies and changes in young people during the first two decades of life. ■

1.1 The Field of Child Development

1.1a Describe the field of child development, along with factors that stimulated its expansion.

1.1b Explain how child development is typically divided into domains and periods.

The questions just listed are not just of scientific interest. Each has *applied,* or practical, importance as well. In fact, scientific curiosity is just one factor that led child development to become the exciting field it is today. Research about development has also been stimulated by social pressures to improve the lives of children. For example, the beginning of public education in the early twentieth century led to a demand for knowledge about what and how to teach children of different ages. The interest of pediatricians and nurses in improving children's health required an understanding of physical growth and nutrition. The social service profession's desire to treat children's emotional and behavior problems and to help them cope with challenging life circumstances, such as the birth of a sibling, parental divorce, poverty, bullying in school, or racial and ethnic prejudices, required information about personality and social development. And parents have continually sought advice about child-rearing practices and experiences that would promote their children's development and well-being.

Our large storehouse of information about child development is *interdisciplinary.* It has grown through the combined efforts of people from many fields. Because of the need to solve everyday problems concerning children, researchers from psychology, sociology, anthropology, biology, and neuroscience have joined forces with those from education, family studies, medicine, public health, and social service, to name just a few. Together, they have created the field of child development as it exists today—a body of knowledge that is not just scientifically important but also relevant and useful.

1.1.1 Domains of Development

To make the vast, interdisciplinary study of human constancy and change more orderly and convenient, development is often divided into three broad domains: *physical, cognitive,* and *emotional and social.* Refer to Figure 1.1 for a description and illustration of each. In this text, we will largely consider the three domains in the order just mentioned. Yet the domains are not really distinct. Rather, they combine in an integrated, holistic fashion to yield the living, growing child. Furthermore, each domain influences and is influenced by the others. For example, in Chapter 5 you will see that new motor capacities, such as reaching, sitting, crawling, and walking (physical), contribute greatly to infants' understanding of their surroundings (cognitive). When babies think and act more competently, adults stimulate them more with games, language, and expressions of delight at their new achievements (emotional and social). These enriched experiences, in turn, promote all aspects of development.

You will encounter instances of the interwoven nature of all domains on nearly every page of this text. In its margins, you will find occasional *Look and Listen* activities—opportunities for you to see everyday illustrations of development by observing what real children say and do or by attending to everyday influences on children. Through these experiences, I hope to make your study of development more authentic and meaningful.

Physical Development

Changes in body size, proportions, appearance, functioning of body systems, perceptual and motor capacities, and physical health

Cognitive Development

Changes in intellectual abilities, including attention, memory, academic and everyday knowledge, problem solving, imagination, creativity, and language

Emotional and Social Development

Changes in emotional communication, self-understanding, knowledge about other people, interpersonal skills, friendships, intimate relationships, and moral reasoning and behavior

FIGURE 1.1   Major domains of development. The three domains are not really distinct. Rather, they overlap and interact.

Also, at the end of major sections, look for *Ask Yourself,* a feature designed to help deepen your understanding. Within it, I have included *Connect* questions, which help you form a coherent, unified picture of child development; *Apply* questions, which encourage you to apply your knowledge to controversial issues and problems faced by parents, teachers, and children; and *Reflect* questions, which invite you to reflect on your own development and that of people you know well.

1.1.2 Periods of Development

Besides distinguishing and integrating the three domains, another dilemma arises in discussing development: how to divide the flow of time into sensible, manageable parts. Researchers usually use the following age periods, each of which brings new capacities and social expectations that serve as important transitions in major theories:

1. *The prenatal period: from conception to birth.* In this nine-month period, the most rapid time of change, a one-celled organism is transformed into a human baby with remarkable capacities for adjusting to life in the surrounding world.
2. *Infancy and toddlerhood: from birth to 2 years.* This period brings dramatic changes in the body and brain that support the emergence of a wide array of motor, perceptual, and intellectual capacities; the beginnings of language; and the first intimate ties to others. Infancy spans the first year. Toddlerhood spans the second, during which children take their first independent steps, marking a shift to greater autonomy.
3. *Early childhood: from 2 to 6 years.* The body becomes longer and leaner, motor skills are refined, and children become more self-controlled and self-sufficient. Make-believe play blossoms, reflecting and supporting many aspects of psychological development. Thought and language expand at an astounding pace, a sense of morality becomes evident, and children establish ties with peers.
4. *Middle childhood: from 6 to 11 years.* Children learn about the wider world and master new responsibilities that increasingly resemble those they will perform as adults. Hallmarks of this period are improved athletic abilities; participation in organized games with rules; more logical thought processes; mastery of fundamental reading, writing, math, and other academic knowledge and skills; and advances in understanding the self, morality, and friendship.
5. *Adolescence: from 11 to 18 years.* This is the intervening period between childhood and adulthood. Puberty leads to an adult-sized body and sexual maturity. Thought becomes increasingly complex, abstract, and idealistic, and schooling is directed toward entry into higher education and the world of work. During this period, young people establish autonomy from the family and define personal values and goals.

For many contemporary youths in industrialized nations, the transition to adult roles has become increasingly prolonged—so much so that some researchers have proposed an additional period of development called *emerging adulthood* that extends from age 18 to the mid- to late-twenties. Although emerging adults have moved beyond adolescence, they have not yet fully assumed adult responsibilities. Rather, during the college years and sometimes beyond, these young people intensify their exploration of options in love, career, and personal values before making enduring commitments (Arnett, 2015). Perhaps emerging adulthood is your period of development.

With this introduction in mind, let's turn to some basic issues that have captivated, puzzled, and sparked debate among child development theorists. Then our discussion will trace the emergence of the field and survey major theories. We will return to each contemporary theory in greater depth in later chapters.

© UWE OMMER, *1,000 FAMILIES*, TASCHEN

To make sense of the timetable of child development, researchers divide it into manageable periods. This large South African family includes children in infancy (child in arms), early childhood (seated boys), middle childhood (girl standing in front row), and adolescence (boy standing at far left).

1.2 Basic Issues

Research on child development did not begin until the late nineteenth and early twentieth centuries. But ideas about how children grow and change have a much longer history. As these speculations combined with research, they inspired the construction of *theories* of development. A **theory** is an orderly, integrated set of statements that describes, explains, and predicts behavior. For example, a good theory of infant–caregiver attachment would (1) *describe* the behaviors of babies around 6 to 8 months of age, when they start to actively seek the affection and comfort of a familiar adult, (2) *explain* how and why infants develop this strong desire to bond with a familiar caregiver, and (3) *predict* the consequences of this emotional bond for future relationships.

Theories are vital tools for two reasons. First, they provide organizing frameworks for our observations of children. In other words, they *guide and give meaning* to what we see. Second, theories that are verified by research often serve as a sound basis for practical action. Once a theory helps us *understand* development, we are in a much better position *to know how to improve* the welfare and treatment of children.

As we will see later, theories are influenced by the cultural values and belief systems of their times. But theories differ in one important way from mere opinion or belief: A theory's continued existence depends on *scientific verification.* Every theory must be tested using a fair set of research procedures agreed on by the scientific community, and findings that verify the theory must endure, or be replicated over time.

Within the field of child development, many theories offer different ideas about what children are like and how they change. The study of child development provides no ultimate truth because investigators do not always agree on the meaning of what they see. Also, children are complex beings; they change physically, cognitively, emotionally, and socially. No single theory has explained all these aspects. But the existence of many theories helps advance knowledge because researchers are continually trying to support, contradict, and integrate these different points of view.

Although there are many theories, we can easily organize them by looking at the stand they take on three basic issues: (1) Is the course of development continuous or discontinuous? (2) Does one course of development characterize all children, or are there many possible courses? (3) What are the roles of genetic and environmental factors in development? Let's look closely at each of these issues.

1.2 Identify three basic issues on which theories of child development take a stand.

1.2.1 Continuous or Discontinuous Development?

A mother reported with amazement that her 20-month-old son Angelo had pushed a toy car across the living room floor while making a motorlike sound, "Brmmmm, brmmmm," for the first time. When he hit a nearby wall with a bang, Angelo let go of the car, exclaimed, "C'ash!" and laughed heartily.

"How come Angelo can pretend, but he couldn't a few months ago?" his mother asked. "And I wonder what 'Brmmmm, brmmmm' and 'Crash!' mean to Angelo. Does he understand motorlike sounds and collision the same way I do?"

Angelo's mother has raised a puzzling issue about development: How can we best describe the differences in capacities and behavior between small infants, young children, adolescents, and adults? As Figure 1.2 on page 7 illustrates, most major theories recognize two possibilities.

One view holds that infants and preschoolers respond to the world in much the same way as adults do. The difference between the immature and the mature being is one of *amount or complexity.* For example, little Angelo's thinking may be just as logical and well-organized as our own. Perhaps (as his mother reports) he can sort objects into simple categories, recognize whether he has more of one kind than of another, and remember where he left his favorite toy at child care the week before. Angelo's only limitation may be that he cannot perform these skills with as much information and precision as we can. If this is so, then Angelo's development is **continuous**—a process of gradually adding more of the same types of skills that were there to begin with.

FIGURE 1.2 **Is development continuous or discontinuous?** (a) Some theorists believe that development is a smooth, continuous process. Children gradually add more of the same types of skills that were there to begin with. (b) Other theorists think that development takes place in discontinuous stages. Children change rapidly as they step up to a new level and then change very little for a while. With each step, the child interprets and responds to the world in a qualitatively different way.

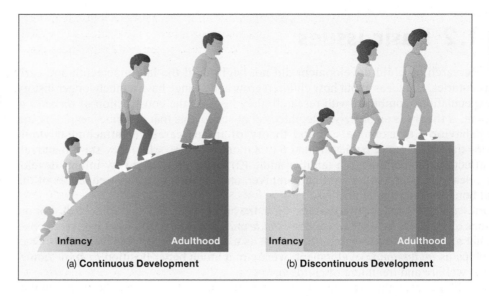

(a) **Continuous Development**   (b) **Discontinuous Development**

According to a second view, Angelo's thoughts, emotions, and behavior differ considerably from those of adults. His development is **discontinuous**—a process in which new ways of understanding and responding to the world emerge at specific times. From this perspective, Angelo is not yet able to organize objects or remember and interpret experiences as we do. Instead, he will move through a series of developmental steps, each with unique features, until he reaches the highest level of functioning.

Theories that accept the discontinuous perspective regard development as taking place in **stages**—*qualitative* changes in thinking, feeling, and behaving that characterize specific periods of development. In stage theories, development is much like climbing a staircase, with each step corresponding to a more mature, reorganized way of functioning. The stage concept also assumes that children undergo periods of rapid transformation as they step up from one stage to the next, alternating with plateaus during which they stand solidly within a stage. In other words, change is fairly sudden rather than gradual and ongoing.

Does development actually occur in a neat, orderly sequence of stages? This ambitious assumption has faced significant challenges (Collins & Hartup, 2013). Later in this chapter, we will review some influential stage theories.

1.2.2 One Course of Development or Many?

Stage theorists assume that people everywhere follow the same sequence of development. For example, in the domain of cognition, a stage theorist might try to identify the common influences that lead children to represent their world through language and make-believe play in early childhood, to think more logically and systematically in middle childhood, and to reason more systematically and abstractly in adolescence.

At the same time, the field of child development is becoming increasingly aware that children grow up in distinct **contexts**—unique combinations of personal and environmental circumstances that can result in different paths of change. For example, a shy child who fears social encounters develops in very different contexts from those of an outgoing agemate who readily seeks out other people. Children in non-Western village societies have experiences in their families and communities that differ sharply from those of children in large Western cities. These varying circumstances foster different intellectual capacities, social skills, and feelings about the self and others (Kagan, 2013a; Mistry & Dutta, 2015).

As you will see, contemporary theorists regard the contexts that shape development as many-layered and complex. On the personal side, these include heredity and biological makeup. On the environmental side, they include both immediate settings (home, child-care center, school, neighborhood) and circumstances that are more remote from children's everyday lives (community resources, societal values, historical time period). Furthermore, new evidence is increasingly emphasizing *mutually influential relations* between individuals and their contexts: Children not only are affected by but also contribute to the contexts in which they develop (Elder, Shanahan, & Jennings, 2015). Finally, researchers today are more conscious than ever before of cultural diversity in development.

1.2.3 Relative Influence of Nature and Nurture?

In addition to describing the course of child development, each theory takes a stand on a major issue about its underlying causes: how to characterize the relative influence of genetic and environmental factors in development? This is the age-old **nature–nurture controversy.** By *nature,* we mean the hereditary information we receive from our parents at the moment of conception. By *nurture,* we mean the complex forces of the physical and social world that influence our biological makeup and psychological experiences before and after birth.

Although all theories grant roles to both nature and nurture, they vary in emphasis. Consider the following questions: Is the older child's ability to think in more complex ways largely the result of a built-in timetable of growth, or is it heavily influenced by stimulation from parents and teachers? Do children acquire language because they are genetically predisposed to do so or because parents intensively teach them from an early age? And what accounts for the vast individual differences among children in height, weight, physical coordination, cognitive abilities, personality traits, and social skills? Is nature or nurture more responsible?

A theory's position on the roles of nature and nurture affects how it explains individual differences. Theorists who emphasize *stability*—that children who are high or low in a characteristic (such as verbal ability, anxiety, or sociability) will remain so at later ages—typically stress the importance of *heredity.* If they regard environment as important, they usually point to *early experiences* as establishing a lifelong pattern of behavior. Powerful negative events in the first few years, they argue, cannot be fully overcome by later, more positive ones (Bowlby, 1980; Sroufe, Coffino, & Carlson, 2010). Other theorists, taking a more optimistic view, see development as having substantial **plasticity** throughout life—as being open to change in response to influential experiences (Baltes, Lindenberger, & Staudinger, 2006; Overton & Molenaar, 2015).

Throughout this book, you will see that investigators disagree, often sharply, on the question of *stability versus plasticity.* Their answers have great applied significance. If you believe that development is largely due to nature, then providing experiences aimed at promoting change would seem to be of little value. If, on the other hand, you are convinced of the importance of early experience, then you would intervene as soon as possible, offering high-quality stimulation and support to ensure that children develop at their best. Finally, if you think that environment is profoundly influential throughout development, you would provide assistance any time children or adolescents face difficulties, in the belief that, with the help of favorable life circumstances, they can recover from negative events.

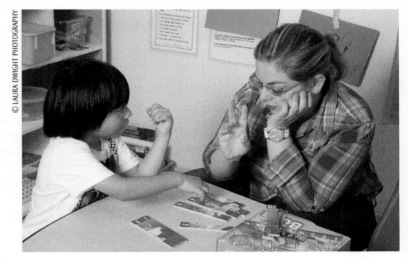

A special education teacher works with a child in a preschool classroom. Providing high-quality stimulation and support to children at risk for learning difficulties reflects the view that development has substantial *plasticity*.

1.2.4 A Balanced Point of View

So far, we have discussed basic issues of child development in terms of solutions favoring one side or the other. But as we trace the unfolding of the field in the rest of this chapter, you will see that the positions of many theorists have softened. Today, some theorists believe that both continuous and discontinuous changes occur. Many acknowledge that development has both universal features and features unique to the individual and his or her contexts. And a growing number regard heredity and environment as inseparably interwoven, each affecting the potential of the other to modify the child's traits and capacities (Lerner et al., 2014; Overton

Biology and Environment | Resilient Children

John and his best friend, Gary, grew up in a rundown, crime-ridden urban neighborhood. By age 10, each had experienced years of family conflict followed by parental divorce. Reared from then on in mother-headed households, John and Gary rarely saw their fathers. Both dropped out of high school and were in and out of trouble with the police.

Then their paths diverged. By age 30, John had fathered two children with women he never married, had spent time in prison, was unemployed, and drank alcohol heavily. In contrast, Gary had returned to finish high school, had studied auto mechanics at a community college, and became manager of a gas station and repair shop. Married with two children, he had saved his earnings and bought a home. He was happy, healthy, and well-adapted to life.

A wealth of evidence shows that environmental risks—poverty, negative family interactions and parental divorce, job loss, mental illness, and drug abuse—predispose children to future problems (Masten, 2013). Why did Gary "beat the odds" and come through unscathed?

Research on **resilience**—the ability to adapt effectively in the face of threats to development—is receiving increased attention as investigators look for ways to protect young people from the damaging effects of stressful life conditions (Wright & Masten, 2015). This interest has been inspired by several long-term studies on the relationship of life stressors in childhood to competence and adjustment in adolescence and adulthood. In each study, some individuals were shielded from negative outcomes, whereas others had lasting problems (Werner, 2013). Four broad factors seemed to offer protection from the damaging effects of stressful life events.

Personal Characteristics

A child's genetically influenced characteristics can reduce exposure to risk or lead to experiences that compensate for early stressful events. High intelligence and socially valued talents (in music or athletics, for example) increase the chances that a child will have rewarding experiences at school and in the community that offset the impact of a stressful home life. Temperament is particularly powerful. Children who have easygoing, sociable dispositions and who can readily inhibit negative emotions and impulses tend to have an optimistic outlook on life and a special capacity to adapt to change—qualities that elicit positive responses from others. In contrast, emotionally reactive and irritable children often

tax the patience of people around them (Wang & Deater-Deckard, 2013). For example, both John and Gary moved several times during their childhoods. Each time, John became anxious and angry, whereas Gary looked forward to making new friends.

A Warm Parental Relationship

A close relationship with at least one parent who provides warmth, appropriately high expectations, monitoring of the child's activities, and an organized home environment fosters resilience (Shonkoff & Garner, 2012). But this factor (as well as other sources of social support) is not independent of children's personal characteristics. Children who are self-controlled, socially responsive, and able to deal with change are easier to rear and more likely to enjoy positive relationships with parents and other people. At the same time, children may develop more attractive dispositions as a result of parental warmth and attention (Luthar, Crossman, & Small, 2015).

Social Support Outside the Immediate Family

The most consistent asset of resilient children is a strong bond with a competent, caring adult. For children who are not close to either parent, a grandparent, aunt, uncle, or teacher who forms a special relationship with the child can promote resilience (Masten, 2013). Gary received support in adolescence from his grandfather, who listened to Gary's concerns and helped him solve problems.

Associations with rule-abiding peers who value school achievement are also linked to resilience (Furman & Rose, 2015). But children who have positive relationships with adults are far more likely to establish these supportive peer ties.

Community Resources and Opportunities

Community supports—good schools, convenient and affordable health care and social services,

A 16-year-old student at a high school for the arts walks off stage after performing a musical number and is congratulated by a returning student with a leading role in the successful show, "Motown the Musical." Personal characteristics (such as exceptional talent), a strong bond with an adult (like this successful performer), and skill-building extra-curricular activities foster resilience in this teenager.

libraries, and recreation centers—foster both parents' and children's well-being. In addition, engaging in extracurricular activities at school and religious youth groups, scouting, and other organizations teach important social skills, such as cooperation, leadership, and contributing to others' welfare. As participants acquire these competencies, they gain in self-reliance, self-esteem, and community commitment (Leventhal, Dupéré, & Shuey, 2015). As a college student, Gary volunteered for Habitat for Humanity, joining a team building affordable housing in low-income neighborhoods. Community involvement offered Gary opportunities to form meaningful relationships, which further strengthened his resilience.

Research on resilience highlights the complex connections between heredity and environment (Masten, 2016). Armed with positive characteristics, which stem from native endowment, favorable rearing experiences, or both, children and adolescents can act to reduce stressful situations. But when many risks pile up, they are increasingly difficult to overcome (Evans, Li, & Sepanski Whipple, 2013). To fortify children against the negative effects of risk, interventions must not only reduce risks but also enhance children's protective relationships at home, in school, and in the community.

& Molenaar, 2015). We will discuss these contemporary ideas about nature and nurture in Chapter 2.

Finally, as you will see later in this text, the relative impact of early and later experiences varies greatly from one domain of development to another and even—as the Biology and Environment box on page 10 indicates—across individuals! Because of the complex network of factors contributing to developmental change and the challenges of isolating the effects of each, more researchers are envisioning it from a *developmental systems perspective*—as a perpetually ongoing process that is molded by a complex network of genetic/biological, psychological, and social influences (Lerner, 2015). Our review of child development theories will conclude with influential systems theories.

ASK YOURSELF

Connect ■ Provide an example of how one domain of development (physical, cognitive, or emotional/social) can affect development in another domain.

Apply ■ Review Reiko's story in the introduction to this chapter. What factors likely contributed to her resilience in the face of wartime persecution, relocation, and internment?

Reflect ■ Describe an aspect of your development that differs from a parent's or a grandparent's when she or he was your age. How might differing *contexts* be responsible?

1.3 Historical Foundations

Contemporary theories of child development are the result of centuries of change in Western cultural values, philosophical thinking about children, and scientific progress. To understand the field as it exists today, we must return to its early beginnings—to ideas about children that long preceded scientific child study but that linger as important forces in current theory and research.

1.3 Describe major historical influences on theories of child development.

1.3.1 Medieval Times

At least since medieval times—the sixth through the fifteenth centuries—childhood has been regarded as a separate period of life. Medieval painters often depicted children wearing loose, comfortable gowns, playing games, and looking up to adults. Written texts contained terms that distinguished children under age 7 or 8 from other people and that recognized even young teenagers as not fully mature. By the fourteenth century, manuals offering advice on many aspects of child care, including health, feeding, clothing, and games, were common (Heywood, 2013; Lett, 1997). Laws recognized that children needed protection from people who might mistreat them, and courts exercised leniency with lawbreaking youths because of their tender years (Hanawalt, 1993).

KUNSTHISTORISCHES MUSEUM, VIENNA, AUSTRIA/ ALI MEYER/THE BRIDGEMAN IMAGES

At least since medieval times, adults have viewed childhood as a distinct developmental period. In this detail from a sixteenth-century painting by Pieter Bruegel the Elder, children wearing loose, comfortable clothing play lively outdoor games. [*Children's Games (Kinderspiele)*: Detail of bottom center, 1560 (oil on panel) (detail of 68945), Bruegel, Pieter the Elder (c. 1525–69).]

In sum, in medieval times, if not before, clear awareness existed of children as vulnerable beings. Religious writings, however, contained contradictory depictions of children's basic nature, sometimes portraying them as possessed by the devil and in need of purification, at other times as innocent and close to angels (Hanawalt, 2003). Both ideas foreshadowed later views of childhood.

1.3.2 The Reformation

In the sixteenth century, the Puritan belief in original sin gave rise to the view that children were born evil and stubborn and had to be civilized (Heywood, 2013). Harsh, restrictive child-rearing practices were recommended to tame the depraved child. Children were dressed in stiff, uncomfortable clothing that held them in adultlike postures, and disobedient students were routinely beaten by their schoolmasters. Nevertheless, love and affection for their children prevented most Puritan parents from using extremely repressive measures (Moran & Vinovskis, 1986).

As the Puritans emigrated from England to the New World, they brought the belief that child rearing was one of their most important obligations. Although they continued to regard the child's soul as tainted by original sin, they tried to teach their sons and daughters to use reason to tell right from wrong (Clarke-Stewart, 1998). As they trained their children in self-reliance and self-control, Puritan parents gradually adopted a moderate balance between severity and permissiveness.

1.3.3 Philosophies of the Enlightenment

The seventeenth-century Enlightenment brought new philosophies that emphasized ideals of human dignity and respect. Conceptions of childhood were more humane than those of the past.

John Locke   The writings of British philosopher John Locke (1632–1704) served as the forerunner of a twentieth-century perspective that we will discuss shortly: behaviorism. Locke viewed the child as a *tabula rasa*—Latin for "blank slate." According to this idea, children begin as nothing at all; their characters are shaped entirely by experience. Locke (1690/1892) saw parents as rational tutors who can mold the child in any way they wish through careful instruction, effective example, and rewards for good behavior. He was ahead of his time in recommending child-rearing practices that present-day research supports—for example, the use of adult attention and approval as rewards, rather than money or sweets. He also opposed physical punishment: "The child repeatedly beaten in school cannot look upon books and teachers without experiencing fear and anger." Locke's philosophy led to a change from harshness toward children to kindness and compassion.

Look carefully at Locke's ideas, and you will see that he regarded development as *continuous:* Adultlike behaviors are gradually built up through the warm, consistent teachings of parents. His view of the child as a tabula rasa led him to champion *nurture*—the power of the environment to shape the child. And his faith in nurture suggests the possibility of *many courses of development* and of *high plasticity at later ages* due to new experiences. Finally, Locke's philosophy characterizes children as doing little to influence their own destiny, which is written on "blank slates" by others. This vision of a passive child has been discarded. All contemporary theories view children as active, purposeful beings who contribute substantially to their own development.

Jean-Jacques Rousseau   In the eighteenth century, French philosopher Jean-Jacques Rousseau (1712–1778) introduced a new view of childhood. Children, Rousseau claimed, are not blank slates to be filled by adult instruction. Instead, they are *noble savages,* naturally endowed with a sense of right and wrong and an innate plan for orderly, healthy growth. Unlike Locke, Rousseau believed that children's built-in moral sense and unique ways of thinking and feeling would only be harmed by adult training. His was a child-centered philosophy in which the adult should be receptive to the child's needs at each of four stages: infancy, childhood, late childhood, and adolescence.

Rousseau's philosophy includes two influential concepts. The first is the concept of *stage,* which we discussed earlier. The second is the concept of **maturation,** which refers to a genetically determined, naturally unfolding course of growth. In contrast to Locke, Rousseau saw children as determining their own destinies. And he viewed development as a *discontinuous, stagewise* process that follows a *single, unified course* mapped out by *nature.*

1.3.4 Scientific Beginnings

The study of child development evolved quickly in the late nineteenth and early twentieth centuries. Early observations of children were soon followed by improved methods and theories. Each advance contributed to the firm foundation on which the field rests today.

Darwin: Birth of Scientific Child Study   British naturalist Charles Darwin (1809–1882) joined an expedition to distant parts of the world, where he observed infinite variation among plant and animal species. He also saw that within a species, no two individuals are exactly alike. From these observations, he constructed his famous *theory of evolution.*

The theory emphasized two related principles: *natural selection* and *survival of the fittest.* Darwin (1859/2003) explained that certain species survive in particular parts of the world because they have characteristics that fit with, or are adapted to, their surroundings. Other species die off because they are less well-suited to their environments. Individuals within a species who best meet the environment's survival requirements live long enough to reproduce and pass their more beneficial characteristics to future generations. Darwin's emphasis on the adaptive value of physical characteristics and behavior eventually found its way into important developmental theories.

During his explorations, Darwin discovered that early prenatal growth is strikingly similar in many species. Other scientists concluded from Darwin's observation that the development of the human child followed the same general plan as the evolution of the human species. Although this belief eventually proved inaccurate, efforts to chart parallels between child growth and human evolution prompted researchers to make careful observations of all aspects of children's behavior. Out of these first attempts to document an idea about development, scientific child study was born.

The Normative Period   G. Stanley Hall (1844–1924), one of the most influential American psychologists of the early twentieth century, is generally regarded as the founder of the child-study movement (Cairns & Cairns, 2006). Inspired by Darwin's work, Hall and his well-known student Arnold Gesell (1880–1961) devised theories based on evolutionary ideas. They regarded development as a *maturational process*—a genetically determined series of events that unfold automatically, much like a flower (Gesell, 1933; Hall, 1904).

Hall and Gesell are remembered less for their one-sided theories than for their intensive efforts to describe all aspects of child development. They launched the **normative approach,** in which measures of behavior are taken on large numbers of individuals, and age-related averages are computed to represent typical development. Using this procedure, Hall constructed elaborate questionnaires asking children of different ages almost everything they could tell about themselves—interests, fears, imaginary playmates, dreams, friendships, everyday knowledge, and more. Similarly, through observations and parent interviews, Gesell collected detailed normative information on the motor achievements, social behaviors, and personality characteristics of infants and children.

Gesell was also among the first to make knowledge about child development meaningful to parents by telling them what to expect at each age. If, as he believed, the timetable of development is the product of millions of years of evolution, then children are naturally knowledgeable about their needs. His child-rearing advice, in the tradition of Rousseau, recommended sensitivity to children's cues (Thelen & Adolph, 1992). Along with *Dr. Spock's Baby and Child Care,* Gesell's books became a central part of a rapidly expanding popular literature for parents.

LOOK and LISTEN

Examine several recently published parenting-advice books, and identify the stance each takes on the three basic issues about child development.

The Mental Testing Movement   While Hall and Gesell were developing their theories and methods in the United States, French psychologist Alfred Binet (1857–1911) was also taking a normative approach to child development, but for a different reason. In the early 1900s, Binet and his colleague Theodore Simon were asked by Paris school officials to find a way to identify children with learning problems who needed to be placed in special classes. To address these practical educational concerns, Binet and Simon constructed the first successful intelligence test.

Binet began with a well-developed theory of intelligence. Capturing the complexity of children's thinking, he defined intelligence as good judgment, planning, and critical reflection (Sternberg & Jarvin, 2003). Then he created age-graded test items that directly measured these abilities.

In 1916, at Stanford University, Binet's test was adapted for use with English-speaking children. Since then, the English version has been known as the *Stanford-Binet Intelligence Scale.* Besides providing a score that could successfully predict school achievement, the Binet test sparked tremendous interest in individual differences in development. Comparisons of the scores of children who vary in gender, ethnicity, birth order, family background, and other characteristics became a major focus of research. And measures of intelligence rose quickly to the forefront of the nature–nurture controversy.

1.4 Mid-Twentieth-Century Theories

1.4 Describe theories that influenced child development research in the mid-twentieth century.

In the mid-twentieth century, the field of child development expanded into a legitimate discipline. A variety of theories emerged, each of which continues to have followers today. In these theories, the European concern with the child's inner thoughts and feelings contrasts sharply with the North American academic focus on scientific precision and concrete, observable behavior.

1.4.1 The Psychoanalytic Perspective

By the 1930s and 1940s, parents on both sides of the Atlantic increasingly sought professional help in dealing with children's emotional difficulties. The earlier normative movement had answered the question, What are children like? Now another question had to be addressed: How and why do children become the way they are? To treat psychological problems, psychiatrists and social workers turned to an emerging approach to personality development that emphasized each child's unique history.

According to the **psychoanalytic perspective,** children move through a series of stages in which they confront conflicts between biological drives and social expectations. How these conflicts are resolved determines the person's ability to learn, to get along with others, and to cope with anxiety. Among the many contributors to the psychoanalytic perspective, two were especially influential: Sigmund Freud, founder of the psychoanalytic movement, and Erik Erikson.

Freud's Theory   Freud (1856–1939), a Viennese physician, sought a cure for emotionally troubled adults by having them talk freely about painful events of their childhoods. Working with these recollections, he examined his patients' unconscious motivations and constructed his **psychosexual theory,** which emphasizes that how parents manage their child's sexual and aggressive drives in the first few years is crucial for healthy personality development.

In Freud's theory, three parts of the personality—id, ego, and superego—become integrated during five stages, summarized in Table 1.1. The *id,* the largest portion of the mind, is the source of basic biological needs and desires. The *ego,* the conscious, rational part of personality, emerges in early infancy to redirect the id's impulses so they are discharged in acceptable ways. Between 3 and 6 years of age, the *superego,* or conscience, develops as parents insist

TABLE 1.1　Freud's Psychosexual Stages and Erikson's Psychosocial Stages Compared

APPROXIMATE AGE	FREUD'S PSYCHOSEXUAL STAGE	ERIKSON'S PSYCHOSOCIAL STAGE
Birth–1 year	**Oral:** If oral needs are not met through sucking from breast or bottle, the individual may develop such habits as thumb sucking, fingernail biting, overeating, or smoking.	**Basic trust versus mistrust:** From warm, responsive care, infants gain a sense of trust that the world is good. Mistrust occurs if infants are neglected or handled harshly.
1–3 years	**Anal:** Toddlers and preschoolers enjoy holding and releasing urine and feces. If parents toilet train before children are ready or make too few demands, conflicts about anal control may appear in the form of extreme orderliness or disorder.	**Autonomy versus shame and doubt:** Using new mental and motor skills, children want to decide for themselves. Parents can foster autonomy by permitting reasonable free choice and not forcing or shaming the child.
3–6 years	**Phallic:** As preschoolers take pleasure in genital stimulation, Freud's Oedipus conflict for boys and Electra conflict for girls arise: Children feel a sexual desire for the other-sex parent. To avoid punishment, they give up this desire and adopt the same-sex parent's characteristics and values. As a result, the superego is formed, and children feel guilty when they violate its standards.	**Initiative versus guilt:** Through make-believe play, children gain insight into the person they can become. Initiative—a sense of ambition and responsibility—develops when parents support their child's sense of purpose. If parents demand too much self-control, children experience excessive guilt.
6–11 years	**Latency:** Sexual instincts die down, and the superego strengthens as the child acquires new social values from adults and same-sex peers.	**Industry versus inferiority:** At school, children learn to work and cooperate with others. Inferiority develops when negative experiences at home, at school, or with peers lead to feelings of incompetence.
Adolescence	**Genital:** With puberty, sexual impulses reappear. Successful development during earlier stages leads to marriage, mature sexuality, and child rearing.	**Identity versus role confusion:** By exploring values and vocational goals, young people form a personal identity. The negative outcome is confusion about future adult roles.
Early adulthood		**Intimacy versus isolation:** Young adults establish intimate relationships. Because of earlier disappointments, some individuals cannot form close bonds and remain isolated.
Middle adulthood		**Generativity versus stagnation:** Generativity means giving to the next generation through child rearing, caring for others, or productive work. The person who fails in these ways feels an absence of meaningful accomplishment.
Old age		**Integrity versus despair:** Integrity results from feeling that life was worth living as it happened. Older people who are dissatisfied with their lives fear death.

© JON ERIKSON/THE IMAGE WORKS

Erik Erikson

that children conform to the values of society. Now the ego faces the increasingly complex task of reconciling the demands of the id, the external world, and conscience—for example, the id impulse to grab an attractive toy from a playmate versus the superego's warning that such behavior is wrong. According to Freud, the relations established between id, ego, and superego during the preschool years determine the individual's basic personality.

Freud (1938/1973) believed that during childhood, sexual impulses shift their focus from the oral to the anal to the genital regions of the body. In each stage, parents walk a fine line between permitting too much or too little gratification of their child's basic needs. If parents strike an appropriate balance, children grow into well-adjusted adults with the capacity for mature sexual behavior and investment in family life.

Freud's theory was the first to stress the influence of the early parent–child relationship on development. But his perspective was eventually criticized. First, it overemphasized the influence of sexual feelings in development. Second, because it was based on the problems of sexually repressed, well-to-do adults in nineteenth-century Victorian society, it did not apply in other cultures. Finally, Freud had not studied children directly.

A child of the Kazakh people of Mongolia learns from her grandfather how to train an eagle to hunt small animals, essential for the meat-based Kazakh diet. As Erikson recognized, this parenting practice is best understood in relation to the competencies valued and needed in Kazakh culture.

Erikson's Theory   Several of Freud's followers improved on his vision. The most important is Erik Erikson (1902–1994), who expanded the picture of development at each stage. In his **psychosocial theory,** Erikson emphasized that in addition to mediating between id impulses and superego demands, the ego makes a positive contribution to development, acquiring attitudes and skills that make the individual an active, contributing member of society. A basic psychological conflict, which is resolved along a continuum from positive to negative, determines healthy or maladaptive outcomes at each stage. As Table 1.1 shows, Erikson's first five stages parallel Freud's stages, but Erikson added three adult stages. He was one of the first to recognize the lifespan nature of development.

Unlike Freud, Erikson pointed out that normal development must be understood in relation to each culture's life situation. For example, in the 1940s, he observed that the Yurok Indians of the U.S. northwest coast deprived newborns of breastfeeding for the first 10 days, instead feeding them a thin soup. At age 6 months, infants were abruptly weaned—if necessary, by having the mother leave for a few days. From our cultural vantage point, these practices may seem cruel. But Erikson explained that because the Yurok depended on salmon, which fill the river just once a year, the development of self-restraint was essential for survival. In this way, he showed that child rearing is responsive to the competencies valued and needed by the child's society.

Contributions and Limitations of the Psychoanalytic Perspective   A special strength of the psychoanalytic perspective is its emphasis on understanding the individual's unique life history. Consistent with this view, psychoanalytic theorists favor the *clinical,* or *case study, method,* which synthesizes information from a variety of sources into a detailed picture of the personality of a single child. (We will discuss this method at the end of this chapter.) Psychoanalytic theory has also inspired a wealth of research on many aspects of emotional and social development, including infant–caregiver attachment, aggression, sibling relationships, child-rearing practices, morality, gender roles, and adolescent identity.

Despite its extensive contributions, the psychoanalytic perspective is no longer in the mainstream of child development research. Psychoanalytic theorists may have become isolated from the rest of the field because they were so strongly committed to the clinical approach that they failed to consider other methods. In addition, many psychoanalytic ideas, such as psychosexual stages and ego functioning, are too vague to be tested empirically (Miller, 2016). Nevertheless, Erikson's broad outline of psychosocial change captures the essence of personality development during childhood and adolescence. Consequently, we will return to it in later chapters.

1.4.2 Behaviorism and Social Learning Theory

As the psychoanalytic perspective gained prominence, child study was also influenced by a very different perspective. According to **behaviorism,** directly observable events—stimuli and responses—are the appropriate focus of study. North American behaviorism began in the early twentieth century with the work of psychologist John Watson (1878–1958), who wanted to create an objective science of psychology.

Traditional Behaviorism   Watson was inspired by Russian physiologist Ivan Pavlov's studies of animal learning. Pavlov knew that dogs release saliva as an innate reflex when they are given food. But he noticed that his dogs started salivating before they tasted any food—when they saw the trainer who usually fed them. The dogs, Pavlov reasoned, must have learned to associate a neutral stimulus (the trainer) with another stimulus (food) that produces a reflexive response (salivation). Because of this association, the neutral stimulus alone could bring about a response resembling the reflex. Eager to test this idea, Pavlov successfully taught dogs to salivate at the sound of a bell by pairing it with the presentation of food. He had discovered *classical conditioning.*

In a historic experiment that applied classical conditioning to children's behavior, Watson taught Albert, an 11-month-old infant, to fear a neutral stimulus—a soft white rat—by presenting it several times with a sharp, loud sound, which naturally scared the baby. Little Albert, who at first had reached out eagerly to touch the furry rat, began to cry and turn his head away at the sight of it (Watson & Raynor, 1920). In fact, Albert's fear was so intense that researchers eventually challenged the ethics of studies like this one. Consistent with Locke's tabula rasa, Watson concluded that environment is the supreme force in development and that adults can mold children's behavior by carefully controlling stimulus–response associations. He viewed development as continuous—a gradual increase with age in the number and strength of these associations.

Another form of behaviorism was B. F. Skinner's (1904–1990) *operant conditioning theory.* Skinner showed that the frequency of a behavior can be increased by following it with a wide variety of *reinforcers,* such as food, praise, or a friendly smile, or decreased through *punishment,* such as disapproval or withdrawal of privileges. As a result of Skinner's work, operant conditioning became a broadly applied learning principle. We will consider these basic learning capacities further in Chapter 5.

Social Learning Theory Psychologists wondered whether behaviorism might offer a more direct and effective explanation of the development of children's social behavior than the less precise concepts of psychoanalytic theory. This sparked approaches that built on the principles of conditioning, offering expanded views of how children and adults acquire new responses.

Several kinds of **social learning theory** emerged. The most influential, devised by Albert Bandura (1925–), emphasizes *modeling,* also known as *imitation* or *observational learning,* as a powerful source of development. The baby who claps her hands after her mother does so, the child who angrily hits a playmate in the same way that he has been punished at home, and the teenager who wears the same clothes and hairstyle as her friends are all displaying observational learning. In his early research, Bandura found that diverse factors influence children's motivation to imitate: their own history of reinforcement or punishment for the behavior, the promise of future reinforcement or punishment, and even observations of the model being reinforced or punished.

Bandura's work continues to influence much research on children's social development. But today, his theory stresses the importance of *cognition,* or thinking. Bandura has shown that children's ability to listen, remember, and abstract general rules from complex sets of observed behaviors affects their imitation and learning. In fact, the most recent revision of Bandura's (1992, 2001) theory places such strong emphasis on how children think about themselves and other people that he calls it a *social-cognitive* rather than a social learning approach.

In Bandura's revised view, children gradually become more selective in what they imitate. From watching others engage in self-praise and self-blame and through feedback about the worth of their own actions, children develop *personal standards* for behavior and a *sense of self-efficacy*—the belief that their own abilities and characteristics will help them succeed. These cognitions guide responses in particular situations (Bandura, 2011, 2016). For example, imagine a parent who often remarks, "I'm glad I kept working on that task, even though it was hard," and who encourages persistence by saying, "I know you can do a good job on that homework!" Soon the child starts to view herself as hardworking and high-achieving and selects people with these characteristics as models. In this way, as children acquire attitudes, values, and convictions about themselves, they control their own learning and behavior.

© LAURA DWIGHT PHOTOGRAPHY

A child intently observes and imitates as her mother shows her how to make tortillas. Social learning theory emphasizes that children acquire many skills through modeling.

Contributions and Limitations of Behaviorism and Social Learning Theory
Behaviorism and social learning theory have had a major impact on practices with children. **Applied behavior analysis** consists of observations of relationships between behavior and environmental events, followed by systematic changes in those events based on procedures of conditioning and modeling. The goal is to eliminate undesirable behaviors and increase desirable responses. It has been used to relieve a wide range of difficulties in children and adults, ranging from poor time management and unwanted habits to serious problems such as language delays, persistent aggression, and extreme fears (Heron, Hewar, & Cooper, 2013).

Nevertheless, behaviorism and social learning theory offer too narrow a view of important environmental influences. These extend beyond immediate reinforcement, punishment, and modeled behaviors to children's rich physical and social worlds. Behaviorism and social learning theory have also been criticized for underestimating children's contributions to their own development. Bandura, with his emphasis on cognition, is unique among theorists whose work grew out of the behaviorist tradition in granting children an active role in their own learning.

1.4.3 Piaget's Cognitive-Developmental Theory

No single individual has had more influence on the contemporary field of child development than Swiss cognitive theorist Jean Piaget (1896–1980). North American investigators had been aware of Piaget's work since 1930. But they did not grant it much attention until the 1960s, mainly because Piaget's ideas were at odds with behaviorism, which dominated North American psychology in the mid-twentieth century (Watrin & Darwich, 2012). Piaget did not believe that children's learning depends on reinforcers, such as rewards from adults. According to his **cognitive-developmental theory,** children actively construct knowledge as they manipulate and explore their world.

Piaget's Stages   Piaget's view of development was greatly influenced by his early training in biology. Central to his theory is the biological concept of *adaptation* (Piaget, 1971). Just as structures of the body are adapted to fit with the environment, so structures of the mind develop to better fit with, or represent, the external world. In infancy and early childhood, Piaget claimed, children's understanding is different from adults'. For example, he believed that young babies do not realize that an object hidden from view—a favorite toy or even the parent—continues to exist. He also concluded that preschoolers' thinking is full of faulty logic. For example, children younger than age 7 commonly say that the amount of a liquid changes

In Piaget's sensorimotor stage, infants learn by acting on the world. As this 1-year-old bangs a wooden spoon on a coffee can, he discovers that his movements have predictable effects on objects, and that objects influence one another in regular ways.

In Piaget's preoperational stage, preschoolers represent their earlier sensorimotor discoveries with symbols, and language and make-believe play develop rapidly. These Cambodian children pretend to purchase items at a store.

TABLE 1.2   Piaget's Stages of Cognitive Development

STAGE	PERIOD OF DEVELOPMENT	DESCRIPTION
Sensorimotor	Birth–2 years	Infants "think" by acting on the world with their eyes, ears, hands, and mouth. As a result, they invent ways of solving sensorimotor problems, such as pulling a lever to hear the sound of a music box, finding hidden toys, and putting objects into and taking them out of containers.
Preoperational	2–7 years	Preschool children use symbols to represent their earlier sensori-motor discoveries. Development of language and make-believe play takes place. However, thinking lacks the logic of the two remaining stages.
Concrete operational	7–11 years	Children's reasoning becomes logical and better organized. School-age children understand that a certain amount of lemonade or play dough remains the same even after its appearance changes. They also organize objects into hierarchies of classes and sub-classes. However, children think in a logical, organized fashion only when dealing with concrete information they can perceive directly.
Formal operational	11 years on	The capacity for abstract, systematic thinking enables adolescents, when faced with a problem, to start with a hypothesis, deduce testable inferences, and isolate and combine variables to see which inferences are confirmed. Adolescents can also evaluate the logic of verbal statements without referring to real-world circumstances.

© BETTMANN/GETTY IMAGES

Jean Piaget

when it is poured into a different-shaped container. According to Piaget, children eventually revise these incorrect ideas in their ongoing efforts to achieve an *equilibrium,* or balance, between internal structures and information they encounter in their everyday worlds.

In Piaget's theory, as the brain develops and children's experiences expand, they move through four broad stages, each characterized by qualitatively distinct ways of thinking. Table 1.2 provides a brief description of Piaget's stages. Cognitive development begins in the *sensorimotor stage* with the baby's use of the senses and movements to explore the world. These action patterns evolve into the symbolic but illogical thinking of the preschooler in

In Piaget's concrete operational stage, school-age children think in an organized, logical fashion about concrete objects. This 7-year-old understands that the quantity of pie dough remains the same after he changes its shape from a ball to a flattened circle.

In Piaget's formal operational stage, adolescents think systematically and abstractly. These high school students grapple with abstract principles in a discussion of medical ethics in a science class.

the *preoperational stage.* Then cognition is transformed into the more organized, logical reasoning of the school-age child in the *concrete operational stage.* Finally, in the *formal operational stage,* thought becomes the abstract, systematic reasoning system of the adolescent and adult.

Piaget devised special methods for investigating how children think. Early in his career, he carefully observed his three infant children and also presented them with everyday problems, such as an attractive object that could be grasped, mouthed, kicked, or searched for. From their responses, Piaget derived his ideas about cognitive changes during the first two years. To study childhood and adolescent thought, Piaget adapted the clinical method of psychoanalysis, conducting open-ended *clinical interviews* in which a child's initial response to a task served as the basis for Piaget's next question.

Contributions and Limitations of Piaget's Theory

Piaget convinced the field that children are active learners whose minds consist of rich structures of knowledge. Besides investigating children's understanding of the physical world, Piaget explored their reasoning about the social world. His stages have sparked a wealth of research on children's conceptions of themselves, other people, and social relationships. In practical terms, Piaget's theory encouraged the development of educational philosophies and programs that emphasize children's discovery learning and direct contact with the environment.

Despite Piaget's overwhelming contributions, his theory has been challenged. Research indicates that Piaget underestimated the competencies of infants and preschoolers. When young children are given tasks scaled down in difficulty and relevant to their everyday experiences, their understanding appears closer to that of the older child and adult than Piaget assumed. Also, adolescents generally reach their full intellectual potential only in areas of endeavor in which they have had extensive education and experience. These findings have led many researchers to conclude that cognitive maturity depends heavily on the complexity of knowledge sampled and the individual's familiarity with the task (Miller, 2016).

Furthermore, children's performance on Piagetian problems can be improved with training—findings that call into question Piaget's assumption that discovery learning rather than adult teaching is the best way to foster development (Klahr, Matlin, & Jirout, 2013). Critics also point out that Piaget's stagewise account pays insufficient attention to social and cultural influences—and the resulting wide variation in thinking among children and adolescents of the same age.

Today, the field of child development is divided over its loyalty to Piaget's ideas. Those who continue to find merit in Piaget's stages often accept a modified view—one in which changes in children's thinking take place more gradually than Piaget believed (Case, 1998; Halford & Andrews, 2011; Mascolo & Fischer, 2015). Among those who disagree with Piaget's stage sequence, some have embraced an approach that emphasizes continuous gains in children's cognition: information processing. And still others have been drawn to theories that highlight the role of children's social and cultural contexts (Lourenço, 2016). We take up these approaches in the next section.

 ASK YOURSELF

Connect ■ What aspect of behaviorism made it attractive to critics of psychoanalytic theory? How did Piaget's theory respond to a major limitation of behaviorism?

Apply ■ A 4-year-old becomes frightened of the dark and refuses to go to sleep at night. How would a psychoanalyst and a behaviorist differ in their views of how this problem developed?

Reflect ■ Illustrate Bandura's ideas by describing a personal experience in which you observed and received feedback from another person that strengthened your self-efficacy. How did that person's message influence your self-perceptions and choice of models?

1.5 Recent Theoretical Perspectives

New ways of understanding the child are constantly emerging—questioning, building on, and enhancing the discoveries of earlier theories. Today, a burst of fresh approaches and research emphases is broadening our understanding of children's development.

1.5.1 Information Processing

In the 1970s and 1980s, researchers turned to the field of cognitive psychology for ways to understand the development of children's thinking. The design of digital computers that use mathematically specified steps to solve problems suggested to psychologists that the human mind might also be viewed as a symbol-manipulating system through which information flows—a perspective called **information processing.** From the time information is presented to the senses at *input* until it emerges as a behavioral response at *output,* information is actively coded, transformed, and organized.

Information-processing researchers often design flowcharts to map the precise steps individuals use to solve problems and complete tasks, much like the plans devised by programmers to get computers to perform a series of "mental operations." They seek to clarify how both task characteristics and cognitive limitations—for example, memory capacity or available knowledge—influence performance (Birney & Sternberg, 2011). To see the usefulness of this approach, let's look at an example.

In a study of problem solving, a researcher gave school-age children a pile of blocks varying in size, shape, and weight and asked them to build a bridge across a "river" (painted on a floor mat) that was too wide for any single block to span (Thornton, 1999). Whereas older children easily built successful bridges, only one 5-year-old did. Careful tracking of her efforts revealed that she repeatedly tried unsuccessful strategies, such as pushing two planks together and pressing down on their ends to hold them in place. But eventually, her experimentation triggered the idea of using the blocks as counterweights, as shown in Figure 1.3. Her mistaken procedures helped her understand why the counterweight approach worked. Although this child had no prior understanding of counterweight and balance, she arrived at just as effective a solution as older children, who started with considerable task-relevant knowledge. Her own actions within the task triggered new insights that facilitated problem solving.

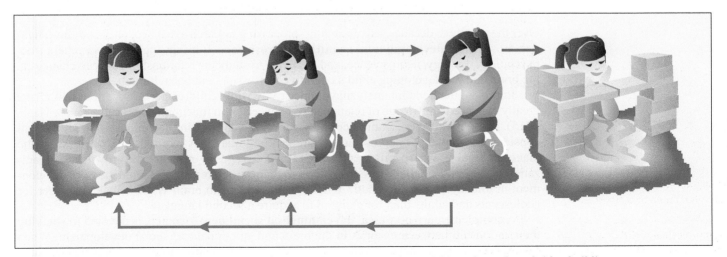

FIGURE 1.3 **Information-processing flowchart showing the steps that a 5-year-old used to solve a bridge-building problem.** Her task was to use blocks varying in size, shape, and weight, some of which were planklike, to construct a bridge across a "river" (painted on a floor mat) too wide for any single block to span. The child discovered how to counterweight and balance the bridge. The arrows reveal that even after building a successful counterweight, she returned to earlier, unsuccessful strategies, which seemed to help her understand why the counterweight approach worked. (Based on Thornton, 1999.)

Many information-processing models exist. Some, like the one just considered, track children's mastery of one or a few tasks. Others describe the human cognitive system as a whole (Gopnik & Tenenbaum, 2007; Ristic & Enns, 2015; Westermann et al., 2006). These general models are used as guides for asking questions about broad age changes in children's thinking: Does a child's ability to solve problems become more organized and "planful" with age? What strategies do younger and older children use to remember new information, and how do those strategies affect children's recall?

The information-processing approach has also been used to clarify the processing of social information. For example, flowcharts exist that track the steps children use to solve social problems (such as how to enter an ongoing play group) and acquire gender-linked preferences and behaviors (Liben & Bigler, 2002; Rubin, Begle, & McDonald, 2012). If we can identify how social problem solving and gender stereotyping arise in childhood, then we can design interventions that promote more favorable social development.

Like Piaget's theory, the information-processing approach regards children as active, sense-making beings who modify their own thinking in response to environmental demands (Halford & Andrews, 2011). But unlike Piaget's theory, it does not divide development into stages. Rather, most information-processing researchers regard the thought processes studied—perception, attention, memory, categorization of information, planning, problem solving, and comprehension of written and spoken prose—as similar at all ages but present to a lesser or greater extent. The view of development is one of continuous change.

A great strength of the information-processing approach is its commitment to rigorous research methods. Because it has provided precise accounts of how children and adults tackle many cognitive tasks, its findings have important implications for education. Currently, researchers are intensely interested in the development of an array of "executive" processes that enable children and adults to manage their thoughts, emotions, and actions. These capacities—variously labeled executive function, self-control, self-regulation, delay of gratification, and more—are essential for attaining our goals in challenging situations (Carlson, Zelazo, & Faja, 2013; Chevalier, 2015; Müller & Kerns, 2015). Executive processes are consistent predictors of both academic achievement and socially competent behavior.

Nevertheless, information processing has fallen short in some respects. It has been better at analyzing thinking into its components than at putting them back together into a comprehensive theory. And it has had little to say about aspects of children's cognition that are not linear and logical, such as imagination and creativity (Birney & Sternberg, 2011).

1.5.2 Developmental Neuroscience

Over the past three decades, as information-processing research expanded, an area of investigation arose called **developmental cognitive neuroscience.** It brings together researchers from psychology, biology, neuroscience, and medicine to study the relationship between changes in the brain and the developing child's cognitive processing and behavior patterns.

Improved methods for analyzing brain activity while children perform various tasks have greatly enhanced knowledge of relationships between brain functioning and behavior (de Haan, 2015). Armed with these brain electrical-recording and imaging techniques (which we will consider in Chapter 5), neuroscientists are tackling questions like these: How does genetic makeup combine with specific experiences at various ages to influence the growth and organization of the child's brain? How do changes in brain structures support rapid memory development in infancy and toddlerhood? What transformations in brain systems make it harder for adolescents and adults than for children to acquire a second language?

A complementary new area, **developmental social neuroscience,** is devoted to studying the relationship between changes in the brain and emotional and social development. When researchers started to tap convenient measures that are sensitive to psychological state, such as heart rate, blood pressure, and hormone levels detected in saliva, an explosion of social-neuroscience investigations followed.

Active areas of study include identification of the neural systems underlying infant gains in perception of facial expressions, adolescent risk-taking behavior, and individual differences in sociability, anxiety, aggression, and depression. One particularly energetic focus is the negative impact of extreme adversity, such as early rearing in deprived orphanages or child abuse and neglect, on brain development and cognitive, emotional, and social skills (Anderson & Beauchamp, 2013; Gunnar, Doom, & Esposito, 2015). Another burgeoning interest is uncovering the neurological bases of *autism*—the disrupted brain structures and networks that lead to the impaired social skills, language delays, and repetitive motor behavior associated with this disorder (Stoner et al., 2014). As these efforts illustrate, researchers are forging links between cognitive and social neuroscience, identifying brain systems that affect both domains of development.

Rapid progress in clarifying the types of experiences that support or undermine brain development at diverse ages is contributing to effective interventions for enhancing cognitive and social functioning. Today, researchers are examining the impact of various treatment techniques on both brain functioning and behavior (Johnson & de Haan, 2015; Lustig & Lin, 2016). Although much remains to be discovered, developmental neuroscience is broadening our understanding of development and yielding major practical applications.

Neuroscience research has so captivated the field that it poses the risk that brain properties underlying children's behavior will be granted undue importance over powerful environmental influences, such as parenting, education, and economic inequalities in families and communities. Although most neuroscientists are mindful of the complex interplay between heredity, individual experiences, and brain development, their findings have too often resulted in excessive emphasis being placed on biological processes (Kagan, 2013b). Consequently, psychological outcomes in children have sometimes been wrongly attributed mostly or entirely to genetic and brain-based causes.

Fortunately, an advantage of having many theories is that they encourage researchers to attend to previously neglected dimensions of children's lives. The final four perspectives we will discuss focus on *contexts* for development. The first of these views emphasizes that the environments to which humans have been exposed over their long evolutionary history influence the development of many capacities.

A therapist works with a 6-year-old who has autism to improve impaired social skills associated with this disorder. Developmental social neuroscientists are intensely interested in identifying the neurological bases of autism and using those findings to devise effective interventions.

1.5.3 Ethology and Evolutionary Developmental Psychology

Ethology is concerned with the adaptive, or survival, value of behavior and its evolutionary history. Its roots can be traced to the work of Darwin. Two European zoologists, Konrad Lorenz and Niko Tinbergen, laid its modern foundations. Watching diverse animal species in their natural habitats, Lorenz and Tinbergen observed behavior patterns that promote survival. The best known of these is *imprinting,* the early following behavior of certain baby birds, such as geese, which ensures that the young will stay close to the mother and be fed and protected from danger (Lorenz, 1952). Imprinting takes place during an early, restricted period of development. If the mother goose is absent during this time but an object resembling her in important features is present, young goslings may imprint on it instead.

Observations of imprinting led to a major concept in child development: the *critical period*. It is a limited time span during which the child is biologically prepared to acquire certain adaptive behaviors but needs the support of an appropriately stimulating environment. Many researchers have investigated whether complex cognitive and social behaviors must be learned during certain periods. For example, if children are deprived of adequate physical and social stimulation during their early years, will their intelligence, emotional responsiveness, and social skills be impaired?

In later chapters, we will discover that the term *sensitive period* applies better to human development than the strict notion of a critical period (Knudsen, 2004). A **sensitive period** is a time that is biologically optimal for certain capacities to emerge because the individual is

Ethology focuses on the adaptive, or survival, value of behavior and its evolutionary history, as reflected in similarities between human behavior and that of other species, including our primate relatives. Observing this chimpanzee mother cuddling her infant helps us understand the human infant–caregiver relationship.

especially responsive to environmental influences. However, its boundaries are less well-defined than are those of a critical period. Development can occur later, but it is harder to induce.

Inspired by observations of imprinting, British psychoanalyst John Bowlby (1969) applied ethological theory to understanding the human infant–caregiver relationship. He argued that infant smiling, babbling, grasping, and crying are built-in social signals that encourage the caregiver to approach, care for, and interact with the baby. By keeping the parent near, these behaviors help ensure that the infant will be fed, protected from danger, and provided with the stimulation and affection necessary for healthy growth. The development of attachment in human infants is a lengthy process involving changes in psychological structures that lead the baby to form a deep affectionate tie with the caregiver. In Chapter 7, we will consider how infant, caregiver, and family context contribute to attachment and how attachment influences later development.

Observations by ethologists have shown that many aspects of children's social behavior, including emotional expressions, aggression, cooperation, and social play, resemble those of our primate relatives. Recently, researchers have extended this effort in a new area of research called **evolutionary developmental psychology.** It seeks to understand the adaptive value of species-wide cognitive, emotional, and social competencies as those competencies change with age (King & Bjorklund, 2010; Lickliter & Honeycutt, 2013; Tomasello & Gonzales-Cabrera, 2017). Evolutionary developmental psychologists ask questions like these: What role does the newborn's visual preference for facelike stimuli play in survival? Does it support older infants' capacity to distinguish familiar caregivers from unfamiliar people? How does an early appearing "helping motive"—evident in toddlers' sharing, expressions of comfort, and efforts to assist others to attain a goal—contribute to the development of uniquely human cooperative skills? What do children learn from playing in gender-segregated peer groups that might lead to adult gender-typed behaviors, such as male dominance and female investment in caregiving?

As these examples suggest, evolutionary psychologists are not just concerned with the genetic and biological roots of development. They recognize that humans' large brain and extended childhood resulted from the need to master an increasingly complex environment, so they are also interested in the roles of experience and learning. In sum, evolutionary developmental psychology aims to understand the entire *person–environment system* (Bjorklund & Ellis, 2014). The next contextual perspective we will discuss, Vygotsky's sociocultural theory, serves as an excellent complement to the evolutionary viewpoint because it highlights the social and cultural dimensions of children's experiences.

1.5.4 Vygotsky's Sociocultural Theory

The field of child development has recently seen a dramatic increase in research demonstrating that development and culture are closely interwoven (Mistry & Dutta, 2015). The contributions of Russian psychologist Lev Vygotsky (1896–1934) and his followers have played a major role in this trend. Although Vygotsky proposed his ideas in the 1920s and early 1930s, they remained virtually unknown in North America until the 1980s, when questioning of Piaget's theory spurred psychologists and educators to search for alternative approaches to understanding cognitive development.

Vygotsky's (1934/1987) perspective, commonly referred to as **sociocultural theory,** focuses on how culture—the values, beliefs, customs, and skills of a social group—is transmitted to the next generation. According to Vygotsky, social interaction—in particular, cooperative dialogues with more knowledgeable members of society—is necessary for children to acquire the ways of thinking and behaving that make up a community's culture. Vygotsky

(1934/1987) believed that as adults and more expert peers help children master culturally meaningful activities, the communication between them becomes part of children's thinking. As children internalize features of these dialogues, they can use the language within them to guide their own thoughts and actions and to acquire new skills (Fernyhough, 2016; Lourenço, 2012). The young child instructing herself while working a puzzle or preparing a table for dinner has begun to produce the same kinds of guiding comments that an adult previously used to help her master important tasks.

Vygotsky agreed with Piaget that children are active, constructive beings. But whereas Piaget emphasized children's independent efforts to make sense of their world, Vygotsky viewed cognitive development as a *socially mediated process,* in which children depend on assistance from others as they tackle new challenges.

In Vygotsky's theory, children undergo certain stagewise changes. For example, when they acquire language, they gain in ability to participate in dialogues with others, and mastery of culturally valued competencies surges forward. When children enter school, they spend much time discussing language, literacy, and other academic concepts—experiences that encourage them to reflect on their own thinking (Kozulin, 2003). As a result, they gain dramatically in reasoning and problem solving.

At the same time, Vygotsky stressed that dialogues with experts lead to continuous changes in thinking that vary greatly from culture to culture. Consistent with this view, a major finding of cross-cultural research is that cultures select different tasks for children's learning, and social interaction surrounding those tasks leads to competencies essential for success in a particular culture. For example, in industrialized nations, teachers help people learn to read, drive a car, or use a computer. Among the Zinacanteco Indians of southern Mexico, adult experts guide young girls as they master complicated weaving techniques (Greenfield, 2004). In Brazil, child candy sellers with little or no schooling develop sophisticated mathematical abilities as the result of buying candy from wholesalers, pricing it in collaboration with adults and experienced peers, and bargaining with customers on city streets (Saxe, 1988).

According to Lev Vygotsky, shown here with his daughter, many cognitive processes and skills are socially transferred from more knowledgeable members of society to children. Vygotsky's sociocultural theory helps explain the wide cultural variation in cognitive competencies.

Research stimulated by Vygotsky's theory reveals that children in every culture develop unique strengths. Nevertheless, Vygotsky's emphasis on culture and social experience led him to neglect the biological side of development. Although he recognized the importance of heredity and brain growth, he said little about their role in cognitive change. Furthermore, Vygotsky's focus on social transmission of knowledge meant that, compared with other theorists, he placed less emphasis on children's capacity to shape their own development.

Followers of Vygotsky stress that children strive for social connection, actively participating in the conversations and social activities from which their development springs. From these joint experiences, they not only acquire culturally valued practices but also modify and transform those practices (Daniels, 2011; Rogoff, 2003). Contemporary sociocultural theorists grant the individual and society balanced, mutually influential roles.

With her father's guidance, a child from the Kamtsa ethnic group in Colombia learns to make a papier mâché doll to carry in a community festival. Consistent with Vygotsky's theory, she acquires a culturally valued skill through interaction with an adult expert.

1.5.5 Ecological Systems Theory

Urie Bronfenbrenner (1917–2005) is responsible for an approach to child development that moved to the forefront of the field because it offers the most differentiated and complete account of interrelated contextual influences on children's development. **Ecological systems theory** views the child as developing within a complex *system* of relationships affected by multiple levels of the surrounding environment. Because the child's biologically influenced

FIGURE 1.4   **Structure of the environment in ecological systems theory.** The *microsystem* concerns relations between the child and the immediate environment; the *mesosystem,* connections among immediate settings; the *exosystem,* social settings that affect but do not contain the child; and the *macrosystem,* the values, laws, customs, and resources of the culture that affect activities and interactions at all inner layers. The *chronosystem* (not pictured) is not a specific context. Instead, it refers to the dynamic, ever-changing nature of the child's environment.

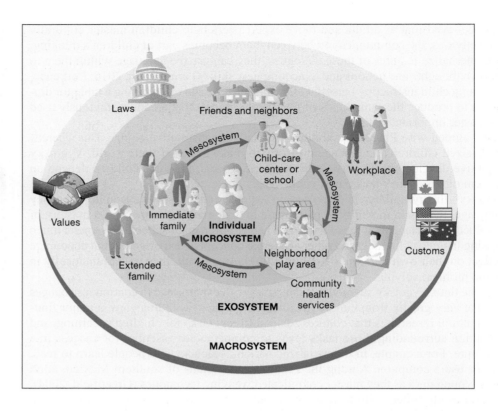

dispositions join with environmental forces to mold development, Bronfenbrenner characterized his perspective as a *bioecological model* (Bronfenbrenner & Morris, 2006).

Bronfenbrenner envisioned the environment as a series of interrelated, nested structures that form a complex functioning whole, or *system.* These include but also extend beyond the home, school, and neighborhood settings in which children spend their everyday lives (see Figure 1.4). Each level joins with the others to powerfully affect development.

The Microsystem   The innermost level of the environment, the **microsystem,** consists of activities and interaction patterns in the child's immediate surroundings. Bronfenbrenner emphasized that to understand child development at this level, we must keep in mind that all relationships are *bidirectional:* Adults affect children's behavior, but children's biologically and socially influenced characteristics—their physical attributes, personalities, and capacities—also affect adults' behavior. A friendly, attentive child is likely to evoke positive, patient reactions from parents, whereas an easily upset, emotionally negative child is more likely to receive impatience, restriction, and punishment (Streit et al., 2017). When these reciprocal interactions occur often over time, they have an enduring impact on development.

Third parties—other individuals in the microsystem—also affect the quality of any two-person relationship. If they are supportive, interaction is enhanced. For example, when parents encourage each other in their child-rearing roles, each engages in more effective parenting. In contrast, marital conflict is associated with inconsistent discipline and hostility toward children. In response, children often react with fear and anxiety or anger and aggression, and their well-being suffers (Cummings & Davies, 2010; Low & Stocker, 2012). Similarly, children can affect their parents' relationship in powerful ways. In one investigation, parental reports of child-rearing stressors predicted worsening couple communication, in the form of criticism, defensiveness, anger, and other expressions of negativity, which undermined parents' relationship satisfaction (Zemp et al., 2017).

The Mesosystem   The second level of Bronfenbrenner's model, the **mesosystem,** encompasses connections between microsystems, such as home, school, neighborhood, and child-care center. For example, a child's academic progress depends not just on activities that take place in classrooms but also on parent involvement in school life and on the extent to which academic learning is carried over into the home (Wang & Sheikh-Khalil, 2014). Similarly, parent–child interaction at home is likely to affect caregiver–child interaction in the child-care setting, and vice versa. Each relationship is more likely to support development when links are forged between home and child care, in the form of visits and cooperative exchanges of information.

The Exosystem   The **exosystem** consists of social settings that do not contain children but that nevertheless affect children's experiences in immediate settings. These can be formal organizations, such as parents' workplaces, their religious institutions, and community health and welfare services. Flexible work schedules, paid maternity and paternity leave, and sick leave for parents whose children are ill are examples of ways that work settings can support child rearing and, indirectly, enhance children's development. Exosystem supports also can be informal, such as parents' social networks—friends and extended-family members who provide advice, companionship, and even financial assistance.

Research confirms the negative impact of a breakdown in exosystem activities. Families who are affected by unemployment or who are socially isolated, with few personal or community-based ties, show increased rates of conflict and child abuse (Tomyr, Ouimet, & Ugnat, 2012). Refer to the Social Issues: Health box on page 28 for an additional illustration of the power of the exosystem to affect family functioning and children's development.

The Macrosystem   The outermost level of Bronfenbrenner's model, the **macrosystem,** consists of cultural values, laws, customs, and resources. The priority that the macrosystem gives to children's needs affects the support they receive at inner levels of the environment. For example, in countries that require generous workplace benefits for employed parents and high-quality standards for child care, children are more likely to have favorable experiences in their immediate settings. As you will see in later chapters, such programs are far less available in the United States than in other industrialized nations (Pew Research Center, 2013a).

An Ever-Changing System   The environment is not a static force that affects children in a uniform way. Instead, it is ever-changing. Important life events, such as the birth of a sibling, the beginning of school, a move to a new neighborhood, or parents' divorce, modify existing relationships between children and their environments, producing new conditions that affect development. In addition, the timing of environmental change affects its impact. The arrival of a new sibling has very different consequences for a homebound toddler than for a school-age child with many relationships and activities beyond the family.

Bronfenbrenner called the temporal dimension of his model the **chronosystem** (the prefix *chrono-* means "time"). Life changes can be imposed on the child, as in the examples just given. Alternatively, they can arise from within the child because as children get older, they select, modify, and create many of their own settings and experiences. How they do so depends on their physical, intellectual, and personality characteristics and their environmental opportunities. Therefore, in ecological systems theory, development is neither entirely controlled by environmental circumstances nor driven solely by inner dispositions. Rather, children and their environments form a network of interdependent effects. Notice how our discussion of resilient children on pages 9–11 illustrates this idea. You will see many more examples in later chapters.

1.5.6 Development as a Dynamic System

Today, researchers recognize both consistency and variability in children's development and want to do a better job of explaining variation. Consequently, a new wave of systems theorists focuses on how children, in interacting with their complex contexts, alter their behavior to attain more advanced functioning. According to this **dynamic systems perspective,** the child's mind, body, and physical and social worlds form an *integrated system* that guides mastery of new skills. The system is *dynamic,* or constantly in motion. A change in any part of it—from

LOOK and LISTEN

Ask a parent to explain his or her most worrisome child-rearing challenge. Describe one source of support at each level of Bronfenbrenner's model that could ease parental stress and promote child development.

Social Issues: Health | Family Chaos Undermines Children's Well-Being

All of us can recall days during our childhoods when family routines—regular mealtime, bedtime, homework time, and parent–child reading and playtime—were disrupted, perhaps because of a change in a parent's job, a family illness, or a busy season of after-school sports. In some families, however, absence of daily structure is nearly constant, yielding a chaotic home life that interferes with healthy development (Fiese & Winter, 2010). An organized family life provides a supportive context for warm, involved parent–child interaction, which is essential to children's well-being.

Family chaos is linked to economic disadvantage—especially, single mothers with limited incomes struggling to juggle the challenges of transportation, shift jobs, unstable child-care arrangements, and other daily hassles. But chaos is not limited to such families. Across income levels and ethnic groups, mothers and fathers, but especially mothers, report more multitasking while caring for children—for example, preparing dinner while helping with homework, or reading to children while checking emails (Craig & Brown, 2017; Radesky et al., 2016). Parents who frequently multitask experience greater psychological stress.

Parental multitasking disrupts family routines. For example, only about half of U.S. families of school-age children report eating together regularly (Child Trends, 2014b). Frequency of family meals is associated with wide-ranging positive outcomes—in childhood, enhanced language development and academic achievement and fewer behavior problems; and in adolescence, reduced sexual risk taking, alcohol and drug use, and mental health problems. Shared mealtimes also increase the likelihood of a healthy diet and protect against obesity and adolescent eating disorders (Fiese & Schwartz, 2008; Lora et al., 2014). As these findings suggest, regular mealtimes are a general indicator of an organized family life and positive parent involvement.

A chaotic home life interferes with warm, relaxed parent–child interaction and contributes to behavior problems. Exosystem influences, such as excessive workplace pressures, can trigger disorganized family routines.

But family chaos can prevail even when families do engage in joint activities. Disorganized family meals involving harsh or lax parental discipline and hostile, disrespectful communication are associated with children's adjustment difficulties (Fiese, Foley, & Spagnola, 2006; Nomaguchi & Milkie, 2016). As family time becomes pressured, its orderly structure diminishes, and parental stress escalates while warm parent–child engagement disintegrates.

Diverse circumstances can trigger a pileup of limited parental emotional resources, breeding family chaos. In addition to *microsystem* and *mesosystem* influences (parents with mental health problems, parental separation and divorce, single parents with few or no supportive relationships), the *exosystem* is powerful: When family time is at the mercy of external forces—parents commuting several hours a day to and from work, child-care arrangements often failing, parents

experiencing excessive workplace pressures or job loss—family routines are threatened.

Family chaos contributes to children's behavior problems, above and beyond its negative impact on parenting effectiveness (Fiese & Winter, 2010; Martin, Razza, & Brooks-Gunn, 2012). Chaotic surroundings induce in children a sense of being hassled and feelings of powerlessness, which engender anxiety and low self-esteem.

Exosystem and macrosystem supports—including work settings with favorable family policies and high-quality child care that is affordable and reliable—can help prevent escalating demands on families that give way to chaos. In one community, a child-care center initiated a take-home dinner program. Busy parents could special-order a healthy, reasonably priced family meal, ready to go at day's end to aid in making the family dinner a routine that enhances children's development.

brain growth to physical or social surroundings—disrupts the current organism–environment relationship. When this happens, the child actively reorganizes his or her behavior so the various components of the system work together again but in a more complex, effective way (Mascolo & Fischer, 2015; Spencer, Perone, & Buss, 2011; Thelen & Smith, 2006).

Researchers adopting a dynamic systems perspective try to find out just how children attain new levels of organization by studying their behavior while they are in transition (Thelen & Corbetta, 2002). For example, when presented with an attractive toy, how does a 3-month-old baby who engages in many, varied hand and arm movements discover how to reach for it?

On hearing a new word, how does a 2-year-old figure out the category of objects or events to which it refers?

Dynamic systems theorists acknowledge that a common human genetic heritage and basic regularities in children's physical and social worlds yield certain universal, broad outlines of development. But children's biological makeup, interests and goals, everyday tasks, and the people who support children in mastery of those tasks vary greatly, leading to wide individual differences in specific skills. Even when children master the same skills, such as walking, talking, or adding and subtracting, they often do so in unique ways. And because children build competencies by engaging in real activities in real contexts, different skills vary in maturity within the same child. From this perspective, development cannot be characterized as a single line of change. As Figure 1.5 shows, it is more like a web of fibers branching out in many directions, each representing a different skill area that may undergo both continuous and stagewise transformations (Fischer & Bidell, 2006; Mascolo & Fischer, 2015).

The dynamic systems view has been inspired by other scientific disciplines, especially biology and physics. It also draws on information-processing and contextual theories—evolutionary developmental psychology, sociocultural theory, and ecological systems theory. Dynamic systems research is still in its early stages. The perspective has largely been applied to children's motor and cognitive skills, but investigators are increasingly turning to it to explain emotional and social development as well (Kloep et al., 2016; Kunnen, 2012). Consider the young teenager, whose body and reasoning powers are changing massively and who also is confronting a multiplicity of new academic and social challenges. Researchers following parent–child interaction over time found that the transition to adolescence disrupted family communication. It became unstable and variable for several years—a mix of positive, neutral, and negative exchanges (Granic et al., 2003). Gradually, as parent and adolescent devised new, more mature ways of relating to one another, the system reorganized and stabilized. Once again, interaction became predictable and mostly positive.

As dynamic systems research illustrates, today investigators are tracking and analyzing development in all its complexity. In doing so, they hope to move closer to an all-encompassing approach to understanding change.

The dynamic systems perspective views the child's mind, body, and physical and social worlds as a continuously reorganizing, integrated system. In response to the physical and psychological changes of adolescence, this teenager and his mother must develop a new, more mature relationship.

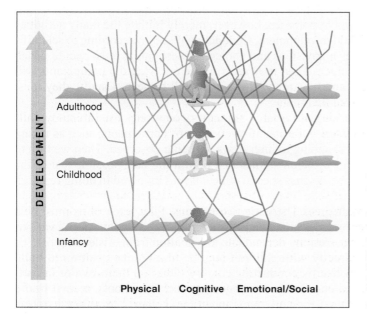

FIGURE 1.5 **The dynamic systems view of development.** Rather than envisioning a single line of stagewise or continuous change (refer to Figure 1.2 on page 8), development from a dynamic systems view is more like a web of fibers branching out in many directions. Each strand in the web represents a skill within the major domains of development—physical, cognitive, and emotional/social. The differing directions of the strands signify possible variations in paths and outcomes as the child masters skills necessary to participate in diverse contexts. The interconnections of the strands at each row of "hills" portray stagelike changes—periods of major transformation in which various skills work together as a functioning whole. As the web expands, skills become more numerous, complex, and effective. (Based on Fischer & Bidell, 2006.)

ASK YOURSELF

Connect ■ Explain how each recent theoretical perspective regards children as active contributors to their own development.

Apply ■ Mario wants to find out precisely how children of different ages recall stories. Desiree is interested in how adult–child communication in different cultures influences children's storytelling. Which theoretical perspective has Mario probably chosen? How about Desiree? Explain.

Reflect ■ To illustrate the chronosystem in ecological systems theory, select an important event from your childhood, such as a move to a new neighborhood, a class with an inspiring teacher, or parental divorce. How did the event affect you? How might its impact have differed had you been five years younger? How about five years older?

 # 1.6 Comparing Child Development Theories

1.6 Identify the stand taken by each major theory on the basic issues of child development.

In the preceding sections, we reviewed major theoretical perspectives in child development research that differ in many respects. First, they focus on different domains of development. Some, such as the psychoanalytic perspective and ethology, emphasize emotional and social development. Others, such as Piaget's cognitive-developmental theory, information processing, and Vygotsky's sociocultural theory, stress changes in thinking. The remaining approaches—behaviorism, social learning theory, evolutionary developmental psychology, ecological systems theory, and the dynamic systems perspective—encompass many aspects of children's functioning. Second, every theory contains a point of view about child development.

As we conclude our review of theoretical perspectives, identify the stand that each theory takes on the basic issues presented at the beginning of this chapter. Then check your analysis of the theories against Table 1.3 on page 31.

1.7 Studying the Child

1.7a Describe research methods commonly used to study children.

1.7b Distinguish between correlational and experimental research designs, noting strengths and limitations of each.

1.7c Describe designs for studying development, noting strengths and limitations of each.

LOOK and LISTEN

Ask a teacher, counselor, social worker, or nurse to describe a question about development he or she would like researchers to address. After reading the rest of this chapter, recommend research strategies best suited to answering that question, citing their strengths and limitations.

In every science, research usually begins with a *hypothesis*—a prediction drawn directly from a theory. Theories and hypotheses, however, merely initiate the many activities that result in sound evidence on child development. Conducting research according to scientifically accepted procedures involves many steps and choices. Investigators must decide which participants, and how many, to include. Then they must figure out what the participants will be asked to do and when, where, and how many times each will be seen. Finally, they must examine and draw conclusions from their data.

In the following sections, we look at research strategies commonly used to study children. We begin with *research methods*—the specific activities of participants, such as taking tests, answering questionnaires, responding to interviews, or being observed. Then we turn to *research designs*—overall plans for research studies that permit the best possible test of the investigator's hypothesis. Finally, we discuss special ethical issues involved in doing research on children.

Why learn about research strategies? There are two reasons. First, each of us must be a wise and critical consumer of knowledge. Knowing the strengths and limitations of various research strategies is important in separating dependable information from misleading results. Second, individuals who work directly with children may be in a unique position to build bridges between research and practice by conducting studies, either on their own or in partnership with experienced investigators. Community agencies such as schools, mental health facilities, museums, and parks and recreation programs sometimes collaborate with researchers

TABLE 1.3   Stances of Major Theories on Basic Issues in Child Development

THEORY	CONTINUOUS OR DISCONTINUOUS DEVELOPMENT?	ONE COURSE OF DEVELOPMENT OR MANY?	RELATIVE INFLUENCE OF NATURE AND NURTURE?
Psychoanalytic perspective	*Discontinuous:* Psychosexual and psycho-social development takes place in stages.	*One course:* Stages are assumed to be universal.	*Both nature and nurture:* Innate impulses are channeled and controlled through child-rearing experiences. *Early experiences* set the course of later development.
Behaviorism and social learning theory	*Continuous:* Development involves an increase in learned behaviors.	*Many possible courses:* Behaviors reinforced and modeled may vary from child to child.	*Emphasis on nurture:* Development results from conditioning and modeling. *Both early and later experiences* are important.
Piaget's cognitive-developmental theory	*Discontinuous:* Cognitive development takes place in stages.	*One course:* Stages are assumed to be universal.	*Both nature and nurture:* Development occurs as the brain grows and children exercise their innate drive to discover reality in a generally stimulating environment. *Both early and later experiences* are important.
Information processing	*Continuous:* Children gradually improve in perception, attention, memory, and problem-solving skills.	*One course:* Changes studied characterize most or all children.	*Both nature and nurture:* Children are active, sense-making beings who modify their thinking as the brain grows and they confront new environmental demands. *Both early and later experiences* are important.
Ethology and evolutionary developmental psychology	*Both continuous and discontinuous:* Children gradually develop a wider range of adaptive behaviors. Sensitive periods occur, in which qualitatively distinct capacities emerge fairly suddenly.	*One course:* Adaptive behaviors and sensitive periods apply to all members of a species.	*Both nature and nurture:* Heredity combines with experiences and learning to influence the development of adaptive behaviors. In sensitive periods, *early experiences* set the course of later development.
Vygotsky's socio-cultural theory	*Both continuous and discontinuous:* Language acquisition and schooling lead to stagewise changes. Dialogues with more expert members of society also lead to continuous changes that vary from culture to culture.	*Many possible courses:* Socially mediated changes in thought and behavior vary from culture to culture.	*Both nature and nurture:* Heredity, brain growth, and dialogues with more expert members of society jointly contribute to development. *Both early and later experiences* are important.
Ecological systems theory	*Not specified.*	*Many possible courses:* Children's characteristics join with environmental forces at multiple levels to mold development in unique ways.	*Both nature and nurture:* Children's characteristics and the reactions of others affect each other in a bidirectional fashion. Layers of the environment influence child-rearing experiences. *Both early and later experiences* are important.
Dynamic systems perspective	*Both continuous and discontinuous:* Change in the system is always ongoing. Stagelike transformations occur as children reorganize their behavior so components of the system work as a functioning whole.	*Many possible courses:* Biological makeup, everyday tasks, and social experiences vary, yielding wide individual differences in specific skills.	*Both nature and nurture:* The child's mind, body, and physical and social surroundings form an integrated system that guides mastery of new skills. *Both early and later experiences* are important.

in designing, implementing, and evaluating interventions aimed at enhancing children's development (Tseng, Easton, & Supplee, 2017). To broaden these efforts, a basic understanding of the research process is essential.

1.7.1 Common Research Methods

How does a researcher choose a basic approach to gathering information about children? Common methods include systematic observation, self-reports (such as questionnaires and interviews), clinical or case studies of a single child, and ethnographies of the life circumstances of a specific group of children. Table 1.4 summarizes the strengths and limitations of these methods.

TABLE 1.4 Strengths and Limitations of Common Research Methods

METHOD	DESCRIPTION	STRENGTHS	LIMITATIONS
Systematic Observation			
Naturalistic observation	Observation of behavior in natural contexts.	Reflects participants' everyday behaviors.	Cannot control conditions under which participants are observed.
Structured observation	Observation of behavior in a laboratory, where conditions are the same for all participants.	Grants each participant an equal opportunity to display the behavior of interest. Permits study of behaviors rarely seen in everyday life.	May not yield observations typical of participants' behavior in everyday life.
Self-Reports			
Clinical interview	Flexible interviewing procedure in which the investigator obtains a complete account of the participant's thoughts.	Comes as close as possible to the way participants think in everyday life. Great breadth and depth of information can be obtained in a short time.	May not result in accurate reporting of information. Flexible procedure makes comparing individuals' responses difficult.
Structured interview, questionnaires, and tests	Self-report instruments in which each participant is asked the same questions in the same way.	Permits comparisons of participants' responses and efficient data collection. Researchers can specify answer alternatives that participants might not think of in an open-ended interview.	Does not yield the same depth of information as a clinical interview. Responses are still subject to inaccurate reporting.
Clinical, or Case Study, Method			
	A full picture of one individual's psychological functioning, obtained by combining interviews, observations, and sometimes test scores.	Provides rich, descriptive insights into processes of development.	May be biased by researchers' theoretical preferences. Findings cannot be applied to individuals other than the participant.
Ethnography			
	Participant observation of a culture or distinct social group. By making extensive field notes, the researcher tries to capture the culture's unique values and social processes.	Provides a more complete and accurate description than can be derived from a single observational visit, interview, or questionnaire.	May be biased by researchers' values and theoretical preferences. Findings cannot be applied to individuals and settings other than the ones studied.

Systematic Observation   Observations of the behavior of children, and of adults who are important in their lives, can be made in different ways. One approach is to go into the field, or natural environment, and observe the behavior of interest—a method called **naturalistic observation.**

A study of preschoolers' responses to their peers' distress provides a good example of this technique (Farver & Branstetter, 1994). Observing 3- and 4-year-olds in child-care centers, the researchers recorded each instance of a child crying and the reactions of nearby children— whether they ignored, watched curiously, commented on the child's unhappiness, scolded or teased, or shared, helped, or expressed sympathy. Caregiver behaviors—explaining why a child was crying, mediating conflict, or offering comfort—were noted to see if adult sensitivity was related to children's caring responses. A strong relationship emerged. The great strength of naturalistic observation is that investigators can see directly the everyday behaviors they hope to explain.

Naturalistic observation also has a major limitation: Not all children have the same opportunity to display a particular behavior in everyday life. In the study just described, some children might have witnessed a child crying more often than others or been exposed to more cues for positive social responses from caregivers. For this reason, they might have displayed more compassion.

Researchers commonly deal with this difficulty by making **structured observations,** in which the investigator sets up a laboratory situation that evokes the behavior of interest so that every participant has an equal opportunity to display the response. In one such study, 2-year-olds' emotional reactions to harm they thought they had caused were observed. Each child was asked to take care of a rag doll that had been modified so its leg would fall off when the child picked it up. Then, to make the child feel at fault when the leg detached, an adult "talked for" the doll by saying, "Ow!" Researchers recorded children's facial expressions of sadness and concern for the injured doll, efforts to help the doll, and body tension—responses that indicated remorse and a desire to make amends. In addition, mothers were asked to engage in brief conversations about emotions with their children (Garner, 2003). Toddlers whose mothers more often explained the causes and consequences of emotion were more likely to express concern for the injured doll.

Structured observation permits greater control over the research situation than does naturalistic observation. In addition, the method is especially useful for studying behaviors—such as parent–child or friendship interactions—that

In naturalistic observation, the researcher goes into the field and records the behavior of interest. Here, a research assistant observes children at preschool. She may be focusing on their playmate choices, cooperation, helpfulness, or conflicts.

investigators rarely have an opportunity to see in everyday life. When aggressive and nonaggressive 10-year-old boys were observed playing games with their best friend in a laboratory, the aggressive boys and their friends more often violated game rules, cheated, and encouraged each other to engage in these dishonest acts. In addition, observers rated these boys' interactions as angrier and less cooperative than the interactions of nonaggressive boys and their friends (Bagwell & Coie, 2004). The researchers concluded that aggressive boys' close peer ties provide a context in which they practice hostility and other negative behaviors, which may contribute to their antisocial behavior.

In this study, antisocial boys' laboratory interactions were probably similar to their natural behaviors. The boys acted negatively even though they knew they were being observed. But the great disadvantage of structured observations is that most of the time, we cannot be certain that participants behave in the laboratory as they do in their natural environments.

Systematic observation provides invaluable information on how children and adults behave, but it tells us little about the reasoning behind their responses. For this kind of information, researchers must turn to self-report techniques.

Self-Reports   Self-reports ask research participants to provide information on their perceptions, thoughts, abilities, feelings, attitudes, beliefs, and past experiences. They range from relatively unstructured interviews to highly structured interviews, questionnaires, and tests.

In a **clinical interview,** a flexible, conversational style is used to probe for the participant's point of view. In the following example, Piaget questioned a 5-year-old child about his understanding of dreams:

> *Where does the dream come from?*—I think you sleep so well that you dream.—*Does it come from us or from outside?*—From outside.—*When you are in bed and you dream, where is the dream?*—In my bed, under the blanket. I don't really know. If it was in my stomach, the bones would be in the way and I shouldn't see it.—*Is the dream there when you sleep?*—Yes, it is in the bed beside me. (Piaget, 1926/1930, pp. 97–98)

Although a researcher conducting clinical interviews with more than one child would typically ask the same first question to establish a common task, individualized prompts are used to provide a fuller picture of each child's reasoning.

The clinical interview has two major strengths. First, it permits people to display their thoughts in terms that are as close as possible to the way they think in everyday life. Second, the clinical interview can provide a large amount of information in a fairly brief period (Sharp et al., 2013). For example, in an hour-long session, we can obtain a wide range of child-rearing information from a parent—much more than we could capture by observing for the same amount of time.

A major limitation of the clinical interview has to do with the accuracy with which people report their thoughts, feelings, and experiences. Some participants, wishing to please the interviewer, may make up answers. When asked about past events, some may have trouble recalling exactly what happened. And because the clinical interview depends on verbal ability and expressiveness, it may underestimate the capacities of individuals who have difficulty putting their thoughts into words.

The clinical interview has also been criticized because of its flexibility. When questions are phrased differently for each participant, variations in responses may reflect the manner of interviewing rather than real differences in the way people think about a topic. **Structured interviews** (including tests and questionnaires), in which each participant is asked the same questions in the same way, eliminate this problem. These instruments are also much more efficient. Answers are briefer, and researchers can obtain written responses from an entire group at the same time. Furthermore, by listing answer alternatives, researchers can indicate the specific activities and behaviors of interest—ones that participants might not think of in an open-ended clinical interview. For example, when parents were asked what they considered "the most important thing for children to prepare them for life," over 60 percent checked "to think for themselves" when this alternative appeared on a list. Yet only 5 percent thought of it during a clinical interview (Schwarz, 2008).

Nevertheless, structured interviews do not yield the same depth of information as a clinical interview. And they can still be affected by inaccurate reporting.

The Clinical, or Case Study, Method   An outgrowth of psychoanalytic theory, the **clinical,** or **case study, method** brings together a wide range of information on one child, including interviews, observations, and sometimes test scores. The aim is to obtain as complete a picture as possible of that child's psychological functioning and the experiences that led up to it.

The clinical method is well-suited to studying the development of certain types of individuals who are few in number but vary widely in characteristics. For example, the method has been used to find out what contributes to the accomplishments of *prodigies*—extremely gifted children who attain adult competence in a field before age 10.

In one investigation, researchers conducted case studies of eight child prodigies nationally recognized for talents in such areas as art, music, and mathematics (Ruthsatz & Urbach,

2012). One child began playing the violin at 28 months, had won regional competitions as a 5-year-old, and by age 7 had performed as a soloist at New York's Carnegie Hall and Lincoln Center. Another child started reading as an infant, took college-level classes beginning at age 8, and published a paper in a mathematics journal at 13. Across the eight cases, the researchers noticed interesting patterns, including above-average intelligence and exceptionally high scores on tests of memory and attention to detail. Notably, several prodigies in the study had relatives with autism, a condition that also involves intense attention to detail. The researchers concluded that although child prodigies generally do not display the social and cognitive deficits of individuals with autism, the two groups may share an underlying genetic trait that affects the functioning of certain brain regions, heightening perception and attention.

The clinical method yields richly detailed case narratives that offer valuable insights into the multiplicity of factors affecting development. Nevertheless, like all other

Using the clinical, or case study, method, this researcher interacts with a 3-year-old during a visit to her preschool. Interviews and observations will contribute to an in-depth picture of this child's psychological functioning.

© LAURA DWIGHT PHOTOGRAPHY

methods, it has drawbacks. Because information often is collected unsystematically and subjectively, researchers' theoretical preferences may bias their observations and interpretations. In addition, investigators cannot assume that their conclusions apply, or generalize, to anyone other than the child or children studied (Simons, 2014). Even when patterns emerge across several cases, as occurred in the study of child prodigies, it is wise to confirm these with other research strategies.

Methods for Studying Culture   To study the impact of culture on child development, researchers adjust the methods just considered or tap procedures specially devised for cross-cultural and multicultural research. Which approach investigators choose depends on their research goals.

Sometimes researchers are interested in characteristics that are believed to be universal but that vary in degree from one culture to the next: Are parents warmer or more directive in some cultures than in others? How strong are gender stereotypes in different nations? In each instance, several cultural groups will be compared, and all participants must be questioned or observed in the same way. Therefore, researchers draw on the observational and self-report procedures we have already considered, adapting them through translation so they can be understood in each cultural context. For example, to study cultural variation in parent–adolescent relationships, the same questionnaire, asking for ratings on such items as "I often start a conversation with my parents about what happens in school" or "My parents can tell when I'm upset about something," is given to all participants (Qin & Pomerantz, 2013). Still, investigators must be mindful of cultural differences in familiarity with self-report instruments that may bias their findings (van de Vijver, 2011).

A Western researcher working with Zinacantec Mayan children in Chiapas, Mexico, uses the ethnographic method to gather information about how they learn through everyday activities.

At other times, researchers want to uncover the *cultural meanings* of children's and adults' behaviors by becoming as familiar as possible with their way of life. To achieve this goal, researchers rely on a method borrowed from the field of anthropology—**ethnography.** Like the clinical method, ethnographic research is a descriptive, qualitative technique. But instead of aiming to understand a single individual, it is directed toward understanding a culture or a distinct social group through *participant observation.* Typically, the researcher spends months and sometimes years in the cultural community, participating in its daily life. Extensive field notes are gathered, consisting of a mix of observations, self-reports from members of the culture, and careful interpretations by the investigator (Case, Todd, & Kral, 2014). Later, these notes are put together into a description of the community that tries to capture its unique values and social processes.

The ethnographic method assumes that by entering into close contact with a social group, researchers can understand the beliefs and behaviors of its members in a way not possible with an observational visit, interview, or questionnaire. Some ethnographies take in many aspects of children's experience, as one researcher did in describing what it is like to grow up in an isolated mountain village in Peru. Others focus on one or a few settings and issues—for example, youth resilience in an economically disadvantaged Alaska-Native community (Bolin, 2006; Rasmus, Allen, & Ford, 2014). Researchers may supplement traditional self-report and observational methods with ethnography if they suspect that unique meanings underlie cultural differences, as the Cultural Influences box on page 36 reveals.

Ethnographers strive to minimize their influence on the culture they are studying by becoming part of it. Nevertheless, as with clinical research, investigators' cultural values and theoretical commitments sometimes lead them to observe selectively or misinterpret what they see. Finally, the findings of ethnographic studies cannot be assumed to generalize beyond the people and settings in which the research was conducted.

Cultural Influences | Immigrant Youths: Adapting to a New Land

Over the past several decades, increasing numbers of immigrants have come to the United States, fleeing war and persecution in their homelands or seeking better life chances. Today, one-fourth of U.S. children and adolescents have foreign-born parents, mostly originating from Latin American, the Caribbean, Asia, and Africa. Although some move with their parents, nearly 90 percent of young people from immigrant families are U.S.-born citizens (Migration Policy Institute, 2015).

How well are these youths—now the fastest growing sector of the U.S. youth population—adapting to their families' new country? To find out, researchers use multiple research methods: academic testing, questionnaires assessing psychological adjustment, and in-depth ethnographies.

Academic Achievement and Adjustment

Although educators and laypeople often assume that the transition to a new country has a negative impact on psychological well-being, many children of immigrant parents adapt amazingly well. Students who are first generation (foreign-born) or second generation (American-born, with immigrant parents) often achieve in school as well as or better than students of native-born parents (Hao & Woo, 2012; Hernandez, Denton, & Blanchard, 2011). And compared with their agemates, adolescents from immigrant families are less likely to commit delinquent and violent acts, use drugs and alcohol, have early sex, miss school because of illness, or suffer from obesity (Saucier et al., 2002; Supple & Small, 2006).

These outcomes are strongest for Chinese, Filipino, Japanese, Korean, and East Indian youths (Fuligni, 2004; Louie, 2001; Portes & Rumbaut, 2005). Variation in adjustment is greater among Mexican, Central American, and Southeast Asian (Hmong, Cambodian, Laotian, Thai, and Vietnamese) young people, who show elevated rates of school failure and dropout, delinquency, teenage parenthood, and drug use (Gurrola, Ayón, & Moya Salas, 2016; Pong & Landale, 2012). Disparities in parental economic resources, education, English-language proficiency, and support of children contribute to these trends.

Still, many first- and second-generation youths whose parents face considerable financial hardship and who speak little English are successful (Suárez-Orozco, Abo-Zena, & Marks, 2015). Factors other than income are responsible—notably, family values and strong ethnic-community ties.

These children prepare to take part in the Parade of Nations that is part of the annual DC Latino Festival in the U.S. capital. Cultural values that engender allegiance to family and community promote high achievement and protect many immigrant youths from involvement in risky behaviors.

Family and Ethnic-Community Influences

Ethnographies reveal that immigrant parents view education as the surest way to improve life chances (Feliciano & Lanuza, 2015). Aware of the challenges their children face, they typically emphasize trying hard. They remind their children that, because educational opportunities were not available in their native countries, they themselves are often limited to menial jobs.

Adolescents from these families internalize their parents' valuing of academic achievement, endorsing it more strongly than agemates with native-born parents. Recall from the chapter introduction, for example, how Reiko amused herself playing "school" and "library" while confined in an internment camp. Because minority ethnicities usually stress allegiance to family and community over individual goals, first- and second-generation young people often feel a strong sense of obligation to their parents. They view school success as both their own and their parents' success and as an important way of repaying their parents for the hardships they have endured (van Geel & Vedder, 2011; Burgos, Al-Adeimi, & Brown, 2017). Both family relationships and school achievement protect these youths from risky behaviors.

Immigrant parents of successful youths typically develop close ties to an ethnic community, which exerts additional control through a high consensus on values and constant monitoring of young people's activities. The following comments capture the power of these family and community forces:

- *A 16-year-old girl from Central America describes the supportive adults in her neighborhood:* They ask me if I need anything for school. If we go to a store and I see a notebook, they ask me if I want it. They give me advice, tell me that I should be careful of the friends I choose. They also tell me to stay in school to get prepared. They tell me I am smart. They give me encouragement. (Suárez-Orozco, Pimental, & Martin, 2009, p. 733).

- *A teenage boy from Mexico discusses the importance of family in his culture:* A really big part of the Hispanic population [is] being close to family, and the family being a priority all the time. I hate people who say, "Why do you want to go to a party where your family's at? Don't you want to get away from them?" You know, I don't really get tired of them. I've always been really close to them. That connection to my parents, that trust that you can talk to them, that makes me Mexican. (Bacallao & Smokowski, 2007, p. 62)

The experiences of well-adjusted immigrant youths are not problem-free. Many encounter racial and ethnic prejudices and experience tensions between family values and the new culture. In the long term, however, family and community cohesion, supervision, and high expectations promote favorable outcomes.

ASK YOURSELF

1.7.2 General Research Designs

In deciding on a research design, investigators choose a way of setting up a study that permits them to test their hypotheses with the greatest degree of certainty possible. Two main designs are used in all research on human behavior: *correlational* and *experimental.*

Correlational Design   In a **correlational design,** researchers gather information on individuals, generally in natural life circumstances without altering their experiences. Then they look at relationships between participants' characteristics and their behavior or development. Suppose we want to answer the following questions: Do parents' styles of interacting with their children have any bearing on children's intelligence? How do child abuse and neglect affect children's feelings about themselves and their relationships with peers? In these and many other instances, the conditions of interest are difficult or impossible to arrange and control and must be studied as they currently exist.

Correlational studies have one major limitation: We cannot infer cause and effect. For example, if we were to find that parental interaction is related to children's intelligence, we would not know whether parents' behavior actually *causes* intellectual differences among children. In fact, the opposite is possible. The behaviors of highly intelligent children may be so attractive that they cause parents to interact more favorably. Or a third variable that we did not even consider, such as the amount of noise and distraction in the home, may cause changes in both parental interaction and children's intelligence.

In correlational studies, and in other types of research designs, investigators often examine relationships by using a **correlation coefficient**—a number that describes how two measures, or variables, are associated with each other. We will encounter the correlation coefficient in discussing research findings throughout this book, so let's look at what it is and how it is interpreted: A correlation coefficient can range in value from +1.00 to −1.00. The *magnitude,* or *size, of the number* shows the *strength of the relationship.* A zero correlation indicates no relationship; the closer the value is to either +1.00 or −1.00, the stronger the relationship (see Figure 1.6). For instance, a correlation of −.78 is high, −.52 is moderate, and −.18 is low. Note, however that correlations of +.52 and −.52 are equally strong. The *sign of the number* refers to the *direction of the relationship.* A positive sign (+) means that as one variable *increases,* the other also *increases.* A negative sign (−) indicates that as one variable *increases,* the other *decreases.*

Let's look at some examples of how a correlation coefficient works. One researcher reported a +.57 correlation between the variety of words mothers used when conversing with their children at age 2½ and the size of the children's vocabularies a year later, at age 3½ (Rowe, 2012). This is a moderate correlation, which indicates that mothers whose conversations contained a greater diversity of words had preschoolers who were more advanced in language development. In two other studies, child-rearing practices were related to toddlers' compliance in consistent ways. First, maternal warmth and sensitivity during play correlated positively with 2-year-olds' willingness to comply with their mother's directive to clean up toys, at +.34 (Feldman & Klein, 2003). Second, the extent to which mothers spoke harshly, interrupted, and controlled their 4-year-olds' play correlated negatively with children's compliance, at −.31 for boys and −.42 for girls (Smith et al., 2004).

All these investigations found a relationship between parenting and young children's behavior. Are you tempted to conclude that parenting influenced children's responses?

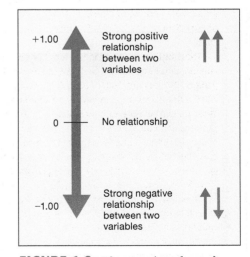

FIGURE 1.6 The meaning of correlation coefficients. The magnitude of the number indicates the *strength* of the relationship. The sign of the number (+ or −) indicates the *direction* of the relationship.

Although the researchers in these studies suspected this was so, they could not be sure of cause and effect. Can you think of other possible explanations? Finding a relationship in a correlational study suggests that tracking down its cause—using a more powerful experimental strategy, if possible—would be worthwhile.

Experimental Design   An **experimental design** permits inferences about cause and effect because researchers use an evenhanded procedure to assign people to two or more treatment conditions. In an experiment, the events and behaviors of interest are divided into two types: independent and dependent variables. The **independent variable** is the one the investigator expects to cause changes in another variable. The **dependent variable** is the one the investigator expects to be influenced by the independent variable. Cause-and-effect relationships can be detected because the researcher directly *controls* or *manipulates* changes in the independent variable by exposing participants to the treatment conditions. Then the researcher compares their performance on measures of the dependent variable.

In one *laboratory experiment,* researchers explored the impact of teaching families to engage in healthy, respectful communication (independent variable) on parents' efforts at conflict resolution and teenage children's adjustment (dependent variables) (Miller-Graff, Cummings, & Bergman, 2016). Family triads, composed of two parents and their adolescent child, were randomly assigned to one of three groups: (1) *parents-only communication training,* consisting of four weekly sessions in which parents, guided by specially trained research assistants, discussed and practiced techniques aimed at improving family communication, (2) *parents plus adolescent communication training,* also four sessions, in which adolescent children participated with their parents, and (3) *self-study control,* in which parents were given a syllabus to guide them through four weeks of readings on effective family relationships.

As Figure 1.7 shows, at the conclusion of the sessions, parents in both training groups showed greater gains than controls in observed constructive conflict resolution. Furthermore, at a six-month follow-up, parents who had improved in conflict resolution as the result of training viewed their teenagers as having fewer emotional and behavior problems. The experiment revealed that even a brief family program emphasizing interactive learning can improve family relationships.

In experimental studies, investigators must take special precautions to control for participants' characteristics that could reduce the accuracy of their findings. For example, in the study just described, if more children from homes high in parental conflict ended up in the self-study control group, we would not be able to tell what produced the results—the independent variable or the children's home experiences. Level of parental conflict would be a **confounding variable**—so closely associated with the independent variable that the researcher cannot tell which one is actually responsible for changes in the dependent variable. To protect against this problem, researchers engage in **random assignment** of participants to treatment conditions. By using an unbiased procedure, such as drawing numbers out of a hat or flipping a coin, investigators increase the chances that participants' characteristics will be equally distributed across treatment groups.

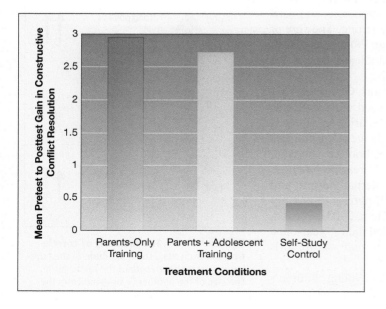

FIGURE 1.7   Impact of training in effective family communication on parents' constructive conflict resolution. A laboratory experiment revealed that training aimed at improving family interaction, either with parents-only or with parents plus their adolescent child, led to greater gains in parents' constructive conflict resolution than did a self-study control condition, in which parents merely read about effective family relationships. (Based on Miller-Graff, Cummings, & Bergman, 2016.)

Sometimes researchers combine random assignment with another technique called *matching.* In this procedure, participants are measured before the experiment on the factor in question—in our example, exposure to parental conflict. Then children high and low on that factor are assigned in equal numbers to each treatment condition. In this way, the experimental groups are deliberately matched, or made equivalent, on characteristics that are likely to distort the results.

Modified Experimental Designs: Field and Natural Experiments   Most experiments are conducted in laboratories, where researchers can achieve the maximum possible control over treatment conditions. But as we have already indicated, findings obtained in laboratories may not apply to natural situations. In *field experiments,* investigators assign participants randomly to treatment conditions in natural settings. In the experiment just described, we can conclude that inducing effective family communication in the laboratory yields improved parent-rated child adjustment. But do findings like these carry over to everyday life?

Another study sheds light on this question. Ethnically diverse, poverty-stricken families with a 2-year-old child were scheduled for a home visit, during which researchers assessed family functioning and child problem behaviors by asking parents to respond to questionnaires and videotaping parent–child interaction. Then the families were randomly assigned to either an intervention condition, called the Family Check-Up, or a no-intervention control group. The intervention consisted of three home-based sessions in which a consultant gave parents feedback about their child-rearing practices and their child's adjustment, explored parents' willingness to improve, identified community services appropriate to each family's needs, and offered follow-up sessions on parenting practices and other concerns (Brennan et al., 2013; Dishion et al., 2008; Shaw et al., 2016). Findings showed that families assigned to the Family Check-Up (but not controls) gained in positive parenting, which predicted a reduction in child problem behaviors and higher academic achievement when the children reached school age. Lessening of aggression was greatest for children living in neighborhoods with the deepest poverty.

Often researchers cannot randomly assign participants and manipulate conditions in the real world, as these investigators were able to do. Sometimes they can compromise by conducting *natural,* or *quasi-, experiments.* Treatments that already exist, such as different family environments, child-care centers, or schools, are compared. These studies differ from correlational research only in that groups of participants are carefully chosen to ensure that their characteristics are as much alike as possible. In this way, investigators do their best to rule out alternative explanations for their treatment effects. But despite these efforts, natural experiments cannot achieve the precision and rigor of true experimental research.

To help you compare correlational and experimental designs, Table 1.5 on page 40 summarizes their strengths and limitations. It also includes an overview of designs for studying development, to which we turn next.

1.7.3 Designs for Studying Development

Scientists interested in child development require information about the way research participants change over time. To answer questions about development, they must extend correlational and experimental approaches to include measurements at different ages using longitudinal and cross-sectional designs.

The Longitudinal Design   In a **longitudinal design,** participants are studied repeatedly, and changes are noted as they get older. The time spanned may be relatively short (a few months to several years) or very long (a decade or even a lifetime).

The longitudinal approach has two major strengths. First, because it tracks the performance of each person over time, researchers can identify common patterns as well as individual differences in development. Second, longitudinal studies permit investigators to examine relationships between early and later events and behaviors. Let's illustrate these ideas.

TABLE 1.5   Strengths and Limitations of Research Designs

DESIGN	DESCRIPTION	STRENGTHS	LIMITATIONS
General			
Correlational	The investigator obtains information on participants without altering their experiences.	Permits study of relationships between variables.	Does not permit inferences about cause-and-effect relationships.
Experimental	Through random assignment of participants to treatment conditions, the investigator manipulates an independent variable and examines its effect on a dependent variable. Can be conducted in the laboratory or in the natural environment.	Permits inferences about cause-and-effect relationships.	When conducted in the laboratory, findings may not generalize to the real world. In *field experiments,* control over the treatment is usually weaker than in the laboratory. In *natural,* or *quasi-, experiments,* lack of random assignment substantially reduces the precision of research.
Developmental			
Longitudinal	The investigator studies the same group of participants repeatedly at different ages.	Permits study of common patterns and individual differences in development and relationships between early and later events and behaviors.	Age-related changes may be distorted because of biased sampling, selective attrition, practice effects, and cohort effects.
Cross-sectional	The investigator studies groups of participants differing in age at the same point in time.	More efficient than the longitudinal design. Not plagued by such problems as participant dropout and practice effects.	Does not permit study of individual developmental trends. Age differences may be distorted because of cohort effects.
Sequential	The investigator conducts several similar cross-sectional or longitudinal studies (called sequences). These might study participants over the same ages but in different years, or they might study participants over different ages but during the same years.	When the design includes longitudinal sequences, permits both longitudinal and cross-sectional comparisons. Also reveals cohort effects. Permits tracking of age-related changes more efficiently than the longitudinal design.	May have the same problems as longitudinal and cross-sectional strategies, but the design itself helps identify difficulties.
Microgenetic	The investigator presents children with a novel task and follows their mastery over a series of closely spaced sessions.	Offers insights into how change occurs.	Requires intensive study of participants' moment-by-moment behaviors. The time required for participants to change is difficult to anticipate. Practice effects may distort developmental trends.

A group of researchers wondered whether children who display extreme personality styles—either angry and explosive or shy and withdrawn—retain the same dispositions when they become adults. In addition, the researchers wanted to know what kinds of experiences promote stability or plasticity in personality and what consequences explosiveness and shyness have for long-term adjustment. To answer these questions, the researchers delved into the archives of the Guidance Study, a well-known longitudinal investigation initiated in 1928 at the University of California, Berkeley, that continued for several decades (Caspi, Elder, & Bem, 1987, 1988).

Results revealed that the two personality styles were moderately stable. Between ages 8 and 30, a good number of individuals remained the same, whereas others changed substantially. When stability did occur, it appeared to be due to a "snowballing effect," in which children evoked responses from adults and peers that acted to maintain their dispositions. Explosive youngsters were likely to be treated with anger, whereas shy children were apt to be ignored. As a result, the two types of children came to view their social worlds differently. Explosive children tended to view others as hostile; shy children regarded them as unfriendly (Caspi & Roberts, 2001). Together, these factors led explosive children to sustain or increase their unruliness and shy children to continue to withdraw.

Persistence of extreme personality styles affected many areas of adult adjustment. For men, the results of early explosiveness were most apparent in their work lives, in the form of conflicts with supervisors, frequent job changes, and unemployment. Since few women in this sample of an earlier generation worked after marriage, their family lives were most affected. Explosive girls grew up to be hotheaded wives and mothers who were especially prone to divorce. Sex differences in the long-term consequences of shyness were even greater. Men who had been withdrawn in childhood were delayed in marrying, becoming fathers, and developing stable careers. However, because a withdrawn, unassertive style was socially acceptable for females in the mid-twentieth century, women with shy personalities showed no special adjustment problems.

Problems in Conducting Longitudinal Research   Despite their strengths, longitudinal investigations pose a number of problems. For example, *biased sampling*—the failure to enlist participants who adequately represent the population of interest—is a common problem. People who willingly participate in research that requires them to be observed and tested over many years are likely to have distinctive characteristics—perhaps a special appreciation for the scientific value of research, or a unique need or desire for medical, mental health, or educational services provided by the investigators. Furthermore, longitudinal samples generally become more biased as the investigation proceeds because of *selective attrition.* Participants may move away or drop out of the study for other reasons, and the ones who remain may differ in important ways from the ones who do not continue. Also, from repeated study, participants may become "test-wise." Their performance may improve as a result of *practice effects*—better test-taking skills and increased familiarity with the test—not because of factors commonly associated with development.

The most widely discussed threat to the accuracy of longitudinal findings is cultural–historical change, commonly called **cohort effects.** Longitudinal studies examine the development of *cohorts*—children born at the same time, who are influenced by particular cultural and historical conditions. Results based on one cohort may not apply to children developing at other times. For example, look back at the findings on female shyness described in the preceding section, which were gathered in the 1950s. Today's shy adolescent girls and young women tend to be poorly adjusted—a difference that may be due to changes in gender roles in Western societies. Persistently shy individuals, whether male or female, feel more anxious, depressed, have fewer social supports, and do less well in educational and career attainment than their agemates (Karevold et al., 2012; Poole, Van Lieshout, & Schmidt, 2017; Schmidt et al., 2017). Similarly, a longitudinal study of social development carried out in the second decade of the twenty-first century would probably have resulted in quite different findings had it been conducted around the time of World War II or during the Great Depression of the 1930s.

Cohort effects don't just operate broadly on an entire generation. They also occur when specific experiences influence some children but not others in the same generation, as Reiko's internment as a Japanese-American during World War II illustrates. Children who witnessed the terrorist attacks of September 11, 2001—either because they were near Ground Zero or because they saw injury and death on TV—provide another example. They were far more likely than other children to display persistent emotional problems, including intense fear, anxiety, and depression (Mullett-Hume et al., 2008; Rosen & Cohen, 2010).

Finally, longitudinal research, especially when conducted over multiple years, requires large investments of

© SPENCER PLATT/GETTY IMAGES

These refugees being helped ashore in Greece are among millions of Syrians who have been displaced by or have fled their country's civil war. Their lives have been dramatically altered by their wartime and migration experiences—a cohort effect deemed the largest humanitarian crisis of contemporary times.

time, effort, and resources. To maximize the benefits of these costly endeavors, investigators are increasingly carrying out massive longitudinal projects that gather information from large, representative samples on many aspects of development. Then they create multipurpose longitudinal data banks, which any researcher can access.

For example, the Early Childhood Longitudinal Study (ECLS), sponsored by the U.S. Department of Education in collaboration with other federal agencies, includes several nationally representative samples with thousands of participants, some followed from birth to kindergarten and others from kindergarten through eighth grade. The ECLS data bank has been used to study a wide variety of topics, including predictors of childhood obesity, effects of maternal stress during pregnancy on early development, the impact of family and preschool experiences on kindergarten readiness, and the influence of elementary school teaching practices on later academic performance. Investigations like the ECLS are enabling much more research to capitalize on the unique strengths of the longitudinal design.

The Cross-Sectional Design   The length of time it takes for many behaviors to change, even in limited longitudinal studies, has led researchers to turn to a more efficient strategy for studying development. In the **cross-sectional design,** groups of people differing in age are studied at the same point in time. Because participants are measured only once, researchers need not be concerned about such difficulties as participant dropout or practice effects.

An investigation in which students in grades 3, 6, 9, and 12 filled out a questionnaire about their sibling relationships provides a good illustration (Buhrmester & Furman, 1990). Findings revealed that sibling interaction was characterized by greater equality and less power assertion with age. Also, feelings of sibling companionship declined during adolescence. Several factors likely contributed to these age differences. As later-born children become more competent and independent, they no longer need, and are probably less willing to accept, direction from older siblings. And as adolescents move from psychological dependence on the family to greater involvement with peers, they may have less time and emotional need to invest in siblings (Hindle & Sherwin-White, 2014). As you will see in Chapter 13, subsequent research has confirmed these intriguing ideas about the development of sibling relationships.

Problems in Conducting Cross-Sectional Research   Despite its convenience, cross-sectional research does not provide evidence about change at the level at which it actually occurs: the individual. For example, in the cross-sectional study of sibling relationships just discussed, comparisons are limited to age-group averages. We cannot tell if important individual differences exist. Indeed, longitudinal findings reveal that adolescents vary considerably in the changing quality of their sibling relationships. Although many become more distant, others become more supportive and intimate, still others more rivalrous and antagonistic (Dirks et al., 2015; Dunn, 2014).

Cross-sectional studies—especially those that cover a wide age span—have another problem. Like longitudinal research, they can be threatened by cohort effects. For example, comparisons of 5-year-old cohorts and 15-year-old cohorts—groups born and reared in different years—may not really represent age-related changes. Instead, they may reflect unique experiences associated with the time period in which the age groups were growing up.

1.7.4 Improving Developmental Designs

Researchers have devised ways of building on the strengths and minimizing the weaknesses of longitudinal and cross-sectional approaches. Several modified developmental designs have resulted.

Sequential Designs   To overcome some of the limitations of traditional developmental designs, investigators sometimes use **sequential designs,** in which they conduct several similar cross-sectional or longitudinal studies (called *sequences*). The sequences might study participants over the same ages but in different years, or they might study participants over

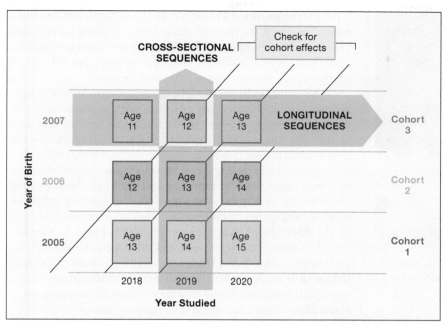

FIGURE 1.8 **Example of a sequential design.** Three cohorts, born in 2005 (blue), 2006 (orange), and 2007 (pink), respectively, are followed longitudinally for three years. Testing the cohorts at overlapping ages enables researchers to check for cohort effects by comparing participants born in different years when they reach the same age (see diagonals). In a study using this design, same-age adolescents who were members of different cohorts scored similarly on a questionnaire assessing family harmony, indicating no cohort effects. By following each cohort for just three years, the investigator could infer a developmental trend across five years, from ages 11 to 15.

different ages but during the same years. As the illustration in Figure 1.8 reveals, some sequential designs combine longitudinal and cross-sectional strategies, an approach that has three advantages:

● We can find out whether cohort effects are operating by comparing participants of the same age who were born in different years. In Figure 1.8, for example, we can compare the longitudinal samples at ages 12, 13, and 14. If they do not differ, we can rule out cohort effects.

● We can make both longitudinal and cross-sectional comparisons. If outcomes are similar, we can be especially confident about the findings.

● The design is efficient. In our example, we can find out about change over a five-year period by following each cohort for three years.

In a study that used a design similar to the one depicted in Figure 1.8, researchers wanted to find out if family harmony changed as young people experienced the dramatic physical and psychological changes of adolescence (Baer, 2002). A questionnaire assessing emotional bonding among family members was given to three adolescent cohorts, each born a year apart. In longitudinal follow-ups, each cohort again responded to the questionnaire during the following two years. Findings for the three cohorts converged: All reported (1) a slight decline in family harmony with age and (2) similar levels of family harmony as they reached the same age, confirming that there were no cohort effects. Therefore, the researcher concluded that family closeness diminishes steadily from sixth to tenth grade, noting, however, that the change is mild—not enough to threaten supportive family ties.

When sequential designs do uncover cohort effects, they help explain diversity in development. Yet to date, only a small number of sequential studies have been conducted.

© LAURA DWIGHT PHOTOGRAPHY

How do these kindergarteners make use of manipulatives to master arithmetic? A microgenetic design, which permits researchers to follow children's mastery of a challenging task, is uniquely suited to answering this question.

The Microgenetic Design   In the examples of developmental research we have discussed, observations of children are fairly widely spaced. When we observe once a year or every few years, we can describe development, but we cannot easily capture the processes that produce it.

The **microgenetic design,** an adaptation of the longitudinal approach, presents children with a novel task and tracks their mastery over a series of closely spaced sessions. Within this "microcosm" of development, researchers observe how change occurs (Flynn & Siegler, 2007; Kuhn, 1995). The microgenetic design has been used to trace infants' mastery of motor skills, such as crawling and walking; the strategies children use to acquire new knowledge in reading, math, or science; and gains in children's social competence (Adolph et al., 2012; Booker & Dunsmore, 2017; Laski & Siegler, 2014). Investigators try to conduct microgenetic research on participants who are in transition—ready to master the particular skill being studied. Because of their interest in studying developmental change as it takes place, dynamic systems researchers often choose the microgenetic design.

Microgenetic studies are difficult to carry out. Researchers must pore over hours of recorded information, analyzing each participant's behavior many times. Also, the time required for children to change is hard to anticipate. It depends on a careful match between the child's capabilities and the demands of the task. Finally, as in other longitudinal research, practice effects can distort microgenetic findings. When researchers overcome these challenges, they reap the benefits of seeing development as it takes place.

Combining Experimental and Developmental Designs   Perhaps you noticed that all the examples of longitudinal and cross-sectional research we have considered permit only correlational, not causal, inferences. Sometimes researchers can explore the causal link between experiences and development by experimentally manipulating the experiences. If, as a result, development improves, then we have strong evidence for a causal association. Today, research that combines an experimental strategy with either a longitudinal or a cross-sectional approach, with the aim of enhancing development, is becoming increasingly common.

1.8 Ethics in Research on Children

1.8 Discuss special ethical concerns that arise in doing research on children.

Research into human behavior creates ethical issues because, unfortunately, the quest for scientific knowledge can sometimes exploit people. When children take part in research, the ethical concerns are especially complex. Children are more vulnerable than adults to physical and psychological harm. In addition, immaturity makes it difficult or impossible for children to evaluate for themselves what participation in research will mean. For these reasons, special ethical guidelines for research on children have been developed by the federal government, by funding agencies, and by research-oriented associations such as the American Psychological Association (2017) and the Society for Research in Child Development (2007).

Table 1.6 presents a summary of children's basic research rights drawn from these guidelines. After examining them, read about the following research situations, each of which poses a serious ethical dilemma. What precautions do you think should be taken in each instance? Is either so threatening to children's well-being that it should not be carried out?

- In a study of moral development, an investigator wants to assess children's ability to resist temptation by videotaping their behavior without their knowledge. She promises 7-year-olds an attractive prize for solving difficult puzzles but tells them not to look at

TABLE 1.6 **Children's Research Rights**

RESEARCH RIGHT	DESCRIPTION
Protection from harm	Children have the right to be protected from physical or psychological harm in research. If in doubt about the harmful effects of research, investigators should seek the opinion of others. When harm seems possible, investigators should find other means for obtaining the desired information or abandon the research.
Informed consent/assent	All participants, including children, have the right to have explained to them, in language appropriate to their level of understanding, all aspects of the research that may affect their willingness to participate. When children are participants, informed consent of parents as well as others who act on the child's behalf (such as school officials) should be obtained, preferably in writing, along with the child's written or verbal assent (agreement) for participation. Children, and the adults responsible for them, have the right to discontinue participation in the research at any time.
Privacy	Children have the right to concealment of their identity on all information collected in the course of research. They also have this right with respect to written reports and any informal discussions about the research.
Knowledge of results	Children and the adults responsible for them have the right to be informed of the results of research in language that is appropriate to their level of understanding.
Beneficial treatments	If experimental treatments believed to be beneficial are under investigation, children in control groups have the right to alternative beneficial treatments (if available) or to the same treatment (if found to be effective) once the research is complete.

Sources: American Psychological Association, 2017; Society for Research in Child Development, 2007.

a classmate's correct solutions, which are deliberately placed at the back of the room. Informing children ahead of time that cheating is being studied or that their behavior is being monitored will defeat the purpose of the study.

- A researcher is interviewing fifth graders about their experiences with bullying. One child describes frequent name-calling and derogatory comments by her older sister. Although the child is unhappy, she wants to handle the problem on her own. If the researcher alerts the child's parents to provide protection and help, he will violate his promise to keep participants' responses private.

Virtually every organization that has devised ethical principles for research has concluded that conflicts arising in research situations do not have simple right or wrong answers. The ultimate responsibility for the ethical integrity of research lies with the investigator. But researchers are advised—and often required—to seek advice from others. Committees for this purpose, called *institutional review boards (IRBs),* exist in colleges, universities, and other institutions, which follow U.S. federal guidelines for the protection of human subjects. If any risks to the safety and welfare of participants outweigh the worth of the research for advancing knowledge and improving life conditions, then preference is always given to the participants' interests.

The ethical principle of *informed consent* requires special interpretation when participants cannot fully appreciate the research goals and activities. Parental consent is meant to protect the safety of children. In addition, researchers should obtain the agreement of other individuals who act on children's behalf, such as institutional officials when research is conducted in schools, child-care centers, or hospitals. This is especially important when research includes special groups, such as abused children, whose parents may not always represent their best interests.

Extra steps must be taken to protect children's research rights. Although this 8-year-old responds to the interviewer's questions, she may not know that she has the right to withdraw from the study at any time without negative consequences.

As soon as they are old enough to appreciate the purpose of the research, and certainly by age 7, children's own informed *assent,* or agreement, should be obtained in addition to parental consent. Around age 7, changes in children's thinking permit them to better understand basic scientific principles and the needs of others. Researchers should respect and enhance these capacities by giving school-age children a full explanation of research activities in language they can understand (Birbeck & Drummond, 2015).

Extra care must be taken when telling children that the information they provide will be kept confidential and that they can end their participation at any time. Even adolescents may not understand, and sometimes do not believe, these promises (Bruzzese & Fisher, 2003). In certain ethnic minority communities, where deference to authority, maintaining pleasant relationships, and meeting the needs of a guest (the researcher) are highly valued, children and parents may be particularly likely to consent or assent when they would rather not do so (Fisher et al., 2002).

Careful attention to informed consent and assent helps resolve dilemmas about revealing children's responses to parents, teachers, or other authorities when those responses suggest that the child's welfare is at risk. Children can be told in advance that if they report that someone is harming them, the researcher will tell an appropriate adult to take action to ensure the child's safety (Jennifer & Cowie, 2009).

Finally, all ethical guidelines advise that special precautions be taken in the use of deception and concealment, as occurs when researchers observe children from behind one-way mirrors, give them false feedback about their performance, or misrepresent the real purpose of the research. When these procedures are used with adults, *debriefing,* in which the researcher provides a full account and justification of the activities, occurs after the research session is over. Debriefing should also be done with children, and it sometimes works well. But young children often lack the cognitive skills to understand the reasons for deceptive procedures and, despite explanations, even older children may leave the research situation questioning the honesty of adults. Ethical standards permit deception if investigators satisfy IRBs that such practices are necessary. Nevertheless, because deception may have serious emotional consequences for some children, many experts in research ethics believe that investigators should use it only if the risk of harm is minimal.

ASK YOURSELF

Connect ■ Review the study of the Family Check-Up, described on page 39. Why is it ethically important for researchers to offer the intervention to the no-intervention control group after completion of the study? (Hint: Refer to Table 1.6 on page 45.)

Apply ■ A researcher compares children who attended summer leadership camps with children who attended athletic camps. She finds that those who attended leadership camps are friendlier. Should the investigator tell parents that sending children to leadership camps will make them more sociable? Why or why not?

Reflect ■ Suppose a researcher asks you to enroll your baby in a 10-year longitudinal study. What factors would lead you to agree and stay involved? Do your answers shed light on why longitudinal studies often have biased samples? Explain.

SUMMARY

1.1 The Field of Child Development (p. 4)

1.1a Describe the field of child development, along with factors that stimulated its expansion.

- **Child development** is a field of study devoted to understanding constancy and change from conception through adolescence. It is part of a larger interdisciplinary field known as **developmental science,** which includes all changes we experience throughout the lifespan. Both scientific curiosity and social pressures to better children's lives have stimulated research on child development.

1.1b Explain how child development is typically divided into domains and periods.

- Development is often divided into physical, cognitive, and emotional and social domains. These domains combine in an integrated, holistic fashion.

- Researchers generally divide child development into the following age periods: (1) prenatal (conception to birth), (2) infancy and toddlerhood (birth to 2 years), (3) early childhood (2 to 6 years), (4) middle childhood (6 to 11 years), and (5) adolescence (11 to 18 years).

1.2 Basic Issues (p. 7)

1.2 Identify three basic issues on which theories of child development take a stand.

- Each **theory** of child development takes a stand on three fundamental issues: (1) development as a **continuous** process or a series of **discontinuous stages;** (2) one course of development characterizing all children, or many possible courses due to mutually influential relations between children and their **contexts;** (3) development influenced more by genetic or environmental factors (the **nature–nurture controversy**), and stable or characterized by substantial **plasticity?**

- Recent theories have shifted toward a balanced stand on these issues. Contemporary investigators realize that answers may vary across domains of development and even, as research on **resilience** indicates, across individuals. More researchers are endorsing a developmental systems perspective, which views development as shaped by a complex network of genetic/biological, psychological, and social influences.

1.3 Historical Foundations (p. 11)

1.3 Describe major historical influences on theories of child development.

- At least since medieval times, childhood has been regarded as a separate phase of life. In the sixteenth and seventeenth centuries, the Puritan conception of original sin led to a harsh philosophy of child rearing.

- The seventeenth-century Enlightenment brought a new emphasis on human dignity and respect that led to more humane views of childhood. Locke's notion of the child as a tabula rasa ("blank slate") foreshadowed twentieth-century behaviorism, while Rousseau's view of children as noble savages foreshadowed the concepts of stage and **maturation**.

- Darwin's theory of evolution influenced important developmental theories and inspired the beginning of scientific child study in the late nineteenth and early twentieth centuries. Hall and Gesell introduced the **normative approach,** which measured behaviors of large groups to yield descriptions of typical development.

- Binet and Simon constructed the first successful intelligence test, which sparked interest in individual differences and made measures of intelligence central to the nature–nurture controversy.

1.4 Mid-Twentieth-Century Theories (p. 14)

1.4 Describe theories that influenced child development research in the mid-twentieth century.

- In the 1930s and 1940s, psychiatrists and social workers turned to the **psychoanalytic perspective** for help in treating children's psychological problems. In Freud's **psychosexual theory,** children move through five stages, during which three portions of the personality—id, ego, and superego—become integrated.

- Erikson's **psychosocial theory** builds on Freud's theory, emphasizing the development of culturally relevant attitudes and skills and the lifespan nature of development.

- **Behaviorism** focuses on directly observable events (stimuli and responses). Pavlov's studies of animal learning led to the discovery of classical conditioning. Skinner's work led operant conditioning to become a broadly applied learning principle.

- A related approach, Albert Bandura's **social learning theory,** views modeling as a major means of acquiring new responses. Its most recent revision takes a social-cognitive approach, stressing the role of cognition, or thinking, in children's imitation and learning.

- Behaviorism and social learning theory gave rise to **applied behavior analysis,** in which procedures of conditioning and modeling are used to eliminate undesirable behaviors and increase desirable responses.

- According to Piaget's **cognitive-developmental theory,** children actively construct knowledge as they progress through four stages, beginning with the baby's sensorimotor action patterns and ending with the abstract, systematic reasoning system of the adolescent and adult. Piaget's work has stimulated a wealth of research on children's thinking and has encouraged educational programs that emphasize children's discovery learning.

1.5 Recent Theoretical Perspectives (p. 21)

1.5 Describe recent theoretical perspectives on child development.

■ According to the **Information processing** perspective, the mind is a complex symbol-manipulating system through which information flows. Because it has provided precise accounts of how children and adults tackle many cognitive tasks—including "executive" processes used to manage thoughts, emotions, and actions—information processing has important implications for education.

■ Researchers in **developmental cognitive neuroscience** study the relationship between changes in the brain and the developing child's cognitive processing and behavior patterns. Investigators in **developmental social neuroscience** examine relationships between changes in the brain and social development. Findings on the types of experiences that support or undermine brain development are leading to effective interventions for enhancing cognitive and social functioning.

■ Four contemporary perspectives emphasize contexts for development. **Ethology,** which focuses on the adaptive value and evolutionary history of behavior, inspired the **sensitive period** concept. In **evolutionary developmental psychology,** which extends this emphasis, researchers seek to understand the adaptive value of species-wide competencies as they change with age.

■ Vygotsky's **sociocultural theory,** which focuses on how culture is transmitted from one generation to the next through social interaction, views cognitive development as a socially mediated process. Through cooperative dialogues with more expert members of society, children come to use language to guide their own thoughts and actions and acquire culturally relevant knowledge and skills.

■ **Ecological systems theory** views the child as developing within a complex system of relationships affected by multiple, nested layers of the surrounding environment—**microsystem, mesosystem, exosystem,** and **macrosystem.** The **chronosystem** represents the dynamic, ever-changing nature of children and their experiences.

■ According to the **dynamic systems perspective,** the child's mind, body, and physical and social worlds form an integrated system that guides mastery of new skills. A change in any part of the system prompts the child to reorganize his or her behavior so the various components work together again but in a more complex, effective way. The dynamic systems perspective aims to better understand variability in children's development.

1.6 Comparing Child Development Theories (p. 30)

1.6 Identify the stand taken by each major theory on the basic issues of child development.

■ Major theories vary in their focus on different domains of development, in their view of how development occurs, and in their strengths and weaknesses. (For a full summary, see Table 1.3 on page 31.)

1.7 Studying the Child (p. 30)

1.7a Describe research methods commonly used to study children.

■ **Naturalistic observations,** gathered in everyday environments, permit researchers to see directly the everyday behaviors they hope to explain. **Structured observations,** in contrast, take place in laboratories, where every participant has an equal opportunity to display the behaviors of interest.

■ Self-report methods can be flexible and open-ended like the **clinical interview.** Alternatively, in **structured interviews**—including tests and questionnaires—each participant is asked the same questions in the same way.

■ Investigators use the **clinical,** or **case study, method** to obtain an in-depth understanding of a single child.

■ Researchers have adapted observational and self-report methods to permit direct comparisons of cultures. To understand the unique values and social processes of a culture or distinct social group, researchers rely on **ethnography,** engaging in participant observation.

1.7b Distinguish between correlational and experimental research designs, noting strengths and limitations of each.

■ The **correlational design** examines relationships between variables, generally as they occur in natural life circumstances, without altering participants' experiences. A **correlation coefficient** is often used to measure the association between variables. Correlational studies do not permit inferences about cause and effect, but they can be helpful in identifying relationships that are worth exploring with a more powerful experimental strategy.

■ An **experimental design** permits inferences about cause and effect. Researchers manipulate an **independent variable** by exposing participants to two or more treatment conditions. Then they determine what effect this variable has on a **dependent variable. Random assignment** and matching reduce the chances that characteristics of participants and treatment conditions do not operate as **confounding variables,** reducing the accuracy of experimental findings.

■ In field experiments, researchers randomly assign participants to treatment conditions in the real world. Natural, or quasi-, experiments, which compare treatments that already exist in natural environments, are less rigorous than true experimental research.

1.7c Describe designs for studying development, noting strengths and limitations of each.

■ The **longitudinal design** permits researchers to identify common patterns as well as individual differences in development and to examine the relationship between early and later events and behaviors. Problems for longitudinal research include biased sampling, selective attrition, practice effects, and **cohort effects**—difficulty generalizing to children developing under different historical conditions. Longitudinal research also requires large investments of time and resources.

■ The **cross-sectional design** is more efficient than the longitudinal design, but it is limited to comparisons of age-group averages and vulnerable to cohort effects.

■ **Sequential designs** can determine whether cohort effects are operating by comparing participants of the same age who were born in different years. When sequential designs combine longitudinal and cross-sectional strategies, researchers can see if outcomes are similar, for added confidence in their findings.

■ In the **microgenetic design,** researchers present children with a novel task and track their mastery over a series of closely spaced sessions, seeking to capture processes of development. However, the time required for children to change is hard to anticipate, and practice effects can bias findings.

■ Combining experimental and developmental designs can help identify causal influences on development.

1.8 Ethics in Research on Children (p. 44)

1.8 *Discuss special ethical concerns that arise in doing research on children.*

■ Because of their immaturity, children are especially vulnerable to harm and often cannot evaluate the risks and benefits of research participation. Ethical guidelines and institutional review boards that weigh the risks and benefits of research help ensure that children's research rights are protected.

■ Besides obtaining consent from parents and others who act on children's behalf, researchers should seek the informed assent of children 7 years and older. The use of deception in research with children is especially risky because it may undermine their basic faith in the honesty of adults.

IMPORTANT TERMS AND CONCEPTS

applied behavior analysis (p. 18)
behaviorism (p. 16)
child development (p. 4)
chronosystem (p. 27)
clinical interview (p. 33)
clinical, or case study, method (p. 34)
cognitive-developmental theory (p. 18)
cohort effects (p. 41)
confounding variable (p. 38)
contexts (p. 8)
continuous development (p. 7)
correlational design (p. 37)
correlation coefficient (p. 37)
cross-sectional design (p. 42)
dependent variable (p. 38)
developmental cognitive neuroscience (p. 22)
developmental social neuroscience (p. 22)
developmental science (p. 4)

discontinuous development (p. 8)
dynamic systems perspective (p. 27)
ecological systems theory (p. 25)
ethnography (p. 35)
ethology (p. 23)
evolutionary developmental psychology (p. 24)
exosystem (p. 27)
experimental design (p. 38)
independent variable (p. 38)
information processing (p. 21)
longitudinal design (p. 39)
macrosystem (p. 27)
maturation (p. 13)
mesosystem (p. 26)
microgenetic design (p. 44)
microsystem (p. 25)
naturalistic observation (p. 32)
nature–nurture controversy (p. 9)

neurobiological methods (p. 00)
normative approach (p. 13)
plasticity (p. 9)
psychoanalytic perspective (p. 14)
psychosexual theory (p. 14)
psychosocial theory (p. 16)
random assignment (p. 38)
resilience (p. 10)
sensitive period (p. 23)
sequential design (p. 42)
social learning theory (p. 17)
sociocultural theory (p. 24)
stage (p. 8)
structured interview (p. 34)
structured observation (p. 33)
theory (p. 7)

Genetic and Environmental Foundations

Save Our Environment
F. N. Mithila, 12 years, Bangladesh

Children and adults enjoy themselves, embedded in the supportive context of an idyllic urban landscape. Chapter 2 considers how heredity and multiple layers of the surrounding environment jointly influence child development.

Reprinted with permission from The International Museum of Children's Art, Oslo, Norway

"It's a girl!" announces the doctor, holding up the squalling newborn baby as her parents gaze with amazement at their miraculous creation.

"A girl! We've named her Sarah!" exclaims the proud father to eager relatives waiting for news of their new family member.

As we join these parents in thinking about how this wondrous being came into existence and imagining her future, we are struck by many questions. How did this baby, equipped with everything necessary for life outside the womb, develop from the union of two tiny cells? What ensures that Sarah will, in due time, roll over, reach for objects, walk, talk, make friends, learn, imagine, and create—just like other typical children born before her? Why is she a girl and not a boy, dark-haired rather than blond, calm and patient rather than energetic and distractible? What difference will it make that Sarah is given a name and place in one family, community, nation, and culture rather than another?

To answer these questions, this chapter takes a close look at the foundations of development: heredity and environment. Because nature has prepared us for survival, all humans have features in common. Yet each of us is also unique. Think about several children you know well, and jot down the most obvious physical and behavioral similarities between them and their parents. Did you find that one child shows combined features of both parents, another resembles just one parent, whereas a third is not like either parent? These directly observable characteristics are called **phenotypes.** They depend in part on the individual's **genotype**—the complex blend of genetic information that determines our species and influences all our unique characteristics. Yet phenotypes are also affected by each person's lifelong history of experiences.

We begin our discussion with a review of basic genetic principles that help explain similarities and differences among children in appearance and behavior. Then we turn to aspects of the environment that play powerful roles in children's lives. As our discussion proceeds, some findings may surprise you. For example, many people are convinced that when children inherit unfavorable characteristics, little can be done to help them. Others believe that the damage done to children by a harmful environment can easily be corrected. As we will see, neither of these assumptions is accurate. Rather, heredity and environment continuously collaborate, each modifying—for better or for worse—the power of the other to influence the course of development. ■

What's Ahead in Chapter 2

2.1 Genetic Foundations

Within each of the trillions of cells in the human body (except red blood cells) is a control center, or *nucleus,* that contains rodlike structures called **chromosomes,** which store and transmit genetic information. Human chromosomes come in 23 matching pairs; an exception is the XY pair in males, which we will discuss shortly. Each member of a pair corresponds to the other in size, shape, and genetic functions. One chromosome is inherited from the mother and one from the father (see Figure 2.1 on page 52).

2.1.1 The Genetic Code

Chromosomes are made up of a chemical substance called **deoxyribonucleic acid, or DNA.** As Figure 2.2 on page 52 shows, DNA is a long, double-stranded molecule that looks like a twisted ladder. Each rung of the ladder consists of a specific pair of chemical substances called *bases.* It is this sequence of base pairs that provides

2.1a Explain what genes are and how they are transmitted from one generation to the next.

2.1b Describe various patterns of gene–gene interaction.

2.1c Describe major chromosomal abnormalities, and explain how they occur.

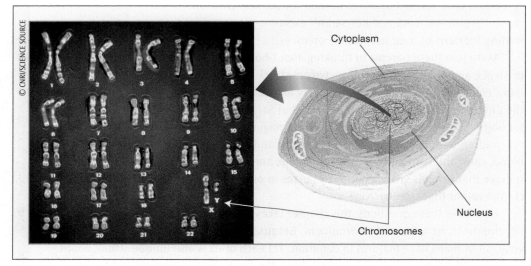

FIGURE 2.1 **A karyotype, or photograph, of human chromosomes.** The 46 chromosomes shown on the left were isolated from a human cell, stained, greatly magnified, and arranged in pairs according to decreasing size of the upper "arm" of each chromosome. The twenty-third pair, XY, reveals that the cell donor is a genetic male. In a genetic female, this pair would be XX.

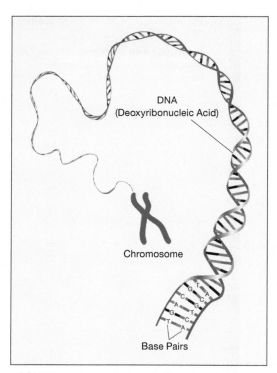

FIGURE 2.2 **DNA's ladderlike structure.**
A gene is a segment of DNA along the length of the chromosome, varying from perhaps 100 to several thousand ladder rungs long. The pairings of bases across the rungs of the ladder are very specific: Adenine (A) always appears with thymine (T), and cytosine (C) always appears with guanine (G).

genetic instructions. Although the bases always pair up in the same way across the ladder rungs—A with T and C with G—they can occur in any order along its sides. A **gene** is a segment of DNA along the length of the chromosome. Genes can be of different lengths—perhaps 100 to several thousand ladder rungs long. An estimated 19,000 to 20,000 **protein-coding genes,** which directly affect our body's characteristics, lie along the human chromosomes (Ezkurdia et al., 2014). They send instructions for making a rich assortment of proteins to the *cytoplasm,* the area surrounding the cell nucleus. Proteins, which trigger chemical reactions throughout the body, are the biological foundation on which our characteristics are built. An additional 18,000 **regulator genes** modify the instructions given by protein-coding genes, greatly complicating their genetic impact (Pennisi, 2012).

We share some of our DNA with even the simplest organisms, such as bacteria and molds, and most of it with other mammals, especially primates. About 99 percent of chimpanzee and human DNA is identical. And the genetic variation from one human to the next is even less: Individuals around the world are about 99.6 percent genetically identical (Tishkoff & Kidd, 2004; Wong, 2014). But these straightforward comparisons are misleading. Many human DNA segments that appear like those of chimpanzees have undergone duplications and rearrangements with other segments. So in actuality, the species-specific genetic material responsible for the attributes that make us human, from our upright gait to our extraordinary language and cognitive capacities, is extensive (Sudmant et al., 2015). Furthermore, it takes a change in only a single DNA base pair to influence human traits. And such tiny changes generally combine in unique ways across multiple genes, amplifying human variability.

How do humans, with far fewer genes than scientists once thought, manage to develop into such complex beings? The answer lies in the proteins our genes make, which break up and reassemble in staggering variety—about 10 to 20 million altogether. Simpler species have far fewer proteins. Furthermore, the communication system between the cell nucleus and cytoplasm, which fine-tunes gene activity, is more intricate in humans than in simpler organisms. Finally, within the cell, environmental factors modify gene expression. Many such effects are unique to humans and influence brain development (Lussier, Islam, & Kobor, 2018). So even at this microscopic level, biological events of profound developmental significance are the result of *both* genetic and nongenetic forces.

2.1.2 The Sex Cells

New individuals are created when two special cells called **gametes,** or sex cells—the sperm and ovum—combine. A gamete contains only 23 chromosomes, half as many as a regular body cell. Gametes are formed through a cell division process called **meiosis,** which halves the number of chromosomes normally present in body cells. When sperm and ovum unite at conception, the resulting cell, called a **zygote,** will again have 46 chromosomes. Meiosis ensures that a constant quantity of genetic material is transmitted from one generation to the next.

In meiosis, the chromosomes pair up and exchange segments, so that genes from one are replaced by genes from another. This shuffling of genes creates new hereditary combinations. Then chance determines which member of each pair will gather with others and end up in the same gamete. These events make the likelihood that nontwin siblings will be genetically identical about 1 in 700 trillion, or virtually nil. The genetic variability produced by meiosis is adaptive: It increases the chances that at least some members of a species will cope with ever-changing environments and will survive.

In the male, the cells from which sperm arise are produced continuously throughout life, so a healthy man can father a child at any age after sexual maturity. The female is born with a bank of ova already present in her ovaries, though recent findings suggest that new ova may arise from ovarian stem cells later on (Virant-Klun, 2015). Still, there are plenty of female sex cells. About 1 to 2 million are present at birth, 40,000 remain at adolescence, and approximately 350 to 450 female sex cells will mature during a woman's childbearing years (Moore, Persaud, & Torchia, 2016).

2.1.3 Sex Determination

Return to Figure 2.1 and note that 22 of the 23 pairs of chromosomes are matching pairs, called **autosomes** (meaning *not* sex chromosomes). The twenty-third pair consists of **sex chromosomes.** In females, this pair is called XX; in males, it is called XY. The X is a relatively long chromosome, whereas the Y is short and carries little genetic material. When gametes form in males, the X and Y chromosomes separate into different sperm cells. The gametes that form in females all carry an X chromosome. Therefore, the genetic sex of the new organism is determined by whether an X-bearing or a Y-bearing sperm fertilizes the ovum. In fact, scientists have isolated a gene on the Y chromosome that initiates the formation of male sex organs during the prenatal period (Sekido & Lovell-Badge, 2009). Additional genes, some yet to be identified, are involved in the development of sexual characteristics.

Biologists caution that human sexual diversity is much wider than a simple male–female dichotomy. As a result of variations in genes or chance events in development, some individuals' sex chromosomes do not match their sexual anatomy. An estimated 1 in every 100 people are affected, usually mildly but occasionally substantially (Ainsworth, 2015). The existence of people with intersex traits, many of whom go through life unaware of their condition unless they seek treatment for infertility or another medical issue, is redefining sex as a spectrum.

2.1.4 Multiple Offspring

Ruth and Peter, a couple I know well, tried for several years to have a child, without success. Eventually, Ruth's doctor prescribed a fertility drug, and twins—Jeannie and Jason—were born. Jeannie and Jason are **fraternal,** or **dizygotic, twins,** the most common type of multiple offspring, resulting from the release and fertilization of two ova. Genetically, they are no more alike than ordinary siblings. Table 2.1 on page 254 summarizes genetic and environmental factors that increase the chances of giving birth to fraternal twins. Older maternal age, fertility drugs, and in vitro fertilization are major causes of the dramatic rise in fraternal twinning and other multiple births in industrialized nations over the past several decades. Currently, fraternal twins account for 1 in about every 33 births in the United States (Martin et al., 2017).

TABLE 2.1   Maternal Factors Linked to Fraternal Twinning

FACTOR	DESCRIPTION
Heredity	Occurs more often among women whose families contain fraternal twins, suggesting a genetic influence. Two recently identified genes, one that augments hormone levels and another that may heighten the ovaries' responsiveness to hormones, increase the chances of fraternal twinning.
Geographic region	Occurs in 6 per 1,000 births in Asia and Latin America, 9 to 12 per 1,000 births in White Europeans, and 40 per 1,000 births among Black Africans[a]
Age	Rises with maternal age, peaking between 35 and 39 years, and then rapidly falls
Body build	Occurs more often among women who are tall and overweight or of normal weight as opposed to slight body build
Number of births	Is more likely with each additional birth
Fertility drugs and in vitro fertilization	Is more likely with fertility hormones and in vitro fertilization (see page 61), which also increase the chances of bearing higher-order multiples

[a] Worldwide rates, not including multiple births resulting from use of fertility drugs.

Sources: Hoekstra et al., 2008, 2010; Kulkarni et al., 2013; Smits & Monden, 2011; Mbarek et al., 2016.

Twins can also be created when a zygote that has started to duplicate separates into two clusters of cells that develop into two individuals. These are called **identical,** or **monozygotic, twins** because they have the same genetic makeup. The frequency of identical twins is the same around the world—about 3 to 4 per 1,000 births (Kulkarni et al., 2013). Animal research has uncovered environmental influences that prompt this type of twinning, including temperature changes, variation in oxygen levels, and late fertilization of the ovum (Lashley, 2007). In a minority of cases, identical twinning runs in families, but this occurs so rarely that it is likely due to chance rather than heredity.

During their early years, children of single births often are healthier and develop more rapidly than twins. Jeannie and Jason, like most twins, were born several weeks prematurely and required special care in the hospital. When the twins came home, Ruth and Peter had to divide time between them. Perhaps because neither baby received as much attention as the average single infant, Jeannie and Jason walked and talked several months later than most children their age, though like most twins they caught up in development by middle childhood (Lytton & Gallagher, 2002; Nan et al., 2013; Raz et al., 2016). Parental energies are further strained after the birth of triplets, whose early development is slower than that of twins (Feldman, Eidelman, & Rotenberg, 2004).

2.1.5 Patterns of Gene–Gene Interaction

Jeannie has her parents' dark, straight hair; Jason is curly-haired and blond. The way genes from each parent interact helps explain these outcomes. Recall that except for the XY pair in males, all chromosomes come in matching pairs. Two forms of each gene occur at the same place on the chromosomes, one inherited from the mother and one from the father. Each form of a gene is called an **allele.** If the alleles from both parents are alike, the child is **homozygous** and will display the inherited trait. If the alleles differ, then the child is **heterozygous,** and relationships between the alleles influence the phenotype.

© RAY EVANS/ALAMY STOCK PHOTO

These identical, or monozygotic, twins were created when a duplicating zygote separated into two clusters of cells, which developed into two individuals with the same genetic makeup.

Dominant–Recessive Pattern In many heterozygous pairings, **dominant–recessive inheritance** occurs: Only one allele affects the child's characteristics. It is called *dominant;* the second allele, which has no effect, is called *recessive.* Hair color is an example. The allele for dark hair is dominant (we can represent it with a capital *D*), whereas the one for blond hair is recessive (symbolized by a lowercase *b*). Both a child who inherits a homozygous pair of dominant alleles *(DD)* and a child who inherits a heterozygous pair *(Db)* will be dark-haired, even though their genotypes differ. Blond hair (like Jason's) can result only from having two recessive alleles *(bb)*. Still, heterozygous individuals with just one recessive allele *(Db)* can pass that trait to their children. Therefore, they are called **carriers** of the trait.

Most recessive alleles—like those for blond hair, pattern baldness, or nearsightedness—are of little developmental importance. But some cause serious disabilities and diseases. One well-known recessive disorder is *phenylketonuria,* or *PKU,* which affects the way the body breaks down proteins contained in many foods. Infants born with two recessive alleles lack an enzyme that converts one of the basic amino acids that make up proteins (phenylalanine) into a byproduct essential for body functioning (tyrosine). Without this enzyme, phenylalanine quickly builds to toxic levels that damage the central nervous system, causing permanent intellectual disability.

Despite its potentially damaging effects, PKU illustrates that inheriting unfavorable genes does not always lead to an untreatable condition. All U.S. states require that each newborn be given a blood test for PKU. If the disease is found, doctors place the baby on a diet low in phenylalanine. Children who receive this treatment nevertheless show mild deficits in control of attention, memory, planning, decision making, and problem solving, because even small amounts of phenylalanine interfere with brain functioning (Fonnesbeck et al., 2013; Jahja et al. 2014). But as long as dietary treatment begins early and continues, children with PKU usually attain an average level of intelligence and have a normal lifespan.

In dominant–recessive inheritance, if we know the genetic makeup of the parents, we can predict the percentage of children in a family who are likely to display or carry a trait. Figure 2.3 illustrates this for PKU. For a child to inherit the condition, each parent must have a recessive allele. But because of the action of regulator genes, children vary in the degree to which phenylalanine accumulates in their tissues and in the extent to which they respond to treatment.

Only rarely are serious diseases due to dominant alleles. Think about why this is so. Children who inherit the dominant allele always develop the disorder. They seldom live long enough to reproduce, so the harmful dominant allele is eliminated from the family's heredity in a single generation. Some dominant disorders, however, do persist. One is *Huntington disease,* a condition in which the central nervous system degenerates. Its symptoms usually do not appear until age 35 or later, after the person may have passed the dominant allele to his or her children.

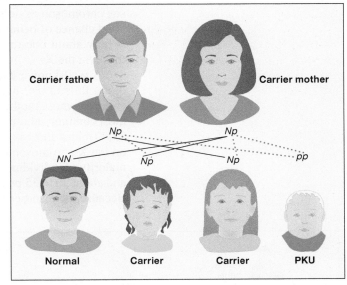

FIGURE 2.3 **Dominant–recessive mode of inheritance, as illustrated by PKU.** When both parents are heterozygous carriers of the recessive gene *(p)*, we can predict that 25 percent of their offspring are likely to be normal *(NN)*, 50 percent are likely to be carriers *(Np)*, and 25 percent are likely to inherit the disorder *(pp)*. Notice that the child with PKU, in contrast to his siblings, has light hair. The recessive gene for PKU affects more than one trait. It also leads to fair coloring.

Incomplete-Dominance Pattern In some heterozygous circumstances, the dominant–recessive relationship does not hold completely. Instead, we see **incomplete dominance,** a pattern of inheritance in which both alleles are expressed in the phenotype, resulting in a combined trait, or one that is intermediate between the two.

The *sickle cell trait,* a heterozygous condition present in many Black Africans, provides an example. *Sickle cell anemia* occurs in full form when a child inherits two recessive alleles. They cause the usually round red blood cells to become sickle (crescent-moon) shaped, especially under low-oxygen conditions. The sickled cells clog the blood vessels and block the flow of blood, causing intense pain, swelling, and tissue damage. Despite medical advances that today allow 85 percent of affected children to survive to adulthood, North Americans with sickle cell anemia have an average life expectancy of only 55 years (Chakravorty & Williams,

2015). Heterozygous individuals are protected from the disease under most circumstances. However, when they experience oxygen deprivation—for example, at high altitudes or after intense physical exercise—the single recessive allele asserts itself, and a temporary, mild form of the illness occurs.

The sickle cell allele is common among Black Africans for a special reason. Carriers of it are more resistant to malaria than are individuals with two alleles for normal red blood cells. In Africa, where malaria is common, these carriers survived and reproduced more frequently than others, leading the gene to be maintained in the Black population. But in regions of the world where the risk of malaria is low, the frequency of the gene is declining. For example, only 8 percent of African Americans are carriers, compared with 20 percent of Black Africans (Centers for Disease Control and Prevention, 2017h).

X-Linked Pattern Males and females have an equal chance of inheriting recessive disorders carried on the autosomes. When a harmful allele is carried on the X chromosome, however, **X-linked inheritance** applies, making males more likely to be affected because their sex chromosomes do not match. In females, any recessive allele on one X chromosome has a good chance of being suppressed by a dominant allele on the other X. But the Y chromosome is only about one-third as long and therefore lacks many corresponding alleles to override those on the X.

A well-known example of X-linked inheritance is *hemophilia,* a disorder in which the blood fails to clot normally. Figure 2.4 shows its greater likelihood of inheritance by male children whose mothers carry the abnormal allele. Another example is *fragile X syndrome,* the most common inherited cause of intellectual disability. In this disorder, which affects about 1 in 2,000 males and 1 in 6,000 females, an abnormal repetition of a sequence of DNA bases occurs on the X chromosome, damaging a particular gene. In addition to cognitive impairments, the majority of individuals with fragile X syndrome suffer from attention deficits and high anxiety, and about 30 to 35 percent also have symptoms of autism (Wadell, Hagerman, & Hessl, 2013). Because the disorder is X-linked, males are more often affected.

Besides X-linked disorders, many sex differences reveal the male to be at a disadvantage. Rates of miscarriage, infant and childhood deaths, birth defects, learning disabilities, behavior disorders, and intellectual disability all are higher for boys (Boyle et al., 2011; MacDorman & Gregory, 2015). It is possible that these sex differences can be traced to the genetic code. The female, with two X chromosomes, benefits from a greater variety of genes. Nature, however, seems to have adjusted for the male's disadvantage. Worldwide, about 103 boys are born for every 100 girls, and an even greater number of males are conceived (United Nations, 2017).

In cultures with strong gender-biased attitudes that induce expectant parents to prefer a male child, the male-to-female birth sex ratio is often much larger. In China, for example, the spread of ultrasound technology (which enables prenatal sex determination) and enforcement of a one-child family policy to control population growth—both of which began in the 1980s—led to a dramatic increase in sex-selective abortion. In 2015, China ended its one-child policy, substituting a two-child policy. Nevertheless, many Chinese couples continue to say they desire just one child (Basten & Jiang, 2015; Jiang, Li, & Sanchez-Barricarte, 2016). Today, China's birth sex ratio is 117 boys for every 100 girls—a gender imbalance with adverse social consequences, such as rising crime rates and male competition for marriage partners.

In contrast, in Europe, the Middle East, and North America, the proportion of male births has declined in recent decades. Some researchers attribute this trend to a rise in stressful living conditions, which heighten spontaneous abortions, especially of male fetuses

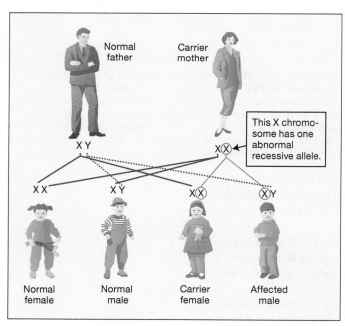

FIGURE 2.4 X-linked inheritance. In the example shown here, the allele on the father's X chromosome is normal. The mother has one normal and one abnormal recessive allele on her X chromosomes. By looking at the possible combinations of the parents' alleles, we can predict that 50 percent of these parents' male children are likely to have the disorder and 50 percent of their female children are likely to be carriers of it.

(Catalano et al., 2010). In support of this hypothesis, dips in the male-to-female birth ratio have been documented after armed conflicts, environmental disasters, and financial crises, such as the economic recession of 2007–2009 (Catalano et al., 2009; Grech, 2014).

In sum, social and cultural factors can modify the male-to-female birth sex ratio, in either direction. And they can readily undermine the ratio's assumed evolutionary role: compensating for males' greater genetic vulnerability.

Genomic Imprinting   More than 1,000 human characteristics follow the rules of dominant–recessive and incomplete-dominance inheritance (McKusick-Nathans Institute of Genetic Medicine, 2018). For these traits, whichever parent contributes a gene to the new individual, the gene responds similarly. Geneticists, however, have identified some exceptions. In **genomic imprinting**, alleles are imprinted, or chemically marked, within the ovum or sperm in such a way that one pair member (either the mother's or the father's) is silenced, leaving the other to be expressed regardless of its makeup (Perez, Rubinstein, & Dulac, 2016). The imprint may be passed to the next generation or be temporary, erased in the next generation.

A 9-year-old who has fragile X syndrome participates in an art class with typical students. This disorder—the most common inherited cause of intellectual disability—results from an abnormal repetition of a sequence of DNA bases that damages a gene on the X chromosome.

The number of genes subjected to genomic imprinting is believed to be small—less than 1 percent. Nevertheless, these genes have a significant impact on brain development and physical health, as disruptions in imprinting reveal. For example, imprinting is involved in several childhood cancers and in *Prader-Willi syndrome,* a rare disorder with symptoms of intellectual disability, delays in language motor development, small stature, and severe obesity (Zoghbi & Beaudet, 2016). Imprinting also may explain why children are more likely to develop diabetes if their father, rather than their mother, suffers from it, and why people with asthma or hay fever tend to have mothers, not fathers, with the illness (Ishida & Moore, 2013).

Mutation   Although less than 3 percent of pregnancies result in the birth of a baby with a hereditary abnormality, these children account for about 20 percent of infant deaths and contribute substantially to lifelong impaired physical and mental functioning (Martin et al., 2017). How are harmful genes created in the first place? The answer is **mutation,** a sudden but permanent change in a segment of DNA. A mutation may affect only one or two genes, or it may involve many genes, as in the chromosomal disorders we will discuss shortly. Some mutations occur spontaneously, simply by chance. Others are caused by hazardous environmental agents.

Ionizing (high-energy) radiation is an established cause of mutation. Women who receive repeated doses before conception are more likely to miscarry or give birth to children with hereditary defects. The incidence of genetic abnormalities, such as physical malformations and childhood cancer, is also higher in children whose fathers are exposed to radiation in their occupations. However, infrequent and mild exposure to radiation generally does not cause genetic damage (Adelstein, 2014). Rather, moderate to high doses over an extended time can impair DNA.

The examples just given illustrate *germline mutation,* which takes place in the cells that give rise to gametes. When the affected individual mates, the defective DNA is passed on to the next generation. In a second type, called *somatic mutation,* normal body cells mutate, an event that can occur at any time of life. The DNA defect appears in every cell derived from the affected body cell, eventually causing disease (such as cancer) or disability.

It is easy to see how disorders that run in families can result from germline mutation. But somatic mutation may be involved in these disorders as well. Some people harbor a genetic susceptibility that causes certain body cells to mutate easily in the presence of triggering events (Insel, 2014). This helps explain why certain individuals develop serious illnesses (such as cancer) as a result of smoking, exposure to pollutants, or psychological stress, while others do not.

Although virtually all mutations that have been studied are harmful, some spontaneous ones (such as the sickle cell allele in malaria-ridden regions of the world) are necessary and desirable. By increasing genetic variation, they help individuals adapt to unexpected environmental challenges. Scientists, however, seldom go looking for mutations that contribute to favorable traits, such as an exceptional talent or sturdy immune system. They are far more concerned with identifying and eliminating unfavorable genes that threaten health and survival.

Polygenic Inheritance   So far, we have discussed patterns of gene–gene interaction in which people either display a particular trait or do not. These cut-and-dried individual differences are much easier to trace to their genetic origins than are characteristics that vary on a continuum among people, such as height, weight, intelligence, and personality. These traits are due to **polygenic inheritance,** in which many genes affect the characteristic in question. Polygenic inheritance is complex, and much about it is still unknown. In the final section of this chapter, we will discuss how researchers infer the influence of heredity on human attributes when they do not know the precise patterns of inheritance.

2.1.6 Chromosomal Abnormalities

Besides harmful recessive alleles, abnormalities of the chromosomes are a major cause of serious developmental problems. Most chromosomal defects result from mistakes during meiosis, when the ovum and sperm are formed. A chromosome pair does not separate properly, or part of a chromosome breaks off. Because these errors involve far more DNA than problems due to single genes, they usually produce many physical and mental symptoms.

Down Syndrome   The most common chromosomal disorder, occurring in 1 out of every 700 live births, is *Down syndrome.* In 95 percent of cases, it results from a failure of the twenty-first pair of chromosomes to separate during meiosis, so the new individual receives three of these chromosomes rather than the normal two. For this reason, Down syndrome is sometimes called *trisomy 21.* In other, less frequent forms, an extra broken piece of a twenty-first chromosome is attached to another chromosome (called *translocation* pattern). Or an error occurs during early prenatal cell duplication, causing some but not all body cells to have the defective chromosomal makeup (called *mosaic* pattern) (U.S. Department of Health and Human Services, 2017). Because the mosaic type involves less genetic material, symptoms may be less extreme.

The consequences of Down syndrome include intellectual disability, memory and speech problems, limited vocabulary, and slow motor development. EEG measures of brain activity reveal substantial disruption in connectivity among brain regions. This indicates that the brains of individuals with Down syndrome function in a less coordinated fashion than the brains of typical individuals (Ahmadlou et al., 2013). The disorder is also associated with distinct physical features—a short, stocky build, a flattened face, a protruding tongue, almond-shaped eyes, and (in 50 percent of cases) an unusual crease running across the palm of the hand. In addition, infants with Down syndrome are often born with eye cataracts, hearing loss, and heart and intestinal defects (U.S. Department of Health and Human Services, 2017).

Because of medical advances, life expectancy of individuals with Down syndrome has increased greatly: Today, it is about 60 years. However, about 70 percent of affected people who live past age 40 show symptoms of *Alzheimer's disease,* the most common form of dementia (Hartley et al., 2015). Genes on chromosome 21 are linked to this disorder.

Infants with Down syndrome smile less readily, show poor eye-to-eye contact, have weak muscle tone, and explore

© LAURA DWIGHT PHOTOGRAPHY

An 8-year-old with Down syndrome, at right, plays with a typically developing classmate. Despite impaired intellectual development, this child benefits from exposure to stimulating environments and from opportunities to interact with peers.

objects less persistently (Slonims & McConachie, 2006). But when parents encourage them to engage with their surroundings, children with Down syndrome develop more favorably. They also benefit from infant and preschool intervention programs, although emotional, social, and motor skills improve more than intellectual performance (Roizen, 2013). Clearly, environmental factors affect how well children with Down syndrome fare.

As Figure 2.5 shows, the risk of bearing a baby with Down syndrome, as well as other chromosomal abnormalities, rises dramatically with maternal age. Chromosomal analyses of ova from older women reveal errors during meiosis in the pairing up of chromosomes and exchange of segments between the pairs (Herbert et al., 2015). In about 5 percent of cases, the extra genetic material originates with the father (Vranekovic et al., 2012).

Abnormalities of the Sex Chromosomes   Other disorders of the autosomes usually disrupt development so severely that miscarriage occurs. When such babies are born, they rarely survive beyond early childhood. In contrast, sex chromosome disorders often are not recognized until adolescence when, in some deviations, puberty is delayed. The most common problems involve the presence of an extra chromosome (either X or Y) or the absence of one X in females.

Research has discredited a variety of myths about individuals with sex chromosome disorders. For example, males with *XYY syndrome* are not necessarily more aggressive and antisocial than XY males (Re & Birkhoff, 2015). And most children with sex chromosome disorders do not suffer from intellectual disability but, rather, have specific cognitive challenges. Verbal difficulties—for example, with reading and vocabulary—are common among girls with *triple X syndrome* and boys with *Klinefelter syndrome,* both of whom inherit an extra X chromosome. In contrast, girls with *Turner syndrome,* who are missing an X, have trouble with spatial relationships—for example, drawing pictures, following travel directions, and noticing changes in facial expressions (Otter et al., 2013; Ross et al., 2012; Temple & Shephard, 2012). Brain-imaging evidence confirms that adding to or subtracting from the usual number of X chromosomes alters the development of certain brain structures, yielding particular intellectual deficits (Hong et al., 2014).

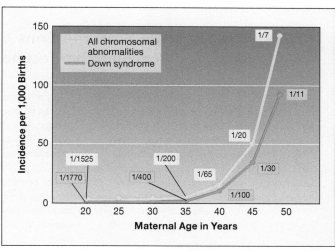

FIGURE 2.5   **Risk of Down syndrome and all chromosomal abnormalities by maternal age.** Risk rises sharply after age 35. (From R. L. Schonberg, 2012, "Birth Defects and Prenatal Diagnosis," from *Children with Disabilities*, 7th ed., M. L. Batshaw, N. J. Roizen, & G. R. Lotrecchiano, eds., p. 50. Baltimore: Paul H. Brookes Publishing Co, Inc. Adapted by permission.)

ASK YOURSELF

Connect ■ Referring to ecological systems theory (Chapter 1, pages 25–27), explain why parents of children with genetic disorders often experience increased stress. What factors, within and beyond the family, can help these parents support their children's development?

Apply ■ Gilbert's genetic makeup is homozygous for dark hair. Jan's is homozygous for blond hair. What proportion of their children are likely to be dark-haired? Explain.

Reflect ■ Provide illustrations from our discussion, and from individuals you know with genetic disorders, of environmental influences on development.

2.2 Reproductive Choices

In the past, many couples with genetic disorders in their families chose not to bear a child at all rather than risk the birth of a baby with abnormalities. Today, genetic counseling and prenatal diagnosis help people make informed decisions about conceiving, carrying a pregnancy to term, or adopting a child.

2.2 Discuss counseling, medical procedures, and reproductive options that can assist prospective parents in having healthy children.

Social Issues: Health | The Pros and Cons of Reproductive Technologies

Some people decide not to risk pregnancy because of a history of genetic disease. Many others—12 percent of all couples who try to conceive—discover that they are infertile (Centers for Disease Control and Prevention, 2016). And some never-married adults and lesbian and gay couples want to bear children. Today, increasing numbers of individuals are turning to alternative methods of conception—technologies that have become the subject of heated debate.

Donor Insemination and In Vitro Fertilization

Donor insemination—injection of sperm from an anonymous man into a woman—is often used to overcome male reproductive difficulties. It also permits women without a male partner to become pregnant. Donor insemination is 70 percent successful, resulting in about 40,000 deliveries and 52,000 newborn babies in the United States each year (Rossi, 2014).

In vitro fertilization is another commonly used reproductive technology. About 1 percent of all children in developed countries—65,000 babies in the United States—are conceived through this technique annually (Sunderam et al., 2015). A woman is given hormones that stimulate ripening of several ova. These are removed surgically and placed in a dish of nutrients, to which sperm are added. Once an ovum is fertilized and duplicates into several cells, it is injected into the woman's uterus.

By mixing and matching gametes, pregnancies can be brought about when either or both partners have a reproductive problem. Usually, in vitro fertilization is used to treat women whose fallopian tubes are permanently damaged. But a single sperm can now be injected directly into an ovum, thereby overcoming most male fertility problems. And a "sex sorter" method helps ensure that couples who carry X-linked diseases (which usually affect males) have a daughter.

Nevertheless, the success of assisted reproduction declines steadily with age, from 55 percent in women ages 31 to 35 to 8 percent in women age 43 (Cetinkaya, Siano, & Benadiva, 2013; Gnoth et al., 2011). Furthermore, assisted reproduction is associated with an elevated risk of pregnancy complications, miscarriage, and birth defects, due to the biological effects of in vitro techniques and the older age of many people seeking treatment.

Children conceived through these methods may be genetically unrelated to one or both of their parents. Does lack of genetic ties or secrecy interfere with parent–child relationships? Perhaps because of a strong desire for parenthood, caregiving is actually somewhat warmer for young children conceived through donor insemination or in vitro fertilization. Also, these children and adolescents are as well-adjusted as their naturally conceived counterparts (Punamaki, 2006; Wagenaar et al., 2011). Children whose parents

feel comfortable telling them about their gamete-donor origins are particularly advantaged in parent–child relationship quality and psychological well-being. Telling children early, by age 7, appears most beneficial (Ilioi et al., 2017; Rueter et al., 2016). Perhaps older children's more complex appreciation of the meaning of being genetically unrelated to at least one parent leads them to be less accepting.

Although reproductive technologies have many benefits, serious questions have arisen about their use. In many countries, including the United States, doctors are not required to keep records of donor characteristics, though information about the child's genetic background might be critical in the case of serious disease (Murphy, 2013). Another concern is that the in vitro "sex sorter" method enables parental sex selection, thereby eroding the moral value that boys and girls are equally precious.

In vitro fertilization poses greater risks than natural conception to infant survival and healthy development. About 26 percent of in vitro procedures result in multiple births. Most are twins, but 3 percent are triplets and higher-order multiples. Consequently, among in vitro babies, the rate of low birth weight is nearly four times as high as in the general population. In response, doctors have reduced the number of fertilized ova injected into a woman's uterus, typically to no more than two (Kulkarni et al., 2013; Sunderam et al., 2015). Risk of pregnancy complications, miscarriage, and major birth defects also rises, due to the biological effects of in vitro techniques and the older age of many people seeking treatment.

2.2.1 Genetic Counseling

Genetic counseling is a communication process designed to help couples assess their chances of giving birth to a baby with a hereditary disorder and choose the best course of action in view of risks and family goals. Individuals likely to seek counseling are those who have had difficulties bearing children—for example, repeated miscarriages—or who know that genetic problems exist in their families.

In addition, adults who delay childbearing are often candidates because as maternal age rises beyond age 35, the rates of chromosomal abnormalities increase sharply. Older paternal age elevates risk of DNA mutations as well. After age 40, it is associated with increased incidence of several serious psychological disorders. These include *autism* (see page 23 in Chapter 1); *schizophrenia,* characterized by hallucinations, delusions, and irrational behavior; and *bipolar disorder,* marked by alternating periods of elation and depression (Zitzmann, 2013). But because younger parents have children in far higher numbers than older parents, they still bear the majority of babies with genetic defects. Therefore, some experts argue that parental needs, not age, should determine referral for genetic counseling (Berkowitz, Roberts, & Minkoff, 2006).

If prospective parents have a family history of intellectual disability, psychological disorders, physical defects, or inherited diseases, the genetic counselor interviews them and prepares

Surrogate Motherhood

An even more controversial form of medically assisted conception is *surrogate motherhood.* In this procedure, in vitro fertilization may be used to impregnate a woman (called a surrogate) with a couple's fertilized ovum. Alternatively, sperm from a man whose partner is infertile may be used to inseminate the surrogate, who agrees to turn the baby over to the father. The child is then adopted by his partner. In both cases, the surrogate is paid a fee for her childbearing services.

Most surrogate arrangements proceed smoothly, and the limited evidence available suggests that families usually function well and stay in touch with the surrogate, especially if she is genetically related to the child (Golombok et al., 2011, 2013; Jadva, Casey, & Golombok, 2012). The small number of children who have been studied are generally well-adjusted. Nevertheless, because surrogacy typically involves the wealthy as contractors for infants and the less economically advantaged as surrogates, it may promote exploitation of financially needy women (Frankford, Bennington, & Ryan, 2015).

Reproductive Frontiers

Experts are debating the ethics of other reproductive options. Doctors have used donor ova from younger women in combination with in vitro fertilization to help postmenopausal women become pregnant. Most recipients are in their forties, but some in their fifties and sixties, and a few in their early seventies, have given birth. These cases magnify health risks to mother and baby and bring children into the world whose parents may not live to see them reach adulthood.

Today, customers at donor banks can select ova or sperm on the basis of physical characteristics and even IQ. And scientists are devising ways to alter the DNA of human ova, sperm, and embryos to protect against hereditary disorders—techniques that could be used to engineer other desired characteristics. Many worry that these practices are dangerous steps toward "designer babies"—controlling offspring traits by manipulating genetic makeup.

Although reproductive technologies permit many barren adults to become parents, laws are needed to regulate such practices. In Australia, New Zealand, and Europe, in vitro gamete donors and applicants for the procedure must undergo highly regulated screening. Denmark, France, and Italy prohibit in vitro fertilization for women past menopause (Cutas & Smajdor, 2015; Murphy, 2013). Pressure from those working in the field of assisted reproduction may lead to similar policies in the United States.

The ethical problems of surrogate motherhood are so complex that 18 U.S. states and the District of Columbia sharply restrict or ban the practice. Most European nations, along with Australia and Canada, allow only "altruistic" surrogacy, in which the surrogate has no financial gain. More research on how such children grow up, including later-appearing medical conditions and feelings about their origins, is important for weighing the pros and cons of these techniques.

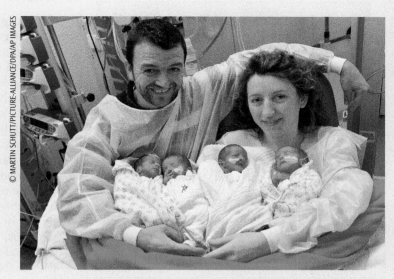

Fertility drugs and in vitro fertilization often lead to multiple births and increase the risk of low birth weight and birth defects. These quadruplets required extended care before they were able to leave the hospital.

a *pedigree,* a picture of the family tree in which affected relatives are identified. The pedigree is used to estimate the likelihood that a child will be affected by a disorder. For many disorders traceable to a single gene, molecular genetic testing using a sample of blood, saliva, or body tissue can reveal whether the parent is a carrier of the harmful allele.

Autism, schizophrenia, and bipolar disorder have each been linked to an array of DNA-sequence deviations (called *genetic markers*) distributed across multiple chromosomes. New *genomewide testing methods,* which look for these genetic markers, enable genetic counselors to estimate risk for these conditions and other psychological disorders. But estimates are generally low because the genetic markers are found in only a minority of affected people. Also, the genetic markers are not associated with mental illness every time they appear. Their expression—as we will illustrate at the end of this chapter—may depend on environmental conditions. Recently, geneticists have begun to identify rare repeats and deletions of DNA bases that are more consistently related to mental illness (Vissers, Gilissen, & Veltman, 2016). These discoveries may lead to more accurate prediction of the likelihood of passing a psychological disorder from parent to child.

When all the relevant hereditary information is in, genetic counselors help people consider appropriate options. These include taking a chance and conceiving or choosing from among a variety of reproductive technologies (see the Social Issues: Health box starting on page 60).

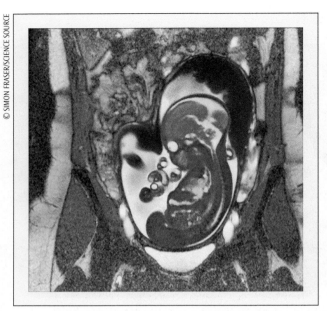

© SIMON FRASER/SCIENCE SOURCE

FIGURE 2.6   Ultrafast MRI of a fetus, showing body structures. Ultrafast MRI is increasingly being used as a supplement to ultrasound because it records detailed pictures of body structures, permitting greater diagnostic accuracy. In this colorized MRI of a 26-week-old fetus, the yellow area highlights a brain abnormality.

2.2.2 Prenatal Diagnosis

Several **prenatal diagnostic methods**—medical procedures that permit detection of developmental problems before birth—are available to couples at risk of bearing a child with abnormalities who decide to conceive (see Table 2.2). Women of advanced maternal age are prime candidates for *amniocentesis* or *chorionic villus sampling. Ultrasound,* commonly used during pregnancy to track fetal growth, permits detection of gross structural abnormalities. When ultrasound suggests problems but diagnosis is uncertain, *ultrafast fetal magnetic resonance imaging,* in which a scanner magnetically records detailed pictures of fetal structures, can be used for greater accuracy (see Figure 2.6). Except for *maternal blood analysis,* prenatal diagnostic methods should not be used routinely because of injury risks to the developing organism.

Prenatal diagnosis has led to advances in fetal medicine. For example, by inserting a needle into the uterus, doctors can administer drugs to the fetus. Surgery has been performed to repair such problems as heart, lung, and diaphragm malformations, urinary tract obstructions, and neural defects (Nassr et al., 2018). Fetuses with blood disorders have been given blood transfusions. And those with immune deficiencies have received bone marrow transplants that succeeded in creating a normally functioning immune system (Deprest et al., 2010).

These techniques frequently result in complications, the most common being premature labor and miscarriage (Danzer & Johnson, 2014). Yet parents may be willing to try almost any option, even one with only a

TABLE 2.2   Prenatal Diagnostic Methods

METHOD	DESCRIPTION
Amniocentesis	The most widely used technique. A hollow needle is inserted through the abdominal wall to obtain a sample of fluid in the uterus. Cells are examined for genetic defects. Can be performed by the 14th week after conception; 1 to 2 more weeks are required for test results. Small risk of miscarriage.
Chorionic villus sampling	A procedure that can be used if results are desired or needed very early in pregnancy. A thin tube is inserted into the uterus through the vagina, or a hollow needle is inserted through the abdominal wall. A small plug of tissue is removed from the end of one or more chorionic villi, the hairlike projections on the membrane surrounding the developing organism. Cells are examined for genetic defects. Can be performed at 9 weeks after conception; results are available within 24 hours. Entails a slightly greater risk of miscarriage than amniocentesis and is also associated with a small risk of limb deformities.
Fetoscopy	A small tube with a light source at one end is inserted into the uterus to inspect the fetus for defects of the limbs and face. Also allows a sample of fetal blood to be obtained, permitting diagnosis of such disorders as hemophilia and sickle cell anemia, as well as neural defects (see below). Usually performed between 15 and 18 weeks after conception but can be done as early as 5 weeks. Entails some risk of miscarriage.
Maternal blood analysis	By the second month of pregnancy, some of the developing organism's cells enter the maternal bloodstream. An elevated level of alpha-fetoprotein may indicate kidney disease, abnormal closure of the esophagus, or neural tube defects, such as *anencephaly* (absence of most of the brain) and *spina bifida* (bulging of the spinal cord from the spinal column). Isolated cells can be examined for genetic defects.
Ultrasound	High-frequency sound waves are beamed at the uterus; their reflection is translated into a picture on a video screen that reveals the size, shape, and placement of the fetus. By itself, permits assessment of fetal age, detection of multiple pregnancies, and identification of gross physical defects. Also used to guide amniocentesis, chorionic villus sampling, and fetoscopy. When used five or more times, may increase the chances of low birth weight.
Ultrafast magnetic resonance imaging (MRI)	Sometimes used as a supplement to ultrasound, where brain or other abnormalities are detected and MRI can provide greater diagnostic accuracy. Uses a scanner to magnetically record detailed pictures of fetal structures. The ultrafast technique overcomes image blurring due to fetal movements. No evidence of adverse effects.
Preimplantation genetic diagnosis	After in vitro fertilization and duplication of the zygote into a cluster of cells, one or two cells are removed and examined for genetic defects. Only if that sample is normal is the fertilized ovum implanted in the woman's uterus.

Sources: Akolekar et al., 2015; Griffin et al., 2017; Jokhi & Whitby, 2011; Kollmann et al., 2013; Moore, Persaud, & Torchia, 2016.

APPLYING WHAT WE KNOW

Steps Prospective Parents Can Take Before Conception to Increase the Chances of a Healthy Baby

RECOMMENDATION	EXPLANATION
Arrange for a physical exam.	A physical exam before conception permits getting up to date on vaccinations and detection of diseases and other medical conditions that might reduce fertility, be difficult to treat during pregnancy, or affect the developing organism.
Consider your genetic makeup.	Find out if anyone in your family has had a child with a genetic disease or disability. If so, seek genetic counseling before conception.
Reduce or eliminate toxins under your control.	Because the developing organism is highly sensitive to damaging environmental agents during the early weeks of pregnancy, couples trying to conceive should avoid drugs, alcohol, cigarette smoke, radiation, pollution, chemical substances in the home and workplace, and exposure to infectious diseases. They should also stay away from ionizing radiation, which poses risks for mutations.
Ensure proper nutrition.	A doctor-recommended vitamin–mineral supplement, begun before conception, helps prevent many prenatal problems. It should include folic acid, which reduces the chances of neural tube defects, prematurity, and low birth weight (see Chapter 3, page 00).
Consult your doctor after 12 months of unsuccessful efforts at conception.	Long periods of infertility may be due to undiagnosed spontaneous abortions, which can be caused by genetic defects in either partner. If a physical exam reveals a healthy reproductive system, seek genetic counseling.

slim chance of success. Currently, the medical profession is struggling with how to help parents make informed decisions about fetal surgery.

Advances in *genetic engineering* also offer hope for correcting hereditary defects. As part of the Human Genome Project—an ambitious international research program, extending from 1990 to 2003, that identified the sequence of DNA bases in the human genome—thousands of genes have been identified, including those involved in disorders of the heart, blood, eyes, lungs, digestive and nervous systems, and in many forms of cancer (National Institutes of Health, 2018b). As a result, new treatments are being explored.

One such approach is *gene therapy*—correcting genetic abnormalities by delivering DNA carrying a functional gene to the cells. Testing of gene therapies for treating severe immune system dysfunction, several forms of cancer, and certain blood disorders has been encouraging (Kaufmann et al., 2013). In a recent breakthrough, researchers successfully replaced an abnormal gene with a normal one in the red blood cells of young children with *beta thalassemia,* a disease in which low levels of hemoglobin cause life-threatening anemia and widespread organ damage (Thompson et al., 2018). In another approach, called *proteomics,* that shows special promise for treating heart disease and cancer, scientists modify gene-specified proteins involved in particular diseases (Lippolis & De Angelis, 2016).

Despite some successes, genetic treatments are still some distance away for most single-gene defects and farther off for diseases involving multiple genes that combine in complex ways with each other and the environment. Applying What We Know above summarizes steps that prospective parents can take before conception to protect the genetic health of their child.

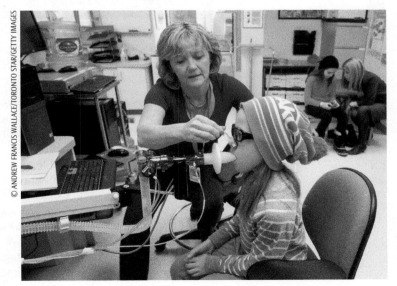

© ANDREW FRANCIS WALLACE/TORONTO STAR/GETTY IMAGES

A 9-year-old with cystic fibrosis undergoes a breathing test to assess lung functioning. This recessive disorder causes the lungs, liver, and pancreas to secrete large amounts of thick mucus, leading to breathing and digestive difficulties. Worsening lung disease causes premature death in early adulthood. Today, researchers are testing gene therapies aimed at regenerating the lining of the lungs.

2.2.3 Adoption

Adults who are infertile or likely to pass along a genetic disorder, same-sex couples, and single adults who want a family are turning to adoption in increasing numbers. Couples who have children by birth, too, sometimes choose to expand their families through adoption. Because the availability of healthy babies has diminished (fewer young unwed mothers give up their babies than in the past), Americans, and people in other Western nations, often seek to adopt internationally. But despite a dramatic rise in orphaned, abandoned, and voluntarily surrendered children worldwide, intercountry adoption has declined substantially, due to host-country and U.S. adoption policies. Rising numbers of children are being adopted from U.S. foster care (Jones & Placek, 2017). And more families are accepting children who are past infancy or who have known developmental problems.

Adopted children and adolescents—whether or not born in their adoptive parents' country—tend to have more learning and emotional difficulties than other children, a difference that increases with the child's age at time of adoption (Askeland et al., 2017; Diamond et al., 2015; van den Dries et al., 2009). Various explanations exist for adoptees' more problematic childhoods. The biological mother may have been unable to care for the child because of problems believed to be partly genetic, such as alcoholism or severe depression, and may have passed this tendency to her offspring. Or perhaps she experienced stress, poor diet, or inadequate medical care during pregnancy—factors that can affect the child. Furthermore, children adopted after infancy often have a preadoptive history of conflict-ridden family relationships, lack of parental affection, neglect and abuse, or deprived institutional rearing. Finally, adoptive parents and children, who are genetically unrelated, are less alike in intelligence and personality than are biological relatives—differences that may threaten family harmony.

Adoption is one option for adults who want a family but are infertile or have a family history of genetic disorders. This father and his 15-month-old daughter attend a reunion of families who traveled together to adopt babies from China. As she gets older, parental warmth and openness about her adoption will promote this child's adjustment.

Despite these risks, most adopted children fare well, and those with preexisting problems who experience sensitive parenting usually make rapid progress (Arcus & Chambers, 2008; Juffer & van IJzendoorn, 2012). Overall, international adoptees develop much more favorably than birth siblings or institutionalized agemates who remain in their birth country (Christoffersen, 2012). And children with troubled family histories who are adopted at older ages generally improve in feelings of trust and affection for their adoptive parents as they come to feel loved and supported (Veríssimo & Salvaterra, 2006). As we will see in Chapter 5, however, later-adopted children—especially those with multiple early-life adversities—are more likely than their agemates to have persistent cognitive, emotional, and social problems.

By adolescence, adoptees' lives are often complicated by unresolved curiosity about their roots. As they try to integrate aspects of their birth family and their adoptive family into their emerging identity, teenagers face a challenging process of defining themselves. When parents have been warm, open, and supportive in their communication about adoption, their children typically forge a positive sense of self and display fewer emotional and behavior problems (Brodzinsky, 2011; LeMare & Audet, 2014). Also, as long as parents took steps to help them learn about their birth heritage in childhood, young people adopted into a different ethnic group or culture generally develop identities that are healthy blends of their birth and rearing backgrounds (Barn, 2013; Thomas & Tessler, 2007). At the same time, intercountry adoptees who express a strong host-culture identity also tend to be well adjusted (Boivin & Hassan, 2015). If parents do not know enough about their child's birth heritage to transmit it, adoptees may explore it later, in adulthood.

 **A S K   Y O U R S E L F**

Connect ■ Why is genetic counseling called a communication process? Who should seek it, and why?

Apply ■ Imagine that you must counsel a couple considering in vitro fertilization using donor ova to overcome infertility. What medical and ethical risks would you raise?

Reflect ■ Suppose you are a carrier of fragile X syndrome and want to have children. Would you choose pregnancy, adoption, or surrogacy? If you became pregnant, would you opt for prenatal diagnosis? Explain your decisions.

 # 2.3 Environmental Contexts for Development

Just as complex as genetic inheritance is the surrounding environment—a multi-layered set of influences that combine to help or hinder physical and psychological well-being. Jot down a brief description of events and people that have significantly influenced your development. Do the items on your list resemble those of my students, who mostly mention experiences that involve their families? This emphasis is not surprising, since the family is the first and longest-lasting context for development. Other influences that make most students' top ten are friends, neighbors, school, and community and religious organizations.

Return to Bronfenbrenner's ecological systems theory, discussed in Chapter 1. It emphasizes that environments extending beyond the *microsystem*—the immediate settings just mentioned—also powerfully affect development. Indeed, my students rarely mention one important context. Its impact is so pervasive that we seldom stop to think about it in our daily lives. This is the *macrosystem,* or broad social climate of society—its values and programs that support and protect children's development. All families need help in rearing children—through affordable housing and health care, safe neighborhoods, good schools, well-equipped recreational facilities, and high-quality child care and other services that permit them to meet both work and family responsibilities. And some families, because of poverty or special tragedies, need considerably more help than others.

In the following sections, we take up these contexts for development. Because they affect every age and aspect of change, we will return to them in later chapters. For now, our discussion emphasizes that environments, as well as heredity, can enhance or create risks for development.

2.3 Discuss aspects of children's multi-layered environment that influence their development and well-being.

2.3.1 The Family

In power and breadth of influence, no other microsystem context equals the family. The family creates unique bonds among people. Attachments to parents and siblings are usually lifelong and serve as models for relationships in the wider world. Within the family, children learn the language, skills, and social and moral values of their culture. Furthermore, research conducted in over 20 countries across six continents with tens of thousands of children and adults reveals that warm, affectionate family ties, especially with parents, consistently predict physical and psychological health throughout development (Khaleque & Rohner, 2012). In contrast, parental rejection—coldness, hostility, or indifference—is generally associated with developmental problems.

Contemporary researchers view the family as a network of interdependent relationships (Bronfenbrenner & Morris, 2006; Russell, 2014). Recall from ecological systems theory that family members exert *bidirectional influences* on one another, the behaviors of each affecting those of others. Indeed, the very term *system* implies that the responses of family members are related. These system influences operate both directly and indirectly.

This family is a network of interdependent relationships, in which each person's behavior influences that of the others. As parents and children play a game, warm, considerate parental communication encourages children's cooperation, which promotes further parental warmth and caring.

Direct Influences   The next time you have a chance to observe family members interacting, watch carefully. You are likely to see that kind, patient communication evokes cooperative, harmonious responses, whereas harshness and impatience engender angry, resistive behavior. Each of these reactions, in turn, forges a new link in the interactive chain. In the first instance, a positive message tends to follow; in the second, a negative or avoidant one is likely.

These observations fit with a wealth of research on the family system. Studies of families of diverse ethnicities show that when parents are firm but warm, children tend to comply with their requests. And when children cooperate, their parents are likely to be warm and gentle in the future. In contrast, children whose parents discipline harshly and impatiently are likely to refuse and rebel. And because children's misbehavior is stressful, parents may increase their use of punishment, leading to more unruliness by the child (Lorber & Egeland, 2011; Shaw, Hyde, & Brennan, 2012). In each case, the behavior of one family member helps sustain a form of interaction in the other that either promotes or undermines children's psychological well-being.

LOOK and LISTEN

Observe several parent–young child pairs in a supermarket or department store, where parents are likely to place limits on children's behavior. How does the quality of parent communication seem to influence the child's response? How does the child's response affect the parent's subsequent interaction?

Indirect Influences   The impact of family relationships on development becomes even more complicated when we consider that interaction between any two members is affected by others present in the setting. Recall from Chapter 1 that Bronfenbrenner called these indirect influences the effect of *third parties.*

Third parties can serve to enhance or impede development. For example, when a marital relationship is warm and considerate, parents are more likely to engage in **coparenting,** or coordination of parenting roles, that is mutually supportive and collaborative. Such parents are warmer, praise and stimulate their children more, and nag and scold them less (Morrill et al., 2010). In contrast, parents whose marriage is tense and hostile often coparent ineptly. They interfere with each other's child-rearing efforts, are less responsive to children's needs, and are more likely to criticize, express anger, and punish (Palkovitz, Fagan, & Hull, 2013; Stroud et al., 2015).

Children who are chronically exposed to angry, unresolved parental conflict have serious behavior problems resulting from disrupted emotional security (Cummings & Miller-Graff, 2015). These include both *internalizing difficulties,* such as feeling anxious and fearful and trying to repair their parents' relationship, and *externalizing difficulties,* including anger and aggression (Goeke-Morey, Papp, & Cummings, 2013; Stroud et al., 2015).

Adapting to Change   Think back to the *chronosystem* in ecological systems theory (see page 27 in Chapter 1). The interplay of forces within the family is dynamic and ever-changing as each member adapts to the development of other members.

For example, as children acquire new skills, parents adjust the way they treat their more competent youngsters. Consider the way a parent relates to a young infant compared to a walking, talking toddler. During the first few months, parents spend much time feeding, bathing, and cuddling the baby. Within a year, things change dramatically. The 1-year-old points, shows, names objects, and explores the household cupboards. In response, parents devote more time to talking, playing games, and disciplining. These new ways of interacting, in turn, encourage the child's expanding motor, cognitive, and social skills.

Parents' development affects children as well. The rise in parent–child conflict that often occurs in early adolescence is not solely due to teenagers' striving for independence. This is a time when most parents have reached middle age and—conscious that their children will soon leave home and establish their own lives—are reconsidering their own commitments (Steinberg & Silk, 2002). While the adolescent presses for greater autonomy, the parent presses for more togetherness. This imbalance promotes friction, which parent and teenager gradually resolve by accommodating to changes in each other.

Historical time period also contributes to a dynamic family system. In recent decades, a declining birth rate, a high divorce rate, expansion of women's roles, increased acceptance of same-sex relationships, and postponement of parenthood have led to a smaller family size and a greater number of single parents, remarried parents, lesbian and gay parents, employed mothers, and dual-earner families. Clearly, families in industrialized nations have become more diverse than ever before. In later chapters, we will take up these family forms, examining how each affects family relationships and children's development.

Nevertheless, some general patterns in family functioning do exist. In the United States and other industrialized nations, one important source of these consistencies is socioeconomic status.

2.3.2 Socioeconomic Status and Family Functioning

People in industrialized nations are stratified on the basis of what they do at work and how much they earn for doing it—factors that determine their social position and economic well-being. Researchers assess a family's standing on this continuum through an index called **socioeconomic status (SES),** which combines three related, but not completely overlapping, variables: (1) years of education and (2) the prestige of one's job and the skill it requires, both of which measure social status; and (3) income, which measures economic status. As SES rises and falls, families face changing circumstances that profoundly affect children's development and well-being.

SES is linked to timing of parenthood and to family size. People who work in skilled and semiskilled manual occupations (for example, construction workers, truck drivers, and custodians) tend to marry and have children earlier as well as give birth to more children than people in professional and technical occupations. The two groups also differ in child-rearing values and expectations. When more than 200,000 parents in 90 nations around the world were asked about personal qualities they desire for their children, lower-SES parents more often emphasized obedience, whereas higher-SES parents placed greater weight on independence (Park & Lau, 2016). In other research, low-SES parents tended to stress external characteristics, such as politeness, neatness, and cleanliness. In contrast, higher-SES parents focused on psychological traits, such as curiosity, happiness, self-esteem, self-direction, and cognitive and social maturity (Duncan & Magnuson, 2003; Hoff, Laursen, & Tardif, 2002).

These differences are reflected in family interaction. Parents higher in SES talk to, read to, and otherwise stimulate their infants and preschoolers more and grant them greater freedom to explore. With older children and adolescents, higher-SES parents use more warmth, explanations, and verbal praise; set higher academic and other developmental goals; and allow their children to make more decisions. Commands ("You do that because I told you to"), criticism, and physical punishment occur more often in low-SES households (Bush & Peterson, 2008; Mandara et al., 2009).

Education contributes substantially to these variations. Higher-SES parents' interest in providing verbal stimulation, nurturing inner traits, and promoting academic achievement is supported by years of schooling, during which they learned to think about abstract, subjective ideas and, thus, to invest in their children's cognitive and social development (Mistry et al., 2008). At the same time, greater economic security enables parents to devote more time, energy, and material resources to fostering their children's psychological characteristics (Duncan, Magnuson, & Votruba-Drzal, 2015). In diverse cultures around the world, as the Social Issues: Education box on page 68 makes clear, education of women in particular fosters patterns of thinking and behaving that greatly improve quality of life, for both parents and children.

Because of limited education and low social status, many low-SES parents feel a sense of powerlessness in their relationships beyond the home. At work, for example, they must obey rules made by others in positions of authority. When they get home, they often expect the same unquestioning obedience from their children (Belsky, Schlomer, & Ellis, 2012; Conger & Donnellan, 2007). High levels of stress sparked by economic insecurity contribute to low-SES parents' reduced provision of stimulating interaction and activities as well as greater use of coercive discipline.

Social Issues: Education | Worldwide Education of Girls: Transforming Current and Future Generations

In 2012, Malala Yousafzai, a Pakistani teenager, rose to international prominence after surviving an assassination attempt by a Taliban gunman for her persuasive activism favoring girls' right to education. Three years earlier, at age 11, Malala had begun writing a blog for the BBC, using a pseudonym to protect her safety. The blog reported her experiences under Taliban rule, which had at times banned girls in her province from attending school. After the New York Times released a documentary about Malala's life and courage, she began giving interviews that were broadcast around the world. In retaliation, the Taliban gunned her down on a school bus.

Malala's recovery from life-threatening gunshot wounds sparked worldwide support for her cause. Among the outcomes were a 2012 United Nations petition called "I am Malala," advocating school enrollment for all the world's children, and a UNESCO fund directed at expanding girls' access to high-quality, safe learning environments, especially in countries affected by conflict and disaster. These initiatives led to Pakistan's first compulsory education law, which guarantees free education to all children between ages 5 and 16.

From 1950 to 2010, the percentage of children in developing nations attending school increased from a small minority of boys to a majority of all children in most regions. Recently, however, progress has slowed. Today, 63 million (9 percent) of the world's children of elementary-school age are not in school, a rate that climbs to 61 million (16 percent) at the middle-school level and 263 million (36 percent) at the high-school level (UNESCO, 2018). Although gender differences have declined, more girls than boys remain out of school, especially in the poorest countries. Two-thirds of the world's 750 million illiterate adults are women.

In research carried out in four nations—Mexico, Nepal, Venezuela, and Zambia—investigators examined the impact of variations in maternal language and literacy skills on family health, mother–child interaction, and young children's literacy skills (LeVine et al., 2012). Participating mothers' average levels of schooling ranged from 5 years in Nepal to 8 years in Zambia, with some having attended for as little as 1 year and most having left by age 13.

Findings in each country, and across rural and urban areas, were the same. Educating girls had a powerful impact on the welfare of children and families. The diverse benefits largely accrued in two ways: (1) through enhanced verbal skills—reading, writing, and oral communication; and (2) through the cognitive abilities that literacy promotes. Together, these capacities enable girls, as they become adults and mothers, to navigate health and educational settings more effectively and to teach their children in ways that foster school success.

Child Health

Maternal education in developing countries is the most important contributor to steady, worldwide gains in children's health over the past several decades (Denno & Paul, 2017). In the four-countries study, the higher mothers' school attainment and literacy level, the better their comprehension of radio and TV health messages and the more easily they could explain their children's illness symptoms to health professionals.

Clearly, education gives women the knowledge and communication skills to benefit from public health information. As a result, it strongly predicts preventive health behaviors, including prenatal visits, child immunizations, and healthy diet. Also, because women with more schooling have more life opportunities, they are more likely to take advantage of family planning services, delay childbearing, and have more widely spaced and fewer children (Günes, 2015). All these practices are linked to improvements in child survival and health.

As early as the second year of life, higher SES is associated with enhanced cognitive and language development and with reduced incidence of behavior problems. And throughout childhood and adolescence, children from higher-SES families, on average, do better in school (Bradley & Corwyn, 2003; Hoff, 2013; Melby et al., 2008; Noble et al., 2015a). As a result, they usually attain higher levels of education, which greatly enhances their opportunities for a prosperous adult life.

2.3.3 Affluence

Despite their advanced education and great material wealth, affluent parents—those in prestigious and high-paying occupations—too often fail to engage in family interaction and parenting that promote favorable development. In several studies, researchers tracked the adjustment of youths growing up in wealthy suburbs. By seventh grade, many showed serious problems that worsened in high school (Luthar & Barkin, 2012; Racz, McMahon, & Luthar, 2011). Their school grades were poor, and they were more likely than youths in general to engage in alcohol and drug use, to commit delinquent acts, and to report high levels of anxiety and depression.

Why are so many affluent youths troubled? Compared to their better-adjusted counterparts, poorly adjusted affluent young people report less emotional closeness, less supervision, and fewer serious consequences for misbehaviors from their parents, who lead professionally and socially demanding lives. As a group, wealthy parents are nearly as physically and emotionally unavailable to their youngsters as parents coping with serious financial strain. At the same time,

Mother–Child Interaction and Children's Literacy Skills

Making home observations, researchers in the four-countries study found that schooling and literacy skills were positively associated with mothers' verbal responsiveness to their infants' and toddlers' vocalizations. Follow-ups as the children grew older revealed that mothers who talked more had children with larger vocabularies. The more literate mothers had adopted a style of interaction that promoted language development.

In Nepal, the investigators looked closely at literacy-related parenting behaviors in the preschool and early school years. Mothers with more education—especially those with better literacy skills—reported more often teaching their children academic skills, enriching the home with literacy materials, modeling literacy behaviors, and having higher expectations for their children's education. These home supports, in turn, predicted children's language and literacy progress.

Implications

Educating girls is the most effective means of combating the most profound, global threats to children's development: poverty, child mortality, disease, gender inequality, and economic and social instability in the world's poorest countries (Tao, 2018). Even the limited educational doses available to women in the four-countries study were influential. But because of cultural beliefs about gender roles, reluctance to give

Pakastani girls attend class on the first anniversary of the near-fatal shooting of Malalah Yousafzai, a teenage activist who advocates forcefully for education for girls. Within weeks of the assassination attempt, a shocked Pakistan enacted its first compulsory education legislation. After recovering, Malalah resumed her activism. In 2014, she was awarded the Nobel Peace Prize and, in 2017, was named a United Nations Messenger of Peace.

up a daughter's work at home, or war and social upheaval, parents may resist sending their daughters to school.

An even greater barrier is that many low-income countries continue to charge parents a fee for each child enrolled in school. Consequently, poverty-stricken parents—if they send any

children—tend to send only sons. When governments abolish enrollment fees, provide information about the benefits of education for girls, and create employment possibilities for women, the overwhelming majority of parents—including the very poor—choose to send their daughters to school and are willing to make sacrifices to do so.

these parents often make excessive demands for achievement and are critical when their children perform less than perfectly (Luthar, Barkin, & Crossman, 2013). Adolescents whose parents value their accomplishments more than their character are more likely to have academic and emotional problems.

For both affluent and low-SES youths, a simple routine—eating dinner with parents—is associated with a reduction in adjustment difficulties, even after many other aspects of parenting are controlled (see Figure 2.7) (Luthar & Latendresse, 2005). Interventions that make wealthy parents aware of the high costs of a competitive lifestyle, weak involvement in children's lives, and unrealistically high expectations are badly needed.

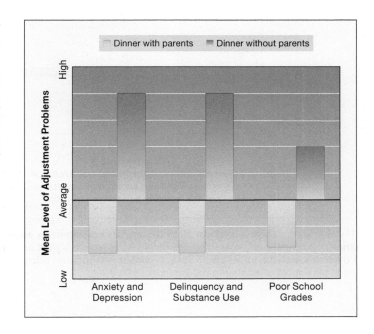

FIGURE 2.7 **Relationship of regularly eating dinner with parents to affluent youths' adjustment problems.** Among several hundred affluent sixth graders, those who rarely ate dinner with their parents, compared with those who often did so, were far more likely to display anxiety and depression, delinquency and substance use, and poor school grades, even after many other aspects of parenting were controlled. In this study, frequent family mealtimes also protected low-SES youths from delinquency and substance use and from classroom learning problems. (Based on Luthar & Latendresse, 2005a.)

2.3.4 Poverty

When families slip into poverty, development is seriously threatened. In a TV documentary on childhood poverty, a PBS filmmaker explored the daily lives of several American children, along with the struggles of their families (Frontline, 2012). Asked what being poor is like, 10-year-old Kaylie replied, "We don't get three meals a day…. Sometimes we have cereal but no milk and have to eat it dry." Kaylie said she felt hungry much of the time, adding, "I'm afraid if we can't pay our bills, me and my brother will starve."

Kaylie lives with her 12-year-old brother Tyler and their mother, who suffers from depression and panic attacks and cannot work. The children sometimes gather discarded tin cans from around their rural neighborhood and sell them for a small amount. When money to pay rent ran out, the family moved from its small house to an extended-stay motel. Before the move, Kaylie and Tyler tearfully gave up their pet dog to a shelter.

With family belongings piled haphazardly around her in the cramped motel room, Kaylie complained, "I have no friends, no places to play. I pass the time by." Kaylie and Tyler had few books and indoor games; no outdoor play equipment such as bicycles, bats and balls, and roller skates; and no scheduled leisure pursuits. Asked to imagine her future, Kaylie wasn't hopeful. "I see my future poor, on the streets, in a box, asking for money from everyone, stealing stuff…. I'd like to explore the world, but I'm never going to be able to do that."

Today, 12.7 percent of the U.S. population—nearly 41 million Americans—live in poverty. Among those hit hardest are parents under age 25 with young children, one-fourth of whom are poor. Poverty is also magnified among ethnic minorities and women. For example, 18 percent of U.S. children younger than age 18—about 12 million—live in families with incomes below the federal poverty level, the income judged necessary for a minimum living standard (about $25,000 for a family of four). Poverty rates climb to 27 percent for Hispanic children, 31 percent for African-American children, and 34 percent for Native-American children. For single mothers with preschool children, the poverty rate is close to 50 percent (Semega, Fontenot, & Kollar, 2017; U.S. Census Bureau, 2017a).

As we will see later, government programs with insufficient resources to meet family needs are responsible for these disheartening statistics. The U.S. poverty rate is higher among children than any other age group. And of all Western nations, the United States has the highest percentage of extremely poor children. Eight percent of U.S. children live in deep poverty (at less than half the poverty threshold, the income level judged necessary for a minimum living standard). In contrast, in most economically advanced nations, child poverty rates have remained well below the U.S. poverty rate for several decades (see Figure 2.8), and extreme poverty is rare (UNICEF, 2017c). The earlier poverty begins, the deeper it is, and the longer it lasts, the more devastating are its effects. Children of poverty are more likely than other children to suffer from lifelong poor

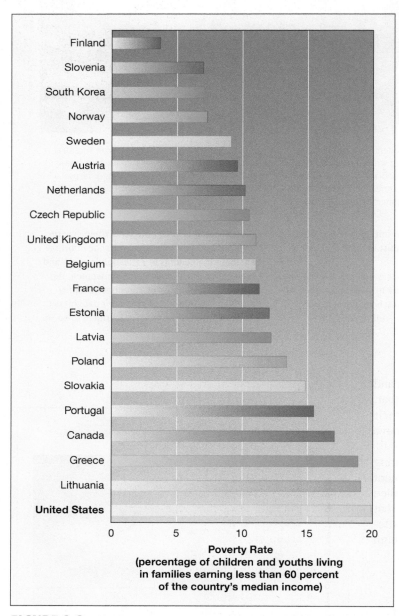

FIGURE 2.8 **Child poverty in 20 of the world's economically advanced nations.** Among the countries listed, the United States has the highest percentage of children and youths under age 18 living in families with incomes below 60 percent of the national median income. (Based on OECD, 2018.)

physical health, persistent deficits in cognitive develop-ment and academic achievement, high school dropout, mental illness, and impulsivity, aggression, and antiso-cial behavior (Duncan, Magnuson, & Votruba-Drzal, 2015; Yoshikawa, Aber, & Beardslee, 2012).

The constant stressors that accompany poverty gradually weaken the family system. Poor families have many daily hassles: loss of welfare and unemployment payments, basic services—phone, TV, electricity, hot water—being shut off because of inability to pay bills, and limited or uncertain access to food, to name just a few. When daily crises arise, family members become depressed, irritable, and distracted; hostile interactions increase; and children's development suffers (Conger & Donnellan, 2007; Kohen et al., 2008).

Negative outcomes are especially severe in single-parent families and in families who must live in run-down, overcrowded housing and dangerous neigh-borhoods—conditions that make everyday existence even more difficult while reducing social supports that help people cope with economic hardship (Leventhal, Dupéré, & Shuey, 2015). On average, poverty rates are higher, neighborhood disorganization greater, and community services scarcer in rural com-munities—like the one where Kaylie, Tyler, and their mother live—than in urban areas (Hicken et al., 2014; Vernon-Feagans & Cox, 2013). These circumstances heighten risks for disrupted family functioning and physical and psychological adjustment difficulties.

Homelessness poses enormous challenges for maintaining positive family relationships and physical and mental health. This mother and her three young children prepare to move out of the motel room they share with her boyfriend and her father.

A related problem has reduced the life chances of substantial numbers of children: More than 3 percent—nearly 2.5 million—experienced homelessness in the most recently reported year (Bassuk et al., 2014). Most homeless families consist of women with children under age 5. Besides health problems (which affect the majority of homeless people), many homeless children suffer from developmental delays and chronic emotional stress due to harsh, insecure daily lives (Kilmer et al., 2012). Homeless children achieve less less well academically than other poverty-stricken children because of poor school attendance, frequent moves from school to school, and physical and emotional health problems (Cutuli et al., 2010; National Coalition for the Homeless, 2012).

Although gaps in overall health and achievement between poverty-stricken children and their economically better-off peers are substantial, a considerable number of children from financially stressed families are resilient, faring well. A host of interventions have emerged to help children and youths surmount the risks of poverty. Some address family functioning and parenting. In a study of one such program, poverty-stricken families with preschool through adolescent children were randomly assigned to a family-strengthening intervention or to a no-intervention control group. The intervention involved 14 hours of intensive parent training devoted to learning about and practicing effective strategies for coping with stress, solving everyday problems, and engaging in positive family communication and parenting. Compared with controls, participating parents reported an improved capacity to manage stressful situ-ations, lessening of economic strain, warmer parent–child interaction, and fewer depressive symptoms—benefits that translated into a reduction in child internalizing and externalizing difficulties (Wadsworth et al., 2013). These positive outcomes were still evident 18 months after the intervention ended.

Other interventions directly target children's academic, emotional, and social skills in child-care centers, preschools, and elementary and secondary schools. And more programs recognize that because poverty-stricken children often experience multiple adversities, they benefit most from multifaceted efforts that focus on family, parenting, and children's needs at once (Kagan, 2013a). We will discuss many such interventions later in this text.

2.3.5 Beyond the Family: Neighborhoods and Schools

As the concepts of *mesosystem* and *exosystem* in ecological systems theory make clear, connections between family and community are vital for psychological well-being. From our discussion of poverty, perhaps you can see why: In poverty-stricken areas, community life is often disrupted. Families move often, parks and playgrounds are in disarray, and community centers providing organized leisure-time activities do not exist. In poor urban neighborhoods, family violence, child abuse and neglect, child and youth internalizing and externalizing difficulties, and adult criminal behavior are widespread (Chen, Howard, & Brooks-Gunn, 2011; Dunn, Schaefer-McDaniel, & Ramsay, 2010; Ingoldsby et al., 2012; Lang et al., 2008). And in poor rural communities, family isolation and scarcity of supportive services are especially high (Vernon-Feagans & Cox, 2013). In contrast, strong family ties to the surrounding social context—as indicated by frequent contact with relatives and friends and regular church, synagogue, temple, or mosque attendance—reduce stress and enhance adjustment.

Neighborhoods   Neighborhoods offer resources and social ties that play an important part in children's development. In an experimental study of neighborhood mobility, low-SES families were randomly assigned vouchers to move out of public housing into neighborhoods varying widely in affluence. Compared with their peers who remained in poverty-stricken areas, children and youths who moved into low-poverty neighborhoods and remained there for at least several years showed better physical and mental health and school achievement. Children exposed to advantaged neighborhoods consistently, from early childhood into adolescence, benefit the most academically (Anderson & Leventhal, 2014; Leventhal & Brooks-Gunn, 2003; Leventhal & Dupéré, 2011). The ability of low-income families to integrate into the social life of their new neighborhoods is also key to favorable outcomes.

Neighborhood resources have a greater impact on economically disadvantaged than on well-to-do young people. Higher-SES families can afford to transport their children to lessons and entertainment and, if necessary, to better-quality schools in distant parts of the community. In low-income neighborhoods, in-school and after-school programs that substitute for lack of other resources by providing art, music, sports, and other enrichment activities are associated with improved academic performance and a reduction in emotional and behavior problems in elementary and middle school (Durlak, Weissberg, & Pachan, 2010; Kataoka & Vandell, 2013; Vandell, Reisner, & Pierce, 2007). Neighborhood organizations, such as religious youth groups and special interest clubs, contribute to favorable development in adolescence, including increased self-confidence, school achievement, and educational aspirations (Barnes et al., 2007).

Yet in dangerous, disorganized neighborhoods, high-quality activities for children and adolescents are scarce. Even when they are available, crime and social disorder limit young people's access, and parents overwhelmed by financial and other stressors are unlikely to encourage their children to participate. In an investigation of a large sample of elementary school students diverse in SES and neighborhood residence, those living in the least stimulating homes and the most chaotic neighborhoods were least likely to enroll in after-school and community-center enrichment activities (Dearing et al., 2009). Thus, the neediest children and youths were especially likely to miss out on these development-enhancing experiences.

Just how do family–neighborhood ties reduce parenting stress and promote children's development? One answer lies in their provision of social support, which leads to the following benefits:

- *Parental self-worth.* A neighbor or relative who listens and tries to relieve a parent's concern enhances her self-esteem. The parent, in turn, is likely to interact in a more sensitive and involved manner with her children.
- *Parental access to valuable information and services.* A friend who suggests where a parent might find a job, housing, and affordable child care and youth activities helps make the multiple roles of spouse, parent, and provider easier to fulfill.

LOOK and LISTEN

Ask several parents to list their school-age children's regular lessons and other enrichment activities. Then inquire about home and neighborhood factors that either encourage or impede their children's participation.

- *Child-rearing controls and role models.* Friends, relatives, and other community members may encourage and demonstrate effective parenting practices and discourage ineffective practices.
- *Direct assistance with child rearing.* As children and adolescents participate in their parents' social networks and in neighborhood settings, other adults can influence children through warmth, stimulation, and exposure to a wider array of competent models. In this way, family–neighborhood ties can reduce the impact of ineffective parenting (Silk et al., 2004). Nearby adults can also intervene when they see young people skipping school or behaving antisocially.

High-school volunteers take part in a program to clean up and revitalize Detroit's distressed Brightmoor neighborhood. Participation in such neighborhood organizations contributes to favorable development of economically disadvantaged adolescents.

The Better Beginnings, Better Futures Project of Ontario, Canada, is a government-sponsored initiative aimed at preventing the dire consequences of neighborhood poverty by strengthening community capacity to create development-enhancing environments for children and families. Using neighborhood elementary schools as its base, Better Beginnings programs provided children ages 4 to 8 years with in-class, before- and after-school, and summer enrichment activities. Program staff also visited each child's parents regularly, informed them about community resources, and encouraged their involvement in the child's school and neighborhood life. And a communitywide component focused on improving neighborhood life by offering leadership training and adult education programs and organizing special events and celebrations (Peters, 2005; Peters, Petrunka, & Arnold, 2003).

Longitudinal follow-ups of Better Beginnings as participants reached grades 3, 6, 9, and 12 revealed wide-ranging benefits compared with children and families living in impoverished neighborhoods without this set of programs (Peters et al., 2010; Worton et al., 2014). Among these were gains in children's academic performance and social adjustment, a reduction in adolescent delinquency and drug use, and parent-reported improved family functioning, child-rearing practices, and sense of community connection.

Schools   Unlike the informal worlds of family and neighborhood, the school is a formal institution designed to transmit knowledge and skills needed to become productive members of society. Children and youths in the developed world spend much time in school—a total of about 14,000 hours, on average, by high school graduation. And today, because many children younger than age 5 attend "school-like" child-care centers or preschools, the impact of schooling begins earlier and is even more powerful than these figures suggest.

Schools are complex social systems that affect many aspects of development. Schools vary in their physical environments—space, equipment, and materials available for work and play. They also differ in their educational philosophies—whether teachers regard students as passive learners to be molded by adult instruction; as active, curious beings who determine their own learning; or as collaborative partners assisted by adult experts, who guide their mastery of new skills. The social life of schools varies as well—in the degree to which students cooperate and compete; in the extent to which students of different abilities and SES and ethnic backgrounds learn together; and in whether they are safe, humane settings or riddled with peer harassment and violence. We will discuss these aspects of schooling in later chapters.

As with SES and family functioning, schooling and academic achievement contribute substantially to life chances and well-being. Furthermore, these contextual influences are interrelated: Children from homes in low-income and poverty-stricken neighborhoods are more likely to attend underfunded schools and experience poorer quality education. For these reasons, educational interventions aimed at upgrading the educational experiences and school performance of economically disadvantaged children are best begun in the early years (Crosnoe & Benner, 2015). But intervening at later periods to target specific educational problems is also helpful—for example, by promoting academic self-confidence and motivation in middle childhood and providing high-quality vocational education to non-college-bound youths.

Students whose parents are involved in their education—through participating in school organizations, volunteering at school, attending parent–teacher conferences, and reinforcing school-based learning at home—show better academic achievement. And when followed up in early adulthood, their educational attainment is higher (Benner, Boyle, & Sadler, 2016). Higher-SES parents, whose backgrounds and values are similar to those of teachers, are more likely to sustain regular educational involvement. In contrast, low-SES parents often feel uncomfortable about coming to school and approaching teachers on behalf of their children's learning, and daily stressors reduce the time and energy they have to do so (Calarco, 2014; Grant & Ray, 2010). Teachers and administrators must take extra steps with low-SES and ethnic minority families to build supportive family–school ties.

2.3.6 The Cultural Context

Our discussion in Chapter 1 emphasized that child development can be fully understood only when viewed in its larger cultural context. In the following sections, we expand on this theme by taking up the role of the *macrosystem* in development. First, we discuss ways that cultural values and practices affect contexts for development. Then we consider how healthy development depends on laws and government programs that shield children from harm and foster their well-being.

Cultural Values and Practices   Cultures shape family interaction and community settings beyond the home—in short, all aspects of daily life. Many of us remain blind to aspects of our own cultural heritage until we see them in relation to the practices of others.

Consider the question, Who should be responsible for rearing young children? How would you answer it? Here are some common responses from my students: "If parents decide to have a baby, then they should be ready to care for it." "Most people are not happy about others intruding into family life." These statements reflect a widely held opinion in the United States—that the care and rearing of children, and paying for that care, are the duty of parents, and only parents. This view has a long history—one in which independence, self-reliance, and the privacy of family life emerged as basic American values (Dodge & Haskins, 2015). It is one reason, among others, that the public has been slow to endorse government-supported benefits for all families, such as high-quality child care and paid employment leave for meeting family needs. It has also contributed to the large number of U.S. children who remain poor, even though their parents are employed (Gruendel & Aber, 2007; UNICEF, 2017c).

Although the culture as a whole may value independence and privacy, not all citizens share the same values. Some belong to **subcultures**—groups of people with beliefs and customs that differ from those of the larger culture. Many ethnic minority groups in the United States have cooperative family structures, illustrated by the active, involved extended-family bonds common in African-American, Asian, Hispanic, and Native-American subcultures. Within these extended families, grandparents play meaningful roles in guiding younger generations; adults who face employment, marital, or parenting difficulties receive assistance and emotional support; and children are better adjusted, academically and socially (Jones & Lindahl, 2011; Washington, Gleeson, & Rulison, 2013). In Hispanic extended families, grandparents are especially likely to share in child rearing—a collaborative parenting arrangement that is consistent with the Hispanic cultural ideal of *familism*, which places a particularly high priority on close, harmonious family relationships. As the Cultural Influences box on page 75 indicates, familism is associated with multiple positive developmental outcomes.

Our discussion so far reflects two broad sets of values on which cultures and subcultures are commonly compared: *collectivism* versus *individualism* (Triandis & Gelfand, 2012). In cultures that emphasize collectivism, people stress group goals over individual goals and value *interdependent* qualities, such as interpersonal harmony, obligations and responsibility to others, and collaborative endeavors. In cultures that emphasize individualism, people are largely concerned with their own personal needs and value *independence*—personal exploration, discovery, achievement, and choice in relationships.

Cultural Influences | Familism Promotes Competence in Hispanic Children and Youths

Here are some responses from Dominican, Mexican, and Puerto Rican parents who were asked to describe their most basic values:

> You have to help each other out, be there for each other, especially when you're growing up or when you have families. I mean that togetherness is very important.

> Your parents are number one but your grandparents are even greater than number one [in reference to extended family members who play a significant role in a child's life].

> When I was growing up, you had to be crazy to talk back to your parents. No one got away with that kind of falta de respeto [lack of respect] (Calzada, 2010).

Each of these statements expresses the Hispanic core cultural value of **familism,** which elevates the needs of family above any concerns of the individual. Familism requires family members to establish loyal, cohesive relationships with one another; to be respectful, especially toward elders; and to provide one another with emotional and material support. Familism also holds that the quality of relationships forged with family members is central to each person's self-esteem and identity. Consequently, frequent contact is the norm in Hispanic extended families (Calzada, Tamis-LeMonda, & Yoshikawa, 2013). As they fulfill the obligations of familism in their everyday lives, many Hispanic adults live in close proximity to or share living arrangements with extended kin.

Parents begin to instill familism in young children by insisting that they interact respectfully with adults through polite greetings, not interrupting, and not challenging what they say (Stein et al., 2014). Mothers strongly committed to familism report greater warmth and closeness with their preschoolers. In one study, the combination of high maternal warmth and valuing of familism predicted better classroom emotional adjustment and peer relations among Mexican-American preschoolers (Gamble & Modry-Mandell,

2008). By emphasizing cohesiveness, support, and respect, familism seems to foster both positive parent–child interaction and preschoolers' favorable social behavior.

From these early parental teachings, school-age children and adolescents internalize the value of familism, which further supports social competence (Bridges et al., 2012). In an investigation of Mexican-American 9- to 13-year-olds, those whose mothers exposed them to social learning opportunities consistent with familism—such as helping with sibling caregiving or meeting elder family members' needs—expressed stronger familism beliefs (Calderón-Tena, Knight, & Carlo, 2011). Together, these parenting practices and children's consequent familism beliefs predicted children's willingness to help and support peers and others outside the family.

As their adolescent children become more autonomous, Hispanic parents engage in many parenting strategies consistent with familism, including closely monitoring teenagers' activities, insisting that they follow reasonable rules, and expressing warmth and support (Stein et al., 2015; Updegraff et al., 2012). Although striving for autonomy typically leads to a decline in familism beliefs over the teenage years, young people nevertheless continue to demonstrate many behaviors consistent with familism, including spending considerable time with family members and willingly fulfilling family obligations (Updegraff et al., 2005).

Adolescents' commitment to familism is linked to diverse aspects of maturity and adjustment. These include greater likelihood of viewing parents as legitimate sources of guidance; higher academic motivation and school grades; greater sense of school belonging; fewer deviant peer associations and risky behaviors; less anxiety and fearfulness; and less anger and aggression (Ayón, Marsiglia, & Bermudez-Parsai, 2010; Sánchez, Colón, & Esparza, 2005; Sánchez et al., 2010; Stein & Polo, 2014; Stein et al., 2015). If family responsibilities become excessive, teenagers can react with stress, depression, and worsening school performance. But overall, familism beliefs seem to make young people more aware of others' needs and the importance of behaving respectfully and responsibly in contexts beyond the home.

Neighborhood familism—the extent to which Hispanic mothers and fathers in the same neighborhood endorse familism—is a stronger predictor of positive adolescent adjustment than family income and neighborhood economic status (Gonzales et al., 2010). Living in a community in which many adults value familism may provide youths with collective supervision and other supports for favorable development.

A grandmother enjoys a warm relationship with her granddaughter as they work together on a baking project. In Hispanic extended families, grandparents are especially likely to share actively in child rearing, reflecting the cultural ideal of familism.

Although it is the most common basis for comparing cultures, the collectivism–individualism distinction is controversial because both sets of values exist in most cultures. As societies change, due to immigration and contact with other cultural, political, and economic systems, the values of their people diversify, yielding varying mixtures of collectivism and individualism (Taras et al., 2014). Integration of the two sets of values is positive for children's development because collectivism fosters access to social support, whereas individualism promotes striving for personal goals (Chen, 2015). Both are vital for psychological well-being.

Nevertheless, consistent cross-national differences in collectivism–individualism remain: The United States is more individualistic than most Western countries, which place greater weight on collectivism. These value priorities affect a nation's approach to protecting the well-being of children and families.

Public Policies and Child Development When widespread social problems arise, such as poverty, hunger, and disease, nations attempt to solve them through devising **public policies**—laws and government programs designed to improve current conditions. In the United States, public policies safeguarding children and youths have lagged behind policies in other developed nations. As Table 2.3 reveals, the United States does not rank well on important key measures of children's health and well-being.

The problems of children and youths extend beyond the indicators in the table. The U.S. Affordable Care Act, signed into law in 2010, extended government-supported health insurance to all children in low-income families. But expanded coverage for low-income adults, including parents, is not mandatory for the states, leaving millions of low-income parents without an affordable coverage option. Largely because uninsured parents lack knowledge of how to enroll their children, 11 percent of children eligible for the federally supported Children's Health Insurance Program (CHIP)—more than 5 million—do not receive coverage (Kaiser Family Foundation, 2015, 2017). Furthermore, the United States has been slow to move toward national standards and funding for child care. Affordable care is in short supply, and much of it is mediocre to poor in quality (Burchinal, 2018; Burchinal et al., 2015). In families affected by divorce, weak enforcement of child support payments heightens poverty in mother-headed households. And 8 percent of 16- to 24-year-olds who dropped out of high school have not returned to earn a diploma (U.S. Department of Education, 2017b).

Why have attempts to help children and youths been difficult to realize in the United States? Cultural values of self-reliance and privacy have made government hesitant to become involved in family matters. Furthermore, good social programs are expensive, and they must compete for a fair share of a country's economic resources. Children can easily remain unrecognized in this process because they cannot vote or speak out to protect their own interests (Ripple & Zigler, 2003). They must rely on the goodwill of others to become an important government priority.

TABLE 2.3 How Does the United States Compare to Other Nations on Indicators of Children's Health and Well-Being?

INDICATOR	U.S. RANK[a]	SOME COUNTRIES THE UNITED STATES TRAILS
Childhood poverty (among 20 economically advanced nations with similar standards of living)	20th	Canada, Iceland, Germany, United Kingdom, Norway, Sweden, Spain
Infant deaths in the first year of life (among 39 industrialized nations considered)	39th	Canada, Greece, Hungary, Ireland, Spain
Teenage birth rate (among 20 industrialized nations considered)	20th	Australia, Canada, Czech Republic, Denmark, Hungary, Iceland, Poland, Slovakia
Public expenditure on elementary education as a percentage of gross domestic product[b] (among 35 industrialized nations considered)	15th	Belgium, France, Iceland, New Zealand, Portugal, Spain, Sweden
Public expenditure on early childhood education as a percentage of gross domestic product[b] (among 28 industrialized nations considered)	21st	Austria, Chile, Germany, Italy, France, Sweden, Slovenia
Public expenditure on health as a percentage of total health expenditure, public plus private (among 35 industrialized nations considered)	35th	Austria, Australia, Canada, France, Hungary, Iceland, Switzerland, New Zealand

[a] 1 = highest, or best, rank.

[b] Gross domestic product is the value of all goods and services produced by a nation during a specified time period. It provides an overall measure of a nation's wealth.

Sources: OECD, 2017a, 2017b; Sedgh et al., 2015; UNICEF, 2017c; U.S. Census Bureau, 2017a; World Bank, 2018a.

Looking Toward the Future   Public policies aimed at fostering children's development can be justified on two grounds. The first is that children are the future—the parents, workers, and citizens of tomorrow. Investing in children yields valuable returns to a nation's quality of life. Second, child-oriented policies can be defended on humanitarian grounds—children's basic rights as human beings.

In 1989, the United Nations General Assembly, with the assistance of experts from many child-related fields, drew up the *Convention on the Rights of the Child,* a legal agreement among nations that commits each cooperating country to work toward guaranteeing environments that foster children's development, protect them from harm, and enhance their community participation and self-determination. Examples of rights include the highest attainable standard of health; an adequate standard of living; free and compulsory education; a happy, understanding, and loving family life; protection from all forms of abuse and neglect; and freedom of thought, conscience, religion, and expression, subject to appropriate parental guidance and national law.

The United States played a key role in drawing up the Convention, yet it is the only country in the world whose legislature has not ratified it. American individualism has stood in the way (Ruck et al., 2014; Scherrer, 2012). Opponents maintain that the Convention's provisions would shift the burden of child rearing from family to state.

Public policies fostering development are vital both on humanitarian grounds and as an investment in the future. Upward Bound—a federally funded educational enrichment program—helps prepare high school students from low-income families for successful admission to college. Here, an Upward Bound 16-year-old (right) attending a university-sponsored program on marine conservation assists a researcher during a shark-tagging expedition.

Although the worrisome state of many children and families persists, efforts are being made to improve their condition. Throughout this book, we will discuss many successful programs that could be expanded. Also, growing awareness of the gap between what we know and what we do to better children's lives has led experts in child development to join with concerned citizens as advocates for more effective policies. As a result, influential interest groups devoted to the well-being of children have emerged.

In the United States, one of the most vigorous is the Children's Defense Fund (CDF), *www.childrensdefense.org,* a nonprofit organization that engages in public education and partners with other organizations, communities, and elected officials to improve policies for children and adolescents. Another energetic advocacy organization is the National Center for Children in Poverty, *www.nccp.org,* dedicated to advancing the economic security, health, and welfare of U.S. children in low-income families.

Besides strong advocacy, public policies that enhance development depend on research that documents needs and evaluates programs to spark improvements. Today, more researchers are collaborating with community and government agencies to enhance the relevance of their investigations to public policies aimed at ensuring children's rights and improving their lives (SRCD Equity and Justice Committee, 2018). Investigators are also doing a better job of disseminating their findings in easily understandable, compelling ways, through reports to government officials, websites aimed at increasing public understanding, and collaborations with the media to ensure accurate and effective reporting. In these ways, researchers are helping to create the sense of immediacy about the condition of children and families that is necessary to spur a society into action.

ASK YOURSELF

Connect ▪ How does poverty affect functioning of the family system, placing all domains of development at risk?

Apply ▪ Check your local newspaper or one or two national news websites to see how often articles appear on the condition of children and families. Why is it important for researchers to communicate with the public about children's needs?

Reflect ▪ Do you agree with the widespread American sentiment that government should not become involved in family life? Explain.

2.4 Understanding the Relationship Between Heredity and Environment

2.4 Explain the various ways heredity and environment may combine to influence complex traits.

Throughout this chapter, we have discussed a wide variety of genetic and environmental influences, each of which has the power to alter the course of development. Yet children who are born into the same family, and who therefore share both genes and environments, are often quite different in characteristics. We also know that some individuals are affected more than others by their homes, neighborhoods, and communities. In some cases, a child who is given many advantages nevertheless does poorly, while another, though exposed to unfavorable rearing conditions, does well. How do scientists explain the impact of heredity and environment when they seem to operate in such varied ways?

Behavioral genetics is a field devoted to uncovering the contributions of nature and nurture to this diversity in human traits and abilities. Although scientists are making progress in identifying the multiple variations in DNA sequences associated with such complex attributes as intelligence and personality, so far these genetic markers explain only a small amount of variation in human behavior, and a minority of cases of most psychological disorders (Plomin et al., 2016; Zhao & Castellanos, 2016). For the most part, scientists are still limited to investigating the impact of genes on these characteristics indirectly.

Some believe that it is useful and possible to answer the question of *how much each factor contributes* to differences among people. A growing consensus, however, regards that question as unanswerable. These investigators believe that heredity and environment are inseparable (Lickliter & Honeycutt, 2015; Moore, 2013). The important question, they maintain, is *how nature and nurture work together.* Let's consider each position in turn.

2.4.1 The Question, "How Much?"

To infer the role of heredity in complex human characteristics, researchers use special methods, the most common being the *heritability estimate.* Let's look closely at the information this procedure yields, along with its limitations.

Heritability **Heritability estimates** measure the extent to which individual differences in complex traits in a specific population are due to genetic factors. We will take a brief look at heritability findings on intelligence and personality here, returning to them in greater detail in later chapters. Heritability estimates are obtained from **kinship studies,** which compare the characteristics of family members. The most common type of kinship study compares identical twins, who share all their genes, with fraternal twins, who, on average, share only half. If people who are genetically more alike are also more similar in intelligence and personality, then the researcher assumes that heredity plays an important role.

Kinship studies of intelligence provide some of the most controversial findings in the field of developmental science. Some experts claim a strong genetic influence, whereas others believe that heredity is barely involved. Currently, most kinship findings support a moderate role for heredity. When many twin studies are examined, correlations between the scores of identical twins are consistently higher than those of fraternal twins. In a summary of more than 10,000 twin pairs of diverse ages, the correlation for intelligence was .85 for identical twins and .60 for fraternal twins (Plomin & Spinath, 2004; Plomin et al., 2016).

Researchers use a complex statistical procedure to compare these correlations, arriving at a heritability estimate ranging from 0 to 1.00. The typical overall heritability estimate for intelligence is about .50 for child and adolescent twin samples in Western industrialized nations, suggesting that differences in genetic makeup explain half the variation in intelligence. However, heritability increases with age, from approximately .20 in infancy, to .40 in childhood, to .55 in adolescence, to .65 in early adulthood (Plomin & Deary, 2015). As we will see later, one explanation is that, compared to children, adolescents and adults exert greater personal control over their intellectual experiences—for example, how much time they spend reading or solving challenging problems. Adopted children's intelligence test scores are more strongly related to their biological parents' scores than to those of their adoptive parents, offering further support for the role of heredity (Petrill & Deater-Deckard, 2004).

Heritability research also reveals that genetic factors are important in personality. For frequently studied traits, such as sociability, anxiety, agreeableness, and activity level, heritability estimates obtained on child, adolescent, and young adult twins are moderate, in the .40s and .50s (van Beijsterveldt et al., 2016; Vukasović & Bratko, 2015). Unlike intelligence, however, heritability of personality does not increase with age (Turkheimer, Pettersson, & Horn, 2014).

Twin studies of schizophrenia, bipolar disorder, and autism generally yield high heritabilities, above .70. Heritabilities for antisocial behavior and major depression are considerably lower, in the .30s and .40s (Ronald & Hoekstra, 2014; Sullivan, Daly, & O'Donovan, 2012). Again, adoption studies are consistent with these results. Biological relatives of adoptees with schizophrenia, bipolar disorder, or autism are more likely than adoptive relatives to share the same disorder (Plomin, DeFries, & Knopik, 2013).

Celena Kopinski (left) and Sarah Heath (right) were born in China and adopted during their first year into different American families. Both were unaware they were related until, during Sarah's first year of college, a classmate called her by the wrong name and sent a photo of her to Celena. Two years later, when the adoptees met, DNA testing confirmed that they are identical twins. About getting to know each other, Celena commented, "It's kind of like looking in the mirror, except there is no mirror!" They discovered striking similarities, including the same taste in fashion. Clearly, heredity contributes to personality, but generalizing from twin evidence to the population is controversial.

Limitations of Heritability   The accuracy of heritability estimates depends on the extent to which the twin pairs studied reflect genetic and environmental variation in the population. Within a population in which all people have very similar home, school, and community experiences, individual differences in intelligence and personality are assumed to be largely genetic, and heritability estimates should be close to 1.00. Conversely, the more environments vary, the more likely they are to account for individual differences, yielding lower heritability estimates. In twin studies, most twin pairs are reared together under highly similar conditions. Even when separated twins are available for study, social service agencies have often placed them in advantaged homes that are alike in many ways (Charney, 2017; Richardson & Norgate, 2006). Because the environments of most twin pairs are less diverse than those of the general population, heritability estimates are likely to exaggerate the role of heredity.

Heritability estimates can easily be misapplied. For example, high heritabilities have been used to suggest that ethnic differences in intelligence test scores, such as the poorer performance of African-American children compared to European-American children, have a genetic basis (Jensen, 1969, 2001; Rushton, 2012). Yet heritabilities computed on mostly White twin samples do not explain test score differences between ethnic groups. We have already seen that large SES differences are involved. In Chapter 12, we will discuss research indicating that when African-American children are adopted into economically advantaged homes at an early age, their scores are well above average and substantially higher than those of children growing up in impoverished families.

Consistent with these findings, the heritability of children's intelligence increases as parental education and income increase—that is, as children grow up in conditions that allow them to make the most of their genetic endowment. In impoverished environments, children are prevented from realizing their potential. Consequently, enhancing these children's experiences through interventions—such as parent education and high-quality preschool or child care—has a greater impact on development (Bronfenbrenner & Morris, 2006; Phillips & Lowenstein, 2011).

2.4.2 The Question, "How?"

Today, most researchers view development as the result of a dynamic interplay between heredity and environment. How do nature and nurture work together? Several concepts shed light on this question.

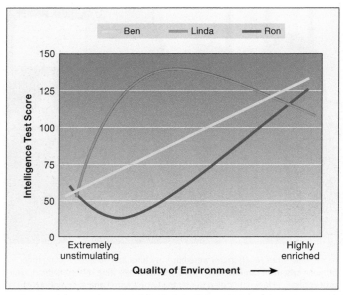

FIGURE 2.9 **Gene–environment interaction, illustrated for intelligence by three children who differ in responsiveness to quality of the environment.** As environments vary from extremely unstimulating to highly enriched, Ben's intelligence test score increases steadily, Linda's rises sharply and then falls off, and Ron's begins to increase only after the environment becomes modestly stimulating.

Gene–Environment Interaction The first of these ideas is **gene–environment interaction,** which means that because of their genetic makeup, individuals differ in their responsiveness to qualities of the environment (Rutter, 2011). Gene–environment interaction can apply to any characteristic; it is illustrated for intelligence in Figure 2.9. Notice that when environments vary from extremely unstimulating to highly enriched, Ben's intelligence increases steadily, Linda's rises sharply and then falls off, and Ron's begins to increase only after the environment becomes modestly stimulating.

Gene–environment interaction highlights two important points. First, it shows that because each of us has a unique genetic makeup, we respond differently to the same environment. Notice in Figure 2.9 how a poor environment results in similarly low scores for all three individuals. But when the environment provides a moderate level of simulations, Linda is by far the best-performing child. In a highly enriched environment, Ben does best, followed by Ron, both of whom now outperform Linda. Second, sometimes different gene–environment combinations can make two people look the same! For example, if Linda is reared in a minimally stimulating environment, her score will be about 100—average for people in general. Ben and Ron can also obtain this score, but to do so, they must grow up in fairly enriched circumstances (Gottlieb, Wahlsten, & Lickliter, 2006).

Recently, researchers have made strides in identifying gene–environment interactions in personality development. In Chapter 7 we will see that young children with certain genes that increase their risk of an emotionally reactive temperament respond especially strongly to variations in parenting quality (Bakermans-Kranenburg & van IJzendoorn, 2015; Halldorsdottir & Binder, 2017). When parenting is supportive, they gain control over their emotions and adjust as well or better than other children. But when parenting is harsh and insensitive, they become increasingly irritable, difficult, and poorly adjusted, more so than children not at genetic risk. Notice how such children are genetically constituted to react to both positive and negative parenting with especially high *plasticity.*

Gene–Environment Correlation A major problem in trying to separate heredity and environment is that they are often correlated (Rutter, 2011; Scarr & McCartney, 1983). According to the concept of **gene–environment correlation,** our genes influence the environments to which we are exposed. The way this happens changes with age.

Passive and Evocative Correlation At younger ages, two types of gene–environment correlation are common. The first is called *passive* correlation because the child has no control over it. Early on, parents provide environments influenced by their own heredity. For example, parents who are good athletes emphasize outdoor activities and enroll their children in swimming and gymnastics. Besides being exposed to an "athletic environment," the children may have inherited their parents' athletic ability. As a result, they are likely to become good athletes for both genetic and environmental reasons.

The second type of gene–environment correlation is *evocative.* Children evoke responses that are influenced by their heredity, and these responses strengthen their original behavior pattern. For example, an active friendly baby is likely to receive more social stimulation than a passive, quiet infant. And a cooperative, attentive child probably receives more sensitive, patient interactions from parents than an inattentive, distractible child. In support of this idea, the more genetically alike siblings are, the more their parents treat them alike, in both warmth and negativity. Parents' treatment of identical twins is highly similar, whereas their treatment of fraternal twins and nontwin biological siblings is only moderately so. And little resemblance exists in parents' warm and negative interactions with unrelated stepsiblings (Reiss, 2003). Likewise, identical-twin pairs—who resemble each other more in sociability than fraternal twins do—tend to be more alike in the degree of friendliness they evoke from new playmates (DiLalla, Bersted, & John, 2015).

Active Correlation At older ages, *active* gene–environment correlation becomes common. As children extend their experiences beyond the immediate family and are given the freedom to make more choices, they actively seek environments that fit with their genetic tendencies. The well-coordinated, muscular child spends more time at after-school sports, while the intellectually curious child is a familiar patron at the local library.

This tendency to actively choose environments that complement our heredity is called **niche-picking** (Scarr & McCartney, 1983). Infants and young children cannot do much niche-picking because adults select environments for them. In contrast, older children and adolescents are increasingly in charge of their own environments.

Niche-picking explains why pairs of identical twins reared apart during childhood and later reunited may find,

A mother imparts her ceramic skills to her daughter, who may have inherited her mother's artistic ability. When heredity and environment are correlated, the influence of one cannot be separated from the influence of the other.

to their surprise, that they have similar hobbies, food preferences, and vocations—a trend that is especially marked when twins' environmental opportunities are similar. Niche-picking also helps us understand why identical twins become somewhat more alike, and fraternal twins and adopted siblings less alike, in intelligence with age (Bouchard, 2004). And niche-picking sheds light on why identical twin pairs—far more often than same-sex fraternal twin pairs—report similar stressful life events influenced by personal decisions and actions, such as failing a course or getting in trouble for drug-taking (Bemmels, et al., 2008).

The influence of heredity and environment is not constant but changes over time. With age, genetic factors may become more important in influencing the environments we experience and choose for ourselves.

Environmental Influences on Gene Expression   Notice how, in the concepts just considered, heredity is granted priority. In gene–environment interaction, it affects responsiveness to particular environments. Similarly, gene–environment correlation is viewed as driven by genetics, in that children's genetic makeup causes them to receive, evoke, or seek experiences that actualize their hereditary tendencies (Rutter, 2011).

A growing number of researchers contend that heredity does not dictate children's experiences or development in a rigid way. For example, in a large Finnish adoption study, children with a genetic tendency for mental illness (based on having a biological mother diagnosed with schizophrenia) but who were being reared by healthy adoptive parents showed little mental illness. In contrast, schizophrenia and other psychological impairments piled up in adoptees whose biological and adoptive parents were both mentally ill (Tienari, Wahlberg, & Wynne, 2006; Tienari et al., 2003).

Furthermore, parents and other caring adults can *uncouple* unfavorable gene–environment correlations by providing children with positive experiences that modify the expression of heredity, yielding positive outcomes. In an investigation that tracked the development of 5-year-old identical twins, pair members tended to resemble each other in level of aggression. The more aggression children displayed, the more maternal anger and criticism they received (a gene–environment correlation). Nevertheless, some mothers treated their twins differently. When followed up at age 7, twins who had been targets of more maternal negativity engaged in even more aggressive behavior. In contrast, their better-treated counterparts showed a reduction in disruptive acts (Caspi et al., 2004). Good parenting protected them from a spiraling, antisocial course of development.

Accumulating evidence reveals that the relationship between heredity and environment is not a one-way street, from genes to environment to behavior. Rather, like other system influences considered in this and the previous chapter, it is *bidirectional:* Genes affect people's

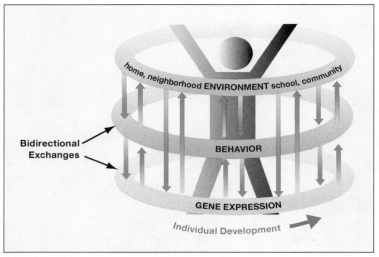

FIGURE 2.10 **Epigenesis.** Development takes place through ongoing, bidirectional exchanges between heredity and all levels of the environment. Genes affect behavior and experiences. Experiences and behavior also affect gene expression. (Based on Gottlieb, 2007.)

behavior and experiences, but their experiences and behavior also affect gene expression. Stimulation both *external* to the child (home, neighborhood, school, and society) and *internal* to the child (activity within the cytoplasm of the cell, hormones released into the bloodstream) modifies gene activity.

This view of the relationship between heredity and environment, depicted in Figure 2.10, is called **epigenesis,** which means development resulting from ongoing, bidirectional exchanges between heredity and all levels of the environment (Cox, 2013; Gottlieb, 1998, 2007). Biologists are clarifying the precise mechanisms through which environment can alter gene expression without changing the DNA sequence—a field of research called *epigenetics.* The most highly studied mechanism is **methylation**—a biochemical process triggered by certain experiences, in which a set of chemical compounds (called a methyl group) lands on top of a gene and changes its impact, reducing or silencing its expression. Methylation levels can be measured, and they help explain why identical twins, though precisely the same in DNA sequencing, sometimes display strikingly different phenotypes with age.

A case study of a pair of identical-twin adults offers an illustration. Researchers reported that they had been highly similar in personality throughout childhood. But after high school, one twin remained close to home, studied law, married, and had children, whereas the other left home, became a journalist, and traveled to war zones around the world, where she repeatedly encountered life-threatening situations. Assessed again in their forties, compared with the "law twin," the "war twin" engaged in more risky behaviors, including drinking and gambling (Kaminsky et al., 2007). DNA analyses revealed greater methylation of a gene known to affect impulse control in the "war twin" than in the "law twin"—a difference much larger than is typical for identical-twin pairs.

Environmental modification of gene expression can occur at any age, even prenatally. Recall our discussion of genomic imprinting on page 57. It is an epigenetic process occurring within the ovum or sperm, often involving methylation. And one way harmful prenatal environmental factors we will address in Chapter 3 may compromise development is through gene methylation (Markunas et al., 2014). As the Biology and Environment box on page 83 illustrates, severe maternal stress during pregnancy is linked to long-term impairment in children's capacity to manage stress, with gene methylation likely contributing to unfavorable outcomes. Furthermore, animal evidence indicates that some methylated genes are passed to offspring at conception, thereby affecting development in subsequent generations (Grossniklaus et al., 2013).

We must keep in mind, however, that epigenetic processes also operate positively: Favorable rearing experiences alter gene expression in ways that enhance development! And some negative epigenetic modifications may be reversible through carefully designed interventions (Boyce & Kobor, 2015; van IJzendoorn, Bakermans-Kranenburg, & Ebstein, 2011). The concept of epigenesis reminds us that the genome is constantly in flux, both reflecting and affecting the individual's ever-changing environment.

Epigenetics is still an emerging field, and clarifying its mechanisms may prove to be even more complex than efforts to understand DNA sequence variations. But from what we already know, one lesson is clear: Development is best understood as a series of complex exchanges between genes and the child's multi-layered, surrounding environment. In this way, epigenesis is consistent with the *developmental systems perspective,* introduced on page 11 in Chapter 1

© KIKE CALVO/V&W/THE IMAGE WORKS

The relationship between heredity and environment is bidirectional. This child's genetic makeup might predispose her to heart disease or obesity. But favorable experiences—such as participation in sports programs that promote regular, vigorous exercise—might alter gene expression in ways that overcome this genetic susceptibility.

Biology and Environment

The Tutsi Genocide and Epigenetic Transmission of Maternal Stress to Children

n 1994, in a genocidal rampage against the Tutsi people of Rwanda, nearly 1 million people perished within a three-month period. The horror was so extreme that in surveys of Rwandans during the years following the genocide, an estimated 40 to 60 percent reported symptoms of *post-traumatic stress disorder (PTSD)* (Neugebauer et al., 2009; Schaal et al., 2011). In PTSD, flashbacks, nightmares, anxiety, irritability, angry outbursts, and difficulty concentrating lead to intense distress, physical symptoms, and loss of interest in relationships and daily life.

Parents with PTSD often have children with PTSD (Brand et al., 2011; Morris, Gabert-Quillen, & Delahanty, 2012). In both children and adults, PTSD is associated with disruptions in the body's stress response system, reflected in abnormal blood levels of the stress hormone cortisol. In appropriate concentrations, cortisol assists our brains in managing stress effectively. In individuals with PTSD, cortisol levels are either too high or (more often) too low, contributing to persistently disturbed stress regulation.

Mounting evidence confirms that exposure to extreme adversity increases methylation of a chromosome-5 gene called *GR*, which plays a central role in stress-hormone regulation. Might this epigenetic process contribute to parent–to–child transmission of PTSD?

To explore this question, researchers identified 50 Tutsi women who had been pregnant during the genocide (Perroud et al., 2014). Half had been directly exposed to the trauma; the other half had been out of the country at the time. Eighteen years later, the mothers and their adolescent children were assessed for PTSD and depression by trained psychologists. Blood samples enabled genetic testing for methylation of the GR gene and assessment of cortisol levels.

Compared with non-exposed mothers, mothers who witnessed the genocidal carnage had substantially higher PTSD and depression scores, and children of the two groups of mothers differed similarly. Also, as Figure 2.11 reveals, exposed mothers and their children displayed stronger GR methylation. And consistent with methylation's dampening effect on gene expression, trauma-exposed mothers and their children had much lower cortisol levels than their non-exposed counterparts.

These findings are consistent with other evidence, in both animals and humans, indicating that prenatal exposure to the biological consequences of severe maternal stress can induce epigenetic changes, through methylation, that impair functioning of the body's stress response system (Daskalakis & Yehuda, 2014; Mueller & Bale, 2008). In the Tutsi

This Rwandan mother gave birth shortly after the Tutsi genocide. Nine years later, she continues to suffer from PTSD caused by first-hand experience of atrocities, including repeated rape and loss of her mother, brother, and two sisters in the massacre. Her daughter's PTSD and depression might be the result of prenatal exposure to severe maternal stress, which can trigger epigenetic changes that disrupt the body's stress response system.

mothers and children, the effects of genocidal trauma were long-lasting, evident in serious psychological disorders nearly two decades later.

As the researchers noted, more remains to be discovered about exactly how maternal trauma exposure compromised the Tutsi children's capacity to manage stress. Epigenetic processes, not just prenatally but also at later ages, may have been largely responsible. Alternatively, poor-quality parenting, resulting from maternal anxiety, irritability, anger, and depression, could have been the major influence. More likely, epigenetic changes, inept parenting, and other unfavorable environmental influences combined to place the Tutsi children at high risk for PTSD and depression. In Chapter 3, we will return to the impact of prenatal stress, including evidence showing that its negative impact can be lessened or prevented through social support.

FIGURE 2.11   Methylation status of the GR gene in trauma-exposed and non-trauma-exposed Tutsi mothers and their children. Mothers who had been directly exposed to the Rwandan Tutsi genocide, as well as their children, showed elevated methylation of the GR gene, which is centrally involved in functioning of the body's stress response system. (Based on Perroud et al., 2014.)

[Bar graph: Mean Extent of *GR* Methylation (y-axis, 0 to 12). Bars for: Trauma-Exposed Mothers (~6.7), Children of Trauma-Exposed Mothers (~9.8), Non-Exposed Mothers (~5), Children of Non-Exposed Mothers (~5.4).]

(Bjorklund & Ellis, 2014). Although people cannot be changed in any way we might desire, environments can modify genetic influences. The success of any attempt to improve development depends on the characteristics we want to change, the genetic makeup of the individual, and the type and timing of our intervention.

ASK YOURSELF

Connect ■ Explain how each of the following concepts supports the conclusion that genetic influences on human characteristics are not constant but change over time: somatic mutation (page 57), niche-picking (page 81), and epigenesis (page 82).

Apply ■ Bianca's parents are accomplished musicians. At age 4, Bianca began taking piano lessons. By age 10, she was accompanying the school choir. At age 14, she asked to attend a special music high school. Explain how gene–environment correlation promoted Bianca's talent.

Reflect ■ What aspects of your own development—for example, interests, hobbies, college major, or vocational choice—are probably due to niche-picking? Explain.

SUMMARY

2.1 Genetic Foundations
(p. 51)

2.1a Explain what genes are and how they are transmitted from one generation to the next.

■ Each individual's **phenotype,** or observable characteristics, is a product of both **genotype** and environment. **Chromosomes,** rodlike structures within the cell nucleus, contain our hereditary endowment. Along their length are **genes,** segments of **deoxyribonucleic acid (DNA).**

■ **Protein-coding genes** directly affect our body's characteristics. **Regulator genes** modify protein-coding genes' instructions. Environmental factors also alter gene expression.

■ **Gametes,** or sex cells, result from a cell division process called **meiosis,** which ensures that each individual receives a unique set of genes from each parent. Once sperm and ovum unite, the resulting **zygote** will then have a full complement of chromosomes.

■ Genetic sex is determined by whether sperm containing an X-bearing or a Y-bearing chromosome fertilizes the ovum.

■ **Fraternal,** or **dizygotic, twins** result when two ova are released from the mother's ovaries and each is fertilized. **Identical,** or **monozygotic, twins** develop when a zygote divides in two during the early stages of cell duplication.

2.1b Describe various patterns of gene–gene interaction.

■ Traits controlled by single genes follow **dominant–recessive** and **incomplete-dominance inheritance**. **Homozygous** individuals have two identical **alleles,** or forms of a gene. **Heterozygous** individuals, with one dominant and one recessive allele, are **carriers** of the recessive trait. In **incomplete dominance,** both alleles are expressed in the phenotype.

■ **X-linked inheritance** applies when recessive disorders are carried on the X chromosome and, therefore, are more likely to affect males.

■ In **genomic imprinting,** alleles are chemically marked within the ovum or sperm, silencing one pair member and leaving the other to be expressed, regardless of its makeup.

■ Harmful genes arise from **mutation,** which can occur spontaneously or be caused by hazardous environmental agents. Germline mutation occurs in the cells that give rise to gametes; somatic mutation can occur in body cells at any time of life.

■ Traits that vary on a continuum, such as intelligence and personality, result from **polygenic inheritance**—the effects of many genes.

2.1c Describe major chromosomal abnormalities, and explain how they occur.

■ Most chromosomal abnormalities result from errors during meiosis. The most common, Down syndrome, leads to intellectual disability, distinctive physical features, and physical defects. **Sex chromosome** disorders are milder than defects of the **autosomes.**

2.2 Reproductive Choices
(p. 59)

2.2 Discuss counseling, medical procedures, and reproductive options that can assist prospective parents in having healthy children.

■ **Genetic counseling** helps couples consider reproductive options when they are at risk for giving birth to children with genetic abnormalities. **Prenatal diagnostic methods** allow early detection of developmental problems. Advances in fetal medicine and genetic engineering offer hope for treating hereditary disorders.

- Reproductive technologies, such as donor insemination, in vitro fertilization, and surrogate motherhood, enable individuals to conceive children who otherwise would not. However, the technologies raise legal and ethical concerns.

- Many adults who cannot conceive or who are likely to transmit a genetic disorder choose adoption. Although adopted children tend to have more learning and emotional problems than children in general, most fare well in the long run. Warm, supportive parenting that includes open communication about adoption contributes to favorable development.

2.3 Environmental Contexts for Development (p. 65)

2.3 Discuss aspects of children's multi-layered environment that influence their development and well-being.

- In the family—the first and most enduring context for development—the behaviors of each member affect those of the others in a dynamic, ever-changing system of direct and indirect influences. Warm, gratifying family ties, which foster effective **coparenting,** help ensure children's psychological health.

- **Socioeconomic status (SES)** profoundly affects family functioning and children's development. Higher-SES parents tend to have smaller families, to value independence, and to engage in warm, verbally stimulating interaction with children. Lower-SES parents tend to value obedience and to use more commands, criticism, and physical punishment.

- In affluent families, parental physical and emotional unavailability may impair youths' adjustment. Poverty and homelessness undermine effective parenting and pose serious threats to children's development.

- Children benefit from supportive ties between the family and community, including stable, socially cohesive neighborhoods that provide constructive leisure and enrichment activities. High-quality schooling and parent involvement in children's education enhance academic achievement, educational attainment, and life chances.

- The values and practices of cultures and **subcultures** affect all aspects of children's daily life. Extended families, common among many ethnic minorities, help protect family members from the negative effects of poverty and other stressful life conditions. The Hispanic cultural value of **familism,** which elevates family needs above individual concerns, is associated with multiple positive developmental outcomes.

© JIM WEST/ALAMY STOCK PHOTO

- Cross-national differences in *collectivism–individualism* powerfully affect **public policies** aimed at addressing social problems. Largely because of its strongly individualistic values, the United States lags behind other developed nations in policies safeguarding children and youths.

2.4 Understanding the Relationship Between Heredity and Environment (p. 78)

2.4 Explain the various ways heredity and environment may combine to influence complex traits.

- **Behavioral genetics** examines the contributions of nature and nurture to diversity in human traits and abilities. **Heritability estimates,** derived from **kinship studies,** attempt to quantify the influence of genetic factors on such complex traits as intelligence and personality. However, the accuracy of this approach has been challenged.

- In **gene–environment interaction,** heredity influences each individual's responsiveness to qualities of the environment. In **gene–environment correlation,** children's genes affect the environments to which they are exposed, at first passively and evocatively. At older ages, children actively choose environments that complement their heredity, a process called **niche-picking.**

- **Epigenesis** reminds us that development is best understood as a series of complex, bidirectional exchanges between heredity and all levels of the environment. Epigenetic research is uncovering biochemical processes—such as **methylation**—through which the environment can modify gene expression.

IMPORTANT TERMS AND CONCEPTS

allele (p. 54)
autosomes (p. 53)
behavioral genetics (p. 78)
carrier (p. 55)
chromosomes (p. 51)
coparenting (p. 66)
deoxyribonucleic acid (DNA) (p. 51)
dominant–recessive inheritance (p. 55)
epigenesis (p. 82)
familism (p. 75)
fraternal, or dizygotic, twins (p. 53)
gametes (p. 53)
gene (p. 52)

gene–environment correlation (p. 80)
gene–environment interaction (p. 80)
genetic counseling (p. 60)
genomic imprinting (p. 57)
genotype (p. 51)
heritability estimate (p. 78)
heterozygous (p. 54)
homozygous (p. 54)
identical, or monozygotic, twins (p. 54)
incomplete dominance (p. 55)
kinship studies (p. 78)
meiosis (p. 53)
methylation (p. 82)

mutation (p. 57)
niche-picking (p. 81)
phenotype (p. 51)
polygenic inheritance (p. 58)
prenatal diagnostic methods (p. 62)
protein-coding genes (p. 52)
public policies (p. 76)
regulator genes (p. 52)
sex chromosomes (p. 53)
socioeconomic status (SES) (p. 67)
subculture (p. 74)
X-linked inheritance (p. 56)
zygote (p. 53)

Giving Birth to Peace

Lotfeh Mohamed El Mari, 11 years, Lebanon

Expectant mothers hope that their nearly full-term fetuses will benefit from and eventually contribute to a world of peace. How is the one-celled organism transformed into a baby with the capacity to participate in family life? What factors support or undermine this earliest period of development? Chapter 3 provides answers to these questions.

Reprinted with permission from The International Child Art Foundation, Washington, DC

One fall, Yolanda and Jay enrolled in an evening section of my child development course, when Yolanda was just two months pregnant. In their early thirties, married for several years, and their careers well under way, they had decided to have a baby. Each week, they arrived for class full of questions: "How does the baby grow before birth?" "When is each organ formed?" "Has its heart begun to beat?" "Can it hear, feel, or sense our presence?"

Most of all, Yolanda and Jay wanted to do everything possible to make sure their baby would be born healthy. Yolanda started to wonder about her diet and whether she should keep up her daily aerobic workouts. And she asked whether an aspirin for a headache, a glass of wine at dinner, or a few cups of coffee during the workday might be harmful.

In this chapter, we answer Yolanda and Jay's questions, along with a great many more that researchers have asked about the events before birth. We begin our discussion with these puzzling questions: Why is it that generation after generation, most couples want to become parents? And what factors influence their decision to have just one child or more than one?

Then we trace prenatal development, addressing both supports for healthy growth and damaging influences that threaten the child's health and survival. Because the changes taking place during these nine months are so astounding, the prenatal environment can exert a powerful, lasting impact—for better or for worse—on physical and mental health. ∎

3.1 Motivations for Parenthood

What, in your view, are the benefits and drawbacks of having children? How large would your ideal family be, and why? Until just a few decades ago, the issue of whether to have children was, for many adults, a biological given or a compelling social expectation. Today, in Western industrialized nations, it is a matter of true individual choice. Effective contraception enables sexually active adults to avoid having children in most instances. And changing cultural values allow people to remain childless with far less fear of social criticism than a generation or two ago.

Nevertheless, the 6 percent of American 18- to 40-year-olds who currently say they do not want children is just slightly higher than the 5 percent who said so three decades ago. The desire for children remains the norm: In a survey of a large, nationally representative sample of U.S. adults of childbearing age, 90 percent said they already have children or are planning to have them (Gallup, 2013). Actually becoming parents, however, is affected by a complex array of contextual factors, including financial circumstances, religious values, partnership changes, career goals, health conditions, and availability of supportive government and workplace family policies (Mills et al., 2011; Vespa, 2017).

3.1.1 Why Have Children?

In addition to the contextual factors just mentioned, vital personal attributes called *childbearing motivations*—positive or negative inclinations toward the idea of parenthood—affect people's decision to have children as well as their psychological adjustment to pregnancy and a baby's arrival. In Western nations, these motivations have changed over time, increasingly emphasizing individual fulfillment and deemphasizing obligation to society (Frejka et al., 2008; Guedes et al., 2015).

When Americans and Europeans are asked about their childbearing motivations, they mention a variety of advantages and disadvantages, listed in Table 3.1. Although some ethnic and regional differences exist, in all groups highly rated reasons for having children include personal fulfillment—for example, the warm, affectionate

3.1 Discuss factors that contribute to contemporary adults' decision making about parenthood, including timing of childbearing and family size.

TABLE 3.1 **Advantages and Disadvantages of Parenthood Mentioned by American and European Adults of Childbearing Age (in General Order of Importance)**

ADVANTAGES	DISADVANTAGES
Giving and receiving warmth and affection and providing care and teaching	Risk of birth complications
Enhancing life's meaning	Constant worries over and responsibility for children's health, safety, and well-being
Nurturing a new person and personality	Fear that children will turn out badly, through no fault of one's own
Creating one's own family	Role overload—not enough time to meet both child-rearing and job responsibilities
Strengthening the couple relationship through a shared project	
Fulfilling a partner's desire for parenthood	Risks of bringing up children in a world plagued by crime, war, and pollution
Carrying on one's family name, lineage, heritage, or values	Financial strain and sacrifices
	Reduced time to spend with partner
Being accepted as a responsible and mature member of the community	Loss of privacy
Having a source of caregiving and economic support in later life	

Sources: Guedes, et al., 2015; Miller, 2009.

LOOK and LISTEN

Interview several parents of infants or preschoolers about the benefits and challenges of parenthood. Ask which issues they considered before starting a family. How deliberate about family planning were they?

relationship and opportunities for care and teaching that children provide. Also frequently mentioned are the deepening of a couple's relationship that comes from sharing in a challenging but important life task, and the sense of future continuity that results from perpetuating a family line and passing on one's heritage and values (Guedes, et al., 2015). Less important but still mentioned are social and economic returns, including being recognized as a family and having children to rely on as sources of caregiving and financial support late in life.

Most adults also realize that having children means years of extra burdens and responsibilities. Among disadvantages of parenthood, they often cite risk of birth complications; constant worries over children's health, safety, and well-being; fear that children will turn out badly; concerns about role overload (not enough time for both family and work responsibilities); and worries about bringing up children in a troubled world. The financial strains and sacrifices of child rearing also rank high. According to a conservative estimate, middle-income parents in the United States today will spend nearly $300,000 to rear a child from birth to age 18, and many will incur substantial additional expense for higher education (U.S. Department of Agriculture, 2017).

Greater freedom to choose whether, when, and how to have children (see the discussion of reproductive choices in Chapter 2) makes contemporary family planning more challenging, as well as intentional, than in past generations. Still, about 30 percent of U.S. births are the result of unintended pregnancies, with most born to low-income, less educated mothers—circumstances associated with delayed prenatal care, premature birth, and child health problems (Bearak et al., 2018). Yet opportunities to explore childbearing motivations in high school, college, and community-based health education classes and through family-planning counseling might encourage more adults to make informed and personally meaningful decisions—a trend that would increase the chances that they would have children when ready, find parenting an enriching experience, and rear physically and mentally healthy children.

Among often-cited reasons for having children are the affectionate relationship and opportunity for care and teaching that a child provides.

3.1.2 How Large a Family?

Prior to the economic recession of 2007–2009, the overall fertility rate, or lifetime births per woman, in developed countries was about 2.1. Since then, the U.S. fertility rate has declined by 16 percent, to 1.8. Fertility rates are similar, or even lower, in other industrialized nations: 1.9 in Sweden, 1.8 in Australia and the United Kingdom, 1.6 in Canada, 1.5 in Germany, 1.4 in Italy and Japan, and 1.3 in Spain (World Bank, 2018b).

A major reason for this drop in births is that increasing numbers of adults of childbearing age are delaying marriage and parenthood until their education is complete, their work lives are under way, and they are more secure economically (Vespa, 2017). As Figure 3.1 shows, the U.S. birthrate decline is substantial for women in their twenties, with small gains in births limited to women ages 35 and older (Centers for Disease Control and Prevention, 2018f; Pew Research Center, 2018e). Starting a family later is associated with having fewer children.

A smaller family size is compatible with the decision of increasing numbers of women to divide their energies between family and career. In addition, popular advice to prospective parents often includes limiting family size in the interests of "child-rearing quality," based on the presumed ability of parents of fewer children to devote more affection, stimulation, and material resources to each child, thus enhancing the intellectual development of all. Do smaller families really make brighter children, as is commonly believed?

For years, researchers thought that earlier birth order and wider spacing might grant children more parental involvement and, therefore, result in more favorable cognitive outcomes. But two decades of research consistently indicates that the relationship of birth order and spacing to children's intelligence is negligible (Damian & Roberts, 2015; Kanazawa, 2012; Rodgers et al., 2000; Wichman, Rodgers, & MacCallum, 2007). Rather, parents' differential treatment of siblings is far more responsive to children's personalities, interests, and behaviors than to these aspects of family structure.

Furthermore, the well-documented association between large family size and lower intelligence test scores of all siblings can be entirely explained by a strong trend for low-SES mothers to give birth to more children. Most of these families suffer from poverty, which threatens all domains of development (see pages 70–71 in Chapter 2). Among children of well-educated, economically advantaged mothers, the family size–intelligence relationship disappears (Guo & VanWey, 1999; Wichman, Rodgers, & MacCallum, 2007). In sum, although many good reasons exist for limiting family size, the concern that additional births will reduce parenting quality and thus impair children's skills and life chances is not warranted.

Average family size has declined in recent decades in most industrialized nations. But, contrary to popular belief, having more children does not reduce the intelligence or life chances of later-born children.

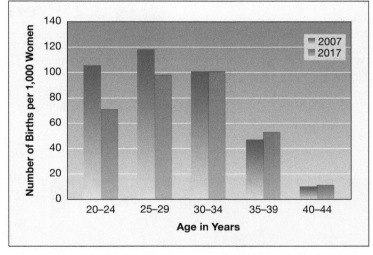

FIGURE 3.1   **Births to U.S. women by age in 2007 and 2017.** Births declined for women in their twenties through mid-thirties while increasing for women 35 and older, reflecting the trend toward delayed parenthood. (Based on Centers for Disease Control and Prevention, 2018f.)

3.1.3 Is There a Best Time During Adulthood to Have a Child?

Yolanda, at age 32, is pregnant for the first time. Many people believe that women should, ideally, have children before 35 because the risk of having a baby with a chromosomal disorder rises sharply from then on. Advanced paternal age is associated with elevated risk of certain genetically influenced disorders as well (see page 60 in Chapter 2).

Reproductive capacity also declines with age. Between ages 25 and 34, 12 percent of women are affected, a figure that escalates to 39 percent for 35- to 39-year-olds and to 47 percent for 40- to 44-year-olds. Similarly, age affects male reproductive capacity. Amount of semen, concentration of sperm in each ejaculation, and quality of sperm decline gradually after age 35 (Chandra, Copen, & Stephen, 2013).

Highly educated women with demanding careers are especially likely to delay parenthood (Pew Research Center, 2015a). Many believe, incorrectly, that if they have difficulty conceiving, they can rely on reproductive technologies. But recall from Chapter 2 that the success of these procedures declines steadily with age. Although no one time during adulthood is best to begin parenthood, individuals who decide to put off pregnancy until their late thirties or early forties risk having fewer biological children than they desire or none at all.

ASK YOURSELF

Connect ■ Why is it incorrect for couples who postpone childbearing until age 35 or later to conclude that medical advances can overcome fertility problems? (See Chapter 2, page 60.)

Apply ■ Rhonda and Mark, a career-oriented couple in their early thirties, are thinking about having a baby. What factors should they keep in mind as they decide whether to add to their family at this time in their lives?

Reflect ■ Ask one of your parents or grandparents to list her or his childbearing motivations. How do those motivations compare with your own? What factors—for example, education or cultural change—might account for any differences?

3.2 Prenatal Development

3.2 List the three periods of prenatal development, and describe the major milestones of each.

The sperm and ovum that unite to form the new individual are uniquely suited for the task of reproduction. The ovum is a tiny sphere, measuring $\frac{1}{175}$ inch in diameter—barely visible to the naked eye as a dot the size of the period at the end of this sentence. But in its microscopic world, it is a giant—the largest cell in the human body, making it a perfect target for the much smaller sperm, which measure only $\frac{1}{500}$ inch.

3.2.1 Conception

About once every 28 days, in the middle of a woman's menstrual cycle, an ovum bursts from one of her *ovaries,* two walnut-sized organs located deep inside her abdomen, and is drawn into one of two *fallopian tubes*—long, thin structures that lead to the hollow, softly lined uterus (see Figure 3.2). While the ovum is traveling, the spot on the ovary from which it was released, now called the *corpus luteum,* secretes hormones that prepare the lining of the uterus to receive a fertilized ovum. If pregnancy does not occur, the corpus luteum shrinks, and the lining of the uterus is discarded two weeks later with menstruation.

The male produces sperm in vast numbers—an average of 300 million a day—in the *testes,* two glands located in the *scrotum,* sacs that lie just behind the penis. In the final process of maturation, each sperm develops a tail that permits it to swim long distances, upstream in the female reproductive tract, through the *cervix* (opening of the uterus) and into the fallopian tube, where fertilization usually takes place. The journey is difficult, and many sperm die. Only 300 to 500 reach their destination. Once in the fallopian tube, sperm live for up to six days and can lie in wait for the ovum, which survives for only

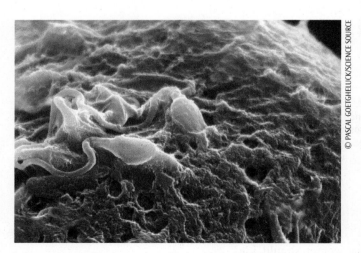

© PASCAL GOETGHELUCK/SCIENCE SOURCE

Conception. In this photo, taken with the aid of a powerful microscope, sperm penetrate the surface of the ovum, the largest cell in the human body. When one sperm succeeds in fertilizing the ovum, the resulting zygote begins to duplicate.

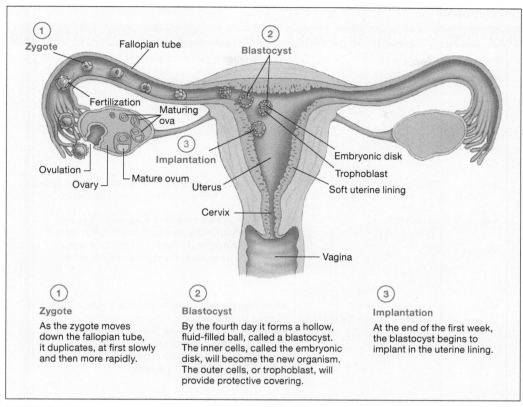

FIGURE 3.2 **Female reproductive organs, showing fertilization, early cell duplication, and implantation.** (From *Before We Are Born*, 9th ed., by K. L. Moore, T. V. N. Persaud, & M G. Torchia, p. 33. Copyright © 2016, adapted with permission from Elsevier, Inc.)

one day after its release from the ovary. However, most conceptions result from intercourse occurring during a three-day period—on the day of ovulation or during the two days preceding it (Mu & Fehring, 2014).

With conception, the story of prenatal development begins to unfold. The vast changes that take place during the 38 weeks of pregnancy are usually divided into three periods: (1) the germinal period, (2) the period of the embryo, and (3) the period of the fetus. As we consider each, you may find it useful to refer to Table 3.2 on page 92, which summarizes milestones of prenatal development.

3.2.2 Germinal Period

The **germinal period** lasts about two weeks, from fertilization and formation of the zygote until the tiny mass of cells drifts down and out of the fallopian tube and attaches itself to the wall of the uterus. The zygote's first cell duplication is long and drawn out, taking about 30 hours. Gradually, new cells are added at a faster rate, forming a hollow, fluid-filled ball called a *blastocyst* that by the fourth day consists of 60 to 70 cells (refer again to Figure 3.2). The cells on the inside of the blastocyst, called the *embryonic disk,* will become the new organism; the outer ring of cells, termed the *trophoblast,* will become the structures that provide protective covering and nourishment.

Implantation   Between the seventh and ninth days, **implantation** occurs: The blastocyst burrows deep into the uterine lining. Surrounded by the woman's nourishing blood, it starts to grow in earnest. At first, the trophoblast (protective outer layer) multiplies fastest. It forms a membrane, called the **amnion,** that encloses the developing organism in *amniotic fluid,* which helps keep the temperature of the prenatal world constant and provides a cushion against any

TABLE 3.2   Milestones of Prenatal Development

TRIMESTER	PRENATAL PERIOD	WEEKS	LENGTH AND WEIGHT	MAJOR EVENTS
First	Germinal	1		The one-celled zygote multiplies and forms a blastocyst.
		2		The blastocyst burrows into the uterine lining. Structures that feed and protect the developing organism begin to form—*amnion, chorion, yolk sac, placenta,* and *umbilical cord.*
	Embryo	3–4	¼ inch (6 mm)	A primitive brain and spinal cord appear. Heart, muscles, ribs, backbone, and digestive tract begin to develop.
		5–8	1 inch (2.5 cm); ½ ounce (4 g)	Many external body structures (face, arms, legs, toes, fingers) and internal organs form, and production and migration of neurons in the brain begin. The sense of touch starts to develop, and the embryo can move.
	Fetus	9–12	3 inches (7.6 cm); less than 1 ounce (28 g)	Rapid increase in size begins. Nervous system, organs, and muscles become organized and connected, touch sensitivity extends to most of the body, and new behavioral capacities (kicking, thumb sucking, mouth opening, and rehearsal of breathing) appear. External genitals are well-formed, and the fetus's sex is evident.
Second		13–24	12 inches (30 cm); 1.8 pounds (820 g)	The fetus continues to enlarge rapidly. In the middle of this period, the mother can feel fetal movements. Vernix and lanugo keep the fetus's skin from chapping in the amniotic fluid. Most of the brain's neurons are in place by 24 weeks. Eyes are sensitive to light, and the fetus reacts to sound.
Third		25–38	20 inches (50 cm); 7.5 pounds (3,400 g)	The fetus has a good chance of survival if born during this time. Size increases. Lungs mature. Rapid brain development, in neural connectivity and organization, enables sensory and behavioral capacities to expand. In the middle of this period, a layer of fat is added under the skin. Antibodies are transmitted from mother to fetus to protect against disease. Most fetuses rotate into an upside-down position in preparation for birth.

Sources: Moore, Persaud, & Torchia, 2016.

Photos (from top to bottom): © Claude Cortier/Science Source; © Dr. G. Moscoso/Science Source; © Claude Edelmann/Science Source; © James Stevenson/Science Source; © Lennart Nilsson, *A Child Is Born*/TT Nyhetsbyrån.

jolts caused by the woman's movement. A *yolk sac* emerges that produces blood cells until the developing liver, spleen, and bone marrow are mature enough to take over this function (Moore, Persaud, & Torchia, 2016).

The events of these first two weeks are delicate and uncertain. As many as 30 percent of zygotes do not survive this period. In some, the sperm and ovum do not join properly. In others, cell duplication never begins. By preventing implantation in these cases, nature eliminates most prenatal abnormalities (Sadler, 2014).

The Placenta and Umbilical Cord By the end of the second week, cells of the trophoblast form another protective membrane—the **chorion,** which surrounds the amnion. From the chorion, tiny fingerlike *villi,* or blood vessels, emerge.[1] As these villi burrow into the uterine wall, the placenta starts to develop. By bringing the embryo's and mother's blood close together, the **placenta** permits food and oxygen to reach the developing organism and waste products to be carried away. A membrane forms that allows these substances to be exchanged but prevents the mother's and embryo's blood from mixing directly (see Figure 3.3).

The placenta is connected to the developing organism by the **umbilical cord,** which first appears as a primitive body stalk and, during the course of pregnancy, grows to a length of 1 to 3 feet. The umbilical cord contains one large vein that delivers blood loaded with nutrients and two arteries that remove waste products. The force of blood flowing through the cord keeps it firm, so it seldom tangles while the embryo, like a space-walking astronaut, floats freely in its fluid-filled chamber (Moore, Persaud, & Torchia, 2016). By the end of the germinal period, the developing organism has found food and shelter.

3.2.3 Period of the Embryo

The period of the **embryo** lasts from implantation through the eighth week of pregnancy. During these brief six weeks, the most rapid prenatal changes take place as the groundwork is laid for all body structures and internal organs. Because all parts of the body are forming, the embryo is especially vulnerable to interference with healthy development. But the short time span of embryonic growth helps limit opportunities for serious harm.

Last Half of the First Month In the first week of this period, the embryonic disk forms three layers of cells: (1) the *ectoderm,* which will become the nervous system and skin; (2) the *mesoderm,* which will develop into the muscles, skeleton, circulatory system, and other internal organs; and (3) the *endoderm,* which will become the digestive system, lungs, urinary tract, and glands. These three layers give rise to all parts of the body.

FIGURE 3.3 **Cross-section of the uterus, showing detail of the placenta.** The embryo's blood flows from the umbilical cord arteries into the chorionic villi and returns via the umbilical cord vein. The mother's blood circulates in spaces surrounding the chorionic villi. A membrane between the two blood supplies permits food and oxygen to be delivered and waste products to be carried away. The two blood supplies do not mix directly. The umbilical arteries carry oxygen-poor blood (shown in blue) to the placenta, and the umbilical vein carries oxygen-rich blood (shown in red) to the fetus. (Adapted from *Before We Are Born,* 9th ed., by K. L. Moore, T. V. N. Persaud, & M. G. Torchia, p. 76. Copyright © 2016, reprinted with permission from Elsevier, Inc.)

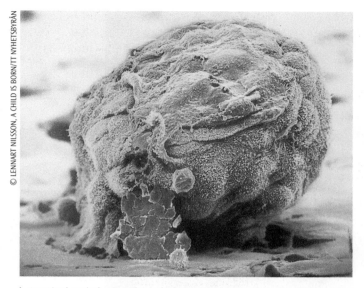

© LENNART NILSSON, A CHILD IS BORN/TT NYHETSBYRÅN

Germinal period: seventh to ninth day. The fertilized ovum duplicates at an increasingly rapid rate, forming a hollow ball of cells, or blastocyst, by the fourth day after conception. Between the seventh and ninth day the blastocyst, as shown here magnified thousands of times, burrows into the uterine lining.

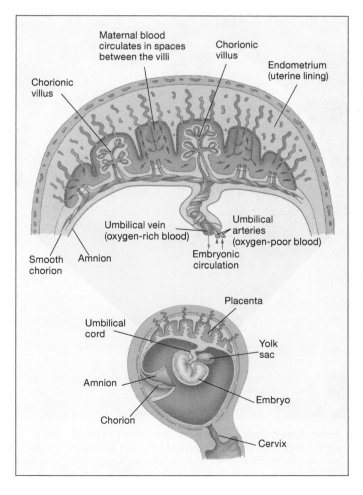

---

[1]Recall from Table 2.2 on page 62 that chorionic villus sampling is the prenatal diagnostic method that can be performed earliest, at nine weeks after conception.

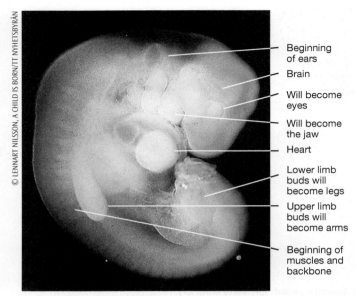

Period of the embryo: fourth week. This 4-week-old embryo is only ¼-inch long, but many body structures have begun to form.

Beginning of ears

Brain

Will become eyes

Will become the jaw

Heart

Lower limb buds will become legs

Upper limb buds will become arms

Beginning of muscles and backbone

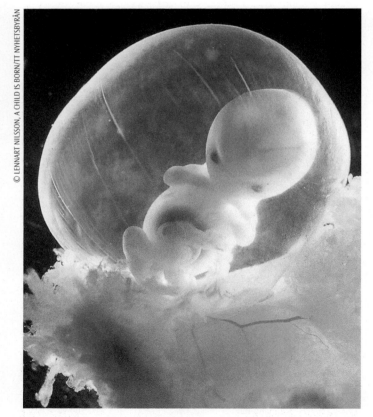

Period of the embryo: seventh week. The embryo's posture is more upright. Body structures—eyes, nose, arms, legs, and internal organs—are more distinct. The embryo now responds to touch and can also move. At less than one inch long and an ounce in weight, it is still too tiny to be felt by the mother.

At first, the nervous system develops fastest. The ectoderm folds over to form the **neural tube,** or primitive spinal cord. At 3½ weeks, the top swells to form the brain. While the nervous system is developing, the heart begins to pump blood, and muscles, backbone, ribs, and digestive tract appear. At the end of the first month, the curled embryo—only ¼ inch long—consists of millions of organized groups of cells with specific functions.

The Second Month   In the second month, growth continues rapidly. The eyes, ears, nose, jaw, and neck form. Tiny buds become arms, legs, fingers, and toes. Internal organs are more distinct: The intestines grow, the heart develops separate chambers, and the liver and spleen take over production of blood cells so that the yolk sac is no longer needed. Changing body proportions cause the embryo's posture to become more upright.

During the fifth week, production of *neurons* (nerve cells that store and transmit information) begins deep inside the neural tube at the astounding pace of more than 250,000 per minute (Jabès & Nelson, 2014). Once formed, neurons begin traveling along tiny threads to their permanent locations, where they will form the major parts of the brain.

By 8 weeks, the testes in the male start to develop and begin secreting the hormone testosterone, which will stimulate differentiation of male internal reproductive organs and the penis and scrotum during the coming month. In the absence of testosterone, female reproductive organs form.

By the end of this period, the embryo—about 1 inch long and ⅐ ounce in weight—can already sense its world. It responds to touch, particularly in the mouth area and on the soles of the feet. And it can move, although its tiny flutters are still too light to be felt by the mother (Moore, Persaud, & Torchia, 2016).

3.2.4 Period of the Fetus

The period of the **fetus,** from the ninth week to the end of pregnancy, is the longest prenatal period. During this "growth and finishing" phase, the organism increases rapidly in size.

The Third Month   In the third month, the organs, muscles, and nervous system start to become organized and connected. Touch sensitivity extends to most of the body (Hepper, 2015). When the brain signals, the fetus kicks, bends its arms, forms a fist, curls its toes, turns its head, opens its mouth, and even sucks its thumb, stretches, and yawns. The tiny lungs begin to expand and contract in an early rehearsal of breathing movements.

By the twelfth week, the external genitals are well-formed, and the sex of the fetus can be detected with ultrasound (Sadler, 2014). Other finishing touches appear, such as fingernails, toenails, tooth buds, and eyelids. The heartbeat can now be heard through a stethoscope.

Prenatal development is sometimes divided into **trimesters,** or three equal time periods. At the end of the third month, the *first trimester* is complete.

The Second Trimester   By the middle of the second trimester, between 17 and 20 weeks, the new being has grown large enough that the mother can feel its movements. Already, the fetus is remarkably active—in motion nearly 30 percent of the time—which helps strengthen the joints and muscles (DiPietro, Costigan, & Voegtline, 2015). A white, cheeselike substance called **vernix** emerges on the skin, protecting it from chapping during the long months spent bathing in the amniotic fluid. White, downy hair called **lanugo** also appears over the entire body, helping the vernix stick to the skin.

At the end of the second trimester, many organs are well-developed. And most of the brain's billions of neurons are in place; few will be produced after this time. However, *glial cells,* which support and feed the neurons, continue to increase rapidly throughout the remaining months of pregnancy, as well as after birth. Consequently, brain weight increases tenfold from the twentieth week until birth (Roelfsema et al., 2004). At the same time, neurons begin forming *synapses,* or connections, at a rapid pace.

Brain growth means new sensory and behavioral capacities. The 20-week-old fetus can be stimulated as well as irritated by sounds. And if a doctor looks inside the uterus using fetoscopy (see Table 2.2 on page 62), fetuses try to shield their eyes from the light with their hands, indicating that sight has begun to emerge (Moore, Persaud, & Torchia, 2016). Still, a fetus born at this time cannot survive. Its lungs are immature, and the brain cannot yet control breathing movements or body temperature.

The Third Trimester During the final trimester, a fetus born early has a chance for survival. The point at which the baby can first survive, called the **age of viability,** occurs sometime between 22 and 26 weeks (Moore, Persaud, & Torchia, 2016). A baby born between the seventh and eighth months, however, usually needs oxygen assistance to breathe. Although the brain's respiratory center is now mature, tiny air sacs in the lungs are not yet ready to inflate and exchange carbon dioxide for oxygen.

The brain continues to make great strides. The *cerebral cortex,* the seat of human intelligence, enlarges. Convolutions and grooves in its surface appear, permitting a dramatic increase in surface area that allows for maximum prenatal brain growth without the full-term baby's head becoming too large to pass through the birth canal. Brain-imaging evidence reveals rapid gains in fetal neural organization: At first, neural connectivity increases *within* brain areas supporting specific functions, such as vision, movement, language, and integration of information. In the last six weeks, connections begin to form *between* these areas, yielding primitive brain networks (Thomason et al., 2014). This pattern of brain growth, which supports coordinated processing of information, will continue after birth.

As neural organization improves, the fetus spends more time awake. At 20 weeks, fetal heart rate reveals no periods of alertness. But by 28 weeks, fetuses are awake about 11 percent of the time, a figure that rises to 16 percent just before birth (DiPietro et al., 1996). Between 30 and 34 weeks, fetuses show rhythmic alternations between sleep and wakefulness that gradually increase in organization (Rivkees, 2003). Around 36 weeks, synchrony between fetal heart rate and motor activity peaks: A rise in heart rate is usually followed within five seconds by a burst of motor activity (DiPietro et al., 2006; DiPietro, Costigan, & Voegtline, 2015). These are clear signs that functioning brain networks have started to take shape in the brain.

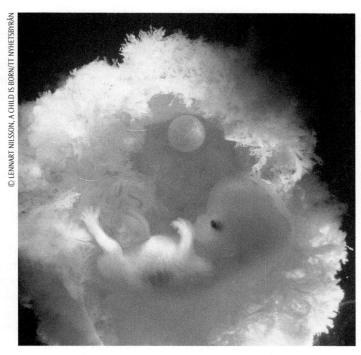

Period of the fetus: eleventh week. The brain and muscles of the rapidly growing fetus are better connected. The fetus can kick, bend its arms, open and close its hands and mouth, and suck its thumb. The yolk sac shrinks as the internal organs assume blood cell production.

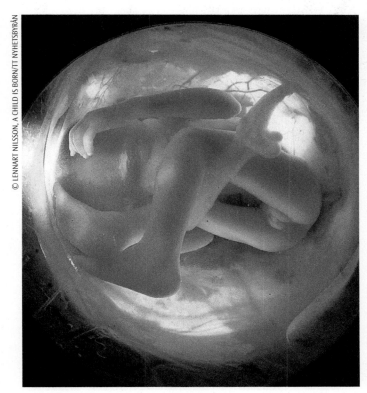

Period of the fetus: twenty-second week. This fetus is almost 1 foot long and weighs slightly more than 1 pound. Its movements can be felt readily by the mother and by others who touch her abdomen. If born now, the fetus would have a slim chance of surviving.

By the end of pregnancy, the fetus takes on the beginnings of a personality. Fetal activity is linked to infant temperament. In one study, more active fetuses during the third trimester became 1-year-olds who could better handle frustration and 2-year-olds who were more active as well as less fearful, in that they more readily interacted with toys and with an unfamiliar adult in a laboratory (DiPietro et al., 2002). Perhaps fetal activity is an indicator of healthy neurological development, which fosters adaptability in childhood. The relationships just described, however, are modest. As we will see in Chapter 6, sensitive caregiving can modify the temperaments of children who have difficulty adapting to new experiences.

The third trimester brings greater responsiveness to external stimulation. As we will see when we discuss newborn capacities in Chapter 4, fetuses acquire taste and odor preferences from bathing in and swallowing amniotic fluid (its makeup is influenced by the mother's diet). Between 23 and 30 weeks, the fetus is clearly sensitive to pain, so painkillers should be used in any surgical procedures (Lee et al., 2005). Around 29 weeks, fetuses can hear. When presented with a repeated auditory stimulus against the mother's abdomen, they initially react with a rise in heart rate, brain-wave activity, and body movements (Kisilevsky, 2016). Then responsiveness gradually declines, indicating *habituation* (adaptation) to the sound. If a new auditory stimulus is introduced, heart rate and brain waves recover to a high level, revealing that the fetus recognizes the new sound as distinct from the original stimulus (Hepper, Dornan, & Lynch, 2012; Muenssinger et al., 2013). This indicates that fetuses can remember for at least a brief period.

Within the next six weeks, fetuses distinguish the tone and rhythm of different voices and sounds—learning that will serve as a springboard for language development. In various studies, they showed systematic heart-rate and brain-wave changes in response to the mother's voice versus the father's or a stranger's, to their native language (English) versus a foreign language (Mandarin Chinese), and to a simple familiar melody (descending tones) versus an unfamiliar melody (ascending tones) (Granier-Deferre et al., 2003; Kisilevsky & Hains, 2011; Kisilevsky et al., 2009; Lecanuet et al., 1993; Lee & Kisilevsky, 2013; Voegtline et al., 2013). In one clever investigation, mothers read aloud Dr. Seuss's lively book *The Cat in the Hat* each day during the last six weeks of pregnancy. After birth, their infants learned to turn on recordings of the mother's voice by sucking on nipples (DeCasper & Spence, 1986). They sucked hardest to hear *The Cat in the Hat*—the sound they had come to know while still in the womb.

On the basis of these findings, would you recommend that expectant mothers provide fetuses with stimulation aimed at enhancing later development? Although specific forms of fetal stimulation, such as reading aloud, contribute to development in the short-term, they are unlikely to have a long-lasting impact because of the child's constantly changing capacities and experiences, which can override the impact of fetal stimulation (Lecanuet, Granier-Deferre, & DeCasper, 2005). In addition, although ordinary stimulation contributes to sensory functioning, excessive input can be hazardous. For example, nonhuman animal studies indicate that a sensitive period (see page 23 in Chapter 1) exists in which the fetal ear is highly susceptible to injury (Pierson, 1996). During that time, prolonged exposure to sounds that are harmless to the mature ear can permanently damage fetal inner-ear structures.

In the final three months, the fetus gains more than 5 pounds and grows 7 inches. During the eighth month, lanugo typically is shed. A layer of fat is added to assist with temperature regulation. The fetus also receives antibodies from the mother's blood that protect against illnesses, since the newborn's immune system will not work well until several months after birth. In the last weeks, most fetuses assume an upside-down position, partly because of the shape of the uterus and partly because the head is heavier than the feet. Growth slows, and birth is about to take place.

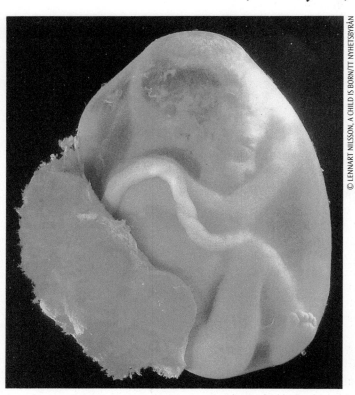

© LENNART NILSSON, A CHILD IS BORN/TT NYHETSBYRÅN

Period of the fetus: thirty-sixth week. This fetus fills the uterus. To nourish it, the umbilical cord and placenta have grown large. Vernix, a cheeselike substance, protects the skin from chapping. The fetus has accumulated fat to aid temperature regulation after birth. In two more weeks, it will be full term.

3.3 Prenatal Environmental Influences

Although the prenatal environment is far more constant than the world outside the womb, many factors can affect the embryo and fetus. Yolanda and Jay learned that parents—and society as a whole—can do a great deal to create a safe environment for development before birth.

3.3a Cite factors that influence the impact of teratogens, and discuss evidence on the impact of known or suspected teratogens.

3.3b Describe the impact of additional maternal factors on prenatal development.

3.3.1 Teratogens

The term **teratogen** (from the Greek word *teras,* meaning "malformation") refers to any environmental agent that causes damage during the prenatal period. The harm done by teratogens is not always simple and straightforward. It depends on the following factors:

- *Dose.* As we discuss particular teratogens, you will see that larger doses over longer time periods usually have more negative effects.
- *Heredity.* The genetic makeup of the mother and the developing organism plays an important role. Some individuals are better able than others to withstand harmful environments.
- *Other negative influences.* The presence of several negative factors at once, such as additional teratogens, poor nutrition, and lack of medical care, can worsen the impact of a harmful agent.
- *Age.* The effects of teratogens vary with the age of the organism at time of exposure. To understand this last idea, think back, once again, to the *sensitive period* concept introduced in Chapter 1. A sensitive period is a limited time span in which a part of the body or a behavior is biologically prepared to develop rapidly. During that time, it is especially sensitive to its surroundings. If the environment is harmful, then damage occurs, and recovery is difficult and sometimes impossible.

Figure 3.4 on page 98 summarizes prenatal sensitive periods. Look at it carefully, and you will see that some parts of the body, such as the brain and eye, have long sensitive periods that extend throughout prenatal development. For other parts, including the limbs and palate, sensitive periods are much shorter. Figure 3.4 also indicates that we can make some general statements about the timing of harmful influences. In the *germinal period,* before implantation, teratogens rarely have any impact. If they do, the tiny mass of cells is usually so damaged that it dies. Serious defects are most likely to arise during the *embryonic period,* when the foundations of all body parts emerge. During the *fetal period,* teratogenic damage is usually minor. However, organs such as the brain, ears, eyes, teeth, and genitals can still be strongly affected.

The effects of teratogens go beyond immediate physical damage. Some health effects may show up years later. Growing evidence indicates that certain teratogens exert long-term effects epigenetically, by modifying gene expression (see page 82 in Chapter 2) (Markunas et al., 2014). Furthermore, delayed psychological consequences can occur indirectly, as a result of physical damage. For example, a defect resulting from drugs the mother took during pregnancy can affect others' reactions to the child as well as the child's ability to explore the environment. Over time, parent–child interaction, peer relations, and cognitive, emotional, and social development may suffer.

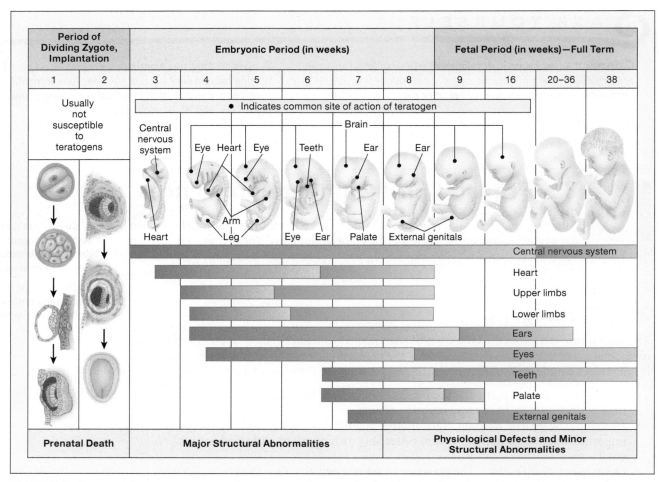

Period of Dividing Zygote, Implantation		Embryonic Period (in weeks)						Fetal Period (in weeks)—Full Term			
1	2	3	4	5	6	7	8	9	16	20–36	38

Usually not susceptible to teratogens

● Indicates common site of action of teratogen

Central nervous system
Eye Heart Eye   Brain
Teeth
Ear
Ear
Arm
Heart   Leg   Eye Ear   Palate   External genitals

Central nervous system
Heart
Upper limbs
Lower limbs
Ears
Eyes
Teeth
Palate
External genitals

Prenatal Death	Major Structural Abnormalities	Physiological Defects and Minor Structural Abnormalities

FIGURE 3.4   **Sensitive periods in prenatal development.** Each organ or structure has a sensitive period, during which its development may be disturbed. Blue horizontal bars indicate highly sensitive periods. Green horizontal bars indicate periods that are somewhat less sensitive to teratogens, although damage can occur. (From *Before We Are Born*, 9th ed., by K. L. Moore, T. V. N. Persaud, & M. G. Torchia, p. 313. Copyright © 2016, adapted with permission from Elsevier, Inc.)

Notice how an important idea about development discussed in earlier chapters is at work here: *bidirectional influences* between child and environment. Now let's look at what researchers have discovered about a variety of teratogens.

Prescription and Nonprescription Drugs   In the early 1960s, the world learned a tragic lesson about drugs and prenatal development. At that time, a sedative called *thalidomide* was widely available in Canada, Europe, and South America. When taken by mothers 4 to 6 weeks after conception, thalidomide produced gross deformities of the embryo's developing arms and legs and, less frequently, damage to the ears, heart, kidneys, and genitals. About 7,000 infants worldwide were affected. Recent evidence suggests that thalidomide may exert its damaging effects through epigenetic mechanisms, including gene methylation (Ross & Desai, 2017). Furthermore, as children exposed to thalidomide grew older, many scored below average in intelligence. Perhaps the drug damaged the central nervous system directly. Or the child-rearing conditions of these youngsters with severe physical deformities may have impaired their intellectual development.

Another medication, a synthetic hormone called *diethylstilbestrol (DES),* was widely prescribed between 1945 and 1970 to prevent miscarriages. As daughters of these mothers reached adolescence and young adulthood, they showed unusually high rates of cancer of the vagina, malformations of the uterus, and infertility. When they tried to have children, their pregnancies more often resulted in prematurity, low birth weight, and miscarriage than those of non-DES-exposed women. Young men showed an increased risk of genital abnormalities and cancer of the testes (Goodman, Schorge, & Greene, 2011; Reed & Fenton, 2013).

Currently, the most widely used, potent teratogenic medication is a vitamin A derivative called *isotretinoin,* prescribed to treat severe acne and taken by hundreds of thousands of women of childbearing age in industrialized nations. Exposure during the first trimester results in eye, ear, skull, brain, heart, and immune system abnormalities (Yook et al., 2012). U.S. regulations for prescribing isotretinoin require female users to commit to avoiding pregnancy by using two methods of birth control.

Any drug with a molecule small enough to penetrate the placental barrier can enter the embryonic or fetal bloodstream. Yet many pregnant women continue to take over-the-counter medications without consulting their doctors. Some research suggests that aspirin use is linked to brain damage leading to impaired motor control, inattention, and overactivity, though other evidence fails to confirm these findings (Barr et al., 1990; Kozer et al., 2003; Thompson et al., 2014; Tyler et al., 2012). Coffee, tea, cola, and cocoa contain another frequently con-

A pregnant woman consults a nurse about her medications and their potential effects on embryonic and fetal development. Before taking any drug—prescription or nonprescription—expectant mothers must seriously consider its risks.

sumed drug, caffeine. High doses increase the risk of low birth weight (Sengpiel et al., 2013). Persistent intake of antidepressant medication is associated with an elevated incidence of premature delivery, low birth weight, respiratory distress at birth, and delayed motor development in infancy, but contrary evidence exists (Grigoriadis et al., 2013; Huang et al., 2014; Robinson, 2015).

Because children's lives are involved, we must take findings like these seriously. At the same time, we cannot be sure that these drugs actually cause the problems just mentioned. Often mothers take more than one drug. If the embryo or fetus is injured, it is hard to tell which drug might be responsible or whether other factors correlated with drug taking are at fault. Until we have more information, the safest course of action is the one Yolanda took: Avoid drugs as far as possible.

Unfortunately, many women do not know that they are pregnant during the early weeks of the embryonic period, when exposure to medications (and other teratogens) can be of greatest threat. In some instances, such as antidepressant use by severely depressed mothers, the benefits of drug treatment may outweigh its risks.

Illegal Drugs   The use of highly addictive mood-altering drugs, such as cocaine and heroin, has become more widespread, especially in poverty-stricken areas where these drugs provide a temporary escape from a daily life of hopelessness. Nearly 6 percent of U.S. pregnant women take these substances (Substance Abuse and Mental Health Services Administration, 2016).

Babies born to users of cocaine, heroin, or methadone (a less addictive drug used to wean people away from heroin) are at risk for a wide variety of problems, including prematurity, low birth weight, brain abnormalities, physical defects, breathing difficulties, and death around the time of birth (Behnke & Smith, 2013). In addition, these infants are born drug-addicted. They are often feverish and irritable and have trouble sleeping, and their cries are abnormally shrill—a common symptom among stressed newborns (Anand & Campbell-Yeo, 2015; Barthell & Mrozek, 2013). When mothers with many problems of their own must care for these babies, who are difficult to calm down, cuddle, and feed, behavior problems are likely to persist.

Throughout the first year, heroin- and methadone-exposed infants are less attentive to the environment than nonexposed babies, and their motor development is slow. After infancy, some children get better, while others remain jittery and inattentive (Hans & Jeremy, 2001). The kind of parenting they receive may explain why problems persist for some but not for others.

Evidence on cocaine suggests that some prenatally exposed babies develop lasting difficulties. Cocaine constricts the blood vessels, causing oxygen delivered to the developing organism to fall for 15 minutes following a high dose. It also can lead to deficits in production of neurons and their synaptic connections, as well as alter the chemical balance in the fetus's brain. These effects may contribute to an array of cocaine-associated physical malformations, especially of the central nervous system and heart; brain hemorrhages and seizures; and delayed physical growth (Cain, Bornick, & Whiteman, 2013; Grewen et al., 2014; Li et al., 2013). An array of studies report perceptual, motor, attention, memory, language, reasoning, and externalizing behavior problems that persist into adolescence (Coyle, 2013; Richardson et al., 2015; Singer et al., 2015).

Other investigations, however, reveal no major negative effects of prenatal cocaine exposure (Ackerman, Riggins, & Black, 2010; Allen et al., 2014; Buckingham-Howes et al., 2013). These contradictory findings illustrate how difficult it is to isolate the precise damage caused by illegal drugs. Cocaine users vary greatly in the amount, potency, and purity of the cocaine they ingest. Also, they often take several drugs, display other high-risk behaviors, suffer from poverty and other stressors, and engage in insensitive caregiving—factors that worsen outcomes for children (Molnar et al., 2014). Researchers have yet to determine exactly what accounts for findings of cocaine-related damage in some studies but not in others.

Another drug, marijuana, has been legalized for medical and recreational use in some U.S. states. Studies have linked prenatal marijuana exposure to increased risk of low birth weight and newborn death and to attention, memory, and academic achievement difficulties; impulsivity and overactivity; and depression as well as anger and aggression in childhood and adolescence (Behnke & Smith, 2013; Goldschmidt et al., 2004; Gray et al., 2005; Hayatabakhsh et al., 2012; Jutras-Aswad et al., 2009). But as with heroin and cocaine, these consequences are not well-established.

However, a growing number of researchers believe that prenatal marijuana exposure delivers an initial, silent "hit" to the fetal brain, inducing epigenetic changes that heighten sensitivity to postnatal environmental stressors. Inadequate parenting, nutritional deprivation, or other stressful conditions may then deliver a second, powerful "hit" that impairs central nervous system functioning profoundly, resulting in long-lasting cognitive and emotional deficits (Calvigioni et al., 2014; Maccarrone et al., 2014; Richardson, Hestor, & McLemore, 2016). Both animal and human longitudinal studies offer support for this hypothesis, though more evidence is needed to confirm it.

Overall, the effects of illegal drugs are less consistent than the impact of two legal substances to which we now turn: tobacco and alcohol.

Tobacco   Although smoking has declined in Western nations, about 7 percent of U.S. women smoke during their pregnancies (Centers for Disease Control and Prevention, 2018b). The best-known effect of smoking during the prenatal period is low birth weight. But the likelihood of other serious consequences, such as miscarriage, prematurity, cleft lip and palate, blood vessel abnormalities, impaired heart rate and breathing during sleep, infant death, and asthma and cancer later in childhood, also increases (Geerts et al., 2012; Havstad et al., 2012; Howell, Coles, & Kable, 2008; Mossey et al., 2009). The more cigarettes a mother smokes, the greater the chances that her baby will be affected. If a pregnant woman stops smoking at any time, even during the third trimester, she reduces the likelihood that her infant will be born underweight and suffer from future problems (Polakowski, Akinbami, & Mendola, 2009). The earlier she stops, the more beneficial the effects.

Even when a baby of a smoking mother appears to be born in good physical condition, slight behavioral abnormalities may threaten the child's development. Newborns of smoking mothers are less attentive to sights and sounds, display more muscle tension, are more emotionally reactive to frustration, and more often have colic (persistent crying). These findings suggest subtle negative effects on brain development (Espy et al., 2011; Shisler et al., 2017 Wiebe et al., 2014). Consistent with this view, prenatally exposed children and adolescents tend to have shorter attention spans, difficulties with impulsivity and overactivity, poorer memories, lower intelligence and achievement test scores, and higher levels of disruptive, aggressive behavior (Espy et al., 2011; Thakur et al., 2013).

Exactly how can smoking harm the fetus? Nicotine, the addictive substance in tobacco, constricts blood vessels, lessens blood flow to the uterus, and causes the placenta to grow abnormally. This reduces the transfer of nutrients, so the fetus gains weight poorly. Also, nicotine raises the concentration of carbon monoxide in the bloodstreams of both mother and fetus. Carbon monoxide displaces oxygen from red blood cells, damaging the central nervous system and slowing fetal body growth (Behnke & Smith, 2013). Other toxic chemicals in tobacco, such as cyanide and cadmium, contribute to its damaging effects. Research also suggests that prenatal exposure to cigarette smoke is a powerful epigenetic modifier of DNA, inducing widespread gene methylation that persists into adulthood (Lee et al., 2015; Tehranifar et al., 2018). These epigenetic changes may contribute to sustained impulsivity, overactivity, and oppositional behavior in childhood, adolescence, and beyond.

From one-third to one-half of nonsmoking pregnant women are "passive smokers" because their partners, relatives, or co-workers use cigarettes. Passive smoking is also related to low birth weight, infant death, childhood respiratory illnesses, and possible long-term attention, learning, and behavior problems (Best, 2009; Hawsawi, Bryant, & Goodfellow, 2015). Clearly, expectant mothers should avoid smoke-filled environments.

Maternal smoking during the prenatal period is associated with many serious consequences, including low birth weight and prematurity. This infant, born many weeks before his due date, breathes with the aid of a respirator.

Alcohol In his moving book *The Broken Cord*, Michael Dorris (1989), a Dartmouth College anthropology professor, described what it was like to rear his adopted son Adam, a Sioux Indian, who was born with **fetal alcohol spectrum disorder (FASD),** a term that encompasses a range of physical, mental, and behavioral outcomes caused by prenatal alcohol exposure. Children with FASD are generally given one of the following four diagnoses, which vary in severity: **fetal alcohol syndrome (FAS), partial fetal alcohol syndrome (p-FAS), alcohol-related neurodevelopmental disorder (ARND),** and **alcohol-related birth defects (ARBD)** (see Table 3.3) (Hoyme et al., 2016).

TABLE 3.3   Diagnostic Criteria for Fetal Alcohol Spectrum Disorder (FASD)

DIAGNOSIS	CRITERIA

Fetal alcohol syndrome (FAS)	• At least two of three characteristic facial abnormalities
	  – Short eyelid openings (measured horizontally)
	  – Thin upper lip
	  – Smooth or flattened philtrum (indentation between the nose and upper lip)
	• Deficient physical growth (height or weight at or below the tenth percentile for child's age)
	• Deficient brain growth or profound brain injury, indicated either by a small head (at or below the tenth percentile) or confirmed through brain imaging
	• Substantial cognitive impairment and behavioral impairment in self-regulation

Partial fetal alcohol syndrome (p-FAS)	• At least two of the three characteristic facial abnormalities • Either deficient physical growth or profound brain injury • Either substantial cognitive impairment or behavioral impairment in self-regulation
Alcohol-related neurodevelopmental disorder (ARND)	• Deficient brain growth or profound brain injury • Either substantial cognitive impairment or behavioral impairment in self-regulation • Typical physical growth and absence of facial abnormalities
Alcohol-related birth defects (ARBD)	• At least two of the three characteristic facial abnormalities • Other alcohol-related physical malformations—for example, of the eyes, ears, heart, urinary tract, or hands • Typical physical growth, absence of brain abnormalities, and absence of cognitive and behavioral deficits

Source: Hoyme et al., 2016.

short eyelid openings

thin upper lip

smooth or flattened philtrum

This child, whose mother drank heavily during pregnancy, has all three of the facial abnormalities characteristic of fetal alcohol syndrome (FAS): short eyelid openings, which make her eyes look widely spaced; a thin upper lip; and a flattened philtrum (the indentation between her nose and upper lip).

Adam was diagnosed as having FAS. As is typical of this disorder, his mother drank heavily during pregnancy. Frequent binge drinking (consuming four or more drinks on a single occasion), especially early in pregnancy, elevates risk for FAS and p-FAS (Popova et al., 2018). For ARND, and ARBD, prenatal alcohol exposure, though confirmed, is usually less pervasive than for FAS and p-FAS (Mattson, Crocker, & Nguyen, 2012).

The brain abnormalities associated with FASD show up in diverse symptoms—for example, poor memory, language and communication, impulse control, attention span, activity level (overactivity), planning and reasoning, motor coordination, and academic and social skills. Additional physical defects—of the eyes, ears, nose, throat, heart, genitals, skeleton, hands, urinary tract, or immune system—may also be present.

Even when provided with enriched diets, babies with FAS or p-FAS fail to catch up in physical size during infancy or childhood. Cognitive and behavioral impairments are also permanent: In his teens and twenties, Adam had trouble concentrating and keeping a routine job, and he suffered from poor judgment. For example, he would buy something and not wait for change or would wander off in the middle of a task. He died at age 23, after being hit by a car. Adolescents and young adults with FAS, p-FAS, or ARND generally display persisting attention, impulse-control, and motor-coordination deficits, school failure, inappropriate social and sexual behaviors, trouble with the law, and mental health problems, including inability to manage stress, depression, and alcohol and drug abuse (Bertrand & Dang, 2012; Hellemans et al., 2010; Roszel, 2015). Still, as the Biology and Environment box on the following page illustrates, some recovery is possible for children with p-FAS and ARND through carefully designed intervention.

How does alcohol produce its devastating effects? First, it interferes with production and migration of neurons in the primitive neural tube. Neuroimaging findings confirm damage to many brain structures and abnormalities in brain functioning, including electrical and chemical activity involved in transferring messages from one part of the brain to another (de la Monte & Kril, 2014; Memo et al., 2013). Second, the body uses large quantities of oxygen to metabolize alcohol. A pregnant woman's heavy drinking draws away oxygen that the developing organism needs for cell growth. Third, both animal and human research reveals widespread epigenetic changes in response to alcohol consumption, including altered methylation of many genes, that contribute to physical and brain abnormalities (Laufer et al., 2017; Lussier et al., 2018; Mandal et al., 2017). Other evidence suggests that paternal alcohol use around the time of conception can also alter gene expression, thereby playing a role in these damaging outcomes (Basavarajappa & Subbanna, 2016).

About 10 percent of U.S. pregnant women report drinking during the previous month, one-third of whom admit to binge drinking. An estimated 3 percent of U.S. infants are affected, with diagnoses of p-FAS, ARND, and ARBD occurring 3 to 4 times more often than full-blown FAS (Centers for Disease Control and Prevention, 2015; Roozen et al., 2016). Globally, an estimated 630,000 infants with FASD are born each year. The incidence is especially high in Eastern Europe, and South Africa has the highest rate in the world, at 11 percent (Lange et al., 2017).

As with heroin and cocaine, alcohol abuse is higher in poverty-stricken women. It is especially high among Native Americans, for whom the risk of a baby born with FAS is 20 to 25 times greater than for the rest of the U.S. population (Rentner, Dixon, & Lengel, 2012). Unfortunately, when affected girls later become pregnant, the poor judgment caused by the syndrome often prevents them from understanding why they themselves should avoid alcohol. Thus, the tragic cycle is likely to be repeated in the next generation.

How much alcohol is safe during pregnancy? Even mild drinking, less than one drink per day, can lead to slow physical growth, brain damage, and cognitive and behavioral impairments (Flak et al., 2014; Martinez-Frias et al., 2004). Recall that other factors—both genetic and environmental—can make some fetuses more vulnerable to teratogens. Therefore, no amount of alcohol is safe. Couples planning a pregnancy and expectant mothers should avoid alcohol entirely.

Biology and Environment

Self-Regulation Therapy for Children with Fetal Alcohol Spectrum Disorder (FASD)

Self-regulation difficulties are so pervasive among children with the brain abnormalities caused by prenatal alcohol exposure that they are now regarded as a core deficit of FASD. A weakened capacity to manage one's thoughts, emotions, and actions is apparent in high emotional reactivity, distractibility, and overactivity as early as infancy and in poor planning, reasoning, and social awareness in childhood. These behaviors are strong predictors of the high levels of mental health problems and law-breaking associated with FASD by adolescence.

Until recently, treatments for FASD have shown either minimal or inconsistent effects (Murawski et al., 2015). But a new approach that targets a central deficit of diagnosed children—impaired self-regulation skills—shows considerable promise.

In several experiments, researchers randomly assigned 8- to 12-year-olds with p-FAS or ARND to either a therapy or a no-treatment control condition. In each investigation, therapy was based on a widely applied self-regulation intervention for school-age children called the Alert Program (Williams & Shellenberger, 1996). In 12 weekly sessions, Alert shows children how to monitor their thoughts, feelings, and behavior, noticing when their arousal level interferes with their ability to engage in everyday learning and social activities.

Using the analogy of a car engine running at different speeds, the Alert therapist helps children recognize when their engines are running "too quickly" (wired) or "too slowly" (sluggish). Then the therapist teaches strategies for adjusting the engine to run "just right" (focused on the task at hand). These include steps for planning ahead, identifying emotions in themselves and others, expressing feelings appropriately, and solving social problems, such as how to cooperate in a game with a peer. Finally, the therapist provides children with practice in selecting strategies independently and applying those strategies appropriately outside the therapeutic situation.

Relative to controls, children experiencing Alert improved considerably in regulation of behavior, especially in ability to inhibit irrelevant actions and control their emotions (Nash et al., 2015). In addition, parents of Alert children rated them as better regulated and as having fewer behavior problems—an outcome still evident at a six-month follow-up.

Furthermore, magnetic resonance imaging (MRI) brain scans gathered before and after the intervention revealed that Alert led to denser *gray matter* (darker tissue consisting mainly of neurons and their connective fibers) in regions of the cerebral cortex crucial for self-regulation, indicating that new synapses had formed (Soh et al., 2015). Treatment children also displayed more efficient functioning in these cerebral regions, which correlated with their ability to inhibit impulsive

The mother of a child with FASD helps her daughter with a homework assignment. School-age children with p-FAS and ARND who experienced Alert self-regulation therapy improved in ability to inhibit irrelevant actions and control their emotions, and their parents viewed them as having fewer behavior problems.

responding while playing a computer game (Nash et al., 2018). These findings suggest that it is possible to modify some of the brain damage caused by fetal alcohol exposure.

The researchers noted that the gains of treatment children were greatest on simple rather than complex self-regulation tasks—findings not surprising, given the significant brain pathology associated with p-FAS and ARND. At the same time, the shift in parents' views of their children following Alert is impressive: It may spark favorable changes in the parent–child relationship that lead to continued progress, especially as therapists equip parents with knowledge of Alert therapeutic techniques.

Radiation In Chapter 2, we saw that ionizing radiation can cause mutation, damaging DNA in ova and sperm. When mothers are exposed to radiation during pregnancy, the embryo or fetus can suffer additional harm. Defects due to ionizing radiation were tragically apparent in children born to pregnant women who survived the bombing of Hiroshima and Nagasaki during World War II. Similar abnormalities surfaced in the nine months following the 1986 Chernobyl, Ukraine, nuclear power plant accident. After each disaster, the incidence of miscarriage and babies born with brain damage, physical deformities, and slow physical growth rose dramatically. The risk of brain injury and intellectual disability is greatest from the end of the first trimester through the second trimester, when production and migration of neurons is especially high (Verreet et al., 2016; Yang, Ren, & Tang, 2017). Evacuation of residents in areas near the Japanese nuclear facility damaged by the March 2011 earthquake and tsunami was intended to prevent these devastating outcomes.

Even when a radiation-exposed baby seems unaffected, problems may appear later. For example, even low-level radiation, resulting from industrial leakage or medical radiation

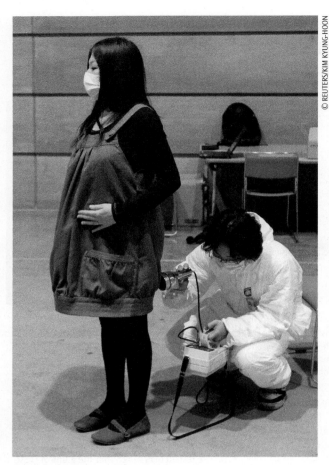

A pregnant woman is tested for exposure to radiation at an evacuation center following the Fukushima, Japan, nuclear power plant disaster in 2011. Radiation can cause devastating harm to the embryo or fetus and is particularly dangerous for the developing brain from the end of the first trimester through the second trimester.

procedures, can increase the risk of childhood cancer (Fushiki, 2013). In middle childhood, prenatally exposed Chernobyl children had abnormal brain-wave activity, lower intelligence test scores, and rates of language and emotional disorders two to three times greater than those of non-exposed children in the surrounding area. Furthermore, the more tension parents reported, due to forced evacuation from their homes and worries about living in irradiated areas, the poorer their children's emotional functioning (Loganovskaja & Loganovsky, 1999; Loganovsky et al., 2008). Stressful rearing conditions seemed to combine with the damaging effects of prenatal radiation to impair children's development.

Women should do their best to avoid medical radiation during pregnancy. If dental, thyroid, chest, or other X-rays are necessary, insisting on the use of an abdominal shield is a key protective measure.

Environmental Pollution   In industrialized nations, an astounding number of potentially dangerous chemicals are released into the environment, and many new pollutants are introduced each year. When 10 newborns were randomly selected from U.S. hospitals for analysis of umbilical cord blood, researchers uncovered a startling array of industrial contaminants—287 in all (Houlihan et al., 2005). They concluded that many babies are "born polluted" by chemicals that not only impair prenatal development but increase the chances of life-threatening diseases and health problems later on.

Certain pollutants cause severe prenatal damage. In the 1950s, an industrial plant released waste containing high levels of *mercury* into a bay providing seafood and water for the town of Minamata, Japan. Many children born at the time displayed physical deformities, intellectual disability, abnormal speech, difficulty in chewing and swallowing, and uncoordinated movements. High levels of prenatal mercury exposure disrupt production and migration of neurons, causing widespread brain damage (Caserta et al., 2013; Hubbs-Tait et al., 2005). Prenatal mercury exposure from maternal seafood diets predicts deficits in speed of cognitive processing, attention, and memory during the school years (Boucher et al., 2010, 2012; Lam et al., 2013). Pregnant women are wise to avoid eating long-lived predatory fish, such as swordfish, albacore tuna, and shark, which are heavily contaminated with mercury.

For many years, *polychlorinated biphenyls (PCBs)* were used to insulate electrical equipment, until research showed that, like mercury, they entered waterways and the food supply. In Taiwan, prenatal exposure to high levels of PCBs in rice oil resulted in low birth weight, discolored skin, deformities of the gums and nails, brain-wave abnormalities, and delayed cognitive development (Chen & Hsu, 1994; Chen et al., 1994). Steady, low-level PCB exposure is also harmful. Women who frequently ate PCB-contaminated fish, compared with those who ate little or no fish, had infants with lower birth weights, smaller heads, persisting attention and memory difficulties, and lower intelligence test scores in childhood (Boucher, Muckle, & Bastien, 2009; Polanska, Jurewicz, & Hanke, 2013; Stewart et al., 2008).

Another teratogen, *lead,* is present in paint flaking off the walls of old buildings and in certain materials used in industrial occupations. High levels of prenatal lead exposure are related to prematurity, low birth weight, brain damage, and a wide variety of physical defects. Even at low levels, affected infants and children show slightly poorer mental and motor development (Caserta et al., 2013; Jedrychowski et al., 2009).

Prenatal exposure to *dioxins*—toxic compounds resulting from incineration and burning of fuels, such as coal or oil—is linked to thyroid abnormalities in infancy and to an increased incidence of breast and uterine cancers in women, perhaps through altering hormone levels (ten Tusscher & Koppe, 2004). Even tiny amounts of dioxin in the paternal bloodstream cause a dramatic change in the sex ratio of offspring: Affected men father nearly twice as many girls as boys (Ishihara et al., 2007). Dioxin seems to impair the fertility of Y-bearing sperm prior to conception.

Finally, persistent air pollution inflicts substantial prenatal harm. Exposure to traffic-related fumes and smog is associated with reduced infant head size, low birth weight, elevated infant death rates, impaired lung and immune-system functioning, and later respiratory illnesses (Proietti et al, 2013; Ritz et al., 2014). In several large-scale studies, prenatal exposure to air pollution was linked to several childhood cancers, including leukemia and tumors of the eye and brain (Ghosh et al., 2013; Lavigne et al., 2017).

Infectious Disease Most infectious illnesses women experience during pregnancy, such as the common cold, seem to have no impact on the embryo or fetus. However, as Table 3.4 illustrates, a few can cause extensive damage.

Viruses In the mid-1960s, a worldwide epidemic of *rubella* (three-day, or German, measles) led to the birth of more than 20,000 U.S. babies with serious defects and to 13,000 fetal and newborn deaths. Consistent with the sensitive period concept, the greatest damage occurs when rubella strikes during the embryonic period. More than 50 percent of infants whose mothers become ill during that time are born with some or all of the following: deafness; eye deformities, including cataracts; heart, genital, urinary, intestinal, bone, and dental defects; and intellectual disability. Infection during the fetal period is less harmful, but low birth weight, hearing loss, and bone defects may still occur. The organ damage inflicted by prenatal rubella often leads to lifelong health problems, including severe mental illness, diabetes, cardiovascular disease, and thyroid and immune-system dysfunction in adulthood (Duszak, 2009; Waldorf & McAdams, 2013). Routine vaccination in infancy and childhood has made new rubella

TABLE 3.4   Effects of Some Infectious Diseases During Pregnancy

DISEASE	MISCARRIAGE	PHYSICAL MALFORMATIONS	INTELLECTUAL DISABILITY	LOW BIRTH WEIGHT AND PREMATURITY
Viral				
Acquired immune deficiency syndrome (AIDS)	✓	?	✓	✓
Chickenpox	✓	✓	✓	✓
Cytomegalovirus	✓	✓	✓	✓
Herpes simplex 2 (genital herpes)	✓	✓	✓	✓
Mumps	✓	✗	✗	✗
Rubella (German measles)	✓	✓	✓	✓
Zika	✓	✓	✓	✓
Bacterial				
Chlamydia	✓	?	✗	✓
Syphilis	✓	✓	✓	?
Tuberculosis	✓	?	✓	✓
Parasitic				
Malaria	✓	✗	✗	✓
Toxoplasmosis	✓	✓	✓	✓

✓ = established finding, ✗ = no present evidence, ? = possible effect that is not clearly established.

Sources: Beckham et al., 2016; Kliegman et al., 2015; Waldorf & McAdams, 2013.

outbreaks unlikely in industrialized nations. But over 100,000 cases of prenatal infection continue to occur each year, primarily in developing countries in Africa and Asia with weak or absent immunization programs (World Health Organization, 2017b).

The *human immunodeficiency virus (HIV),* which can lead to *acquired immune deficiency syndrome (AIDS),* a disease that destroys the immune system, has infected increasing numbers of women over the past three decades. In developing countries, where 95 percent of new infections occur, more than half affect women. In South Africa, for example, 30 percent of all pregnant women are HIV-positive (Burton, Giddy, & Stinson, 2015). Untreated HIV-infected expectant mothers pass the deadly virus to the developing organism 10 to 20 percent of the time.

A Brazilian child lovingly cradles his 1-year-old brother who was born with microcephaly, a condition characterized by a severely damaged brain and unusually small head. The baby's mother contracted the Zika virus during pregnancy.

AIDS progresses rapidly in infants. By 6 months, weight loss, diarrhea, and repeated respiratory illnesses are common. The virus also causes brain damage, as indicated by seizures, gradual loss in brain weight, and delayed cognitive and motor development. Most untreated prenatal AIDS babies die by age 3 (Siberry, 2015). Antiretroviral drug therapy reduces prenatal transmission to less than 1 to 2 percent, and several babies born with HIV for whom aggressive retroviral treatment began within 2 days after birth appeared free of the disease (McNeil, 2014). However, antiretroviral drugs remain unavailable to at least one-third of HIV-infected pregnant women in developing countries (World Health Organization, 2017a).

As Table 3.4 reveals, the developing organism is especially sensitive to the family of herpes viruses, for which no vaccine exists. Among these, *cytomegalovirus* (the most frequent prenatal infection, transmitted through respiratory or sexual contact) and *herpes simplex 2* (transmitted sexually) are especially dangerous. In both, the virus invades the mother's genital tract, infecting babies either during pregnancy or at birth. Both diseases often have no symptoms, very mild symptoms, or symptoms with which people are unfamiliar, thereby increasing the likelihood of contagion. Pregnant women who are not in a mutually monogamous relationship are at greatest risk.

A 2015 outbreak in Brazil of the Zika virus (mainly transmitted by mosquito but also through sexual contact with an infected person) drew widespread attention because of an associated rise in the number of babies born with *microcephaly* (unusually severe brain injury, evident in extremely small head size, as low as the first percentile) and eye deformities (Beckham et al., 2016; Brasil et al., 2016). As the disease spread through Central America, South America, and the Caribbean, Zika was declared a public health emergency. Expectant mothers are advised not to travel to countries or regions with Zika outbreaks. At present, no vaccine is available.

Bacterial and Parasitic Diseases Table 3.4 also includes several bacterial and parasitic diseases. Among the most common is *toxoplasmosis,* caused by a parasite found in many animals. Pregnant women may become infected from handling contaminated soil while gardening, having contact with the feces of infected cats, or eating raw or undercooked meat or unwashed fruits and vegetables. About 40 percent of women who have the disease transmit it to the developing organism. If it strikes during the first trimester, it is likely to cause eye and brain damage. Later infection is linked to mild visual and cognitive impairments (Wallon et al., 2013). Expectant mothers can avoid toxoplasmosis by having pet cats checked for the disease, and turning over the care of litter boxes and the garden to other family members, and making sure that the meat they eat is well-cooked.

3.3.2 Other Maternal Factors

Besides avoiding teratogens, expectant parents can support prenatal development in other ways. In the following sections, we examine the influence of maternal exercise, nutrition, emotional well-being, blood type, and age.

Exercise   In healthy, physically fit women, regular moderate exercise, such as walking, swimming, biking, or an aerobic workout, is related to improved fetal cardiovascular functioning, higher birth weight, and a reduction in risk of certain complications, such as pregnancy-induced maternal diabetes, high blood pressure, and premature birth (Artal, 2015; Jukic et al., 2012). However, frequent, vigorous exercise, especially late in pregnancy, results in lower birth weight than in healthy, nonexercising controls (Clapp et al., 2002; Leet & Flick, 2003). Hospital-sponsored childbirth education programs frequently offer exercise classes and suggest appropriate routines that help prepare for labor and delivery.

During the last trimester, when the abdomen grows very large, mothers have difficulty moving freely and often must cut back on exercise. Most women, however, do not engage in sufficient moderate exercise during pregnancy to promote their own and their baby's health. An expectant mother who remains fit experiences fewer physical discomforts in the final weeks.

Pregnant women with health problems, such as circulatory difficulties or a history of miscarriages, should consult their doctor about a physical fitness routine. For these mothers, exercise (especially the wrong kind) can endanger the pregnancy.

Nutrition   During the prenatal period, when children are growing more rapidly than at any other time, they depend totally on the mother for nutrients. A healthy diet, consisting of a gradual increase in calories that results in a weight gain of 25 to 30 pounds (10 to 13.5 kilograms) helps ensure the health of mother and baby.

Prenatal malnutrition can cause serious damage to the central nervous system. The poorer the mother's diet, the greater the loss in brain weight, especially if malnutrition occurs during the third trimester, when the brain is increasing rapidly in size. An inadequate diet during pregnancy can also distort the structure of the liver, kidney, pancreas, and other organs, predisposing the child to later health problems. As Figure 3.5 illustrates, large-scale studies reveal a consistent link between low birth weight and high blood pressure, cardiovascular disease, and diabetes in adulthood, even after many other prenatal and postnatal health risks were controlled (Johnson & Schoeni, 2011).

Because poor nutrition suppresses development of the immune system, prenatally malnourished babies frequently catch respiratory illnesses. In addition, they are often irritable and unresponsive to stimulation. Like drug-addicted newborns, they have a high-pitched cry that is particularly distressing to their caregivers. In poverty-stricken families, these effects quickly combine with a stressful home life. Delays in motor, attention, and memory development, low intelligence test scores, and serious learning problems become more apparent with age (Monk, Georgieff, & Osterholm, 2013).

Many studies show that providing pregnant women with an adequate quantity of food has a substantial impact on the health of their newborn babies. Vitamin–mineral enrichment is also crucial. For example, taking a folic acid supplement around the time of conception reduces by more than 70 percent abnormalities of the neural tube, such as *anencephaly* and *spina bifida* (see Table 2.2 on page 62). Folic acid supplementation early in pregnancy also lessens the risk of other physical defects, including cleft lip and palate, circulatory system and urinary tract abnormalities, and limb deformities. Furthermore, adequate folic acid intake during the last 10 weeks of pregnancy cuts in half premature delivery and low birth weight (Goh & Koren, 2008; Hovdenak & Haram, 2012).

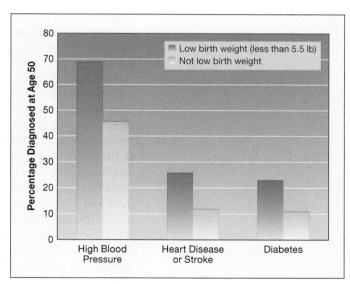

FIGURE 3.5   Relationship of low birth weight to disease risk in adulthood. In a follow-up of more than 2,000 U.S. births at age 50, low birth weight was associated with a greatly increased incidence of high blood pressure, heart disease, stroke, and diabetes after many other prenatal and postnatal health risks were controlled. (Based on Johnson & Schoeni, 2011.)

A government-supported farmers' market nutrition program enables this low-income expectant mother to purchase fruits and vegetables. A maternal diet rich in vitamins and minerals can help protect prenatal brain development and prevent diverse birth defects.

Because of these findings, U.S. government guidelines recommend that all women of childbearing age consume 0.4 milligram of folic acid per day. For women who have previously had a pregnancy affected by a neural tube defect, the recommended amount is 4 milligrams (dosage must be carefully monitored, as excessive intake can be harmful) (Centers for Disease Control and Prevention, 2017d). Because many U.S. pregnancies are unplanned, government regulations mandate that bread, flour, rice, pasta, and other grain products be fortified with folic acid.

Other vitamins and minerals also have established benefits. Enriching women's diets with calcium helps prevent maternal high blood pressure and low birth weight. Adequate magnesium and zinc reduce the risk of many prenatal and birth complications (Hovdenak & Haram, 2012). Fortifying table salt with iodine virtually eradicates *infantile hypothyroidism*—a condition of stunted physical growth and brain injury caused by prenatal iodine deficiency that is a common cause of intellectual disability in many parts of the world (Williams, 2008). And sufficient vitamins C and E and iron beginning early in pregnancy promote placental growth, healthy birth weight, and brain development. Prenatal iron deficiency, in particular, is linked to deficiencies in neural connectivity and structural alterations in the brain. Affected children, adolescents, and young adults score lower on measures of self-regulation, memory, and motor skills (Kennedy et al., 2016; Klemmensen et al., 2009; Lukowski et al., 2010; Monk et al., 2016). Nevertheless, a supplement program should complement, not replace, efforts to improve maternal diets during pregnancy. For women who do not get enough food or an adequate variety of foods, multivitamin tablets are a necessary, but not sufficient, intervention.

Although prenatal malnutrition is highest in developing countries, it also occurs in the industrialized world. The U.S. Special Supplemental Food Program for Women, Infants, and Children (WIC), which provides food packages and nutrition education to low-income pregnant women, reaches about 90 percent of those who qualify because of their extremely low incomes (U.S. Department of Agriculture, 2018). But many U.S. women who need nutrition intervention are not eligible for WIC.

Emotional Stress When women experience severe emotional stress during pregnancy, their babies are at risk for a wide variety of difficulties. Intense anxiety—especially during the first two trimesters—is associated with higher rates of miscarriage, prematurity, low birth weight, physical defects, infant respiratory and digestive illnesses, colic (persistent infant crying), sleep disturbances, and irritability during the child's first three years (Dunkel-Shetter & Lobel, 2012; Glover, Ahmed-Salim, & Capron, 2016; Field, 2011). Prenatal stressors consistently found to impair later physical and psychological well-being include chronic strain due to poverty; partner abuse; major negative life events such as divorce or death of a family member; disasters such as earthquakes or terrorist attacks; and fears specific to pregnancy and childbirth, including persistent anxiety about the health and survival of the baby and oneself. It is important to note that mild to moderate occasional stress has no adverse impact.

How can severe maternal stress affect prenatal development? When we experience fear and anxiety, stress hormones released into our bloodstream—such as *cortisol* and *epinephrine* (adrenaline), known as the "flight or fight" hormones—cause us to be "poised for action." Large amounts of blood are sent to parts of the body involved in the defensive response—the brain, the heart, and the muscles in the arms, legs, and trunk. Blood flow to other organs, including the uterus, may be reduced. As a result, the fetus is deprived of a full supply of oxygen and nutrients.

Maternal stress hormones also cross the placenta, causing a dramatic rise in fetal stress hormones (evident in the amniotic fluid) and, therefore, in fetal heart rate, blood pressure, blood glucose, and activity level (Kinsella & Monk, 2009; Weinstock, 2008). Excessive fetal stress is related to structural alterations in the infant brain that are linked to mood disorders in later life (O'Donnell & Meaney, 2016; Sandman, Glynn, & Davis, 2016). Infants and children of mothers who experienced severe prenatal anxiety display cortisol levels that are either abnormally high or abnormally low, both of which signal reduced physiological capacity to manage stress. Recall from Chapter 2 that prenatal epigenetic changes, through gene methylation, may be partly or largely responsible (Monk et al., 2016).

Maternal emotional stress during pregnancy is associated with diverse negative behavioral outcomes in childhood and adolescence, including anxiety, depression, short attention span, anger, aggression, overactivity, and lower intelligence test scores, above and beyond the impact of other risks, such as maternal smoking during pregnancy, low birth weight, postnatal maternal anxiety, and low SES (Coall et al., 2015; Monk, Georgieff, & Osterholm, 2013). Furthermore, similar to prenatal malnutrition, overwhelming the fetus with maternal stress hormones heightens susceptibility to later illness, including infectious diseases in childhood and cardiovascular disease and diabetes in adulthood (Nielsen et al., 2011; Reynolds, 2013).

However, stress-related prenatal complications are greatly reduced when mothers have partners, other family members, or friends who offer social support (Bloom et al., 2013; Luecken et al., 2013). The relationship of social support to positive pregnancy outcomes and subsequent child development is particularly strong for economically disadvantaged women, who often lead highly stressful lives (see the Social Issues: Health box on page 110).

RH Factor Incompatibility   When inherited blood types of mother and fetus differ, serious problems sometimes result. The most common cause of these difficulties is **Rh factor incompatibility.** When the mother is Rh-negative (lacks the Rh blood protein) and the father is Rh-positive (has the protein), the baby may inherit the father's Rh-positive blood type. (Because Rh-positive blood is dominant and Rh-negative blood is recessive, the chances are good that a baby will be Rh-positive.) If even a little of a fetus's Rh-positive blood crosses the placenta into the Rh-negative mother's bloodstream, she begins to form antibodies to the foreign Rh protein. If these enter the fetus's system, they destroy red blood cells, reducing the oxygen supply to organs and tissues. Intellectual disability, miscarriage, heart damage, and infant death can occur.

It takes time for the mother to produce Rh antibodies, so first-born children are rarely affected. The risk increases with each additional pregnancy. Fortunately, Rh incompatibility can be prevented in most cases. After the birth of each Rh-positive baby, Rh-negative mothers are routinely given a vaccine to prevent the buildup of antibodies. In emergency cases, blood transfusions can be performed immediately after delivery or, if necessary, even before birth.

Maternal Age   First births to women in their thirties and early forties have increased dramatically over the past several decades (Martin et al., 2018b). Many people are delaying childbearing until their education is complete, their careers are established, and they know they can support a child. In Chapter 2, we noted that women who delay childbearing until their thirties or forties face increased risk of infertility, miscarriage, and babies with chromosomal defects. Are other pregnancy complications more common for older mothers? Research indicates that healthy women in their thirties have about the same rates as those in their twenties. Thereafter, as Figure 3.6 reveals, complication rates increase, with a sharp rise among 50- to 55-year-olds—an age at which, because of menopause (end

LOOK and LISTEN

List prenatal environmental factors that can compromise later cognitive and social development. Ask several adults who hope someday to be parents to explain what they know about each factor. How great is their need for prenatal education?

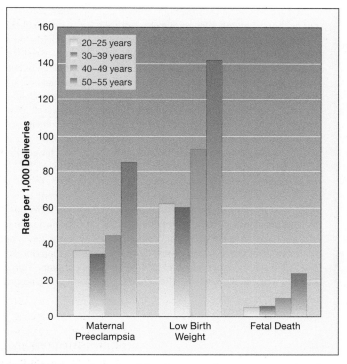

FIGURE 3.6   Relationship of maternal age to prenatal and birth complications. Complications increase after age 40, with a sharp rise between 50 and 55 years. See page 111 for a description of preeclampsia. (Adapted from Salihu et al., 2003.)

Social Issues: Health | The Nurse–Family Partnership: Reducing Maternal Stress and Enhancing Child Development Through Social Support

At age 17, Denise—an unemployed high-school dropout living with her disapproving parents—gave birth to Tara. Having no one to turn to for help during pregnancy and beyond, Denise felt overwhelmed and anxious much of the time. Tara was premature and had breathing difficulties, cried uncontrollably, slept erratically, and suffered from frequent minor illnesses throughout her first year. When she reached school age, she had trouble keeping up academically, and her teachers described her as distractible, unable to sit still, angry, and uncooperative.

The Nurse–Family Partnership—currently implemented in hundreds of counties across 43 U.S. states, in six tribal communities, in the U.S. Virgin Islands, and internationally in Australia, Canada, the Netherlands, and the United Kingdom—is a voluntary home visiting program for first-time, low-income expectant mothers like Denise. Its goals are to reduce pregnancy and birth complications, promote competent early caregiving, and improve family conditions, thereby protecting children from lasting adjustment difficulties.

A registered nurse visits the home weekly during the first month after enrollment, twice a month during the remainder of pregnancy and through the middle of the child's second year, and then monthly until age 2. In these sessions, the nurse provides the mother with intensive social support—a sympathetic ear; assistance in accessing health and other community services and the help of family members (especially fathers and grandmothers); and encouragement to finish high school, find work, and engage in future family planning.

To evaluate the program's effectiveness, researchers randomly assigned large samples of mothers at risk for high prenatal stress (due to teenage pregnancy, poverty, and other negative life conditions) to nurse-visiting or comparison conditions (just prenatal care, or prenatal care plus infant referral for developmental problems). Families were followed through their child's

The Nurse–Family Partnership provides this first-time, low-income mother with regular home visits from a registered nurse. In follow-up research, children of home-visited mothers developed more favorably—cognitively, emotionally, and socially—than comparison children.

school-age years and, in one experiment, into adolescence (Kitzman et al., 2010; Olds et al., 2004, 2007; Rubin et al., 2011).

As kindergartners, Nurse–Family Partnership children obtained higher language and intelligence test scores. And at both ages 6 and 9, the children of home-visited mothers in the poorest mental health during pregnancy exceeded comparison children in academic achievement and displayed fewer behavior problems. Furthermore, from their baby's birth on, home-visited mothers were on a more favorable life course: They had fewer subsequent births, longer intervals between their first and second births, more frequent contact with the child's father, more stable intimate partnerships, less welfare dependence, and a greater sense of control over their lives— key factors in reducing subsequent prenatal stress and in protecting children's development. Perhaps for these reasons, adolescent children of home-visited mothers continued to be advantaged in academic achievement and reported less

alcohol use and drug-taking than comparison-group agemates.

Other findings revealed that professional nurses, compared with trained paraprofessionals, were far more effective in preventing outcomes associated with prenatal stress, including high infant fearfulness to novel stimuli and delayed mental development (Olds et al., 2002). Nurses were probably more proficient in individualizing program guidelines to fit the strengths and challenges faced by each family. They also might have had unique legitimacy as experts in the eyes of stressed mothers, more easily convincing them to take steps to reduce pregnancy complications that can trigger persisting developmental problems—such as those Tara displayed.

The Nurse–Family Partnership is highly cost-effective (Miller, 2015). For every $1 spent, it saves more than five times as much in public spending on pregnancy complications, preterm births, and child and youth health, learning, and behavior problems.

of menstruation) and aging reproductive organs, few women can conceive naturally (Salihu et al., 2003; Usta & Nassar, 2008).

In the case of teenage mothers, does physical immaturity cause prenatal complications? As we will see in Chapter 4, infants born to teenagers have a higher rate of problems, but not directly because of maternal age. Most pregnant teenagers come from low-income backgrounds, where stress, poor nutrition, and health problems are common.

3.4 The Importance of Prenatal Health Care

Yolanda's pregnancy, like most others, was free of complications. But unexpected difficulties can arise, especially if mothers have health problems. For example, an estimated 9 percent of expectant women are diagnosed with *gestational diabetes,* impaired glucose tolerance that emerges during pregnancy (DeSisto, Kim, & Sharma, 2014). All diabetic women need careful prenatal monitoring. Extra glucose in the mother's bloodstream causes the fetus to grow larger than average, making pregnancy and birth problems more common. Furthermore, these infants are at increased risk of becoming overweight or obese and developing type 2 diabetes (Kampmann et al., 2015). Maternal high blood glucose also greatly elevates the chances of physical malformations and compromises prenatal brain development: It is linked to poorer attention, memory, and learning in infancy and early childhood (Hami et al., 2015).

Another complication, experienced by 5 to 10 percent of pregnant women, is *preeclampsia* (sometimes called *toxemia*), in which blood pressure increases sharply and the face, hands, and feet swell in the last half of pregnancy. Untreated preeclampsia can cause brain hemorrhages and kidney failure in expectant mothers, damage to the placenta, and fetal death. Usually, hospitalization, bed rest, and drugs can lower blood pressure to a safe level (Bokslag et al., 2016). If not, the baby must be delivered at once.

Unfortunately, 6 percent of pregnant women in the United States wait until after the first trimester to seek prenatal care or receive none at all. As Figure 3.7 shows, inadequate health care is far more common among low-income, ethnic minority mothers. Their infants are three times more likely to be born underweight and five times more likely to die than babies of mothers who receive early medical attention (Child Trends, 2015). Although government-sponsored health services for low-income pregnant women have expanded, some do not qualify and must

3.4 Explain why early and regular health care is vital during the prenatal period.

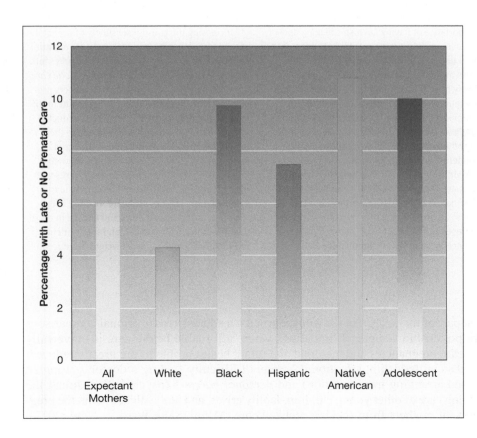

FIGURE 3.7 **Expectant mothers in the United States with late (after the first trimester) or no prenatal care.** From 7 to 11 percent of low-income ethnic minority mothers, and about 10 percent of adolescent mothers, receive inadequate prenatal care. (Based on Child Trends, 2015.)

Cultural Influences | Culturally Sensitive Prenatal Health Care: Perspectives of Expectant Mothers

Compared with their European-American counterparts, low-income, ethnic minority expectant mothers are consistently less likely to access early and regular prenatal care—a difference linked to increased rates of low birth weight, prematurity, newborn death, and other negative birth outcomes (Cox et al., 2011; Kitsantas & Gaffney, 2010). When minority mothers do come in for prenatal appointments, they tend to report more negative experiences with health care providers (Wheatley et al., 2008). They perceive the care they receive to be poor quality, which discourages them from further seeking care, with profound implications for maternal and newborn health.

In several studies, researchers asked ethnic minority mothers who had recently given birth about their prenatal health care experiences. Many highlighted inadequacies in provider–patient communication while expressing a strong desire for culturally sensitive care. Noting that too often, doctors and nurses focused narrowly on completing required tests and conveying results, one mother concluded, "[W]e're numbers and not people" (Coley et al., 2018, p. 161).

Though they readily acknowledged the need for medical procedures, minority mothers regarded the interpersonal side of prenatal visits as essential to quality care. An African-American mother illustrated what culturally sensitive care meant to her: "[for example] being aware of if you have a sickle-cell patient, … really doing your homework on the emotional side of what it means" (p. 161).

Hispanic mothers described provider–patient communication as especially challenging, due to language barriers and the fears of many that seeking prenatal care might threaten their immigrant status. In addition, they perceived doctors and nurses who rushed through appointments while appearing impatient and unfriendly as rude, angry, uncaring, and unreliable. In contrast, they judged those who took time to help

CENTERING HEALTHCARE INSTITUTE

Participants in a group prenatal care program meet after individual checkups to discuss important health issues in a culturally sensitive environment. Compared to mothers receiving traditional brief appointments, group care mothers experience a reduced incidence of prematurity and low birth weight.

reticent or confused patients to be caring and believable (Bergman & Connaughton, 2013). Spanish-speaking mothers consistently stressed the importance of having Spanish-speaking doctors, nurses, or interpreters available to overcome cultural differences, ensure patient understanding, and avoid medical errors.

Many new mothers noted that lack of cultural competence increased the chances that health care providers would harbor biased assumptions and behave disrespectfully. In a survey of several thousand new mothers, 20 percent of minority respondents reported poor treatment by doctors, nurses, or front desk staff due to race, ethnicity, or language (Attanasio & Kozhimannil, 2015). Discrimination in health care settings is associated with an array of negative outcomes, including unraveling of patient trust, reduced patient adherence to treatment recommendations,

missed subsequent appointments, and declines in patient health (Hausmann et al., 2011; Weech-Maldonado et al., 2012).

Increasing the cultural sensitivity of prenatal care by strengthening provider–patient communication is vital for improving health outcomes for babies. In one strategy called *group prenatal care*, after each medical checkup, trained leaders provide low-income ethnic minority expectant mothers with a group discussion session—conducted in their native language—and encourage them to talk about important health issues (Carter et al., 2016; Catling et al., 2015). Compared to mothers receiving traditional brief appointments with little opportunity to ask questions, participants in group prenatal care are more satisfied with their health care experiences and engage in more health-promoting behaviors, and the incidence of prematurity and low birth weight is reduced.

pay for at least part of their care. As we will see when we address cross-national comparisons of health care policies in Chapter 4, in nations where affordable health care is universally available, late-care pregnancies and maternal and infant health problems are greatly reduced.

Besides financial hardship, *situational barriers* (difficulty finding a doctor, getting an appointment, and arranging transportation) and *personal barriers* (psychological stress, the demands of taking care of other young children, family crises, and ambivalence about the pregnancy) can prevent mothers from seeking prenatal care (Mazul, Salm Ward, & Ngui, 2017).

APPLYING WHAT WE KNOW

Do's and Don'ts for a Healthy Pregnancy

DO	DON'T
Do make sure that you have been vaccinated against infectious diseases that are dangerous to the embryo and fetus, such as rubella, before you get pregnant. Most vaccinations are not safe during pregnancy.	Don't take any drugs without consulting your doctor.
Do see a doctor as soon as you suspect that you are pregnant, and continue to get regular medical checkups throughout pregnancy.	Don't smoke. If you have already smoked during part of your pregnancy, cut down or, better yet, quit. If other members of your family smoke, ask them to quit or to smoke outside.
Do eat a well-balanced diet and take vitamin–mineral supplements, as prescribed by your doctor, both prior to and during pregnancy. Gain 25 to 30 pounds gradually.	Don't drink alcohol from the time you decide to get pregnant.
Do obtain literature from your doctor, library, or bookstore about prenatal development. Ask your doctor about anything that concerns you.	Don't engage in activities that might expose your embryo or fetus to environmental hazards, such as radiation or chemical pollutants. If you work in an occupation that involves these agents, ask for a safer assignment or a leave of absence.
Do keep physically fit through moderate exercise. If possible, join a special exercise class for expectant mothers.	Don't engage in activities that might expose your embryo or fetus to harmful infectious diseases, such as toxoplasmosis.
Do avoid emotional stress. If you are a single expectant mother, find a relative or friend on whom you can rely for emotional support.	Don't choose pregnancy as a time to go on a diet.
Do get plenty of rest. An overtired mother is at risk for pregnancy complications.	Don't gain too much weight during pregnancy. A very large weight gain is associated with complications.
Do enroll in a prenatal and childbirth education class with your partner or other companion. When parents know what to expect, the nine months before birth can be one of the most joyful times of life.	

Many also engage in high-risk behaviors, such as smoking and drug abuse, which they do not want to reveal to health professionals.

For these women, assistance in making appointments, drop-in child-care centers, and free or low-cost transportation are vital. As the Cultural Influences box on page 112 reveals, culturally sensitive health-care practices, emphasizing open communication between health-care providers and pregnant women that is respectful of patients' values and needs, are also helpful. Refer to Applying What We Know above, which lists "do's and don'ts" for a healthy pregnancy, based on our discussion of the prenatal environment.

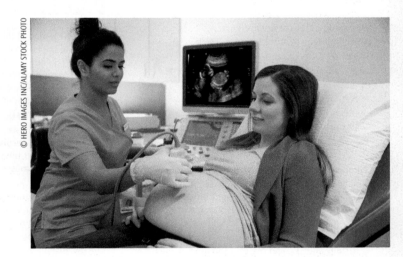

© HERO IMAGES INC/ALAMY STOCK PHOTO

During a routine visit, a woman views an ultrasound image of her developing fetus. All pregnant women need regular prenatal care to protect their health and that of their babies.

ASK YOURSELF

Connect ■ Using what you learned about research strategies in Chapter 1, explain why it is difficult to determine the prenatal effects of many environmental agents, such as drugs and pollution.

Apply ■ Nora, pregnant for the first time, believes that a few cigarettes and a glass of wine a day won't be harmful. Provide Nora with research-based reasons for not smoking or drinking.

Reflect ■ If you had to choose five environmental influences to publicize in a campaign aimed at promoting healthy prenatal development, which ones would you choose, and why?

SUMMARY

3.1 Motivations for Parenthood (p. 87)

3.1 *Discuss factors that contribute to contemporary adults' decision making about parenthood, including timing of childbearing and family size.*

- Compared to a few decades ago, today adults in Western industrialized nations are freer to choose whether, when, and how to have children. Among contextual factors that affect their decision making are financial circumstances, religious values, partnership changes, career goals, and government and workplace family policies.

- Childbearing motivations have also changed over time, increasingly emphasizing individual fulfillment and deemphasizing obligation to society.

- In the United States and other industrialized nations, the overall fertility rate has declined substantially over the past decade, a trend largely due to delayed marriage and parenthood, which results in adults having fewer children.

- Contrary to widespread belief, smaller families do not make brighter children. The higher birth rate of low-SES women accounts for the association between large family size and lower intelligence test scores of all siblings.

- Reproductive capacity declines with age, especially after 35, and risk of chromosomal and other genetically influenced disorders increases. Because highly educated women with demanding careers are especially likely to delay parenthood, they may not realize their childbearing goals.

3.2 Prenatal Development (p. 90)

3.2 *List the three periods of prenatal development, and describe the major milestones of each.*

- The **germinal period** lasts about two weeks, from fertilization through **implantation** of the blastocyst in the uterine lining. Structures that support prenatal growth begin to form, including the **amnion, chorion, placenta,** and **umbilical cord.**

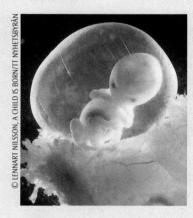

- During the period of the **embryo,** weeks 2 through 8, the foundations for all body structures are laid down. The **neural tube** forms and the nervous system starts to develop. Other organs follow rapidly. By the end of this period, the embryo responds to touch and can move.

- During the period of the **fetus,** the organism increases rapidly in size. By the middle of the second **trimester, vernix** and **lanugo** have emerged to protect the skin. At the end of the second trimester, most of the brain's neurons are in place.

- The fetus reaches the **age of viability** at the beginning of the third trimester, between 22 and 26 weeks. The brain continues to develop rapidly, and new sensory and behavioral capacities emerge, including taste and odor preferences, pain sensitivity, and the ability to distinguish the tone and rhythm of different voices and sounds. Gradually the lungs mature, the fetus fills the uterus, and birth nears.

3.3 Prenatal Environmental Influences (p. 97)

3.3a *Cite factors that influence the impact of teratogens, and discuss evidence on the impact of known or suspected teratogens.*

- The impact of **teratogens** varies with amount and length of exposure, genetic makeup of mother and developing organism, age of the developing organism (serious defects are most likely to occur during embryonic period), and the presence of other negative factors. Growing evidence indicates that certain teratogens exert long-term effects epigenetically.

- The most widely used potent teratogenic medication is isotretinoin, a treatment for severe acne. Evidence on other common medications, such as aspirin, caffeine, and antidepressants, is mixed, and their prenatal impact is hard to separate from other correlated factors.

- Babies born to users of cocaine, heroin, or methadone are at risk for a wide variety of problems, including prematurity, low birth weight, brain abnormalities, physical defects, breathing difficulties, and infant death. Lasting negative effects, however, are not well-established.

- By inducing epigenetic changes that heighten sensitivity to postnatal environmental stressors, prenatal marijuana exposure may lead to long-term cognitive and emotional deficits.

- Infants whose parents use tobacco are often born underweight, may have physical defects, and are at risk for long-term health, attention, learning, and behavior problems.

- Maternal alcohol consumption can lead to **fetal alcohol spectrum disorder (FASD). Fetal alcohol syndrome (FAS)** and **partial fetal alcohol syndrome (p-FAS),** resulting from heavy drinking during pregnancy, involve facial abnormalities, deficient physical growth, brain damage, and substantial cognitive and behavioral impairments. In less severe forms—**alcohol-related neurodevelopmental disorder (ARND)** and **alcohol-related birth defects (ARBD)**—alcohol exposure is usually less pervasive. Self-regulation therapy for school-age children with p-FAS and ARND leads to more efficient neural functioning and gains on simple self-regulation tasks.

- Prenatal exposure to high levels of ionizing radiation, mercury, PCBs, lead, and dioxins leads to physical malformations and severe brain damage. Low-level exposure has been linked to cognitive deficits and emotional and behavioral disorders. Persistent air pollution is associated with low birth weight and impaired lung and immune-system functioning.

- Among infectious diseases, rubella causes wide-ranging abnormalities. Babies with prenatally transmitted HIV rapidly develop AIDS, leading to brain damage and early death. Antiretroviral drug therapy dramatically reduces prenatal transmission. Cytomegalovirus, herpes simplex 2, and toxoplasmosis can also be devastating to the embryo and fetus. Prenatal exposure to the Zika virus is associated with microcephaly and eye deformities.

3.3b *Describe the impact of additional maternal factors on prenatal development.*

- Exercise during pregnancy is linked to improved fetal cardiovascular functioning, higher birth weight, and reduced risk of pregnancy complications.

- Prenatal malnutrition can lead to low birth weight, damage to the brain and other organs, and suppression of immune system development.

- Folic acid supplements can greatly reduce the risk of physical defects, premature delivery, and low birth weight. Other vitamins and minerals also have established benefits.

- Severe maternal emotional stress is linked to pregnancy complications and may impair children's capacity to manage stress, thereby elevating their risk for diverse negative behavioral outcomes and physical illnesses. Providing mothers with social support greatly reduces these consequences.

- **Rh factor incompatibility** can lead to oxygen deprivation, brain and heart damage, and infant death.

- Older mothers face increased risk of miscarriage, babies with chromosomal defects, and, after age 40, a rise in other pregnancy complications. Poor health and environmental risks associated with low income explain higher rates of pregnancy complications in adolescent mothers.

3.4 The Importance of Prenatal Health Care (p. 111)

3.4 *Explain why early and regular health care is vital during the prenatal period.*

- Unexpected complications, such as gestational diabetes and preeclampsia, can threaten any pregnancy. Inadequate prenatal health care is common among adolescent and low-income, ethnic minority mothers, whose babies are more likely to be born underweight and to die than infants of mothers with good prenatal care. Culturally sensitive health-care practices can help overcome the barriers that discourage low-income, ethnic minority mothers from seeking care.

IMPORTANT TERMS AND CONCEPTS

age of viability (p. 95)
alcohol-related birth defects (ARBD) (p. 101)
alcohol-related neurodevelopmental disorder (ARND) (p. 101)
amnion (p. 91)
chorion (p. 93)
embryo (p. 93)

fetal alcohol spectrum disorder (FASD) (p. 101)
fetal alcohol syndrome (FAS) (p. 101)
fetus (p. 94)
germinal period (p. 91)
implantation (p. 91)
lanugo (p. 95)
neural tube (p. 94)

partial fetal alcohol syndrome (p-FAS) (p. 101)
placenta (p. 93)
Rh factor incompatibility (p. 109)
teratogen (p. 97)
trimesters (p. 94)
umbilical cord (p. 93)
vernix (p. 95)

4 | Birth and the Newborn Baby

Welcome

Debjyoti Sakar, 12 years, India

Relatives approach a mother and her newborn to welcome the baby into the family. In Chapter 4, we explore the birth process, the marvelous competencies of the newborn, and the challenges of new parenthood.

Reprinted with permission from The International Museum of Children's Art, Oslo, Norway

Although Yolanda and Jay completed my child development course three months before their baby was born, both agreed to return to share their reactions to birth and new parenthood with next term's class. Two-week-old Joshua came along as well. Yolanda and Jay's story revealed that the birth of a baby is one of the most dramatic and emotional events in human experience. Jay was present throughout Yolanda's labor and delivery. Yolanda explained:

> By morning, we knew I was in labor. It was Thursday, so we went in for my usual weekly appointment. The doctor said, yes, the baby was on the way, but it would be a while. He told us to go home and relax and come to the hospital in three or four hours. We checked in at 3 in the afternoon; Joshua arrived at 2 o'clock the next morning. When, finally, I was ready to deliver, it went quickly. A half hour or so and some good hard pushes, and there he was! His face was red and puffy, and his head was misshapen, but I thought, "Our son! I can't believe he's really here."

Jay was also elated by Joshua's birth. "I wanted to support Yolanda and to experience as much as I could. It was awesome, indescribable," he said, holding little Joshua over his shoulder and patting and kissing him gently.

In this chapter, we explore the experience of childbirth, from both the parents' and the baby's point of view. Today, women in industrialized nations have many choices about where and how they give birth, and hospitals go to great lengths to make the arrival of a new baby a rewarding, family-centered event.

Joshua reaped the benefits of Yolanda and Jay's careful attention to his needs during pregnancy. He was strong, alert, and healthy at birth. Nevertheless, the birth process does not always go smoothly. We will consider the pros and cons of medical interventions, such as pain-relieving drugs and surgical deliveries, designed to ease a difficult birth and protect the health of mother and baby. Our discussion also addresses birth complications, paying special attention to infants who experience oxygen deprivation or who are born underweight or too early.

Finally, Yolanda and Jay spoke candidly about how their lives had changed since Joshua's arrival. "It's exciting and wonderful," reflected Yolanda, "but the adjustments are enormous. I wasn't quite prepared for the intensity of Joshua's 24-hour-a-day demands." In the concluding sections of this chapter, we look closely at the remarkable capacities of newborns to adapt to the external world and to communicate their needs. We also consider how parents adjust to the realities of everyday life with a new baby. ■

4.1 The Stages of Childbirth

It is not surprising that childbirth is often referred to as labor. It is the hardest physical work a woman may ever do. A complex series of hormonal changes initiates the process. As pregnancy advances, the placenta releases increasing amounts of *corticotropin-releasing hormone (CRH),* a hormone involved in the stress response. High levels of CRH trigger additional placental hormone adjustments that induce uterine contractions. And as CRH rises in the fetal bloodstream in the final prenatal weeks, it stimulates fetal production of the stress hormone cortisol, which promotes development of the lungs in preparation for breathing (Li et al., 2014; Vannuccini et al., 2016). An abnormal increase in maternal CRH in the second or third trimesters of pregnancy may be an important, early predictor of premature birth (Latendresse & Ruiz, 2011; Ruiz et al., 2015).

4.1 Describe the three stages of childbirth, the baby's adaptation to labor and delivery, and the newborn baby's appearance.

Several signs let Yolanda know that labor was near:

- She occasionally felt the upper part of her uterus contract. These contractions are often called *false labor* or *prelabor* because they remain brief and unpredictable for several weeks.
- About two weeks before birth, she experienced an event called *lightening:* Joshua's head dropped low into her uterus. Placental hormone changes had caused her cervix to soften, and it no longer supported Joshua's weight so easily.
- When she experienced the *bloody show,* Yolanda knew that labor was only hours or days away. As the cervix began to open, the plug of mucus that sealed it during pregnancy was released, producing a reddish discharge. Soon after, uterine contractions became more frequent, and mother and baby entered the first of three stages of childbirth (see Figure 4.1).

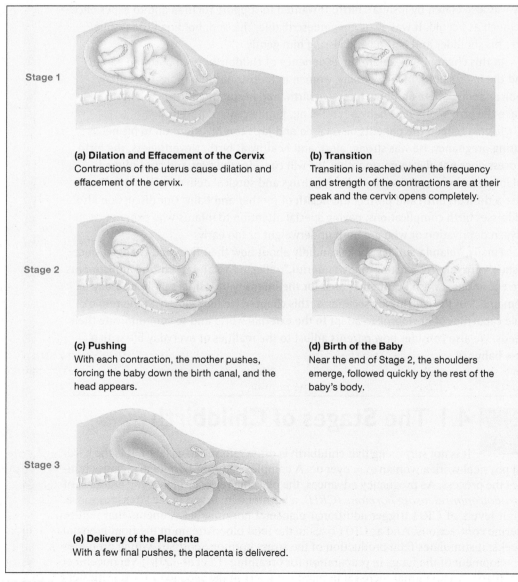

Stage 1

(a) Dilation and Effacement of the Cervix
Contractions of the uterus cause dilation and effacement of the cervix.

(b) Transition
Transition is reached when the frequency and strength of the contractions are at their peak and the cervix opens completely.

Stage 2

(c) Pushing
With each contraction, the mother pushes, forcing the baby down the birth canal, and the head appears.

(d) Birth of the Baby
Near the end of Stage 2, the shoulders emerge, followed quickly by the rest of the baby's body.

Stage 3

(e) Delivery of the Placenta
With a few final pushes, the placenta is delivered.

FIGURE 4.1 **The three stages of childbirth.**

4.1.1 Stage 1: Dilation and Effacement of the Cervix

Stage 1 is the longest, lasting an average of 12 to 14 hours with a first birth and 4 to 6 hours with later births. **Dilation and effacement of the cervix** take place: As uterine contractions gradually become more frequent and powerful, they cause the cervix to open (dilate) and thin (efface), forming a clear channel from the uterus into the birth canal, or vagina. The uterine contractions that open the cervix are forceful and regular, starting at 10 to 20 minutes apart and lasting about 15 to 20 seconds each. Gradually, they get closer together, occurring every 2 to 3 minutes, and become stronger, persisting for as long as 60 seconds each.

During this stage, Yolanda could do nothing to speed up the process. Jay held her hand, provided sips of juice and water, and helped her get comfortable. Throughout the first few hours, Yolanda walked, stood, or sat upright. As the contractions became more intense, she leaned against pillows or lay on her side.

The climax of Stage 1 is a brief phase called **transition,** in which the frequency and strength of contractions are at their peak and the cervix opens completely. Although transition is the most uncomfortable part of childbirth, it is especially important that the mother relax. If she tenses or bears down with her muscles before the cervix is completely dilated and effaced, she may bruise the cervix and slow the progress of labor.

4.1.2 Stage 2: Delivery of the Baby

In Stage 2, which lasts about 50 minutes for a first birth and 20 minutes in later births, the infant is born. Strong contractions of the uterus continue, but the mother also feels a natural urge to squeeze and push with her abdominal muscles. As she does so with each contraction, she forces the baby down and out.

Between contractions, Yolanda dozed lightly. When the doctor announced that the baby's head was *crowning*—the vaginal opening had stretched around the entire head—Yolanda felt renewed energy. She knew that soon the baby would arrive. Quickly, with several more pushes, Joshua's forehead, nose, and chin emerged, then his upper body and trunk. The doctor held him up, wet with amniotic fluid and still attached to the umbilical cord. As air rushed into his lungs, Joshua cried. When the umbilical cord stopped pulsing, it was clamped and cut. A nurse placed Joshua on Yolanda's chest, where she and Jay could see, touch, and gently talk to him. Then the nurse wrapped Joshua snugly to help with temperature regulation.

4.1.3 Stage 3: Birth of the Placenta

Stage 3 brings labor to an end. A few final contractions and pushes cause the placenta to separate from the wall of the uterus and be delivered in about 5 to 10 minutes. Yolanda and Jay were surprised at the large size of the thick 1½-pound red-gray organ, which had taken care of Joshua's basic needs for the previous nine months.

4.1.4 The Baby's Adaptation to Labor and Delivery

At first glance, labor and delivery seem like a dangerous ordeal for the baby. The strong contractions of Yolanda's uterus exposed Joshua's head to a great deal of pressure, and they squeezed the placenta and the umbilical cord repeatedly, temporarily reducing Joshua's supply of oxygen.

Fortunately, healthy babies are equipped to withstand these traumas. The force of the contractions intensifies the baby's production of stress hormones. Unlike during pregnancy, when excessive stress endangers the fetus (see Chapter 3), during childbirth high levels of infant cortisol and other stress hormones are adaptive. They help the baby withstand oxygen deprivation by sending a rich supply of blood to the brain and heart (Gluckman, Sizonenko, & Bassett, 1999). In addition, stress hormones prepare the baby to breathe by causing the lungs to absorb any remaining fluid and by expanding the bronchial tubes (passages leading to the lungs). Finally, stress hormones arouse the infant into alertness. Joshua was born wide-awake, ready to interact with the surrounding world.

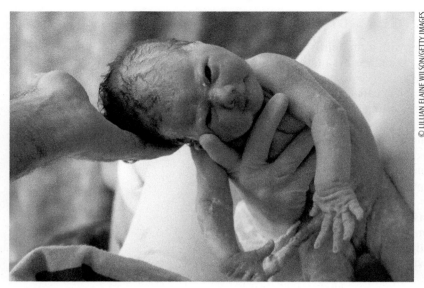

To accommodate the well-developed brain, a newborn's head is large in relation to the trunk and legs. This newborn's body readily turns pink as he takes his first few breaths.

4.1.5 The Newborn Baby's Appearance

Parents are often surprised at the odd-looking newborn—a far cry from the storybook image they may have had in their minds. The average newborn is 20 inches long and 7½ pounds in weight; boys tend to be slightly longer and heavier than girls. The head is large in comparison to the trunk and legs, which are short and bowed. Proportionally, if your head were as large as that of a newborn infant, you would be balancing something about the size of a watermelon between your shoulders! This combination of a large head (with its well-developed brain) and a small body means that human infants learn quickly in the first few months of life. But unlike most other mammals, they cannot get around on their own until much later.

Even though newborn babies may not match parents' idealized image, some features do make them attractive. Their captivating round faces, chubby cheeks, large foreheads, and big eyes generally make adults want to pick them up and cuddle them (Luo et al., 2015).

4.1.6 Assessing the Newborn's Physical Condition: The Apgar Scale

To assess the newborn's physical condition quickly, doctors and nurses use the **Apgar Scale.** As Table 4.1 shows, a rating of 0, 1, or 2 on each of five characteristics is made at 1 minute and again at 5 minutes after birth. A combined Apgar score of 7 or better indicates that the infant is in good physical condition. If the score is between 4 and 6, the baby requires assistance in establishing breathing and other vital signs. If the score is 3 or below, the infant is in serious danger and requires emergency medical attention (Apgar, 1953). Two Apgar ratings are given because some babies have trouble adjusting at first but do quite well after a few minutes.

TABLE 4.1   The Apgar Scale

	RATING		
Sign[a]	**0**	**1**	**2**
Color (**A**ppearance)[b]	Blue body, arms, and legs	Body pink with blue arms and legs	Body, arms, and legs completely pink
Heart rate (**P**ulse)	No heartbeat	Under 100 beats per minute	100 to 140 beats per minute
Reflex irritability (**G**rimacing, sneezing, and coughing)	No response	Weak reflexive response	Strong reflexive response
Muscle tone (**A**ctivity)	Completely limp	Weak movements of arms and legs	Strong movements of arms and legs
Breathing (**R**espiratory effort)	No breathing for 60 seconds	Irregular, shallow breathing	Strong breathing and crying

[a]As an aid for remembering these signs, note that the boldfaced first letter of the words in parentheses—**A**ppearance, **P**ulse, **G**rimacing, **A**ctivity, and **R**espiratory effort—together spell **Apgar.**

[b]It is difficult to apply the pink color criterion to babies with olive to brown skin tones. However, all newborns can be rated for the pinkish glow that results from the flow of oxygen through body tissues.

Source: Apgar, 1953.

ASK YOURSELF

Connect ■ Contrast the positive impact of the baby's production of high levels of stress hormones during childbirth with the negative impact of severe maternal stress on the fetus, discussed on pages 108–109 in Chapter 3.

Apply ■ On seeing her newborn baby for the first time, Caroline exclaimed, "Why is she so out of proportion?" What observations prompted Caroline to ask this question? Explain why her baby's appearance is adaptive.

4.2 Approaches to Childbirth

Childbirth practices, like other aspects of family life, are molded by the society of which mother and baby are a part. In many village and tribal cultures, expectant mothers are well-acquainted with the childbirth process. For example, the Jarara of South America and the Pukapukans of the Pacific Islands treat birth as a vital part of daily life (Lowis & McCaffery, 2004). The Jarara mother gives birth in full view of the entire community, including small children. The Pukapukan girl is so familiar with the events of labor and delivery that she can frequently be seen playing at it. Using a coconut to represent the baby, she stuffs it inside her dress, imitates the mother's pushing, and lets the nut fall at the proper moment.

In most nonindustrialized cultures, women are assisted—though often not by medical personnel—during labor and delivery. Among the Mende of Sierra Leone, birth attendants are appointed by the village chief and are highly respected members of their communities. They visit expectant mothers before and after a birth to provide advice, can be called to help deliver a baby at any time, and practice traditional strategies to promote delivery, including massaging the abdomen and supporting the woman in a squatting position (Dorwie & Pacquiao, 2014). In Bolivia, a Siriono mother delivers her own baby in a hammock with a crowd of women close by, who keep her company. The father cuts the umbilical cord and joins the mother in tending to the newborn for the first few days (Reed, 2005).

In Western nations, childbirth has changed dramatically over the centuries. Before the late 1800s, birth usually took place at home and was a family-centered event. The industrial revolution brought greater crowding to cities, along with new health problems. As a result, childbirth moved from home to hospital, where the health of mothers and babies could be protected (Borst, 1995). Once doctors assumed responsibility for childbirth, women's knowledge of it declined, and relatives and friends no longer participated.

By the 1950s and 1960s, women had begun to question the medical procedures that had come to be used during labor and delivery. Many felt that routine use of strong drugs and delivery instruments had robbed them of a precious experience and was often neither necessary nor safe for the baby. Gradually, a natural childbirth movement arose in Europe and spread to North America. Its purpose was to make hospital birth as comfortable and rewarding for mothers as possible. Today, most hospitals offer birth centers that are family-centered and homelike and that encourage early contact between parents and baby.

Freestanding birth centers also exist. They permit greater maternal control over labor and delivery, including choice of delivery positions and presence of family members and friends, as well as timely transfer to a hospital should an emergency arise. And a small number of North American women reject institutional birth entirely and choose to have their babies at home.

4.2 Describe natural childbirth and home delivery, noting benefits and concerns associated with each.

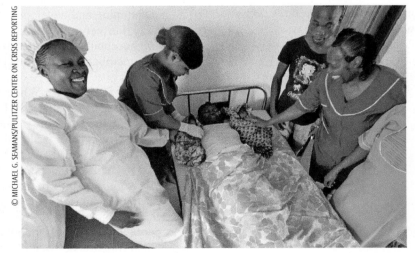

© MICHAEL G. SEAMANS/PULITZER CENTER ON CRISIS REPORTING

In Sierra Leone, a new mother rests comfortably after giving birth to twins. She had her first twin at home, assisted by village birth attendants. After complications arose, the birth attendants took her to a clinic, where they collaborated with nurses in delivering her second twin. Throughout, cultural practices remained a part of this birth experience.

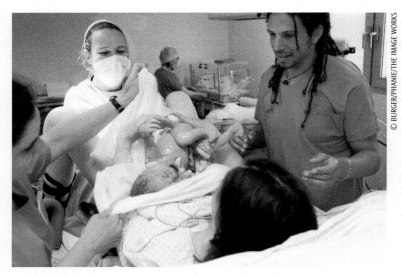

As the father looks on, a mother reaches for her newborn after giving birth. A companion's support is a vital part of natural childbirth, which is associated with shorter labors, fewer complications, and a more rewarding birth experience.

4.2.1 Natural, or Prepared, Childbirth

Yolanda and Jay chose **natural, or prepared, childbirth**— a group of techniques aimed at reducing pain and medical intervention and making childbirth a rewarding experience. Most natural childbirth programs draw on methods developed by Grantly Dick-Read (1959) in England and Fernand Lamaze (1958) in France. These physicians recognized that cultural attitudes had taught women to fear the birth experience. An anxious, frightened woman in labor tenses her muscles, heightening the pain that usually accompanies strong contractions.

In a typical natural childbirth program, the expectant mother and a companion (a partner, relative, or friend) participate in three activities:

- *Classes.* Yolanda and Jay attended a series of classes in which they learned about the anatomy and physiology of labor and delivery. Knowledge about the birth process reduces a mother's fear.
- *Relaxation and breathing techniques.* During each class, Yolanda was taught relaxation and breathing exercises aimed at counteracting the pain of uterine contractions.
- *Labor coach.* Jay learned how to help Yolanda during childbirth by reminding her to relax and breathe, massaging her back, supporting her body, and offering encouragement and affection.

Social Support and Natural Childbirth   Social support is important to the success of natural childbirth. Mothers who are supported during labor and delivery—either by a *doula* (a Greek word referring to a trained lay attendant) or by a relative or friend with doula training—less often have instrument-assisted or cesarean (surgical) deliveries or need medication to control pain. Also, their babies' Apgar scores are higher, and they are more likely to be breastfeeding at a two-month follow-up (Campbell et al., 2006, 2007; Hodnett et al., 2012; McGrath & Kennell, 2008).

The continuous rather than intermittent support of a doula during labor and delivery strengthens these benefits for mothers and babies—outcomes evident in studies conducted in both developing and developed nations and among women of diverse ethnicities (Hodnett et al., 2012). Furthermore, this aspect of natural childbirth makes Western hospital-birth customs more acceptable to women from parts of the world where assistance from family and community members is the norm (Dundek, 2006).

Positions for Delivery   When natural childbirth is combined with delivery in a birth center or at home, mothers often give birth in an upright, sitting position rather than lying flat on their backs with their feet in stirrups (the traditional hospital delivery room practice). When mothers are upright, labor is slightly shorter because contractions are stronger and pushing is more effective (Kopas, 2014). The baby benefits from a richer supply of oxygen because blood flow to the placenta is increased, and fewer infant heartbeat irregularities occur. Compared with those who give birth lying on their backs, women who choose an upright position are less likely to use pain-relieving medication or to have instrument-assisted deliveries (Gupta, Hofmeyr, & Shehmar, 2012; Romano & Lothian, 2008).

In another increasingly popular method, water birth, the mother sits in a warm tub of water, which supports her weight, relaxes her, and provides her with the freedom to move into any position she finds most comfortable. Among mothers at low risk for birth complications, water birth is associated with reduced maternal stress, shorter labor, and greater likelihood of medication-free delivery than both back-lying and seated positions. As long as water birth is

LOOK and LISTEN

Talk to several mothers about social supports available to them during labor and delivery. From the mothers' perspectives, how did those supports (or lack of support) affect the birth experience?

carefully managed by skilled health professionals, it poses no additional risk of infection or safety to mothers or babies (American Association of Birth Centers, 2014; Vanderlaan, Hall, & Lewitt, 2018).

4.2.2 Home Delivery

Home birth has always been popular in certain industrialized nations, such as England, the Netherlands, and Sweden. The number of American women choosing to have their babies at home rose during the 1970s and 1980s but remains small, at less than 1 percent (Martin et al., 2018). Although some home births are attended by doctors, many more are handled by *certified nurse-midwives,* who have degrees in nursing and additional training in childbirth management.

The joys and perils of home delivery are well illustrated by a story told by Don, a father of four. "Our first child was delivered in the hospital," he said. "Even though I was present, Kathy and I found the atmosphere to be rigid and insensitive. We wanted a warmer, more personal birth environment." With a nurse-midwife's coaching, Don delivered their second child, Cindy, at their rural farmhouse. Three years later, when Kathy went into labor with Marnie, a heavy snowstorm prevented the midwife from reaching the house on time, so Don delivered the baby alone. The birth was difficult, and Marnie failed to breathe for several minutes. With great effort, Don revived her. The frightening memory of Marnie's limp, blue body convinced Don and Kathy to return to the hospital to have their last child. By then, the hospital's birth practices had changed, and the event was a rewarding one for both parents.

Don and Kathy's experience raises the question: Is it just as safe to give birth at home as in a hospital? For healthy women who are assisted by a well-trained doctor or midwife, it seems so because complications rarely occur (Cheyney et al., 2014). However, if attendants are not carefully trained and prepared to handle emergencies, the likelihood of infant disability and death is high (Grünebaum et al., 2015). When mothers are at risk for any kind of complication, the appropriate place for labor and delivery is the hospital, where life-saving treatment is available.

After a home birth, the midwife and a lay attendant provide support to the new mother. For healthy women attended by a well-trained doctor or midwife, home birth is as safe as hospital birth.

4.3 Medical Interventions

Medical interventions during childbirth occur in both industrialized and nonindustrialized cultures. For example, some tribal and village societies have discovered foods, oils, and herbs that stimulate labor and have devised surgical techniques to deliver babies (Alliance of African Midwives, 2012; Jordan, 1993). Yet childbirth in North America, more so than elsewhere in the world, is a medically monitored and controlled event. Use of some medical procedures has reached epic proportions—in part because of rising rates of multiple births and other high-risk deliveries, which are associated with increased maternal age and use of fertility treatments. But births unaffected by these factors are also medicalized.

What medical techniques are doctors likely to use during labor and delivery? When are they justified, and what dangers do they pose to mothers and babies?

4.3 List common medical interventions during childbirth, circumstances that justify their use, and any dangers associated with each.

4.3.1 Fetal Monitoring

Fetal monitors are electronic instruments that track the baby's heart rate during labor. An abnormal heartbeat pattern may indicate that the baby is in distress due to **anoxia,** or inadequate

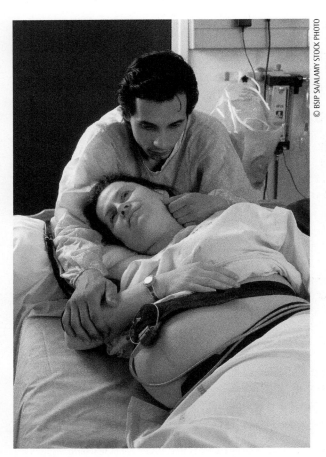

The fetal monitor strapped across this mother's abdomen uses ultrasound to record fetal heart rate throughout labor. In high-risk situations, fetal monitoring saves many lives. But it also may encourage unnecessary instrument and cesarean deliveries.

oxygen supply, and needs to be delivered immediately. Continuous fetal monitoring, which is required in most U.S. hospitals, is used in over 85 percent of U.S. births. The most popular type of monitor is strapped across the mother's abdomen throughout labor. A second, more accurate method involves threading a recording device through the cervix and placing it directly under the baby's scalp.

Fetal monitoring is a safe medical procedure that has saved the lives of many babies in high-risk situations. In healthy pregnancies, however, it does not reduce the already low rates of infant brain damage and death. Furthermore, most infants have some heartbeat irregularities during labor, so critics worry that fetal monitors identify many babies as in danger who, in fact, are not. Monitoring is linked to an increase in the number of instrument and cesarean (surgical) deliveries, practices we will discuss shortly (Mullins, Lees, & Brocklehurst, 2017). In addition, some women complain that the devices are uncomfortable and interfere with the normal course of labor.

Still, fetal monitors will probably continue to be used routinely in the United States, even though they are not necessary in most cases. Doctors fear that they will be sued for malpractice if they cannot show that they did everything they could to avert the death of an infant or the birth of an infant with problems.

4.3.2 Labor and Delivery Medication

Some form of medication is used in over 60 percent of U.S. births (Declercq et al., 2014). *Analgesics,* drugs used to relieve pain, may be given in mild doses during labor to help a mother relax. *Anesthetics* are a stronger type of painkiller that blocks sensation. Currently, the most common approach to controlling pain during labor is *epidural analgesia,* in which a regional pain-relieving drug is delivered continuously through a catheter into a small space in the lower spine. Unlike older spinal block procedures, which numb the entire lower half of the body, epidural analgesia limits pain reduction to the pelvic region. Because the mother retains the capacity to feel the pressure of the contractions and to move her trunk and legs, she is able to push during the second stage of labor.

Although pain-relieving drugs help women cope with childbirth and enable doctors to perform essential medical interventions, they also can cause problems. Epidural analgesia, for example, weakens uterine contractions. As a result, labor is prolonged, and the chances of instrument delivery or cesarean (surgical) birth increase. And because drugs rapidly cross the placenta, exposed newborns are at risk for respiratory distress (Kumar et al., 2014). They also tend to have lower Apgar scores, to be sleepy and withdrawn, to suck poorly during feedings, and to be irritable when awake (Platt, 2014; Törnell et al., 2015). Although no confirmed long-term consequences for development exist, the negative impact of these drugs on the newborn's adjustment supports the current trend to limit their use.

4.3.3 Instrument Delivery

Forceps, metal clamps placed around the baby's head to pull the infant from the birth canal, have been used since the sixteenth century to speed up delivery (see Figure 4.2). A more recent instrument, the *vacuum extractor,* consists of a plastic cup (placed on the baby's head) attached to a suction tube. Instrument delivery is appropriate if the mother's pushing during the second stage of labor does not move the baby through the birth canal in a reasonable period of time.

Instrument use has declined considerably over the past three decades, partly because doctors more often deliver babies surgically when labor problems arise. Today, forceps and (more often) vacuum extractors continue to be used in about 3 percent of U.S. births (Martin et al., 2018).

Using forceps to pull the baby through most or all of the birth canal greatly increases the risk of brain damage. As a result, forceps are seldom used this way today. Low-forceps delivery (carried out when the baby is most of the way through the vagina) is associated with injury to the baby's head and the mother's tissues. Vacuum extractors, which have rapidly replaced forceps as the dominant instrument, are less likely to tear the mother's tissues. Nevertheless, cup suction doubles the risk of bleeding beneath the baby's skin and on the outside of the skull compared with nonassisted deliveries. And the risk of more serious complications, including bleeding beneath the skull and seizures (which can damage the brain), increases tenfold (Ekéus, Högberg, & Norman, 2014; Muraca et al., 2017). Consequently, neither instrument should be used when mothers can be encouraged to deliver normally and there is no special reason to hurry the birth.

4.3.4 Cesarean Delivery

A **cesarean delivery** is a surgical birth; the doctor makes an incision in the mother's abdomen and lifts the baby out of the uterus. Forty years ago, cesarean delivery was rare. Since then, cesarean rates have climbed internationally, reaching 16 percent in Finland, 24 percent in New Zealand, 26 percent in Canada, 32 percent in Australia and Switzerland, and 37 percent in the United States (Martin et al., 2018; OECD, 2017c).

Cesareans have always been warranted by medical emergencies, such as Rh incompatibility, premature separation of the placenta from the uterus, or serious maternal illness or infection (for example, the herpes simplex 2 virus, which can infect the baby during a vaginal delivery). Cesareans are also justified when babies are in **breech position,** turned so that the buttocks or feet would be delivered first (about 1 in every 25 births). The breech position increases the chances of squeezing of the umbilical cord as the large head moves through the birth canal, thereby depriving the infant of oxygen. Head injuries are also more likely. But the infant's exact position makes a difference. Certain breech babies fare just as well with a normal delivery as with a cesarean (Vistad et al., 2013). Sometimes the doctor can gently turn the baby into a head-down position during the early part of labor.

Although previously doctors used the rule, "Once a cesarean, always a cesarean," today many women are offered the option of a trial of labor in subsequent births, and most who attempt a vaginal birth are successful (ACOG, 2017). The recent practice of repeated cesareans, however, cannot account for the rise in cesarean deliveries in Western nations. Instead, medical control over childbirth is largely responsible. Because many needless cesareans are performed, pregnant women should ask questions about the procedure when choosing a doctor. Although the operation itself is safe, mother and baby require more time for recovery. Anesthetic may have crossed the placenta, making cesarean newborns sleepy and unresponsive and putting them at increased risk for breathing difficulties (Kotecha, Gallacher, & Kotecha, 2016; Ramachandrappa & Jain, 2008).

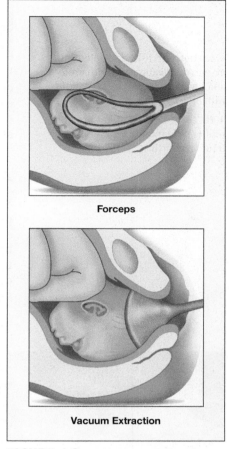

Forceps

Vacuum Extraction

FIGURE 4.2 **Instrument delivery.** The pressure that must be applied to pull the infant from the birth canal with forceps can injure the baby's head. An alternative method, the vacuum extractor, is less likely than forceps to injure the mother's tissues. Nevertheless, risk of infant scalp injuries and internal bleeding in the eyes and skull remains.

ASK YOURSELF

Connect ■ How might natural childbirth positively affect the parent–newborn relationship? Explain how your answer illustrates bidirectional influences between parent and child, emphasized in ecological systems theory.

Apply ■ Sharon, a heavy smoker, has just arrived at the hospital in labor. Which one of the medical interventions discussed in the preceding sections is her doctor justified in using? (For help in answering this question, review the prenatal effects of tobacco on pages 100–101 in Chapter 3.)

Reflect ■ If you were an expectant parent, would you choose home birth? Why or why not?

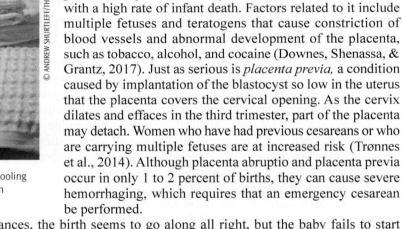

4.4 Birth Complications

4.4a Describe risks associated with oxygen deprivation and with preterm and low-birth-weight infants, along with effective interventions.

4.4b Describe factors that promote resilience in infants who survive a traumatic birth.

We have seen that some infants—in particular, those whose mothers are in poor health, do not receive good medical care, or have a history of pregnancy problems—are especially likely to experience birth complications. Inadequate oxygen, a pregnancy that ends too early, and a baby who is born underweight are serious risks to development that we have touched on many times. A baby remaining in the uterus too long is yet another risk. Let's look at the impact of each complication on later development.

4.4.1 Oxygen Deprivation

Some years ago, I got to know 4-year-old Melinda and her mother, Judy, both of whom participated in a special program for children with disabilities at our laboratory school. Melinda has *cerebral palsy,* a general term for a variety of impairments in muscle coordination caused by brain damage before, during, or just after birth. The disorder can range from very mild tremors to severe crippling and intellectual disability. One out of every 500 American children has cerebral palsy. About 10 percent experienced anoxia as a result of decreased maternal blood supply during labor and delivery (Clark, Ghulmiyyah, & Hankins, 2008; McIntyre et al., 2013).

Melinda walks with a halting, lumbering gait and has difficulty keeping her balance. "Some mothers don't know how the palsy happened," confided Judy, "but I do. I got pregnant accidentally, and my boyfriend didn't want to have anything to do with it. I was frightened and alone most of the time. I arrived at the hospital at the last minute. Melinda was breech, and the cord was wrapped around her neck."

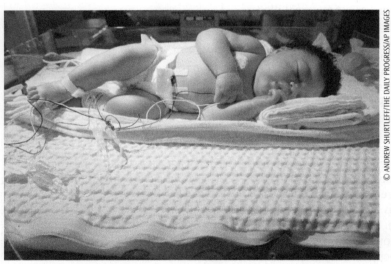

Treatment for this newborn, who experienced oxygen deprivation, includes a cooling water blanket to lower the baby's body temperature, which helps prevent brain damage.

Squeezing of the umbilical cord, as in Melinda's case, is one cause of anoxia. Another cause is *placenta abruptio,* or premature separation of the placenta, a life-threatening event with a high rate of infant death. Factors related to it include multiple fetuses and teratogens that cause constriction of blood vessels and abnormal development of the placenta, such as tobacco, alcohol, and cocaine (Downes, Shenassa, & Grantz, 2017). Just as serious is *placenta previa,* a condition caused by implantation of the blastocyst so low in the uterus that the placenta covers the cervical opening. As the cervix dilates and effaces in the third trimester, part of the placenta may detach. Women who have had previous cesareans or who are carrying multiple fetuses are at increased risk (Trønnes et al., 2014). Although placenta abruptio and placenta previa occur in only 1 to 2 percent of births, they can cause severe hemorrhaging, which requires that an emergency cesarean be performed.

In still other instances, the birth seems to go along all right, but the baby fails to start breathing within a few minutes. Healthy newborns can survive periods of little or no oxygen longer than adults can; they reduce their metabolic rate, thereby conserving the limited oxygen available. Nevertheless, brain damage is likely if regular breathing is delayed more than 10 minutes (Rennie & Rosenbloom, 2011). Can you think of other possible causes of oxygen deprivation that you learned about as you studied prenatal development and birth?

After initial brain injury from anoxia during labor or delivery, another phase of cell death can occur several hours later and last for several days or longer. *Hypothermia treatment,* by placing anoxic newborns in a head-cooling device shortly after birth for 72 hours, substantially reduces this secondary brain damage (detected through brain scans) (Hoehn et al., 2008). Another alternative—whole-body cooling in which anoxic newborns are laid on a precooled water blanket—leads to an impressive reduction in death and disability rates during the first two years (Allen, 2014).

Still, nearly half of newborns treated with hypothermia display persisting motor and cognitive deficits. Those who experienced mild to moderate anoxia often improve over time (Azzopardi et al., 2016; Pappas & Korzeniewski, 2016). In Melinda's case, her physical disability was permanent, but with warm, stimulating intervention services, she was just slightly behind in cognitive and language skills as a preschooler. When development is severely impaired, the anoxia was likely extreme. Perhaps it was caused by prenatal insult to the respiratory system, or it may have happened because the newborn's lungs were not yet mature enough to breathe.

For example, infants born more than six weeks early commonly have *respiratory distress syndrome* (otherwise known as *hyaline membrane disease*). Their tiny lungs are so poorly developed that the air sacs collapse, causing serious breathing difficulties. Although mechanical respirators keep many such infants alive, some suffer permanent brain damage from lack of oxygen, and in other cases their delicate lungs are harmed by the treatment itself. As we will see next, respiratory distress syndrome is just one of many risks for babies born too soon.

4.4.2 Preterm and Low-Birth-Weight Infants

Janet, nearly six months pregnant, and her husband, Rick, boarded a flight in Hartford, Connecticut, on their way to a vacation in Hawaii. During a stopover in San Francisco, Janet told Rick she was bleeding. Rushed to a hospital, she gave birth to Keith, who weighed less than 1½ pounds. Delivered 23 weeks after conception, he had barely reached the age of viability (see page 95 in Chapter 3).

During Keith's first month, he experienced one crisis after another. Three days after birth, an ultrasound suggested that fragile blood vessels feeding Keith's brain had hemorrhaged, a complication that can cause brain damage. Within three weeks, Keith had surgery to close a heart valve that seals automatically in full-term babies. Keith's immature immune system made infections difficult to contain. Repeated illnesses and the drugs used to treat them caused permanent hearing loss. Keith also had respiratory distress syndrome and breathed with the help of a respirator. Soon evidence of lung damage emerged. More than three months of hospitalization passed before Keith's rough course of complications and treatment eased.

Babies born three weeks or more before the end of a full 38-week pregnancy or who weigh less than 5½ pounds (2,500 grams) have for many years been referred to as "premature." Birth weight is the best available predictor of infant survival and healthy development. Many newborns who weigh less than 3½ pounds (1,500 grams) experience persisting difficulties, an effect that becomes stronger as length of pregnancy and birth weight decrease (see Figure 4.3) (Bolisetty et al., 2006; Wilson-Ching et al., 2013). Brain abnormalities, frequent illness, inattention, overactivity, sensory impairments, poor motor coordination, language delays, low intelligence test scores, deficits in school learning, and emotional and behavior difficulties are some of the problems that persist through childhood and adolescence and into adulthood (Breeman et al., 2017; Lemola, 2015; Mathewson et al., 2017).

About 11 percent of American infants are born early, and 8 percent are born underweight. The two risk factors often co-occur, and they can strike unexpectedly, as Keith's case illustrates. But the problem is highest among poverty-stricken women (Martin et al., 2018). These mothers, as indicated in Chapter 3, are more likely to be under stress, undernourished, and exposed to other harmful environmental influences—factors strongly linked to low birth weight. In addition, they often do not receive adequate prenatal care.

African-American infants are especially vulnerable to early and underweight birth: They have about twice the rates of white and

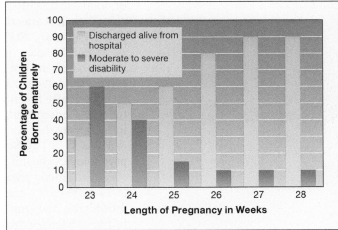

FIGURE 4.3 **Rates of infant survival and child disabilities by length of pregnancy.** In a follow-up of more than 2,300 babies born between 23 and 28 weeks gestation, the percentage who survived decreased and the percentage who displayed moderate to severe disabilities (assessed during the preschool years) increased with reduced length of pregnancy. Severe disabilities included cerebral palsy (unlikely to ever walk), severely delayed mental development, deafness, and blindness. Moderate disabilities included cerebral palsy (able to walk with assistance), moderately delayed mental development, and hearing impairments partially correctable with a hearing aid. (Adapted from Bolisetty et al., 2006.)

Hispanic infants, even after accounting for SES and other potentially contributing factors, such as single parenthood and young maternal age (Martin et al., 2018). Researchers suspect that African-American expectant mothers' greater exposure to multiple chronic stressors, such as job strain (long hours at tiring work), crime-ridden neighborhoods, crowded living conditions, and prejudice and discrimination, is involved (Dunkel-Shetter, 2011; Dunkel-Shetter & Lobel, 2012). Many studies confirm, for example, that African-American women's experience of race-related stressors—biased treatment at school, at work, or in access to housing—predict lower birth weight in their infants (Black, Johnson, & VanHoose, 2015).

Furthermore, low birth weight is often transmitted across generations: Women who were underweight at birth themselves are nearly twice as likely as other women to bear an underweight baby (Collins, Rankin, & David, 2011; Ncube et al., 2017). The possible causes are diverse: They may be genetic, environmental, or epigenetic—for example, excessive prenatal stress may impair offspring's lifelong capacity to manage stress (see page 109 in Chapter 3). When a daughter becomes pregnant, she exposes her fetus to severe emotional stress and its negative consequences.

Recall from Chapter 2 that prematurity is also common in multiple births. About 55 percent of twins and more than 90 percent of triplets are born early and low birth weight (Martin et al., 2018). Because space inside the uterus is restricted, multiples gain less weight than singletons in the second half of pregnancy.

Preterm Versus Small-for-Date Infants   Although preterm and low-birth-weight infants face many obstacles to healthy development, most go on to lead normal lives; about half of those born at 23 to 24 weeks gestation and weighing only a couple of pounds at birth have no disability (refer again to Figure 4.3). To better understand why some babies do better than others, researchers divide them into two groups. **Preterm infants** are born several weeks or more before their due date. Although they are small, their weight may still be appropriate, based on time spent in the uterus. **Small-for-date infants** are below their expected weight considering the length of the pregnancy. Some small-for-date infants are actually full-term. Others are preterm babies who are especially underweight.

Small-for-date infants, especially those who are also preterm, usually have more serious problems. During the first year, they are more likely to die, catch infections, and show evidence of brain damage. By middle childhood, they are smaller in stature, have lower intelligence test scores, are less attentive, achieve more poorly in school, and are socially immature (Katz et al., 2013; Tsai et al., 2015; Wilson-Ching et al., 2013).

Small-for-date infants probably experienced inadequate nutrition before birth. Perhaps their mothers did not eat properly, the placenta did not function normally, or the babies themselves had defects that prevented them from growing as they should. In some of these babies, an abnormally functioning placenta permitted ready transfer of stress hormones from mother to fetus. Consequently, small-for-date infants are especially likely to suffer from neurological impairments that permanently weaken their capacity to manage stress (Osterholm, Hostinar, & Gunnar, 2012). Severe stress, in turn, heightens their susceptibility to later physical and psychological health problems.

Even among preterm newborns whose weight is appropriate for length of pregnancy, just 7 to 14 more days—from 34 to 35 or 36 weeks—greatly reduces rates of illness, costly medical procedures, and lengthy hospital stays (although they need greater medical intervention than full-term babies) (Ananth, Friedman, & Gyamfi-Bannerman, 2013). In longitudinal follow-ups of thousands of births, infants born even 1 or 2 weeks early showed slightly lower kindergarten cognitive and language scores and third-grade reading and math scores than agemates who experienced a full-length prenatal period (Noble et al., 2012; Woythaler et al., 2015). These outcomes persisted even after controlling for other factors linked to achievement, such as birth weight and SES. Yet doctors often induce births several weeks preterm, under the misconception that these babies are developmentally "mature."

Consequences for Caregiving   Imagine a scrawny, thin-skinned infant only a little larger than the size of your hand. You try to play with the baby by stroking and talking softly, but he is sleepy and unresponsive. When you feed him, he sucks poorly. During the short, unpredictable periods in which he is awake, he is usually irritable.

The appearance and behavior of preterm infants—scrawny and thin-skinned, sleepy and unresponsive, irritable when briefly awake—can lead parents to be less sensitive in caring for them. Compared with full-term infants, preterm babies—especially those who are very ill at birth—are less often held close, touched, and talked to gently. At times, mothers of these infants resort to interfering pokes and verbal commands in an effort to obtain a higher level of response from them (Feldman, 2007b; Forcada-Guex et al., 2006). This may explain why preterm babies as a group are at risk for child abuse.

Distressed, emotionally reactive preterm infants are particularly susceptible to the effects of parenting quality: Among a sample of preterm 9-month-olds, the combination of infant negativity and angry or intrusive parenting yielded the highest rates of behavior problems at 2 years of age. But with warm, sensitive parenting, distressed preterm babies' rates of behavior problems were the lowest (Poehlmann et al., 2011).

When preterm infants are born to isolated, poverty-stricken mothers who cannot provide good nutrition, health care, and parenting, the likelihood of unfavorable outcomes increases. In contrast, parents with stable life circumstances and social supports usually can overcome the stresses of caring for a preterm infant (Ment et al., 2003). In these cases, even sick preterm babies have a good chance of catching up in development by middle childhood.

These findings suggest that how well preterm babies develop has a great deal to do with the parent–child relationship. Consequently, interventions directed at supporting both sides of this tie are more likely to help these infants recover.

Interventions for Preterm Infants   A preterm baby is cared for in a special Plexiglas-enclosed bed called an *isolette.* Temperature is carefully controlled because these infants cannot yet regulate their own body temperature effectively. To help protect the baby from infection, air is filtered before it enters the isolette. When a preterm infant is fed through a stomach tube, breathes with the aid of a respirator, and receives medication through an intravenous needle, the isolette can be very isolating indeed! Physical needs that otherwise would lead to close contact and other human stimulation are met mechanically.

Special Infant Stimulation In proper doses, certain kinds of stimulation can help preterm infants develop. In some intensive care nurseries, preterm babies can be seen rocking in suspended hammocks, lying on waterbeds designed to replace the gentle motion they would have received while still in the mother's uterus, or listening to soft music—experiences that promote faster weight gain, improved breathing, more predictable sleep patterns, and greater alertness (Cramer et al., 2018; Marshall-Baker, Lickliter, & Cooper, 1998; Schwilling et al., 2014). In one experiment, extremely preterm newborns, born between the 25th and 32nd prenatal weeks, were exposed either to recordings of their mother's voice and heartbeat for several hours each day or to routine hospital noise. At age 1 month, an ultrasound revealed that auditory areas of the brain had grown substantially larger in the maternal sounds group (see Figure 4.4) (Webb et al., 2015). Listening to womblike, familiar rhythmic maternal sounds, as opposed to the unpredictable din of hospital equipment, promoted brain development.

Touch is an especially important form of stimulation. In baby animals, touching the skin releases certain brain chemicals that support physical growth—effects believed to occur in humans as well. When preterm infants were gently massaged several times each day in the hospital, they gained weight faster and, at the end of the first year, were more advanced in mental and motor development than preterm babies not given this stimulation (Álvarez et al., 2017; Field, Hernandez-Reif, & Freedman, 2004).

In developing countries where hospitalization is not always possible, skin-to-skin "kangaroo care" is the most readily available intervention for promoting the survival and development of preterm babies. It involves placing the infant in a vertical position between the mother's breasts or next to the

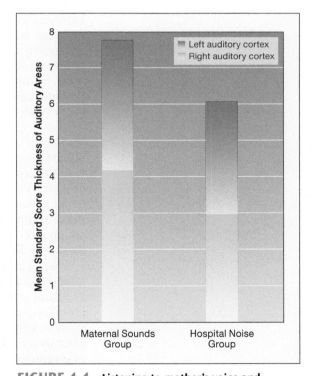

FIGURE 4.4 Listening to mother's voice and heartbeat enhances brain development in extremely preterm newborns. Infants born between the 25th and 32nd prenatal weeks were randomly assigned to hear either recordings of their mother's voice and heartbeat for several hours a day or routine, unpatterned hospital noise. After a month's exposure in the intensive care nursery, ultrasound measures showed that the left and right cerebral auditory areas were substantially thicker in the maternal sounds group than the hospital noise group. In addition to highlighting an effective intervention, the results suggest that exposure to soft, rhythmic maternal sounds during pregnancy enhances early brain growth. (Based on Webb et al., 2015.)

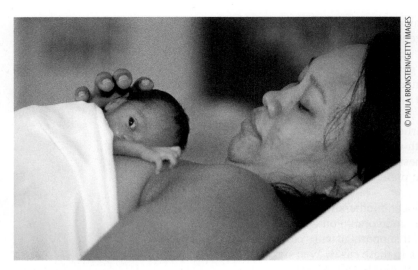

A mother uses skin-to-skin "kangaroo care" to warm and gently stimulate her preterm newborn at a hospital in Manilla, the Philippines. In developing countries, kangaroo care may be the most readily available intervention for promoting the survival of preterm and underweight babies. In Western nations, kangaroo care is often used as a supplement to hospital intensive care.

father's chest (under the parent's clothing) so the parent's body functions as a human incubator. Kangaroo care offers fathers a unique opportunity to increase their involvement in caring for the preterm newborn.

Kangaroo skin-to-skin contact fosters improved oxygenation of the baby's body, temperature regulation, sleep, breastfeeding, alertness, and infant survival (Conde-Agudelo, Belizan, & Diaz-Rossello, 2011; Kaffashi et al., 2013). In addition, the kangaroo position provides the baby with gentle stimulation of all sensory modalities: hearing (through the parent's voice), smell (through proximity to the parent's body), touch (through skin-to-skin contact), and vision (through the upright position). Mothers and fathers practicing kangaroo care feel more confident about caring for their fragile babies, interact more sensitively and affectionately, and feel more attached to them (Dodd, 2005; Feldman, 2007a).

Together, these factors may explain why preterm babies given many hours of kangaroo care in their early weeks, compared to those given little or no such care, are more likely to explore novel toys and score higher on measures of mental and motor development during the first year and beyond (Bera et al., 2014; Feldman, 2007a). In an investigation that followed children born preterm until age 10, those who had experienced two weeks of kangaroo care after birth, compared with matched controls given standard incubator care, displayed a more adaptive cortisol stress response, better organized sleep, more favorable mother–child interaction, and enhanced cognitive development. Favorable neurobiological and cognitive outcomes persisted through middle childhood (Feldman, Rosenthal, & Eidelman, 2014). Because of its diverse benefits, most hospital nurseries in Western nations offer kangaroo care to parents and preterm newborns.

Training Parents in Infant Caregiving Skills Interventions that support parents of preterm infants generally teach them how to recognize and respond to the baby's needs. For parents with the economic and personal resources to care for a preterm infant, just a few sessions of coaching in recognizing and responding to the baby's needs are linked to enhanced parent–infant interaction, reduced infant crying and improved sleep, more rapid language development in the second year, and steady gains in mental test performance that equal those of full-term children by middle childhood (Achenbach, Howell, & Aoki, 1993; Newnham, Milgrom, & Skouteris, 2009).

When preterm infants live in stressed, economically disadvantaged households, long-term intensive intervention is necessary (Guralnick, 2012). In the Infant Health and Development Program, preterm babies born into poverty received a comprehensive intervention aimed at promoting all aspects of their development. It combined medical follow-up, weekly home visits in which mothers received training in infant care and everyday problem solving, and cognitively stimulating child care from 1 to 3 years of age. More than four times as many intervention children as no-intervention controls (39 versus 9 percent) were within normal range at age 3 in intelligence, psychological adjustment, and physical growth (Bradley et al., 1994). In addition, mothers in the intervention group were more affectionate and more often encouraged play and cognitive mastery in their children—one reason their 3-year-olds may have been developing so favorably (McCarton, 1998).

At ages 5 and 8, children who had attended the child-care program regularly—for more than 350 days over the three-year period—continued to show better intellectual functioning. The more they attended, the higher they scored, with greater gains among those whose birth weights were higher—between 4½ and 5½ pounds (2,001 to 2,500 grams) (see Figure 4.5). In contrast, children who attended only sporadically gained little or even lost ground (Hill, Brooks-Gunn, & Waldfogel, 2003). A follow-up at age 18 revealed persisting benefits for the higher-birth-weight participants: They remained advantaged over controls in academic achievement, and they also engaged in fewer risky behaviors such as unprotected sexual activity and alcohol and drug use (McCormick et al., 2006).

These findings confirm that babies who are both preterm and economically disadvantaged require *intensive* intervention. And special strategies, such as extra adult–child interaction both at home and in infant–toddler and early childhood programs, may be necessary to achieve lasting changes in children with the lowest birth weights.

Nevertheless, even the best environments cannot always overcome the enormous biological risks associated with being born extremely preterm and underweight. Think back to Keith, the very sick baby you met at the beginning of this section. Despite advanced medical technology and new ways of helping parents, most infants born as early and with as low a birth weight as Keith either die or end up with serious disabilities (refer again to Figure 4.5). Six months after he was born, Keith died without ever having left the hospital.

Although Keith's premature birth was unavoidable, the high rate of underweight babies in the United States—one of the worst in the industrialized world—can be greatly reduced by improving the health and social conditions described in the Cultural Influences box on page 132. Fortunately, today we can save many preterm babies, but an even better course of action would be to prevent this serious threat to infant survival and development before it happens.

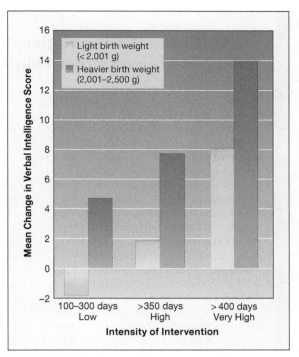

FIGURE 4.5   Influence of intensity of early intervention for low-income, preterm babies on intellectual functioning at age 8. Infants born preterm received cognitively stimulating child care from 1 through 3 years of age. Those who attended the program sporadically gained little in intellectual functioning (heavier-weight babies) or lost ground (lighter-weight babies). The more often children attended, the greater their intellectual gains. Heavier babies consistently gained more than light babies. But boosting the intensity of intervention above 400 days led to a dramatic increase in the performance of the light-weight group. (Adapted from Hill, Brooks-Gunn, & Waldfogel, 2003.)

4.4.3 Birth Complications, Parenting, and Resilience

In the preceding sections, we considered major birth complications. Now let's try to put the evidence together. Can any general principles help us understand how infants who survive a traumatic birth are likely to develop? A landmark study carried out in Hawaii provides answers to this question.

In 1955, Emmy Werner and Ruth Smith began to follow the development of nearly 700 infants on the island of Kauai who experienced either mild, moderate, or severe birth complications. Each was matched, on the basis of SES and ethnicity, with a healthy newborn (Werner & Smith, 1982). The children were monitored in childhood and adolescence and at ages 32 and 40 in adulthood.

Findings revealed that the likelihood of long-term difficulties increased if birth trauma was severe. Among participants with mild to moderate birth complications, those growing up in stable families with sensitive, involved parenting fared almost as well on measures of intelligence and psychological adjustment as those with no birth complications. Children exposed to poverty, family disorganization, and mentally ill parents often developed serious learning difficulties, behavior problems, and emotional disturbance.

The Kauai study tells us that as long as birth injuries are not overwhelming, a supportive home can restore children's development. But the most intriguing cases in this study were the handful of exceptions. A few children with both fairly serious birth complications and troubled family environments grew into competent adults who fared as well as controls in physical and mental health and vocational attainment. Werner and Smith found that these children relied on factors outside the family and within themselves to overcome stress. Some had attractive personalities—cheerfulness, agreeableness, and sociability—that drew positive responses from relatives, neighbors, and peers. In other instances, a grandparent, aunt, uncle, or babysitter provided the needed emotional support (Werner, 2001, 2005; Werner & Smith, 1992).

Do these outcomes remind you of the characteristics of resilient children, discussed in Chapter 1? The Kauai study and other similar investigations reveal that the impact of early biological risks often wanes as children's personal characteristics and social experiences contribute increasingly to their functioning (Werner, 2013). In sum, when the overall balance of life events tips toward the favorable side, children with serious birth problems can develop successfully. And when negative factors outweigh positive ones, even a sturdy newborn can become a lifelong casualty.

Cultural Influences | A Cross-National Perspective on Health Care and Other Policies for Parents and Newborn Babies

Infant mortality—the number of deaths in the first year of life per 1,000 live births—is an index used around the world to assess the overall health of a nation's children. Although the United States has the most up-to-date health-care technology in the world, it has made less progress in reducing infant deaths than many other countries. Over the past three decades, it has slipped in the international rankings, from seventh in the 1950s to thirty-ninth in 2018 (see Figure 4.6). Members of America's poor ethnic minorities are at greatest risk, with African-American infants more than twice as likely as white infants to die in the first year of life (U.S. Census Bureau, 2018b).

Neonatal mortality, the rate of death within the first month of life, accounts for 67 percent of the infant death rate in the United States. Two factors are largely responsible for neonatal mortality. The first is serious physical defects, most of which cannot be prevented. The percentage of babies born with physical defects is about the same in all ethnic and income groups. The second leading cause of neonatal mortality is low birth weight, which is largely preventable.

Widespread poverty and inadequate health-care programs for mothers and young children are largely responsible for these trends. In addition to providing government-sponsored health-care benefits to all citizens, each country in Figure 4.6 that outranks the United States in infant survival takes extra steps to make sure that pregnant mothers and babies have access to good nutrition, high-quality medical care, and social and economic supports that promote effective parenting.

For example, all Western European nations guarantee women a certain number of prenatal visits at very low or no cost. After a baby is born, a health professional routinely visits the home to provide counseling about infant care and to arrange continuing medical services. Home assistance is especially extensive in the Netherlands (Lamkaddem et al., 2014). For a token fee, each mother is granted a specially trained maternity helper, who assists with infant care, shopping, housekeeping, meal preparation, and the care of other children for 8 to 10 days after delivery.

Paid, job-protected employment leave is another vital societal intervention for new parents. Canadian mothers are eligible for 15 weeks maternity leave at 55 percent of prior earnings (up to a maximum of $413 per week), and Canadian mothers or fathers can take an additional 35 weeks of parental leave at the same rate. Sweden has the most generous parental leave program in the world. Mothers can begin maternity leave 60 days prior to expected delivery and extend it to 6 weeks after birth; fathers are granted two weeks of birth leave. In addition, either parent can take full leave for 15 months at 80 percent of prior earnings, followed by an additional three months at a modest flat rate. Each parent is also entitled to another 18 months of unpaid leave. Even economically less well-off nations provide parental leave benefits. In Bulgaria, new mothers are granted 11 months paid leave, and fathers receive 3 weeks (Addati, Cassirer, & Gilchrist, 2014).

Yet in the United States, the federal government mandates *only 12 weeks of unpaid leave* for employees in companies with at least 50 workers. Most women, however, work in smaller businesses, and many of those who work in large enough companies cannot afford to take unpaid leave. And because of financial pressures, many new mothers who are eligible for unpaid work leave take far less

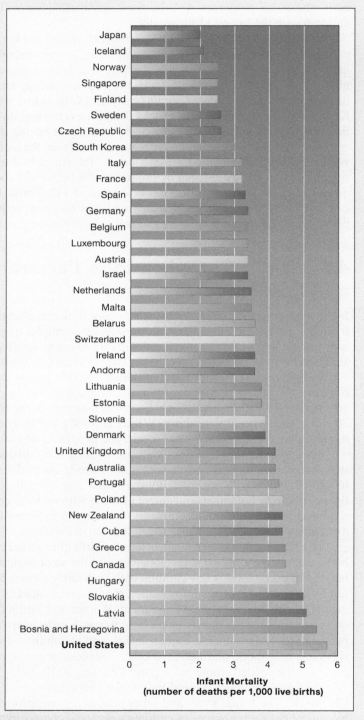

FIGURE 4.6 **Infant mortality in 39 nations.** Despite its advanced health-care technology, the United States ranks poorly. It is thirty-ninth in the world, with a death rate of 5.7 infants per 1,000 births. (Based on U.S. Census Bureau, 2018b.)

than 12 weeks. Similarly, though paternal leave—especially, 2 weeks or more—predicts fathers' increased involvement in child care and is linked to improved cognitive development in the early years, fathers typically take less than 10 days or none at all (Huerta et al., 2013).

In 2002, California became the first state to guarantee a mother or father paid leave—up to 6 weeks at half salary, regardless of the size of the company. Since then, the District of Columbia, Hawaii, New Jersey, New York, Rhode Island, Washington, and the territory of Puerto Rico have passed similar legislation.

Nevertheless, 6 weeks of childbirth leave (the norm in the United States) is not enough. Leaves of 6 to 8 weeks or less are linked to increased maternal anxiety, depression, sense of *role overload* (conflict between work and family responsibilities), and negative interactions with the baby. A leave of 12 weeks or more predicts favorable maternal physical and mental health, supportive marital interaction, and sensitive caregiving (Aitken et al., 2015; Feldman, Sussman, & Zigler, 2004). Single women and their babies are most hurt by the absence of a generous national paid-leave policy. These mothers,

who are usually the sole source of support for their families, can least afford to take time from their jobs.

In countries with low infant mortality rates, expectant parents need not wonder how they will access essential resources for supporting their baby's development. The powerful impact of universal, high-quality health care; generous parental leave; and other social services on maternal and infant well-being provides strong justification for these policies. Responding to these findings, the U.S. Affordable Care Act provides generous grants to the states to cover the cost of evidence-based home-visiting programs that provide comprehensive services to mothers, infants, and young children in high-risk families.

A Swedish father takes advantage of his country's generous parental leave program to care for and bond with his 16-month-old. Paternal leave of 2 weeks or more is linked to improved cognitive development in the early years.

ASK YOURSELF

Connect ■ List factors discussed in this chapter and in Chapter 3 that increase the chances of an infant being born underweight. How many of these factors could be prevented by better health care for expectant mothers?

Apply ■ Cecilia and Anna each gave birth to a 3-pound baby seven weeks preterm. Cecilia is single and on welfare. Anna and her husband are happily married and earn a good income. Plan an intervention appropriate for helping each baby develop.

Reflect ■ Many people object to the use of extraordinary medical measures to save extremely low-birth-weight babies because of their high risk for serious developmental problems. Do you agree or disagree? Explain.

4.5 The Newborn Baby's Capacities

Newborn infants have a remarkable set of capacities that are crucial for survival and for evoking adult attention and care. In relating to the physical and social world, babies are active from the very start.

4.5.1 Reflexes

A **reflex** is an inborn, automatic response to a particular form of stimulation. Reflexes are the newborn baby's most obvious organized patterns of behavior. As Jay placed Joshua on a table in my classroom, we saw several. When Jay bumped the side of the table, Joshua reacted by

4.5a Describe the newborn baby's reflexes and states of arousal, including sleep characteristics and ways to soothe a crying baby.

4.5b Describe the newborn baby's sensory capacities.

4.5c Explain the usefulness of neonatal behavioral assessment.

flinging his arms wide and bringing them back toward his body. As Yolanda stroked Joshua's cheek, he turned his head in her direction. When she put her finger in Joshua's palm, he grabbed on tightly. Look at Table 4.2 and see if you can name the newborn reflexes that Joshua displayed. Let's consider the meaning and purpose of these curious behaviors.

Adaptive Value of Reflexes   Some reflexes have survival value. The rooting reflex helps a breastfed baby find the mother's nipple. Babies display it only when hungry and touched by another person, not when they touch themselves (Rochat & Hespos, 1997). At birth, babies adjust their sucking pressure to how easily milk flows from the nipple (Craig & Lee, 1999). And if sucking were not automatic, our species would be unlikely to survive for a single generation! The swimming reflex helps a baby who is accidentally dropped into water stay afloat, increasing the chances of retrieval by the caregiver.

Other reflexes probably helped babies survive during our evolutionary past. For example, the Moro, or "embracing," reflex is believed to have helped infants cling to their mothers when they were carried about all day. If the baby happened to lose support, the reflex caused the infant to embrace and, along with the palmar grasp reflex (so strong during the first week that it can support the baby's entire weight), regain its hold on the mother's body. Another conjecture is that the Moro embracing motion signals the caregiver to pick up and comfort a startled infant (Rousseau et al., 2017).

TABLE 4.2   Some Newborn Reflexes

REFLEX	STIMULATION	RESPONSE	AGE OF DISAPPEARANCE	FUNCTION
Eye blink	Shine bright light at eyes or clap hand near head.	Infant quickly closes eyelids.	Permanent	Protects infant from strong stimulation
Rooting	Stroke cheek near corner of mouth.	Head turns toward source of stimulation.	3 weeks (becomes voluntary head turning at this time)	Helps infant find the nipple
Sucking	Place finger in infant's mouth.	Infant sucks finger rhythmically.	Replaced by voluntary sucking after 4 months	Permits feeding
Swimming[a]	Occurs when infant is face down in pool of water.	Baby paddles and kicks in swimming motion.	4–6 months	Helps infant survive if dropped into water
Moro	Hold infant horizontally on back and let head drop slightly, or produce a sudden loud sound against surface supporting infant.	Infant makes an "embracing" motion by arching back, extending legs, throwing arms outward, spreading fingers, and then bringing arms in toward the body.	6 months	In human evolutionary past, may have helped infant cling to caregiver or (through extension of arms) signal caregiver to pick up baby
Palmar grasp	Place finger in infant's hand and press against palm.	Spontaneous grasp of finger	3–4 months	Prepares infant for voluntary grasping
Tonic neck	Turn baby's head to one side while infant is lying awake on back.	Infant lies in a "fencing position." One arm is extended in front of eyes on side to which head is turned; other arm is flexed.	4 months	May prepare infant for voluntary reaching
Stepping	Hold infant under arms and permit bare feet to touch a flat surface.	Infant lifts one foot after another in stepping response.	Replaced by voluntary walking at end of the first year	Prepares infant for voluntary walking
Babinski	Stroke sole of foot from toe toward heel.	Toes fan out and curl as foot twists in.	8–12 months	Unknown

[a]Placing infants in a pool of water is dangerous. See discussion on page 136 in this section.

Sources: Knobloch & Pasamanick, 1974; Rousseau et al., 2017; Thelen, Fisher, & Ridley-Johnson, 1984.

Several reflexes help parents and infants establish gratifying interaction. A baby who successfully finds the nipple, sucks easily during feedings, grasps when her hand is touched, or induces the caregiver to pick her up encourages parents to respond lovingly and feel competent as caregivers. Reflexes that help infants control distress can also aid parents in comforting the baby. For example, on outings with Joshua, Yolanda brought along a pacifier. If he became fussy, sucking helped quiet him until she could feed, change, or hold him.

In the Moro reflex, loss of support or a sudden loud sound causes the baby to arch her back, extend her arms outward, and then bring them in toward her body.

Reflexes and the Development of Motor Skills   A few reflexes form the basis for complex motor skills that will develop later. For example, the tonic neck reflex may prepare the baby for voluntary reaching. When infants lie on their backs in this "fencing position," they naturally gaze at the hand in front of their eyes. The reflex may encourage them to combine vision with arm movements and, eventually, reach for objects.

Certain reflexes—such as the palmar grasp, swimming, and stepping—drop out early, but the motor functions involved are renewed later. The stepping reflex, for example, looks like a primitive walking response. Around 2 months, it declines as infants increasingly relax their limbs, flexing their legs at the hip and knees when lowered onto a flat surface, which inhibits stepping. But if babies are held upright in the air, the reflex is clearly evident and persists, over time being integrated into independent walking (Barbu-Roth et al., 2015). Furthermore, when stepping is exercised regularly, babies make more reflexive stepping movements and are likely to walk several weeks earlier than if stepping is not practiced (Zelazo et al., 1993). However, there is no special need for infants to practice the stepping reflex because all typically developing babies walk in due time.

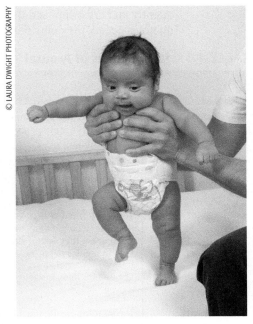

The palmar grasp reflex is so strong during the first week after birth that many infants can use it to support their entire weight.

In the tonic neck reflex, infants lie on their backs in a "fencing position," which may help prepare them for voluntary reaching.

When held upright under the arms, newborn babies show reflexive stepping movements.

In the case of the swimming reflex, trying to build on it is risky. Although young infants placed in a swimming pool will paddle and kick, they swallow large amounts of water. This lowers the sodium concentration in the baby's blood, which can cause brain swelling and seizures. Despite this remarkable reflex, swimming lessons are best postponed until at least 3 years of age.

The Importance of Assessing Newborn Reflexes   Look at Table 4.2 again, and you will see that most newborn reflexes disappear during the first six months. Researchers believe that this is due to a gradual increase in voluntary control over behavior as the cerebral cortex develops.

Pediatricians test reflexes carefully, especially if a newborn has experienced birth trauma, because reflexes can reveal the health of the baby's nervous system. Weak or absent reflexes, overly rigid or exaggerated reflexes, and reflexes that persist beyond the point in development when they should normally disappear can signal brain damage (Schott & Rossor, 2003). However, individual differences in reflexive responses exist that are not cause for concern. An observer must assess reflexes along with other infant attributes to accurately distinguish typical from atypical central nervous system functioning.

4.5.2 States

Throughout the day and night, newborn infants move in and out of the five **states of arousal,** or degrees of sleep and wakefulness, described in Table 4.3. During the first month, these states alternate frequently. The most fleeting is quiet alertness, which usually moves quickly toward fussing and crying. Much to the relief of their fatigued parents, newborns spend the greatest amount of time asleep—about 16 to 18 hours a day. And even those who are as much as 8 weeks preterm are responsive to regular periods of darkness and light in their surroundings, increasingly sleeping more at night than during the day over the early weeks (Figueiredo et al., 2016; Guyer et al., 2015). Nevertheless, young babies' sleep–wake cycles are affected more by fullness–hunger than by darkness–light (Davis, Parker, & Montgomery, 2004).

4.However, striking individual differences in daily rhythms exist that affect parents' attitudes toward and interactions with the baby. A few newborns sleep for long periods, increasing the energy their well-rested parents have for sensitive, responsive care. Other babies wake frequently and cry often, and their parents must exert great effort to soothe them. If these parents do not succeed, they may feel less competent and less positive toward their infant. Babies who

TABLE 4.3   Infant States of Arousal

STATE	DESCRIPTION	DAILY DURATION IN NEWBORN
Regular, or NREM, sleep	The infant is at full rest and shows little or no body activity. The eyelids are closed, no eye movements occur, the face is relaxed, and breathing is slow and regular.	8–9 hours
Irregular, or REM, sleep	Gentle limb movements, occasional stirring, and facial grimacing occur. Although the eyelids are closed, occasional rapid eye movements can be seen beneath them. Breathing is irregular.	8–9 hours
Drowsiness	The infant is either falling asleep or waking up. Body is less active than in irregular sleep but more active than in regular sleep. The eyes open and close; when open, they have a glazed look. Breathing is even but somewhat faster than in regular sleep.	Varies
Quiet alertness	The infant's body is relatively inactive, with eyes open and attentive. Breathing is even.	2–3 hours
Waking activity and crying	The infant shows frequent bursts of uncoordinated body activity. Breathing is very irregular. Face may be relaxed or tense and wrinkled. Crying may occur.	1–4 hours

Source: Wolff, 1966.

spend more time alert probably receive more social stimulation and opportunities to explore and, therefore, may have a slight advantage in cognitive development.

As with adults, sleep contributes to babies' learning and memory. In two studies, eye-movement responses and brain-wave recordings revealed that sleeping newborns readily learned that a tone would be followed by a puff of air to the eye (Fifer et al., 2010; Tarullo et al., 2015). Because young infants spend so much time sleeping, the capacity to learn about external stimuli during sleep may be essential for adaptation to their surroundings.

Of the states listed in Table 4.3, the two extremes—sleep and crying—have been of greatest interest to researchers. Each tells us something about normal and abnormal early development.

Sleep   Observing Joshua as he slept, Yolanda and Jay wondered why his eyelids and body twitched and his rate of breathing varied. Sleep is made up of at least two states. During irregular, or **rapid-eye-movement (REM), sleep,** brain-wave activity is remarkably similar to that of the waking state. The eyes dart beneath the lids; heart rate, blood pressure, and breathing are uneven; and slight body movements occur. The expression "sleeping like a baby" was probably not meant to describe this state! In contrast, during regular, or **non-rapid-eye-movement (NREM), sleep,** the body is almost motionless, and heart rate, breathing, and brain-wave activity are slow and even.

Like children and adults, newborns alternate between REM and NREM sleep. However, they spend far more time in the REM state than they ever will again. REM sleep accounts for 50 percent of the newborn baby's sleep time. By 3 to 5 years, it has declined to an adultlike level of 20 percent (Korotchikova et al., 2016; Louis et al., 1997).

Why do young infants spend so much time in REM sleep? In older children and adults, the REM state is associated with dreaming. Babies probably do not dream, at least not in the same way we do. But researchers believe that the stimulation of REM sleep is vital for growth of the central nervous system (Tarullo, Balsam, & Fifer, 2011). Young infants seem to have a special need for this stimulation because they spend little time in an alert state, when they can get input from the environment. In support of this idea, the percentage of REM sleep is especially great in the fetus and in preterm babies, who are even less able than full-term newborns to take advantage of external stimulation (Peirano, Algarin, & Uauy, 2003).

To soothe his crying infant, this father lifts her to his shoulder, holds her against his gently moving body, and speaks softly to her. This combination of physical contact, upright posture, motion, and gentle sounds causes infants to stop crying and become quietly alert.

Because newborn babies' normal sleep behavior is organized and patterned, observations of sleep states can help identify central nervous system abnormalities. Infants who are brain-damaged or who have experienced birth trauma often have disturbed REM–NREM sleep cycles. Both full-term and preterm babies with poor sleep organization are likely to be behaviorally disorganized and, therefore, to have difficulty learning and eliciting interactions from caregivers that enhance their development. In follow-ups during the preschool years, they show delayed motor, cognitive, and language development (Feldman, 2006; Holditch-Davis, Belyea, & Edwards, 2005; Weisman et al., 2011). And the brain-functioning problems that underlie newborn sleep irregularities may culminate in sudden infant death syndrome, a major cause of infant mortality (see the Social Issues: Health box on page 138).

Crying   Crying is the first way that babies communicate, letting parents know that they need food, comfort, or stimulation. During the weeks after birth, all babies seem to have some fussy periods when they are difficult to console. But most of the time, the nature of the cry, combined with the experiences that led up to it, help guide parents toward its cause. The baby's cry is a complex stimulus that varies in intensity from a whimper to a message of all-out distress (Wood, 2009). As early as the first few weeks, infants can be identified by the unique vocal "signature" of their cries, which helps parents locate their baby from a distance (Gustafson, Green, & Cleland, 1994).

Young infants usually cry because of physical needs, most commonly hunger, but may also cry in response to a change in temperature when undressed, a sudden noise, or a painful stimulus. Newborns (as well as older infants up to

Social Issues: Health | The Mysterious Tragedy of Sudden Infant Death Syndrome

Millie awoke with a start one morning and looked at the clock. It was 7:30, and 3-month-old Sasha had missed both her night waking and her early morning feeding. Wondering if she was all right, Millie tiptoed into Sasha's room. She lay still under her blanket. Sasha had died silently during her sleep.

Sasha was a victim of **sudden infant death syndrome (SIDS)**, the unexpected death, usually during the night, of an infant younger than 1 year of age that remains unexplained after thorough investigation. In industrialized nations, SIDS is the leading cause of infant mortality between 1 and 12 months, accounting for about 20 percent of these deaths in the United States (Centers for Disease Control and Prevention, 2018e).

SIDS victims usually show physical problems from the beginning. Early medical records of SIDS babies reveal higher rates of prematurity and low birth weight, poor Apgar scores, and limp muscle tone. Abnormal heart rate and respiration and disturbances in sleep–wake activity and in REM–NREM cycles while asleep are also involved (Cornwell & Feigenbaum, 2006; Garcia, Koschnitzky, & Ramirez, 2013). At the time of death, many SIDS babies have a mild respiratory infection (Blood-Siegfried, 2009). This seems to increase the chances of respiratory failure in an already vulnerable baby.

Mounting evidence indicates that impaired brain functioning is a major contributor to SIDS. Between 2 and 4 months, when SIDS is most likely to occur, reflexes decline and are replaced by voluntary, learned responses. Neurological weaknesses may prevent SIDS babies from acquiring voluntary behaviors that replace defensive reflexes (Horne, 2017; Rubens & Sarnat, 2013). As a result, when breathing difficulties occur during sleep, these infants do not wake up, shift their position, or cry out for help. Instead, they simply give in to oxygen deprivation and death. In support of this interpretation, autopsies reveal that the brains of SIDS victims contain unusually low levels of serotonin (a brain chemical that assists with arousal when survival is threatened) as well as other abnormalities in centers that control breathing and arousal (Salomonis, 2014).

Several environmental factors are linked to SIDS. Maternal cigarette smoking, both during and after pregnancy, as well as smoking by other caregivers, doubles risk of the disorder. Infants exposed to cigarette smoke arouse less easily from sleep and have more respiratory infections (Blackwell et al., 2015). Prenatal abuse of drugs that depress central nervous system functioning (alcohol, opiates, and barbiturates) increases the risk of SIDS as much as fifteen-fold (Hunt & Hauck, 2006; Maguire et al., 2016).

SIDS babies are also more likely to sleep on their stomachs than on their backs and often are wrapped very warmly in clothing and blankets. Infants who sleep on their stomachs less often wake when their breathing is disturbed, especially if they suffer from biological vulnerabilities (Richardson, Walker, & Horne, 2008). In other cases, healthy babies sleeping face down in soft bedding may suffocate from continually breathing their own exhaled breath, resulting in accidental deaths that would be incorrectly classified as SIDS.

SIDS rates are especially high among poverty-stricken ethnic minorities (Centers for Disease Control and Prevention, 2018e). In these families, parental stress, substance abuse, reduced access to health care, and lack of knowledge about safe sleep practices are widespread.

The U.S. government's Safe to Sleep campaign encourages parents to create safe sleep

Dissemination of information to parents encouraging them to put their infants down on their backs to sleep has helped reduce the incidence of SIDS by more than half.

environments and engage in other protective practices (National Institutes of Health, 2018a). Recommendations include quitting smoking and drug taking, placing infants on their backs in light sleep clothing, providing a firm sleep surface, and eliminating soft bedding. An estimated 20 percent of SIDS cases would be prevented if all infants had smoke-free homes. Dissemination of information to parents about putting infants down on their backs has cut the incidence of SIDS by more than half (Behm et al., 2012). Other protective measures are breastfeeding, perhaps because it offers protection against respiratory infections (see Chapter 5), and pacifier use at bedtime: Sleeping babies who suck arouse more easily in response to breathing and heart-rate irregularities (Alm et al., 2016).

When SIDS does occur, surviving family members require a great deal of help to overcome a sudden and unexpected death. As Millie commented six months after Sasha's death, "It's the worst crisis we've ever been through. What's helped us most are the comforting words of others who've experienced the same tragedy."

age 6 months) often cry at the sound of another crying baby—a response that may reflect an inborn capacity to react to the suffering of others (Dondi, Simion, & Caltran, 1999; Geangu et al., 2010). Furthermore, crying typically increases during the early weeks, peaks at about 4 to 6 weeks, and then declines (Barr, 2001). Because this trend appears in many cultures with vastly different infant care practices, researchers believe that normal readjustments of the central nervous system underlie it.

The next time you hear a baby cry, notice your own reaction. The sound stimulates a sharp rise in alertness, the stress hormone cortisol, and feelings of arousal and discomfort in

APPLYING WHAT WE KNOW

Soothing a Crying Baby

TECHNIQUE	EXPLANATION
Talk softly or play rhythmic sounds.	Continuous, monotonous, rhythmic sounds (such as a clock ticking, a fan whirring, or peaceful music) are more effective than intermittent sounds.
Offer a pacifier.	Sucking helps babies control their own level of arousal.
Massage the baby's body.	Stroking the baby's torso and limbs with continuous, gentle motions relaxes the baby's muscles.
Swaddle the baby.	Restricting movement and increasing warmth often soothe a young infant.
Lift the baby to the shoulder and rock or walk.	This combination of physical contact, upright posture, and motion is an effective soothing technique, causing young infants to become quietly alert.
Take the baby for a short car ride or a walk in a baby carriage; swing the baby in a cradle.	Gentle, rhythmic motion of any kind helps lull the baby to sleep.
Combine several of the methods just listed.	Stimulating several of the baby's senses at once is often more effective than stimulating only one.
If these methods do not work, let the baby cry for a short period.	Occasionally, a baby responds well to just being put down and will, after a few minutes, fall asleep.

Sources: Dayton et al., 2015; Evanoo, 2007; St James-Roberts, 2012.

men and women, parents and nonparents alike (de Cock et al., 2015; Yong & Ruffman, 2014). This powerful response is probably innately programmed to help ensure that babies receive the care and protection they need to survive.

Soothing Crying Infants Although parents do not always interpret their baby's cry correctly, their accuracy improves with experience. At the same time, they vary widely in responsiveness. Parents who are high in empathy (ability to take the perspective of others in distress) and who hold "child-centered" attitudes toward infant care (for example, believe that babies cannot be spoiled by being picked up) are more likely to respond quickly and sensitively (Cohen-Bendahan, van Doornan, & deWeerth, 2014; Leerkes, 2010).

Fortunately, there are many ways to soothe a crying baby when feeding and diaper changing do not work (see Applying What We Know above). The technique that Western parents usually try first, lifting the baby to the shoulder and rocking or walking, is highly effective. Another common soothing method is swaddling—wrapping the baby snugly in a blanket. The Quechua people of the cold, high-altitude desert regions of Peru dress young infants in several layers of clothing and blankets that cover the head and body, a technique that reduces crying and promotes sleep (Tronick, Thomas, & Daltabuit, 1994). It also allows babies to conserve energy for early growth in their harsh environment.

In many tribal and village societies and in non-Western developed nations (such as Japan and Vietnam), young infants are in physical contact with their caregivers nearly continuously. Infants in these cultures show shorter bouts of crying than their American counterparts (Barr, 2001; Murray et al., 2018). When Western parents choose to practice *proximal parenting* by holding their babies extensively and responding swiftly to their cries, the amount of crying in the early months is reduced by about one-third (St James-Roberts, 2012).

© ROBERTHARDING/ALAMY STOCK PHOTO

The Bedouin people of the Middle East tightly swaddle young infants, a practice that reduces crying and promotes sleep.

Abnormal Crying Like reflexes and sleep patterns, the infant's cry offers a clue to central nervous system distress. The cries of brain-damaged babies and those who have experienced prenatal and birth complications are often shrill, piercing, and shorter in duration than the cries of healthy infants (Green, Irwin, & Gustafson, 2000). Even newborns with a fairly common problem—*colic,* or bouts of persistent, hard-to-soothe crying—tend to have high-pitched, harsh-sounding cries. Although the cause of colic is unknown, certain newborns, who react especially strongly to unpleasant stimuli, are susceptible. Because their crying is intense, they find it harder to calm down than other babies (St James-Roberts, 2007). Colic generally subsides between 3 and 6 months.

Most parents try to respond to a crying baby's call for help with extra care and attention, but sometimes the cry is so unpleasant and the infant so difficult to soothe that parents become exhausted, resentful, and angry. Preterm and ill babies are more likely to be abused by highly stressed parents, who sometimes mention a high-pitched, grating cry as one factor that caused them to lose control (Barr et al., 2014; de Weerth & St James-Roberts, 2017). (We will discuss a host of additional influences on child abuse in Chapter 10.)

In a study of a large, nationally representative sample of Dutch infants, excessive crying in the early weeks elevated the risk of child behavior problems at age 5 to 6 years, especially when mothers viewed infant care as burdensome and the crying led them to speak angrily to or slap their baby (Smarius et al., 2017). Support programs for parents can help prevent these negative outcomes. In one intervention, nurses made periodic home visits during which they taught parents to identify early warning signs that their colicky baby was becoming overly aroused, to use effective soothing techniques, and to modify light, noise, and activity in the home to promote predictable sleep–wake cycles (Keefe et al., 2005). Colicky infants in the intervention group spent far less time crying than no-intervention controls—1.3 versus 3 hours per day.

LOOK and LISTEN

In a public setting, watch several parents soothe their crying babies. What techniques did the parents use, and how successful were they?

4.5.3 Sensory Capacities

On his visit to class, Joshua looked wide-eyed at Yolanda's bright pink blouse and readily turned to the sound of her voice. During feedings, he lets Yolanda know by the way he sucks that he prefers the taste of breast milk to a bottle of plain water. Clearly, Joshua has some well-developed sensory capacities. In the following sections, we explore the newborn baby's responsiveness to touch, taste, smell, sound, and visual stimulation.

Touch   In our discussion of preterm infants, we saw that touch helps stimulate early physical growth. And as we will see in Chapter 7, it is vital for emotional development as well. Therefore, it is not surprising that sensitivity to touch is well-developed at birth.

The reflexes listed in Table 4.2 on page 134 in section 4.6.1 reveal that the newborn baby responds to touch, especially around the mouth, on the palms, and on the soles of the feet. During the prenatal period, these areas, along with the genitals, are the first to become sensitive to touch (Humphrey, 1978; Streri, 2005). Newborns, even those born several weeks preterm, use touch to investigate their world. When small objects are placed in their palms, they can distinguish shape (prism versus cylinder) and texture (smooth versus rough), as indicated by their tendency to hold on longer to an object with an unfamiliar shape or texture than to a familiar object (Lejeune et al., 2012; Molina et al., 2015; Sann & Streri, 2007, 2008).

At birth, infants are highly sensitive to pain. If male newborns are circumcised, anesthetic is sometimes not used because of the risk of giving drugs to a very young infant. Babies often respond with a high-pitched, stressful cry and a dramatic rise in heart rate, blood pressure, palm sweating, pupil dilation, and muscle tension (Lehr et al., 2007; Warnock & Sandrin, 2004). Brain-imaging research suggests that because of central nervous system immaturity, preterm and male babies feel the pain of a medical injection especially intensely (Bartocci et al., 2006).

Certain local analgesics for newborns ease the pain of these procedures. As a supplement to pain-relieving medication, offering a nipple that delivers a sugar solution is helpful; it quickly reduces crying and discomfort in young infants, preterm and full-term alike (Roman-Rodriguez et al., 2014). Breast milk is especially effective: Even the smell of the milk of the baby's mother reduces infant stress to a routine blood-test heel stick more readily than the odor of another mother's milk or of formula (Badiee, Asghari, & Mohammadizadeh, 2013; Nishitani et al., 2009). Combining breastfeeding with maternal gentle holding lessens pain even more (Axelin, Salantera, & Lehtonen, 2006; Obeidat & Shuriquie, 2015). Both sweet liquid and physical touch release *endorphins*—painkilling chemicals in the brain.

Allowing a baby to endure severe pain overwhelms the nervous system with stress hormones, which can disrupt the child's developing capacity to handle common, everyday stressors (Walker, 2013). The result is heightened pain sensitivity, sleep disturbances, feeding problems, and difficulty calming down when upset.

Taste and Smell   Facial expressions reveal that newborns can distinguish several basic tastes. Like adults, they relax their facial muscles in response to sweetness, purse their lips when the taste is sour, and show a distinct archlike mouth opening when it is bitter. Similarly, certain odor preferences are present at birth. For example, the smell of bananas or chocolate causes a pleasant facial expression, whereas the odor of rotten eggs makes the infant frown (Steiner, 1979; Steiner et al., 2001). These reactions are important for survival: The food that best supports the infant's early growth is the sweet-tasting milk of the mother's breast. Not until 4 months do babies prefer a salty taste to plain water, a change that may prepare them to accept solid foods (Mennella & Beauchamp, 1998).

During pregnancy, the amniotic fluid is rich in tastes and smells that vary with the mother's diet—early experiences that influence newborns' preferences. In a study carried out in the Alsatian region of France, where anise is frequently used to flavor foods, researchers tested newborns for their reaction to the anise odor (Schaal, Marlier, & Soussignan, 2000). The mothers of some babies had regularly consumed anise during the last two weeks of pregnancy; the other mothers had never consumed it. When presented with the anise odor on the day of birth, the babies of anise-consuming mothers more often displayed facial expressions of interest and liking. In contrast, those of non-anise-consuming mothers were far more likely to turn away with negative facial expressions (see Figure 4.7). These different reactions were still apparent four days later, even though all mothers had refrained from consuming anise during this time.

In some instances, exposure to a flavor, either prenatally in the amniotic fluid or during the weeks after birth in breast milk, can have long-term consequences for odor and taste preferences. Compared to newborns of mothers who rarely drank alcohol during pregnancy, newborns whose mothers had frequently consumed alcoholic drinks more often displayed positive facial expressions to the odor of alcohol in the first two weeks of life—mouthing, sucking, smiling, and sticking out their tongues (Faas et al., 2015). This prenatally influenced attraction to alcohol is still evident in adolescence and early adulthood, even after other factors known to affect alcohol intake are controlled, such as genetic predisposition assessed through family history of alcoholism (Alati et al., 2006; Baer et al., 2003).

At the same time, young infants can learn to prefer a taste that at first evoked either a negative or neutral response. Bottle-fed newborns allergic to cow's milk formula who are given a soy or other vegetable-based substitute (typically very sour and bitter-tasting) soon prefer it to regular formula. When first given solid foods several months later, these infants display an unusual liking for bitter-tasting cereals (Beauchamp & Mennella, 2011). This taste preference is still present at age 4 to 5 years, in more positive responses to foods with sour and bitter tastes than shown by their agemates.

In mammals, including humans, the sense of smell—in addition to playing an important role in feeding—helps mothers and babies identify each other. At 2 to 4 days of age, breastfed

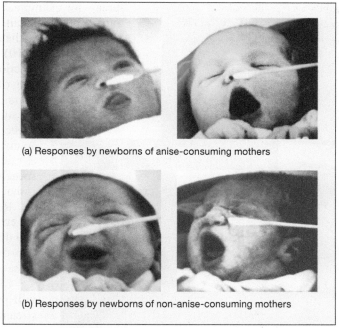

(a) Responses by newborns of anise-consuming mothers

(b) Responses by newborns of non-anise-consuming mothers

FIGURE 4.7   **Examples of facial expressions of newborns exposed to the odor of anise whose mothers' diets differed in anise-flavored foods during late pregnancy.** (a) Babies of anise-consuming mothers spent more time turning toward the odor and sucking, licking, and chewing. (b) Babies of non-anise-consuming mothers more often turned away with a negative facial expression. (From B. Schaal, L. Marlier, & R. Soussignan, 2000, "Human Foetuses Learn Odours from Their Pregnant Mother's Diet," *Chemical Senses, 25,* p. 731. Reprinted by permission of Oxford University Press and Benoist Schaal.)

babies prefer the odor of their own mother's breast and underarm to that of an unfamiliar lactating woman (Cernoch & Porter, 1985; Marin, Rapisardi, & Tani, 2015). And both breast- and bottle-fed 3- to 4-day-olds orient more to the smell of unfamiliar human milk than to formula milk, indicating that (even without postnatal exposure) the odor of human milk is more attractive to newborns (Marlier & Schaal, 2005). Newborns' dual attraction to the odors of their mother and of breast milk helps them locate an appropriate food source and, in the process, begin to distinguish their caregiver from other people.

Hearing   Although conduction of sound through the structures of the ear and transmission of auditory information to the brain are inefficient at birth, newborn infants can hear a wide variety of sounds—sensitivity that improves greatly over the first few months (Johnson & Hannon, 2015). At birth, infants prefer complex sounds, such as noises and voices, to pure tones. And babies only a few days old can tell the difference between a variety of sound patterns: a series of tones arranged in ascending versus descending order; tone sequences with a rhythmic downbeat (as in music) versus those without; utterances with two versus three syllables; the stress patterns of words, such as "*ma*-ma" versus "ma-*ma*"; happy-sounding speech as opposed to speech with negative or neutral emotional qualities; and even two languages spoken by the same bilingual speaker, as long as those languages differ in their rhythmic features—for example, French versus Russian (Mastropieri & Turkewitz, 1999; Ramus, 2002; Sansavini, Bertoncini, & Giovanelli, 1997; Trehub, 2001; Winkler et al., 2009).

Young infants listen longer to human speech than to structurally similar nonspeech sounds (Vouloumanos, 2010). And they can detect the sounds of any human language. Newborns make fine-grained distinctions among many speech sounds. For example, when given a nipple that turns on a recording of the "*ba*" sound, babies suck vigorously for a while and then slow down as the novelty wears off. When the sound switches to "*ga,*" sucking picks up, indicating that infants detect this subtle difference. Using this method, researchers have found only a few speech sounds that newborns cannot discriminate. Their ability to perceive sounds not found in their own language is more precise than an adult's (Jusczyk & Luce, 2002). These capacities, which build on the fetus's sensitivity to human speech in the weeks before birth (see page 96 in Chapter 3), reveal that the baby is marvelously prepared for the awesome task of acquiring language.

Responsiveness to sound also supports the newborn baby's exploration of the environment. Infants as young as 3 days turn their eyes and head in the general direction of a sound. The ability to identify the precise location of a sound improves greatly over the first six months and shows further gains through the preschool years (Litovsky & Ashmead, 1997).

Listen carefully to yourself the next time you talk to a young baby. You will probably speak in ways that highlight important parts of the speech stream—using a slow, high-pitched, expressive voice with a rising tone at the ends of phrases and sentences and pausing before continuing. Adults probably communicate this way with infants because they notice that babies are more attentive when they do so. Indeed, newborns prefer speech with these characteristics: On hearing it, they focus more intently on the speaker's face (Guellaï et al., 2016; Saffran, Werker, & Werner, 2006). They will also suck more on a nipple to hear a recording of their own mother's voice than that of an unfamiliar woman and to hear their native language as opposed to a foreign language (Moon, Cooper, & Fifer, 1993; Spence & DeCasper, 1987). These preferences probably developed from hearing the muffled sounds of the mother's voice before birth.

Vision   Vision is the least-developed of the newborn baby's senses. Visual structures in both the eye and the brain are not yet fully formed at birth. For example, cells in the *retina,* the membrane lining the inside of the eye that captures light and transforms it into messages that are sent to the brain, are not as mature or densely packed as they will be in several months. The optic nerve that relays these messages, and visual centers in the brain that receive them,

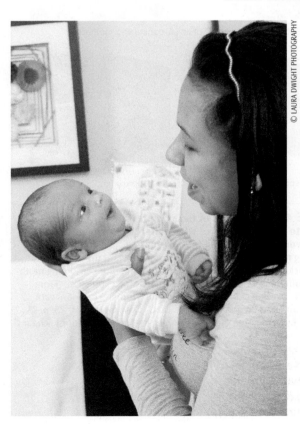

A newborn baby, primed and ready for the awesome task of acquiring language, gazes intently at his mother, listening attentively as she talks to him.

will not be adultlike for several years. And muscles of the *lens,* which permit us to adjust our visual focus to varying distances, are weak (Johnson & Hannon, 2015).

As a result, newborns cannot focus their eyes well, and their **visual acuity,** or fineness of discrimination, is limited. At birth, infants perceive objects at a distance of 20 feet about as clearly as adults do at 600 feet (Slater et al., 2010). In addition, unlike adults (who see nearby objects most clearly), newborn babies see unclearly across a wide range of distances (Banks, 1980; Hainline, 1998). As a result, images such as the parent's face, even from close up, look like the blurry image in Figure 4.8. Nevertheless, as we will see in Chapter 5, newborns can detect human faces. And as with their preference for their mother's smell and voice, from repeated exposures they quickly learn to prefer her face to that of an unfamiliar woman, although they are more sensitive to its broad outlines than its fine-grained, internal features (Bartrip, Morton, & de Schonen, 2001; Walton, Armstrong, & Bower, 1998).

Although they cannot yet see well, newborns actively explore their environment by scanning it for interesting sights and tracking moving objects. However, their eye movements are slow and inaccurate (von Hofsten & Rosander, 1998). Joshua's captivation with my pink blouse reveals that he is attracted to bright objects. Nevertheless, once newborns focus on an object, they tend to look only at a single feature—for example, the corner of a triangle instead of the entire shape. And despite their preference for colored over gray stimuli, newborn babies are not yet good at discriminating colors. It will take about four months for color vision to become adultlike (Johnson & Hannon, 2015).

(a) Newborn View   (b) Adult View

FIGURE 4.8   **View of the human face by the newborn and the adult.** The newborn baby's limited focusing ability and poor visual acuity lead the mother's face, even when viewed from close up, to look much like the fuzzy image in (a) rather than the clear image in (b). Also, newborn infants have some color vision, although they have difficulty discriminating colors. Researchers speculate that colors probably appear similar, but less intense, to newborns than to older infants and adults. (From Kellman & Arterberry, 2006; Slater et al., 2010.)

4.5.4 Neonatal Behavioral Assessment

A variety of instruments permit doctors, nurses, and researchers to assess the behavior of newborn babies. The most widely used of these tests, T. Berry Brazelton's **Neonatal Behavioral Assessment Scale (NBAS),** evaluates the newborn's reflexes, muscle tone, state changes, responsiveness to physical and social stimuli, and other reactions (Brazelton & Nugent, 2011). An instrument consisting of similar items, the *Neonatal Intensive Care Unit Network Neurobehavioral Scale (NNNS),* is specially designed for use with newborns at risk for developmental problems because of low birth weight, preterm delivery, prenatal substance exposure, or other conditions (Tronick & Lester, 2013). Scores are used to recommend appropriate interventions and to guide parents in meeting their baby's unique needs.

The NBAS has been given to many infants around the world, enabling researchers to learn about individual and cultural differences in newborn behavior. For example, compared with scores of European-American infants, NBAS scores of Asian- and Native-American babies reveal less irritability. Mothers in these cultures often encourage their babies' calm dispositions through holding and nursing at the first signs of discomfort (Muret-Wagstaff & Moore, 1989; Small, 1998). The Kipsigis of Kenya, who highly value infant motor maturity, massage babies regularly and begin exercising the stepping reflex shortly after birth. These customs contribute to Kipsigis babies' strong but flexible muscle tone at 5 days of age (Super & Harkness, 2009). Newborns whose mothers experienced depression during pregnancy score considerably lower than those of nondepressed mothers in neurobehavioral maturity (Figueiredo et al., 2017). But with warm, attentive caregiving, NBAS scores can readily improve. In Zambia, Africa, close mother–infant contact throughout the day quickly changed the poor NBAS scores

A Senegalese mother carries her baby in a sling throughout the day, a practice that maintains close physical contact, enables nursing at the first signs of discomfort, and promotes a calm, contented state.

of undernourished newborns (Brazelton, Koslowski, & Tronick, 1976). At age 1 week, these unresponsive infants appeared alert, responsive, and content.

Because newborn behavior and parenting combine to influence development, *changes in scores* over the first week or two of life (rather than a single score) provide the best estimate of the baby's ability to recover from the stress of birth. NBAS "recovery curves" predict intelligence and absence of emotional and behavior problems with moderate success well into the preschool years (Brazelton, Nugent, & Lester, 1987; Ohgi et al., 2003a, 2003b).

In some hospitals, health professionals use the NBAS or the NNNS to help parents get to know their newborns through discussion or demonstration of the capacities these instruments assess. Parents who participate in these programs, compared with no-intervention controls, interact more confidently and effectively with their babies (Browne & Talmi, 2005; Bruschweiler-Stern, 2004). Although lasting effects on development have not been demonstrated, NBAS-based interventions are useful in helping the parent–infant relationship get off to a good start.

ASK YOURSELF

Connect ■ How do the diverse capacities of newborn babies contribute to their first social relationships? Provide as many examples as you can.

Apply ■ After a difficult delivery, Jackie observes her 2-day-old daughter, Kelly, being given the NBAS. Kelly scores poorly on many items. Seeing this, Jackie wonders if Kelly will develop normally. How would you respond to Jackie's concern?

Reflect ■ Are newborns more competent than you thought they were before you read this chapter? Which of their capacities most surprised you?

4.6 The Transition to Parenthood

4.6a Discuss the influence of birth-related hormonal changes and parent–infant contact on emergence of parental affection and concern for the newborn.

4.6b Describe changes in the family after the birth of a baby, along with interventions that foster the transition to parenthood.

Yolanda and Jay's account of Joshua's birth in the opening to this chapter revealed that holding and touching him after delivery was an experience filled with intense emotion. Most parents are overjoyed at their baby's arrival, describe the experience as "awesome," "indescribable," or "unforgettable," and display intense interest in their newborn child—stroking the baby gently, looking into the infant's eyes, and speaking softly.

As we will see, effective caregiving is so crucial for infant survival and optimal development that nature helps prepare mothers and fathers for their new role. Yet biological changes are but one dimension of this transformative time of life. The transition to parenthood is a complex, often stressful process involving profound alterations in family roles, relationships, and responsibilities. Parents who find productive ways of overcoming difficulties adjust well, with great benefits for the parent–infant relationship.

4.6.1 Early Parent–Infant Contact

Toward the end of pregnancy, mothers begin producing higher levels of the hormone *oxytocin*, which causes the breasts to "let down" milk; induces a calm, relaxed mood; and heightens responsiveness to the newborn (Gordon et al., 2010; Gregory et al., 2015). Fathers, too, show hormonal changes around the time of birth that are compatible with those of mothers—specifically, slight increases in *prolactin* (a hormone that stimulates milk production in females), *estrogens* (sex hormones produced in larger quantities in females), and *oxytocin,* and a decrease in *androgens* (sex hormones produced in larger quantities in males) (Storey & Zigler, 2016). These changes, which are induced by a warm couple relationship and fathers' contact with mother and baby, predict paternal involvement and sensitive interactions with infants (Abraham et al., 2014; Edelstein et al., 2017; Feldman, 2014).

Do human parents require close physical contact in the hours after birth for **bonding,** or affection and concern for the infant, to emerge—as many animal species do? Current evidence shows that the human parent–infant relationship does not depend on a precise, early period of togetherness. Some parents report sudden, deep feelings of affection on first holding their babies. For others, these emotions emerge gradually. And as successful adoption reveals (see page 64 in Chapter 2), humans can parent effectively without experiencing birth-related hormonal changes. In fact, when foster and adoptive mothers hold and interact with their nonbiological infants, they typically release oxytocin (Bick et al., 2013; Galbally et al., 2011). The greater their oxytocin production, the more they express affection and pleasure toward the infant.

Human bonding depends on many factors, not just on what happens during a short period after birth. Nevertheless, early contact with the baby may be one of several factors that help build a good parent–infant relationship. Realizing this, today hospitals offer **rooming in,** in which the infant stays in the mother's hospital room all or most of the time. If parents do not choose this option or cannot do so for medical reasons, there is no evidence that their competence as caregivers will be compromised or that the baby will suffer emotionally.

4.6.2 Changes in the Family System

The early weeks after a baby enters the family are a taxing time for new parents. The mother needs to recover from childbirth. If she is breastfeeding, energies must be devoted to working out this intimate relationship. The other parent must become part of what is now a threesome while supporting the mother in her recovery. While all this is going on, the tiny infant is assertive about urgent physical needs, demanding to be fed, changed, and comforted at odd times of the day and night. The family schedule becomes irregular and uncertain, and parental sleep deprivation and consequent daytime fatigue are often major challenges (Insana & Montgomery-Downs, 2012). Yolanda spoke candidly about the changes she and Jay experienced:

A father radiates intense emotion as he gently cradles and kisses his newborn baby. Fathers, like mothers, experience hormonal changes around the time of birth that can heighten involvement and sensitive interactions with the infant.

> When we brought Joshua home, he seemed so small and helpless, and we worried about whether we would be able to take proper care of him. It took us 20 minutes to change the first diaper. I rarely feel rested because I'm up two to four times every night, and I spend a good part of my waking hours trying to anticipate Joshua's rhythms and needs. If Jay weren't so willing to help by holding and walking Joshua, I think I'd find it much harder.

The demands of new parenthood—constant caregiving, added financial responsibilities, and less time for couples to devote to one another—usually cause parents' gender roles to become more traditional (Katz-Wise, Priess, & Hyde, 2010; Yavorsky, Dush, & Schoppe-Sullivan, 2015). This is true even for couples like Yolanda and Jay, who are strongly committed to gender equality and are used to sharing household tasks. Yolanda took a leave of absence from work, whereas Jay's career continued as it had before. As a result, Yolanda spent more time at home with the baby, while Jay focused more on his provider role.

For most new parents, however, the arrival of a baby—though often followed by mild declines in relationship and overall life satisfaction—does not cause significant marital strain. Marriages that are gratifying and supportive tend to remain so (Doss et al., 2009; Luhmann et al., 2012). But troubled marriages usually become more distressed after a baby is born (Houts et al., 2008). And when mothers or fathers perceive their partner as unsupportive in parenting, they experience an especially difficult post-birth adjustment (Don & Mickelson, 2014; Driver et al., 2012). For some new parents, problems are severe (see the Biology and Environment box on page 146).

Violated expectations about division of labor after childbirth powerfully affect family well-being. In dual-earner marriages, the larger the difference between men's and women's

Biology and Environment | Parental Depression and Child Development

About 8 to 10 percent of women experience chronic depression—mild to severe feelings of sadness and withdrawal that continue for months or years. Often, the beginnings of this emotional state cannot be pinpointed. In other instances, depression emerges or strengthens after childbirth but fails to subside (Paulson & Bazemore, 2010). This is called *postpartum depression.*

Although it is less recognized and studied, fathers, too, experience chronic depression. About 5 percent of fathers report symptoms after the birth of a child (Cameron, Sedov, & Tomfohr-Madsen, 2016). Parental depression can interfere with effective parenting and seriously impair children's development. As noted in Chapter 2, genetic makeup increases the risk of depressive illness, but social and cultural factors are also involved.

Maternal Depression

During Julia's pregnancy, her husband, Kyle, showed so little interest in their anticipated baby that Julia worried that having a child might be a mistake. Shortly after Lucy was born, Julia's mood plunged. She felt anxious and weepy, overwhelmed by Lucy's needs, and angry at loss of control over her own schedule. When Julia approached Kyle about her own fatigue and his unwillingness to help with the baby, he snapped that she was overreacting.

Julia's depressed mood quickly affected her baby. In the weeks after birth, infants of depressed mothers sleep poorly, are less attentive to their surroundings, and have elevated levels of the stress hormone cortisol (Fernandes et al., 2015; Goodman et al., 2011; Natsuaki et al., 2014). The more extreme the depression and the greater the number of stressors in a mother's life (such as marital discord, little or no social support, and poverty), the more the parent–child relationship suffers. Julia rarely smiled at, comforted, or talked to Lucy, who responded to her mother's sad, vacant gaze by turning away, crying, and often looking sad or angry herself (Field, 2011; Vaever et al., 2015). Julia, in turn, felt guilty and inadequate, and her depression deepened. By age 6 months, Lucy showed symptoms common in babies of depressed mothers—delays in motor and cognitive development, poor emotion regulation, an irritable mood, and attachment

difficulties (Ibanez et al., 2015; Lefkovics, Baji, & Rigó, 2014; Vedova, 2014).

When maternal depression persists, the parent–child relationship worsens. Depressed parents view their infants negatively, which contributes to their inept caregiving (Lee & Hans, 2015). As their children get older, lack of warmth and involvement is often accompanied by inconsistent discipline—sometimes lax, at other times too forceful (Thomas et al., 2015). As we will see in later chapters, children who experience these maladaptive parenting practices often have serious adjustment problems. Some withdraw into a depressive mood themselves; others become impulsive and aggressive (Rotheram-Fuller et al., 2018).

Paternal Depression

Paternal depression is also linked to dissatisfaction with marriage after childbirth and to other life stressors, including job loss and divorce (Bielawska-Batorowicz & Kossakowska-Petrycka, 2006; Kerstis et al., 2016). In a study of a large representative sample of British parents and babies, researchers assessed depressive symptoms of fathers shortly after birth and again the following year. Then they tracked the children's development into the preschool years (Ramchandani et al., 2008). Persistent paternal depression was, like maternal depression, a strong predictor of child behavior problems—especially overactivity, defiance, and aggression in boys.

Paternal depression is linked to frequent father–child conflict as children grow older (Gutierrez-Galve et al., 2015). Over time, children subjected to parental negativity develop a pessimistic worldview—one in which they lack self-confidence and perceive their parents and other people as threatening. Children who constantly feel in danger are especially likely to become overly aroused in stressful situations, easily losing control in the face of cognitive and social challenges (Sturge-Apple et al., 2008). Although children of depressed parents may inherit a tendency

A mother discusses her postpartum depression with her doctor. Early treatment is vital for preventing parental depression from interfering with the parent–child relationship.

toward emotional and behavior problems, quality of parenting is a major factor in their adjustment.

Interventions

Early treatment is vital to prevent parental depression from interfering with the parent–child relationship. Julia's doctor referred her to a therapist, who helped Julia and Kyle with their marital problems. At times, antidepressant medication is prescribed.

In addition to alleviating parental depression, therapy that encourages depressed parents to revise their negative views of their babies and to engage in emotionally positive, responsive caregiving is vital for reducing developmental problems (Goodman et al., 2015). When a depressed parent does not respond easily to treatment, a warm relationship with the other parent or another caregiver can safeguard children's development.

APPLYING WHAT WE KNOW

How Couples Can Ease the Transition to Parenthood

STRATEGY	DESCRIPTION
Devise a plan for sharing household tasks.	As soon as possible, discuss division of household responsibilities. Decide who does a particular chore based on who has the needed skill and time, not gender. Schedule regular times to reevaluate your plan to fit changing family circumstances.
Begin sharing child care right after the baby's arrival.	For fathers, strive to spend equal time with the baby early. For mothers, refrain from imposing your standards on your partner. Instead, share the role of "child-rearing expert" by discussing parenting values and concerns often. Attend a new-parenthood course together.
Talk over conflicts about decision making and responsibilities.	Face conflict through communication. Clarify your feelings and needs, and express them to your partner. Listen and try to understand your partner's point of view. Then be willing to negotiate and compromise.
Establish a balance between work and parenting.	Critically evaluate the time you devote to work in view of new parenthood. If it is too much, try to cut back.
Press for workplace and public policies that assist parents in rearing children.	Difficulties faced by new parents may be partly due to lack of workplace and societal supports. Encourage your employer to provide benefits that help combine work and family roles, such as paid employment leave, flexible work hours, and on-site, high-quality, affordable child care. Communicate with lawmakers about improving policies for children and families, including paid, job-protected leave to support the transition to parenthood.

responsibilities for caregiving and household chores, the more conflict-ridden their interaction becomes and the more their marital satisfaction suffers, especially for women—with negative consequences for parent–infant interaction (Chong & Mickelson, 2013; Moller, Hwang, & Wickberg, 2008). In contrast, sharing caregiving and other tasks predicts greater parental happiness and sensitivity to the baby. These findings highlight the vital importance of the coparenting relationship for new parents' adjustment and children's development.

Postponing parenthood until the late twenties or thirties, as many couples do today, eases the transition to parenthood. Waiting permits couples to pursue occupational goals, gain life experience, and strengthen their relationship. Under these circumstances, men are more enthusiastic about becoming fathers and therefore more willing to participate. And women whose careers are well under way and whose marriages are happy are more likely to encourage their husbands to share housework and child care, which fosters fathers' involvement (Lee & Doherty, 2007; Schoppe-Sullivan et al., 2008).

A second birth typically requires that fathers take an even more active role in parenting—by caring for the first-born while the mother is recuperating and by sharing in the high demands of tending to both a baby and a young child. Consequently, well-functioning families with a newborn second child typically pull back from the traditional division of responsibilities that occurred after the first birth. In one study, fathers in dual earner families who believed strongly in gender equality tended to be more involved with their first-borns after the second child's arrival, particularly when the births of their two children were closely spaced (Kuo, Volling & Gonzalez, 2018). As we will see in Chapter 7, first-born children—especially those who are toddlers or young preschoolers at the time of the second birth—understandably may feel displaced and react with jealousy and anger. For strategies couples can use to ease the transition to parenthood, refer to Applying What We Know above.

The arrival of a baby profoundly changes family functioning. For couples in gratifying and supportive marriages with a positive coparenting relationship in which caregiving and household chores are shared, the stress of parenthood typically remains manageable, contributing to favorable child development.

4.6.3 Single-Mother Families

About 40 percent of U.S. births are to single mothers, one-third of whom are teenagers (Martin et al., 2018). Although the U.S. adolescent birth rate has undergone a steady decline, it remains high compared with that of other developed nations.

At the other extreme, planned births and adoptions by never-married single 30- to 45-year-old women with at least a bachelor's degree have doubled compared with two decades ago. Nearly one-third have at least one child (Pew Research Center, 2018e). These mothers are generally financially secure, have readily available social support from family members and friends, and adapt to parenthood with relative ease. In fact, older single mothers in well-paid occupations who plan carefully for a new baby may encounter fewer parenting difficulties than married couples, largely because their family structure is simpler: They do not have to coordinate parenting roles with a partner, and they have no unfulfilled expectations for shared caregiving (Tyano et al., 2010). Also, because of their psychological maturity, these mothers are likely to cope effectively with parenting challenges.

The majority of nonmarital births are unplanned and to women in their twenties. Most have incomes below the poverty level and experience a stressful transition to parenthood. Although many live with the baby's father or another partner, cohabiting relationships in the United States, compared with those in Western Europe, involve less commitment and cooperation and are far more likely to break up—especially after an unplanned baby arrives (Guzzo, 2014; Jose, O'Leary, & Moyer, 2010). These single mothers often lack emotional and parenting support—strong predictors of psychological distress and infant caregiving difficulties (Keating-Lefler et al., 2004).

4.6.4 Parent Interventions

Special interventions are available to help parents adjust to life with a new baby. For those who are not at high risk for problems, counselor-led programs that focus on strengthening the couple's relationship and their coparenting skills are particularly successful (Gottman, Gottman, & Shapiro, 2010; Schulz, Cowan, & Cowan, 2006).

In one evaluation of two brief interventions, first-time expectant couples received four 90-minute individualized coaching sessions—two shortly before birth and two 3 months after birth—aimed either at solving relationship challenges or at devising a coparenting plan for mutually supportive, shared caregiving. Compared to control-group women, those randomly assigned to either intervention reported large post-birth benefits in relationship satisfaction and in mutually supportive coparenting that were still evident two years after the birth (see Figure 4.9). Also, women experiencing the interventions were far less likely than controls to report a sharp rise in stress during their baby's first year (Doss et al., 2014). Men also benefitted from the interventions, though not as much as women, perhaps because overall, men experience fewer difficulties during the transition to parenthood.

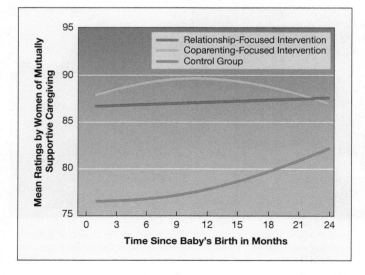

FIGURE 4.9   Impact of parent interventions focusing on the couple's relationship and on supportive coparenting during the transition to parenthood. Ninety couples who were either married or cohabiting were randomly assigned to either a relationship-focused intervention, a coparenting-focused intervention, or a control group receiving written materials about infant care. As shown here, women receiving either intervention reported far more favorable coparenting throughout their baby's first two years than did control-group women. Women's relationship satisfaction with their partners showed similar post-birth trends. (From B. D. Doss et al., 2014, "A Randomized Controlled Trial of Brief Coparenting and Relationship Interventions During the Transition to Parenthood," *Journal of Family Psychology,* p. 490. Copyright © 2014 American Psychological Association. Adapted by permission.)

High-risk parents struggling with poverty or the birth of a baby with disabilities need more intensive interventions. Programs in which a professional intervener visits the home and focuses on enhancing social support and parenting have resulted in improved parent–infant interaction and benefits for children's cognitive and social development into middle childhood (to review one example, return to page 110 in Chapter 3). Many low-income single mothers benefit from interventions that focus on sustaining the father's involvement (Jones, Charles, & Benson, 2013). These parents also require tangible support—money, food, transportation, and affordable child care—to ease stress so they have the psychological resources to engage in sensitive, responsive infant care.

When parents' relationships are positive and cooperative, social support is available, and families have sufficient income, the stress caused by the birth of a baby remains manageable. These family conditions, as we have already seen, consistently contribute to favorable development—in infancy and beyond.

A counselor discusses options with this single mother for continuing her education. Parents struggling with poverty benefit from intensive intervention focusing on social support and effective parenting.

 ASK YOURSELF

Connect ■ Explain how generous employment leave for childbirth—at least 12 weeks of paid time off available to either the mother or father—can ease the transition to parenthood and promote positive parent–infant interaction. (*Hint:* Consult the Cultural Influences box on pages 132–133 in section 4.4.2.)

Apply ■ Derek, father of a 3-year-old and a newborn, reported that he had a harder time adjusting to the birth of his second child than to that of his first. Explain why this might be so.

Reflect ■ If you are a parent, what was the transition to parenthood like for you? What factors helped you adjust? What factors made it more difficult? If you are not a parent, pose these questions to someone you know who recently became a parent.

SUMMARY

4.1 The Stages of Childbirth (p. 117)

4.1 *Describe the three stages of childbirth, the baby's adaptation to labor and delivery, and the newborn baby's appearance.*

■ In the first stage, **dilation and effacement of the cervix** occur as uterine contractions increase in strength and frequency. This stage culminates in **transition,** a brief period of peak contractions in which the cervix opens completely. In the second stage, the mother feels an urge to push the baby through the birth canal, and the baby is born. In the final stage, the placenta is delivered.

■ During labor, infants produce high levels of stress hormones, which help them withstand oxygen deprivation, clear their lungs for breathing, and arouse them into alertness.

■ Newborns may be odd-looking, but their facial features make adults feel like cuddling them.

■ The **Apgar Scale** assesses the baby's physical condition at birth.

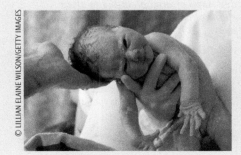

4.2 Approaches to Childbirth (p. 121)

4.2 *Describe natural childbirth and home delivery, noting benefits and concerns associated with each.*

■ In **natural,** or **prepared, childbirth,** the expectant mother and a companion typically attend classes where they learn about labor and delivery, master relaxation and breathing techniques to counteract pain, and prepare for coaching during childbirth. Social support from a doula reduces the need for instrument-assisted births and pain medication and is associated with higher Apgar scores.

- An upright position and water birth are increasingly popular alternatives that ease labor and delivery for both mother and baby, compared to the traditional lying on the back, feet in stirrups hospital position.
- Home birth is safe for healthy mothers assisted by a well-trained doctor or midwife, but mothers at risk for any complication are safer giving birth in a hospital.

4.3 Medical Interventions
(p. 123)

4.3 *List common medical interventions during childbirth, circumstances that justify their use, and any dangers associated with each.*

- **Fetal monitors** help save the lives of many babies at risk for **anoxia** due to pregnancy complications. Used routinely, however, they may identify infants as in danger who are not, contributing to an increase in instrument and cesarean deliveries.
- Use of analgesics and anesthetics to control pain, though sometimes necessary, can prolong labor and compromise newborn adjustment.
- Although appropriate when the mother's pushing is insufficient, instrument delivery can cause serious complications and should be avoided if possible.
- **Cesarean delivery** is warranted for medical emergencies and in some cases of **breech position.** However, many unnecessary cesareans are performed.

4.4 Birth Complications
(p. 126)

4.4a *Describe risks associated with oxygen deprivation and with preterm and low-birth-weight infants, along with effective interventions.*

- Inadequate oxygen supply during labor and delivery can damage the brain, resulting in persisting motor and cognitive deficits that vary in severity with the extent of anoxia. Hypothermia treatment substantially reduces brain damage due to anoxia.

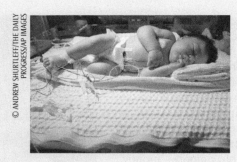

- Low birth weight, most common in infants born to poverty-stricken women, is a major cause of **neonatal** and **infant mortality** and developmental problems.
- Compared with **preterm infants,** whose weight is appropriate for time spent in the uterus, **small-for-date infants** usually have longer-lasting difficulties. However, even minimally preterm babies experience greater rates of illness and persisting, mild intellectual delays.
- Some interventions for preterm infants provide special stimulation in the intensive care nursery. Others teach parents how to care for and interact with their babies. Preterm infants in stressed, low-income households need long-term, intensive intervention. Skin-to-skin "kangaroo care" promotes survival and diverse aspects of development in preterm infants.
- Countries that outrank the United States in infant survival promote prenatal health and effective parenting through government-sponsored high-quality health care and generous, paid employment leave.

4.4b *Describe factors that promote resilience in infants who survive a traumatic birth.*

- When infants experience birth trauma, a supportive family environment or relationships with other caring adults can help restore their growth. Even infants with fairly serious birth complications can recover with the help of positive life events.

4.5 The Newborn Baby's Capacities (p. 133)

4.5a *Describe the newborn baby's reflexes and states of arousal, including sleep characteristics and ways to soothe a crying baby.*

- **Reflexes** are the newborn baby's most obvious organized patterns of behavior. Some have survival value, others help parents and infants establish gratifying interaction, and still others provide the foundation for voluntary motor skills.

- Although newborns move in and out of five **states of arousal,** they spend most of their time asleep. Sleep includes at least two states: **rapid-eye-movement (REM) sleep** and **non-rapid-eye-movement (NREM) sleep.** Newborns spend about 50 percent of their sleep time in REM sleep, far more than they ever will again. REM sleep provides young infants with stimulation essential for central nervous system development. Sleep contributes to babies' learning and memory.
- Disturbed REM–NREM cycles are a sign of central nervous system abnormalities, which may lead to **sudden infant death syndrome (SIDS).**
- A crying baby triggers strong feelings of discomfort in nearby adults. Once feeding and diaper changing have been tried, lifting the baby to the shoulder and rocking or walking is a highly effective soothing technique. Extensive parent–infant physical contact substantially reduces crying in the early months. Support programs can help parents acquire techniques that reduce excessive infant crying.

4.5b *Describe the newborn baby's sensory capacities.*

- The senses of touch, taste, smell, and sound are well-developed at birth. Newborns use touch to investigate their world, are highly sensitive to pain, prefer sweet tastes and smells, and orient toward the odor of their own mother's lactating breast and toward human milk rather than formula milk. Attraction to certain flavors, developed through prenatal exposure to a mother's diet or through breast milk, can, in some instances have long-term consequences for odor and taste preferences.
- Newborns can distinguish a variety of sound patterns as well as nearly all speech sounds. They are especially responsive to human speech, high-pitched expressive voices, their own mother's voice, and speech in their native language.
- Vision is the least developed of the newborn's senses. At birth, focusing ability and **visual acuity** are limited. Nevertheless, newborns can detect human faces and prefer their mother's familiar face to the face of a stranger. In exploring the visual field, they are attracted to bright objects but tend to limit their looking to single features. Newborn babies have difficulty discriminating colors.

4.5c *Explain the usefulness of neonatal behavioral assessment.*

■ The most widely used instrument for assessing the behavior of newborn infants, Brazelton's **Neonatal Behavioral Assessment Scale (NBAS)**, has helped researchers understand individual and cultural differences in newborn behavior.

■ Changes in NBAS scores over the first week or two of life provide the best estimate of the baby's ability to recover from the stress of birth. Sometimes the NBAS is used to teach parents about their baby's capacities.

4.6 The Transition to Parenthood (p. 144)

4.6a *Discuss the influence of birth-related hormonal changes and parent–infant contact on emergence of parental affection and concern for the infant.*

■ Near birth, mothers—as well as fathers in a warm couple relationship—experience hormonal changes associated with sensitivity and responsiveness to the baby. Although human parents do not require close physical contact with the infant immediately after birth for **bonding** to occur, hospital practices that promote parent–infant closeness, such as **rooming in,** may help parents build a good relationship with their newborn.

4.6b *Describe changes in the family after the birth of a baby, along with interventions that foster the transition to parenthood.*

■ In response to the demands of new parenthood, the gender roles of parents usually become more traditional. Parents in gratifying marriages who continue to support each other's needs generally adapt well. But in dual-earner marriages, a large difference between a couple's caregiving responsibilities can threaten marital satisfaction, especially for women, and negatively affect parent–infant interaction. Favorable adjustment to a second birth typically requires that fathers take an even more active role in parenting.

■ Early therapeutic intervention can prevent parental depression from interfering with effective caregiving and the parent–child relationship.

■ Planned births and adoptions by never-married, well-educated women in their thirties and forties have increased dramatically. These mothers typically adapt easily to parenthood. Most non-marital births are unplanned and to poverty-stricken young women experiencing a stressful transition to parenthood.

■ When parents are at low risk for problems, counselor-led interventions that focus on strengthening the couple's relationship and their coparenting skills can ease the transition to parenthood. High-risk parents struggling with poverty or the birth of a baby with disabilities are more likely to benefit from intensive home interventions focusing on enhancing social support and parenting.

IMPORTANT TERMS AND CONCEPTS

anoxia (p. 123)
Apgar Scale (p. 120)
bonding (p. 145)
breech position (p. 125)
cesarean delivery (p. 125)
dilation and effacement of the cervix (p. 119)
fetal monitors (p. 123)
infant mortality (p. 132)

natural, or prepared, childbirth (p. 122)
Neonatal Behavioral Assessment Scale (NBAS) (p. 143)
neonatal mortality (p. 132)
non-rapid-eye-movement (NREM) sleep (p. 137)
preterm infants (p. 128)
rapid-eye-movement (REM) sleep (p. 137)
reflex (p. 133)

rooming in (p. 145)
small-for-date infants (p. 128)
states of arousal (p. 136)
sudden infant death syndrome (SIDS) (p. 138)
transition (p. 119)
visual acuity (p. 143)

Physical Development in Infancy and Toddlerhood

Mother

Shang Meng Lei, 9 years, China

This painting captures a mother and her infant affectionately imitating each other's facial expressions and gestures. During the first year, infants grow rapidly, move on their own, increasingly investigate and make sense of their surroundings, and learn from others.

Reprinted with permission from The International Museum of Children's Art, Oslo, Norway

On a brilliant June morning, 16-month-old Caitlin emerged from her front
door, ready for the short drive to the child-care home where she spent her
weekdays while her mother, Carolyn, and her father, David, worked. Clutch-
ing a teddy bear in one hand and her mother's arm with the other, Caitlin descended
the steps. "One! Two! Threeeee!" Carolyn counted as she helped Caitlin down. "How
much she's changed!" Carolyn thought to herself, looking at the child who, not long
ago, had been a newborn. With her first steps, Caitlin had passed from *infancy* to
toddlerhood—a period spanning the second year of life. At first, Caitlin did, indeed,
"toddle" with an awkward gait, tipping over frequently. But her face reflected the
thrill of conquering a new skill.

As they walked toward the car, Carolyn and Caitlin spotted 3-year-old Eli and his
father, Kevin, in the neighboring yard. Eli dashed toward them, waving a bright yellow envelope. Carolyn bent down to open the envelope and took out a card. It read,
"Announcing the arrival of Grace Ann. Born: Cambodia. Age: 16 months." Carolyn
turned toward Kevin and Eli. "That's wonderful news! When can we see her?"

"Let's wait a few days," Kevin suggested. "Monica's taken Grace to the doctor this
morning. She's underweight and malnourished." Kevin described Monica's first night
with Grace in a hotel room in Phnom Penh. Grace lay on the bed, withdrawn and
fearful. Eventually she fell asleep, gripping crackers in both hands.

Carolyn felt Caitlin's impatient tug at her sleeve. Off they drove to child care,
where Vanessa had just dropped off her 18-month-old son, Timmy. Within moments,
Caitlin and Timmy were in the sandbox, shoveling sand into plastic cups and buckets
with the help of their caregiver, Ginette.

A few weeks later, Grace joined Caitlin and Timmy at Ginette's child-care home.
Although still unable to crawl or walk, she had grown taller and heavier, and her sad,
vacant gaze had given way to an alert expression, a ready smile, and an enthusiastic
desire to imitate and explore. When Caitlin headed for the sandbox, Grace stretched
out her arms, asking Ginette to carry her there, too. Soon Grace was pulling herself
up at every opportunity. Finally, at age 18 months, she walked!

This chapter traces physical growth during the first two years—one of the most
remarkable and busiest times of development. We will see how rapid changes in
the infant's body and brain support learning, motor skills, and perceptual capacities. Caitlin, Grace, and Timmy will join us along the way to illustrate how individual
differences and environmental influences affect physical development. ■

*What's
Ahead in
Chapter 5*

5.1 Body Growth
Changes in Body Size and Muscle–Fat
Makeup • Changes in Body Proportions •
Individual and Group Differences

5.2 Brain Development
Development of Neurons • Measures of
Brain Functioning • Development of the
Cerebral Cortex • Sensitive Periods in Brain
Development • Changing States of Arousal

■ **BIOLOGY AND ENVIRONMENT:** *Brain
Plasticity: Insights from Research on Children
with Brain Injury*

■ **CULTURAL INFLUENCES:** *Cultural Variation
in Infant Sleeping Arrangements*

5.3 Influences on Early Physical Growth
Heredity • Nutrition • Malnutrition •
Emotional Well-Being

■ **SOCIAL ISSUES: HEALTH:** *Lead Exposure
and Children's Development*

5.4 Learning Capacities
Classical Conditioning • Operant
Conditioning • Habituation • Statistical
Learning • Imitation

5.5 Motor Development
The Sequence of Motor Development •
Motor Skills as Dynamic Systems • Fine-Motor
Development: Reaching and Grasping

5.6 Perceptual Development
Hearing • Vision • Object Perception •
Intermodal Perception • Understanding
Perceptual Development

■ **BIOLOGY AND ENVIRONMENT:** *"Tuning
in" to Familiar Speech, Faces, and Music:
A Sensitive Period for Culture-Specific Learning*

5.1 Body Growth

The next time you're walking in your neighborhood park or at the mall,
note the contrast between infants' and toddlers' physical capabilities. One reason for
the vast changes in what children can do over the first two years is that their bodies
change enormously—faster than at any other time after birth.

5.1.1 Changes in Body Size and Muscle–Fat Makeup

By the end of the first year, a typical infant's height is about 32 inches—more than
50 percent greater than at birth. By 2 years, it is 75 percent greater, averaging 36
inches. Similarly, by age 5 months, birth weight has doubled to about 15 pounds. At 1
year it has tripled to 22 pounds, and at 2 years it has quadrupled to about 30 pounds.

5.1 Describe major changes in body growth over the first two years.

Figure 5.1 illustrates this dramatic increase in body size. But rather than making steady gains, infants and toddlers grow in little spurts. In one study, children who were followed over the first 21 months of life went for periods of 7 to 63 days with no growth, then added as much as half an inch in a 24-hour period! Almost always, parents described their babies as irritable, very hungry, and sleeping more on the days before a spurt (Lampl, 1993; Lampl & Johnson, 2011).

One of the most obvious changes in infants' appearance is their transformation into round, plump babies by the middle of the first year. This early rise in "baby fat," which peaks at about 9 months, helps the infant maintain a constant body temperature. In the second year, most toddlers slim down, a trend that continues into middle childhood (Fomon & Nelson, 2002). In contrast, muscle tissue increases very slowly during infancy and will not reach a peak until adolescence. Babies are not very muscular; their strength and physical coordination are limited.

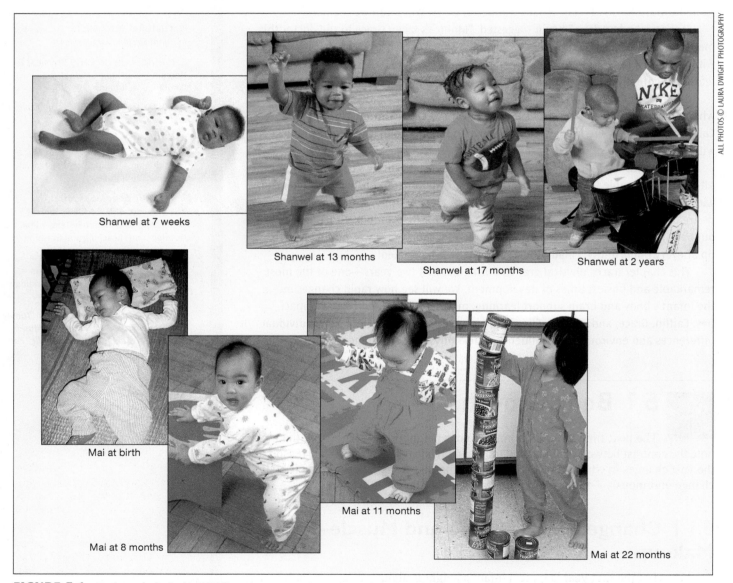

Shanwel at 7 weeks

Shanwel at 13 months

Shanwel at 17 months

Shanwel at 2 years

Mai at birth

Mai at 8 months

Mai at 11 months

Mai at 22 months

ALL PHOTOS © LAURA DWIGHT PHOTOGRAPHY

FIGURE 5.1   Body growth during the first two years. These photos depict the dramatic changes in body size and proportions during infancy and toddlerhood in two children—a boy, Shanwel, and a girl, Mai. In the first year, the head is quite large in proportion to the rest of the body, and height and weight gain are especially rapid. During the second year, the lower portion of the body catches up. Notice how both children added "baby fat" in the early months of life and then slimmed down, a trend that continues into middle childhood.

5.1.2 Changes in Body Proportions

As the child's overall size increases, parts of the body grow at different rates. Two growth patterns describe these changes. The first is the **cephalocaudal trend**—from the Latin for "head to tail." During the prenatal period, the head develops more rapidly than the lower part of the body. At birth, the head takes up one-fourth of total body length, the legs only one-third. Notice how, in Figure 5.1, the lower portion of the body catches up. By age 2, the head accounts for only one-fifth and the legs for nearly one-half of total body length.

In the second pattern, the **proximodistal trend,** growth proceeds, literally, from "near to far"—from the center of the body outward. In the prenatal period, the head, chest, and trunk grow first; then the arms and legs; and finally the hands and feet. During infancy and childhood, the arms and legs continue to grow somewhat ahead of the hands and feet.

5.1.3 Individual and Group Differences

In infancy, girls are slightly shorter and lighter than boys, with a higher ratio of fat to muscle. These small sex differences persist throughout early and middle childhood and are greatly magnified at adolescence. Ethnic differences in body size are apparent as well. Grace was below the *growth norms* (height and weight averages for children her age). Early malnutrition contributed, but even after substantial catch-up, Grace—as is typical for Asian children—remained below North American norms. In contrast, Timmy is slightly above average in size, as African-American children tend to be (Bogin, 2001).

Children of the same age differ in *rate* of physical growth; some make faster progress toward mature body size than others. But current body size is not enough to tell us how quickly a child's physical growth is moving along. Although Timmy is larger and heavier than Caitlin and Grace, he is not physically more mature. In a moment, you will see why.

The best estimate of a child's physical maturity is *skeletal age,* a measure of bone development. It is determined by X-raying the long bones of the body to see the extent to which soft, pliable cartilage has hardened into bone, a gradual process that is completed in adolescence. When skeletal ages are examined, African-American children tend to be slightly ahead of European-American and Hispanic children of the same chronological age. And girls are considerably ahead of boys—the reason Timmy's skeletal age lags behind that of Caitlin and Grace. At birth, the sexes differ by about 4 to 6 weeks, a gap that widens over infancy and childhood (McCormack et al., 2017; Tanner, Healy, & Cameron, 2001). Girls are advanced in development of other organs as well. This greater physical maturity may contribute to girls' greater resistance to harmful environmental influences. As noted in Chapter 2, girls experience fewer developmental problems than boys and have lower infant and childhood mortality rates.

5.2 Brain Development

At birth, the brain is nearer to its adult size than any other physical structure, and it continues to develop at an astounding pace throughout infancy and toddlerhood. We can best understand brain growth by looking at it from two vantage points: (1) the microscopic level of individual brain cells and (2) the larger level of the cerebral cortex, the most complex brain structure and the one responsible for the highly developed intelligence of our species.

5.2a Describe brain development during infancy and toddlerhood, current methods of measuring brain functioning, and appropriate stimulation to support the brain's potential.

5.2b Explain how the organization of sleep and wakefulness changes over the first two years.

5.2.1 Development of Neurons

The typical adult human brain has 100 to 200 billion **neurons,** or nerve cells, that store and transmit information, many of which have thousands of direct connections with other neurons. Unlike other body cells, neurons are not tightly packed together. Between them are tiny gaps, or **synapses,** where fibers from different neurons come close together but do not touch (see

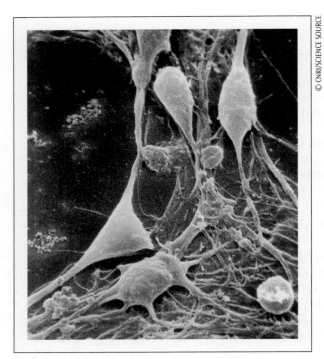

© CNRI/SCIENCE SOURCE

FIGURE 5.2   Neurons and their connective fibers.
This photograph of several neurons, taken with the aid of a powerful microscope, shows the elaborate synaptic connections that form with neighboring cells.

Figure 5.2). Neurons send messages to one another by releasing chemicals called **neurotransmitters,** which cross synapses.

The basic story of brain growth concerns how neurons develop and form this elaborate communication system. Figure 5.3 summarizes major milestones of brain development. In the prenatal period, neurons are produced in the embryo's primitive neural tube. From there, they migrate to form the major parts of the brain (see page 94 in Chapter 3). Once neurons are in place, they differentiate, establishing their unique functions by extending their fibers to form synaptic connections with neighboring cells. During the first two years, neural fibers and synapses increase at an astounding pace (Budday, Steinmann, & Kuhl, 2015; Moore, Persaud, & Torchia, 2016). A surprising aspect of brain growth is **programmed cell death,** which makes space for these connective structures: As synapses form, many surrounding neurons die—40 to 60 percent, depending on the brain region (Jabès & Nelson, 2014). Fortunately, during the prenatal period, the neural tube produces far more neurons than the brain will ever need.

As neurons form connections, *stimulation* becomes vital to their survival. Neurons that are stimulated by input from the surrounding environment continue to establish new synapses, forming increasingly elaborate systems of communication that support more complex abilities. At first, stimulation results in a massive overabundance of synapses, many of which serve identical functions, thereby ensuring that the child will acquire the motor, cognitive, and social skills that our species needs to survive. Neurons that are seldom stimulated soon lose their synapses in a process called **synaptic pruning** that returns neurons not needed at the moment to an uncommitted state so they can support future development. At the same time, pruning allows for rearrangement and strengthening of remaining synapses, which fine-tunes neural circuitry and is essential for effective information processing. In all, about 50 percent of synapses are pruned during childhood and adolescence (Jiang & Nardelli, 2016). For this process to advance, appropriate stimulation of the child's brain is vital during periods in which the formation of synapses is at its peak.

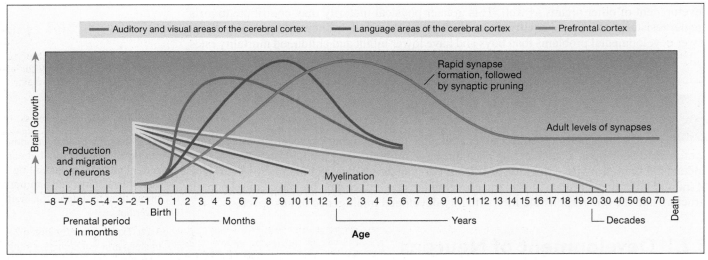

FIGURE 5.3   Major milestones of brain development. Formation of synapses is rapid during the first two years, especially in the auditory, visual, and language areas of the cerebral cortex. The prefrontal cortex, responsible for complex thought (see page 159), undergoes more extended synaptic growth. In each area, overproduction of synapses is followed by synaptic pruning. The prefrontal cortex is among the last regions to attain adult levels of synaptic connections—in mid- to late adolescence. Myelination occurs at a dramatic pace during the first two years, more slowly through childhood, followed by an acceleration at adolescence. The multiple yellow lines indicate that the timing of myelination varies among different brain areas. For example, neural fibers myelinate over a longer period in the language areas, and especially in the prefrontal cortex, than in the auditory and visual areas. (Based on Thompson & Nelson, 2001.)

If few neurons are produced after the prenatal period, what causes the extraordinary increase in brain size during the first two years? About half the brain's volume is made up of **glial cells,** which are responsible for **myelination,** the coating of neural fibers with an insulating fatty sheath (called *myelin*) that improves the efficiency of message transfer. Certain types of glial cells also participate directly in neural communication, by picking up and passing on neuronal signals and releasing neurotransmitters. Glial cells multiply rapidly from the fourth month of pregnancy through the second year of life—a process that continues at a slower pace through middle childhood and accelerates again in adolescence. Gains in neural fibers and myelination account for the overall increase in size of the brain, from nearly 30 percent of its adult weight at birth to 70 percent by age 2 (Budday, Steinmann, & Kuhl, 2015; Terni, López-Murcia, & Llobet, 2017). Growth is especially rapid during the first year, when the brain more than doubles in size.

Brain development can be compared to molding a "living sculpture." First, neurons and synapses are overproduced. Then, cell death and synaptic pruning sculpt away excess building material to form the mature brain—a process jointly influenced by genetically programmed events and the child's experiences. The resulting "sculpture" is a set of interconnected regions, each with specific functions—much like countries on a globe that communicate with one another (Johnston et al., 2001). This "geography" of the brain permits researchers to study its organization and the activity of its regions using neurobiological techniques.

5.2.2 Measures of Brain Functioning

Table 5.1 describes major measures of brain functioning. Among these methods, the two most frequently used detect changes in *electrical activity* in the cerebral cortex. In an *electroencephalogram (EEG),* researchers examine *brain-wave patterns* for stability and organization—signs of mature functioning of the cortex (see Figure 5.4). As a child processes a particular stimulus, *event-related potentials (ERPs)* can detect the general location of brain-wave activity—a technique often used to study preverbal infants' responsiveness to various stimuli, the impact of experience on specialization of specific regions of the cortex, and atypical brain functioning in children at risk for learning and emotional problems (DeBoer, Scott, & Nelson, 2007; Gunnar & de Haan, 2009).

OLI SCARFF/GETTY IMAGES

FIGURE 5.4   Electroencephalogram (EEG) using the geodesic sensor net (GSN). Interconnected electrodes embedded in the head cap record electrical brain-wave activity in the cerebral cortex.

TABLE 5.1   Measuring Brain Functioning

METHOD	DESCRIPTION
Electroencephalogram (EEG)	Electrodes embedded in a head cap record electrical brain-wave activity in the brain's outer layers—the cerebral cortex. Researchers use an advanced tool called a geodesic sensor net (GSN) to hold interconnected electrodes (up to 128 for infants and 256 for children and adults) in place through a cap that adjusts to each person's head shape, yielding high-quality brain-wave detection.
Event-related potentials (ERPs)	Using the EEG, the frequency and amplitude of brain waves in response to particular stimuli (such as a picture, music, or speech) are recorded in multiple areas of the cerebral cortex. Enables identification of general regions of stimulus-induced activity.
Functional magnetic resonance imaging (fMRI)	While the child lies inside a tunnel-shaped apparatus that creates a magnetic field, a scanner magnetically detects increased blood flow and oxygen metabolism in areas of the brain as the individual processes particular stimuli. The scanner typically records images every 1 to 4 seconds; these are combined into a computerized moving picture of activity anywhere in the brain (not just its outer layers). Not appropriate for children younger than age 5 to 6, who cannot remain still during testing.
Positron emission tomography (PET)	After injection or inhalation of a radioactive substance, the person lies on an apparatus with a scanner that emits fine streams of X-rays, which detect increased blood flow and oxygen metabolism in areas of the brain as the person processes particular stimuli. As with fMRI, the result is a computerized image of activity anywhere in the brain. Also like fMRI, not appropriate for children younger than age 5 to 6.
Near-infrared spectroscopy (NIRS)	Using thin, flexible optical fibers attached to the scalp through a head cap, infrared (invisible) light is beamed at the brain; its absorption by areas of the cerebral cortex varies with changes in blood flow and oxygen metabolism as the individual processes particular stimuli. The result is a computerized moving picture of active areas in the cerebral cortex. Unlike fMRI and PET, NIRS is appropriate for infants and young children, who can move within limited range during testing.

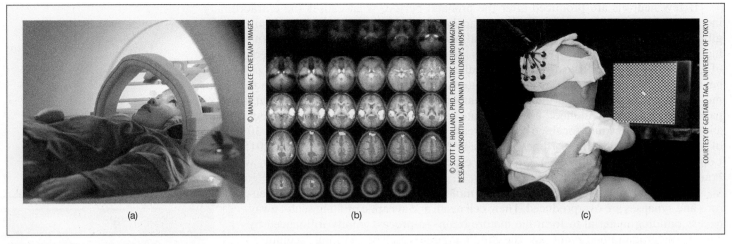

FIGURE 5.5 **Functional magnetic resonance imaging (fMRI) and near infrared spectroscopy (NIRS).** (a) This 6-year-old is part of a study that uses fMRI to find out how his brain processes light and motion. (b) The fMRI image shows which areas of the child's brain are active while he views changing visual stimuli. (c) Here, NIRS is used to investigate a 2-month-old's response to a visual stimulus. During testing, the baby can move freely within a limited range. (Photo (c) from G. Taga, K. Asakawa, A. Maki, Y. Konishi, & H. Koisumi, 2003, "Brain Imaging in Awake Infants by Near-Infrared Optical Topography," *Proceedings of the National Academy of Sciences, 100,* p. 10723. Reprinted by permission.)

Neuroimaging techniques, which yield detailed, three-dimensional computerized pictures of the entire brain and its active areas, provide the most precise information about which brain regions are specialized for certain capacities and about abnormalities in brain functioning. In *positron emission tomography (PET),* the child must lie quietly on a scanner bed, and in *functional magnetic resonance imaging (fMRI),* inside a tunnel-like apparatus. But unlike PET, fMRI does not depend on X-ray photography, which requires injection of a radioactive substance. Rather, when a child is exposed to a stimulus, fMRI detects changes in blood flow and oxygen metabolism throughout the brain magnetically, yielding a colorful, moving picture of parts of the brain used to perform a given activity (see Figure 5.5a and b).

Because PET and fMRI require that the participant lie as motionless as possible for an extended time, they are not suitable for infants and young children. A neuroimaging technique that works well in infancy and early childhood is *near infrared spectroscopy (NIRS)* (refer again to Table 5.1). Because the apparatus consists only of thin, flexible optical fibers attached to the scalp using a head cap, a baby can sit on the parent's lap and move during testing—as Figure 5.5c illustrates. But unlike PET and fMRI, which map activity changes throughout the brain, NIRS examines only the functioning of the cerebral cortex.

The measures just reviewed are powerful tools for uncovering relationships between the brain and psychological development. But like all research methods, they have limitations. Even though a stimulus produces a consistent pattern of brain activity, investigators cannot be certain that an individual has processed it in a certain way (Kagan, 2013b). And a researcher who takes a change in brain activity as an indicator of information processing must make sure that the change was not due instead to hunger, boredom, fatigue, or body movements. Consequently, other methods—both observations and self-reports—must be combined with brain-wave and imaging findings to clarify their meaning. Now let's turn to the developing organization of the cerebral cortex.

5.2.3 Development of the Cerebral Cortex

The **cerebral cortex,** resembling half a shelled walnut, surrounds the rest of the brain. It is the largest brain structure—accounting for 85 percent of the brain's weight and containing the greatest number of neurons and synapses. Each of the 20 billion neurons located in the cerebral cortex has, on average, 7,000 synaptic connections, yielding more than 23,000 miles of myelinated neural fibers (Budday, Steinman, & Kuhl, 2015). Because the cerebral cortex is the last part of the brain to stop growing, it is sensitive to environmental influences for a much longer period than any other part of the brain.

Regions of the Cerebral Cortex Figure 5.6 shows specific functions of regions of the cerebral cortex, such as receiving information from the senses, instructing the body to move, and thinking. The order in which cortical regions develop corresponds to the order in which various capacities emerge in the infant and growing child. For example, a burst of synaptic growth occurs in the auditory and visual cortexes and in areas responsible for body movement over the first year—a period of dramatic gains in auditory and visual perception and mastery of motor skills (Gilmore et al., 2012). Language areas are especially active from late infancy through the preschool years, when language development flourishes (Pujol et al., 2006).

The cortical regions with the most extended period of development are the *frontal lobes*. The **prefrontal cortex,** lying in front of areas controlling body movement, is responsible for complex thought—in particular, consciousness and various "executive" processes, including inhibition of impulses; integration of information; self-regulation of cognition, emotion, and behavior; and memory, reasoning, planning, and problem-solving strategies. From age 2 months on, the prefrontal cortex functions more effectively. But it undergoes especially rapid myelination and formation and pruning of synapses during the preschool and school years, followed by another period of accelerated growth in adolescence, when it reaches an adult level of synaptic connections (Jabès & Nelson, 2014; Jiang & Nardelli, 2016).

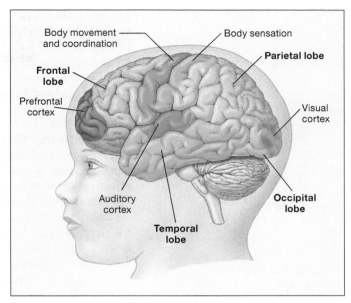

FIGURE 5.6 **The left side of the human brain, showing the cerebral cortex.** The cortex is divided into different lobes, each of which contains a variety of regions with specific functions. Some major regions are labeled here.

Lateralization and Plasticity of the Cerebral Cortex The cerebral cortex has two *hemispheres,* or sides, that differ in their motor, cognitive, and emotional functions. Some tasks are done mostly by the left hemisphere, others by the right—specialization of the hemispheres is called **lateralization.** For example, each hemisphere receives sensory information from the side of the body opposite to it and controls only that side (vision is a complicated exception). For most of us, the left hemisphere is largely responsible for verbal abilities (such as spoken and written language) and positive emotion (such as joy). The right hemisphere handles spatial abilities (judging distances, reading maps, and recognizing geometric shapes) and negative emotion (such as distress) (Banish & Heller, 1998; Nelson & Bosquet, 2000).

Handedness is the most obvious reflection of cerebral lateralization in humans. In longitudinal research on several hundred ethnically diverse U.S. infants, hand preference in reaching for objects was evident for about half between ages 6 and 14 months. An additional one-fourth began to show a hand preference over the second year; the rest as yet showed no preference (Campbell, Marcinowski, & Michel, 2018; Michel et al., 2014). Like adults, most infants who displayed a hand preference preferred the right hand, which is controlled by the left hemisphere. Nevertheless, numerous studies comparing identical and fraternal twins reveal the heritability of left-handedness to be weak (Ooki, 2014; Vuoksimaa et al., 2009). Although many hypotheses about early environmental influences on handedness exist, none is consistently supported by research.

Handedness, however, is not a good indicator of how cognitive functions are organized in the cerebral cortex. The approximately 10 percent of people who are left-handed or to varying degrees mixed-handed usually display the same lateralization pattern for language and spatial abilities as right-handers. For a few non-right-handers, the cortex is less clearly specialized. And a small minority of healthy right- and left-handers display atypical forms of hemispheric specialization (Guadalupe et al., 2014; Mazoyer et al., 2014). These range from lack of lateralization (language governed by both hemispheres) to a reversal of the typical pattern (language in the right hemisphere, spatial abilities in the left).

Why, in the overwhelming majority of humans, does lateralization of cognitive and emotional functions occur? A lateralized brain may have evolved because it

Handedness—as in this 1-year-old's preference for using his left hand—is the most visible reflection of cerebral lateralization. Although handedness becomes increasingly apparent with age, the majority of young left- and right-handers show the same lateralization pattern for cognitive functions.

permits a wider array of functions to be carried out effectively, enabling humans to cope more successfully with changing environmental demands than if both sides processed information in exactly the same way. Studies using fMRI reveal, for example, that the left hemisphere is better at processing information in a sequential, analytic (piece-by-piece) way, useful for dealing with communicative information—both verbal (language) and emotional (a joyful smile). In contrast, the right hemisphere is specialized for processing information in a holistic, integrative manner, ideal for making sense of spatial information and regulating negative emotion (Silbereis et al., 2016).

Nevertheless, the popular notion that lateralization means that there are "right-brained" and "left-brained" people is an oversimplification. The two hemispheres communicate and work together to enhance information processing of all kinds, doing so more rapidly and effectively with age.

Researchers study the timing of brain lateralization to learn more about **brain plasticity.** A *plastic* cerebral cortex, in which many areas are not yet committed to specific functions, has a high capacity for learning. And if a part of the cortex is damaged, other parts can take over the tasks it would have handled. But once the hemispheres lateralize, damage to a specific region means that the abilities it controls cannot be recovered to the same extent or as easily as earlier.

Early in development, the hemispheres have already begun to specialize for cognitive and emotional processing. The majority of newborns show greater activation (detected with either ERP or NIRS) in the left hemisphere while listening to speech sounds or displaying a positive state of arousal. In contrast, the right hemisphere reacts more strongly to nonspeech sounds and to stimuli (such as a sour-tasting fluid) that evoke negative emotion (Hespos et al., 2010).

Nevertheless, research on children and adults who survived brain injuries offers evidence for substantial plasticity in the young brain, summarized in the Biology and Environment box on the following page. Furthermore, early experience greatly influences the organization of the cerebral cortex for language. For example, deaf adults, who as infants and children learned sign language (a spatial skill), depend more than hearing individuals on the right hemisphere for language processing (Neville & Bavelier, 2002). And toddlers who are verbally advanced show greater left-hemispheric specialization for language than their more slowly developing agemates (Bishop et al., 2014; Mills et al., 2005). Apparently, the very process of acquiring language and other skills promotes lateralization.

In sum, the brain is more plastic during the first few years than it will ever be again. An overabundance of synaptic connections supports brain plasticity and, therefore, young children's ability to learn, which is fundamental to their survival. And although the cortex is programmed from the start for hemispheric specialization, experience greatly influences the rate and success of its advancing organization.

5.2.4 Sensitive Periods in Brain Development

Animal studies confirm that early, extreme sensory deprivation results in permanent brain damage and loss of functions—findings that verify the existence of sensitive periods in brain development. For example, early, varied visual experiences must occur for the brain's visual centers to develop normally. If a 1-month-old kitten is deprived of light for just three or four days, these areas of the brain undergo accelerated synapse elimination and degenerate. If the kitten is kept in the dark during the fourth week of life and beyond, the damage is severe and permanent (Crair, Gillespie, & Stryker, 1998). And the general quality of the early environment affects overall brain growth. When animals reared from birth in physically and socially stimulating surroundings are compared with those reared in isolation, the brains of the stimulated animals are larger and show much denser synaptic connections (Sale, Berardi, & Maffei, 2009).

Human Evidence: Victims of Deprived Early Environments   For ethical reasons, we cannot deliberately deprive some infants of normal rearing experiences and observe the impact on their brains and competencies. Instead, we must turn to natural experiments, in which children were victims of deprived early environments that were later rectified. Such studies have revealed some parallels with the animal evidence just described.

Biology and Environment | Brain Plasticity: Insights from Research on Children with Brain Injury

In the first few years of life, the brain is highly plastic. It can reorganize areas committed to specific functions in a way that the mature brain cannot. Adults who suffered focal brain injury (damage to a specific part of the brain) in infancy and early childhood show milder cognitive deficits than adults with similar, later-occurring injury (Huttenlocher, 2002). Nevertheless, the young brain is not totally plastic. When it is injured, its functioning is compromised.

Brain Plasticity in Infancy and Early Childhood

In a large study of children with focal injuries to the cerebral cortex that occurred around the time of birth or in the first six months of life, language and spatial skills were assessed repeatedly into adolescence (Stiles, Reilly, & Levine, 2012; Stiles et al., 2008, 2009). All the children had experienced early brain seizures or hemorrhages. fMRI and PET scans revealed the precise site of damage.

Regardless of whether injury occurred in the left or right cerebral hemisphere, the children showed delays in language development that persisted until about 3½ years of age. That damage to either hemisphere affected early language competence indicates that at first, language functioning is broadly distributed in the brain. But by age 5, the children caught up in vocabulary and grammatical skills. Undamaged areas—in either the left or the right hemisphere—had taken over these language functions.

Compared with language, spatial skills were more impaired after early brain injury. When preschool through adolescent-age youngsters were asked to copy designs, those with early right-hemispheric damage had trouble with holistic processing—accurately representing the overall shape. In contrast, children with left-hemispheric damage captured the basic shape but omitted fine-grained details. Nevertheless, the children improved with age in their drawing skills—gains that did not occur in individuals who experienced similar brain injuries in adulthood (Stiles, Reilly, & Levine, 2012; Stiles et al., 2008, 2009).

Clearly, recovery after early brain injury is greater for language than for spatial skills. Why is this so? Researchers speculate that spatial processing is the older of the two capacities in our evolutionary history and, therefore, more lateralized at birth (Forsyth, 2014). But early focal injury has far less impact than later injury on both language and spatial skills, revealing the young brain's plasticity.

The Price of High Plasticity in the Young Brain

Despite impressive recovery of language and (to a lesser extent) spatial skills, children with early brain injuries show deficits in a wide range of complex mental abilities during the school years. For example, their reading and math progress is slow. In telling stories, they produce simpler narratives than age-mates who had no early brain injuries. And as the demands of daily life increase, they have difficulty with self-regulation—managing homework and other responsibilities (Anderson, Spencer-Smith, & Wood, 2011; Stiles, Reilly, & Levine, 2012).

High brain plasticity, researchers explain, comes at a price. When healthy brain regions take over the functions of damaged areas, a "crowding effect" occurs: Multiple tasks must be done by a smaller-than-usual volume of brain tissue (Fiori & Guzzetta, 2015; Stiles, 2012). Consequently, the brain processes information less quickly and accurately than it would if it were intact. Complex mental abilities of all kinds suffer because performing them well requires the collaboration of many regions in the cerebral cortex. In sum, the full impact of an early brain injury may not be apparent for many years, until higher-order skills are expected to develop.

A System of Influences

In infancy and childhood, the goal of brain growth is to form neural connections that ensure mastery of essential skills. Animal research reveals that plasticity is greatest while the brain is forming many new synapses; it declines during synaptic pruning (Murphy & Corbett, 2009).

At the same time, for reasons not yet fully understood, some children who experienced

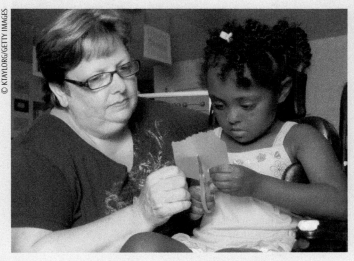

This preschooler, who experienced brain damage in infancy, has been spared massive impairments because of high plasticity of the brain. Here, a teacher encourages her to cut basic shapes to strengthen spatial skills, which remain more impaired than language after early brain injury.

focal brain injury in infancy or early childhood display lasting cognitive deficits (Anderson, Spencer-Smith, & Wood, 2011; Anderson et al., 2014). Accumulating evidence suggests that age combines with an array of other factors to affect extent of plasticity. These include the site of the injury, the severity of injury, and the availability of diverse environmental supports, including a stimulating home environment, warm parenting, access to intervention services, and high-quality schooling (Dennis et al., 2014).

At older ages, specialized brain structures are in place, but after focal injury the brain can still recover to some degree. When an individual practices relevant tasks, the brain strengthens existing synapses and generates new ones. Nevertheless, when brain injury is widespread, recovery for both children and adults is greatly reduced. And when damage occurs to certain regions—for example, the prefrontal cortex—recovery is also limited. Because of its executive role in thinking and widespread connections throughout the brain, prefrontal abilities are difficult to transfer to other cortical areas. Consequently, early prefrontal lesions typically result in persisting, general intellectual deficits (Pennington, 2015). Clearly, plasticity is a complex process that is not equivalent throughout the brain.

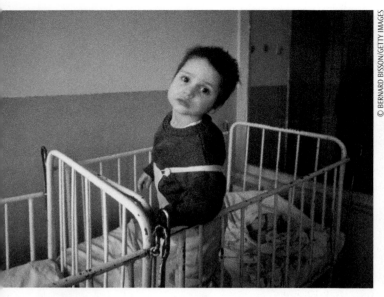

This Romanian orphan receives little adult contact or stimulation. The longer he remains in this barren environment, the greater his risk of brain damage and lasting impairments in all domains of development.

For example, when babies are born with cataracts in both eyes (clouded lenses, preventing clear visual images), those who have corrective surgery within 4 to 6 months show rapid improvement in vision, except for subtle aspects of face perception, which require early visual input to the right hemisphere to develop. The longer cataract surgery is postponed beyond infancy, the less complete the recovery in visual skills (Maurer & Lewis, 2013). If surgery is delayed until adulthood, vision is severely and permanently impaired.

Studies of infants placed in orphanages who were later exposed to family rearing confirm the importance of a generally stimulating environment for healthy psychological development. In one investigation, researchers followed the progress of a large sample of children transferred between birth and 3½ years from extremely deprived Romanian orphanages to adoptive families in Great Britain (Beckett et al., 2006; O'Connor et al., 2000; Rutter et al., 1998, 2004, 2010). On arrival, most were impaired in all domains of development. Cognitive catch-up was impressive for children adopted before 6 months, who consistently attained average mental test scores in childhood and adolescence, performing as well as a comparison group of early-adopted British-born children.

But Romanian children who had been institutionalized for more than the first six months showed substantial intellectual deficits (see Figure 5.7). Although they improved in intelligence test scores during middle childhood and adolescence, they remained well below average. And most displayed at least three serious mental health problems, such as inattention, overactivity, unruly behavior, and autistic-like symptoms (social disinterest, stereotyped behavior) (Kreppner et al., 2007, 2010).

Neurobiological findings indicate that early, prolonged institutionalization leads to a generalized decrease in volume and activity of the cerebral cortex—especially the prefrontal cortex, which governs complex cognition and impulse control. Neural fibers connecting the prefrontal cortex with other brain structures involved in control of emotion are also reduced (Hodel et al., 2015; McLaughlin et al., 2014; Perego, Caputi, & Ogliari, 2016). And activation of the left cerebral hemisphere, governing positive emotion, is diminished relative to right cerebral activation, governing negative emotion (McLaughlin et al., 2011).

Additional evidence confirms that the chronic stress of early, deprived orphanage rearing disrupts the brain's capacity to manage stress. In another investigation, researchers followed the development of children who had spent their first eight months or more in Romanian institutions and were then adopted into Canadian homes (Gunnar & Cheatham, 2003; Gunnar et al., 2001). Compared with agemates adopted shortly after birth, these children showed extreme stress reactivity, as indicated by high concentrations of the stress hormone *cortisol* in their saliva. The longer the children spent in orphanage care, the higher their cortisol levels—even 6½ years after adoption. In other research, orphanage children from diverse regions of the world who were adopted after 1 year of age by American families displayed abnormally low cortisol—a blunted physiological response that is also a sign of impaired capacity to manage stress (Koss et al., 2014; Loman & Gunnar, 2010). Persisting abnormally high or low cortisol levels are linked to later learning, emotional, and behavior problems, including both internalizing (fear and anxiety) and externalizing (anger and aggression) difficulties.

Finally, early deprived rearing may also disrupt the brain's typical response to pleasurable social experiences. After sitting on their

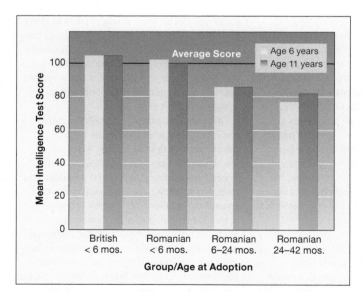

FIGURE 5.7   Relationship of age at adoption to mental test scores at ages 6 and 11 among British and Romanian adoptees. Children transferred from Romanian orphanages to British adoptive homes in the first six months of life attained average scores and fared as well as British early-adopted children, suggesting that they had fully recovered from extreme early deprivation. Romanian children adopted after 6 months of age performed well below average. Although those adopted after age 2 improved between ages 6 and 11, they continued to show serious intellectual deficits. (Adapted from Beckett et al., 2006.)

mother's lap and playing an enjoyable game, preschoolers adopted, on average, at age 1½ years from Romanian orphanages had abnormally low urine levels of *oxytocin*—a hormone released by the brain that evokes calmness and contentment in the presence of familiar, trusted people (Fries et al., 2005). And as we will see in Chapter 7, forming secure attachment relationships with their adoptive parents is more challenging for children who spent their infancy in neglectful institutions.

Appropriate Stimulation   Unlike the orphanage children just described, Grace, whom Monica and Kevin had adopted in Cambodia at 16 months of age, showed favorable progress. Two years earlier, they had adopted Grace's older brother, Eli. When Eli was 2 years old, Monica and Kevin sent a letter and a photo of Eli to his biological mother, describing a bright, happy child. The next day, the Cambodian mother tearfully asked an adoption agency to send her baby daughter to join Eli and his American family.

Although Grace's early environment was very impoverished, her biological mother's loving care—holding her gently, speaking softly, interacting playfully with her, and breastfeeding—likely prevented irreversible damage to her brain. Besides offering gentle, appropriate stimulation, sensitive adult care helps normalize cortisol production in both typically developing and emotionally traumatized infants and young children (Gunnar & Quevedo, 2007; Tarullo & Gunnar, 2006). Good parenting seems to protect the young brain from the potentially damaging effects of both excessive and inadequate stress-hormone exposure.

In the Bucharest Early Intervention Project, 136 institutionalized Romanian babies were randomized into conditions of either care as usual or transfer between 6 and 31 months of age to high-quality foster families. Specially trained social workers provided foster parents with counseling and support. Periodic follow-ups when the children were between 2½ and 12 years old revealed that the foster-care group exceeded the institutional-care group in intelligence test scores, language development, self-regulation skills, emotional responsiveness, social skills, EEG and ERP assessments of brain development, and adaptive cortisol levels. On nearly all measures, earlier entry into foster care predicted better outcomes (Almas et al., 2016; McLaughlin et al., 2015; Nelson, Fox, & Zeanah, 2014; Troller-Renfree et al., 2018). But consistent with an early sensitive period, the foster-care group remained behind never-institutionalized agemates living with Bucharest families.

In addition to impoverished environments, those that overwhelm children with expectations beyond their current capacities also interfere with the brain's potential. In recent years, expensive early learning centers as well as "educational" tablets and DVDs aimed at babies have become widespread. Within these contexts, infants are trained with letter and number flash cards and toddlers are given a full curriculum of reading, math, science, art, and more. There is no evidence that these programs yield smarter "super-babies" (Principe, 2011). To the contrary, trying to prime infants with stimulation for which they are not ready can cause them to withdraw, thereby threatening their interest in learning.

How, then, can we characterize appropriate stimulation during the early years? To answer this question, researchers distinguish between two types of brain development. The first, **experience-expectant brain growth,** refers to the young brain's rapidly developing organization, which depends on ordinary experiences—opportunities to explore the environment, interact with people, and hear language and other sounds. As a result of millions of years of evolution, the brains of all infants, toddlers, and young children *expect* to encounter these experiences and, if they do, grow normally. The second type of brain development, **experience-dependent brain growth,** occurs throughout our lives. It consists of additional growth and the refinement of established brain structures as a result of specific learning experiences that vary widely across individuals and cultures (Greenough & Black, 1992). Reading and writing, playing computer games, weaving an intricate rug, and practicing the violin are examples. The brain of a violinist differs in certain ways from the brain of a poet because each has exercised different brain regions for a long time.

Experience-expectant brain development occurs early and naturally as caregivers offer babies and preschoolers age-appropriate play materials and engage them in enjoyable daily routines—a shared meal, a game of peekaboo, a bath before bed, a picture book to talk about, or a song to sing. The resulting growth provides the foundation for later-occurring,

Experience-expectant brain growth depends on ordinary, stimulating experiences—like this infant's exploration of the textures of a fallen log and pebbly surface. It provides the foundation for experience-dependent brain growth—refinements due to culturally specific learning. But too much emphasis on training at an early age—for example, drill on mastering the ABCs—can interfere with access to everyday experiences the young brain needs to grow optimally.

experience-dependent development (Belsky & de Haan, 2011). No evidence exists for a sensitive period in the first few years of life for mastering skills that depend on extensive training, such as reading, musical performance, or gymnastics. To the contrary, rushing early learning harms the brain by overwhelming its neural circuits, thereby reducing the brain's sensitivity to the everyday experiences it needs for a healthy start in life.

5.2.5 Changing States of Arousal

Rapid brain growth means that the organization of sleep and wakefulness changes substantially between birth and 2 years, and fussiness and crying decline. The newborn baby takes round-the-clock naps that total about 16 to 18 hours. The average 2-year-old still needs 12 to 13 hours of sleep, but periods of sleep and wakefulness become fewer and longer, and the sleep–wake pattern increasingly conforms to a night–day schedule. Most 6- to 9-month-olds take two daytime naps; by about 18 months, children generally need only one nap (Galland et al., 2012). Between ages 3 and 5, napping subsides.

These changing arousal patterns are due to brain development, but they are also affected by cultural beliefs and practices and parents' needs. Dutch parents, for example, view sleep regularity as far more important than U.S. parents do. And whereas U.S. parents regard a predictable sleep schedule as emerging naturally from within the child, Dutch parents believe that a schedule must be imposed, or the baby's development might suffer (Super & Harkness, 2010; Super et al., 1996). At age 6 months, Dutch babies are put to bed earlier and sleep, on average, 2 hours more per day than their U.S. agemates. Furthermore, as the Cultural Influences box on the following page reveals, isolating infants and toddlers in a separate room for sleep is rare around the world.

Motivated by demanding work schedules and other needs, many Western parents try to get their babies to sleep through the night as early as 3 to 4 months by offering an evening feeding. But infants who receive more milk or solid foods during the day are not less likely to wake, though they feed less at night (Brown & Harries, 2015). However, babies just a few weeks old—though they typically wake every two hours—have some capacity to resettle on their own. When infants wake up and cry, parents who in the early weeks wait just a few minutes before initiating feeding, granting the baby an opportunity to settle and return to sleep, have infants who are more likely to sleep for longer nighttime periods at 3 months of age (St James-Roberts et al., 2015, 2017). Around 2 to 3 months, most Western infants begin sleeping 4 to 5 hours at a stretch.

LOOK and LISTEN

Interview a parent of a baby about sleep challenges. What strategies has the parent tried to ease these difficulties? Are the techniques likely to be effective, in view of evidence on infant sleep development?

Cultural Influences | Cultural Variation in Infant Sleeping Arrangements

A Vietnamese mother and child sleep together—a practice common in their culture and around the globe. Hard wooden sleeping surfaces protect cosleeping children from entrapment in soft bedding.

Western child-rearing advice from experts strongly encourages nighttime separation of baby from parent. For example, the most recent edition of Benjamin Spock's *Baby and Child Care* recommends that babies sleep in their own room by 3 months of age, explaining, "By 6 months, a child who regularly sleeps in her parents' room may feel uneasy sleeping anywhere else" (Spock & Needlman, 2011, p. 62). And the American Academy of Pediatrics (2016b) has issued a controversial warning that parent–infant bedsharing increases the risk of sudden infant death syndrome (SIDS) and accidental suffocation.

Yet parent–infant cosleeping—in the same room and often in the same bed—is the norm for approximately 90 percent of the world's population, in cultures as diverse as the Japanese, the rural Guatemalan Maya, the Inuit of northwestern Canada, and the !Kung of Botswana. Japanese and Korean children usually lie next to their mothers throughout infancy and early childhood (Shimizu, Park & Greenfield, 2014; Yang & Hahn, 2002). Bedsharing is also common in U.S. ethnic minority families (McKenna & Volpe, 2007). African-American children, for example, frequently fall asleep with their parents and remain with them for part or all of the night (Buswell & Spatz, 2007).

Cultural values strongly influence infant sleeping arrangements. In one study, researchers interviewed Guatemalan Mayan mothers and American middle-SES mothers about their sleeping practices. Mayan mothers stressed the importance of promoting an *interdependent self*, explaining that cosleeping builds a close parent–child bond, which is necessary for children to learn the ways of people around them. In contrast, American mothers emphasized an *independent self*, mentioning their desire to instill early autonomy, prevent bad habits, and protect their own privacy (Morelli et al., 1992).

Over the past several decades, cosleeping has increased in Western nations, including the United States. In a survey of a large, nationally representative sample of U.S. mothers, 20 percent reported routinely bedsharing with their infants (Smith et al., 2016). Parents who support the practice say that it helps their baby sleep, makes breastfeeding more convenient, reduces infant distress, and provides valuable bonding time (McKenna & Volpe, 2007; Tikotzky et al., 2010).

Babies who sleep with their parents breastfeed three times longer than infants who sleep alone (Huang et al., 2013). Because infants arouse to nurse more often when sleeping next to their mothers, some researchers believe that cosleeping may actually help safeguard babies at risk for SIDS. Consistent with this view, SIDS is rare in Asian nations where bedsharing is widespread, including Cambodia, China, Japan, Korea, Thailand, and Vietnam (McKenna, 2002; McKenna & McDade, 2005).

Critics warn that bedsharing will promote sleep and adjustment problems, especially excessive dependency. Yet in Western societies, bedsharing often emerges in response to children's sleep and emotional difficulties, rather than occurring as a consistent, intentional practice (Mileva-Seitz et al., 2017). A study following children from the end of pregnancy through age 18 years showed that young people who had bedshared in the early years were no different from others in any aspect of adjustment (Okami, Weisner, & Olmstead, 2002).

A more serious concern is that infants might become trapped under the parent's body or in soft bedding and suffocate. Parents who are obese or who use alcohol, tobacco, or illegal drugs do pose a serious risk to bedsharing babies, as does the use of quilts and comforters or an overly soft mattress (Carpenter et al., 2013).

But with appropriate precautions, parents and infants can cosleep safely (Ball & Volpe, 2013). In cultures where cosleeping is widespread, parents and infants usually sleep with light covering on hard surfaces, such as firm mattresses or wooden planks. Alternatively, babies sleep in a cradle or hammock next to the parents' bed.

To protect against SIDS and other sleep-related deaths, the American Academy of Pediatrics (2016b) recommends that parents roomshare but not bedshare for the first year, placing the baby within easy view and reach on a separate surface designed for infants. Currently, the majority of U.S. mothers of infants—65 percent—report usually roomsharing without bedsharing (Smith et al., 2016). However, some researchers point out that placing too much emphasis on separate sleeping may have risky consequences—for example, inducing tired parents to avoid feeding their babies in bed in favor of using dangerously soft sofas (Bartick & Smith, 2014).

In general, when discussing each infant's sleep environment with parents, pediatricians are wise to take into account cultural values and motivations (Ward, 2015). Then they can work within that framework to ensure the sleep environment is a safe one.

At the end of the first year, as REM sleep (the state that usually prompts waking) declines, infants approximate an adultlike sleep–wake schedule. But even after they sleep through the night, they continue to wake occasionally. In studies carried out in Australia, Israel, and the United States, night wakings increased around 6 months and again between 1½ and 2 years (Armstrong, Quinn, & Dadds, 1994; Scher, Epstein, & Tirosh, 2004; Scher et al., 1995). As Chapter 7 will reveal, around the middle of the first year, infants are forming a clear-cut attachment to their familiar caregiver and begin protesting when she or he leaves. And the

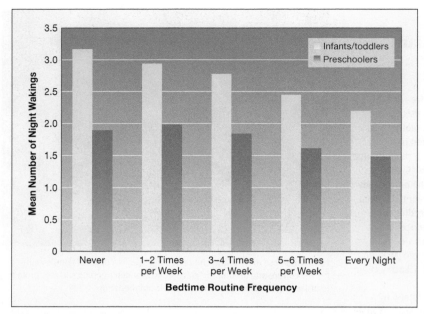

FIGURE 5.8   Relationship of bedtime routines to night-wakings in infancy/ toddlerhood and the preschool years. In a large sample of mothers in 13 Western and Asian nations, the more consistently they used bedtime routines, the less often their infants, toddlers, and preschoolers woke during the night. Findings were similar for ease of falling asleep and amount of nighttime sleep. (From J. A. Mindell, A. M. Li, A. Sadeh, R. Kwon, & D. Y. Goh, 2015, "Bedtime Routines for Young Children: A Dose-Dependent Association with Sleep Outcomes," *Sleep, 38,* p. 720. Copyright © 2015 by permission of the Associated Professional Sleep Societies, LLC. Reprinted by permission.)

challenges of toddlerhood—the ability to range farther from the caregiver and increased awareness of the self as separate from others—often prompt anxiety, evident in disturbed sleep and clinginess. In one study, young babies whose mothers were warm, sensitive, and available to them at bedtime slept more during the night (Philbrook & Teti, 2016). In turn, lower infant nighttime distress predicted greater maternal sensitivity in the following months.

Bedtime routines promote sleep as early as the first two years. In a study carried out in 13 Western and Asian nations, over 10,000 mothers reported on their bedtime practices and their newborn to 5-year-olds' sleep quality (Mindell et al., 2015). Consistently engaging in bedtime routines—for example, rocking and singing in infancy, storybook reading in toddlerhood and early childhood—was associated with falling asleep more readily, waking less often, and getting more nighttime sleep throughout the entire age range (see Figure 5.8).

As noted in Chapter 4 (page 137), restful sleep is vital for infants' learning and memory. For example, compared to 12-month-olds in a no-nap condition, those given an opportunity to nap imitated more adult actions with toys observed earlier that day (Konrad et al., 2016b). Similarly, 6-month-olds who slept well the previous night remembered more than those who woke often (Konrad et al., 2016a). In addition to supporting memory storage, sleep enhanced toddlers' ability to solve a novel problem: figuring out how to efficiently navigate a tunnel to reach a caregiver waiting at the other end (Berger & Scher, 2017).

◎ ASK YOURSELF

Connect ■ Explain how either too little or too much stimulation can impair cognitive and emotional development in the early years.

Apply ■ Which infant enrichment program would you choose: one that emphasizes gentle talking and touching and social games, or one that includes reading and number drills and classical music lessons? Explain.

Reflect ■ What is your attitude toward parent–infant cosleeping? Is it influenced by your cultural background? Explain.

5.3 Influences on Early Physical Growth

5.3 Cite evidence that heredity, nutrition, and parental affection all contribute to early physical growth.

Physical growth, like other aspects of development, results from a continuous and complex interplay between genetic and environmental factors. Good nutrition and relative freedom from disease are essential for young children's healthy development, while environmental pollutants are a threat. The Social Issues: Health box on the following page considers the extent to which one of the most common pollutants, lead, impairs children's brain growth and cognitive functioning and contributes to behavior problems.

Social Issues: Health | Lead Exposure and Children's Development

Lead is a highly toxic element that, at blood levels exceeding 60 µg/dL (micrograms per deciliter), causes brain swelling, hemorrhaging, disrupted functioning of neurons, and widespread cell death. Before 1980, exposure to lead resulted from use of lead-based paints in housing (infants and young children often ate paint flakes) and from use of leaded gasoline (producing a highly breathable form of lead in car exhaust). Laws limiting the lead content of paint and mandating lead-free gasoline led to a sharp decline in U.S. children's lead levels, from an average of 15 µg/dL in 1980 to less than 1 µg/dL today (Tsoi, Cheung, & Cheung, 2016).

Yet in areas near certain airports (because some aviation fuels still contain lead), near industries using lead production processes, or where lead-based paint remains in older homes, children's blood levels are still markedly elevated. Contaminated soil and imported consumer products, such as toys made of leaded plastic, are additional sources of exposure.

In the Flint, Michigan, water crisis of 2014 to 2015, the city began using a new water source without adding corrosion inhibitors, causing lead to leach from aging pipes and contaminate the city's drinking water. This resulted in blood levels of lead above 5 µg/dL—the level deemed high enough by the U.S. government to warrant immediate efforts to reduce exposure—in as many as 5 percent of the city's children (Hannah-Attisha et al., 2016).

Over the past quarter century, longitudinal studies of the consequences of lead have been conducted in multiple countries, including Australia, Mexico, New Zealand, the United Kingdom, and the United States. Each tracked children's lead exposure over an extended time and controlled for factors associated with both lead levels and mental test scores (such as SES, home environmental quality, and nutrition) that might otherwise account for the findings.

Nearly all investigations reported negative relationships between lead exposure and children's intelligence test scores (Canfield et al., 2003; Hubbs-Tait et al., 2005; Lanphear et al., 2005). Impaired cognitive functioning was evident at all levels of exposure— even small quantities. Some studies reported persisting effects into adulthood (Mazumdar et al., 2011; Reuben et al., 2017). Higher blood levels were also associated with distractibility, overactivity, weak academic performance, childhood behavior problems, and adolescent antisocial behavior (Needleman et al., 2002; Nevin, 2006; Stretesky & Lynch, 2004; Wright et al., 2008).

Furthermore, in several investigations, cognitive effects were much greater for low-SES than higher SES children (Bellinger, Leviton, & Sloman, 1990; Ris et al., 2004; Tong, McMichael, & Baghurst, 2000). A stressed, disorganized

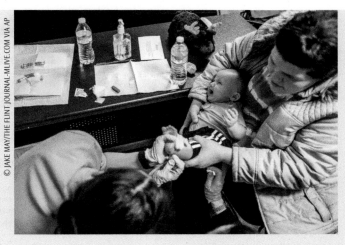

A public health worker pricks a 5-month-old's foot to collect blood as part of a program to monitor children's lead levels in Flint, Michigan. Even at low levels, exposure to lead can impair children's cognitive functioning and contribute to behavior problems.

home life seems to heighten lead-induced brain damage. Dietary factors can also magnify lead's toxic effects. Iron and zinc deficiencies, especially common in low-SES children, increase lead concentration in the blood (Noonan et al., 2003; Wolf, Jimenez, & Lozoff, 2003).

In sum, lead impairs mental development and contributes to behavior problems. Low-SES children are more likely to live in lead-contaminated areas and to experience additional risks that magnify lead-induced damage. Because lead is a stable element, its release into the environment is difficult to reverse. Therefore, in addition to laws that control lead pollution, interventions that reduce the negative impact of lead—through involved parenting, dietary enrichment, better schools, and public education about lead hazards—are vital.

5.3.1 Heredity

Because identical twins are much more alike in body size than fraternal twins, we know that heredity contributes considerably to physical growth (Dubois et al., 2012; Jelenkovic et al., 2016). When diet and health are adequate, height and rate of physical growth are largely governed by heredity. In fact, as long as negative environmental influences such as poor nutrition or illness are not severe, children and adolescents typically show *catch-up growth*—a return to a genetically determined growth path—once conditions improve. After her adoption, Grace grew rapidly until, at age 2, she was nearly average in size by Cambodian standards. Still, the health of the brain and many internal organs may be permanently compromised by malnutrition. (Recall the consequences of inadequate prenatal nutrition for long-term health, discussed on pages 107–108 in Chapter 3.)

Twin studies reveal that genetic makeup also affects body weight (Elks et al., 2012; Kinnunen, Pietilainen, & Rissanen, 2006; Liu et al., 2015). At the same time, environment— in particular, nutrition—plays an especially important role.

APPLYING WHAT WE KNOW

Reasons to Breastfeed

NUTRITIONAL AND HEALTH ADVANTAGES	EXPLANATION
Provides the correct balance of fat and protein	Compared with the milk of other mammals, human milk is higher in fat and lower in protein. This balance, as well as the unique proteins and fats contained in human milk, is ideal for a rapidly myelinating nervous system.
Ensures nutritional completeness	A mother who breastfeeds need not add other foods to her infant's diet until the baby is 6 months old. The milks of all mammals are low in iron, but the iron contained in breast milk is much more easily absorbed by the baby's system. Consequently, bottle-fed infants need iron-fortified formula.
Helps ensure healthy physical growth	One-year-old breastfed babies are leaner (have a higher percentage of muscle to fat), a growth pattern that persists through the preschool years and that is associated with a reduction in later overweight and obesity.
Protects against many diseases	Breastfeeding transfers antibodies and other infection-fighting agents from mother to baby and enhances functioning of the immune system. Compared with bottle-fed infants, breastfed babies have far fewer allergic reactions and respiratory and intestinal illnesses. Breast milk also has anti-inflammatory effects, which reduce the severity of illness symptoms. Breastfeeding in the first four months (especially when exclusive) is linked to lower blood cholesterol levels in adulthood and, thereby, may help prevent cardiovascular disease.
Protects against faulty jaw development and tooth decay	Sucking the mother's nipple instead of an artificial nipple helps avoid malocclusion, a condition in which the upper and lower jaws do not meet properly. It also protects against tooth decay due to sweet liquid remaining in the mouths of infants who fall asleep while sucking on a bottle.
Ensures digestibility	Because breastfed babies have a different kind of bacteria growing in their intestines than do bottle-fed infants, they rarely suffer from constipation or other gastrointestinal problems.
Smooths the transition to solid foods	Breastfed infants accept new solid foods more easily than do formula-fed infants, perhaps because of their greater experience with a variety of flavors, which pass from the maternal diet into the mother's milk.

Sources: American Academy of Pediatrics, 2012; Druet et al., 2012; Owen et al., 2008; Peres et al., 2015; UNICEF, 2017a.

5.3.2 Nutrition

Nutrition is especially crucial for development in the first two years because the baby's brain and body are growing so rapidly. Pound for pound, an infant's energy needs are at least twice those of an adult. Twenty-five percent of infants' total caloric intake is devoted to growth, and babies need extra calories to keep rapidly developing organs functioning properly (Meyer, 2009).

Breastfeeding Versus Formula-Feeding   Babies need both enough food and the right kind of food. In early infancy, breast milk is ideally suited to their needs, and bottled formulas try to imitate it. Applying What We Know above summarizes major nutritional and health advantages of breastfeeding.

Because of these benefits, breastfed babies in poverty-stricken regions of the world are much less likely to be malnourished and 6 to 14 times more likely to survive the first year of life. The World Health Organization recommends breastfeeding until age 2 years, with solid foods added at 6 months. These practices, if widely followed, would save the lives of more than 800,000 infants annually (World Health Organization, 2017d). Even breastfeeding for just a few weeks offers some protection against respiratory and intestinal infections, which are devastating to young children in developing countries. Also, because a nursing mother is less likely to get pregnant, breastfeeding helps increase spacing among siblings, a major factor in reducing infant and childhood deaths in nations with widespread poverty. (Note, however, that breastfeeding is not a reliable method of birth control.)

Yet many mothers in the developing world do not know about these benefits. In Africa, the Middle East, and Latin America, most babies get some breastfeeding, but fewer than 40 percent are exclusively breastfed for the first six months, and one-third are fully weaned from the breast before 1 year (UNICEF, 2017a). In place of breast milk, mothers give their babies commercial formula or low-grade nutrients, such as rice water or highly diluted cow or goat milk. Contamination of these foods as a result of poor sanitation is common and often leads to illness and infant death. The United Nations has encouraged all hospitals and maternity units in developing countries to promote breastfeeding as long as mothers do not have viral or bacterial infections (such as HIV or tuberculosis) that can be transmitted to the baby. Today, most developing countries have banned the practice of giving free or subsidized formula to new mothers.

Partly as a result of the natural childbirth movement, breastfeeding has become more common in industrialized nations, especially among well-educated women. Today, 83 percent of American mothers begin breastfeeding after birth, but nearly one-third stop by 6 months. And despite the health benefits of breast milk, only 50 percent of preterm infants are breastfed at hospital discharge (Centers for Disease Control and Prevention, 2018a). Breastfeeding a preterm baby presents special challenges, including maintaining a sufficient milk supply with artificial pumping until the baby is mature enough to suck at the breast and providing the infant with enough sucking experience to learn to feed successfully. Kangaroo care (see page 129 in Chapter 4) and the support of health professionals are helpful.

Mothers breastfeeding their infants at a health clinic in Senegal offer one another support. Breastfeeding is especially important in developing countries, where it helps protect babies against life-threatening infections and early death.

Breast milk is so easily digestible that a breastfed infant becomes hungry quite often—every 1½ to 2 hours, compared to every 3 or 4 hours for a bottle-fed baby. This makes breastfeeding inconvenient for many employed women. Not surprisingly, mothers who return to work sooner wean their babies from the breast earlier. But mothers who cannot be with their babies all the time can still breastfeed, and they are more likely to do so if their workplace provides supports, such as private places for breastfeeding and onsite or nearby child care (Smith & Forrester, 2013; Spitzmueller et al., 2016). The U.S. Department of Health and Human Services (2014a) advises exclusive breastfeeding for the first 6 months and inclusion of breast milk in the baby's diet until at least 1 year.

Women who do not breastfeed sometimes worry that they are depriving their baby of an experience essential for healthy psychological development. Yet breastfed and bottle-fed infants in industrialized nations do not differ in quality of the mother–infant relationship or in later emotional adjustment (Jansen, de Weerth, & Riksen-Walraven, 2008; Lind et al., 2014). A growing number of studies report a slight advantage in intelligence test scores for children and adolescents who were breastfed, after controlling for maternal intelligence, SES, and other factors (Bernard et al., 2017; Horta, Loret de Mola, & Victoria, 2015; Luby et al., 2016). Other studies, however, find no cognitive benefits (Walfisch et al., 2013).

Are Chubby Babies at Risk for Later Overweight and Obesity?

From early infancy, Timmy was an enthusiastic eater who nursed vigorously and gained weight quickly. By 5 months, he began reaching for food on his parents' plates. Vanessa wondered: Was she overfeeding Timmy and increasing his chances of long-term overweight?

Most chubby babies thin out during toddlerhood and early childhood, as weight gain slows and they become more active. But recent evidence does indicate a strengthening relationship between rapid weight gain in infancy and later obesity (Nanri et al., 2017). The trend may be due to the rise in overweight adults, who engage in unhealthy feeding practices in the first year. Their babies, some of whom may be genetically prone to overeat, establish an early pattern of excessive unhealthy food consumption that persists (Llewellyn & Wardle, 2015). Interviews with large, nationally representative samples of U.S. parents revealed that many routinely served their older infants and toddlers French fries, pizza, candy, sugary fruit drinks, and soda (Miles & Siega-Riz, 2017; Siega-Riz et al., 2010). As many as one-fourth ate no fruits or vegetables.

How can parents prevent their infants from becoming overweight children and adults? One way is to breastfeed for the first six months, which is associated with slower early weight gain and 10 to 20 percent reduced obesity risk in later life (Koletzko et al., 2013). Another strategy is for parents to avoid giving babies foods loaded with sugar, salt, and saturated fats.

LOOK and LISTEN

Ask several parents of 1- to 2-year-olds to keep a diary of all the foods and drinks they offer their toddler over a weekend. How healthy are the toddlers' diets? Did any of the parents report heightened awareness of family nutrition as a result of the diary exercise?

A WIC counselor meets with breastfeeding mothers to provide nutrition education and enhanced food packages—incentives that have nearly doubled the incidence of breastfeeding among low-income mothers.

Public policies directed at low-income families, where breastfeeding rates are lowest and unhealthy feeding practices are highest, are a vital child health measure. The U.S. Special Supplemental Nutrition Program for Women, Infants and Children (WIC) provides nutrition education and food to low-income mothers and their children from birth to age 5. New mothers who opt to breastfeed receive enhanced food packages with a greater variety of healthy foods for themselves during their baby's first year—a policy that has nearly doubled the incidence of breastfeeding among low-income women (Whaley et al., 2012).

Finally, once toddlers learn to walk, climb, and run, parents can provide plenty of opportunities for energetic play. And as Chapter 11 will reveal, because excessive television viewing is linked to lack of exercise, unhealthy eating, and overweight in older children, parents should begin limiting time devoted to TV and other screen media in the first two years.

5.3.3 Malnutrition

In developing countries and war-torn areas where food resources are limited, malnutrition is widespread. Malnutrition contributes to nearly half of worldwide infant and early childhood deaths—about 2.6 million children annually. It is also responsible for growth stunting of nearly one-fifth of the world's children under age 5 (UNICEF, 2018). The 8 percent who are severely affected suffer from two dietary diseases, marasmus and kwashiorkor.

Marasmus is a wasted condition of the body caused by a diet low in all essential nutrients. It usually appears in the first year of life when a baby's mother is too malnourished to produce enough breast milk and bottle-feeding is also inadequate. Her starving baby becomes painfully thin and is in danger of dying.

Kwashiorkor is caused by an unbalanced diet very low in protein. The disease usually strikes after weaning, between 1 and 3 years of age. It is common in regions where children get just enough calories from starchy foods but little protein. The child's body responds by breaking down its own protein reserves, which causes hair loss, skin rash, swelling of the abdomen, ankles, and feet due to fluid retention, and irritable, listless behavior.

Children who survive these extreme forms of malnutrition often grow to be smaller in all body dimensions and suffer from lasting damage to the brain, heart, liver, pancreas, and other organs (Müller & Krawinkel, 2005; Spoelstra et al., 2012). When their diets do improve, they tend to gain excessive weight (Black et al., 2013). A malnourished body protects itself by establishing a low basal metabolism rate, which may endure after nutrition improves. Also,

The baby on the left, of Niger, Africa, has marasmus, a wasted condition caused by a diet low in all essential nutrients. The swollen abdomen of the toddler on the right, also from Niger, is a symptom of kwashiorkor, which results from a diet very low in protein. If these children survive, they are likely to suffer stunted growth and lasting organ damage as well as serious cognitive and emotional impairments.

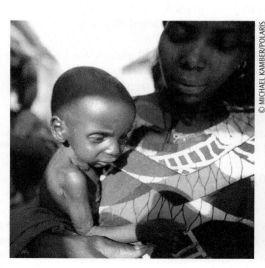

malnutrition may disrupt appetite control centers in the brain, causing the child to overeat when food becomes plentiful.

Children who experienced marasmus or kwashiorkor show poor fine-motor coordination, have difficulty paying attention, often display conduct problems, and show persisting low scores on intelligence tests (Galler et al., 2012; Venables & Raine, 2016; Waber et al., 2014). In one study, these dietary diseases were associated with increased methylation of many genes involved in brain development—epigenetic changes that predicted cognitive impairments decades later, in mature adulthood (Peter et al., 2016).

The passivity and irritability of malnourished children worsen the impact of poor diet. These behaviors may appear even when protein–calorie deprivation is only mild to moderate. They also accompany *iron-deficiency anemia,* a condition affecting up to half of children younger than age 5 worldwide that interferes with many central nervous system processes (Wang, 2016). Withdrawal and listlessness reduce the nutritionally deprived child's ability to pay attention, explore, and evoke sensitive caregiving from parents, whose lives are already disrupted by poverty and stressful living conditions (Corapci, Radan, & Lozoff, 2006). These children score lower than their nonanemic counterparts in intellectual development, with iron supplementation alone failing to correct the difference (Lukowski et al., 2010). For this reason, interventions for malnourished children must improve the family situation as well as the child's diet.

Inadequate nutrition is not confined to developing countries. Because government-supported supplementary food programs do not reach all families in need, an estimated 16 percent of U.S. children suffer from *food insecurity*—uncertain access to enough food for a healthy, active life. Food insecurity is especially high among single-mother families (30 percent) and low-income ethnic minority families—for example, Hispanic and African American (18 and 21 percent, respectively) (Coleman-Jensen, et al., 2018). Although few of these children have marasmus or kwashiorkor, their physical growth and ability to learn are still affected.

5.3.4 Emotional Well-Being

We may not think of affection as necessary for healthy physical growth, but it is as vital as food. **Weight faltering** is a term applied to infants and young children whose weight (but not height) is substantially below age-related growth norms and who are withdrawn and apathetic. Although the immediate cause is usually inadequate caloric intake, contributing factors are generally complex. As many as half of such cases involve a disturbed parent–child relationship. Nearly 10 percent of U.S. infants and young children are affected (Black, 2005; Homan, 2016). If undernutrition is allowed to continue, it soon impairs overall growth, including height and head circumference.

Lana, an observant nurse at a public health clinic, became concerned about 8-month-old Melanie, who was 3 pounds lighter than she had been at her last checkup. Lana noted that Melanie kept her eyes on nearby adults, anxiously watching their every move, and rarely smiled at her mother. During feeding and diaper changing, Melanie's mother sometimes appeared depressed and distant, at other times impatient and hostile. Melanie tried to protect herself by tracking her mother's whereabouts and, when she approached, avoiding her gaze.

Often intense parental stressors, such as an unhappy marriage, financial strain, or lack of social support; parental psychological disturbance; or poor parenting skills contribute to weight faltering. Most of the time, affected infants and young children are irritable and display abnormal feeding behaviors, such as poor sucking or vomiting, that both interfere with weight gain and lead parents to feel anxious and helpless, which stress the parent–child relationship further (Batchelor, 2008).

In Melanie's case, her alcoholic father was out of work, and her parents argued constantly. Melanie's mother had little energy to meet Melanie's psychological needs. When treated early, by intervening in feeding problems, helping parents with life challenges, and encouraging sensitive caregiving, children show quick catch-up growth. But if the disorder is not corrected promptly, most remain small and show lasting cognitive and emotional difficulties (Crookston et al., 2013; Shields, Wacogne, & Wright, 2012).

ASK YOURSELF

Connect ■ Explain why breastfeeding can have lifelong, favorable consequences for the development of infants in poverty-stricken regions of the world.

Apply ■ Eight-month-old Shaun is well below average in height and painfully thin. What serious dietary disease does he likely have, and what types of intervention, in addition to dietary enrichment, can help restore his development?

Reflect ■ Imagine that you are the parent of a newborn baby. Describe feeding and other practices you would use in the first two years, and ones you would avoid, to prevent overweight and obesity.

5.4 Learning Capacities

5.4 Discuss infant learning capacities, the conditions under which they occur, and the unique value of each.

Learning refers to changes in behavior as the result of experience. Babies come into the world with built-in learning capacities that permit them to profit from experience immediately. Infants are capable of two basic forms of learning, which we introduced in Chapter 1: classical and operant conditioning. They also learn through their natural preference for novel stimulation. And they have an amazing capacity to learn by analyzing streams of perceptual information for consistent patterns. Finally, shortly after birth, babies appear to learn by observing and imitating the facial expressions and gestures of adults. As we will see, however, newborns' imitative capacity is hotly debated.

5.4.1 Classical Conditioning

Newborn reflexes, discussed in Chapter 4, make **classical conditioning** possible in the young infant. In this form of learning, a neutral stimulus is paired with a stimulus that leads to a reflexive response. Once the baby's nervous system makes the connection between the two stimuli, the neutral stimulus produces the behavior by itself. Classical conditioning helps infants recognize which events usually occur together in the everyday world, so they can anticipate what is about to happen next. As a result, the environment becomes more orderly and predictable. Let's take a closer look at the steps of classical conditioning.

As Carolyn settled down in the rocking chair to nurse Caitlin, she often stroked Caitlin's forehead. Soon Carolyn noticed that each time she did this, Caitlin made active sucking movements. Caitlin had been classically conditioned. Figure 5.9 shows how it happened:

1. Before learning takes place, an **unconditioned stimulus (UCS)** must consistently produce a *reflexive,* or **unconditioned, response (UCR).** In Caitlin's case, sweet breast milk (UCS) resulted in sucking (UCR).
2. To produce learning, a *neutral stimulus* that does not lead to the reflex is presented just before, or at about the same time as, the UCS. Carolyn stroked Caitlin's forehead as each nursing period began. The stroking (neutral stimulus) was paired with the taste of milk (UCS).
3. If learning has occurred, the neutral stimulus by itself produces a response similar to the reflexive response. The neutral stimulus is then called a **conditioned stimulus (CS),** and the response it elicits is called a **conditioned response (CR).** We know that Caitlin has been classically conditioned because stroking her forehead outside the feeding situation (CS) results in sucking (CR).

If the CS is presented alone enough times, without being paired with the UCS, the CR will no longer occur, an outcome called extinction. In other words, if Carolyn repeatedly strokes Caitlin's forehead without feeding her, Caitlin will gradually stop sucking in response to stroking.

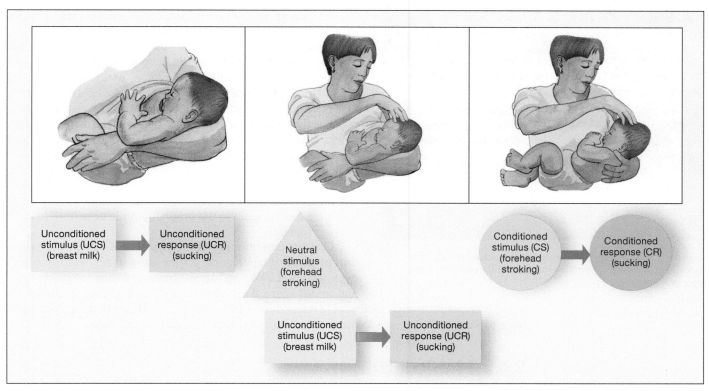

FIGURE 5.9   The steps of classical conditioning. This example shows how a mother classically conditioned her baby to make sucking movements by stroking the baby's forehead at the beginning of feedings.

Young infants can be classically conditioned most easily when the association between two stimuli has survival value. In the example just described, learning which stimuli regularly accompany feeding improves the infant's ability to get food and survive (Blass, Ganchrow, & Steiner, 1984).

In contrast, some responses, such as fear, are very difficult to classically condition in young babies. Until infants have the motor skills to escape unpleasant events, they have no biological need to form these associations. After age 6 months, however, fear is easy to condition. Return to page 17 in Chapter 1 to review John Watson's well-known experiment in which he conditioned Little Albert to withdraw and cry at the sight of a furry white rat. Then test your knowledge of classical conditioning by identifying the UCS, UCR, CS, and CR in Watson's study.

5.4.2 Operant Conditioning

In classical conditioning, babies build expectations about stimulus events in the environment, but they do not influence the stimuli that occur. In **operant conditioning,** infants act, or *operate,* on the environment, and stimuli that follow their behavior change the probability that the behavior will occur again. A stimulus that increases the occurrence of a response is called a **reinforcer.** For example, sweet liquid *reinforces* the sucking response in young infants. Removing a desirable stimulus or presenting an unpleasant one to decrease the occurrence of a response is called **punishment.** A sour-tasting fluid *punishes* the sucking response, causing babies to purse their lips and stop sucking entirely.

Many stimuli besides food can serve as reinforcers of infant behavior. For example, newborns will suck faster on a nipple when their rate of sucking produces interesting sights and sounds, including visual designs, music, or human voices (Floccia, Christophe, & Bertoncini, 1997). As these findings suggest, operant conditioning is a powerful tool for finding out what stimuli babies can perceive and which ones they prefer.

As this baby and a teenage brother imitate each other's facial expressions and bubbling sounds, the behavior of each reinforces that of the other, sustaining their pleasurable interaction.

As infants' motor control improves, operant conditioning expands to include a wider range of behaviors and stimuli. For example, researchers have hung special mobiles over the cribs of 2- to 6-month-olds. When the baby's foot is attached to the mobile with a long cord, the infant can, by kicking, make the mobile move. Under these conditions, it takes only a few minutes for infants to start kicking more forcefully and quickly to produce the reinforcing sights and sounds of the dancing mobile (Merz et al., 2017; Rovee-Collier & Barr, 2001). As Chapter 6 will reveal, operant conditioning with mobiles is frequently used to study young infants' memory and their ability to group similar stimuli into categories. Once babies learn the kicking response, researchers see how long and under what conditions they retain it when exposed again to the original mobile or to mobiles with varying features.

Operant conditioning also plays a vital role in the formation of social relationships. As the baby gazes into the adult's eyes, the adult looks and smiles back, and then the infant looks and smiles again. As the behavior of each partner reinforces the other, both continue their pleasurable interaction. In Chapter 7, we will see that this contingent responsiveness contributes to the development of infant–caregiver attachment.

5.4.3 Habituation

At birth, the human brain is set up to be attracted to novelty. Infants tend to respond more strongly to a new element that has entered their environment, an inclination that ensures that they will continually add to their knowledge base. **Habituation** refers to a gradual reduction in the strength of a response due to repetitive stimulation. Time spent looking at the stimulus, heart rate, respiration rate, and brain activity may all decline, indicating a loss of interest. Once this has occurred, a new stimulus—a change in the environment—causes responsiveness to return to a high level, an increase called **recovery.** For example, when you walk through a familiar space, you notice things that are new and different—a recently hung picture on the wall or a piece of furniture that has been moved. Habituation and recovery make learning more efficient by focusing our attention on those aspects of the environment we know least about.

Researchers investigating infants' understanding of the world rely on habituation and recovery more than any other learning capacity. For example, a baby who first *habituates* to a visual pattern (a photo of a baby) and then *recovers* to a new one (a photo of a bald man) appears to remember the first stimulus and perceive the second one as new and different from it. This method of studying infant perception and cognition, illustrated in Figure 5.10, can be used with newborns, including preterm infants (Kavšek & Bornstein, 2010). It has even been used to study the fetus's sensitivity to external stimuli in the third trimester of pregnancy—for example, by measuring changes in fetal heart rate or brain waves when various repeated sounds are presented, followed by a different sound (see page 96 in Chapter 3).

Recovery to a new stimulus, or *novelty preference,* assesses infants' *recent memory.* Think about what happens when you return to a place you have not seen for a long time. Instead of attending to novelty, you are likely to focus on aspects that are familiar: "I recognize that— I've been here before!" Like adults, infants shift from a novelty preference to a *familiarity preference* as more time intervenes between habituation and test phases in research. That is, babies recover to the familiar stimulus rather than to a novel stimulus (see Figure 5.10) (Colombo, Brez, & Curtindale, 2013; Flom & Bahrick, 2010). By focusing on that shift, researchers can also use habituation to assess *remote memory,* or memory for stimuli to which infants were exposed weeks or months earlier.

With age, babies habituate and recover to stimuli more quickly, indicating that they process information more efficiently (Kavšek & Bornstein, 2010). As the next section on statistical learning, along with our later discussion of perceptual development will illustrate, habituation and recovery have been used to assess a wide range of infant perceptual and cognitive

FIGURE 5.10 **Using habituation to study infant perception and cognition.** In the habituation phase, infants view a photo of a baby until their looking declines. In the test phase, infants are again shown the baby photo, but this time it appears alongside a photo of a bald-headed man. (a) When the test phase occurs soon after the habituation phase (within minutes, hours, or days, depending on the age of the infants), participants who remember the baby face and distinguish it from the man's face show a *novelty preference;* they recover to (spend more time looking at) the new stimulus. (b) When the test phase is delayed for weeks or months, infants who continue to remember the baby face shift to a *familiarity preference;* they recover to the familiar baby face rather than to the novel man's face.

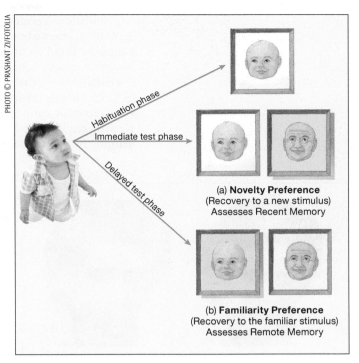

PHOTO © PRASHANT ZI/FOTOLIA

Habituation phase

Immediate test phase

Delayed test phase

(a) Novelty Preference
(Recovery to a new stimulus)
Assesses Recent Memory

(b) Familiarity Preference
(Recovery to the familiar stimulus)
Assesses Remote Memory

capacities, including speech perception, musical and visual pattern perception, and object perception. But despite the strengths of habituation research, its findings are not clear-cut. When looking, sucking, heart rate, or brain activity declines and recovers, what babies consciously know about the stimuli to which they responded is not always clear. We will return to this difficulty in Chapter 6.

5.4.4 Statistical Learning

Infants are continuously exposed to rich, temporal streams of auditory and visual information as their caregivers speak, sing, and play music and as they view their surroundings. A wealth of research verifies that infants engage in **statistical learning,** readily detecting the fundamental structure of this complex flow of information by extracting frequently occurring patterns and doing so fairly automatically, without feedback from others.

Most studies of infants' statistical learning have focused on the speech stream (Saffran, 2017). On average, babies say their first words around age 12 months, so by the end of the first year they must have determined from the flow of speech spoken by their caregivers where one word ends and the next word begins. In an early study, researchers exposed 8-month-olds to an unfamiliar artificial language consisting of sequences of three syllables that always occur together and, thus, form words—for example, *pa-bi-ku go-la-tu.* At the same time, the language included syllables that less often occur together because they span word boundaries— in the previous word sequence, *ku go-la* (Saffran, Aslin, & Newport, 1996). When tested, infants' patterns of attention revealed a clear ability to isolate the perfectly predictable three-syllable words from the statistically less consistent syllable sequences. The infants did so after just a minute or two of exposure to a language they had never heard before.

Infants engage in similar statistical learning when presented with sequences of musical tones and visual shapes (Dawson & Gerken, 2009; Johnson et al., 2009). For example, 9-month-olds prefer to look at pairs of shapes that previously occurred together consistently, rather than pairs of shapes that did not co-occur consistently (Fiser & Aslin, 2002). Furthermore, statistical learning is not limited to temporal streams of information. Infants also use it with visual stimuli in spatial arrangements that are presented to them all at once (Wu et al., 2011).

Even newborns are capable of statistical learning from speech and visual information (Bulf, Johnson, & Valenza, 2011; Teinonen et al., 2009). Statistical learning from speech is also evident in other species, such as rats, who will never acquire language (Toro & Trobalon, 2005). These findings suggest that statistical learning is a built-in, broadly applied capacity that is functional at birth and that operates across sensory modalities, time and space, and species.

© ELLEN B. SENISI

As a mother sings to her 11-month-old, the baby uses her capacity for statistical learning to detect melodic and rhythmic regularities in the tune. Statistical learning appears to be a built-in, powerful means of learning that operates across sensory modalities.

Statistical learning helps explain the speed with which infants sift through the immense quantity of stimulation they encounter daily, extracting regularities that they then use to acquire language, build an organized visual world, and solve other tasks (Aslin, 2017). Although a powerful capacity, statistical learning must also be constrained, or young learners would be overwhelmed by the vast number of statistical patterns in their surroundings and retain few of them. Infants do some of this limiting themselves: Research shows that they are biased to attend to information that is neither too simple nor too complex (Kidd et al., 2012). Also, as we will see in this and later chapters, caregivers provide much support for infant statistical learning by appropriately adjusting the complexity of stimulation to which infants are exposed.

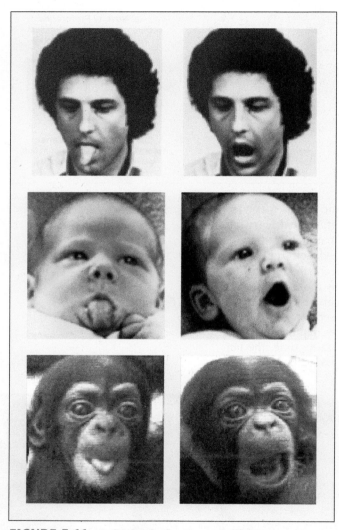

FIGURE 5.11 Imitation by human and chimpanzee newborns. The human infants in the middle row imitating (left) tongue protrusion and (right) mouth opening are 2 to 3 weeks old. The chimpanzee imitating both facial expressions is 2 weeks old. (From A. N. Meltzoff & M. K. Moore, 1977, "Imitation of Facial and Manual Gestures by Human Neonates," *Science, 198,* p. 75. Copyright © 1977 by AAAS. Reprinted by permission of the American Association for the Advancement of Science conveyed through Copyright Clearance Center, Inc., and Dr. Andrew Meltzoff. And from M. Myowa-Yamakoshi et al., 2004, "Imitation in Neonatal Chimpanzees [Pan Troglodytes]." *Developmental Science, 7,* p. 440. Copyright © 2004 by John Wiley and Sons. Reprinted with permission of John Wiley and Sons conveyed through Copyright Clearance Center, Inc.)

5.4.5 Imitation

Babies seem to come into the world with a primitive ability to learn through **imitation**—by copying the behavior of another person. For example, Figure 5.11 shows a human newborn imitating two adult facial expressions (Meltzoff & Moore, 1977). Newborn imitation extends to certain gestures, such as head and index-finger movements, and has been demonstrated in many ethnic groups and cultures (Meltzoff & Kuhl, 1994; Nagy, Pal, & Orvos, 2014). As the figure reveals, even newborn primates, including chimpanzees (our closest evolutionary relatives), imitate some behaviors (Ferrari et al., 2006; Myowa-Yamakoshi et al., 2004; Paukner et al., 2014).

Nevertheless, some studies have failed to reproduce the human findings (see, for example, Anisfeld, 2005). And because newborn mouth and tongue movements occur with increased frequency to almost any arousing change in stimulation (such as lively music or flashing lights), some researchers argue that certain newborn "imitative" responses are actually mouthing—a common early exploratory response to interesting stimuli (Jones, 2009). Furthermore, imitation is harder to induce in babies 2 to 3 months old than just after birth. Therefore, skeptics believe that newborns' apparent imitative behaviors are no more than automatic responses to arousing stimuli (such as adult faces) that decline with age, much like reflexes (Keven & Aikins, 2017).

Others claim that newborns imitate a variety of facial expressions and head movements with effort and determination, even after short delays—when the adult is no longer demonstrating the behavior (Meltzoff, 2017; Meltzoff & Williamson, 2013; Paukner, Ferrari, & Suomi, 2011). Furthermore, these investigators argue that imitation—unlike reflexes—does not decline. Rather, they claim, human babies several months old often do not imitate an adult's behavior right away because they first try to play familiar social games—mutual gazing, cooing, smiling, and waving their arms. But when an adult models a gesture repeatedly, older human infants soon get down to business and imitate (Meltzoff & Moore, 1994). Similarly, imitation declines in baby chimps around 9 weeks of age, when mother–baby mutual gazing and other face-to-face exchanges increase.

According to Andrew Meltzoff, newborns imitate much as older children and adults do—by actively trying to match body movements they *see* with ones they *feel* themselves make. With successive tries, they imitate a modeled gesture with greater accuracy (Meltzoff & Williamson, 2013; Nagy, Pal, & Orvos, 2014). Later we will encounter evidence that young babies are remarkably adept at coordinating information across sensory systems.

Scientists have identified specialized cells in motor areas of the cerebral cortex in primates—called **mirror neurons**—that may underlie early imitation. Mirror neurons fire identically when a primate hears or sees an action and when it carries out that action on its own (Ferrari & Coudé, 2011). Humans have especially elaborate neural mirroring systems, which are believed to be the biological basis of a variety of interrelated, complex social abilities, including imitation, empathic sharing of emotions, and understanding others' intentions (Simpson et al., 2014). A growing number of studies report that infants age 6 months and older and adults show a similar, unique change in a particular EEG brain-wave pattern when observing a model perform an action and when engaging in the action themselves (Marshall & Meltzoff, 2014). The consistency of these findings suggests a functioning neural mirroring system in the first year of life.

Still, Meltzoff's view of newborn imitation as a flexible, voluntary capacity remains highly controversial. Some critics staunchly contend that newborns cannot imitate, arguing that that only gradually do babies learn to engage in imitation through rich social experiences (Jones, 2017; Ray & Heyes, 2011). Others who believe that newborns have some ability to imitate use simpler accounts to explain it, such as a natural tendency for newborn perceptions to elicit corresponding actions (Vincini et al., 2017). These investigators agree that months of opportunities to watch others' responses, to see oneself act, and to engage in imitative games with caregivers are required for infants to become proficient imitators. Consistent with this view, the human neural mirroring system, though possibly functional at birth, undergoes an extended period of development (Ferrari et al., 2013). And as we will see in Chapter 6, the capacity to imitate expands greatly over the first two years.

However limited it is at birth, imitation is a powerful means of learning. Using imitation, infants explore their social world, learning from other people. As they notice similarities between their own actions and those of others, they experience other people as "like me" and learn about themselves (Meltzoff, 2017). By tapping into infants' ability to imitate, adults can get infants to exhibit desirable behaviors. Finally, caregivers take great pleasure in a baby who participates in imitative exchanges, which strengthen the parent–infant bond.

ASK YOURSELF

Connect ▪ Which learning capacities contribute to an infant's first social relationships? Explain, providing examples.

Apply ▪ Nine-month-old Byron has a toy with large, colored push buttons on it. Each time he pushes a button, he hears a nursery tune. Which learning capacity is the manufacturer of this toy taking advantage of? What can Byron's play with the toy reveal about his perception of sound patterns?

5.5 Motor Development

Carolyn, Monica, and Vanessa each kept a baby book, filled with proud notations about when their children held up their heads, reached for objects, sat by themselves, and walked alone. Parents are understandably excited about these new motor skills, which allow babies to master their bodies and the environment in new ways. For example, reaching permits babies to find out about objects by acting on them. Sitting and standing give infants a far more expansive visual perspective on their surroundings. And when infants can move on their own, their opportunities for exploration multiply.

Babies' motor achievements have a powerful effect on their social relationships. When Caitlin crawled at 7½ months, Carolyn and David began to restrict her movements by saying no and expressing mild impatience. When she walked three days after her first birthday, the

5.5 Describe dynamic systems theory of motor development, along with factors that influence motor progress in the first two years.

first "testing of wills" occurred (Biringen et al., 1995). Despite her mother's warnings, she sometimes pulled items from shelves that were off limits. "I said, 'Don't do that!'" Carolyn would repeat firmly, taking Caitlin's hand and redirecting her attention.

At the same time, newly walking babies more actively attend to and initiate social interaction (Clearfield, 2011; Karasik, Tamis-LeMonda, & Adolph, 2011). Caitlin frequently toddled over to her parents to express a greeting, give a hug, or show them an object of interest. Carolyn and David, in turn, increased their expressions of affection, and playful activities. And when Caitlin encountered risky situations, such as a sloping walkway or a dangerous object, Carolyn and David intervened, combining emotional warnings with rich verbal and gestural information that helped Caitlin notice critical features of her surroundings, regulate her motor actions, and acquire language (Karasik et al., 2008; Walle & Campos, 2014). Caitlin's delight as she worked on new motor skills triggered pleasurable reactions in others, which encouraged her efforts further. Motor, social, cognitive, and language competencies developed together and supported one another.

5.5.1 The Sequence of Motor Development

Gross-motor development refers to control over actions that help infants get around in the environment, such as crawling, standing, and walking. *Fine-motor development* has to do with smaller movements, such as reaching and grasping. Table 5.2 shows the average ages at which U.S. infants and toddlers achieve a variety of gross- and fine-motor skills. It also presents the

TABLE 5.2   Gross- and Fine-Motor Development in the First Two Years

MOTOR SKILL	AVERAGE AGE ACHIEVED	AGE RANGE IN WHICH 90 PERCENT OF INFANTS ACHIEVE THE SKILL
When held upright, holds head erect and steady	6 weeks	3 weeks–4 months
When prone, lifts self by arms	2 months	3 weeks–4 months
Rolls from side to back	2 months	3 weeks–5 months
Grasps cube	3 months, 3 weeks	2–7 months
Rolls from back to side	4½ months	2–7 months
Sits alone	7 months	5–9 months
Crawls	7 months	5–11 months
Pulls to stand	8 months	5–12 months
Plays pat-a-cake	9 months, 3 weeks	7–15 months
Stands alone	11 months	9–16 months
Walks alone	11 months, 3 weeks	9–17 months
Builds tower of two cubes	11 months, 3 weeks	10–19 months
Scribbles vigorously	14 months	10–21 months
Walks up stairs with help	16 months	12–23 months
Jumps in place	23 months, 2 weeks	17–30 months
Walks on tiptoe	25 months	16–30 months

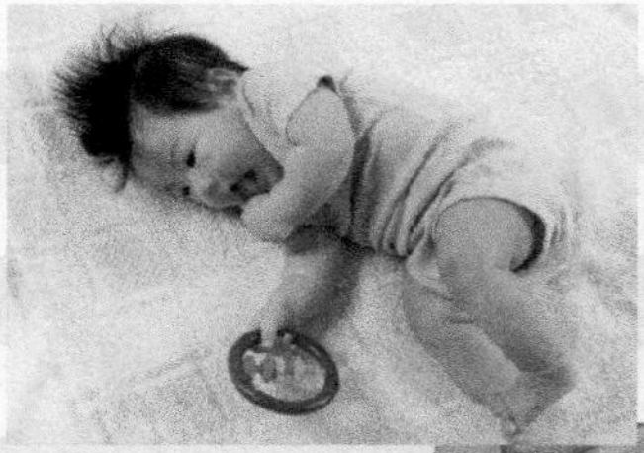

© LAURA DWIGHT PHOTOGRAPHY

© LAURA DWIGHT PHOTOGRAPHY

© BSIP SA/ALAMY STOCK PHOTO

Note: These milestones represent overall age trends. Individual differences exist in the precise age at which each milestone is attained.

Sources: Bayley, 1969, 1993, 2005.

age range during which most babies accomplish each skill, indicating large individual differences in *rate* of motor progress. Also, a baby who is a late reacher will not necessarily be a late crawler or walker. We would be concerned about a child's development only if many motor skills were seriously delayed.

Historically, researchers assumed that motor milestones emerged in a fixed sequence governed by a built-in maturational timetable. This view has long been discredited. Rather, motor skills are interrelated: Each is a product of earlier motor attainments and a contributor to new ones. Also, children acquire motor skills in highly individual ways (Adolph & Robinson, 2013). For example, before her adoption, Grace spent most of her days lying in a hammock. Because she rarely was placed on her tummy and on firm surfaces that enabled her to move on her own, she did not try to crawl. As a result, she pulled to a stand and walked before she crawled! Babies display such skills as rolling, sitting, crawling, and walking in diverse orders rather than in the sequence implied by motor norms (Adolph, Karasik, & Tamis-LeMonda, 2010).

Many influences—both internal and external to the child—combine to support the vast transformations in motor competencies of the first two years. The *dynamic systems perspective,* introduced in Chapter 1 (see pages 27–29), helps us understand how motor development takes place.

5.5.2 Motor Skills as Dynamic Systems

According to **dynamic systems theory of motor development,** mastery of motor skills involves acquiring increasingly complex *systems of action.* When motor skills work as a system, separate abilities blend together, each cooperating with others to produce more effective ways of exploring and controlling the environment. For example, control of the head and upper chest combine into sitting with support. Kicking, rocking on all fours, and reaching combine to become crawling. Then crawling, standing, and stepping are united into walking (Adolph & Robinson, 2015; Thelen & Smith, 1998).

Each new skill is a joint product of the following factors: (1) central nervous system development, (2) the body's movement capacities, (3) the goals the child has in mind, (4) the child's perceptual and cognitive capacities, which are essential for planning and guiding actions, and (5) environmental supports for the skill. Change in any element makes the system less stable, and the child starts to explore and select new, more effective motor patterns. Postural control is fundamental to all other motor actions. Control of the head, shoulders, torso, and trunk must be stable enough to allow babies to turn in different directions, sit up, and move their arms and legs purposefully to pursue various goals, such as interacting with the caregiver, retrieving and manipulating objects, or crossing a room, At the same time, infants' movements are inseparable from their environmental contexts (Adolph & Franchak, 2017). Parental encouragement or restriction of movement and availability of objects and spaces to explore join with infant attributes to influence the form of new skills and how quickly they are acquired.

The broader physical environment also profoundly influences motor development. Infants with stairs in their home learn to crawl up stairs at an earlier age and also more readily master a back-descent strategy—the safest but also the most challenging position because the baby must turn around at the top, give up visual guidance of her goal, and crawl backward (Berger, Theuring, & Adolph, 2007). And if children were reared on the moon with its reduced gravity, they would prefer jumping to walking or running!

When a skill is first acquired, infants must refine it. For example, in trying to crawl, Caitlin often collapsed on her tummy and moved backward. Soon she figured out how to propel herself forward by alternately pulling with her arms and pushing with her feet, "belly-crawling" in various ways for several weeks. As they attempt a new skill, most babies move back and forth between its presence and absence: An infant might roll over, sit, crawl, or take a few steps but not do so again until the following week. And related, previously mastered skills often become less secure. As the novice walker experiments with balancing the body vertically over two small moving feet, balance during sitting may become temporarily less

LOOK and LISTEN

Spend an hour observing a newly crawling or walking baby. Note the goals that motivate the baby to move, along with the baby's effort and motor experimentation. Describe parenting behaviors and features of the environment that promote mastery of the skill.

stable (Chen et al., 2007). This variability is evidence of loss of stability in the system—in dynamic systems theory, a necessary transition between a less mature and a more mature stable state.

Motor mastery involves intense practice. In learning to walk, for example, toddlers practice six or more hours a day, traveling the length of 29 football fields! They fall, on average, 17 times per hour but rarely cry, returning to motion within a few seconds (Adolph et al., 2012). Gradually their ability to balance the body on one leg as the other leg swings forward improves, their small unsteady steps change to a longer stride, their feet move closer together, their toes point to the front, and their legs become symmetrically coordinated (Adolph, Vereijken, & Shrout, 2003). As movements are repeated thousands of times, they promote new synaptic connections in the brain that govern motor patterns.

In tackling challenging motor tasks, babies are steadfast problem solvers, taking into account multiple sources of information. They explore ways of adapting to varied surfaces and openings, such as sliding down a steep slope and turning sideways to fit through a narrow doorway (Franchak & Adolph, 2012; Gill, Adolph, & Vereijken, 2009). And when conditions are uncertain—for instance, a ledge that may not be passable—toddlers are more likely to back off when the penalty for error is high (a fall). In these situations, they also place greater weight on caregivers' advice (Adolph, Karasik, & Tamis-LeMonda, 2010). If the parent says "go," they usually proceed; if she says "no," they avoid.

Dynamic systems theory shows us why motor development cannot be genetically determined. Because it is motivated by exploration and the desire to master new tasks and varies with context, heredity can map it out only at a general level. Rather than being *hardwired* into the nervous system, motor behaviors are *softly assembled* from multiple components, allowing for different paths to the same motor skill (Adolph & Robinson, 2015; Spencer, Perone, & Buss, 2011).

Dynamic Motor Systems in Action   To find out how infants acquire motor capacities, researchers conduct microgenetic studies (see page 44 in Chapter 1), following babies from their first attempts at a skill until it becomes smooth and effortless. In one such study, researchers held sounding toys alternately in front of infants' hands and feet, from the time they first showed interest until they engaged in well-coordinated reaching and grasping. As Figure 5.12 illustrates, the infants violated the normative sequence of arm and hand control preceding leg and foot control, shown in Table 5.2 (Galloway & Thelen, 2004). They first explored the toys with their feet—as early as 8 weeks of age, at least a month before reaching with their hands!

Why did the infants reach "feet first"? Because the hip joint constrains the legs to move less freely than the shoulder joint constrains the arms, infants could more easily control their leg movements. Consequently, foot reaching required far less practice than hand reaching. As these findings confirm, rather than following a strict, predetermined pattern, the order in which motor skills develop depends on the anatomy of the body part being used, the surrounding environment, and the baby's efforts.

Furthermore, in building a more effective dynamic system, babies often use advances in one motor skill to support others. For example, beginning to walk frees the hands for carrying, and new walkers like to fetch distant objects and transport them—often just for the fun of carrying but also to share with their caregivers (Karasik, Tamis-LeMonda, & Adolph, 2011). Observations of new walkers reveal that, surprisingly, they fall less often when carrying objects than when their hands are empty (Karasik et al., 2012). Even though combining walking with carrying is a more attention-demanding task, toddlers integrate object carrying into their emerging "walking system," using it to improve their balance (see Figure 5.13).

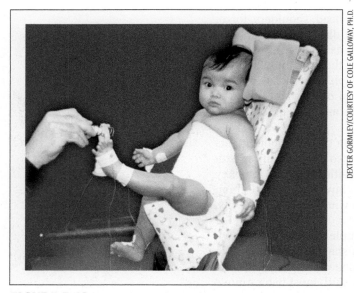

DEXTER GORMLEY/COURTESY OF COLE GALLOWAY, PH.D.

FIGURE 5.12   Reaching "feet first." When sounding toys were held in front of babies' hands and feet, they reached with their feet as early as 8 weeks of age, a month or more before they reached with their hands. This 2½-month-old skillfully explores an object with her foot.

FIGURE 5.13   New walkers fall less often when carrying objects. *Left:* When toddlers are first beginning to walk, carrying objects helps them focus attention and steady their balance. *Right:* An empty-handed new walker easily tips over.

Cultural Variations in Motor Development   Cultural variations in infant-rearing customs affect motor development. To ensure safety and ease toileting while parents work in the fields, mothers in rural northeastern China place infants on their backs in bags of sand (similar to kitty litter) for most of the day, continuing this practice into the second year. Compared with diapered infants in the same region, sandbag-reared babies are greatly delayed in sitting and walking (Mei, 1994). Among the Zinacanteco Indians of southern Mexico and the Gusii of Kenya, adults view babies who walk before they know enough to keep away from cooking fires and weaving looms as dangerous to themselves and disruptive to others (Greenfield, 1992). As a result, Zinacanteco and Gusii parents actively discourage infants' gross-motor progress.

In contrast, among the Kipsigis of Kenya and the West Indies of Jamaica, babies hold their heads up, sit alone, and walk considerably earlier than North American infants. In both societies, parents emphasize early motor maturity, practicing formal exercises to stimulate particular skills (Adolph, Karasik, & Tamis-LeMonda, 2010). In the first few months, infants are seated in holes dug in the ground, with rolled blankets to keep them upright. Walking is promoted by frequently standing babies in adults' laps, bouncing them on their feet, and exercising the stepping reflex (see page 135 in Chapter 4) (Hopkins & Westra, 1988; Super, 1981). As parents in these cultures support babies in upright postures and rarely put them down on the floor, their infants usually skip crawling—a motor skill regarded as crucial in Western nations!

Finally, because it decreases exposure to "tummy time," the current Western practice of having babies sleep on their backs to protect them from SIDS (see page 138 in Chapter 4) delays gross-motor milestones of rolling, sitting, and crawling (Majnemer & Barr, 2005). Regularly exposing infants to the tummy-lying position during waking hours, even for just a few minutes a day, prevents these delays.

The West Indies of Jamaica believe that exercise helps infants grow up strong and physically attractive. This mother "walks" her baby up her body—an activity that contributes to earlier mastery of walking.

5.5.3 Fine-Motor Development: Reaching and Grasping

Of all motor skills, reaching may play the greatest role in infant cognitive development. By grasping things, turning them over, and seeing what happens when they are released, infants learn a great deal about the sights, sounds, and feel of objects. Because certain gross-motor attainments vastly increase infants' view of their surroundings, they promote manual coordination. When babies sit, and even more so when they stand and walk, they see the panorama of an entire room (Kretch, Franchak, & Adolph, 2014). In these positions, they focus mainly on nearby objects and want to explore them.

Reaching and grasping, like many other motor skills, start out as gross, diffuse activity and move toward mastery of fine movements. Figure 5.14 illustrates some milestones of reaching over the first nine months. Newborns will actively work to bring their hands into their field of vision: In a dimly lit room, they keep their hand within a narrow beam of light, moving the hand when the light beam moves (van der Meer, 1997). Newborns also make poorly coordinated swipes, called **prereaching,** toward an object in front of them, but because of poor arm and hand control they rarely contact the object. Like newborn reflexes, prereaching drops out around 7 weeks of age, when babies improve in eye movements involved in tracking and fixating on objects, which are essential for accurate reaching (von Hofsten, 2004). Yet these early behaviors suggest that babies are biologically prepared to coordinate hand with eye in the act of exploring.

At about 3 to 4 months, as infants develop the necessary eye, head, and shoulder control, reaching reappears as purposeful, forward arm movements in the presence of a nearby toy and gradually improves in accuracy (Bhat, Heathcock, & Galloway, 2005). By 5 to 6 months, infants reach for an object in a room that has been darkened during the reach by switching off the lights—a skill that improves over the next few months (McCarty & Ashmead, 1999). This indicates that the baby does not need to use vision to guide the arms and hands in reaching. Rather, reaching is largely controlled by *proprioception*—our sense of movement and location in space, arising from stimuli within the body. When vision is freed from the basic act of reaching, it can focus on more complex adjustments, such as fine-tuning actions to fit the distance and shape of objects.

Reaching improves as depth perception advances, as infants gain greater control of body posture and arm and hand movements, and as they encounter experiences that motivate them to reach. Providing 3-month olds with many reinforcing reaching opportunities—such as nearby toys that move and sound when the baby's hand makes contact—results in faster development of reaching (Williams & Corbetta, 2016). Interacting with responsive toys leads infants to

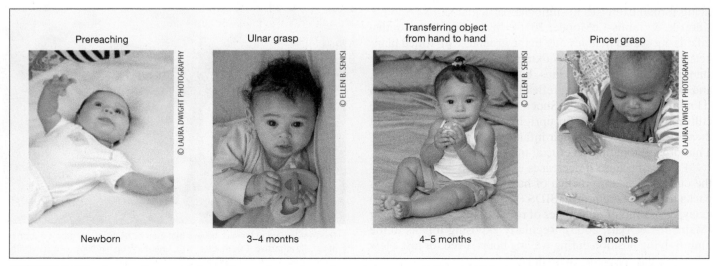

FIGURE 5.14 **Some milestones of reaching and grasping.** The average age at which each skill is attained is given. (Ages from Bayley, 1969; Rochat, 1989.)

attend more closely to their hand–toy contacts, which helps them refine their movements into successful reaches.

As infants gain in reaching experience, they adjust their movements to the demands of reaching tasks. Four-month-olds aim their reaches ahead of a moving object so they can catch it (von Hofsten, 1993). Around 5 months, babies reduce their efforts when an object is moved beyond their reach (Robin, Berthier, & Clifton, 1996). By 7 months, the arms become more independent: Infants reach for an object by extending one arm rather than both (Fagard & Pezé, 1997). During the next few months, infants become more efficient at reaching for moving objects—ones that spin, change direction, and move sideways, closer, or farther away (Fagard, Spelke, & von Hofsten, 2009; Wentworth, Benson, & Haith, 2000).

Once infants can reach, they modify their grasp. The newborn's grasp reflex is replaced by the **ulnar grasp,** a clumsy motion in which the young infant's fingers close against the palm. Still, even 4- to 5-month-olds modify their grasp to suit an object's size, shape, and texture (rigid versus soft)—a capacity that improves over the second half-year as infants adjust the hand more precisely and do so in advance of contacting the object (Ransburg et al., 2017; Witherington, 2005). Around 4 to 5 months, when infants begin to sit up, both hands become coordinated in exploring objects. Babies of this age can hold an object in front of their eyes with one hand while the other scans it with the tips of the fingers, and they frequently transfer objects from hand to hand (Soska & Adolph, 2014). By the end of the first year, infants use the thumb and index finger in a well-coordinated **pincer grasp.** Then the ability to manipulate objects greatly expands. The 1-year-old can pick up raisins and blades of grass, turn knobs, and open and close small boxes.

Between 8 and 11 months, reaching and grasping are well-practiced. As a result, attention is released from the motor skill to events that occur before and after obtaining the object. For example, 10-month-olds easily modify their reach to anticipate their next action. They reach for a ball faster when they intend to throw it than when they intend to push it down a narrow tube (Kayed & Van der Meer, 2009). Around this time, too, infants begin to solve simple problems that involve reaching, such as searching for and finding a hidden toy. And in the second year, they gradually become more skilled at using tools, such as rakes and hooks, to acquire out-of-reach objects (Rat-Fischer, O'Regan, & Fagard, 2012).

Finally, the capacity to reach for and manipulate an object increases infants' attention to the way an adult reaches for and plays with that same object (Hauf, Aschersleben, & Prinz, 2007). As babies watch what others do, they broaden their understanding of others' behaviors and of the range of actions that can be performed on various objects, incorporating those possibilities into their own object-related behaviors.

As with other motor milestones, environmental contexts affect infant reaching. In cultures where mothers carry their infants on their hips or in slings for most of the day, babies have rich opportunities to explore with their hands. Among the !Kung of Botswana, infants grasp their mothers' colorful, beaded necklaces to steady themselves while breastfeeding as the mother moves. While riding along, they frequently swipe at and manipulate the mother's jewelry and other dangling objects (Konner, 1977). As a result, !Kung infants are advanced in development of reaching and grasping. And because babies of Mali and Uganda spend half or more of their day held in sitting or standing positions, which facilitate reaching, they, too, develop manual skills earlier than Western infants, who spend much of their day lying down (Adolph, Karasik, & Tamis-LeMonda, 2010).

To explore the surface of this uniquely textured ball, a 6-month-old coordinates both hands—and uses her mouth as well!

 ASK YOURSELF

Connect ■ Provide several examples of how motor development influences infants' and toddlers' social experiences. How do social experiences, in turn, influence motor development?

Apply ■ List features of everyday contexts that support infants' progress in reaching, grasping, sitting, and crawling. Why should caregivers place young infants in a variety of waking-time body positions?

Reflect ■ Do you favor early, systematic training of infants in motor skills such as crawling, walking, running, hopping, and stair climbing? Why or why not?

5.6 Perceptual Development

In Chapter 4, you learned that the senses of touch, taste, smell, and hearing—but not vision—are remarkably well-developed at birth. Recall that we used the term *sensation* to talk about these capacities. That term suggests a fairly passive process—what the baby's receptors detect when exposed to stimulation. Now let's turn to a related issue: How does *perception* change over the first year? *Perception,* in contrast to *sensation,* is an active process: When we perceive, we organize and interpret what we sense. Because hearing and vision are the focus of nearly all research on perception, our discussion will address only those two senses.

As we review the perceptual achievements of infancy, you may find it hard to tell where perception leaves off and thinking begins. For this reason, the research we are about to discuss provides an excellent bridge to the topic of Chapter 6—cognitive development during the first two years.

5.6.1 Hearing

Like most mothers and many fathers as well, Vanessa often sang to Timmy. As his first birthday approached, she bought several CDs of nursery songs and lullabies and played one each afternoon at naptime. The simplicity, slowed tempo, repetitiveness, and playful or soothing quality of the music attracted Timmy's attention (Trehub, 2016). Soon Timmy let Vanessa know his favorite tune. If she put on "Twinkle, Twinkle," he stood up in his crib and whimpered until she replaced it with "Jack and Jill."

Around 4 months, infants display a sense of musical phrasing. They prefer Mozart minuets with pauses between phrases to those with awkward breaks (Jusczyk & Krumhansl, 1993). At 6 to 7 months, they can distinguish musical tunes on the basis of variations in rhythmic patterns, including beat structure (duple or triple) and accent structure (emphasis on the first note of every beat unit or at other positions) (Hannon & Johnson, 2004). They are also sensitive to features conveying the purpose of familiar types of songs, preferring to listen to high-pitched playsongs (aimed at entertaining) and low-pitched lullabies (used to soothe) (Tsang & Conrad, 2010). By the end of the first year, infants recognize the same melody when it is played in different keys (Trehub, 2001).

These achievements illustrate the greatest change in hearing over the first year: Using the remarkable statistical learning capacity we discussed earlier (see page 175), babies detect increasingly complex, predictable sound patterns, in speech as well as in music.

Speech Perception   Recall from Chapter 4 that newborns can distinguish nearly all sounds in human languages and that they prefer listening to speech over nonspeech sounds and to their native tongue rather than a rhythmically distinct foreign language. Brain-imaging evidence indicates that in young infants, discrimination of speech sounds activates *both* auditory and motor areas in the cerebral cortex. Furthermore, when researchers used teething toys to restrain the position and movement of 6-month-olds' tongues so they could not produce certain speech sounds, the infants had difficulty isolating those sounds from the speech stream (Bruderer et al., 2015; Kuhl et al., 2014). While listening to speech, babies seem to generate internal motor plans that help them perceive particular sounds and that prepare them for producing those sounds.

As infants listen to people talk, they learn to focus on meaningful sound variations. ERP brain-wave recordings reveal that around 5 months, infants become sensitive to syllable stress patterns in their own language (Weber et al., 2004). Between 6 and 8 months, they start to "screen out" sounds not used in their native tongue (Curtin & Werker, 2007). Bilingual infants do so in both their native languages, though slightly later, between 8 and 9 months, due to the challenges of processing the sounds of two languages. But once bilingual babies begin distinguishing native from nonnative sounds, they do so more rapidly and effectively than their monolingual agemates. Their richer linguistic experience seems to induce heightened

Biology and Environment | "Tuning in" to Familiar Speech, Faces, and Music: A Sensitive Period for Culture-Specific Learning

To share experiences with members of their family and community, babies must become skilled at making perceptual discriminations that are meaningful in their culture. As we have seen, at first infants are sensitive to virtually all speech sounds, but around 6 months, they narrow their focus, limiting the distinctions they make to the language they hear and will soon learn.

The ability to perceive faces shows a similar **perceptual narrowing effect**—perceptual sensitivity that becomes increasingly attuned with age to information most often encountered. After habituating to one member of each pair of faces in Figure 5.15, 6-month-olds were shown the familiar face and the novel face side by side. For both pairs, they recovered to (looked longer at) the novel face, indicating that they could discriminate the individual faces of both humans and monkeys equally well. But at 9 months, infants no longer showed a novelty preference when viewing the monkey pair (Pascalis, de Haan, & Nelson, 2002). Like adults, they distinguished only the human faces. Similar findings emerge with sheep faces: Four- to 6-month-olds easily distinguish them, but 9- to 11-month-olds no longer do (Simpson et al., 2011).

This perceptual narrowing effect appears again in musical rhythm perception. Western adults are accustomed to the even-beat pattern of Western music—repetition of the same rhythmic structure in every measure of a tune—and easily notice rhythmic changes that disrupt this familiar beat. But present them with music that does not follow this typical Western rhythmic form—Baltic folk tunes, for example—and they fail to pick up on rhythmic-pattern deviations. In contrast, 6-month-olds can detect such disruptions in both typically Western and nontypically Western melodies. By 12 months, however, after added exposure to Western music, babies are no longer aware of deviations in foreign musical rhythms, although their sensitivity to Western rhythmic structure remains unchanged (Hannon & Trehub, 2005b).

Several weeks of regular interaction with a foreign-language speaker and of daily opportunities to listen to non-Western music fully restore 12-month-olds' sensitivity to wide-ranging speech sounds and music rhythms (Hannon & Trehub, 2005a; Kuhl, Tsao, & Liu, 2003). Similarly, 12-month-olds who are given additional exposure and testing for discrimination of monkey faces regain their ability to discriminate such faces (Fair et al., 2012). Adults given similar experiences, by contrast, show little improvement in perceptual sensitivity.

Taken together, these findings suggest a heightened capacity—or sensitive period—in the second half of the first year, when infants are biologically prepared to "zero in" on socially meaningful perceptual distinctions. Notice how, between 6 and 12 months, learning is especially rapid across several domains (speech, faces, and music) and is easily modified by experience. This suggests a broad neurological change—perhaps a special time of experience-expectant brain growth (see page 160) in which babies analyze everyday stimulation of all kinds similarly, in ways that prepare them to participate in their cultural community.

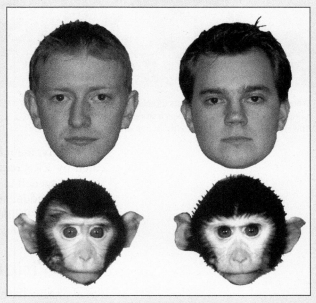

FIGURE 5.15   Discrimination of human and monkey faces. Which of these pairs is easiest for you to tell apart? After habituating to one of the photos in each pair, infants were shown the familiar and the novel face side by side. For both pairs, 6-month-olds recovered to (looked longer at) the novel face, indicating that they could discriminate human and monkey faces equally well. By 9 months, babies lost their ability to distinguish the monkey faces. Like adults, they showed a novelty preference only to human stimuli. (From O. Pascalis et al., 2002, "Is Face Processing Species-Specific During the First Year of Life?" *Science, 296*, p. 1322. Copyright © 2002 by AAAS. Republished with permission of American Association for the Advancement of Science conveyed through Copyright Clearance Center, Inc.)

sensitivity to the details of language sounds (Liu & Kager, 2015, 2016; Ramírez et al., 2017). As the Biology and Environment box above explains, this increased responsiveness to native-language sounds is part of a general "tuning" process in the second half of the first year—a possible sensitive period in which infants acquire a range of perceptual skills for picking up socially important information.

Soon after, infants focus on larger speech units that are critical to figuring out meaning. They recognize familiar words in spoken passages and listen longer to speech with clear clause and phrase boundaries (Johnson & Seidl, 2008; Soderstrom et al., 2003). Around 7 to 9 months, infants extend this sensitivity to speech structure to individual words: They begin to divide the speech stream into wordlike units (Jusczyk, 2002; MacWhinney, 2015).

When speaking to babies, parents often use a single word followed by the same word embedded in the speech stream ("Doggie! Pat the doggie."). This style of communicating helps infants with word discrimination.

Analyzing the Speech Stream   Applying their statistical learning capacity, older infants rapidly locate words in adult speech by discriminating syllables that often occur together (indicating that they belong to the same word) from syllables that seldom occur together (indicating a word boundary; see page 175 to review). For example, after hearing the English word sequence *pretty baby* several times in a brief segment of speech (about 60 words), 8-month-olds can distinguish the word-internal syllable pair *(pret-ty)* from the word-external syllable pair *(ty ba)* (Saffran & Thiessen, 2003). They prefer to listen to new speech that preserves the word-internal pattern.

Once infants begin locating words, they focus on the words and discover additional statistical cues that signal word boundaries (Thiessen, Kronstein, & Hufnagle, 2012). Seven- to 8-month-olds detect regular syllable-stress patterns—for example, in English and Dutch, that the onset of a strong syllable (*hap*-py, *rab*-bit) often signals a new word (Thiessen & Saffran, 2007). By 10 months, babies can detect words that start with weak syllables, such as "sur*prise*," by listening for sound regularities before and after the words (Kooijman, Hagoort, & Cutler, 2009).

Finally, the more rapidly 10-month-olds detect words within the speech stream (as indicated by ERP recordings), the larger their vocabulary at age 2 years (Junge et al., 2012). Parents' speech to babies, which often contains single-word utterances followed by the same words embedded in the speech stream ("Doggie!" "See the big doggie?") aids word discrimination (Lew-Williams, Pelucchi, & Saffran, 2011). As we will see in Chapter 6, adults' style of communicating with infants facilitates analysis of the structure of speech.

5.6.2 Vision

For exploring the environment, humans depend on vision more than any other sense. Although at first a baby's visual world is fragmented, it undergoes extraordinary changes during the first seven to eight months of life.

Visual development is supported by rapid maturation of the eye and visual centers in the cerebral cortex. Around 2 months, infants can focus on objects about as well as adults can, and their color vision is adultlike by 4 months (Johnson & Hannon, 2015). *Visual acuity* (fineness of discrimination) increases steadily, reaching 20/80 by 6 months and an adult level of about 20/20 by 4 years (Slater et al., 2010). Scanning the environment and tracking moving objects also improve over the first half-year as infants better control their eye movements and as they build an organized perceptual world, which enables them to scan more thoroughly and systematically (Johnson, Slemmer, & Amso, 2004).

As babies explore their visual field, they figure out the characteristics of objects and how they are arranged in space. To understand how they do so, let's examine the development of three aspects of vision: depth, pattern, and object perception.

Depth Perception   *Depth perception* is the ability to judge the distance of objects from one another and from ourselves. It is important for understanding the layout of the environment and for guiding motor activity.

Figure 5.16 shows the *visual cliff,* designed by Eleanor Gibson and Richard Walk (1960) and used in the earliest studies of depth perception. It consists of a Plexiglas-covered table with a platform at the center, a "shallow" side with a checkerboard pattern just under the glass, and a "deep" side with a checkerboard several feet below the glass. The researchers found that crawling babies readily crossed the shallow side, but most avoided the deep side. They concluded that around the time infants crawl, most distinguish deep from shallow surfaces and steer clear of drop-offs.

The visual cliff shows that crawling and avoidance of drop-offs are linked, but not how they are related or when depth perception first appears. Recent research has looked at babies' ability to detect specific depth cues, using methods that do not require that they crawl.

Emergence of Depth Perception How do we know when an object is near rather than far away? Try these exercises to find out. Pick up a small object (such as your cup) and move it toward and away from your face. Did its image grow larger as it approached and smaller as it receded? Next time you take a bike or car ride, notice that nearby objects move past your field of vision more quickly than those far away.

Motion is the first depth cue to which infants are sensitive. Babies 3 to 4 weeks old blink their eyes defensively when an object moves toward their face as though it is going to hit them (Nánez & Yonas, 1994). *Binocular depth cues* arise because our two eyes have slightly different views of the visual field. The brain blends these two images, resulting in perception of depth. Research in which two overlapping images are projected before the baby, using a computer-assisted device that ensures each eye receives only one image, reveals that sensitivity to binocular cues emerges at about 8 weeks and improves gradually over the next few months (Kavšek, 2013; Kavšek & Braun, 2016). Finally, beginning at 3 to 4 months and strengthening between 5 and 7 months, babies display sensitivity to *pictorial depth cues*—the ones artists often use to make a painting look three-dimensional. Examples include receding lines that create the illusion of perspective, changes in texture (nearby textures are more detailed than faraway ones), and overlapping objects (an object partially hidden by another object is perceived to be more distant) (Kavšek, Yonas, & Granrud, 2012).

Why does perception of depth cues emerge in the order just described? Researchers speculate that motor development is involved. For example, control of the head during the early weeks of life may help infants notice motion and binocular cues. Around 5 to 6 months, the ability to turn, poke, and feel the surface of objects may promote perception of pictorial cues (Bushnell & Boudreau, 1993; Soska, Adolph, & Johnson, 2010). And as we will see next, one aspect of motor progress—independent movement—plays a vital role in refinement of depth perception.

FIGURE 5.16   The visual cliff. Plexiglas covers the deep and shallow sides. By refusing to cross the deep side and showing a preference for the shallow side, this infant demonstrates the ability to perceive depth.

Independent Movement and Depth Perception At 6 months, Timmy started crawling. "He's fearless!" exclaimed Vanessa. "If I put him down in the middle of my bed, he crawls right over the edge. The same thing happens by the stairs." Will Timmy become wary of the side of the bed and the staircase as he becomes a more experienced crawler? Research suggests that he will. Infants with more crawling experience (regardless of when they started to crawl) are far more likely to avoid the deep side of the visual cliff (Campos et al., 2000). And only after many weeks of crawling will infants hesitate at the edge of a real drop-off that has no safety glass to protect them from falling.

From extensive everyday experience, babies gradually figure out how to use depth cues to detect the danger of falling. But because the loss of body control that leads to falling differs greatly for each body position, infants must undergo this learning separately for each posture (Adolph & Franchak, 2017). In one study, 9-month-olds, who were experienced sitters but novice crawlers, were placed on the edge of a shallow drop-off that could be widened (Adolph, 2002, 2008). While in the familiar sitting position, infants avoided leaning out for an attractive toy at distances likely to result in falling. But in the unfamiliar crawling position, they headed over the edge, even when the distance was extremely wide! And newly walking babies will step repeatedly over a risky drop-off (Kretch & Adolph, 2013a). They will also careen down slopes and over uneven surfaces without making necessary postural adjustments (Adolph et al., 2008; Joh & Adolph, 2006). Thus, they fall frequently.

Even experienced crawlers and walkers encounter new depth-at-an-edge situations that require additional learning. When researchers encouraged crawling and walking babies to cross bridges varying in width over drop-offs (with

Infants must learn to use depth cues to detect the danger of falling separately for each posture—sitting, crawling, and walking. This novice crawler proceeding headlong over a short staircase risks tumbling awkwardly to the landing. With more crawling experience, he will discover that backing down is more secure.

FIGURE 5.17 **An experienced walker crosses a narrow bridge over a drop-off.** This 14-month-old has figured out how to turn his body sideways to accommodate the narrow passageway. (From K. S. Kretch & K. E. Adolph, 2013b, "No Bridge Too High: Infants Decide Whether to Cross Based on the Probability of Falling Not the Severity of the Potential Fall," *Developmental Science, 16,* p. 338. © 2013 Blackwell Publishing Ltd. Reprinted by permission of John Wiley and Sons, Inc., conveyed through Copyright Clearance Center, Inc.)

an adult following alongside to catch infants if they began to fall), most avoided crossing impossibly narrow bridges. And the greater their experience, the narrower the bridge both crawlers and walkers attempted to cross. Nevertheless, walkers perceived the likelihood of falling from a narrow bridge more accurately than crawlers. While crossing, crawlers could not easily see and adjust the placement of their hind limbs to prevent falls. In contrast, experienced walkers had figured out how to turn their body to accommodate the narrow passageway (see Figure 5.17) (Kretch & Adolph, 2013b). As infants and toddlers discover how to avoid falling in different postures and situations, their understanding of depth expands.

Independent movement promotes other aspects of three-dimensional understanding. For example, seasoned crawlers are better than their inexperienced age-mates at remembering object locations, finding hidden objects, and recognizing the identity of a previously viewed object from a new angle (Campos et al., 2000; Schwarzer, Freitag, & Schum, 2013). Why does crawling make such a difference? Compare your own experience of the environment when you are driven from one place to another with what you experience when you walk or drive yourself. When you move on your own, you are much more aware of landmarks and routes of travel, and you take more careful note of what things look like from different points of view. The same is true for infants.

Pattern Perception Even newborns prefer to look at patterned rather than plain stimuli (Fantz, 1961). As they get older, they prefer more complex patterns. For example, 3-week-olds look longest at black-and-white checkerboards with a few large squares, whereas 8-week-olds prefer those with many small squares. Because of their poor vision, very young babies cannot resolve the small features in the complex checkerboard, which appears blurred. Around 2 months, when detection of fine-grained detail has improved, infants can detect the features of complex patterns and spend more time looking at them (Gwiazda & Birch, 2001).

In the early weeks of life, infants respond to the separate parts of a pattern. They stare at single high-contrast features, generally on the edges, and have difficulty shifting their gaze away toward other interesting stimuli (Hunnius & Geuze, 2004a, 2004b). At 2 to 3 months, when scanning ability has improved, infants thoroughly explore a pattern's internal features, pausing briefly to look at each part (Bronson, 1994).

Once babies can take in all aspects of a pattern, they integrate the parts into a unified whole. Around 4 months, infants are so good at detecting pattern organization that they perceive subjective boundaries that are not really present. For example, they perceive a square in the center of Figure 5.18a, just as you do (Kavšek, 2009). Older infants carry this sensitivity to subjective form further. For example, 9-month-olds look much longer at an organized series of moving lights that resembles a human being walking than at an upside-down or scrambled version (Proffitt & Bertenthal, 1990). At 12 months, infants can detect familiar objects represented by incomplete drawings, even when as much as two-thirds of the drawing is missing (see Figure 5.18b) (Rose, Jankowski, & Senior, 1997). As these findings reveal, infants' increasing knowledge of objects and actions supports pattern perception.

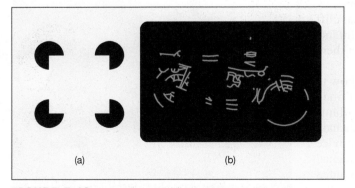

FIGURE 5.18 **Subjective boundaries in visual patterns.** (a) Do you perceive a square in the middle of the figure? By 4 months of age, infants do, too. (b) What does the image, missing two-thirds of its outline, look like to you? By 12 months, infants detect a motorcycle. After habituating to the incomplete motorcycle image, they were shown an intact motorcycle figure paired with a novel form. Twelve-month-olds recovered to (looked longer at) the novel figure, indicating that they recognized the motorcycle pattern on the basis of very little visual information. (Based on Kavšek, 2009; Rose, Jankowski, & Senior, 1997.)

Face Perception Infants' tendency to search for structure in a patterned stimulus applies to face perception. Newborns prefer to look at photos and simplified drawings of faces with features arranged naturally (upright) rather than unnaturally (upside down or sideways) (see Figure 5.19a and b) (Cassia, Turati, & Simion, 2004; Simion et al., 2001). They also track a facelike pattern moving across their visual field farther than they track other stimuli

FIGURE 5.19 **Early face perception.** Newborns prefer to look at the photo of a face and the simple pattern resembling a face over the upside-down versions (a and b). (c) When the complex drawing of a face on the left and the equally complex, scrambled version on the right are moved across newborns' visual field, they follow the face longer. But if the two stimuli are stationary, infants show no preference for the face until around 2 months of age. (From Cassia, Turati, & Simion, 2004; Johnson, 1999; Mondloch et al., 1999.)

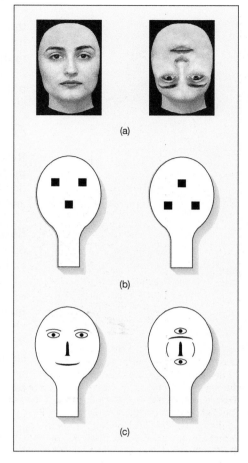

(Johnson, 1999). And although they rely more on outer features (hairline and chin) than inner features to distinguish real faces, newborns prefer photos of faces with eyes open and a direct gaze (Farroni et al., 2002; Turati et al., 2006). Yet another amazing capacity is their tendency to look longer at both human and animal faces judged by adults as attractive—a preference that may be the origin of the widespread social bias favoring physically attractive people (Quinn et al., 2008; Slater et al., 2010).

Some researchers claim that these behaviors reflect a built-in capacity to orient toward members of one's own species, just as many newborn animals do (Slater et al., 2011). Others assert that newborns simply prefer any stimulus in which the most salient elements are arranged horizontally in the upper part of a pattern—like the "eyes" in Figure 5.19b. Indeed, newborns do prefer patterns with these characteristics over other arrangements (Cassia, Turati, & Simion, 2004; Simion et al., 2001). Still other researchers argue that from birth on, infants are exposed to faces more often than to other stimuli—experiences that promote newborns' early sensitivity to faces and facelike stimuli (Johnson, 2011).

Despite newborns' responsiveness to faces, they cannot discriminate a complex facial pattern from other, equally complex patterns (see Figure 5.19c). But from repeated exposures to their mother's face, they quickly learn to prefer her face to that of an unfamiliar woman, though they mostly attend to its broad outlines (Bushnell, 2001). Around 2 months, when infants can combine pattern elements into an organized whole, they prefer a complex drawing of the human face to other equally complex stimulus arrangements (Dannemiller & Stephens, 1988). And they clearly prefer their mother's detailed facial features to those of another woman (Bartrip, Morton, & de Schonen, 2001).

Around 3 months, infants readily make fine distinctions among the features of different faces—for example, between photographs of two strangers, even when the faces are moderately similar (Farroni et al., 2007). At 5 months, infants perceive emotional expressions as meaningful wholes. They treat positive faces (happy and surprised) as different from negative ones (sad and fearful) (Bornstein & Arterberry, 2003). And by 7 months, they discriminate among a wider range of facial emotional expressions, including happiness, surprise, sadness, fearfulness, and anger (Safar & Moulson, 2017; Witherington et al., 2010).

Experience with particular faces influences face processing, leading babies to form group biases at a tender age. As early as 3 months, infants prefer and more easily discriminate among female faces than among male faces (Liu et al., 2015; Ramsey-Rennels & Langlois, 2006). The greater time spent with female adults explains this effect, as infants with a male primary caregiver prefer male faces. Furthermore, 3-month-olds exposed mostly to members of their own race prefer to look at the faces of members of that race, and between 6 and 9 months their ability to discriminate other-race faces weakens (Fassbender, Teubert, & Lohaus, 2016; Kelly et al., 2007, 2009). This own-race bias is absent in infants who have frequent contact with members of other races or who view picture books of other-race faces, and it can be reversed in older infants through exposure to racial diversity (Anzures et al., 2013; Heron-Delaney et al., 2011). Notice how early experience promotes *perceptual narrowing* with respect to gender and racial information in faces, as occurs for species information, discussed in the Biology and Environment box on page 185.

Exposure to racial diversity in her child-care center means that this baby is unlikely to have developed a preference for faces of her own race. When infants have limited social experiences, group biases emerge early.

Although key aspects of face identification develop in infancy, it continues to improve throughout childhood (Stiles et al., 2015). In line with these findings, despite a right-hemispheric bias for processing faces by the middle of the first year, infants and children show more broadly distributed neural activity to faces than do adolescents and adults (Otsuka et al., 2007; Turati & Quadrelli, 2017). Not until late adolescence does rapid, accurate discrimination of highly similar faces reach an adultlike level of proficiency.

5.6.3 Object Perception

Research on pattern perception involves only two-dimensional stimuli, but our environment is made up of stable, three-dimensional objects. Do young infants perceive a world of independently existing objects—knowledge essential for distinguishing among the self, other people, and things?

Size and Shape Constancy   As we move around the environment, the images that objects cast on our retina constantly change in size and shape. To perceive objects as stable and unchanging, we must translate these varying retinal images into a single representation.

Size constancy—perception of an object's size as the same, despite changes in the size of its retinal image—is evident in the first week of life. To test for it, researchers habituated infants to a small cube at varying distances from the eye in an effort to desensitize them to changes in the cube's retinal image size and direct their attention to the object's actual size. When the small cube was presented together with a new, large cube—but at different distances so they cast retinal images of the same size—all babies recovered to (looked longer at) the novel large cube, indicating that they distinguished objects on the basis of actual size, not retinal image size (Slater et al., 2010).

Perception of an object's shape as stable, despite changes in the shape projected on the retina, is called **shape constancy.** Habituation research reveals that it, too, is present within the first week of life, long before babies can actively rotate objects with their hands and view them from different angles (Slater & Johnson, 1999).

Both size and shape constancy seem to be built-in capacities that assist infants in detecting a coherent world of objects. Yet they provide only a partial picture of young infants' object perception.

Perception of Object Identity   At first, infants rely heavily on motion and spatial arrangement to distinguish objects. When researchers strategically use these cues, even new-born babies can bind together separate elements in a visual display and perceive a unified object. As Figure 5.20 reveals, they realize that a moving rod whose center is hidden behind a moving rectangular box is a complete rod rather than two rod pieces (Valenza & Bulf, 2011). Like size and shape constancy, perception of object unity appears to be a built-in property of the human perceptual system.

Nevertheless, infants have much to learn about the cues signifying boundaries between objects in their visual field, including shape, color, and pattern. When two objects varying in these cues are touching and either stand still or move in unison, babies younger than 4 months

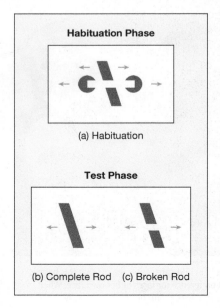

Habituation Phase

(a) Habituation

Test Phase

(b) Complete Rod   (c) Broken Rod

FIGURE 5.20   Testing newborn infants' ability to perceive object unity. (a) Supported in front of a screen, infants were habituated to a gray rod moving back and forth behind a white rectangular box with ends highlighted by two incomplete circular shapes. The box plus circular shapes also moved back and forth in unison, but out of phase with the rod. Instead of typical continuous motion, the researchers used strobo-scopic motion (a rapid series of images of the rod and box along their brief movement paths), which attracts newborns' attention and adjusts to their weak ability to track moving stimuli. (b) Following habituation, the infants viewed a side-by-side display of a complete rod and a broken rod with a gap corresponding to the location of the box. Each stimulus moved with the same stroboscopic motion as the rod in the habituation phase. Infants recovered to (looked longer at) the broken rod than the complete rod. Their novelty prefer-ence suggests that they perceived the rod behind the box in the first display as a single unit. (From E. Valenza & H. Bulf, 2011, "Early Development of Object Unity: Evidence for Perceptual Completion in Newborns," *Developmental Science,* 14, p. 801. Copyright © John Wiley & Sons, adapted by permission.)

have difficulty distinguishing them. As infants become familiar with many objects and as gains in scanning assist them in integrating each object's features into a unified whole, they rely more on shape, color, and pattern and less on motion (Johnson, 2011; Slater et al., 2010). By 4½ months, they can discriminate two touching objects on the basis of their features in very simple, easy-to-process situations. And prior exposure to one of the test objects enhances 4½-month-olds' ability to discern the boundary between two touching objects—a finding that highlights the role of experience (Dueker, Modi, & Needham, 2003; Needham, 2001).

In everyday life, objects frequently move in and out of sight, so infants must keep track of their disappearance and reappearance to perceive their identity. Habituation research, in which a ball moves back and forth behind a screen, reveals that at age 4 months, infants first perceive the ball's path as continuous (Johnson et al., 2003). Between 4 and 5 months, infants can monitor more intricate paths of objects. As indicated by their future-oriented eye movements (looking ahead to where they expect an object to reappear from behind a barrier), 5-month-olds even keep track of an object that travels on a curvilinear course at varying speeds (Rosander & von Hofsten, 2004). Again, experience—the opportunity to track a moving object along a fully visible path of movement just before testing—enhances predictive eye tracking (Johnson & Shuwairi, 2009).

From 4 to 11 months, infants increasingly use featural information to detect the identity of an object traveling behind a screen. At first, they need strong featural cues—a change in two features (size and shape, or shape and color)—to signify that a disappearing object is distinct from an emerging object. Later in the first year, change in a single feature is sufficient (Bremner et al., 2013; Wilcox & Woods, 2009). And as before, experience—in particular, physically manipulating the object—boosts older infants' attention to its surface features.

In sum, perception of object identity is mastered gradually over the first year. We will consider a related attainment, infants' understanding of object permanence—awareness that an object still exists when hidden—in Chapter 6.

5.6.4 Intermodal Perception

Our world provides rich, continuous *intermodal stimulation*—simultaneous input from more than one *modality,* or sensory system. In **intermodal perception,** we make sense of these running streams of light, sound, tactile, odor, and taste information, perceiving them as integrated wholes. We know, for example, that an object's shape is the same whether we see it or touch it, that lip movements are closely coordinated with the sound of a voice, and that dropping a rigid object on a hard surface will cause a sharp, banging sound.

Infants perceive input from different sensory systems in a unified way by detecting **amodal sensory properties,** information that is not specific to a single modality but that overlaps two or more sensory systems, such as rate, rhythm, duration, intensity, temporal synchrony (for vision and hearing), and texture and shape (for vision and touch). Consider the sight and sound of a bouncing ball or the face and voice of a speaking person. In each event, visual and auditory information are conveyed simultaneously and with the same rate, rhythm, duration, and intensity.

Even newborns are impressive perceivers of amodal properties. After touching an object (such as a cylinder) placed in their palms, they recognize it visually, distinguishing it from a different-shaped object (Sann & Streri, 2007). And they require just one exposure to learn the association between the sight and sound of a toy, such as a rhythmically jangling rattle (Morrongiello, Fenwick, & Chance, 1998).

Within the first half-year, infants master a remarkable range of intermodal relationships. Three- to 5-month-olds can match faces with voices on the basis of lip–voice synchrony, emotional expression, and even age and gender of the speaker. Around 6 months,

This toddler exploring a tambourine readily detects amodal relations in the synchronous sounds and visual appearance of its metal jingles.

infants can perceive and remember the unique face–voice pairings of unfamiliar adults (Flom, 2013). And around 7 months, they readily learn associations between arbitrary speech sounds and object motions (Marcus, Fernandes, & Johnson, 2012).

How does intermodal perception develop so quickly? Young infants seem biologically primed to focus on amodal information. Their detection of amodal relations—for example, the common tempo and rhythm in sights and sounds—precedes and provides the basis for detecting more specific intermodal matches, such as the relation between a particular person's face and the sound of her voice or between an object and its verbal label (Bahrick, 2010).

Intermodal sensitivity is crucial for perceptual development. In the first few months, it enables babies to notice meaningful correlations between sensory inputs and rapidly make sense of their surroundings. As a result, inexperienced perceivers notice a unitary event, such as a hammer's tapping, without being distracted by momentarily irrelevant aspects of the situation, such as the hammer's color or orientation.

In addition to easing perception of the physical world, intermodal perception facilitates social and language processing. For example, as 3- to 4-month-olds gaze at an adult's face, they initially require both vocal and visual input to distinguish positive from negative emotional expressions (Flom & Bahrick, 2007). Only later do infants discriminate positive from negative emotion in each sensory modality—first in voices (around 5 months), later (from 7 months on) in faces (Bahrick, Hernandez-Reif, & Flom, 2005). Furthermore, in speaking to infants, parents often provide temporal synchrony between words, object motions, and touch—for example, saying "doll" while moving a doll and having it touch the infant (Gogate & Bahrick, 2001). This greatly increases the chances that babies will remember the association between the word and the object.

In sum, intermodal stimulation fosters all aspects of psychological development. When caregivers provide many concurrent sights, sounds, and touches, babies process more information and learn faster (Bahrick, 2010). Intermodal perception is yet another fundamental capacity that assists infants in their active efforts to build an orderly, understandable world.

LOOK and LISTEN

While watching a parent and infant playing, list instances of parental intermodal stimulation and communication. What is the baby likely learning about people, objects, or language from each intermodal experience?

5.6.5 Understanding Perceptual Development

Now that we have reviewed the development of infant perceptual capacities, how can we put together this diverse array of amazing achievements? Widely accepted answers come from the work of Eleanor and James Gibson. According to the Gibsons' **differentiation theory,** infants actively search for *invariant features* of the environment—those that remain stable—in a constantly changing perceptual world. In pattern perception, for example, young babies search for features that stand out and orient toward faces. Soon they explore a stimulus more thoroughly, noticing *stable relationships* among its features, detecting patterns, such as complex designs and individual faces. Similarly, infants analyze the speech stream for regularities, detecting words, word-order sequences, and—within words—syllable-stress patterns. The development of intermodal perception also reflects this principle (Bahrick & Lickliter, 2012). Babies seek out invariant relationships—first, amodal properties, such as common rate and rhythm, in a voice and face, later more detailed associations, such as unique voice–face matches.

The Gibsons described their theory as *differentiation* (where *differentiate* means "analyze" or "break down") because over time the baby detects finer and finer invariant features among stimuli. In addition to pattern perception and intermodal perception, differentiation applies to depth and object perception: Recall how in each, sensitivity to motion precedes detection of fine-grained features. So one way of understanding perceptual development is to think of it as a built-in tendency to seek order and consistency—a capacity that becomes increasingly fine-tuned with age (Gibson, 1970; Gibson, 1979).

Acting on the environment contributes to perceptual differentiation. According to the Gibsons, perception is enhanced by the discovery of **affordances**—the action possibilities that a situation offers an organism with certain motor capabilities (Gibson, 2003). Infants constantly look for ways in which the environment *affords possibilities for action.* By exploring their surroundings, they figure out which objects can be grasped, squeezed, bounced, or stroked and which surfaces are safe to cross or present the possibility of falling. And from handling objects, babies become more aware of a variety of observable object properties (Perone et al., 2008). As a result, they differentiate their world in new ways.

To illustrate, recall how infants' changing capabilities for independent movement affect their perception. When babies crawl, and again when they walk, they gradually realize that a sloping surface *affords the possibility* of falling (see Figure 5.21). With added practice of each skill, they hesitate to crawl or walk down a risky incline. Experience in trying to keep their balance on various surfaces makes crawlers and walkers more aware of the consequences of their movements. Crawlers come to detect when surface slant places so much body weight on their arms that they will fall forward, and walkers come to sense when an incline shifts body weight so their legs and feet can no longer hold them upright.

FIGURE 5.21 **Babies' changing motor skills transform the way they perceive surfaces.** *Left:* A 12-month-old who has just begun to walk proceeds feet-first down a steep incline, unaware of the high risk of falling. *Right:* An 18-month-old with extensive experience walking knows that it's best to sit and scoot down the incline.

Infants do not transfer their learning about slopes or drop-offs from crawling to walking because the affordances for each posture are different (Adolph, Kretch, & LoBue, 2014). Learning takes time because newly crawling and walking babies cross many types of surfaces in their homes each day. As they experiment with balance and postural adjustments to accommodate each, they perceive surfaces in new ways that guide their movements. As a result, they act more competently.

As we conclude this chapter, it is only fair to note that some researchers believe that babies do more than make sense of experience by searching for invariant features and action possibilities: They also *impose meaning* on what they perceive, constructing categories of objects and events in the surrounding environment (Johnson & Hannon, 2015). We have seen the glimmerings of this *cognitive* point of view in this chapter. For example, older babies *interpret* a familiar face as a source of pleasure and affection and a pattern of blinking lights as a human being walking. This cognitive perspective also has merit in understanding the achievements of infancy. In fact, many researchers combine these two positions, regarding infant development as proceeding from a perceptual to a cognitive emphasis over the first year of life.

 ASK YOURSELF

Connect ■ According to differentiation theory, perceptual development reflects infants' active search for invariant features. Provide examples from research on hearing, pattern perception, object perception, and intermodal perception.

Apply ■ Ben, age 13 months, has just started to walk. Using the concept of affordances, explain why he is likely to step over risky drop-offs.

Reflect ■ Are young infants more competent than you thought they were before you read this chapter? List the capacities that most surprised you.

S U M M A R Y

5.1 Body Growth (p. 153)

5.1 *Describe major changes in body growth over the first two years.*

■ Height and weight gains are greater during the first two years than at any other time after birth. Body fat develops quickly during the first nine months, whereas muscle development is slow and gradual.

■ Body proportions change as growth follows the **cephalocaudal** and **proximodistal trends.**

■ Assessments of skeletal age reveal that girls are ahead of boys in physical maturity, and African-American children tend to be ahead of European-American and Hispanic children.

5.2 Brain Development (p. 155)

5.2a *Describe brain development during infancy and toddlerhood, current methods of measuring brain functioning, and appropriate stimulation to support the brain's potential.*

■ At birth, the brain is nearer its adult size than any other physical structure. **Neurons** rapidly form **synapses** and release **neurotransmitters** to send messages to one another. During the peak period of synaptic growth in any brain region, many surrounding neurons die through **programmed cell death.** Neurons that are seldom stimulated lose their synapses in a process called **synaptic pruning. Glial cells,** responsible for **myelination,** multiply rapidly through the second year, contributing to large gains in brain weight.

■ Measures of brain functioning include those that detect changes in electrical activity in the cerebral cortex (EEG, ERPs), neuroimaging techniques (PET, fMRI), and NIRS, which uses infrared light.

■ The **cerebral cortex** is the largest, most complex brain structure and the last to stop growing. Its regions develop in the general order in which various capacities emerge in the growing child. The frontal lobes, including the **prefrontal cortex** (responsible for complex thought) have the most extended period of development. The hemispheres of the cerebral cortex develop specialized functions, a process called **lateralization. Brain plasticity,** which decreases with age, enables other parts of the brain to take over functions of damaged areas.

■ Stimulation of the brain is essential during sensitive periods. Prolonged early deprivation like that experienced by infants in impoverished orphanages, can disrupt brain growth and interfere with the brain's capacity to manage stress, with long-term psychological consequences.

■ Appropriate early stimulation promotes **experience-expectant brain growth** through ordinary experiences. No evidence exists for a sensitive period in the first few years for **experience-dependent brain growth,** which relies on specific learning experiences. In fact, environments that overwhelm children with inappropriately advanced expectations also interfere with the brain's potential.

© CHRISTINE SCHNEIDER/GETTY IMAGES

5.2b *Explain how the organization of sleep and wakefulness changes over the first two years.*

■ Infants' changing arousal patterns are primarily affected by brain growth, but the social environment also plays a role. Periods of sleep and wakefulness become fewer but longer over the first two years, conforming to a night–day schedule. Most parents in Western nations try to get their babies to sleep through the night much earlier than parents throughout most of the world, who are more likely to cosleep with their babies. Bedtime routines help promote sleep.

5.3 Influences on Early Physical Growth (p. 166)

5.3 *Cite evidence that heredity, nutrition, and parental affection all contribute to early physical growth.*

■ Twin and adoption studies reveal that heredity contributes to body size and rate of physical growth.

■ Breast milk is ideally suited to infants' growth needs. Breastfeeding protects against disease and prevents malnutrition and infant death in poverty-stricken areas of the world.

■ Most infants and toddlers can eat nutritious foods freely without risk of becoming overweight. However, the relationship between rapid weight gain in infancy and obesity at older ages is strengthening, perhaps because of a rise in unhealthy early feeding practices.

■ **Marasmus** and **kwashiorkor** are dietary diseases caused by malnutrition that affect many children in developing countries and, if prolonged, can permanently stunt body growth and brain development. **Weight faltering** illustrates the importance of parental affection and early emotional well-being for normal physical growth.

5.4 Learning Capacities (p. 172)

5.4 *Discuss infant learning capacities, the conditions under which they occur, and the unique value of each.*

■ **Classical conditioning** helps infants associate events that usually occur together in the everyday world. Infants can be classically conditioned most easily when the pairing of an **unconditioned stimulus** (UCS) and a **conditioned stimulus** (CS) has survival value.

■ In **operant conditioning,** infants act on their environment and their behavior is followed by either **reinforcers,** which increase the occurrence of a preceding behavior, or **punishment,** which either removes a desirable stimulus or presents an unpleasant one to decrease the occurrence of a response. In young infants, interesting sights and sounds and pleasurable caregiver interaction serve as effective reinforcers.

■ **Habituation** and **recovery** reveal that at birth, babies are attracted to novelty. Novelty preference (recovery to a novel stimulus) assesses recent memory, whereas familiarity preference (recovery to the familiar stimulus) assesses remote memory.

© ELLEN B. SENISI

■ Infants have a built-in capacity for **statistical learning,** the ability to extract frequently occurring patterns—in speech, music, and visual shapes—from the complex flow of information in their surroundings.

■ Although hotly contested, the capacity for **imitation,** a powerful means of learning that contributes to the parent–infant bond, may be present at birth, as reflected in the apparent ability of newborns to imitate adults' expressions and gestures. Scientists have identified specialized cells called **mirror neurons** that may underlie early imitation.

5.5 Motor Development
(p. 177)

5.5 Describe dynamic systems theory of motor development, along with factors that influence motor progress in the first two years.

■ According to **dynamic systems theory of motor development,** children acquire new motor skills by combining existing skills into increasingly complex systems of action. Each new skill is a joint product of central nervous system development, the body's movement capacities, the child's goals and perceptual and cognitive capacities, and environmental supports for the skill.

■ Cultural values and infant-rearing customs contribute to the emergence and refinement of early motor skills.

■ During the first year, infants perfect their reaching and grasping. The poorly coordinated **prereaching** of the newborn gradually becomes more flexible and accurate, and the clumsy **ulnar grasp** is transformed into a refined **pincer grasp.**

5.6 Perceptual Development (p. 184)

5.6a Identify changes in hearing and in depth, pattern, object, and intermodal perception during infancy.

■ Infants organize sounds into increasingly complex patterns. In the middle of the first year, as part of the **perceptual narrowing effect,** they become more sensitive to the sounds of their own language. Infants' capacity for statistical learning enables them to detect speech regularities for which they will later learn meanings.

■ Rapid maturation of the eye and visual centers in the cerebral cortex supports the development of focusing, color discrimination, and visual acuity during the first few months. The ability to scan the environment and track moving objects also improves.

■ Motion is the first depth cue to which infants are sensitive, followed by sensitivity to binocular and then to pictorial depth cues. Experience in crawling enhances depth perception, but babies must learn to use depth cues for each body position in order to avoid drop-offs.

■ Newborns prefer to look at patterned rather than plain stimuli. Once able to take in all aspects of a pattern, infants integrate its parts into a unified whole. With age, they prefer more complex, meaningful patterns.

■ Newborns prefer to look at photos and simplified drawings of faces with features arranged naturally. They quickly learn to prefer their mother's face to that of an unfamiliar woman, and at 3 months, they make fine-grained distinctions among the features of different faces. At 5 months, they perceive emotional expressions as meaningful wholes. Early experience promotes perceptual narrowing with respect to gender and racial information in faces.

■ From birth, **size** and **shape constancy** and perception of object unity help babies detect a coherent world of objects. At first, infants depend on motion and spatial arrangement to identify objects. After 4 months of age, they rely more on shape, color, and pattern. Soon they can monitor increasingly intricate paths of objects, and they look for featural information to detect the identity of moving objects.

■ From the start, infants are capable of **intermodal perception**—combining information across sensory modalities. Detection of **amodal sensory properties,** such as common rate, rhythm, or intensity, or texture and shape, provides the basis for detecting many intermodal matches.

5.6b Explain differentiation theory of perceptual development.

■ According to **differentiation theory,** perceptual development involves detecting increasingly fine-grained invariant features in a constantly changing perceptual world. Perceptual differentiation is guided by discovery of **affordances**—the action possibilities that a situation offers the individual.

IMPORTANT TERMS AND CONCEPTS

affordances (p. 192)
amodal sensory properties (p. 191)
brain plasticity (p. 160)
cephalocaudal trend (p. 155)
cerebral cortex (p. 158)
classical conditioning (p. 172)
conditioned response (CR) (p. 172)
conditioned stimulus (CS) (p. 172)
differentiation theory (p. 192)
dynamic systems theory of motor development (p. 179)
experience-dependent brain growth (p. 163)
experience-expectant brain growth (p. 163)
glial cells (p. 157)
habituation (p. 174)

imitation (p. 176)
intermodal perception (p. 191)
kwashiorkor (p. 170)
lateralization (p. 159)
marasmus (p. 170)
mirror neurons (p. 177)
myelination (p. 157)
neurons (p. 155)
neurotransmitters (p. 156)
operant conditioning (p. 173)
perceptual narrowing effect (p. 185)
pincer grasp (p. 183)
prefrontal cortex (p. 159)
prereaching (p. 182)
programmed cell death (p. 156)

proximodistal trend (p. 155)
punishment (p. 173)
recovery (p. 174)
reinforcer (p. 173)
shape constancy (p. 190)
size constancy (p. 190)
statistical learning (p. 175)
synapses (p. 155)
synaptic pruning (p. 156)
ulnar grasp (p. 183)
unconditioned response (UCR) (p. 172)
unconditioned stimulus (UCS) (p. 172)
weight faltering (p. 171)

chapter

6 | Cognitive Development in Infancy and Toddlerhood

The Birds Are Back

Lene Margrethe Linnerud, 12 years, Norway

Children greet a returning flock of birds while their baby sibling plays nearby. In Chapter 6, you will see that a stimulating environment and the guidance of more mature members of their culture ensure that infants' and toddlers' cognition will develop at its best.

Reprinted with permission from The International Museum of Children's Art, Oslo, Norway

W   hen 19-month-olds Caitlin and Grace and 21-month-old Timmy gathered
       at Ginette's child-care home, the playroom was alive with activity. The
       three spirited explorers were bent on discovery. Grace dropped shapes
through holes in a plastic box that Ginette held and adjusted so the more difficult
ones would fall smoothly into place. Once a few shapes were inside, Grace grabbed
the box and shook it, squealing with delight as the lid fell open and the shapes scattered around her. The clatter attracted Timmy, who picked up a shape, carried it to
the railing at the top of the basement steps, dropped it overboard, and then followed
it with a teddy bear, a ball, his shoe, and a spoon.

Meanwhile, Caitlin pulled open a drawer, unloaded a set of wooden bowls,
stacked them in a pile, knocked it over, and then banged two bowls together. With
each action, the children seemed to be asking, "How do things work? What makes
interesting events happen? Which ones can I control?"

As the toddlers experimented, I could see the beginnings of spoken language—
a whole new way of influencing the world. "Baw!" Caitlin exclaimed as Timmy tossed
the bright red ball down the basement steps. "Bye-bye," Grace chimed in, waving as
the ball rolled out of sight. Later that day, Grace revealed that she could pretend.
"Night-night," she said, hugging her teddy bear, putting her head down, briefly closing her eyes, then "awakening" and exclaiming, "No more nap!"

Over the first two years, the small, reflexive newborn baby becomes a self-
assertive, purposeful being who solves simple problems and starts to master the
most amazing human ability: language. Parents wonder, "How does all this happen
so quickly?" This question has also captivated researchers, yielding a wealth of findings along with vigorous debate over how to explain the astonishing pace of infant
and toddler cognitive development.

In this chapter, we take up three perspectives: Piaget's *cognitive-developmental
theory, information processing,* and Vygotsky's *sociocultural theory.* We also consider
the usefulness of tests that measure infants' and toddlers' intellectual progress.
Finally, we look at the dawning of language. We will see how toddlers' first words
build on early cognitive achievements and how, very soon, new words and expressions greatly increase the speed and flexibility of thinking. Throughout development,
cognition and language mutually support each other. ■

What's Ahead in Chapter 6

6.1 Piaget's Cognitive-Developmental Theory

Swiss theorist Jean Piaget inspired a vision of children as busy, motivated explorers whose thinking develops as they act directly on the environment. Influenced by his background in biology, Piaget believed that the child's mind forms and modifies psychological structures so they achieve a better fit with external reality. Recall from Chapter 1 that in Piaget's theory, children move through four stages between infancy and adolescence. During these stages, Piaget claimed, all aspects of cogni-tion develop in an integrated fashion, changing in a similar way at about the same time.

Piaget's **sensorimotor stage** spans the first two years of life. Piaget believed that infants and toddlers "think" with their eyes, ears, hands, and other sensorimotor equipment. They cannot yet carry out many activities inside their heads. But by the end of toddlerhood, children can solve everyday practical problems and represent their experiences in speech, gesture, and play. To appreciate Piaget's view of how these vast changes take place, let's consider some important concepts.

6.1.1 Piaget's Ideas About Cognitive Change

According to Piaget, specific psychological structures—organized ways of making sense of experience called **schemes**—change with age. At first, schemes are sensorimotor action patterns. For example, at 6 months, Timmy dropped objects in a fairly rigid way, simply letting go of a rattle or teething ring and watching with interest. By 18 months, his "dropping scheme" had become deliberate and creative. In tossing objects down the basement stairs, he threw some in the air, bounced others off walls, released some gently and others forcefully. Soon, instead of just acting on objects, he will show evidence of thinking before he acts. For Piaget, this change marks the transition from sensorimotor to preoperational thought.

In Piaget's theory, two processes, *adaptation* and *organization,* account for changes in schemes.

In Piaget's theory, first schemes are sensorimotor action patterns. As this 12-month-old experiments with his dropping scheme, his behavior becomes more deliberate and varied.

Adaptation   The next time you have a chance, notice how infants and toddlers tirelessly repeat actions that lead to interesting effects. **Adaptation** involves building schemes through direct interaction with the environment. It consists of two complementary activities: *assimilation* and *accommodation.* During **assimilation,** we use our current schemes to interpret the external world. For example, when Timmy dropped objects, he was assimilating them to his sensorimotor "dropping scheme." In **accommodation,** we create new schemes or adjust old ones after noticing that our current ways of thinking do not capture the environment completely. When Timmy dropped objects in different ways, he modified his dropping scheme to take account of the varied properties of objects.

According to Piaget, the balance between assimilation and accommodation varies over time. When children are not changing much, they assimilate more than they accommodate—a steady, comfortable state that Piaget called cognitive *equilibrium.* During times of rapid cognitive change, children are in a state of *disequilibrium,* or cognitive discomfort. Realizing that new information does not match their current schemes, they shift from assimilation to accommodation. After modifying their schemes, they move back toward assimilation, exercising their newly changed structures until they are ready to be modified again.

Each time this back-and-forth movement between equilibrium and disequilibrium occurs, more effective schemes are produced. Because the times of greatest accommodation are the earliest ones, the sensorimotor stage is Piaget's most complex period of development.

Organization   Schemes also change through **organization,** a process that occurs internally, apart from direct contact with the environment. Once children form new schemes, they rearrange them, linking them with other schemes to create a strongly interconnected cognitive system. For example, eventually Timmy will relate "dropping" to "throwing" and to his developing understanding of "nearness" and "farness." According to Piaget, schemes truly reach equilibrium when they become part of a broad network of structures that can be jointly applied to the surrounding world (Piaget, 1936/1952).

In the following sections, we will first describe infant development as Piaget saw it, noting research that supports his observations. Then we will consider evidence demonstrating that in some ways, babies' cognitive competence is more advanced than Piaget believed.

6.1.2 The Sensorimotor Stage

The difference between the newborn baby and the 2-year-old child is so vast that Piaget divided the sensorimotor stage into six substages, summarized in Table 6.1. Piaget based this sequence on a very small sample: He observed his own three children carefully and also presented them with everyday problems (such as hidden objects) that helped reveal their understanding of the world.

TABLE 6.1 **Summary of Piaget's Sensorimotor Stage**

SENSORIMOTOR SUBSTAGE	TYPICAL ADAPTIVE BEHAVIORS
1. Reflexive schemes (birth–1 month)	Newborn reflexes (see Chapter 4, page 134)
2. Primary circular reactions (1–4 months)	Simple motor habits centered around the infant's own body; limited anticipation of events
3. Secondary circular reactions (4–8 months)	Actions aimed at repeating interesting effects in the surrounding world; imitation of familiar behaviors
4. Coordination of secondary circular reactions (8–12 months)	Intentional, or goal-directed, behavior; ability to find a hidden object in the first location in which it is hidden (object permanence); improved anticipation of events; imitation of behaviors slightly different from those the infant usually performs
5. Tertiary circular reactions (12–18 months)	Exploration of the properties of objects by acting on them in novel ways; imitation of novel behaviors; ability to search in several locations for a hidden object (accurate A–B search)
6. Mental representation (18 months–2 years)	Internal depictions of objects and events, as indicated by sudden solutions to problems; ability to find an object that has been moved while out of sight (invisible displacement); deferred imitation; and make-believe play

According to Piaget, at birth infants know so little that they cannot explore purposefully. The **circular reaction** provides a special means of adapting their first schemes. It involves stumbling onto a new experience caused by the baby's own motor activity. The reaction is "circular" because, as the infant tries to repeat the event again and again, a sensorimotor response that originally occurred by chance strengthens into a new scheme. Consider Caitlin, who at age 2 months accidentally made a smacking sound after a feeding. Intrigued, she tried to repeat it until, after a few days, she became quite expert at smacking her lips.

The circular reaction initially centers on the infant's own body and later turns outward, toward manipulation of objects. In the second year, it becomes experimental and creative, aimed at producing novel outcomes. Infants' difficulty stopping themselves from repeating new and interesting behaviors may underlie the circular reaction. This immaturity in inhibition seems to be adaptive, helping to ensure that new skills will not be interrupted before they strengthen (Carey & Markman, 1999). Piaget considered revisions in the circular reaction so important that, as Table 6.1 shows, he named the sensorimotor substages after them.

Repeating Chance Behaviors Piaget saw newborn reflexes as the building blocks of sensorimotor intelligence. In Substage 1, babies suck, grasp, and look in much the same way, no matter what experiences they encounter. Around 1 month, as they enter Substage 2, they start to gain voluntary control over their actions through the *primary circular reaction,* by repeating chance behaviors largely motivated by basic needs. This leads to some simple motor habits, such as sucking their fists or thumbs. Babies of this substage also begin to vary their behavior in response to environmental demands. For example, they open their mouths differently for a nipple than for a spoon. And they start to anticipate events. On awaking from a nap hungry, 3-month-old Timmy would stop crying as soon as Vanessa entered the room—a sign that feeding time was near.

This 3-month-old repeats a newly discovered action—sucking her toes—in a primary circular reaction that helps her gain voluntary control over her behavior.

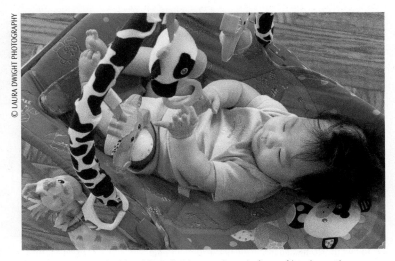

When this 4-month-old accidentally hits a toy hung in front of her, her action causes it to swing. Using the secondary circular reaction, she tries to recapture this interesting effect. In the process, she forms a new "hitting scheme."

During Substage 3, from 4 to 8 months, infants sit up and reach for and manipulate objects. These motor attainments strengthen the *secondary circular reaction,* through which babies try to repeat interesting events in the surrounding environment that are caused by their own actions. For example, 4-month-old Caitlin accidentally knocked a toy hung in front of her, producing a fascinating swinging motion. Over the next three days, Caitlin tried to repeat this effect, gradually forming a new "hitting" scheme.

Improved control over their own behavior permits infants to imitate others' behavior more effectively. Piaget noted, however, that 4- to 8-month-olds cannot adapt flexibly and quickly enough to imitate novel behaviors. Although they enjoy watching an adult demonstrate a game of pat-a-cake, they are not yet able to participate.

Intentional Behavior   In Substage 4, 8- to 12-month-olds combine schemes into new, more complex action sequences. As a result, actions that lead to new schemes no longer have a random, hit-or-miss quality—*accidentally* bringing the thumb to the mouth or *happening* to hit the toy. Instead, 8- to 12-month-olds can engage in **intentional,** or **goal-directed, behavior,** coordinating schemes deliberately to solve simple problems. Consider Piaget's famous object-hiding task, in which he shows the baby an attractive toy and then hides it behind his hand or under a cover. Infants of this substage can find the object by coordinating two schemes— "pushing" aside the obstacle and "grasping" the toy. Piaget regarded these *means–end action sequences* as the foundation for all problem solving.

Retrieving hidden objects reveals that infants have begun to master **object permanence,** the understanding that objects continue to exist when they are out of sight. But this awareness is not yet complete. Babies make the **A-not-B search error:** If they reach several times for an object at a first hiding place (A) and then see it moved to a second (B) hiding place, they still search for it in the first hiding place (A). Consequently, Piaget concluded that they do not have a clear image of the object as persisting when hidden from view.

Infants in Substage 4, who can better anticipate events, sometimes use their capacity for intentional behavior to try to change those events. At 10 months, Timmy crawled after Vanessa when she put on her coat, whimpering to keep her from leaving. Also, babies can now imitate behaviors slightly different from those they usually perform. After watching someone else, they try to stir with a spoon, push a toy car, or drop raisins into a cup (Piaget, 1945/1951).

In Substage 5, from 12 to 18 months, the *tertiary circular reaction* emerges, in which toddlers repeat behaviors with variation. Recall how Timmy dropped objects over the basement steps, trying this action, then that, then another. This deliberately exploratory approach makes 12- to 18-month-olds better problem solvers. For example, Grace figured out how to fit a shape through a hole in a container by turning and twisting it until it fell through and how to use a stick to get an out-of-reach toy. According to Piaget, this capacity to experiment leads toddlers to look for a hidden toy in several locations, displaying an accurate A–B search. Their more flexible action patterns also permit them to imitate many more behaviors, such as stacking blocks, scribbling on paper, and making funny faces.

To find the toy hidden inside the pot, a 10-month-old engages in intentional, goal-directed behavior—the basis for all problem solving.

Using a tertiary circular reaction, this baby twists, turns, and pushes until a block fits through its matching hole in a shape sorter. Between 12 and 18 months, toddlers take a deliberately experimental approach to problem solving.

Mental Representation   Substage 6 brings the ability to create **mental representations**—internal depictions of information that the mind can manipulate. Our most powerful mental representations are of two kinds: (1) *images*—mental pictures of objects, people, and spaces; and (2) *concepts*—categories in which similar objects or events are grouped together. We use a mental image to retrace our steps when we've misplaced something or to imitate someone's behavior long after observing it. By thinking in concepts and labeling them (for example, "ball" for all rounded, movable objects used in play), we become more efficient thinkers, organizing our diverse experiences into meaningful, manageable, and memorable units.

Piaget noted that 18- to 24-month-olds arrive at solutions suddenly rather than through trial-and-error behavior. In doing so, they seem to experiment with actions inside their heads—evidence that they can mentally represent their experiences. For example, at 19 months, Grace—after bumping her new push toy against a wall—paused for a moment as if to "think," and then immediately turned the toy in a new direction.

Representation enables older toddlers to solve advanced object permanence problems involving *invisible displacement*—finding a toy moved while out of sight, such as into a small box while under a cover. It also permits **deferred imitation**—the ability to remember and copy the behavior of models who are not present. And it makes possible **make-believe play,** in which children act out everyday and imaginary activities. As the sensorimotor stage draws to a close, mental symbols have become major instruments of thinking.

The capacity for mental representation enables this 20-month-old to engage in first acts of make-believe.

6.1.3 Follow-Up Research on Infant Cognitive Development

Many studies suggest that infants display a wide array of understandings earlier than Piaget believed. Recall the operant conditioning research reviewed in Chapter 5, in which newborns sucked vigorously on a nipple to gain access to interesting sights and sounds. This behavior, which closely resembles Piaget's secondary circular reaction, shows that babies try to explore and control the external world long before 4 to 8 months. In fact, they do so as soon as they are born.

To discover what infants know about hidden objects and other aspects of physical reality, researchers often use the **violation-of-expectation method.** They may *habituate* babies to a physical event (expose them to the event until their looking declines) to familiarize them with a situation in which their knowledge will be tested. Or they may simply show babies an *expected event* (one that is consistent with reality) and an *unexpected event* (a variation of the first event that violates reality). Heightened attention to the unexpected event suggests that the infant is "surprised" by a deviation from physical reality and, therefore, is aware of that aspect of the physical world.

The violation-of-expectation method is controversial. Some researchers believe that it indicates limited, implicit (nonconscious) awareness of physical events—not the full-blown, conscious understanding that was Piaget's focus in requiring infants to act on their surroundings, as in searching for hidden objects (Campos et al., 2008). Others maintain that the method reveals only babies' perceptual preference for novelty, not their knowledge of the physical world. According to these researchers, infants may look longer at the novel (unexpected) event simply because it requires more time to make sense of than the expected event (Dunn & Bremner, 2017; Bremner, Slater, & Johnson, 2015). Let's examine this debate in light of recent evidence.

Object Permanence   In a series of studies using the violation-of-expectation method, Renée Baillargeon and her collaborators claimed to have found evidence for object permanence in the first few months of life. Figure 6.1 on page 202 describes and illustrates one of these studies, in which infants exposed to both an expected and an unexpected object-hiding event looked longer at the unexpected event (Aguiar & Baillargeon, 2002; Baillargeon & DeVos, 1991).

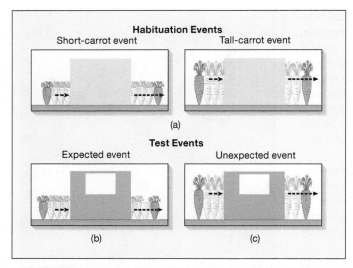

FIGURE 6.1 **Testing young infants for awareness of object permanence using the violation-of-expectation method.** (a) First, infants were habituated to two events: a short carrot and a tall carrot moving behind a yellow screen on alternate trials. Next, the researchers presented two test events. The color of the screen was changed to help infants notice its window. (b) In the *expected event,* the carrot shorter than the window's lower edge moved behind the blue screen and reappeared on the other side. (c) In the *unexpected event,* the carrot taller than the window's lower edge moved behind the screen and did not appear in the window, but then emerged intact on the other side. Infants as young as 2½ to 3½ months looked longer at the *unexpected event,* suggesting that they had some awareness of object permanence. (Adapted from R. Baillargeon & J. DeVos, 1991, "Object Permanence in Young Infants: Further Evidence," *Child Development, 62,* p. 1230. © 1991, John Wiley and Sons. Reprinted with permission of John Wiley & Sons Ltd. conveyed through Copyright Clearance Center, Inc.)

Additional violation-of-expectation studies yielded similar results, suggesting that infants look longer at a wide variety of unexpected events involving hidden objects (Wang, Baillargeon, & Paterson, 2005). Still, several researchers using similar procedures failed to confirm some of Baillargeon's findings (Cohen & Marks, 2002; Schöner & Thelen, 2006; Sirois & Jackson, 2012). And, as previously noted, critics question what babies' looking preferences tell us about what they actually understand.

Another type of looking behavior suggests that young infants are aware that objects persist when out of view. Four- and 5-month-olds will track a ball's path of movement as it disappears and reappears from behind a barrier, even gazing ahead to where they expect it to emerge. As further support for such awareness, 5- to 9-month-olds more often engaged in such predictive tracking when a ball viewed on a computer screen gradually rolled behind a barrier than when it disappeared instantaneously or imploded (rapidly decreased in size) at the barrier's edge (Bertenthal, Gredebäck, & Boyer, 2013; Bertenthal, Longo, & Kenny, 2007). With age, babies are more likely to fixate on the predicted place of the ball's reappearance and wait for it—evidence of an increasingly secure grasp of object permanence.

If young infants do have some notion of object permanence, how do we explain Piaget's finding that even infants capable of reaching do not try to search for hidden objects before 8 months of age? Compared with looking reactions in violation-of-expectation tasks, searching for a hidden object is far more cognitively demanding: The baby must figure out where the hidden object is. Consistent with this idea, infants solve some object-hiding tasks before others. For example, 10-month-olds search for an object placed on a table and covered by a cloth before they search for an object that a hand deposits under a cloth. Experience with partially hidden objects—common in infants' everyday lives—may help them grasp that the cloth-covered object has not been replaced by the cloth but, rather, continues to exist and can be retrieved. In the second, more difficult task, infants seem to expect the object to reappear in the hand from which it initially disappeared (Moore & Meltzoff, 1999, 2008). Not until 14 months can most babies infer that the hand deposited the object under the cloth.

Searching for Objects Hidden in More Than One Location

Once 8- to 12-month-olds search for hidden objects, they make the A-not-B search error. Some research suggests that they search at A (where they found the object on previous reaches) instead of B (its most recent location) because they have trouble inhibiting a previously rewarded motor response (Diamond, Cruttenden, & Neiderman, 1994; Johansson, Forssman, & Bohlin, 2014). Another possibility is that after finding the object several times at A, babies do not attend closely when it is hidden at B (Ruffman & Langman, 2002).

A more comprehensive explanation is that a complex, dynamic system of factors—having built a habit of reaching toward A, continuing to look at A, having the hiding place at B appear similar to the one at A, and maintaining a constant body posture—increases the chances that the baby will make the A-not-B search error. Disrupting any one of these factors induces 10-month-olds to think more flexibly, increasing their accurate searching at B (Thelen et al., 2001). In addition, older infants are still perfecting reaching and grasping (see Chapter 5) (Berger, 2010). If these motor skills are challenging, babies have little attention left to focus on inhibiting their habitual reach toward A.

Around 12 months, infants respond to an adult's verbal prompts to search for a hidden object ("Find the ball!") by looking at and gesturing toward where they last saw it (Saylor, Ganea, & Vásquez, 2011). But they do so only if the object is easily accessible. If an adult places the container in which the object is hidden in an inaccessible location (on an out-of-reach shelf), 12-month-olds won't look, point, or move toward the container (Osina, Saylor, &

Ganea, 2017). Their difficulty is not that they have forgotten about the hidden object, because if the adult moves the container to an accessible location, 12-month-olds promptly recover the object. Rather, making a hidden object inaccessible seems to inhibit their willingness to search. By 16 months, searching is no longer affected by object accessibility. As toddlers grow taller and walk more securely, they may modify their representations of hidden objects, viewing those beyond their immediate reach as retrievable.

In sum, mastery of object permanence is a gradual achievement. Babies' understanding becomes increasingly complex with age: They must perceive an object's identity by integrating feature and movement information (see pages 190–191 in Chapter 5), distinguish the object from the barrier concealing it and the surface on which it rests, keep track of the object's whereabouts, and use this knowledge to obtain the object (Bremner, Slater, & Johnson, 2015). A wide variety of experiences perceiving, remembering, acting on, and communicating about objects undoubtedly contributes to the emergence of these capabilities.

Mental Representation   In Piaget's theory, before about 18 months, infants are unable to mentally represent experience. Yet 8- to 10-month-olds' recall the location of hidden objects after delays of more than a minute and 14-month-olds' after delays of a day or more, clearly indicating that babies construct mental representations of objects and their whereabouts (McDonough, 1999; Moore & Meltzoff, 2004). In studies of deferred imitation and problem solving, representational thought is evident even earlier. And toddlers make impressive strides in symbolic understanding, as their grasp of words and photos reveals.

Deferred and Inferred Imitation   Piaget studied imitation by noting when his three children demonstrated it in their everyday behavior. Under these conditions, a great deal must be known about the infant's daily life to be sure that deferred imitation—which requires infants to represent a model's past behavior—has occurred.

Laboratory research, in contrast, suggests that deferred imitation is present at 6 weeks of age! Infants who watched an unfamiliar adult's facial expression imitated it when exposed to the same adult the next day (Meltzoff & Moore, 1994). As motor capacities improve, infants copy actions with objects. In one study, an adult showed 6- and 9-month-olds a novel series of actions with a puppet: taking its glove off, shaking the glove to ring a bell inside, and replacing the glove. When tested a day later, infants who had seen the novel actions were far more likely to imitate them (see Figure 6.2). And when the adult paired a second, motionless puppet

LOOK and LISTEN

Using an attractive toy and cloth, try several object-hiding tasks with 8- to 14-month-olds. Is their search behavior consistent with research findings?

(a)   (b)

FIGURE 6.2   Testing infants for deferred imitation. After researchers performed a novel series of actions with a puppet, this 6-month-old imitated the actions a day later: (a) removing the glove; (b) shaking the glove to ring a bell inside. With age, gains in recall are evident in deferred imitation of others' behaviors over longer delays.

COURTESY OF CAROLYN ROVEE-COLLIER

with the first puppet 1 to 6 days before the demonstration, 6- to 9-month-olds generalized the actions to this new, very different-looking puppet (Barr, Marrott, & Rovee-Collier, 2003; Giles & Rovee-Collier, 2011). Even more impressive, after having seen Puppet A paired with B and Puppet B paired with C on successive days, infants transferred modeled actions from A to C and from C to A, although they had not directly observed this pair together (Townsend & Rovee-Collier, 2007). Already, infants can form flexible mental representations that include chains of relevant associations.

Gains in recall, expressed through deferred imitation, are accompanied by changes in brain-wave activity during memory tasks, as measured by event-related potentials (ERPs). This suggests that improvements in memory storage in the cerebral cortex contribute to these advances (Bauer et al., 2006). Between 12 and 18 months, toddlers use deferred imitation skillfully to enrich their range of schemes. They retain modeled behaviors for at least several months, copy the actions of peers as well as adults, and imitate across a change in context—for example, enact at home a behavior seen at child care (Meltzoff & Williamson, 2010; Patel, Gaylord, & Fagen, 2013). The ability to recall modeled behaviors in the order they occurred— evident as early as 6 months—also strengthens over the second year (Bauer, Larkina, & Deocampo, 2011; Rovee-Collier & Cuevas, 2009). And when toddlers imitate in correct sequence, they remember more behaviors.

Older infants and toddlers even imitate rationally, by *inferring* others' intentions! They are more likely to imitate purposeful than accidental or arbitrary behaviors on objects. And they adapt their imitative acts to a model's goals (Kolling, Óturai, & Knopf, 2014; Zmyj & Buttelmann, 2014). If 12-month-olds see an adult perform an unusual action for fun (make a toy dog enter a miniature house by jumping through the chimney, even though its door is wide open), they copy the behavior. But if the adult engages in the odd behavior because she *must* (she makes the dog go through the chimney only after first trying to use the door and finding it locked), 12-month-olds typically imitate the more efficient action (putting the dog through the door) (Schwier et al., 2006).

Between 14 and 18 months, toddlers become increasingly adept at imitating actions an adult *tries* to produce, even if these are not fully realized (Bellagamba, Camaioni, & Colonnesi, 2006; Olineck & Poulin-Dubois, 2009). On one occasion, Ginette attempted to pour some raisins into a small bag but missed, spilling them onto the counter. A moment later, Grace began dropping the raisins into the bag, indicating that she had inferred Ginette's goal.

Though advanced in terms of Piaget's predictions, toddlers' ability to represent others' intentions—a cornerstone of social understanding and communication—has roots in earlier sensorimotor activity (Rosander & von Hofsten, 2011). Infants' skill at engaging in goal-directed actions—reaching for objects at 3 to 4 months, pointing to objects at 9 months— predicts their awareness of an adult's similar behavior as goal-directed (Gerson & Woodward, 2010; Woodward, 2009). And the better 10-month-olds are at detecting the goals of others' gazes and reaches, the more successful they are four months later at inferring an adult's intention from her incomplete actions in an imitation task (Olineck & Poulin-Dubois, 2009).

Problem Solving As Piaget indicated, around 7 to 8 months, infants develop intentional means–end action sequences that they use to solve sensorimotor problems, such as pulling on a cloth to obtain an out-of-reach toy resting on it or grasping a handle to secure a toy attached to its far end (Fagard et al., 2015; Willatts, 1999). Out of these explorations of object-to-object relations, the capacity for tool use in problem solving—manipulating an object (tool) as a means to a goal—emerges (Keen, 2011).

For example, 12-month-olds who were repeatedly presented with a spoon containing food, oriented so its handle pointed toward their preferred hand (usually the right), adapted their grip when the spoon's handle was presented in the opposite orientation (to the left). As a result, they succeeded in transporting the food to their mouths most of the time (McCarty & Keen, 2005). With age, babies increasingly adjusted their grip to fit the spoon's orientation in advance, planning ahead for what they wanted to do with the tool.

In each of the tasks just mentioned, the tool and the object were physically linked. Not until the middle of the second year can toddlers engage in tool use when an unfamiliar tool and an object they want are spatially separated. In several studies, an adult presented 14- to

22-month-olds with an out-of-reach toy and a small rake that was placed to the side of the toy. Around 18 months, toddlers spontaneously began using the rake to get the toy, with the number doing so rising gradually with age (Fagard, Rat-Fischer, & O'Regan, 2014; Rat-Fischer, O'Regan, & Fagard, 2012). A demonstration of how to use the tool, in which the adult first highlighted her goal by stretching her arm and hand toward the toy and saying, "I can't get it," led 16-month-olds to try harder to rake in the toy, though they often did not succeed (Esseily et al., 2013; Fagard et al., 2016). Merely showing toddlers how to use the rake had little impact until 18 months, the age at which they began discovering the tool's use on their own.

These findings suggest that around the middle of the second year, infants begin forming mental representations of how to use an unfamiliar tool to secure a desired object. As Piaget suggested, they have some ability to move beyond trial-and-error experimentation and represent a solution to a problem mentally.

Symbolic Understanding One of the most momentous early attainments is the realization that words can be used to cue mental images of things not physically present—a symbolic capacity called **displaced reference** that emerges around the first birthday. It greatly enhances toddlers' capacity to learn about the world through communicating with others. As we saw in our discussion of objects hidden in more than one location, 12-month-olds respond to the verbal label of an absent toy by looking at and gesturing toward a nearby spot where they last saw it. And on hearing the name of a parent or sibling who has just left the room, most 13-month-olds turn toward the door (DeLoache & Ganea, 2009). The more experience toddlers have with an object and its verbal label, the more likely they are to call up a mental representation when they hear the object's name. As memory and vocabulary improve, skill at displaced reference expands.

But at first, toddlers have difficulty using language to acquire new information about an absent object—an ability that is essential for learning from symbols. In one study, an adult taught 19- and 22-month-olds a name for a stuffed animal—"Lucy"—a frog. Then, with the frog out of sight, each toddler was told that some water had spilled, so "Lucy's all wet!" Finally, the adult showed the toddler three stuffed animals—a wet frog, a dry frog, and a pig—and said, "Get Lucy!" (Ganea et al., 2007). Although all the children remembered that Lucy was a frog, only the 22-month-olds identified the wet frog as Lucy. This capacity to use language as a flexible symbolic tool—to modify an existing mental representation—improves into the preschool years.

A beginning awareness of the symbolic function of pictures emerges in the first year, strengthening in the second. By 9 months, the majority of infants touch, rub, or pat a color photo of an object but rarely try to grasp it (Ziemer, Plumert, & Pick, 2012). These behaviors suggest that 9-month-olds do not mistake a picture for the real thing, though they may not yet comprehend it as a symbol. By the middle of the second year, toddlers clearly treat pictures symbolically, as long as the pictures strongly resemble real objects. After hearing a novel label ("blicket") applied to a color photo of an unfamiliar object, most 15- to 24-month-olds—when presented with both the real object and its picture and asked to indicate the "blicket"—gave a symbolic response (Ganea et al., 2009). They selected either the real object or both the object and its picture, not the picture alone.

Around this time, toddlers frequently use pictures as vehicles for communicating with others and acquiring new knowledge. They point to, name, and talk about pictures, and they can apply something learned from a book with realistic-looking pictures to real objects, and vice versa (Ganea, Ma, & DeLoache, 2011; Simcock, Garrity, & Barr, 2011).

Picture-rich environments in which caregivers often direct babies' attention to the link between pictures and their referents promote pictorial understanding. In non-Western cultures where pictures are rare, symbolic understanding of pictures is delayed (Callaghan et al., 2011). In a study carried out in a village community in Tanzania, Africa, where children receive no exposure to pictures

© ELLEN B. SENISI

A 17-month-old points to a picture in a book, revealing her beginning awareness of the symbolic function of pictures. But pictures must be highly realistic for toddlers to treat them symbolically.

Social Issues: Education | Baby Learning from Screen Media: The Video Deficit Effect

Children first become TV and video viewers in early infancy, as they are exposed to programs watched by parents and older siblings or to ones specially aimed at baby viewers. U.S. parents report that 50 percent of 2-month-olds watch TV and videos, a figure that rises to 90 percent by 2 years of age. Smart phone and tablet use by children under age 2, who often view videos on these devices, is similar. Average screen time increases from 55 minutes per day at 6 months to just under 1½ hours per day at age 2 (Anand et al., 2014; Cespedes et al., 2014; Kabali et al., 2015). Although parents assume that babies learn from videos, research indicates that babies cannot take full advantage of them.

Initially, infants respond to videos of people as if viewing people directly—smiling, moving their arms and legs, and (by 6 months) imitating the actions of a televised adult (Barr, Muentener, & Garcia, 2007). But when shown videos of attractive toys, 9-month-olds touch and grab at the screen, suggesting that they confuse the images with the real thing. By the middle of the second year, manual exploration declines in favor of pointing at the images (Pierroutsakos & Troseth, 2003). Nevertheless, toddlers have difficulty applying what they see on video to real situations.

In a series of studies, some 2-year-olds watched through a window while an adult hid an object in an adjoining room, while others watched the same event on a video screen. Children in the direct-viewing condition retrieved the toy easily; those in the video condition had difficulty (Troseth, 2003). This **video deficit effect**—poorer performance after a video than a live demonstration—has also been found for 2-year-olds' deferred imitation, word learning, and means–end problem solving (Bellagamba et al., 2012; Hayne, Herbert, & Simcock, 2003; Roseberry et al., 2009).

Making sense of complex video, even when it depicts familiar events, is cognitively challenging for toddlers, who require more time to process two-dimensional images than their three-dimensional real-life equivalents (Kirkorian, 2018; Kirkorian & Choi, 2017). In addition, video typically lacks social cues that support toddlers' everyday learning, such as caregivers looking at and conversing with them directly and establishing a shared focus on objects.

In one study, researchers provided 12- to 25-month olds with a series of tablet sessions involving either real-time video chat through FaceTime or noninteractive, prerecorded videos. The two types of sessions were similar in content: An adult introduced herself, labeled novel toys, and read a book with a give-and-take verbal pattern. After a week of six 8- to 12-minute tablet sessions, only participants in the FaceTime condition recognized and preferred to play with their video partner in real life. The FaceTime condition also resulted in greater learning from book reading and, among the oldest toddlers, mastery of more novel words (Myers et al., 2017). In another investigation comparing an interactive video experience on closed circuit TV with a noninteractive video, 2-year-olds in the interactive condition were far more successful in using a verbal cue from an adult on video to retrieve a hidden toy in real life (Troseth, Saylor, & Archer, 2006).

Around age 2½, the video deficit effect declines. The American Academy of Pediatrics (American Academy of Pediatrics, 2016a) recommends against screen media exposure before 1½ to 2 years of age and, between 2 and 5 years, limiting it to one hour per day with parental coviewing. In support of this advice, amount of TV viewing is negatively related to toddlers' language progress (Zimmerman, Christakis, & Meltzoff, 2007). And 1- to 3-year-old heavy viewers tend to have attention, memory, and reading difficulties in the early school years (Christakis et al., 2004; Zimmerman & Christakis, 2005).

When toddlers do watch TV or video, it is likely to work best as a teaching tool when it is rich in social cues (Lauricella, Gola, & Calvert, 2011). These include use of familiar characters

An 18-month-old reaches toward a sad character in a children's cartoon. Perhaps he has difficulty making sense of the image because the character does not look like his real-life social partners or converse with him directly, as adults do.

and close-ups in which the character looks directly at the camera, addresses questions to viewers, and pauses to invite a response. Interactive touchscreens may also help toddlers transfer information on the screen to real life, but only if their interactive elements direct toddlers' attention to relevant features of word-learning and object-retrieval tasks (Kirkorian, Choi, & Pempek, 2016; Choi & Kirkorian, 2016).

Finally, video chat offers an exception to the video deficit effect. Toddlers readily learn from its socially contingent format, which helps them make connections between video and reality. Parents report often using video chat formats, such as Skype and FaceTime, to connect with their young children while separated from them and to promote relationships with distant relatives (McClure et al., 2015). Media experts recommend that video chat be exempt from restrictive screen media rules for infants and toddlers.

---

before they start school, an adult taught 1½- to 3-year-olds a new name for an unfamiliar object during picture-book interaction (Walker, Walker, & Ganea, 2013). When later asked to pick the named object from arrays of pictures and real objects, not until 3 years of age did the Tanzanian children perform as well as U.S. 15-month-olds.

But even after coming to appreciate the symbolic nature of pictures, young children continue to have difficulty grasping the distinction between some pictures (such as line drawings) and their referents, as we will see in Chapter 8. How do infants and toddlers interpret another ever-present, pictorial medium—video? See the Social Issues: Education box above to find out.

6.1.4 Evaluation of the Sensorimotor Stage

Table 6.2 summarizes the remarkable cognitive attainments we have just considered. Compare this table with Piaget's description of the sensorimotor substages in Table 6.1 on page 199. You will see that infants anticipate events, actively search for hidden objects, master the A–B object search, flexibly vary their sensorimotor schemes, mentally represent solutions to problems, engage in make-believe play, and treat pictures and video images symbolically within Piaget's time frame. Yet other capacities—including secondary circular reactions, understanding of object properties, first signs of object permanence, deferred imitation, and displaced reference of words—emerge earlier than Piaget expected. These findings show that the cognitive attainments of infancy and toddlerhood do not develop together in the neat, stepwise fashion that Piaget predicted.

Recent research raises questions about Piaget's view of how infant development takes place. Consistent with Piaget's ideas, sensorimotor action helps infants construct some forms of knowledge. For example, as we saw in Chapter 5, crawling enhances depth perception and ability to find hidden objects, and handling objects fosters awareness of object properties. Yet we have also seen that infants comprehend a great deal before they are capable of the motor behaviors that Piaget assumed led to those understandings. How can we account for babies' amazing cognitive accomplishments?

Alternative Explanations   Unlike Piaget, who thought babies constructed all mental representations out of sensorimotor activity, most researchers now believe that infants have some built-in cognitive equipment for making sense of experience. But intense disagreement exists over the extent of this initial understanding. As we have seen, much evidence on young infants' cognition rests on the violation-of-expectation method. Researchers who lack confidence in this method argue that babies' cognitive starting point is limited (Bremner, Slater, & Johnson, 2015; Cohen, 2010; Kagan, 2013c). For example, some believe that newborns begin life with a set of biases for attending to certain information and with general-purpose learning procedures—such as powerful techniques for analyzing complex perceptual information (Bahrick, 2010; MacWhinney, 2015; Rakison, 2010). Together, these capacities enable infants to construct a wide variety of schemes.

Others, convinced by violation-of-expectation findings, believe that infants start out with impressive understandings. According to this **core knowledge perspective,** babies are born with a set of innate knowledge systems, or *core domains of thought.* Each of these prewired understandings permits a ready grasp of new, related information and therefore supports early, rapid development (Carey, 2009; Leslie, 2004; Spelke, 2016; Spelke & Kinzler, 2013). Core

TABLE 6.2   **Some Cognitive Attainments of Infancy and Toddlerhood**

AGE	COGNITIVE ATTAINMENTS
Birth–1 month	Secondary circular reactions using limited motor skills, such as sucking a nipple to gain access to interesting sights and sounds
1–4 months	Awareness of object permanence, object solidity, and gravity, as suggested by violation-of-expectation findings; deferred imitation of an adult's facial expression over a short delay (one day)
4–8 months	Improved knowledge of object properties and basic numerical knowledge, as suggested by violation-of-expectation findings; deferred imitation of an adult's novel actions on objects over a short delay (one to three days)
8–12 months	Improved anticipation of events (such as parent's departure) and efforts to change those events; ability to search for a hidden object when covered by a cloth
12–18 months	Ability to search for a hidden object when it is moved from one location to another (accurate A–B search); deferred imitation of an adult's novel actions on objects after long delays (at least several months) and across a change in context (from child care to home); rational imitation, inferring the model's intentions; displaced reference of words
18 months–2 years	Ability to find an object moved while out of sight (invisible displacement); deferred imitation of actions an adult tries to produce, even if these are not fully realized; beginnings of make-believe play; ability to mentally represent the solution to a problem, in using an unfamiliar tool to secure an object; increasing awareness of pictures and video as symbols of reality

Did this toddler learn to build a tower of cans by repeatedly acting on objects, as Piaget assumed? Or did he begin life with innate knowledge that helps him understand objects and their relationships quickly, with little hands-on exploration?

knowledge theorists argue that infants could not make sense of the complex stimulation around them without having been genetically "set up" in the course of evolution to comprehend its crucial aspects.

Researchers have conducted many studies of infants' *physical knowledge,* including object permanence, object solidity (that one object cannot move through another), and gravity (that an object will fall without support). Violation-of-expectation findings suggest that in the first few months, infants have some awareness of all these basic object properties and quickly build on this knowledge (Baillargeon et al., 2011). Core knowledge theorists also assume that an inherited foundation of *linguistic knowledge* enables swift language acquisition in early childhood—a possibility we will consider later in this chapter. Furthermore, these theorists argue, infants' early orientation toward people initiates rapid development of *psychological knowledge*— in particular, understanding of mental states, such as intentions, emotions, desires, and beliefs, which we will address further in Chapter 7.

Research even suggests that infants have basic *numerical knowledge.* In the best-known study, 5-month-olds saw a screen raised to hide a single toy animal and then watched a hand place a second toy behind the screen. Finally, the screen was removed to reveal either one or two toys. If infants kept track of the two objects (requiring them to add one object to another), then they should look longer at the unexpected, one-toy display—which is what they did (see Figure 6.3) (Wynn, 1992). These findings and others suggest that babies can discriminate quantities up to three and use that knowledge to perform simple arithmetic—both addition and subtraction (in which two objects are covered and one object is removed) (Kobayashi, Hiraki, & Hasegawa, 2005; Walden et al., 2007; Wynn, Bloom, & Chiang, 2002). As further support, ERP brain-wave recordings taken while infants view correct and incorrect simple arithmetic solutions reveal a response pattern identical to the pattern adults show when detecting errors (Berger, Tzur, & Posner, 2006).

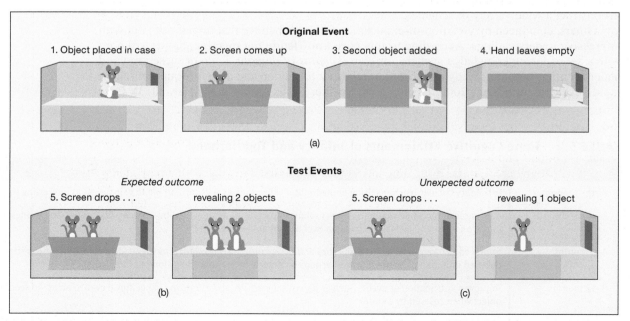

FIGURE 6.3 **Testing infants for basic number concepts.** (a) First, infants saw a screen raised in front of a toy animal. Then an identical toy was added behind the screen. Next, the researchers presented two outcomes. (b) In the *expected outcome,* the screen dropped to reveal two toy animals. (c) In the *unexpected outcome,* the screen dropped to reveal one toy animal. Five-month-olds shown the unexpected outcome looked longer than did 5-month-olds shown the expected outcome. The researchers concluded that infants can discriminate the quantities "one" and "two" and use that knowledge to perform simple addition: 1+1=2. A variation of this procedure suggested that 5-month-olds could also do simple subtraction: 2−1=1. (From K. Wynn, 1992, "Addition and Subtraction by Human Infants," *Nature, 358,* p. 749. © 1992, Nature Publishing Group. Adapted with permission of Nature Publishing Group in the format "Republish in a book" via Copyright Clearance Center.)

Additional evidence suggests that 6-month-olds can distinguish among large sets of items, as long as the difference between those sets is very great—at least a factor of two. For example, they can tell the difference between 8 and 16 dots but not between 8 and 12 (Lipton & Spelke, 2003; Xu, Spelke, & Goddard, 2005). Furthermore, 6-month-olds' factor-of-two discrimination capacity is similar across quantitative dimensions. It also applies to the area of spatial surfaces and the duration of tones (Brannon, Lutz, & Cordes, 2006; Lipton & Spelke, 2003; VanMarle & Wynn, 2006). Consequently, some researchers believe that in addition to making small-number discriminations, infants can represent approximate large-number values and that their ability to do so reflects a more general quantitative understanding.

But as with other violation-of-expectation results, this evidence is controversial. Skeptics question whether other aspects of object displays, rather than numerical sensitivity, are responsible for the findings (Bremner, Slater, & Johnson, 2015; Clearfield & Westfahl, 2006). Indisputable evidence for built-in core knowledge requires that it be demonstrated at birth or close to it—in the absence of relevant opportunities to learn. Yet findings on newborns' ability to process small and large numerical values are inconsistent (Coubart et al., 2014; Izard et al., 2009). And critics point out that claims for infants' number knowledge are surprising, in view of other research indicating that before 14 to 16 months, toddlers have difficulty making less-than and greater-than comparisons between small sets. As we will see in Chapter 9, not until the preschool years do children add and subtract small sets correctly.

The core knowledge perspective, while emphasizing native endowment, acknowledges that experience is essential for children to extend this initial knowledge. But so far, it has said little about which experiences are most important in each core domain and how those experiences advance children's thinking. Despite these limitations, core knowledge investigators have sharpened the field's focus on clarifying the starting point for human cognition and on carefully tracking the changes that build on it.

Piaget's Legacy   Current research on infant cognition yields broad agreement on two issues. First, many cognitive changes of infancy are not abrupt and stagelike but gradual and continuous (Bjorklund & Causey, 2018). Second, rather than developing together, various aspects of infant cognition change unevenly because of the challenges posed by different types of tasks and infants' varying experiences with them. These ideas serve as the basis for another major approach to cognitive development—*information processing*—which we take up next.

Before we turn to this alternative point of view, let's recognize Piaget's enormous contributions. Piaget's work inspired a wealth of research on infant cognition, including studies that challenged his theory. Today, researchers are far from consensus on how to modify or replace his account of infant cognitive development, and some believe that his general approach continues to make sense and fits most of the evidence (Cohen, 2010; Lourenço, 2016). Piaget's observations also have been of great practical value. Teachers and caregivers continue to look to the sensorimotor stage for guidelines on how to create developmentally appropriate environments for infants and toddlers.

Now that you are familiar with some milestones of the first two years, what play materials do you think would support the development of sensorimotor and early representational schemes? Prepare a list, justifying it by referring to the cognitive attainments described in the previous sections. Then compare your suggestions to the ones given in Applying What We Know on page 210.

ASK YOURSELF

Connect ■ Which of the capacities listed in Table 6.2 indicate that mental representation emerges earlier than Piaget concluded?

Apply ■ Several times, after her father hid a teething biscuit under a red cup, 12-month-old Mimi retrieved it easily. Then Mimi's father hid the biscuit under a nearby yellow cup. Why did Mimi persist in searching for it under the red cup?

Reflect ■ What advice would you give the typical U.S. parent about permitting an infant or toddler to watch as much as 1 to 1½ hours of TV or video per day? Explain.

APPLYING WHAT WE KNOW

Play Materials That Support Infant and Toddler Cognitive Development

FROM 2 MONTHS	FROM 6 MONTHS	FROM 1 YEAR
Crib mobile	Squeeze toys	Large dolls, toy dishes, toy telephone
Rattles and other handheld sound-making toys, such as a bell on a handle	Nesting cups	Cars and trucks
	Clutch and texture balls	Large blocks, cardboard boxes
Adult-operated music boxes and music recordings with gentle, regular rhythms, songs, and lullabies	Stuffed animals and soft-bodied dolls	Hammer-and-peg toy
	Filling and emptying toys	Pull and push toys, riding toys that can be pushed with feet
	Large and small blocks	Rhythm instruments for shaking and banging, such as bells, cymbals, and drums
	Pots, pans, and spoons from the kitchen	Simple puzzles
	Simple, floating objects for the bath	Sandbox, shovel, and pail
	Picture books with realistic color images	Shallow wading pool and water toys
		Balls of various sizes

6.2 Information Processing

6.2a Describe the information-processing view of cognitive development and the general structure of the information-processing system.

6.2b Describe changes in attention, memory, and categorization over the first two years.

6.2c Explain the strengths and limitations of the information-processing approach to early cognitive development.

Advocates of the information-processing approach agree with Piaget that children are active, inquiring beings. However, instead of proposing a single, unified theory of cognitive development, they focus on many aspects of thinking, from attention, memory, and categorization skills to complex problem solving. Furthermore, information-processing researchers are not satisfied with general concepts, such as assimilation and accommodation, to explain how children think. Rather, they want to know exactly what individuals of different ages do when faced with a task or problem (Birney & Sternberg, 2011). As we saw in Chapter 1, the information-processing perspective often relies on computerlike flowcharts to model the human cognitive system. This way of representing thinking is attractive because it is explicit and precise.

6.2.1 Assumptions of the Information-Processing Perspective

Information-processing researchers generally assume that we hold information in three parts of the cognitive system for processing: the *sensory store,* the *short-term memory store,* and the *long-term memory store* (see Figure 6.4). Initially, most viewed processing as occurring in a *serial,* step-by-step fashion, with information moving through the stores in the order just mentioned. Today, investigators realize that information is often held and processed in the three stores *simultaneously* (Bjorklund & Causey, 2016). For example, when putting together a complex jigsaw puzzle, you might continuously refer to a visual image held in long-term memory as a "big picture" guide to which puzzle pieces to focus on in the sensory store and how to manipulate the selected pieces in the short-term memory store.

As information flows between the stores, we use *mental strategies* to operate on and transform it, increasing the chances that we will retain the information; use it efficiently and flexibly, adapting it to changing circumstances; and pass it to the next store, eventually producing an effective response. To understand this more clearly, let's look at each aspect of the cognitive system.

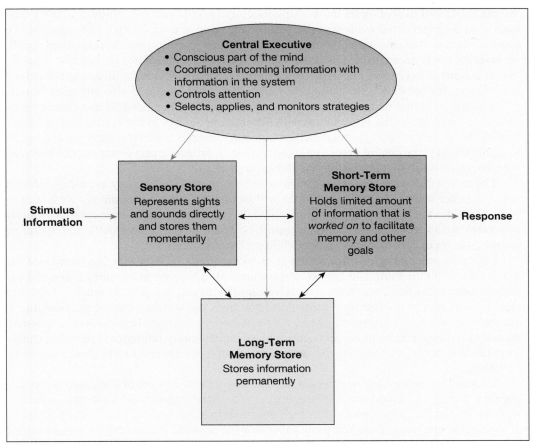

FIGURE 6.4 **The information-processing system.** Information is held and often simultaneously processed in three parts of the cognitive system: the *sensory store,* the *short-term memory store,* and the *long-term memory store.* In each, mental strategies can be used to manipulate information, increasing the efficiency and flexibility of thinking and the chances that information will be retained. The *central executive* is the conscious, reflective part of working memory. It coordinates incoming information already in the system, decides what to attend to, and oversees the use of strategies.

In the **sensory store,** sights and sounds in the surrounding world are represented directly and stored momentarily. Look around you, and then close your eyes. An image of what you saw persists for a few seconds, but then it decays, or disappears, unless you use mental strategies to preserve it. For example, by *attending to* some information more carefully than to other information, you increase the chances that it will transfer to the other stores.

As information enters the **short-term memory store,** we retain it briefly so we can actively "work" on it to reach our goals. One way of looking at the short-term store is in terms of its *basic capacity,* often referred to as *short-term memory:* the number of pieces of information a person can hold in mind at once for a few seconds. But most researchers endorse a contemporary view of the short-term store, which is a more meaningful indicator of its capacity, called **working memory**—the number of items a person can briefly hold in mind while also engaging in some effort to monitor or manipulate those items. Working memory can be thought of as a "mental workspace" that we use to accomplish many activities in daily life. From childhood on, researchers assess changes in its capacity by presenting individuals with lists of items (such as numerical digits or short sentences), asking them to "work on" the items (for example, repeat the digits backward or remember the final word of each sentence in correct order), and seeing how well they do.

The sensory store can take in a wide panorama of information. Short-term and working memory are far more restricted, though their capacity increases steadily from early childhood through adolescence—from about two to seven items on a verbatim numerical digit-span task to about two to five items on working-memory tasks (Cowan & Alloway, 2009). Still, individual differences are evident at all ages. By engaging in a variety of basic cognitive procedures, such as focusing attention on relevant items and repeating (rehearsing) them rapidly, we increase the chances that information will be retained and accessible to ongoing thinking.

The **central executive** manages the cognitive system's activities, directing the flow of information, implementing the basic procedures just mentioned, and also engaging in more sophisticated activities that enable complex, flexible thinking. For example, the central executive coordinates incoming information with information already in the system, and it selects, applies, and monitors strategies that facilitate memory storage, comprehension, reasoning, and problem solving. The central executive is the conscious, reflective part of our cognitive system. It ensures that we think purposefully to attain our goals.

The more effectively the central executive joins with working memory to process information, the better learned cognitive activities will be and the more *automatically* we can apply them. Consider the richness of your thinking while you automatically drive a car. **Automatic processes** are so well-learned that they require no space in working memory and, therefore, permit us to focus on other information while performing them.

Effective processing of information in working memory increases the likelihood that it will transfer to the third, and largest, storage area—the **long-term memory store,** our permanent knowledge base, which has a massive capacity. In fact, we store so much in long-term memory that *retrieval*—getting information back from the system—can be problematic. To aid retrieval, we apply strategies, just as we do in memory storage. Information in long-term memory is *categorized* by its contents, much like a digital library reference system that enables us to retrieve items by following the same network of associations used to store them in the first place.

Information-processing researchers believe that several aspects of the cognitive system improve during childhood and adolescence: (1) the *basic capacity* of its stores, especially working memory; (2) the *speed* with which information is worked on; and (3) the *functioning of the central executive.* Together, these changes make possible more complex forms of thinking with age (Halford & Andrews, 2011).

Gains in working-memory capacity are due in part to brain development, but greater processing speed also contributes. Fast, fluent thinking frees working-memory resources to support storage and manipulation of additional information. Furthermore, researchers have become intensely interested in studying the development of **executive function**—the diverse cognitive operations and strategies that enable us to achieve our goals in cognitively challenging situations (Zelazo & Carlson, 2012). These include controlling attention by inhibiting impulses and irrelevant actions and by flexibly directing thought and behavior to suit the demands of a task; coordinating information in working memory; and planning—capacities governed by the prefrontal cortex and its elaborate connections to other brain regions (Chevalier, 2015). Measures of executive function predict important cognitive and social outcomes in childhood, adolescence, and adulthood, such as task persistence, self-control, academic achievement, and interpersonal acceptance (Carlson, Zelazo, & Faja, 2013; Müller & Kerns, 2015).

Gains in aspects of executive function are under way in the first two years. Dramatic strides will follow in childhood and adolescence.

6.2.2 Attention

Newborns show a primitive ability to control attention, evident in their preference for looking at simplified but coherent stimuli—for example, upright rather than inverted faces (see page 189 in Chapter 5) (Daum, 2016). Recall, also, that around 2 to 3 months of age, infants shift from focusing on single, high-contrast features to exploring objects and patterns more thoroughly (Frank, Amso, & Johnson, 2014). When presented with a complex scene, such as a Charlie Brown cartoon video, infants transitioned between 3 and 9 months from scattered attention to areas of changing color, brightness, and motion throughout the screen to more narrowly focused attention to characters' faces (Frank, Vul, & Johnson, 2009). With age, infants seemed better able to inhibit attending to distracting background stimuli and to focus on socially meaningful information.

Besides improving in attentional control, infants gradually become more efficient at managing their attention, taking in information more quickly. Habituation research reveals that preterm and newborn babies require a long time—about three to four minutes—to habituate and recover to novel visual stimuli. But by 4 or 5 months, they need as little as 5 to 10 seconds to take in a complex visual stimulus and recognize it as different from a previous one (Colombo, Kapa, & Curtindale, 2011).

At the end of the first year, as the prefrontal cortex improves in its executive role and babies become increasingly capable of intentional behavior (refer to Piaget's Substage 4), attraction to novelty declines (but does not disappear) and *sustained attention* increases (Posner et al., 2012). This change is especially evident when children play with toys. A toddler who engages even in simple goal-directed behavior, such as stacking blocks or putting them in a container, must sustain attention to reach the goal. As plans and activities gradually become more complex, the duration of attention expands.

Adults can foster sustained attention by encouraging babies' current interest ("Oh, you like that bell!") and prompting the child to stay focused ("See, it makes a noise!"). Consistently helping infants focus attention at 10 months predicts higher intelligence test scores at 18 months (Bono & Stifter, 2003). Also, from age 3 months on, infants looking at faces are especially attracted to human eyes, and gradually they become more interested in what others are attending to (Dupierrix et al., 2014). Later we will see that this joint attention between caregiver and child is important for language development.

By encouraging her toddler's goal-directed play, this mother promotes sustained attention.

6.2.3 Memory

Methods devised to assess infants' short-term memory, which require keeping in mind an increasingly longer sequence of very briefly presented visual stimuli, reveal that retention increases from one visual item at age 6 months to two to four visual items at 12 months (Oakes, Ross-Sheehy, & Luck, 2007; Kwon, Luck, & Oakes, 2014). Furthermore, using a clever technique requiring infants to momentarily retain two visual stimuli while also monitoring their unique locations, researchers reported that working memory emerges between 8 and 10 months of age (Kaldy, Guillory, & Blaser, 2016).

Operant conditioning and habituation techniques, which grant babies more time to process information, provide windows into early development of long-term memory. Both methods show that retention of visual events improves greatly with age.

Operant Conditioning Research   Using operant conditioning, researchers study infant memory by teaching 2- to 6-month-olds to move a mobile by kicking a foot tied to it with a long cord. Two-month-olds remember how to activate the mobile for one to two days after training, and 3-month-olds for one week. By 6 months, memory increases to two weeks (Rovee-Collier, 1999; Rovee-Collier & Bhatt, 1993). Around the middle of the first year, babies can manipulate switches or buttons to control stimulation. When 6- to 18-month-olds pressed a lever to make a toy train move around a track, duration of memory continued to increase with age; 13 weeks after training, 18-month-olds still remembered how to press the lever (Hartshorn et al., 1998b). Figure 6.5 on page 214 shows this dramatic rise in retention of operant responses over the first year and a half.

Even after 2- to 6-month-olds forget an operant response, they need only a brief prompt—an adult who shakes the mobile—to reinstate the memory (Hildreth & Rovee-Collier, 2002; Fagen, Ohr, & Boller, 2016). And when 6-month-olds are given a chance to reactivate the response themselves for just a couple of minutes—jiggling the mobile by kicking or moving the train by lever-pressing—their memory not only returns but also extends dramatically to about

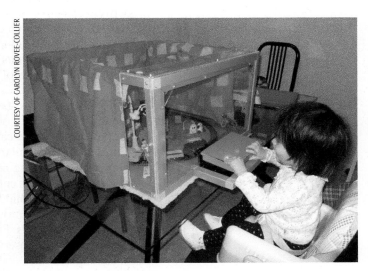

Memory for operant responses improves dramatically over the first 18 months. This 12-month-old has learned to press a lever to make a toy train move around a track—an operant response she is likely to remember when re-exposed to the task many weeks later.

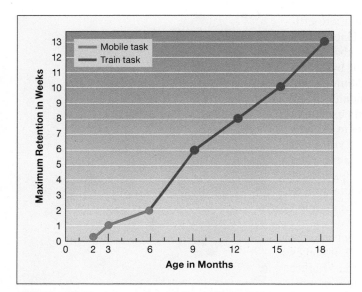

FIGURE 6.5 **Increase in retention in two operant conditioning tasks from 2 to 18 months.** Two- to 6-month-olds were trained to make a kicking response that turned a mobile. Six- to 18-month-olds were trained to press a lever that made a toy train move around a track. Six-month-olds learned both responses and retained them for an identical length of time, indicating that the tasks are comparable. Consequently, researchers could plot a single line of gains in retention from 2 to 18 months of age. The line shows that memory improves dramatically. (From C. Rovee-Collier & R. Barr, 2001, "Infant Learning and Memory," in G. Bremner & A. Fogel [Eds.], *Blackwell Handbook of Infant Development,* Oxford, U.K.: Blackwell, p. 150. © 2001, 2004 by Blackwell Publishing Ltd.)

17 weeks (Rovee-Collier & Cuevas, 2009). Perhaps permitting the baby to generate the previously learned behavior strengthens memory because it re-exposes the child to more aspects of the original learning situation. Furthermore, with just five widely spaced adult-provided reminders of the train task extending over 1½ years, infants trained at age 6 months still remembered the response after reaching their second birthday (Hartshorn, 2003).

At first, infants' memory for operant responses is highly *context-dependent.* If on the day after training 2- to 6-month-olds are not tested in the same situation in which training took place—with the same mobile and crib bumper and in the same room—they remember poorly (Hayne, 2004). After 9 months, the importance of context declines. Older infants and toddlers remember how to make the toy train move even when its features are altered and testing takes place in a different room (Hartshorn et al., 1998a; Learmonth, Lamberth, & Rovee-Collier, 2004). Crawling is strongly associated with 9-month-olds' formation of an increasingly context-free memory (Herbert, Gross, & Hayne, 2007). As infants move on their own and experience frequent changes in context, they apply learned responses more flexibly, generalizing them to relevant new situations.

Habituation Research Habituation studies show that infants learn and retain a wide variety of information just by watching objects and events, without being physically active. Sometimes they do so for much longer time spans than in operant conditioning studies. Babies are especially attentive to the movements of objects and people. For example, 3-month-olds' retention of the unusual movements of objects (such as a metal nut swinging on the end of a string) persists for at least three months (Bahrick, Hernandex-Reif, & Pickens, 1997). By contrast, infants' memory for the faces of unfamiliar people and the features of objects is short-lived—24 hours at 3- to 5-months, extending to just several days to a few weeks at the end of the first year (Fagan, 1973; Pascalis, de Haan, & Nelson, 1998).

By 10 months, infants remember both novel actions and features of objects involved in those actions equally well (Baumgartner & Oakes, 2011). Thus, over the second half-year, sensitivity to object appearance increases. This change, as noted earlier, is fostered by infants' increasing ability to manipulate objects, which helps them learn about objects' observable properties.

Habituation research confirms that infants need not be physically active to acquire new information. Nevertheless, as illustrated by research presented in Chapter 5 on the facilitating role of crawling in infants' ability to find hidden objects (see page 188), motor activity does promote certain aspects of learning and memory.

Recall Memory So far, we have discussed only **recognition**—noticing when a stimulus is identical or similar to one previously experienced. It is the simplest form of memory: All babies have to do is indicate (by kicking, pressing a lever, or looking) whether a new experience is identical or similar to a previous one. **Recall** is more challenging because it involves remembering something not present. To recall, you must generate a mental image of the past experience. Can infants engage in recall? By the middle of the first year, they can, as indicated by their ability to find hidden objects and engage in deferred imitation.

Recall memory improves steadily with age, with older infants recalling more information over longer time periods. For example, 1-year-olds can retain short sequences of adult-modeled behaviors they have observed several times for up to three months, and 1½-year-olds can do so for as long as 12 months. The ability to recall a sequence of modeled behaviors in the order in which the actions occurred—evident at 9 months—strengthens over the second year (Bauer, 2013; Bauer, Larkina, & Deocampo, 2011; Lukowski, Wiebe, & Bauer, 2009). And when toddlers imitate in correct sequence, processing not just separate actions but relations between actions, they remember more (Knopf, Kraus, & Kressley-Mba, 2006).

Long-term recall depends on connections among multiple regions of the cerebral cortex, especially with the prefrontal cortex. Formation of these neural circuits is under way in infancy and toddlerhood and will accelerate in early childhood (Jabès & Nelson, 2014). The evidence as a whole indicates that infants' memory processing is remarkably similar to that of older children and adults: Babies have distinct short-term and long-term memories and display both recognition and recall. And they acquire information quickly and retain it over time, doing so more effectively with age (Howe, 2015). Furthermore, recall assessed through deferred imitation tasks at age 20 months predicts performance on memory tests at age 6, suggesting continuity of memory functions over time (Riggins et al., 2013). Yet a puzzling finding is that older children and adults no longer recall their earliest experiences! See the Biology and Environment box on page 216 for a discussion of *infantile amnesia.*

6.2.4 Categorization

Even young infants can *categorize,* grouping similar objects and events into a single representation (Rakison & Lawson, 2013). Categorization reduces the enormous amount of new information infants encounter every day, helping them learn and remember.

Creative variations of operant conditioning research with mobiles have been used to investigate infant categorization. One such study of 3-month-olds is described and illustrated in Figure 6.6. Similar investigations reveal that in the first few months, babies categorize stimuli on the basis of shape, size, and other physical properties (Wasserman & Rovee-Collier, 2001). By 6 months of age, they can categorize on the basis of two correlated features—for example, the shape and color of an alphabet letter (Bhatt et al., 2004). This ability to categorize using clusters of features prepares babies for acquiring many complex everyday categories.

Infant categorization has also been studied using habituation. Researchers show babies a series of pictures belonging to one category and then see whether they recover to (look longer at) a picture that is not a member of the category (see Figure 6.8 on page 217). Findings reveal that in the second half of the first year, infants group familiar objects into an impressive array of categories—food items, furniture, birds, land animals, air animals, sea animals, plants, vehicles, kitchen utensils, and spatial location ("above" and "below," "on" and "in") (Bornstein, Arterberry, & Mash, 2010; Casasola & Park, 2013; Sloutsky, 2015). Besides organizing the physical world, infants of this age categorize their emotional and social worlds. They sort people and their voices by gender and age, have begun to distinguish emotional expressions, can separate people's natural actions (walking) from other motions, and expect people (but not inanimate objects) to move spontaneously (Spelke, Phillips, & Woodward, 1995; see also page 188 in Chapter 5).

Babies' earliest categories are based on similar overall appearance or prominent object part: legs for animals, wheels for vehicles. But as infants approach their first birthday, more categories appear to be based on subtle sets of features (Mandler, 2004; Quinn, 2008). Older infants can even make categorical distinctions when the perceptual contrast between two categories is minimal (birds versus airplanes).

As they gain experience in comparing to-be-categorized items in varied ways and their store of verbal labels expands, toddlers start to categorize flexibly: When 14-month-olds are given four balls and four blocks, some made of soft rubber and some of rigid plastic, their sequence of object touching reveals that after classifying by shape, they can switch to classifying by material (soft versus hard) if an adult calls their attention to the new basis for grouping (Ellis & Oakes, 2006).

In addition to touching and sorting, toddlers' categorization skills are evident in their imitative and play behaviors. After watching an adult give a toy dog a drink from a cup, most 9- to 14-month-olds shown a rabbit

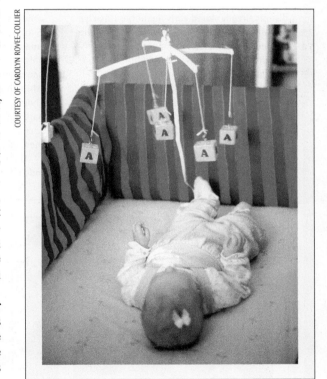

COURTESY OF CAROLYN ROVEE-COLLIER

FIGURE 6.6 **Investigating infant categorization using operant conditioning.** Three-month-olds were taught to kick to move a mobile that was made of small blocks, all with the letter *A* on them. After a delay, kicking returned to a high level only if the babies were shown a mobile whose blocks were labeled with the same form (the letter *A*). If the form was changed (from *A*s to *2*s), infants no longer kicked vigorously. While making the mobile move, the babies had grouped together its features. They associated the kicking response with the category *A* and, at later testing, distinguished it from the category *2*. (Bhatt, Rovee-Collier, & Weiner, 1994; Hayne, Rovee-Collier, & Perris, 1987).

Biology and Environment | Infantile Amnesia

If infants and toddlers recall many aspects of their everyday lives, how do we explain **infantile amnesia**—that most of us can retrieve few, if any, events that happened to us before age 2½ to 3? The reason cannot be merely the passage of time because we can recall many personally meaningful one-time events from both the recent and the distant past: the day a sibling was born or a move to a new house—recollections known as **autobiographical memory**.

Several explanations of infantile amnesia have been proposed. One theory credits brain development, pointing to the *hippocampus* (located just under the temporal lobes of the cerebral cortex), which plays a vital role in the formation of new memories. Though its overall structure is formed prenatally, the hippocampus continues to add new neurons well after birth. Integrating those neurons into existing neural circuits is believed to disrupt already stored early memories (Josselyn & Frankland, 2012). In support of this view, the decline in production of hippocampal neurons—in monkeys and rats as well as in humans—coincides with the ability to form stable, long-term memories of unique experiences.

Another conjecture is that older children and adults often use verbal means for storing information, whereas infants' and toddlers' memory processing is largely nonverbal—an incompatibility that may prevent long-term retention of early experiences. To test this idea, researchers sent two adults to the homes of 2- to 4-year-olds with an unusual toy that the children were likely to remember: The Magic Shrinking Machine, shown in Figure 6.7. One adult showed the child how, after inserting an object in an opening on top of the machine and turning a crank that activated flashing lights and musical sounds, the child could retrieve a smaller, identical object (discreetly dropped down a chute by the second adult) from behind a door on the front of the machine.

A day later, the researchers tested the children to see how well they recalled the event. Their nonverbal memory—based on acting out the "shrinking" event and recognizing the "shrunken" objects in photos—was excellent. But even when they had the vocabulary, children younger than age 3 had trouble describing features of the "shrinking" experience. Verbal recall increased sharply between ages 3 and 4—the period during which children "scramble over the amnesia barrier" (Simcock & Hayne, 2003, p. 813). In a follow-up study, which assessed verbal recall 6 years later, only 19 percent—including two children who had been younger than age 3— remembered the "shrinking" event (Jack, Simcock, & Hayne, 2012). Those who recalled were more likely to have participated in conversations about the experience with a parent, which could have helped them gain verbal access to the memory.

These findings help us reconcile infants' and toddlers' remarkable memory skills with infantile amnesia. During the first few years, children rely heavily on nonverbal memory techniques, such as visual images and motor actions. As language emerges, their ability to use it to refer to preverbal memories requires considerable support from adults. After age 3, when children increasingly represent autobiographical events in verbal form, they use language-based cues to retrieve them, which strengthens the accessibility of memories at later ages (Peterson, Warren, & Short, 2011).

Other evidence indicates that the advent of a clear self-image contributes to the end of infantile amnesia. For example, among children and adolescents, the average age of earliest memory is around age 2 to 2½ (Howe, 2014; Tustin & Hayne, 2010). Though these recollections are sparse in information recalled, their timing coincides with the age at which toddlers display firmer self-awareness, reflected in pointing to themselves in photos and referring to themselves by name.

Very likely, both neurological change and social experience contribute to the decline of infantile amnesia. Brain development and adult–child interaction may jointly foster self-awareness, language, and improved memory, which enable children to talk with adults about significant past experiences (Howe, 2015). As a result, preschoolers begin to construct a long-lasting autobiographical narrative of their lives and enter into the history of their family and community.

(a)

(b)

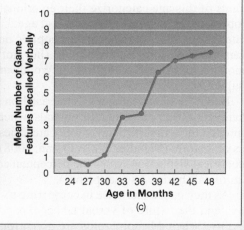
(c)

FIGURE 6.7 **The Magic Shrinking Machine, used to test young children's verbal and nonverbal memory of an unusual event.** After being shown how the machine worked, the child participated in selecting objects from a polka-dot bag, dropping them into the top of the machine (a), and turning a crank, which produced a "shrunken" object (b). When tested the next day, 2- to 4-year-olds' nonverbal memory for the event was excellent. But below 36 months, verbal recall was poor, based on the number of features recalled about the game during an open-ended interview (c). Recall improved between 36 and 48 months, the period during which infantile amnesia subsides. (From G. Simcock & H. Hayne, 2003, "Age-Related Changes in Verbal and Nonverbal Memory During Early Childhood," *Developmental Psychology, 39*(5), pp. 807, 809. Copyright © 2003 by the American Psychological Association. *Photos:* Ross Coombes/Courtesy of Harlene Hayne.)

and a motorcycle offered the drink only to the rabbit. Similarly, after watching an adult start a toy car with a key, older infants and toddlers imitated the action with a truck but not a rabbit (Mandler & McDonough, 1996, 1998). They clearly understood that certain actions are appropriate for some categories of items (animals) but not for others (vehicles).

By the end of the second year, toddlers' grasp of the animate–inanimate distinction expands. Nonlinear motions are typical of animates (a person or a dog jumping), and linear motions of inanimates (a car or a table pushed along a surface). At 18 months, toddlers more often imitate a nonlinear motion with a toy that has animatelike parts (legs), even if it represents an inanimate (a bed). At 22 months, displaying a fuller understanding, they imitate a nonlinear motion only with toys in the animate category (a cat but not a bed) (Rakison, 2005). They seem to realize that whereas animates are self-propelled and therefore have varied paths of movement, inanimates move only when acted on in highly restricted ways.

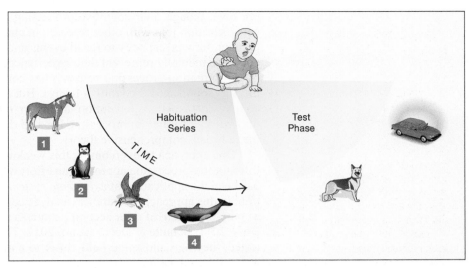

FIGURE 6.8   Using habituation to study infant categorization. After habituating to a series of items belonging to one category (in this example, animals), infants are shown two novel items, one that is a member of the category (dog) and one that is not (car). If infants recover to (look longer at or spend more time manipulating) the out-of-category item (car), this indicates that they distinguish it from the set of within-category items (animals). Habituating another group of infants to a series of vehicles and seeing if, when presented with the two test items above, they recover to the dog confirms that babies can distinguish animals from vehicles. This pattern of responding has been found in many infant categorization studies.

Researchers disagree on how babies arrive at these impressive attainments. One view holds that older infants and toddlers categorize more effectively because they become increasingly sensitive to fine-grained perceptual features and to stable relations among those features—for example, objects with flapping wings and feathers belong to one category; objects with rigid wings, windows, and a smooth surface belong to another category (Madole, Oakes, & Rakison, 2013; Schultz, 2011). An alternative view is that before the end of the first year, babies undergo a fundamental shift from a perceptual to a conceptual basis for constructing categories, increasingly grouping objects by their common function or behavior (birds versus airplanes, cars versus trucks, dogs versus cats) (Mandler, 2004; Träuble & Pauen, 2011).

But all acknowledge that exploration of objects and expanding knowledge of the world contribute (Mash & Bornstein, 2012). In addition, adult labeling of a set of objects with a consistently applied word—"Look at the car!" "Do you see the car?"—calls babies' attention to commonalities among objects, fostering categorization as early as 3 to 4 months of age (Althaus & Plunkett, 2016; Ferry, Hespos, & Waxman, 2010). Toddlers' vocabulary growth, in turn, promotes categorization by highlighting new categorical distinctions (Cohen & Brunt, 2009).

By age 2, toddlers can use conceptual similarity to guide behavior in increasingly novel situations, which greatly enhances the flexibility of their problem solving. In one study, 24-month-olds watched as an adult constructed a toy animal resembling a monkey using wooden, Velcro, and plastic pieces and then labeled it a "thornby." A day later, the toddlers were given a different set of wooden, Velcro, and plastic materials that, when put together, resembled a rabbit (Hayne & Gross, 2015). Those asked to make a "thornby" out of "these other things" readily formed a category and applied the adult's actions with the first animal to constructing the second, novel animal. A control group not presented with verbal cues performed poorly.

LOOK and LISTEN

Observe a toddler playing with a variety of small toys—some representing animals and some representing household objects. What play behaviors reveal the child's ability to categorize?

6.2.5 Evaluation of Information-Processing Findings

The information-processing perspective underscores the continuity of human thinking from infancy into adult life. In attending to the environment, remembering everyday events, and categorizing objects, Caitlin, Grace, and Timmy think in ways that are remarkably similar to our own, though their cognitive processing is far from proficient. Findings on memory and categorization join with other research in challenging Piaget's view of early cognitive development. Infants' capacity to recall events and to categorize stimuli attests, once again, to their ability to mentally represent their experiences.

Information-processing research has contributed greatly to our view of infants and toddlers as sophisticated cognitive beings. But its central strength—analyzing cognition into its components, such as perception, attention, memory, and categorization—is also its greatest drawback: Information processing has had difficulty putting these components back together into a broad, comprehensive theory.

One approach to overcoming this weakness has been to combine Piaget's theory with the information-processing approach, an effort we will explore in Chapter 12. A more recent trend has been the application of a *dynamic systems view* (see page 29 in Chapter 1) to early cognition. In this approach, researchers analyze each cognitive attainment to see how it results from a complex system of prior accomplishments and the child's current goals (Spencer, Perone, & Buss, 2011; Schutte & DeGirolamo, 2017; Thelen & Smith, 2006). Once these ideas are fully tested, they may move the field closer to a more powerful view of how the minds of infants and children develop.

6.3 The Social Context of Early Cognitive Development

6.3 Explain how Vygotsky's concept of the zone of proximal development expands our understanding of early cognitive development.

Recall the description at the beginning of this chapter of Grace dropping shapes into a container. Notice that she learns about the toy with Ginette's help. With adult support, Grace will become better at matching shapes to openings and dropping them into the container, gradually performing this and similar activities on her own. Throughout this chapter, we have seen other examples of how adult support fosters early cognitive attainments—using tools to access objects, understanding screen media, sustaining attention, retrieving autobiographical memories, and forming categories,

Lev Vygotsky's sociocultural theory emphasizes that children live in rich social and cultural contexts that affect the way their cognitive world is structured (Bodrova & Leong, 2007; Lourenço, 2012). Vygotsky believed that complex mental activities, including voluntary attention, deliberate memory, categorization, and problem solving, have their origins in social interaction. Through joint activities with more mature members of their society, children master activities and think in ways that have meaning in their culture.

A special Vygotskian concept explains how this happens. The **zone of proximal** (or potential) **development** refers to a range of tasks that the child cannot yet handle alone but can do with the help of more skilled partners. To understand this idea, think about how a sensitive adult (such as Ginette) introduces a child to a new activity. The adult picks a task that the child can master but that is challenging enough that the child cannot do it by herself. Or the adult capitalizes on an activity that the child has chosen. The adult guides and supports, adjusting the level of support offered to fit the child's current performance. As the child joins in the interaction and picks up mental strategies, her competence increases, and the adult steps back, permitting the child to take more responsibility for the task (Mermelshtine, 2017). This form of teaching—known as *scaffolding*—promotes learning at all ages, and we will consider it further in Chapter 9.

Vygotsky's ideas have been applied mostly to preschool and school-age children, who are more skilled in language and social communication. Recently, however, his theory has been extended to infancy and toddlerhood. Picture an adult helping a baby figure out how a jack-in-the-box works. In the early months, the adult demonstrates and, as the clown pops out, tries to capture the infant's attention by saying something like "See what happened!" By the end of the first year, when cognitive and motor skills have improved, interaction centers on how to use the toy: The adult guides the baby's hand in turning the crank. During the second year, the adult helps from a distance using gestures and verbal prompts, such as making a turning motion and verbally prompting, "Turn it!" Research indicates that this fine-tuned support is related to advanced play, language, and problem solving during the second year—for example, transferring how a simple toy works on a touchscreen to the same toy in real life, which is highly challenging for toddlers (Bornstein et al., 1992; Charman et al., 2001; Zack & Barr, 2016).

As early as the first year, cultural variations in social experiences affect mental strategies. In the jack-in-the-box example, adults and children focus on a single activity. This strategy, common in Western middle-SES homes, is well-suited to lessons in which children master skills apart from everyday situations in which they will later use those skills. In contrast, infants and young children in Guatemalan Mayan and other Native American and indigenous communities often attend to several events at once. For example, one 12-month-old skillfully put objects in a jar while watching a passing truck and blowing into a toy whistle (Correa-Chavez, Roberts, & Perez, 2011).

Attending to several competing events simultaneously may be vital in cultures where children learn largely through keen observation of others' ongoing activities. In a comparison of 18-month-olds from German middle-SES homes and Nso farming villages in Cameroon, the Nso toddlers copied far fewer experimenter-demonstrated actions on toys than did the German toddlers (Borchert et al., 2013). Nso caregivers rarely create such child-focused teaching situations. Rather, they expect children to imitate observed behaviors without adult prompting. Nso children are motivated to do so because they want to be included in the major activities of their community.

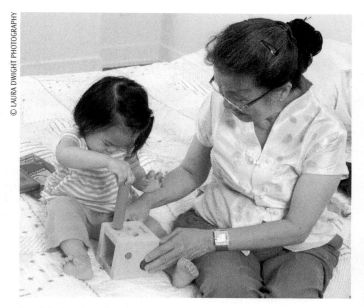

By bringing the task within the child's zone of proximal development and adjusting her communication to suit the child's needs, a grandmother transfers mental strategies to her granddaughter, promoting her cognitive development.

Earlier we saw how infants and toddlers create new schemes by acting on the physical world (Piaget) and how certain skills become better-developed as children represent their experiences more efficiently and meaningfully (information processing). Vygotsky adds a third dimension to our understanding by emphasizing that many aspects of cognitive development are socially mediated. The Cultural Influences box on page 220 presents additional evidence for this idea, and we will see even more evidence in the next section.

ASK YOURSELF

Connect ■ List techniques that parents can use to *scaffold* development *of categorization* in infancy and toddlerhood, and explain why each is effective.

Apply ■ When Timmy was 18 months old, his mother stood behind him, helping him throw a large ball into a box. As his skill improved, she stepped back, letting him try on his own. Using Vygotsky's ideas, explain how Timmy's mother is supporting his cognitive development.

Reflect ■ Describe your earliest autobiographical memory. How old were you when the event occurred? Do your responses fit with research on infantile amnesia?

6.4 Individual Differences in Early Mental Development

At age 22 months, Timmy had only a handful of words in his vocabulary, played in a less mature way than Caitlin and Grace, and seemed restless and overactive. Worried about Timmy's progress, Vanessa arranged for a psychologist to give him one of many tests available for assessing mental development in infants and toddlers.

6.4a Describe the mental testing approach, the meaning of intelligence test scores, and the extent to which infant tests predict later performance.

6.4b Discuss environmental influences on early mental development, including home, child care, and early intervention for at-risk infants and toddlers.

Cultural Influences | Social Origins of Make-Believe Play

One of the activities my husband, Ken, used to do with our two young sons was to bake pineapple upside-down cake, a favorite treat. One Sunday afternoon when a cake was in the making, 21-month-old Peter stood on a chair at the kitchen sink, busily pouring water from one cup to another.

"He's in the way, Dad!" complained 4-year-old David, trying to pull Peter away from the sink.

"Maybe if we let him help, he'll give us room," Ken suggested. As David stirred the batter, Ken poured some into a small bowl for Peter, moved his chair to the side of the sink, and handed him a spoon.

"Here's how you do it, Petey," instructed David, with a superior air. Peter watched as David stirred, then tried to copy his motion. When it was time to pour the batter, Ken helped Peter hold and tip the small bowl.

"Time to bake it," said Ken.

"Bake it, bake it," repeated Peter, watching Ken slip the pan into the oven.

Several hours later, Ken observed one of Peter's earliest instances of make-believe play. He got his pail from the sandbox and, after filling it with a handful of sand, carried it into the kitchen and put it down on the floor in front of the oven. "Bake it, bake it," Peter called to Ken. Together, father and son placed the pretend cake in the oven.

Piaget and his followers concluded that toddlers discover make-believe independently, once they are capable of representational schemes. Vygotsky's theory has challenged this view. He believed that society provides children with opportunities to represent culturally meaningful activities in play. Make-believe, like other complex mental activities, is first learned under the guidance of experts (Meyers & Berk, 2014). In the example just described, Peter extended his capacity to represent daily events when Ken drew him into the baking task and helped him act it out in play.

Current evidence supports the idea that early make-believe is the combined result of children's readiness to engage in it and social experiences that promote it. In Western middle-SES families, play is culturally cultivated and scaffolded by adults (Gaskins, 2015). Mothers, especially, offer toddlers a rich array of cues that they are pretending—looking and smiling at the child more, making more exaggerated movements, and using more "we" talk (acknowledging that pretending is a joint endeavor) than they do during the same real-life event (Lillard et al., 2007). These cues encourage toddlers to join in and probably facilitate their ability to distinguish pretend from real acts, which strengthens over the second and third years.

When adults participate, toddlers' make-believe is more elaborate (Keren et al., 2005). They are more likely to combine pretend acts into complex sequences, as Peter did when he put the sand in the bucket (making the batter), carried it into the kitchen, and, with Ken's help, put it in the oven (baking the cake). The more parents pretend with their toddlers, the more time their children devote to make-believe (Cote & Bornstein, 2009).

In some cultures, such as those of Indonesia and Mexico, where play is viewed as solely a child's activity and sibling caregiving is common, make-believe is more frequent and more complex with older siblings than with mothers. As early as age 3 to 4, children provide rich, challenging stimulation to their younger brothers and sisters, take these teaching responsibilities seriously, and, with age, become better at them (Lancy, 2014; Zukow-Goldring, 2002). In a study of Zinacanteco Indian children of southern Mexico, by age 8, sibling teachers were highly skilled at showing 2-year-olds how to play at everyday tasks, such as washing and cooking (Maynard, 2002). They often guided toddlers verbally and physically through the task and provided feedback.

As we will see in Chapters 9 and Chapter 10, make-believe play is an important means through which children enhance their cognitive and social skills and learn about important activities in their culture (Nielsen, 2012). Vygotsky's theory, and the findings that support it, tell us that providing a stimulating physical environment is not enough to promote early cognitive development. In addition, toddlers must be invited and encouraged by more skilled members of their culture to participate in the social world around them. Parents and teachers can enhance early make-believe by playing often with toddlers, guiding and elaborating their make-believe themes.

In cultures where sibling caregiving is common, make-believe play is more frequent and complex with older siblings than with mothers. These Afghan children play "wedding," dressing the youngest as a bride.

The cognitive theories we have just discussed try to explain the *process* of development—how children's thinking changes. Mental tests, in contrast, focus on *individual differences*: They measure variations in developmental progress, arriving at scores that *predict* future performance, such as later intelligence and school achievement. This concern with prediction arose over a century ago, when French psychologist Alfred Binet designed the first successful intelligence test, which predicted school achievement (see Chapter 1). It inspired the design of many new tests, including ones that measure intelligence at very early ages.

6.4.1 Infant and Toddler Intelligence Tests

Accurately measuring infants' intelligence is a challenge because they cannot answer questions or follow directions. All we can do is present them with stimuli, coax them to respond, and observe their behavior. As a result, most infant tests emphasize perceptual and motor responses. But increasingly, tests are being developed that also tap early language, cognition, and social behavior, especially with older infants and toddlers.

One commonly used test, the *Bayley Scales of Infant and Toddler Development,* is suitable for children between 1 month and 3½ years. The most recent edition, the Bayley-III, has three main subtests: (1) the Cognitive Scale, which includes such items as attention to familiar and unfamiliar objects, looking for a fallen object, and pretend play; (2) the Language Scale, which taps understanding and expressions of language—for example, recognition of objects and people, following simple directions, and naming objects and pictures; and (3) the Motor Scale, which includes gross- and fine-motor skills, such as grasping, sitting, stacking blocks, and climbing stairs (Bayley, 2005).

Two additional Bayley-III scales depend on parental report: (4) the Social-Emotional Scale, which asks caregivers about such behaviors as ease of calming, social responsiveness, and imitation in play; and (5) the Adaptive Behavior Scale, which asks about adaptation to the demands of daily life, including communication, self-control, following rules, and getting along with others.

A trained examiner administers a test based on the Bayley Scales of Infant Development to a 1-year-old in her mother's lap. Current Bayley-III Cognitive and Language Scales predict preschool mental test performance better than earlier versions.

Computing Intelligence Test Scores   Intelligence tests for infants, children, and adults are scored in much the same way—by computing an **intelligence quotient (IQ),** which indicates the extent to which the raw score (number of items passed) deviates from the typical performance of same-age individuals. To make this comparison possible, test designers engage in **standardization**—giving the test to a large, representative sample and using the results as the *standard* for interpreting scores. The standardization sample for the Bayley-III included 1,700 infants, toddlers, and young preschoolers, reflecting the U.S. population in SES and ethnic diversity.

Within the standardization sample, performances at each age level form a **normal distribution,** in which most scores cluster around the mean, or average, with progressively fewer falling toward the extremes (see Figure 6.9). This *bell-shaped distribution* results whenever researchers measure individual differences in large samples. When intelligence tests are standardized, the mean IQ is set at 100. An individual's IQ is higher or lower than 100 by an amount that reflects how much his or her test performance deviates from the standardization-sample mean.

The IQ offers a way of finding out whether an individual is ahead, behind, or on time (average) in mental development compared with others of the same age. For example, if Timmy's score is 100, then he did better than 50 percent of his agemates. A child with an IQ of 85 did better than only 16 percent, whereas a child with an IQ of 130 outperformed 98 percent. The IQs of 96 percent of individuals fall between 70 and 130; only a few achieve higher or lower scores.

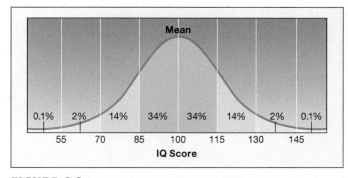

FIGURE 6.9   Normal distribution of intelligence test scores. To determine what percentage of same-age individuals in the population a person with a certain IQ outperformed, add the figures to the left of that IQ score. For example, an 8-year-old child with an IQ of 115 scored better than 84 percent of the population of 8-year-olds.

Predicting Later Performance from Infant Tests   Despite careful construction, most infant tests—including previous editions of the Bayley—predict later intelligence poorly. Infants and toddlers easily become distracted, fatigued, or bored during testing, so their scores often do not reflect their true abilities. And infant perceptual and motor items differ from the tasks given to older children, which increasingly emphasize verbal, conceptual, and problem-solving skills. In contrast, the Bayley-III Cognitive and Language Scales, which better dovetail with childhood tests, are good predictors of preschool mental test performance (Albers & Grieve, 2007; Bode et al., 2014). But because most infant test scores do not tap the same dimensions of intelligence measured at older ages, they usually are conservatively labeled **developmental quotients (DQs)** rather than IQs.

Infant tests are somewhat better at making long-term predictions for extremely low-scoring babies. Today, they are largely used for *screening*—helping to identify for further observation and intervention babies who are likely to have developmental problems.

As an alternative to infant tests, some researchers have turned to information-processing measures, such as habituation, to assess early mental progress. Their findings show that speed of habituation and recovery to novel visual stimuli are among the best available infant predictors of IQ from early childhood to early adulthood, with correlations ranging from the .30s to the .60s (Fagan, Holland, & Wheeler, 2007; Kavšek, 2004). Habituation and recovery seem to be an especially effective early index of intelligence because they assess memory as well as quickness and flexibility of thinking, which underlie intelligent behavior at all ages (Colombo et al., 2004). The consistency of these findings has prompted designers of the Bayley-III to include items that tap such cognitive skills as habituation, object permanence, and categorization.

6.4.2 Early Environment and Mental Development

In Chapter 2, we indicated that intelligence is a complex blend of hereditary and environmental influences. As we consider evidence on the relationship of environmental factors to infant and toddler mental test scores, you will encounter findings that highlight the role of heredity as well.

Home Environment   The **Home Observation for Measurement of the Environment (HOME)** is a checklist for gathering information about the quality of children's home lives through observation and parental interview (Caldwell & Bradley, 1994). Applying What We Know on the following page lists the factors measured by the HOME Infant–Toddler Subscales—the most widely used home environment measure during the first three years. A briefer, exclusively observational HOME instrument is also available (Rijlaarsdam et al., 2012).

Each HOME subscale is positively related to toddlers' mental test performance. Furthermore, within diverse SES and ethnic groups, an organized, stimulating physical setting and parental affection, involvement, and encouragement of new skills repeatedly predict better language and IQ scores in toddlerhood and early childhood (Bornstein, 2015; Fuligni, Han, & Brooks-Gunn, 2004; Linver, Martin, & Brooks-Gunn, 2004; Ronfani et al., 2015; Tong et al., 2007). The extent to which parents talk to infants and toddlers is particularly important. It contributes strongly to early language progress, which, in turn, predicts intelligence and academic achievement in elementary school (Hart & Risley, 1995; Hoff, 2013).

Yet we must interpret these correlational findings cautiously. In all the studies, children were reared by their biological parents, with whom they share not just a common environment but also a common heredity. Parents who are genetically more intelligent may provide better experiences while also giving birth to genetically brighter children, who evoke more stimulation from their parents. Research supports this hypothesis, which refers to *gene–environment correlation* (see pages 80–81 in Chapter 2) (Hadd & Rodgers, 2017; Saudino & Plomin, 1997). But parent–child shared heredity does not account for the entire association between home environment and mental test scores. Family living conditions—both HOME scores and affluence of the surrounding neighborhood—continue to predict children's IQ beyond the contribution of parental IQ and education (Chase-Lansdale et al., 1997; Klebanov et al., 1998).

A father plays actively with his baby. Parental warmth, attention, and verbal communication predict better language and IQ scores in toddlerhood and early childhood.

© ROBERTO WESTBROOK/BLEND IMAGES/GETTY IMAGES

APPLYING WHAT WE KNOW

Features of a High-Quality Home Life for Infants and Toddlers: The HOME Infant–Toddler Subscales

HOME SUBSCALE	SAMPLE ITEM
Organization of the physical environment	Child's play environment appears safe and free of hazards.
Provision of appropriate play materials	Parent provides toys or interesting activities for child during observer's visit.
Emotional and verbal responsiveness of the parent	Parent caresses or kisses child at least once during observer's visit.
	Parent spontaneously speaks to child twice or more (excluding scolding) during observer's visit.
Parental acceptance of the child	Parent does not interfere with child's actions or restrict child's movements more than three times during observer's visit.
Parental involvement with the child	Parent tends to keep child within view and to look at child often during observer's visit.
Opportunities for variety in daily stimulation	Child eats at least one meal per day with mother and/or father, according to parental report.
	Child frequently has a chance to get out of house (for example, accompanies parent on trips to grocery store).

Sources: Bradley, 1994; Bradley et al., 2001. A brief, exclusively observational HOME instrument taps the first three subscales only (Rijlaarsdam et al., 2012).

How can the research summarized so far help us understand Vanessa's concern about Timmy's development? Ben, the psychologist who tested Timmy, found that he scored only slightly below average. Ben talked with Vanessa about her child-rearing practices and watched her play with Timmy. A single parent who worked long hours, Vanessa had little energy for Timmy at the end of the day. Ben also noticed that Vanessa, anxious about Timmy's progress, was intrusive: She interfered with his active behavior and bombarded him with directions: "That's enough ball play. Stack these blocks."

Children who experience intrusive parenting are likely to be distractible and withdrawn and do poorly on mental tests—negative outcomes that persist unless parenting improves (Clincy & Mills-Koonce, 2013; Rubin, Coplan, & Bowker, 2009). Ben coached Vanessa in how to interact sensitively with Timmy while assuring her that responsive parenting that builds on toddlers' current capacities is a much better indicator of how children will do later than an early mental test score.

Infant and Toddler Child Care　　Today, about 60 percent of U.S. mothers with a child under age 2 are employed (U.S. Bureau of Labor Statistics, 2018). Child care for infants and toddlers has become common, and its quality—though not as influential as parenting—affects mental development.

Research consistently shows that young children exposed to poor-quality child care—whether they come from middle- or low-SES homes—score lower on measures of cognitive, language, academic, and social skills during the preschool, elementary, and secondary school years (Belsky et al., 2007; Burchinal et al., 2015; Dearing, McCartney, & Taylor, 2009; NICHD Early Child Care Research Network, 2000b, 2001, 2003b, 2006; Vandell et al., 2010).

WALTRAUDÀ GRUBITZSCH/PICTURE ALLIANCE/GETTY IMAGES

With support from their caregivers, toddlers at a child-care center in Leipzig, Germany, explore the look and feel of colorful paints. High-quality child care—a generous caregiver–child ratio, well-trained caregivers, and developmentally appropriate activities—benefits children of all SES levels, especially those from low-SES homes.

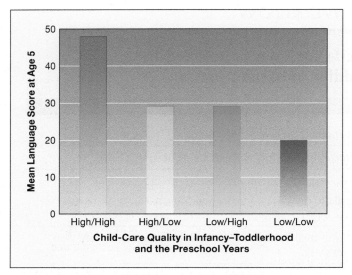

FIGURE 6.10 **Relationship of child-care quality in infancy–toddlerhood and the preschool years to language development at age 5.** When a nationally representative sample of more than 1,300 children was followed over the first five years, language scores were highest for those experiencing high-quality child care in both infancy–toddlerhood and the preschool years, intermediate for those experiencing high-quality care in just one of these periods, and lowest for those experiencing poor-quality care in both periods. Cognitive, literacy, and math scores also showed this pattern. (Based on Li et al., 2013.)

LOOK and LISTEN

Ask several employed parents of infants or toddlers to describe what they sought in a child-care setting, along with challenges they faced in finding child care. How knowledgeable are the parents about the ingredients of high-quality care?

In contrast, good child care can reduce the negative impact of a stressed, poverty-stricken home life and it sustains the benefits of growing up in an economically advantaged family (Burchinal, Kainz, & Cai, 2011; McCartney et al., 2007). As Figure 6.10 illustrates, the Early Childhood Longitudinal Study—consisting of a large sample of U.S. children diverse in SES and ethnicity followed from birth through the preschool years (see page 42 in Chapter 1)—confirmed the importance of continuous high-quality child care from infancy through the preschool years (Li et al., 2013).

Unlike child care in most European countries and Australia and New Zealand, which is nationally regulated and funded to ensure its quality, child care in the United States raises serious concerns. Standards are set by the individual states and vary widely. In studies of quality, only 20 to 25 percent of child-care centers and family child-care homes provided infants and toddlers with sufficiently positive, stimulating experiences to promote healthy psychological development. Most settings offered substandard care (NICHD Early Child Care Research Network, 2000a, 2004). And the cost of child care in the United States is high: On average, full-time center-based care for one infant consumes 15 percent of the median income for couples and 50 percent for single parents (Child Care Aware, 2017). The cost of a family child-care home is about two-thirds of center-based care.

Unfortunately, many U.S. children from low-income families experience inadequate child care (Torquati et al., 2011). But U.S. settings providing the very worst care tend to serve middle-income families. These parents are especially likely to place their children in for-profit centers, where quality tends to be lowest. Economically disadvantaged children more often attend publicly subsidized, nonprofit centers, which are better equipped with learning materials and have smaller group sizes and more favorable teacher–child ratios (Johnson, Ryan, & Brooks-Gunn, 2012), Still, many low-income children experience substandard child care.

See Applying What We Know on the following page for signs of high-quality child care for infants and toddlers based on standards for **developmentally appropriate practice** devised by the U.S. National Association for the Education of Young Children. These standards specify program characteristics that serve young children's developmental and individual needs, based on both current research and consensus among experts.

Child care in the United States is affected by a macrosystem of individualistic values and weak government regulation and funding. Furthermore, many parents think that their children's child-care experiences are better than they really are (Torquati et al., 2011). Unable to identify good care or without the financial means to purchase it, they do not demand it. In recent years, the U.S. federal government and some states have allocated additional funds to subsidize child-care costs, especially for low-income families (Matthews, 2014). Though far from meeting the need, this increase in resources has had a positive impact on child-care quality and accessibility.

6.4.3 Early Intervention for At-Risk Infants and Toddlers

Children living in persistent poverty are likely to show gradual declines in intelligence test scores and to achieve poorly when they reach school age (Schoon et al., 2012). These problems are largely due to stressful home environments that undermine children's ability to learn and increase the likelihood that they will remain poor as adults. A variety of intervention programs have been developed to break this tragic cycle of poverty. Although most begin during the preschool years (we will discuss these in Chapter 9), some start during infancy and continue through early childhood.

APPLYING WHAT WE KNOW

Signs of Developmentally Appropriate Infant and Toddler Child Care

PROGRAM CHARACTERISTIC	SIGNS OF QUALITY
Physical setting	Indoor environment is clean, in good repair, well-lighted, and well-ventilated. Fenced outdoor play space is available. Setting does not appear overcrowded when children are present.
Toys and equipment	Play materials are appropriate for infants and toddlers and are stored on low shelves within easy reach. Cribs, highchairs, infant seats, and child-sized tables and chairs are available. Outdoor equipment includes small riding toys, swings, slide, and sandbox.
Caregiver–child ratio	In child-care centers, caregiver–child ratio is no greater than 1 to 3 for infants and 1 to 6 for toddlers. Group size (number of children in one room) is no greater than 6 infants with two caregivers and 12 toddlers with two caregivers. In family child-care homes, caregiver is responsible for no more than 6 children; within this group, no more than 2 are infants or toddlers. Staffing is consistent, so infants and toddlers can form relationships with particular caregivers.
Daily activities	Daily schedule includes times for active play, quiet play, naps, snacks, and meals. It is flexible rather than rigid, to meet the needs of individual children. Atmosphere is warm and supportive, and children are never left unsupervised.
Interactions among adults and children	Caregivers respond promptly to infants' and toddlers' distress; hold, talk to, sing, and read to them; and interact with them in a manner that respects the individual child's interests and tolerance for stimulation.
Caregiver qualifications	Caregiver has some training in child development, first aid, and safety.
Relationships with parents	Parents are welcome anytime. Caregivers talk frequently with parents about children's behavior and development.
Licensing and accreditation	Child-care setting, whether a center or a home, is licensed by the state. In the United States, voluntary accreditation by the National Association for the Education of Young Children, *www.naeyc.org/accreditation,* or the National Association for Family Child Care, *www.nafcc.org,* is evidence of an especially high-quality program.

Source: Copple & Bredekamp, 2009.

In center-based interventions, children attend an organized child-care or preschool program where they receive educational, nutritional, and health services, and their parents receive child-rearing and other social service supports. In home-based interventions, a skilled adult visits the home and works with parents, providing social support and teaching them how to stimulate a young child's development. In most programs of either type, participating children score higher than untreated controls on mental tests by age 2. The earlier intervention begins, the longer it lasts, and the greater its scope and intensity (for example, year-round high-quality child care plus generous support services for parents), the better participants' cognitive and academic performance throughout childhood and adolescence (Ramey, Ramey, & Lanzi, 2006).

The Carolina Abecedarian Project illustrates these positive outcomes. In the 1970s, more than 100 infants from poverty-stricken families, ranging in age from 3 weeks to 3 months, were randomly assigned to either a treatment group or a control group. Treatment infants were enrolled in full-time, year-round child care through the preschool years. There they received carefully planned educational experiences aimed at promoting motor, cognitive, language, and social skills and, after age 3, literacy and math concepts. Special emphasis was placed on rich, responsive adult–child verbal communication. All children received nutrition and health services; the primary difference between treatment and controls was the intensive child-care experience.

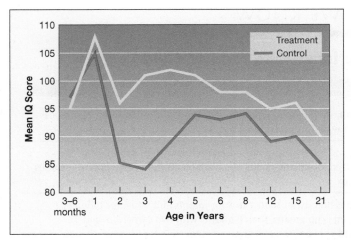

FIGURE 6.11   **IQ scores of treatment and control children from infancy to 21 years in the Carolina Abecedarian Project.**
At 1 year of age, treatment children outperformed controls, an advantage consistently maintained through age 21. The IQ scores of both groups declined gradually during childhood and adolescence—a trend probably due to the damaging impact of poverty on mental development. (Based on Campbell et al., 2001.)

This Early Head Start program provides rich, educational experiences for toddlers plus parent education and family social supports. The most favorable outcomes of Early Head Start result from mixing center- and home-visiting services.

As Figure 6.11 shows, by 12 months of age, the IQs of the two groups diverged. Treatment children sustained an advantage until last tested—at age 21. In addition, throughout their years of schooling, treatment youths achieved considerably higher scores in reading and math. These gains translated into reduced enrollment in special education, more years of schooling completed, higher rates of college enrollment and employment in skilled jobs, and lower rates of drug use and adolescent parenthood (Campbell & Ramey, 2010; Campbell et al., 2001, 2002, 2012).

Recognition of the power of intervening as early as possible led the U.S. Congress to provide limited funding for intervention services directed at infants and toddlers who already have serious developmental problems or who are at risk for problems because of poverty. Early Head Start, begun in 1995, currently has 1,000 sites serving about 110,000 low-income children and their families (Walker, 2014). It offers an array of coordinated services—child care, educational experiences for infants and toddlers, parenting education, family social support, and health care—delivered through a center-based, home-based, or mixed approach, depending on community needs.

An evaluation, conducted when children reached age 3, showed that Early Head Start led to warmer, more supportive and stimulating parenting, a reduction in harsh discipline, gains in cognitive and language development, and lessening of child aggression (Love, Chazan-Cohen, & Raikes, 2007; Love et al., 2005; Paschall & Mastergeorge, 2018; Raikes et al., 2010). Also, Early Head Start offered some protection from the negative effects of parental insensitivity, which led to less harmful outcomes among children in the program than among no-intervention controls (Ayoub et al., 2014). The strongest effects occurred at sites mixing center- and home-visiting services.

By age 5, however, most benefits of Early Head Start had declined or disappeared, and a follow-up in fifth grade showed no persisting cognitive gains (U.S. Department of Health and Human Services, 2006; Vogel et al., 2010). One speculation is that more intentional educational experiences extending through the preschool years—as in the Abecedarian project—would increase the lasting impact of Early Head Start (Barnett, 2011). Also, some evidence suggests that the cognitive benefits of Early Head Start are greater for certain children—in particular, those who receive little stimulation at home (Bradley, McKelvey, & Whiteside-Mansell, 2011). Although Early Head Start is in need of refinement, it is a promising beginning at providing U.S. infants and toddlers living in poverty with publicly supported intervention.

ASK YOURSELF

Connect ■ Using what you learned about brain development in Chapter 5, explain why it is best to initiate intervention for children living in poverty in the first two years rather than later.

Apply ■ Fifteen-month-old Joey's developmental quotient (DQ) is 115. His mother wants to know exactly what this means and what she should do to support his intellectual development. How would you respond?

Reflect ■ Suppose you were seeking a child-care setting for your baby. What would you want it to be like, and why?

6.5 Language Development

Advances in perception and cognition during infancy pave the way for an extraordinary human achievement—language. In Chapter 5, we saw that by the second half of the first year, infants make dramatic progress in distinguishing the basic sounds of their language and in segmenting the flow of speech into word and phrase units. They also start to comprehend some word meanings and, around 12 months of age, say their first word. Sometime between 1½ and 2 years, toddlers combine two words (MacWhinney, 2015). By age 6, children understand the meaning of about 14,000 words, speak in elaborate sentences, and are skilled conversationalists.

To appreciate this awesome task, think about the many abilities involved in your own flexible use of language. When you speak, you must select words that match the underlying concepts you want to convey. To be understood, you must pronounce words correctly. Then you must combine them into phrases and sentences using a complex set of grammatical rules. Finally, you must follow the rules of everyday conversation, taking turns, making comments relevant to what your partner just said, and using an appropriate tone of voice.

How do infants and toddlers make such remarkable progress in launching these skills? To address this question, let's examine several prominent theories of language development.

6.5a Describe theories of language development, and indicate the emphasis each places on innate abilities and environmental influences.

6.5b Describe major language milestones in the first two years, individual and cultural differences, and ways adults can support early language development.

6.5.1 Theories of Language Development

In the 1950s, researchers did not take seriously the idea that very young children might be able to figure out important properties of language. Children's regular and rapid attainment of language milestones suggested a process largely governed by maturation, inspiring the nativist perspective on language development. In recent years, new evidence has spawned the interactionist perspective, which emphasizes the joint roles of children's inner capacities and communicative experiences.

The Nativist Perspective According to linguist Noam Chomsky's (1957) *nativist* theory, language is a uniquely human accomplishment, etched into the structure of the brain. Focusing on grammar, Chomsky reasoned that the rules of sentence organization are too complex to be directly taught to or discovered by even a cognitively sophisticated young child. Rather, he proposed that all children have a **language acquisition device (LAD),** an innate system that contains a *universal grammar,* or set of rules common to all languages. It enables children, no matter which language they hear, to understand and speak in a rule-oriented fashion as soon as they pick up enough words.

Are children innately primed to acquire language? Recall from Chapter 4 that newborn babies are remarkably sensitive to speech sounds. And children everywhere attain major language milestones in a similar sequence (Parish-Morris, Golinkoff, & Hirsh-Pasek, 2013). Also, the ability to master a grammatically complex language system seems to be unique to humans, as efforts to teach language to nonhuman primates—using either specially devised artificial symbol systems or sign language—have met with only limited success. Even after extensive training, chimpanzees (who are closest to humans in terms of evolution) master only a basic vocabulary and short word combinations, and they produce these combinations far less consistently than human preschoolers do (Tomasello, Call, & Hare, 2003).

Evidence for specialized language areas in the brain and a sensitive period for language development have also been interpreted as supporting Chomsky's theory. Let's take a closer look at these findings.

Language Areas in the Brain Recall from Chapter 5 that for most individuals, language is housed largely in the left hemisphere of the cerebral cortex. Within it are two important language-related structures (see Figure 6.12 on page 228). To clarify their functions, researchers have, for several decades, studied adults who experienced damage to these structures and display *aphasias,* or communication disorders. *Broca's area,* located in the left frontal

© LAURA DWIGHT PHOTOGRAPHY

Infants communicate from the very beginning of life. How will this child become a fluent speaker of her native language within just a few years? Theorists disagree sharply.

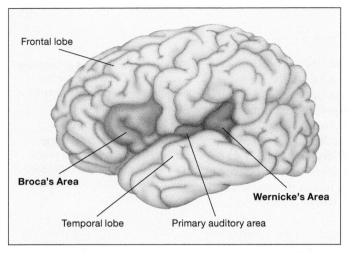

FIGURE 6.12   Broca's and Wernicke's areas, in the left hemisphere of the cerebral cortex. Broca's area, located in the frontal lobe, supports grammatical processing and language production. Wernicke's area, located in the temporal lobe, is involved in comprehending word meaning. Contrary to what was once believed, however, neither area is solely or even mainly responsible for these functions.

lobe, supports grammatical processing and language production. *Wernicke's area,* located in the left temporal lobe, plays a role in comprehending word meaning.

But brain-imaging research suggests that the relationship between these brain structures and language functions is complicated. Neither area is solely, or even mainly, responsible for specific language capacities (Ardila, Bernal, & Rosselli, 2016). Furthermore, the impaired pronunciation and grammar of patients with Broca's aphasia and the meaningless speech streams of patients with Wernicke's aphasia involve the spread of injury from those areas to nearby cortical areas. In addition, the brain damage triggers widespread abnormal activity elsewhere in the left cerebral hemisphere (Bates et al., 2003; Keller et al., 2009).

The broad association of language functions with left-hemispheric regions is consistent with Chomsky's notion of a brain prepared to process language. But critics point out that at birth, the brain is not fully lateralized; it is highly plastic. Language areas in the cerebral cortex *develop* as children acquire language (Bishop et al., 2014; Mills & Conboy, 2005). Although the left hemisphere is biased for language processing, if it is injured in the first few years, other regions take over language functions, and most affected children eventually attain typical language competence. Thus, left-hemispheric localization, though the norm, is not necessary for effective language processing.

Nevertheless, when the young brain allocates language to the right hemisphere—as a result of left-hemispheric damage or the learning of sign language (see pages 160–161 in Chapter 5)—it localizes it in roughly the same regions that typically support language in the left hemisphere (Stiles, Reilly, & Levine, 2012). This suggests that those brain structures are uniquely disposed for language processing.

A Sensitive Period for Language Development Must language be acquired early in life, during an age span in which the brain is particularly responsive to language stimulation? Evidence for a sensitive period would support the view that language development has unique biological properties.

To test this idea, researchers examined the language competence of deaf adults who acquired their first language—American Sign Language (ASL), a gestural system just as complex as any spoken language—at different ages. The later learners, whose hearing parents chose to educate them through the oral method, which relies on speech and lip-reading, acquired little spoken language because of their profound deafness. Consistent with the sensitive-period notion, those who learned ASL in adolescence or adulthood never became as proficient, especially at ASL grammar, as those who learned it in childhood (Mayberry, 2010; Singleton & Newport, 2004).

The age at which children with hearing impairment start receiving language input emerges repeatedly in research as a powerful influence on language outcomes. Deaf children of deaf parents, who from birth were exposed to rich language stimulation through sign language, show typical language progress. Among hearing impaired children of hearing parents, language development depends on the age at which they were fitted with an effective hearing device—either a hearing aid or a *cochlear implant,* an electronic mechanism surgically inserted into the ear that converts sounds into signals to stimulate the auditory nerve. In one series of studies, children born with limited or no hearing showed typical mastery of complex grammatical structures in middle childhood only if they were exposed to language input during the first year of life after receiving such a device (Friedmann & Haddad-Hanna, 2014; Friedmann & Szterman, 2011; Szterman & Friedmann, 2014). In contrast, children who lost their hearing after their first year and were fitted with hearing devices at varying later ages showed no difficulties with grammatical development (Friedmann & Rusou, 2015).

These findings suggest that infancy is a sensitive period for acquiring grammar, even though infants are not yet able to understand and produce sentences. Some researchers speculate that capacities evident in infancy, such as statistical learning of native-language speech

Biology and Environment | Thiamine Deficiency in the First Year and Later Language Impairment

Thiamine (vitamin B1) is essential for normal brain development and functioning, including synapse formation, production of neurotransmitters, myelination, and maintenance of neuronal structures. Because the body continuously uses available thiamine, storing it only briefly, adults show central nervous system symptoms—poor memory, sleep difficulties, mental confusion, vision problems, and muscle cramps and weakness—after just two to three weeks of dietary thiamine deficiency, recovering if adequate thiamine is soon restored (Kloss, Eskin, & Suh, 2018). Insufficient thiamine intake also affects the infant brain, though symptoms are difficult to recognize and often confused with indicators of other diseases.

Vitamin enrichment of basic foods has made thiamine deficiency rare, except in poverty-stricken regions of the world with food shortages (Hiffler et al., 2016). Errors in food enrichment, however, can cause widespread deficiency, even in nations with plentiful, healthy food.

In 2003, a manufacturer in Israel mistakenly released a defective infant formula, failing to include in it a thiamine additive. An estimated 600 to 1,000 infants regularly consumed the formula. Though many showed no neurological symptoms, they were nevertheless considered high-risk for developmental problems and monitored over time. As they reached 2 to 3 years of age, an evaluation of 20 children revealed substantial delays in language comprehension and production (Fattal-Valevski et al., 2009).

A subsequent follow-up of 59 affected children at age 5 to 7 examined complex language skills (Fattal, Friedmann, & Fattal-Valevski, 2011). The researchers assessed mastery of grammatical structures in several ways. For example, the children were asked to select from pairs of pictures the one that matched the meaning of sentences containing relative clauses (see Figure 6.13 for an example). They were also asked to repeat sentences with intricate grammatical structures (such as, "Which teacher does the boy like?"), a challenging task that requires both understanding of each structure and the ability to produce it. Furthermore, to assess vocabulary recall, the children had to label pictures that depicted various word classes, including objects, object parts, adjectives, verbs, adverbs, and prepositions.

Results revealed that 97 percent of children who had been thiamine-deficient in their first year displayed language deficits in grammar, vocabulary recall, or both, even though their thiamine intake had been adequate from toddlerhood on. In contrast, same-age controls, recruited from the same communities as the thiamine-deficient children, performed well: Only 9 percent displayed language deficits, the same rate as in the general population.

The thiamine-deficient children attained typical scores on the Bayley Scales (with the exception of language) at age 2 to 3 and on assessments of conceptual understanding at 5 to 7. Therefore, their language impairment could not be attributed to low intelligence.

Thiamine deficiency in adulthood, after brain development is complete, does not affect language abilities (Sechi et al., 2016). But when thiamine is lacking in infancy, its impact on language persists, seriously impairing children's grammatical and word recall skills. These findings support the conclusion that the first year of life is a sensitive period for development of brain structures crucial for acquiring language.

FIGURE 6.13　An example of a pair of pictures used in the relative-clause comprehension task. A relative clause has a subject and verb that elaborate on the noun that precedes them, as in "Show me the girl *that the woman is drawing.*" The child was shown a pair of pictures and asked to point to the one that matches the meaning of this sentence. (From I. Fattal, N. Friedman, & A. Fattal-Valevski, 2011, "The Crucial Role of Thiamine in the Development of Syntax and Lexical Retrieval: A Study of Infantile Thiamine Deficiency," *Brain, 134,* p. 1725. Copyright © 2011 Oxford University Press. Reprinted by permission.)

units (see page 175 in Chapter 5), combined with the young brain's openness to detecting those units, may be vital for later mastery of grammar (Thiessen, Girard, & Erickson, 2016). The importance of the first year for later language proficiency is also evident in children who suffered from an early dietary deficiency that is crucial for brain development, as the Biology and Environment box above reveals.

Is acquiring a second language also harder after a sensitive period has passed? In several studies, researchers selected immigrants from non-English-speaking countries who had resided in the United States for at least six years, to ensure that they had accomplished most of their English learning. As age of immigration increased from infancy and early childhood into adulthood, proficiency in both English pronunciation and grammar declined (Hakuta, Bialystok, & Wiley, 2003; Huang, 2014). Furthermore, ERP and fMRI measures of brain activity indicate that second-language processing is less lateralized in older than in younger learners (Neville & Bruer, 2001). However, second-language competence does not drop sharply at a certain age. Rather, a continuous, age-related decrease occurs.

An Ethiopian father attends an English-as-a-second-language class with his daughter. Evidence that second-language proficiency declines with age suggests that he will never be as proficient an English speaker as she will.

In sum, research on both first- and second-language learning reveals a biologically based timeframe for optimum language development. However, the boundaries of the sensitive period for second language learning remain unclear.

Limitations of the Nativist Perspective Chomsky's theory has had a major impact on current views of language development. It is now widely accepted that humans have a unique, biologically based capacity to acquire language. Still, the theory has been contested on several grounds.

First, researchers have had great difficulty specifying Chomsky's universal grammar. A major problem is the absence of a complete description of these abstract grammatical rules or even an agreed-on list of how many exist or the best examples of them. Chomsky's critics doubt that one set of rules can account for the extraordinary variation in grammatical forms among the world's 5,000 to 8,000 languages (Cole, Hermon, & Yanti, 2015; Dabrowska, 2015). How children manage to link such rules with the strings of words they hear is also unclear.

Second, Chomsky's assumption that grammatical knowledge is innately determined does not fit with certain observations of language development. Once children begin to use an innate grammatical structure, we would expect them to apply it to all relevant instances in their language. But children refine and generalize many grammatical forms gradually, engaging in much piecemeal learning and making errors along the way (Evans & Levinson, 2009; MacWhinney, 2015). For example, one 3-year-old, in grappling with prepositions, initially added *with* to the verb *open* ("You open with scissors") but not to the verb *hit* ("He hit me stick") (Tomasello, 2006). As we will see in Chapter 12, complete mastery of some grammatical forms, such as the passive voice, is not achieved until well into middle childhood. This suggests that more experimentation and learning are involved than Chomsky assumed.

The Interactionist Perspective Recent ideas about language development emphasize *interactions* between inner capacities and environmental influences. One type of interactionist theory applies the information-processing perspective to language development. A second type emphasizes social interaction.

Some information-processing theorists assume that children make sense of their complex language environments by applying powerful cognitive capacities of a general kind (Joanisse & McClelland, 2015; MacWhinney, 2015; Samuelson & McMurray, 2017). These theorists note that regions of the brain housing language also govern similar perceptual and cognitive abilities, such as the capacity to analyze musical and visual patterns (Saygin, Leech, & Dick, 2010).

Other theorists blend this information-processing view with Chomsky's nativist perspective. They argue that general cognitive capacities probably are not sufficient to account for mastery of higher-level aspects of language, such as intricate grammatical structures (Aslin & Newport, 2012). They also point out that grammatical competence may depend more on specific brain structures than the other components of language. When 2- to 2½-year-olds and adults listened to short sentences—some grammatically correct, others with grammatical errors—both groups showed similarly distinct ERP brain-wave patterns for each sentence type in the left frontal and temporal lobes of the cerebral cortex (Oberecker & Friederici, 2006). This suggests that 2-year-olds process sentence structures using the same neural system as adults do.

Still other interactionists emphasize that children's social skills and language experiences are centrally involved in language development. In this *social-interactionist* view, an active child strives to communicate, which cues her caregivers to provide appropriate language experiences. These experiences, in turn, help the child relate the content and structure of language to its social meanings (Bohannon & Bonvillian, 2013; Chapman, 2006).

Social interactionists disagree over whether or not children are equipped with specialized language structures (Hsu, Chater, & Vitányi, 2013; Lidz, 2007; Tomasello, 2006). Nevertheless, as we chart the course of language development, we will encounter much support for their shared central premise—that children's social competencies and language experiences greatly

TABLE 6.3   Milestones of Language Development During the First Two Years

APPROXIMATE AGE	MILESTONE
2 months	Infants coo, making pleasant vowel sounds.
4 months on	Infants observe with interest as the caregiver plays turn-taking games, such as pat-a-cake and peekaboo.
6 months on	Infants babble, adding consonants to their cooing sounds and repeating syllables. By 7 months, babbling starts to include many sounds of spoken languages.
	Infants begin to comprehend a few commonly heard words.
8–12 months	Infants become more accurate at establishing joint attention with the caregiver, who often verbally labels what the baby is looking at.
	Infants actively participate in turn-taking games, trading roles with the caregiver.
	Infants use preverbal gestures, such as showing and pointing, to influence others' goals and behavior and to convey information.
12 months	Babbling includes sound and intonation patterns of the child's language community.
	Speed and accuracy of word comprehension increase rapidly.
	Toddlers say their first recognizable word.
18–24 months	Spoken vocabulary expands from about 50 words to 200–250 words.
	Toddlers combine two words.

affect their language progress. In reality, native endowment, cognitive-processing strategies, and social experience probably operate in different balances with respect to each aspect of language: pronunciation, vocabulary, grammar, and communication skills. Table 6.3 provides an overview of early language milestones that we will examine in the next few sections.

6.5.2 Getting Ready to Talk

Before babies say their first word, they make impressive progress toward understanding and speaking their native tongue. They listen attentively to human speech, and they make speech-like sounds. As adults, we can hardly help but respond.

Cooing and Babbling   Around 2 months, babies begin to make vowel-like noises, called **cooing** because of their pleasant "oo" quality. Gradually, consonants are added, and around 6 months **babbling** appears, in which infants repeat consonant–vowel combinations. With age, they increasingly babble in long strings, such as "babababababa" or "nanananana," perhaps to gain control over producing particular sounds (Fagan, 2015).

Babies everywhere (even those who are deaf) start babbling at about the same age and produce a similar range of early sounds. But for babbling to develop further, infants must be able to hear human speech. In hearing-impaired babies, these speechlike sounds are greatly delayed and limited in diversity of sounds (Bass-Ringdahl, 2010). And a deaf infant not exposed to sign language will stop babbling entirely (Oller, 2000). As we saw in our discussion of a sensitive period, if language input is not restored in the first year, children remain substantially behind in language development.

Babies initially produce a limited number of sounds and then expand to a much broader range. Around 7 months, babbling starts to include many sounds of spoken languages. As caregivers respond to infant babbles, older infants modify their babbling to include sound patterns like those in the adult's speech. And at 8 to 10 months, infants shift their gaze from the eyes to the mouth of an adult speaker and try to match the speaker's oral movements (de Boisferon et al., 2017; Diepstra et al., 2017). On hearing this more mature babbling, mothers increase their responsiveness, imitating babbles and labeling objects the baby is looking at even more

© CHRISTINA KENNEDY/ALAMY STOCK PHOTO

Even babies who are deaf begin babbling at around 2 months. Those exposed to sign language from birth, as this child has been, babble with their hands, much as hearing babies do through speech.

(Albert, Schwade, & Goldstein, 2018). Around this time, infant babbling reflects the sound and intonation patterns of the baby's language community—an attainment that predicts the timing of first spoken words (Boysson-Bardies & Vihman, 1991; McGillion et al., 2017).

The next time you hear an older baby babbling, notice how certain sounds appear in particular contexts—for example, when the child is exploring objects, looking at books, or walking upright (Blake & Boysson-Bardies, 1992). Infants seem to be experimenting with the sound system and meaning of language, using parental feedback to acquire native-language forms. Toddlers continue babbling for four or five months after they say their first words.

Deaf infants exposed to sign language from birth babble with their hands much as hearing infants do through speech (Petitto & Marentette, 1991). Furthermore, hearing babies of deaf, signing parents produce babblelike hand motions with the rhythmic patterns of natural sign languages (Petitto et al., 2001, 2004). This sensitivity to language rhythm—evident in both spoken and signed babbling—supports both discovery and production of meaningful language units.

Becoming a Communicator At birth, infants are prepared for some aspects of conversational behavior. For example, newborns initiate interaction through eye contact and terminate it by looking away. By 3 to 4 months, infants start to gaze in the same general direction adults are looking—a skill that becomes more accurate at 10 to 11 months, as babies realize that others' focus offers information about their communicative intentions (to talk about an object) or other goals (to obtain an object) (Brooks & Meltzoff, 2005; Senju, Csibra, & Johnson, 2008). Around their first birthday, infants realize that a person's visual gaze signals a vital connection between the viewer and his or her surroundings, and they want to participate.

This **joint attention,** in which the child attends to the same object or event as the caregiver, who often labels it, contributes importantly to early language development. Infants and toddlers who frequently experience it sustain attention to named objects longer, comprehend more language, produce meaningful gestures and words earlier, and show faster vocabulary development through 2 years of age (Brooks & Meltzoff, 2008; Flom & Pick, 2003; Yu, Suanda, & Smith, 2019). Gains in joint attention at the end of the first year enable babies to establish a "common ground" with the adult, through which they can figure out the meaning of the adult's verbal labels.

Around 2 to 3 months, interactions between caregivers and babies begin to include *give-and-take.* Infants and mothers mutually imitate the pitch, loudness, and duration of each other's sounds, with mothers taking the lead, imitating about twice as often as infants (Gratier & Devouche, 2011). Between 4 and 6 months, imitation extends to social games, as in pat-a-cake and peekaboo. At first, the parent starts the game and the baby is an amused observer. Gradually, infants join in. By 12 months, infants participate actively, trading roles with the caregiver. Through these imitative exchanges, babies practice the turn-taking pattern of human conversation, a vital context for acquiring language.

At the end of the first year, infants use *preverbal gestures* to direct adults' attention, influence their behavior, and convey helpful information (Tomasello, Carpenter, & Liszkowski, 2007). For example, Caitlin held up a toy to show it, pointed to the cupboard when she wanted a cookie, and pointed at her mother's car keys lying on the floor. Carolyn responded to these gestures and also labeled them ("That's your bear!" "You want a cookie!" "Oh, there are my keys!"). In this way, toddlers learn that using language leads to desired results.

Besides using preverbal gestures to serve their own goals, 12-month-olds adapt these gestures to the needs of others. In one study, they pointed more often to an object whose location a searching adult did not know than to an object whose location the adult did know (Liszkowski, Carpenter, & Tomasello, 2008). They also understand what an adult means when she points to the location of a hidden toy (Behne et al., 2012). Already, the cooperative processes essential for effective communication are under way—namely, modifying messages to suit others' intentions and knowledge and recognizing when others have done the same.

This baby uses a preverbal gesture to direct his father's attention. The father's verbal response ("I see that squirrel!") promotes the baby's transition to spoken language.

The more time caregivers and infants spend in joint activity with objects, the earlier and more often babies use preverbal gestures (Salomo & Liszkowski, 2013). Over time, some of these gestures become explicitly symbolic. For example, a toddler might flap her arms to indicate "butterfly" or raise her palms to signal "all gone." Soon toddlers integrate words with gestures, using the gesture to expand their verbal message, as in pointing to a toy while saying "give" (Capirci et al., 2005). Gradually, gestures recede, and words become dominant. But the greater the number of items toddlers gesture about and the earlier they form word–gesture combinations, the faster their vocabulary growth, the sooner toward the end of the second year they begin to produce two-word utterances, and the more complex their sentences are at age 3½ (Rowe & Goldin-Meadow, 2009).

6.5.3 First Words

In the middle of the first year, infants begin to understand word meanings; for example, they respond to their own name and, on hearing the words "Mommy" or "Daddy," look longer at the named parent (Luche et al., 2017; Tincoff & Jusczyk, 1999). At 9 months, after hearing a word paired with an object, infants looked longer at other objects in the same category than at those in a different category. They also expect different speakers of their native language to use object labels consistently, indicating that they grasp the shared nature of word meanings (Balaban & Waxman, 1997; Henderson & Woodward, 2012). Furthermore, by the end of the first year, babies know that the purpose of speech, even if unfamiliar, is to communicate (Martin, Onisha, & Vouloumanos, 2012). These understandings undoubtedly contribute to their motivation to use words in conventional ways.

First recognizable spoken words, around 1 year, build on the sensorimotor foundations Piaget described and on categories infants have formed. In a study tracking the first 10 words used by several hundred U.S. and Chinese (both Mandarin- and Cantonese-speaking) babies, important people ("Mama," "Dada"), common objects ("ball," "bread"), and sound effects ("woof-woof," "vroom") were uttered most often. Action words ("hit," "grab," "hug") and social routines ("hi," "bye"), though also appearing in all three groups, were more often produced by Chinese than U.S. babies, and the Chinese babies also named more important people—differences we will consider shortly (Tardif et al., 2008). Other investigations concur that earliest words usually include people, objects that move, foods, animals (in families with pets), familiar actions, outcomes of such actions ("hot," "wet"), and social terms (Hart, 2004; Nelson, 1973). In their first 50 words, toddlers rarely name things that just *sit there,* like "table" or "vase."

When toddlers first learn words, they sometimes apply them too narrowly, an error called **underextension.** At 16 months, Caitlin used "bear" only to refer to the worn and tattered teddy bear she carried nearly constantly. As vocabulary expands, a more common error is **overextension**—applying a word to a wider collection of objects and events than is appropriate. For example, Grace used "car" for buses, trains, trucks, and fire engines. Toddlers' overextensions reflect their sensitivity to categories (MacWhinney, 2005). They apply a new word to a group of similar experiences: "car" to wheeled objects, "open" to opening a door, peeling fruit, and untying shoelaces. This suggests that children often overextend deliberately because they have difficulty recalling or have not acquired a suitable word. As vocabulary expands and pronunciation improves, overextensions gradually decline.

Overextensions illustrate another important feature of language development: the distinction between language *production* (the words and word combinations children use) and language *comprehension* (the language they understand). At all ages comprehension develops ahead of production. Think back to the distinction made earlier in this chapter between two types of memory: recognition and recall. Comprehension requires only that children recognize the meaning of a word. But for production, children must recall, or actively retrieve from their memories both the word and the concept for which it stands.

Still the two capacities are related. The speed and accuracy of toddlers' comprehension of spoken language increase dramatically over the second year. And toddlers who are faster and more accurate in comprehension show more rapid growth in words understood and produced over the following year (Fernald & Marchman, 2012). Quick comprehension frees space in working memory for picking up new words and using them to communicate.

LOOK and LISTEN

Observe a toddler for 30 to 60 minutes at home or in child care. Jot down preverbal gestures, words, and word–gesture combinations that the baby produces. Do the toddler's language skills fit with research findings?

6.5.4 The Two-Word Utterance Phase

Young toddlers add to their spoken vocabularies at a rate of one to three words per week. Because gains in word production between 18 and 24 months are so impressive (one or two words per day), many researchers concluded that toddlers undergo a *spurt in vocabulary*—a transition from a slower to a faster learning phase. In actuality, most children show a steady increase in rate of producing new words that continues through the preschool years (Ganger & Brent, 2004). As a result, vocabulary growth seems to explode in the latter half of the second year.

How do toddlers build their vocabularies so quickly? In the second year, they improve in ability to categorize experience, recall words, and grasp others' social cues to meaning, such as eye gaze, pointing, and handling objects (Golinkoff & Hirsh-Pasek, 2006; Liszkowski, Carpenter, & Tomasello, 2007). Furthermore, as toddlers' experiences broaden, they have a wider range of interesting objects and events to label. For example, children approaching age 2 more often mention places to go ("park," "store"). And as they construct a clearer self-image, they add more words that refer to themselves ("me," "mine," "Katy") and to their own and others' bodies and clothing ("eyes," "mouth," "jacket") (Hart, 2004). In Chapter 9, we will consider the diverse strategies young children use to figure out word meanings.

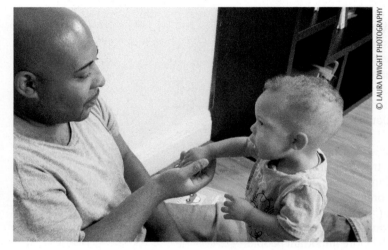

This 13-month-old has just begun to utter his first words ("car"). As his experiences broaden, he will label more objects and events with single words and then, between 18 ad 24 months, combine two words ("Go car" "Daddy car") in telegraphic speech.

Once toddlers produce 200 to 250 words, they start to combine two words: "Mommy shoe," "go car," "more cookie." These two-word utterances are called **telegraphic speech** because, like a telegram, they focus on high-content words, omitting smaller, less important ones ("can," "the," "to"). Children the world over use them to express an impressive variety of meanings.

Two-word speech consists largely of simple formulas ("more + *X*," "eat + *X*"), with different words inserted in the "*X*" position. Toddlers rarely make gross grammatical errors, such as saying "chair my" instead of "my chair." But their word-order regularities are usually copies of adult word pairings, as when Carolyn remarked to Caitlin, "How about *more sandwich?*" or "Let's see if you can *eat the berries.*" (Tomasello, 2003; Tomasello & Brandt, 2009). When 18- to 23-month-olds were taught noun and verb nonsense words (for example, "meek" for a doll and "gop" for a snapping action), they easily combined the new nouns with words they knew well ("more meek"). But they seldom formed word combinations with the new verbs (Tomasello, 2000; Tomasello et al., 1997). This suggests that they cannot yet flexibly form novel sentences that express subject–verb and verb–object relations, which are the foundation of grammar.

In sum, toddlers are absorbed in figuring out word meanings and using their limited vocabularies in whatever way possible to get their thoughts across. At first, they rely on "concrete pieces of language" they often hear, gradually generalizing from those pieces to word-order and other grammatical rules (Bannard, Lieven, & Tomasello, 2009; MacWhinney, 2015). As we will see in Chapter 9, they make steady progress over the preschool years.

6.5.5 Individual and Cultural Differences

Although children typically produce their first word around their first birthday, the range is large, from 8 to 18 months—variation due to a complex blend of genetic and environmental influences. Earlier we saw that Timmy's spoken language was delayed, in part because of Vanessa's tense, directive communication with him. But Timmy is also a boy, and research indicates that girls are slightly ahead of boys in early vocabulary growth (Frota et al., 2016; Van Hulle, Goldsmith, & Lemery, 2004). The most common explanation is girls' faster rate of physical maturation, which is believed to promote earlier development of the left cerebral hemisphere.

Temperament matters, too. Highly sociable toddlers tend to be advanced in language progress (Pérez-Pereira et al., 2016). Shy toddlers often wait until they understand a great deal before trying to speak. Once they do speak, their vocabularies increase rapidly, although they remain slightly behind their agemates (Spere et al., 2004). Emotionally negative toddlers also acquire language more slowly because their high reactivity diverts them from processing linguistic information (Salley & Dixon, 2007).

Caregiver–child conversation—especially, the richness of adults' vocabularies—also plays a strong role (Huttenlocher et al. 2010; Rowe, 2012). Commonly used words for objects appear early in toddlers' speech, and the more often their caregivers use a particular noun, the sooner young children produce it (Goodman, Dale, & Li, 2008). Parents talk more to toddler-age girls than to boys, and they converse less often with shy than with sociable children (Leaper, Anderson, & Sanders, 1998; Mascaro et al., 2017; Patterson & Fisher, 2002).

Compared to their higher-SES agemates, children from low-SES homes usually have smaller vocabularies. By 18 to 24 months, they are slower at word comprehension and produce 30 percent fewer words (Fernald, Marchman & Weisleder, 2013). Limited parent–child conversation and book reading are major factors. Higher-SES parents typically interact more with their children, using a richer vocabulary, than do low-SES parents (Golinkoff et al., 2019; Hoff, 2006; Ramírez-Esparza, García-Sierra, & Kuhl, 2014). And on average, a middle-SES child is read to for 1,000 hours between 1 and 5 years, a low-SES child for only 25 hours (Neuman, 2003). Rate of early vocabulary growth is a strong predictor of low-SES children's vocabulary size at kindergarten entry, which forecasts their later literacy skills and academic success (Rowe, Raudenbush, & Goldin-Meadow, 2012). Higher-SES toddlers who lag behind their agemates in word learning have more opportunities to catch up in early childhood.

Young children have distinct styles of early language learning. The vocabularies of Caitlin and Grace, like most toddlers, consisted mainly of words that refer to objects. A smaller number of toddlers produce many more social formulas and pronouns ("thank you," "done," "I want it") (Bates et al., 1994). The vocabularies of object-naming toddlers grow faster because all languages contain many more object labels than social phrases.

Chinese toddlers use more words for actions and social routines than their English-speaking agemates. In Cantonese and Mandarin, verbs are emphasized. And perhaps because of cultural values, Chinese parents frequently use social formulas ("Thank you," "It's no trouble"), which their children acquire early.

What accounts for a toddler's language style? Rapidly developing children with a vocabulary of many object words often have an especially active interest in exploring their surroundings. They also eagerly imitate their parents' frequent naming of objects, and their parents imitate back, which helps children remember new labels (Masur & Rodemaker, 1999). Toddlers who emphasize pronouns and social formulas tend to have parents who frequently use verbal routines that support social relationships ("How are you?" "It's no trouble").

The two language styles are also linked to culture. Object words (nouns) are particularly common in the vocabularies of English-speaking toddlers, whereas Chinese, Japanese, and Korean toddlers use more words for actions (verbs) and social routines. Mothers' speech in each culture reflects this difference (Chan, Brandone, & Tardif, 2009; Choi & Gopnik, 1995; Fernald & Morikawa, 1993; Hao et al., 2015). American mothers frequently label objects when interacting with their babies. Asian mothers, perhaps because of a cultural emphasis on the importance of group membership, more often use words for actions and social routines. Also, in Cantonese, Mandarin, and Korean, nouns are often dropped from sentences when context leads them to be understood, leaving verbs to be produced more frequently (Gogate & Hollich, 2016). Consequently, action words are especially salient to toddlers acquiring these languages.

At what point should parents become concerned if their child talks very little or not at all? If a toddler's language is greatly delayed when compared with the norms in Table 6.3 (page 231), then parents should consult the child's doctor or a speech and language therapist. Late babbling, gesturing, and spoken words may be signs of slow language development that can be prevented with early intervention (Hsu & Iyer, 2016). Some toddlers who do not follow simple directions or who, after age 2, have difficulty putting their thoughts into words may suffer from a language disorder that requires immediate treatment.

APPLYING WHAT WE KNOW

Supporting Early Language Learning

STRATEGY	CONSEQUENCE
Respond to coos and babbles with speech sounds and words.	Encourages experimentation with sounds that can later be blended into first words Provides experience with the turn-taking pattern of human conversation
Establish joint attention and comment on what child sees.	Predicts earlier onset of preverbal gestures and words and faster vocabulary development
Play social games, such as pat-a-cake and peekaboo.	Provides experience with the turn-taking pattern of human conversation
Engage toddlers in joint make-believe play.	Promotes all aspects of conversational dialogue
Engage toddlers in frequent conversations.	Predicts faster early language development and academic success during the school years
Read to toddlers often, engaging them in dialogues about picture books.	Provides exposure to many aspects of language, including vocabulary, grammar, communication skills, and information about written symbols and story structures

6.5.6 Supporting Early Language Development

Consistent with the interactionist view, a rich social environment builds on young children's natural readiness to speak their native tongue. For a summary of how caregivers can consciously support early language learning, see Applying What We Know above. Caregivers also do so unconsciously—through a special style of speech.

Adults in many cultures speak to young children in **infant-directed speech (IDS),** a form of communication made up of short sentences with high-pitched, exaggerated expression, clear pronunciation, distinct pauses between speech segments, clear gestures to support verbal meaning, and repetition of new words in a variety of contexts ("See the *ball.*" "The *ball* bounced!") (Fernald et al., 1989; O'Neill et al., 2005). Deaf parents use a similar style of communication when signing to their deaf babies (Masataka, 1996). From birth on, infants prefer IDS over other kinds of adult talk, and by 5 months they are more emotionally responsive to it (Aslin, Jusczyk, & Pisoni, 1998). The features of IDS facilitate statistical learning of speech sounds and other speech units throughout the first year (Bosseler et al., 2016; Thiessen & Saffran, 2003).

IDS builds on several communicative strategies we have already considered: joint attention, turn-taking, and caregivers' sensitivity to babies' preverbal gestures. In this example, Carolyn uses IDS with 15-month-old Caitlin:

Caitlin:	"Car."
Carolyn:	"Go in the car. Where's your jacket?"
Caitlin:	*[Looks around; walks to the closet.]* "Dackit!" *[Points to her jacket.]*
Carolyn:	"There's that jacket! *[She helps Caitlin into the jacket.]* On it goes! Let's zip up. *[Zips up the jacket.]* Say bye-bye to Grace."
Caitlin:	"Bye-bye." *[Waves good-bye.]* "G-ace!"
Carolyn:	"Where's your bear?"
Caitlin:	*[Looks around.]*
Carolyn:	*[Pointing.]* "By the sofa." *[Caitlin gets the bear.]*

Notice how Carolyn kept her utterance length brief, just ahead of Caitlin's, creating a sensitive match between language stimulation and Caitlin's current capacities. Parents constantly fine-tune the length and content of their utterances in IDS to fit infants' and toddlers' needs—adjustments that promote vocabulary development in the second year, in monolingual and bilingual babies alike (Ma, Golinkoff, et al., 2011; Ramírez-Esparza, Kuhl, & García-Sierra, 2017; Rowe, 2008). (We will take up development of bilingualism in Chapter 12.)

As we saw earlier, caregiver–child conversation strongly predicts language development and later academic success. It provides many examples of speech adjusted to the child's current level and a sympathetic environment in which children can try out new skills. Dialogues about picture books are particularly effective. They expose children to great breadth of language and literacy knowledge, from vocabulary, grammar, and communication skills to information about written symbols and story structures. From the end of the first year through early childhood, children who experience regular adult–child book reading are substantially ahead of their agemates in language skills (Karrass & Braungart-Rieker, 2005; Whitehurst & Lonigan, 1998).

Research also suggests that one-on-one interaction with an adult is better suited to spurring early language development than speech directed to an infant or toddler in the presence of two or more adults (Ramírez-Esparza, Kuhl, & García-Sierra, 2017). The one-on-one context increases opportunities for sensitive, responsive interaction. Also, noisy background speech interferes with toddlers' ability to acquire new words, though by age 2½, children are better language users and sufficiently experienced with noisy environments to learn from conversation despite distracting talk nearby (Dombroski & Newman, 2014; McMillan & Saffran, 2016).

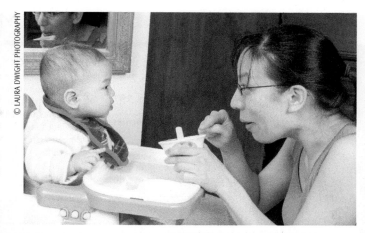

A mother speaks to her baby in short, clearly pronounced sentences with high-pitched, exaggerated intonation. This form of communication, called infant-directed speech, eases language learning for infants and toddlers.

Furthermore, live adult–toddler communication promotes language progress far more effectively than most media sources. After a month's regular exposure to a commercial video for babies that labeled common household objects, 12- to 18-month-olds did not add any more words to their vocabulary than nonviewing controls. Rather, toddlers in a comparison group whose parents spent time teaching them the words in everyday activities learned best (DeLoache et al., 2010). Consistent with these findings, recall that a video chat format such as FaceTime, which enables an adult to interact responsively with a toddler, is an effective context for acquiring new words (see page 206).

Similarly, toddlers are able to learn new words from a touchscreen tablet only if the program allows them to participate in contingent interaction. In one study, 2½-year-olds acquired names of objects in a tablet presentation when their screen-touching enabled them to control the emergence of each object from a box and hear its spoken name, not when their touching merely advanced the screen and they watched as each object popped out of its box and was named (Kirkorian, Choi, & Pempek, 2016). Viewers younger than age 3 acquire little language from TV or video alone—even from programs specially designed for them (Krcmar, Grela, & Lin, 2007; Roseberry et al., 2009). Note how these findings illustrate the *video deficit effect* discussed earlier in this chapter.

Do social experiences that promote early language development remind you of those that strengthen cognitive development in general? IDS and parent–child conversation create a *zone of proximal development* in which children's language expands. In contrast, adult behaviors that are unresponsive to children's needs or impatient with their efforts to talk result in immature language skills (Cabrera, Shannon, & Tamis-LeMonda, 2007). In the next chapter, we will see that adult sensitivity supports infants' and toddlers' emotional and social development as well.

 ## ASK YOURSELF

Connect ■ Cognition and language are interrelated. List examples of how cognition fosters language development. Next, list examples of how language fosters cognitive development.

Apply ■ Fran frequently corrects her 17-month-old son Jeremy's attempts to talk and—fearing that he won't use words—refuses to respond to his gestures. How might Fran be contributing to Jeremy's slow language progress?

Reflect ■ Find an opportunity to interact with an infant or toddler. Did you use IDS? What features of your speech are likely to promote early language development, and why?

SUMMARY

6.1 Piaget's Cognitive-Developmental Theory (p. 197)

6.1a *Explain how, in Piaget's theory, schemes change over the course of development.*

- By acting on the environment, children move through four stages in which psychological structures, or **schemes,** achieve a better fit with external reality.

- Schemes change in two ways: through **adaptation,** which consists of two complementary activities—**assimilation** and **accommodation;** and through **organization,** the internal rearrangement of schemes into a strongly interconnected cognitive system.

6.1b *Describe major cognitive attainments of the sensorimotor stage.*

- In the **sensorimotor stage,** the **circular reaction** provides a means of adapting first schemes, and the newborn's reflexes gradually transform into the more flexible action patterns of the older infant. Around 8 months, infants develop **intentional,** or **goal-directed, behavior** and begin to understand **object permanence.**

- Twelve- to 18-month-olds engage in more deliberate, varied exploration and no longer make the **A-not-B search error.** Between 18 and 24 months, **mental representation** is evident in sudden solutions to sensorimotor problems, mastery of object-permanence problems involving invisible displacement, **deferred imitation,** and **make-believe play.**

6.1c *Explain the implications of follow-up research on infant cognitive development for the accuracy of Piaget's sensorimotor stage.*

- Many studies suggest that infants display a variety of understandings earlier than Piaget believed. Some awareness of object permanence, as revealed by the **violation-of-expectation method** and object-tracking research, may be evident in the first few months.

- Furthermore, young infants display deferred imitation, an attainment that requires mental representation. Older infants and toddlers even imitate rationally, by inferring others' intentions. Around the middle of the second year, toddlers begin forming mental representations of how to use an unfamiliar tool to secure a desired object.

- The capacity for **displaced reference**—use of words to cue mental images of things not physically present—is a major advance in symbolic understanding that emerges around the first birthday. The use of language to modify mental representations improves from the end of the second into the preschool years. Awareness of the symbolic function of pictures emerges in the first year and strengthens in the second. Around 2½ years, the **video deficit effect** declines, and children grasp the symbolic meaning of video.

- Today, researchers believe that newborns have more built-in equipment for making sense of their world than Piaget assumed, although they disagree on how much initial understanding infants have. According to the **core knowledge perspective,** infants are born with core domains of thought—including physical, psychological, linguistic, and numerical knowledge—that support rapid cognitive development.

- Broad agreement exists that many cognitive changes of infancy are continuous rather than stagelike and that various aspects of cognition develop unevenly, rather than in an integrated fashion.

6.2 Information Processing (p. 210)

6.2a *Describe the information-processing view of cognitive development and the general structure of the information-processing system.*

- Information-processing researchers generally assume that we hold and process information in three parts of the cognitive system: the **sensory store;** the **short-term memory store;** and the **long-term memory store.** The **central executive** joins with **working memory**—our "mental workspace"—to process information effectively. Well-learned **automatic processes** require no space in working memory.

- Gains in **executive function**—including inhibition of impulses and irrelevant actions, flexible thinking, coordination of information in working memory, and planning—predict important cognitive and social outcomes.

6.2b *Describe changes in attention, memory, and categorization over the first two years.*

- With age, infants gain attentional control and take information in more quickly. In the second year, attraction to novelty declines and sustained attention improves.

- Short-term memory increases from 6 months on, and working memory emerges at the end of the first year. Operant conditioning and habituation research show that long-term retention of visual events increases greatly with age.

- By the middle of the first year, infants can engage in **recall** as well as **recognition** memory.

- A combination of factors—neurological changes, increasing reliance on verbal means for storing information, and firmer self-awareness—may account for the decline of **infantile amnesia** and the emergence of **autobiographical memory.**

- Infants group stimuli into an expanding array of categories. In the second year, toddlers begin to categorize flexibly, switching their basis of object sorting, and their grasp of the animate–inanimate distinction expands. Babies' exploration of objects, expanding knowledge of the world, and advancing language skills foster categorization.

6.2c *Explain the strengths and limitations of the information-processing approach to early cognitive development.*

- Information-processing findings challenge Piaget's view of infants as purely sensorimotor beings who cannot mentally represent experiences. But information processing has not yet provided a broad, comprehensive theory of children's thinking.

6.3 The Social Context of Early Cognitive Development (p. 218)

6.3 *Explain how Vygotsky's concept of the zone of proximal development expands our understanding of early cognitive development.*

- Vygotsky believed that children master tasks within the **zone of proximal development**—ones just ahead of their current capacities—through the support and guidance of more skilled partners. As early as the first year, cultural variations in social experiences affect mental strategies.

6.4 Individual Differences in Early Mental Development (p. 219)

6.4a Describe the mental testing approach, the meaning of intelligence test scores, and the extent to which infant tests predict later performance.

■ The mental testing approach measures intellectual development in an effort to predict future performance. Scores are arrived at by computing an **intelligence quotient (IQ),** which compares an individual's performance with that of a **standardization** sample of same-age individuals, whose performances form a **normal distribution.**

■ Infant tests consisting largely of perceptual and motor responses predict later intelligence poorly. As a result, scores on infant tests are called **developmental quotients (DQs),** rather than IQs. Speed of habituation and recovery to novel visual stimuli is among the best available predictors of future IQ.

6.4b Discuss environmental influences on early mental development, including home, child care, and early intervention for at-risk infants and toddlers.

■ Research with the **Home Observation for Measurement of the Environment (HOME)** shows that an organized, stimulating home environment and parental affection, involvement, and encouragement repeatedly predict better language and IQ scores. Although the HOME–IQ relationship is partly due to heredity, family living conditions also affect mental test scores.

■ Quality of infant and toddler child care influences cognitive, language, academic, and social skills. Standards for **developmentally appropriate practice** specify program characteristics that meet young children's developmental needs.

■ Intensive intervention beginning in infancy and extending through early childhood can help prevent the gradual declines in intelligence and the poor academic performance evident in many poverty-stricken children.

6.5 Language Development (p. 227)

6.5a Describe theories of language development, and indicate the emphasis each places on innate abilities and environmental influences.

■ According to Chomsky's nativist theory, language is a uniquely human capacity made possible by a **language acquisition device (LAD),** an innate system containing a universal grammar underlying all languages.

■ Evidence for specialized language areas in the brain and for a sensitive period of language development support Chomsky's theory. Challenges include the inability to specify the rules of universal grammar and evidence that children's language development involves more experimentation and learning than Chomsky assumed.

■ Interactionist theories suggest that language development results from interactions between inner capacities and environmental influences. Some interactionists apply the information-processing perspective to language development. Others emphasize the importance of children's social skills and language experiences.

6.5b Describe major language milestones in the first two years, individual and cultural differences, and ways adults can support early language development.

■ Infants begin **cooing** at 2 months and **babbling** around 6 months. Around 10 to 11 months, their skill at establishing **joint attention** improves, and at the end of the first year they use preverbal gestures.

■ Around 12 months, toddlers say their first word. As they learn new words, they make errors of **underextension** and **overextension.** At all ages, comprehension develops ahead of production. Vocabulary typically increases at a steady rate, and once it reaches about 200 to 250 words, toddlers begin producing two-word utterances called **telegraphic speech.**

■ Girls acquire early vocabulary faster than boys, and both shy and emotionally negative toddlers acquire language more slowly than others. Low-SES children, who receive less verbal stimulation than higher-SES children, have smaller vocabularies—a strong predictor of later weak literacy skills and academic performance.

■ The vocabularies of most toddlers consist mainly of words that refer to objects. A smaller number produce more social phrases, and their vocabularies grow more slowly. These differences are linked to toddlers' individual attributes and to culture.

■ Adults in many cultures speak to babies in **infant-directed speech (IDS),** a simplified form of communication that is well-suited to their learning needs. Live interaction with a responsive adult is better suited to early spurring language progress than are media sources, which are effective only if they permit contingent interaction.

IMPORTANT TERMS AND CONCEPTS

accommodation (p. 198)
adaptation (p. 198)
A-not-B search error (p. 200)
assimilation (p. 198)
autobiographical memory (p. 216)
automatic processes (p. 212)
babbling (p. 231)
central executive (p. 212)
circular reaction (p. 199)
cooing (p. 231)
core knowledge perspective (p. 207)
deferred imitation (p. 201)
developmentally appropriate practice (p. 224)
developmental quotient (DQ) (p. 222)
displaced reference (p. 205)

executive function (p. 212)
Home Observation for Measurement of the Environment (HOME) (p. 222)
infant-directed speech (IDS) (p. 236)
infantile amnesia (p. 216)
intelligence quotient (IQ) (p. 221)
intentional, or goal-directed, behavior (p. 200)
joint attention (p. 232)
language acquisition device (LAD) (p. 227)
long-term memory store (p. 212)
make-believe play (p. 201)
mental representation (p. 201)
normal distribution (p. 221)
object permanence (p. 200)
organization (p. 198)

overextension (p. 233)
recall (p. 214)
recognition (p. 214)
scheme (p. 198)
sensorimotor stage (p. 197)
sensory store (p. 211)
short-term memory store (p. 211)
standardization (p. 221)
telegraphic speech (p. 234)
underextension (p. 233)
video deficit effect (p. 206)
violation-of-expectation method (p. 201)
working memory (p. 211)
zone of proximal development (p. 218)

Emotional and Social Development in Infancy and Toddlerhood

Motherhood
Camona Angelico, 13 years, Mexico

A mutual embrace reflects the strong, affectionate bond between this mother and child. Chapter 7 considers the importance of parental love and sensitivity for infants' and toddlers' feelings of security and competence.

Reprinted with permission from The International Museum of Children's Art, Oslo, Norway

When Caitlin reached 8 months of age, her parents, Carolyn and David, noticed that she had become more fearful. One evening, as they were about to leave her with a babysitter, she wailed as they headed for the door—an experience she had accepted easily a few weeks earlier. Caitlin's caregiver Ginette had also noticed an increasing wariness of strangers in Caitlin and also in Timmy, Vanessa's 10-month-old son. At the mail carrier's knock at the door, they clung to Ginette's legs, reaching out to be picked up.

At the same time, each baby seemed more willful. When 10-month-old Timmy managed to reach a table knife that Vanessa quickly took from him, he burst into angry screams and could not be easily consoled or distracted.

All Monica and Kevin knew about Grace's first year in Cambodia was that she had been deeply loved by her destitute, homeless mother, who had tearfully given her up for adoption. Separation from her, followed by the long journey to her new U.S. home, had left Grace in shock. At first she was extremely sad, turning away when Monica or Kevin picked her up. But as Grace's adoptive parents held her close, spoke gently, and satisfied her craving for food, Grace returned their affection. Two weeks after her arrival, her despondency gave way to a sunny, easygoing disposition. She burst into a wide grin at the sight of Monica and Kevin and laughed at her older brother Eli's funny faces. Among her first English words were the names of family members—"Eli," "Mama," and "Dada." As her second birthday approached, she pointed to herself, exclaiming "Gwace!" and laid claim to treasured possessions: "Gwace's teddy bear!"

Taken together, the children's reactions reflect two related aspects of personality that develop during the first two years: close ties to others and a sense of self. In this chapter, we begin by tracing the course of early emotional development. As we do so, we will discover why fear and anger became more apparent in Caitlin's and Timmy's range of emotions by the end of the first year. Our attention then turns to the foundation of personality: temperament. We will examine genetic and environmental contributions to individual differences in temperament and the consequences of those differences for future development.

Next, we take up attachment to the caregiver, the child's first affectionate tie. We will see how the feelings of security that grow out of this important bond support the child's exploration, sense of independence, and expanding social relationships.

Finally, we focus on early self-development. By the end of toddlerhood, Grace recognized herself in mirrors and photographs, labeled herself with her own name, and showed the beginnings of self-control. "Don't touch!" she instructed herself one day as she resisted the desire to pull a lamp cord out of its socket. Cognitive advances combine with social experiences to produce these changes during the second year. ■

What's Ahead in Chapter 7

7.1 Emotional Development

Observe several infants and toddlers, noting the emotions each displays, the cues you rely on to interpret the baby's emotional state, and how caregivers respond. Researchers have conducted many such observations to find out how babies convey their emotions and interpret those of others. They have discovered that emotions play powerful roles in organizing key developmental attainments of the first two years: formation of first social relationships, exploration of the environment, and discovery of the self (Saarni et al., 2006).

Think back to the *dynamic systems perspective* introduced in Chapters 1 and 5. As you read about early emotional development in the sections that follow, notice how emotions are an integral part of young children's dynamic systems of action.

Compare the uncertain expression of a startled 3-month-old (left) to the unmistakable expression of surprise of a startled 5-month-old (right). Only gradually do infants' expressions of emotion become clear, well-organized signals.

7.1a Describe the development of basic emotions over the first year, noting the adaptive function of each.

7.1b Summarize changes during the first two years in understanding of others' emotions, expression of self-conscious emotions, and emotional self-regulation.

Emotions energize development. At the same time, they are an aspect of the system that develops, becoming more varied and complex as children reorganize their behavior to attain new goals (Campos, Frankel, & Camras, 2004; Camras, 2011).

Because infants cannot describe their feelings, determining exactly which emotions they are experiencing is a challenge. Although vocalizations and body movements provide some information, facial expressions offer the most reliable cues. Cross-cultural evidence reveals that people around the world associate photographs of different facial expressions with emotions in the same way (Ekman & Friesen, 1972; Ekman & Matsumoto, 2011). These findings inspired researchers to analyze infants' facial patterns to determine the range of emotions they display at different ages.

Nevertheless, assuming a close correspondence between a pattern of behavior and an underlying emotional state can lead to error. Infants, children, and adults use diverse responses to express a particular emotion. For example, babies placed on the visual cliff (see page 187 in Chapter 5) generally do not display a fearful facial expression, though they do show signs of avoidance—drawing back and refusing to crawl over the deep side. And the emotional expressions of blind babies, who cannot make eye contact, are muted, prompting parents to withdraw. When therapists show parents how blind infants express emotions through finger movements, parents become more interactive (Fraiberg, 1971; Saarni et al., 2006). Furthermore, the same general response can express several emotions. Depending on the situation, a smile might convey joy, embarrassment, contempt, or a social greeting.

In line with the dynamic systems view, emotional expressions vary with the individual's developing capacities, goals, and contexts. To infer babies' emotions as accurately as possible, researchers must attend to multiple interacting expressive cues—vocal, facial, and gestural—and see how they vary across situations believed to elicit different emotions (Camras & Shuster, 2013). With these ideas in mind, let's chart the course of early emotional development.

7.1.1 Basic Emotions

Basic emotions—happiness, interest, surprise, fear, anger, sadness, and disgust—are universal in humans and other primates and have a long evolutionary history of promoting survival. Do infants come into the world with the ability to express basic emotions? Although signs of some emotions are present, babies' earliest emotional life consists of little more than two global arousal states: attraction to pleasant stimulation and withdrawal from unpleasant stimulation (Camras et al., 2003). Only gradually do emotions become clear, well-organized signals.

The dynamic systems perspective helps us understand how this happens: Children coordinate separate skills into more effective, emotionally expressive systems as the central nervous system develops and the child's goals and experiences change (Camras & Shuster, 2013;

Camras & Shutter, 2010). Videotaping the facial expressions of her daughter from 6 to 14 weeks, Linda Camras (1992) found that in the early weeks, the baby displayed a fleeting angry face as she was about to cry and a sad face as her crying waned. At first, these expressions appeared on the way to or from full-blown distress and were not clearly linked to the baby's experiences and desires. With age, she was better able to sustain an angry signal when she encountered a blocked goal and a sad signal when she could not overcome an obstacle.

According to one view, sensitive, contingent caregiver communication, in which parents selectively mirror aspects of the baby's diffuse emotional behavior, helps infants construct emotional expressions that more closely resemble those of adults (Gergely & Watson, 1999). With age, the face, gaze, voice, and posture combine into organized patterns that vary meaningfully with environmental events. For example, 8-month-old Caitlin typically responded to her parents' playful interaction with a joyful face, pleasant babbling, and a relaxed posture, as if to say, "This is fun!" In contrast, an unresponsive parent often evokes a sad face, fussy sounds, and a drooping body (sending the message, "I'm despondent") or an angry face, crying, and "pick-me-up" gestures (as if to say, "Change this unpleasant event!") (Mesman, van IJzendoorn, & Bakermans-Kranenburg, 2009; Vieites & Reeb-Sutherland, 2017). Gradually, emotional expressions become well-organized and specific—and therefore provide more precise information about the infant's internal state.

Four basic emotions—happiness, anger, sadness, and fear—have received the most research attention. Let's see how they develop.

Happiness Happiness—expressed first in blissful smiles, later through exuberant laughter—contributes to many aspects of development. When infants achieve new skills, they smile and laugh, displaying delight in motor and cognitive mastery. The baby's smile encourages caregivers to smile responsively and to be affectionate and stimulating, and then the baby smiles even more (Bigelow & Power, 2014). Happiness binds parent and baby into a warm, supportive relationship that fosters the infant's motor, cognitive, and social competencies.

During the early weeks, newborn babies smile when full, during REM sleep, and in response to gentle touches and sounds, such as stroking of the skin, rocking, and a parent's soft, high-pitched voice. By the end of the first month, infants smile at dynamic, eye-catching sights, such as a bright object jumping suddenly across their field of vision. As infants and parents engage in face-to-face mutual gazing while the parent talks and smiles, babies knit their brows, open their mouths, and move their arms and legs excitedly, gradually becoming more emotionally positive until, between 6 and 10 weeks, the parent's communication evokes a broad grin called the **social smile** (Lavelli & Fogel, 2005; Super & Harkness, 2010). These changes parallel the development of infant perceptual capacities—in particular, sensitivity to visual patterns, including the human face (see Chapter 5). And social smiling becomes better-organized and stable as babies learn to use it to evoke and sustain pleasurable face-to-face interaction with the parent.

Development of the social smile, however, varies substantially with culture. The Nso people, a rural farming society of Cameroon, highly value infant calmness, so Nso caregivers discourage emotional expressiveness of all kinds and, instead, emphasize soothing behaviors, such as holding, stroking, and patting (Keller & Otto, 2009). In contrast, Western middle-SES parents, who value self-expression, enthusiastically promote active social engagement in their babies. In line with these differences, observations of Nso and urban German mother–infant pairs between 6 and 12 weeks revealed that the Nso mothers participated in far fewer face-to-face imitative exchanges, including smiling. As a result, frequency of Nso infant smiling lagged behind that of German infants with age (see Figure 7.1) (Wörmann et al., 2012, 2014). The smiling of Nso babies was also muted—vastly shorter in duration.

Laughter, which typically appears around 3 to 4 months, reflects faster processing of information than smiling. But as with smiling, first laughs occur in response to very active stimuli, such as the parent

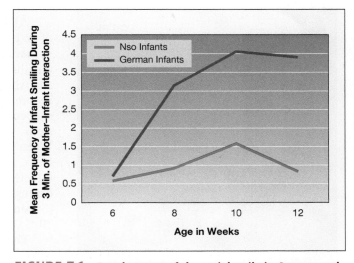

FIGURE 7.1   Development of the social smile in German and Nso infants. At 6 weeks, frequency of social smiling among Nso and German infants was similar. Among Nso infants, who experienced far fewer face-to-face imitative exchanges with their mothers, social smiling lagged behind that of German infants, whose smiling rose sharply with age. (Based on Wörmann et al., 2014.)

saying playfully, "I'm gonna get you!" and kissing the baby's tummy. As infants understand more about their world, they laugh at events with subtler elements of surprise, such as a silent game of peekaboo. Soon they pick up on parents' facial and vocal cues to humor, laughing in the presence of those cues at absurd events, such as an adult wearing a ball as a clown's nose. From 5 months on, infants laugh at absurd events in the absence of parental cues (Mireault et al., 2015, 2017). This suggests that they can independently appraise such events as funny on the basis of their cognitive features.

Babies just a few months old smile and laugh more often when interacting with familiar people, a preference that strengthens the parent–child bond. Between 8 and 10 months, infants interrupt their play with an interesting toy to relay their delight to an attentive adult (Venezia et al., 2004). And like adults, 10- to 12-month-olds have several smiles, which vary with context—a broad, "cheek-raised" smile in response to a parent's greeting; a reserved, muted smile for a friendly stranger; and a "mouth-open" smile during stimulating play (Messinger & Fogel, 2007). By the end of the first year, the smile has become a deliberate social signal.

Anger and Sadness   Newborn babies respond with generalized distress to a variety of unpleasant experiences, including hunger, painful medical procedures, changes in body temperature, and too much or too little stimulation (see Chapter 4). From 4 to 6 months into the second year, angry expressions increase in frequency and intensity (Braungart-Rieker, Hill-Soderlund, & Karrass, 2010). Older infants also react with anger in a wider range of situations—when an interesting object or event is removed, their play is interrupted, their arms are restrained, the caregiver leaves for a brief time, or they are put down for a nap (Camras et al., 1992; Sullivan & Lewis, 2003).

Why do angry reactions increase with age? As infants become capable of intentional behavior (see Chapter 6), they want to control their own actions and the effects they produce (Mascolo & Fischer, 2007). Furthermore, older infants are better at identifying who blocked their goals or caused them pain. Their anger is particularly intense when a caregiver from whom they have come to expect warm behavior causes discomfort. And increased parental limit-setting once babies crawl and walk contributes to babies' angry responses (Roben et al., 2012).

The rise in anger is also adaptive. Infants who at 5 months reacted with greater anger to interruption of their play are more persistent during play with toys at age 2 years (Lewis, Sullivan, & Kim, 2015). Anger seems to motivate them to overcome obstacles. Finally, anger spurs caregivers to relieve infant distress and, in the case of separation, may discourage them from leaving again soon.

Although expressions of sadness also occur in response to pain, removal of an object, and brief separations, they are less frequent than anger. However, sadness occurs often when infants are deprived of a familiar, loving caregiver (as illustrated by Grace's despondency after separation from her birth mother) and when parent–infant interaction is seriously disrupted. In a widely used procedure, researchers had parents interact with their 2- to 7-month-olds and then, suddenly, assume a still-faced, unreactive pose. The infants tried facial expressions, vocalizations, and body movements to get the parent to respond again. When these efforts failed, they turned away, frowned, and cried (Adamson & Frick, 2003; Provenzi et al, 2015). After parents resumed typical interaction, infants showed a brief carryover effect: partial recovery of positive emotional expressions mixed with negative affect and reduced interaction with the parent (Mesman, van Ijzendoorn, & Bakermans-Kranenburg, 2009; Montirosso et al., 2015).

The still-face reaction is identical among American, Canadian, and Chinese babies, suggesting that it is a built-in sad, withdrawn reaction to caregivers' lack of communication (Kisilevsky et al., 1998). Return to page 146 in Chapter 4, and note that infants of depressed parents respond this way. When allowed to persist, a sad, vacant outlook heightens infant stress reactivity, as indicated by elevated cortisol levels, and poses risks to all aspects of early development (Provenzi, Giusti, & Montirosso, 2016).

© LAURA DWIGHT PHOTOGRAPHY

A 12-month-old erupts in anger when frustrated during play. From 4 to 6 months into the second year, angry expressions increase in frequency and intensity.

Fear   Like anger, fear rises during the second half of the first year into the second year (Braungart-Rieker, Hill-Soderlund, & Karrass, 2010; Brooker et al., 2013). Older infants, for example, look wary, hesitating before playing with a new toy. But the most frequent expression of fear is to unfamiliar adults, a response called **stranger anxiety.** Many infants and toddlers react fearfully to strangers, although not always. Whether or not the reaction occurs depends on several factors: temperament (some babies are generally more fearful), past experiences with strangers, and the current situation. When an unfamiliar adult picks up the infant in a new situation, stranger anxiety is likely. If the adult sits still while the baby moves around and a parent is nearby, infants often show positive and curious behavior (Horner, 1980). The stranger's style of interaction—expressing warmth, holding out an attractive toy, playing a familiar game, and approaching slowly rather than abruptly—reduces the baby's fear.

Cross-cultural research reveals that infant-rearing practices can modify stranger anxiety. Among the Aka of the Central African Republic and the Nso of Cameroon, infants experience a collective caregiving system in which many adults are responsible for their safety and well-being. Aka and Nso babies' interaction with diverse caregivers—up to 20 each day—influences their response to unfamiliar people: They show little stranger anxiety (Meehan & Hawks, 2014b; Otto & Keller, 2015). In contrast, the Bedouins of southern Israel, who live in makeshift tents and shacks in impoverished villages without public services, frequently experience the destruction of their homes by Israeli soldiers. Bedouin mothers largely care for their own babies, keeping them physically close to protect them from danger, and by the end of the first year, most Bedouin infants display stranger anxiety (Marey-Sarwan, Keller, & Otto, 2016).

The overall rise in fear after age 6 months keeps newly mobile babies' enthusiasm for exploration in check. Once wariness develops, infants use the familiar caregiver as a **secure base,** or point from which to explore, venturing into the environment and then returning for emotional support. As part of this adaptive system, encounters with unfamiliar objects and people lead to two conflicting tendencies: approach (indicated by interest) and avoidance (indicated by fear). The infant's behavior is a blend of the two.

As cognitive development permits toddlers to discriminate more effectively between threatening and nonthreatening situations, stranger anxiety and other fears of the first two years decline. Fear also wanes as children acquire a wider array of strategies for coping with it, as we will see when we discuss emotional self-regulation.

Stranger anxiety appears in many infants after 6 months of age. This baby, though safe in her mother's arms, observes her doctor with cautious curiosity.

LOOK and LISTEN

While observing an 8- to 18-month-old with his or her parent, gently approach the baby, offering a toy. Does the baby respond with stranger anxiety? To better understand the baby's behavior, ask the parent to describe his or her temperament and past experiences with strangers.

7.1.2 Understanding and Responding to the Emotions of Others

Infants' emotional expressions are closely tied to their ability to interpret the emotional cues of others. We have seen that in the first few months, babies match the feeling tone of the caregiver in face-to-face communication. Around 2 to 3 months, infants become sensitive to the structure and timing of face-to-face interactions (see page 232 in Chapter 6). When they gaze, smile, or vocalize, they now expect their social partner to respond in kind, and they reply with positive vocal and emotional reactions (Bigelow & Power, 2014; Lavelli & Fogel, 2013). Within these exchanges, babies become increasingly aware of the range of emotional expressions (Montague & Walker-Andrews, 2001).

By 4 to 5 months, infants distinguish positive from negative emotion in voices and, soon after, in facial expressions, gradually discriminating a wider range of emotions (see Chapter 5). At about the same time, they match specific facial and vocal displays of emotion. Infants look longer at an appropriate face–voice pairing (such as a happy face with a happy voice) than at an inappropriate one (a happy face with an angry voice) (de Haan & Matheson, 2009; Vaillant-Molina, Bahrick, & Flom, 2013).

A 5-month-old reacts to his grandmother's cheerful voice and broad smile with similar emotion, and he expects her to respond again in kind. Within these face-to-face interactions, infants gradually detect a wider range of emotions.

LOOK and LISTEN

Observe a toddler and parent at a playground, park, or shopping mall, noting circumstances that trigger social referencing. How does the parent convey emotional information? How does the toddler respond?

In responding to emotional expressions as organized wholes, babies indicate that these signals are becoming meaningful to them. From 7 months on, event-related potentials (ERPs) recorded while infants attend to facial expressions reveal reorganized brain-wave patterns resembling those of adults, suggesting enhanced processing of emotional cues (Grossmann, Striano, & Friederici, 2007). By 8 months, infants use body expressions of emotion as aids to processing corresponding facial expressions (Rajhans et al., 2016). And as skill at establishing joint attention improves (see Chapter 6), infants realize that an emotional expression not only has meaning but is also a meaningful reaction to a specific object or event.

Once these understandings are in place, 8- to 10-month-olds start to engage in **social referencing**—actively seeking emotional information from a trusted person in an uncertain situation (Mumme et al., 2007). Many studies show that a caregiver's emotional expression (happy, angry, or fearful) influences whether a 1-year-old will be wary of strangers, play with an unfamiliar toy, or cross the deep side of the visual cliff (de Rosnay et al., 2006; Mireault et al., 2014; Stenberg, 2017; Striano & Rochat, 2000). The adult's voice—either alone or combined with a facial expression—is more effective than a facial expression alone (Kim, Walden, & Knieps, 2010; Vaish & Striano, 2004). The voice conveys both emotional and verbal information, so the baby can focus on evaluating a novel event without the need to turn toward the adult.

As toddlers start to appreciate that others' emotional reactions may differ from their own, social referencing allows them to compare their own and others' assessments of events. In one study, an adult showed 14- and 18-month-olds broccoli and crackers and acted delighted with one food but disgusted with the other (Repacholi & Gopnik, 1997). When asked to share the food, 18-month-olds gave the adult whichever food she appeared to like, regardless of their own preferences.

In sum, in social referencing, toddlers use others' emotional messages to evaluate the safety and security of their surroundings, to guide their own actions, and to gather information about others' intentions and preferences. These experiences, along with cognitive and language development, probably help toddlers refine the meanings of emotions of the same valence—for example, happiness versus surprise, anger versus fear—during the second year (Gendler, Witherington, & Edwards, 2008; Ruba et al., 2017).

7.1.3 Emergence of Self-Conscious Emotions

Besides basic emotions, humans are capable of a second, higher-order set of feelings, including guilt, shame, embarrassment, envy, and pride. These are called **self-conscious emotions** because each involves injury to or enhancement of our sense of self. We feel guilt when we know that we have harmed someone and want to correct the wrongdoing. Envy arises when we desire something that another possesses, so we try to restore our sense of self-worth by securing that possession. When we are ashamed or embarrassed, we have negative feelings about our behavior, and we want to retreat so others will no longer notice our failings. In contrast, pride reflects delight in the self's achievements, and we are inclined to tell others what we have accomplished and to take on further challenges (Lewis, 2014).

Self-conscious emotions appear in the middle of the second year, as 18- to 24-month-olds become firmly aware of the self as a separate, unique individual. Toddlers show shame and embarrassment by averting their eyes, hanging their heads, and hiding their faces with their hands. They show guiltlike reactions, too. After noticing Grace's unhappiness, 22-month-old Caitlin returned a toy she had grabbed and patted her upset playmate. Pride and envy also emerge around age 2 (Muris & Meesters, 2014; Lewis, 2014).

Besides self-awareness, self-conscious emotions require an additional ingredient: adult instruction in *when* to feel proud, ashamed, or guilty. Parents begin this tutoring early when they say, "Look how far you can throw that ball!" or "You should feel ashamed for grabbing that toy!" Self-conscious emotions play important roles in children's achievement-related and moral behaviors. The situations in which adults encourage these feelings vary from culture to culture. In Western nations, most children are taught to feel pride over personal achievement—throwing a ball the farthest, winning a game, and (later on) getting good grades. In cultures such as China and Japan, which promote an interdependent self, calling attention to individual success evokes embarrassment and self-effacement. And violating cultural standards by failing to show concern for others—especially authority figures, such as a parent or teacher—sparks intense shame (Lewis, 2014).

7.1.4 Beginnings of Emotional Self-Regulation

Besides expressing a wider range of emotions, infants and toddlers begin to manage their emotional experiences. **Emotional self-regulation** refers to the strategies we use to adjust our emotional state to a comfortable level of intensity so we can accomplish our goals (Thompson & Goodvin, 2007). When you remind yourself that an anxiety-provoking event will be over soon, suppress your anger at a friend's behavior, or decide not to see a scary horror film, you are engaging in emotional self-regulation.

Emotional self-regulation requires voluntary, effortful management of emotions. It improves rapidly in early childhood, as the result of a *dynamic system* of influences. These include development of the prefrontal cortex and its network of connections to brain areas involved in emotional reactivity and support from caregivers, who help children manage intense emotion and (as cognitive, language, and motor skills advance) teach them strategies for doing so on their own (Rothbart et al., 2014; Thompson, 2015). Individual differences in control of emotion are

This 2-year-old's older sister praises his success at tower building. To experience self-conscious emotions, such as pride, young children need self-awareness as well as instruction in when to feel proud of an accomplishment.

already evident in infancy and, by early childhood, play such a vital role in adjustment that—as we will see later—they are viewed as a major dimension of temperament called *effortful control*. A good start in regulating emotion during the first two years contributes greatly to mastery of cognitive and social skills. Poorly regulated toddlers, by contrast, are at risk for long-lasting adjustment difficulties (Eisenberg et al., 2014).

In the early months, infants have only a limited capacity to regulate their emotional states. When their feelings get too intense, they are easily overwhelmed. They depend on soothing interventions of caregivers—being lifted to the shoulder, rocked, gently stroked, and talked to softly—for distraction and reorienting of attention.

More effective functioning of the prefrontal cortex increases the baby's tolerance for stimulation. Between 2 and 4 months, caregivers build on this capacity by initiating face-to-face play and attention to objects. In these interactions, parents arouse pleasure in the baby while adjusting the pace of their own behavior so the infant does not become overwhelmed and distressed (Kopp & Neufeld, 2003). As a result, the baby's tolerance for stimulation increases further.

From 3 months on, the ability to shift attention away from unpleasant events and to engage in self-soothing helps infants control emotion. Beginning around 6 months, infants improve at communicating their need for help in regulating emotion by gesturing and vocalizing to the caregiver (Ekas, Lickenbrock, & Braungart-Rieker, 2013). And crawling and walking, which permit babies to approach or retreat from various situations, foster more effective self-regulation. Also, around the end of the first year, further gains in attention involving greater reliance on the prefrontal cortex enable infants and toddlers to be less diverted by captivating stimuli and to exert more controlled, sustained interest in events and play activities (Posner et al., 2012).

As caregivers help infants regulate their emotional states, they contribute to the child's style of emotional self-regulation. Infants whose parents are highly involved in caregiving and play and who "read" and respond contingently and sympathetically to their emotional cues tend to be better at self-distraction and self-soothing, to express more pleasurable emotion, and to be more interested in exploration (Braungart-Rieker, Hill-Soderlund, & Karrass, 2010; Crockenberg & Leerkes, 2004; Planalp & Braungart-Rieker, 2015). In contrast, parents

A mother of the Baka people of the Central African rainforest antici-pates her baby's discomfort, soothing before he begins to cry. Many non-Western cultures that highly value social harmony discourage the expression of strong emotion in infants.

who respond impatiently or angrily or who wait to intervene until the infant has become extremely agitated reinforce the baby's rapid rise to intense distress. This makes it harder for parents to soothe the baby in the future—and for the baby to learn to calm herself. When caregivers fail to regulate stressful experiences for infants who cannot yet regulate them for themselves, brain structures that buffer stress may fail to develop properly, resulting in an anxious, reactive child who has a reduced capac-ity for managing emotional problems (Blair & Raver, 2012; Frankel et al., 2015).

Caregivers also provide lessons in socially approved ways of express-ing feelings. Beginning in the first few months, parents encourage infants to suppress negative emotion by imitating their expressions of interest, happiness, and surprise more often than their expressions of anger and sadness. Boys get more of this training than girls, in part because boys have a harder time regulating negative emotion (Else-Quest et al., 2006; Malatesta et al., 1986). As a result, the well-known sex difference—females as emotionally expressive and males as emotionally controlled—is promoted at a tender age.

Cultures that highly value social harmony place particular emphasis on socially appropriate emotional behavior while discouraging expres-sion of individual feelings. Compared with Western parents, Chinese and Japanese parents, and parents in many non-Western village cultures, dis-courage the expression of strong emotion in babies. For example, as noted earlier in this chapter, Nso mothers of rural Cameroon spend less time imitating infant social smiling than do German mothers. Nso mothers are also especially quick to quiet infant distress through soothing and breastfeeding. Chinese, Japanese, and Nso babies, in turn, smile, laugh, and cry less than their Western agemates (Friedlmeier, Corapci, & Cole, 2011; Gartstein et al., 2010; Kärtner, Holodynski, & Wörmann, 2013).

In the second year, growth in representation and language leads to new ways of regulat-ing emotions. A vocabulary for talking about feelings—"happy," "love," "surprised," "scary," "yucky," "mad"—develops rapidly after 18 months, but toddlers are not yet good at using language to manage their emotions. Temper tantrums tend to occur because toddlers cannot control the intense anger that often arises when an adult rejects their demands, particularly when they are fatigued or hungry (Mascolo & Fischer, 2007). When parents are emotionally sympathetic but set limits (by not giving in to tantrums), distract the child by offering accept-able alternatives, and later suggest better ways to solve the initial problem, children display more effective anger-regulation strategies and social skills during the preschool years (LeCuyer & Houck, 2006; Scrimgeour, Davis, & Buss, 2016).

Patient, sensitive parents also talk about emotions and encourage toddlers to describe their internal states. Then, when 2-year-olds feel distressed, they can guide caregivers in helping them (Cole, Armstrong, & Pemberton, 2010). For example, while listening to a story about monsters, Grace whimpered, "Mommy, scary." Monica put the book down and gave Grace a comforting hug.

ASK YOURSELF

Connect ■ Why do children of depressed parents have difficulty regulating emotion (see page 146 in Chapter 4)? What implications do their weak self-regulatory skills have for their response to cognitive and social challenges?

Apply ■ At age 14 months, Reggie built a block tower and glee-fully knocked it down. At age 2, he called to his mother and pointed proudly to his tall block tower. What explains this change in Reggie's emotional behavior?

Reflect ■ How do you typically manage negative emotion? How might your early experiences, gender, and cultural background have influenced your style of emotional self-regulation?

7.2 Temperament and Development

From early infancy, Caitlin's sociability was unmistakable. She smiled and laughed while interacting with adults and, in her second year, readily approached other children. Meanwhile, Monica marveled at Grace's calm, relaxed disposition. At 19 months, she sat contentedly in a highchair through a two-hour family celebration at a restaurant. In contrast, Timmy was active and distractible. Vanessa found herself chasing him as he dropped one toy, moved on to the next, and climbed on chairs and tables.

When we describe one person as cheerful and upbeat, another as active and energetic, and still others as calm, cautious, or prone to angry outbursts, we are referring to **temperament**—early-appearing, stable individual differences in reactivity and self-regulation. *Reactivity* refers to quickness and intensity of emotional arousal, attention, and motor activity. *Self-regulation,* as we have seen, refers to strategies that modify that reactivity (Chen & Schmidt, 2015; Rothbart, 2011; Rothbart, Sheese, & Posner, 2014). The psychological traits that make up temperament are believed to form the cornerstone of the adult personality.

In 1956, Alexander Thomas and Stella Chess initiated the New York Longitudinal Study, a groundbreaking investigation of the development of temperament that followed 141 children from early infancy well into adulthood. Results showed that temperament can increase a child's chances of experiencing psychological problems or, alternatively, protect a child from the negative effects of a highly stressful home life. At the same time, Thomas and Chess (1977) discovered that parenting practices can modify temperament considerably.

These findings stimulated a growing body of research on temperament, including its stability, biological roots, and interaction with child-rearing experiences. Let's begin to explore these issues by looking at the structure, or makeup, of temperament and how it is measured.

7.2.1 The Structure of Temperament

Thomas and Chess's model of temperament inspired all others that followed. When detailed descriptions of infants' and children's behavior obtained from parental interviews were rated on nine dimensions of temperament, certain characteristics clustered together, yielding three types of children:

- The **easy child** (40 percent of the sample) quickly establishes regular routines in infancy, is generally cheerful, and adapts easily to new experiences.
- The **difficult child** (10 percent of the sample) is irregular in daily routines, is slow to accept new experiences, and tends to react negatively and intensely.
- The **slow-to-warm-up child** (15 percent of the sample) is inactive, shows mild, low-key reactions to environmental stimuli, is negative in mood, and adjusts slowly to new experiences.

Note that 35 percent of the children did not fit any of these categories. Instead, they showed unique blends of temperamental characteristics.

The difficult child pattern has sparked the most interest because children who display it are at high risk for adjustment problems—both anxious withdrawal and aggressive behavior in early and middle childhood (Bates, Wachs, & Emde, 1994; Ramos et al., 2005; Trentacosta et al., 2011). Use of the label "difficult" is problematic, however, because judgments of child difficulty vary widely across caregivers and cultures. Compared with difficult children, slow-to-warm-up children present fewer problems initially. However, they tend to show excessive fearfulness and slow, constricted behavior in the late preschool and school years, when they are expected to respond actively and quickly in classrooms and peer groups (Chess & Thomas, 1984; Schmitz et al., 1999).

Today, the most influential model of temperament is Mary Rothbart's, described in Table 7.1 on page 250. It combines related traits proposed by Thomas and Chess and other researchers, yielding a concise list of just six dimensions. For example, distractibility and persistence are considered opposite ends of the same dimension, which is labeled "attention span/persistence." A unique feature of Rothbart's model is inclusion of both "fearful distress" and "irritable distress," which distinguish between reactivity triggered by fear and reactivity due

7.2a Explain the meaning of temperament and how it is measured.

7.2b Discuss the roles of heredity and environment in the stability of temperament, including the goodness-of-fit model.

TABLE 7.1 Rothbart's Model of Temperament

DIMENSION	DESCRIPTION
Reactivity	
Activity level	Level of gross-motor activity
Attention span/persistence	Duration of orienting or interest
Fearful distress	Wariness and distress in response to intense or novel stimuli, including time to adjust to new situations
Irritable distress	Extent of fussing, crying, and distress when desires are frustrated
Positive affect	Frequency of expression of happiness and pleasure
Self-Regulation	
Effortful control	Capacity to voluntarily suppress a dominant, reactive response in order to plan and execute a more adaptive response
	In the first two years, called *orienting/regulation,* which refers to the capacity to engage in self-soothing, shift attention from unpleasant events, and sustain interest for an extended time

© ELLEN B. SENISI

A mother calmly waits out her toddler's tantrum at having to go on an errand, offering brief words of explanation and reassurance that they'll return soon. Patient, supportive parenting can help him modify his biologically based temperament and better manage his reactivity.

to frustration (Rothbart, 2011; Rothbart, Ahadi, & Evans, 2000). And Rothbart's model excludes such overly broad dimensions in Thomas and Chess's model as regularity of routines and intensity of reaction. A child who is regular in sleeping is not necessarily regular in eating or bowel habits. And a child who smiles and laughs intensely is not necessarily intense in fear, irritability, or motor activity.

Rothbart's dimensions represent the three underlying components included in the definition of temperament: (1) *emotion* ("fearful distress," "irritable distress," "positive affect"), (2) *attention* ("attention span/persistence"), and (3) *action* ("activity level"). According to Rothbart, individuals differ not just in their reactivity on each dimension but also in the self-regulatory dimension of temperament, **effortful control**—the capacity to voluntarily suppress a dominant response in order to plan and execute a more adaptive response (Rothbart, 2011, 2015; Rothbart & Bates, 2006). Variations in effortful control are evident in how effectively a child can focus and shift attention, inhibit impulses, and manage negative emotion.

The capacity for effortful control in early childhood predicts favorable development and adjustment in diverse cultures, with some studies showing long-term effects into adolescence and adulthood (Chen & Schmidt, 2015). Positive outcomes include persistence, task mastery, academic achievement, moral maturity (such as concern about wrongdoing and willingness to apologize), and social behaviors of cooperation, sharing, and helpfulness, which contribute to positive relationships with adults and peers (Eisenberg, 2010; Kochanska & Aksan, 2006; Posner & Rothbart, 2007b; Valiente, Lemery-Chalfant, & Swanson, 2010).

Turn back to page 212 in Chapter 6 to review the concept of executive function, and notice its resemblance to effortful control. These converging concepts, which are associated with similar positive outcomes, reveal that the same mental activities lead to effective regulation in both the cognitive and emotional/social domains.

7.2.2 Measuring Temperament

Temperament is often assessed through interviews or questionnaires given to parents. Behavior ratings by pediatricians, teachers, and others familiar with the child and laboratory observations by researchers have also been used. Parental reports are convenient and take advantage of parents' depth of knowledge about their child across many situations (Chen & Schmidt, 2015). Although information from parents has been criticized as being biased, parental reports are moderately related to researchers' observations of children's behavior (Majdandčžić &

van den Boom, 2007; Mangelsdorf, Schoppe, & Buur, 2000). And parent perceptions are vital for understanding how parents view and respond to their child.

Observations by researchers in the home or laboratory avoid the subjectivity of parent reports but can lead to other inaccuracies. In homes, observers find it hard to capture rare but important events, such as infants' response to frustration. And in the unfamiliar lab setting, fearful children who calmly avoid certain experiences at home may become too upset to complete the session (Rothbart, 2011). Still, researchers can better control children's experiences in the lab. And they can conveniently combine observations of behavior with neurobiological measures to gain insight into the biological basis of temperament.

Most neurobiological research has focused on children who fall at opposite extremes of the positive-affect and fearful-distress dimensions of temperament: **inhibited,** or **shy, children,** who react negatively to and withdraw from novel stimuli, and **uninhibited,** or **sociable, children,** who display positive emotion and approach novel stimuli. As the Biology and Environment box on page 252 reveals, biologically based reactivity—evident in heart rate, hormone levels, and measures of brain activity—differentiates children with inhibited and uninhibited temperaments.

7.2.3 Stability of Temperament

Young children who score low or high on attention span, irritability, sociability, shyness, or effortful control tend to respond similarly when assessed again several months to a few years later and, occasionally, even into the adult years (Casalin et al., 2012; Caspi et al., 2003; Kochanska & Knaack, 2003; Majdandcžić & van den Boom, 2007; van den Akker et al., 2010). However, when assessed across wider intervals of several months or more, the stability of temperament is low to moderate in infancy and toddlerhood. And stability across intervals of several years is moderate from the preschool years on, with a tendency for traits to become more stable with age (Bornstein et al., 2015; Parade et al., 2015; Shiner, 2015).

Why isn't temperament more stable? A major reason is that temperament itself develops over time. To illustrate, let's look at irritability and activity level. Recall from Chapter 4 that the early months are a period of fussing and crying for most babies. As infants better regulate their attention and emotions, many who initially seemed irritable become calm and content. In the case of activity level, the meaning of the behavior changes. At first, an active, wriggling infant tends to be highly aroused and uncomfortable, whereas an inactive baby is often alert and attentive. Once infants move on their own, the reverse is so! An active crawler is usually alert and interested in exploration, whereas an inactive baby may be fearful and withdrawn.

These discrepancies help us understand why long-term prediction from early temperament is best achieved after age 3, when children's styles of responding are better established (Dyson et al., 2015; Roberts & DelVecchio, 2000). In line with this idea, between ages 2½ and 3, children improve substantially and also perform more consistently across a wide range of tasks requiring effortful control, such as waiting for a reward, lowering their voice to a whisper, succeeding at games like "Simon Says," and selectively attending to one stimulus while ignoring competing stimuli (Kochanska, Murray, & Harlan, 2000; Li-Grining, 2007). Around this time, areas in the prefrontal cortex involved in suppressing impulses develop rapidly (Rothbart, 2011).

Nevertheless, the ease with which children manage their reactivity in early childhood depends on the type and strength of the reactive emotion involved. Preschoolers who were highly fearful as toddlers score slightly better than their agemates in effortful control. In contrast, angry, irritable toddlers tend to be less effective at effortful control at later ages (Bridgett et al., 2009; Kochanska & Knaack, 2003). Other evidence confirms that child rearing plays an important role in modifying temperamental traits. Toddlers and young preschoolers who have fearful or negative, irritable temperaments but experience patient, supportive parenting gain most in capacity to manage their reactivity (Bates, Schermerhorn, & Petersen, 2012; Kim & Kochanska, 2012). But if exposed to insensitive or unresponsive parenting, these emotionally negative children are especially likely to score low in effortful control, placing them at risk for adjustment problems.

In sum, diverse personal factors affect the extent to which a child's temperament remains stable, including development of the biological systems on which temperament is based, the

Biology and Environment | Development of Shyness and Sociability

© LAURA DWIGHT PHOTOGRAPHY

Two 4-month-old babies, Larry and Mitch, visited the laboratory of Jerome Kagan, who observed their reactions to a variety of unfamiliar experiences. When exposed to new sights and sounds, such as a moving mobile decorated with colorful toys, Larry tensed his muscles, moved his arms and legs with agitation, and began to cry. In contrast, Mitch remained relaxed and quiet, smiling and cooing at the excitement around him.

As toddlers, Larry and Mitch returned to the laboratory, where they experienced a variety of procedures designed to induce uncertainty. Electrodes were placed on their bodies and blood pressure cuffs on their arms to measure heart rate; toy robots, animals, and puppets moved before their eyes; and unfamiliar people entered and behaved in unexpected ways or wore novel costumes. While Larry whimpered and quickly withdrew, Mitch watched with interest, laughed at the strange sights, and approached the toys and strangers.

On a third visit, at age 4½ Larry barely talked or smiled during an interview with an unfamiliar adult. In contrast, Mitch was outgoing, asking questions and communicating his pleasure at each new activity the adult suggested. In a playroom with two unfamiliar peers, Larry pulled back and watched, while Mitch made friends quickly.

In longitudinal research on several hundred European-American infants followed into adolescence, Kagan found that about 20 percent of 4-month-olds were, like Larry, easily upset by novelty; another 40 percent, like Mitch, were comfortable, even delighted, with new experiences. About 20 to 25 percent of these extreme groups retained their temperamental styles as they grew older (Kagan, 2003, 2013d; Kagan et al., 2007). But most children's dispositions became less extreme over time. Genetic makeup and child-rearing experiences jointly influenced stability and change in temperament.

Neurobiological Correlates of Shyness and Sociability

Individual differences in arousal of the *amygdala,* an inner brain structure devoted to processing of novelty and emotional information, contribute to these contrasting temperaments. In shy, inhibited children, novel stimuli easily excite the amygdala and its connections to the prefrontal cortex and the sympathetic nervous system, which prepares the body to act in the face of threat. In sociable, uninhibited children, the same level of stimulation evokes minimal neural excitation (Schwartz et al., 2012). And additional neurobiological responses known to be affected by arousal of the amygdala distinguish these two emotional styles:

■ *Heart rate.* From the first few weeks of life, the heart rates of shy children are consistently higher than those of sociable children, and they speed up further in response to unfamiliar events (Schmidt et al., 2007). In addition, *vagal tone*—naturally occurring variation in heart rate during each resting-state breathing cycle (a rise with inhalation, a decline with exhalation)—tends to be reduced in shy children. Low vagal tone is a sign of persistent stress (Chen & Schmidt, 2015).

■ *Cortisol.* Saliva concentrations of the stress hormone cortisol tend to be higher, and to rise more in response to a stressful event, in shy than in sociable children (Schmidt et al., 1999; Zimmermann & Stansbury, 2004).

■ *Pupil dilation, blood pressure, and skin surface temperature.* Compared with sociable children, shy children show greater pupil dilation, rise in blood pressure, and cooling of the fingertips when faced with novelty (Kagan et al., 2007).

Another physiological correlate of approach–withdrawal to people and objects is the pattern of brain waves in the frontal lobes of the cerebral cortex. Shy infants and preschoolers show greater EEG activity in the right frontal lobe, which is associated with negative emotional reactivity. In contrast, sociable children display greater activity in the left frontal lobe, which is linked to expressions of joy (Diaz & Bell, 2012; Fox et al., 2008). Inhibited children also show a stronger ERP brain-wave response to unfamiliar visual scenes (Kagan, 2013d). Neural activity in the amygdala, which is transmitted to the frontal lobes, probably contributes to these differences.

Child-Rearing Practices

According to Kagan, most extremely shy or sociable children inherit a physiology that biases them toward a particular temperamental style (Kagan, 2013d). Yet experience, too, has a powerful impact.

A strong physiological response to uncertain situations prompts this child to cling to her father. With patient, insistent encouragement, her parents can help her overcome the urge to retreat from unfamiliar events.

Child-rearing practices affect the chances that an emotionally reactive baby will become a fearful child. Warm, supportive parenting reduces shy infants' and preschoolers' intense physiological reaction to novelty, whereas cold, intrusive parenting that punishes or denies children's feelings heightens anxiety (Davis & Buss, 2012; Kiel, Premo, & Buss, 2016). And if parents overprotect infants and young children who dislike novelty, they make it harder for the child to overcome an urge to retreat. Parents who make appropriate demands for their child to approach new experiences help shy youngsters develop strategies for regulating fear (Chronis-Tuscano et al., 2015).

When inhibition persists, it leads to excessive cautiousness, low self-esteem, and loneliness. In adolescence, it increases the risk of severe anxiety, depression, and other internalizing problems, including unrealistic worries about harm, illness, and criticism for mistakes as well as social phobia—intense fear of being humiliated in social situations (Kagan, 2013d; Karevold et al., 2012). For inhibited children to acquire effective social skills, parenting must be tailored to their temperaments—a theme we will encounter again in this and later chapters.

child's capacity for effortful control, and the success of her efforts, which depend on the quality and intensity of her emotional reactivity. In addition, child rearing can modify biologically based temperamental traits considerably, and children with certain traits, such as negative emotionality, are especially susceptible to the influence of parenting—a finding we will return to shortly.

When we consider the evidence as a whole, the low to moderate stability of temperament makes sense. Let's look more closely at genetic and environmental contributions to temperament and personality.

7.2.4 Genetic and Environmental Influences

The word *temperament* implies a genetic foundation for individual differences in personality. Identical twins are more similar than fraternal twins across a wide range of temperamental traits (activity level, attention span, difficultness, shyness/sociability, irritability, and effortful control) and personality measures (introversion/extroversion, anxiety, agreeableness, curiosity and imaginativeness, and impulsivity) (Caspi & Shiner, 2006; Micalizzi, Wang, & Saudino, 2017; Saudino & Micalizzi, 2015). In Chapter 2, we noted that heritability estimates derived from twin studies suggest a moderate role for genetic factors in temperament and personality: About half of individual differences have been attributed to differences in genetic makeup.

Although genetic influences on temperament are clear, environment is also powerful. Recall from Chapter 5 that children exposed to severe malnutrition in infancy remain more distractible and irritable than their agemates, even after dietary improvement. And infants reared in deprived orphanages are easily overwhelmed by stressful events. Their poor regulation of emotion results in inattention and weak impulse control, including frequent expressions of fear and anger (see pages 162 and 171 in Chapter 5).

Furthermore, heredity and environment often jointly contribute to temperament, since a child's initial approach to the world can be intensified or lessened by experience. To illustrate, let's begin by looking closely at ethnic and gender differences in temperament.

Ethnic and Gender Differences   Compared with European-American infants, Chinese and Japanese babies tend to be less active, irritable, and vocal; more easily soothed when upset; and better at quieting themselves (Kagan, 2013d; Lewis, Ramsay, & Kawakami, 1993). East Asian babies are also more attentive and less distractible, and as 2-year-olds, they are more compliant and cooperative with adults and higher in effortful control—for example, able to wait longer to play with an attractive toy (Chen et al., 2003; Gartstein et al., 2006). Grace's capacity to remain contentedly seated in her highchair through a long family event at a restaurant certainly fits with this evidence. Chinese and Japanese babies are also more fearful and inhibited (Chen, Wang, & DeSouza, 2006; Slobodskaya et al., 2013). They remain closer to their mothers in an unfamiliar playroom and display more anxiety on encountering a stranger.

These variations may have genetic roots, but they are supported by cultural beliefs and practices, yielding possible *gene–environment correlations*. Japanese mothers, for example, usually say that babies come into the world as independent beings who must learn to rely on their parents through close physical contact. European-American mothers, in contrast, typically believe that they must wean their babies away

At a Hong Kong playground, a 2-year-old assists her mother in wiping sand off a seesaw before climbing aboard. Compared to their European-American counterparts, East Asian babies are more compliant, less distractible, and higher in effortful control.

from dependency toward autonomy. Consistent with these beliefs, East Asian mothers interact gently, soothingly, and gesturally with their infants, whereas European-American mothers use a more active, stimulating, verbal approach (Kagan, 2010). Also, recall from our discussion of emotional self-regulation that Chinese and Japanese adults discourage babies from expressing strong emotion, which contributes further to their infants' tranquility.

Similarly, gender differences in temperament are evident as early as infancy, suggesting a genetic foundation. Boys are more active and daring, less fearful, more irritable when

LOOK and LISTEN

In her first two years, Grace experienced a cultural mix of caregiving—by her East Asian birth mother for 16 months and by her European-American adoptive parents thereafter. How might this mix affect Grace's developing temperament?

frustrated, more likely to express high-intensity pleasure in play, and slightly more impulsive than girls—factors that contribute to boys' higher injury rates throughout childhood and adolescence. Girls, in contrast, tend to be more anxious and timid. And girls' large advantage in effortful control undoubtedly contributes to their greater compliance and cooperativeness, better school performance, and lower incidence of behavior problems (Else-Quest, 2012; Olino et al., 2013). At the same time, parents more often encourage their young sons to be physically active and their daughters to seek help and physical closeness—through activities they encourage and through more positive reactions when their child exhibits temperamental traits consistent with gender stereotypes (Bryan & Dix, 2009; Hines, 2015). Perhaps for this reason, gender differences in some temperamental traits widen by adolescence.

Differential Susceptibility to Rearing Experiences   Earlier we discussed findings indicating that emotionally reactive toddlers function worse than other children when exposed to ineffective parenting yet benefit more from good parenting. Researchers have become increasingly interested in temperamental differences in children's susceptibility (or responsiveness) to environmental influences (Pluess & Belsky, 2011; Slagt et al., 2016). Using molecular genetic testing, they are clarifying how these *gene–environment interactions* operate.

Consistently, young children with a chromosome 7 gene containing a certain repetition of DNA base pairs called short 5-HTTLPR—which interferes with functioning of the inhibitory neurotransmitter serotonin and, thus, greatly increases the risk of self-regulation difficulties—are highly susceptible to the effects of parenting quality. Those exposed to maladaptive parenting readily develop externalizing behavior problems (anger and aggression). But when parenting is kind and supportive, children with this genetic marker fare exceedingly well in adjustment (Kochanska et al., 2011, 2015; van Ijzendoorn, Belsky, & Bakermans-Kranenburg, 2012). Among children without the 5-HTTLPR genotype, parenting—whether positive or negative—has minimal impact on adjustment.

Findings from a two-year follow-up of 1-year-olds from poverty-stricken families provide an impressive illustration (see Figure 7.2) (Davies & Cicchetti, 2014). Toddlers with the high-risk 5-HTTLPR genotype subjected to hostile, rejecting maternal parenting became increasingly emotionally reactive to their mother's behavior, responding with distress, anger, and uncontrolled screaming. Their negative emotionality, in turn, predicted a sharp rise in defiance and aggression by age 3. In contrast, high-risk toddlers of affectionate, involved, and encouraging mothers displayed effective emotion regulation and far less anger and aggression than children with a low-risk genotype! Low-risk children barely reacted to variation in parenting quality.

As these outcomes reveal, children with the short 5-HTTLPR genetic marker show unusually high early *plasticity* (see page 9 in Chapter 1 to review). Their emotion regulation is particularly susceptible to the effects of both positive and negative parenting. Because young children with this "susceptibility attribute" fare better than other children when parenting is supportive, they are likely to benefit most from interventions aimed at reducing parental stress and promoting responsive child rearing.

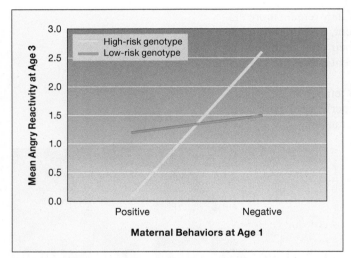

FIGURE 7.2   Angry reactivity at age 3 in response to positive and negative maternal behaviors for children with and without the short 5-HTTLPR genotype. Children with a high-risk genotype (with the genetic marker) were highly susceptible to parenting quality—both good and bad. They displayed little anger when exposed to maternal affection and encouragement but high anger to maternal insensitivity and hostility. Children with a low-risk genotype (without the genetic marker) responded little to quality of maternal behavior. (From P. T. Davies and D. Cicchetti, 2014, "How and Why Does the 5-HTTLPR Gene Moderate Associations Between Maternal Unresponsiveness and Children's Disruptive Problems?" *Child Development, 85,* p. 494. Adapted by permission of John Wiley & Sons.)

Siblings' Unique Experiences   In families with several children, another influence on temperament is at work. When asked to describe their children's personalities, parents often focus on differences: "She's a lot more active." "He's more sociable." "She's far more persistent." As a result, they often view siblings as more distinct than other observers do.

In a large study of 1- to 3-year-old twin pairs, parents rated identical twins as less alike in temperament than researchers' ratings indicated. And whereas researchers rated fraternal twins as moderately similar, parents viewed them as somewhat opposite in temperament—one shy and the other sociable, one active and the other restrained, one persistent and the other distractible (Saudino, 2003). This tendency to exaggerate each child's unique qualities affects parenting practices. Each child, in turn, evokes responses from caregivers that are consistent with parental beliefs and with the child's developing temperament.

Besides different experiences within the family, siblings have distinct experiences with teachers, peers, and others in their community that affect development. And as we will see in Chapter 13, in middle childhood and adolescence, siblings often seek ways to differ from one another. For all these reasons, both identical and fraternal twins tend to become increasingly dissimilar in personality with age (Loehlin & Martin, 2001). In sum, temperament and personality can be understood only in terms of complex interdependencies between genetic and environmental factors.

LOOK and LISTEN

Ask several parents of siblings to describe their children's temperaments, along with child-rearing practices they use with each. Do the parents tend to emphasize differences? Do their child-rearing practices reflect their views of each child's unique qualities?

7.2.5 Temperament and Child Rearing: The Goodness-of-Fit Model

Thomas and Chess (1977) proposed a **goodness-of-fit model** to explain how temperament and environment can together produce favorable outcomes. Goodness of fit involves creating child-rearing environments that recognize each child's temperament while simultaneously encouraging more adaptive functioning. If a child's disposition interferes with learning or getting along with others, adults must gently but consistently counteract the child's maladaptive style.

Difficult children (who withdraw from new experiences and react negatively and intensely) frequently experience parenting that fits poorly with their dispositions. As infants, they are less likely to receive sensitive caregiving. By the second year, their parents tend to resort to angry, punitive discipline, which undermines the development of effortful control. As the child reacts with defiance and disobedience, parents become increasingly stressed. As a result, they continue their coercive tactics and also discipline inconsistently, at times rewarding the child's noncompliance by giving in to it (Lee et al., 2012; Micalizzi, Wang, & Saudino, 2017; Pesonen et al., 2008). These practices sustain and even increase the child's irritable, conflict-ridden style.

In contrast, positive and sensitive parenting helps infants and toddlers—especially those who are emotionally reactive—regulate emotion, reducing difficultness by age 2 or 3 (Raikes et al., 2007). In toddlerhood and childhood, parental sensitivity, support, clear expectations, and limits foster effortful control, lessening the likelihood that difficultness will persist and lead to emotional and social difficulties (Cipriano & Stifter, 2010).

Effective parenting of difficult children, however, also depends on life conditions—good parental mental health, marital happiness, and favorable economic conditions (Schoppe-Sullivan et al., 2007). In comparisons of the temperaments of Russian and U.S. babies, Russian infants were more emotionally negative, fearful, and upset when frustrated (Gartstein, Slobodskaya, & Kinsht, 2003; Slobodskaya et al., 2013). At the time of these investigations, Russian parents faced a severely depressed national economy compared to that of the United States. Because of financial worries and longer work hours, Russian parents may have lacked time and energy for patient parenting.

Cultural values also affect the fit between parenting and child temperament, as research in China illustrates. In the past, high valuing of social harmony, which discourages self-assertion, led Chinese adults to evaluate shy children positively. But, rapid expansion of a market economy, which requires assertiveness and sociability for success, prompted a reversal in Chinese parents' and teachers' attitudes toward childhood shyness (Chen, Wang, & DeSouza, 2006; Yu, 2002). Whereas shyness was positively correlated with academic competence, peer acceptance, and leadership in the early 1990s, these correlations gradually weakened and became negative, until they mirrored findings of Western research. Today, shyness in Chinese children is linked to maladjustment—poor achievement, internalizing difficulties (anxiety and loneliness), and peer relationship problems (Chen et al., 2005; Coplan et al., 2016; Liu et al., 2017). Nevertheless, positive valuing of shyness has persisted in rural areas

This parent's firm but affectionate approach to discipline is "a good fit" with his son's difficult temperament, helping the toddler gain in effortful control and manage negative emotion.

of China, where many shy children continue to be well-adjusted (Chen, Wang, & Cao, 2011). Cultural context makes a difference in whether shy children receive support or disapproval and whether they adjust well or poorly.

An effective match between rearing conditions and child temperament is best accomplished early, before unfavorable temperament–environment relationships produce maladjustment. Recall from Chapter 6 that Vanessa often behaved in an overly directive way with Timmy in an effort to contain his high activity level. A poor fit between her intrusive parenting and Timmy's active temperament may have contributed to his tendency to move from one activity to the next with little involvement.

The goodness-of-fit model reminds us that babies have unique dispositions that adults must accept. Parents can neither take full credit for their children's virtues nor be blamed for all their faults. But parents can turn an environment that exaggerates a child's problems into one that builds on the child's strengths. As we will see, goodness of fit is also at the heart of infant–caregiver attachment. This first intimate relationship grows out of interaction between parent and baby, to which the emotional styles of both partners contribute.

ASK YOURSELF

Connect ■ Explain how findings on ethnic and gender differences in temperament illustrate gene–environment correlation, discussed on page 80 in Chapter 2.

Apply ■ Mandy and Jeff are parents of 2-year-old inhibited Sam and 3-year-old irritable Maria. Explain the importance of effortful control to Mandy and Jeff, and suggest ways they can strengthen it in each of their children.

Reflect ■ How would you describe your temperament as a young child? Do you think it has remained stable, or has it changed? What factors might be involved?

7.3 Development of Attachment

7.3a Describe the features of ethological theory of attachment and its view of the development of attachment during the first two years.

7.3b Describe techniques for measuring attachment security, the stability of attachment patterns, and cultural variations in attachment behavior.

7.3c Discuss factors that influence early attachment security, infants' and toddlers' formation of multiple attachments, and how attachment paves the way for peer sociability.

7.3d Discuss the relationship of attachment patterns in infancy and of caregiving quality from infancy through adolescence to children's long-term adjustment.

Attachment is the strong affectionate tie we have with special people in our lives that leads us to experience pleasure when we interact with them and to be comforted by their nearness in times of stress. By the second half-year, infants have become attached to familiar people who have responded to their needs. Consider how babies of this age single out their parents for special attention: When the parent enters the room, the baby breaks into a broad, friendly smile. When she picks him up, he pats her face, explores her hair, and snuggles against her. When he feels anxious or afraid, he crawls into her lap and clings closely.

Sigmund Freud first suggested that the infant's emotional tie to the mother is the foundation for all later relationships. Contemporary research indicates that—although the infant–parent bond is vitally important—later development is influenced not just by early attachment experiences but also by the continuing quality of the parent–child relationship.

Attachment has also been the subject of intense theoretical debate. Recall from Chapter 1 that the *psychoanalytic perspective* regards feeding—satisfying the baby's oral needs—as the central context in which caregivers and babies build this close emotional bond. Erik Erikson's psychosocial theory expanded Freud's view of the oral stage, pointing out that a positive outcome in infancy depends not on the amount of oral stimulation offered but rather on quality of caregiving. When the parent relieves the baby's discomfort promptly and sensitively, holds the infant gently, and waits patiently until the baby has had enough milk, the infant acquires a *sense of trust* in the caregiver and the surrounding world. *Behaviorism,* too, emphasizes feeding as central in the development of attachment, but for different reasons. According to a well-known behaviorist account, infants learn to prefer the mother's soft caresses, warm smiles, and tender words because these events are paired with tension relief as she satisfies the baby's hunger.

Although feeding is an important context for building a close relationship, attachment does not depend on hunger satisfaction. In the 1950s, a famous experiment showed that rhesus monkeys reared with terry-cloth and wire-mesh "surrogate mothers" clung to the soft terry-cloth substitute, even though the wire-mesh "mother" held the bottle and infants had to climb onto it to be fed (Harlow & Zimmerman, 1959). Human infants, too, become attached to family members who seldom feed them, including fathers, siblings, and grandparents. And toddlers in Western cultures who sleep alone and experience frequent daytime separations from their parents sometimes develop strong emotional ties to cuddly objects, such as blankets and teddy bears, that play no role in infant feeding!

Both psychoanalytic and behaviorist accounts of attachment have another problem: They emphasize the caregiver's contribution to the attachment relationship but pay little attention to the importance of the infant's characteristics.

7.3.1 Bowlby's Ethological Theory

Today, **ethological theory of attachment,** which recognizes the infant's emotional tie to the caregiver as an evolved response that promotes survival, is the most widely accepted view. John Bowlby (1969), who first applied this perspective to the infant–caregiver bond, retained the psychoanalytic idea that quality of attachment to the caregiver has profound implications for the child's feelings of security and capacity to form trusting relationships.

At the same time, Bowlby was inspired by Konrad Lorenz's studies of imprinting in baby geese (see Chapter 1). Bowlby believed that the human infant, like the young of other animal species, is endowed with a set of built-in behaviors that keep the parent nearby to protect the infant from danger and to provide support for exploring and mastering the environment. Contact with the parent also ensures that the baby will be fed, but Bowlby maintained that feeding is not the basis for attachment. Rather, attachment can best be understood in an evolutionary context in which survival of the species—through ensuring both safety and competence—is of utmost importance.

According to Bowlby, the infant's relationship with the parent begins as a set of innate signals that call the adult to the baby's side. Over time, a true affectionate bond forms, supported by new cognitive and emotional capacities as well as by a history of warm, sensitive care. In Bowlby's theory, attachment develops in four phases:

1. *Preattachment phase (birth to 6 weeks).* Built-in signals—grasping, smiling, crying, and gazing into the adult's eyes—help bring newborn babies into close contact with other humans, who comfort them. Infants of this age recognize their own mother's smell, voice, and face (see Chapter 4). But they are not yet attached to her, since they do not mind being left with an unfamiliar adult.
2. *"Attachment in the making" phase (6 weeks to 6–8 months).* During this phase, infants respond differently to a familiar caregiver than to a stranger. For example, at 4 months, Timmy smiled, laughed, and babbled more freely when interacting with his mother than with other adults and quieted more quickly when she picked him up. As infants learn that their own actions affect the behavior of those around them, they begin to develop a *sense of trust*—the expectation that the caregiver will respond when signaled—but they still do not protest when separated from her.
3. *"Clear-cut" attachment phase (6–8 months to 18 months–2 years).* Now attachment to the familiar caregiver is evident. Babies display **separation anxiety,** becoming upset when their trusted caregiver leaves. Like stranger anxiety (see page 245), separation anxiety does not always occur; it depends on infant temperament and the current context. But in many cultures, separation anxiety increases between 6 and 15 months, suggesting that infants have developed a clear understanding that the caregiver continues to exist when not in view. Besides protesting the parent's departure, older infants and toddlers try hard to maintain her presence. They approach, follow, and climb on her in preference to others. And they use the familiar caregiver as a secure base from which to explore.
4. *Formation of a reciprocal relationship (18 months to 2 years and on).* By the end of the second year, rapid growth in representation and language enables toddlers to

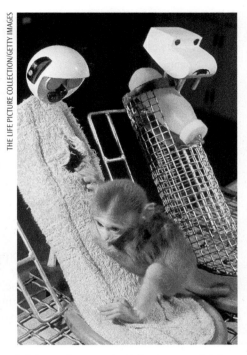

Baby monkeys reared with "surrogate mothers" preferred to cling to a soft terry-cloth "mother" instead of a wire-mesh "mother" that held a bottle. These findings contradict explanations of infant–caregiver attachment that assume the relationship is based on feeding.

With gentle encouragement, this toddler reaches for her familiar caregiver's hand, separating from her mother with little protest at child care. As language and representational skills increase, enabling toddlers to predict the parent's return, separation anxiety declines.

understand some of the factors that influence the parent's coming and going and to predict her return. As a result, separation protest declines. Children of this age are able to negotiate with the caregiver, using requests and persuasion to alter her goals. For example, at age 2, Caitlin asked Carolyn and David to read her a story before leaving her with a babysitter. The extra time with her parents, along with a better understanding of where they were going ("to have dinner with Uncle Sean") and when they would be back ("right after you go to sleep"), helped Caitlin withstand her parents' absence.

According to Bowlby (1980), out of their experiences during these four phases, children construct an enduring affectionate tie to the caregiver that they can use as a secure base in the parent's absence. This image serves as an **internal working model,** or set of expectations about the availability of attachment figures, their likelihood of providing support during times of stress, and the self's interaction with those figures. The internal working model becomes a vital part of personality, serving as a guide for all future close relationships (Bretherton & Munholland, 2008).

Consistent with these ideas, as early as the second year, toddlers form attachment-related expectations about parental comfort and support. In several studies, securely attached 12- to 16-month-olds looked longer at a video of an unresponsive caregiver (inconsistent with their expectations) than a video of a responsive caregiver. Insecurely attached agemates, in contrast, either looked longer at the responsive caregiver or did not distinguish between the two (see Figure 7.3) (Johnson, Dweck, & Chen, 2007; Johnson et al., 2010). The researchers concluded that the toddlers' visual responses reflected "surprise" at caregiver behavior at odds with their own internal working model. With age, children continually revise and expand their internal working model as their cognitive, emotional, and social capacities increase and as they interact with parents and form other close bonds with adults, siblings, and friends.

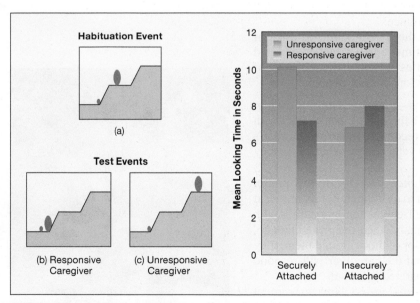

FIGURE 7.3   Testing toddlers for internal working models of attachment. (a) First, 12- to 16-month-olds were habituated to a video of two animated shapes, one large (the "caregiver") and one small (the "child"). The caregiver traveled halfway up an incline to a plateau, and the child began to "cry," depicted by pulsing and bouncing paired with an infant cry. Next the researchers presented two test events: (b) In the *responsive caregiver outcome,* the caregiver returned to the child. (c) In the *unresponsive caregiver outcome,* the caregiver continued up the slope away from the child. Securely attached toddlers looked longer at the unresponsive outcome, depicting caregiver behavior inconsistent with their expectations. Insecurely attached toddlers did not differentiate between the two test events. (Based on Johnson, Dweck, & Chen, 2007.)

7.3.2 Measuring the Security of Attachment

Although all family-reared babies become attached to a familiar caregiver by the second year, the quality of this relationship varies. Some infants appear relaxed and secure in the presence of their caregiver; they know they can count on the familiar adult for protection and support. Others seem anxious and uncertain.

A widely used laboratory technique for assessing the quality of attachment between 1 and 2 years of age is the **Strange Situation.** In designing it, Mary Ainsworth and her colleagues reasoned that securely attached infants and toddlers should use the parent as a secure base from which to explore in an unfamiliar playroom. In addition, when the parent leaves and an unfamiliar adult enters the room, the baby should be less comforted by the stranger than by the parent. The Strange Situation takes the baby through eight short episodes in which brief separations from and reunions with the parent occur (see Table 7.2).

Observing infants' responses to these episodes, researchers identified a secure attachment pattern and three patterns of insecurity; a few babies could not be classified (Ainsworth et al., 1978; Main & Solomon, 1990; Thompson, 2013). Although separation anxiety varies among the groups, the baby's reunion responses largely define attachment quality. From the description at the beginning of this chapter, which pattern do you think Grace displayed after adjusting to her adoptive family?

TABLE 7.2   Episodes in the Strange Situation

EPISODE	EVENTS	ATTACHMENT BEHAVIOR OBSERVED
1	Researcher introduces parent and baby to playroom and then leaves.	
2	Parent is seated while baby plays with toys.	Parent as a secure base
3	Stranger enters, is seated, and talks to parent.	Reaction to unfamiliar adult
4	Parent leaves room. Stranger responds to baby and offers comfort if baby is upset.	Separation anxiety
5	Parent returns, greets baby, and offers comfort if necessary. Stranger leaves room.	Reaction to reunion
6	Parent leaves room.	Separation anxiety
7	Stranger enters room and offers comfort.	Ability to be soothed by stranger
8	Parent returns, greets baby, offers comfort if necessary, and tries to reinterest baby in toys.	Reaction to reunion

Note: Episode 1 lasts about 30 seconds; each of the remaining episodes lasts about 3 minutes. Separation episodes are cut short if the baby becomes very upset. Reunion episodes are extended if the baby needs more time to calm down and return to play.

Source: Ainsworth et al., 1978.

- **Secure attachment.** These infants use the parent as a secure base. When separated, they may or may not cry, but if they do, it is because the parent is absent and they prefer her to the stranger. When the parent returns, they convey clear pleasure—some expressing joy from a distance, others asking to be held until settling down to return to play—and crying is reduced immediately. About 60 percent of North American infants in middle-SES families show this pattern. (In low-SES families, a smaller proportion of babies show the secure pattern, with higher proportions falling into the insecure patterns.)
- **Insecure–avoidant attachment.** These infants seem unresponsive to the parent when he is present. When the parent leaves, they usually are not distressed, and they react to the stranger in much the same way as to the parent. During reunion, they avoid or are slow to greet the parent, and when picked up, they often fail to cling. About 15 percent of North American infants in middle-SES families show this pattern.
- **Insecure–resistant attachment.** Before separation, these infants seek closeness to the parent and often fail to explore. When the parent leaves, they are usually distressed, and on her return they combine clinginess with angry, resistive behavior (struggling when held, hitting, and pushing) or with an anxious focus on the parent. Many continue to cry after being picked up and cannot be comforted easily. About 10 percent of North American infants in middle-SES families show this pattern.
- **Disorganized/disoriented attachment.** This pattern reflects the greatest insecurity. At reunion, these infants show confused, contradictory behaviors—for example, looking away while the parent is holding them or approaching the parent with flat, depressed emotion. Most display a dazed facial expression, and a few cry out unexpectedly after having calmed down or display odd, frozen postures. About 15 percent of North American infants in middle-SES families show this pattern.

An alternative method, the **Attachment Q-Sort,** suitable for children between 1 and 5 years, depends on home observations (Waters et al., 1995). Either the parent or a highly trained observer sorts 90 behaviors—such as "Child greets mother with a big smile when she enters the room," "If mother moves very far, child follows along," and "Child uses mother's facial expressions as a good source of information when something looks risky or threatening"—into nine categories ranging from "highly descriptive" to "not at all descriptive" of the child. Then a score, ranging from high to low in security, is computed.

Because the Q-Sort is based on lengthy, naturalistic home observations and taps a wider array of attachment-related behaviors than the laboratory-based Strange Situation, it may better reflect the parent–infant relationship in everyday life. However, the Q-Sort method is time-consuming, requiring a nonparent informant to spend several hours observing the child before sorting the descriptors, and it does not differentiate between types of insecurity. The Q-Sort responses of expert observers correspond moderately well with babies' secure-base behavior in the Strange Situation. In contrast, associations between parents' Q-Sorts and infants' Strange Situation reactions are weak (Cadman, Diamond, & Fearon, 2015; van IJzendoorn et al., 2004). Parents of insecure children, especially, may have difficulty accurately reporting their child's attachment behaviors.

7.3.3 Stability of Attachment

Research on the stability of attachment patterns between 1 and 2 years of age yields a wide range of findings. In some studies, as many as 70 to 90 percent of children remain the same in their reactions to parents; in others, only 30 to 40 percent do. A careful look at which babies stay the same and which ones change yields a more consistent picture. Quality of attachment is usually secure and stable for middle-SES babies experiencing favorable life conditions. And infants who move from insecurity to security typically have well-adjusted mothers with positive family and friendship ties (Pinquart, Feufner, & Ahnert, 2013; Thompson, 2006, 2013). Perhaps many became parents before they were psychologically ready but, with social support, grew into the role.

In contrast, in low-SES families with many daily stresses, attachment generally moves away from security or changes from one insecure pattern to another (Fish, 2004; Levendosky et al., 2011). In follow-ups extending from infancy to late adolescence and early adulthood, shifts from security to insecurity were associated with single parenthood, maternal depression, and poor family functioning and parenting, including child maltreatment (Booth-LaForce et al., 2014; Weinfield, Sroufe, & Egeland, 2000; Weinfield, Whaley, & Egeland, 2004).

These findings indicate that securely attached babies more often maintain their attachment status than insecure babies, whose relationship with the caregiver is, by definition, fragile and uncertain. The exception is disorganized/disoriented attachment, an insecure pattern that is either highly stable or that consistently predicts insecurity of another type (Groh et al., 2014; Weinfeld, Whaley, & Egeland, 2004). Furthermore, adults with histories of attachment disorganization are at increased risk of having children who display disorganized/disoriented attachment (Raby et al., 2015). As you will soon see, many disorganized/disoriented infants experience extremely negative caregiving, which may disrupt emotional self-regulation so severely that confused, ambivalent feelings toward parents persist, impairing child rearing in the next generation.

7.3.4 Cultural Variations

Though broadly accepted as a brief, convenient laboratory procedure for assessing attachment security, the Strange Situation has been criticized for not taking into account family cultural context. Some researchers claim that that the attachment patterns derived from the Strange Situation, which are based on the primacy Bowlby accorded to a close infant–parent (mostly maternal) attachment bond, are inappropriate for children in non-Western cultures (Vicedo, 2017). Even when parents are the main caregivers, variations in their child-rearing beliefs and goals can modify children's attachment-related behaviors.

In hunting-and-gathering and subsistence farming societies, nonmaternal caregivers, called *allomothers,* often share responsibility for infants, even assisting with breastfeeding (Meehan & Hawks, 2014b). Caregivers carry infants while they work and grant them few opportunities to independently explore. Consequently, their infants express secure base behavior through observing their surroundings and manipulating nearby objects rather than venturing away from the caregiver and returning for emotional support (Keller & Chaudhary, 2017; Mesman, van Ijzendoorn, & Sagi-Schwartz, 2016; Morelli et al., 2017). Furthermore, as we saw earlier in our discussion of Nso and Aka cultures, collective caregiving results in low levels of stranger anxiety—a key indicator of Western infants' attachment security.

© TON KOENE/ALAMY STOCK PHOTO

The Samburu, a nomadic people of northern Kenya, practice a form of shared caregiving in which grandmothers, acting as allomothers, care for infants while mothers forage for food and assist with herding of livestock. As a result, Samburu infants become attached to a network of caregivers.

In Nso, Aka, and other similar societies, the infant's attachment to a *caregiving network,* in addition to parents, must be considered.

Research in diverse Western and non-Western developed nations using the Strange Situation also indicates that attachment behaviors can have distinct, cultural meanings. For example, as Figure 7.4 shows, German infants show considerably more avoidant attachment than American babies do. But German parents value independence and encourage their infants to be nonclingy, so the baby's behavior may be an intended outcome of cultural beliefs and practices (Grossmann et al., 1985).

Japanese infants, in contrast, rarely show avoidant attachment (refer again to Figure 7.4). Rather, many are resistantly attached, but this reaction may not represent true insecurity. The Japanese ideal of *amae,* emphasizing interdependency and oneness between infant and mother, leads Japanese mothers to seldom leave their babies in others' care, so the Strange Situation probably induces greater distress in them than in infants who frequently experience maternal separations (Takahashi, 1990). Also, Japanese parents view the attention seeking that is part of resistant attachment as a normal indicator of infants' efforts to satisfy dependency and security needs (Rothbaum, Morelli, & Rusk, 2011).

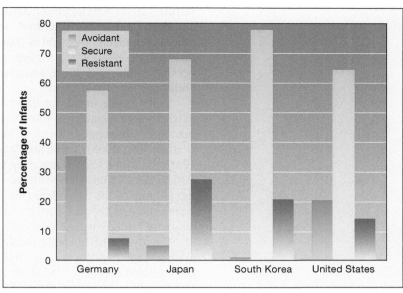

FIGURE 7.4 **A cross-cultural comparison of infants' reactions in the Strange Situation.** A high percentage of German babies seem avoidantly attached, whereas a substantial number of Japanese and Korean infants appear resistantly attached. Note that these responses may not reflect true insecurity. Instead, they are probably due to cultural differences in child-rearing practices. (Based on Jin et al., 2012; van IJzendoorn & Kroonenberg, 1988; van IJzendoorn & Sagi-Schwartz, 2008.)

Likewise, Figure 7.4 indicates that resistant attachment is high among Korean infants, while almost none are avoidantly attached. The Korean concept of *maternal dew* stresses the importance of a strong bond between infant and mother, who is seen as having special healing powers. For example, many Korean mothers believe that if their baby has an upset stomach, merely touching it will help the infant recover (Jin et al., 2012). Korean mothers are highly attentive to their babies' needs and, like Japanese mothers, rarely separate from them.

In sum, infants' ways of expressing attachment and exploration differ widely across cultures. Although the secure pattern is the most common attachment quality in all societies studied to date, culturally specific definitions and research methods are needed to achieve a more complete understanding of infant–caregiver attachment relationships around the world (Morelli et al., 2017; van IJzendoorn & Sagi-Schwartz, 2008).

7.3.5 Factors That Affect Attachment Security

What factors might influence attachment security? Researchers have looked closely at four important influences: (1) early availability of a consistent caregiver, (2) quality of caregiving, (3) the baby's characteristics, and (4) family context, including parents' internal working models.

Early Availability of a Consistent Caregiver What happens when a baby does not have the opportunity to establish a close tie to any caregiver? To find out, researchers followed the development of infants in British institutions with good caregiver–child ratios and a rich selection of books and toys but with such rapid staff turnover that the average child had 50 caregivers by age 4½ Many of these children became "late adoptees" who were placed in homes after age 4. Most developed deep ties with their adoptive parents, indicating that a first attachment can develop as late as 4 to 6 years of age (Hodges & Tizard, 1989; Tizard & Rees, 1975). But these children were more likely to display attachment difficulties, including an excessive desire for adult attention, "overfriendliness" to unfamiliar adults and peers, failure to check back with the parent in anxiety-arousing situations, and few friendships.

Although adopted children who spent their first year or more in deprived Eastern European orphanages are able to bond with their adoptive parents, they show greatly elevated rates of attachment insecurity, especially disorganized/disoriented attachment (Lionetti, Pastore, &

Barone, 2015; Smyke et al., 2010; van den Dries et al., 2009). They are also at high risk for emotional and social difficulties. Many are indiscriminately friendly toward unfamiliar adults; others are sad, anxious, and withdrawn; and still others are angry and aggressive (Bakermans-Kranenburg et al., 2011; Kreppner et al., 2010; O'Connor et al., 2003). Symptoms tend to persist over time and are associated with wide-ranging mental health problems in middle childhood and adolescence.

Furthermore, institutionalized children as young as 7 months show reduced ERP brain waves in response to facial expressions of emotion and have trouble discriminating such expressions—outcomes that suggest disrupted formation of neural structures involved in "reading" emotions (Parker et al., 2005). These problems are still evident in preschoolers adopted during the second year, who find it hard to match appropriate facial expressions with situations in stories (Fries & Pollak, 2004). Consistent with these findings, in adopted children with longer institutional stays, the volume of the *amygdala* (see page 252) is atypically large. The larger the amygdala, the worse adopted children perform on tasks assessing understanding of emotion, the greater their emotional reactivity, and the poorer their emotional self-regulation (Tottenham, 2012).

Finally, formerly institutionalized children and youths often show weak executive function skills, which contribute to lasting emotional problems. Brain-imaging evidence reveals that the prefrontal cortex of these children is reduced in volume, myelination, and neural activity (McLaughlin, Sheridan, & Nelson, 2017; Merz et al., 2016). Lack of early opportunities to form attachments combined with inadequate early stimulation are believed to be responsible. Overall, the evidence indicates that fully normal emotional development depends on establishing a close tie with a caregiver early in life.

Quality of Caregiving   Dozens of studies report that **sensitive caregiving**—responding promptly, consistently, and appropriately to infants and holding them tenderly and carefully—is moderately related to attachment security in both biological and adoptive mother–infant pairs and in diverse cultures and SES groups (Belsky & Fearon, 2008; Cassidy, Jones, & Shaver, 2013; van IJzendoorn et al., 2004). In contrast, insecurely attached infants tend to have mothers who engage in less physical contact, handle them awkwardly or "routinely," and are resentful and rejecting (Ainsworth et al., 1978; McElwain & Booth-LaForce, 2006).

Cultures, however, vary greatly in their view of sensitivity toward infants. In Western societies that highly value independence, sensitive caregivers follow the baby's lead by noticing infant cues, interpreting these signals accurately, and responding contingently to them, especially when the infant is distressed (Feeney & Woodhouse, 2016). For example, when Caitlin fussed and cried, Carolyn picked her up, carried her to the rocking chair, and whispered soothingly, "Are you sleepy?" When Caitlin excitedly shook a rattle, Carolyn smiled broadly and encouraged enthusiastically, "That-a-girl!" Also, mothers of securely attached babies in Western nations frequently refer to their infants' mental states and motives: "You really *like* that swing!" "Do you *remember* Grandma?" This *maternal mind-mindedness*—the tendency to treat the baby as a person with inner thoughts and feelings—seems to promote sensitive responsiveness (Shai & Meins, 2018; Zeegers et al., 2017).

In non-Western village communities and Asian cultures that emphasize interdependence, *proximal care*—keeping the baby physically close, dampening emotional expressiveness by anticipating the infants' physical needs (feeding before the baby starts to cry), and orienting infants to face toward others so as to notice their wants and needs—is deemed sensitive because it advances the child's connectedness to their social group and promotes social harmony (Keller et al., 2018; Morelli, 2015). Among the Gusii people of Kenya, for example, mothers are quick to quiet their infants and satisfy their physical needs, but they rarely interact contingently or playfully with them. Yet most Gusii infants appear securely attached (LeVine et al., 1994). Puerto Rican mothers, who highly value obedience and socially appropriate behavior, often physically direct and limit their babies' actions—a caregiving style linked to attachment security in Puerto Rican culture (Carlson & Harwood, 2003). Yet typically in Western cultures, such physical control and restriction of exploration are viewed as intrusive and predict insecurity (Whipple, Bernier, & Mageau, 2011).

Compared with securely attached infants, avoidant babies tend to receive overstimulating, intrusive care. Their mothers might, for example, talk energetically to them while they are looking away or falling asleep. By avoiding the mother, these infants appear to be escaping from overwhelming interaction. Mothers of resistant infants often engage in inconsistent care. At times, they are sensitively responsive to infant signals; at other times, they are insensitive or unresponsive (Cassidy & Berlin, 1994; Vondra, Shaw, & Kevenides, 1995). The baby seems to react with impatience and anger to the mother's unreliable behavior.

Highly inadequate caregiving is a powerful predictor of disruptions in attachment. Child abuse and neglect (topics we will consider in Chapter 10) are associated with all three forms of attachment insecurity. Among maltreated infants, disorganized/disoriented attachment is especially high (Cyr et al., 2010; Doyle & Cicchetti, 2017). Persistently depressed mothers, mothers with very low marital satisfaction, and parents suffering from a traumatic event, such as serious illness or loss of a loved one, also tend to promote the uncertain behaviors of this pattern (Campbell et al., 2004; Madigan et al., 2006). And some mothers of disorganized/disoriented infants engage in frightening, contradictory, and unpleasant behaviors, such as looking scared, teasing the baby, holding the baby stiffly at a distance, roughly pulling the baby by the arm, or seeking reassurance from the upset child (Hesse & Main, 2006; Solomon & George, 2011). Perhaps the baby's disorganized behavior reflects a conflicted reaction to the parent, who sometimes comforts but at other times arouses fear.

Infant Characteristics Because attachment is the result of a *relationship* between two partners, infant characteristics should affect how easily it is established. In Chapters 3 and 4 we saw that prematurity, birth complications, and newborn illness make caregiving more taxing. In families under stress, these difficulties are linked to attachment insecurity. In one study, the *combination* of preterm birth with either socioeconomic risk (poverty, single parenthood, high-school dropout) or maternal psychological risk (depression, high emotional stress)—but not preterm birth alone—reduced maternal sensitivity, which predicted insecure attachment at 12 months (Candelaria, Teti, & Black, 2011). Infants with special needs probably require greater parental sensitivity, which stressed parents often cannot provide. At-risk newborns whose parents have adequate time and patience to care for them fare quite well in attachment security (Brisch et al., 2005; Cox, Hopkins, & Hans, 2000).

With respect to temperament, combined analyses of many studies with thousands of infant and young child participants diverse in SES and ethnicity reveal only a weak relationship between temperament and attachment, with one exception: An emotionally reactive temperament is modestly associated with attachment insecurity (Groh et al., 2017; van IJzendoorn et al., 2004; Vaughn, Bost, & Van IJzendoorn, 2008). Again, however, evidence highlighting gene–environment interactions suggests that parental mental health and caregiving are involved.

In several investigations, babies with emotionally reactive temperaments, or with genetic markers predisposing them to emotional reactivity (including the short 5-HTTLPR gene, see page 254), were more likely than infants with low-risk genotypes to exhibit insecure attachment, but only when their mothers displayed negative parenting characteristics (Kim et al., 2017; Luijk et al., 2011; Spangler et al., 2009). With exposure to sensitive caregiving, these babies tended to be more secure. In other research, mothers' experience of relationship trauma was associated with attachment disorganization, but only in infants with a chromosome-11 gene having a certain repetition of DNA base pairs (called DRD4 7-repeat), which disrupts the inhibitory effects of the neurotransmitter dopamine and is linked to impulsive, overactive behavior (Bakermans-Kranenburg & van Ijzendoorn, 2016; van IJzendoorn & Bakermans-Kranenburg, 2006). Infants with this genetic marker, who face special self-regulation challenges, appeared more susceptible to the negative impact of maternal adjustment problems.

If children's temperaments alone determined attachment quality, we would expect attachment, like temperament, to be at least moderately heritable. Yet twin comparisons reveal that

© CULTURA RM/ALAMY STOCK PHOTO

© CHRISTOPHER HERWIG/ROBERT HARDING

Top photo: A father responds contingently to his baby's signals, "reading" the infant's joy and smiling exuberantly in return—a form of sensitivity common in Western societies. Bottom photo: In non-Western village communities and Asian cultures, parental sensitivity is expressed through physical closeness, calmness, and promptly meeting the infant's physical needs.

the heritability of attachment is virtually nil (Roisman & Fraley, 2008). Rather, babies with certain genotypes are at increased risk for attachment insecurity when they also experience insensitive parenting. Consistent with this conclusion, about two-thirds of siblings establish similar attachment patterns with their parents, although the siblings often differ in temperament (Cole, 2006). This suggests that most parents try to adjust their caregiving to each child's individual needs.

Interventions that teach parents to interact sensitively with difficult-to-care-for infants and toddlers enhance both sensitive caregiving and attachment security (van IJzendoorn & Bakermans-Kranenburg, 2015). One program that focused on both maternal sensitivity and effective discipline was particularly effective in reducing irritable distress and disruptive behavior in toddlers with the DRD4 7-repeat gene (Bakermans-Kranenburg & van IJzendoorn, 2011; Bakermans-Kranenburg et al., 2008a, 2008b). These findings suggest that the DRD4 7-repeat—like the short 5-HTTLPR gene—makes children more susceptible to the effects of both negative and positive parenting.

Family circumstances are linked to attachment quality. Observing her parents' heated quarrels may undermine this child's sense of emotional security.

Family Circumstances   Shortly after Timmy's birth, his parents divorced, and his father moved to a distant city. Anxious and distracted, Vanessa placed Timmy in Ginette's child-care home and began working 50-hour weeks to make ends meet. On days Vanessa stayed late at the office, a babysitter picked Timmy up, gave him dinner, and put him to bed. Once or twice a week, Vanessa retrieved Timmy from child care. As he neared his first birthday, Vanessa noticed that unlike the other children, who reached out, crawled, or ran to their parents, Timmy ignored her.

Timmy's behavior reflects a repeated finding: Job loss, a failing marriage, financial difficulties, or parental psychological problems (such as anxiety or depression) can undermine attachment indirectly by interfering with parental sensitivity. These stressors can also negatively affect babies' sense of security directly, by altering the emotional climate of the family (for example, exposing them to angry adult interactions) or by disrupting familiar daily routines (Feeney & Monin, 2016; Thompson, 2013). Social support can foster attachment security by reducing parental stress and improving the quality of parent–child communication (Moss et al., 2005). Ginette's sensitivity toward Timmy was helpful, as was the parenting advice Vanessa received from Ben, a psychologist. As Timmy turned 2, his relationship with his mother seemed warmer.

Parents' Internal Working Models   Parents bring to the family context their own history of attachment experiences, from which they construct internal working models that they apply to the bonds they establish with their babies. Monica, who recalled her mother as tense and preoccupied, expressed regret that they had not had a closer relationship. Is her image of parenthood likely to affect Grace's attachment security?

To assess parents' internal working models, researchers ask them to evaluate childhood memories of attachment experiences (Main & Goldwyn, 1998). Parents who discuss their childhoods with objectivity and balance, regardless of whether their experiences were positive or negative, tend to behave sensitively and have securely attached infants. In contrast, parents who dismiss the importance of early relationships or describe them in angry, confused ways usually have insecurely attached children and are less warm, sensitive, and encouraging of learning and mastery. However, the relationship between parents' internal working models and sensitivity toward their own infants is only modest (McFarland-Piazza et al., 2012; Shafer et al., 2015; Verhage et al., 2016; Whipple, Bernier, & Mageau, 2011). As we have seen, family circumstances and infant characteristics also influence caregiving quality.

Furthermore, we must not assume any direct transfer of parents' childhood experiences to quality of attachment with their own children. Internal working models are *reconstructed memories* affected by many factors, including relationship experiences over the life course, personality, and current life satisfaction. Longitudinal research reveals that negative life events can weaken the link between attachment security in infancy and a secure internal working model in adulthood. And insecurely attached babies who become adults with insecure internal working models often have lives that, based on self-reports in adulthood, are filled with family crises (Waters et al., 2000; Weinfield, Sroufe, & Egeland, 2000).

In sum, our own early rearing experiences do not destine us to become either sensitive or insensitive parents. Rather, the way we *view* our childhoods—our ability to come to terms with negative events, to integrate new information into our working models, and to look back on our own parents in an understanding, forgiving way—is more influential in how we rear our children than the actual history of care we received.

Attachment in Context   Carolyn and Vanessa returned to work when their babies were 2 to 3 months old. Monica did the same a few weeks after Grace's adoption. When parents divide their time between work and parenting and place their infants and toddlers in child care, is quality of attachment and child adjustment affected? See the Social Issues: Health box on page 266 for research that addresses this issue.

After reading the box, consider each factor that influences the development of attachment—infant and parent characteristics, parents' relationship with each other, outside-the-family stressors, the availability of social supports, parents' views of their attachment history, and child-care arrangements. Although attachment builds within the warmth and intimacy of caregiver–infant interaction, it can be fully understood only from an ecological systems perspective. Return to pages 25–27 in Chapter 1, to review Bronfenbrenner's ecological systems theory. Notice how research confirms the importance of each level of the environment for attachment security.

7.3.6 Multiple Attachments

As we have indicated, babies develop attachments to a variety of familiar people—not just mothers, but also fathers, grandparents, siblings, and professional caregivers. Although Bowlby (1969) believed that infants are predisposed to direct their attachment behaviors to a single special person (usually the mother), especially when they are distressed, his theory allows for attachments to other familiar adults.

Fathers   An anxious, unhappy 1-year-old who is permitted to choose between the mother and the father as a source of comfort and security will usually choose the mother. But this preference typically declines over the second year. And when babies are not distressed, they approach, vocalize to, and smile equally often at both parents, who in turn are equally responsive to their infant's social overtures (Bornstein, 2015; Parke, 2002).

Fathers' sensitivity toward infants predicts attachment security, but less strongly than mothers'. Security is less common in infant ties with fathers than with mothers, perhaps because fathers typically spend less time with their infants (Brown, Mangelsdorf, & Neff, 2012; Fuertes et al., 2016; Lucassen et al., 2011). At the same time, interventions aimed at increasing parental sensitivity and attachment security, though successful with both mothers and fathers, appear more effective with fathers (Bakermans-Kranenburg, Van IJzendoorn, & Juffer, 2003). As infancy progresses, mothers and fathers in many cultures, including Australia, Canada, Germany, India, Israel, Italy, Japan, and the United States, tend to interact differently with their babies: Mothers devote more time to physical care and expressing affection, and fathers to playful interaction (Freeman & Newland, 2010; Pleck, 2012).

Also, mothers and fathers tend to play differently. Mothers more often provide toys, talk to infants, and gently play conventional games like pat-a-cake and peekaboo. In contrast, fathers—especially with their infant sons—tend to engage in highly stimulating physical play with bursts of excitement and surprise (Feldman, 2003). As long as fathers are also sensitive, this stimulating, startling play style helps babies regulate emotion in intensely arousing situations and may prepare them to venture confidently into active, unpredictable contexts, including novel physical environments and play with peers (Cabrera et al., 2007; Hazen et al., 2010). Fathers' sensitive, challenging play with preschoolers is associated with favorable emotional and social adjustment from early childhood to early adulthood (Bureau et al., 2017; Grossmann et al, 2008; StGeorge, Wroe, & Cashin, 2018). In contrast, paternal insensitivity during play is linked to preschoolers' attachment insecurity and externalizing problems, even after other factors related to these outcomes (such as SES and parental stress) have been controlled.

LOOK and LISTEN

Observe parents at play with infants at home or a family gathering, and describe both similarities and differences in mothers' and fathers' behaviors. Are your observations consistent with research findings?

Social Issues: Health | Does Child Care in Infancy Threaten Attachment Security and Later Adjustment?

A caregiver supports exploration and social interaction in toddlers, one with cerebral palsy. High-quality child care, with generous caregiver–child ratios, small group sizes, and knowledgeable caregivers, can be part of a system that promotes all aspects of development, including attachment security.

Are infants who experience daily separations from their employed parents and early placement in child care at risk for attachment insecurity and developmental problems? Evidence from the U.S. National Institute of Child Health and Development (NICHD) Study of Early Child Care—the largest longitudinal investigation of the effects of child care to date, which included more than 1,300 infants and their families—confirmed that nonparental care by itself does not affect attachment quality (NICHD Early Child Care Research Network, 2001). Rather, the relationship between child care and emotional well-being depends on both family and child-care experiences.

Family Circumstances

We have seen that family conditions affect children's attachment security and later adjustment. The NICHD Study showed that parenting quality, based on a combination of maternal sensitivity and HOME scores (see page 222 in Chapter 6), exerts a more powerful impact on children's adjustment than does exposure to child care (NICHD Early Childhood Research Network, 1998; Watamura et al., 2011).

For employed parents, balancing work and caregiving can be stressful. Mothers who are fatigued and anxious because they feel overloaded by work and family pressures may respond less sensitively to their babies, thereby risking the infant's security. As paternal involvement in caregiving has risen (see page 267), many more U.S. fathers in dual-earner families also report role overload (Pew Research Center, 2018a).

Quality and Extent of Child Care

Nevertheless, poor-quality child care may contribute to a higher rate of insecure attachment. In the NICHD Study, when babies were exposed to combined home and child-care risk factors—insensitive caregiving at home along with insensitive caregiving in child care, long hours in child care, or more than one child-care arrangement—the rate of attachment insecurity increased. Overall, mother–child interaction was more favorable when children attended higher-quality child care and also spent fewer hours in child care (NICHD Early Child Care Research Network, 1997, 1999).

Furthermore, when these children reached age 3, a history of higher-quality child care predicted better social skills (NICHD Early Child Care Research Network, 2002b). However, at ages 4½ to 5, children averaging more than 30 child-care hours per week displayed more externalizing problems, especially defiance, disobedience, and aggression (NICHD Early Child Care Research Network, 2003a, 2006).

This does not necessarily mean that child care causes behavior problems. Rather, heavy exposure to substandard care, which is widespread in the United States, may promote these difficulties, especially when combined with family risk factors. A closer look at the NICHD participants during the preschool years revealed that those in both poor-quality home and child-care environments fared worst in social skills and problem behaviors, whereas those in both high-quality home and child-care environments fared best. In between were preschoolers in high-quality child care but poor-quality homes (Watamura et al., 2011). These children benefited from the *protective influence* of high-quality child care.

Evidence from other industrialized nations confirms that full-time child care need not harm children's development. For example, amount of time spent in child care in Norway, which offers high-quality, government-subsidized center-based care, is unrelated to children's behavior problems (Zachrisson et al., 2013). And when family income drops, Norwegian children who don't attend child care show more behavior problems than children who do attend (Zachrisson & Dearing, 2015).

Still, some children may be particularly stressed by long child-care hours. Many infants, toddlers, and preschoolers attending child-care centers for full days show a mild increase in saliva concentrations of the stress hormone cortisol across the day—a pattern that does not occur on days they spend at home. Children rated as highly fearful by their caregivers experience an especially sharp increase in cortisol levels (Gunnar et al., 2011; O'Brien, Franco, & Dunn, 2014). Inhibited children may find the constant company of large numbers of peers particularly stressful. Nevertheless, a secure attachment to a professional caregiver is protective (Badanes, Dmitrieva, & Watamura, 2012). It is associated with falling cortisol levels across the child-care day.

Conclusions

Taken together, research suggests that some infants may be at risk for attachment insecurity and adjustment problems due to inadequate child care, long hours in such care, and parental role overload. But it is inappropriate to use these findings to justify a reduction in child-care services. When family incomes are limited or mothers who want to work are forced to stay at home, children's emotional security is not promoted.

Instead, it makes sense to increase the availability of high-quality child care and to relieve role overload by providing parents with paid employment leave (see pages 132–133 in Chapter 4) and opportunities for part-time work. Longer employment leaves in the first year are linked to more sensitive maternal interaction with infants and, in turn, to increased attachment security in the second year (Plotka & Busch-Rossnagel, 2018). Similarly, part-time (as opposed to full-time) employment is associated with maternal sensitivity and a higher-quality home environment, which predicts more favorable development in early childhood (Brooks-Gunn, Han, & Waldfogel, 2010).

Finally, the professional caregiver's relationship with the baby is vital. When caregiver–child ratios are generous, group sizes are small, and caregivers are educated about child development, caregivers' interactions are more positive, their attachments to babies are more secure, and children develop more favorably—cognitively, emotionally, and socially (Biringen et al., 2012; Howes, 2016). Child care with these characteristics can become part of an ecological system that relieves parental and child stress, thereby promoting healthy attachment and development.

Play is a vital context in which fathers build secure attachments. It may be especially influential in cultures where long work hours prevent most fathers from sharing in infant caregiving, such as Japan (Ishii-Kuntz, 2013). In many Western nations, however, a strict division of parental roles—mother as caregiver, father as playmate—has changed over the past several decades in response to women's workforce participation and to cultural valuing of gender equality.

National surveys of thousands of U.S. married couples with children reveal that although their involvement continues to fall far short of mothers', today's fathers spend more than triple the amount of time caring for children as fathers did in 1965 (see Figure 7.5) (Pew Research Center, 2018a, 2018b). Paternal availability to children is fairly similar across U.S. SES and ethnic groups, with one exception: Hispanic fathers spend more time engaged with their infants and young children, probably because of the particularly high value that Hispanic cultures place on family involvement (Cabrera, Aldoney, & Tamis-LeMonda, 2014; Hofferth, 2003).

A warm marital bond and supportive coparenting (see page 66 in Chapter 2) promote both parents' sensitivity and involvement and children's attachment security, but they are especially important for fathers. See the Cultural Influences box on page 268 for cross-cultural evidence documenting this conclusion—and also highlighting the powerful role of paternal involvement in children's development.

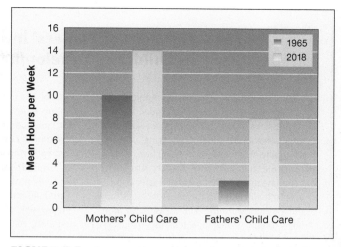

FIGURE 7.5 **Average hours per week U.S. mothers and fathers reported caring for children in 1965 and 2018.** In national surveys of thousands of married couples, mothers' time spent caring for children between birth and age 18 years increased moderately from 1965 to 2018. Though falling far short of mothers', fathers' time devoted to children more than tripled. (Based on Pew Research Center, 2018a, 2018b.)

Grandparent Primary Caregivers   Nearly 1.8 million U.S. grandparents live with grandchildren but apart from the children's parents in *skipped-generation families* (U.S. Census Bureau, 2016). The number of grandparents with primary responsibility for rearing grandchildren has increased over the past two decades, with an especially sharp rise during the economic recession of 2007 to 2009. The arrangement occurs in all ethnic groups, but more often in African-American, Hispanic, and Native-American families than in European-American families. Although grandparent caregivers are more likely to be women than men, many grandfathers participate (Ellis & Simmons, 2014; Fuller-Thomson & Minkler, 2005, 2007). As we saw in Chapter 2, in U.S. ethnic minority groups that highly value close, supportive extended family ties, grandparents often share in child rearing (see page 74). But grandparents who fully assume the child-rearing role generally do so when parents' troubled lives—severe financial hardship, substance abuse, child abuse and neglect, family violence, or physical or mental illness—threaten children's safety and security (Smith, 2016). Often these families take in two or more children.

As a result, grandparents in skipped-generation families engage in child rearing under highly stressful life circumstances. Unfavorable child-rearing experiences have left their mark on the children, who show high rates of learning, emotional, and behavior problems. Absent parents' adjustment difficulties strain family relationships. Grandchildren also introduce financial burdens into households that often are already low-income (Hayslip, Blumenthal, & Garner, 2014; Henderson & Bailey, 2015). All these factors heighten grandparents' emotional distress.

Grandparent caregivers, at a time when they anticipated having more time for spouses, friends, and leisure, instead have less. Many report feeling emotionally drained, depressed, and worried about what will happen to the children if their own health fails (Henderson & Bailey, 2015). Nevertheless, because they provide physical and emotional care for an extended time and are invested in the child's well-being, grandparent caregivers forge significant attachment relationships with their grandchildren. Warm grandparent–grandchild bonds help protect children from worsening adjustment problems, even under conditions of great hardship (Hicks & Goedereis, 2009). Still, grandparent caregivers have a tremendous need for social and financial support and intervention services for their at-risk grandchildren.

Despite stressful family conditions, grandparents who provide long-term physical and emotional care form deep attachments with their grandchildren.

Siblings   Despite declines in family size, nearly 80 percent of U.S. children grow up with at least one sibling (U.S. Census Bureau, 2017a). The arrival of a new baby is a challenging experience for most preschoolers, who—realizing that they must now share their parents'

Cultural Influences

The Role of Fathers' Involvement in Children's Development

In studies of many societies and ethnic groups around the world, researchers coded fathers' expressions of love and nurturance—evident in such behaviors as cuddling, hugging, comforting, playing, verbally expressing love, and praising the child's behavior. Fathers' sustained affectionate involvement predicted later cognitive, emotional, and social competence as strongly as did mothers' warmth—and occasionally more strongly (Daniel, Madigan, & Jenkins, 2016; Veneziano, 2003). In Western cultures, paternal warmth and secure attachment are associated with higher academic achievement, better social skills, and a reduction in child and adolescent behavior problems (Bornstein, 2015; Lamb & Lewis, 2013; Michiels et al., 2010).

What factors promote fathers' involvement? Cross-cultural research reveals a consistent association between the amount of time fathers spend near infants and toddlers and their expressions of caring and affection (Rohner & Veneziano, 2001). Consider the Aka of the Central African Republic, where fathers spend more time in physical proximity to their babies than in any other known

society. Aka fathers are within arm's reach of infants more than half the day, and they pick up, cuddle, and play with their babies at least five times as often as fathers in other hunting-and-gathering societies. Why are Aka fathers so involved? The bond between Aka husband and wife is unusually cooperative and intimate. Throughout the day, couples share hunting, food preparation, and social and leisure activities (Hewlett, 1992). The more time Aka parents are together, the greater the father's loving interaction with his baby.

In Western cultures as well, happily married fathers whose partners coparent cooperatively with them spend more time with and interact more effectively with infants. In contrast, marital dissatisfaction is associated with insensitive paternal care (Brown et al., 2010; Sevigny & Loutzenhiser, 2010). Clearly, fathers' relationships with their partners and their babies are closely linked. Evidence for the power of fathers' involvement, reported in virtually every culture and ethnic group studied, is reason to encourage and support their nurturing care of young children.

In both Western and non-Western nations, fathers' affectionate, sustained involvement predicts long-term favorable cognitive, emotional, and social development.

---

attention and affection—often display a temporary increase in aggressive behavior and become demanding, clingy, deliberately naughty, and less affectionate with their parents for a time. Attachment security may also decline, especially for children over age 2 (old enough to feel threatened and displaced) and for those with mothers under stress (Teti et al., 1996; Volling, 2012; Volling et al., 2017).

Yet resentment is only one feature of the rich emotional relationship that starts to build between siblings after a baby's birth. Older children also show affection and concern—kissing

The arrival of a new baby is a difficult experience for most preschoolers. Maternal warmth toward both children assures the older sibling of continuing parental love, models affectionate caring, and is related to positive sibling interaction.

and patting the baby and calling out, "Mom, he needs you," when the infant cries. By the end of the first year, babies typically spend much time with older siblings and are comforted by the presence of a preschool-age brother or sister during short parental absences. Throughout childhood, children continue to treat older siblings as attachment figures, turning to them for comfort in stressful situations when parents are unavailable (Seibert & Kerns, 2009). And in the second year, as toddlers imitate and join in play with their brothers and sisters, siblings start to become gratifying sources of companionship (Barr & Hayne, 2003).

Nevertheless, individual differences in sibling relationships emerge early. Temperament plays an important role. High emotional reactivity on the part of the older child increases the likelihood of angry, aggressive reactions after the baby's arrival and rising sibling conflict (Dunn, 1994; Kolak & Volling, 2013). And maternal warmth toward both children is related to positive sibling interaction and to preschoolers' support of a distressed younger sibling (Volling, 2001; Volling & Belsky, 1992). In contrast, maternal harshness and lack of involvement are linked to antagonistic

APPLYING WHAT WE KNOW

Encouraging Affectionate Ties Between Infants and Their Preschool Siblings

SUGGESTION	DESCRIPTION
Spend extra time with the older child.	Parents can minimize the older child's feelings of being deprived of affection and attention by setting aside time to spend with the child. Fathers can be especially helpful, planning special outings with the preschooler and taking over care of the baby so the mother can be with the older child.
Handle sibling misbehavior with patience.	When parents respond patiently to the older sibling's misbehavior and demands for attention, these reactions are usually temporary. Parents can give the preschooler opportunities to feel proud of being more grown-up than the baby—for example, by encouraging the older child to assist with feeding, bathing, dressing, and offering toys, and showing appreciation for these efforts.
Discuss the baby's wants and needs.	By helping the older sibling understand the baby's point of view, parents can promote friendly, considerate behavior. They can say, for example, "He's so little that he just can't wait to be fed" or "He's trying to reach his rattle, and he can't."
Express positive emotion toward your partner and engage in joint problem solving.	When parents mutually support each other's parenting behavior, their good communication helps the older sibling cope adaptively with jealousy and conflict.

sibling relationships (Howe, Aquan-Assee, & Bukowski, 2001). However, older siblings who remain securely attached to their fathers after the baby's arrival are less likely to experience worsening conflict with their mothers and are more likely to forge positive sibling ties later in the first year (Volling et al., 2017). A close father–child bond seems to support children in adjusting to siblinghood.

Finally, a good marriage and effective coparenting are correlated with the capacity of older preschool siblings—especially those high in emotional reactivity—to cope adaptively with jealousy and conflict (Kolak & Volling, 2013; Volling et al., 2017). Perhaps good communication between parents serves as a model of effective problem solving. It may also foster a generally happy family environment, giving children less reason to feel jealous.

Refer to Applying What We Know above for ways to promote positive relationships between infants and their preschool siblings. Siblings offer a rich social context in which children learn and practice a wide range of skills, including affectionate caring, conflict resolution, and control of hostile and envious feelings.

7.3.7 From Attachment to Peer Sociability

In cultures where agemates have regular contact during the first year of life, peer sociability begins early. By age 6 months, Caitlin and Timmy occasionally looked, reached, smiled, and babbled when they saw each other. These isolated social acts increase until, by the end of the first year, infant peers occasionally exchange smiles, laughs, gestures, and imitations of one another's behavior (Vandell & Mueller, 1995).

Between 1 and 2 years, as toddlers appreciate that others have intentions, desires, and emotions distinct from their own, they increasingly view one another as playmates (Brownell & Kopp, 2007). As a result, coordinated interaction occurs more often, largely in the form of offering each other objects, sharing positive emotions, and mutual imitation of play behaviors (Vandell et al., 2006; Williams, Mastergeorge, & Ontai, 2010). As they approach age 2, toddlers use words to talk about and influence a peer's behavior, as when Caitlin said to Grace, "Let's play

As toddlers approach age 2, advances in peer sociability are evident in increasing use of language to talk about and influence one another's behavior.

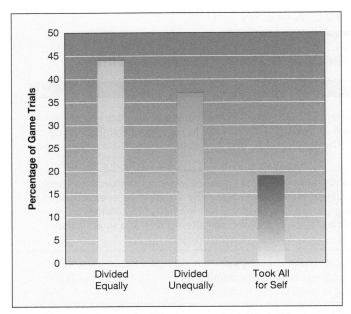

FIGURE 7.6 **Toddlers' willingness to divide colorful marbles for playing a game with a peer.** Pairs of 18- and 24-month-olds were shown four colorful marbles in a container and told the marbles could be used to play "the jingle game." An adult then demonstrated the game by throwing a marble into "the jingle box," which caused a jingling sound. During four game trials, toddlers' spontaneous divisions of the marbles were recorded. They seldom behaved selfishly, taking all the marbles for themselves. Rather, on most trials, they divided the marbles equally or divided them so that each pair member got some. (Based on Ulber, Hamann, & Tomasello, 2015.)

chase," and after the game got going, encouraged, "Hey, good running!" (Eckerman & Peterman, 2001).

These reciprocal exchanges promote peer engagement and probably facilitate joint understandings, including toddlers increasing sensitivity to playmates' needs evident in helping and sharing. In one investigation, 18-month-olds spontaneously helped an agemate continue playing a game by providing the peer with the necessary objects, which were accessible only to the helping child (Hepach, Kante, & Tomasello, 2017). Toddlers readily helped even when the game was not engaging to them (its attractive features were visible only to the game-playing peer) and when the peer did not ask for assistance! In another study, when pairs of 18- and 24-month-olds were exposed to attractive play materials (colorful marbles for playing a game) that neither owned ahead of time, they seldom tried to monopolize the materials, taking all of them for themselves. Rather, they divided them so each child got some and often divided them equally (see Figure 7.6) (Ulber, Hamann, & Tomasello, 2015). An opportunity to collaborate with a peer partner in playing a game to secure the marbles further increased toddlers' willingness to give each player an equal share.

Early peer sociability is promoted by the caregiver–child bond. Toddlers who have a warm parental relationship or who attend high-quality child care with small group sizes and generous caregiver–child ratios—features that promote warm, stimulating caregiving and gentle support for interacting with peers—engage in more positive and extended peer exchanges. These children, in turn, display more socially competent behavior as preschoolers (Deynoot-Schaub & Riksen-Walraven, 2006a, 2006b; Williams, Mastergeorge, & Ontai, 2010).

7.3.8 Attachment and Later Development

According to Erikson's psychosocial theory and Bowlby's ethological theory, the inner feelings of affection and security that result from an early, healthy attachment relationship should promote many favorable aspects of emotional and social development. The most extensive longitudinal study conducted to date, which followed children from infancy to age 34, yielded outcomes consistent with this prediction. On reaching the preschool years, children who had been securely attached in the first two years were rated by teachers as higher in self-esteem, social skills, and empathy than were their insecurely attached counterparts, who displayed more behavior problems. When followed up at age 11 in summer camp, children who had been secure as infants and toddlers had more positive peer ties, closer friendships, and better social skills, as judged by camp counselors. And as these well-functioning school-age children became adolescents and young adults, they continued to benefit from more supportive social networks, formed more stable and gratifying romantic relationships, and attained higher levels of education (Elicker, Englund, & Sroufe, 1992; Sroufe, 2002, 2016; Sroufe et al., 2005).

The more favorable social relationships of children and youths with a secure attachment history are consistent with Bowlby's conviction that attachment security supports healthy psychological development through children's internal working models of their social world. A wealth of research confirms that an early, secure child–parent bond predicts diverse, interrelated aspects of social competence: a more confident and complex self-concept, more advanced emotional understanding of self and other, more effective emotional self-regulation, greater skill in relating to peers and forming gratifying friendships, a stronger sense of moral responsibility, more positive relationships with teachers, and higher motivation to achieve in school (Drake, Belsky, & Fearon, 2014; Groh et al., 2014; Thompson, 2015, 2016; Viddal et al., 2015).

At the same time, the evidence indicates that early attachment security is more strongly associated with favorable outcomes when children experience parental sensitivity and security not just in infancy but also in later years (Lamb et al., 1985; Thompson, 2013). In contrast, children whose parents are persistently insensitive or who, over a long period, are exposed to a negative family climate tend to establish enduring patterns of avoidant, resistant, or disorganized behavior that heighten their risk for lasting developmental difficulties.

A close look at relationships of early parenting and attachment quality to children's later adjustment supports the importance of *continuity of good caregiving and attachment security* for long-term, favorable adjustment. Disorganized/disoriented attachment, a pattern associated with serious parental psychological problems and extended, highly maladaptive caregiving, is strongly linked to internalizing and externalizing behavior problems in childhood (Moss et al., 2006; Steele & Steele, 2014). And when researchers tracked a large sample of children from ages 1 to 3 years, those with histories of secure attachment followed by sensitive parenting scored highest in cognitive, emotional, and social outcomes. Those with histories of insecure attachment followed by insensitive parenting scored lowest, while those with mixed histories of attachment and maternal sensitivity scored in between (Belsky & Fearon, 2002). Specifically, insecurely attached infants whose mothers became more positive and supportive in early childhood showed signs of developmental recovery.

Does this trend remind you of our discussion of *resilience* in Chapter 1? A child whose parental caregiving improves or who has other compensating affectionate ties can bounce back from adversity. In contrast, a child who experiences tender care in infancy but lacks sympathetic ties later on is at risk for problems.

Although secure attachment in infancy does not guarantee continued good parenting, it does launch the parent–child relationship on a positive path. But the effects of early attachment security are *conditional*—dependent on the quality of the baby's future close relationships. Finally, as we will see again in later chapters, attachment is just one of the complex influences on children's psychological development.

ASK YOURSELF

Connect ■ Review research on emotional self-regulation on pages 247–248. How do the caregiving experiences of securely attached infants promote emotional self-regulation?

Apply ■ What attachment pattern did Timmy display when Vanessa picked him up from child care, and what factors probably contributed to it?

Reflect ■ How would you characterize your internal working model? What factors, in addition to your early relationships with parents, might have influenced it?

7.4 Self-Development

Infancy is a rich formative period for the development of physical and social understanding. In Chapter 6, you learned that infants develop an appreciation of the permanence of objects. And in this chapter, we have seen that over the first year, infants recognize and respond appropriately to others' emotions and distinguish familiar from unfamiliar people. That both objects and people achieve an independent, stable existence for the infant implies that knowledge of the self as a separate, permanent entity is also emerging.

7.4 Describe the development of self-awareness in infancy and toddlerhood, along with the emotional and social capacities it supports.

7.4.1 Self-Awareness

After Caitlin's bath, Carolyn often held her in front of the bathroom mirror. As early as the first few months, Caitlin smiled and returned friendly behaviors to her image. At what age did she realize that the charming baby gazing and grinning back was herself?

Beginnings of Self-Awareness   At birth, infants sense that they are physically distinct from their surroundings. For example, newborns display a stronger rooting reflex in response to external stimulation (an adult's finger touching their cheek) than to self-stimulation (their

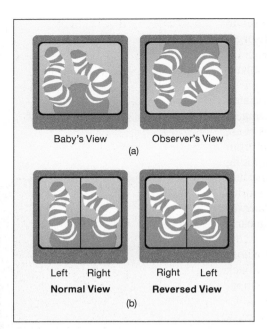

FIGURE 7.7   Three-month-olds' emerging self-awareness, as indicated by reactions to video images. (a) When shown two side-by-side views of their kicking legs, babies looked longer at the novel, observer's view than at their own view. (b) When shown a normal view of their leg positions alongside a reversed view, infants looked longer at the novel, reversed view. (Based on Rochat, 1998.)

own hand contacting their cheek) (Rochat & Hespos, 1997). Newborns' remarkable capacity for intermodal perception (see page 191 in Chapter 5) supports the beginnings of self-awareness (Rochat, 2015). As they feel their own touch, feel and watch their limbs move, and feel and hear themselves cry, babies experience intermodal matches that differentiate their own body from surrounding bodies and objects.

Over the first few months, infants distinguish their own visual image from other stimuli, but their self-awareness is limited—expressed only in perception and action. When shown two side-by-side video images of their kicking legs, one from their own perspective (camera behind the baby) and one from an observer's perspective (camera in front of the baby), 3-month-olds looked longer at the observer's view (see Figure 7.7a). In another video-image comparison, they looked longer at a reversal of their leg positions than at a normal view (see Figure 7.7b) (Rochat, 1998). This suggests that young babies have a sense of their own body as a distinct entity, since they have habituated to it, as indicated by their interest in novel views of the body.

This discrimination of a normal view of one's own limbs from novel views in real-time video presentations reflects an *implicit sense of self–world differentiation.* Implicit self-awareness is also evident in young infants' social expectations. Recall that as early as 2 to 3 months, infants start to engage in exchanges of smiles and vocalizations with their caregivers, and they protest or withdraw when give-and-take with a responsive adult is disrupted. Within these turn-taking interactions, infants display a sense of their own agency in relating to others, which suggests an emerging sense of self distinct from other people. By 4 months, they look and smile more at video images of others than video images of themselves, indicating that they treat another person (as opposed to the self) as a potential social partner (Rochat & Striano, 2002). These early signs of self-experience serve as the foundation for development of *explicit self-awareness*—conscious realization that the self is a unique object in a world of objects.

Explicit Self-Awareness   During the second year, toddlers become consciously aware of the self's physical features. In several studies, 9- to 28-month-olds were placed in front of a mirror. Then, under the pretext of wiping the baby's face, each mother rubbed red dye on her child's nose or forehead. Younger babies touched the mirror as if the red mark had nothing to do with them. But the majority of those older than 18 to 20 months touched or rubbed their noses or foreheads, indicating awareness of their unique facial appearance (Lewis, 2017; Lewis & Brooks-Gunn, 1979). And some toddlers act silly or coy in front of the mirror, playfully experimenting with the way the self looks (Bullock & Lutkenhaus, 1990).

Around age 2, *self-recognition*—identification of the self as a physically unique being—is well under way. Children point to themselves in photos and refer to themselves by name or with a personal pronoun ("I" or "me") (Lewis & Ramsay, 2004). Soon they identify themselves in images with less detail and fidelity than mirrors. Around age 2½ when they see themselves in a live video with a sticker on top of their heads that had been surreptitiously placed there, most reach for the sticker, and around age 3 most recognize their own shadow (Cameron & Gallup, 1988; Suddendorf, Simcock, & Nielsen, 2007).

As self-recognition takes shape, older toddlers also construct an explicit *body self-awareness.* At the end of the second year, they realize that their own body can serve as an obstacle, are able to locate their own body parts, and know how their body parts are spatially organized (Brownell et al., 2010; Moore et al., 2007). Toddlers who are more advanced at recognizing themselves in mirrors and photos attain these milestones sooner, and they also have larger body-part vocabularies (Waugh & Brownell, 2015). This suggests that firmer self-awareness contributes to toddlers' developing understanding of the features of their own body.

Nevertheless, toddlers make **scale errors,** attempting to do things that their body size makes impossible. For example, they will try to put on dolls' clothes, sit in a doll-sized chair, or walk through a doorway too narrow for them to pass through (Brownell, Zerwas, & Ramani, 2007; DeLoache et al., 2013). Possibly, toddlers lack an accurate understanding of their own body dimensions. Alternatively, they may simply be exploring the consequences of squeezing into restricted spaces, which they are far less likely

© ELLEN B. SENISI

This 18-month-old makes silly faces in a mirror, a playful response to her reflection that indicates she is aware of herself as a separate being and recognizes her unique physical features.

to try when the risk of harming themselves is high (for example, if the too-narrow doorway is next to a ledge where they could fall) (Franchak & Adolph, 2012). Other evidence suggests that toddlers, in focusing intently on how they can act on objects, often ignore size information (Grzyb et al., 2017). Scale errors decline gradually, between ages 2 and 4. Young preschoolers are still learning to process physical information when acting with their own bodies.

Influences on Self-Awareness According to many theorists, self-awareness and self-recognition develop as infants and toddlers increasingly realize that their own actions cause objects and people to react in predictable ways (Nadel, Prepin, & Okanda, 2005; Rochat, 2013). Sensitive caregiving seems to play an important role. Compared to their insecurely attached agemates, securely attached toddlers display more complex self-related actions during play, such as making a doll labeled as the self (with the child's own name) take a drink or kiss a teddy bear. They also show greater body self-awareness—for example, in labeling body parts (Pipp, Easterbrooks, & Brown, 1993; Pipp, Easterbrooks, & Harmon, 1992). And 18-month-olds who often establish joint attention with their caregivers are advanced in mirror self-recognition (Nichols, Fox, & Mundy, 2005). Joint attention offers toddlers many opportunities to engage in social referencing—to compare their own and others' reactions to objects and events—which may enhance their awareness of their own physical uniqueness.

Cultural variations exist in early self-development. In one investigation, urban middle-SES German and East Indian toddlers attained mirror self-recognition earlier than toddlers of non-Western farming communities, such as the Nso people of rural Cameroon and rural families of East India (see Figure 7.8) (Kärtner et al., 2012). Urban German and, to a lesser extent, urban East Indian mothers placed considerable emphasis on *autonomous child-rearing goals,* including promoting personal talents and interests and expressing one's own preferences, which strongly predicted earlier mirror self-recognition. In contrast, Nso and East Indian rural mothers valued *relational child rearing goals*—doing what parents say and sharing with others. In related research, Nso toddlers, though delayed in mirror self-recognition, displayed an earlier capacity to comply with adult requests than did middle-SES urban Greek toddlers, whose mothers encouraged child autonomy (Keller et al., 2004).

Self-Awareness and Early Emotional and Social Development Self-awareness quickly becomes a central part of children's emotional and social lives. Recall that self-conscious emotions depend on a strengthening sense of self. Self-awareness also leads to first efforts to understand another's perspective. We have seen that toddlers increasingly appreciate others' intentions, feelings, and desires—knowledge that provides the motivational basis for positive social behaviors that become more common over the second year.

Already, 15- to 18-month-olds display a sense of fairness: They expect adults to divide resources and rewards equally among participants (Sloane, Baillargeon, & Premack, 2012; Sommerville et al., 2013). And as we saw in our discussion of peer sociability, toddlers soon act in accord with this expectation. When 2-year-olds assert ownership over toys with the refrain, "Mine!," they mostly limit this claim to their own possessions (Ross, Friedman, & Field, 2015). They also say, "Yours!," often handing over toys that belong to their playmates.

Older toddlers who have experienced sensitive caregiving and emotionally available parents draw on their advancing capacity to distinguish what happens to themselves from what happens to others to express first signs of **empathy**—the ability to understand another's emotional state and *feel with* that person, or respond emotionally in a

Ask several parents of 1½- to 3-year-olds if they have observed any instances of scale errors. Have the parent hand the toddler doll-sized clothing (hat, jacket, or shoe) or furniture (table, slide, or car) and watch for scale errors.

A toddler guides her younger sibling in community dancing in a village of the San people of the Kalahari Desert, South Africa. Like many non-Western farming societies, the San value relational child rearing that encourages doing what parents say and sharing with others.

FIGURE 7.8 **Mirror self-recognition at 19 months in four cultures.** Urban middle-SES German and East Indian toddlers attained mirror self-recognition earlier than Nso toddlers of rural Cameroon and toddlers of rural East India—a finding that held even after toddlers were provided considerable experience in seeing themselves in mirrors. Urban German and East Indian mothers emphasized autonomous child-rearing goals, which strongly predicted earlier self-recognition. In contrast, rural Nso and East Indian mothers valued relational child-rearing goals. (Based on Kärtner et al., 2012.)

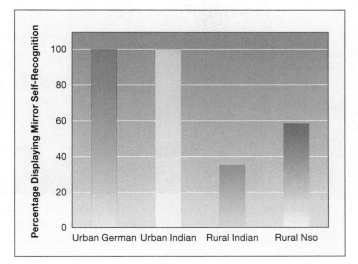

similar way (Bischoff-Köhler, 2012; Moreno, Klute, & Robinson, 2008). They communicate concern when others are distressed and may offer what they themselves find comforting—a hug, a reassuring comment, or a favorite doll or blanket.

At the same time, toddlers demonstrate clearer awareness of how to upset others. One 18-month-old heard her mother talking to another adult about an older sibling: "Anny is really frightened of spiders. In fact, there's a particular toy spider that we've got that she just hates" (Dunn, 1989, p. 107). The innocent-looking toddler ran to the bedroom, returned with the toy spider, and pushed it in front of Anny's face!

7.4.2 Categorizing the Self

By the end of the second year, language becomes a powerful tool in self-development. Between 18 and 30 months, children develop a **categorical self** as they classify themselves and others on the basis of age ("baby," "boy," or "man"), sex ("boy" or "girl"), physical characteristics ("big," "strong"), and even goodness versus badness ("I good girl." "Tommy mean!"). They also start to refer to the self's competencies ("Did it!" "I can't") (Stipek, Gralinski, & Kopp, 1990).

Toddlers use their limited understanding of these social categories to organize their own behavior. As early as their first birthday, they select and play in a more involved way with toys that are stereotyped for their own gender—dolls and tea sets for girls, trucks and cars for boys. Once toddlers can label their own gender, these play preferences rise sharply. Then parents encourage gender-typed behavior further by responding more positively when toddlers display it (Hines, 2015; Zosuls et al., 2009). As we will see in Chapter 10, gender typing increases dramatically during early childhood.

7.4.3 Self-Control

Self-awareness also contributes to *effortful control,* the extent to which children can inhibit impulses, manage negative emotion, and behave in socially acceptable ways. To behave in a self-controlled fashion, children must think of themselves as separate, autonomous beings who can direct their own actions. And they must have the representational and memory capacities to recall a caregiver's earlier directive ("Caitlin, don't touch that light socket!") and apply it to their current behavior.

As these capacities emerge between 12 and 18 months, toddlers first become capable of **compliance:** They show clear awareness of caregivers' wishes and expectations and can obey simple requests and commands. And, as every parent knows, they can also decide to do just the opposite! Although defiance in preschoolers is associated with negative parent–

This father encourages compliance and the beginnings of self-control. The toddler joins in dusting snow off the family car with an eager, willing spirit, which suggests he is adopting the adult's directive as his own.

child relationships and poor adjustment, toddlers who sometimes strongly resist parental demands tend to have sensitive, supportive parents with whom they interact positively. These parents recognize the young child's need for self-assertion and autonomy (Dix et al., 2007).

Indeed, active resistance in toddlerhood does not predict later, persisting defiance. Rather, for most toddlers, assertiveness and opposition occur alongside compliance with an eager, willing spirit, which suggests that the child is beginning to adopt the adult's directives as her own (Kochanska, Murray, & Harlan, 2000). Compliance quickly leads to toddlers' first consciencelike verbalizations—for example, correcting the self by saying "No, can't" before reaching for a treat or jumping on the sofa.

Researchers often study the early emergence of self-control by giving children tasks that, like the situations just mentioned, require **delay of gratification**—waiting for an appropriate time and place to engage in a tempting act. Between ages 1½ and 4, children show an increasing capacity to wait before eating a treat, opening a present, or playing with a toy (Cole, LeDonne, & Tan,

APPLYING WHAT WE KNOW

Helping Toddlers Develop Compliance and Self-Control

SUGGESTION	RATIONALE
Respond to the toddler with sensitivity and encouragement.	Toddlers whose parents are sensitive and supportive sometimes actively resist, but they are also more compliant and self-controlled.
Provide advance notice when the toddler must stop an enjoyable activity.	Toddlers find it more difficult to stop a pleasant activity that is already under way than to wait before engaging in a desired action.
Offer many prompts and reminders.	Toddlers' ability to remember and comply with rules is limited; they need continuous adult oversight and patient assistance.
Respond to self-controlled behavior with verbal and physical approval.	Praise and hugs reinforce appropriate behavior, increasing the likelihood that it will occur again.
Encourage selective and sustained attention (see page 213 in Chapter 6).	Development of attention is related to self-control. Children who can shift attention from a captivating stimulus and focus on a less attractive alternative are better at controlling their impulses.
Support language development (see pages 236–237 in Chapter 6).	In the second year, children begin to use language to remind themselves of adult expectations and to delay gratification.
Gradually increase rules in a manner consistent with the toddler's developing capacities.	As cognition and language improve, toddlers can follow more rules related to safety, respect for people and property, family routines, manners, and simple chores.

2013; Vaughn, Kopp, & Krakow, 1984). Children who are advanced in development of attention, language, and suppressing negative emotion tend to be better at delaying gratification—findings that help explain why girls are typically more self-controlled than boys (Else-Quest, 2012). Some toddlers already use verbal and other attention-diverting techniques—talking to themselves, singing, or looking away—to keep from engaging in prohibited acts.

Like effortful control in general, young children's capacity to delay gratification is influenced by both temperament and quality of caregiving. Inhibited children find it easier to wait than angry, irritable children do. But toddlers and preschoolers who experience parental warmth and gentle encouragement are more likely to be cooperative and to resist temptation (Feng & Hooper, 2017; Kochanska & Aksan, 2006). Recall that such parenting—which encourages and models patient, nonimpulsive behavior—is particularly important for emotionally reactive children. And in our consideration of ethnic differences in temperament, we saw that East Asian children, whose mothers emphasize gentle soothing and proximal care, are advanced in effortful control and ability to delay gratification (see page 253). Nso children of rural Cameroon, as well, are ahead of their Western agemates in delay of gratification (Lamm et al., 2017). From an early age, Nso parents expect children to control their own emotions and behavior.

As self-control improves, parents gradually expand the rules they expect toddlers to follow, from safety and respect for property and people to family routines, manners, and simple chores (Gralinski & Kopp, 1993). Still, toddlers' control over their own actions depends on constant parental oversight and reminders. Several prompts ("Remember, we're going to go in just a minute") and gentle insistence were usually necessary to get Caitlin to stop playing so that she and her parents could go on an errand. Applying What We Know above summarizes ways to help toddlers develop compliance and self-control.

As the second year of life drew to a close, Caitlin, Timmy, and Grace's parents were delighted with their children's progress in acquiring the rules of social life. As we will see in Chapter 10, advances in cognition and language, along with parental warmth and reasonable demands for maturity, lead preschoolers to make tremendous strides in this area.

ASK YOURSELF

Connect ■ What type of early parenting fosters the development of emotional self-regulation, secure attachment, and self-control? Why, in each instance, is it effective?

Apply ■ Len, a caregiver of 1- and 2-year-olds, wonders whether toddlers recognize themselves. List signs of self-recognition in the second year that Len can observe. What behaviors reveal that toddlers are still forming objective representations of their own physical features?

Reflect ■ In view of research findings on emotional and social development in the second year, do you think the expression "the terrible twos"—commonly used to characterize typical toddler behavior—is an apt description? Explain.

SUMMARY

7.1 Emotional Development (p. 241)

7.1a Describe the development of basic emotions over the first year, noting the adaptive function of each.

■ During the first half-year, **basic emotions** gradually become clear, well-organized signals. The **social smile** appears between 6 and 10 weeks, though its frequency thereafter varies by culture. Laughter emerges around 3 to 4 months. Happiness strengthens the parent–child bond and fosters physical, cognitive, and social competencies.

© CATTIE COYLE/ALAMY STOCK PHOTO

■ Anger and fear increase in the second half of the first year. **Stranger anxiety** varies with infant-rearing practices. Newly mobile babies use the familiar caregiver as a **secure base.** Sadness often occurs when infants are deprived of a loving caregiver.

7.1b Summarize changes during the first two years in understanding of others' emotions, expression of self-conscious emotions, and emotional self-regulation.

■ **Social referencing** appears at 8 to 10 months as infants' ability to detect the meaning of emotional expressions improves. By the middle of the second year, toddlers realize that others' emotional reactions may differ from their own.

■ During toddlerhood, self-awareness and adult instruction provide the foundation for **self-conscious emotions:** guilt, shame, embarrassment, envy, and pride.

■ **Emotional self-regulation** emerges as the prefrontal cortex functions more effectively, as caregivers sensitively assist infants in adjusting their emotional reactions, and as infants' ability to shift attention improves. In the second year, growth in representation and language leads to more effective ways of regulating emotion.

7.2 Temperament and Development (p. 249)

7.2a Explain the meaning of temperament and how it is measured.

■ Children differ greatly in **temperament.** The pioneering New York Longitudinal Study identified three patterns: the **easy child,** the **difficult child,** and the **slow-to-warm-up child.** Rothbart's influential model of temperament includes dimensions representing emotion, attention, and action along with **effortful control.**

© LAURA DWIGHT PHOTOGRAPHY

■ Temperament is assessed through parental reports, behavior ratings by others familiar with the child, and laboratory observations. Most neurobiological research has focused on distinguishing **inhibited,** or **shy, children** from **uninhibited,** or **sociable, children.**

7.2b Discuss the roles of heredity and environment in the stability of temperament, including the goodness-of-fit model.

■ Temperament has low to moderate stability: It develops with age and can be modified by experience. Long-term prediction from early temperament is best achieved after age 3, when effortful control improves substantially.

■ Temperament has a genetic foundation, but child rearing and cultural beliefs and practices have much to do with maintaining or changing it.

■ Children with self-regulation difficulties function worse than other children when exposed to ineffective parenting but benefit more from good parenting. Parents' tendency to exaggerate siblings' differences also affects development of temperament.

■ According to the **goodness-of-fit model,** parenting practices that fit well with the child's temperament help children achieve adaptive functioning.

7.3 Development of Attachment (p. 256)

7.3a Describe the features of ethological theory of attachment and its view of the development of attachment during the first two years.

■ **Ethological theory of attachment** recognizes the infant's emotional tie to the caregiver as an evolved response that promotes survival. In early infancy, built-in signals help bring infants into close contact with other humans.

■ Around 6 to 8 months, **separation anxiety** and use of the caregiver as a secure base indicate a true attachment bond. As representation and language develop, separation anxiety declines. From early caregiving experiences, children construct an **internal working model** that guides future close relationships.

7.3b Describe techniques for measuring attachment security, the stability of attachment patterns, and cultural variations in attachment behavior.

■ Using the **Strange Situation,** a laboratory technique for assessing the quality of attachment between 1 and 2 years of age, researchers have identified four attachment patterns: **secure, insecure-avoidant, insecure-resistant,** and **disorganized/disoriented attachment.** The **Attachment Q-Sort,** based on home observations of children between ages 1 and 5, yields a score ranging from low to high security.

■ Securely attached babies in middle-SES families with favorable life conditions more often maintain their attachment pattern than insecure babies. However, the disorganized/disoriented pattern is highly stable.

■ Wide cultural variations in infants' ways of expressing attachment reflect cultural differences in child-rearing beliefs and goals.

7.3c Discuss factors that influence early attachment security, infants' and toddlers' formation of multiple attachments, and how attachment paves the way for peer sociability.

■ Attachment security is influenced by early availability of a consistent caregiver, quality of caregiving, the fit between the baby's temperament and parenting practices, and family circumstances.

■ Late adoption from institutionalized settings is associated with high rates of attachment insecurity and emotional and social difficulties.

■ In Western cultures that value independence, **sensitive caregiving** involves responding contingently to infant signals and "reading" the baby's mental states. In non-Western village communities and Asian cultures that value interdependence, proximal care is deemed sensitive because it promotes connection to the social group.

■ Babies genetically predisposed to emotional reactivity are at increased risk for insecure attachment, but only when exposed to negative parenting. With exposure to sensitive caregiving, these infants are more likely to be securely attached.

■ Parents' internal working models are modestly related to their sensitive caregiving and own infants' attachment security. However, parents' childhood experiences do not transfer directly to quality of attachment with their children.

■ Infants develop strong affectionate ties to fathers, who tend to engage in more exciting physical play than do mothers. In Western cultures, paternal warmth and secure attachment are associated with higher academic achievement, better social skills, and a reduction in child and adolescent behavior problems.

© LAURA DWIGHT PHOTOGRAPHY

■ Despite highly stressful life circumstances, grandparents who serve as primary caregivers for grandchildren forge significant attachment ties that help protect children from worsening adjustment problems.

■ Early in the first year, infants start to form rich emotional relationships with siblings that combine rivalry and resentment with affection and sympathetic concern. Temperament, parenting, and marital quality affect individual differences in quality of sibling relationships.

■ Peer sociability begins in infancy with isolated social acts followed by reciprocal exchanges that promote peer engagement and increasing sensitivity to playmates' needs. A warm caregiver–child bond supports peer sociability.

7.3d Discuss the relationship of attachment patterns in infancy and of caregiving quality from infancy through adolescence to children's long-term adjustment.

■ Children's long-term, favorable adjustment is promoted by continuity of good caregiving and attachment security. With improved caregiving, insecurely attached infants show signs of developmental recovery.

7.4 Self-Development (p. 271)

7.4 Describe the development of self-awareness in infancy and toddlerhood, along with the emotional and social capacities it supports.

■ At birth, infants sense that they are physically distinct from their surroundings, an implicit self-awareness that serves as the foundation for explicit self-awareness. Toward the end of the second year, self-recognition is evident in toddlers' awareness of their own unique facial appearance.

■ Soon after, body self-awareness is apparent in toddlers' ability to locate and name body parts. However, they make **scale errors,** attempting to do things their body size makes impossible.

■ Self-awareness leads to toddlers' first efforts to appreciate others' perspectives, including expectations of fairness in dividing resources and early signs of **empathy.** Between 18 and 30 months, as language develops, children develop a **categorical self,** classifying themselves and others on the basis of age, sex, physical characteristics, and competencies.

■ Self-awareness also contributes to gains in self-control. **Compliance** emerges between 12 and 18 months, followed by **delay of gratification,** which strengthens between 1½ and 4 years. Toddlers who experience parental warmth and gentle encouragement are likely to be advanced in self-control.

IMPORTANT TERMS AND CONCEPTS

attachment (p. 256)
Attachment Q-Sort (p. 259)
basic emotions (p. 242)
categorical self (p. 274)
compliance (p. 274)
delay of gratification (p. 274)
difficult child (p. 249)
disorganized/disoriented attachment (p. 259)
easy child (p. 249)
effortful control (p. 250)
emotional self-regulation (p. 247)

empathy (p. 273)
ethological theory of attachment (p. 257)
goodness-of-fit model (p. 255)
inhibited, or shy, child (p. 251)
insecure–avoidant attachment (p. 259)
insecure–resistant attachment (p. 259)
internal working model (p. 258)
scale errors (p. 272)
secure attachment (p. 259)
secure base (p. 245)
self-conscious emotions (p. 246)

sensitive caregiving (p. 262)
separation anxiety (p. 257)
slow-to-warm-up child (p. 249)
social referencing (p. 246)
social smile (p. 243)
stranger anxiety (p. 245)
Strange Situation (p. 258)
temperament (p. 249)
uninhibited, or sociable, child (p. 251)

Development in Infancy and Toddlerhood

BIRTH–6 MONTHS

ELECTRA K. VASILEADOU/GETTY IMAGES

Physical

- Height and weight increase rapidly. (153–154)
- Newborn reflexes decline. (136)
- Distinguishes basic tastes and odors; shows preference for sweet-tasting foods. (141)
- Responses can be classically and operantly conditioned. (172–174)
- Habituates to unchanging stimuli; recovers to novel stimuli. (174–175)
- Sleep–wake schedule increasingly organizes into a night–day pattern. (164)
- Holds head up, rolls over, and grasps objects. (178)
- Shows sensitivity to motion, then binocular, and finally pictorial depth cues. (186–187)
- Recognizes and prefers human facial pattern; recognizes features of mother's face. (188–189)
- Perceives auditory and visual stimuli as organized patterns. (184, 188)
- Moves from relying on motion and spatial arrangement to using featural information—shape, color, and pattern—to visually detect the identity of an object. (190–191)
- Masters a wide range of intermodal (visual, auditory, and tactile) relationships. (191–192)

Cognitive

- Engages in immediate and deferred imitation of adults' facial expressions. (176, 203)
- Repeats chance behaviors that lead to pleasurable and interesting results. (199–200)
- Has some awareness of many physical properties (including object permanence) and basic numerical knowledge. (201–203, 208)
- Attention becomes more efficient and focused. (212–213)
- Recognition memory for visual events improves. (213–214)
- Forms categories based on objects' similar physical properties. (215)

Language

- Coos and, by the end of this period, babbles. (231)
- Begins to establish joint attention with caregiver, who labels objects and events. (232)

Emotional/Social

- Social smile and laughter emerge. (243)
- Matches feeling tone of caregiver in face-to-face communication; later, expects matched responses. (245)
- Distinguishes positive from negative emotion in voices and facial expressions. (245)
- Emotional expressions become well organized and meaningfully related to environmental events (243)

© RADIUS IMAGES/ALAMY IMAGES

- Regulates emotion by shifting attention and self-soothing. (247)
- Smiles, laughs, and babbles more to caregiver than to a stranger. (257)
- Awareness of self as physically distinct from surroundings increases. (271–272)

7–12 MONTHS

Physical

- Approaches adultlike sleep–wake schedule. (164)
- Sits alone, crawls, and walks. (178)

© ELLEN B. SENISI

- Reaching and grasping improve in flexibility and accuracy; shows refined pincer grasp. (182–183)
- Discriminates among a wider range of facial expressions, including happiness, surprise, sadness, fearfulness, and anger. (189)
- Increasingly uses featural information to detect the identity of an object. (191)
- Intermodal perception continues to improve. (192)

Cognitive

- Engages in intentional, or goal-directed, behavior. (200)
- Finds an object hidden in an initial location. (200)

© LAURA DWIGHT PHOTOGRAPHY

- Recall memory improves, as indicated by gains in deferred imitation of adults' actions with objects. (203–204)
- Capacity for tool use in problem solving emerges. (204)
- Categorizes objects on the basis of subtle sets of features, even when the perceptual contrast between categories is minimal. (215)

Language

- Babbling expands to include many sounds of spoken languages and patterns of the child's language community. (231–232)
- Joint attention with caregiver becomes more accurate. (232)
- Takes turns in games, such as pat-a-cake and peekaboo. (232)

© GERI ENGBERG/THE IMAGE WORKS

- Uses preverbal gestures (showing, pointing) to influence others' behavior and convey information. (232)

Note: Numbers in parentheses indicate the page or pages on which each milestone is discussed.

- Comprehends some word meanings. (233)
- Around end of this period, understands displaced reference of words and says first words. (207, 233)

Emotional/Social

- Smiling and laughter increase in frequency and expressiveness. (243–244)
- Anger and fear increase in frequency and intensity. (244–245)
- Stranger anxiety and separation anxiety appear. (245, 257)
- Uses caregiver as a secure base for exploration. (245)
- Shows "clear-cut" attachment to a familiar caregiver. (257)
- Increasingly detects the meaning of others' emotional expressions and engages in social referencing. (245–246)
- Regulates emotion by approaching and retreating from stimulation. (247)

13–18 MONTHS

Physical

- Height and weight gain are rapid, but not as great as in first year; toddlers slim down. (153–154)
- Walking is better coordinated (180)
- Manipulates small objects with improved coordination. (183)

Cognitive

- Explores the properties of objects by acting on them in novel ways. (199)
- Searches in several locations for a hidden object. (199, 202–203)
- Engages in deferred imitation of adults' actions with objects over longer delays and across a change in context—for example, from child care to home. (204)
- Sustained attention increases. (213)
- Recall memory improves further. (214)
- Categorizes objects flexibly, switching basis for grouping. (215)
- Realizes that pictures can symbolize real objects. (205)

Language

- Steadily adds to vocabulary. (234)
- By end of this period, produces 50 words. (231)

Emotional/Social

- Joins in play with siblings and peers. (268, 269)
- Realizes that others' emotional reactions may differ from one's own. (246)

- Complies with simple directives. (274)

19–24 MONTHS

Physical

- Walks up stairs with help, jumps, and walks on tiptoe. (178–180)

- Manipulates small objects with good coordination. (183)

Cognitive

- Solves simple problems suddenly, through mental representation. (201)
- Finds a hidden object that has been moved while out of sight. (201)
- Engages in make-believe play, using simple actions experienced in everyday life. (201)

- Engages in deferred imitation of actions an adult tries to produce, even if not fully realized. (204)
- Categorizes objects conceptually, on the basis of common function or behavior. (217)
- Begins to use language as a flexible symbolic tool, to modify existing mental representations. (205)

Language

- Produces 200 to 250 words. (231, 234)
- Combines two words. (234)

Emotional/Social

- Self-conscious emotions (shame, embarrassment, guilt, envy, and pride) emerge. (246)
- Acquires a vocabulary for talking about feelings. (248)
- Begins to use language to assist with emotional self-regulation. (248)
- Begins to tolerate caregiver's absences more easily; separation anxiety declines. (257–258)
- Recognizes image of self and, by end of this period, uses own name or personal pronoun to refer to self. (272)

- Less often makes scale errors. (272–273)
- Shows signs of empathy. (273)
- Categorizes self and others on the basis of age, sex, physical characteristics, goodness and badness, and competencies. (274)
- Shows gender-stereotyped toy preferences. (274)
- Starts to use words to influence a playmate's behavior. (269–270)
- Helps and shares with peers. (270)
- Self-control, as indicated by delay of gratification, emerges. (274–275)

Note: Numbers in parentheses indicate the page or pages on which each milestone is discussed.

Physical Development in Early Childhood

My Back Yard

Andy Laing, 6 years, USA

This artist depicts early childhood just as it is often described: "the play years."
Chapter 8 highlights the close connections between physical growth and other
aspects of young children's development.

*Reprinted with permission from Children's Museum of the Arts Permanent Collection,
New York, NY*

For more than a decade, my fourth-floor office windows overlooked the preschool and kindergarten play yard of our university laboratory school. On mild fall and spring mornings, classroom doors swung open, and sand table, easels, and large blocks spilled out into a small courtyard. Alongside the building was a grassy area with jungle gyms, swings, a playhouse, and a flower garden planted by the children; beyond the garden, a circular path lined with tricycles and wagons could be seen. Each day, the setting was alive with activity.

Even from my distant vantage point, the physical changes of early childhood were evident. Children's bodies were longer and leaner than they had been a year or two earlier. The awkward gait of toddlerhood had disappeared in favor of more refined movements that included running, climbing, jumping, galloping, and skipping. Children scaled the jungle gym, raced across the lawn, turned somersaults, and vigorously pedaled tricycles. Just as impressive as these gross-motor achievements were gains in fine-motor skills. At the sand table, children built hills, valleys, caves, and roads and prepared trays of pretend cookies and cupcakes. And as they grew older, their paintings at outdoor easels took on greater structure and detail, with family members, houses, trees, birds, sky, monsters, and letterlike forms appearing in the colorful creations.

The years from 2 to 6 are often called "the play years"—aptly so, because play blossoms during this time, becoming increasingly complex, flexible, and symbolic. Our discussion of early childhood opens with the physical attainments of this period—body and brain growth, improvements in motor coordination, and refinements in perception. We pay special attention to genetic and environmental factors that support these changes and to their intimate connection with other domains of development. The children I came to know well, first by watching from my office window and later by observing at close range in their classrooms, provide many of the examples of developmental trends and individual differences used in this chapter. ■

What's Ahead in Chapter 8

8.1 A Changing Body and Brain

In early childhood, the rapid increase in body size of the first two years tapers off into a slower growth pattern. On average, children add 2 to 3 inches in height and about 5 pounds in weight each year. Boys continue to be slightly larger than girls. As the "baby fat" that began to decline in toddlerhood drops off further, children gradually become thinner, although girls retain somewhat more body fat than boys, who are slightly more muscular (Fomon & Nelson, 2002). As the torso lengthens and widens, internal organs tuck neatly inside, and the spine straightens. As Figure 8.1 on page 282 shows, by age 5 the top-heavy, bowlegged, potbellied toddler has become a more streamlined, flat-tummied, longer-legged child with body proportions similar to those of an adult. Consequently, posture and balance improve—changes that foster gains in motor coordination.

Individual differences in body size become more apparent in early childhood. Speeding around the bike path in the play yard, 5-year-old Darryl—at 48 inches tall and 55 pounds—towered over his kindergarten classmates. (The average North American 5-year-old boy is 43 inches tall and weighs 42 pounds.) Priti, an Asian-Indian child, was unusually small because of genetic factors linked to her cultural ancestry. And Hal, a European-American child from a poverty-stricken home, was well below average for reasons we will discuss shortly.

The existence of these variations in body size reminds us that growth norms for one population are not good standards for children elsewhere in the world.

8.1 Describe body growth and brain development in early childhood.

Consider the Efe of the Republic of Congo, whose typical adult height is less than 5 feet. For genetic reasons, the impact of hormones controlling body size is reduced in Efe children (Le Bouc, 2017). By age 5, the average Efe child is shorter than more than 97 percent of North American and European agemates, and Efe children reach puberty and stop growing at an earlier age than U.S. comparison children. Researchers disagree on why the Efe's small size evolved. Some suggest that it reduces their caloric requirements in the face of food scarcity in the rain forests of Central Africa, others that it permits easy movement through the dense forest underbrush, and still others that it enables earlier childbearing to compensate for the Efe's extremely high mortality rate (Verdu, 2016). Efe children's short stature is not a sign of growth or health problems. But for other children, such as Hal, extremely slow growth is cause for concern.

Wilson at 3 years

Wilson at 3½ years

Wilson at 4½ years

Wilson at 5 years

Mariel at 2½ years

Mariel at 4 years

Mariel at 4½ years

Mariel at 5 years

PHOTOS OF WILSON: DIAHANNE LUCAS; PHOTOS OF MARIEL: © JIM WEST/JIMWESTPHOTO.COM

FIGURE 8.1 **Body growth during early childhood.** During the preschool years, children grow more slowly than in infancy and toddlerhood. Wilson and Mariel's bodies became more streamlined, flat-tummied, and longer-legged. Boys continue to be slightly taller, heavier, and more muscular than girls. But generally, the two sexes are similar in body proportions and physical capacities.

8.1.1 Skeletal Growth

The skeletal changes of infancy continue throughout early childhood. Between ages 2 and 6, approximately 45 new *epiphyses,* or growth centers in which cartilage hardens into bone, emerge in various parts of the skeleton. Other epiphyses will appear in middle childhood. X-rays of these growth centers enable doctors to estimate children's *skeletal age,* or progress toward physical maturity (see page 155 in Chapter 5)—information helpful in diagnosing growth disorders.

By the end of the preschool years, children start to lose their primary, or "baby," teeth. The age at which they do so is heavily influenced by genetic factors. For example, girls, who are ahead of boys in physical development, lose their primary teeth sooner. Cultural ancestry also makes a difference. North American children typically get their first secondary (permanent) tooth at 6½ years, children in Ghana at just over 5 years, and children in Hong Kong around the sixth birthday (Burns, 2000). But nutritional factors also

Like Efe children, these children of the Batwa people of Central Africa's Great Lakes region are genetically short-statured, expected to reach a typical adult height of less than 5 feet. They remind us that growth norms for one population are not good standards for children elsewhere in the world.

influence dental development. Prolonged malnutrition delays the appearance of permanent teeth, whereas overweight and obesity accelerate it (Costacurta et al., 2012; Heinrich-Weltzien et al., 2013).

Diseased baby teeth can affect the health of permanent teeth, so preventing decay in primary teeth is essential—by brushing consistently, avoiding sugary foods, drinking fluoridated water, and getting topical fluoride treatments and sealants (plastic coatings that protect tooth surfaces). Another factor is exposure to tobacco smoke, which suppresses children's immune systems, including the ability to fight bacteria responsible for tooth decay. The risk associated with this suppression is greatest in infancy and early childhood, when the immune system is not yet fully mature. Young children in homes with regular smokers are at increased risk for decayed teeth (Hanioka et al., 2011; Wen et al., 2017).

An estimated 23 percent of U.S. preschoolers have tooth decay, a figure that rises to 50 percent in middle childhood and 60 percent by age 18. Causes include poor diet and inadequate health care—factors that are more likely to affect children from low-SES homes. One-fourth of U.S. children living in poverty have untreated dental cavities (U.S. Department of Health and Human Services, 2018b).

8.1.2 Brain Development

Between ages 2 and 6, the brain increases from 70 percent of its adult weight to 90 percent. At the same time, preschoolers improve in a wide variety of skills—physical coordination, perception, attention, memory, language, logical thinking, and imagination. In addition to increasing in volume, the cerebral cortex undergoes much reshaping and refining.

Development of the Cerebral Cortex   By age 4 to 5, many parts of the cerebral cortex have overproduced synapses. In some regions, such as the prefrontal cortex, the number of synapses is nearly double the adult value. Together, synaptic growth and myelination of neural fibers result in a high energy need. In fact, brain-imaging evidence reveals that energy metabolism in the cerebral cortex reaches a peak around this age (Jabès & Nelson, 2014; Jiang & Nardelli, 2016).

Recall from Chapter 5 that overabundance of synaptic connections supports *plasticity* of the young brain, helping to ensure that the child will acquire certain abilities even if some areas are damaged. *Synaptic pruning* follows: Neurons that are seldom stimulated lose their connective fibers, and the number of synapses gradually declines (see page 156 in Chapter 5). As the structures of stimulated neurons become more elaborate and require more space, surrounding neurons die, and brain plasticity declines. Between ages 8 and 10, energy consumption

Learning to program their own interactive stories and games challenges these 5-year-olds' capacity to remember, think flexibly, and plan—aspects of executive function supported by rapid growth of the prefrontal cortex from early to middle childhood.

of most cortical regions diminishes to near-adult levels (Lebel & Beaulieu, 2011). In addition, cognitive functions are no longer as widely distributed in the cerebral cortex. Rather, they increasingly localize in distinct neural systems that become better integrated, reflecting a developmental shift toward a more lateralized, fine-tuned, and efficient neural organization (Bathelt et al., 2013; Markant & Thomas, 2013).

Measures of neural activity—electroencephalography (EEG), near infrared spectroscopy (NIRS), and functional magnetic resonance imaging (fMRI)—reveal especially rapid growth from early to middle childhood in prefrontal-cortical areas devoted to various aspects of executive function. These include inhibition of impulses and irrelevant behaviors, working memory, flexibility of thinking, and planning—capacities that advance markedly during the preschool years (Müller & Kerns, 2015). Furthermore, for most children, the left cerebral hemisphere is especially active between 3 and 6 years and then levels off. In contrast, activity in the right hemisphere increases steadily throughout early and middle childhood, with a slight spurt between ages 8 and 10 (Thatcher, Walker, & Giudice, 1987; Thompson et al., 2000).

These findings fit nicely with what we know about several aspects of cognitive development. Early childhood is a time of marked gains on tasks that depend on the prefrontal cortex—ones that require improved attentional control and thoughtful reflection (Rothbart, 2011). Further, language skills (typically housed in the left hemisphere) increase at an astonishing pace in early childhood, and they support children's increasing control over behavior, also mediated by the prefrontal cortex. In contrast, spatial skills (usually located in the right hemisphere), such as giving directions, drawing pictures, and recognizing geometric shapes, develop gradually over childhood and adolescence.

Advances in Other Brain Structures   Besides the cerebral cortex, several other areas of the brain make strides during early childhood (see Figure 8.2). All of these changes involve establishing links between parts of the brain, increasing the coordinated functioning of the central nervous system.

At the rear and base of the brain is the **cerebellum,** a structure that aids in balance and control of body movement. Fibers linking the cerebellum to the cerebral cortex grow and myelinate from birth through the preschool years, contributing to dramatic gains in motor coordination: By the end of the preschool years, children can play hopscotch, throw a ball with well-coordinated movements, and print letters of the alphabet. Cerebellar–cortical neural circuits also support thinking. And because damage to the cerebellum in infancy is associated with impaired growth of the cerebral cortex, they appear to be crucial for typical brain development (Stoodley, 2016). Children with injury to the cerebellum usually display both motor and cognitive deficits, including problems with memory, planning, and language (Hoang et al., 2014; Noterdaeme et al., 2002).

The **reticular formation,** a structure in the brain stem that maintains alertness and consciousness, generates synapses and myelinates throughout early childhood and into adolescence (Sampaio & Truwit, 2001). Neurons in the reticular formation send out fibers to other areas of the brain. Many go to the prefrontal cortex, contributing to improvements in sustained, controlled attention.

An inner brain structure called the **hippocampus,** which plays a vital role in memory and in images of space that help us find our way, undergoes rapid synapse formation and myelination in the second half of the first year, when recall memory and independent movement emerge. Over the preschool and elementary school years

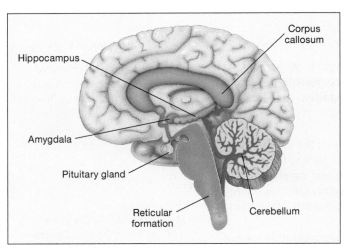

FIGURE 8.2   Cross-section of the human brain, showing the location of the cerebellum, the reticular formation, the hippocampus, the amygdala, and the corpus callosum. These structures undergo considerable development during early childhood. Also shown is the pituitary gland, which secretes hormones that control body growth (see page 286).

and into early adolescence, the hippocampus and surrounding areas of the cerebral cortex continue to develop swiftly, establishing connections with one another and with the prefrontal cortex and lateralizing toward greater right-sided activation (Blankenship et al., 2017; Hopf et al., 2013). These changes make possible the dramatic gains in memory and spatial understanding of early and middle childhood—ability to use strategies to store and retrieve information, expansion of autobiographical memory (which brings an end to infantile amnesia), and drawing and reading of maps (which we will take up in Chapter 9). Advances in hippocampal development in school-age children and adolescents are associated with higher scores on measures of general intelligence and, in particular, with diverse memory skills (Daugherty, Flinn, & Ofen, 2017; Keresztes et al., 2017; Tamnes et al., 2018).

Also located in the inner brain, adjacent to the hippocampus, is the **amygdala,** a structure that plays a central role in processing of novelty and emotional information. The amygdala is sensitive to facial emotional expressions, especially fear (Adolphs, 2010). It also enhances memory for emotionally salient events, thereby ensuring that information relevant for survival—stimuli that signify fear or safety—will be retrieved on future occasions. This capacity for emotional learning seems to emerge in early childhood: Extensive damage to the amygdala in the first few years leads to loss of ability to learn about fear and safety signals and wide-ranging socially inappropriate behaviors (Shaw, Brierley, & David, 2005). Throughout childhood and adolescence, connections between the amygdala and the prefrontal cortex, which governs regulation of emotion, form and myelinate (Gabard-Durnam et al., 2014; Tottenham, Hare, & Casey, 2009). Recall from Chapter 7 that in socially anxious children, the amygdala is overly reactive to threatening situations (see page 252 in Chapter 7).

The **corpus callosum** is a large bundle of fibers connecting the two cerebral hemispheres. Production of synapses and myelination of the corpus callosum are especially rapid in infancy and early childhood, then continue at a slower pace through middle childhood and adolescence (Tanaka-Arakawa et al., 2015). The corpus callosum supports smooth coordination of movements on both sides of the body and integration of many aspects of thinking, including perception, attention, memory, language, and problem solving. The more complex the task, the more essential is communication between the hemispheres.

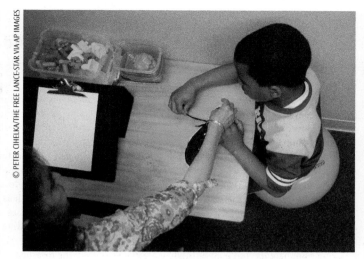

This child has been diagnosed with a rare condition in which part of the corpus callosum is absent. He has difficulty with tasks that have multiple steps and that require coordinated movements on both sides of the body. Here, a therapist helps him learn to tie shoes.

ASK YOURSELF

Connect ■ What aspects of brain development support the tremendous gains in language, thinking, and motor control of early childhood?

Apply ■ Dental checkups revealed a high incidence of untreated tooth decay in a U.S. preschool program serving low-income children. Using findings presented in this and previous chapters, list possible contributing factors.

8.2 Influences on Physical Growth and Health

As we consider factors affecting growth and health in early childhood, you will encounter some familiar themes. Heredity remains influential, but environmental factors are also essential. In the sections that follow, we focus on the importance of sufficient restful sleep, good nutrition, relative freedom from disease, and physical safety. The limited material resources and constant stressors experienced by children growing up in poverty result in family conditions that are

8.2a Describe the effects of heredity, restful sleep, nutrition, and infectious disease on physical growth and health in early childhood.

8.2b Cite factors that increase the risk of unintentional injuries, and explain how childhood injuries can be prevented.

Biology and Environment | Childhood Poverty and Brain Development

The profound threats posed to all domains of development by persistent childhood poverty are well documented: poorer physical health, impaired cognitive functioning, and emotional and behavior problems emerging in the early years that, without effective intervention, pose lifelong risks to overall competence and well-being (Duncan et al., 2012). Clear evidence also exists that environmental adversities associated with poverty—chronic high life stress; inadequate affection, involvement, and appropriate stimulation from parents; and poor nutrition—affect brain development.

Recall from Chapter 2 that 18 percent of U.S. children and adolescents live in families with incomes below the federal poverty level (the income judged necessary for a minimum living standard). Among children between birth and age 5, the U.S. poverty rate is even higher, at 21 percent, and it escalates to 50 percent in single-mother families with young children (U.S. Census Bureau, 2017a). While poverty negatively affects children of all ages, young children are particularly at risk. As we have seen in Chapter 5 and in this chapter, infancy and early childhood are sensitive periods during which brain structures governing cognitive and emotional abilities are developing especially rapidly, making them especially vulnerable to the effects of deficient experiences.

In a groundbreaking study, researchers asked whether atypical patterns of brain development might account for the link between childhood poverty and poorer cognitive outcomes. To answer this question, they capitalized on the rich data bank of the U.S. National Institutes of Health (NIH) Magnetic Resonance Imaging Study of Normal Brain Development (Hair et al., 2015). Nearly 400 4- to 18-year-olds, varying widely in family income and ethnicity, were assessed three times at two-year intervals. On each occasion, information

on family background was gathered, and participants underwent MRI brain scans and took an array of cognitive tests. Factors that could otherwise explain a poverty–impaired brain development association, such as birth weight, family size, and maternal education, were carefully controlled.

The investigators focused on the volume of *gray matter* (darker tissue consisting mainly of neurons and their connective fibers) in several brain structures with lengthier periods of development and therefore likely to be vulnerable to adverse early experiences. They chose the *frontal lobes*, including the prefrontal cortex, important for executive processes such as control of attention, self-regulation, and thoughtful reflection; the *temporal lobe*, which supports language development; and the *hippocampus*, because of its crucial role in memory and processing of spatial information. At each age, participants' gray matter volumes were compared to averages reflecting typical development, based on large numbers of individuals of the same age and sex.

Results revealed that children and adolescents growing up in the poorest families (those persistently below the federal poverty level) had gray matter volumes in the brain structures of interest that were 8 to 10 percent below average. Furthermore, atypical brain development accounted for 15 to 20 percent of their lower cognitive scores, when compared to the scores of economically better-off peers, on measures of vocabulary, verbal and spatial reasoning, concept formation, and reading and math achievement.

The children in this single-parent family are growing up in a southern Texas county with one of the lowest average incomes per person in the United States. Persistent poverty can compromise brain structures crucial for learning, school success, and a satisfying adult life.

The NIH Study, along with similar investigations, confirms that persistent childhood poverty can compromise brain structures crucial for learning, school success, and a satisfying adult life (Johnson, Riis, & Noble, 2016; Noble et al., 2015). In other research, the effects of poverty on the developing brain were apparent as early as infancy, in reduced gray matter volumes and EEG brain-wave activity in the cerebral cortex (Hanson et al., 2013; Tomalski et al., 2013).

Of course, not all children living in poverty display the deficits in brain development and cognitive outcomes just described. Those with personal attributes and environmental supports that foster resilience often develop favorably (return to page 10 in Chapter 1 to review). Nevertheless, the power of poverty to undermine children's optimal neurological and psychological functioning offers one of the strongest justifications for public policies aimed at reducing poverty and for early interventions that improve the environments of economically disadvantaged children.

often deficient in these and other ways. As the Biology and Environment box above reveals, the extent to which poverty negatively affects brain structures undergoing rapid development in early childhood is the focus of intensive research.

8.2.1 Heredity and Hormones

Children's physical size and rate of growth are related to those of their biological parents and siblings, making the impact of heredity on physical growth evident throughout childhood (Stulp & Barrett, 2016). Genes influence growth by controlling the body's production of and sensitivity to hormones. Figure 8.2 on page 284 shows the **pituitary gland,** located at the base of the brain, which plays a critical role by releasing two hormones that induce growth.

The first, **growth hormone (GH),** is necessary from birth on for development of almost all body tissues. GH acts directly but also accomplishes its task with the help of an intermediary. It stimulates the liver and epiphyses of the skeleton to release another hormone called *insulin-like growth factor 1 (IGF-1),* which triggers cell duplication throughout the body, especially the skeleton, muscles, nerves, bone marrow (origin of blood cells), liver, kidney, skin, and lungs.

About 2 percent of children suffer from inherited conditions that cause either GH deficiency or IGF-1 deficiency (in which GH fails to stimulate IGF-1). Without medical intervention, such children reach an average mature height of only 4 to 4½ feet. When treated early with injections of GH or IGF-1 (depending on the disorder), they show catch-up growth and then grow at a typical rate, with most reaching an adult height within normal range (Pfäffle et al., 2018; Ranke & Wit, 2018).

The availability of synthetic GH has also made it possible to treat short, normal-GH children with hormone injections, in hopes of increasing their final height. Thousands of parents, concerned that their children will suffer social stigma because of their shortness, have sought this GH therapy. But most normal-GH children given GH treatment grow only slightly taller than their previously predicted mature height (Loche et al., 2014). And contrary to popular belief, normal-GH short children are not deficient in self-esteem or other aspects of psychological adjustment (Gardner & Sandberg, 2011). So despite the existence of "heightism" in Western cultures, little justification exists for medically intervening in short stature that is merely the result of biologically normal human diversity.

A second pituitary hormone, **thyroid-stimulating hormone (TSH),** prompts the thyroid gland in the neck to release *thyroxine,* which is necessary for brain development and for GH to have its full impact on body size. Infants born with inadequate thyroxine must receive it at once, or they will be intellectually disabled. Once the most rapid period of brain development is complete, children with too little thyroxine grow at a below-average rate, but the central nervous system is no longer affected (Wassner, 2017). With prompt treatment, such children catch up in body growth and eventually reach normal size.

These preschoolers are the same age but differ greatly in body size. Early treatment of growth hormone (GH) deficiency leads to substantial gains in height, but little justification exists for intervention with normal-GH children whose short stature simply reflects human diversity.

8.2.2 Sleep Habits and Problems

Because GH is released during the child's sleeping hours, sleep contributes to body growth. And a well-rested child is better able to play, learn, and contribute positively to family functioning. Many studies confirm that sleep difficulties are associated with impaired cognitive performance, including decreased attention, slower speed of thinking, poorer memory, and lower intelligence and achievement test scores, as well as with internalizing behavior problems (fear and anxiety) and externalizing behavior problems (anger and aggression). The impact of disrupted sleep on cognitive functioning and emotional adjustment is more pronounced for low-SES children. Perhaps insufficient sleep heightens the impact of other environmental stressors prevalent in their daily lives (Calhoun et al., 2017; Cellini, 2017; El-Sheikh et al., 2010, 2013). Also, children who sleep poorly disturb their parents' sleep, which can generate significant family stress—a major reason that sleep difficulties are among the most frequent concerns parents raise with their preschooler's doctor.

Total sleep declines in early childhood; on average, 2- and 3-year-olds sleep 11 to 12 hours, 4- to 6-year-olds 10 to 11 hours. But these averages encompass substantial individual variability, with lesser- or greater-than-average sleep remaining fairly stable over time (Jenni & Carskadon, 2012). Younger preschoolers typically take a 1- to 2-hour nap in the early afternoon, although daytime sleep need also varies widely. Some continue to take two naps, as they did in toddlerhood; others give up napping entirely.

Most European-American children stop napping between ages 3 and 4, although a quiet rest period after lunch helps them rejuvenate for the rest of the day. Perhaps because of greater cultural acceptance, napping remains common among African-American, Asian, and Hispanic children throughout early childhood, balanced by a tendency toward later bedtimes and less nighttime sleep (Crosby, LeBourgeois, & Harsh, 2005; Mindell et al., 2013). And napping at preschool enhances memories acquired earlier in the day, especially for children who nap

In early childhood, as in toddlerhood, storybook reading and other bedtime routines are linked to reduced nighttime waking and longer total sleep times.

regularly at home (Kurdziel, Duclos, & Spencer, 2013). Consequently, replacing nap opportunities with additional learning activities in early childhood programs may be counterproductive.

The majority of Western parents engage in bedtime routines with their preschoolers, though in the United States this is slightly more common among European-American than African-American and Hispanic parents. As noted in Chapter 5, bedtime routines are linked to reduced nighttime waking and longer total sleep time (see page 166). As in infancy and toddlerhood, during early childhood, European-American children are less likely to cosleep with their parents than their African-American and Hispanic agemates. European-American children more often go to bed with a security object, which may help them adjust to feelings of uneasiness at being left by themselves in a darkened room. In most cases, parent–child cosleeping is not associated with problems during the preschool years, other than more frequent night wakings of parents due to children's movements (Worthman, 2011). Western cosleeping children generally ask to sleep in their own bed by age 6 or 7.

Difficulty falling asleep—calling to the parent or asking for another drink of water—is common in early childhood, occurring in about one-third of preschoolers. But European-American parents more often express concern about their child falling asleep at a regular time than do African-American parents, who, as just noted, report later bedtimes, shorter nighttime sleep durations, and more napping during the day (Milan, Snow, & Belay, 2007; Patrick, Millet, & Mindell, 2016). Perhaps European-American parents more highly value a scheduled bedtime and tend to view falling asleep without protest as a sign of their child's maturity—expectations likely to be unmet at least occasionally.

Sleep problems frequently result from inadequate parental control over young children's TV, computer, video game, tablet, and smart phone use. As Figure 8.3 shows, the more weekly hours young children devote to screen media, the greater their number of parent-reported sleep disturbances—difficulty falling asleep, night wakings, restless sleep, inconsistent bedtimes and hours of sleep from night to night, and daytime fatigue (Mindell et al., 2013; Parent, Sanders, & Forehand, 2016). Among older children and adolescents, a similar relationship exists between screen media time and sleep disturbances. However, it takes fewer screen-time hours to disrupt young children's sleep.

Sleep difficulties may also stem from a mismatch between parental demands and children's biology. The parent may step up pressure on the child, who vigorously resists because of a lower-than-average need for sleep. Consequently, sleep interventions should include parent education about individual differences in young children's sleep requirements (Johnson & Mindell, 2011). Intense bedtime struggles sometimes result from family turmoil, as children worry about how their parents may get along when they are asleep and not available to distract them. In these cases, addressing family stress and conflict is key to improving children's sleep.

Finally, most children waken during the night from time to time, but those who cannot return to sleep on their own may suffer from a sleep disorder. Because young children have vivid imaginations and difficulty separating fantasy from reality, *nightmares* are common; half of 3- to 6-year-olds occasionally experience them. And about 4 percent of children are frequent sleepwalkers, who are unaware of their wanderings during the night. Gently awakening and returning the child to bed helps avoid self-injury. *Sleep terrors,* which affect 3 percent of young children, are perhaps the most upsetting sleep problem to parents. In these panic-stricken arousals from deep sleep, the child may scream, thrash, speak incoherently, show a sharp rise in

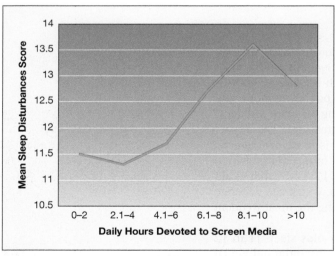

FIGURE 8.3   Relationship between hours devoted to screen media and sleep disturbances among young children. Several hundred parents of 3- to 7-year-olds were asked how much daily time over a typical week their child spent watching TV or videos, using a computer, playing video games, using a tablet, and using a smartphone for activities other than talking on the phone. Parents also rated their child's frequency of sleep disturbances for the most recent typical week. A positive relationship between screen time and sleep disturbances emerged, with a steep increase in parent-reported sleep problems after six daily hours devoted to screen media. (Based on Parent, Sanders, & Forehand, 2016.)

heart rate and breathing, and initially be unresponsive to parents' attempts to comfort. Sleep-walking and sleep terrors tend to run in families, suggesting a genetic influence (Moore & Mindell, 2012; Ophoff et al., 2018). But they can also be triggered by stress or extreme fatigue.

Fortunately, sleep disorders of early childhood usually subside without treatment. In the few cases that persist, children require a medical and psychological evaluation. Their disturbed sleep may be a sign of neurological or emotional difficulties.

8.2.3 Nutrition

As children approach age 2, many become unpredictable, picky eaters. One father I know wistfully recalled how his son as a toddler eagerly sampled Chinese food: "He ate rice, chicken chow mein, egg rolls—and now, at age 3, the only thing he'll try is the ice cream!"

Preschoolers' appetites decline because their growth has slowed. Their wariness of new foods is also adaptive: If they stick to familiar foods, they are less likely to swallow dangerous substances when adults are not around to protect them. With the transition to middle childhood, picky eating usually subsides (Birch & Fisher, 1995; Cardona Cano et al., 2015). Parents need not worry about variations in amount eaten from meal to meal. Over the course of a day, preschoolers compensate for eating little at one meal by eating more at a later one (Hursti, 1999).

Though they eat less, preschoolers need a high-quality diet, including the same variety of foods adults need, but in smaller amounts. These include milk and milk products, meat or meat alternatives (such as eggs, dried peas or beans, and peanut butter), vegetables and fruits, and breads and cereals. Fats, oils, and salt are best kept to a minimum because of their link to high blood pressure and heart disease in adulthood. And foods high in sugar should be eaten only in small amounts to prevent tooth decay and protect against overweight and obesity—a topic we will take up in Chapter 11.

Children tend to imitate the food choices and eating practices of people they admire, both adults and peers. For example, in Mexico, where children see family members delighting in the taste of peppery foods, preschoolers enthusiastically eat chili peppers, whereas most U.S. children reject them. Simply offering a new food, with repeated, unpressured opportunities to taste it over 5 to 15 mealtime exposures, is highly effective in getting young children to accept it (Lam, 2015). And pleasant prompts combined with reasoning can boost preschoolers' willingness to eat a new vegetable: "This squash tastes like sweet potatoes, so you might like it" (Edelson, Mokdad, & Martin, 2016).

Providing occasions for children to become visually familiar with the food is helpful as well. In one study, researchers randomly assigned parents varying in SES to a treatment in which they joined their preschooler in looking at a picture book featuring an unfamiliar vegetable once a day for two weeks. Over a second two-week period, the parents offered their child a daily taste of the food. Compared to a no-book control group, parents in the picture-book group reported experiencing more pleasure at introducing their child to the new vegetable, and their children were more willing to taste it, expressed greater liking for it, and ate more of it (Houston-Price et al., 2019). At a three-month follow-up, children in the picture-book group continued to eat more of the food.

Unfortunately, parents who dislike vegetables and other healthy foods usually don't offer them to their children (Boles et al., 2014). Children in such families consume a restricted variety of foods and eat a less healthy diet. Yet mothers who say they don't like vegetables but still offer them regularly generally report that their child likes them (Kaar et al., 2016).

The emotional climate at mealtimes has a powerful impact on children's eating habits. When parents are worried about how well their preschoolers are eating, meals can become unpleasant and stressful. Coercing children to eat—for example, by offering bribes, such as "Finish your vegetables, and you can have an

A preschooler helps his mother prepare a traditional treat for a Chinese festival: sweet rice dumplings wrapped in bamboo leaves. Children tend to imitate the food preferences of those they admire—both adults and peers.

APPLYING WHAT WE KNOW

Encouraging Good Nutrition in Early Childhood

SUGGESTION	DESCRIPTION
Offer a varied, healthy diet.	Provide a well-balanced variety of nutritious foods that are colorful and attractively served. Avoid including sweets and "junk" foods in the child's regular food environment.
Offer predictable meals as well as several snacks each day.	Preschoolers' stomachs are small, and they may not be able to eat enough in three meals to satisfy their energy requirements. They benefit from extra opportunities to eat.
Offer small portions, and permit the child to serve him- or herself and to ask for seconds.	When too much food is put on the plate, preschoolers (like adults) often overeat, increasing the risk of obesity. On average, preschoolers consume 25 percent less at a meal when permitted to serve themselves.
Offer healthy new foods early in a meal and repeatedly at subsequent meals, and respond with patience if the child rejects the food.	Introduce healthy new foods before the child's appetite is satisfied. Let children see you eat and enjoy the new food. When prompting the child to try the food, use reasoning: "Prunes are like big raisins, so you might like them." If the child rejects the food, accept the refusal and serve it again at another meal. As foods become more familiar, they are more readily accepted.
Keep mealtimes pleasant, include the child in mealtime conversations, and refrain from coercing the child to eat.	A pleasant, relaxed eating environment helps children develop positive attitudes about food. Refrain from constantly offering food, pressuring the child to eat, or engaging in confrontations over disliked foods and table manners—practices associated with children's refusal to eat.
Avoid using food as a reward and restricting access to certain foods.	Saying "No dessert until you clean your plate" tells children that they must eat even if they are not hungry and that dessert is the best part of the meal. Restricting access to a food increases children's valuing of that food and efforts to obtain it.

Sources: Jansen et al., 2012; Kaar et al., 2016.

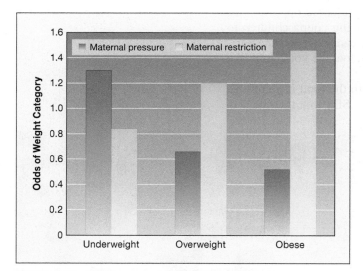

FIGURE 8.4 **Relationship of maternal feeding practices to underweight, overweight, and obesity among preschoolers.** In a Dutch study of nearly 5,000 4-year-olds, mothers who pressured their child to eat were more likely to have an underweight child. Mothers who restricted their child's eating increased their chances of having an overweight or obese child. These relationships held even after controlling for many factors that could have influenced maternal feeding practices and preschoolers' weight gain, including parents' SES, ethnicity, height and weight, and children's enjoyment of eating. (Based on Jansen et al., 2012.)

extra cookie"—leads children to like the healthy food less and the treat more (Birch, Fisher, & Davison, 2003). Similarly, restricting access to tasty foods focuses children's attention on those foods and increases their desire to eat them. In a study of nearly 5,000 Dutch 4-year-olds, maternal feeding practices were strongly associated with children's unhealthy weight, in both directions. The more mothers reported pressuring their child to eat, the greater the likelihood of an underweight child. And the more mothers reported restricting their child's eating, the greater the chances of an overweight or obese child (see Figure 8.4) (Jansen et al., 2012). Too much parental control over eating seems to interfere with children's responsiveness to hunger cues, resulting either in withdrawal from food or in excessive eating.

Food preferences and eating patterns acquired in early childhood remain relatively stable through adolescence and adulthood (Mikkila et al., 2005; Northstone & Emmett, 2008). Thus, the preschool years are a window of opportunity for establishing good eating practices, with potentially lifelong health benefits. For ways to encourage healthy, varied eating in young children, refer to Applying What We Know above.

Finally, as indicated in earlier chapters, many children in the United States and in developing countries lack access to sufficient high-quality food to support healthy growth. Five-year-old Hal rode a bus from a poverty-stricken neighborhood to our laboratory preschool. His mother's paycheck barely covered her rent, let alone food. Hal's diet was deficient in protein and in essential vitamins and minerals—iron (to prevent anemia), calcium (to support development of bones and teeth), zinc (to support immune system functioning, neural communication, and cell duplication), vitamin A (to help maintain eyes, skin, and a variety of internal organs), and vitamin C (to facilitate iron absorption and wound healing). These are the most common dietary deficiencies of the preschool years (Yousafzai, Yakoob, & Bhutta, 2013).

Hal was small for his age, pale, inattentive, and disruptive at preschool. Throughout childhood and adolescence, a nutritionally deficient diet is associated with shorter stature, attention and memory difficulties, poorer intelligence and achievement test scores, and hyperactivity and aggression, even after family factors that might account for these relationships (such as stressors, parental psychological health, education, warmth, and stimulation of the child) are controlled (Lukowski et al., 2010; Prado & Dewey, 2014).

8.2.4 Infectious Disease

One day, I noticed that Hal had been absent from the play yard for several weeks, so I asked Leslie, his preschool teacher, what was wrong. "Hal's been hospitalized with the measles," she explained. "He's had difficulty recovering—lost weight when there wasn't much to lose in the first place." In well-nourished children, ordinary childhood illnesses have no effect on physical growth. But when children are undernourished, disease interacts with malnutrition in a vicious spiral, with potentially severe consequences.

Infectious Disease and Malnutrition   Hal's reaction to the measles is commonplace in developing nations, where a large proportion of the population lives in poverty and children do not receive routine immunizations. Illnesses such as measles and chickenpox, which typically do not appear until after age 3 in industrialized nations, occur much earlier. Poor diet depresses the body's immune system, making children far more susceptible to disease. Of the 5.9 million annual deaths of children under age 5 worldwide, 98 percent are in developing countries, and about half are due to infectious diseases (UNICEF, 2017b).

Disease, in turn, is a major contributor to malnutrition, hindering both physical growth and cognitive development. Illness reduces appetite and limits the body's ability to absorb foods, especially in children with intestinal infections. In developing countries, widespread diarrhea, resulting from unsafe water and contaminated foods, leads to stunted growth and an estimated 400,000 to 700,000 childhood deaths each year, with children under age 5 most affected (Glass & Stoll, 2018; Mokomane et al., 2018). Studies carried out in low-income countries reveal that the more persistent diarrhea is in early childhood, the shorter children are in height and the lower their intelligence test scores during the school years (Black, 2017; Pinkerton et al., 2016).

Most developmental impairments and deaths due to diarrhea can be prevented with nearly cost-free *oral rehydration therapy (ORT)*, in which sick children are given a glucose, salt, and water solution that quickly replaces fluids the body loses. Since 1990, public health workers have taught many families in the developing world how to administer ORT. Also, low-cost supplements of zinc (essential for immune system functioning) substantially reduce the incidence of

A public health worker teaches a Haitian mother how to prepare oral rehydration therapy (ORT) for her child, who is suffering from diarrhea. This nearly cost-free treatment saves the lives of millions of children in developing countries each year.

severe and prolonged diarrhea, especially when combined with ORT (World Health Organization, 2018). Through these interventions, the lives of millions of children are saved each year.

Immunization   In industrialized nations, childhood diseases have declined dramatically during the past half century, largely as a result of widespread immunization of infants and young children. Hal got the measles because, unlike his classmates from more advantaged homes, he did not receive a full program of immunizations.

In the United States, routine childhood immunizations have prevented an estimated 20 million illnesses and 40,000 deaths each year (Ventola, 2016). Yet about 28 percent of U.S. 1½- to 3-year-olds lack one or more essential immunizations. The rate rises to 32 percent

LOOK and LISTEN

Arrange to join a family with at least one preschooler for a meal, and closely observe parental mealtime practices. Are they likely to promote healthy eating habits? Explain.

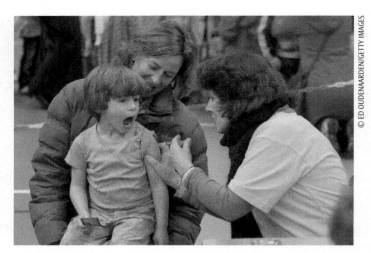

A 4-year-old in the Netherlands reacts to receiving an essential immunization at a mass vaccination event in his community. The Netherlands has one of the highest early childhood vaccination rates in the world.

for poverty-stricken children, many of whom do not receive full protection until ages 5 or 6, when it is required for school entry (Centers for Disease Control and Prevention, 2017c). In contrast, fewer than 10 percent of preschoolers lack immunizations in Australia, Denmark, and Norway, and fewer than 5 percent in Canada, the Netherlands, Sweden, and the United Kingdom (World Health Organization, 2017b).

Why does the United States lag behind these countries in immunization? Although the U.S. Affordable Care Act of 2010 greatly improved health insurance coverage for American children, many low-income children remain without coverage (see page 76 in Chapter 2) and, therefore, may not receive timely vaccinations. Beginning in 1994, all U.S. children whose parents are unable to pay were guaranteed free immunizations, a program that has led to gains in immunization rates.

Inability to afford vaccines is not the only cause of inadequate immunization. Parents with little education and with stressful daily lives often fail to schedule vaccination appointments. Some parents have been influenced by media reports—now widely discredited—suggesting a link between the measles–mumps–rubella vaccine and a rise in the number of children diagnosed with autism. In fact, numerous large-scale studies show no association (Maglione et al., 2014; Ventola, 2016). Other parents have religious or philosophical objections—for example, the belief that children should develop immunities naturally.

In areas where many parents refuse to immunize their children, disease outbreaks have occurred, with life-threatening consequences (Salmon et al., 2015). Public education programs directed at increasing parental knowledge about the importance and safety of timely immunizations, and convenient opportunities to obtain them free or at low cost, are badly needed. The Netherlands achieves its high child immunization rate by giving parents of every newborn baby a written schedule that shows exactly when and where the child should be immunized (Lernout et al., 2013). If a parent does not bring the child at the specified time, a public health nurse goes to the home to ensure that the child remains in step with the schedule.

A final point regarding communicable disease in early childhood deserves mention. Childhood illness rises with child-care attendance. On average, an infant or toddler in child care becomes sick 9 to 10 times a year, a preschooler 6 to 7 times. The diseases that spread most rapidly are those most frequently suffered by young children—diarrhea and respiratory infections (Shope, 2014). The risk that a respiratory infection will result in *otitis media,* or middle ear infection, is greatly elevated. To learn about the consequences of otitis media and how to prevent it, consult the Social Issues: Health box on the following page.

8.2.5 Childhood Injuries

More than any other child in the preschool classroom, 3-year-old Tommy had trouble sitting still and paying attention. Instead, he darted from one place and activity to another. One day, he narrowly escaped serious injury when he put his mother's car in gear while she was outside scraping ice from its windows. The vehicle rolled through a guardrail and over the side of a 10-foot concrete underpass, where it hung until rescue workers arrived. Police charged Tommy's mother with failing to use a restraint seat for a child younger than age 8.

Unintentional injuries are the leading cause of childhood mortality in industrialized nations. Although U.S. childhood injury fatalities have declined steadily over the past four decades due to state laws and community policies aimed at improving child safety, the United States nevertheless ranks poorly among Western nations in these largely preventable events. About 29 percent of U.S. deaths between ages 1 and 14 and 75 percent of deaths between ages 15 and 19 result from injuries, causing about 8,000 children and youths to die annually (Centers for Disease Control and Prevention, 2018c). Among the hundreds of thousands who survive, many suffer pain, brain damage, and permanent physical disabilities.

Social Issues: Health | Otitis Media and Development

During his first year in child care, 2-year-old Alex caught five colds, had the flu on two occasions, and experienced repeated otitis media (middle-ear infection). Alex is not unusual. By age 3, 80 percent of children have had respiratory illnesses that resulted in at least one bout of otitis media; nearly half of these have had three or more bouts (Marom et al., 2014). Although antibiotics eliminate the bacteria responsible for otitis media, they do not reduce fluid buildup in the middle ear, which causes mild to moderate hearing loss that can last for weeks or months.

The incidence of otitis media is greatest between 6 months and 3 years, when children are first acquiring language. Frequent infections predict delayed language progress in early childhood, and poorer academic performance (including reading deficits) after school entry (Racanello & McCabe, 2010).

How might otitis media disrupt language and academic progress? Difficulties in perceiving and processing speech sounds, particularly in noisy settings, may be responsible. Children with many bouts are less attentive to others' speech and less persistent at tasks (Asbjornsen et al., 2005; Cai & McPherson, 2017; Carroll & Breadmore, 2018). Their distractibility may result from an inability to make out what people around them are saying—which, in turn, may reduce the quality of others' interactions with them.

Because otitis media is so widespread, current evidence argues strongly in favor of early prevention. Crowded living conditions and exposure to cigarette smoke and other pollutants are linked to the disease, probably accounting for its high incidence among low-SES children (Bartholomew, 2015; Jang, Jun, & Park, 2016). And compared with children remaining at home, rates of otitis media nearly double in children who attend child-care centers, where severe, antibacterial-resistant strains of respiratory infections can easily develop and spread. Risk increases further with the number of daily child-care settings a child experiences, which magnifies the number of peers with whom the child comes in contact (Morrissey, 2013).

Early otitis media can be prevented in the following ways:

- *Frequent screening for the disease, followed by prompt medical intervention.* Plastic tubes that drain the narrow Eustachian tubes of the middle ear often are used to treat repeated episodes of otitis media in children, although their effectiveness is uncertain (Venekamp et al., 2018).

- *Child-care settings that control infection.* Because infants and young children often put toys in their mouths, these objects should be rinsed frequently with a disinfectant. Pacifier

Otitis media is widespread among children who attend child-care centers, where close contact leads to rapid spread of respiratory infections.

use has also been linked to a greater risk of otitis media (Nelson, 2012). Spacious, well-ventilated rooms and small group sizes help limit spread of the disease.

- *Verbally stimulating adult–child interaction.* Developmental problems associated with otitis media are reduced or eliminated in high-quality child-care centers (Vernon-Feagans et al., 2007). When caregivers are verbally stimulating and keep noise to a minimum, children have more opportunities to hear, and benefit from, spoken language.

- *Vaccines.* Many cases of otitis media are associated with pneumonia and influenza infection, making pneumonia immunization in infancy and annual flu vaccination effective preventive measures (Principi, Baggi, & Esposito, 2012; Sigurdsson et al., 2018).

Auto and traffic accidents, suffocation, drowning, and poisoning are the most common injuries resulting in childhood deaths (Safe Kids Worldwide, 2015). Motor vehicle collisions are by far the most frequent overall source of injury. They rank as the second leading U.S. cause of mortality from birth to age 5 (after suffocation among infants and drowning among toddlers and preschoolers) and as the leading cause among school-age children and adolescents.

Factors Related to Childhood Injuries   The common view of childhood injuries as "accidental" suggests that they are due to chance and cannot be prevented. In fact, these injuries occur within a complex *ecological system* of individual, family, community, and societal influences—and we can do something about them.

As Tommy's case suggests, individual differences exist in the safety of children's behaviors. Because of their higher activity level and greater impulsivity and risk taking, boys are nearly twice as likely as girls to be injured, and their injuries are more severe (Merrick, 2016). Parents realize that they need to take more steps to protect their young sons than daughters from injury, and most do so. Still, mothers judge that they are less likely to succeed in preventing injuries in sons than in daughters (Morrongiello & Kiriakou, 2004; Morrongiello, Ondejko, & Littlejohn, 2004). This belief may keep them from sufficiently monitoring the most injury-prone boys.

Childhood injury rates are highest in areas with extensive poverty, lack of high-quality child care, and weak parental vigilance, as illustrated by these children's makeshift playground.

Children with certain temperamental and personality characteristics—inattentiveness, overactivity, irritability, defiance, and aggression—are also at greater risk for injuries (Ordonana, Caspi, & Moffitt, 2008; Schwebel & Gaines, 2007). As we saw in Chapter 7, these children present child-rearing challenges. They are likely to protest when placed in auto seat restraints, to refuse to take a companion's hand when crossing the street, and to disobey after repeated instruction and discipline.

Poverty, single parenthood, and low parental education are also strongly associated with injury (Dudani, Macpherson, & Tamim, 2010; Schwebel & Brezausek, 2007). Parents who must cope with many daily stressors often have little time or energy to monitor the safety of their children. And their homes and neighborhoods are likely to be noisy, crowded, and rundown, posing further risks.

Broad societal conditions also affect childhood injury. In developing countries, the rate of childhood deaths from injuries is far greater than in developed nations and soon may exceed disease as the leading cause of childhood mortality (Kahn et al., 2015). Rapid population growth, overcrowding in cities, and heavy road traffic combined with weak safety measures are major causes. Safety devices, such as car safety seats and bicycle helmets, are neither readily available nor affordable.

Childhood injury rates are high in the United States because of extensive poverty, shortages of high-quality child care (to supervise children in their parents' absence), and a high rate of births to teenagers, who are neither psychologically nor financially ready for parenthood (Child Trends, 2014a; Höllwarth, 2013). But U.S. children from economically advantaged families are also at considerably greater risk for injury than children in other Western nations. This indicates that besides reducing poverty and teenage parenthood and upgrading the status of child care, additional steps are needed to ensure children's safety.

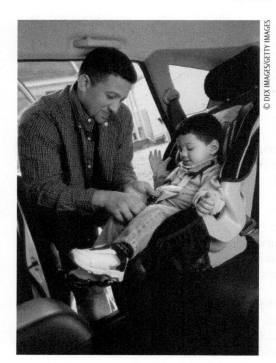

Parental attention to straightforward precautions—such as properly securing children in car safety seats—can substantially reduce childhood injury rates.

Preventing Childhood Injuries   Childhood injuries have many causes, so a variety of approaches are needed to control them. Laws prevent many injuries, for example, by requiring car safety seats, child-resistant caps on medicine bottles, flameproof clothing, and fencing around backyard swimming pools—the site of 50 percent of early childhood drownings. Communities can help by modifying their physical environments. Providing inexpensive and widely available public transportation can reduce the amount of time that children spend in cars. Playgrounds, a common site of injury, can be covered with protective surfaces. Free, easily installed window guards can be given to families in high-rise apartment buildings to prevent falls. And media campaigns can inform parents and children about safety issues.

But even though they know better, many parents and children behave in ways that compromise safety. During the past several decades, U.S. parents have changed very little in how much they do to protect their children, citing such reasons as "the chances of serious injury are slim," taking necessary steps "is a hassle," and (among low-income families) safety devices (such as home fire extinguishers and bicycle helmets) "cost too much." For example, about 27 percent of U.S. parents (like Tommy's mother) fail to place their children in car safety seats, and nearly 75 percent of infant seats and 40 percent of child booster seats are improperly used (Macy et al., 2015). Yet research confirms that young children properly restrained in car safety seats have a 70 to 80 percent reduced risk of injury in a crash (Centers for Disease Control and Prevention, 2017b). American parents, especially, seem willing to ignore familiar safety practices, perhaps because of the high value they place on individual rights and personal freedom.

Furthermore, many parents overestimate young children's knowledge of safety rules and consequently pull back from monitoring and controlling their access to

APPLYING WHAT WE KNOW

Reducing Unintentional Injuries in Early Childhood

SUGGESTION	DESCRIPTION
Provide age-appropriate supervision and safety instruction.	Despite gains in understanding and self-control, preschoolers need nearly constant supervision. To encourage children to remember and obey safety rules, establish the rules, explain the reasons behind them, consistently enforce them, and praise children for following them.
Know the child's temperament.	Children who are unusually active, distractible, negative, or curious have more than their share of injuries and need extra monitoring.
Eliminate the most serious dangers from the home.	Examine all spaces for safety. For example, in the kitchen, store dangerous products in high cabinets out of sight, and keep sharp implements in a latched drawer. Remove guns; if that is impossible, store them unloaded in a locked cabinet. Always accompany young preschoolers to the bathroom, and keep all medicines in containers with safety caps.
During automobile travel, always restrain the child properly in the back seat of the car.	Use an age-appropriate, properly installed car safety seat or booster seat until the child is at least 4 feet 9 inches tall and 8 to 12 years of age, and strap the child in correctly every time. Children should always ride in the back seat; passenger-side air bags in the front seat deploy so forcefully that they can cause injury or death to a child. Never leave a child alone in a car, even on a cool, sunny day; a child's core body temperature increases 3 to 5 times faster than an adult's, with risk of permanent injury or death.
Select safe playground equipment and sites.	Make sure sand, wood chips, or rubberized matting has been placed under swings, see-saws, slides, and jungle gyms and that all playground equipment is well-maintained. Check yards for dangerous plants. Always supervise outdoor play.
Be extra cautious around water.	Constantly observe children during water play; even shallow, inflatable pools are frequent sites of drownings. While they are swimming, young children's heads should not be immersed in water; they may swallow so much that they develop water intoxication, which can lead to convulsions and death.
Practice safety around animals.	Wait to get a pet until the child is mature enough to handle and help care for it—usually around ages 5 or 6. Never leave a young child alone with an animal; bites often occur during playful roughhousing. Model and teach humane pet treatment.

Source: Centers for Disease Control and Prevention, 2017f.

hazards—a premature transition associated with a rise in home injuries. When parents teach safety rules to preschoolers, they often do so as a reaction to unsafe behaviors, rather than as an advance preventive. And they frequently fail to explain the basis for the rules—despite evidence that explanations enhance children's retention, understanding, and compliance (Morrongiello, Ondejko, & Littlejohn, 2004; Morrongiello et al., 2014). Even with well-learned rules, preschoolers need supervision to ensure that they comply.

Interventions aimed at parents that highlight risk factors and that model and reinforce safety practices are effective in reducing home hazards and childhood injuries (Kendrick et al., 2008). Family conditions associated with childhood injuries must be similarly addressed: relieving crowding in the home, providing social supports to ease parental stress, and teaching parents to use effective discipline—a topic we will take up in Chapter 10. Positive parenting— an affectionate, supportive relationship with the child; consistent, reasonable expectations for maturity; and oversight to ensure safety-rule compliance—substantially reduces injury rates, especially in overactive, emotionally reactive, and impulsive children. And in two-parent households, effective coparenting combined with both parents' involvement with young children are helpful as well (Nepomnyaschy & Donnelly, 2015; Schwebel & Gaines, 2007). But to implement these strategies, parents must have sufficient time and emotional resources along with relevant knowledge and skills. Refer to Applying What We Know above for ways to minimize unintentional injuries in early childhood.

ASK YOURSELF

8.3a Cite major milestones of gross- and fine-motor development in early childhood.

8.3b Describe individual differences in preschoolers' motor skills and ways to enhance motor development in early childhood.

8.3 Motor Development

Observe several 2- to 6-year-olds at play in a neighborhood park, preschool, or child-care center. You will see that an explosion of new motor skills occurs in early childhood, each of which builds on the simpler movement patterns of toddlerhood.

During the preschool years, children continue to integrate previously acquired skills into more complex, *dynamic systems.* Then they revise each new skill as their bodies grow larger and stronger, their central nervous systems develop, their environments present new challenges, and they set new goals, aided by gains in perceptual and cognitive capacities.

8.3.1 Gross-Motor Development

As children's bodies become more streamlined and less top-heavy, their center of gravity shifts downward, toward the trunk. As a result, balance improves greatly, paving the way for new motor skills involving large muscles of the body. By age 2, preschoolers' gaits become smooth and rhythmic—secure enough that soon they leave the ground, at first by running and later by jumping, hopping, galloping, and skipping.

As children become steadier on their feet, their arms and torsos are freed to experiment with new skills—throwing and catching balls, steering tricycles, and swinging on horizontal bars and rings. Then upper- and lower-body skills combine into more refined actions. Five- and 6-year-olds simultaneously steer and pedal a tricycle and flexibly move their whole body when throwing, catching, hopping, and jumping. By the end of the preschool years, all skills are performed with greater speed and endurance. Table 8.1 provides a closer look at gross-motor development in early childhood.

Changes in ball skills provide an excellent illustration of preschoolers' gross-motor progress. Young preschoolers stand still, facing the target, throwing with their arm thrust forward (see Figure 8.5a). Catching is equally awkward. Two-year-olds extend their arms and hands rigidly, using them as a single unit to trap the ball. By age 3, children flex their elbows enough to trap the ball against the chest. But if the ball arrives too quickly, they cannot adapt, and it may bounce off the body (Haywood & Getchell, 2014).

Gradually, children call on the shoulders, torso, trunk, and legs to support throwing and catching. By age 4, children rotate the body and take a step forward to add force to their throw. Around 5 to 6 years, they begin by shifting their weight to a rear foot in a preparatory backswing and then shift forward, rotating the trunk and stepping into the throw as they release the ball (see Figure 8.5b). As a result, the ball travels faster and farther. When the ball is returned, older preschoolers predict its place of landing by moving forward, backward, or sideways. Soon, they can catch the ball with their hands and fingers, "giving" with arms and body to absorb the force of the ball.

LOOK and LISTEN

Play a game of catch with a 2- to 3-year-old, then with a 4- to 6-year-old. What differences in movement and coordination are evident?

TABLE 8.1   Changes in Gross- and Fine-Motor Skills During Early Childhood

AGE	GROSS-MOTOR SKILLS	FINE-MOTOR SKILLS
2–3 years	Walks more rhythmically; hurried walk changes to run Jumps, hops, throws, and catches with rigid upper body Pushes riding toy with feet; little steering	Puts on and removes simple items of clothing Zips and unzips large zippers Uses spoon effectively
3–4 years	Walks up stairs, alternating feet, and down stairs, leading with one foot Jumps and hops, flexing upper body Throws and catches with slight involvement of upper body; still catches by trapping ball against chest Pedals and steers tricycle	Fastens and unfastens large buttons Serves self food without assistance Uses scissors Copies vertical line and circle Draws first picture of person, using tadpole image
4–5 years	Walks down stairs, alternating feet Runs more smoothly Gallops and skips with one foot Throws ball with increased body rotation and transfer of weight from one foot to the other; catches ball with hands Rides tricycle rapidly, steers smoothly	Uses fork effectively Cuts with scissors following line Copies triangle, cross, and some letters
5–6 years	Increases running speed to 12 feet per second Gallops more smoothly; engages in true skipping Displays mature throwing and catching pattern Rides bicycle with training wheels	Uses knife to cut soft food Ties shoes Draws person with six parts Copies some numbers and simple words

Sources: Haywood & Getchell, 2014; Malina & Bouchard, 1991.

8.3.2 Fine-Motor Development

Like gross-motor development, fine-motor skills take a giant leap forward in the preschool years. As control of the hands and fingers improves, young children put puzzles together, build with small blocks, cut and paste, string beads, and use touch screens adeptly. To parents, fine-motor progress is most apparent in two areas: (1) children's care of their own bodies, and (2) the drawings and paintings that fill the walls at home, child care, and preschool.

Throwing style typical of young preschoolers
(a)

Throwing style typical of older children
(b)

FIGURE 8.5   Changes in throwing during early childhood. At age 2 to 3, children stand still, simply bringing the hand back and throwing rigidly without taking a step. Gradually, they involve the entire body. By age 5 to 6, they typically engage in arm, leg, and trunk rotation and preparatory action before executing the throw. Integrated throwing movements become increasingly refined and adapted to the throwing situation during middle childhood. (Adapted figures drawn from film tracings taken in the Motor Development and Child Study Laboratory, University of Wisconsin–Madison and now available from the Motor Development Film Collection, Kinesiology Division, Bowling Green State University. © Mary Ann Roberton. Reprinted by permission of Mary Ann Roberton).

Preschoolers gradually become more proficient at self-help skills of dressing and feeding themselves. Most master shoe tying, the most complex self-help skill, around age 6.

Self-Help Skills   As Table 8.1 shows, young children gradually become self-sufficient at dressing and feeding. Two-year-olds put on and take off simple items of clothing. By age 3, children can dress and undress well enough to take care of toileting needs by themselves. Between ages 4 and 5, children can dress and undress without supervision. At mealtimes, young preschoolers use a spoon well, and they can serve themselves. By age 4 they are adept with a fork, and around 5 to 6 years they can use a knife to cut soft foods. Roomy clothing with large buttons and zippers and child-sized eating utensils help children master these skills.

Preschoolers get great satisfaction from managing their own bodies. They are proud of their independence, and their new skills also make life easier for adults. But parents must be patient about these abilities: When tired and in a hurry, young children often revert to eating with their fingers. And the 3-year-old who dresses himself in the morning sometimes ends up with his shirt on inside out, his pants on backward, and his left snow boot on his right foot! Perhaps the most complex self-help skill of early childhood is shoe tying, mastered around age 6. Success requires a longer attention span, sufficient working memory to hold in mind an intricate series of hand movements, and the dexterity to perform them. Shoe tying illustrates the close connection between motor and cognitive development, as do two other skills: drawing and writing.

Drawing   When given crayon and paper, even toddlers scribble in imitation of others. And after being shown by an adult how to use a smartphone drawing app to select a color from a palette and draw on the screen, children as young as age 2 can use it to scribble (Yadav & Chakraborty, 2017). As the young child's ability to mentally represent the world expands, markings on the page or screen take on meaning. A variety of factors combine with fine-motor control in the development of children's artful representations (Golomb, 2004). These include the realization that pictures can serve as symbols, improved planning and spatial understanding, and the emphasis that the child's culture places on artistic expression.

Typically, drawing progresses through the following sequence:

1. *Scribbles.* As long as drawing materials are available, many children begin to draw during the second year. At first, the intended representation is contained in gestures rather than in the resulting marks on the page. For example, one 22-month-old rapidly made some dots on a page and explained, "Crayon running!"

    Recall from Chapter 6 that 2-year-olds treat realistic-looking pictures symbolically (see page 205 in Chapter 6). However, they have difficulty interpreting line drawings. When an adult held up a drawing indicating which of two objects preschoolers should drop down a chute, 3-year-olds used the drawing as a symbol to guide their behavior, but 2-year-olds did not (Callaghan, 1999).

2. *First representational forms.* Around age 3, children's scribbles start to become pictures. Often children make a gesture with the crayon, notice that they have drawn a recognizable shape, and then label it. In one case, a 2-year-old made some random scribbles and then, realizing the resemblance between his scribbles and noodles, named the creation "chicken pie and noodles" (Winner, 1986).

    Few 3-year-olds spontaneously draw so others can tell what their picture represents. However, after an adult demonstrated how drawings can be used to stand for objects in a game, more 3-year-olds drew recognizable forms (Callaghan & Rankin, 2002). Western parents and teachers spend much time promoting 2- and 3-year-olds' language and make-believe play but relatively little time showing them how they can use drawings to represent their world (Cohn, 2014). When adults draw with children and point out resemblances between drawings and objects, preschoolers' pictures become more comprehensible and detailed (Braswell & Callanan, 2003).

FIGURE 8.6 **Examples of young children's drawings.** The universal tadpolelike shape that children use to draw their first picture of a person is shown on the left. The tadpole soon becomes an anchor for details such as arms, fingers, toes, and facial features that sprout from the basic shape. By the end of the preschool years, children produce more complex, differentiated pictures like the one on the right by a 5-year-old child. (*Left:* From H. Gardner, 1980, *Artful Scribbles: The Significance of Children's Drawing*, New York: Basic Books, p. 64. Copyright © 1980 by Howard Gardner. Reprinted by permission of Basic Books, an imprint of Perseus Books, conveyed through Copyright Clearance Center. *Right:* © Children's Museum of the Arts New York, Permanent Collection.)

LOOK and LISTEN

Visit a preschool or child-care center where artwork by 3- to 5-year-olds is plentiful. Note developmental progress in drawings of human and animal figures and in the complexity of children's pictures.

A major milestone in drawing occurs when children use lines to represent the boundaries of objects, enabling 3- and 4-year-olds to draw their first picture of a person. Fine-motor and cognitive limitations lead preschoolers to reduce the figure to the simplest form that still looks human: the universal "tadpole" image, a circular shape with lines attached, shown on the left in Figure 8.6, produced by children from widely differing cultures (Gernhardt, Rübeling, & Keller, 2014; Rübeling, 2014). Four-year-olds add features, such as eyes, nose, mouth, hair, fingers, and feet, as the tadpole drawings illustrate.

3. *More realistic drawings.* Five- and 6-year-olds create more complex drawings, like the one on the right in Figure 8.6, containing more conventional human and animal figures, with the head and body differentiated. Older preschoolers' drawings still contain perceptual distortions because they have just begun to represent depth. Use of depth cues, such as overlapping objects, smaller size for distant than for near objects, diagonal placement, and converging lines, increases during middle childhood (Nicholls & Kennedy, 1992).

Realism in drawing appears gradually, with improvements in visual perception, fine-motor skills, symbolic understanding, and the working memory capacity needed to combine these components into a representation (Morra & Panesi, 2017; Riggs, Jolley, & Simpson, 2013; Toomela, 2002). Drawing of geometric objects follows the steps illustrated in Figure 8.7. (1) Three- to 7-year olds draw a single unit to stand for an object. To represent a cube, they draw a square; to represent a cylinder, they draw a circle, an oval, or a rectangle. (2) During the late preschool and school years, children represent salient object parts. They draw several squares to stand for a cube's sides and draw two circles and some lines to represent a cylinder. However, the parts are not joined properly. (3) Older school-age children and adolescents integrate object parts into a realistic whole (Toomela, 1999).

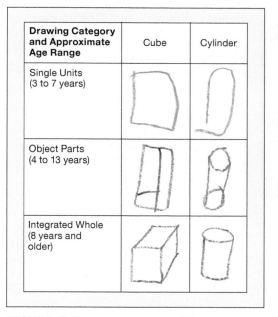

Drawing Category and Approximate Age Range	Cube	Cylinder
Single Units (3 to 7 years)		
Object Parts (4 to 13 years)		
Integrated Whole (8 years and older)		

FIGURE 8.7 **Development of children's drawings of geometric objects—a cube and a cylinder.** As these examples show, drawings change from single units to representation of object parts. Then the parts are integrated into a realistic whole. (Based on Toomela, 2003.)

Cultural Influences | Why Are Children from Asian Cultures Advanced in Drawing Skills?

Observations of young children's drawings in Asian cultures, such as China, Japan, Korea, the Philippines, Taiwan, and Vietnam, reveal skills that are remarkably advanced over those of their Western agemates. What explains such early artistic ability?

To answer this question, researchers examined cultural influences on children's drawings, comparing China to the United States. Artistic models offered by the culture, teaching strategies, valuing of the visual arts, and expectations for children's artistic development have a notable impact on the art that children produce.

In China's 4,000-year-old artistic tradition, adults showed children how to draw, teaching the precise steps required to depict people, butterflies, fish, birds, and other images. When taught to paint, Chinese children follow prescribed brush strokes, at first copying their teacher's model. To learn to write, they must concentrate hard on the unique details of each Chinese character—a requirement that likely enhances their drawing ability. Chinese parents and teachers believe that children can be creative only after they have acquired a foundation of artistic knowledge and technique (Golomb, 2004). To that end, China has devised a national art curriculum with standards and teaching materials extending from age 3 through secondary school.

The United States, as well, has a rich artistic tradition, but its styles and conventions are enormously diverse compared with those of Asian cultures. Children everywhere try to imitate the art around them as a way to acquire their culture's "visual language." But American children face a daunting imitative task, much like a child growing

up in a context where each person speaks a different language (Cohn, 2014). Furthermore, U.S. art education emphasizes independence—finding one's own style. American teachers typically assume that copying others' drawings stifles creativity, so they discourage children from doing so (Copple & Bredekamp, 2009). Rather than promoting correct ways to draw, U.S. teachers, and parents as well, emphasize imagination and self-expression. While one American father and his 5-year-old daughter drew pictures side-by-side, he commented, "There aren't any rules when you draw, so you can do it any way you want. That's what's fun about drawing."

Does the Chinese method of teaching drawing skills beginning in the preschool years interfere with children's creativity? To find out, researchers followed a group of Chinese-American children of immigrant parents and a group of European-American children, all from middle-SES two-parent families, from ages 5 to 9. At two-year intervals, the children's human-figure drawings were rated for maturity and originality (inclusion of novel elements) (Huntsinger et al., 2011). On each occasion, the Chinese-American children's drawings were judged more advanced and also more creative.

Interviews revealed that European-American parents more often provided their children with a rich variety of art materials, whereas Chinese-American parents more often enrolled their children in art lessons, viewing the development of artistic competence as more important. The Chinese-American children also spent more time as preschoolers and kindergartners in focused practice of fine-motor tasks, including drawing.

A 3-year-old in a Beijing preschool follows her teacher's directions in an artistic exercise aimed at improving control of the crayon while experimenting with color combinations. Systematic teaching of artistic knowledge and technique combined with adult expectations that young children learn to draw well contributes to Chinese children's advanced drawing skills.

And the more time they spent practicing, especially when their parents taught and modeled drawing at home, the more mature their drawing skills. At the same time, Chinese-American children's artistic creativity flourished under this systematic approach to promoting artistic maturity. Once they succeeded at drawing basic forms, they spontaneously added unusual details of their own.

In sum, even though young Chinese children are taught how to draw, their artistic products are original. Once they succeed at drawing basic forms, they spontaneously add unusual details of their own. Although Western children may come up with rich ideas about what to draw, until they acquire the necessary skills, they cannot implement those ideas. Cross-cultural research indicates that children benefit from adult guidance in learning to draw, just as they do in learning to talk.

Cultural Variations in Development of Drawing   In cultures that have rich artistic traditions and that highly value artistic competence, children create elaborate drawings that reflect the conventions of their culture. Adults encourage young children by guiding them in mastering basic drawing skills, modeling ways to draw, and discussing their pictures. Peers, as well, talk about one another's drawings and copy from one another's work (Boyatzis, 2000; Braswell, 2006). All of these practices enhance young children's drawing progress. And as the Cultural Influences box above reveals, they help explain why, from an early age, children in Asian cultures are advanced over Western children in drawing skills.

In cultures with little interest in art, even older children and adolescents produce only simple forms. In the Jimi Valley, a remote region of Papua New Guinea with no indigenous pictorial art, many children do not go to school and therefore have little opportunity to develop drawing skills. When a Western researcher asked nonschooled Jimi 10- to 15-year-olds to draw a human figure for the first time, most produced nonrepresentational scribbles and shapes or simple "stick" or "contour" images (see Figure 8.8) (Martlew & Connolly, 1996). These forms, which resemble those of preschoolers, seem to be a universal beginning in drawing. Once children realize that lines must evoke human features, they find solutions to figure drawing that vary somewhat from culture to culture but, overall, follow the sequence described earlier.

Early Printing   When preschoolers first try to write, they scribble, making no distinction between writing and drawing. As they experiment with lines and shapes, notice print in storybooks, and observe people writing, they attempt to print letters and, later, words. Around age 4, children's writing shows some distinctive features of print, such as separate forms arranged in a line on the page. But children often include picturelike devices. For example, they might use a circular shape to write "sun." Or they might call a large scribble the word *lion,* a small scribble the word *caterpillar,* and a red scribble the word *apple* (Ehri & Roberts, 2006; Levin & Bus, 2003). Applying their understanding of the symbolic function of drawings, 4-year-olds asked to write typically make a "drawing of print." Only gradually, between ages 4 and 6, as they learn to name alphabet letters and link them with language sounds, do children realize that writing stands for language.

Preschoolers' first attempts to print often involve their name, generally using a single letter. "How do you make a *D?*" my older son David asked at age 3½. When I printed a large uppercase *D,* he tried to copy. "*D* for David," he proclaimed, quite satisfied with his backward, imperfect creation. A year later, David added several letters, and around age 5, he printed his name clearly enough that others could read it.

Between ages 3 and 5, children acquire skill in gripping a pencil. As Figure 8.9 shows, 3-year-olds display diverse grip patterns and pencil angles, varying their grip depending on the direction and location of the marks they want to make. By trying out different forms of pencil-holding, they discover the grip and angle that maximize stability and writing efficiency (Greer & Lockman, 1998). By age 5, most children use an adult grip pattern and a fairly constant pencil angle across a range of drawing and writing conditions.

(a)   (b)

FIGURE 8.8   Human figure drawings produced by nonschooled 10- to 15-year-olds of the Jimi Valley of Papua New Guinea. Many produced (a) "stick" figures or (b) "contour" figures, which resemble the tadpole form of young preschoolers. (From M. Martlew & K. J. Connolly, 1996, "Human Figure Drawings by Schooled and Unschooled Children in Papua New Guinea," *Child Development, 67,* pp. 2750–2751. © The Society for Research in Child Development. Adapted with permission of John Wiley and Sons, Inc., conveyed through Copyright Clearance Center, Inc.)

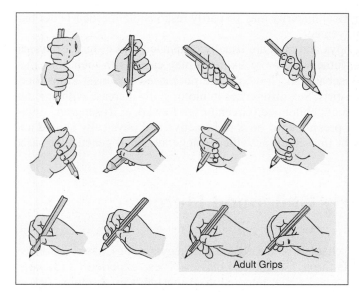

FIGURE 8.9   Variations in 3-year-olds' pencil grip. Through experimenting with different grips, preschoolers gradually discover an adult grip with one or two fingers on top of the pencil, which maximizes writing stability and efficiency. (Based on Greer & Lockman, 1998.)

Adult Grips

© LAURA DWIGHT PHOTOGRAPHY

Gains in fine-motor control and perception, along with experience with written materials, contribute to this 4-year-old's emerging skill at gripping a marker and printing his name.

In addition to gains in fine-motor control, advances in perception contribute to the ability to print. Like many children, David continued to reverse letters until well into second grade. Once preschoolers distinguish writing from nonwriting around age 4, they make progress in identifying individual letters. Many preschoolers confuse letter pairs that are alike in shape with subtle distinctive features, such as *C* and *G, E* and *F,* and *M* and *W* (Bornstein & Arterberry, 1999). Mirror-image letter pairs (*b* and *d, p* and *q*) are especially hard to discriminate. Until children start to read, they do not find it especially useful to notice the difference between these forms.

The ability to tune in to mirror images and to scan a printed line from left to right improves as children gain experience with written materials (Casey, 1986). Besides providing practice with a vital fine-motor skill, writing requires children to use their letter–sound knowledge to decide which marks, and in what order, to place on the page. The more parents and teachers assist preschoolers and kindergartners in their efforts to print, the more advanced children are in writing and other aspects of early literacy development. Furthermore, many studies confirm that being able to write letters and one's own name by kindergarten predicts better reading and spelling achievement during the school years (Aram & Levin, 2011; Shanahan & Lonigan, 2010). We will consider early childhood literacy in greater detail in Chapter 9.

8.3.3 Individual Differences in Motor Skills

Wide individual differences exist in the ages at which children reach motor milestones. A tall, muscular child tends to move more quickly and to acquire certain gross-motor skills earlier than a short, stocky youngster. And as in other domains, parents and teachers probably provide more encouragement to children with genetically based motor-skill advantages.

Sex differences in motor skills are evident in early childhood. Boys are ahead of girls in skills that emphasize force and power. By age 5, they can broad-jump slightly farther, run slightly faster, and throw a ball about 5 feet farther. Girls have an edge in fine-motor skills and in certain gross-motor skills that require a combination of good balance and foot movement, such as hopping and skipping (Fischman, Moore, & Steele, 1992; Haywood & Getchell, 2014). Boys' greater muscle mass and, in the case of throwing, slightly longer forearms contribute to their skill advantages. And girls' greater overall physical maturity may be partly responsible for their better balance and precision of movement.

From an early age, boys and girls are usually channeled into different physical activities. For example, fathers are more likely to play catch with their sons than with their daughters. Baseballs and footballs are purchased for boys, jump ropes and sewing materials for girls. Sex differences in motor skills increase with age, but they remain small throughout childhood (Greendorfer, Lewko, & Rosengren, 1996). This suggests that social pressures for boys to be active and physically skilled and for girls to play quietly at fine-motor activities exaggerate small genetically based sex differences.

Sex differences in motor development are already apparent in early childhood. Girls have an edge in skills that require balance and precision of movement, like jumping rope, but boys benefit from greater encouragement to improve their throwing, catching, and running skills.

8.3.4 Enhancing Early Childhood Motor Development

Many Western parents provide preschoolers with early training in gymnastics, tumbling, dance, soccer, and other movement skills through organized classes. These experiences can offer excellent opportunities for exercise and social interaction. But aside from throwing (where direct instruction is helpful), formal lessons during the preschool years have little added impact on gross-motor progress. Rather, children master the gross-motor skills of early childhood through everyday play.

When play spaces (left) are properly designed and equipped, young children respond eagerly to gross-motor challenges and develop new skills through informal play. Fine-motor skills benefit from environments richly stocked with puzzles, construction sets, and tools for sculpting, cutting, pasting, drawing, painting, and writing (above).

Nevertheless, the physical environment in which play takes place can affect mastery of complex motor skills. The Society of Health and Physical Educators (2009a) recommends that preschoolers engage in at least 60 minutes of adult-planned physical experiences in which parents and teachers provide enjoyable games and other playful activities, and up to several hours of child-directed physical activity, every day. When children have play spaces and equipment appropriate for running, climbing, jumping, and throwing and are encouraged to use them, they respond eagerly to these challenges. But if balls are too large and heavy to be properly grasped and thrown, or jungle gyms, ladders, and horizontal bars are suitable for only the largest and strongest children, then preschoolers cannot easily acquire new motor skills. Playgrounds must offer a range of equipment to meet the diverse needs of individual children.

Similarly, development of fine-motor skills can be supported through daily routines, such as dressing and pouring juice, and through richly equipped early childhood environments that include puzzles, construction sets, drawing, painting, sculpting, cutting, pasting, and writing. And as our discussion revealed, adults who guide and support children in drawing and writing foster not just their fine-motor mastery but their general artistic and literacy progress, respectively.

Finally, the social climate created by adults can enhance or dampen preschoolers' motor development. When parents and teachers criticize a child's performance, push specific motor skills, or promote a competitive attitude, they risk undermining children's self-confidence and, in turn, their motor mastery (Berk, 2006). Adult involvement in young children's motor activities should focus on fun rather than on winning or perfecting the "correct" technique.

ASK YOURSELF

Connect ■ How are experiences that best support preschoolers' gross-motor development consistent with experience-expectant brain growth of the early years? (Return to page 163 in Chapter 5 to review.)

Apply ■ Mabel and Chad want to do everything they can to support their 3-year-old daughter's motor development. What advice would you give them?

Reflect ■ Do you think that American children should be provided with systematic instruction in drawing skills beginning in early childhood, similar to the direct teaching Chinese children receive? Explain.

SUMMARY

8.1 A Changing Body and Brain (p. 281)

8.1 Describe body growth and brain development in early childhood.

- Gains in body size taper off in early childhood as children become longer and leaner, and individual differences in body size and rate of growth become more apparent.

DIAHANNE LUCAS

- New epiphyses emerge in the skeleton, and by the end of the preschool years, children start to lose their primary teeth. Care of primary teeth is essential because diseased baby teeth can affect the health of permanent teeth. Childhood tooth decay is common, especially among low-SES children.

- By age 4 to 5, many parts of the cerebral cortex have overproduced synapses, and synaptic pruning occurs. To make room for the connective structures of stimulated neurons, many surrounding neurons die, leading to reduced brain plasticity.

- Prefrontal-cortical areas devoted to various aspects of executive function develop rapidly from early to middle childhood. For most children, the left cerebral hemisphere is especially active, supporting rapidly expanding language skills.

- Changes in other areas of the brain involve establishing links between brain structures. Fibers linking the **cerebellum** to the cerebral cortex grow and myelinate, enhancing motor coordination and cognition. Also developing rapidly are the **reticular formation,** responsible for alertness and consciousness; the **hippocampus,** which plays a vital role in memory and understanding of space; the **amygdala,** which plays a central role in processing novelty and emotional information; and the **corpus callosum,** which connects the two cortical hemispheres.

- Persistent childhood poverty can compromise brain structures crucial for learning, thereby contributing to the lower cognitive scores of poverty-stricken children relative to their financially better-off agemates.

8.2 Influences on Physical Growth and Health (p. 285)

8.2a Describe the effects of heredity, restful sleep, nutrition, and infectious disease on physical growth and health in early childhood.

- Genes influence physical growth by controlling production and release of two vital hormones from the **pituitary gland: growth hormone (GH),** which affects the development of almost all body tissues, and **thyroid-stimulating hormone (TSH),** which affects brain growth and body size.

- Because GH is released during the child's sleeping hours, sleep contributes to body growth. Sleep difficulties are associated with impaired cognitive functioning and emotional adjustment, especially for low-SES children. Total sleep declines in early childhood, but with substantial individual variability.

© GURPAL DUTTA/INDIAPICTURE/ALAMY STOCK PHOTO

- Sleep problems frequently stem from inadequate parental control over young children's use of screen media, as well as a mismatch between parental demands and children's sleep needs. Many preschoolers have difficulty falling asleep, and most waken occasionally at night. A few suffer from sleep disorders, such as sleep-walking or sleep terrors, which run in families, suggesting a genetic influence. These problems can also be triggered by stress or extreme fatigue. Most subside with age.

- As growth rate slows, preschoolers' appetites decline, and they often become wary of new foods. Providing preschoolers unpressured opportunities to taste new foods can promote healthy, varied eating. In contrast, excessive parental control over children's food intake interferes with children's responsiveness to hunger cues and can lead to eating problems.

- Dietary deficiencies are associated with attention and memory difficulties, academic and behavior problems, and greater susceptibility to infectious diseases. Diseases also contribute to malnutrition, especially those that cause persistent diarrhea. In developing countries, inexpensive oral rehydration therapy (ORT) and zinc supplements can prevent most developmental impairments and deaths due to diarrhea.

- Immunization rates are lower in the United States than in other industrialized nations because many low-income children lack access to adequate health care. Parental stress and misconceptions about vaccine safety also contribute.

- Child-care attendance increases the risk of exposure to infectious diseases. Because repeated bouts of otitis media can disrupt language development and later academic performance, early prevention is important.

8.2b Cite factors that increase the risk of unintentional injuries, and explain how childhood injuries can be prevented.

- Unintentional injuries are the leading cause of childhood mortality in industrialized nations. Injury victims are more likely to be boys; to be temperamentally irritable, inattentive, overactive, and aggressive; and to live in stressed, poverty-stricken, crowded family environments.

- Effective injury prevention includes passing laws that promote child safety; creating safer home, travel, and play environments; relieving sources of family stress; and changing parent and child behaviors.

© DEX IMAGES/GETTY IMAGES

8.3 Motor Development

(p. 296)

8.3a *Cite major milestones of gross- and fine-motor development in early childhood.*

■ As preschoolers' center of gravity shifts toward the trunk, balance improves and gaits become smooth and rhythmic, paving the way for such new gross-motor achievements as running, jumping, hopping, galloping, skipping, and throwing and catching.

■ Increasing control of the hands and fingers leads to dramatic improvements in fine-motor skills. Preschoolers gradually become adept at self-help skills such as dressing themselves and using a fork and knife.

■ As perceptual, cognitive, and fine-motor capacities improve, children's drawings progress from 1- to 2-year-olds' scribbles to 3- and 4-year-olds' representational forms and 5- and 6-year-olds' more realistic drawings.

■ Children's artistic traditions also influence their drawings. In Asian cultures, early teaching of how to draw produces results that are remarkably advanced without dampening children's creativity.

■ Between 3 and 5 years, children experiment with pencil grip; by age 5, most use an adult-like grip that maximizes stability and writing efficiency.

■ Improved perception and exposure to written materials contribute to progress in discriminating and accurately printing individual letters. When parents and teachers support children's efforts to print, preschoolers are more advanced in writing and other aspects of literacy development. The ability to write letters and one's own name by kindergarten predicts better reading and spelling achievement during the school years.

8.3b *Describe individual differences in preschoolers' motor skills and ways to enhance motor development in early childhood.*

■ Body build and opportunity for physical play affect early childhood motor development. Sex differences that favor boys in skills requiring force and power and girls in skills requiring good balance and fine movements are partly genetic, but social pressures exaggerate them.

■ Children master the motor skills of early childhood through informal play experiences, with little benefit from exposure to formal training. Motor development during the preschool years is best promoted through richly equipped play environments that offer pleasurable physical activities and accommodate a wide range of abilities.

© BLEND IMAGES/ALAMY STOCK PHOTO

IMPORTANT TERMS AND CONCEPTS

amygdala (p. 285)
cerebellum (p. 284)
corpus callosum (p. 285)

growth hormone (GH) (p. 287)
hippocampus (p. 284)
pituitary gland (p. 286)

reticular formation (p. 284)
thyroid-stimulating hormone (TSH) (p. 287)

chapter

9

Cognitive Development in Early Childhood

Working in the Garden

Aljay van der Merwe, 6 years, South Africa

Cultivating a garden requires the ability to resist distraction, focus attention on what's important at the moment, and plan—components of executive function that improve during early childhood, contributing greatly to cognitive and social development.

Reprinted with permission from Children's Museum of the Arts Permanent Collection, New York, NY

One rainy morning, as I observed in our laboratory preschool, Leslie, the children's teacher, joined me at the back of the room. "Preschoolers' minds are such a blend of logic, fantasy, and faulty reasoning," Leslie reflected. "Every day, I'm startled by the maturity and originality of what they say and do. Yet at other times, their thinking seems limited and inflexible."

Leslie's comments sum up the puzzling contradictions of early childhood cognition. That day, for example, 3-year-old Sammy looked up, startled, after a loud crash of thunder outside. "A magic man turned on the thunder!" he pronounced. Even when Leslie patiently explained that thunder is caused by lightning, not by a person turning it on, Sammy persisted: "Then a magic lady did it."

In other respects, Sammy's thinking was surprisingly advanced. At snack time, he accurately counted, "One, two, three, four!" and then got four cartons of milk, one for each child at his table. Sammy's keen memory and ability to categorize were also evident. He could recite by heart *The Very Hungry Caterpillar*, a story he had heard many times. And he could name and classify dozens of animals.

But when his snack group included more than four children, Sammy's counting broke down. And some of his notions about quantity seemed as fantastic as his understanding of thunder. After Priti dumped out her raisins, scattering them on the table, Sammy asked, "How come you got lots, and I only got this little bit?" He didn't realize that he had just as many raisins; his were simply all bunched up in a tiny red box.

While Priti was washing her hands after snack, Sammy stuffed her remaining raisins back in the box and placed it in her cubby. When Priti returned and looked for her raisins, Sammy insisted, "You know where they are!" He failed to consider that Priti, who hadn't seen him move the raisins, would expect them to be where she had left them.

In this chapter, we explore early childhood cognition, drawing on three theories with which you are already familiar. To understand Sammy's reasoning, we turn first to Piaget's and Vygotsky's theories along with evidence highlighting the strengths and limitations of each. Then we examine additional research on young children's cognition inspired by the information-processing perspective. Next, we address factors that contribute to individual differences in mental development—the home environment, the quality of preschool and child care, and the many hours young children spend with screen media. Our chapter concludes with the dramatic expansion of language in early childhood. ■

What's Ahead in Chapter 9

9.1 Piaget's Theory: The Preoperational Stage
Advances in Mental Representation • Make-Believe Play • Symbol–Real-World Relations • Limitations of Preoperational Thought • Follow-Up Research on Preoperational Thought • Evaluation of the Preoperational Stage • Piaget and Education

■ **SOCIAL ISSUES: EDUCATION:** *Children's Gestures Facilitate Cognitive Change*

9.2 Vygotsky's Sociocultural Theory
Private Speech • Social Origins of Early Childhood Cognition • Vygotsky and Early Childhood Education • Evaluation of Vygotsky's Theory

■ **CULTURAL INFLUENCES:** *Children in Village and Tribal Cultures Observe and Participate in Adult Work*

9.3 Information Processing
Executive Function • Memory • Problem Solving • The Young Child's Theory of Mind • Early Literacy and Mathematical Development

■ **BIOLOGY AND ENVIRONMENT:** *Autism and Theory of Mind*

9.4 Individual Differences in Mental Development
Early Childhood Intelligence Tests • Home Environment and Mental Development • Preschool, Kindergarten, and Child Care • Educational Screen Media

■ **SOCIAL ISSUES: EDUCATION:** *Teaching Through Guided Play*

9.5 Language Development
Vocabulary • Grammar • Conversation • Supporting Language Learning in Early Childhood

---

9.1 Piaget's Theory: The Preoperational Stage

As children move from the sensorimotor to the **preoperational stage,** which spans the years 2 to 7, the most obvious change is an extraordinary increase in representational, or symbolic, activity. Recall that infants and toddlers have an impressive ability to mentally represent their world. In early childhood, this capacity blossoms.

9.1.1 Advances in Mental Representation

Piaget acknowledged that language is our most flexible means of mental representation. By detaching thought from action, rapid gains in language permit far more efficient thinking than was possible during the first two years. When we think in words, we overcome the limits of our momentary experiences. We can deal with

9.1a Describe advances in mental representation, and limitations of thinking, during the preoperational stage.

9.1b Explain the implications of follow-up research on early childhood cognitive development for the accuracy of Piaget's preoperational stage.

9.1c Describe educational principles that can be derived from Piaget's theory.

past, present, and future at once and combine concepts in unique ways, as when we imagine a hungry caterpillar eating bananas or monsters flying through the forest at night.

Despite the power of language, Piaget did not regard it as a primary ingredient in childhood cognitive change. Instead, he believed that sensorimotor activity leads to internal images of experience, which children then label with words (Piaget, 1936/1952). In support of Piaget's view, recall from Chapter 6 that children's first words have a strong sensorimotor basis. Also, infants and toddlers acquire an impressive range of categories long before they use words to label them (see page 215 in Chapter 6). But as we will see, Piaget underestimated the power of language to spur children's cognition.

9.1.2 Make-Believe Play

Make-believe play is another excellent example of the development of representation in early childhood. Piaget believed that through pretending, young children practice and strengthen newly acquired representational schemes. Drawing on his ideas, several investigators have traced changes in make-believe play during the preschool years.

Development of Make-Believe One day, Sammy's 20-month-old brother, Dwayne, visited the classroom. Dwayne wandered around, picked up a toy telephone receiver, eyed his mother, said, "Hi, Mommy," and then dropped it. Next, he found a cup, pretended to drink, and then toddled off again. Meanwhile, Sammy joined Vance and Priti in the block area for a space shuttle launch.

"That can be our control tower," Sammy suggested, pointing to a corner by a bookshelf. "Countdown!" he announced, speaking into his "walkie-talkie"—a small wooden block. "Five, six, two, four, one, blastoff!" Priti made a doll push a pretend button, and the rocket was off!

Comparing Dwayne's pretend play with Sammy's, we see three important changes that reflect the preschool child's growing symbolic mastery:

- *Play detaches from the real-life conditions associated with it.* In early pretending, toddlers use only realistic objects—a toy telephone to talk into or a cup to drink from. Their earliest pretend acts usually imitate adults' actions and are not yet flexible. Children younger than age 2, for example, will pretend to drink from a cup but refuse to pretend a cup is a hat (Rakoczy, Tomasello, & Striano, 2005). They have trouble using an object (cup) that already has an obvious use as a symbol of another object (hat).

  After age 2, children pretend with less realistic toys—for example, a block for a telephone receiver. Gradually, they can imagine objects and events without any support from the real world, as Sammy's imaginary control tower illustrates. And by age 3, they flexibly understand that an object (a yellow stick) may take on one fictional identity (a toothbrush) in one pretend game and another fictional identity (a carrot) in a different pretend game (Wyman, Rakoczy, & Tomasello, 2009).

- *Play becomes less self-centered.* At first, make-believe is directed toward the self. For example, Dwayne pretends to feed only himself. Soon, children begin to direct pretend actions toward objects, as when a child feeds a doll. Early in the third year, they become detached participants, making a doll feed itself or pushing a button to launch a rocket (McCune, 1993). Increasingly, preschoolers realize that agents and recipients of pretend actions can be independent of themselves.

- *Play includes more complex combinations of schemes.* Dwayne can pretend to drink from a cup, but he does not yet combine drinking with pouring. Later, children combine schemes with those of peers in **sociodramatic play,** the make-believe with others that is under way by the end of the second year and that increases rapidly in complexity during early childhood (Jing & Li, 2015; Kavanaugh, 2006). Already, Sammy and his classmates can create and coordinate several roles in an elaborate plot. By the end of the preschool years, children have a sophisticated understanding of role relationships and story lines.

© ELLEN B. SENISI

Make-believe play increases in sophistication during the preschool years. Children pretend with less realistic toys and increasingly coordinate make-believe roles, such as school bus driver and passengers.

In sociodramatic play, children as young as age 2 display awareness that make-believe is a representational activity. They distinguish make-believe from real experiences and grasp that pretending is a deliberate effort to act out imaginary ideas—an understanding that strengthens over early childhood (Rakoczy, Tomasello, & Striano, 2004; Sobel, 2006). Listen closely to a group of preschoolers as they assign roles and negotiate make-believe plans: "*You pretend to be* the astronaut, *I'll act like* I'm operating the control tower!" "Wait, *I gotta set up* the space-ship." In communicating about pretend, children think about their own and others' fanciful representations—evidence that they have begun to reason about people's mental activities, a topic we will return to later in this chapter.

Benefits of Make-Believe   Today, many researchers regard Piaget's view of make-believe as mere practice of representational schemes as too limited. In their view, play not only reflects but also contributes to children's cognitive and social skills. Sociodramatic play has been studied most thoroughly. Compared with social nonpretend activities (such as drawing or putting puzzles together), during sociodramatic play preschoolers' interactions last longer, show more involvement, draw more children into the activity, and are more cooperative (Creasey, Jarvis, & Berk, 1998).

It is not surprising, then, that preschoolers who devote a lot of time to sociodramatic play are rated by observers as more socially competent than their peers a year later (Lindsey & Colwell, 2013). And many studies reveal that make-believe predicts a wide variety of cognitive capacities, including executive function, memory, logical reasoning, language and literacy (including story comprehension and storytelling skills), math computation skills, imagination, creativity, and the ability to reflect on one's own thinking, regulate emotions, and take another's perspective (Berk & Meyers, 2013; Buchsbaum et al., 2012; Carlson & White, 2013; Melzer & Palermo, 2016; Mottweiler & Taylor, 2014; Nicolopoulou & Ilgaz, 2013; Roskos & Christie, 2013; Wallace & Russ, 2015).

Critics, however, point out that the evidence just summarized is largely correlational, with too many studies failing to control all factors that might alternatively explain their findings (Lillard et al., 2013). In response, play investigators note that decades of research are consistent with a positive role for make-believe play in development and that new, carefully conducted research strengthens that conclusion (Berk, 2015; Carlson, White, & Davis-Unger, 2014; Thibodeau et al., 2016). Furthermore, make-believe is difficult to study experimentally, by training children to engage in it. Besides alterations of reality, true make-believe *play* involves spontaneous qualities, including intrinsic motivation (doing it for fun, not to please an adult), positive emotion, and child control of the experience (Bergen, 2013).

Finally, much make-believe takes place when adults are not around to observe it! An estimated 25 to 45 percent of preschoolers and young school-age children spend much time in solitary make-believe, creating imaginary companions—special fantasized friends endowed with humanlike qualities. For example, one preschooler created Nutsy and Nutsy, a pair of boisterous birds who lived outside her bedroom window and often went along on family outings (Gleason, Sebanc, & Hartup, 2000; Taylor et al., 2004). Imaginary companions were once viewed as a sign of maladjustment, but research challenges this assumption. Children with imaginary companions display more complex and imaginative make-believe play; more often describe others in terms of their internal states, including desires, thoughts, and emotions; and are more sociable with peers (Bouldin, 2006; Davis, Meins, & Fernyhough, 2014; Gleason, 2013, 2017). Imaginary companions seem to offer children rich opportunities to enact events and practice social skills that might occur in real relationships.

Applying What We Know on page 310 lists ways to enhance preschoolers' make-believe play. Later we will return to the origins and consequences of make-believe from an alternative perspective—that of Vygotsky.

9.1.3 Symbol–Real-World Relations

To engage in symbolic representation, as in make-believe and drawing—and to understand other forms of symbolic representation, such as photographs, models, and maps—children must realize that symbols correspond to something specific in everyday life. In Chapter 6, we

LOOK and LISTEN

Observe the make-believe play of several 2- to 4-year-olds at a family gathering, a preschool or child-care center, or in another community setting. Describe pretend acts that illustrate important developmental changes.

APPLYING WHAT WE KNOW

Enhancing Make-Believe Play in Early Childhood

STRATEGY	DESCRIPTION
Provide sufficient space and play materials.	Generous space and materials allow for many play options and reduce conflict.
Encourage children's play without controlling it.	Model, guide, and build on young preschoolers' play themes. Provide open-ended suggestions ("I wonder whether the animals want to walk or take a train ride."), and talk with the child about the thoughts, motivations, and emotions of play characters. These forms of adult support lead to more elaborate pretending. Refrain from directing the child's play; excessive adult control destroys the creativity and pleasure of make-believe.
Offer a variety of both realistic materials and materials without clear functions.	Children use realistic materials, such as trucks, dolls, tea sets, dress-up clothes, and toy scenes (house, farm, garage, airport) to act out everyday roles in their culture. Materials without clear functions (such as blocks, cardboard cylinders, paper bags, and sand) inspire fantastic role play, such as "pirate" and "creature from outer space."
Ensure that children have many rich, real-world experiences to inspire positive fantasy play.	Opportunities to participate in real-world activities with adults and to observe adult roles in the community provide children with rich social knowledge to integrate into make-believe. Restricting time devoted to screen media, especially access to programs and video games with violent content, limits the degree to which violent themes and aggressive behavior become part of children's play. (See pages 379–380 in Chapter 10.)
Help children solve social conflicts constructively.	Cooperation is essential for sociodramatic play. Guide children toward positive relationships with peers by helping them resolve disagreements constructively. For example, ask, "What can you do if you want a turn?" If the child cannot think of possibilities, suggest options and assist the child in implementing them.

Sources: Nielsen & Christie, 2008; Weisberg et al., 2013.

saw that by the middle of the second year, children grasp the symbolic function of realistic-looking pictures and, around age 2½, of TV and video. When do children comprehend other challenging symbols—for example, three-dimensional scale models of real-world spaces?

In one study, 2½- and 3-year-olds watched an adult hide a small toy (Little Snoopy) in a scale model of a room and then were asked to retrieve it. Next, they had to find a larger toy (Big Snoopy) hidden in the room that the model represented. Not until age 3 could most children use the model as a guide to finding Big Snoopy in the real room (DeLoache, 1987). The 2½-year-olds did not realize that the model could be both *a toy room* and *a symbol of another room.* They had trouble with **dual representation**—viewing a symbolic object as both an object in its own right and a symbol. In support of this interpretation, when researchers made the model room less prominent as an object, by placing it behind a window and preventing children from touching it, more 2½-year-olds succeeded at the search task (DeLoache, 2002). Recall, also, that in make-believe play, 1½- to 2-year-olds cannot use an object that has an obvious use (cup) to stand for another object (hat).

How do children grasp the dual representation of symbolic objects? When adults point out similarities between models and real-world spaces, 2½-year-olds perform better on the find-Snoopy task (Peralta de Mendoza & Salsa, 2003). And 3-year-olds who can use a model of a room to locate Big Snoopy readily transfer their understanding to a simple map (Marzolf & DeLoache, 1994). Similarly, opportunities to make drawings and label them, and to observe peers and adults doing the same, help children grasp that line drawings can represent real-world objects—an understanding first evident between ages 2½ and 3 (Preissler & Bloom, 2008). By age 4, children flexibly realize that an ambiguous drawing, such as a circular shape,

These 4-year-olds understand dual representation—that the structure they are building is both an object in its own right and a potential model of a real-world structure.

can serve as a symbol for more than one object, such as a balloon or a lollipop (Allen, Nurm-soo, & Freeman, 2016). They are also aware that which object the drawing actually stands for depends on the intention of the artist.

In sum, experiences with diverse symbols—photographs, drawings, make-believe, and maps—strengthen preschoolers' understanding that one object can stand for another. With age, children comprehend a wider range of symbols that have little physical similarity to what they represent. As a result, doors open to vast realms of knowledge.

9.1.4 Limitations of Preoperational Thought

Aside from gains in representation, Piaget described preschoolers in terms of what they *cannot* understand. As the term *pre*operational suggests, he compared them to older, more compe-tent children who have reached the concrete operational stage. According to Piaget, young children are not capable of *operations*—mental representations of actions that obey logical rules. Rather, their thinking is rigid, limited to one aspect of a situation at a time, and strongly influenced by the way things appear at the moment.

Egocentrism   For Piaget, the most fundamental deficiency of preoperational thinking is **egocentrism**—failure to distinguish oth-ers' symbolic viewpoints from one's own. He believed that when children first mentally represent the world, they tend to focus on their own viewpoint and simply assume that others perceive, think, and feel the same way they do.

Piaget's most convincing demonstration of egocentrism involves his *three-mountains problem,* described in Figure 9.1. He also regarded egocentrism as responsible for preoperational chil-dren's *animistic thinking*—the belief that inanimate objects have lifelike qualities, such as thoughts, wishes, feelings, and intentions (Piaget, 1926/1930). Recall Sammy's insistence that someone must have turned on the thunder. According to Piaget, because young children egocentrically assign human purposes to physical events, magical thinking is common during the preschool years.

Piaget believed that preschoolers' egocentric bias prevents them from *accommodating,* or reflecting on and revising their faulty rea-soning in response to their physical and social worlds. To understand this shortcoming, let's consider some additional tasks that Piaget gave to children.

FIGURE 9.1   **Piaget's three-mountains problem.** Each moun-tain is distinguished by its color and by its summit. One has a red cross, another a small house, and the third a snow-capped peak. Children at the preoperational stage respond egocentrically. They cannot select a picture that shows the mountains from the doll's perspective. Instead, they simply choose the photo that reflects their own vantage point.

Inability to Conserve   Piaget's famous conservation tasks reveal a variety of deficiencies of preoperational thinking. **Conservation** refers to the idea that certain physical characteristics of objects remain the same, even when their outward appearance changes. At snack time, Priti and Sammy had identical boxes of raisins, but when Priti spread her raisins out on the table, Sammy was convinced that she had more.

In another conservation task, involving liquid, the child is shown two identical tall glasses of water and asked if they contain equal amounts. Once the child agrees, an adult pours the water in one glass into a short, wide container, changing its appearance but not its amount. Then the adult asks the child whether the amount of water is the same or has changed. Pre-operational children think the quantity has changed. They explain, "There is less now because the water is way down here" (that is, its level is so low) or, "There is more now because it is all spread out." Figure 9.2 on page 312 illustrates other conservation tasks that you can try with children.

The inability to conserve highlights several related aspects of preoperational children's thinking. First, their understanding is *centered,* or characterized by **centration.** They focus on one aspect of a situation, neglecting other important features. In conservation of liquid, the child *centers* on the height of the water, failing to realize that changes in width compensate for the changes in height. Second, children are easily distracted by the *perceptual appearance* of

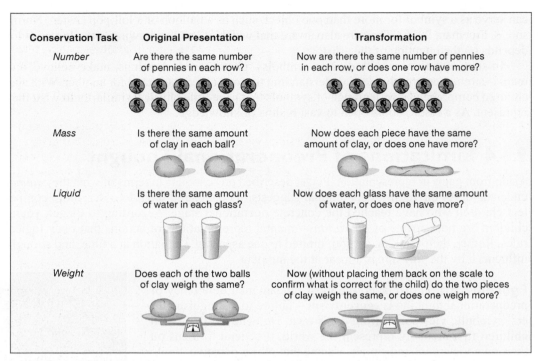

FIGURE 9.2   Some Piagetian conservation tasks. Children at the preoperational stage cannot yet conserve. These tasks are mastered gradually over the concrete operational stage. Children in Western nations typically acquire conservation of number, mass, and liquid sometime between 6 and 7 years and conservation of weight between 8 and 10 years.

objects. Third, children treat the initial and final states of the water as unrelated events, ignoring the *dynamic transformation* (pouring of water) between them.

The most important illogical feature of preoperational thought is its **irreversibility**—an inability to mentally go through a series of steps in a problem and then reverse direction, returning to the starting point. *Reversibility* is part of every logical operation. After Priti spills her raisins, Sammy cannot reverse by thinking, "I know Priti doesn't have more raisins than I do. If we put them back in that little box, her raisins and mine would look just the same."

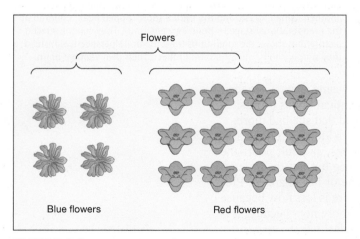

FIGURE 9.3   A Piagetian class inclusion problem. Children are shown 16 flowers, 4 of which are blue and 12 of which are red. When asked, "Are there more red flowers or flowers?" the preoperational child responds, "More red flowers," failing to realize that both red and blue flowers are included in the category "flowers."

Lack of Hierarchical Classification   Preoperational children have difficulty with **hierarchical classification**—the organization of objects into classes and subclasses on the basis of similarities and differences. Piaget's famous *class inclusion problem,* illustrated in Figure 9.3, demonstrates this limitation. Preoperational children *center* on the overriding feature, red. They do not think reversibly, moving from the whole class (flowers) to the parts (red and blue) and back again.

9.1.5 Follow-Up Research on Preoperational Thought

Over the past several decades, researchers have challenged Piaget's view of preschoolers as cognitively deficient. Because many Piagetian problems contain unfamiliar elements or too many pieces of information for young children to handle at once, preschoolers' responses often do not reflect their true abilities. Piaget also missed many naturally occurring instances of effective reasoning by preschoolers. Let's look at some examples.

Egocentric, Animistic, and Magical Thinking When researchers use simplified tasks with familiar objects, 3-year-olds show clear awareness of others' vantage points, such as recognizing how something appears to another person who is looking at it through a color filter (Moll & Meltzoff, 2011). Even 2-year-olds realize that what they see sometimes differs from what another person sees. When asked to help an adult look for a lost object, 24-month-olds (but not 18-month-olds) handed her a toy resting behind a bucket that was within their line of sight but not the adult's (Moll & Tomasello, 2006).

Nonegocentric responses also appear in young children's everyday interactions. For example, 4-year-olds use shorter, simpler expressions when talking to 2-year-olds than to agemates or adults (Gelman & Shatz, 1978). Furthermore, in describing objects, children do not use such words as "big" and "little" in a rigid, egocentric fashion. Instead, they *adjust* their descriptions to allow for context. By age 3, children judge a 2-inch shoe as little when seen by itself (because it is much smaller than most shoes) but as big for a tiny 5-inch-tall doll (Ebeling & Gelman, 1994). And research described in previous chapters reveals that even toddlers have begun to infer others' intentions and perspectives. In his later writings, Piaget (1945/1951) described preschoolers' egocentrism as a *tendency* rather than an inability. As we revisit the topic of perspective taking, we will see that it develops gradually throughout childhood and adolescence.

Piaget also overestimated preschoolers' animistic beliefs. By age 2½, children give psychological explanations ("he likes to" or "she wants to") for people and occasionally for other animals, but rarely for objects (Hickling & Wellman, 2001). In addition, preschoolers seldom attribute biological properties (like eating and growing) to objects, including robots, indicating that they are well aware that even a self-moving object with lifelike features is not alive. But unlike adults, they often say that robots have perceptual and psychological capacities—for example, seeing, thinking, and remembering (Jipson & Gelman, 2007; Subrahmanyam, Gelman, & Lafosse, 2002). These responses result from incomplete knowledge about certain objects, and they decline with age.

Similarly, preschoolers think that magic accounts for events they otherwise cannot explain—fairies, goblins, and for Sammy, thunder in the opening to this chapter. But their notions of magic are flexible and appropriate. For example, older 3-year-olds and 4-year-olds are more likely to say that a magical process—wishing—caused an event (an object to appear in a box) when a person made the wish before the event

Three- to 5-year-olds distinguish between animate and inanimate and realize, for example, that a robot with lifelike features cannot eat or grow. But because of incomplete knowledge, they often claim that robots have perceptual and psychological capacities, such as seeing, thinking, and remembering.

occurred, the event was consistent with the wish (the wished-for object rather than another object appeared in the box), and no alternative causes were apparent (Woolley, Browne, & Boerger, 2006). These features of causality are the same ones preschoolers rely on in ordinary situations.

Between ages 4 and 8, as children gain familiarity with physical events and principles, their magical beliefs decline. They question the reality of Santa Claus and the Tooth Fairy, realize that magicians' feats are due to trickery, and say that characters and events in fantastical stories aren't real (Shtulman & Yoo, 2015; Woolley & Cornelius, 2013; Woolley & Cox, 2007). Still, because children entertain the possibility that something they imagine might materialize, they may react with anxiety to scary stories, TV shows, and nightmares.

Culture and religion play a role in children's fantastic and supernatural ideas. The more live Santas children encounter in their everyday lives and the more they observe their parents vouching for Santa's existence, the less likely they are to question who live Santa really is (Goldstein & Woolley, 2016). This helps explain why Jewish children are more likely than their Christian agemates to express disbelief in Santa Claus, and the Tooth Fairy as well. Having heard at home that Santa is imaginary, Jewish children generalize this attitude to other unseen agents (Woolley, 1997). And cultural myths about wishing—for example, the custom

LOOK and LISTEN

Try the conservation of number and mass tasks in Figure 9.2 with a 3- or 4-year-old. Next, simplify conservation of number by reducing the number of pennies, and relate conservation of mass to the child's experience by pretending the clay is baking dough and transforming it into cupcakes. Did the child perform more competently?

of making a wish before blowing out birthday candles—probably underlie the conviction of most 3- to 6-year-olds that by wishing, you can sometimes make your desires come true (Woolley, 2000).

In actuality, adults as well as children often attribute hard-to-explain events to both supernatural and natural causes. Children, however, prefer natural over supernatural explanations, even in cultures that strongly endorse supernatural beliefs (Woolley, Cornelius, & Lacey, 2011). In one study, researchers asked 5- to 15-year-olds living in South African communities where witchcraft beliefs were widespread to explain why certain people got AIDS. Children of all ages—even 5-year-olds—more often gave biological explanations (contact with a sick person, exposure to germs) than bewitchment explanations (a neighbor cast a spell). Bewitchment accounts increased in middle childhood, as children acquired their culture's belief system, but they did not replace biological explanations (Legare & Gelman, 2008). And children mentioned witchcraft as a cause of serious illness far less often than did adults!

Logical Thought Many studies show that when preschoolers are given tasks that are simplified and made relevant to their everyday lives, they do not display the illogical characteristics that Piaget saw in the preoperational stage. For example, when a conservation-of-number task is scaled down to include only three items instead of six or seven, 3-year-olds perform well (Gelman, 1972). And when preschoolers are asked carefully worded questions about what happens to substances (such as sugar) after they are dissolved in water, most 3- to 5-year-olds know that the substance is conserved—that it continues to exist, can be tasted, and makes the liquid heavier, even though it is invisible in the water (Au, Sidle, & Rollins, 1993; Rosen & Rozin, 1993).

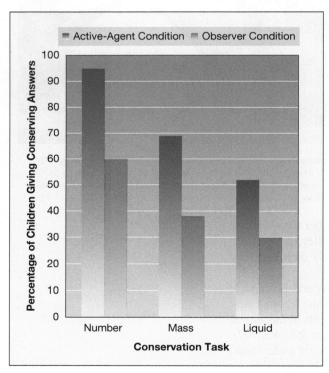

FIGURE 9.4 **Influence of children's active transformation of materials on conservation performance.** Six-year-olds randomly assigned to an active-agent condition, in which they actively transformed the materials in conservation tasks, performed much better than children in an observer condition who experienced typical task procedures in which an adult demonstrated the transformations for them. (From M. Lozada & N. Carro, 2016, "Embodied Action Improves Cognition in Children: Evidence from a Study Based on Piagetian Conservation Tasks," *Frontiers in Psychology*, 7, Art. No. 393. Adapted by permission.)

Notice in our description on page 311 that in a typical conservation task, the child observes while an adult demonstrates the transformation. In one study, 6-year-olds were randomly assigned to either an observer condition or an active-agent condition, in which they actively transformed the conservation materials. For example, in a conservation of mass task, the adult asked the child to form two identical balls with the same amount of clay and then roll one ball into a thinner, longer shape. As Figure 9.4 shows, actively manipulating the materials through the transformation process greatly facilitated learning, increasing children's conservation performance across multiple conservation tasks, including number, mass, and liquid (Lozada & Carro, 2016). Furthermore, in this investigation and others, children often used both speech and gesture when explaining their answers. As the Social Issues: Education box on the following page reveals, gesture offers an additional illustration of the vital role of action in advancing children's cognition.

Young children's ability to reason about transformations is evident on problems other than conservation. For example, they can engage in impressive *reasoning by analogy* about physical changes. When presented with the picture-matching problem "Play dough is to cut up play dough as apple is to …," even 3-year-olds choose the correct answer (a cut-up apple) from a set of alternatives, several of which (a bitten apple, a cut-up loaf of bread) share physical features with the right choice (Goswami, 1996). These findings indicate that in familiar contexts, preschoolers can overcome appearances and think logically about cause and effect.

Categorization Despite their difficulty with Piagetian class inclusion tasks, preschoolers organize their everyday knowledge into nested categories at an early age. By the beginning of early childhood, children's categories include objects that go together because of their common function, behavior, or natural kind (animate versus inanimate), challenging Piaget's assumption that preschoolers' thinking is wholly governed by perceptual appearances.

Social Issues: Education | Children's Gestures Facilitate Cognitive Change

A 4-year-old gestures dramatically as she explains an event in a story—a combination of speech and action that promotes learning.

After agreeing that two identical tall, narrow glasses held the same amount of water, 5-year-old Kerry watched as an adult poured the water from one into a short, wide glass. She then confidently asserted that the amount of water had changed. When asked to explain, she replied, "It's less because this one's lower than that one," gesturing with her hands to highlight the discrepant water levels. With this *speech–gesture match*, Kerry conveyed the same nonconserving information in both speech and gesture.

Kerry's classmate Noelle, also a nonconserver, responded differently, with a *speech–gesture mismatch*. While claiming that the short, wide glass held less water, she expressed contrary information in gesture, designating the differing widths of the two glasses with her hands.

Although Piaget believed that action plays a central role in cognitive development, he overlooked the importance of the gestures children produce as they explain their solutions to problems. If we merely listen to Kerry and Noelle, they appear to reason identically. But if we look at their gestures, we can predict which of the two children is most likely to benefit from teaching. When researchers divided 5- to 8-year-olds into those producing speech–gesture matches and those producing mismatches and gave both groups the same training in conservation, those who produced mismatches before instruction were more likely to gain in understanding (Church & Goldin-Meadow, 1986; Ping & Goldin-Meadow, 2008).

Speech–gesture mismatches are common, occurring spontaneously in children of all ages and in adults as well. They have been studied in preschoolers explaining a game, counting objects, and assigning numbers to small and large sets; school-age children solving math problems and puzzles; and adults engaged in a wide variety of activities. Children who produce speech–gesture mismatches appear to be in cognitive transition or, as Piaget expressed it, a state of disequilibrium (see page 198 in Chapter 6). Their behavior indicates that they are considering two contradictory strategies at once, a sign of readiness to learn. On diverse tasks, children and adults who displayed speech–gesture mismatches were more likely than others to gain in performance as the result of teaching (Goldin-Meadow, 2015).

Gestures seem to provide a window into the thoughts of learners as they move from lesser to greater mastery of a problem. But beyond insight into children's thinking, gesturing can facilitate their reasoning, helping them work out their ideas.

In one study, children who were told to gesture while explaining solutions to math problems generated more new and accurate ideas in their gestures than control-group agemates told not to gesture or given no gesturing instructions (Broaders et al., 2007). When later taught how to solve the problems, the children who had been told to gesture displayed greater gains.

Furthermore, training children to produce either type of speech–gesture strategy (a match or a mismatch) while acquiring a concept promotes greater learning than asking them to produce only correct speech (Goldin-Meadow, Cook, & Mitchell, 2009; Wakefield & James, 2015).

Why does gesture promote learning? One conjecture is that it brings together two forms of representation, one in action and the other in speech, enabling the former to influence the latter. Consistent with this view, brain-imaging evidence suggests that gesturing during learning establishes sensorimotor representations in the cerebral cortex that learners reactivate during subsequent encounters with the task (Wakefield et al., 2014).

Parents and teachers can use children's gestures to provide teaching at the most opportune moments. And adults who gesture while teaching encourage children to gesture, which enhances learning (Goldin-Meadow, 2015).

Indeed, 2- to 5-year-olds readily draw appropriate inferences about nonobvious, inner features shared by category members. For example, even without detailed biological or mechanical knowledge, they realize that the insides of animals are responsible for causing certain behaviors (such as making oneself move) that are impossible for nonliving things, such as machines (Gelman, 2003). And after being told that a bird has warm blood and that a stegosaurus (dinosaur) has cold blood, preschoolers infer that a pterodactyl (labeled a dinosaur) has cold blood, even though it closely resembles a bird (Gopnik & Nazzi, 2003).

Nevertheless, when most instances of a category have a certain perceptual property (such as long ears), preschoolers readily categorize on the basis of perceptual features. This indicates that they flexibly use both nonobvious and perceptual information to classify, depending on the situation (Rakison & Lawson, 2013). Watching others interact with objects influences how preschoolers' categorize. When 3- and 4-year-olds observed an adult reveal a nonobvious property of a set of small containers (shaking them to see whether or not they made a sound), most preferred to sort the containers by the nonobvious property, even though they could have sorted by color (Yu & Kushnir, 2016). The children also generalized their bias for sorting by the nonobvious property to a new set of objects. This suggests that by watching the adult, they acquired a categorization strategy that they readily applied to new situations.

These preschoolers understand that a category ("dinosaurs") can be based on underlying characteristics ("cold-blooded"), not just on perceptual features such as upright posture and scaly skin.

Children's own past experience also influences how they categorize. A comparison of Native-American 5-year-olds growing up on the Menominee Reservation in northern Wisconsin with European-American 5-year-olds growing up in Boston revealed that the Menominee children often categorized animals according to their relation to the natural world. For example, they grouped together wolves and eagles because of their shared forest habitat (Ross et al., 2003). In contrast, the European-American children mostly categorized animals according to their common features.

During the second and third years, and perhaps earlier, children discriminate many *basic-level categories*—ones at an intermediate level of generality, such as "chairs," "tables," and "beds." By the third year, children easily move back and forth between basic-level categories and *general categories,* such as "furniture." And they break down basic-level categories into *subcategories,* such as "rocking chairs" and "desk chairs."

Preschoolers' rapidly expanding vocabularies and general knowledge support their impressive skill at categorizing, and they benefit greatly from conversations with adults, who frequently label and explain categories to them. When adults use the word *bird* for hummingbirds, turkeys, and swans, they signal to children that something other than physical similarity binds these instances together (Gelman & Kalish, 2006). Children also ask many questions about their world, the majority of which are information-seeking: "What's that?" "What does it do?" (Chouinard, 2007). Usually parents give informative answers that advance children's conceptual understanding. Picture-book reading is an especially rich context for category learning. In conversing about books, parents provide information that guides children's inferences about the structure of categories: "Penguins live at the South Pole, swim, catch fish, and have thick layers of fat and feathers that help them stay warm."

In sum, although preschoolers' category systems are less complex than those of older children and adults, they already have the capacity to classify hierarchically and on the basis of nonobvious properties. And they use logical, causal reasoning to identify the features that form the basis of a category and to classify new members.

9.1.6 Evaluation of the Preoperational Stage

Table 9.1 provides an overview of the cognitive attainments of early childhood just considered. Compare them with Piaget's description of the preoperational child on pages 311–312. The evidence as a whole indicates that Piaget was partly wrong and partly right about young children's cognitive capacities. When given simplified tasks based on familiar experiences, preschoolers show the beginnings of logical thinking. How can we make sense of the contradictions between Piaget's conclusions and the findings of recent research?

That preschoolers display logical understandings that strengthen with age indicates they attain logical operations gradually. Over time, children rely on increasingly effective mental (as opposed to perceptual) approaches to solving problems. For example, children who cannot use counting to compare two sets of items do not conserve number. Rather, they use perceptual cues to compare the amounts in two sets of items (Rouselle, Palmers, & Noël, 2004). Once preschoolers can count, they apply this skill to conservation-of-number tasks involving just a few items. As counting improves, they extend the strategy to problems with more items. Eventually, they realize that number remains the same after a transformation in the length and spacing of a set of items as long as nothing is added or taken away (Halford & Andrews, 2011). Consequently, they no longer need to count to verify their answer.

Evidence that preschool children can be trained to perform well on Piagetian problems also supports the idea that operational thought is not absent at one point in time and present at another (Siegler & Svetina, 2006). Children who possess some understanding would naturally benefit from training, unlike those with no understanding at all. The gradual development of logical operations poses a serious challenge to Piaget's assumption of abrupt change toward logical reasoning around age 6 or 7. Does a preoperational stage really exist? Some researchers no longer think so. Recall from Chapter 6 that according to the information-processing

TABLE 9.1   **Some Cognitive Attainments of Early Childhood**

APPROXIMATE AGE		COGNITIVE ATTAINMENTS
2–4 years		Shows a dramatic increase in representational activity, as reflected in the development of language, make-believe play, understanding of dual representation, and categorization
		Takes the perspective of others in simplified, familiar situations and in everyday, face-to-face communication
		Distinguishes animate beings from inanimate objects; prefers natural over supernatural explanations for events
		Grasps conservation, notices transformations, reverses thinking, and understands many cause-and-effect relationships in simplified, familiar situations
		Categorizes objects on the basis of common function, behavior, and natural kind as well as perceptual features, depending on context; uses nonobvious, inner features to categorize objects varying widely in external appearance
		Sorts familiar objects into hierarchically organized categories
4–7 years		Becomes increasingly aware that make-believe and other thought processes are representational activities
		Replaces beliefs in magical creatures and events with plausible explanations
		Passes Piaget's conservation of number, mass, and liquid problems

© LAURA DWIGHT PHOTOGRAPHY

© RYAN MCVAY/PHOTODISC/GETTY IMAGES

perspective, children work out their understanding of each type of task separately, and their thought processes are basically the same at all ages—just present to a greater or lesser extent.

Other experts think the stage concept is still valid, with modifications. For example, some *neo-Piagetian theorists* combine Piaget's stage approach with the information-processing emphasis on task-specific change (Case, 1998; Halford & Andrews, 2011). They believe that Piaget's strict stage definition must be transformed into a less tightly knit concept, one in which a related set of competencies develops over an extended period, depending on brain development and specific experiences. These investigators point to evidence that as long as the complexity of tasks and children's exposure to them are carefully controlled, children approach those tasks in similar, stage-consistent ways (Andrews & Halford, 2002; Case & Okamoto, 1996). For example, in drawing pictures, preschoolers depict objects separately, ignoring their spatial arrangement (return to the drawing in Figure 8.6 on page 299 in Chapter 8). In understanding stories, they grasp a single story line but have trouble with a main plot plus one or more subplots.

This flexible stage notion recognizes the unique qualities of early childhood thinking. At the same time, it provides a better account of why, as Leslie put it, "Preschoolers' minds are such a blend of logic, fantasy, and faulty reasoning."

9.1.7 Piaget and Education

Three educational principles derived from Piaget's theory continue to influence teacher training and classroom practices, especially those for young children:

● *Discovery learning.* In a Piagetian classroom, children are encouraged to discover for themselves through spontaneous interaction with the environment. Instead of presenting ready-made knowledge verbally, teachers provide a rich variety of activities designed to promote exploration and discovery, including art, puzzles, table games, dress-up clothing, building blocks, books, measuring tools, natural science tasks, and musical instruments.

- *Sensitivity to children's readiness to learn.* In a Piagetian classroom, teachers introduce activities that build on children's current thinking, challenging their incorrect ways of viewing the world. But they do not try to speed up development by imposing new skills before children indicate they are interested and ready.
- *Acceptance of individual differences.* Piaget's theory assumes that all children go through the same sequence of development, but at different rates. Therefore, teachers must plan activities for individual children and small groups, not just for the whole class. In addition, teachers evaluate educational progress in relation to each child's previous development, rather than on the basis of normative standards, or average performance of same-age peers.

Like his stages, educational applications of Piaget's theory have met with criticism, especially his insistence that young children learn primarily through acting on the environment (Bjorklund & Causey, 2016). As we have already seen, children also use language-based routes to knowledge—a point emphasized by Vygotsky's sociocultural theory, to which we now turn. Nevertheless, Piaget's influence on education has been powerful. He gave teachers new ways to observe, understand, and enhance young children's development and offered strong theoretical justification for child-oriented approaches to classroom teaching and learning.

⊙ ASK YOURSELF

Connect ■ Select two of the following features of preoperational thought: egocentrism, a focus on perceptual appearances, difficulty reasoning about transformations, and lack of hierarchical classification. Present evidence indicating that preschoolers are more capable thinkers than Piaget assumed.

Apply ■ Three-year-old Will understands that his tricycle isn't alive and can't feel or move on its own. But at the beach, while watching the sun dip below the horizon, Will exclaimed, "The sun is tired. It's going to sleep!" What explains this apparent contradiction in Will's reasoning?

Reflect ■ Did you have an imaginary companion as a young child? If so, what was your companion like, and why might you have created it? Were your parents aware of your companion? What was their attitude toward it?

9.2a Describe Vygotsky's perspective on the social origins and developmental significance of children's private speech.

9.2b Describe applications of Vygotsky's theory to education, and evaluate his major ideas.

⊙ 9.2 Vygotsky's Sociocultural Theory

Piaget's de-emphasis on language as a source of cognitive development brought on yet another challenge, this time from Vygotsky's sociocultural theory, which stresses the social context of cognitive development. In Vygotsky's view, the child and the social environment collaborate to mold cognition in culturally adaptive ways. During early childhood, rapid expansion of language broadens preschoolers' participation in social dialogues with more knowledgeable individuals, who encourage them to master culturally meaningful tasks. Soon children start to communicate with themselves in much the same way they converse with others. This greatly enhances their thinking and ability to control their own behavior. Let's see how this happens.

9.2.1 Private Speech

Watch preschoolers as they play and explore the environment, and you will see that they frequently talk out loud to themselves. For example, as Sammy worked a puzzle, he said, "Where's the red piece? I need the red one. Now, a blue one. No, it doesn't fit. Try it here."

Piaget (1923/1926) called these utterances *egocentric speech,* reflecting his belief that young children have difficulty taking the perspectives of others. Their talk, he said, is often "talk for self" in which they express thoughts in whatever form they happen to occur, regardless of whether a listener can understand. Piaget believed that cognitive development and certain social experiences eventually bring an end to egocentric speech. Specifically, through disagreements with peers, children see that others hold viewpoints different from their own. As a result, egocentric speech declines in favor of social speech, in which children adapt what they say to their listeners.

Vygotsky (1934/1987) disagreed with Piaget's conclusions. He maintained that language helps children think about their mental activities and behavior and select courses of action, thereby serving as the foundation for all higher cognitive processes, including controlled attention, deliberate memorization and recall, categorization, planning, problem solving, and self-reflection. In Vygotsky's view, children speak to themselves for self-guidance. As they get older and find tasks easier, their self-directed speech is internalized as silent, *inner speech*—the internal verbal dialogues we carry on while thinking and acting in everyday situations.

Because nearly all studies support Vygotsky's perspective, children's self-directed speech is now called **private speech** instead of egocentric speech. Research indicates that children use more of it when tasks are appropriately challenging (neither too easy nor too hard), after they make errors, or when they are confused about how to proceed. For example, Figure 9.5 shows how 5- and 6-year-olds' private speech increased as researchers made a problem-solving task moderately difficult, then decreased as the task became very difficult (Fernyhough & Fradley, 2005).

With age, as Vygotsky predicted, private speech goes underground, changing into whispers and silent lip movements. Furthermore, children who freely use private speech during a challenging activity are more attentive and involved and perform better than their less talkative agemates (Alarcón-Rubio, Sánchez-Medina, & Prieto-Garcia, 2014; Benigno et al., 2011; Lidstone, Meins, & Fernyhough, 2010). Private speech seems to play an important role in diverse activities in which children must manage their thinking and behavior, including regulating emotions, communicating clearly with others, strengthening autobiographical memories, and thinking flexibly, imaginatively, and creatively (Alderson-Day & Fernyhough, 2015).

Compared with their agemates, children with learning and behavior problems engage in more private speech over a longer period of development (Berk, 2001; Bono & Bizri, 2014; Ostad, 2015; Winsler et al., 2007). They seem to use private speech to help compensate for challenges with attention and cognitive processing that make many tasks more difficult for them.

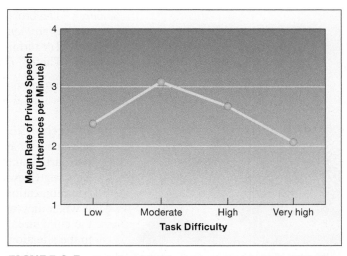

FIGURE 9.5   Relationship of private speech to task difficulty among 5- and 6-year-olds. Researchers increased the difficulty of a problem-solving task. Private speech rose as the task became moderately difficult, then declined as it became highly difficult. Children are more likely to use private speech for self-guidance when tasks are within their zone of proximal development, or range of mastery. (Adapted from Fernyhough & Fradley, 2005.)

A 4-year-old talks to herself as she attempts to mount a toy car on a tow truck. Research supports Vygotsky's theory that children use private speech to guide their thinking and behavior during challenging tasks.

9.2.2 Social Origins of Early Childhood Cognition

Where does private speech come from? Recall from Chapter 6 that Vygotsky believed that children's learning takes place within the *zone of proximal development*—a range of tasks too difficult for the child to do alone but possible with the help of others. Consider the joint activity of Sammy and his mother, who helps him put together a difficult puzzle:

Sammy: "I can't get this one in." *[Tries to insert a piece in the wrong place.]*

Mother: "Which piece might go down here?" *[Points to the bottom of the puzzle.]*

Sammy: "His shoes." *[Looks for a piece resembling the clown's shoes but tries the wrong one.]*

Mother: "Well, what piece looks like this shape?" *[Pointing again to the bottom of the puzzle.]*

Sammy: "The brown one." *[Tries it, and it fits; then attempts another piece and looks at his mother.]*

Mother: "Try turning it just a little." *[Gestures to show him.]*

Sammy: "There!" *[Puts in several more pieces while his mother watches.]*

By questioning, prompting, and suggesting strategies, Sammy's mother keeps the puzzle within his zone of proximal development, at a manageable level of difficulty.

A father engages in scaffolding as his 4-year-old son uses blocks to lay out the streets of a miniature town. As the child gains in competence, his father will gradually withdraw support, permitting his son to take more responsibility for the task.

LOOK and LISTEN

Ask a preschooler to join you in working a difficult puzzle or mastering another challenging task. How did you scaffold the child's progress? Did the child display any self-guiding private speech?

Effective Social Interaction To promote cognitive development, social interaction must have two vital features. The first is **intersubjectivity,** the process by which two participants who begin a task with different understandings arrive at a shared understanding (Newson & Newson, 1975). Intersubjectivity creates a common ground for communication, as each partner adjusts to the other's perspective. Adults try to promote it when they translate their own insights in ways that are within the child's grasp. As the child stretches to understand the adult, she is drawn into a more mature approach to the situation.

The capacity for intersubjectivity is present early, in parent–infant mutual gaze, exchange of vocal and emotional signals, imitation, and joint play with objects; and in toddlers' capacity to infer others' intentions (Brugué & Burriel, 2016; Csibra, 2010). Later, language facilitates intersubjectivity. As conversational skills improve, preschoolers increasingly seek others' help and direct that assistance to ensure that it is beneficial. Between ages 3 and 5, children strive for intersubjectivity in dialogues with peers, as when they affirm a playmate's message, add new ideas, and make contributions to ongoing play to sustain it. They can also be heard saying, "I think [this way]. What do you think?"—evidence of a willingness to share viewpoints (Berk, 2001; Garte, 2015). In these ways, children create zones of proximal development for one another.

A second important feature of social experience is **scaffolding**—adjusting the support offered during a teaching session to fit the child's current level of performance. When the child has little notion of how to proceed, the adult uses direct instruction, breaking the task into manageable units, suggesting strategies, and offering rationales for using them. As the child's competence increases, effective scaffolders—like Sammy's mother—gradually and sensitively withdraw support, turning over responsibility to the child. Then children take the language of these dialogues, make it part of their private speech, and use this speech to organize their independent efforts. Although preschoolers freely use private speech when alone or when others are nearby, they use more in the presence of others (McGonigle-Chalmers, Slater, & Smith, 2014). This suggests that some private speech retains a social purpose, perhaps as an indirect appeal for renewed scaffolding should the child need additional help.

Scaffolding captures the form of teaching interaction that occurs as children work on school or school-like tasks, such as puzzles, model building, conversing about picture books, and (later) academic assignments. It may not apply to other contexts that are equally vital for cognitive development—for example, play or everyday activities, during which adults usually support children's efforts without deliberately teaching.

Research on Social Interaction and Cognitive Development What evidence supports Vygotsky's ideas on the social origins of cognitive development? In previous chapters, we reviewed evidence indicating that when adults establish intersubjectivity by being stimulating, responsive, and supportive, they foster many competencies—attention, language, complex play, and understanding of others' perspectives. In several studies, children whose parents were effective scaffolders used more private speech, were more likely to succeed when attempting challenging tasks on their own, and were more advanced in executive function and overall intellectual performance than children of less effective scaffolders (Berk & Spuhl, 1995; Conner & Cross, 2003; Fay-Stammbach, Hawes, & Meredith, 2014). Improved scaffolding also helps explain why many home-based interventions aimed at enhancing parenting skills in poverty-stricken families result in cognitive gains in early childhood (Guttentag et al., 2014).

Effective scaffolding, however, can take different forms in different cultures. An investigation of Hmong families who had emigrated from Southeast Asia to the United States found, like other studies, that parental cognitive support was associated with children's advanced reasoning skills. But unlike European-American parents, who emphasize independence by encouraging their children to think of ways to approach a task, Hmong parents—who highly value interdependence and child obedience—frequently tell their children what to do (for example, "put this block piece here, then this piece on top of it") (Stright, Herr, & Neitzel, 2009). Among European-American kindergartners, such directive scaffolding is associated with lack of self-control and behavior problems (Neitzel & Stright, 2003). Among the Hmong kindergartners, it is linked to greater rule following, organization, and task completion.

9.2.3 Vygotsky and Early Childhood Education

Both Piagetian and Vygotskian classrooms emphasize active participation and acceptance of individual differences. But a Vygotskian classroom goes beyond independent discovery to promote *assisted discovery.* Teachers guide children's learning with explanations, demonstrations, and verbal prompts, tailoring their interventions to each child's zone of proximal development. Assisted discovery is aided by *peer collaboration,* as children with varying abilities work in groups, teaching and helping one another.

Vygotsky (1935/1978) saw make-believe play as the ideal social context for fostering cognitive development in early childhood. As children create imaginary situations, they learn to follow internal ideas and social rules rather than their immediate impulses. For example, a child pretending to go to sleep follows the rules of bedtime behavior. A child imagining himself as a father and a doll as a child conforms to the rules of parental behavior (Meyers & Berk, 2014). According to Vygotsky, make-believe play is a unique, broadly influential zone of proximal development in which children try out a wide variety of challenging activities and acquire many new competencies. (Turn back to page 309 to review evidence on the contributions of make-believe play to cognitive and social development.)

Make-believe play is also rich in private speech—a finding that supports its role in helping children bring action under the control of thought (Berk & Meyers, 2013). Preschoolers who spend more time engaged in sociodramatic play are better at inhibiting impulses, thinking flexibly, regulating emotion, and taking personal responsibility for following classroom rules (Elias & Berk, 2002; Kelly & Hammond, 2011; Lemche et al., 2003; Thibodeau et al., 2016). These findings support the role of make-believe in children's increasing self-control.

In this Vygotsky-inspired classroom, preschoolers benefit from peer collaboration as they jointly create an elaborate block structure.

9.2.4 Evaluation of Vygotsky's Theory

In granting social experience a fundamental role in cognitive development, Vygotsky's theory underscores the vital role of teaching and helps us understand the wide cultural variation in children's cognitive skills. Nevertheless, his ideas have not gone unchallenged. In some cultures, verbal dialogues are not the only—or even the most important—means through which children learn. When Western parents scaffold their young children's mastery of challenging tasks, they assume much responsibility for children's motivation by frequently giving verbal instructions and conversing with the child. Their communication resembles the teaching that occurs in school, where their children will spend years preparing for adult life. In cultures that place less emphasis on schooling and literacy, parents often expect children to take greater responsibility for acquiring new skills through keen observation and participation in community activities (Rogoff, Correa-Chavez, & Silva, 2011). See the Cultural Influences box on page 322 for research illustrating this difference.

Finally, Vygotsky's theory says little about how basic motor, perceptual, attention, memory, and problem-solving skills, discussed in Chapters 5 and 6, contribute to socially transmitted higher cognitive processes. For example, his theory does not address how these elementary capacities spark changes in children's social experiences, from which more advanced

Cultural Influences | Children in Village and Tribal Cultures Observe and Participate in Adult Work

In Western societies, children are largely excluded from participating in adult work, which generally takes place outside the home. The role of equipping children with the skills they need to become competent workers is assigned to school. In early childhood, middle-SES parents' interactions with children emphasize child-focused activities designed to prepare children to succeed academically—especially adult–child conversations and play that enhance language, literacy, and other school-related knowledge. In village and tribal cultures, children receive little or no schooling, spend their days in contact with or participating in adult work, and start to assume mature responsibilities in early childhood (Gaskins, 2014). Consequently, parents have little need to rely on conversation and play to teach children.

A study comparing 2- and 3-year-olds' daily lives in four cultures—two U.S. middle-SES suburbs, the Efe hunters and gatherers of the Republic of Congo, and a Mayan agricultural town in Guatemala—documented these differences (Morelli, Rogoff, & Angelillo, 2003). In the U.S. communities, young children had little access to adult work and spent much time conversing and playing with adults. In contrast, the Efe and Mayan children rarely engaged in these child-focused activities. Instead, they spent their days close to—and frequently observing—adult work, which often took place in or near the Efe campsite or the Mayan family home.

An ethnography of a remote Mayan village in Yucatán, Mexico, shows that when young children are legitimate onlookers and participants in a daily life structured around adult work, their competencies differ from those of Western preschoolers (Gaskins, 1999; Gaskins, Haight, & Lancy, 2007). Yucatec Mayan adults are subsistence farmers. Men tend cornfields, aided by sons age 8 and older. Women prepare meals, wash clothes, and care for the livestock and garden, assisted by daughters and by sons too young to work in the fields. Children join in these activities from the second year on. When not participating, they are expected to be self-sufficient.

Young children make many nonwork decisions for themselves—how much to sleep and eat, what to wear, when to take their daily bath, and even when to start school. As a result, Yucatec Mayan preschoolers are highly competent at self-care. In contrast, their make-believe play is limited; when it occurs, they usually imitate adult work. Otherwise, they watch others—for hours each day.

Yucatec Mayan parents rarely converse or play with preschoolers or scaffold their learning. Rather, when children imitate adult tasks, parents conclude that they are ready for more responsibility. Then they assign chores, selecting tasks the child can do with little help so that adult work is not disturbed. If a child cannot do a task, the adult takes over and the child observes, reengaging when able to contribute.

Expected to be autonomous and helpful, Yucatec Mayan children seldom display attention-getting behaviors or ask others for something interesting to do. From an early age, they can sit quietly for long periods—through a lengthy religious service or a three-hour truck ride. And when an adult interrupts their activity and directs them to do a chore, they respond eagerly to the type of command that Western children frequently avoid or resent. By age 5, Yucatec Mayan children spontaneously take responsibility for tasks beyond those assigned.

In a South African village, a young child intently watches his mother grind grain. Children in village and tribal cultures observe and participate in the work of their community from an early age.

© DANITA DELIMONT/ALAMY STOCK PHOTO

cognition springs (Bjorklund & Causey, 2016; Daniels, 2011). Piaget paid far more attention than Vygotsky to the development of basic cognitive processes. It is intriguing to speculate about the broader theory that might exist today had Piaget and Vygotsky—the two twentieth-century giants of cognitive development—had a chance to meet and weave together their extraordinary accomplishments.

⊙ ASK YOURSELF

Connect ■ Explain how Piaget's and Vygotsky's theories complement each other. How would classroom practices inspired by these theories be similar? How would they differ?

Apply ■ Tanisha sees her 5-year-old son Toby talking aloud to himself as he plays. She wonders whether she should discourage this behavior. Use Vygotsky's theory to explain why Toby talks to himself. How would you advise Tanisha?

Reflect ■ When do you use private speech? Does it serve a self-guiding function for you, as it does for children? Explain.

9.3 Information Processing

Return to the model of information processing discussed on pages 210–212 in Chapter 6. Recall that information processing focuses on cognitive operations and mental strategies that children use to transform stimuli flowing into their mental systems. As we have already seen, early childhood is a period of dramatic strides in mental representation. And the various components of *executive function* that enable children to succeed in cognitively challenging situations—inhibiting impulses and distracting stimuli, flexibly shifting attention depending on task demands, coordinating information in working memory, and planning—show impressive gains (Carlson, Zelazo, & Faja, 2013). Preschoolers also become more aware of their own mental life and begin to acquire academically relevant knowledge important for school success.

9.3a Describe changes in executive function and memory during early childhood.

9.3b Describe the young child's theory of mind.

9.3c Summarize children's literacy and mathematical knowledge during early childhood.

9.3.1 Executive Function

As parents and teachers know, preschoolers—compared with school-age children—spend shorter times involved in tasks and are more easily distracted. Control of attention improves substantially during early childhood, as studies of inhibition and flexible shifting reveal. As we will see, expansion of working memory supports these attainments. The components of executive function are closely interrelated in the preschool years, and they contribute vitally to academic and social skills from early childhood on (Nelson et al., 2016; Shaul & Schwartz, 2014).

Inhibition   With age, preschoolers gain steadily in ability to inhibit impulses and keep their mind on a competing goal. Consider a task in which the child must tap once when the adult taps twice and tap twice when the adult taps once or must say "night" to a picture of the sun and "day" to a picture of the moon with stars. As Figure 9.6 shows, 3- and 4-year-olds make many errors. But by age 6 to 7, children find such tasks easy (Diamond, 2004; Montgomery & Koeltzow, 2010). They can resist the "pull" of their attention toward a dominant stimulus—a skill that predicts social maturity as early as age 3 to 5 and reading and math achievement from kindergarten through high school (Allan et al., 2014; Duncan et al., 2007; Rhoades, Greenberg, & Domitrovich, 2009).

Flexible Shifting of Attention   In preschoolers and school-age children, the ability to shift one's focus of attention, depending on what's important at the moment, is often studied through rule-use tasks (Zelazo et al., 2013). In a commonly used procedure, the *Dimensional Change Card Sort,* children are asked to switch the rules they use to sort picture cards in the face of conflicting cues. For example, a child might first be told to sort pictures of boats and flowers using color rules, by placing all the blue boats and flowers in a box marked with a blue boat and all the red boats and flowers in a box marked with a red flower. Then the child is asked to switch to shape rules, placing all the boats (irrespective of color) into the box marked with the blue boat and all the flowers into the box marked with the red flower. Three-year-olds persist in sorting by color, whereas most 5-year-olds switch rules flexibly (Zelazo et al., 2013). But when researchers increase the complexity of the rules—for example, requiring children to shift from color to shape rules only on a subset of picture cards with an added black border—most 6-year-olds have difficulty (Henning, Spinath, & Aschersleben, 2011).

As these findings indicate, flexible shifting improves greatly during the preschool years, with gains continuing in middle childhood. Notice how inhibition contributes to preschoolers' flexible shifting (Kirkham, Cruess, & Diamond, 2003; Zelazo et al., 2013).

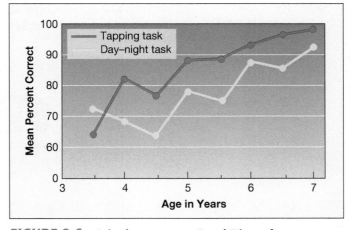

FIGURE 9.6   Gains between ages 3 and 7 in performance on tasks requiring children to inhibit an impulse and focus on a competing goal. In the tapping task, children had to tap once when the adult tapped twice and tap twice when the adult tapped once. In the day–night task, children had to say "night" to a picture of the sun and "day" to a picture of the moon with stars. (From A. Diamond, 2004, "Normal Development of Prefrontal Cortex from Birth to Young Adulthood: Cognitive Functions, Anatomy, and Biochemistry," as appeared in D. T. Stuss & R. T. Knight, [Eds.], *Principles of Frontal Lobe Function,* New York: Oxford University Press, p. 474. Reprinted by permission of Adele Diamond.)

By playing a game of Simon Says, these 3- and 4-year-olds practice inhibition, refraining from acting when their teacher's command omits "Simon Says." Improved inhibition along with gains in working memory contributes to preschoolers' increasing capacity to flexibly shift attention and engage in more complex problem solving.

To switch rules, children must inhibit attending to the previously relevant dimension while focusing on the dimension they had just ignored.

Working Memory Gains in working memory, enabling preschoolers to hold in mind and manipulate more information at once (see page 211 in Chapter 6), contribute to control of attention. A larger working memory permits preschoolers to generate increasingly complex play and problem-solving goals, which require concentration to attain (Senn, Espy, & Kaufmann, 2004). Greater working-memory capacity also eases effort in keeping several rules in mind, ignoring ones not currently important, and flexibly shifting one's focus to new rules, thereby improving performance.

With age, the ability to hold and combine information in working memory becomes increasingly important in problem solving. In one study, both inhibition and working-memory scores predicted 2½- to 6-year-olds' solutions to a problem-solving task requiring multistep planning. But working memory was a stronger predictor for the 4- to 6-year-olds than for the younger children (Senn, Espy, & Kaufman, 2004). Older preschoolers were able to deploy their larger working memories to solve more challenging problems involving planning.

Planning As the findings just described suggest, early childhood is a time of marked gains in **planning**—thinking out a sequence of acts ahead of time and performing them accordingly to reach a goal. Because successful planning requires that basic executive processes be integrated with other cognitive operations, it is regarded as a complex executive function activity (Müller & Kerns, 2015). As long as tasks are not too difficult, older preschoolers can follow a plan.

Consider a task, devised to resemble real-world planning, in which 3- to 5-year-olds were shown a doll named Molly, a camera, and a miniature zoo with a path, along which were three animal cages. The first and third cages had storage lockers next to them; the middle cage, with no locker, housed a kangaroo (see Figure 9.7). The children were told that Molly could follow the path only once and that she wanted to take a picture of the kangaroo. Then they were asked, "What locker could you leave the camera in so Molly can get it and take a photo of the

FIGURE 9.7 **Miniature zoo used to assess children's planning.** After having been told that Molly wanted to take a picture of the kangaroo but could follow the path only once, preschoolers were asked which locker the camera should be left in so Molly could get it and take the photo. Not until age 5 did children plan, more often selecting the first locker. (Based on McColgan & McCormack, 2008.)

kangaroo?" (McColgan & McCormack, 2008). Not until age 5 were children able to plan effectively, selecting the locker at the first cage.

On this and other planning tasks, younger preschoolers have difficulty (McCormack & Atance, 2011). By the end of early childhood, children make strides in postponing action in favor of mapping out a sequence of future moves, evaluating the consequences of each, and adjusting their plan to fit task requirements.

Parenting, Socioeconomic Status, and Development of Executive Function   Parental sensitivity, encouragement, and scaffolding foster preschoolers' executive function skills, as many investigations reveal (Carlson, Zelazo, & Faja, 2013; Devine, Bignardi, & Hughes, 2016). In one study, parental scaffolding of 2- and 3-year-olds while jointly solving a challenging puzzle predicted higher scores on diverse executive function tasks at age 4 (Hammond et al., 2012). Among the 2-year-olds, effective scaffolding led to gains in language, which in turn promoted executive function, perhaps by augmenting children's ability to verbally regulate their behavior through private speech.

With respect to planning, children learn much from cultural tools that support it—directions for playing games, diagrams for construction, recipes for cooking—especially when they collaborate with expert planners who offer scaffolded assistance. In another investigation, mothers were observed jointly using a diagram to construct a structure out of interlocking blocks with their 3-year-olds. Those who pointed out the overall goal of the task, modeled the successive steps needed to reach the goal, and encouraged planning ("Do you want to look at the picture and see what pieces you need first?") had children who scored higher in math achievement when they reached first grade (Lombardi et al., 2017). Parents who take advantage of many opportunities to promote planning in everyday activities, from loading the dishwasher to packing for a vacation, help their children plan more effectively while also enhancing their academic success.

Children learn much from cultural tools that support planning. This preschooler consults a box-top illustration to decide which pieces he should insert next into a partially completed puzzle.

A wealth of evidence confirms that from early childhood on, children from low-SES families score less well on measures of executive function than their higher-SES counterparts—a difference that contributes to SES variations in achievement throughout middle childhood and adolescence (Hackman et al., 2015; Lawson & Farah, 2017). Conditions more common in low-SES homes—reduced parental scaffolding, negative parent–child interactions, and fewer informal learning opportunities—interfere with the development of preschoolers' executive function, thereby diminishing their literacy and math skills and thus their readiness for formal schooling (Devine, Bignardi, & Hughes, 2016).

Poverty exerts an especially negative impact on executive function, in part through maladaptive parenting practices and chronic stress (Lawson et al., 2016). In a sample diverse in SES and ethnicity, poverty-stricken mothers more often interacted harshly and intrusively with their 7- to 24-month-olds—parenting behaviors associated with children's elevated cortisol levels and with poor executive function scores during a follow-up at age 3 (Blair et al., 2011). As the authors noted, poverty and negative parenting undermined early stress regulation, promoting "reactive and inflexible rather than reflective and flexible forms of behavior and cognition" (p. 1980).

Factors that compromise young children's executive function are prime targets for early intervention. In an investigation conducted in rural Pakistan, where extreme poverty is widespread, mothers were randomly assigned to either a parenting intervention or a control group receiving only food supplements during their child's first two years. During monthly group meetings and home visits, trained health workers taught intervention-group mothers about child development and coached them on how to engage in appropriate play and communication activities with their children (Obradović et al., 2016; Yousafzai et al., 2014). Follow-ups revealed that the parenting intervention led to improved home stimulation and maternal scaffolding, which predicted gains in children's cognitive skills, including executive function, at age 4.

As we will see later, preschool intervention is another route to strengthening executive function (Blair, 2016). These approaches may be among the best ways to protect young children from the adverse effects of poverty on brain development, discussed in Chapter 8.

9.3.2 Memory

The memory changes that infants and toddlers experience during the first two years are largely *implicit,* taking place without conscious awareness. In contrast, preschoolers have the language skills to describe what they remember, and they can follow directions on simple memory tasks. This enables researchers to focus on *explicit,* or conscious, memory, which undergoes the greatest change throughout development.

Recognition and Recall   Show a young child a set of 10 pictures of objects. Then mix them up with some unfamiliar items, and ask the child to point to the ones in the original set. You will find that preschoolers' *recognition* memory—ability to tell whether a stimulus is the same as or similar to one they have seen before—is remarkably good. In fact, 4- and 5-year-olds perform nearly perfectly.

Now keep the items out of view, and ask the child to name the ones she saw. This more demanding task requires *recall*—generating a mental image of an absent stimulus. Young children's recall is much poorer than their recognition. At age 2, they can recall no more than one or two items, and at age 4 only about three or four (Perlmutter, 1984).

Gains in recall in early childhood are strongly associated with language development, which greatly enhances long-lasting representations of both lists of items and past experiences (Melby-Lervag & Hulme, 2010). But even preschoolers with good language skills recall poorly because they are not skilled at using **memory strategies**—deliberate mental activities that improve our chances of remembering. Preschoolers do not yet *rehearse,* or repeat items over and over, to remember. Nor do they *organize,* intentionally grouping items that are alike (all the animals together, all the vehicles together) so they can easily retrieve those items by thinking of their similar characteristics—even after they are trained to do so (Bauer, 2013). Memory strategies tax the limited working memories of preschoolers, who have difficulty holding onto pieces of information and applying a strategy at the same time.

Memory for Everyday Experiences   Think about the difference between your recall of listlike information and your memory for everyday experiences—what researchers call **episodic memory.** In remembering everyday experiences, you recall information in context—linked to a particular time, place, or person. In remembering lists, you recall isolated pieces—information removed from the context in which it was first learned that has become part of your general knowledge base. Researchers call this type of memory **semantic memory.**

Between 3 and 6 years, children improve sharply in memory for relations among stimuli. For example, in a set of photos, they remember not just the animals they saw but also their contexts, such as a bear emerging from a tunnel or a zebra tied to a tree on a city street (Lloyd, Doydum, & Newcombe, 2009). The capacity to *bind together stimuli* supports the development of an increasingly rich episodic memory.

Memory for Routine Events Like adults, preschoolers remember familiar, everyday events—what you do when you go to child care or have dinner—in terms of **scripts,** general descriptions of what occurs and when it occurs in a particular situation. Young children's scripts begin as a structure of main acts. For example, when asked to tell what happens at a restaurant, a 3-year-old might say, "You go in, get the food, eat, and then pay." Although children's first scripts contain only a few acts, as long as events in a situation take place in logical order, they are almost always recalled in correct sequence (Bauer, 2006, 2013). With age, scripts become more elaborate, as in this 5-year-old's account of going to a restaurant: "You go in. You can sit in a booth or at a table. Then you tell the waitress what you want. You eat. If you want dessert, you can have some. Then you pay and go home" (Hudson, Fivush, & Kuebli, 1992).

Scripts help children (and adults) organize, interpret, and predict routine experiences. Once formed, scripts can be used to predict what will happen on similar

Like adults, preschoolers remember familiar, repeated events, such as brushing teeth, in terms of scripts. Over time, children construct more elaborate scripts: "You squeeze out the toothpaste and brush your teeth. You rinse your mouth and then your toothbrush."

occasions in the future. Children rely on scripts to assist recall when listening to and telling stories. They also act out scripts in make-believe play as they pretend to put the baby to bed, go on a trip, or play school. And scripts support children's planning by helping them represent sequences of actions that lead to desired goals (Hudson & Mayhew, 2009).

Memory for One-Time Events In addition to memory for routine events, a second type of episodic memory, which we considered in Chapter 6, is *autobiographical memory*—representations of personally meaningful, one-time events. As preschoolers' cognitive and conversational skills improve, their descriptions of special events become better organized in time, more detailed, enriched with a personal perspective, and related to the larger context of their lives. A young preschooler simply reports, "I went camping." Older preschoolers include specifics: where and when the event happened and who was present. And with age, preschoolers increasingly include subjective information—why, for example, an event was exciting, funny, sad, or made them feel proud or embarrassed—that explains the event's personal significance (Bauer, 2013; Pathman et al., 2013). For example, they might say, "I *loved* sleeping all night in the tent!"

As this 3-year-old talks about past experiences while exploring a family photo album, her mother responds in an elaborative style, asking varied questions and contributing her own recollections and evaluations of events. Elaborative-style conversations enrich young children's autobiographical memories.

Adults use two styles to elicit children's autobiographical narratives. In the *elaborative style,* they follow the child's lead, ask varied questions, add information to the child's statements, and volunteer their own recollections and evaluations of events, assisting the child in weaving together a story. For example, after a field trip to the zoo, Leslie asked, "What was the first thing we did? Why weren't the parrots in their cages? I thought the lion was scary. What did you think?" In this way, she helped the children reestablish and reorganize their memory of the field trip. In contrast, adults who use the *repetitive style* provide little information and keep repeating the same questions, regardless of the child's interest: "Do you remember the zoo? What did we do at the zoo? What did we do there?" Elaborative-style parents *scaffold* the autobiographical memories of their young children, who recall more information about past events and also produce more organized and detailed personal stories when followed up later in childhood and in adolescence (Reese, 2002; Valentino et al., 2014).

As children talk with adults about the past, they not only improve their autobiographical memories but also create a shared history that strengthens close relationships and self-understanding. Parents and preschoolers with secure attachment bonds engage in more elaborative reminiscing (Bost et al., 2006). And 5- and 6-year-old children of elaborative-style parents describe themselves in clearer, more consistent ways (Bird & Reese, 2006).

Girls tend to produce more organized and detailed personal narratives than boys. Compared with East Asian children, Western children produce narratives with more talk about their own thoughts and emotions. These differences fit with variations in parent–child conversations. Parents reminisce in greater detail and talk more about the emotional significance of events with daughters (Fivush & Zaman, 2014). And cultural valuing of an interdependent self leads many East Asian parents to discourage children from talking about themselves (Fivush & Wang, 2005).

Consistent with these early experiences, women report an earlier age of first memory and more vivid early memories than men. And Western adults' autobiographical memories include earlier, more detailed events that focus more on their own roles than do the memories of Asians, who tend to highlight the roles of others (Wang, 2008).

Finally, parents can be trained to use an elaborative style, which increases the richness of their preschoolers' episodic memories (Reese & Newcombe, 2007). And preschoolers with elaborative-style parents also display more strategylike behaviors (naming and pointing) and attain higher scores on listlike memory tasks (recall of a just-viewed set of objects) (Langley, Coffman, & Ornstein, 2017). By providing children with many opportunities to search their memories, elaborative-style parents seem to give them practice in skills needed to succeed on memory tasks they will encounter often in school.

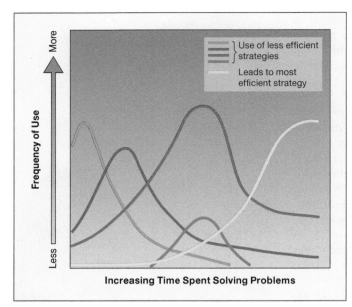

FIGURE 9.8 Overlapping-waves pattern of strategy use in problem solving. When given challenging problems, a child generates a variety of strategies, each represented by a wave. The waves overlap because the child tries several different strategies at the same time. Use of each strategy, depicted by the height of the wave, is constantly changing. As the child observes which strategies work best, which work less well, and which are ineffective, the strategy that results in the most rapid, accurate solutions wins out. (From R. S. Siegler, 1996, *Emerging Minds: The Process of Change in Children's Thinking.* Copyright © 1996 by Oxford University Press, Inc. Adapted by permission of Oxford University Press, Inc.)

9.3.3 Problem Solving

How do preschoolers use their cognitive competencies to discover new problem-solving strategies? To find out, let's look in on 5-year-old Darryl as he adds marbles tucked into pairs of small bags that Leslie set out on a table.

As Darryl tries to add each pair, his strategies vary. Sometimes he guesses, without applying any strategy. At other times, he counts from one on his fingers. For example, for bags containing 2 + 4 marbles, his fingers pop up one by one as he exclaims, "One, two, three, four, five, six!" On still other occasions, he starts with the lower digit, 2, and "counts on" ("two, three, four, five, six"). Or he begins with the higher digit, 4, and "counts on" ("four, five, six")—a strategy called *min* because it minimizes the work. Sometimes, he simply retrieves the answer from memory.

To study children's problem solving, Robert Siegler (1996, 2006) used the microgenetic research design (see page 44 in Chapter 1), presenting children with many problems over an extended time. He found that children experiment with diverse strategies on many types of problems—basic math facts, numerical estimation, conservation, memory for lists of items, reading first words, spelling, even tic-tac-toe. And their strategy use follows the overlapping-waves pattern shown in Figure 9.8. According to **overlapping-waves theory,** when given challenging problems, children try out various strategies and observe which work best, which work less well, and which are ineffective. Gradually, they select strategies on the basis of two criteria: *accuracy* and *speed*—for basic addition, the *min* strategy. As children home in on effective strategies for solving the problems at hand, correct solutions become more strongly associated with problems in long-term memory, and children display the most efficient strategy—automatic retrieval of the answer.

How do children move from less to more effective strategies? Often they discover faster, more accurate strategies by using more time-consuming techniques. For example, by repeatedly counting on fingers, Darryl began to recognize the number of fingers he held up. Also, certain problems dramatize the need for a better strategy. When Darryl opened a pair of bags, one containing ten marbles and the other with only two, he realized that *min* would be best. Teaching children to reason logically with concepts relevant to the problems is also helpful (Alibali, Phillips, & Fischer, 2009; Siegler & Svetina, 2006). Once Darryl understood that he got the same result regardless of the order in which he combined two sets (3 + 6 = 9 and 6 + 3 = 9), he more often used *min* and arrived at correct answers. Finally, a large improvement in the accuracy of a newly discovered strategy over previous strategies generally leads to rapid adoption of the new approach (Siegler, 2006).

As children transition to automatic retrieval, functional magnetic resonance imaging (fMRI) reveals reorganized and better integrated activity in networks of brain regions involved in memory-based problem solving (Cho et al., 2011; Qin et al., 2014). These include the prefrontal cortex, the hippocampus, and other areas in the cerebral cortex known to support long-term retention. Augmented brain functioning, in turn, likely enhances future problem solving.

Many factors, including practice, tasks with new challenges, adult scaffolding, and problem-relevant knowledge, contribute to gains in problem solving (Chu et al., 2018). And experimenting with less mature strategies lets children see the limitations of those strategies. In sum, overlapping-waves theory emphasizes that trying many strategies is vital for developing new, more effective solution techniques. The overlapping-waves pattern characterizes problem solving across a wide range of ages. And in the tradition of the information-processing approach, the theory views development as occurring gradually, rather than in discontinuous stages.

9.3.4 The Young Child's Theory of Mind

As mental representation, memory, and problem solving improve, children start to reflect on their own thought processes and construct a *theory of mind,* or coherent set of ideas about mental activities. These understandings are also known as **metacognition,** or "thinking about thought" (the prefix *meta-* means "beyond" or "higher"). As adults, we have a complex appreciation of our inner mental worlds, which we use to interpret our own and others' behavior and to improve our performance on various tasks. How early are children aware of their mental lives, and how complete and accurate is their knowledge?

Awareness of Mental Life   At the end of the first year, babies view people as intentional beings who can share and influence one another's mental states, a milestone that opens the door to new forms of communication—joint attention, social referencing, preverbal gestures, and spoken language. These early milestones serve as the foundation for later mental understandings. In longitudinal research, 8- to 10-month-olds' ability to engage in joint attention and grasp others' intentions predicted theory-of-mind competence at age 4 (Brooks & Meltzoff, 2015; Wellman et al., 2008).

As they approach age 2, children display a clearer grasp of others' emotions and desires, evident in their realization that people often differ from one another and from themselves in likes, dislikes, wants, needs, and wishes ("Mommy like broccoli. Daddy like carrots. I no like carrots."). As 2-year-olds' vocabularies expand, their first verbs include such mental-state words as *want, think, remember,* and *pretend* (Wellman, 2011).

By age 3, children realize that thinking takes place inside their heads and that a person can think about something without seeing, touching, or talking about it (Flavell, Green, & Flavell, 1995). But 2- to 3-year-olds' verbal responses indicate that they think people always behave in ways consistent with their *desires;* they do not understand that less obvious, more interpretive mental states, such as *beliefs,* also affect behavior. Between ages 3 and 4, children use *think* and *know* to refer to their own and others' thoughts and beliefs (Wellman, 2011). And from age 4 on, they realize that both *beliefs* and *desires* determine behavior.

Dramatic evidence for this advance comes from games that test whether preschoolers realize that *false beliefs*—ones that do not represent reality accurately—can guide people's behavior. For example, show a child two small closed boxes—a familiar Band-Aid box and a plain, unmarked box (see Figure 9.9). Then say, "Pick the box you think has the Band-Aids in it." Children usually pick the marked container. Next, open the boxes and show the child that, contrary to her own belief, the marked one is empty, and the unmarked one contains the Band-Aids. Finally, introduce the child to a hand puppet and explain, "Here's Pam. She has a cut, see? Where do you think she'll look for Band-Aids? Why would she look in there? Before you looked inside, did you think that the plain box contained the Band-Aids? Why?" (Bartsch & Wellman, 1995). Only a handful of 3-year-olds can explain Pam's—and their own—false beliefs, but many 4-year-olds can.

Some researchers claim that the procedures just described, which require verbal responses, grossly underestimate younger children's ability to attribute false beliefs to others. Relying on the violation-of-expectation method (which depends on looking behavior), these investigators assert that children comprehend others' false beliefs by age 15 months (Baillargeon, Scott, & He, 2010). But like other violation-of-expectation evidence, this conclusion is controversial (see page 201 in Chapter 6) (Siroiss & Jackson, 2007).

Yet in a study relying on active behavior (helping), most 18-month-olds—after observing an adult reach for a box previously used for blocks that now contains a spoon—based their choice of how to help her on her false belief about the contents of the box: They gave her a block rather than a spoon (Buttelmann et al., 2014). This indicates that toddlers *implicitly* grasp that

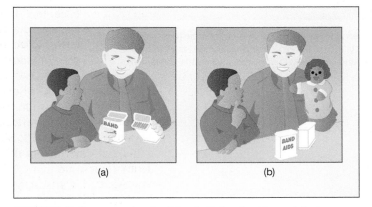

FIGURE 9.9   **Example of a false-belief task.** (a) An adult shows a child the contents of a Band-Aid box and of an unmarked box. The Band-Aids are in the unmarked container. (b) The adult introduces the child to a hand puppet named Pam and asks the child to predict where Pam would look for the Band-Aids and to explain Pam's behavior. The task reveals whether children understand that without having seen that the Band-Aids are in the unmarked container, Pam will hold a false belief.

people's actions can be guided by a false belief—a sensitivity that may be prerequisite for a mature theory of mind. But the striking contrast between toddlers' success on nonverbal tasks and 3-year-olds' consistent failure on verbal assessments suggests that toddlers' appreciation of false beliefs is minimal (Butterfill & Apperly, 2013; Ruffman, 2014).

Among children of diverse cultural and SES backgrounds, *explicit* false-belief understanding, assessed with verbal tasks, strengthens after age 3½, becoming more secure between ages 4 and 6 (Wellman, 2012). During that time, it becomes a powerful tool for reflecting on the thoughts and emotions of oneself and others and a good predictor of social skills (Hughes, Ensor, & Marks, 2010). Understanding the mind contributes to *selective trust*—the realization that some people are more credible sources of information than others. For example, preschoolers' developing grasp of mental states, including false belief, predicts greater willingness to follow the advice of a helpful person as opposed to a trickster, which emerges around age 5 (Vanderbilt, Liu, & Heyman, 2011).

Finally, mastery of false belief is associated with early reading ability, probably because it helps children comprehend story narratives (Astington & Pelletier, 2005). To follow a story line, children generally must link plot actions with characters' motives and beliefs.

Factors Contributing to Preschoolers' Theory of Mind　How do children develop a theory of mind beginning at such a young age? Research indicates that language, executive function, make-believe play, and social experiences all contribute.

Because their language lacks mental state terms, Quechua children of the Peruvian highlands take longer to master false-belief tasks than children in industrialized nations.

Language and Verbal Reasoning　The prefrontal cortex seems to play a crucial role in theory-of-mind development. Brain-wave recordings obtained while 4- to 6-year-olds reasoned about others' beliefs revealed that children who pass false-belief tasks (as opposed to those who fail) display a distinct pattern of activity in the left prefrontal cortex (Liu et al., 2009). This left-prefrontal pattern also appears when adults reason verbally about mental concepts.

Understanding the mind requires the ability to reflect on thoughts, which language makes possible. Many studies indicate that language ability strongly predicts preschoolers' grasp of false belief (Milligan, Astington, & Dack, 2007). Grammatical competence and use of mental-state terms in conversation are associated with passing false-belief tasks, likely because these linguistic features help clarify the differing perspectives people bring to the same event—for example, "Heidi thought that peanut butter was in the jar, but Isra knew it was really tahini" (Brooks & Meltzoff, 2015; de Villiers & de Villiers, 2014; San Juan & Astington, 2012).

Children with language impairments are often delayed in mastery of false belief (Stanzione & Schick, 2014). And native language attributes make a difference, too. The Quechua people of the Peruvian highlands refer to mental states such as "think" and "believe" indirectly because their language lacks mental-state terms. Quechua children have difficulty with false-belief tasks for years after children in industrialized nations have mastered them (Vinden, 1996).

Executive Function　Several aspects of preschoolers' executive function—inhibition, flexible shifting of attention, and planning—predict mastery of false belief because they enhance children's ability to reflect on people's experiences and mental states (Benson et al., 2013; Marcovitch et al., 2015; Müller et al., 2012). Inhibition is strongly related to mastery of false belief and other theory of mind tasks, perhaps because each requires suppression of the tendency to assume that others' perspectives are the same as one's own (Carlson, Claxton, & Moses, 2015; Carlson, Moses, & Claxton, 2004).

Make-Believe Play　Make-believe offers a rich context for thinking about the mind. As children act out roles, they often express the thoughts and emotions of the characters they portray and then reason about their implications (Saracho, 2014). Preschoolers who engage in extensive fantasy play or who have imaginary companions—and, thus, are deeply absorbed in creating make-believe characters—are advanced in understanding false belief and other aspects of the mind (Astington & Jenkins, 1995; Lalonde & Chandler, 1995). And as theory of mind develops, it may enhance the richness of children's make-believe.

Social Interaction Social experiences promote understanding of the mind. In longitudinal research, the maternal "mind-mindedness" experienced by securely attached babies (frequent commentary on their mental states) was positively associated with later performance on false-belief and other theory-of-mind tasks (Laranjo et al., 2010; Meins et al., 2003; Ruffman et al., 2006). And as we saw earlier, secure attachment is also related to more elaborative parent–child narratives, which often include discussions of mental states that help preschoolers think about their own and others' mental lives (Ontai & Thompson, 2008; Taumoepeau & Ruffman, 2006).

Also, preschoolers with siblings who are children (but not infants)—especially those with older siblings or two or more siblings—tend to be more aware of false beliefs because they are exposed to more family talk about varying thoughts, beliefs, and emotions (Devine & Hughes, 2018; Hughes et al., 2010; McAlister & Peterson, 2013). Similarly, preschool friends who often engage in mental-state talk are advanced in false-belief and other mental-state understandings (de Rosnay & Hughes, 2006). These exchanges offer children extra opportunities to talk about their own and others' inner states.

Children with cultural backgrounds emphasizing interdependence, where talk about one's own opinions and emotions is discouraged, are delayed in passing false-belief tasks in relation to Western children. Preschoolers growing up in China and Iran, for example, attain a grasp of explicit false belief somewhat later than their Australian and American agemates (Shahaeian et al., 2011; Wellman et al., 2006). Both Chinese and Iranian parents teach children to respect their elders' authority and to avoid disagreeing with the viewpoints of parents and other family members.

Core knowledge theorists (see pages 207–209 in Chapter 6) believe that to profit from the social experiences just described, children must be biologically prepared to develop a theory of mind. They claim that children with *autism,* for whom mastery of false belief is either greatly delayed or absent, are deficient in the brain mechanism that enables humans to detect mental states. See the Biology and Environment box on page 332 to find out more about the biological basis of reasoning about the mind.

Interaction with siblings, especially older siblings, contributes to preschoolers' awareness of others' perspectives and, therefore, promotes understanding of false belief.

Limitations of the Young Child's Theory of Mind   Though surprisingly advanced, preschoolers' awareness of mental activities is far from complete. For example, 3- and 4-year-olds are unaware that people continue to think while they wait, look at pictures, listen to stories, or read books—that is, when there are no obvious cues that they are thinking. Preschoolers also do not realize that when two people view the same object, their trains of thought will differ because of variations in their knowledge and other characteristics (Eisbach, 2004; Flavell, Green, & Flavell, 1995, 2000).

A major reason for these findings is that children younger than age 6 pay little attention to the *process* of thinking. When asked about subtle distinctions between mental states, such as *know* and *forget,* they express confusion. And they often insist that they have always known information they just learned (Lyon & Flavell, 1994; Taylor, Esbenson, & Bennett, 1994). Finally, they believe that all events must be directly observed to be known. They do not understand that *mental inferences* can be a source of knowledge (Miller, Hardin, & Montgomery, 2003).

These findings suggest that preschoolers view the mind as a passive container of information. Consequently, they greatly underestimate the amount of mental activity that people engage in and are poor at inferring what people know or are thinking about. As they move into middle childhood, they will increasingly view the mind as an active, constructive agent—a change we will consider in Chapter 12.

9.3.5 Early Literacy and Mathematical Development

Researchers are studying how children's information-processing capacities affect the development of basic reading, writing, and mathematical skills that prepare them for school. The way preschoolers begin to master these complex activities gives us additional information about their cognitive strengths and limitations—knowledge we can use to foster early literacy and mathematical development.

Biology and Environment | Autism and Theory of Mind

Michael stood at the water table in Leslie's classroom, repeatedly filling a plastic cup and dumping out its contents—dip-splash, dip-splash—until Leslie came over and redirected his actions. Without looking at Leslie's face, Michael moved to a new repetitive pursuit: pouring water from one cup into another and back again. As other children entered the play space and conversed, Michael hardly noticed. He rarely spoke, and when he did, he usually used words to get things he wanted, not to exchange ideas.

Michael has *autism,* a term meaning "absorbed in the self." Autism varies in severity along a continuum, called *autism spectrum disorder.* Michael's difficulties are substantial. Like other similarly affected children, by age 3 he displayed deficits in two core areas of functioning. First, he had only limited ability to engage in social interaction—evident in his difficulty with nonverbal communication, such as eye gaze, facial expressions, gestures, imitation, and give-and-take, and in his delayed and stereotyped language: He used words to echo what others said and to get things he wanted, not to exchange ideas. Second, his interests were narrow and overly intense. For example, one day he sat for more than an hour spinning a toy Ferris wheel. And Michael showed another typical feature of autism: He engaged in much less make-believe play than other children (American Psychiatric Association, 2013; Tager-Flusberg, 2014).

Researchers agree that autism stems from abnormal brain functioning, usually due to genetic or prenatal environmental causes. Beginning in the first year, children with the disorder have larger-than-average brains, with the greatest excess in brain-region volume occurring in the prefrontal cortex (Courchesne et al., 2011). This brain overgrowth is believed to result from lack of synaptic pruning, which accompanies typical development of cognitive, language, and communication skills. Furthermore, preschoolers with autism show a deficient left-hemispheric response to speech sounds (Eyler, Pierce, & Courchesne, 2012). Failure of the left hemisphere of the cerebral cortex to

lateralize for language may underlie these children's language deficits.

The amygdala, devoted to emotion processing (see page 252 in Chapter 7), also grows abnormally large in childhood, followed by a greater than average reduction in size in adolescence and adulthood. This deviant growth pattern is believed to contribute to deficits in emotion processing and social interaction involved in the disorder (Allely, Gillberg, & Wilson, 2014). fMRI studies reveal that autism is associated with reduced activity in areas of the cerebral cortex involved in emotional and social responsiveness and with weaker connections between the amygdala and the temporal lobes (important for processing facial expressions) (Monk et al., 2010).

Mounting evidence reveals that children with autism are impaired in theory of mind. As early as the first two years, they show deficits in capacities believed to contribute to an understanding of mental life, including interest in observing people's actions, joint attention, and social referencing (Chawarska, Macari, & Shic, 2013; Warreyn, Roeyers, & De Groote, 2005). Long after they reach the intellectual level of an average 4-year-old, they have great difficulty with false belief. Most find it hard to attribute mental states to themselves or others (Hoogenhout & Malcolm-Smith, 2017). They rarely use mental-state words such as *believe, think, know, feel,* and *pretend.*

Do these findings indicate that autism is due to impairment in an innate, core brain function that leaves the child unable to detect others' mental states and therefore deficient in human sociability? Some researchers think so (Baron-Cohen, 2011; Baron-Cohen & Belmonte, 2005). Others point out that individuals with general intellectual disability but not autism also do poorly on tasks assessing mental understanding (Yirmiya et al., 1998). This suggests that cognitive deficits are largely responsible.

One hypothesis with growing research support is that children with autism are impaired in executive function (Kimhi et al., 2014; Kouklari

A teacher works with this child, who has autism, on social skills such as making eye contact. Researchers disagree on whether the deficiencies accompanying autism result from a basic inability to detect others' mental states, an impairment in executive function, or a style of information processing that focuses on parts rather than patterns and coherent wholes.

et al., 2017; Pugliese et al., 2016). This leaves them deficient in skills involved in flexible, goal-oriented thinking, including inhibiting irrelevant responses, shifting attention, and generating plans.

Another possibility is that children with autism display a peculiar style of information processing, preferring to process the parts of stimuli over patterns and coherent wholes (Booth & Happé, 2016). Deficits in thinking flexibly and in holistic processing of stimuli would each interfere with understanding the social world because social interaction requires quick integration of information from various sources and evaluation of alternative possibilities.

It is not clear which of these hypotheses is correct. Perhaps several biologically based deficits underlie the tragic social isolation of children like Michael.

Literacy   One week, Leslie's students created a make-believe grocery store. They placed empty food boxes on shelves in the classroom, labeled items with prices, made shopping lists, and wrote checks at the cash register. A sign at the entrance announced the daily specials: "APLS BNS 5¢" ("apples bananas 5¢").

As their play reveals, preschoolers understand a great deal about written language long before they learn to read or write in conventional ways. This is not surprising: Children in industrialized nations live in a world filled with written symbols. Each day, they observe and participate in activities involving storybooks, calendars, lists, and signs. Children's active efforts to construct literacy knowledge through informal experiences are called **emergent literacy.**

Young preschoolers search for units of written language as they "read" memorized versions of stories and recognize familiar signs ("PIZZA"). But they do not yet understand the symbolic function of the elements of print (Bialystok & Martin, 2003). Many preschoolers think that a single letter stands for a whole word or that each letter in a person's signature represents a separate name. Initially, as we noted in Chapter 8, preschoolers do not distinguish between drawing and writing but often believe that letters (like pictures) resemble the meanings they represent. For example, one child explained that the word sun begins with the letter O because that letter is shaped like the sun; to demonstrate, he drew an O surrounded with rays to produce a picture of the sun.

Children revise these ideas as their perceptual and cognitive capacities improve, as they encounter writing in many contexts, and as adults help them with written communication. Gradually, preschoolers notice more features of written language and depict writing that varies in function, as in the "story" and "grocery list" in Figure 9.10.

(a)   (b)

FIGURE 9.10   **A story (a) and a grocery list (b) written by a 4-year-old child.** This child's writing has many features of real print. It also reveals an awareness of different kinds of written expression. (From McGee, Lea M., & Richgels, Donald J., 2004, *Literacy's Beginnings: Supporting Young Readers and Writers,* 4th Ed. Copyright © 2004. Reprinted and electronically reproduced by permission of Pearson Education, Inc., Upper Saddle River, New Jersey.)

Eventually children figure out that letters are parts of words and are linked to sounds in systematic ways, as 5- to 7-year-olds' invented spellings illustrate. At first, children rely on sounds in the names of letters: "ADE LAFWTS KRMD NTU A LAVATR" ("eighty elephants crammed into a[n] elevator"). Over time, they grasp sound–letter correspondences and learn that some letters have more than one common sound and that context affects their use (*a* is pronounced differently in "cat" than in "table") (McGee & Richgels, 2012).

Literacy development builds on a broad foundation of spoken language and knowledge about the world (Dickinson, Golinkoff, & Hirsh-Pasek, 2010). **Phonological awareness**—the ability to reflect on and manipulate the sound structures of spoken language, as indicated by sensitivity to changes in sounds within words, to rhyming, and to incorrect pronunciation—is a strong predictor of emergent literacy and later reading and spelling achievement (Gillon, 2018). When combined with sound–letter knowledge, it enables children to isolate speech segments and link them with their written symbols. Vocabulary and grammatical knowledge are also influential. And preschoolers' narrative competence, assessed through having them retell stories, fosters diverse language skills essential for literacy progress, including phonological awareness (Gardner-Neblett & Iruka, 2015; Piasta et al., 2018). Coherent storytelling requires attention to large language structures, such as character, setting, problem, and resolution. This seems to support the smaller-scale analysis involved in awareness of sound structures.

The more informal literacy experiences young children have, the better their language and emergent literacy development and their later reading and writing skills (Aram & Levin, 2014; Dickinson & McCabe, 2001). Pointing out letter–sound correspondences and playing language–sound games enhance children's awareness of the sound structures of language and how they are represented in

Preschoolers acquire literacy knowledge informally by participating in everyday activities involving written symbols. These young chefs "write down" orders they need to fill.

print (Ehri & Roberts, 2006; Foy & Mann, 2003). *Interactive reading,* in which adults discuss storybook content with preschoolers, promotes many aspects of language and literacy development. And adult-supported writing activities that focus on narrative, such as preparing a letter or a story, also have wide-ranging benefits (Purcell-Gates, 1996; Wasik & Bond, 2001). In longitudinal research, each of these literacy experiences is linked to improved reading achievement in middle childhood (Hood, Conlon, & Andrews, 2008; Senechal & LeFevre, 2002; Storch & Whitehurst, 2001; Wasik, Hindman, & Snell, 2016).

Preschoolers from low-SES families have fewer home and preschool language and literacy learning opportunities—a gap that translates into large differences in emergent literacy skills at kindergarten entry and into widening disparities in reading achievement during the school years (Cabell et al., 2013; Strang & Piasta, 2016). Age-appropriate books, for example, are scarce in their environments, and parents read to their children far less often than in higher-SES families, in part because many low-SES parents' own language and literacy skills are less well developed (Puglisi et al., 2017). Over time, skilled readers acquire wide-ranging knowledge more efficiently, progressing more rapidly than poor readers in all achievement areas (Neuman, 2006). In this way, literacy deficiencies at the start of school contribute to widening achievement disparities between economically advantaged and disadvantaged children that often persist into high school.

High-quality intervention can reduce the SES gap in early literacy development substantially. Providing low-SES parents with children's books, along with guidance in how to stimulate emergent literacy, greatly enhances literacy activities in the home (Huebner & Payne, 2010). And when teachers are shown how to engage in effective early childhood instruction of diverse literacy skills, low-SES preschoolers gain in emergent literacy components included in their classroom experiences (Hilbert & Eis, 2014; Lonigan et al., 2013). For ways to support early childhood literacy development, refer to Applying What We Know on the following page.

Mathematical Reasoning   Mathematical reasoning, like literacy, builds on informal knowledge. Between 14 and 16 months, toddlers display a beginning grasp of **ordinality,** or order relationships between quantities—for example, that 3 is more than 2, and 2 is more than 1. In the early preschool years, children attach verbal labels (*lots, little, big, small*) to amounts and sizes. Sometime in the third year, they begin to count. By the time children turn 3, most can count rows of about five objects, although they do not yet know what the words mean. For example, when asked for *one,* they give one item, but when asked for *two, three, four,* or *five,* they usually give a larger, but incorrect, amount. Nevertheless, 2½- to 3½-year-olds realize that a number word refers to a unique quantity (Sarnecka & Gelman, 2004). They know that when a number label changes (for example, from *five* to *six*), the number of items should also change. Soon they comprehend the meaning of the first three to four number words.

A 3½-year-old counts blocks of different colors. Grasping the principle of cardinality—that the last number word in a sequence indicates the quantity of items in a set—spurs development of numerical knowledge and skills.

By age 3½ to 4, most children have mastered the numbers up to *ten,* count correctly, and grasp the vital principle of **cardinality**—that the last number word in a counting sequence indicates the quantity of items in the set, and each additional number word is one more than the preceding number (Sarnecka & Wright, 2013). In the preschool scene described in the opening of this chapter, Sammy showed an understanding of cardinality when he counted four children at his snack table and then retrieved four milk cartons. Grasping cardinality seems to spur development of crucial numerical knowledge and skills. Once preschoolers attain this insight, they show improved understanding of the quantities and relative magnitudes (7 is more than 4, 12 is more than 10) that number words represent, and their counting increases in accuracy and efficiency (Geary & vanMarle, 2018; Knudsen, Fischer, & Aschersleben, 2015).

Around age 4, children use counting to solve simple arithmetic problems. At first, their strategies are tied to the order of numbers presented; to add 2 + 4, they count on from 2 (Bryant & Nunes, 2002). But soon they experiment with other strategies and master

APPLYING WHAT WE KNOW

Supporting Emergent Literacy in Early Childhood

STRATEGY	EXPLANATION
Provide literacy-rich home and preschool environments.	Homes and preschools with abundant reading and writing materials—including a wide variety of children's storybooks, some relevant to children's ethnic backgrounds—open the door to a wealth of language and literacy experiences. Make-believe play in which children have many opportunities to use newly acquired literacy skills in meaningful ways spurs literacy development.
Engage in interactive book reading.	When adults discuss story content, ask open-ended questions about story events, explain the meaning of words, and point out features of print, they promote language development, comprehension of story content, knowledge of story structure, and awareness of units of written language.
Provide outings to libraries, museums, parks, zoos, and other community settings.	Visits to child-oriented community settings enhance children's general knowledge and offer many opportunities to see how written language is used in everyday life. They also provide personally meaningful topics for narrative conversation, which promote many language skills essential for literacy development.
Point out letter–sound correspondences, play rhyming and other language–sound games, and read rhyming poems and stories.	Experiences that help children isolate the sounds in words foster phonological awareness—a powerful predictor of early childhood literacy knowledge and later reading and spelling achievement.
Support children's efforts at writing, especially narrative products.	Assisting children in their efforts to write—especially letters, stories, and other narratives—fosters many language and literacy skills.
Model literacy activities.	When children see adults engaged in reading and writing activities, they better understand the diverse everyday functions of literacy skills and the knowledge and pleasure that literacy brings. As a result, children's motivation to become literate strengthens.

Sources: McGee & Richgels, 2012.

the *min* strategy, a more efficient approach (see page 328)—in this example, beginning with 4, the higher digit. Around this time, children realize that subtraction cancels out addition. Knowing, for example, that $4 + 3 = 7$, they infer without counting that $7 - 3 = 4$ (Rasmussen, Ho, & Bisanz, 2003). Grasping basic arithmetic rules greatly facilitates rapid, accurate computation. With enough practice, children recall answers automatically and gradually extend their knowledge to larger numbers.

Understanding basic arithmetic makes possible beginning estimation—the ability to generate approximate answers, which are useful for evaluating the accuracy of exact answers. After watching several doughnuts being added to or removed from a plate of four to ten doughnuts, 3- and 4-year-olds make sensible predictions about how many are on the plate (Zur & Gelman, 2004). Still, children can estimate only just beyond their calculation competence. For example, preschoolers who can solve addition problems with sums up to 10 can estimate answers with sums up to about 20 (Dowker, 2003). And as with arithmetic operations, children try out diverse estimation strategies, gradually moving to more efficient, accurate techniques.

The arithmetic knowledge just described emerges universally around the world. But when adults provide occasions for counting, comparing quantities, and talking about numbers, children acquire these understandings sooner (Ginsburg, Lee, & Boyd, 2008). In one study, preschoolers' grasp of number concepts was enhanced by just a brief, 5-minute teaching session in which an adult modeled counting and labeling of the number of items in a set beyond which the child could currently count (Posid & Cordes, 2018).

Numerical knowledge at age 4—especially, understanding the cardinal value of number words—is strongly related to math knowledge and skills at school entry, after diverse factors that might otherwise explain the relationship (such as IQ, executive function, and parental education) are controlled (Geary & vanMarle, 2016; Geary et al., 2018). Math proficiency

LOOK and LISTEN

Ask several parents of preschoolers what they routinely do to help their children learn about math. Then ask what they do to support literacy. Do the parents promote math as much as literacy learning?

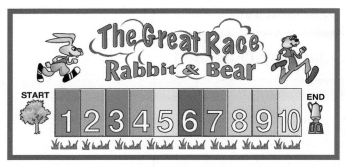

FIGURE 9.11 **A number board game.** An adult and child took turns using a spinner with a "1" section and a "2" section, which indicated how far to move a token on each turn. Children were asked to say the number spun and the numbers on the spaces as they moved. For example, a child on 5 who spun 2 would say "6, 7." Compared with agemates who played a color version of the game (it had only colored spaces on the board and a spinner with matching color sections), low-SES 4-year-olds who played the number board game showed large gains in number concepts and counting proficiency from 1 to 10. (From R. S. Siegler, 2009, "Improving Preschoolers' Number Sense Using Information-Processing Theory," in O. A. Barbarin & B. H. Wasik, eds., *Handbook of Child Development and Early Education.* New York: Guilford, p. 438. Reprinted by permission of Guilford Publications, Inc.)

at school entry, in turn, predicts math achievement years later, in elementary and secondary school (Duncan et al., 2007; Romano et al., 2010).

As with emergent literacy, children from low-SES families receive less stimulation and support at home for acquiring numerical concepts and skills and, thus, begin kindergarten with considerably less math knowledge than their economically advantaged agemates (Elliott, 2018). In several studies, just a few sessions devoted to playing number board games with an adult (see Figure 9.11 for an example) led to dramatic improvements in low-SES 4- to 5-year-olds' numerical understanding and proficiency at counting (Siegler, 2009; Siegler & Braithwaite, 2017). And in an early childhood math curriculum called *Building Blocks,* materials that promote math concepts and skills through three types of media—computers, manipulatives, and print—enable teachers to weave math into many preschool daily activities, from block-building to art and stories (Clements et al., 2011). Compared with agemates randomly assigned to other preschool programs, low-SES preschoolers experiencing Building Blocks showed substantially greater year-end gains in math concepts and skills, including counting, sequencing, arithmetic computation, and knowledge of geometric shapes.

ASK YOURSELF

Connect ■ Cite evidence on the development of preschoolers' executive function, memory, theory of mind, and literacy and mathematical understanding that is consistent with Vygotsky's sociocultural theory.

Apply ■ Lena wonders why her 4-year-old son Gregor's teacher provides extensive playtime in learning centers during each preschool day. Explain to Lena how adult-supported play can promote literacy and math skills essential for academic success.

Reflect ■ Describe informal experiences important for literacy and math development that you experienced while growing up.

9.4 Individual Differences in Mental Development

9.4 Describe early childhood intelligence tests and the impact of home, preschool and kindergarten programs, child care, and educational media on mental development.

Psychologists and educators typically measure how well preschoolers are developing mentally by giving them intelligence tests. Scores are computed in the same way as they are for infants and toddlers (return to page 221 in Chapter 6 to review). But tests for preschoolers sample a much wider range of mental abilities. Understanding the link between early childhood experiences and intelligence test performance is essential for identifying ways to intervene in support of children's cognitive development.

9.4.1 Early Childhood Intelligence Tests

Five-year-old Hal sat in a small, unfamiliar testing room while Sarah gave him an intelligence test. Some of Sarah's questions were *verbal*. For example, she showed Hal a picture of a shovel and said, "Tell me what this is"—an item measuring vocabulary. She tested Hal's working memory by asking him to repeat lists of letters and numbers backward. She probed his quantitative knowledge and problem solving by seeing if he could count and solve simple addition and subtraction problems. Finally, to assess Hal's spatial reasoning, Sarah used *nonverbal* tasks: Hal copied designs with special blocks, figured out the pattern in a series of shapes, and indicated what a piece of paper folded and cut would look like when unfolded (Roid, 2003; Wechsler, 2012).

The questions Sarah asked Hal tap knowledge and skills that not all children have equal opportunity to learn. In Chapter 12, we will take up the hotly debated issue of *cultural bias* in mental testing. For now, keep in mind that intelligence tests do not sample all human abilities, and performance is affected by cultural and situational factors. Nevertheless, test scores remain important: By age 6 to 7, they are good predictors of later IQ and academic achievement, which are related to adult vocational success in industrialized societies. Let's see how the environments in which children spend their days—home, preschool, and child care—affect mental test performance.

9.4.2 Home Environment and Mental Development

A special version of the *Home Observation for Measurement of the Environment (HOME)*, covered in Chapter 6, assesses aspects of 3- to 6-year-olds' home lives that foster intellectual growth. Research with the HOME early childhood subscales reveals that preschoolers who develop well intellectually have homes rich in educational toys and books. Their parents are warm and affectionate, stimulate language and academic skills, and arrange interesting outings. They also make reasonable demands for socially mature behavior—for example, that the child perform simple chores and behave courteously toward others. And these parents resolve conflicts with reason instead of physical force and punishment (Bradley & Caldwell, 1982; Espy, Molfese, & DiLalla, 2001; Roberts, Burchinal, & Durham, 1999).

When low-SES parents manage, despite low education and income, to obtain high HOME scores, their preschoolers do substantially better on tests of intelligence, language, and emergent literacy skills (Berger, Paxson, & Waldfogel, 2009; Mistry et al., 2008). In a study of African-American 3- and 4-year-olds from low-income families, HOME cognitive stimulation and emotional support subscales predicted reading achievement four years later (Zaslow et al., 2006). These findings (along with others we will discuss in Chapter 12) highlight the vital contribution of home environmental quality to children's overall intellectual development.

Parents who arrange interesting outings, such as a visit to an aquarium, encourage their children's intellectual development.

9.4.3 Preschool, Kindergarten, and Child Care

Largely because of the rise in maternal employment, over the past several decades the number of young children enrolled in preschool or child care has steadily increased to more than 65 percent in the United States (U.S. Bureau of Labor Statistics, 2019). The line between preschool and child care is fuzzy. Parents often select a preschool as a child-care option. And in response to the needs of employed parents, many U.S. preschools, as well as most public school kindergartens, have increased their hours from half to full days (U.S. Department of Education, 2018).

With age, preschoolers tend to shift from home-based to center-based early childhood programs. In the United States, children of higher-income parents and children of very low-income parents are especially likely to attend preschools or child-care centers (U.S. Department of Education, 2018). Many low-income working parents rely on care by relatives because they are not eligible for public preschool or government-subsidized child-care centers. A few states offer government-funded prekindergarten programs located within public schools to all 4-year-olds. The goal of these universal prekindergartens is to ensure that as many children as possible, from all SES levels, enter kindergarten prepared to succeed.

Types of Preschool and Kindergarten   Preschool and kindergarten programs range along a continuum from child-centered to teacher-directed. In **child-centered programs,** teachers provide activities from which children select, and much learning takes place through play. In contrast, in **academic programs,** teachers structure children's learning, teaching letters, numbers, colors, shapes, and other academic skills through formal lessons, often using repetition and drill.

Despite evidence that formal academic training undermines young children's motivation and emotional well-being, early childhood teachers have felt increased pressure to take this approach. Preschoolers and kindergartners who spend much time in large-group, teacher-directed academic instruction and completing worksheets—as opposed to being actively engaged in learning centers by warm, responsive teachers—display more stress behaviors (such as wiggling and rocking), have less confidence in their abilities, prefer less challenging tasks, and are less advanced in motor, academic, language, and social skills at the end of the school year (Stipek, 2011; Stipek et al., 1995). Follow-ups reveal lasting effects through elementary school in poorer study habits and lower achievement test scores (Burts et al., 1992; Hart et al., 1998; Stipek, 2004; Stipek et al., 2017). These outcomes are strongest for low-SES children, with whom teachers more often use a directive, academic approach—a disturbing trend in view of its negative impact on motivation and learning.

Although government spending for universal prekindergarten is controversial in the United States, in Western Europe such programs are widespread and child-centered in their daily activities. Enrolled preschoolers of all SES backgrounds show gains in cognitive and social development still evident in elementary and secondary school (Rindermann & Ceci, 2008; Waldfogel & Zhai, 2008). Findings on some U.S. universal prekindergarten programs that meet rigorous state standards of quality—especially, provision of rich teacher–child interactions and stimulating learning activities—reveal up to a one-year advantage in kindergarten and first-grade language, literacy, and math scores relative to those of children not enrolled (Gormley & Phillips, 2009; Weiland & Yoshikawa, 2013). Children from low-SES families benefit most.

Five-year-olds in a Montessori classroom benefit cognitively and socially from specially designed teaching materials that permit them to learn at their own pace and from ample time for both individual and small-group learning.

A special type of child-centered approach is Montessori education, devised more than a century ago by Italian physician and child development researcher Maria Montessori, who originally applied her method to poverty-stricken children. Features of Montessori schooling include multiage classrooms, long time periods for individual and small-group learning in child-chosen activities, teaching materials specially designed to enable children to move from easier to more complex tasks at their own pace and skill level, and equal emphasis on academic content and social development (Lillard, 2008). In a study that followed children diverse in ethnicity and family income from ages 3 to 6, researchers compared the development of those randomly assigned to either Montessori or other public preschools. From age 4 on, the Montessori children outperformed their other-preschool agemates in language, literacy, and math knowledge; mastery motivation (preference for solving a challenging rather than easy puzzle); and theory of mind, including false belief (Lillard et al., 2017). Especially impressive, the Montessori preschools substantially reduced the gap in academic knowledge typically found between low- and higher-SES children.

Montessori children also reported greater liking of academic tasks, perhaps because of the leeway they have to select their own activities. Children and adults alike tend to be more satisfied when they are given options, which grants them a sense of self-determination (Ryan & Deci, 2017). Another educational approach that combines child autonomy with focused learning is *guided play.* See the Social Issues: Education box on the following page for evidence on its effectiveness.

As for the dramatic rise in U.S. full-day preschools and kindergartens, the longer school day is associated with better academic achievement in elementary school for children of all SES backgrounds, though gains generally diminish over time. And findings for social development are mixed (Ansari, 2018; Brownell et al., 2015; Cooper et al., 2010; Thompson & Sonnenschein, 2015). In some studies, children in full-day as opposed to half-day have more behavior problems, whereas other studies report social benefits or no difference.

Social Issues: Education | Teaching Through Guided Play

"Play is the core of my teaching approach because it's hands-on. It keeps the children engaged, excited about learning, and supports the development of so many important capacities," Leslie explained to the parents of her preschool students during an open house. "But I also need to intervene in that play to make sure my students acquire the knowledge and skills they'll need to succeed in school."

Like Leslie, many early childhood teachers seek a middle ground between child-controlled playful exploration and teacher-directed academic tutoring. **Guided play,** which integrates child autonomy and playful exploration with adult-guided instruction, enables teachers to preserve the voluntary, engaging, and flexible features of play while ensuring that children focus on content relevant to learning goals (Weisberg et al., 2016). Adults can implement guided play in two ways.

In the first, teachers arrange activities by setting out a limited, carefully chosen set of materials that emphasizes a learning goal. Then they permit children to explore those materials relatively freely while keeping the learning goal in mind. For example, when an adult showed 4- to 9-year-olds evidence that conflicted with their belief that only the size of an object affects the size of its shadow, all children (even preschoolers) experimented successfully while playing with a "shadow machine," varying the distance of two equal-size objects from a light source to verify that distance also influences shadow size (van Schijndel et al., 2015). In comparison, only half the children who received evidence confirming their initial belief discovered the importance of distance.

In a second approach to guided play, adults observe child-controlled, playful activities, making comments and suggestions and asking questions that extend children's knowledge and deepen their curiosity. In an investigation that took place in kindergarten classrooms, children were divided into small groups and given miniature toys and letter tiles to be used to promote phonological awareness (word rhyming and sounds of initial letters in words). In groups assigned to a guided play condition, a teacher assisted the children in collaboratively making up a game through which they practiced the skills using the objects. In groups serving as controls, a teacher told the children how to practice the skills. Students experiencing guided play showed greater gains in literacy knowledge that extended well beyond the skills taught. The guided-play condition also offered other benefits, including practice in social skills such as negotiating with peers and (since most games involved fanciful pretend scenarios) in imagination, humor, and creativity (Cavanaugh et al., 2017). Children experiencing guided play so enjoyed the experience that they continued to play the games they had invented during recess and at other times.

Notice how in guided play, adult *scaffolding* promotes progress toward a learning goal while capitalizing on the power of play to spur children's motivation to learn. A growing number of studies report that guided play leads to more favorable outcomes in early childhood than other types of learning. It exceeds direct instruction, resulting in greater transfer of acquired knowledge to new situations while cultivating children's enthusiasm for learning (Alfieri et al., 2011; Fisher et al., 2013). And although free play promotes many skills in early childhood, children often must be pointed toward relevant aspects of a play situation to learn from it. By integrating adult scaffolding with child exploration, guided play offers an optimal means of doing so.

© LAURA DWIGHT PHOTOGRAPHY

Guided play combines adult scaffolding of learning with the pleasurable, motivating features of play. As these preschoolers explore pieces of a tree trunk, a teacher makes comments and suggestions that enhance the children's knowledge and curiosity.

Early Educational Intervention for At-Risk Preschoolers In the 1960s, as part of the "War on Poverty" in the United States, many intervention programs for low-SES preschoolers were initiated in an effort to address learning problems prior to school entry. The most extensive of these federal programs, **Project Head Start,** began in 1965. A typical Head Start center provides children with a year or two of preschool, along with nutritional and health services. Parent involvement is central to the Head Start philosophy. Parents serve on policy councils, contribute to program planning, work directly with children in classrooms, attend special programs on parenting and child development, and receive services directed at their own emotional, social, and vocational needs. Currently, Head Start serves about 1 million children and their families across the nation (Office of Head Start, 2018).

Benefits of Preschool Intervention Several decades of research have established the long-term benefits of preschool intervention. The most extensive study combined data from seven programs implemented by universities or research foundations. Results showed that

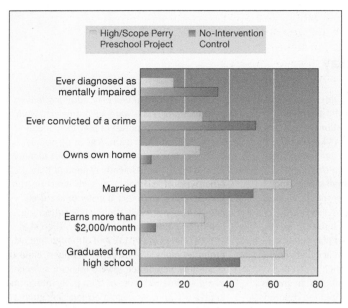

FIGURE 9.12 **Some outcomes of the High/Scope Perry Preschool Project on follow-up at age 27.** Although two years of a cognitively enriching preschool program did not eradicate the effects of growing up in poverty, children who received intervention were advantaged over no-intervention controls on all measures of life success when they reached adulthood. (Adapted from Schweinhart, 2010; Schweinhart et al., 2005.)

poverty-stricken children who attended programs scored higher in IQ and achievement than no-intervention controls during the first two to three years of elementary school. After that, differences declined (Lazar & Darlington, 1982). But on real-life measures of school adjustment, children and adolescents who had received intervention remained ahead. They were less likely to be placed in special education or retained in grade, and a greater number graduated from high school.

A separate report on one program—the High/Scope Perry Preschool Project—revealed benefits lasting well into adulthood. Two years' exposure to cognitively enriching preschool was associated with increased employment and reduced pregnancy and delinquency rates in adolescence. At age 27, those who had attended preschool were more likely than their no-preschool counterparts to have earned both high school and college degrees, have higher incomes, be married, and own their own home—and less likely to have been involved with the criminal justice system (see Figure 9.12). In the most recent follow-up, at age 40, the intervention group sustained its advantage on all measures of life success, including education, income, family life, and law-abiding behavior (Schweinhart, 2010; Schweinhart et al., 2005).

Do effects on school adjustment of these excellent interventions generalize to Head Start and other community-based preschool interventions? Gains are similar, though not as strong, because the quality of services provided often does not equal that of model university-based programs (Barnett, 2011). But community-based interventions of documented high quality are associated with diverse life-success outcomes, including higher rates of high school graduation and college enrollment and lower rates of school absenteeism, grade retention, and adolescent drug use and delinquency (Yoshikawa et al., 2013).

A consistent finding is that gains in IQ and achievement test scores from attending Head Start and other interventions quickly dissolve. In the Head Start Impact Study, a nationally representative sample of 5,000 Head Start eligible 3- and 4-year-olds was randomly assigned to one year of Head Start or to a control group that could attend other types of preschool programs, though half were cared for by a parent or other relative (Puma et al., 2012; U.S. Department of Health and Human Services, 2010, 2014b). By year's end, Head Start 3-year-olds exceeded controls in vocabulary, emergent literacy, and math skills; Head Start 4-year-olds were ahead in vocabulary, emergent literacy, and color identification. Head Start 3-year-olds also benefited socially, displaying declines in overactivity and withdrawn behavior. But except for language skills, academic test-score advantages were no longer evident by the end of first grade. And Head Start graduates did not differ from controls on any achievement measures at the end of third grade.

What explains these disappointing results? Head Start programs vary considerably in quality, and children who attend typically enter inferior public schools in poverty-stricken neighborhoods, which undermine the benefits of preschool intervention (Ramey, Ramey, & Lanzi, 2006). In one evaluation of a Head Start program of especially high quality, achievement gains in math were still evident in middle school (Phillips, Gormley, & Anderson, 2016).

Furthermore, in the Head Start Impact Study and other research, children from higher-risk families (single-parent, low education, non-English-speaking, deeper poverty, parental psychological problems) benefitted most from Head Start, academically and socially. And children who experienced two years (entering at age 3) rather than just one year displayed greater academic gains at the end of

© LAURA DWIGHT PHOTOGRAPHY

Project Head Start provides preschoolers from poverty-stricken families with preschool education and nutritional and health services. High-quality early educational intervention is associated with diverse life success outcomes, including reduced need for special education assistance and higher rates of high school graduation and college enrollment.

their Head Start experience (Cooper & Lanza, 2014; Lee, 2011). Recall from Chapter 6 that when high-quality intervention begins in infancy and is sustained through the preschool years, IQ gains are more likely to endure into adulthood (see pages 224–226 in Chapter 6).

The long-term, improved school adjustment that results from attending a one- or two-year high-quality preschool education program is especially impressive. Program effects on parents may contribute: The more involved parents are in Head Start, the better their child-rearing practices and the more stimulating their home learning environments. These factors are positively related to preschoolers' independence, task persistence, and year-end academic, language, and social skills (Bulotsky-Shearer et al., 2012; Marcon, 1999; McLoyd, Aikens, & Burton, 2006).

Strengthening Preschool Intervention A few supplementary programs have responded to the need to intensify preschool intervention to augment its impact. One of the most widely implemented is *Head Start REDI-C* (Research-Based Developmentally Informed classroom program), an enrichment curriculum designed for integration into existing Head Start classrooms. Before preschool begins, Head Start teachers—27 percent of whom do not have a bachelor's degree in early childhood education or a related field—take workshops in which they learn research-based strategies for enhancing language, literacy, and social skills. Throughout the school year, they receive one-to-one mentoring from master teachers, aimed at ensuring effective delivery of REDI-C. An additional parent program, REDI-P, provides home visits before and after the transition to kindergarten, during which parents learn how to engage their children in educational games, interactive storybook reading, and guided play and to use positive child-rearing practices.

This teacher integrates Head Start REDI-C into her preschool classroom. By delivering extra educational enrichment, Head Start REDI yields greater gains in language, literacy, executive function, and social skills than typical Head Start classrooms.

Relative to typical Head Start classrooms, Head Start plus REDI-C yields higher year-end language, literacy, executive function, and social development scores—advantages still evident in third grade (Bierman et al., 2014; Nix et al., 2016; Sasser et al., 2017). REDI-C's powerful impact on teaching quality is believed to be responsible. Teachers trained in REDI-C converse with preschoolers in more cognitively complex ways and more often use management strategies that prevent disruptive behavior (Domitrovich et al., 2009). Combining REDI-P with REDI-C further strengthens academic and social skills gains in the early elementary school years (Bierman et al., 2017).

Children who experience Head Start are less likely later in life to require special education assistance and be involved with the criminal justice system and more likely to be employed, making the program highly cost-effective. Because of limited funding, however, only 46 percent of 3- and 4-year-olds living in poverty attend preschool, with Head Start serving only about half of these children (Friedman-Krauss et al., 2018).

Child Care As noted in Chapter 6, however, much child care in the United States is substandard. Preschoolers exposed to it, especially for long hours, tend to score lower in cognitive and social skills and higher in teacher-rated behavior problems (Burchinal et al., 2015; NICHD Early Child Care Research Network, 2003b, 2006). Economically advantaged children in substandard care, for example, are especially likely to display externalizing difficulties (anger and aggression) that endure into the school years (Belsky et al., 2007; Huston, Bobbitt, & Bentley, 2015; Vandell et al., 2010). Children from low-income families, however, more often attend better-quality, publicly subsidized nonprofit child-care centers (see page 224 in Chapter 6), which may offset the negative impact of their stressful home lives.

In contrast to poor-quality care, good child care enhances cognitive, language, and social development, particularly for low-SES children—effects that persist into elementary school and, for academic achievement, into adolescence (Burchinal et al., 2015; Dearing, McCartney, & Taylor, 2009; Vandell et al., 2010). Center-based care is more strongly associated with cognitive gains than are other child-care arrangements (Abner et al., 2013). Child-care centers are more likely than family child-care homes to provide a systematic educational program.

LOOK and LISTEN

Arrange to observe at a child-care center and to talk to its director. Jot down signs of quality, referring to Applying What We Know on page 342. How would you rate the center's overall quality?

APPLYING WHAT WE KNOW

Signs of Developmentally Appropriate Early Childhood Programs

PROGRAM CHARACTERISTIC	SIGNS OF QUALITY
Physical setting	Indoor environment is clean, in good repair, and well-ventilated. Classroom space is divided into richly equipped activity areas, including make-believe play, blocks, science, math, games and puzzles, books, art, and music. Fenced outdoor play space is equipped with swings, climbing equipment, tricycles, and sandbox.
Group size	In preschools and child-care centers, group size is no greater than 18 to 20 children with two teachers.
Teacher–child ratio	In preschools and child-care centers, teacher is responsible for no more than 8 to 10 children. In family child-care homes, caregiver is responsible for no more than 6 children.
Daily activities	Children select many of their own activities and learn through experiences relevant to their own lives, mainly in small groups or individually. Teachers facilitate children's involvement, accept individual differences, and adjust expectations to children's developing capacities.
Interactions between adults and children	Teachers move among groups and individuals, asking questions, offering suggestions, and adding more complex ideas. Teachers use positive guidance techniques, such as modeling and encouraging expected behavior and redirecting children to more acceptable activities.
Teacher qualifications	Teachers have college-level specialized preparation in early childhood development, early childhood education, or a related field.
Relationships with parents	Parents are encouraged to observe and participate. Teachers talk frequently with parents about children's behavior and development.
Licensing and accreditation	Preschool and child-care programs are licensed by the state. Voluntary accreditation by the National Association for the Education of Young Children (*www.naeyc.org/academy*) or the National Association for Family Child Care (*www.nafcc.org*) is evidence of an especially high-quality program.

Sources: Copple & Bredekamp, 2009.

© ELLEN B. SENISI

Ingredients of high-quality child care include small group size, generous caregiver-child ratios, richly equipped activity areas, and well-educated caregivers. Child care that meets these criteria enhances development, especially for low-SES preschoolers.

Applying What We Know above summarizes characteristics of high-quality early childhood programs, based on standards for developmentally appropriate practice devised by the U.S. National Association for the Education of Young Children. These standards offer a set of worthy goals as the United States strives to upgrade child-care, preschool, and kindergarten services for young children.

9.4.4 Educational Screen Media

Besides home and preschool, young children spend much time in another learning environment: screen media. In the industrialized world, nearly all homes have at least one television set, and most have two or more. Similarly, the overwhelming majority—again, over 90 percent—have access to a computer and one or more mobile devices, usually smartphones but also tablets, with access to the Internet (Rideout, 2018; U.S. Census Bureau, 2018a).

Educational Television and Videos   Sammy's favorite TV program, *Sesame Street,* uses lively visual and sound effects to convey basic literacy and number concepts and presents engaging puppet and human characters to teach general knowledge, emotional and social understanding, and social skills. Today, *Sesame Street* is broadcast in more than 140 countries, making it the most widely viewed children's program in the world (Sesame Workshop, 2018).

Time devoted to watching children's educational programs, including *Sesame Street,* is associated with gains in early literacy and math skills and with academic progress in elementary school (Fisch, 2015; Mares & Pan, 2013). One study reported a link between preschool viewing of *Sesame Street* (and similar educational programs) and getting higher grades, reading more books, and placing more value on achievement in high school (Anderson et al., 2001).

Children's programs with slow-paced action and easy-to-follow narratives are associated with improved executive function, greater recall of program content, gains in vocabulary and reading skills, and more elaborate make-believe play than programs presenting quick, disconnected bits of information (Lillard & Peterson, 2011; Linebarger & Piotrowski, 2010). Narratively structured educational TV and video ease processing demands, facilitating sustained attention and freeing up space in working memory for applying program content to real-life situations.

Despite the spread of computers and mobile devices, television remains the dominant form of youth media. On average, U.S. 2- to 8-year-olds watch TV programs and videos 1½ hours a day. In addition, the typical child of this age range devotes about one hour to smartphone and tablet use, mostly to view videos, access apps, or play games (Rideout, 2018). Children's time on mobile devices has tripled since 2013 and may soon overtake time devoted to TV.

As Figure 9.13 shows, children from low-income families devote substantially more time to screen media than their higher-income agemates, a difference that has recently widened. It is largely explained by a rise in low-income children's TV viewing; middle- and high-income children's TV viewing has declined in favor of use of mobile devices. On the positive side, preschoolers from low-income families watch as much educational programming on TV as their economically advantaged agemates (Rideout, 2013, 2018). But parents with limited education are more likely to engage in practices that increase TV viewing of all kinds, including leaving the TV on all day and eating family meals in front of it (Masur, Flynn, & Olson, 2015; Rideout, Foehr, & Roberts, 2010).

Over 40 percent of U.S. parents of children age 8 and younger report that the TV is on in their home "most of the time" or "always" (Rideout, 2018). Background TV impairs young children's sustained attention to play activities, reduces quantity and quality of parent–child interaction, and is associated with delayed motor, cognitive, and language development during toddlerhood and early childhood (Courage & Howe, 2010; Lin et al., 2015; Masur, Flynn, & Olson, 2016).

About 30 percent of U.S. preschoolers and school-age children have a TV set in their bedroom, and 16 percent have a mobile device or laptop in their room on "most" nights or "every night." These children spend an estimated 85 additional minutes per day watching programs, usually with no parental restrictions on what they view (Kabali et al., 2015; Rideout, 2018).

Does extensive screen media viewing take children away from worthwhile activities? The more preschool and school-age children watch prime-time shows and cartoons, the weaker their executive function skills, the less time they spend reading and interacting with others, and the poorer their academic skills (Ennemoser & Schneider, 2007; Munzer et al., 2018; Ribner, Fitzpatrick, & Blair, 2017). Whereas educational media experiences can be beneficial, viewing entertainment media—especially heavy viewing—detracts from children's school success and social experiences.

Learning Through Interactive Digital Media   The majority of 2- to 6-year-olds use interactive digital media (requiring an action on the part of the child), doing so more often on mobile devices than computers. Although nearly all young children from higher-income families have access to a computer with a high-speed Internet connection at home, only about 70 percent of those from low-income families do. The family-income gap is also considerable for access to tablets: 85 percent higher-income versus 60 percent low-income (Rideout, 2018).

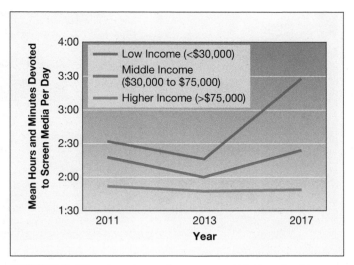

FIGURE 9.13   **Time devoted to screen media per day by children age 8 and younger, by family income.** Surveys of large, representative samples of U.S. parents of children ages 8 and younger in 2011, 2013, and 2017 revealed a recent widening of the family-income difference in screen media use. Compared to children from higher-income families, children from low-income families devoted substantially more time to screen media in 2017—on average, nearly 3½ hours per day. The rise is mostly due to an increase in TV viewing by economically disadvantaged children, who are therefore more susceptible to the detrimental effects of heavy TV use. (From V. Rideout, 2018, *The Common Sense Census: Media Use by Kids Age Zero to Eight,* p. 4. San Francisco: Common Sense Media. Adapted by permission.)

Kindergarten children use a simplified computer language to design a fanciful structure on a tablet. With adult support, programming activities foster many cognitive skills, including reasoning, mathematical and spatial abilities, and creative thinking.

Because interactive media can have rich educational benefits, most early childhood classrooms include learning centers equipped with tablets or computers. As long as adults scaffold children's efforts, well-designed literacy and math apps expand children's general knowledge and enhance diverse language, literacy, and math skills, and their interactivity heightens attention and interest. Tablet-based ebooks are also effective at improving a range of literacy outcomes (Anderson & Subrahmanyam, 2017; Calvert, Strong, & Gallagher, 2005; Neumann & Neumann, 2017; Reich, Yau, & Warschauer, 2016). And kindergartners who use apps to draw or write produce more elaborate pictures and text, make fewer writing errors, and edit their work much as older children do.

Still, in several studies, shared reading of a paper book led to higher-quality parent–child conversation than did shared reading of an ebook. The ebook format resulted in more interaction about the mechanics of using the tablet than about story content, thereby reducing recall of story details (Chiong et al., 2012; Krcmar & Cingel, 2014; Moody, Justice, & Cabell, 2010). Ebooks that are enhanced with too many features, such as animation, music, and hotspots to tap, can also divert children from the text and hinder learning.

Simplified computer languages that can be used to make designs or build structures introduce children as young as kindergarten age to programming skills. With adult support, these activities promote metacognition (awareness of thought processes), reasoning, mathematical and spatial abilities, and creative thinking. To get their programs to work, young programmers must use these skills, which they often transfer to other activities (Scherer, Siddiq, & Viveros, 2019). Furthermore, while programming, children are especially likely to help one another and persist in the face of challenge (Resnick & Silverman, 2005; Tran & Subrahmanyam, 2013).

As with television, children spend much time using interactive digital media for entertainment—especially game playing. Parental reports suggest that about one-third of U.S. preschoolers play electronic games at least occasionally, though typically for just a few minutes per day (Rideout, 2018). As we will see in Chapter 12, playing video games can have cognitive benefits. However, much TV and game media are rife with gender stereotypes and violence, a topic we will consider in the next chapter.

ASK YOURSELF

Connect ■ Explain how guided play is consistent with educational implications of both Piaget's and Vygotsky's theories.

Apply ■ Your senator has heard that IQ and achievement gains resulting from Head Start do not last, so she plans to vote against additional funding. Write a letter explaining why she should support Head Start.

Reflect ■ How much and what kinds of screen media use did you engage in as a child? How do you think your home media environment influenced your development?

9.5a Trace the development of vocabulary, grammar, and conversational skills in early childhood.

9.5b Cite factors that support language learning in early childhood.

9.5 Language Development

Language is intimately related to virtually all the cognitive changes discussed in this chapter. Between ages 2 and 6, children make momentous advances in language. Their remarkable achievements, as well as their mistakes along the way, reveal their active, rule-oriented approach to mastering their native tongue.

9.5.1 Vocabulary

At age 2, Sammy had a spoken vocabulary of about 250 words. By age 6, he will comprehend around 10,000 words and produce several thousand (Byrnes & Wasik, 2009). To accomplish this feat, Sammy will learn about five new words each day. How do children build their vocabularies so quickly? Research shows that they can connect new words with their underlying concepts after only a brief encounter, a process called **fast-mapping.** Even toddlers comprehend new labels remarkably quickly, although they need to hear a word used more times than do preschoolers, who process speech-based information faster and are better able to categorize and recall it (Akhtar & Montague, 1999; Brady & Goodman, 2014). Still, fast-mapping does not imply that children immediately acquire adultlike word meanings.

Types of Words   One day, Leslie announced to the children that they would soon take a field trip. That night, Sammy excitedly told his mother, "We're going on a field trip!" When she asked where the class would go, Sammy responded matter-of-factly, "To a field!" Sammy's error suggests that young children fast-map some words more easily than others.

Children in many language communities fast-map labels for objects especially rapidly because these refer to concepts that are easy to perceive (McDonough et al., 2011; Parish-Morris et al., 2010). When adults point to, label, and talk about an object, they help the child figure out and retain the word's meaning. Soon children add verbs *(go, run, broke),* which require understandings of relationships between objects and actions. Preschoolers speaking quite different languages take longer to extend a new verb ("*push* the bike") to other instances of the same action ("*push* the box") than they do to extend a novel noun to other objects in the same category (Imai et al., 2008; Scott & Fisher, 2012). The explanation most often given for this evidence is that learning verbs is more cognitively challenging.

However, children learning Chinese, Japanese, and Korean—languages in which nouns are often omitted from adults' sentences, while verbs are stressed—acquire verbs much sooner (early in the second year) and more readily than their English-speaking agemates (Chan et al., 2011; Tardif, 2006). Besides increased exposure to verbs, Chinese-speaking children hear a greater variety of verbs denoting physical actions, which are visually obvious and therefore easily mastered (Ma et al., 2009). For example, Mandarin Chinese has several verbs for *carry,* each referring to a different way of carrying, such as on one's back, in one's arms, or with one's hands.

These findings suggest that verb meanings might not be inherently harder to learn than noun meanings. In mastering both, young children benefit from multiple examples of the same word used in a consistent manner in different contexts. But in many languages (such as English), nouns are especially frequent in everyday conversation and verbs less so, making verbs seem more difficult to acquire during early vocabulary development (Gogate & Hollich, 2016).

As young children acquire verbs, they also add modifiers *(red, round, sad).* First, they make general distinctions *(big–small),* and then more specific ones *(tall–short, high–low, wide–narrow)* (Stevenson & Pollitt, 1987). During their third year, children of both "noun-friendly" and "verb-friendly" languages become adept learners of a variety of word types.

Strategies for Word Learning   Preschoolers figure out the meanings of words by contrasting them with words they already know and assigning the new label to a gap in their vocabulary. On hearing a new word, 2-year-olds repeat the word or acknowledge it with "yeah" or "uh-huh" in their next verbalization 60 percent of the time (Clark, 2007). This suggests that they assign the word a preliminary meaning and often start to use it right away. Over time, they refine its meaning, striving to match its conventional use in their language community.

When learning a new noun, toddlers and preschoolers acquiring diverse languages tend to assume it refers to an object category at the basic level—an intermediate level of generality (see page 316). This preference helps young children narrow the range of possible meanings. Once they acquire a basic-level name *(dog),* they add names at other hierarchical levels—both more general *(animal)* and more specific *(beagle, greyhound)* (Imai & Haryu, 2004; Waxman & Lidz, 2006).

To engage in effective verbal communication, preschoolers must master and combine principles of word meaning, grammar, and everyday conversation. How they accomplish this feat so rapidly is the focus of intensive research and debate.

How do children discover which concept each word picks out? This process is not yet fully understood. Early in vocabulary growth, children adopt a **mutual exclusivity bias**—the assumption that words refer to entirely separate (nonoverlapping) categories (Markman, 1992). Use of mutual exclusivity to connect new words with objects increases after age 2 (Bion, Borovsky, & Fernald, 2013). Young children are especially likely to use mutual exclusivity when the objects named are perceptually distinct—for example, differ clearly in shape. After hearing the labels for two distinct novel objects (for example, *clip* and *horn*), 2-year-olds assigned each word correctly, to the whole object, not just a part of it (Waxman & Senghas, 1992).

Indeed, children's first several hundred nouns refer mostly to objects well-organized by shape. In a study in which toddlers repeatedly played with and heard names for novel objects of different shapes ("That's a *wif*") over a nine-week period, they soon formed the generalization that only similar-shaped objects have the same name (Smith et al., 2002; Yoshida & Smith, 2003). Toddlers with this training added more than three times as many object names to their vocabularies outside the laboratory as did untrained controls. Because shape is a perceptual property relevant to most object categories for which they have already learned names, this *shape bias* helps preschoolers master additional names of objects as well as their distinctly shaped features (*blade* of a knife, *branch* of a tree) (Perry, Axelsson, & Horst, 2016; Vlach, 2016). As a result, vocabulary accelerates.

Once the name of a whole object is familiar, on hearing a new name for that object, 2- and 3-year-olds set aside the mutual exclusivity assumption. For example, if the object *(bottle)* has a part that stands out *(spout),* children readily apply the new label to it (Hansen & Markman, 2009). In these instances, mutual exclusivity helps limit the possibilities the child must consider. Still, mutual exclusivity and object shape cannot account for preschoolers' remarkably flexible responses when objects have more than one name.

By age 3, preschoolers' memory, categorization, and language skills have expanded, and they assign multiple labels to many objects. For example, they refer to a sticker of a gray goose as "sticker," "goose," and "gray." To do so, children often call on other aspects of language. According to one proposal, preschoolers discover many word meanings by observing how words are used in syntax, or the structure of sentences—a strategy called **syntactic bootstrapping** (Gleitman et al., 2005; Naigles & Swenson, 2007). Consider an adult who says, "This is a *citron* one," while showing the child a yellow car. Two- and 3-year-olds conclude that a new word used as an adjective for a familiar object (car) refers to a property of that object (Imai & Haryu, 2004). As children hear the word in various sentence structures ("That lemon is bright *citron*"), they use syntactic information to refine the word's meaning.

In addition to information about the meaning of individual words, sentence structure helps children grasp word relationships. For example, on hearing the sentences, "The *cat* drank the *milk*" and "The *dog* drank the *water*," 2½ -year-olds with sufficient grammatical knowledge begin to realize that pairs of words used in the same position—*dog* and *cat, milk* and *water*—have features in common (Wojcik & Saffran, 2015). Preschoolers' capacity to use syntactic cues to discern word meanings predicts vocabulary growth in diverse languages (Abend et al., 2017; McBride-Chang et al., 2008).

Young children also take advantage of rich social information that adults frequently provide, while drawing on their own expanding ability to infer others' intentions, desires, and perspectives. In one study, an adult performed an action on an object and then used a new label while looking back and forth between the child and the object, as if inviting the child to play. Two-year-olds concluded that the label referred to the action, not the object (Tomasello & Akhtar, 1995). Relying on their expanding theory of mind, by age 3 children can even use a speaker's recently expressed desire ("I really want to play with the *riff*") to figure out a word's meaning (Saylor & Troseth, 2006). And adults often inform children directly about word meanings: "That's not a birdie. It's a seal."

Furthermore, to fill in for words they have not yet learned, children as young as age 3 coin new words using ones they already know—"plant-man" for a gardener, "crayoner" for a child using crayons. Preschoolers also extend language meanings through metaphors based on concrete sensory comparisons: "Clouds are pillows," "Leaves are dancers." Once vocabulary and general knowledge expand, children also appreciate nonsensory comparisons: "Friends are like magnets," "Time flies by" (Özçalişkan, 2005; Pouscoulous, 2014). Metaphors permit young children to communicate in amazingly vivid and memorable ways.

Explaining Vocabulary Development   Children acquire vocabulary so efficiently and accurately that some theorists believe that they are innately biased to induce word meanings using certain principles, such as mutual exclusivity and syntactic bootstrapping (Lidz, Gleitman, & Gleitman, 2004). But critics observe that a small set of built-in, fixed principles cannot account for the varied, flexible manner in which children master vocabulary (Parish-Morris, Golinkoff, & Hirsh-Pasek, 2013). And many word-learning strategies cannot be innate because children acquiring different languages use different approaches to mastering the same meanings.

An alternative view is that vocabulary growth is governed by the same cognitive strategies that children apply to nonlinguistic information. In one account, children draw on a *coalition* of cues—perceptual, social, and linguistic—which shift in importance with age (Golinkoff & Hirsh-Pasek, 2006, 2008). Infants rely solely on perceptual features. Toddlers and young preschoolers, while still sensitive to perceptual features (such as object shape and physical action), increasingly attend to social cues—the speaker's direction of gaze, gestures, and expressions of intention and desire (Hollich, Hirsh-Pasek, & Golinkoff, 2000; Pruden et al., 2006). And as language develops further, linguistic cues—sentence structure and intonation (stress, pitch, and loudness)—play larger roles.

Preschoolers are most successful at figuring out new word meanings when several kinds of information are available (Parish-Morris, Golinkoff, & Hirsh-Pasek, 2013). Researchers have just begun to study the multiple cues that children use for different kinds of words and how their combined strategies change with development.

As this child observes her father creating a sculpture, she attends to a variety of perceptual, social, and linguistic cues to grasp the meanings of unfamiliar words, such as *plaster, statue, base, form, sculpt, mold,* and *studio.*

9.5.2 Grammar

Between ages 2 and 3, English-speaking children use simple sentences that follow a basic subject–verb–object word order. Children learning other languages adopt the word orders of the adult speech to which they are exposed.

Basic Rules   Toddlers' greater looking times at scenes that match sentences they hear reveal that they comprehend the meaning of basic grammatical structures that they cannot yet produce, such as "Big Bird is tickling Cookie Monster" or "What did the ball hit?" (Seidl, Hollich, & Jusczyk, 2003). First use of grammatical rules, however, is piecemeal—limited to just a few verbs. As children listen for familiar verbs in adults' speech, they expand their own utterances containing those verbs, relying on adult speech as their model (Gathercole, Sebastián, & Soto, 1999). Sammy, for example, added the preposition *with* to the verb *open* ("You open with scissors") because he often heard his parents say "open with." But he failed to add *with* to the verb *hit* ("He hit me stick").

To test preschoolers' ability to generate novel sentences that conform to basic English grammar, researchers had them use a new verb in the subject–verb–object form after hearing it in a different construction, such as passive: "Ernie is getting *gorped* by the dog." When children were asked what the dog was doing, the percentage who could respond, "He's *gorping* Ernie," rose steadily with age. But not until age 3½ to 4 could the majority of children apply the fundamental subject–verb–object structure broadly, to newly acquired verbs (Chan et al., 2010; Tomasello, 2003, 2006).

Once children form three-word sentences, they make small additions and changes in words that enable speakers to express meanings flexibly and efficiently. For example, they add -*ing* for ongoing actions *(playing)*, add -*s* for plural *(cats)*, use prepositions *(in* and *on)*, and form various tenses of the verb *to be (is, are, were, has been, will)*. English-speaking children master these grammatical markers in a regular sequence, from the simplest meanings and structures *(-ing, in* and *on, -s)* to the most complex (tenses of the verb *to be*) (Brown, 1973). As with basic word order, comprehension of these small units proceeds ahead of production (Soderstrom, 2008; Wood, Kouider, & Carey, 2009). Even 1½- to 2-year-olds can discriminate an adult's correct from incorrect application of the plural -*s* months in advance of using it themselves.

When preschoolers acquire these markers, they sometimes overextend the rules to words that are exceptions, a type of error called **overregularization.** "We each got two *foots"* and "My toy car *breaked"* are expressions that appear between ages 2 and 3 and persist into middle childhood (Maratsos, 2000). Children less often make this error on frequently used irregular verbs, such as the past tense of *go (went)* and *say (said)*, which they hear often enough to learn by rote. For rarely used verbs, such as *grow* and *sing,* children alternate for months—or even several years—between overregularized forms *(growed, singed)* and correct forms, until the irregular form eventually wins out. Overregularization provides evidence that children apply grammatical rules creatively.

Complex Structures   Gradually, preschoolers master more complex grammatical structures, although they do make mistakes. Question asking remains variable for several years. An analysis of one child's questions revealed that he inverted the subject and verb when asking certain questions ("What she will do?" "Why he can go?") but not others. The correct expressions were the ones he heard most often in his mother's speech (Rowland & Pine, 2000). And sometimes children produce errors in subject–verb agreement ("Where does the dogs play?") and subject case ("Where can me sit?") (Rowland, 2007).

Similarly, children have trouble with some passive sentences. When told, "The car is pushed by the truck," young preschoolers often make a toy car push a truck. By age 4½, they understand such expressions, whether they contain familiar or novel verbs (Dittmar et al., 2014). But full mastery of the passive form is not complete until the end of middle childhood.

Nevertheless, preschoolers' grasp of language structures is remarkable. By age 4 to 5, they form embedded sentences ("I think *he will come"*), tag questions ("Dad's going to be home soon, *isn't he?"*), and indirect objects ("He showed *his friend* the present") (Zukowski, 2013). As the preschool years draw to a close, children use most of the grammatical constructions of their language competently.

Explaining Grammatical Development   Evidence that grammatical development is an extended process has raised questions about Chomsky's *language acquisition device* (LAD), which assumes that children have innate knowledge of grammatical rules (see page 227 in Chapter 6). Some experts believe that grammar is a product of general cognitive development—children's tendency to search the environment for consistencies and patterns of all sorts (Bloom, 1999; Chang, Dell, & Bock, 2006; Tomasello, 2011). Over time, they group words into grammatical categories and use them appropriately in sentences. Yet among these theorists, debate continues over just how children master grammar.

According to one view, young children rely on *semantics,* or word meanings, to figure out grammatical rules—an approach called **semantic bootstrapping.** For example, children might begin by grouping together words with "agent qualities" (things that cause actions) as subjects and words with "action qualities" as verbs. Then they merge these categories with observations of how words are used in sentences (Bates & MacWhinney, 1987; Braine, 1994).

Others believe that children master grammar through direct observation of the structure of language: These *information-processing theorists* propose that children notice which words appear in the same positions in sentences and are combined in the same way with other words (Howell & Becker, 2013; MacWhinney, 2015; Tomasello, 2011). Over time, they group words into grammatical categories and use them appropriately in sentences (Bannard, Lieven, & Tomasello, 2009; Chang, Dell, & Bock, 2006).

Still other theorists agree with the essence of Chomsky's theory. One idea accepts semantic bootstrapping but proposes that the grammatical categories into which children group word meanings are innate—present at the outset (Pinker, 1999; Tien, 2013). Critics, however, point out that toddlers' two-word utterances do not reflect a flexible grasp of grammar and that preschoolers make many errors in their gradual mastery of grammar. In sum, controversy persists over whether a universal, built-in language-processing device exists or whether children draw on general cognitive-processing procedures, devising unique strategies adapted to the specific language they hear.

9.5.3 Conversation

Besides acquiring vocabulary and grammar, children must learn to engage in effective and appropriate communication—by taking turns, staying on the same topic, stating their messages clearly, and conforming to cultural rules for social interaction. This practical, social side of language is called **pragmatics,** and preschoolers make considerable headway in mastering it.

As early as age 2, children are skilled conversationalists. In face-to-face interaction, they take turns and respond appropriately to their partner's remarks, adding new information. With age, the number of turns over which children can sustain interaction and their ability to respond in a timely fashion, maintain a topic over a sequence of turns, and answer requests for clarification increase (Casillas, 2014; Clark, 2014). By age 3, children can infer a speaker's intention when the speaker expresses it indirectly. For example, most know that an adult who responds to an offer of cereal by saying, "We have no milk," is declining the cereal (Schulze, Grassmann, & Tomasello, 2013). These surprisingly advanced abilities grow out of early interactive experiences with parents and other adults (Callanan & Siegel, 2014; Filipi, 2014).

These preschoolers likely use more assertive language when speaking for a male puppet than they would if speaking for a female puppet. In doing so, they reveal their early grasp of stereotypic features of social roles.

The presence of a sibling also seems conducive to acquiring the pragmatics of language. Preschoolers closely monitor conversations between their twin or older siblings and parents, and they often try to join in. When they do, these verbal exchanges last longer, with each participant taking more turns (Barton & Strosberg, 1997; Barton & Tomasello, 1991). As they listen to these conversations, young language learners pick up important skills, such as use of personal pronouns (*I* versus *you*), which are more common in the early vocabularies of later-born than of firstborn siblings (Pine, 1995). Furthermore, older siblings' remarks to a younger brother or sister often focus on regulating interaction: "Do you like Kermit?" "OK, your turn" (Oshima-Takane & Robbins, 2003). This emphasis probably contributes to younger siblings' conversational skills.

By age 4, children adjust their speech to fit the age, gender, and social status of their listeners. For example, in acting out roles with hand puppets, they show that they understand the stereotypic features of different social positions. They use more commands when playing socially dominant and male roles (teacher, doctor, father) but speak more politely and use more indirect requests when playing less dominant and female roles (student, patient, mother) (Andersen, 2000).

Preschoolers' conversational skills occasionally do break down—for example, when talking on the phone. Here is an excerpt from one 4-year-old's phone conversation with his grandfather:

Grandfather: "How old will you be?"
John: "Dis many." *[Holding up four fingers.]*
Grandfather: "Huh?"
John: "Dis many." *[Again holding up four fingers.]* (Warren & Tate, 1992, pp. 259–260)

Young children's conversations appear less mature in highly demanding situations in which they cannot see their listeners' reactions or rely on typical conversational aids, such as gestures and objects to talk about. But when asked to tell a listener how to solve a simple puzzle, 3- to 6-year-olds give more specific directions over the phone than in person, indicating that they realize that more verbal description is necessary on the phone (Cameron & Lee, 1997). Between ages 4 and 8, both conversing and giving directions over the phone improve greatly.

9.5.4 Supporting Language Learning in Early Childhood

How can adults foster preschoolers' language development? As in toddlerhood, interaction with more skilled speakers remains vital in early childhood. Conversational give-and-take with adults, either at home or in preschool, is consistently related to language progress (Justice, Jiang, & Strasser, 2018; Weisleder & Fernald, 2013). In one investigation, the more conversational turns with adults 4- to 6-year-olds' experienced during storybook reading at home, the greater the activation of Broca's area in the left frontal cortex (which supports grammatical processing and word production), as measured by fMRI. Increased activation of Broca's area, in turn, predicted more advanced language skills, even after SES and IQ were controlled (Romeo et al., 2018). Enhanced brain functioning appears to play an important role in the association between adult–child conversation and language progress in early childhood.

Sensitive, caring adults use additional techniques that promote language skills. When children use words incorrectly or communicate unclearly, they give helpful, direct feedback: "I can't tell which ball you want. Do you mean a large or small one or a red or green one?" But they do not overcorrect, especially when children make grammatical mistakes. Criticism discourages children from freely using language in ways that lead to new skills.

Instead, adults often provide indirect feedback about grammar by using two strategies, often in combination: **recasts**—restructuring inaccurate speech into correct form, and **expansions**—elaborating on children's speech, increasing its complexity (Bohannon & Stanowicz, 1988; Chouinard & Clark, 2003). For example, if a child says, "I gotted new red shoes," the parent might respond, "Yes, you got a pair of new red shoes." After such corrective input, young children often shift to correct forms (Cleave et al., 2015; Saxton, Backley, & Gallaway, 2005). However, these techniques are not used in all cultures, and in some investigations they had no impact on children's grammar. Rather than eliminating errors, perhaps expansions and recasts model grammatical alternatives and encourage children to experiment with them.

Do the findings just described remind you once again of Vygotsky's theory? In language, as in other aspects of cognitive development, parents and teachers gently prompt young children to take the next developmental step forward. Children strive to master language because they want to connect with other people. Adults, in turn, respond to children's desire to become competent speakers by listening attentively, elaborating on what children say, modeling correct usage, and stimulating children to talk further. In the next chapter, we will see that this combination of warmth and encouragement of mature behavior is at the heart of early childhood emotional and social development as well.

© LAURA DWIGHT PHOTOGRAPHY

Adults can support preschoolers' grammatical learning through indirect feedback, including recasts and expansions, which model grammatical alternatives to incorrect constructions.

LOOK and LISTEN

Observe a parent conversing with a 2- or 3-year-old child during play or picture-book reading. List examples of how the parent promotes the child's vocabulary, grammar, and pragmatic skills.

ASK YOURSELF

Connect ■ Explain how children's strategies for word learning support the interactionist perspective on language development, described on page 230 in Chapter 6.

Apply ■ Sammy's mother explained to him that the family would take a vacation in Miami. The next morning, Sammy announced, "I gotted my bags packed. When are we going to Your-ami?" What explains Sammy's errors?

SUMMARY

9.1 Piaget's Theory: The Preoperational Stage (p. 307)

9.1a Describe advances in mental representation, and limitations of thinking, during the preoperational stage.

- Rapid advances in mental representation, notably language and make-believe play, mark the beginning of Piaget's **preoperational stage.** With age, make-believe becomes increasingly complex and flexibly symbolic, evident in **sociodramatic play** with peers. Although critics question the certainty of the evidence, many studies suggest that make-believe supports diverse aspects of cognitive and social development.

- **Dual representation** improves rapidly over the third year of life as children realize that models, drawings, and simple maps correspond to circumstances in the real world.

- Aside from representation, Piaget described preschoolers in terms of deficits rather than strengths. Because **egocentrism** prevents them from reflecting on their own thinking and accommodating, it contributes to animistic thinking, **centration**, and **irreversibility.** These difficulties cause preschoolers to fail **conservation** and **hierarchical classification** tasks.

9.1b Explain the implications of follow-up research on early childhood cognitive development for the accuracy of Piaget's preoperational stage.

- When young children are given simplified tasks relevant to their experiences, their performance appears more mature than Piaget assumed. Preschoolers recognize differing perspectives, distinguish animate from inanimate objects, have flexible and appropriate notions of magic, and notice and reason about transformations and cause-and-effect relations. They also show impressive skill at flexibly categorizing on the basis of both perceptually apparent and nonobservable characteristics.

- These findings indicate that logical operations develop gradually rather than abruptly, suggesting a less strictly defined preoperational stage than Piaget assumed.

- Combining gestures with speech during problem solving facilitates learning.

9.1c Describe educational principles that can be derived from Piaget's theory.

- A Piagetian classroom promotes discovery learning, sensitivity to children's readiness to learn, and acceptance of individual differences.

9.2 Vygotsky's Sociocultural Theory (p. 318)

9.2a Describe Vygotsky's perspective on the social origins and developmental significance of children's private speech.

- Unlike Piaget, Vygotsky regarded language as the foundation for all higher cognitive processes. **Private speech** emerges out of social communication as adults and more skilled peers help children master challenging tasks within the zone of proximal development. Children use private speech for self-guidance, eventually internalizing it as silent, inner speech.

- **Intersubjectivity** and **scaffolding** are two features of social interaction that promote cognitive development in children.

9.2b Describe applications of Vygotsky's theory to education, and evaluate his major ideas.

- A Vygotskian classroom emphasizes assisted discovery, in which both teacher guidance and peer collaboration are vitally important. Make-believe play is a unique, broadly influential zone of proximal development in early childhood.

- Vygotsky's theory helps us understand the wide cultural variation in cognitive skills. In some cultures, verbal communication is not the only means—or even the most important means—through which children learn.

9.3 Information Processing (p. 323)

9.3a Describe changes in executive function and memory during early childhood.

- Children show impressive gains in executive function during the preschool years. They gain steadily in inhibition, flexible shifting of attention, and working-memory capacity, which contribute vitally to cognitive and social skills. Older preschoolers also improve in **planning,** a complex executive function activity.

- Parental sensitivity, encouragement, and scaffolding foster preschoolers' performance on executive function tasks, whereas conditions common in low-SES homes compromise development of executive function. Poverty exerts an especially negative impact through maladaptive parenting and chronic stress.

- Young children's recognition memory is remarkably accurate. But their recall of listlike information is poor because they use **memory strategies** less effectively than older children.

- **Episodic memory,** or memory for everyday experiences, improves greatly in early childhood, supported by improvements in memory for contextual relations among stimuli. Like adults, preschoolers remember recurring events as **scripts,** which become more elaborate with age.

- As cognitive and conversational skills improve, children's autobiographical memories become more organized, detailed, and related to the larger context of their lives, especially when adults use an elaborative style to talk about the past.

- According to **overlapping-waves theory,** children try out various strategies to solve challenging problems, gradually selecting those that result in rapid, accurate solutions.

9.3b *Describe the young child's theory of mind.*

- Preschoolers begin to construct a theory of mind, indicating that they are capable of **metacognition,** or thinking about thought. Their performance on verbal false belief tasks indicates that from age 4 on, they realize that beliefs as well as desires can influence behavior. False-belief understanding enhances children's capacity to reflect on the thoughts and emotions of themselves and others.

- Language, executive function, make-believe play, and mental-state talk with adults, older siblings, and friends contribute to young children's awareness of false belief and other mental-state understandings.

- Preschoolers regard the mind as a passive container of information. As a result, they have difficulty inferring what people know or are thinking about.

- Children with autism are impaired in theory of mind, including mastery of false belief.

9.3c *Summarize children's literacy and mathematical knowledge during early childhood.*

- Young children's **emergent literacy** reveals that they revise incorrect ideas about the meaning of written language as their perceptual and cognitive capacities improve, as they encounter writing in many contexts, and as adults help them with written information.

- **Phonological awareness** is a strong predictor of emergent literacy and later reading and spelling achievement. Preschoolers' vocabulary, grammatical knowledge, and narrative competence are also influential. Informal literacy experiences, including adult–child interactive storybook reading, foster literacy development.

- Toddlers' beginning grasp of **ordinality** serves as the basis for early childhood mathematical understandings. By age 3½ to 4, preschoolers grasp the principle of **cardinality,** which spurs the development of crucial numerical knowledge and skills. When adults provide many occasions for counting and comparing quantities, children grasp number concepts sooner.

- High-quality intervention can reduce the gap between preschoolers from low-SES and high-SES families in both early literacy and mathematical development.

9.4 Individual Differences in Mental Development (p. 336)

9.4 *Describe early childhood intelligence tests and the impact of home, preschool and kindergarten programs, child care, and educational media on mental development.*

- Although intelligence test scores are affected by cultural and situational factors, by age 6 to 7 they are nevertheless good predictors of later IQ and academic achievement.

- A warm, stimulating home and parental reasonable demands for mature behavior promote children's intellectual development.

- Preschools and kindergartens range along a continuum from **child-centered programs** to **academic programs.** Emphasizing formal academic training undermines children's motivation and negatively influences later achievement.

- **Guided play** classrooms seek a middle ground between child-centered and academic programs. Montessori education is another approach that combines child autonomy with focused learning through specially designed teaching materials.

- **Project Head Start** is the most extensive federally funded preschool program for low-income children in the United States. High-quality preschool intervention results in immediate IQ and achievement gains and long-term improvements in school adjustment, educational attainment, and life success. Parental involvement in Head Start, and the implementation of Head Start REDI-C and REDI-P yield higher academic, language, and social skills.

- Poor-quality child care undermines preschoolers' cognitive and social skills. In contrast, good child care enhances cognitive, language, and social development, especially for low-SES children.

- Children's educational TV programs and videos are associated with improved executive function and academic gains. However, the more preschool and school-age children watch prime-time TV and cartoons, the less time they spend reading and interacting with others and the poorer their academic skills.

- As long as adults scaffold children's efforts, well-designed interactive media, including literacy and math apps, tablet-based ebooks, and simplified computer programming languages, can have rich educational benefits.

9.5 Language Development (p. 344)

9.5a *Trace the development of vocabulary, grammar, and conversational skills in early childhood.*

- Supported by **fast-mapping,** preschoolers' vocabularies increase dramatically. Children learning many languages (including English) fast-map nouns more rapidly than verbs. But in languages in which verbs are stressed (such as Chinese, Japanese, and Korean), children acquire verbs earlier and more readily than their English-speaking counterparts.

- Early in vocabulary development, children induce word meanings using a **mutual exclusivity bias. In syntactic bootstrapping,** they observe how words are used in the structure of sentences to figure out their meanings.

- Some researchers believe that children are innately biased to use these principles. Another view is that children use the same cognitive strategies to acquire vocabulary that they apply to nonlinguistic information. In one account, preschoolers draw on a coalition of cues—perceptual, social, and linguistic—which shift in importance with age.

- Between ages 2 and 3, children adopt the basic word order of their language. As they gradually master grammatical rules, they sometimes overextend them in an error called **overregularization.** By the end of the preschool years, children have acquired complex grammatical forms.

- According to one view, children engage in **semantic bootstrapping,** relying on word meanings to figure out grammatical rules. Alternatively, information-processing theorists propose that children master grammar through direct observation of the structure of language. Still others agree with the essence of Chomsky's theory that children's brains are innately tuned for acquiring grammar.

- **Pragmatics** refers to the practical, social side of language. In face-to-face interaction with peers, young preschoolers are already skilled conversationalists. By age 4, they adapt their language to social expectations.

9.5b *Cite factors that support language learning in early childhood.*

- Conversational give-and-take with more skilled speakers activates Broca's area and fosters preschoolers' language progress. Adults provide direct feedback on the clarity of children's utterances. With respect to grammar, they often give indirect feedback through **recasts** and **expansions.**

IMPORTANT TERMS AND CONCEPTS

academic programs (p. 338)
cardinality (p. 334)
centration (p. 311)
child-centered programs (p. 337)
conservation (p. 311)
dual representation (p. 310)
egocentrism (p. 311)
emergent literacy (p. 333)
episodic memory (p. 326)
expansions (p. 350)
fast-mapping (p. 345)
guided play (p. 339)

hierarchical classification (p. 312)
intersubjectivity (p. 320)
irreversibility (p. 312)
memory strategies (p. 326)
metacognition (p. 329)
mutual exclusivity bias (p. 346)
ordinality (p. 334)
overlapping-waves theory (p. 328)
overregularization (p. 348)
phonological awareness (p. 333)
planning (p. 324)
pragmatics (p. 349)

preoperational stage (p. 307)
private speech (p. 319)
Project Head Start (p. 339)
recasts (p. 350)
scaffolding (p. 320)
scripts (p. 326)
semantic bootstrapping (p. 348)
semantic memory (p. 326)
sociodramatic play (p. 308)
syntactic bootstrapping (p. 346)

chapter 10
Emotional and Social Development in Early Childhood

My Family

Kyan Swa Lin, 9 years, Myanmar

Parental warmth, involvement, and playfulness are linked to children's emotional and social competence. And as this image makes clear, gender typing is well underway during the preschool years. Chapter 10 considers these and other facets of early childhood emotional and social development.

Reprinted with permission from The International Museum of Children's Art, Oslo, Norway

As the children in Leslie's classroom moved through the preschool years, their personalities took on clearer definition. By age 3, they voiced firm likes and dislikes as well as new ideas about themselves. "Stop bothering me," Sammy said to Mark, who had reached for Sammy's beanbag as Sammy aimed it toward the mouth of a large clown face. "See, I'm great at this game," Sammy announced with confidence, an attitude that kept him trying, even though he missed most of the throws.

The children's conversations also revealed early notions about morality. Often they combined statements about right and wrong with forceful attempts to defend their own desires. "You're 'posed to share," stated Mark, grabbing the beanbag out of Sammy's hand.

"I was here first! Gimme it back," demanded Sammy, pushing Mark. The two boys struggled until Leslie intervened, provided an extra set of beanbags, and showed them how they could both play.

As the interaction between Sammy and Mark reveals, preschoolers quickly become complex social beings. Young children argue, grab, and push, but cooperative exchanges are far more frequent. Between ages 2 and 6, first friendships form, in which children converse, act out complementary roles, and learn that their own desires for companionship and toys are best met when they consider others' needs and interests.

The children's developing understanding of their social world was especially apparent in their growing attention to the dividing line between male and female. While Priti and Karen cared for a sick baby doll in the housekeeping area, Sammy, Vance, and Mark transformed the block corner into a busy intersection. "Green light, go!" shouted police officer Sammy as Vance and Mark pushed large wooden cars and trucks across the floor. Already, the children preferred peers of their own gender, and their play themes mirrored their culture's gender stereotypes.

This chapter is devoted to the many facets of early childhood emotional and social development. We begin with children's concepts of themselves and their changing understanding and expression of emotion. Then we consider their expanding insights into their social and moral worlds, their susceptibility to gender typing, and their increasing ability to manage their emotional and social behaviors. Finally, we discuss the ingredients of effective child rearing, including the complex conditions that support it and those that lead it to break down, contributing to the serious and widespread problems of child abuse and neglect. ■

10.1 Self-Understanding

In Chapter 9, we noted that preschoolers acquire a vocabulary for talking about their inner mental lives and refine their understanding of mental states. As self-awareness strengthens, children focus more intently on qualities that make the self unique. They begin to develop a **self-concept,** the set of attributes, abilities, attitudes, and values that an individual believes defines who he or she is. This mental representation of the self has profound implications for children's emotional and social lives, influencing, as Erik Erikson expressed it, their sense of *initiative:* eagerness to tackle new tasks, capacity to join in activities with peers, and willingness to discover what they can do with the help of adults.

10.1 Describe the development of self-concept and self-esteem in early childhood.

10.1.1 Foundations of Self-Concept

Ask 3- to 5-year-olds to tell you about themselves, and you are likely to hear descriptions like this: "I'm Dana. I'm 4 years old. I can wash my hair all by myself. I have a new Lego set, and I made this big, big tower." Preschoolers' self-concepts largely consist of observable characteristics, such as their name, physical appearance, possessions, and everyday behaviors (Harter, 2012).

When asked to tell about themselves, preschoolers typically mention observable characteristics—physical appearance, possessions, and everyday behaviors, such as "I can button my jacket." They also have an emerging grasp of their unique psychological characteristics—for this 4-year-old, determination!

By age 3½, children also describe themselves in terms of typical emotions and attitudes ("I'm happy when I play with my friends"; "I don't like scary TV programs"; "I usually do what Mommy says"), suggesting a beginning understanding of their unique psychological characteristics (Eder & Mangelsdorf, 1997). And by age 5, children's degree of agreement with a battery of such statements coincides with maternal reports of their personality traits, indicating that older preschoolers have a sense of their own timidity, agreeableness, and positive or negative affect (Brown et al., 2008). As further support for this emerging grasp of personality, when given a trait label ("nice," "mean"), 4-year-olds can appropriately link it to behavioral descriptions of others. For example, they know that a child who would pull a dog's tail is mean, and they can predict that a nice child would share toys with a playmate (Chen, Corriveau, & Harris, 2016). But most preschoolers do not yet spontaneously say, "I'm nice" or "I'm shy." Direct references to personality traits must wait for greater cognitive maturity.

A warm, sensitive parent–child relationship fosters a positive, coherent early self-concept. In one study, 4-year-olds with a secure attachment to their mothers were more likely than their insecurely attached agemates to describe themselves in favorable terms at age 5—with statements reflecting agreeableness and positive affect (Goodvin et al., 2008). Also, recall from Chapter 9 that securely attached preschoolers participate in more elaborative parent–child conversations about personally experienced events, which help them understand themselves (see page 327 in Chapter 9). When, in past-event conversations, a child discovers that she finds swimming, getting together with friends, and going to the zoo fun, she can begin to connect these specific experiences into a general understanding of "what I enjoy" (Fivush, 2011). The result is a clearer image of herself.

Elaborative reminiscing that focuses on young children's *internal states*—their thoughts, feelings, and subjective experiences—plays an especially important role in early self-concept development. Although preschoolers rarely refer to personality traits, they are more likely to mention traits ("I'm smart," "I'm really strong!") and typical emotions ("My brother makes me feel cranky") if their parents talk to them about causes and consequences of internal states ("Tell mommy why you were crying") (Wang, Doan, & Song, 2010). Also, when parents reminisce with preschoolers about times they successfully resolved upsetting feelings, 4- and 5-year-olds describe their emotional tendencies more favorably ("I'm not scared, not me!") (Goodvin & Romdall, 2013). By emphasizing the personal meaning of past events, conversations about internal states facilitate development of self-knowledge.

As early as age 2, parents use narratives of past events to impart rules, standards for behavior, and evaluative information about the child: "You added the milk when we made the mashed potatoes. That's a very important job!" (Nelson, 2003). As the Cultural Influences box on the following page reveals, these self-evaluative narratives are a major means through which caregivers imbue the young child's self-concept with cultural values.

As they talk about personally significant events and as their cognitive skills advance, preschoolers gradually come to view themselves as persisting over time—a change evident in their ability to anticipate their own future states and needs, which increases sharply from age 3 to 4 (Atance & Meltzoff, 2005; Povinelli, 2001). By age 5, children better understand that their future preferences are likely to differ from their current ones. Most agree that when they grow up, they will prefer reading newspapers to reading picture books and drinking coffee to drinking grape juice (Bélanger et al., 2014). By the end of the preschool years, children can set aside their current state of mind and take a future perspective.

Cultural Influences

Cultural Variations in Personal Storytelling: Implications for Early Self-Concept

© RONNIE KAUFMAN/GETTY IMAGES

Preschoolers of many cultural backgrounds participate in personal storytelling with their parents. The way parents select and interpret events in these narratives differs strikingly by culture, affecting the way children view themselves.

In one study, researchers spent hundreds of hours over a two-year period studying the storytelling practices of six middle-SES Irish-American families in Chicago and six middle-SES Chinese families in Taiwan. From extensive videotapes of adults' conversations with the children from age 2½ to 4, the investigators identified personal stories and coded them for content, quality of their endings, and evaluation of the child (Miller, Fung, & Mintz, 1996; Miller et al., 1997; 2012).

Parents in both cultures discussed pleasurable holidays and family excursions in similar ways and with similar frequency. But five times more often than the Irish-American parents, the Chinese parents told long stories about their preschoolers' previous misdeeds—using impolite language, writing on the wall, or playing in an overly rowdy way. These narratives, often sparked by a current misdeed, were conveyed with warmth and caring, stressed the impact of misbehavior on others ("You made Mama lose face"), and often ended with direct teaching of proper behavior ("Saying

dirty words is not good"). By contrast, in the few instances in which Irish-American stories referred to transgressions, parents downplayed their seriousness, attributing them to the child's spunk and assertiveness.

Early narratives about the child launch preschoolers' self-concepts on culturally distinct paths (Miller, 2014). Influenced by Confucian traditions of strict discipline and social obligations, Chinese parents integrated these values into their stories, affirming the importance of not disgracing the family and explicitly conveying expectations in the story's conclusion. By contrast, although Irish-American parents disciplined their children, they rarely dwelt on misdeeds in storytelling. In the few instances in which Irish-American stories referred to transgressions, parents interpreted these acts positively, perhaps to promote self-esteem (Miller, 2014; Miller et al., 1997; 2012).

Whereas most Americans believe that favorable self-esteem is crucial for healthy development, Chinese adults generally see it as unimportant or even negative—as impeding the child's willingness to listen and be corrected (Miller et al., 2002). Consistent with this view, the Chinese parents did little to cultivate their child's individuality. Instead, they used storytelling to guide the child

A Chinese mother speaks gently to her child about proper behavior. Chinese parents often use storytelling to point out how their child's misdeeds affect others. The Chinese child's self-concept, in turn, emphasizes social obligations.

toward socially responsible behavior. Hence, by the end of the preschool years, the Chinese child's self-image emphasizes a sense of belonging and obligations to others ("I belong to the Lee family"; "I like to help my mom wash dishes"), whereas the American child's is more autonomous, consisting largely of personal descriptions ("I do lots of puzzles"; "I like hockey") (Wang, 2004; Wang, Doan, & Song, 2010).

10.1.2 Emergence of Self-Esteem

Another aspect of self-concept emerges in early childhood: **self-esteem,** the judgments we make about our own worth and the feelings associated with those judgments. Make a list of your own self-judgments. Notice that, besides a global appraisal of your worth as a person, you have a variety of separate self-evaluations concerning different activities. These evaluations are among the most important aspects of self-development because they affect our emotional experiences, future behavior, and long-term psychological adjustment.

By age 4, preschoolers have several self-judgments—for example, about learning things well in school, making friends, getting along with parents, and treating others kindly (Marsh, Ellis, & Craven, 2002). But young children lack the cognitive maturity necessary to develop a global sense of self-esteem. They are not yet able to integrate the judgments of other people, and they cannot combine information about their competencies in different domains. Thus, their self-appraisals are fragmented. Also, because they have difficulty distinguishing between their desired and their actual competence, they usually rate their own ability as extremely high and often underestimate task difficulty, as Sammy did when he asserted, despite his many misses, that he was great at beanbag throwing (Harter, 2012).

High self-esteem contributes greatly to preschoolers' initiative during a period in which they must master many new skills. By age 3, children whose parents patiently encourage while offering information about how to succeed are enthusiastic and highly motivated. In contrast, children whose parents criticize their worth and performance give up easily when

© LAURA DWIGHT PHOTOGRAPHY

This preschooler confidently prepares to slide down the pole of a playground jungle gym. Her high self-esteem contributes greatly to her initiative in mastering new skills.

faced with challenges and express shame and despondency after failing (Kelley, Brownell, & Campbell, 2000). Adults can avoid promoting these self-defeating reactions by adjusting their expectations to children's capacities, scaffolding children's attempts at difficult tasks, and pointing out effort and improvement in children's work or behavior.

10.2 Emotional Development

10.2 Identify changes in understanding and expressing emotion during early childhood, citing factors that influence those changes.

Gains in representation, language, and self-concept support emotional development in early childhood. Between ages 2 and 6, children make strides in the emotional abilities that, collectively, researchers refer to as *emotional competence* (Denham et al., 2011). First, preschoolers gain in emotional understanding, becoming better able to talk about feelings and to respond appropriately to others' emotional signals. Second, they become better at emotional self-regulation—in particular, at coping with intense negative emotion. Finally, preschoolers more often experience *self-conscious emotions* and *empathy,* which contribute to their developing sense of morality.

Parenting strongly influences preschoolers' emotional competence. Emotional competence, in turn, is vital for successful peer relationships and overall mental health.

10.2.1 Understanding Emotion

Preschoolers' vocabulary for talking about emotion expands rapidly, and they use it skillfully to reflect on their own and others' behavior. Here are some excerpts from conversations in which 2-year-olds and 6-year-olds commented on emotionally charged experiences:

> *Two-year-old: [After father shouted at child, she became angry, shouting back.]* "I'm mad at you, Daddy. I'm going away. Good-bye."
>
> *Two-year-old: [Commenting on another child who refused to nap and cried.]* "Mom, Annie cry. Annie sad."
>
> *Six-year-old: [In response to mother's comment, "It's hard to hear the baby crying."]* "Well, it's not as hard for me as it is for you." [*When mother asked why*] "Well, you like Johnny better than I do! I like him a little, and you like him a lot, so I think it's harder for you to hear him cry."
>
> *Six-year-old: [Trying to comfort a small boy in church whose mother had gone up to communion.]* "Aw, that's all right. She'll be right back. Don't be afraid. I'm here." (Bretherton et al., 1986, pp. 536, 540, 541)

Cognitive Development and Emotional Understanding As these examples show, young preschoolers refer to causes, consequences, and behavioral signs of emotion, and over time their understanding becomes more accurate and complex (Thompson, Winer, & Goodvin, 2011). By age 4 to 5, emotion labeling differentiates: Children use *happy, sad, angry, afraid,* and *surprised* accurately (Widen, 2013). Older preschoolers also correctly judge the causes of diverse basic emotions ("He's surprised because his mom's hair is pink," "He's sad because his goldfish died"). Their explanations tend to emphasize external factors over internal states, a balance that changes with age (Rieffe, Terwogt, & Cowan, 2005). In Chapter 9, we saw that after age 4, children appreciate that both desires and beliefs motivate behavior. Once these understandings are secure, children's grasp of how internal factors can trigger emotion expands.

Three- to 5-year-olds are good at inferring how others are feeling based on their behavior. For example, they can tell that a child who jumps up and down and claps his hands is probably happy, and that a child who is tearful and withdrawn is sad (Widen & Russell, 2011). They also realize that thinking and feeling are interconnected—that focusing on negative thoughts ("I broke my arm, so now I have to wear this itchy cast that makes it hard to play") is likely to make a person feel worse, but thinking positively ("Now I have a cool cast my friends can write their names on!") can help a person feel better (Bamford & Lagattuta, 2012). And they are aware that being reminded of a past experience or anticipating a future experience can influence one's current emotions, an understanding that strengthens with age (Lagattuta, 2014). Furthermore, preschoolers come up with effective ways to relieve others' negative emotions, such as hugging to reduce sadness (Fabes et al., 1988). Overall, they have an impressive ability to interpret, predict, and change others' feelings.

At the same time, preschoolers have difficulty interpreting situations that offer conflicting cues about how a person is feeling. When shown a picture of a happy-faced child with a broken bicycle, 4- and 5-year-olds tended to rely only on the emotional expression: "He's happy because he likes to ride his bike." Older children more often reconciled the two cues: "He's happy because his father promised to help fix his broken bike" (Gnepp, 1983; Hoffner & Badzinski, 1989). As in their approach to Piagetian tasks, young children focus on the most obvious aspect of a complex emotional situation to the neglect of other relevant information.

Social Experience and Emotional Understanding   The more parents label emotions, explain them, and express warmth and enthusiasm when conversing with preschoolers, the more "emotion words" children use and the better developed their emotional understanding (Fivush & Haden, 2005; Laible & Song, 2006). Discussions focusing on negative experiences or involving disagreements are particularly helpful.

In one study, mothers engaged in more detailed dialogues about causes of emotion and more often validated their preschoolers' feelings when discussing negative (as opposed to positive) topics. And the more elaborative the discussions, the higher the children scored in emotional understanding (Laible, 2011). In another study, when mothers explained feelings, negotiated, and compromised during conflicts with their 2½-year-olds, their children, at age 3, were advanced in emotional understanding and used similar strategies to resolve disagreements (Laible & Thompson, 2002). Such dialogues seem to help children reflect on the causes and consequences of emotion while also modeling mature communication skills. Furthermore, preschoolers who are securely attached better understand emotion (Cooke et al., 2016). A secure attachment relationship allows for open parent–child communication about feelings along with sensitive responsiveness to the child's range of emotional expressions. And as we have seen, attachment security is related to more elaborative parent–child narratives, including discussions that highlight the emotional significance of past events.

Warm, elaborative conversations in which parents label and explain emotions enhance preschoolers' emotional understanding.

Knowledge about emotion helps children in their efforts to get along with others. As early as 3, it is related to friendly, considerate behavior (such as sharing, helping), constructive responses to disputes with agemates, and perspective-taking ability (Hughes & Ensor, 2010; O'Brien et al., 2011; Sette, Spinrad, & Baumgartner, 2017). As children learn about emotion from interacting with adults, they engage in more emotion talk with siblings and friends (Hughes & Dunn, 1998). Referring to feelings and exchanging positive emotion when interacting with playmates, in turn, predicts better liking by peers (Fabes et al., 2001; Lindsey, 2017). Children seem to recognize that acknowledging others' emotions and explaining their own enhance the quality of relationships.

10.2.2 Emotional Self-Regulation

Language, along with preschoolers' growing understanding of emotion, contributes to gains in *emotional self-regulation,* or ability to manage the experience and expression of emotion (Blankson et al., 2013; Thompson, 2015). By age 3 to 4, children verbalize a variety of strategies for alleviating negative emotion that they tailor to specific situations (Davis et al., 2010; Dennis & Kelemen, 2009). For example, they know they can restrict sensory input (cover their eyes or ears to block out a scary sight or sound), talk to themselves ("Mommy said she'll

By covering their ears to protect themselves from the noise of an imaginary explosion, these 4-year-olds reveal their awareness of a strategy for coping with scary sounds.

be back soon"), change their goals (decide that they don't want to play anyway after being excluded from a game), or repair a relationship ("stop fighting and share" to resolve a conflict with a peer). The effectiveness of preschoolers' suggested strategies improves with age.

As children use these strategies, emotional outbursts decline. Gains in executive function—in particular, inhibition and flexible shifting of attention—contribute greatly to managing negative emotion. Preschoolers who can distract themselves when upset and focus on how to handle their feelings tend to become cooperative kindergartners with few problem behaviors, yielding benefits for academic as well as social competence. And their effective management of emotion predicts further gains in emotion understanding (Denham et al., 2012; von Salisch, Haenel, & Denham, 2015). Over time, emotional self-regulation and understanding of emotion seem to mutually support each other.

By age 3, skill at emotional self-regulation predicts children's ability to portray an emotion they do not feel—for example, reacting cheerfully after receiving an undesirable gift (Kieras et al., 2005). These emotional "masks" are largely limited to the positive feelings of happiness and surprise. Children of all ages (and adults as well) find it harder to act sad, angry, or disgusted than pleased (Denham, 1998). To promote good social relations, most cultures teach children to communicate positive feelings and inhibit unpleasant ones.

Temperament affects the development of emotional self-regulation. Children who experience negative emotion intensely find it harder to inhibit feelings and shift attention away from disturbing events. They are more likely to be anxious and fearful, respond with irritation to others' distress, react angrily or aggressively when frustrated, and get along poorly with teachers and peers (Eisenberg, Smith, & Spinrad, 2011; Raikes et al., 2007).

To avoid social difficulties, emotionally reactive children must develop effective emotion-regulation strategies. By watching parents manage their feelings, children learn strategies for regulating their own. Parents who are in tune with their own emotional experiences tend to be supportive and patient with their preschoolers, offering suggestions and explanations of emotion-regulation strategies that strengthen children's capacity to handle stress (Meyer et al., 2014; Morris et al., 2011).

In contrast, when parents rarely express positive emotion, dismiss children's feelings as unimportant, and fail to control their own anger, children's emotion management and psychological adjustment suffer (Hill et al., 2006; Thompson & Goodman, 2010). And because emotionally reactive children become increasingly difficult to rear, they are often targets of ineffective parenting, which compounds their poor self-regulation. Children in economically disadvantaged families with an accumulation of risks—low parental education, unemployment, single parenting, frequent moves, crowded households—are especially susceptible to emotional self-regulation difficulties (Cadima et al, 2016; Sturge-Apple et al., 2017).

Conversations in which adults prepare children for difficult experiences by discussing what to expect and ways to handle negative feelings contribute to children's effective emotional self-regulation (Thompson & Goodman, 2010). Nevertheless, preschoolers' vivid imaginations and incomplete grasp of the distinction between fantasy and reality make fears common in early childhood. Consult Applying What We Know on the following page for ways adults can help young children manage fears.

10.2.3 Self-Conscious Emotions

One morning in Leslie's classroom, a group of children crowded around for a bread-baking activity. Leslie asked them to wait patiently while she got a baking pan. But Sammy reached over to feel the dough, and the bowl tumbled off the table. When Leslie returned, Sammy looked at her, then covered his eyes with his hands, and said, "I did something bad." He felt ashamed and guilty.

APPLYING WHAT WE KNOW

Helping Children Manage Common Fears of Early Childhood

FEAR	SUGGESTION
Monsters, ghosts, and darkness	Reduce exposure to frightening stories and TV programs until the child is better able to understand that fantastical beings are not real. "Search" the child's room for monsters, showing him that none are there. Use a night-light, sit by the child's bed until the child falls asleep, and tuck in a favorite toy for protection.
Preschool or child care	If the child resists going to preschool but seems content once there, the fear is probably separation. Provide a sense of warmth and caring while gently encouraging independence. If the child fears being at preschool, find out why—the teacher, the children, or a crowded, noisy environment. Provide support by accompanying the child and gradually lessening the amount of time you stay.
Animals	Do not force the child to approach a dog, cat, or other animal that arouses fear. Let the child move at her or his own pace. Demonstrate how to hold and pet the animal, showing that when treated gently, the animal is friendly. If the child is larger than the animal, emphasize this: "You're so big. That kitty is probably afraid of *you!*"
Intense fears	If a child's fear is intense, persists for a long time, interferes with daily activities, and cannot be reduced in any of the ways just suggested, it has reached the level of a *phobia*. Some phobias are linked to family problems and require counseling. Other phobias diminish without treatment as the child's emotional self-regulation improves.

As their self-concepts develop, preschoolers become increasingly sensitive to praise and blame or (as Sammy did) to the possibility of such feedback. As a result, they more often experience *self-conscious emotions*—feelings that involve injury to or enhancement of their sense of self (see Chapter 7). Around age 3, self-conscious emotions become clearly linked to self-evaluation (Lagattuta & Thompson, 2007; Lewis, 1995). But because preschoolers are still developing standards of excellence and conduct, they depend on messages from parents, teachers, and others who matter to them to know *when* to feel proud, ashamed, or guilty ("That block tower is so tall. You're a great tower builder!" "Don't grab crayons from Adrian. If you want that color, you need to wait for a turn.") (Thompson, Meyer, & McGinley, 2006).

Furthermore, it takes time before children recognize self-conscious emotions in themselves and others. For example, when 3- to 6-year-olds were shown photos of a happy, sad, surprised, and proud child after building a block tower taller than that of an adult and labeled as the fastest tower-builder in the world, not until age 5 to 6 did most select the photo depicting pride as the emotion they felt. And whereas many 4-year-olds can point to a photo of an unfamiliar peer that conveys pride when asked to do so, nearly all 5- and 6-year-olds can do so (Garcia, Janis, & Flom, 2015; Tracy, Robins, & Lagatutta, 2005). Children seem to identify a photo expressing another's pride before they recognize the emotion in themselves.

When parents repeatedly comment on the worth of the child and her performance ("That's a bad job! I thought you were a good girl"), children experience self-conscious emotions intensely—more shame after failure, more pride after success. In contrast, when parents focus on how to improve performance ("You did it this way; now try doing it that way"), they induce moderate, more adaptive levels of shame and pride and greater persistence on difficult tasks (Kelley, Brownell, & Campbell, 2000; Lewis, 1998).

Among Western children, intense shame is associated with feelings of personal inadequacy ("I'm stupid"; "I'm a terrible person") and with maladjustment—withdrawal and depression as well as intense anger and aggression toward those who shamed them (Muris & Meesters, 2014). In contrast, guilt—when it occurs in appropriate circumstances and is neither excessive nor accompanied by shame—is related to good adjustment. Guilt helps children resist harmful impulses, and as early as age 2½ it motivates a misbehaving child to confess, repair the damage, and behave kindly and helpfully toward others in the future (Drummond et al., 2017; Mascolo & Fischer, 2007). But overwhelming guilt—involving such high emotional distress that the child cannot make amends—is linked to depressive symptoms as early as age 3 (Luby et al., 2009).

Finally, the consequences of shame for children's adjustment may vary across cultures. As illustrated in the Cultural Influences box on page 357, people in Asian societies, who tend to define themselves in relation to their social group, view shame as an adaptive reminder of an interdependent self and of the importance of others' judgments (Friedlmeier, Corapci, & Cole, 2011).

10.2.4 Empathy and Sympathy

Empathy is another emotional capacity that becomes more common in early childhood. It serves as a motivator of **prosocial behavior**—actions aimed at benefitting others (Eisenberg, Spinrad, & Knafo-Noam, 2015). Compared with toddlers, preschoolers rely more on words to communicate empathic feelings, a change that indicates a more reflective level of empathy. When a 4-year-old received a Christmas gift that she hadn't included on her list for Santa, she assumed it belonged to another little girl and pleaded with her parents, "We've got to give it back—Santa's made a big mistake. I think the girl's crying 'cause she didn't get her present!"

Preschoolers' growing understanding of the causes of others' distress influences their empathic responsiveness. As early as age 3, they are more likely to display empathic concern when another's upset emotional reaction is clearly justified—appropriate to the harm experienced rather than an overreaction to a minor inconvenience or without any apparent cause (Hepbach, Vaish, & Tomasello, 2013). As the ability to take the perspective of others improves with age, empathic responding increases.

As children's language skills and capacity to take the perspective of others improve, empathy also increases, motivating prosocial behavior.

© LAURA DWIGHT PHOTOGRAPHY

Yet for some children, empathizing—*feeling with* an upset adult or peer and responding emotionally in a similar way—does not yield acts of kindness and helpfulness but, instead, escalates into *personal distress.* In trying to reduce their negative feelings, these children focus on their own anxiety rather than on the person in need. As a result, empathy does not lead to **sympathy**—feelings of concern or sorrow for another's plight.

Temperament plays a role in whether empathy prompts sympathetic, prosocial behavior or a personally distressed, self-focused response. Children who are sociable, assertive, and good at regulating emotion are more likely to help, share, and comfort others in distress. But poor emotion regulators less often display sympathetic concern and prosocial behavior (Eisenberg, Spinrad, & Knafo-Noam, 2015; Valiente et al., 2004). When faced with someone in need, they react with behavioral and physiological distress—frowning, lip biting, thumb sucking, comfort seeking, a rise in heart rate, and a sharp increase in electroencephalogram (EEG) brain-wave activity in the right cerebral hemisphere, which houses negative emotion—indications that they are overwhelmed by their feelings (Liew et al., 2010; Pickens, Field, & Nawrocki, 2001).

Preschoolers' empathic concern strengthens in the context of a secure parent–child attachment relationship (Murphy & Laible, 2013). When parents are warm, show sensitive, empathic concern for their preschoolers' feelings, and promote effective emotion-regulation strategies, children are more likely to react with concern to others' distress—a response that persists into adolescence and early adulthood (Michalik et al., 2007; Newton et al., 2014; Taylor et al., 2013). In addition, parents can teach children the importance of kindness and can intervene when they display inappropriate emotion—practices that predict high levels of sympathetic responding (Eisenberg, 2003).

In contrast, angry, punitive parenting can disrupt the development of empathy and sympathy at an early age—particularly among children who are poor emotion regulators and who therefore respond to parental hostility with especially high personal distress (Knafo & Plomin, 2006; Valiente et al., 2004). Physically abused preschoolers, who experience negative parenting to an extreme, rarely express concern at a peer's unhappiness but, rather, are likely to withdraw or react with verbal and physical attacks (Anthonysamy & Zimmer-Gembeck, 2007). Their behavior resembles their parents' insensitive responding to the suffering of others.

ASK YOURSELF

Connect ■ Cite ways that parenting contributes to preschoolers' self-concept, self-esteem, emotional understanding, emotional self-regulation, self-conscious emotions, and empathy and sympathy. Do you see any patterns? Explain.

Apply ■ On a hike with his family, 5-year-old Ryan became frightened when he reached a steep section of the trail. His father gently helped him climb up while saying, "Can you be brave? Being brave is when you feel scared but you do it anyway." What aspect of emotional development is Ryan's father trying to promote, and why is his intervention likely to help Ryan?

Reflect ■ When you were a child, did your parents actively promote your self-esteem? How did their efforts reflect your family's cultural background? Explain.

10.3 Peer Relations

As children become increasingly self-aware and better at communicating and understanding the thoughts and feelings of others, their skill at interacting with peers improves rapidly. Peers provide young children with learning experiences they can get in no other way. Because peers interact on an equal footing, they must keep a conversation going, cooperate, and set goals in play. With peers, children form friendships—special relationships marked by attachment and common interests. Let's look at how peer interaction changes over the preschool years.

10.3 Describe peer sociability, friendship, and social problem solving in early childhood, along with cultural and parental influences on early peer relations.

10.3.1 Advances in Peer Sociability

Mildred Parten (1932), one of the first to study peer sociability among 2- to 5-year-olds, noticed a dramatic rise with age in joint, interactive play. She concluded that social development proceeds in a three-step sequence. It begins with **nonsocial activity**—unoccupied, onlooker behavior and solitary play. Then it shifts to **parallel play,** a limited form of social participation in which a child plays near other children with similar materials but does not try to influence their behavior. At the highest level are two forms of true social interaction—associative play and cooperative play. In **associative play,** children engage in separate activities but exchange toys and comment on one another's behavior. In **cooperative play,** a more advanced type of interaction, children orient toward a common goal, such as acting out a make-believe theme.

Four-year-olds *(left)* engage in parallel play. Cooperative play *(right)* develops later than parallel play, but preschoolers continue to move back and forth between the two types of sociability. They often use parallel play as a respite from the complex demands of cooperation.

LOOK and LISTEN

Observe several 3- to 5-year-olds during a free-play period in a preschool or child-care program. How much time does each child devote to nonsocial activity, parallel play, and socially interactive play? Do children seem to use parallel play as a way station between activities?

Follow-Up Research on Peer Sociability   Longitudinal evidence indicates that these play forms emerge in the order Parten suggested but that later-appearing ones do not replace earlier ones in a developmental sequence (Rubin, Bukowski, & Parker, 2006). Rather, all types coexist in early childhood.

During classroom free-play periods, preschoolers often transition from onlooker to parallel to cooperative play and back again (Robinson et al., 2003). They seem to use parallel play as a way station. To successfully join the ongoing play of peers, they often first engage in parallel play nearby, easing into the group's activities—a strategy that increases the likelihood of being accepted. Later, they may return to parallel play as a respite from the high demands of complex social interaction and as a crossroad to new activities.

Although nonsocial activity declines with age, it is still the most frequent form among 3- to 4-year-olds. Even among kindergartners, it continues to occupy about one-third of children's free-play time. Both solitary and parallel play remain fairly stable from 3 to 6 years of age, accounting for as much of the young child's play as highly social, cooperative interaction (Rubin, Fein, & Vandenberg, 1983).

We now understand it is the *type,* not the amount, of solitary and parallel play that changes during early childhood. In studies of preschoolers' play in Taiwan and the United States, researchers rated the *cognitive maturity* of nonsocial, parallel, and cooperative play, using the categories shown in Table 10.1. Within each of Parten's play types, older children displayed more cognitively mature behavior than younger children (Pan, 1994; Rubin, Watson, & Jambor, 1978).

Often parents wonder whether a preschooler who spends large amounts of time playing alone is developing normally. But only *certain types* of nonsocial activity—aimless wandering, hovering near peers but not joining in, and functional play involving immature, repetitive motor action—are cause for concern. Children who behave reticently, by watching peers without playing, are usually temperamentally shy and inhibited—high in social anxiety (Coplan & Ooi, 2014). Their parents tend to overprotect them, criticize their social awkwardness, and unnecessarily control their play activities instead of patiently encouraging them to approach other children and helping them form at least one rewarding friendship, which protects against persisting adjustment problems (Guimond et al., 2012; Rubin, Bukowski, & Parker, 2006; Rubin, Burgess, & Hastings, 2002). And preschoolers who engage in solitary, repetitive behavior (banging blocks, making a doll jump up and down) tend to be immature, impulsive children who find it difficult to regulate anger and aggression (Coplan et al., 2001). In the classroom, both reticent and impulsive children experience peer ostracism, with boys at greater risk for rejection than girls (Coplan & Arbeau, 2008).

Other preschoolers with low rates of peer interaction do not display socially anxious or impulsive behavior. Most simply prefer to play alone, and their solitary activities are positive and constructive. When they do play with peers, such children, at least when studied in North America, show socially skilled behavior and form positive friendships (Coplan, Ooi, & Nocita, 2015). Also, Chinese-American preschoolers with shy dispositions whose immigrant mothers promote culturally valued modesty seem to develop social skills that protect them from peer rejection (Balkaya et al., 2018). In avoiding attention for themselves and politely complying with playmates' wishes, these children seem to regulate their social anxiety by behaving in an unassuming, agreeable, peer-supportive manner.

TABLE 10.1   **Developmental Sequence of Cognitive Play Categories**

PLAY CATEGORY	DESCRIPTION	EXAMPLES
Functional play	Simple, repetitive motor movements with or without objects, especially common during the first 2 years	Running around a room, rolling a car back and forth, kneading clay with no intent to make something
Constructive play	Creating or constructing something, especially common between 3 and 6 years	Making a house out of toy blocks, drawing a picture, putting together a puzzle
Make-believe play	Acting out everyday and imaginary roles, especially common between 2 and 6 years	Playing house, school, or police officer; acting out storybook or television characters

Source: Rubin, Fein, & Vandenberg, 1983.

Still, a few North American preschoolers who engage in age-appropriate solitary play—again, more often boys—are rebuffed by peers (Coplan et al., 2001, 2004). Perhaps because quiet play is inconsistent with the "masculine" gender role, boys who engage in it are at risk for negative reactions from their male classmates.

As noted in Chapter 9, *sociodramatic play*—an advanced form of cooperative play—becomes especially common over the preschool years. In joint make-believe, preschoolers act out and respond to one another's pretend feelings. They also explore and gain control of fear-arousing experiences when they play doctor or pretend to search for monsters in a magical forest. As a result, they can better understand others' feelings and regulate their own (Meyers & Berk, 2014). Finally, preschoolers spend much time negotiating roles and rules in sociodramatic play. To create and manage complex plots, they must resolve disputes through discussion and compromise.

When researchers observed free-play periods in preschools, they found that girls participated more in sociodramatic play, whereas boys participated more in friendly, vigorous interactions called *rough-and-tumble play.* Each type of play was associated with expressions of positive emotion and predicted children's emotional understanding and self-regulation one year later (Lindsey & Colwell, 2013). Both sociodramatic play and rough-and-tumble play require children to exercise self-control and respond to peers' verbal and nonverbal emotional cues. We will return to the topic of rough-and-tumble play in Chapter 11.

Cultural Variations   Peer sociability takes different forms, depending on the relative importance cultures place on group harmony as opposed to individual autonomy (Chen, 2012). For example, children in India generally play in large groups. Much of their behavior is imitative, occurs in unison, and involves close physical contact—a play style requiring high levels of cooperation (Roopnarine et al., 1994). In a game called Bhatto Bhatto, children act out a script about a trip to the market, touching one another's elbows and hands as they pretend to cut and share a tasty vegetable.

The group-oriented play reflected in this example, which is characteristic of non-Western cultures that highly value interdependence, may make the unsociability of children who prefer to play alone unacceptable. Consistent with this idea, preference for solitary activities in school-age children is associated with poor academic and social adjustment in China, where it seems to be viewed as self-focused and impolite (Chen, 2010; Liu et al., 2015). In Western cultures, solitary play is better accepted, perhaps because it is often regarded as an expression of independence, or personal choice.

Cultural beliefs about the importance of play also affect early peer associations. Caregivers who view play as mere entertainment are less likely to provide props or to encourage pretend than those who value its cognitive and social benefits (Gaskins, 2014). Recall the description of children's daily lives in village and tribal cultures, described on page 322 in Chapter 9. Mayan parents, for example, do not promote children's play—yet Mayan children are socially competent. When Mayan children do pretend, their play themes are *interpretive* of daily life—involving a limited number of scripts that reflect everyday roles and experiences. Children in industrialized, urban contexts more often engage in *inventive* play, generating make-believe scenarios unconstrained by actual experience (Gaskins, 2013, 2015). Perhaps Western-style sociodramatic play, with its elaborate materials and wide-ranging imaginative themes, is particularly important for social development in societies where the worlds of adults and children are distinct. It may be less crucial in village cultures where children participate in adult activities from an early age.

Masai children of Kenya cooperatively construct a model of a village dwelling using twigs and mud. Group-oriented play is characteristic of non-Western cultures that value interdependence and harmony over individual autonomy.

10.3.2 First Friendships

As preschoolers interact, first friendships form that serve as important contexts for emotional and social development. To adults, friendship is a mutual relationship involving companionship, sharing, understanding of thoughts and feelings, and caring for and comforting each other in times of need. In addition, mature friendships endure over time and survive occasional conflicts.

Preschoolers understand something about the uniqueness of friendship. They say that a friend is someone "who likes you" and with whom you spend a lot of time playing. Yet their ideas about friendship are far from mature. Four- to 7-year-olds regard friendship as pleasurable play and sharing of toys. But friendship does not yet have a long-term, enduring quality based on mutual trust (Damon, 1988; Hartup, 2006). "Mark's my best friend," Sammy would declare on days when they got along well. But when a dispute arose, he would reverse himself: "Mark, you're not my friend!" Nevertheless, preschool friendships can be remarkably stable across early childhood, as long as peers remain in the same social group. In one study, 40 percent mentioned the same best friends—the children they like to play with most—a year later (Dunn, 2004; Eivers et al., 2012).

Already, interactions between preschoolers who mutually name each other as friends are especially positive, reflecting greater support and intimacy than do other peer relationships (Furman & Rose, 2015; Hartup, 2006). Preschoolers give far more reinforcement—greetings, praise, and compliance—to their friends, and they also receive more from them. Friends also play together in more complex ways and are more cooperative and emotionally expressive—talking, laughing, and looking at each other more often than nonfriends do.

As early as the preschool years, children with a mutual friendship are better adjusted and more socially competent (Shin et al., 2014). Furthermore, children entering kindergarten who have friends in their class or who readily make new friends adjust to school more favorably (Ladd, Birch, & Buhs, 1999; Proulx & Poulin, 2013). Perhaps the company of friends serves as a secure base from which to develop new relationships, enhancing children's feelings of comfort in the new classroom.

10.3.3 Peer Relations and School Readiness

The ease with which children make new friends and are accepted by classmates predicts cooperative participation in classroom activities, task persistence, and academic skills in preschool, which carry over to better academic performance in kindergarten and the early school grades (Bell et al., 2016; Walker & Henderson, 2012; Ziv, 2013). Of course, kindergartners with friendly, prosocial behavioral styles make new friends easily, whereas those with weak emotional self-regulation skills and argumentative, aggressive, or peer-avoidant styles establish poor-quality relationships and make few friends.

In Chapter 7, we indicated that certain genetically influenced temperamental traits—negative mood, emotional reactivity, and weak effortful control—place children at risk for adjustment problems, including peer difficulties (Boivin et al., 2013). But recall, also, that environment—in particular, parenting quality—contributes profoundly to outcomes for these children. Early childhood classroom contexts also make a difference. In research in which identical-twin pair members' kindergarten experiences differed, those encountering peer rejection or conflict-ridden teacher relationships performed less well academically in first grade than their twin counterparts with more favorable classroom social experiences (Vitaro et al., 2012).

The capacity to form mutually rewarding friendships, cooperate with peers, and build positive ties with teachers enables young children to integrate themselves into classroom environments in ways that foster both academic and social competence. Socially competent preschoolers are more motivated and persistent, consistently exceeding their less socially skilled peers in language, literacy, and math scores in the early school grades (Walker & Henderson, 2012; Ziv, 2013). Because social maturity in early childhood contributes to academic performance, readiness for kindergarten must be assessed in terms of not only academic skills but also social skills.

Young children's positive peer interactions occur most often within child-controlled, playful pursuits, making it important for early childhood programs to provide space, time, materials, and adult

In evaluating readiness for school, children's capacity for friendly, cooperative interaction is just as important as their academic skills.

scaffolding to support free-play and guided-play activities (Booren, Downer, & Vitiello, 2012; Shearer et al., 2016). Warm, responsive teacher–child interaction is also vital, especially for shy children and for impulsive, emotionally negative, and aggressive children, who are at high risk for social difficulties (Brendgen et al., 2011; Vitaro et al., 2012). Recall from Chapter 9 that by strengthening teacher training, REDI-C, a supplementary preschool intervention, enhances both academic and social skills of children enrolled in Head Start (see page 341 in Chapter 9). Along with excellent teacher preparation, other indicators of program quality—small group sizes, generous teacher–child ratios, and developmentally appropriate daily activities—create classroom conditions that make positive teacher and peer relationships more likely.

10.3.4 Social Problem Solving

As noted earlier, children, even those who are best friends, come into conflict—events that provide invaluable learning experiences in resolving disputes constructively. Preschoolers' disagreements only rarely result in hostile encounters. Although friends argue more than other peers do, they are also more likely to work out their differences through negotiation and to continue interacting (Laursen & Adams, 2018).

At your next opportunity, observe preschoolers' play, noting disputes over objects ("That's mine!" "I had it first!"), entry into and control over play activities ("I'm on your team, Jerry." "No, you're not!"), and disagreements over facts, ideas, and beliefs ("I'm taller than he is." "No, you aren't!"). These social conflicts, which children take quite seriously, provide repeated occasions for **social problem solving**—generating and applying strategies that prevent or resolve disagreements, resulting in outcomes that are both acceptable to others and beneficial to the self. To engage in social problem solving, children must bring together diverse social understandings.

The Social Problem-Solving Process The most influential model of the social problem-solving process organizes it into the circular series of steps shown in Figure 10.1 (Crick & Dodge, 1994). Notice how this flowchart takes an *information-processing approach,* clarifying exactly what a child must do to grapple with and solve a social problem. It enables identification of processing deficits, so intervention can be tailored to meet individual needs.

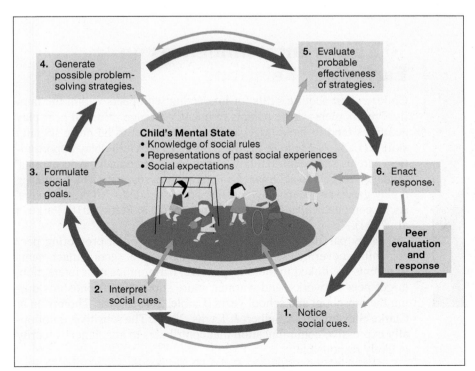

FIGURE 10.1 An information-processing model of social problem solving. The model is circular because children often engage in several information-processing activities at once—for example, interpreting information as they notice it and continuing to consider the meaning of another's behavior while they generate and evaluate problem-solving strategies. The model also takes into account the impact of mental state on social information processing—in particular, children's knowledge of social rules, their representations of past social experiences, and their expectations for future experiences. Peer evaluations and responses to enacted strategies are also important factors in social problem solving. (Adapted from N. R. Crick & K. A. Dodge, 1994, "A Review and Reformulation of Social Information-Processing Mechanisms in Children's Social Adjustment," *Psychological Bulletin, 115,* 74–101, Figure 2 [adapted], p. 76. Copyright © 1994 by the American Psychological Association. Reprinted with permission of the American Psychological Association.)

Social problem solving profoundly affects peer relations. Children who get along well with agemates interpret social cues accurately, formulate goals (helping or cooperating with peers) that enhance relationships, and have a repertoire of effective problem-solving strategies—for example, politely asking to play, requesting an explanation when they do not understand a peer's behavior, and working out a compromise when faced with peer disagreement. In contrast, children with peer difficulties often hold biased social expectations. They attend selectively to social cues (such as hostile acts) and misinterpret others' behavior (view an unintentional jostle as hostile). Their social goals (satisfying an impulse, getting even with or avoiding a peer) frequently lead to strategies that damage relationships (Dodge, Coie, & Lynam, 2006; Meece & Mize, 2011). They might barge into a play group without asking, use threats and physical force, or fearfully hover around peers' activities.

Children improve greatly in social problem solving over the preschool and early school years. With age, they increasingly negotiate with peers through persuasion and compromise, think of alternative strategies when an initial one does not work, and resolve disagreements without adult intervention (Mayeux & Cillessen, 2003; Walker et al., 2013). By kindergarten, the accuracy and effectiveness of each component of social problem solving are related to socially competent behavior (Dodge et al., 1986).

Enhancing Social Problem Solving   Interventions in preschool programs aimed at equipping children with the knowledge, attitudes and skills depicted in Figure 10.1 yield consistent gains in children's social competence and reductions in externalizing behavior problems (anger and aggression). Because of their increased risk for social adjustment difficulties, most of these efforts focus on economically disadvantaged children (Barnes, Wang, & O'Brien, 2017). But preschoolers from financially secure homes also benefit.

In one intervention—the *Promoting Alternative Thinking Strategies (PATHS)* curriculum for preschool children—teachers use stories, puppet characters, discussion, and role-play demonstrations to teach such skills as detecting others' feelings, planning sequences of action, generating effective strategies, and anticipating probable outcomes. In evaluations of PATHS, children in Head Start classrooms and other preschool programs who completed weekly lessons over an academic year scored higher than no-intervention controls in accurately "reading" others' emotions, inferring how others are likely to feel based on situational cues, selecting competent solutions to social conflicts, and cooperating and communicating with peers (Bierman et al., 2008; Bilir Seyhan et al., 2019; Domitrovich, Cortes, & Greenberg, 2007).

Parents' play with children, especially same-sex children, contributes to social competence. By playing with his father as he would a peer, this child acquires social skills that facilitate peer interaction.

10.3.5 Parental Influences on Early Peer Relations

Children first acquire skills for interacting with peers within the family. Preschoolers whose parents frequently arrange informal peer play activities tend to have larger peer networks and to be more socially skilled (Ladd, LeSieur, & Profilet, 1993). In providing play opportunities, parents show children how to initiate peer contacts. And parents' guidance on how to act toward others, such as suggestions for entering a play group and managing conflict, are associated with preschoolers' social competence and peer acceptance (Mize & Pettit, 2010; Parke et al., 2004).

Many parenting behaviors not directly aimed at promoting peer sociability nevertheless influence it. For example, secure attachments to parents are linked to more responsive, harmonious peer interaction, larger peer networks, and warmer, more supportive friendships during the preschool and school years (Laible, 2007; Lucas-Thompson & Clarke-Stewart, 2007; Seibert & Kerns, 2015). The sensitive, emotionally expressive communication that contributes to attachment security is likely responsible.

© LAURA DWIGHT PHOTOGRAPHY

Warm, collaborative parent–child play seems particularly effective for promoting peer interaction skills. During play, parents interact with their child on a "level playing field," much as peers do. And perhaps because parents play more with children of their own sex, mothers' play is more strongly linked to daughters' competence, fathers' play to sons' competence (Lindsey & Mize, 2000; Pettit et al., 1998).

As we have seen, some preschoolers already have great difficulty with peer relations. In Leslie's classroom, Robbie was one of them. Wherever he happened to be, comments like "Robbie ruined our block tower" and "Robbie hit me for no reason" could be heard. As we take up moral development in the next section, you will learn more about how parenting contributed to Robbie's peer problems.

ASK YOURSELF

Connect ■ How does emotional self-regulation affect the development of empathy and sympathy? Why are these emotional capacities vital for positive peer relations?

Apply ■ Three-year-old Ben lives in the country, with no other preschoolers nearby. His parents wonder whether it is worth driving Ben into town once a week to participate in a peer play group. What advice would you give Ben's parents, and why?

Reflect ■ What forms of play do you recall engaging in as a young child? In what ways might those early experiences reflect your gender, culture, and family background?

10.4 Foundations of Morality and Aggression

Young children's behavior provides many examples of their budding moral sense. In Chapter 4, we noted that newborn (and older) infants often cry in response to the cries of other babies, a possible precursor of empathy. And after watching scenes in which one puppet helps another by returning a dropped ball while a second puppet takes the ball away, babies as young as 3 months overwhelmingly preferred (looked longer at) the helpful character over the hinderer. And 6-month-olds expressed a similar preference for the "nice" guy over the "mean" guy by reaching more often for the helper than the hinderer (Hamlin, 2013; Hamlin & Wynn, 2011). They seemed implicitly drawn to prosocial over antisocial behavior.

Morally relevant inclinations and behaviors appear so early that some researchers have proposed the existence of an innate moral sense that serves as the springboard for development of more complex moral cognitions and emotions (Wynn & Bloom, 2014). Other investigators caution that more evidence is needed to be certain that young infants are responding to moral (rather than irrelevant) properties of scenes in the research just described (Buon, Habib, & Frey, 2017). And still others point to social experiences that offer early, relevant learning opportunities.

Of course, the possibility of a built-in moral sense does not preclude social experiences and cognitive factors from strongly influencing moral development. As we saw in Chapter 7, moral acts are evident by the middle of the second year: Toddlers willingly divide attractive play materials, often giving another player in a game an equal share. They also expect others to behave fairly, by dividing resources and rewards equally among recipients (see page 273 in Chapter 7). As children reach age 2, they often use language to evaluate their own and others' actions: "I naughty. I wrote on the wall" or (after being hit by another child) "Connie not nice." And we have seen that children of this age help, share, and cooperate with others—early indicators of considerate, responsible, prosocial attitudes.

10.4a Identify the central features of psychoanalytic, social learning, and cognitive-developmental approaches to moral development.

10.4b Describe the development of aggression in early childhood, including family and media influences and effective approaches to reducing aggressive behavior.

Adults everywhere take note of this developing capacity to distinguish right from wrong and to accommodate the needs of others. Some cultures have special terms for it. The Utku Indians of Hudson Bay say the child develops *ihuma* (reason). The Fijians believe that *vakayalo* (sense) appears. In response, parents hold children more responsible for their actions (Dunn, 2005). By the end of early childhood, children can state many moral rules: "Don't take someone's things without asking." "Tell the truth!" In addition, they argue over matters of justice: "You sat there last time, so it's my turn." "It's not fair. He got more!"

All theories of moral development recognize that conscience begins to take shape in early childhood. And most agree that at first, the child's morality is *externally controlled* by adults. Gradually, it becomes regulated by *inner standards.* Truly moral individuals do not do the right thing just to conform to others' expectations. Rather, they have developed compassionate concerns and principles of good conduct, which they follow in many situations.

Each major perspective on moral development emphasizes a different aspect of morality. The psychoanalytic perspective stresses the *emotional side* of conscience development—in particular, identification and guilt as motivators of good conduct. Social learning theory focuses on how *moral behavior* is learned through reinforcement and modeling. And the cognitive-developmental perspective emphasizes *thinking*—children's ability to reason about justice and fairness.

10.4.1 The Psychoanalytic Perspective

Recall that according to Freud, young children form a *superego,* or conscience, by *identifying* with the same-sex parent, whose moral standards they adopt. Children obey the superego to avoid *guilt,* a painful emotion that arises each time they are tempted to misbehave. Moral development, Freud believed, is largely complete by 5 to 6 years of age.

Today, most researchers disagree with Freud's view of conscience development. In his theory (see page 15 in Chapter 1), fear of punishment and loss of parental love motivate conscience formation and moral behavior. Yet children whose parents frequently use threats, commands, or physical force tend to violate standards often and feel little guilt, whereas parental warmth and responsiveness predict greater guilt following transgressions (Kochanska et al., 2005, 2008). And if a parent withdraws love after misbehavior—for example, refuses to speak to or states a dislike for the child—children often respond with high levels of self-blame, thinking "I'm no good" or "Nobody loves me." Eventually, to protect themselves from overwhelming guilt, these children may deny the emotion and, as a result, also develop a weak conscience (Kochanska, 1991; Rudy et al., 2014).

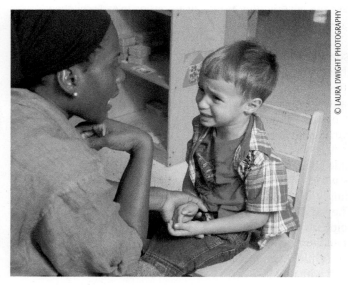

This teacher uses inductive discipline to explain to a distressed child how his misbehavior affects others. She indicates how the child should behave, encouraging empathy and sympathetic concern.

Inductive Discipline In contrast, conscience formation is promoted by a type of discipline called **induction,** in which an adult helps make the child aware of feelings by pointing out the effects of the child's misbehavior on others, especially noting their distress and making clear that the child caused it. For example, a parent might say, "If you keep pushing him, he'll fall down and cry" or "She's crying because you won't give back her doll" (Hoffman, 2000). When generally warm parents provide explanations that match the child's capacity to understand, while firmly insisting that the child listen and comply, induction is effective as early as age 2. Preschoolers whose parents use it are more likely to refrain from wrongdoing, confess and repair damages after misdeeds, and display prosocial behavior (Choe, Olson, & Sameroff, 2013; Volling, Mahoney, & Rauer, 2009).

The success of induction may lie in its power to motivate children's active commitment to moral standards, in the following ways:

- Induction gives children information about how to behave that they can use in future situations.
- By emphasizing the impact of the child's actions on others, induction encourages empathy and sympathetic concern, which motivate prosocial behavior.

- Giving children reasons for changing their behavior encourages them to adopt moral standards because those standards make sense.
- Children who consistently experience induction may form a *script* for the negative emotional consequences of harming others: Child causes harm, inductive message points out harm, child feels empathy for victim, child makes amends (Hoffman, 2000). The script deters future transgressions.

In contrast, discipline that relies too heavily on threats of punishment or withdrawal of love makes children so anxious and frightened that they cannot think clearly enough to figure out what they should do. As a result, these practices do not get children to internalize moral rules and—as noted earlier—also interfere with empathy and prosocial responding (Eisenberg, Spinrad, & Knafo-Noam, 2015). Nevertheless, warnings, disapproval, and commands are occasionally necessary to get an unruly child to listen to an inductive message.

The Child's Contribution   Although good discipline is crucial, children's characteristics affect the success of parenting techniques. Twin studies suggest a moderate to strong genetic contribution to empathy (Knafo et al., 2009; Knafo-Noam et al., 2015). More empathic children evoke less power assertion and are more responsive to induction.

Temperament is also influential. Mild, patient tactics—requests, suggestions, and explanations—are sufficient to prompt guilt reactions and conscience development in anxious, inhibited preschoolers (Kochanska et al., 2002). But with fearless, impulsive children, gentle discipline has little impact. As a result, parents of preschoolers with these attributes seldom use induction, relying instead on power assertive methods including physical punishment. But power assertion also works poorly. It undermines the child's capacity for emotional self-regulation, which strongly predicts good conduct, empathy, sympathy, and prosocial behavior (Kochanska & Aksan, 2006). Parents of impulsive children can foster conscience development by ensuring a warm, harmonious relationship and combining firm correction of misbehavior with induction (Kim et al., 2014; Kochanska & Kim, 2014). When children are so low in anxiety that parental disapproval causes them little discomfort, a close parent–child bond provides an alternative foundation for morality. It motivates children to listen to parents as a means of preserving an affectionate, supportive relationship.

In sum, to foster early moral development, parents must tailor their disciplinary strategies to their child's personality. Does this remind you of *goodness of fit,* discussed in Chapter 7? Return to page 255 to review this idea.

The Role of Guilt   Although little support exists for Freudian ideas about conscience development, Freud was correct that guilt motivates moral action. Preschoolers' assertions reveal that they anticipate feeling guilty when they consider violating parental standards and have internalized the parent's moral voice: "Didn't you hear my mommy? We'd better not play with these toys."

Inducing *empathy-based* guilt (expressions of personal responsibility and regret, such as "I'm sorry I hurt him") by explaining that the child is harming someone and has disappointed the parent is a particularly effective means of influencing children without using coercion. Empathy-based guilt reactions are associated with stopping harmful actions, repairing damage caused by misdeeds, and engaging in future prosocial behavior (Eisenberg, Eggum, & Edwards, 2010).

But contrary to what Freud believed, guilt is not the only force that compels us to act morally. Nor is moral development complete by the end of early childhood. Rather, it is a gradual process that extends into adulthood.

10.4.2 Social Learning Theory

According to social learning theory, morality does not have a unique course of development. Rather, moral behavior is acquired through modeling and reinforcement.

Importance of Modeling   Many prosocial acts—sharing, helping, comforting an unhappy playmate—occur so rarely at first that reinforcement, in the form of approval, affection, and other rewards, cannot explain their rapid development in early childhood. Rather, social learning theorists believe that children learn to behave morally largely through *modeling*—by observing and imitating people who demonstrate appropriate behavior. Once children acquire a moral response, such as sharing or telling the truth, reinforcement in the form of praise for the act ("That was a very nice thing to do") and for the child's character ("You're very kind and considerate") can increase its frequency, and parents say they commonly reinforce their 3- to 5-year-olds in these ways (Bower & Casas, 2016; Mills & Grusec, 1989).

Nevertheless, certain characteristics of models affect children's willingness to imitate:

- *Warmth and responsiveness.* Preschoolers are more likely to copy prosocial acts of warm, responsive (as opposed to cold, distant) adults (Yarrow, Scott, & Waxler, 1973). Warmth seems to make children more attentive and receptive to the model and is itself an example of a prosocial response.
- *Competence and power.* Children admire and therefore tend to imitate competent, powerful models—especially older peers and adults (Bandura, 1977).
- *Consistency between assertions and behavior.* When models say one thing and do another—for example, announce that "it's important to help others" but rarely engage in helpful acts—children generally choose the most lenient standard of behavior (Mischel & Liebert, 1966).

Models are most influential in the early years. In one study, toddlers' eager, willing imitation of their mothers' behavior predicted moral conduct (not cheating in a game) and guilt following transgressions at age 3 (Forman, Aksan, & Kochanska, 2004). At the end of the preschool years, children who have had consistent exposure to caring adults tend to behave prosocially whether or not a model is present (Mussen & Eisenberg-Berg, 1977). They have internalized prosocial rules from repeated observations of and encouragement by others.

At the same time, reinforcing young children with parental attention or praise appears unnecessary to induce them to help others. Most 2-year-olds will readily help an unfamiliar adult obtain an out-of-reach object, regardless of whether their parent offers encouragement and approval (Warneken & Tomasello, 2013). The most effective reinforcers for prosocial acts appear to be natural outcomes, such as positive emotional experiences, sustained social interactions, and peer acceptance. Furthermore, giving children material rewards for helping undermines their prosocial responding (Henderlong & Lepper, 2002; Warneken & Tomasello, 2009). Material rewards induce children to expect something in return for helping, so they rarely help spontaneously out of kindness to others.

A 3-year-old observes attentively as her teacher comforts a sad classmate. The teacher's warmth and responsiveness increase the likelihood that the onlooker will imitate this model of prosocial behavior.

© LAURA DWIGHT PHOTOGRAPHY

Effects of Punishment A sharp reprimand or physical force to restrain or move a child is justified when immediate obedience is necessary—for example, when a 3-year-old is about to harm another or run into the street. In fact, parents are most likely to use forceful methods under these conditions. But to foster long-term goals, such as acting kindly toward others, they tend to rely on warmth and reasoning (Dahl & Chan, 2017; Lansford et al., 2012). And in response to serious transgressions, such as lying and stealing, they often combine power assertion with reasoning (Grusec, 2006).

Frequent harsh punishment promotes immediate compliance but not lasting changes in behavior. For example, Robbie's parents often punished by shouting, criticizing, hitting, and spanking. But as soon as they stopped punishing and turned away, Robbie—like most children subjected to corporal punishment—misbehaved again (Holden, Williamson, & Holland, 2014). The more harsh threats, angry physical control, and physical punishment children experience, the more likely they are to develop serious, lasting problems. These include weak internalization of moral rules; depression, aggression, antisocial behavior, and poor academic performance in childhood and adolescence; and depression, alcohol abuse, criminality, physical health problems, and family violence (including child maltreatment) in adulthood (Afifi, Ford, & Gershoff, 2017; Bender et al., 2007; Gershoff & Grogan-Kaylor, 2016).

Repeated harsh punishment has undesirable side effects:

- Parents often spank in response to children's aggression. Yet the punishment itself models aggression!
- Harshly treated children react with anger, resentment, and a chronic sense of being personally threatened, which prompts a focus on the self's distress rather than a sympathetic orientation to others' needs.
- Children who are frequently punished develop a conflict-ridden, defiant relationship with the punitive parent, whom they avoid as a means of self-protection (Kim & Kochanska, 2015; Shaw, Lacourse, & Nagin, 2005). Consequently, the parent's effectiveness at teaching desirable behaviors is substantially reduced.
- By stopping children's misbehavior temporarily, harsh punishment gives adults immediate relief, reinforcing them for using coercive discipline. For this reason, a punitive parent is likely to punish with greater frequency over time, a course of action that can spiral into serious abuse.
- Children, adolescents, and adults whose parents used *corporal punishment*—physical force that inflicts pain but not injury—are more accepting of such discipline (Deater-Deckard et al., 2003; Vitrup & Holden, 2010). In this way, use of physical punishment may transfer to the next generation.

Although corporal punishment spans the SES spectrum, its frequency and harshness are elevated among less educated, economically disadvantaged parents (Giles-Sims, Straus, & Sugarman, 1995; Lansford et al., 2009). And consistently, parents with conflict-ridden marriages and with mental health problems (who are emotionally reactive, depressed, or aggressive) are more likely to be punitive and also to have hard-to-manage children (Berlin et al., 2009; Taylor et al., 2010). But even after controlling for child, parenting, and family characteristics that might otherwise account for the relationship, the link between physical punishment and later child and adolescent aggression remains (Lansford et al., 2011; Lee, Altschul, & Gershoff, 2015; MacKenzie et al., 2013).

Nevertheless, children exposed to corporal punishment vary in the extent to which they display externalizing behavior problems, suggesting additional factors play a role in this relationship. The association between physical punishment and aggression is greater when parents are low in warmth and responsiveness and high in angry, critical, rejecting behaviors (Grusec et al., 2017; Kim & Kochanska, 2015; Mendez et al., 2016). Temperament is also influential: In a longitudinal study extending from 15 months to 3 years, early corporal punishment was a stronger predictor of externalizing difficulties in temperamentally difficult than easy children (Mulvaney & Mebert, 2007). Similar findings emerged in a twin study in which physical punishment was most detrimental for children at high genetic risk for behavior problems (Boutwell et al., 2011).

When we consider the evidence as a whole, the widespread use of corporal punishment by American parents is cause for concern. Surveys of nationally representative samples of U.S. households reveal that although corporal punishment typically increases from infancy to age 5 and then declines, it is high at all ages (see Figure 10.2) (Gershoff et al., 2012; Straus & Stewart, 1999; Zolotor et al., 2011). Among U.S. parents who physically punish their children, more than one-fourth report having used a hard object, such as a brush or a belt.

Over the past three decades, the percentage of U.S. adults agreeing that "it is sometimes necessary to give a child a good, hard spanking" has declined by 20 percent in women and 8 percent in men. Still, the majority of women (66 percent) and men (76 percent) continue to endorse spanking (Child Trends, 2018a). A prevailing American belief is that corporal punishment, if implemented

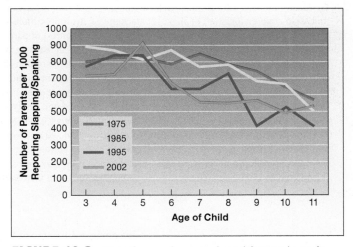

FIGURE 10.2   Prevalence of corporal punishment in early and middle childhood by year of survey. Five large surveys of U.S. parents show little change in use of corporal punishment over nearly three decades. Estimates are based on the number of parents per 1,000 reporting one or more instances of spanking or slapping their child during the past year. Rates are not shown for infants and toddlers, though other evidence indicates that 50 to 80 percent experience physical punishment. (From A. J. Zolotor, A. D. Theodore, D. K. Runyan, J. J. Chang, & A. L. Laskey, 2011, "Corporal Punishment and Physical Abuse: Population-Based Trends for Three- to 11-Year-Old Children in the United States," *Child Abuse Review, 20,* p. 61. Reprinted by permission of John Wiley & Sons, Ltd.)

Cultural Influences | Ethnic Differences in the Consequences of Physical Punishment

In an African-American community, six older adults, who had volunteered to serve as mentors for parents facing child-rearing challenges, met to discuss parenting issues at a social service agency. Their attitudes toward discipline were strikingly different from those of the European-American social workers who had brought them together. Each mentor argued that successful child rearing required appropriate physical discipline. At the same time, they voiced strong disapproval of screaming or cursing at children, calling such out-of-control parenting behavior "abusive." Ruth, the oldest and most respected member of the group, characterized good parenting as a complex combination of warmth, teaching, talking nicely, and disciplining physically. She related how an older neighbor advised her to handle her own children when she was a young parent:

> She said to me says, don't scream … you talk to them real nice and sweet and when they do something ugly … get a nice little switch and you won't have any trouble with them and from that day that's the way I raised 'em. (Mosby et al., 1999, pp. 511–512)

In several studies, corporal punishment predicted externalizing problems similarly among European-American, African-American, Hispanic, and Asian children (Gershoff et al., 2012; MacKenzie et al., 2013). Yet other studies point to ethnic variations. In one longitudinal investigation, researchers followed several hundred families, collecting information from mothers on disciplinary strategies and from teachers on children's problem behaviors from kindergarten through fourth grade (Lansford et al., 2012). Regardless of ethnicity, reasoning was the most common approach to discipline, spanking the least common. But predictors and consequences of spanking differed by family ethnicity.

Among European-American families, externalizing behavior in kindergarten predicted parental physical punishment in first through third grades, which in turn led to more externalizing behavior by fourth grade. In contrast, among African-American families, kindergarten externalizing behavior was unrelated to later physical punishment, and physical punishment did not augment externalizing behavior. The investigators concluded that European-American parents more often use physical discipline in reaction to challenging behaviors, causing those behaviors to escalate. African-American parents, in contrast, appear to use physical punishment to prevent child difficulties, thereby reducing its negative consequences.

Consistent with this interpretation, African-American and European-American parents report meting out physical punishment differently. In African-American families, physical discipline is typically culturally approved, mild, delivered in a context of parental warmth, accompanied by verbal teaching, and aimed at helping children become responsible adults. When European-American parents resort to physical punishment, they are often highly agitated and rejecting of the child and view the harshness of their discipline as wrong (Dodge, McLoyd, & Lansford, 2006; LeCuyer et al., 2011; Su et al., 2019).

Consequently, most African-American children may view spanking as a practice carried out with their best interests in mind, whereas

© LAURA DWIGHT PHOTOGRAPHY

In African-American families, physical discipline is often culturally approved, generally mild, and delivered in a context of parental warmth. As a result, children may view it as an effort to encourage maturity, not as an act of aggression.

European-American children may regard it as an act of aggression. In support of this view, in an investigation of nearly 900 African-American families, spanking predicted depressive symptoms only among a small number of children whose mothers tended to use it when they were highly angry and frustrated (McLoyd et al., 2007).

These findings are not an endorsement of physical punishment. Other forms of discipline, such as time out, withdrawal of privileges, and the positive parenting strategies listed on the following page are far more effective. In adolescence, ethnic differences in physical punishment fade: It is broadly associated with depression and misconduct among teenagers (Wang & Kenny, 2014). But it is noteworthy that the meaning and impact of physical discipline to children can vary sharply with its intensity level, context of warmth and support, and cultural approval.

by caring parents, is harmless, perhaps even beneficial. But as the Cultural Influences box above reveals, this assumption is valid only under conditions of limited use in certain social contexts.

Alternatives to Harsh Punishment   Alternatives to criticism, slaps, and spankings can reduce the side effects of punishment. A technique called **time out** involves removing children from the immediate setting—for example, by sending them to their rooms—until they are ready to act appropriately. When a child is out of control, a few minutes in time out can be enough to change behavior while also giving angry parents time to cool off (Morawska & Sanders, 2011). Another approach is *withdrawal of privileges,* such as playing outside or watching a favorite TV program. Like time out, removing privileges allows parents to avoid using harsh techniques that can easily intensify into violence.

APPLYING WHAT WE KNOW

Positive Parenting

STRATEGY	EXPLANATION
Use transgressions as opportunities to teach.	When a child engages in harmful or unsafe behavior, intervene firmly, and then use induction, which motivates children to make amends and behave prosocially.
Reduce opportunities for misbehavior.	On long car trips, bring back-seat activities that relieve children's restlessness. At the supermarket, converse with children and let them help with shopping. Children then learn to occupy themselves constructively when options are limited.
Provide reasons for rules.	When children appreciate that rules are rational, not arbitrary, they are more likely to strive to follow the rules.
Arrange for children to participate in family routines and duties.	By joining with adults in preparing a meal, washing dishes, or raking leaves, children develop a sense of responsible participation in family and community life and acquire many practical skills.
When children are obstinate, try compromising and problem solving.	When a child refuses to obey, express understanding of the child's feelings ("I know it's not fun to clean up"), suggest a compromise ("You put those away, I'll take care of these"), and help the child think of ways to avoid the problem in the future. Responding firmly but kindly and respectfully increases the likelihood of willing cooperation.
Encourage mature behavior.	Express confidence in children's capacity to learn and appreciation for effort and cooperation, as in "You gave that your best!" "Thanks for cleaning up on your own!" Adult encouragement fosters pride and satisfaction in succeeding, thereby inspiring children to improve further.
Be sensitive to children's physical and emotional resources.	When children are tired, ill, or bored, they are likely to engage in attention-getting, disorganized, or otherwise improper behavior as a reaction to discomfort. In these instances, meeting the child's needs makes more sense than disciplining.

Sources: Grogan-Kaylor, Ma, & Graham-Bermann, 2018; Grusec, 2006.

When parents do decide to use punishment, they can increase its effectiveness in three ways:

- *Consistency.* Permitting children to act inappropriately on some occasions but scolding them on others confuses children, and the unacceptable act persists (Acker & O'Leary, 1996).
- *A warm parent–child relationship.* Children of involved, caring parents find the interruption in parental affection that accompanies punishment especially unpleasant. They want to regain parental warmth and approval as quickly as possible.
- *Explanations.* Providing reasons for mild punishment helps children relate the misdeed to expectations for future behavior. This approach leads to far greater reduction in misbehavior than using punishment alone (Larzelere et al., 1996).

Positive Relationships, Positive Parenting   The most effective forms of discipline encourage good conduct—by building a mutually respectful bond with the child, letting the child know ahead of time how to act, and praising mature behavior ("You helped clear the dishes. That was thoughtful"). When sensitivity, cooperation, and shared positive emotion are evident in joint activities between parents and preschoolers, children show firmer conscience development—expressing empathy after transgressions, behaving responsibly, playing fairly in games, and considering others' welfare (Kochanska et al., 2008; Thompson, 2014). Parent–child closeness leads children to heed parental demands because children feel a sense of commitment to the relationship.

See Applying What We Know above for ways to parent positively. After experiencing a training program in these strategies, parents diverse in SES felt more confident about their ability to handle child-rearing challenges and were less approving of physical punishment

(Durrant et al., 2014). When parents focus on promoting children's cooperation, social problem solving, and consideration for others, they greatly reduce the need for punishment.

10.4.3 The Cognitive-Developmental Perspective

The psychoanalytic and social learning approaches to morality focus on how children acquire ready-made standards of good conduct from adults. In contrast, the cognitive-developmental perspective regards children as *active thinkers* about social rules. As early as the preschool years, children make moral judgments, deciding what is right or wrong on the basis of concepts they construct about justice and fairness (Gibbs, 2019; Killen & Smetana, 2015).

Preschoolers' Moral Understanding   Young children have some well-developed ideas about morality. As long as researchers emphasize people's intentions, 3-year-olds say that a person with bad intentions—someone who deliberately frightens, embarrasses, or otherwise hurts another—is more deserving of punishment than a well-intentioned person. They also protest when they see one person harming another (Helwig, Zelazo, & Wilson, 2001; Vaish, Missana, & Tomasello, 2011). Around age 4, children know that a person who expresses an insincere intention—saying, "I'll come over and help you rake leaves," while not intending to do so—is lying (Maas, 2008). And 4-year-olds approve of telling the truth and disapprove of lying, even when a lie remains undetected (Bussey, 1992).

A Laotian preschooler protects her younger sister from harm by helping her navigate the wet front steps of their home. Young children in diverse cultures understand the importance of protecting others' rights and welfare.

© KEITH LEVIT/ALAMY STOCK PHOTO

Furthermore, preschoolers in diverse cultures distinguish **moral imperatives,** which protect people's rights and welfare, from two other types of rules and expectations: **social conventions,** customs determined solely by consensus, such as table manners and politeness rituals (saying "please" and "thank you"); and **matters of personal choice,** such as choice of friends, hairstyle, and leisure activities, which do not violate rights and are up to the individual (Killen, Margie, & Sinno, 2006; Nucci & Gingo, 2011; Smetana, 2006). Interviews with 3- and 4-year-olds reveal that they consider moral violations (unprovoked hitting, stealing an apple) as more wrong and deserving of punishment than violations of social conventions (eating ice cream with your fingers). They also say that moral violations would still be wrong even if an adult did not see them and no rules existed to prohibit them, because they harm others (Smetana et al., 2012). And preschoolers' concern with personal choice, conveyed through statements like "I'm gonna wear *this* shirt," serves as the springboard for moral concepts of individual rights, which will expand greatly in middle childhood and adolescence.

Preschoolers' moral reasoning tends to be *rigid,* emphasizing salient features and consequences while neglecting other important information. For example, they have difficulty distinguishing between accidental and intentional transgressions (Killen et al., 2011). And they are more likely than older children to claim that stealing and lying are always wrong, even when a person has a morally sound reason for engaging in these acts (Lourenço, 2003; Poplinger, Talwar, & Crossman, 2011). Furthermore, their explanations for why hitting others is wrong are simplistic and centered on physical harm: "When you get hit, it hurts, and you start to cry" (Nucci, 2009).

Children's commitment to the wrongness of moral transgressions builds on their early concern for others' welfare. When they see a peer cause another harm, preschoolers as young as age 3 often tattle to a caregiver, a behavior generally viewed as undesirable and discouraged by adults. Yet children do not tattle because they believe that they themselves might be wrongly blamed for the transgression. Even when they know they cannot be blamed, they tattle nonetheless (Yucel & Vaish, 2018). Their tattling indicates that they care enough about moral imperatives to try to ensure that others also follow them.

With language and cognitive development—especially in theory of mind and understanding of emotion—older preschoolers begin to reason morally by referring to others' perspectives and feelings. In several studies, understanding of false belief was associated with 4- and 5-year-olds' moral justifications that focused on the harmed individual's emotional distress and diminished well-being (Dunn, Cutting, & Demetriou, 2000; Lane et al., 2010). But advances in theory of mind, though influencing preschoolers' explanations, are not sufficient to account for gains in moral understanding.

Social Experiences and Moral Understanding Morally relevant social experiences are vital for moral progress in early childhood, contributing to gains in both theory of mind and moral understanding and to their integration (Killen & Smetana, 2015). Disputes with siblings and peers over rights, possessions, and property allow preschoolers to express emotions and perspectives, negotiate, compromise, and work out their first ideas about justice and fairness. Children also learn from warm, sensitive parental communication and from observing how adults respond to children's rule violations. And they benefit greatly from adult–child discussions of moral issues (Killen & Dahl, 2018). Children who are advanced in moral thinking tend to have parents who adapt their communications about fighting, honesty, and ownership to what their children can understand, tell stories with moral implications, point out injustices, encourage prosocial behavior, and gently stimulate the child to think further, without being hostile or critical (Dunn, 2014; Janssens & Deković, 1997).

Preschoolers and school-age children who verbally and physically assault others, often with little or no provocation, are delayed in moral reasoning (Ciu et al., 2016; Helwig & Turiel, 2004). Without special help, such children show long-term disruptions in moral development, deficits in self-control, and ultimately an antisocial lifestyle.

10.4.4 Development of Aggression

Beginning in late infancy, all children display aggression from time to time, and as opportunities to interact with siblings and peers increase, aggressive outbursts occur more often (Nærde et al., 2014). By the second year, aggressive acts with two distinct purposes emerge. Initially, the most common is **proactive** (or *instrumental*) **aggression,** in which children act to fulfill a need or desire—to obtain an object, privilege, space, or social reward, such as adult or peer attention—and unemotionally attack a person to achieve their goal. The other type, **reactive** (or *hostile*) **aggression,** is an angry, defensive response to provocation or a blocked goal and is meant to hurt another person (Eisner & Malti, 2015; Vitaro & Brendgen, 2012).

Proactive and reactive aggression come in three forms, which are the focus of most research:

- **Physical aggression** harms others through physical injury—pushing, hitting, kicking, or punching others, or destroying another's property.
- **Verbal aggression** harms others through threats of physical aggression, name-calling, or hostile teasing.
- **Relational aggression** damages another's peer relationships through social exclusion, malicious gossip, or friendship manipulation.

Although verbal aggression is always direct, physical and relational aggression can be either *direct* or *indirect.* For example, hitting injures a person directly, whereas destroying property indirectly inflicts physical harm. Similarly, saying, "Do what I say, or I won't be your friend," conveys relational aggression directly, while spreading rumors, refusing to talk to a peer, or manipulating friendship by saying behind someone's back, "Don't play with her; she's a nerd," does so indirectly.

Physical aggression emerges by the end of the first year as infants become capable of pushing, pulling, hitting, kicking, or otherwise forcefully striking others. It rises sharply between ages 1 and 3 and then diminishes as verbal aggression replaces it (Hay, 2017; Tremblay, 2015). Proactive aggression also declines as preschoolers' improved capacity to delay gratification enables them to resist grabbing others' possessions. But reactive aggression in verbal and relational forms tends to rise over early and middle childhood (Côté et al., 2007; Tremblay, 2000). Older children are better able to recognize malicious intentions and, as a result, more often retaliate in hostile ways.

By age 17 months, boys are more physically aggressive than girls—a difference found throughout childhood in many cultures

These preschoolers display proactive aggression, pushing and grabbing as they argue over a game. Proactive aggression declines with age as children's capacity to delay gratification improves.

(Baillargeon et al., 2007; Björkqvist, 2018; Lussier, Corrado, & Tzoumakis, 2012). The sex difference is due in part to biology—in particular, to male sex hormones (androgens) and temperamental traits (activity level, irritability, impulsivity) on which boys score higher (Book, Starzyk, & Quinsey, 2001). Parental gender-role attitudes are also important. In a longitudinal study carried out in the Netherlands, fathers with strong gender-stereotyped attitudes responded with more physical coercion (restraining, pushing, yanking the child's arm) to their preschool sons' than daughters' disobedience—forceful parenting practices associated with elevated aggressive behavior in boys a year later (Endendijk et al., 2017). In contrast, fathers with gender-equitable attitudes engaged in more physical coercion with their daughters, which subsequently predicted greater aggression in girls than boys.

Although girls have a reputation for being both verbally and relationally more aggressive than boys, the sex difference is small (Crick, Ostrov, & Werner, 2006; Crick et al., 2006). Beginning in the preschool years, girls concentrate most of their aggressive acts in the relational category. Boys inflict harm in more variable ways. Physically and verbally aggressive boys also tend to be relationally aggressive (Card et al., 2008). Therefore, boys display overall rates of aggression that are much higher than girls'.

At the same time, girls more often use indirect relational tactics that—in disrupting intimate bonds especially important to girls—can be particularly mean. Whereas physical attacks are usually brief, acts of indirect relational aggression may extend for hours, weeks, or even months (Nelson, Robinson, & Hart, 2005; Underwood, 2003). In one instance, a 6-year-old girl formed a "pretty-girls club" and—for nearly an entire school year—convinced its members to exclude several classmates by saying they were "dirty and smelly."

An occasional aggressive exchange between preschoolers is normal. Children sometimes assert their sense of self through these encounters, which become important learning experiences as adults intervene and teach social problem solving. But preschoolers who are emotionally negative, impulsive, and defiant and who score low in cognitive abilities—especially, language and executive function skills necessary for self-regulation—are at risk for early, high rates of physical or relational aggression (or both) that can persist. Persistent aggression, in turn, predicts later internalizing and externalizing difficulties and social skills deficits, including loneliness, anxiety, depression, peer relationship problems, and antisocial activity in middle childhood and adolescence (Eisner & Malti, 2015; Hay, 2017; Tremblay, 2015).

The Family as Training Ground for Aggressive Behavior   "I can't control him; he's impossible," Robbie's mother, Nadine, complained to Leslie one day. When Leslie asked if Robbie might be troubled by something happening at home, she discovered that his parents fought constantly and resorted to harsh, inconsistent discipline. The same child-rearing practices that undermine moral internalization—love withdrawal, power assertion, physical punishment, negative comments and emotions, and inconsistency—are linked to aggression from early childhood through adolescence, in children of both sexes and in many cultures, with most of these practices predicting both physical and relational forms (Côté et al., 2007; Gershoff et al., 2010; Kuppens et al., 2013; Nelson et al., 2013; Olson et al., 2011).

In families like Robbie's, anger and punitiveness quickly create a conflict-ridden family atmosphere and an "out-of-control" child. The pattern begins with forceful discipline, which occurs more often with stressful life experiences (such as economic hardship or an unhappy marriage), a parent with an unstable personality, or a temperamentally difficult child (Baydar & Akcinar, 2018; Eisner & Malti, 2015). Typically, the parent threatens, criticizes, and punishes, and the child angrily resists until the parent "gives in." At the end of each exchange, both parent and child get relief from stopping the unpleasant behavior of the other, so the behaviors repeat and escalate.

As these cycles become more frequent, they generate anxiety and irritability among other family members, who soon join in the hostile interactions. Compared with siblings in typical families, those with critical, punitive parents are more aggressive toward one another (Dickson et al., 2015). Physically, verbally, and relationally destructive sibling conflict, in turn, quickly spreads to peer relationships, contributing to poor impulse control and antisocial behavior by the early school years (Garcia et al., 2000; Miller et al., 2012; Ostrov, Crick, & Stauffacher, 2006).

Overall, boys are more likely than girls to be targets of harsh, inconsistent discipline because they are more active and impulsive and therefore harder to control. In longitudinal research, boys with a gene predisposing them to weak regulation of emotion and behavior were far more likely to display childhood aggression and engage in violent acts once they reached adolescence and adulthood if they had a history severe family adversity, such as child abuse, domestic violence, or parental mental illness (Enoch et al., 2010; Fergusson et al., 2011). These boys seemed especially susceptible to the negative effects of harsh, inept parenting. When frustrated, angry, or disappointed, they lashed out at others.

Social Information-Processing Deficits   Children subjected to these family processes acquire a distorted view of the social world. Those who are high in reactive aggression often see hostile intent where it does not exist—in situations where peers' intentions are unclear, where harm is accidental, and even where peers are trying to be helpful. As a result, they make many unprovoked attacks, which trigger aggressive retaliations (Healy et al., 2015; Orbio de Castro et al., 2002).

Children high in proactive aggression have different social information-processing deficits. Compared with agemates, they believe that there are more benefits and fewer costs for engaging in destructive acts (Arsenio, 2010). They are also delayed in moral understanding. As preschoolers, they show a reduced capacity to differentiate moral imperatives from social conventions—a distinction that serves as an early foundation for appreciating fairness and justice (Jambon & Smetana, 2018). Some, who conclude that aggression "works" to access rewards and control others, callously use it to advance their own goals and are relatively unconcerned about causing suffering in others—an aggressive style associated with later, more severe conduct problems, violent behavior, and delinquency (Marsee & Frick, 2010).

Return to the information-processing model of social problem solving in Figure 10.1 on page 367. Notice how reactive aggression is linked to deficiencies in recognizing and interpreting social cues. In contrast, proactive aggression is associated with deficiencies in formulating social goals (caring more about satisfying one's own needs than getting along with others) and in generating and evaluating strategies (engaging in aggression and evaluating it favorably) (Arsenio, 2010). A substantial number of aggressive children engage in both reactive and proactive acts, while others largely display one type (Fite et al., 2008).

Highly aggressive children tend to be rejected by peers, to fail in school, and (by adolescence) to seek out deviant peers. Together, these factors contribute to the long-term stability of aggression.

Media Violence and Aggression   In the United States, an estimated 60 percent of television programs contain violent scenes, often portraying repeated aggressive acts that go unpunished. TV victims of violence are rarely shown experiencing serious harm, and few programs condemn violence or depict other ways of solving problems (Calvert, 2015). Violent content is 10 percent above average in children's TV and video programs, with cartoons being the most violent. And over the past several decades, violent video games have become increasingly realistic (Hartmann, Möller, & Krause, 2015). Many portray extreme, graphic violence.

Assessing the findings of thousands of studies using a wide variety of designs and methods, the overwhelming majority of researchers have concluded that violent screen media—including TV and video programs, movies, and video games—increase the likelihood of hostile thoughts and emotions and of verbally, physically, and relationally aggressive behavior (Anderson et al., 2015; Anderson & Bushman, 2018; Bushman, Gollwitzer, & Cruz, 2015; Krahé, 2016). The link between violent media and aggression is remarkably consistent across different countries. Although young people of all ages are susceptible, preschool and young school-age children may be especially likely to imitate screen media violence because they believe that much of it is real and accept what they see uncritically.

Violent screen media of all kinds, video games included, increase the likelihood of hostile thoughts and emotions and aggressive behavior.

In addition to creating short-term difficulties in parent and peer relations, violent media can have lasting negative consequences. In several longitudinal studies, exposure to violent media in childhood and adolescence predicted aggressive behavior in early adulthood, after other factors linked to viewing (such as prior child and parent aggression, IQ, parent education, family income, and neighborhood crime) were controlled (Graber et al., 2006; Huesmann et al., 2003; Johnson et al., 2002). And in a longitudinal investigation of over 3,000 children and adolescents, violent video game play led to an increase in aggressive thoughts a year later, which in turn predicted a rise in aggressive behavior the following year (Gentile et al., 2014).

Aggressive children and adolescents have a greater appetite for violent media fare. And boys devote more time to violent media than girls, in part because of male-oriented themes of conquest and adventure and use of males as lead characters. But even in nonaggressive children, media violence sparks hostile thoughts and behavior (Anderson et al., 2015). Its impact is simply less intense.

Furthermore, media violence "hardens" children to aggression, making them more willing to tolerate it in others (Anderson & Bushman, 2018; Anderson et al., 2010). Viewers quickly habituate, responding with reduced arousal to the pain and suffering of victims and with greater acceptance of violence when exposed to real-world instances.

Preschoolers, as we saw in Chapter 9, spend much time watching educational programs for young children. Although beneficial for cognitive and academic progress, high exposure to educational programs is associated with a rise in relational aggression in young children (Ostrov, Gentile, & Mullins, 2013). The likely reason is that these programs often present social-conflict scenes, in a well-intentioned effort to model social problem solving. But preschoolers have difficulty connecting characters' conflicts to their eventual favorable resolutions, so they readily imitate the relationally aggressive acts they see.

As a result, parents bear most responsibility for regulating their children's exposure to media violence and other inappropriate content. In the United States, TV programs are rated for violent and sexual content, and since 2000 new TV sets have been required to contain the V-chip, which allows parents to block undesired material. And parents can control children's Internet access by using filters or programs that monitor website visits.

Although surveys of U.S. parents indicate that nearly 80 percent are "somewhat or very concerned" about their children's exposure to media violence, 20 to 30 percent of preschoolers and about half of school-age children experience no limits on TV, computer, or tablet use at home. Some children begin visiting websites without parental supervision as early as age 4 (Rideout, 2018; Rideout & Hamel, 2006; Varnhagen, 2007). And parents often model excessive, inappropriate screen media use. In observations of adults with children in fast-food restaurants, almost one-third of the adults spent the entire meal absorbed with mobile devices rather than engaged with the children in their care (Radesky et al., 2014).

To help parents improve their preschoolers' "media diet," one group of researchers devised a year-long intervention in which they guided parents in replacing violent programs with age-appropriate educational and prosocial programs. Compared to a control group, children in intervention families displayed lower rates of externalizing behavior and improved social competence (Christakis et al., 2013). Applying What We Know on the following page lists strategies parents can use to regulate children's screen media use.

Helping Children and Parents Control Aggression

Treatment for aggressive children is best begun early, before their antisocial behavior becomes well-practiced and difficult to change. Breaking the cycle of hostilities between family members and promoting effective ways of relating to others are crucial. The coercive cycles of punitive parents and aggressive children are so persistent that these children often are punished even when they do behave appropriately!

Leslie suggested that Robbie's parents enroll in a training program aimed at improving the parenting of children at risk for or showing conduct problems. Many such programs based on social learning theory are highly effective with preschool and elementary school children (Piquero et al., 2016; Vlahovicova et al., 2017).

In one approach called Incredible Years, parents complete 18 weekly group sessions facilitated by two professionals, who teach positive parenting techniques for promoting children's

LOOK and LISTEN

Watch a half-hour of children's cartoons and a prime-time movie on TV, and tally the number of violent acts, including those that go unpunished. How often did violence, especially without consequences, occur in each type of program?

APPLYING WHAT WE KNOW

Regulating Screen Media Use

STRATEGY	EXPLANATION
Limit TV, computer, and tablet use.	Parents should provide clear rules limiting children's TV, computer, and tablet use and stick to the rules. The American Academy of Pediatrics (2016a) recommends no more than 1 hour per day of high-quality programming for 2- to 5-year-olds. Screen media should not be used as a babysitter. Placing a TV, computer, or tablet in a child's bedroom substantially increases use and makes the child's activity hard to monitor.
Avoid using screen media as a reward.	When media access is used as a reward or withheld as punishment, children become increasingly attracted to it.
Watch programs and other screen media content with children, helping them understand what they see.	By raising questions about realism in media depictions, expressing disapproval of on-screen behavior, and encouraging discussion, adults help children understand and critically evaluate screen media content.
Link screen media content to everyday learning experiences.	Parents can extend screen media learning in ways that encourage children to engage actively with their surroundings. For example, a program on animals might spark a trip to the zoo, a visit to the library for books about animals, or new ways of observing and caring for the family pet.
Model good media practices.	Parents' media behavior influences children's behavior. Parents should avoid excessive media use, limit their own exposure to harmful content, and limit mobile device use during family interactions.
Use a warm, rational approach to child rearing.	Children of warm parents who make reasonable demands for mature behavior prefer media experiences with educational and prosocial content and are less attracted to violent programming.

academic, emotional, and social skills and for managing disruptive behaviors. Sessions include coaching, modeling, and practicing effective parenting behaviors—experiences aimed at interrupting parent–child destructive interaction while promoting positive relationships and competencies (Webster-Stratton & Reid, 2010). For example, Robbie's parents learned to impose clear limits on his unacceptable behaviors rather than giving in to him, to pair commands with reasons, and to replace verbal insults and spankings with more effective punishments, such as time out and withdrawal of privileges. A special focus is positive parenting, including warmth, attention, encouragement, and praise for prosocial behaviors.

Numerous evaluations in which families with aggressive children were randomly assigned to either Incredible Years or control groups reveal that the program increases use of effective parenting practices, reduces child behavior problems, and promotes prosocial behaviors (Leijten et al., 2018; Menting, Orobio de Castro, & Mathys, 2013). Children with high levels of hostile, unruly behavior tend to benefit most. And in one long-term follow-up, positive outcomes endured: Among 3- to 8-year-olds with serious conduct problems whose parents participated in Incredible Years, 75 percent appeared well-adjusted as teenagers (Webster-Stratton, Rinaldi, & Reid, 2011).

At preschool, Leslie began teaching Robbie more successful ways of relating to peers, had him practice these skills, and praised him for using them. As opportunities arose, she encouraged Robbie to talk about playmates' feelings and to express his own. As he increasingly took the perspective of others, empathized, and felt sympathetic concern, his lashing out at peers declined (Izard et al., 2008). Robbie also participated in a social problem-solving intervention (return to page 368 to review).

Finally, relieving stressors that stem from poverty and neighborhood disorganization and providing families with social supports help prevent childhood aggression (Bugental, Corpuz, & Schwartz, 2012). When parents better cope with difficulties in their own lives, interventions aimed at reducing children's aggression are even more effective.

ASK YOURSELF

Connect ■ What must parents do to foster conscience development in fearless, impulsive children? How does this illustrate the concept of goodness of fit (see page 255 in Chapter 7)?

Apply ■ Alice and Wayne want their two young children to become morally mature, caring individuals. List some parenting practices they should use and some they should avoid.

Reflect ■ Which types of punishment for a misbehaving preschooler do you endorse, and which types do you reject? Why?

10.5a Discuss biological and environmental influences on preschoolers' gender-stereotyped beliefs and behavior.

10.5b Describe and evaluate major theories that explain the emergence of gender identity.

10.5 Gender Typing

Gender typing refers to any association of objects, activities, roles, or traits with one sex or the other in ways that conform to cultural stereotypes (Blakemore, Berenbaum, & Liben, 2009). In Leslie's classroom, girls tended to spend more time in the housekeeping, art, and reading corners, while boys gathered more often in spaces devoted to blocks, woodworking, and active play. Already, the children had acquired many gender-linked beliefs and preferences and more often played with peers of their own sex.

Two theoretical perspectives—*social learning theory,* with its emphasis on modeling and reinforcement, and *cognitive-developmental theory,* with its focus on children as active thinkers about their social world—offer insights into the early development of gender typing. But neither perspective by itself provides a sufficient account. A third perspective has gained favor: *gender schema theory,* which combines elements of both social learning and cognitive-developmental theory. And as we will also see, a growing body of evidence confirms that *biological influences,* especially prenatal exposure to sex hormones, contribute as well.

10.5.1 Gender-Stereotyped Beliefs and Behaviors

Even before children can label their own sex, they have begun to acquire subtle associations with gender that most of us hold. An investigation of infants' play patterns showed that gender-stereotyped toy preferences are evident as early as 12½ months: In a play session in which dolls and trucks were available, girls more often chose the dolls and boys more often chose the trucks (Boe & Woods, 2018). The types of toys in the infants' homes predicted these preferences, suggesting that toy familiarity contributes to these early gender-typed choices.

By the middle of the second year, toddlers display the glimmerings of gender-stereotyped attitudes. In another study, 18-month-olds' looking behaviors revealed that they linked rough and sharp items (such as a fir tree and hammer) with males, although they had not yet learned to associate round and soft items (heart shape and dress) with females (Eichstedt et al., 2002). Recall from Chapter 7 that around age 2, children use such words as *boy, girl, lady,* and *man* appropriately. As soon as children become consciously aware of gender categories, gender-stereotyping of activities and behaviors accelerates.

Most preschoolers explicitly associate particular toys, types of clothing, tools, household items, games, occupations, colors (pink and blue), and behaviors (physical and relational aggression) with one gender or the other (Banse et al., 2010; Giles & Heyman, 2005; Weisgram, Fulcher, & Dinella, 2014). And their actions reflect their beliefs, not only in play preferences but in personality traits as well. As we have seen, boys tend to be more active, impulsive, assertive, and physically aggressive. Girls tend to be more fearful, dependent, emotionally sensitive, compliant, advanced in effortful control, and skilled at understanding self-conscious emotions and at inflicting indirect relational aggression (Else-Quest, 2012).

During early childhood, gender-stereotyped beliefs strengthen—so much so that many children apply them as blanket rules rather than flexible guidelines (Halim, Ruble, & Tamis-LeMonda, 2013). When asked whether gender stereotypes could be violated, half or more of

3- and 4-year-olds answered "no" to clothing, hairstyle, certain play styles (girls playing roughly), and play with certain toys (Barbie dolls and G.I. Joes) (Blakemore, 2003). Furthermore, most 3- to 6-year-olds are firm about not wanting to be friends with a child who violates a gender stereotype (a boy who wears nail polish, a girl who plays with trucks) or to attend a school where such violations are allowed (Ruble et al., 2007).

The rigidity of preschoolers' gender stereotypes helps us understand some commonly observed everyday behaviors. When Leslie showed her class a picture of a Scottish bagpiper wearing a kilt, the children exclaimed, "Men don't wear skirts!" And many insisted on wearing gender-stereotypical clothing themselves—dresses and the color pink among girls; sports jerseys, superhero T-shirts, and "not pink" among boys (Halim et al., 2016). During free play, the children frequently asserted that girls can't be police officers and boys don't take care of babies.

These one-sided judgments are a joint product of gender stereotyping in young children's environments and their cognitive limitations—in particular, their difficulty coordinating conflicting sources of information (Halim, 2016; Trautner et al., 2005). Most preschoolers do not yet realize that characteristics *associated with* one's sex—activities, toys, occupations, hairstyle, and clothing—do not *determine* whether a person is male or female. They have trouble understanding that males and females can be different in terms of their bodies but similar in many other ways.

Gender typing is well under way in the preschool years. Girls tend to play with girls and are drawn to toys and activities that emphasize nurturance, cooperation, and physical attractiveness.

10.5.2 Biological Influences on Gender Typing

The sex differences in play preferences and personality traits just described appear in many cultures (Dinella & Weisgram, 2018; Halim, 2016; Todd et al., 2017). Certain ones—male activity level and physical aggression, female emotional sensitivity, and preference for same-sex playmates—are widespread among mammalian species (de Waal, 2001). According to an evolutionary perspective, the adult life of our male ancestors was oriented toward competing for mates, and that of our female ancestors toward rearing children. Therefore, males became genetically primed for dominance and females for intimacy, responsiveness, and cooperativeness (Konner, 2010; Maccoby, 2002). Evolutionary theorists claim that family and cultural forces can influence the intensity of genetically based sex differences, leading some individuals to be more gender-typed than others. But experience cannot eradicate aspects of gender typing that served adaptive functions in human history.

Experiments with nonhuman mammals reveal that prenatally administered testosterone (the major androgen hormone in males) increases active play and physical aggression toward unfamiliar animals and suppresses maternal caregiving in females. The larger the dose of testosterone, the greater the impact on behavior (Arnold, 2009). In contrast, removing testosterone from prenatally developing male animals has the reverse effect, reducing "masculine" behaviors and increasing "feminine" behaviors.

Many studies of humans reveal similar patterns. Girls exposed prenatally to high levels of androgens (including testosterone), due to normal variation in hormone levels, a genetic defect, or medically prescribed hormones during pregnancy, show more "masculine" behavior—a preference for trucks and blocks over dolls, for active over quiet play, and for boys as playmates—even when parents encourage them to engage in gender-typical play (Berenbaum & Beltz, 2011; Hines, 2015; Hines & Davis, 2018). Likewise, boys with diminished prenatal androgen exposure, either because production by the testes is reduced or because body cells are androgen insensitive, tend to engage in "feminine" behaviors, including toy choices, play behaviors, and preference for girl playmates (Jürgensen et al., 2007; Lamminmaki et al., 2012).

As with findings in nonhuman mammals, the greater the deviation from typical prenatal hormone exposure in boys and girls, the larger the impact on behavior. Also, girls exposed to markedly elevated levels of prenatal androgens (similar to those of male fetuses) are usually born with masculinized genitals (Hines & Davis, 2018). And boys who are androgen insensitive are born with feminized genitals.

Some researchers argue that biologically based sex differences, which affect children's play styles, lead children to seek out same-sex playmates whose interests and behaviors are compatible with their own (Maccoby, 1998; Mehta & Strough, 2009). Preschool girls like to play in pairs with other girls because they share a preference for quieter activities involving cooperative roles. Boys prefer larger-group play with other boys, due to a shared desire to run, climb, play-fight, compete, and build up and knock things down (Fabes, Martin, & Hanish, 2003).

Research confirms that preschoolers are drawn to peers who engage in similar levels of gender-typed activities. But they also like to spend time with same-sex peers regardless of type of activity—perhaps because they expect a playmate who is like themselves in so basic a way to be more enjoyable (Martin et al., 2013). At age 4, children spend three times as much time with same-sex as with other-sex playmates. By age 6, this ratio has climbed to 11 to 1 (Martin & Fabes, 2001).

10.5.3 Environmental Influences on Gender Typing

A wealth of evidence reveals that environmental forces—at home, at school, with peers, and in the community—build on biological influences to promote vigorous gender typing in early childhood.

The Family   Beginning at birth, parents have different expectations of sons than of daughters. They tend to describe active behavior, competition, achievement, and control of emotion as appropriate for sons and warmth, polite behavior, and closely supervised activities as important for daughters (Brody, 1999; Endendijk et al., 2013; Turner & Gervai, 1995). Furthermore, parents usually prefer that their children play with gender-stereotyped and gender-neutral toys (Kollmeyer et al., 2018; Weisgram & Bruun, 2018).

Actual parenting practices reflect these beliefs. Parents give their sons toys that stress action and competition (cars, tools, footballs) and their daughters toys that emphasize nurturance, cooperation, and physical attractiveness (dolls, tea sets, jewelry) (Brown & Stone, 2018). Fathers of preschoolers report more physical activities (chasing, playing ball, playing outdoors) with sons, and more literacy activities (singing, reading, storytelling) with daughters (Leavell et al., 2011). And both mothers and fathers tend to react more positively when a son plays with cars and trucks, demands attention, runs and climbs, or tries to take toys from others. When interacting with daughters, they more often direct play activities, provide help, encourage participation in household tasks, make supportive statements (approval, praise, and agreement), and discuss emotions (Aznar & Tenenbaum, 2014; Denham, Bassett, & Wyatt, 2010; Fagot & Hagan, 1991; Leaper, 2000).

Parents also teach children about gender stereotypes through the language they use. In research on picture book reading with toddlers and preschoolers, mothers made many positive comments about story characters engaging in activities consistent with gender stereotypes ("She likes playing with that doll"). And both mothers and fathers frequently expressed *generic utterances,* which referred to nearly all same-sex individuals as alike, ignoring exceptions ("Boys can be sailors," "Most girls don't like trucks") (Endendijk et al., 2014; Gelman, Taylor, & Nguyen, 2004). Children readily picked up these generic expressions from parental speech, often receiving an affirming response (Child: "Only boys can drive trucks." Mother: "Okay").

Of the two sexes, boys are more gender-typed. Fathers, especially, are more insistent that boys conform to gender roles. As Figure 10.3 shows, in a survey of a large, nationally representative sample of U.S. parents, fathers were less likely than mothers to agree that it is "a very or somewhat good thing" for parents to encourage boys/girls to play with toys or participate in activities typically associated with the [other] gender" (Pew Research Center, 2018a). Both parents, though more so fathers, particularly felt this way about boys. Consistent with these trends, research repeatedly indicates that fathers differentiate more than mothers when it comes to children's "cross-gender" behavior: They are much more concerned when a boy acts like a "sissy" than when a girl acts like a "tomboy" (Blakemore & Hill, 2008; Kollmeyer et al., 2018).

Yet as Figure 10.3 indicates, at least half of fathers express flexible views about boys' activities. And recognizing the negative effects of other restrictive expectations for males, some fathers want their sons to be comfortable expressing feelings. As one father explained: "I'm more reserved than my wife emotionally. I realize that it is better to have our son be more open emotionally…. So, that's a challenge. You want him to open up, and you have to do the same thing. I'm not used to doing that" (Parker et al., 2012, p. 61).

Parents who hold nonstereotyped values and who behave accordingly have children who are less gender-typed (Tenenbaum & Leaper, 2002). Children of lesbian parents tend to be less gender-typed than their agemates of heterosexual or gay parents (Goldberg & Garcia, 2016; Goldberg, Kashy, & Smith, 2012). Lesbian mothers, due to their female gender and sexual minority status, may be especially accepting of "cross-gender" behavior in their children.

Other family members may also reduce gender typing. For example, children with older, other-sex siblings have many more opportunities to imitate and participate in "cross-gender" activities. As a result, they are less gender-typed in play preferences, attitudes, and personality traits than their agemates with older, same-sex siblings or no siblings (McHale et al., 2001; Rust et al., 2000).

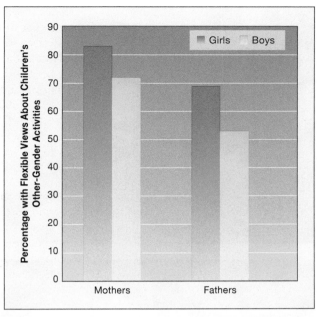

FIGURE 10.3 U.S. parents' views of whether it is "a very or somewhat good thing" to encourage children to participate in other-gender activities. In a survey of a nationally representative sample of several thousand parents, fathers expressed more resistance than mothers to steering children, especially boys, to play with toys and participate in activities typically associated with the other gender. (Based on Pew Research Center, 2018a.)

Teachers Teachers often act in ways that extend gender-role learning. Several times, Leslie caught herself emphasizing gender distinctions when she called out, "Will the girls line up on one side and the boys on the other?" or pleaded "Boys, I wish you'd quiet down like the girls!" These practices increase preschoolers' gender-stereotyped beliefs while reducing their liking for and willingness to play with other-sex peers (Hilliard & Liben, 2010).

Like parents, preschool teachers encourage girls to participate in adult-structured activities. Girls frequently cluster around the teacher, following directions, while boys are more attracted to play areas where adults are minimally involved (Campbell, Shirley, & Candy, 2004). As a result, boys and girls engage in different social behaviors. Compliance and bids for help occur more often in adult-structured contexts; assertiveness, leadership, and creative use of materials in unstructured pursuits.

As early as kindergarten, teachers give more overall attention (both positive and negative) to boys than girls—a difference evident in diverse countries, including China, England, and the United States. They praise boys more for their academic knowledge but also use more disapproval and controlling discipline with them (Chen & Rao, 2011; Davies, 2008; Swinson & Harrop, 2009). Teachers seem to expect boys to misbehave more often—a belief based partly on boys' actual behavior and partly on gender stereotypes.

In this preschool classroom, girls cluster around the teacher while boys play independently. As a result, children practice gender-typed behaviors—compliance and bids for attention by girls, assertiveness and leadership in boys.

Children develop different styles of interaction in gender-segregated play. Boys more often use commands and physical force to get their way. Girls, out of greater concern for their playmate's feelings, rely on polite requests and persuasion.

Peers   Children's same-sex peer associations make the peer context an especially potent source of gender-role learning. The more preschoolers play with same-sex partners, the more their behavior becomes gender-typed—in toy choices, activity level, aggression, and adult involvement (Martin et al., 2011, 2013).

By age 3, same-sex peers positively reinforce one another for gender-typed play by praising, imitating, or joining in. In contrast, when preschoolers engage in "cross-gender" activities—for example, when boys play with dolls or girls with cars and trucks—peers criticize them. Boys are especially intolerant of cross-gender play in other boys (Thorne, 1993). A boy who frequently crosses gender lines is likely to be ignored by other boys, even when he does engage in "masculine" activities!

Children also develop different styles of social influence in gender-segregated peer groups. To get their way in large-group play, boys often rely on commands, threats, and physical force. Girls' preference for playing in pairs leads to greater concern with a partner's needs, evident in girls' use of polite requests, persuasion, and acceptance. When girls communicate assertively with commands, other girls tend to respond with aggression (Hanish et al., 2012). Girls soon find that gentle tactics succeed with other girls but not with boys, who ignore their courteous overtures (Leaper, 1994; Leaper, Tenenbaum, & Shaffer, 1999). Boys' unresponsiveness gives girls another reason to stop interacting with them.

Over time, children come to believe in the "correctness" of gender-segregated play and to perceive themselves as more similar to same-sex than other-sex peers, which further strengthens gender segregation and gender-stereotyped activities (Martin et al., 2011). As boys and girls separate, *in-group favoritism*—more positive evaluations of members of one's own gender—becomes another factor that sustains the separate social worlds of boys and girls, resulting in "two distinct subcultures" of shared knowledge, beliefs, interests, and behaviors (Maccoby, 2002; Ruble, Martin, & Berenbaum, 2006).

The Broader Social Environment   Although children's everyday environments have changed to some degree, they continue to present many examples of gender typing—in occupations, leisure activities, and achievements. Screen media powerfully convey gender stereotypes, depicting them in diverse settings and formats. For example, although today's TV and video programs include more career-oriented women than in the past, female characters continue to be young, physically attractive, caring, emotional, and victimized and to be seen in romantic and family contexts. In contrast, male characters are usually dominant and powerful. Stereotypes are especially prevalent in video games, cartoons, and animated films for children (Calvert, 2015; Leaper, 2013).

These images contribute to young children's biased beliefs about roles and behaviors suitable for males and females. For example, introducing commercial princess costumes based on Disney animated films (such as Cinderella and Sleeping Beauty) into dramatic play areas in preschool classrooms led the pretend play themes of 3- to 5-year-old girls to emphasize beauty, clothing, accessories, and body movements (twirling, ballroom dancing, and hand posing) that the girls associated with princesses (Golden & Jacoby, 2018). These themes almost never appeared in girls' play with non-princess costumes. Princess play also intensified girls' exclusion of boys.

Many children's toys are explicitly marketed as "for boys" or "for girls" through TV and online advertising, through their gender-typed packaging, and by the stores where they are sold, as the doll and princess aisles and the superhero and vehicle aisles in major toy stores

LOOK and LISTEN

While observing 3- to 5-year-olds during a free-play period in a preschool or child-care program, note the extent of gender segregation and gender-typed play. Did styles of social influence differ in boys' and girls' gender-segregated groups? Jot down examples.

Many children's toys are explicitly marketed as "for boys" or "for girls" through gender-typed packaging and store displays—for example, Disney Princess dolls and Star Wars toys in segregated aisles.

illustrate (Auster & Mansbach, 2012). As we will see next, children do more than imitate the many gender-linked responses they observe. They soon come to view not just their social surroundings but also themselves through a "gender-biased lens"—a perspective that can seriously restrict their interests and learning opportunities.

10.5.4 Gender Identity

As adults, each of us has a **gender identity**—an image of oneself as relatively masculine or feminine in characteristics. By middle childhood, researchers can measure gender identity by asking children to rate themselves on personality traits. A child or adult with a "masculine" identity scores high on traditionally masculine items (such as *ambitious, competitive,* and *self-sufficient*) and low on traditionally feminine items (such as *affectionate, cheerful,* and *soft-spoken*). Someone with a "feminine" identity does the reverse. And a substantial minority (especially females) have a gender identity called **androgyny,** scoring high on both masculine and feminine personality characteristics.

Gender identity is a good predictor of psychological adjustment. "Masculine" and androgynous children and adults have higher self-esteem than "feminine" individuals, perhaps because many typically feminine traits are not highly valued by society (DiDonato & Berenbaum, 2011; Harter, 2012). Also, androgynous individuals are more flexible: They can show either "masculine" independence or "feminine" sensitivity, depending on the requirements of their situation (Huyck, 1996; Taylor & Hall, 1982). The existence of an androgynous identity demonstrates that children can acquire a mixture of positive qualities traditionally associated with each gender and use them adaptively to fit their current circumstances—an orientation that may best help them realize their potential.

Consistent with this idea, new assessments of androgyny ask children age 6 and older about the extent to which they feel similar to both boys and girls in appearance, behaviors, activities, and playmates. Although the majority identify more closely with their own group, about one-third also feel moderately similar to other-sex peers (Martin, Cook, & Andrews, 2017; Martin et al., 2017). These flexible, dual gender-identity children display certain mental health and social advantages. They feel more accepted by agemates of both sexes, are more likely to have other-sex friends, and hold fewer negative biases against children of the other sex.

Yet as with their gender-stereotyped attitudes and behavior, the overwhelming majority of 3- to 5-year-olds are quite unbending in their early sense of gender identity. They typically report that being a girl or a boy is "very important" to them and feel "very happy" with their own gender and gender group (Halim, Bryant, & Zucker, 2016). And for most, this positive regard for their gender strengthens during early childhood.

Emergence of Gender Identity   How do children begin to develop a gender identity? According to *social learning theory,* behavior comes before self-perceptions. Preschoolers first acquire gender-typed responses through modeling and reinforcement and only later organize these behaviors into gender-linked ideas about themselves. In contrast, *cognitive-developmental theory* maintains that self-perceptions come before behavior. Over the preschool years, children acquire **gender constancy**—a full understanding of the biologically based permanence of their gender, including the realization that sex remains the same over time, even if clothing, hairstyle, and play activities change (Kohlberg, 1966). Then children use this knowledge to guide their behavior.

When 3- to 5-year-olds are asked such questions as "When you (a girl) grow up, could you ever be a daddy?" or "Could you be a boy if you wanted to?" they freely answer yes. And children younger than age 6 who watch an adult dressing a doll in "other-gender" clothing typically insist that the doll's sex has also changed (Chauhan, Shastri, & Mohite, 2005; Fagot, 1985). Indeed, gender identity in early childhood is closely associated with a focus on physical appearance. In an investigation of 3- to 6-year-olds, the more important and positive the children considered their gender to be, the more likely they were to insist on wearing gender-typed clothing (Halim et al., 2014).

Mastery of gender constancy follows a three-step sequence: *gender labeling* (correct naming of one's own and others' sex), *gender stability* (understanding that gender remains the same over time), and *gender consistency* (realizing that gender is not altered by superficial changes in clothing or activities). Full attainment of gender constancy is strongly related to ability to pass Piagetian conservation tasks (De Lisi & Gallagher, 1991). Indeed, gender constancy tasks can be considered a type of conservation problem, in that children must conserve a person's sex despite a superficial change in that person's outward appearance.

Is cognitive-developmental theory correct that gender constancy is responsible for children's gender-typed behavior? Evidence for this assumption is weak. Although outcomes are not entirely consistent, some findings suggest that attaining gender constancy actually contributes to the emergence of more flexible gender-role attitudes in the early school years, perhaps because children then realize that engaging in gender-atypical behavior cannot cause their sex to change (Ruble et al., 2007). But overall, the impact of gender constancy on gender typing is not great. As research in the following section reveals, gender-role adoption is more powerfully affected by children's beliefs about how close the connection must be between their own gender and their behavior.

Gender Schema Theory   **Gender schema theory** is an information-processing approach to gender typing that combines social learning and cognitive-developmental features. It explains how environmental pressures and children's cognitions work together to shape gender-role development (Martin & Halverson, 1987; Martin, Ruble, & Szkrybalo, 2002). At an early age, children pick up gender-stereotyped preferences and behaviors from others. At the same time, they organize their experiences into *gender schemas,* or masculine and feminine categories, that they use to interpret their world. As soon as preschoolers can label their own gender, they select gender schemas consistent with it ("Only boys can be doctors" or "Cooking is a girl's job") and apply those categories to themselves. Their self-perceptions then become gender-typed and serve as additional schemas that children use to process information and guide their own behavior.

We have seen that individual differences exist in the extent to which children endorse gender-typed views. Figure 10.4 shows different cognitive pathways for children who often apply gender schemas to their experiences and those who rarely do (Liben & Bigler, 2002). Consider Billy, who encounters a doll. If Billy is a *gender-schematic child,* his *gender-salience filter* immediately makes gender highly relevant. Drawing on his prior learning, he asks himself, "Should boys play with dolls?" If he answers "yes" and the toy interests him, he will approach it, explore it, and learn more about it. If he answers "no," he will avoid the "gender-inappropriate" toy. But if Billy is a *gender-aschematic child*—one who seldom views the world in gender-linked terms—he simply asks himself, "Do I like this toy?" and responds on the basis of his interests.

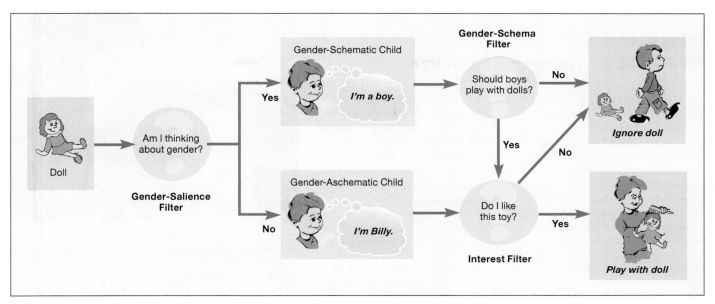

FIGURE 10.4   Cognitive pathways for gender-schematic and gender-aschematic children. In *gender-schematic children,* the gender-salience filter immediately makes gender highly relevant: Billy sees a doll and thinks, "I'm a boy. Should boys play with dolls?" Drawing on his experiences, he answers "yes" or "no." If he answers "yes" and the doll interests him, he plays with the doll. If he answers "no," he avoids the "gender-inappropriate" toy. *Gender-aschematic children* rarely view the world in gender-linked terms. Billy simply asks, "Do I like this toy?" and responds on the basis of his interests. (Reprinted by permission of Rebecca Bigler.)

To examine the consequences of gender-schematic processing, investigators often present preschoolers with gender-neutral toys, labeling them as either "for boys" or "for girls." Most children respond with gender-schematic reasoning, preferring toys labeled for their gender, predicting that same-sex peers would also like those toys, and rejecting toys labeled for the other gender (Dinella & Weisgram, 2018).

In one such study conducted in China, some 5- to 7-year-olds were provided with gender labels before playing with a tangram—a Chinese puzzle consisting of a square divided into seven shapes that can be rearranged to make various patterns. Compared to no gender labeling, labeling the task as either "for boys" or "for girls" resulted in boys correctly placing more tangram pieces (see Figure 10.5) (Yeung & Wong, 2018). Even when gender labeled for girls, this task—which relies on spatial skills that children and adults alike often view males as better at—seemed to heighten boys' awareness of their gender identity ("I'm a boy. I'm good at this kind of puzzle!"). This probably increased boys' liking for the task, self-confidence and motivation to succeed, and ultimately their performance. The findings illustrate the power of gender schemas to influence children's gender-role behavior and learning opportunities.

Gender-schematic thinking is so influential that when children see others behaving in "gender-inconsistent" ways, they often distort their memory to make it "gender-consistent." For example, when shown a picture of a male nurse, they may remember him as a doctor (Martin & Ruble, 2004). And because gender-schematic preschoolers typically conclude, "What I like, children of my own sex will also like," they often use their own preferences to add to their gender biases (Liben & Bigler, 2002). For example, a girl who dislikes oysters may declare, "Only boys like oysters!" even though she has never actually been given information promoting such a stereotype. At least partly for this reason, young children's gender

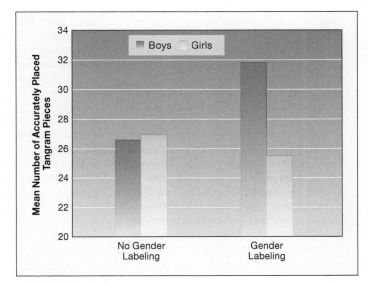

FIGURE 10.5   Influence of gender labeling on Chinese children's tangram performance. Five- to 7-year-olds were randomly assigned to either a no gender-labeling or a gender-labeling condition. In the no gender-labeling group, girls and boys played with a tangram, performing similarly. In the gender-labeling group, prior to playing with the tangram, an adult provided a gender label—either "for boys" or "for girls." Gender labeling led to a marked increase in boys' (but not girls') performance on this task, which relies on spatial skills. (Based on Yeung & Wong, 2018.)

Biology and Environment | Transgender Children

Jacob, who began life as a girl named Mia, firmly insisted at age 2, "I am a boy!" in opposition to his parents' suggestion that he was merely "pretending." At preschool, he became increasingly angry at being identified as a girl. When his teacher asked him to write his name, he would print M-I-A but then vigorously cross it out. Gradually, his parents sensed the strength of his expressed identity. With guidance from a therapist, they began following his lead, providing boys' clothes, a short haircut, toy cars, and superhero action figures. At age 4, at his parents' suggestion, he affirmed that he wanted to change his name to Jacob and go to a different school, where he could start a new public life as a boy (Lemay, 2015). "I want to be a boy always," Jacob declared. His problematic behavior at home and school quickly subsided.

The number of transgender children, adolescents, and adults in Western nations, though few, has risen recently—perhaps because more stories like Jacob's are appearing in the media and because seeking treatment has become more acceptable. Individuals dissatisfied with their birth sex who strongly identify as the other gender experience substantial distress—a condition called *gender dysphoria*. Estimates based on adults in treatment suggest that 1 in 12,000 to 21,000 males and 1 in 30,000 to 48,000 females suffer from gender dysphoria (Zucker & Lawrence, 2009). In the general population, the prevalence of gender dysphoria may be considerably greater—according to one survey, perhaps as high as ½ of 1 percent (Conron et al., 2012). Many do not receive support from their families or from health professionals.

Individuals who change gender in adulthood often trace the emergence of their gender dysphoria to early childhood. Although contributing factors are not well understood, the prenatal hormone environment seems to play a role. For example, genetic females known to have been exposed to high levels of prenatal androgens are more likely than other women to be transgender (Dessens, Slijper, & Drop, 2005). But many females

prenatally exposed to high androgen levels, and many males exposed to low levels, do not express discomfort with their birth sex.

Although some studies claim that most cases of childhood gender dysphoria subside in adolescence and adulthood, their samples failed to distinguish between gender-dysphoric children and children who merely display gender-nonconforming behavior. Children who are severely troubled over the mismatch between their birth sex and core gender identity, who insist that they *are* the other gender, and who also engage in high levels of "other-gender" behavior generally experience persisting dysphoria (Newhook et al., 2018; Ristori & Steensma, 2016). These persisters are likely to transition mostly or entirely—as Jacob did—to their desired gender role.

Transgender preschoolers and school-age children are not pretending, confused, or delayed in gender understanding. When questioned about their peer preferences, gender-typed toy choices, and gender identity, their responses are similar to those of nontransgender agemates who share their expressed gender (Fast & Olson, 2018; Olson, Key, & Eaton, 2015). Understandably, however, transgender preschoolers are less likely than their cisgender agemates to view gender as a stable trait in other people (Fast & Olson, 2018).

During early adolescence, gender dysphoria typically deepens as persisters encounter changes in their bodies and first feelings of sexual attraction (Leibowitz & de Vries, 2016). Some desire, and may be deemed eligible for, psychological and medical sex-change treatment, involving suppression of pubertal sex hormones, cross-sex hormone treatment after age 16, and surgery after age 18. Others go through a period of questioning, including hesitancy over invasive treatments, and take additional time to assess their feelings about transitioning physically (Steensma & Cohen-Kettenis, 2015). A number of these young people

Jacob, who began life as a girl, changed his name and transitioned to living as a boy in early childhood. Transgender children whose parents support their desire to express their identified gender are more content and better-adjusted.

find their gender dysphoria so overwhelming that they eventually decide on treatment in their twenties and thirties.

Controversy exists over therapies for gender-dysphoric children. One approach is directed at lessening their other-gender identity and behavior and increasing their comfort with their birth sex. These therapies, however, have yielded poor results (Adelson, 2012; Olson, 2016). Gender-dysphoric children react with heightened distress to efforts to suppress or deny their identified gender.

Increasing numbers of health professionals are convinced that therapies must be aimed at permitting children to follow their gender-identity inclinations and helping parents protect their children from the negative reactions of others. They are motivated by the tragic circumstances of many contemporary transgender adults, who experienced family rejection and social ostracism from childhood on and who face high rates of unemployment, poverty, homelessness, depression, and suicide. Current evidence suggests that embracing transgender children's expressed identity leads to contented, better-adjusted children and adolescents (Durwood, McLaughlin, & Olson, 2017; Edwards-Leeper, Leibowitz, & Sangganjanavanich, 2016; Spivey & Edwards-Leeper, 2019). Follow-up research is needed to assess long-term outcomes in the coming generation of transgender adults.

schemas contain both culturally standard and nonstandard ideas (Tenenbaum et al., 2010). Not until well into the school years do children's gender schemas fully resemble those of adults.

For most children, development of gender identity involves constructing self-perceptions that accept the sex they were assigned at birth—a compatibility commonly referred to as *cisgender*. A few children express great discomfort with their birth sex and want to live as the other gender, saying so as early as the preschool years. For research on development of gender identity in these *transgender* children, refer to the Biology and Environment box above.

Also, recall from our earlier discussion of children exposed to atypical levels of prenatal sex hormones that their genital characteristics may differ from their chromosomally determined genetic sex. And regardless of genetic sex, gender identity may be more or less "masculine," more or less "feminine," or an androgynous mixture of both. For all these reasons, child development researchers are increasingly recognizing the importance of inclusive conceptions of biological sex and gender identity that are not dichotomies (male versus female, masculine versus feminine) but rather are characterized as a spectrum.

10.5.5 Reducing Gender Stereotyping in Young Children

How can we help young children avoid rigid gender schemas that restrict their behavior and learning opportunities? No easy recipe exists. Biology clearly affects children's gender typing, channeling boys, on average, toward active, competitive play and girls toward quieter, more intimate interaction. At the same time, differential expectations and treatment of boys and girls begin in infancy, amplifying biologically based tendencies and promoting many aspects of gender typing that are unrelated to human nature (Hines, 2015).

Because young children's cognitive limitations lead them to assume that cultural practices determine gender, parents and teachers are wise to delay preschoolers' exposure to gender-stereotyped messages. Adults can begin by limiting adherence to traditional gender roles in their own behavior and by providing children with counterstereotypic alternatives. For example, parents can take turns making dinner, bathing children, and driving the family car, and they can give sons and daughters both trucks and dolls and both pink and blue clothing. Teachers can ensure that all children spend time in mixed-gender play activities and unstructured pursuits because children's behavior tends to be less gender-typed in these contexts (Goble et al., 2012).

Finally, adults can avoid language that conveys gender stereotypes and can shield children from media presentations that do the same. In one study, just two minutes of exposure to magazine models of counterstereotypic toy play—pictures of a girl playing with a car and a boy playing with a stuffed animal (pony), with each toy described as the child's favorite—increased 4- to 7-year-olds' willingness to endorse an array of gender-stereotyped toys as appropriate for both genders (Spinner, Cameron, & Calogero, 2018). The counterstereotypic magazine images also increased the children's willingness to choose the other-gender child as their preferred playmate.

Once children notice the vast array of gender stereotypes in their environment, adults can point out exceptions. They can arrange for children to see men and women pursuing nontraditional careers and can explain that interests and skills, not gender, should determine a person's job—reasoning that reduces children's gender-biased views of occupations. By middle childhood, children who hold flexible beliefs about what boys and girls can do are more likely to notice instances of gender discrimination (Brown & Bigler, 2004). As we will see in the next section, a rational approach to child rearing promotes healthy, adaptable functioning in many other areas as well.

Parents and teachers can reduce preschoolers' gender stereotyping by modeling nonstereotyped behaviors and providing nontraditional alternatives. For this boy, making cookies is not "for girls." It's an activity he and his mother enjoy together.

ASK YOURSELF

Connect ■ In addition to gender-stereotyped beliefs, what other aspects of preschoolers' social understanding tend to be rigid and one-sided?

Apply ■ List findings indicating that language and communication—between parents and children, between teachers and children, and between peers—powerfully affect children's gender typing. What recommendations would you make to counteract these influences?

Reflect ■ Would you describe your own gender identity as "masculine," "feminine," or "androgynous"? What biological and social factors might have influenced your gender identity?

10.6 Child Rearing and Emotional and Social Development

10.6a Describe the impact of child-rearing styles on development, and explain why authoritative parenting is effective.

10.6b Discuss the multiple origins of child maltreatment, its consequences for development, and prevention strategies.

In this and previous chapters, we have seen how parents can foster children's competence—by building a parent–child relationship based on affection and cooperation, by modeling and reinforcing mature behavior, by using reasoning and inductive discipline, and by guiding and encouraging mastery of new skills. Now let's put these practices together into an overall view of effective parenting.

10.6.1 Styles of Child Rearing

Child-rearing styles are combinations of parenting behaviors that occur over a wide range of situations, creating an enduring child-rearing climate. In a landmark series of studies, Diana Baumrind gathered information on child rearing by watching parents interact with their preschoolers (Baumrind, 1971). Her findings, and those of others who have extended her work, reveal three features that consistently differentiate an effective style from less effective ones: (1) acceptance and involvement, (2) control, and (3) autonomy granting (Gray & Steinberg, 1999; Hart, Newell, & Olsen, 2003). Table 10.2 shows how child-rearing styles differ in these features. Let's discuss each style in turn.

Authoritative Child Rearing The **authoritative child-rearing style**—the most successful approach—involves high acceptance and involvement, adaptive control techniques, and appropriate autonomy granting. Authoritative parents are warm, attentive, and sensitive to their child's needs. They establish an enjoyable, emotionally fulfilling parent–child relationship that draws the child into close connection. At the same time, authoritative parents exercise firm, reasonable control over children's behavior: They insist that the child act sensibly and responsibly, give reasons for their expectations, and use disciplinary encounters as "teaching moments" to promote the child's self-regulation. Finally, authoritative parents engage in gradual, appropriate *autonomy granting,* allowing the child to make decisions in

TABLE 10.2 Features of Child-Rearing Styles

CHILD-REARING STYLE	ACCEPTANCE AND INVOLVEMENT	CONTROL	AUTONOMY GRANTING
Authoritative	Is warm, responsive, attentive, and sensitive to the child's needs	Engages in adaptive behavioral control: Makes reasonable demands for mature behavior and consistently enforces and explains them	Permits the child to make decisions in accord with readiness Encourages the child to express thoughts, feelings, and desires If parent and child disagree, engages in joint decision making when possible
Authoritarian	Is cold and rejecting and frequently degrades the child	Engages in coercive behavioral control: Makes excessive demands for mature behavior, uses force and punishment Often uses psychological control, withdrawing love and manipulating and intruding on the child's individuality and attachment to parents	Makes decisions for the child Rarely listens to the child's point of view
Permissive	Is warm but overindulgent or inattentive	Is lax in behavioral control: Makes few or no demands for mature behavior	Permits the child to make many decisions before the child is ready
Uninvolved	Is emotionally detached and withdrawn	Is lax in behavioral control: Makes few or no demands for mature behavior	Is indifferent to the child's decision making and point of view

areas where she is ready to do so (Baumrind, 2013; Kuczynski & Lollis, 2002; Russell, Mize, & Bissaker, 2004).

Throughout childhood and adolescence, authoritative parenting is linked to many aspects of competence—an upbeat mood, self-control, task persistence, cooperativeness, positive self-esteem, advanced theory-of-mind understanding, social and moral maturity, and favorable school performance (Amato & Fowler, 2002; Gonzalez & Wolters, 2006; Jaffe, Gullone, & Hughes, 2010; Kuppens & Ceulemans, 2018; Mackey, Arnold, & Pratt, 2001; Milevsky et al., 2007; O'Reilly & Peterson, 2014).

Authoritarian Child Rearing   The **authoritarian child-rearing style** is low in acceptance and involvement, high in coercive control, and low in autonomy granting. Authoritarian parents appear cold and rejecting. To exert control, they yell, command, criticize, and threaten. "Do it because I said so!" is their attitude. They make decisions for their child and expect their child to accept their word unquestioningly. If the child resists, authoritarian parents resort to force and punishment.

Children of authoritarian parents are more likely to be anxious, unhappy, and low in self-esteem and self-reliance. When frustrated, they tend to react with hostility and, like their parents, use force to get their way. Boys, especially, show high rates of anger and defiance. Although girls also engage in acting-out behavior, they are more likely to be dependent, lacking interest in exploration, and overwhelmed by challenging tasks (Hart, Newell, & Olsen, 2003; Kakihara et al., 2010; Thompson, Hollis, & Richards, 2003). Children and adolescents exposed to the authoritarian style typically do poorly in school. However, because of their parents' concern with control, they tend to achieve better and to commit fewer antisocial acts than agemates with undemanding parents—that is, those whose parents use one of the two styles we will consider next (Steinberg, Blatt-Eisengart, & Cauffman, 2006).

In addition to unwarranted direct control, authoritarian parents engage in a more subtle type called **psychological control,** in which they attempt to take advantage of children's psychological needs by intruding on and manipulating their verbal expressions, individuality, and attachments to parents. These parents frequently interrupt or put down the child's ideas, decisions, and choice of friends. When they are dissatisfied, they withdraw love, making their affection contingent on the child's compliance, and often shame the child ("You're not as good as your sister"). Children subjected to psychological control exhibit adjustment problems involving high stress reactivity (indicated by elevated cortisol levels) and both anxious, withdrawn behavior and defiance and aggression—including the relational form, which (like parental psychological control) damages relationships through manipulation and exclusion (Barber & Xia, 2013; Doan et al., 2017; Kuppens et al., 2013; Nelson et al., 2013).

Permissive Child Rearing   The **permissive child-rearing style** is warm and accepting but uninvolved. Permissive parents are either overindulgent or inattentive and, thus, engage in little control. Instead of gradually granting autonomy, they allow children to make many of their own decisions at an age when they are not yet capable of doing so. Their children can eat meals and go to bed when they feel like it and watch as much television as they want. They do not have to learn good manners or do any household chores. Although some permissive parents truly believe in this approach, many others simply lack confidence in their ability to influence their child's behavior (Oyserman et al., 2005).

Children of permissive parents are impulsive, disobedient, and rebellious. They are also overly demanding and dependent on adults, and they show less persistence on tasks, poorer school achievement, and more antisocial behavior. The link between permissive parenting and dependent, nonachieving, rebellious behavior is especially strong for boys (Barber & Olsen, 1997; Steinberg, Blatt-Eisengart, & Cauffman, 2006).

Uninvolved Child Rearing   The **uninvolved child-rearing style** combines low acceptance and involvement with little control and general indifference to issues of autonomy. Often these parents are emotionally detached and depressed and so overwhelmed by life stress that they have little time and energy for children. At its extreme, uninvolved parenting is a form of child maltreatment called *neglect.* Especially when it begins early, it disrupts virtually all aspects of development (see page 146 in Chapter 4). Even with less extreme parental disengagement, children and adolescents display many problems—poor emotional self-regulation, school achievement difficulties, depression, and antisocial behavior (Aunola, Stattin, & Nurmi, 2000; Schroeder et al., 2010).

10.6.2 What Makes Authoritative Child Rearing Effective?

LOOK and LISTEN

Ask several parents to explain their style of child rearing, inquiring about acceptance and involvement, control, and autonomy granting. Look, especially, for variations in amount and type of control over children's behavior along with parents' rationales.

Like other correlational findings, the association between authoritative parenting and children's competence is open to interpretation. Perhaps parents of well-adjusted children are authoritative because their youngsters have especially cooperative dispositions. Yet combined evidence from many longitudinal studies reveals a bidirectional relationship between children's attributes and parenting styles: Children who are impulsive, overactive, defiant, or aggressive are more likely to evoke authoritarian parenting, including both coercive and psychological control. At the same time, authoritative parenting is associated with a decline in these externalizing behavior problems, whereas authoritarian and permissive parenting predict that they will worsen (Larzelere, Cox, & Mandara, 2013; Pinquart, 2017). For children with internalizing difficulties (fear and anxiety), parents must suppress their tendency to be overprotective. Rather, inhibited children's adjustment improves with extra encouragement to be assertive and to express their autonomy (Chronis-Tuscano et al., 2015).

The warmth and caring that authoritative parents accord their children are linked to favorable child functioning in many cultures, suggesting that this feature of child rearing is universally necessary (Khaleque & Rohner, 2002). And a variant of authoritativeness in which parents exert strong control over their child's behavior—becoming directive but not coercive—yields just as favorable long-term outcomes as a more democratic approach (Baumrind, Larzelere, & Owens, 2010). Indeed, some children, because of their dispositions, require "heavier doses" of certain authoritative features.

In sum, authoritative child rearing seems to create a positive emotional context for parental influence in the following ways:

A preschooler searches a shelf in her local library to select a book on her own. By adjusting autonomy granting to children's capacities, authoritative parents convey to children that they can do things successfully for themselves.

- Warm, involved parents who are secure in the standards they hold for their children model caring concern as well as confident, self-controlled behavior.
- Children are far more likely to comply with and internalize control that appears fair and reasonable, not arbitrary.
- By adjusting demands and autonomy granting to children's capacities, authoritative parents convey to children that they are competent and can do things successfully for themselves. In this way, parents foster favorable self-esteem and cognitive and social maturity.
- Supportive aspects of the authoritative style, including parental acceptance, involvement, and rational control, are a powerful source of *resilience,* protecting children from the negative effects of family stress and poverty (Luthar, Crossman, & Small, 2015).

10.6.3 Cultural Variations

Although authoritative parenting is broadly advantageous, ethnic minority parents often have distinct child-rearing beliefs and practices reflecting cultural values. Let's look at some examples.

Compared with Western parents, Chinese parents describe their parenting as more controlling. In their efforts to foster self-discipline and high achievement, they are more directive in teaching their children and in scheduling their time. Chinese parents may appear less warm than Western parents because they withhold praise, which they believe results in self-satisfied, poorly motivated children (Cheah & Li, 2010; Ng, Pomerantz, & Deng, 2014). High control reflects the Confucian belief in strict discipline, respect for elders, and socially desirable behavior, taught by deeply involved parents.

Chinese parents report expressing affection and concern and using induction and other reasoning-oriented discipline as much as American parents do, but they more often shame a misbehaving child, withdraw love, and use physical punishment (Cheah et al., 2009; Chen, Sun, & Yu, 2017). When these practices become excessive, resulting in an authoritarian style high in coercive or psychological control, Chinese children and adolescents display the same negative outcomes as Western children: poor academic achievement, anxiety, impaired self-regulation, and aggressive behavior (Chan, 2010; Lee et al., 2012; Sorkhabi & Mandara, 2013; Zhang et al., 2017).

In Hispanic families, Asian Pacific Island families, and Caribbean families of African and East Indian origin, firm insistence on respect for parental authority is typically paired with high parental warmth—a combination suited to promoting cognitive, academic, and social competence and family loyalty (Kim et al., 2018; Roopnarine, 2016; Tamis-LeMonda & McFadden, 2010). Hispanic fathers often spend much time with their children and are warm and sensitive (Cabrera & Bradley, 2012). In Caribbean families that immigrated to the United States, fathers' authoritativeness—but not mothers'—predicted preschoolers' literacy and math skills, probably because Caribbean fathers take a larger role in guiding their children's academic progress than Caribbean mothers do (Roopnarine et al., 2006).

Although wide variation exists, low-SES African-American parents tend to expect immediate obedience. Many believe strict parenting fosters self-control and vigilance in risky surroundings. African-American parents who use controlling strategies tend to have cognitively and socially competent children who view parental control as a sign of love and concern. And among African-American youths, controlling parenting, when combined with warmth and responsiveness, protects against delinquency and disruptive behaviors at school (Pezzella, Thornberry, & Smith, 2016; Roche, Ensminger, & Cherlin, 2007). Recall, also, that a history of mild physical punishment seems to prevent later externalizing problems in African-American children (refer to the Cultural Influences box on page 374). Most African-American parents who practice strict, "no-nonsense" discipline use physical punishment sparingly and combine it with warmth and reasoning.

These cultural variations remind us that child-rearing styles must be viewed in their larger context. As we have seen, many factors contribute to good parenting: personal characteristics of both child and parent, SES, access to extended family and community supports, cultural values and practices, and public policies.

As we turn to the topic of child maltreatment, our discussion will underscore, once again, that effective child rearing is sustained not just by the desire of mothers and fathers to be good parents. Almost all want to be. Unfortunately, when vital supports for parenting break down, children—as well as parents—can suffer terribly.

In Caribbean families of African or East Indian origins, respect for parental authority is paired with high parental warmth—a combination that promotes competence and family loyalty.

10.6.4 Child Maltreatment

Child maltreatment is as old as human history, but only in recent decades has the problem been widely acknowledged and studied. Perhaps public concern has increased because child maltreatment is especially common in large industrialized nations. In 2016, nearly 700,000 U.S. children (10 out of every 1,000) were identified as victims (U.S. Department of Health and Human Services, 2018a). Because most cases go unreported, the true figures are much higher.

Child maltreatment takes the following forms:

- *Physical abuse.* Assaults, such as kicking, biting, shaking, punching, or stabbing, that inflict physical injury
- *Sexual abuse.* Fondling, intercourse, exhibitionism, commercial exploitation through prostitution or production of pornography, and other forms of sexual exploitation
- *Emotional abuse.* Acts that could cause serious emotional harm, including social isolation, repeated unreasonable demands, ridicule, humiliation, intimidation, or terrorizing
- *Neglect.* Failure to meet a child's basic needs for food, clothing, medical attention, education, or supervision

Neglect occurs in about 75 percent of reported cases, physical abuse in 18 percent, emotional abuse in 9 percent, and sexual abuse in 8 percent (U.S. Department of Health and Human Services, 2018a). Many children experience more than one form.

Parents commit 90 percent of abusive incidents. Other relatives account for about 5 percent, and the remainder are perpetrated by parents' unmarried partners, child-care providers, or other adults. Infants, toddlers, and preschoolers are at greatest risk for neglect, physical abuse, and emotional abuse. Sexual abuse is perpetrated more often against school-age and early adolescent children. But each type occurs among children of every age (U.S. Department of Health and Human Services, 2019). Because many sexual abuse victims are identified in middle childhood, we will pay special attention to this form of maltreatment in Chapter 13.

Origins of Child Maltreatment   Early findings suggested that child maltreatment was rooted in adult psychological disturbance (Kempe et al., 1962). But although child maltreatment is more common among disturbed parents, it soon became clear that a single "abusive personality type" does not exist. Parents who were abused as children do not necessarily become abusers (Jaffee et al., 2013). And sometimes even "normal" parents harm their children!

For help in understanding child maltreatment, researchers turned to *ecological systems theory* (see Chapters 1 and 2). They discovered that many interacting variables—at the family, community, and cultural levels—contribute. The more risks present, the greater the likelihood that abuse or neglect will occur. Table 10.3 summarizes factors associated with child maltreatment.

The Family Within the family, children whose characteristics make them more challenging to rear are more likely to become targets of abuse. These include premature or very sick babies and children who are temperamentally difficult, are inattentive and overactive, or have other developmental problems. Child factors, however, only slightly increase the risk of abuse

TABLE 10.3   Factors Related to Child Maltreatment

FACTOR	DESCRIPTION
Parent characteristics	Psychological disturbance; alcohol and drug abuse; history of abuse as a child; belief in harsh physical discipline; desire to satisfy unmet emotional needs through the child; unreasonable expectations for child behavior; young age (most under 30); low educational level; lack of parenting skills
Child characteristics	Preterm or very sick baby; difficult temperament; inattentiveness and overactivity; other developmental problems
Family characteristics	Low income or poverty; homelessness; marital instability; social isolation; partner abuse; frequent moves; large families with closely spaced children; overcrowded living conditions; presence of nonbiologically related caregivers; disorganized household; lack of steady employment; other signs of high life stress
Community	Characterized by violence and social isolation; few parks, child-care centers, preschool programs, recreation centers, or religious institutions to serve as family supports
Culture	Approval of physical force and violence as ways to solve problems

Sources: U.S. Department of Health and Human Services, 2019; Miyamoto et al., 2017; Whipple, 2006.

(Jaudes & Mackey-Bilaver, 2008; Sidebotham et al., 2003). Whether such children are maltreated largely depends on parents' characteristics.

Maltreating parents are less skillful than other parents in handling discipline confrontations and getting children to cooperate in working toward common goals. They also suffer from biased thinking about their child. For example, they often attribute their baby's crying or their child's misdeeds to a stubborn or bad disposition, evaluate children's transgressions as worse than they are, and feel powerless in parenting—perspectives that lead them to resort quickly to physical force (Bugental & Happaney, 2004; Crouch et al., 2008).

Most parents have enough self-control not to respond with abuse to their child's misbehavior or developmental problems. Rather, other factors combine with the child's characteristics to prompt an extreme response. Unmanageable parental stress is strongly associated with maltreatment. Abusive parents respond to stressful situations with high emotional arousal. And low income, low education (less than a high school diploma), unemployment, alcohol and drug use, partner conflict, overcrowded living conditions, frequent moves, and extreme household disorganization are common in abusive and neglectful homes (Dakil et al., 2012; Wulczyn, 2009). These conditions increase the chances that parents will be too overwhelmed to meet basic child-rearing responsibilities or will vent their frustrations by lashing out at their children.

The Community The majority of abusive and neglectful parents are isolated from both formal and informal social supports. Because of their life histories, many have learned to mistrust and avoid others and are poorly skilled at establishing and maintaining positive relationships. Also, maltreating parents are more likely to live in unstable, rundown neighborhoods that provide few links between family and community, such as parks, recreation centers, and religious institutions (Guterman et al., 2009; Tomyr, Ouimet, & Ugnat, 2012). They lack "lifelines" to others and have no one to turn to for help during stressful times.

The Larger Culture Cultural values, laws, and customs profoundly affect the chances that child maltreatment will occur when parents feel overburdened. Societies that view violence as an appropriate way to solve problems set the stage for child abuse.

Although the United States has laws to protect children from maltreatment, support for the use of physical force is widespread (refer back to page 373). Fifty-seven countries in diverse regions of the globe—including Austria, Brazil, Costa Rica, Croatia, Finland, Israel, Kenya, Latvia, Nepal, New Zealand, Spain, and Togo—have outlawed corporal punishment, a measure that reduces both physical discipline and abuse (duRivage et al., 2015; Zolotor & Puzia, 2010). Yet corporal punishment of children by parents remains legal in all 50 U.S. states. Furthermore, all industrialized nations except the United States prohibit corporal punishment in schools. The U.S. Supreme Court has twice upheld the right of school officials to use corporal punishment. Fortunately, 31 U.S. states and the District of Columbia have passed laws that prohibit it in public schools, though just two states extend this ban to private schools.

Consequences of Child Maltreatment   The family circumstances of maltreated children impair the development of attachment security, emotional self-regulation, empathy and sympathy, self-concept, social skills, and academic motivation. Over time, these youngsters show serious adjustment problems—cognitive deficits including impaired executive function, school failure, difficulties in processing emotional and social signals, peer relationship problems, severe depression, aggressive behavior, substance abuse, and violent crime (Cicchetti & Toth, 2015; Nikulina & Widom, 2013; Stronach et al., 2011).

How do these damaging consequences occur? Recall our earlier discussion of hostile cycles of parent–child interaction. For abused children, these are especially severe. Also, a family characteristic strongly associated with child abuse is partner abuse (Graham-Bermann & Howell, 2011). Clearly, the home lives of abused children overflow with adult conduct that leads to profound distress, including emotional insecurity (see page 66 in Chapter 2), and to aggression as a way of solving problems.

Furthermore, the sense of abandonment conveyed by neglectful parenting and the humiliating, terrorizing behaviors of abusive adults result in low self-esteem, high anxiety, self-blame, and efforts to escape from extreme psychological pain—at times severe enough to lead to post-traumatic stress disorder (PTSD) and attempted suicide in adolescence (Nikulina, Widom, & Czaja, 2011; Wolfe, 2005). A cascade of additional forms of victimization increases the chances of these outcomes. At school, maltreated children's noncompliance, cognitive immaturity, poor academic motivation, and social skills deficits increase their risk for bullying by peers. And in the community, they are four times more likely than their nonmaltreated agemates to experience physical and sexual assault by nonfamilial perpetrators (Hamby et al., 2017).

Finally, chronic abuse is associated with central nervous system damage, including abnormal EEG brain-wave activity; reduced size and impaired functioning of the cerebral cortex, corpus callosum, cerebellum, and hippocampus, as detected with functional magnetic resonance imaging (fMRI); and atypical production of the stress hormone cortisol—initially too high but, after months of abuse, often too low. Over time, the massive trauma of persistent abuse seems to blunt children's normal physiological response to stress (Cicchetti & Toth, 2015; Jaffee & Christian, 2014). These neurobiological effects make it more likely that cognitive and emotional problems will endure.

Preventing Child Maltreatment   Because child maltreatment is embedded in families, communities, and society as a whole, efforts to prevent it must be directed at each of these levels. Many approaches have been suggested, from teaching high-risk parents effective child-rearing strategies to developing broad social programs aimed at improving economic conditions and community services.

We have seen that providing social supports to families is effective in easing parental stress. This approach sharply reduces child maltreatment as well. A trusting relationship with another person is the most important factor in preventing mothers with childhood histories of abuse from repeating the cycle with their own children (Egeland, Jacobvitz, & Sroufe, 1988). Parents Anonymous, a U.S. organization with affiliate programs around the world, helps child-abusing parents learn constructive parenting practices, largely through social supports. Its local chapters offer self-help group meetings, daily phone calls, and regular home visits to relieve social isolation and teach responsible child-rearing skills.

Interventions aimed at strengthening both child and parent competencies can improve parenting practices, thereby preventing child maltreatment. Through its intensive parent training sessions that reduce child conduct problems, Incredible Years, discussed on pages 380–381, also prevents child abuse and neglect (Swenson & Logan, 2017).

Some interventions begin at a much earlier age. Healthy Families America, a program that began in Hawaii and has spread to 430 sites across the United States and Canada, identifies families at risk for maltreatment during pregnancy or at birth. Each receives three years of home visitation, in which a trained worker helps parents manage crises, encourages effective child rearing, and puts parents in touch with community services to meet their own and their children's needs (Healthy Families America, 2011). In evaluations of sites verified to provide high-quality program delivery, parents randomly assigned to Healthy Families home visitation, compared with no-intervention controls, more often engaged their child in developmentally supportive activities and used effective discipline strategies; less often displayed harsh, coercive tactics; and reported less parenting stress—factors that reduce the risk of child maltreatment (Green et al., 2014; LeCroy & Krysik, 2011). Another home-visiting program that prevents child abuse and neglect is the Nurse–Family Partnership, discussed on page 110 in Chapter 3 (Olds et al., 2009).

Still, many experts believe that child maltreatment cannot be eliminated as long as violence is widespread and harsh physical punishment is regarded as acceptable. In addition, combating poverty and its diverse correlates—family stress and disorganization, inadequate food and medical care, teenage parenthood, low-birth-weight babies, and parental hopelessness—would protect many children.

Each year, fourth to sixth graders across Los Angeles County enter a poster contest to celebrate Child Abuse Prevention Month. This recent winner depicts the profound emotional pain caused by physical abuse. (Ricky Sosa-Alvarez, Ramona Middle School, La Verne, CA. Courtesy ICAN Associates, Los Angeles County Inter-Agency Council on Child Abuse & Neglect, ican4kids.org.)

Although more cases reach the courts than in decades past, child maltreatment is difficult to prove. Usually, the only witnesses are the child victims or other loyal family members. And even when the evidence is strong, judges hesitate to impose the ultimate safeguard against further harm: permanently removing the child from the family. There are several reasons for their reluctance. First, in the United States, government intervention into family life is viewed as a last resort. Second, despite destructive family relationships, maltreated children and their parents usually are attached to one another, and neither desires separation. Finally, the U.S. legal system tends to regard children as parental property rather than as human beings in their own right, and this also has stood in the way of court-ordered protection.

Despite intensive treatment, some adults persist in their abusive acts. An estimated 1,600 to 1,800 U.S. children, most of them infants and preschoolers, die from maltreatment annually. Nearly half suffered from physical abuse, including beatings, drownings, suffocation, or *shaken baby syndrome,* in which shaking an infant or young child inflicts brain and neck injuries. About 75 percent were severely neglected. The overwhelming majority of cases involve parents acting alone, together, or with other individuals (U.S. Department of Health and Human Services, 2018a). When parents are unlikely to change their behavior, the drastic step of separating parent from child and legally terminating parental rights is the only justifiable course of action.

Child maltreatment is a sad note on which to end our discussion of a period of childhood that is so full of excitement, awakening, and discovery. But there is reason to be optimistic. Great strides have been made over the past several decades in understanding and preventing child maltreatment.

 ASK YOURSELF

Connect ■ Is the concept of authoritative child rearing useful for understanding effective parenting across cultures? Explain.

Apply ■ Chandra heard a news report about 10 severely neglected children, living in squalor in an inner-city tenement. She wondered, "Why would parents so mistreat their children?" How would you answer Chandra?

Reflect ■ How would you classify your parents' child-rearing styles? What factors might have influenced their approach to parenting?

SUMMARY

10.1 Self-Understanding
(p. 355)

10.1 Describe the development of self-concept and self-esteem in early childhood.

■ As self-awareness strengthens, preschoolers construct a **self-concept** that consists largely of observable characteristics and typical emotions and attitudes. Older preschoolers add an emerging grasp of their own and others' personalities.

■ Secure attachment fosters a positive, coherent self-concept. Elaborative parent–child conversations about past events and internal states contribute to self-understanding.

■ Preschoolers' **self-esteem** consists of several self-judgments. Their typically high self-esteem contributes to initiative during a period in which they must master many new skills.

10.2 Emotional Development (p. 358)

10.2 Identify changes in understanding and expressing emotion during early childhood, citing factors that influence those changes.

■ Preschoolers' increasingly accurate understanding of the causes, consequences, and behavioral signs of emotions is supported by cognitive development, secure attachment, and conversations about feelings.

■ Supported by gains in emotion understanding and executive function, by age 3 to 4 children voice various strategies for regulating negative emotion. Temperament, parental modeling, and parental communication about coping strategies influence preschoolers' capacity for emotional self-regulation.

■ As their self-concepts become better developed, preschoolers more often experience self-conscious emotions. However, they depend on parental feedback to know when to feel these emotions. And it takes time before they recognize them in themselves and others.

■ Empathy also becomes more common in early childhood. The extent to which empathy leads to **sympathy** and results in **prosocial behavior** depends on temperament and parenting.

10.3 Peer Relations (p. 363)

10.3 *Describe peer sociability, friendship, and social problem solving in early childhood, along with cultural and parental influences on early peer relations.*

■ During early childhood, peer interaction increases as **nonsocial activity** gives way to **parallel play** and then **associative** and **cooperative play.** Nevertheless, nonsocial and parallel play remain common.

■ Both sociodramatic and rough-and-tumble play are associated with gains in emotional understanding and self-regulation.

■ Compared with Western cultures that promote independence, cultures that highly value interdependence may be less accepting of children who engage in solitary play.

■ Preschoolers view friendship as pleasurable play. Compared to other peer interactions, their interactions with friends are more cooperative and emotionally expressive. Early childhood friendship and peer acceptance contribute to later academic and social competence.

■ Social conflicts offer occasions for **social problem solving,** which improves over the preschool and early school years. By kindergarten, each of its information-processing components is related to socially competent behavior.

■ Parents influence early peer relations both directly, through attempts to influence their children's interactions with peers, and indirectly, through parent–child communication and play.

10.4 Foundations of Morality and Aggression (p. 369)

10.4a *Identify the central features of psychoanalytic, social learning, and cognitive-developmental approaches to moral development.*

■ Controversial evidence of morally relevant inclinations in infants suggests to some the existence of an innate moral sense. All theories of moral development recognize that conscience begins to take shape in early childhood.

■ The psychoanalytic perspective emphasizes identification and guilt as motivators of good conduct. Guilt is an important motivator of moral action, but contrary to Freud, discipline promoting fear of punishment and loss of parental love does not foster conscience development. **Induction** is far more effective.

■ Social learning theory focuses on how children learn moral behavior through reinforcement and modeling. Effective adult models of morality are warm, powerful, and consistent in what they say and do.

■ Harsh punishment has numerous undesirable side effects, including child and adolescent externalizing behavior problems. Certain social contexts may modify the consequences of physical punishment, as research on African-American children reveals.

■ When parents use such punishments as **time out** and withdrawal of privileges, they can increase their effectiveness by being consistent, maintaining a warm parent–child relationship, and offering explanations. The most effective discipline encourages good conduct by building a mutually respectful bond with the child.

■ The cognitive-developmental perspective views children as active thinkers about social rules. By age 4, children consider intentions in making moral judgments and distinguish truthfulness from lying. Preschoolers also distinguish **moral imperatives** from **social conventions** and **matters of personal choice.**

■ With gains in language, theory of mind, and understanding of emotion, older preschoolers begin to reason morally by referring to others' perspectives and feelings. Morally relevant social experiences, including interactions with parents, siblings, and peers, are also influential.

10.4b *Describe the development of aggression in early childhood, including family and media influences and effective approaches to reducing aggressive behavior.*

■ During early childhood, **proactive aggression** declines while **reactive aggression** increases. Proactive and reactive aggression come in three forms: **physical aggression** (more common in boys), **verbal aggression,** and **relational aggression.** Both biology and parental gender-role attitudes contribute to gender differences in aggression.

■ Ineffective discipline and a conflict-ridden family atmosphere promote children's aggression. Children high in reactive aggression see hostility where it does not exist, making many unprovoked attacks. Those high in proactive aggression tend to callously use it to advance their own goals—a style that predicts severe conduct problems. Media violence also triggers aggression.

■ Teaching parents effective child-rearing practices, intervening to enhance children's emotional and social skills, relieving family stress through social supports, and shielding children from violent media reduce aggressive behavior.

10.5 Gender Typing (p. 382)

10.5a *Discuss biological and environmental influences on preschoolers' gender-stereotyped beliefs and behavior.*

■ Preschoolers acquire a wide range of **gender-typed** beliefs, which operate as blanket rules rather than flexible guidelines for behavior.

■ Prenatal hormones contribute to boys' higher activity level and rowdier play and to children's preference for same-sex playmates. But parents, same-sex older siblings, teachers, peers, and the broader social environment encourage many gender-typed responses. Parents, especially fathers, apply more pressure for gender-role conformity to sons.

10.5b *Describe and evaluate major theories that explain the emergence of gender identity.*

■ Although most people have a traditional **gender identity,** some are **androgynous,** combining both masculine and feminine characteristics. Androgynous children display mental health and social advantages.

■ According to social learning theory, preschoolers first acquire gender-typed responses through modeling and reinforcement and then organize them into gender-linked ideas about themselves. Cognitive-developmental theory suggests that **gender constancy** must be mastered before children develop gender-typed behavior, but evidence for this assumption is weak.

■ **Gender schema theory** combines features of social learning and cognitive-developmental perspectives. As children acquire gender-stereotyped preferences and behaviors, they form masculine and feminine categories, or gender schemas, that they apply to themselves and their world.

■ Embracing transgender children's expressed identity predicts better adjustment.

10.6 Child Rearing and Emotional and Social Development (p. 392)

10.6a *Describe the impact of child-rearing styles on development, and explain why authoritative parenting is effective.*

■ Three features distinguish the major **child-rearing styles:** (1) acceptance and involvement, (2) control, and (3) autonomy granting. Compared with the **authoritarian, permissive, and uninvolved styles,** the **authoritative style** promotes cognitive, emotional, and social competence. Warmth, reasonable control rather than coercive control, and gradual autonomy granting account for the effectiveness of the authoritative style. **Psychological control** is associated with authoritarian parenting and contributes to adjustment problems.

© JAMES QUINE/ROBERTHARDING

■ Certain ethnic groups, including Chinese, Hispanic, Asian Pacific Island, and African-American, combine parental warmth with high levels of control. But when control becomes harsh and excessive, it impairs academic and social competence.

10.6b *Discuss the multiple origins of child maltreatment, its consequences for development, and prevention strategies.*

■ Child maltreatment is related to factors within the family, community, and larger culture. Maltreating parents use ineffective discipline and hold a negatively biased view of their child.

■ Unmanageable parental stress, lack of access to social supports, and social approval of force and violence for solving problems all increase the likelihood of abuse and neglect.

■ Maltreated children are impaired in attachment security, emotional self-regulation, empathy and sympathy, self-concept, social skills, and academic motivation, and are at risk for central nervous system damage. A cascade of additional forms of victimization increases the chances of negative developmental outcomes.

■ Successful prevention of child maltreatment requires efforts at the family, community, and societal levels.

IMPORTANT TERMS AND CONCEPTS

androgyny (p. 387)
associative play (p. 363)
authoritarian child-rearing style (p. 393)
authoritative child-rearing style (p. 392)
child-rearing styles (p. 392)
cooperative play (p. 363)
gender constancy (p. 388)
gender identity (p. 387)
gender schema theory (p. 388)
gender typing (p. 382)

induction (p. 370)
matters of personal choice (p. 376)
moral imperatives (p. 376)
nonsocial activity (p. 363)
parallel play (p. 363)
permissive child-rearing style (p. 393)
physical aggression (p. 377)
proactive aggression (p. 377)
prosocial behavior (p. 362)
psychological control (p. 393)

reactive aggression (p. 377)
relational aggression (p. 377)
self-concept (p. 355)
self-esteem (p. 357)
social conventions (p. 376)
social problem solving (p. 367)
sympathy (p. 362)
time out (p. 374)
uninvolved child-rearing style (p. 393)
verbal aggression (p. 377)

MiLESTONES

Development in
Early Childhood

2 YEARS

Physical

- Throughout early childhood, height and weight increase more slowly than in toddlerhood. (281)
- Balance improves; walking becomes smooth and rhythmic; running emerges. (296–297)

- Jumps, hops, throws, and catches with rigid upper body. (297)
- Puts on and removes simple items of clothing. (297–298)
- Uses spoon effectively. (297)
- First drawings are gestural scribbles. (298)

Cognitive

- Increasingly uses language as a flexible symbolic tool, to modify existing mental representations. (307–308)
- Make-believe becomes less dependent on realistic objects, less self-centered, and more complex; sociodramatic play increases. (308)
- Takes the perspective of others in simplified, familiar situations and in face-to-face communication. (313, 329)
- Recognition memory is well developed. (326)
- Shows awareness of mental states, such as want, think, remember, and pretend. (329)
- Attaches verbal labels to amounts and sizes; begins to count. (334)

Language

- Vocabulary increases rapidly. (345)
- Uses a coalition of cues—perceptual and, increasingly, social and linguistic—to figure out word meanings. (347)
- Speaks in simple sentences that follow basic word order of native language. (347)
- Adds grammatical markers. (348)
- Displays effective conversational skills. (349)

Emotional/Social

- Understands causes, consequences, and behavioral signs of basic emotions. (358)
- Begins to develop self-concept and self-esteem. (356–358)
- Shows early signs of developing moral sense—verbal evaluations of own and others' actions and efforts to relieve others' stress. (369)
- May display proactive (instrumental) and reactive (hostile) aggression. (377)
- Gender-stereotyped beliefs and behavior increase. (382)

3–4 YEARS

Physical

- May no longer need a daytime nap. (287)
- Running, jumping, hopping, throwing, and catching become more refined, with flexible upper body. (296–297)
- Galloping and one-foot skipping appear. (297)
- Pedals and steers tricycle. (297)

- Uses scissors. (297)
- Uses fork effectively. (297)
- Draws first picture of a person, using tadpole image. (299)
- Distinguishes writing from nonwriting. (302)

Cognitive

- Understands the symbolic function of drawings and of models of real-world spaces. (298, 310)
- Grasps conservation, reasons about transformations, and understands cause-and-effect relationships in simplified, familiar situations. (314)
- Organizes everyday knowledge into hierarchically organized categories. (314–316)
- Grasps dual representation. (310–311, 317)
- Uses private speech to guide behavior during challenging tasks. (319)
- Gains in executive function, including inhibition, flexible shifting of attention, and working-memory capacity. (323–324)
- Uses scripts to recall routine events. (326)
- Understands that beliefs can determine behavior. (329)
- Knows meaning of numbers up to ten, counts correctly, and grasps cardinality. (334)

Note: Numbers in parentheses indicate the page or pages on which each milestone is discussed.

Language

- Aware of some meaningful features of written language. (333)
- Coins new words based on known words; extends language meanings through metaphor. (347)

- Masters increasingly complex grammatical structures, occasionally overextending grammatical rules to exceptions. (347–348)
- Adjusts speech to fit the age, gender, and social status of listeners. (313, 349)

Emotional/Social

- Describes self in terms of observable characteristics and typical emotions and attitudes. (356)
- Has several self-esteems, such as learning things in school, making friends, getting along with parents, and treating others kindly. (357)
- Emotional self-regulation improves. (359)
- Experiences self-conscious emotions more often. (361)
- Relies more on language to express empathy. (362)
- Engages in associative and cooperative play with peers, in addition to parallel play. (363–364)

- Proactive aggression declines, while reactive aggression (verbal and relational) increases. (377)
- Forms first friendships, based on pleasurable play and sharing of toys. (365–366)
- Distinguishes moral imperatives from social conventions and matters of personal choices. (376)
- Preference for same-sex playmates strengthens. (384)

5–6 YEARS

Physical

- Starts to lose primary teeth. (283)
- Increases running speed, gallops more smoothly, and engages in true skipping. (297)
- Displays mature, flexible throwing and catching patterns. (297–298)
- Uses knife to cut soft foods. (297, 298)
- Ties shoes. (297, 298)
- Draws more complex pictures. (299)

- Uses an adult pencil grip, writes name, copies some numbers and simple words, and discriminates letters of the alphabet. (297, 301–302)

Cognitive

- Magical beliefs decline. (313)
- Passes Piaget's conservation of number, mass, and liquid problems. (312, 314)
- Gains further in executive function, including planning. (323–325)

- Improves in recognition, recall, scripted memory, and autobiographical memory. (326–327)

- Understanding of false belief strengthens. (329)

Language

- Understands that letters and sounds are linked in systematic ways. (333)
- Uses invented spellings. (333)
- By age 6, comprehends about 10,000 words and produces several thousand. (345)
- Uses most grammatical constructions competently. (348)

Emotional/Social

- Improves in understanding of emotion, including the ability to interpret, predict, and influence others' emotional reactions. (358–359)

- Becomes better at social problem solving. (368)
- Has acquired many morally relevant rules and behaviors and can argue over matters of justice. (370)
- Gender-stereotyped beliefs and behavior, and preference for same-sex playmates, continue to strengthen. (382–384)
- Understands gender constancy. (388)

Physical Development in Middle Childhood

Playing with Mum and Dad in the Pool

Ohmmar Coates, 9 years, New Zealand

Aided by gains in strength, flexibility, and agility, children at a community pool dive, swim, and toss beach balls. Chapter 11 takes up the diverse physical attainments of middle childhood and their close connection with other domains of development.

Reprinted with permission from The International Museum of Children's Art, Oslo, Norway

"I'm on my way, Mom!" hollered 10-year-old Joey as he stuffed the last bite of toast into his mouth, slung his book bag over his shoulder, dashed out the door, jumped on his bike, and headed down the street for school. Joey's 8-year-old sister Lizzie followed, pedaling furiously until she caught up with Joey.

"They're branching out," Rena, the children's mother and one of my colleagues at the university, commented to me over lunch that day as she described the children's expanding activities and relationships. Homework, household chores, soccer teams, music lessons, scouting, and friends at school and in the neighborhood were all part of the children's routine. "It seems the basics are all there; I don't have to monitor Joey and Lizzie so constantly anymore. Being a parent is still challenging, but it's more a matter of refinements—helping them become independent, competent, and productive individuals."

Joey and Lizzie have entered middle childhood—the years from 6 to 11. Around the world, children of this age are assigned new responsibilities. For children in industrialized nations, middle childhood is often called the "school years" because its onset is marked by the start of formal schooling. In village and tribal cultures, the school may be a field or a jungle. But universally, mature members of society guide children of this age period toward real-world tasks that increasingly resemble those they will perform as adults.

This chapter focuses on physical growth in middle childhood—changes less spectacular than those of earlier years. By age 6, the brain has reached 90 percent of its adult weight, and the body continues to grow slowly. In this way, nature gives school-age children the mental powers to master challenging tasks as well as added time—before reaching physical maturity—to acquire the knowledge and skills essential for life in a complex social world.

We begin by reviewing typical growth trends and special health concerns. Then we turn to rapid gains in motor abilities, which support practical everyday activities, athletic skills, and participation in organized games. We will see that each of these attainments is affected by and also contributes to cognitive, emotional, and social development. Our discussion will echo a familiar theme—that all domains are interrelated. ■

11.1 Body Growth

Physical growth during the school years continues at the slow, regular pace of early childhood. At age 6, the average North American child weighs about 45 pounds and is 3½ feet tall. Over the next few years, children will add about 2 to 3 inches in height and 5 pounds in weight each year (see Figure 11.1 on page 406). Between ages 6 and 8, girls are slightly shorter and lighter than boys. By age 9, this trend reverses. Already, Rena noticed, Lizzie was starting to catch up with Joey in physical size as she approached the dramatic adolescent growth spurt, which occurs two years earlier in girls than in boys.

Because the lower portion of the body is growing fastest, Joey and Lizzie appeared longer-legged than they had in early childhood. They grew out of their jeans more quickly than their jackets and frequently needed larger shoes. As in early childhood, girls have slightly more body fat and boys more muscle. After age 8, girls begin accumulating fat at a faster rate, and they will add even more during adolescence (Hauspie & Roelants, 2012).

11.1a Describe changes in body size, proportions, and skeletal maturity during middle childhood.

11.1b Describe brain development in middle childhood.

Mai at 6 years   Mai at 8 years   Mai at 10 years

Henry at 6 years   Henry at 8 years   Henry at 10 years

FIGURE 11.1 **Body growth during middle childhood.** Mai and Henry display a continuing slow, regular pattern of growth that began in early childhood. Around age 9, girls begin to grow at a faster rate than boys as the adolescent growth spurt draws near.

Body size sometimes results from evolutionary adaptations to a particular climate. These boys live near the equator on Kenya's tropical coast. Their long, lean physiques permit their bodies to cool easily.

11.1.1 Worldwide Variations in Body Size

Glance into any elementary school classroom, and you will see wide individual differences in body growth. Diversity in physical size is especially apparent when we travel to different nations. Worldwide, a 9-inch gap separates the shortest and tallest 8-year-olds. The shortest children are found among populations in parts of South America, Asia, the Pacific Islands, and parts of Africa, and the tallest among populations in Australia, North America, northern and central Europe, and, again, Africa (Meredith, 1978; Ruff, 2002). These findings remind us that growth norms (age-related averages for height and weight) must be applied cautiously, especially in countries with high immigration rates and many ethnic minorities.

What accounts for these large differences in physical size? Both heredity and environment are involved. Body size sometimes reflects evolutionary adaptations to a particular climate. Long, lean physiques are typical in hot, tropical regions and short, stocky ones in cold, Arctic areas (Katzmarzyk & Leonard, 1998; Stulp & Barrett, 2016).

Also, children who grow tallest usually live in developed countries, where food is plentiful and infectious diseases are largely controlled. Physically small children tend to live in less developed regions, where poverty, hunger, inadequate health care, and disease are common (Karra, Subramanian, & Fink, 2017). When families move from poor to wealthy nations, their children not only grow taller but also change to a longer-legged body shape. (Recall that during childhood, the legs are growing fastest.) For example, U.S.-born school-age children of immigrant Guatemalan Mayan parents are, on average, 4½ inches taller, with legs nearly 3 inches longer, than their agemates in Guatemalan Mayan villages (Bogin & Varela-Silva, 2010; Bogin, Hermanussen, & Scheffler, 2018).

11.1.2 Secular Trends in Physical Growth

In industrialized nations, height has been increasing for 150 years (Fudvoye & Parent, 2017). This **secular trend in physical growth**—systematic change from one generation to the next in body size and in the timing of the attainment of growth milestones—appears in the first two years, expands during childhood and early adolescence, and then pulls back as mature body size is reached. The pattern suggests that the larger size of today's children is mostly due to a faster rate of physical development.

Once again, improved nutrition and health are largely responsible for these growth gains. As developing nations make socioeconomic progress, they also show secular gains (Ji & Chen, 2008). Secular increases are smaller for low-income children, who have poorer diets and are more likely to suffer from growth-stunting

Although varying considerably in physical size, these fourth graders are taller than previous generations were at the same age. Improved health and nutrition account for this secular trend.

illnesses. And in regions with widespread poverty, famine, and disease, either no secular change or a secular decrease in body size has occurred (Bogin, 2013). In most industrialized nations, the secular gain in height has slowed in recent decades. But as we will see later, overweight and obesity have reached epic proportions.

11.1.3 Skeletal Growth

During middle childhood, the bones of the body lengthen and broaden. However, ligaments are not yet firmly attached to bones. This, combined with increasing muscle strength, gives children unusual flexibility of movement. School-age children often seem like "physical contortionists," turning cartwheels and doing splits and handstands. As their bodies become stronger, many children experience a greater desire for physical exercise. Early evening or nighttime "growing pains"—stiffness and aches in the legs—are common (Lehman & Carl, 2017). These subside as bones strengthen to accommodate increased physical activity and as muscles adapt to an enlarging skeleton.

Between ages 6 and 12, all 20 primary teeth are lost and replaced by permanent ones, with girls losing their teeth slightly earlier than boys. The first teeth to go are the lower and then upper front teeth, giving many first and second graders a "toothless" smile. For a while, the permanent teeth seem much too large. Gradually, growth of the facial bones, especially those of the jaw and chin, causes the child's face to lengthen and the mouth to widen, accommodating the newly erupting teeth.

Care of the teeth is essential during the school years because dental health affects the child's appearance, speech, and ability to chew properly. Parents need to remind children to brush their teeth thoroughly, and most children need help with flossing until about 9 years of age. More than 50 percent of U.S. school-age children have at least some tooth decay. Low-SES children have especially high levels, with one-fourth having at least one untreated decayed tooth (Centers for Disease Control and Prevention, 2019a). As decay progresses, children experience pain, embarrassment at damaged teeth, distraction from play and learning, and school absences due to dental-related illnesses.

Malocclusion, a condition in which the upper and lower teeth do not meet properly, occurs in one-third of school-age children. In about 14 percent of cases, serious difficulties in biting and chewing result. Malocclusion can be caused by thumb sucking after permanent teeth erupt. School-age children who continue to engage in the habit may require gentle but persistent encouragement to give it up (Garde et al., 2014). A more frequent cause of malocclusion is crowding of permanent teeth. In some children, this problem clears up as the jaw grows. Others need braces, a common sight by the end of elementary school.

11.1.4 Brain Development

The weight of the brain increases by only 10 percent during middle childhood and adolescence. Nevertheless, considerable growth occurs in certain brain structures. Using fMRI, researchers can detect the volume of two general types of brain tissue: *white matter,* consisting largely of myelinated nerve fibers, and *gray matter,* consisting mostly of neurons and their connective fibers. White matter rises steadily throughout childhood and adolescence, especially in the prefrontal cortex (responsible for complex thought), in the parietal lobes (supporting spatial abilities), and in the corpus callosum (leading to more efficient communication between the two cortical hemispheres) (Genc et al., 2018; Giedd et al., 2009; Smit et al., 2012). Because interconnectivity among distant regions of the cerebral cortex increases, the prefrontal cortex becomes a more effective "executive"—coordinating the integrated functioning of various areas.

In middle childhood, the prefrontal cortex becomes a more effective "executive," coordinating integrated functioning of various brain regions. These changes support the sustained attention and motor coordination this novice skater needs to become proficient at his new sport.

As children acquire more complex abilities, stimulated neurons increase in synaptic connections, and their neural fibers become more elaborate and myelinated. As a result, gray matter peaks in middle childhood and then declines as synaptic pruning (reduction of unused synapses) and death of surrounding neurons proceed (Markant & Thomas, 2013; Silk & Wood, 2011). Recall from Chapter 5 that about 50 percent of synapses are pruned during childhood and adolescence. Pruning and accompanying reorganization and selection of brain circuits lead to more optimized functioning of specific brain regions and, thus, to more effective information processing. In particular, children gain in executive function, including sustained attention, inhibition, working memory capacity, and organized, flexible thinking.

Additional brain development likely takes place at the level of neurotransmitters, chemicals that permit neurons to communicate across synapses (see page 156 in Chapter 5). Over time, neurons become increasingly selective, responding only to certain chemical messages. This change may add to school-age children's more efficient thinking. Secretions of particular neurotransmitters are related to cognitive performance, social and emotional adjustment, and ability to withstand stress. When neurotransmitters are not present in appropriate balances, children may suffer serious developmental problems, such as inattention and overactivity, emotional disturbance, and epilepsy (an illness involving brain seizures and loss of motor control) (Brooks et al., 2006; Kurian et al., 2011; Weller, Kloos, & Weller, 2006).

Researchers also believe that brain functioning may change in middle childhood because of the influence of hormones. Around age 7 to 8, an increase in androgens (male sex hormones), secreted by the adrenal glands (located on top of the kidneys), occurs in children of both sexes. Androgens will rise further among boys at puberty, when the testes release them in large amounts. Androgens affect brain organization and behavior in many animal species, including humans (Stark & Gibb, 2018). Recall from Chapter 10 that androgens contribute to boys' higher activity level and physical aggression. They may also promote social dominance and play-fighting, topics we will take up at the end of this chapter.

ASK YOURSELF

Connect ■ Relate secular trends in physical growth to the concept of cohort effects, discussed on page 41 in Chapter 1.

Apply ■ Joey complained to his mother that it wasn't fair that his younger sister Lizzie was almost as tall as he was. He worried that he wasn't growing fast enough. How should Rena respond to Joey's concern?

Reflect ■ How does your height compare with that of your parents and grandparents when they were your age? Do your observations illustrate secular trends?

11.2 Health Issues

Children from economically advantaged homes, like Joey and Lizzie, are at their healthiest in middle childhood, full of energy and play. Growth in lung size permits more air to be exchanged with each breath, so children are better able to exercise vigorously without tiring. The cumulative effects of good nutrition, combined with rapid development of the body's immune system, offer greater protection against disease. In fact, children who spent much time in child-care centers during infancy and early childhood, and therefore experienced more respiratory, ear, and intestinal infections, are sick less often than their agemates later on (Côté et al., 2010; de Hoog et al., 2014; Hullegie et al., 2016). Their increased immunity may grant them a learning advantage because they miss fewer days of school.

Not surprisingly, poverty continues to be a powerful predictor of poor health during middle childhood. Because economically disadvantaged U.S. children often lack health insurance or are publicly insured (see page 76 in Chapter 2), they generally receive a lower standard of care, and many do not have regular access to a doctor. A substantial number also lack such basic necessities as a comfortable home and regular meals.

11.2a Describe the causes and consequences of serious nutritional problems in middle childhood, giving special attention to obesity.

11.2b List factors that contribute to illness during the school years, and explain how these health challenges can be reduced.

11.2c Describe changes in the occurrence of unintentional injuries during middle childhood, and cite effective interventions.

11.2.1 Nutrition

Children need a well-balanced, plentiful diet to provide energy for successful learning in school and greater physical activity. With their increasing focus on play, friendships, and new activities, many children spend little time at the table. Joey's hurried breakfast, described at the beginning of this chapter, is a common event in middle childhood. The percentage of U.S. children who eat meals with their families drops sharply between ages 9 and 14. Family dinnertimes have waned in general over the past two decades. Yet eating an evening meal with parents leads to a diet higher in fruits, vegetables, grains, and milk products and lower in soft drinks and fast foods (Hammons & Fiese, 2011; Lopez et al., 2018).

School-age children report that they "feel better" and "focus better" after eating healthy foods and that they feel sluggish, "like a blob," after eating junk foods. In longitudinal studies of large samples of preschool children, a parent-reported diet high in sugar, salt, fat, and processed foods in early childhood predicted slightly lower IQ at middle childhood, after many factors that might otherwise account for this association were controlled (Leventakou et al., 2016; Northstone et al., 2012). Even mild nutritional deficits can affect cognitive functioning. Among school-age children from middle- to high-SES families, insufficient dietary iron and folate are related to poorer concentration and mental test performance (Arija et al., 2006; Low et al., 2013). Children say that a major barrier to healthy eating is the ready availability of unhealthy options, even in their homes. As one sixth grader commented, "When I get home from school, I think, 'I'll have an apple,' but then I see the bag of chips."

Recall from Chapter 8 that food familiarity and food preferences are strongly linked: Children like best the foods they have eaten repeatedly in the past. Readily available, healthy between-meal snacks—such as fruit, raw vegetables, and peanut butter—can help meet school-age children's nutritional needs and increase their liking for healthy foods.

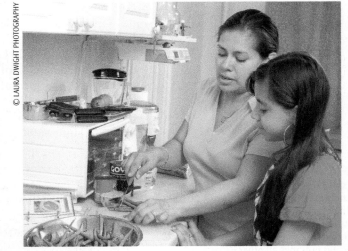

A mother and daughter prepare a healthy meal together. School-age children need a well-balanced, plentiful diet to provide energy for successful learning and greater physical activity. Even mild nutritional deficits can compromise cognitive functioning.

As we saw in earlier chapters, many poverty-stricken children in developing countries and in the United States suffer from serious and prolonged malnutrition. By middle childhood, the effects are apparent in delayed physical growth, impaired motor coordination, inattention, and low IQ. The negative impact of malnutrition on learning and behavior may intensify as children encounter new academic and social challenges at school. First, as in earlier years, growth-stunted school-age children show greater stress reactivity, as indicated by a sharper rise in heart rate and in saliva levels of the stress hormone cortisol (Fernald et al., 2003). Second, a deficient diet alters the production of neurotransmitters in the brain—an effect that can disrupt all aspects of psychological functioning (Goyal, Iannotti, & Raichle, 2018).

Unfortunately, malnutrition that persists from infancy or early childhood into the school years usually results in lasting physical, cognitive, and mental health problems (Liu et al., 2003; Schoenmaker et al., 2015). Government-sponsored supplementary food programs from the early years through adolescence can prevent these effects.

11.2.2 Overweight and Obesity

Mona, a heavy child in Lizzie's class, often watched from the sidelines during recess. When she did join in games, she was slow and clumsy, the target of unkind comments: "Move it, Tubs!" When Mona's classmates chose partners for special activities, she was among the last to be selected. Most afternoons, she walked home alone while her schoolmates gathered in groups, talking, laughing, and chasing. At home, Mona sought comfort in high-calorie snacks.

Mona suffers from **obesity,** a greater-than-20-percent increase over healthy weight, based on *body mass index (BMI)*—a ratio of weight to height associated with body fat. A BMI above the 85th percentile for a child's age and sex is considered *overweight,* and a BMI above the 95th percentile *obese*. During the past four decades, as adult overweight and obesity has climbed around the globe, so too has childhood overweight and obesity, which has risen ten-fold. The largest population weight gains have occurred in Canada, England, Mexico, and—the leading nation—the United States (see Figure 11.2). Today, 31 percent of U.S. children and adolescents are overweight, more than half of them extremely so: 17 percent are obese (Kann et al., 2018; Ogden et al., 2016). Other industrialized nations, including France, Switzerland, Italy, and South Korea, have seen smaller increases. Yet as Figure 11.2 reveals, without widespread effective intervention, obesity rates even in less-affected countries are expected to continue to rise until at least 2030 (OECD, 2017b).

Obesity rates have also risen in developing countries, where urbanization is shifting populations toward sedentary lifestyles and diets high in meats and energy-dense refined foods (NCD-RisC, 2017). In China, for example, where obesity was nearly nonexistent a generation ago, today 25 percent of children are overweight and 9 percent obese, with two to three times as many boys as girls affected (Jia et al., 2017). In addition to lifestyle changes, a prevailing belief in Chinese culture that excess body fat signifies prosperity and health—carried over from a half-century ago, when famine caused millions of deaths—has contributed to this alarming upsurge. High valuing of sons may induce Chinese parents and grandparents to offer boys

FIGURE 11.2 **Adult obesity rates (solid lines) and projected further increases (dashed lines) until 2030 in selected industrialized nations.** At about 40 percent in 2020 and a projected 47 percent in 2030, the United States outranks all other developed nations in pervasiveness of obesity in the adult population, defined here according to the widely accepted adult standard of a BMI of 30 and above. Even in countries with relatively low rates, obesity is expected to increase until at least 2030. (From OECD, 2017b. *Obesity Update*. Copyright© 2017 OECD. Adapted by permission.)

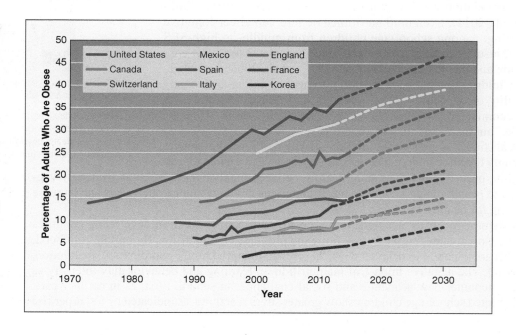

especially generous portions of meat, dairy products, and other energy-dense foods that were once scarce but are now widely available.

As Figure 11.3 reveals, overweight rises with age, and more than half of U.S. overweight school-age children, adolescents, and adults are obese (Centers for Disease Control and Prevention, 2018d; Ogden et al., 2014). Overweight preschoolers are more than five times more likely than their normal-weight peers to be overweight at age 12 (Nader et al., 2006). And most persistently overweight adolescents become overweight or obese adults (Patton et al., 2011; Simmonds et al., 2016).

Cause of Obesity

Childhood obesity is a complex physical disorder with multiple causes. As Table 11.1 reveals, not all children are equally at risk for excessive weight gain. Identical twins are more likely than fraternal twins to resemble each other in BMI, and adopted children tend to resemble their biological parents (Min, Chiu, & Wang, 2013). But heredity accounts for only a *tendency* to gain weight (Kral & Faith, 2009). Genes influence biological processes responsible for metabolism and sensations of fullness, but these factors are also modified by experience. Growing evidence suggests that excessive food intake, especially of unhealthy foods, induces epigenetic modifications in expression of genes affecting metabolism and weight gain (Lopomo, Burgio, & Migliore, 2016). Alterations in gene expression may underlie the persistence of child and adolescent overweight and obesity into adulthood.

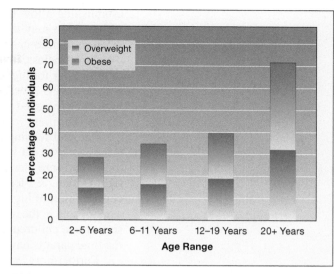

FIGURE 11.3   Age-related increase in U.S. overweight and obesity. In early childhood, nearly half of overweight children are obese. From middle childhood on, more than half of overweight individuals are obese. (Based on U.S. Department of Health and Human Services, 2018b.)

The importance of environment is also evident in the consistent relationship of low SES to overweight and obesity in industrialized nations, especially among ethnic minorities—in the United States, African-American, Hispanic, and Native-American children and adults (Newton, Braithwaite, & Akinyemiju, 2017; Ogden et al., 2016). Factors involved include lack of knowledge about healthy diet; a tendency to buy high-fat, low-cost foods; and family stress, which can prompt overeating.

As noted in Chapter 5, children who were undernourished in their early years are at risk for later excessive weight gain. Studies in many poverty-stricken regions of the world reveal that growth-stunted children are more likely to be overweight than their nonstunted agemates (de Onis, 2017). In industrialized nations, children whose mothers smoked during pregnancy and who therefore are often born underweight (see Chapter 3) are at elevated risk for later overweight and obesity (Rayfield & Plugge, 2017). A malnourished body protects itself by

TABLE 11.1   Factors Contributing to Childhood Obesity

FACTOR	DESCRIPTION
Heredity	Obese children are likely to have at least one obese parent, and identical twins are more likely than fraternal twins to share the disorder.
Socioeconomic status	Obesity is more common in low-SES families.
Early growth pattern	Infants who gain weight rapidly are at greater risk for obesity, probably because their parents promote unhealthy eating habits (see Chapter 5).
Family eating habits	When parents purchase high-calorie fast foods, treats, and junk food; use them as rewards; anxiously overfeed; or control their children's intake, their children are more likely to be obese.
Responsiveness to food cues	Obese children often decide when to eat on the basis of external cues, such as taste, smell, sight, time of day, and food-related words, rather than hunger.
Physical activity	Obese children are less physically active than their normal-weight peers.
Television viewing	Children who spend many hours watching television are more likely to become obese.
Early malnutrition	Early, severe malnutrition that results in growth stunting increases the risk of later obesity.

establishing a low basal metabolism rate, which may endure after nutrition improves. Also, malnutrition may disrupt appetite control centers in the brain, causing the child to overeat when food becomes plentiful.

Nevertheless, in the developing world (unlike industrialized countries), obesity risk tends to be greater for higher-SES families, likely because of greater food availability and reduced activity levels (Ford, Patel, & Narayan, 2017). But as countries improve economically and high-fat, processed foods become plentiful, the burden of obesity shifts from wealthy to low-income families.

Parental feeding practices also contribute to childhood obesity. Overweight children are more likely to eat larger quantities of high-calorie sugary and fatty foods, perhaps because these foods are plentiful in the diets offered by their parents, who also tend to be overweight (Kit, Ogden, & Flegal, 2014). Frequent eating out—which increases parents' and children's consumption of high-calorie fast foods—is linked to overweight. And eating out likely plays a major role in the relationship between mothers' employment hours and elevated BMI among school-age children (Morrissey, Dunifon, & Kalil, 2011). Demanding work schedules reduce the time parents have for healthy meal preparation.

Furthermore, some parents anxiously overfeed, interpreting almost all their child's discomforts as a desire for food—a practice common among immigrant parents and grandparents who, as children themselves, may have survived periods of food deprivation. Still other parents are overly controlling, restricting when, what, and how much their child eats and worrying about weight gain (Couch et al., 2014; Jansen et al., 2012). In each case, parents undermine children's ability to regulate their own food intake.

These experiences contribute to obese children's maladaptive eating habits. They are more responsive than normal-weight individuals to external stimuli associated with food—taste, sight, smell, time of day, and food-related words—and less responsive to internal hunger cues (Temple et al., 2007). And temperament—in particular, weak effortful control and delay of gratification (ability to wait for a reward) during the preschool years—increases the likelihood that children will gain excessive weight in middle childhood (Fiese & Bost, 2016). At the same time, a stressful family life contributes to children's diminished self-regulatory capacity, amplifying uncontrolled eating (see the Social Issues: Health box on the following page).

Another factor implicated in weight gain is insufficient sleep (Hakim, Kheirandish-Gozal, & Gozall, 2015). A follow-up of more than 2,000 U.S. 3- to 12-year-olds revealed that children who got less nightly sleep were more likely to be overweight five years later (Snell, Adam, & Duncan, 2007). Reduced sleep may increase time available for eating while leaving children too fatigued for physical activity. It also disrupts the brain's regulation of hunger and metabolism.

Overweight children are less physically active than their normal-weight peers, and inactivity is both cause and consequence of their excessive weight gain (Kellou et al., 2014). Research reveals that the rise in childhood obesity is due in part to the many hours children devote to screen media. In several longitudinal investigations, more hours per day spent watching TV in childhood and adolescence consistently predicted the likelihood of overweight and obesity in adulthood (Robinson et al., 2017). Many children routinely eat while viewing, and TV and Internet ads encourage unhealthy snacking: The more ads they watch, the greater their consumption of high-calorie snack foods. Screen media may also distract children from attending to sensations of fullness. Children permitted to have a TV in their bedroom—a practice linked to especially high TV viewing—are at even greater risk for weight gain (Borghese et al., 2015; Soos et al., 2014).

Finally, the broader food environment affects the incidence of obesity. The Pima Indians of Arizona, who two decades ago changed from a traditional diet of plant foods to a high-fat, typically American diet, have one of the world's highest obesity rates. Compared with descendants of their ancestors living in the remote Sierra Madre region of Mexico, the Arizona Pima have body weights 50 percent greater. The Pima have a genetic susceptibility to overweight, but it emerges only under Western dietary conditions (Schulz & Chaudhari, 2015). Other ethnic groups with a hereditary tendency to gain weight are Pacific Islanders, including native Hawaiians and Samoans (Subica et al., 2017). Many now eat an Americanized diet of high-calorie processed foods, and over 80 percent are overweight.

LOOK and LISTEN

Observe in the check-out area of a supermarket for an hour on a weekend, recording the percentage of families with children whose carts contain large quantities of high-calorie processed foods and soft drinks. In how many of these families are parents and children overweight?

Social Issues: Health | Family Stressors and Childhood Obesity

In response to chronic stress, many adults and children increase their food consumption—especially foods high in sugar and fat—and gain excessive weight. How can a stressful daily life prompt overeating?

One route is through elevated stress hormones, including cortisol, which signal the body to increase energy expenditure and the brain, in turn, to boost caloric intake (Fiese & Bost, 2016). In a second pathway, chronic stress triggers insulin resistance—a prediabetic condition that frequently induces a raging appetite (Qi & Ding, 2016).

Furthermore, the effort required to manage persistent stress can easily strain self-regulatory capacity, leaving the individual unable to limit excessive eating (Blair, 2010). In several studies, the greater the number of home-life stressors in school-age children's lives, the poorer their regulation of negative emotion and behavior (Evans et al., 2005; Garasky, 2009). Impaired self-regulation, then, might be a major intervening factor in the link between childhood chronic stress and obesity.

To find out, researchers followed several hundred children from economically disadvantaged families, assessing family stressors and self-regulatory ability at age 9 and change in BMI four years later, at age 13 (Evans, Fuller-Rowell, & Doan, 2012). Number of stressors experienced—including poverty, single-parent household, residential crowding, noise, household clutter, lack of books and play materials, child separation from the family, and exposure to violence—strongly predicted impaired self-regulation, as indicated by children's delay of gratification. Poor self-regulation, in turn, largely accounted for the relationship between family stressors and gain in BMI over time.

This 9-year-old, living in shelter housing with her mother, is at high risk for obesity. Home-life stressors, including poverty, single-parenthood, noise, crowding, and clutter, contribute to overeating by impairing children's capacity for self-regulation.

In obesity prevention programs, children given self-regulation training—instructions to "stop and think" in eating situations—show beneficial outcomes in terms of improved eating behaviors and weight loss (Epstein & Anzman-Frasca, 2017; Johnson, 2000). But such training is likely to be fully effective only when stressors in children's family lives are manageable, not overwhelming.

Consequences of Obesity Obese children are at risk for lifelong health problems. Symptoms that begin to appear in the early school years—high blood pressure, high cholesterol levels, respiratory abnormalities, insulin resistance, and inflammatory reactions—are powerful predictors of heart disease, circulatory difficulties, type 2 diabetes, gallbladder disease, sleep and digestive disorders, many forms of cancer, and early death. Furthermore, obesity has caused a dramatic rise in cases of diabetes in children, sometimes leading to early, severe complications, including stroke, kidney failure, and circulatory problems that heighten the risk of eventual blindness and leg amputation (Biro & Wien, 2010; Yanovski, 2015). U.S. Pima Indian children who are obese display double the rate of illness-related premature deaths after they reach adulthood as their normal-weight peers.

Unfortunately, physical attractiveness is a powerful predictor of social acceptance. In Western societies, both children and adults rate obese youngsters as unattractive, unhappy, self-doubting, deceitful, lazy, and less successful (Grant, Mizzi, & Anglim, 2016; Harrison, Rowlinson, & Hill, 2016; Di Pasquale & Celsi, 2017). In school, obese children and adolescents are often socially isolated. They report more emotional, social, and school difficulties, including peer teasing, rejection, victimization by bullies, and consequent low self-esteem (Stensland et al., 2015; van Grieken et al., 2013). They also tend to achieve less well than their healthy-weight agemates (Carey et al., 2015).

Because unhappiness and overeating contribute to each other, the child remains overweight. Persistent obesity from childhood into adolescence predicts elevated rates of serious psychological disorders, including severe anxiety and depression, defiance and aggression, and suicidal thoughts and behavior (Lopresti & Drummond, 2013; Puhl & Latner, 2007). Furthermore, overweight girls are more likely to reach puberty early, increasing their risk for early sexual activity and other adjustment problems (Rubin et al., 2009; Stattin & Skoog, 2016). The psychological consequences of obesity combine with continuing discrimination to further impair physical health and reduce life chances of forming close relationships and gaining satisfying employment.

This mother and son reinforce each other's efforts to lose weight and get in shape. The most effective interventions for childhood obesity focus on changing the family's behaviors, emphasizing fitness and healthy eating.

Treating Obesity   Childhood obesity is difficult to treat because it is a family disorder. In Mona's case, the school nurse suggested that Mona and her obese mother enter a weight-loss program together. But Mona's mother, unhappily married for many years, had her own reasons for overeating. She rejected this idea, claiming that Mona would eventually decide to lose weight on her own. About 50 to 70 percent of U.S. parents judge their overweight or obese child to have a normal weight (Hansen et al., 2014; McKee et al., 2016). Consistent with these findings, fewer than 20 percent of obese children get any treatment. Although many try to slim down in adolescence, they often go on crash diets that make matters worse. Temporary starvation leads to physical stress, discomfort, and fatigue. Soon the child returns to old eating patterns, and weight rebounds to a higher level. Then, to protect itself, the body burns calories more slowly and becomes more resistant to future weight loss.

The most effective interventions are family-based and focus on changing behaviors (Seburg et al., 2015). In one program, both parent and child revised eating patterns, exercised daily, and reinforced each other with praise and points for progress, which they exchanged for special activities and times together. The more weight parents lost, the more their children lost. Follow-ups after 5 and 10 years showed that children maintained their weight loss more effectively than adults—a finding that underscores the importance of early intervention (Epstein, Roemmich, & Raynor, 2001; Wrotniak et al., 2004). Monitoring dietary intake and physical activity is important. Small wireless sensors that sync with mobile devices, enabling individualized goal-setting and tracking of progress through game-like features, are effective (Calvert, 2015; Seburg et al., 2015). But these interventions work best when parents' and children's weight problems are not severe.

Children consume one-third of their daily energy intake at school. Therefore, schools can help reduce obesity by serving healthier meals and ensuring regular physical activity. Because obesity is expected to rise further without broad prevention strategies, many U.S. states and cities have passed obesity-reduction legislation. Among measures taken are weight-related school screenings for all children, improved nutrition standards, additional recess time and physical education, and obesity awareness and weight-reduction programs as part of school curricula. Reviews of school-based efforts reveal impressive benefits (Bleich et al., 2018; Shirley et al., 2015). Obesity prevention in schools is more successful in reducing children's BMIs than programs delivered in other community settings, perhaps because schools are better able to provide long-term, comprehensive intervention.

Finally, obesity prevention and reduction have become priorities in U.S. federal, state, and local government policies. Among current efforts are the following:

- Increased public education about healthy nutrition and physical activity, including limiting time devoted to screen media
- Greater access to healthy, affordable foods in low-income neighborhoods, where overweight and obesity are highest
- Laws mandating improved labels on foods and menus specifying nutritional content and calories
- Improved quality of publicly-supported school breakfasts and lunches
- Expanded opportunities for physical activity in schools as well as in communities, by building more parks, recreation centers, and walking and bike paths

LOOK and LISTEN

Contact your state and local governments to find out about their childhood obesity prevention legislation. Can policies be improved?

11.2.3 Vision and Hearing

The most common vision problem in middle childhood is *myopia,* or nearsightedness. In most developed nations for which evidence is available, the incidence of myopia increases steadily over middle childhood and adolescence and into adulthood (Rudnicka et al., 2016). Myopia rates, however, vary widely from country to country.

Heritability estimates based on comparisons of twins and other family members reveal a moderate genetic influence (Guggenheim et al., 2015). Worldwide, myopia occurs far more frequently in children and adolescents of East Asian than European ancestry: By high school graduation, 80 percent of Chinese and Japanese children are affected, compared with just under 25 percent of their North American and European counterparts (Rudnicka et al., 2016). Early biological trauma can also induce myopia. School-age children with low birth weights show an especially high rate, believed to result from immaturity of visual structures, slower eye growth, and a greater incidence of eye disease (Molloy et al., 2013).

When parents warn their children not to read in dim light or sit too close to the TV or computer screen, their concern ("You'll ruin your eyes!") is well-founded. In diverse cultures, the more time children spend reading, writing, using the computer, and doing other close work, the more likely they are to be myopic. Conversely, in school-age children who spend more time playing outdoors, the incidence of myopia is reduced (Russo et al., 2014). Researchers believe that the increased time children in East Asian countries spend in school, after-school classes, and doing homework contributes to their higher myopia rates (Sun et al., 2018). Myopia is one of the few health conditions to increase with SES, and it has become more prevalent in recent generations. Fortunately, myopia can be overcome easily with corrective lenses.

During middle childhood, the Eustachian tube (canal that runs from the inner ear to the throat) becomes longer, narrower, and more slanted, preventing fluid and bacteria from traveling so easily from the mouth to the ear. As a result, *otitis media* (middle ear infection), common in infancy and early childhood (see Chapter 8), becomes less frequent. Still, about 3 to 4 percent of the U.S. school-age population, and as many as 20 percent of low-SES children, develop some hearing loss as a result of repeated infections (Aarhus et al., 2015; Ryding et al., 2002). With regular screening for both vision and hearing, defects can be corrected before they lead to serious learning difficulties.

11.2.4 Bedwetting

One Friday afternoon, Terry called Joey to see if he could sleep over, but Joey refused. "I can't," said Joey anxiously, without offering an explanation.

"Why not? We can take our sleeping bags out in the backyard. Come on, it'll be cool!"

"My mom won't let me," Joey responded, unconvincingly. "I mean, well, I think we're busy. We're doing something tonight."

"Gosh, Joey, this is the third time you've said no. See if I'll ask you again!" snapped Terry as he hung up the phone.

Joey is one of 15 percent of school-age children in industrialized nations who suffer from **nocturnal enuresis,** or bedwetting during the night. Twice as many boys as girls are affected. In the overwhelming majority of cases, the problem has biological roots. Heredity is a major contributing factor: Parents with a history of bedwetting are far more likely to have a child with the problem, and identical twins are more likely than fraternal twins to share it (Sarici et al., 2016; von Gontard, Heron, & Joinson, 2011). Most often, enuresis is caused by a failure of muscular responses that inhibit urination or by a hormonal imbalance that permits too much urine to accumulate during the night. Some children also have difficulty awakening to the sensation of a full bladder (Becker, 2013). Punishing a school-age child for wetting makes matters worse.

Difficult temperament in infancy and early childhood elevates risk for later nocturnal enuresis in middle childhood (Joinson et al., 2016; Vasconcelos et al., 2017). The self-regulatory challenges experienced by emotionally reactive young children may contribute directly to urinary incontinence. Alternatively, temperamentally difficult children may be more resistant to parental toilet training, which results in persisting continence problems.

To treat enuresis, doctors often prescribe a synthetic hormone called desmopressin, which reduces the amount of urine produced. Although medication is a short-term solution for children attending camp or visiting a friend's house, once children stop taking it, they typically begin wetting again. The most effective treatment is a urine alarm that wakes the child at the first sign of dampness and works according to conditioning principles. Success rates of about 75 percent occur after four months of treatment (Mellon & Houts, 2018; Rittig et al., 2014). The few children who relapse achieve dryness after trying the alarm a second time.

Treating nocturnal enuresis has immediate, positive psychological consequences. It leads to gains in restful sleep, parents' evaluation of their child's behavior, and children's self-esteem (Longstaffe, Moffatt, & Whalen, 2000). Although many children outgrow enuresis without intervention, this generally takes years.

11.2.5 Illnesses

Children experience a somewhat higher rate of illness during the first two years of elementary school than later, because of exposure to sick children and an immune system that is still developing. Typically, illness causes children to miss from one to five days of school per year (National Survey of Children's Health, 2016). Longer absences usually can be traced to a few students with chronic health problems.

About 20 to 25 percent of U.S. children living at home have chronic diseases and conditions (including physical disabilities) (Centers for Disease Control and Prevention, 2017e). By far the most common—accounting for about one-third of childhood chronic illness and the most frequent cause of school absence and childhood hospitalization—is *asthma,* in which the bronchial tubes (passages that connect the throat and lungs) are highly sensitive (Basinger, 2013). In response to a variety of stimuli, such as cold weather, infection, exercise, allergies, and emotional stress, they fill with mucus and contract, leading to coughing, wheezing, and serious breathing difficulties.

The prevalence of asthma in the United States has increased steadily over the past several decades. It is now at its highest level, with nearly 8 percent of children and adolescents affected. Although heredity contributes to asthma, researchers believe that environmental factors are necessary to spark the illness. Boys, African-American children, and children who were born underweight, whose parents smoke, or who live in poverty are at greatest risk (Centers for Disease Control and Prevention, 2017a). Pollution in urban areas (which triggers allergic reactions), stressful home lives, and lack of access to good health care contribute substantially to the higher rates and greater severity of asthma among low-SES African-American and other poverty-stricken children. Childhood obesity is also linked to asthma (Hampton, 2014; Kranjac et al., 2017). High levels of blood-circulating inflammatory substances associated with body fat and the pressure of excess weight on the chest wall seem to be responsible.

© PAT GREENHOUSE/THE BOSTON GLOBE VIA GETTY IMAGES

These children, who live in an impoverished community where asthma is common, use a meter to measure the daily concentration of air pollutants. The device will warn them when pollution reaches a level likely to trigger asthma attacks.

About 2 percent of U.S. children have more severe chronic illnesses, such as sickle cell anemia, cystic fibrosis, diabetes, arthritis, cancer, and acquired immune deficiency syndrome (AIDS). Painful medical treatments, physical discomfort, and changes in appearance often disrupt the chronically sick child's daily life, making it difficult to concentrate in school and separating the child from peers. As the illness worsens, family and child stress increases (Rodriguez, Dunn, & Compas, 2012). For these reasons, chronically ill children are at risk for academic, emotional, and social difficulties. In adolescence, they are more likely than their agemates to suffer from low self-esteem and depression and report more often smoking cigarettes, using illegal drugs, and thinking about and attempting suicide (Champaloux & Young, 2015; Erickson et al., 2005).

A strong link exists between good family functioning and child well-being for chronically ill children, just as it does for physically healthy children (Leeman et al., 2016). Interventions that foster positive family relationships help parent and child cope effectively with the disease and improve adjustment. These include:

- Health education, in which parents and children learn about the illness and get training in how to manage it
- Home visits by health professionals, who offer counseling and social support to enhance parents' and children's strategies for managing the stress of chronic illness
- Schools that accommodate children's special health and education needs
- Disease-specific summer camps, which teach children self-help skills and give parents time off from the demands of caring for an ill child
- Parent and peer support groups

11.2.6 Unintentional Injuries

As we conclude our discussion of threats to school-age children's health, let's turn to the topic of unintentional injuries (discussed in detail in Chapter 8). As Figure 11.4 shows, injury fatalities increase from middle childhood into adolescence, with rates for boys rising considerably above those for girls. Poverty and either rural or urban residence—factors associated with dangerous environments and reduced parental monitoring of children—are also linked to high injury rates (Birken et al., 2006; Ovalle et al., 2016).

Motor vehicle accidents, involving children as passengers or pedestrians, continue to be the leading cause of injury, followed by bicycle accidents (Centers for Disease Control and Prevention, 2019b). School-age children should remain in car booster seats until they reach at least 4 feet 9 inches in height and are between ages 8 and 12, when adult seat belts alone are likely to fit them correctly. Although following these standards reduces serious injury by 45 percent, more than 80 percent of parents fail to do so consistently (Durbin & Hoffman, 2018; Hafner et al., 2017). Pedestrian accidents most often result from midblock dart-outs, and bicycle accidents from disobeying traffic signals and rules. When many stimuli impinge on them at once, young school-age children often fail to think before they act. They need frequent reminders, supervision, and prohibitions against venturing into busy traffic on their own.

Even older school-age children express unrealistic optimism about their likelihood of experiencing commonly occurring injuries—for example, as the result of a bicycle or pedestrian accident. They view themselves as less at risk than their peers (Joshi, Maclean, & Stevens, 2018). Yet a study that tracked routine supervision provided to middle-SES 7- to 10-year-olds at home revealed that the children were unsupervised 35 percent of the time (Morrongiello, Kane, Zdzieborski, 2011). Both nonsupervision and indirect supervision (parent checking on the child intermittently) were associated with increased injuries.

As children range farther from home, safety education related to their widening world becomes important. Effective school- and community-based prevention programs use extensive modeling and rehearsal of safety practices, give children feedback about their performance along with praise and tangible rewards for acquiring safety skills, and provide occasional booster sessions. Targeting specific injury risks (such as traffic safety) rather than many risks at once yields longer-lasting results (Nauta et al., 2014).

One vital safety measure is legally requiring that children wear protective helmets while bicycling, in-line skating, skateboarding, or using scooters. This precaution leads to a 9 percent reduction in head injuries, a leading cause of permanent physical disability and death in school-age children (Karkhaneh et al., 2013). Combining helmet use with preventive education and other community-based prevention strategies is especially effective. In one multifaceted prevention program, children in impoverished urban neighborhoods attended bicycle safety clinics, during which helmets were distributed. They also received traffic safety education in their classrooms and in a simulated traffic environment. In addition, existing playgrounds were improved

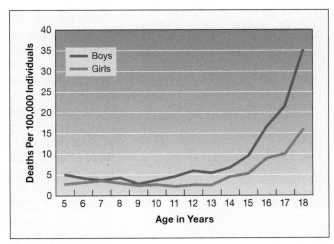

FIGURE 11.4 U.S. rates of injury mortality from middle childhood to adolescence. Injury fatalities increase from middle childhood into adolescence, and the gap between boys and girls expands. Motor vehicle (passenger and pedestrian) accidents are the leading cause, with bicycle injuries next in line. (Based on Centers for Disease Control and Prevention, 2019b.)

© HERO IMAGES INC/ALAMY STOCK PHOTO

By wearing helmets, these bike riders reduce their risk of head injuries, a leading cause of permanent disability and death in school-age children.

and new ones constructed to provide expanded off-street play areas, and more community-sponsored, supervised recreational activities were offered (Durkin et al., 1999; Taylor et al., 2018). As a result, motor vehicle and bicycle injuries declined by 36 percent.

Not all children respond to efforts to increase their safety. By middle childhood, the greatest risk-takers tend to be those whose parents do not act as safety-conscious models, rarely supervise their children's activities, fail to teach safety precautions, or use punitive or inconsistent discipline to enforce rules (Morrongiello, McArthur, & Spence, 2016; Rowe, Maughan, & Goodman, 2004; Tuchfarber, Zins, & Jason, 1997). These child-rearing tactics, as we saw in Chapter 10, spark children's defiance, reduce their willingness to comply, and actually promote high-risk behavior.

Highly active, impulsive children, many of whom are boys, remain particularly susceptible to injury in middle childhood. Although they have just as much safety knowledge as their peers, they are far less likely to implement it. Parents tend to be particularly lax in intervening in the dangerous behaviors of such children, especially under conditions of persistent marital conflict or other forms of stress (Schwebel et al., 2011, 2012). The greatest challenge for injury-control programs is reaching these children, altering high-risk factors in their families, and reducing the dangers to which they are exposed.

11.3 Health Education

11.3 Identify steps that parents and teachers can take to encourage good health practices in school-age children.

Psychologists, educators, and pediatricians are intensely interested in finding ways to help school-age children understand their bodies, acquire mature conceptions of health and illness, and develop behaviors that foster health throughout life. Furthermore, the dramatic physical transformations of puberty are not far off. Older school-age children need accurate information about what changes to expect; about reproduction, pregnancy, and childbirth; about the risks of early sexual activity; and about how to avoid unsafe social situations, including online (National Child Traumatic Stress Network, 2009). Middle childhood is an especially important time for fostering healthy lifestyles because of the child's growing independence, increasing cognitive capacities, and rapidly developing self-concept, which includes a sense of physical well-being.

School-age children can comprehend a wide range of health information—about the structure and functioning of their bodies, about good nutrition, and about the causes and consequences of physical injuries and diseases. When given scientific facts, they build on basic biological concepts acquired during the preschool years, and their understanding advances. For example, a 5-year-old is likely to say, "You get a cold when your friend sneezes and gives you her germs" (Legare, Zhu, & Wellman, 2013). A 10-year-old, in contrast, offers a deeper, more detailed explanation: "You get a cold when your sinuses fill with mucus. Sometimes your lungs do, too, and you get a cough. Colds come from viruses. They get into the bloodstream and make your platelet count go down" (Myant & Williams, 2005).

Without effective teaching, however, school-age children readily generalize their knowledge of familiar health conditions to less familiar ones. As a result, they may conclude that risk factors for colds (getting sneezed on, sharing a Coke) can cause AIDS or that cancer (like a cold) is contagious (González-Rivera & Bauermeister, 2007). Furthermore, supernatural accounts of illness widespread in certain cultures—such as "Maybe his sickness is punishment for bad behavior"—must be gently countered with scientific facts (Raman & Gelman, 2004). Otherwise, these incorrect ideas can lead to unnecessary anxiety about getting a serious disease.

APPLYING WHAT WE KNOW

Strategies for Fostering Healthy Lifestyles in School-Age Children

STRATEGY	DESCRIPTION
Increase health-related knowledge and encourage healthy behaviors.	Provide health education that imparts scientific information about health concepts and healthy lifestyles and that includes modeling, role playing, rehearsal, and reinforcement of good health practices.
Involve parents in supporting health education.	Communicate with parents about health education goals in school, encouraging them to extend these efforts at home. Teach parents about unhealthy dietary practices and how to create healthy food environments at home. Promote proper parental supervision by providing information on children's age-related safety capacities. Inform parents about the importance of educating children about pubertal changes and sexuality.
Provide healthy environments in schools.	Ask school administrators to ensure that school breakfasts and lunches follow widely accepted dietary guidelines. Limit access to vending machines with junk food. Work for daily recess periods in elementary school and mandatory daily physical education at all grade levels. Begin sex education in elementary school, offering information that informs children about and helps them cope with pubertal changes.
Make voluntary screening for risk factors available as part of health education.	Offer periodic measures of height, weight, body mass, blood pressure, and adequacy of diet. Educate children about the meaning of each index, and encourage improvement.
Promote pleasurable physical activity.	Provide opportunities for regular, vigorous physical exercise through activities that de-emphasize competition and that stress skill building and personal and social enjoyment.
Teach children to be critical of media advertising.	Besides teaching children to be skeptical of ads for unhealthy foods on TV and other screen media, reduce such advertising in schools—for example, on sports scoreboards.
Work for safer, healthier community environments for children.	Form community action groups to improve child safety, school nutrition, and play environments, and initiate community programs that foster healthy physical activity.

Nevertheless, most efforts to impart health information to school-age children have little impact on behavior (Tinsley, 2003). Several related reasons underlie this gap between knowledge and practice:

- Health is seldom an important goal for children, who feel good most of the time. They are far more concerned about schoolwork, friends, and play.
- Children do not yet have an adultlike time perspective that relates past, present, and future. They cannot see the connection between engaging in preventive behaviors now and experiencing later health consequences.
- Much health information given to children is contradicted by other sources, such as media advertising and the examples of adults and peers.

Consequently, teaching school-age children health-related facts, though crucial, must be supplemented by other efforts. As we have seen, a powerful means of fostering children's health is to reduce hazards, such as pollution, an unhealthy diet, and inadequate medical and dental care. At the same time, environments will never be totally free of health risks, so parents and teachers must coach children in good health practices and model and reinforce these behaviors. Refer to Applying What We Know above for ways to foster healthy lifestyles in school-age children.

© JIM WEST/ALAMY STOCK PHOTO

A visiting doctor discusses biological information about the human body with fifth graders. When school-age children are provided with scientific facts, they gain in understanding of health and illness.

ASK YOURSELF

Connect ■ Select one of the following health problems of middle childhood: obesity, myopia, bedwetting, asthma, or unintentional injuries. Explain how both genetic and environmental factors contribute to it.

Apply ■ Nine-year-old Talia is afraid to hug and kiss her grandmother, who has cancer. What might explain Talia's mistaken belief that the same behaviors that cause colds to spread might lead her to catch cancer? What would you do to change her thinking?

Reflect ■ List unintentional injuries that you experienced as a child. Were you injury-prone? Why or why not?

11.4 Motor Development and Play

11.4a Cite major changes in gross- and fine-motor development during middle childhood.

11.4b Describe individual differences in motor performance during middle childhood.

11.4c Describe qualities of children's play that are evident in middle childhood.

11.4d Identify steps that schools can take to promote physical fitness in middle childhood.

Visit a park on a pleasant weekend afternoon, and watch several preschool and school-age children at play. You will see that gains in body size and muscle strength support improved motor coordination during middle childhood. And greater cognitive and social maturity enables older children to use their new motor skills in more complex ways. A major change in children's play takes place at this time.

11.4.1 Gross-Motor Development

During the school years, running, jumping, hopping, and ball skills become more refined. At Joey and Lizzie's school, I watched during the third to sixth graders' recess. Children burst into sprints as they raced across the playground, jumped quickly over rotating ropes, engaged in intricate hopscotch patterns, kicked and dribbled soccer balls, batted at balls pitched by their classmates, and balanced adeptly as they walked heel-to-toe across narrow ledges. Table 11.2 summarizes gross-motor achievements between 6 and 12 years of age. These diverse skills reflect gains in four basic motor capacities:

Improved physical flexibility, balance, agility, and force, along with more efficient information processing, promote gains in school-age children's gross motor skills.

- *Flexibility.* Compared with preschoolers, school-age children are physically more pliable and elastic, a difference evident as they swing bats, kick balls, jump over hurdles, and execute tumbling routines.
- *Balance.* Improved balance supports many athletic skills, including running, hopping, skipping, throwing, kicking, and the rapid changes of direction required in many team sports.
- *Agility.* Quicker and more accurate movements are evident in the fancy footwork of dance and cheerleading and in the forward, backward, and sideways motions used to dodge opponents in tag and soccer.
- *Force.* Older children can throw and kick a ball harder and propel themselves farther off the ground when running and jumping than they could at earlier ages (Haywood & Getchell, 2014).

Along with body growth, more efficient information processing plays a vital role in improved gross-motor performance. Younger children often have difficulty with skills that require rapid responding, such as dribbling and batting. During middle childhood, the capacity to react only to relevant information increases. And steady gains in reaction time occur, including anticipatory responding to repeated visual stimuli, such as a thrown ball in a game of catch or a turning rope in a game of jump rope: Ten-year-olds react twice as quickly as 5-year-olds (Debrabant et al., 2012; Kail, 2003). These differences in speed of reaction have practical implications for physical education. Because 5- to 7-year-olds are seldom successful at batting a thrown

TABLE 11.2 **Changes in Gross-Motor Skills During Middle Childhood**

	SKILL	DEVELOPMENTAL CHANGE
	Running	Running speed increases from 12 feet per second at age 6 to more than 18 feet per second at age 12.
	Other gait variations	Skipping improves. Sideways stepping appears around age 6 and becomes more continuous and fluid with age.
	Vertical jump	Height jumped increases from 4 inches at age 6 to 12 inches at age 12.
	Standing broad jump	Distance jumped increases from 3 feet at age 6 to more than 5 feet at age 12.
	Precision jumping and hopping (on a mat divided into squares)	By age 7, children can accurately jump and hop from square to square, a performance that improves until age 9 and then levels off.
	Throwing	Throwing speed, distance, and accuracy increase for both sexes, but much more for boys than for girls. At age 6, a ball thrown by a boy travels 39 feet per second, and one by a girl, 29 feet per second. At age 12, a ball thrown by a boy travels 78 feet per second, and one by a girl, 56 feet per second.
	Catching	Ability to catch small balls thrown over greater distances improves with age.
	Kicking	Kicking speed and accuracy improve, with boys considerably ahead of girls. At age 6, a ball kicked by a boy travels 21 feet per second, and one by a girl, 13 feet per second. At age 12, a ball kicked by a boy travels 34 feet per second, and one by a girl, 26 feet per second.
	Batting	Batting motions become more effective with age, increasing in speed and accuracy and involving the entire body.
	Dribbling	Style of hand dribbling gradually changes, from awkward slapping of the ball to continuous, relaxed, even stroking.

Sources: Haywood & Getchell, 2014; Malina & Bouchard, 1991.

ball, T-ball is more appropriate for them than baseball. Similarly, handball, four-square, and kickball should precede instruction in tennis, basketball, and football.

Children's gross-motor activity not only benefits from but contributes to cognitive development. Physical fitness predicts improved executive function, memory, and academic achievement in middle childhood (Chaddock et al., 2011). Exercise-induced changes in the brain seem to be responsible: Brain-imaging research reveals that structures supporting attentional control and memory are larger, and myelination of neural fibers within them greater, in better-fit than in poorly-fit children (Chaddock et al., 2010a, 2010b; Chaddock-Heyman et al., 2014). Furthermore, children who are physically fit—and those assigned to a yearlong, one-hour-per-day school fitness program—activate these brain structures more effectively while performing executive function tasks (Chaddock et al., 2012; Chaddock-Heyman et al., 2013). Mounting evidence supports the role of vigorous exercise in optimal brain and cognitive functioning in childhood—a relationship that persists throughout the lifespan.

11.4.2 Fine-Motor Development

Fine-motor development also improves over the school years. On rainy afternoons, Joey and Lizzie experimented with yo-yos, built model airplanes, and wove potholders on small looms. Like many children, they took up musical instruments, which demand considerable fine-motor control.

Gains in fine-motor skill are especially evident in children's writing and drawing. By age 6, most children can print the alphabet, their first and last names, and the numbers from 1 to

FIGURE 11.5 **Increase in organization, detail, and depth cues in school-age children's drawings.** Compare both drawings to the one by a 5-year-old in Figure 8.6 on page 299. In the drawing by an 8-year-old on the left, notice how all parts are depicted in relation to one another and with greater detail. Integration of depth cues increases dramatically over the school years, as shown in the drawing on the right, by an 11-year-old. Here, depth is indicated by overlapping objects, diagonal placement, and converging lines, as well as by making distant objects smaller than near ones.

10 with reasonable clarity. Their writing is large, however, because they make strokes using the entire arm rather than just the wrist and fingers. Children usually master uppercase letters first because their horizontal and vertical motions are easier to control than the small curves of the lowercase alphabet. Legibility of writing gradually increases as children produce more accurate letters with uniform height and spacing.

Children's drawings show dramatic gains in organization, detail, and representation of depth during middle childhood. By the end of the preschool years, children can accurately copy many two-dimensional shapes, and they integrate these into their drawings. Some depth cues have also begun to appear, such as making distant objects smaller than near ones (Braine et al., 1993). Yet recall from Chapter 8 that before age 8, children have trouble accurately copying a three-dimensional form, such as a cube or cylinder (see page 299 in Chapter 8). Around 9 to 10 years, the third dimension is clearly evident through overlapping objects, diagonal placement, and converging lines. Furthermore, as Figure 11.5 shows, school-age children not only depict objects in considerable detail but also relate them to one another as part of an organized whole (Case & Okamoto, 1996).

11.4.3 Individual Differences in Motor Skills

As at younger ages, school-age children show marked individual differences in motor capacities that are influenced by both heredity and environment. Body build is influential: Taller, more muscular children excel at many motor tasks. And children whose parents encourage physical exercise tend to enjoy it more and also to be more skilled.

Family income affects children's access to lessons needed to develop abilities in areas such as ballet, tennis, gymnastics, and instrumental music. For children from low-SES homes, school and community provisions for nurturing athletics and other motor skills by making lessons, equipment, and opportunities for regular practice available and affordable are crucial. When these experiences combine with parental encouragement, many low-SES children become highly skilled.

Sex differences in motor skills that appeared during the preschool years extend into middle childhood and, in some instances, become more pronounced. Girls have an edge in fine-motor skills of handwriting and drawing and in gross-motor capacities that depend on balance and agility, such as hopping and skipping (Haywood & Getchell, 2014). But boys outperform girls on all other skills listed in Table 11.2, especially throwing and kicking.

School-age boys' genetic advantage in muscle mass is not large enough to account for their gross-motor superiority. Rather, the social environment plays a larger role. Research confirms that parents hold higher expectations for boys' athletic performance, and children readily absorb these messages. From first through twelfth grades, girls are less positive than boys about the value of sports and their own sports ability—differences explained in part by parental beliefs (Anderson, Hughes, & Fuemmeler, 2009; Fredricks & Eccles, 2002; Noordstar et al., 2016). The more strongly girls believe that females are incompetent at sports (such as hockey or soccer), the lower they judge their own ability and the poorer they actually perform (Belcher et al., 2003; Chalabaev, Sarrazin, & Fontayne, 2009).

Educating parents about the minimal differences between school-age boys' and girls' physical capacities and sensitizing them to unfair biases against promotion of girls' athletic ability may help increase girls' self-confidence and participation in athletics. Greater emphasis on skill training for girls, along with increased attention to their athletic achievements, is also likely to help. As a positive sign, compared with a generation ago, many more girls now participate in individual and team sports such as gymnastics

Fourth graders gather in their schoolyard for a pick-up game of basketball. School-age children show marked individual differences in motor capacities that are influenced by both heredity and environment.

and soccer, though their involvement continues to lag behind boys' (Bassett et al., 2015; Kanters et al., 2013; Sabo & Veliz, 2011). Middle childhood is a crucial time to encourage girls' sports participation because during this period, children start to discover what they are good at and make some definite skill commitments.

11.4.4 Games with Rules

The physical activities of school-age children reflect an important advance in quality of play: Games with rules become common. Children around the world engage in an enormous variety of informally organized games, including variants on popular sports such as soccer, baseball, and basketball. In addition to the best-known childhood games, such as tag, jacks, and hopscotch, children have also invented hundreds of other games, including red rover, statues, leapfrog, kick the can, and prisoner's base.

Gains in perspective taking—in particular, the ability to understand the roles of several players in a game—permit this transition to rule-oriented games. These play experiences, in turn, contribute greatly to emotional and social development. Child-invented games usually rely on simple physical skills and a sizable element of luck. As a result, they rarely become contests of individual ability. Instead, they permit children to try out different styles of cooperating, competing, winning, and losing with little personal risk. Also, in their efforts to organize a game, children discover why rules are necessary and which ones work well. In fact, they often spend as much time working out the details of how a game should proceed as they do playing the game! As we will see in Chapter 13, these experiences help children form more mature concepts of fairness and justice.

Compared with past generations, school-age children today spend less time engaged in informal outdoor play—a change that reflects parental concern about neighborhood safety as well as competition for children's time from TV and other screen media. Another factor is the rise in adult-organized sports, such as Little League baseball and soccer and hockey leagues, which fill many hours that children from economically advantaged families used to devote to spontaneous play.

In village societies in developing countries and in many low-SES communities in industrialized nations, children's informal sports and games remain

Children of the Samburu people of Kenya join in a spontaneous game of soccer. In village societies in developing countries and in many low-SES communities in industrialized nations, children's informal sports and games remain common.

common. In an ethnographic study in two communities—a refugee camp in Angola, Africa, and a Chicago public housing complex—the overwhelming majority of 6- to 12-year-olds engaged in child-organized games at least once a week, and half or more did so nearly every day. Play in each context reflected distinct cultural values (Guest, 2013). In the Angolan community, games emphasized imitation of social roles—soccer moves of admired professional players, the intricate operation of a cooking spice shop. Games in Chicago, in contrast, were competitive and individualistic. In ballgames, for example, children often made sure peers noticed when they batted or fielded balls particularly well.

11.4.5 Adult-Organized Youth Sports

More than half of U.S. children—62 percent of boys and 52 percent of girls—participate in organized sports outside of school hours at some time between ages 6 and 12 (Aspen Institute, 2018). Children in low-SES communities, however, are profoundly underserved, with girls and ethnic minorities having especially limited opportunities. In a comparison of two neighborhoods in Oakland, California, 67 percent of teenage girls in a well-to-do area were members of athletic teams (Team Up for Youth, 2014). Just a few miles away, in a poverty-stricken, largely minority part of the city, a mere 11 percent were involved in organized sports. The high cost of equipment and uniforms (and, at times, travel) keeps many economically disadvantaged children from participating.

Joining community sports teams is associated with increased athletic and social skills, yielding benefits for participants' self-esteem (Cronin, 2015; Wagnsson, Lindwall, & Gustafsson, 2014). Among shy children, sports participation seems to play a protective role, fostering self-confidence and a decline in social anxiety, perhaps because it provides a sense of group belonging and a basis for communicating with peers (Findlay & Coplan, 2008). And children who view themselves as good at sports are more likely to continue playing, which predicts greater participation in sports and other physical fitness activities in adolescence and early adulthood (Duncan, Strycker, & Chaumeton, 2015; Kjønniksen, Anderssen, & Wold, 2009; Marsh et al., 2007).

In some cases, though, the arguments of critics—that youth sports overemphasize competition and substitute adult control for children's natural experimentation with rules and strategies—are valid. When coaches make winning paramount, weaker performers generally experience social ostracism. Children who experience poor-quality relationships with their coach and teammates enjoy sports participation less and soon drop out (Gardner, Magee, & Vella, 2017; Stryer, Tofler, & Lapchick, 1998). And those who join teams so early that the necessary skills are beyond their abilities also lose interest.

Parents, even more than coaches, influence children's athletic attitudes and abilities. Positive parenting is consistently associated with children's persistence and skill gains, whereas high parental pressure sets the stage for emotional difficulties and dislike of sports (Knight, Berrow, & Harwood, 2017). At the extreme are parents who value sports so highly that they punish their child for making mistakes, insist that the child keep playing after injury, hold the child back in school to ensure a physical advantage, or even seek medical interventions to improve the child's performance.

In most organized youth sports, health and safety rules help ensure that injuries are infrequent and mild. An exception is football, which has a high incidence of serious injury. Eight- to 12-year-old boys in tackle football leagues experience rates of concussion—brain injuries resulting from a blow to the head or body—that equal those of high school and college players (Kontos et al., 2013). And in any sport, frequent, intense practice can lead to painful "overuse" injuries

© ELAINE THOMPSON/AP PHOTO IMAGES

A mother—who is also the coach of her daughter's youth basketball team—runs a drill with the 10-year-old while her younger brother looks on. Positive parenting is consistently associated with children's skill gains and persistence at sports.

APPLYING WHAT WE KNOW

Providing Developmentally Appropriate Organized Sports in Middle Childhood

STRATEGY	DESCRIPTION
Build on children's interests.	Permit children to select from among appropriate activities the ones that suit them best. Do not push children into sports they do not enjoy.
Teach age-appropriate skills.	For children younger than age 9, emphasize basic skills, such as kicking, throwing, and batting, and simplified games that grant all participants adequate playing time.
Emphasize enjoyment.	Permit children to progress at their own pace and to play for the fun of it, whether or not they become expert athletes.
Limit the frequency and length of practices.	Adjust practice time to children's attention spans and need for unstructured time with peers, with family, and for homework. Two practices a week, each no longer than 30 minutes for younger school-age children and 60 minutes for older school-age children, are sufficient.
Focus on personal and team improvement.	Emphasize effort, skill gains, and teamwork rather than winning. Avoid criticism for errors and defeat, which promotes anxiety and avoidance of athletics.
Discourage unhealthy competition.	Avoid all-star games and championship ceremonies that recognize individuals. Instead, acknowledge all participants.
Permit children to contribute to rules and strategies.	Involve children in decisions aimed at ensuring fair play and teamwork. To strengthen desirable responses, reinforce compliance rather than punishing noncompliance.

that, in extreme cases, cause stress-related fractures that impair physical growth (Brown, Patel, & Darmawan, 2017). On highly competitive teams with year-round training, overuse injuries are common.

When parents and coaches emphasize effort, improvement, participation, and teamwork, young athletes enjoy sports more, exert greater effort to improve their skills, and perceive themselves as more competent at their chosen sport (Ross, Mallett, & Parkes, 2015). See Applying What We Know above for ways to ensure that athletic leagues provide children with positive learning experiences.

11.4.6 Shadows of Our Evolutionary Past

While watching children in your neighborhood park, notice how they occasionally wrestle, roll, hit, and run after one another, alternating roles while smiling and laughing. This friendly chasing and play-fighting is called **rough-and-tumble play.** It emerges in the preschool years and peaks in middle childhood, and children in many cultures engage in it with peers whom they like especially well (Pellegrini, 2004). After a rough-and-tumble episode, children continue interacting rather than separating, as they do after an aggressive encounter.

Children's rough-and-tumble play resembles the social behavior of many other young mammals. It seems to originate in parents' physical play with babies, especially fathers' play with sons (see page 265 in Chapter 7). And it is more common among boys, probably because prenatal exposure to androgens predisposes boys toward active play (see page 378 in Chapter 10). Boys' rough-and-tumble largely consists of playful wrestling and hitting, whereas girls tend to engage in running and chasing, with only brief physical contact. In middle childhood, rough-and-tumble accounts for as much as 10 percent of free-play behavior.

© CLEVE BRYANT/PHOTOEDIT

In our evolutionary past, rough-and-tumble play—which can be distinguished from aggression by its friendly quality—may have been important for developing fighting skill and establishing dominance hierarchies.

In our evolutionary past, rough-and-tumble play may have been important for developing fighting skill. It also helps children form a **dominance hierarchy**—a stable ordering of group members that predicts who will win when conflict arises. Observations of arguments, threats, and physical attacks between children reveal a consistent lineup of winners and losers that becomes increasingly stable in middle childhood and adolescence, especially among boys. Once school-age children establish a dominance hierarchy, hostility is rare. Children seem to use play-fighting as a safe context to assess the strength of a peer before challenging that peer's dominance (Fry, 2014; Roseth et al., 2007).

Rough-and-tumble play offers lessons in how to handle combative interactions with restraint. And as long as fathers' physical play is warm, energetic, and appropriately challenging, it is associated with children's favorable emotional and social adjustment and self-regulation (St George, Fletcher, & Palazzi, 2017; Fletcher, St George, & Freeman, 2013). High-quality rough-and-tumble seems to provide valuable opportunities for children to practice reading emotions, inhibiting impulses (such as hitting), and coping with frustration.

As children reach puberty, individual differences in strength become apparent, and rough-and-tumble play declines. When it does occur, its meaning changes: Adolescent boys' rough-and-tumble is linked to aggression (Pellegrini, 2003). Unlike children, teenage rough-and-tumble players "cheat," hurting their opponent. In explanation, boys often say that they are retaliating, apparently to reestablish dominance. Thus, a play behavior that limits aggression in childhood becomes a context for hostility in adolescence.

11.4.7 Physical Education

Physical activity supports many aspects of children's development—their health, their sense of self-worth as physically active and capable beings, and the cognitive and social skills necessary for getting along with others. A large body of evidence links school-based physical activity to improved academic achievement (Centers for Disease Control and Prevention, 2017g; Donnelly et al., 2016). Yet to devote more time to academic instruction, U.S. elementary schools have cut back on recess (see the Social Issues: Education box on the following page).

Similarly, although most U.S. states require some physical education, only six require it in every grade, and only one mandates at least 30 minutes per school day in elementary school and 45 minutes in middle and high school. Nearly half of U.S. elementary and secondary school students do not attend any physical education classes during a typical school week. Not surprisingly, physical inactivity among children and adolescents is pervasive. Fewer than 30 percent of 6- to 17-year-olds engage in at least moderate-intensity activity for 60 minutes per day, including some vigorous activity (involving breathing hard and sweating) on three of those days—the U.S. government recommendations for good health (Centers for Disease Control and Prevention, 2014b; Society of Health and Physical Educators, 2016). With the transition to adolescence, physical activity declines, more for girls than for boys.

Many experts believe that schools should not only offer more frequent physical education classes but also change the content of these programs. Training in competitive sports, often a high priority, is unlikely to reach the least physically fit youngsters, who avoid activities demanding a high level of skill. Instead, programs should emphasize enjoyable, informal games and individual exercise (walking, running, jumping, tumbling, and climbing)—pursuits most likely to endure. Furthermore, children of varying skill levels are more likely to sustain physical activity when teachers focus on each child's personal progress and contribution to team accomplishment (Society of Health and Physical Educators, 2009b). Then physical education fosters a healthy sense of self while satisfying school-age children's need to participate with others.

© JEFF MOREHEAD/AP IMAGES

In a lively game of barnyard tag, "animals" scatter to avoid being tagged by "farmers." Many experts believe that physical education classes should emphasize informal games, as well as individual exercise and personal progress, rather than competitive sports.

Social Issues: Education | School Recess—A Time to Play, a Time to Learn

When 7-year-old Whitney's family moved to a new city, she left a school with three daily recess periods for one with just a single 15-minute break per day, which her second-grade teacher canceled if any child misbehaved. Whitney, who had previously enjoyed school, complained daily of headaches and an upset stomach. Her mother, Jill, thought, "My child is stressing out because she can't move all day!" After Jill and other parents successfully appealed to the school board to add a second recess period, Whitney's symptoms vanished.

Over the past two decades, recess—along with its rich opportunities for child-organized play and peer interaction—has diminished or disappeared in many U.S. schools. Under the assumption that extra time for academics will translate into achievement gains, nearly one-third of school districts no longer require a daily recess for public school students (Centers for Disease Control and Prevention, 2017e).

Yet rather than subtracting from classroom learning, recess periods boost it! Research dating back more than 100 years confirms that extending cognitively demanding tasks over a longer time by introducing regular breaks, rather than consolidating intensive effort within one period, enhances attention and performance at all ages. Such breaks are particularly important for young children.

In a series of studies, school-age children were more attentive in the classroom after recess than before it—an effect that was greater for second than fourth graders (Pellegrini, Huberty, & Jones,

1995). And relative to non-participating agemates, second and third graders randomly assigned to a program of 10-minute periods of physical activity distributed across the school day scored substantially higher in academic achievement at a three-year follow-up (Donnelly et al., 2009). Teacher ratings of classroom disruptive behavior also decline for children who have more than 15 minutes of recess a day (Barros, Silver, & Stein, 2009).

In another investigation, kindergartners' and first graders' engagement in peer conversation and games during recess positively predicted later academic achievement, even after other factors that might explain the relationship (such as previous achievement) were controlled (Pellegrini et al., 2002). Consistent with these findings, industrialized nations offering more recess in elementary school tend to have students who attain higher achievement test scores when they reach high school (Yogman et al., 2018).

Recall from Chapter 10 that children's social maturity contributes substantially to early academic competence. Recess is one of the few remaining contexts devoted to child-organized games that provide practice in vital social

Fifth-graders play an energetic game of gaga ball (a variant of dodge ball) during recess. By providing regular opportunities for play and games, recess promotes physical, academic, and social competence.

skills—cooperation, leadership, followership, and inhibition of aggression—under adult supervision rather than direction. As children transfer these skills to the classroom, they may join in discussions, collaborate, follow rules, and enjoy academic pursuits more—factors that enhance motivation and achievement.

Finally, school yards with spacious grassy play areas, a variety of playground equipment, and physically active adult models enhance children's moderate-to-vigorous exercise during recess. Girls, who are less active than boys during recess, benefit especially from encouragement to engage in physically active games (Martin et al., 2012; Woods et al., 2015). In sum, regular, unstructured recess promotes children's health and competence—physically, academically, and socially.

Physically fit children take great pleasure in their rapidly developing motor skills. As a result, they develop rewarding interests in physical activity and sports and are more likely to become active adolescents and adults who reap many benefits (Kjønniksen, Torsheim, & Wold, 2008). These include greater physical strength, resistance to many illnesses (from colds and flu to cancer, diabetes, and heart disease), enhanced psychological well-being, and a longer life.

ASK YOURSELF

Connect ■ On Saturdays, 10-year-old Darnell gathers with friends on the driveway of his house to play basketball. Besides improved ball skills, what else is he learning?

Apply ■ Nine-year-old Jasmine thinks she isn't good at sports, and she doesn't like physical education class. Suggest strategies her teacher can use to improve her pleasure and involvement in physical activity.

Reflect ■ Did you participate in adult-organized sports as a child? If so, what kind of climate for learning did coaches and parents create? What impact do you think your experiences had on your development?

SUMMARY

11.1 Body Growth (p. 405)

11.1a Describe changes in body size, proportions, and skeletal maturity during middle childhood.

- School-age children's growth extends the slow, regular pace of early childhood, although with substantial individual and geographic variation. By age 9, girls overtake boys in physical size.

- In industrialized nations, final height has been increasing for the past 150 years, a **secular trend in physical growth** due mostly to improved nutrition and health.

- Bones continue to lengthen and broaden, and permanent teeth replace primary teeth. Tooth decay affects more than half of U.S. school-age children, with especially high levels among low-SES children. One-third of school-age children suffer from **malocclusion**, requiring braces for some.

11.1b Describe brain development in middle childhood.

- Brain weight increases by only 10 percent during middle childhood, but white matter rises steadily and gray matter peaks and then declines as a result of synaptic pruning. The resulting increase in interconnectivity among distant regions of the cerebral cortex and accompanying reorganization and selection of brain circuits leads to more effective information processing and, in particular, to gains in executive function.

11.2 Health Issues (p. 409)

11.2a Describe the causes and consequences of serious nutritional problems in middle childhood, giving special attention to obesity.

- Poverty-stricken children in developing countries and in the United States suffer from serious and prolonged malnutrition, which can result in lasting physical, cognitive, and mental health problems.

- Overweight and **obesity** have increased dramatically in both industrialized and developing nations. Although heredity contributes to obesity, environmental factors, including family stress, parental feeding practices, maladaptive eating habits, insufficient sleep, physical inactivity, excessive screen media use, and the broader food environment play substantial roles.

- Obese children are at risk for lifelong health problems. Often socially rejected, they also display elevated rates of serious psychological disorders.

- Family-based interventions aimed at changing parents' and children's eating patterns and lifestyles are the most effective approaches to treating childhood obesity. Schools can help by ensuring regular physical activity and serving healthier meals.

11.2b List factors that contribute to illness during the school years, and explain how these health challenges can be reduced.

- The most common vision problem, myopia, is influenced by heredity, early biological trauma, and time spent reading, writing, and doing other close work. Although ear infections decline during the school years, repeated infections, particularly among low-SES children, result in some hearing loss.

- Heredity is a major contributor to **nocturnal enuresis**, though early difficult temperament elevates risk for the problem. The most effective treatment is a urine alarm that works according to conditioning principles.

- The prevalence of asthma, the most frequent cause of school absence and hospitalization in U.S. children, has been steadily increasing. Urban pollution, stressful home lives, childhood obesity, and lack of access to good health care contribute to the illness. Its rate and severity are greatest among boys and children who live in poverty.

- Children with severe chronic illnesses are at risk for academic, emotional, and social difficulties, but positive family relationships improve adjustment.

11.2c Describe changes in the occurrence of unintentional injuries during middle childhood, and cite effective interventions.

- Unintentional injuries increase over middle childhood and adolescence, especially for boys, with motor vehicle and bicycle accidents accounting for most of the rise. Children are unrealistically optimistic about their likelihood of injury, making parental supervision key to injury prevention.

- Effective school- and community-based safety education programs use modeling and rehearsal of safety practices and reward children for good performance. Insisting that children wear protective bicycle helmets dramatically reduces the risk of serious head injury.

11.3 Health Education (p. 418)

11.3 Identify steps that parents and teachers can take to encourage good health practices in school-age children.

- Besides providing health-related information, adults must reduce health hazards in children's environments, coach children in good health practices, and model and reinforce these behaviors.

11.4 Motor Development and Play (p. 420)

11.4a Cite major changes in gross- and fine-motor development during middle childhood.

- Gains in flexibility, balance, agility, and force contribute to improved athletic performance during middle childhood.

- More efficient information processing plays a vital role in children's improved gross-motor performance. Physical exercise, in turn, enhances brain and cognitive functioning.

- Fine-motor development also improves. Handwriting becomes more legible, and children's drawings show dramatic increases in organization, detail, and representation of depth.

11.4b Describe individual differences in motor performance during middle childhood.

- Wide individual differences in children's motor capacities reflect the influence of both heredity and environment, including such factors as body build, parental encouragement, and access to lessons and athletic equipment.

- Gender stereotypes, which affect parental expectations for children's athletic performance, largely account for school-age boys' superiority on a wide range of gross-motor skills. Greater emphasis on skill training for girls and attention to their athletic achievements can help increase their involvement and performance.

11.4c *Describe qualities of children's play that are evident in middle childhood.*

- Games with rules become common during the school years, contributing to emotional and social development. Participation in adult-organized youth sports programs is associated with increased self-esteem and social competence in most players, but low-SES children have limited access to such programs. Adult pressure to perform and overemphasis on competition promote undue anxiety and avoidance of sports in children.

- Some features of children's physical activity reflect our evolutionary past. **Rough-and-tumble play** may once have been important for developing fighting skill and helps children establish a **dominance hierarchy.** In middle childhood, dominance hierarchies become increasingly stable, especially among boys, and serve the adaptive function of limiting aggression among group members. Warm, energetic rough-and-tumble play with fathers is associated with children's favorable adjustment and self-regulation.

11.4d *Identify steps that schools can take to promote physical fitness in middle childhood.*

- In addition to providing an opportunity for physical activity, school recess is a rich context for child-organized games and social interaction.

- U.S. elementary schools have cut back on recess and physical education classes, despite the benefits that exercise and play offer for physical health, academic achievement, social skills, and psychological well-being.

IMPORTANT TERMS AND CONCEPTS

dominance hierarchy (p. 426)
malocclusion (p. 407)

nocturnal enuresis (p. 415)
obesity (p. 410)

rough-and-tumble play (p. 425)
secular trends in physical growth (p. 407)

Cognitive Development in Middle Childhood

Historical Theme

Shkelen Agimi, 11 years, Albania

This artist's vibrant, detailed rendering of a naval battle reflects the dramatic gains in planning, memory, categorization, spatial reasoning, and problem solving of middle childhood.

Reprinted with permission from the International Museum of Children's Art, Oslo, Norway

"Finally!" 6-year-old Lizzie exclaimed the day Rena enrolled her in elementary school. "Now I get to go to real school, just like Joey!" Lizzie confidently walked into a combined kindergarten–first-grade class in her neighborhood school, pencils, crayons, and writing pad in hand, ready for a more disciplined approach to learning than she had experienced previously. As a preschooler, Lizzie had loved playing school, giving assignments as the "teacher" and pretending to read and write as the "student." Now she was eager to master the tasks that had sparked her imagination as a 4- and 5-year-old.

Walking into that classroom, Lizzie entered a whole new world of challenging activities. In a single morning, she and her classmates might meet in reading groups, write in journals, work on addition and subtraction, and sort leaves gathered for a science project. As Lizzie and Joey moved through the elementary school grades, they tackled increasingly complex projects, became more accomplished at reading, writing, and math, and broadened their general knowledge of the world.

To understand the cognitive attainments of middle childhood, we turn to research inspired by Piaget's theory and the information-processing approach. And we look at expanding definitions of intelligence that help us appreciate individual differences in mental development. We also discuss genetic and environmental contributions to IQ scores, which often influence important educational decisions. Our discussion continues with language, which blossoms further in these years. Finally, we consider the role of schools in children's development. ■

12.1 Piaget's Theory: The Concrete Operational Stage

When Lizzie visited my child development class at age 4, Piaget's conservation problems confused her (see page 312 in Chapter 9). For example, after water was poured from a tall, narrow container into a short, wide one, she insisted that the amount of water had changed. When Lizzie returned at age 8, she found this task easy. "Of course it's the same!" she exclaimed. "The water's shorter, but it's also wider. Pour it back," she instructed. "You'll see, it's the same amount!"

12.1.1 Attainments of the Concrete Operational Stage

Lizzie has entered Piaget's **concrete operational stage,** which extends from about 7 to 11 years. Compared with cognition in early childhood, thinking in middle childhood is more logical, flexible, and organized.

Conservation   The ability to pass *conservation tasks* provides clear evidence of *operations*—mental actions that obey logical rules. Notice how Lizzie is capable of **decentration,** focusing on several aspects of a problem and relating them, rather than centering on just one. She also demonstrates **reversibility,** the capacity to think through a series of steps and then mentally reverse direction, returning to the starting point. Recall from Chapter 9 that reversibility is part of every logical operation. It is solidly achieved in middle childhood.

Classification   Between ages 7 and 10, children pass Piaget's *class inclusion problem* (see page 312 in Chapter 9). This indicates that they are more aware of classification hierarchies. Children of this age are better able to inhibit their habitual

12.1a Describe advances in thinking and cognitive limitations during the concrete operational stage.

12.1b Discuss follow-up research on concrete operational thought.

strategy of perceptually comparing two specific categories (blue flowers and yellow flowers) in favor of relating each specific category to its less obvious general category (flowers) (Borst et al., 2013). School-age children's enhanced classification skills are evident in their enthusiasm for collecting treasured objects. At age 10, Joey spent hours sorting and re-sorting his baseball cards, grouping them first by league and team and then by playing position and batting average. He could separate the players into a variety of classes and subclasses and easily rearrange them.

An improved ability to categorize underlies children's interest in collecting objects during middle childhood. This 10-year-old sorts and organizes his extensive rock and mineral collection.

Seriation The ability to order items along a quantitative dimension, such as length or weight, is called **seriation.** To test for it, Piaget asked children to arrange sticks of different lengths from shortest to longest. Older preschoolers can put the sticks in a row to create the series, but they do so haphazardly, making many errors. In contrast, 6- to 7-year-olds create the series efficiently, moving in an orderly sequence from the shortest stick to the longest.

The concrete operational child can also seriate mentally, an ability called **transitive inference.** In a well-known transitive inference problem, Piaget showed children pairings of sticks of different colors. From observing that stick *A* is longer than stick *B* and that stick *B* is longer than stick *C*, children must infer that *A* is longer than C and, also, that A is the longest of the three sticks. Like Piaget's class inclusion task, transitive inference requires children to integrate three relations at once—in this instance, *A–B, B–C,* and *A–C.* As long as they receive help in remembering the premises (*A–B* and *B–C*), 7- to 8-year-olds can grasp transitive inference (Wright, 2006). And when the task is made relevant to children's everyday experiences—for example, based on winners of races between pairs of cartoon characters—6-year-olds perform well, though not on a par with older children (Wright, Robertson, & Hadfield, 2011; Wright & Smailes, 2015).

Spatial Reasoning Piaget found that school-age children's understanding of space is more accurate than that of preschoolers. To illustrate, let's consider children's **cognitive maps**—their mental representations of spaces, such as a classroom, school, or neighborhood. Drawing or reading a map of a large-scale space (school or neighborhood) requires considerable perspective-taking skill. Because the entire space cannot be seen at once, children must infer its overall layout by relating its separate parts.

Preschoolers and young school-age children include *landmarks* on maps they draw of a single room, but their arrangement is not always accurate. They do better when asked to place stickers showing the location of furniture and people on a map of the room. But if the map is rotated to a position other than the room's orientation, they have difficulty (Liben & Downs, 1993). However, giving 7-year-olds the opportunity to walk through the room ahead of time improves their ability to locate landmarks on a rotated map (Lehnung et al., 2003). Actively exploring the room permits them to experience landmarks from different vantage points, which fosters a more flexible mental representation.

With respect to large-scale outdoor environments, not until age 9 can many children accurately place stickers on a map to indicate the location of landmarks. Children who spontaneously use strategies that help them align the map with their current location in the space—rotating the map or tracing their route on it—show better performance (Liben et al., 2013). Around this age, the maps children draw of large-scale spaces become better organized, showing landmarks along an *organized route of travel.* Around age 10, children become less dependent on landmarks to learn a route of travel (Lingwood et al., 2015). Most can give directions for getting from one place to another using only left-turn, right-turn, and straight-ahead directions.

At the end of middle childhood, most children can integrate two or more routes, enabling them to form an *integrative, overall view of a large-scale space.* And they readily draw and read maps, even when the orientation of the map and the space it represents do not match (Liben, 2009; Nazareth et al., 2018). Ten- to 12-year-olds also grasp the notion of *scale*—the proportional relation between a space and its map representation (Liben, 2006). And they appreciate that in interpreting map symbols, a mapmaker's assigned meaning supersedes physical resemblance—for example, that green dots (not red dots) may indicate where red fire trucks are located (Myers & Liben, 2008).

Throughout the school years, substantial individual differences exist in children's cognitive maps, influenced by perspective-taking and mental rotation skills and ability to integrate various sources of information. Map-related experiences enhance children's map skills. When teachers asked fourth graders to write down the clues they used to decide where stickers (signifying landmark locations) should go on a map of an outdoor space, children's performance improved (Kastens & Liben, 2007). Such self-generated explanations seem to induce learners to reflect on and revise their own thinking, sparking gains in many types of problem solving from elementary school through college. And a computer-based curriculum called *Where Are We*, consisting of 12 map-reading and map-making lessons, led to substantial improvements in second to fourth graders' performance on diverse mapping tasks (Liben, Kastens, & Stevenson, 2002).

Cultural contexts influence children's map making. In many non-Western communities, people rarely use maps to find their way but rely on information from neighbors, street vendors, and shopkeepers. Also, compared to their Western agemates, non-Western children less often ride in cars and more often walk, which results in intimate neighborhood knowledge. When a researcher had 12-year-olds in small cities in India and in the United States draw maps of their neighborhoods, the Indian children represented a rich array of landmarks and aspects of social life, such as people and vehicles, in a small area surrounding their home. The U.S. children, in contrast, drew a more formal, extended space, highlighting main streets and key directions (north–south, east–west) but including few landmarks (see Figure 12.1) (Parameswaran, 2003). Although the U.S. children's maps scored higher in cognitive maturity, this difference reflected cultural interpretations of the task: When asked to create a map to "help people find their way," the Indian children drew spaces as far-reaching and organized as the U.S. children's.

This young sightseer consults a map of Amsterdam's city center to locate herself in relation to major landmarks. Development of map-related skills reflects school-age children's advancing mental representations of large-scale spaces.

LOOK and LISTEN

Ask a 6- to 8-year-old and a 9- to 12-year-old to draw a neighborhood map showing important landmarks, such as the school, a friend's house, or a shopping area. In what ways do the children's maps differ?

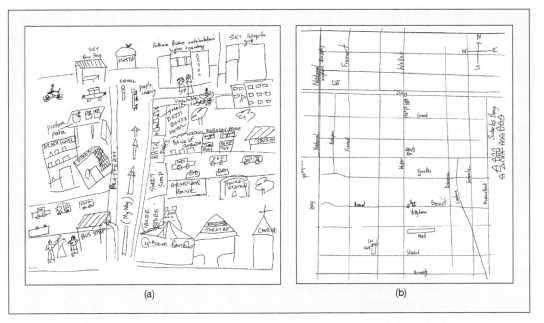

(a)   (b)

FIGURE 12.1 **Maps drawn by older school-age children from India and the United States.** (a) The Indian child depicted many landmarks and features of social life in a small area near her home. (b) The U.S. child drew a more extended space and highlighted main streets and key directions. (From G. Parameswaran, 2003, "Experimenter Instructions as a Mediator in the Effects of Culture on Mapping One's Neighborhood," *Journal of Environmental Psychology, 23*, pp. 415–416. Copyright © 2003, reprinted with permission from Elsevier, Ltd., conveyed through Copyright Clearance Center, Inc.)

12.1.2 Limitations of Concrete Operational Thought

As the name of this stage suggests, concrete operational thinking suffers from one important limitation: Children think in an organized, logical fashion only when dealing with concrete information they can perceive directly. Their mental operations work poorly with abstract ideas—ones not apparent in the real world. Consider children's solutions to transitive inference problems. When shown pairs of sticks of unequal length, Lizzie easily engaged in transitive inference. But she had great difficulty with a hypothetical version of this task: "Susan is taller than Sally, and Sally is taller than Mary. Who is the tallest?" Not until age 11 or 12 can children typically solve this problem.

That logical thought is at first tied to immediate situations helps account for a special feature of concrete operational reasoning. Children master concrete operational tasks step by step, not all at once. For example, they usually grasp conservation of number first, followed by length, liquid, and mass, and then weight. This *continuum of acquisition* (or gradual mastery) of logical concepts is another indication of the limitations of concrete operational thinking (Fischer & Bidell, 1991). Rather than coming up with general logical principles that they apply to all relevant situations, children seem to work out the logic of each problem separately.

12.1.3 Follow-Up Research on Concrete Operational Thought

According to Piaget, brain development combined with experience in a rich and varied external world should lead children everywhere to reach the concrete operational stage. Yet research indicates that cultural and school practices are influential (Rogoff, 2003). And information-processing research helps explain the gradual mastery of logical concepts in middle childhood.

A Zinacanteco Indian girl of southern Mexico learns the centuries-old practice of backstrap weaving. Although Zinacanteco children might do poorly on Piaget's tasks, they are adept at the complex mental transformations involved in converting warp strung on a loom into woven cloth.

© LAUREN GREENFIELD/INSTITUTE FOR ARTIST MANAGEMENT

The Impact of Culture and Schooling   The very experience of going to school seems to promote mastery of certain Piagetian tasks. For example, when children of the same age are tested, those who have been in school longer do better on transitive inference problems (Artman & Cahan, 1993). Opportunities to seriate objects, to learn about order relations, and to remember the parts of complex problems are probably responsible. Yet certain informal, nonschool experiences can also foster operational thought. Around age 7 to 8, Zinacanteco Indian girls of southern Mexico, who learn to weave elaborately designed fabrics as an alternative to schooling, engage in mental transformations to figure out how a warp strung on a loom will turn out as woven cloth—reasoning expected at the concrete operational stage (Maynard & Greenfield, 2003). North American children of the same age, who do much better than Zinacanteco children on Piagetian spatial tasks requiring mental transformations, have great difficulty with these weaving problems.

On the basis of such findings, some investigators have concluded that the forms of logic required by Piagetian tasks do not emerge spontaneously in children but, rather, are heavily influenced by training, context, and cultural conditions. Does this view remind you of Vygotsky's sociocultural theory, which we discussed in earlier chapters?

An Information-Processing View of Concrete Operational Thought   The gradual mastery of logical concepts in middle childhood raises a familiar question about Piaget's theory: Is an abrupt stagewise transition to logical thought the best way to describe cognitive development in middle childhood?

Some *neo-Piagetian theorists* argue that the development of operational thinking can best be understood in terms of expansion of information-processing capacity rather than a sudden shift to a new stage. For example, Robbie Case (1996, 1998) proposed that with brain development and practice, cognitive schemes demand less attention and are applied more rapidly, becoming automatic. This frees up space in working memory (see page 211 in Chapter 6) so children can focus on combining old schemes and generating new ones. For instance, as children's understanding that the height of a liquid changes after it is poured into a differently shaped container becomes routine, they notice that the width of the liquid changes as well. Soon they coordinate these observations, and they grasp conservation of liquid. Then, as this logical idea becomes well-practiced, children transfer it to more demanding situations, such as conservation of weight.

Once the schemes of a Piagetian stage are sufficiently automatic, enough working memory is available to integrate them into an improved, broadly applicable representation. As a result, children transition from concrete operations to the complex, systematic reasoning of formal operational thought, which characterizes adolescence.

Case's theory, along with other similar neo-Piagetian perspectives, helps explain why many understandings appear in specific situations at different times rather than being mastered all at once (Barrouillet & Gaillard, 2011a). First, different forms of the same logical insight, such as the various conservation tasks, vary in their processing demands, with those mastered later requiring more space in working memory. Second, children's experiences with different types of tasks vary widely, affecting their performance. Compared with Piaget's theory, neo-Piagetian approaches better account for unevenness in cognitive development (Andrews & Halford, 2011). When tasks make similar processing demands, such as Piaget's class inclusion and transitive inference problems (each of which requires children to consider three relations at once), children with relevant experiences master those tasks at about the same time.

In a practical application of conservation of liquid, a 6-year-old pours milk from a jar into a pitcher. With repeated experience, children notice how a poured liquid changes in height and width. Eventually they coordinate these observations and grasp conservation of liquid.

12.1.4 Evaluation of the Concrete Operational Stage

Piaget was correct that school-age children approach many problems in more organized, rational ways than preschoolers. But as our discussion of the neo-Piagetian approach to development of concrete operational thought suggests, disagreement continues over whether this difference reflects a *continuous* improvement in logical skills or a *discontinuous* restructuring of children's thinking (as Piaget's stage idea assumes). Many researchers think that both types of change may be involved (Andrews & Halford, 2011; Barrouillet & Gaillard, 2011b; Case, 1998; Mascolo & Fischer, 2015).

During the school years, children apply logical schemes to many more tasks. In the process, their thought seems to change qualitatively—toward a more comprehensive grasp of the underlying principles of logical thought. Piaget himself recognized this possibility in evidence for gradual mastery of conservation and other tasks. So perhaps some blend of Piagetian and information-processing ideas holds the greatest promise for explaining cognitive development in middle childhood.

 ASK YOURSELF

Connect ■ Explain how advances in perspective taking contribute to school-age children's improved ability to draw and use maps.

Apply ■ Nine-year-old Adrienne spends many hours helping her father build furniture in his woodworking shop. How might this experience facilitate Adrienne's advanced performance on Piagetian seriation problems?

Reflect ■ Which aspects of Piaget's description of the concrete operational child do you accept? Which do you doubt? Explain, citing research evidence.

12.2 Information Processing

In contrast to Piaget's focus on overall cognitive change, the information-processing perspective examines separate aspects of thinking. As noted in our discussion of Case's theory, capacity of working memory continues to increase in middle childhood, as does speed of thinking. And school-age children make strides in other facets of executive function, including control of attention and planning. Dramatic gains also occur in acquisition of memory strategies and in self-regulation. Each contributes vitally to academic learning.

12.2.1 Executive Function

As noted in Chapter 11, the school years are a time of continued development of the prefrontal cortex and its connections to other brain areas, yielding more coordinated functioning of neural networks. Consequently, executive function undergoes marked improvement (Xu et al., 2013). Children handle increasingly difficult tasks that require the integration of working memory, inhibition, and flexible thinking, which, in turn, support gains in planning, strategic thinking, and self-monitoring and self-correction of behavior.

Heritability evidence suggests substantial genetic influence on executive function (Polderman et al., 2009; Young et al., 2009). And molecular genetic analyses are identifying specific genes related to severely deficient executive-function components, such as inhibition and flexible thinking, which (as we will soon see) contribute to learning and behavior disorders, including attention-deficit hyperactivity disorder (ADHD) (refer to the Biology and Environment box on the following page).

But in both typically and atypically developing children, heredity combines with environmental factors to influence executive function. In Chapter 3, we reviewed evidence indicating that prenatal teratogens can impair impulse control, attention, planning, and other executive processes. And as we saw in Chapter 9, poverty—through stressful living conditions and maladaptive parenting practices—can undermine executive function, with powerfully negative consequences for academic achievement and social competence (Blair & Raver, 2012). As we turn now to an array of executive processes, our discussion will confirm once more that supportive home and school experiences are essential for their optimal development.

School-age children gain markedly in executive function. They can perform increasingly complex tasks—such as this science project on how flood plains form—that require the integration of working memory, inhibition, and flexible shifting of attention.

Inhibition and Flexible Shifting of Attention   School-age children become better at deliberately attending to relevant aspects of a task and inhibiting irrelevant responses. One way researchers study this increasing selectivity of attention is by introducing irrelevant stimuli into a task to see how well children attend to its central elements. For example, they might present a series of pictures of animals, each of which is either congruent with the animal's real size (a large dinosaur, a small bird) or incongruent with its real size (a large mouse, a small elephant). The child's task is to name the size of each animal in "real life"—large or small. Findings indicate that inhibition improves sharply between ages 6 and 10, with gains continuing through adolescence (Gomez-Perez & Ostrosky-Solis, 2006; Macdonald et al., 2014; Vakil et al., 2009).

Older children are also better at flexibly shifting their attention in response to task requirements. When given the *Dimensional Change Card Sort,* which requires them to switch the rules they use to sort picture cards containing conflicting cues (see page 323 in Chapter 9), schoolchildren gain steadily with age in the complexity of rules they can keep in mind and in the speed and accuracy with which they shift between the rules. Recall that flexible shifting benefits from gains in inhibition, which enables children to ignore rules that are momentarily irrelevant. Expansion of working memory is also vital: To succeed on tasks with complex rule shifting, children must keep in mind a greater number of relevant rules and update that information after each rule switch.

Biology and Environment | Children with Attention-Deficit Hyperactivity Disorder

While the other fifth graders worked quietly at their desks, Calvin squirmed, dropped his pencil, looked out the window, fiddled with his shoelaces, and talked aloud. "Hey Joey," he yelled across the room, "wanna play ball after school?" The other children weren't eager to play with Calvin, who was physically awkward and failed to follow the rules of the game. He had trouble taking turns at bat. In the outfield, he tossed his mitt up in the air and looked elsewhere when the ball came his way. Calvin's desk was a chaotic mess. He often lost pencils, books, and other school materials, and he had difficulty remembering assignments and due dates.

Symptoms of ADHD

Calvin is one of 5 to 8 percent of North American school-age children with **attention-deficit hyperactivity disorder (ADHD),** which involves inattention, impulsivity, and excessive motor activity resulting in academic and social problems (American Psychiatric Association, 2013; Danielson et al., 2018; Hauck et al., 2017). Boys are diagnosed two to three times as often as girls. However, many girls with ADHD seem to be overlooked, either because their symptoms are less flagrant or because of a gender bias: A difficult, disruptive boy is more likely to be referred for treatment (Owens, Cardoos, & Hinshaw, 2015).

Children with ADHD cannot stay focused on a task that requires mental effort for more than a few minutes. They often act impulsively, ignoring social rules and lashing out with hostility when frustrated. Many, though not all, are *hyperactive*, exhausting parents and teachers and irritating other children with their excessive motor activity. For a child to be diagnosed with ADHD, these symptoms must have appeared before age 12 as a persistent problem.

Because of their difficulty concentrating, ADHD children score lower in IQ than other children, though the difference is mostly accounted for by a small subgroup with substantially below-average scores (Biederman et al., 2012). Researchers agree that deficient executive function underlies ADHD symptoms. Children with ADHD are impaired in the ability to inhibit distracting behaviors and irrelevant information, and they score low in working-memory capacity (Antshel, Hier, & Barkley, 2015). Consequently, they have difficulty with sustained attention, planning, memory, reasoning, and problem solving in academic and social situations and often fail to manage frustration and intense emotion.

Origins of ADHD

ADHD runs in families and is highly heritable. Identical twins more often share the disorder than fraternal twins do, and full siblings more often share it than half-siblings (Eilertsen et al., 2019; Polderman et al., 2015). Children with ADHD show abnormal brain functioning, including reduced electrical and blood-flow activity and structural abnormalities in the prefrontal cortex and in other areas involved in attention, inhibition of behavior, and other aspects of motor control (Mackie et al., 2007). Also, the brains of children with ADHD grow more slowly and are about 3 percent smaller in overall volume, with a thinner cerebral cortex, than the brains of unaffected agemates (Narr et al., 2009; Shaw et al., 2007). Several genes that disrupt functioning of the neurotransmitters serotonin (involved in inhibition and self-control) and dopamine (required for effective cognitive processing) have been implicated in the disorder (Akutagava-Martins et al., 2013).

At the same time, ADHD is associated with environmental factors. Prenatal teratogens—such as tobacco, alcohol, illegal drugs, and environmental pollutants—are linked to inattention and hyperactivity (see Chapter 3). Furthermore, children with ADHD are more likely to have parents with psychological disorders and to come from homes where family stress is high (Law et al., 2014). These circumstances often intensify the child's preexisting difficulties.

Treating ADHD

Calvin's doctor eventually prescribed stimulant medication—the most common treatment for ADHD, taken by nearly two-thirds of U.S. children diagnosed with the disorder. Stimulant medication seems to increase activity in the prefrontal cortex, thereby lessening impulsivity and hyperactivity and improving attention in most children who take it (Connor, 2015; Danielson et al., 2018). However, if stimulant treatment is initiated late, after age 9 or 10, it does not reduce the decline in academic performance associated with ADHD (Zoëga et al., 2012).

By itself, drug treatment is insufficient for helping children compensate for inattention and impulsivity in everyday situations. So far, the most effective treatments combine medication with interventions that provide training in executive function skills and that model and reinforce appropriate academic and social behavior (Smith & Shapiro, 2015; Tamm, Nakonezny, & Hughes, 2014). Some evidence suggests that initiating these cognitive and behavioral interventions prior to medication treatment not only yields more favorable outcomes but also reduces the necessary dose of medication, thereby protecting children from its dose-related side effects (sleep problems, decreased appetite, and temporary slowing of physical growth) (Pelham, 2016). Some children do so well under this treatment protocol that they can stop taking low-dose medication within a year.

Family intervention is also vital. Inattentive, hyperactive children strain the patience of parents, who are likely to react punitively and inconsistently—a child-rearing style that strengthens defiant, aggressive behavior. In fact, in 50 to 75 percent of cases, these two sets of behavior problems occur together (Goldstein, 2011a).

ADHD is usually a lifelong disorder. Affected individuals are at risk for persistent antisocial behavior, depression, alcohol and drug abuse, and other problems (Wender & Tomb, 2017). Adults with ADHD continue to need help in structuring their environments, regulating negative emotion, selecting appropriate careers, and understanding their condition as a biological deficit rather than a character flaw.

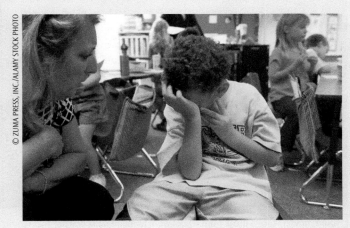

This child frequently engages in disruptive behavior at school. Children with ADHD have great difficulty staying on task and often act impulsively, ignoring social rules.

Two 7-year-olds play Uno, a game requiring executive-function skills that improve over middle childhood—the ability to keep track of changing rules of play, to inhibit irrelevant rules, and to shift attention flexibly among rules to select an appropriate card to play.

In sum, selectivity and flexibility of attention become better controlled and more efficient over middle childhood (Carlson, Zelazo, & Faja, 2013). Children can adapt their attention more quickly in the face of increasingly complex distractors—skills that contribute to more organized, strategic approaches to challenging tasks.

Working Memory   As Case's theory emphasizes, working memory profits from increased efficiency of thinking. In diverse cultures, time needed to process information on a wide variety of cognitive tasks declines rapidly between ages 6 and 12, likely due to myelination and connectivity among regions of the cerebral cortex (Kail & Ferrer, 2007; Kail et al., 2013). A faster thinker can hold on to and operate on more information at once. Still, individual differences in working-memory capacity exist, and they are of particular concern because they predict intelligence test scores and academic achievement in many subjects (DeMarie & Lopez, 2014; Nicolaou et al., 2017).

Observations of elementary school children with limited working memories revealed that they often did poorly on school assignments that made heavy memory demands (Alloway et al., 2009). They could not follow complex instructions, lost their place in tasks with multiple steps, and frequently gave up before finishing their work. The children struggled because they could not hold in mind sufficient information to complete assignments.

Children from poverty-stricken families are especially likely to score low on working-memory tasks. In one study, years of childhood spent in poverty predicted reduced working memory in early adulthood (Evans & Schamberg, 2009). Childhood neurobiological measures of stress—elevated blood pressure and levels of stress hormones, including cortisol—largely explained this poverty–working-memory association. Chronic stress, as we saw in Chapter 5, can impair brain structure and function, especially in the prefrontal cortex and its connections with the hippocampus, which govern working-memory capacity.

About 15 percent of children have very low working-memory scores (Holmes, Gathercole, & Dunning, 2010). Scaffolding in which parents and teachers modify tasks to reduce memory load is essential for these children to learn. Effective approaches include communicating in short sentences with familiar vocabulary, repeating task instructions, breaking complex tasks into manageable parts, and encouraging children to use external memory aids—for example, lists of useful spellings while writing or number lines while doing math (Gathercole & Alloway, 2008).

Training Executive Function   Children's executive function skills can be improved through training, yielding both academic and social benefits (Müller & Kerns, 2015). Both direct and indirect training approaches are effective.

To enhance control of attention and working memory, researchers often embed direct training in interactive electronic games. In one study, 10-year-olds with learning difficulties who played a game providing working-memory training four times a week for eight weeks showed substantially greater improvement in working-memory capacity, IQ, and spelling and math achievement than agemates who played less often or did not play at all (Alloway, Bibile, & Lau, 2013). Working memory, IQ, and spelling gains were still evident eight months after the training ended.

Executive function can also be enhanced indirectly, by increasing children's participation in activities—such as exercise—known to promote it (see page 421 in Chapter 11). Another indirect method is *mindfulness training,* which—similar to meditation- and yoga-based exercises for adults—encourages children to focus attention on their current thoughts, feelings, and sensations, without judging them.

Fourth graders take a break from school work to meditate, a practice that requires focused attention and reflection. Mindfulness training such as meditation leads to gains in executive function, school grades, prosocial behavior, and positive peer relations.

For example, children might be asked to attend to their own breathing or to manipulate an object held behind their backs while noticing how it feels (Zelazo & Lyons, 2012). If their attention wanders, they are told to bring it back to the current moment. Mindfulness training leads to gains in executive function, school grades, prosocial behavior, and positive peer relations (Schonert-Reichl & Lawlor, 2010; Schonert-Reichl et al., 2015). The sustained attention and reflection that mindfulness requires seem to help children avoid snap judgments, distracting thoughts and emotions, and impulsive behavior.

Planning Planning on multistep tasks improves over the school years. Older children make decisions about what to do first and what to do next in a more orderly fashion. Effective planning, however, often goes beyond implementing a sequence of moves: In many instances, children must evaluate the entire sequence *in advance* to see if it will get them to their goal.

To assess both sequential and advance planning, 4- to-10-year-olds were presented with the paddle-box illustrated in Figure 12.2. On each trial, they had to get a small item from the paddle on which an adult placed it to the open goal at the bottom of the box. The paddles could be rotated to three positions: flat, diagonal left, or diagonal right. On sequential trials, children could rotate the start paddle first and still succeed. On advance-planning trials, to prevent the object from being trapped, children needed to preset one or two other paddles before rotating the start paddle (Tecwyn, Thorpe, & Chappell, 2014). Many of the younger children succeeded at sequential planning but had difficulty with advance planning. Not until age 9 to 10 did children consistently perform well on advance-planning trials.

The development of planning illustrates how attention becomes coordinated with other cognitive processes. Children must postpone action in favor of weighing alternatives, organizing an efficient sequence of steps, and remembering the steps so they can attend to each one. Along the way, they must monitor how well the plan works and revise it if necessary.

As Chapter 9 revealed, children learn much about planning by collaborating with more expert planners. With age, they take more responsibility in these joint endeavors, such as suggesting planning strategies and organizing task materials. The demands of school tasks—and

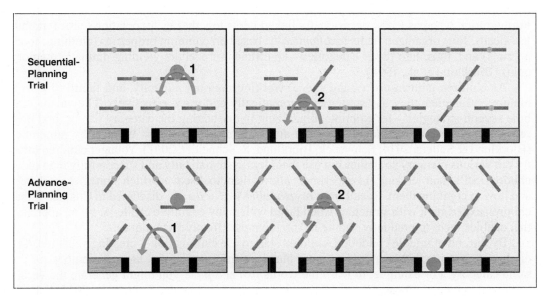

FIGURE 12.2 **Examples of sequential- and advance-planning solutions using the paddle box.**
An adult placed a small item on one of the horizontal paddles within the box, visible to the child through its transparent cover. Children had to get the item to the open goal at the bottom of the box. The paddles could be rotated to three positions—flat, diagonal left, or diagonal right—using handles extending out the front of the box. (a) In sequential planning, rotating the start paddle first, without presetting other paddles, leads to success. (b) In advance planning, children must preset at least one other paddle before rotating the start paddle. (From E. C. Tecwyn, S. K. S. Thorpe, & J. Chappell, 2014, "Development of Planning in 4- to 10-Year-Old Children: Reducing Inhibitory Demands Does Not Improve Performance," *Journal of Experimental Child Psychology, 125,* p. 92. Copyright © 2014 with permission from Elsevier, Ltd., conveyed through Copyright Clearance Center, Inc.)

teachers' explanations of how to plan—also contribute to gains in planning. As early as first grade, planning skills predict later reading and math achievement (Friedman et al., 2014).

But adult-controlled activities may rob children of opportunities to plan. In one study, researchers videotaped small groups of first and second graders devising plays that they would perform for their class (Baker-Sennett, Matusov, & Rogoff, 2008). Some groups were child-led; others were led by adult volunteers. Child-led groups engaged in extensive planning—brainstorming themes and working out the details of their improvisations. But when adults planned the play in advance, the children spent most of their time in nonplanning pursuits, such as rehearsing lines and making play props. The adults missed a rich opportunity to scaffold learning (see page 320 in Chapter 9) by turning over responsibility for play planning to the children and guiding and supporting, as needed.

12.2.2 Memory Strategies

As attention improves, so do *memory strategies,* the deliberate mental activities we use to store and retain information. When 6-year-old Lizzie had a list of things to learn, such as the state capitals of the United States or the names of geometric shapes, she immediately used **rehearsal**—repeating the information to herself. Attention supports rehearsal by enabling children to focus on memory traces of the items they are learning. And language proficiency predicts the emergence of rehearsal in the early school years, perhaps because a certain vocabulary size and the ability to automatically name items is necessary for children to use the strategy (Bebko et al., 2014; Oftinger & Camos, 2018). Around 8 to 9 years, a second strategy typically appears when adults prompt children to use it: **organization**—grouping related items together (for example, all animals, tools, vehicles), an approach that greatly improves recall (Schleepen & Jonkman, 2014).

Perfecting memory strategies requires time and effort. For example, Lizzie rehearsed in a piecemeal fashion. After being given the word cat in a list of words, she said, "Cat, cat, cat." But 10-year-old Joey combined previous words with each new item, saying, "Desk, man, yard, cat, cat." This active, cumulative approach, in which neighboring words create contexts for each other that trigger recall, yields much better memory (Lehman & Hasselhorn, 2012). Furthermore, whereas Lizzy occasionally linked items together by association (carrot–rabbit, hat–head), Joey organized items *taxonomically,* based on common properties (clothing, food, animals) and, thus, into fewer categories—an efficient procedure yielding dramatic memory gains (Bjorklund et al., 1994).

As children gain in processing speed, working-memory capacity, and familiarity with memory strategies, they use strategies automatically and more effectively. They also combine several strategies—for example, organizing items, stating the category names, and then rehearsing. The more strategies children apply simultaneously, the better they remember (Bjorklund & Sellers, 2014; Schwenck, Bjorklund, & Schneider, 2007). Younger children often try out various memory strategies but use them less systematically and successfully than older children. Still, their tendency to experiment allows them to discover which strategies work best and how to combine them. Recall from *overlapping-waves theory,* discussed in Chapter 9, that children experiment with strategies when faced with many cognitive challenges—an approach that enables them to gradually "home in" on the most effective techniques.

By the end of middle childhood, children start to use **elaboration**—creating a relationship, or shared meaning, between two or more pieces of information that are not members of the same category. For example, to learn the words *fish* and *pipe,* you might generate the verbal statement or mental image, "The fish is smoking a pipe" (Schneider & Ornstein, 2015; Schneider & Pressley, 1997). This highly effective memory technique, which requires considerable effort and space in working memory, becomes increasingly common in adolescence.

Because organization and elaboration combine items into *meaningful chunks,* they permit children to hold onto much more information and, as a result, further expand working memory. In addition, when children link a new item to information they already know, they can *retrieve* it easily by thinking of other items associated with it. As we will see, this also contributes to improved memory during the school years.

12.2.3 Knowledge and Memory

During middle childhood, children's general knowledge base, or *semantic memory*, grows larger and becomes organized into increasingly elaborate, hierarchically structured networks. This rapid growth of knowledge helps children use strategies to remember (Schneider, 2002). Knowing more about a topic makes new information more meaningful and familiar, so it is easier to store and retrieve.

To investigate this idea, school-age children who were expert chess players were tested on how well they could remember complex chessboard arrangements. Then their performance was compared with that of adults who knew how to play chess but were not especially knowledgeable. The children's expert knowledge enabled them to reproduce the chessboard configurations considerably better than the adults could (Bédard & Chi, 1992).

In another study, researchers classified fourth graders as either experts or novices in knowledge of soccer and then gave both groups lists of soccer and nonsoccer items to learn. Experts remembered far more items on the soccer list (but not on the nonsoccer list) than novices. And during recall, the experts' listing of items was better organized, as indicated by clustering of items into categories (Schneider & Bjorklund, 1992). This superior organization at retrieval suggests that highly knowledgeable children organize information in their area of expertise with little or no effort—by rapidly associating new items with the large number they already know. Consequently, experts can devote more working-memory resources to using recalled information to reason and solve problems.

But knowledge is not the only important factor in children's strategic memory processing. Children who are expert in an area are usually highly motivated. As a result, they not only acquire knowledge more quickly but also *actively use what they know* to add more. In contrast, academically unsuccessful children often fail to ask how previously stored information can clarify new material. This, in turn, interferes with the development of a broad knowledge base (Schneider & Bjorklund, 1998). So extensive knowledge and use of memory strategies support each other.

12.2.4 Culture, Schooling, and Memory Strategies

Rehearsal, organization, and elaboration are techniques that children and adults usually use when they need to remember information for its own sake. On many other occasions, memories form as a natural byproduct of participation in daily activities. For example, Joey can spout a wealth of facts about baseball teams and players—information he picked up from watching ball games, discussing the games, and trading baseball cards with his friends. And without prior rehearsal, he can recount the story line of an exciting movie or novel—narrative material that is already meaningfully organized.

A repeated finding is that people in village cultures who have little formal schooling do not use or benefit from instruction in memory strategies because they see no practical reason to use them (Rogoff, 2003). Tasks requiring children to engage in isolated recall, which are common in classrooms, strongly motivate memory strategies. In fact, children in developed nations get so much practice with this type of learning that they do not refine techniques that rely on cues available in everyday life, such as spatial location and arrangement of objects. For example, Guatemalan Mayan 9-year-olds do slightly better than their U.S. agemates when told to remember the placement of 40 familiar objects in a play scene (Rogoff & Waddell, 1982). U.S. children often rehearse object names when it would be more effective to keep track of spatial relations, as Mayan children do.

Societal modernization, as indicated by the presence of communication, literacy, and other economically advantageous resources in homes—such as books, writing tablets, electricity, radio, TV, computers, and car ownership—is

A teacher in Bafoussam, Cameroon, guides 7- to 10-year-olds in the use of educational software. Societal modernization—access to contemporary resources for communication and literacy—is broadly associated with cognitive skills valued in industrialized nations.

broadly associated with performance on cognitive tasks commonly administered to children in industrialized nations. In an investigation in which researchers rated towns in Belize, Kenya, Nepal, and American Samoa for degree of modernization, Belize and American Samoa exceeded Kenya and Nepal (Gauvain & Munroe, 2009). Modernity predicted both extent of schooling and 5- to 9-year-olds' cognitive scores—on a memory test plus an array of other measures.

In sum, the development of memory strategies and other cognitive skills valued in complex societies is not just a product of a more competent information-processing system. It also depends on task demands, schooling, and cultural circumstances.

12.2.5 The School-Age Child's Theory of Mind

During middle childhood, children's *theory of mind,* or set of beliefs about mental activities, becomes much more elaborate and refined. Recall from Chapter 9 that this awareness of thought is often called *metacognition.* Children's improved ability to reflect on their own mental life is another reason that their thinking and problem solving advance.

Knowledge of Cognitive Capacities   Unlike preschoolers, who view the mind as a passive container of information, older children regard it as an active, constructive agent that selects and transforms information (Astington & Hughes, 2013). Consequently, they have a much better understanding of cognitive processes and the impact of psychological factors on performance. For example, with age, elementary school children become increasingly aware of effective memory strategies and why they work (Alexander et al., 2003). And they gradually grasp relationships between mental activities—for example, that remembering is crucial for understanding and that understanding strengthens memory (Schwanenflugel, Henderson, & Fabricius, 1998).

Furthermore, school-age children's understanding of sources of knowledge expands. They are aware that people can extend their knowledge not only by directly observing events and talking to others but also by making *mental inferences* (Miller, Hardin, & Montgomery, 2003). This grasp of inference enables knowledge of *false belief* to expand. In several studies, researchers told children complex stories involving one character's belief about a second character's belief. Then the children answered questions about what the first character thought the second character would do (see Figure 12.3). By age 6 to 7, children were aware that people form beliefs about other people's beliefs and that these *second-order beliefs* can be wrong!

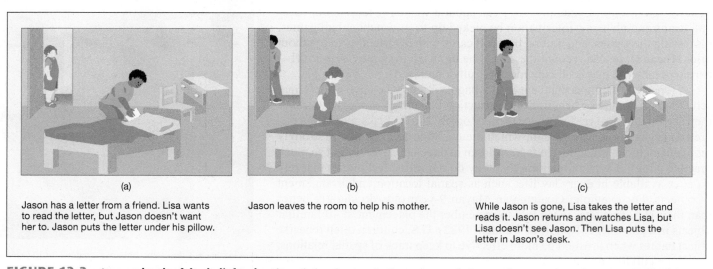

(a)   (b)   (c)

Jason has a letter from a friend. Lisa wants to read the letter, but Jason doesn't want her to. Jason puts the letter under his pillow.

Jason leaves the room to help his mother.

While Jason is gone, Lisa takes the letter and reads it. Jason returns and watches Lisa, but Lisa doesn't see Jason. Then Lisa puts the letter in Jason's desk.

FIGURE 12.3   A second-order false belief task. After relating the story in the sequence of pictures, the researcher asks a second-order false-belief question: "Where does Lisa think Jason will look for the letter? Why?" Around age 7, children answer correctly—that Lisa thinks Jason will look under his pillow because Lisa doesn't know that Jason saw her put the letter in the desk. (Adapted from Astington, Pelletier, & Homer, 2002.)

Appreciation of *second-order false belief* enables children to pinpoint the reasons that another person arrived at a certain belief (Miller, 2013). Notice how it requires the ability to view a situation from at least two perspectives—that is, to reason simultaneously about what two or more people are thinking, a form of perspective taking called **recursive thought.** We think recursively when we make such statements as, *"Lisa believes* that *Jason believes* the letter is under his pillow, but that's *not what Jason really believes; he knows* the letter is in the desk."

The capacity for recursive thought greatly assists children in appreciating that people can harbor quite different interpretations of the same situation. For example, 6- to 7-year-olds understand that when two people view the same object, their trains of thought will differ because of variations in their knowledge, experiences, or other characteristics (Eisbach, 2004). They realize that the same reality can legitimately be construed in multiple ways. Indeed, children's newfound awareness of varying viewpoints is so powerful that, at first, they over-extend it (Lagattuta, Sayfan, & Blattman, 2010). Six- and 7-year-olds are especially likely to overlook the fact that people with differing past experiences sometimes agree! Not surprisingly, school-age children who score higher on theory-of-mind tasks are rated by their teachers as more socially competent (Devine et al., 2016).

Electrical brain-wave and neuroimaging evidence reveals that from age 6 to 11, children become increasingly selective in the brain regions they recruit when thinking about another's mental states (Bowman et al., 2012; Gweon et al., 2012). In addition to the prefrontal cortex, they activate an area connecting the right temporal and parietal lobes (known to play a crucial role in theory-of-mind processes), just as adults do.

Schooling contributes to a more reflective, process-oriented view of the mind. In a study of rural children of Cameroon, Africa, those who attended school performed much better on theory-of-mind tasks (Vinden, 2002). In school, teachers often call attention to the workings of the mind when they remind children to pay attention, remember mental steps, share points of view with peers, and evaluate their own and others' reasoning. As recursive perspective taking becomes more secure, children more often use persuasive strategies to try to change others' viewpoints (Bartsch, London, & Campbell, 2007). They also grasp complex, recursive verbal expressions, such as irony and sarcasm, as we will see later when we address language development.

Knowledge of Strategies   Consistent with their more active view of the mind, school-age children are far more conscious of mental strategies than preschoolers. When shown video clips depicting two children using different recall strategies and asked which one is likely to produce better memory, kindergarten and young elementary school children knew that rehearsing or organizing is better than looking or naming (Justice, 1986; Schneider, 1986). Older children were aware of more subtle differences—that organizing is better than rehearsing.

Between third and fifth grade, children develop a much better appreciation of how and why strategies work (Alexander et al., 2003). Consequently, fifth graders are consider-ably better than younger children at discriminating good from bad reasoning. When given examples varying in quality, fifth graders consistently rated "good" reasoning as based on weighing of possibilities (rather than jumping to conclusions) and gathering of evidence (rather than ignoring important facts), even if such reasoning led to an unfavorable result (Amsterlaw, 2006).

12.2.6 Cognitive Self-Regulation

Although metacognition expands, school-age children frequently have difficulty putting what they know about thinking into action. They are not yet good at **cognitive self-regulation,** the process of continuously monitoring progress toward a goal, checking outcomes, and redirect-ing unsuccessful efforts. For example, Lizzie is aware that she should attend closely to her teacher's directions, group items when memorizing, reread a complicated paragraph to make sure she understands it, and relate new information to what she already knows. But she does not always engage in these activities.

LOOK and LISTEN

Watch a teacher explain a learning activity to 6- to 8-year-olds. How often did the teacher call attention to the workings of the mind?

A second grader helps a classmate complete a project. Providing school-age children with opportunities to teach others promotes deeper learning and increased self-regulation.

To study cognitive self-regulation, researchers sometimes look at the impact of children's awareness of memory strategies on how well they remember. By second grade, the more children know about memory strategies, the more they recall—a relationship that strengthens over middle childhood (DeMarie et al., 2004; Geurten, Catale, & Meulemans, 2015). And when children apply a strategy consistently, their knowledge of strategies strengthens, resulting in a bidirectional relationship between metacognition and strategic processing that enhances self-regulation (Schlagmüller & Schneider, 2002).

Why does cognitive self-regulation develop gradually? Monitoring learning outcomes is cognitively demanding, requiring constant evaluation of effort and progress. Throughout elementary and secondary school, self-regulation predicts academic success (Zimmerman & Labuhn, 2012). Students who do well in school know when their learning is going well and when it is not. If they encounter obstacles, they take steps to address them—for example, organize the learning environment, review confusing material, or seek support from more-expert adults or peers (Schunk & Zimmerman, 2013). This active, purposeful approach contrasts sharply with the passive orientation of students who achieve poorly.

Parents and teachers can foster self-regulation. In one study, researchers observed parents instructing their children on a problem-solving task during the summer before third grade. Parents who patiently pointed out important features of the task, suggested strategies, and explained why they were helpful had children who, in the classroom, more often discussed ways to approach problems and monitored their own performance (Stright et al., 2002).

Providing school-age children with opportunities to teach academic content to others is also effective. In another investigation, 11-year-olds were randomly assigned to a preparing-to-teach or a learning-for-learning (control) condition and then given a complex, multistep math problem to solve. Those in the preparing-to-teach group displayed a more organized and detailed understanding of the problem and more effective self-regulation, including monitoring the effectiveness of their strategies and changing direction as needed. As a result, they arrived at higher-quality solutions (Muis et al., 2015). In an effort to ensure they would be able to explain what they knew to others, the children preparing to teach engaged in deeper learning.

Children who acquire effective self-regulatory skills develop a sense of *academic self-efficacy*—confidence in their own ability, which supports future self-regulation (Fernandez-Rio et al., 2017). Unfortunately, some children receive messages from parents and teachers that seriously undermine their academic self-esteem and self-regulatory skills. We will consider these *learned-helpless* students, along with ways to help them, in Chapter 13.

12.2.7 Applications of Information Processing to Academic Learning

When Joey completed kindergarten, he recognized some familiar written words, used what he knew about letter–sound relations to decode simple words, predicted what might happen next in a beginning-reader story, and could retell its main events in sequence. In second grade, he read grade-level books independently, used story context to help identify unfamiliar words, and read aloud with expression. By fourth grade, he was a proficient reader who understood different types of texts, including biographies, fiction, and poetry.

In math, as a new first grader Joey counted to 100 by ones and tens, performed one-digit addition and subtraction with ease, and could decompose the numbers from 11 to 19 to determine, "How many more than 10" as the foundation for understanding place value. In third grade, he used his grasp of place value to perform two-digit arithmetic, multiplied and divided within 100, and had begun to master fractions and percentages.

Fundamental discoveries about the development of information processing have been applied to children's learning of reading and mathematics. Researchers are identifying the cognitive ingredients of skilled performance, tracing their development, and distinguishing good from poor learners by pinpointing differences in cognitive skills. They hope, as a result, to design teaching methods that will improve children's learning.

Reading   Reading makes use of many skills at once, taxing all aspects of our information-processing systems. We must perceive single letters and letter combinations, translate them into speech sounds, recognize the visual appearance of many common words, hold chunks of text in working memory while interpreting their meaning, and combine the meanings of various parts of a text passage into an understandable whole. Because reading is so demanding, most or all of these skills must be done automatically. If one or more are poorly developed, they will compete for resources in our limited working memories, and reading performance will decline.

As children make the transition from emergent literacy to conventional reading, *phonological awareness,* vocabulary growth, and narrative competence (see page 333 in Chapter 9) continue to facilitate their progress. Other information-processing skills also contribute. Gains in processing speed foster children's rapid conversion of visual symbols into sounds (Moll et al., 2014). Visual scanning and discrimination play important roles and improve with reading experience (Rayner, Pollatsek, & Starr, 2003). Performing these skills efficiently releases working memory for higher-level activities involved in comprehending the text's meaning.

Until recently, researchers were involved in an intense debate over how to teach beginning reading. The *whole-language approach* exposes children to text in its complete form—stories, poems, letters, posters, and lists. It assumes that by keeping reading whole and meaningful, children will be motivated to discover the specific skills they need. The *phonics approach,* in contrast, is grounded in the view that word reading skills must be explicitly taught to beginning readers. It coaches children on the basic rules for translating written symbols into sounds before giving them complex reading material.

Many studies show that children learn best with a mixture of both approaches. In kindergarten, first, and second grades, teaching that includes phonics boosts reading scores, especially for children who lag behind in reading progress (Brady, 2011; Henbest & Apel, 2017). Coaching in letter–sound relationships enables children to *decode,* or decipher, words they have never seen before. Children who enter school low in phonological awareness make far better reading progress when given training in phonics (Casalis & Cole, 2009). Soon they detect new letter–sound relations while reading on their own, and as their fluency in decoding words increases, they are freer to attend to text meaning. Without early phonics training, such children (many of whom come from low-SES families) are substantially behind their age-mates in text comprehension skills by third grade (Foster & Miller, 2007).

Yet too much emphasis on basic skills may cause children to lose sight of the goal of reading: understanding. Children who read aloud fluently without registering meaning

In this second-grade classroom, teaching of phonics is embedded in captivating stories. In the early school grades, coaching in letter–sound relationships enhances children's fluency in decoding words, so they are freer to attend to text meaning.

know little about effective reading strategies—for example, that they must read more carefully if they will be tested than if they are reading for pleasure, that relating ideas in the text to personal experiences and general knowledge will deepen understanding, and that explaining a passage in one's own words is a good way to assess comprehension. Teaching aimed at increasing awareness and use of reading strategies enhances reading performance from third grade on (Lonigan, 2015; McKeown & Beck, 2009).

Furthermore, acquiring the English spelling system strengthens reading comprehension. It helps children distinguish the many words with different meanings that sound the same (such as *here* and *hear*) (Bowers & Bowers, 2017). Likewise, spelling similarities help children identify word meanings (for example, the similar spellings of *here, there,* and *where* specify location, whereas the spelling of *hear* links it to the word *ear*). Lessons in such spelling regularities are especially effective in enhancing the reading progress of children struggling with reading and those learning English as a second language (Goodwin & Ahn, 2010, 2013).

TABLE 12.1 **Sequence of Reading Development**

GRADE/AGE	DEVELOPMENT
Preschool 2–5 years	"Pretends" to read; recognizes some familiar signs ("ON," "OFF," "PIZZA"); "pretends" to write; prints own name and other words
Kindergarten 5–6 years	Knows the most frequent letter–sound correspondences; recognizes some familiar written words; decodes simple, one-syllable words; retells story main events in sequence
Grades 1 and 2 6–7 years	Knows letter–sound correspondences for common double consonants; decodes regularly spelled one-syllable words; recognizes some irregularly spelled words; reads grade-level texts with increasing accuracy on repeated readings
Grades 2 and 3 7–8 years	Reads grade-level stories more fluently; knows letter–sound correspondences for common vowel combinations; decodes multisyllable words and an increasing number of irregularly spelled words; reads grade-level stories more fluently and expressively, while also comprehending
Grades 4 to 9 9–15 years	Reads to acquire new knowledge, usually without questioning the reading material; understands different types of texts, including biographies, fiction, and poetry
Grades 10 to 12 15–18 years	Reads more widely, tapping materials with diverse viewpoints

Source: Chall, 1983; Common Core, 2019.

Table 12.1 charts the general sequence of reading development. Notice the major shift, around age 7 to 8, from "learning to read" to "reading to learn" (Melzi & Schick, 2013). As decoding and comprehension skills reach a high level of efficiency, older readers become actively engaged with the text. They adjust the way they read to fit their current purpose—sometimes seeking new facts and ideas, sometimes questioning, agreeing with, or disagreeing with the writer's viewpoint.

Mathematics Mathematics teaching in elementary school builds on and greatly enriches children's informal knowledge of number concepts and counting. Written notation systems and formal computational techniques enhance children's ability to represent numbers and compute. Over the early elementary school years, children acquire basic math facts through a combination of frequent practice, experimentation with diverse computational procedures (through which they discover faster, more accurate techniques), reasoning about number concepts, and teaching that conveys effective strategies. (Return to pages 334–336 in Chapter 9 for research supporting the importance of both extended practice and a grasp of concepts.)

Eventually children apply their basic knowledge to more complex problems. A vital foundation of their mathematical development is the gradual expansion of a *mental number line,* which they first extend to the right with larger whole numbers, next start to fill in with fractions, and then extend to the left with negative numbers (see Figure 12.4). As children gain counting and computation experience with ranges of numbers—typically, 0–10 in early childhood, 0–100 between ages 5 and 7, and 0–1,000 between ages 7 and 12—this spatial representation of numerical magnitudes enlarges and becomes more accurate (Siegler, 2016). Studies carried out in North America, Europe, and East Asia reveal that the quality of children's mental number lines predicts current and later math achievement, even after other relevant factors such as IQ, executive function, and SES are controlled (Bailey et al., 2015; Resnick et al., 2016; Siegler et al., 2012).

Arguments about how to teach mathematics resemble those about reading, pitting drill in computing against conceptual understanding. As with reading, a blend of both approaches is most beneficial (Rittle-Johnson, Schneider, & Star, 2015). In learning basic math, poorly performing students use cumbersome, error-prone techniques or try to retrieve answers from memory too soon. They have not sufficiently experimented with strategies to see which are most effective or to reorganize their observations in logical, efficient ways—for example,

FIGURE 12.4 Typical mental number lines of school-age children. During the elementary school years, children's mental number lines expand to the right to include larger whole numbers, in between to include fractions, and to the left to include negative numbers. (From R. S. Siegler, 2016, "Magnitude Knowledge: The Common Core of Numerical Development," *Developmental Science, 19*, p. 353. Copyright © 2016 John Wiley & Sons, Ltd. Adapted by permission.)

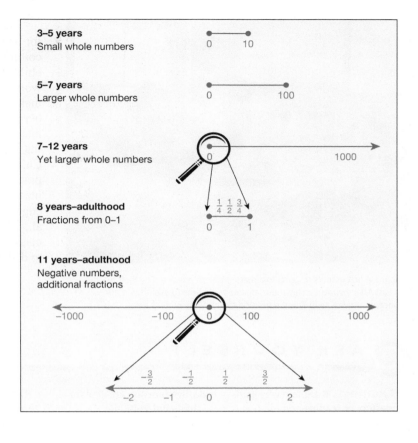

noticing that multiplication problems involving 2 (2×8) are equivalent to addition doubles ($8 + 8$). On tasks assessing their grasp of math concepts, their performance is weak (Clements & Sarama, 2012). This suggests that teaching math concepts, including the reasons certain computation strategies work well, is essential for solid mastery of basic math.

A similar picture emerges for more complex skills, such as carrying in addition, borrowing in subtraction, and operating with decimals and fractions. Children taught by rote cannot apply the procedure to new problems. Instead, they persistently make mistakes, often following a "math rule" that they recall incorrectly because they do not understand it (Carpenter et al., 1999). Look at the following subtraction errors:

$$
\begin{array}{r}
427 \\
-138 \\
\hline
311
\end{array}
\qquad
\begin{array}{r}
7002 \\
-5445 \\
\hline
1447
\end{array}
$$

In the first problem, the child consistently subtracts a smaller from a larger digit, regardless of which is on top. In the second, the child skips columns with zeros in a borrowing operation and, whenever there is a zero on top, writes the bottom digit as the answer.

Children who are given rich opportunities to build an understanding of numerical magnitudes, experiment with problem solving, appreciate the reasons behind strategies, and evaluate solution techniques by explaining them to others seldom make such errors (Fuchs et al., 2016). In one study, second graders taught in these ways not only mastered correct procedures but even invented their own successful strategies, some of which were superior to standard, school-taught methods (Fuson & Burghard, 2003). Consider this solution:

$$
\begin{array}{cccc}
3 & 15 & 14 & 12 \\
\cancel{4} & \cancel{6} & \cancel{5} & \cancel{2} \\
-1 & 9 & 6 & 8 \\
\hline
2 & 6 & 8 & 4
\end{array}
$$

In subtracting, the child performed all trades first, flexibly moving either from right to left or from left to right, and then subtracted all four columns—a highly efficient, accurate approach.

Children with a solid grasp of math concepts draw on their knowledge of relationships between operations (for example, that the inverse of division is multiplication) to generate efficient, flexible procedures: To solve the division problem 360/9, they might multiply $9 \times 40 = 360$. And because such children have been encouraged to estimate answers, if they go down the wrong track in computation, they are usually self-correcting. Furthermore, they appreciate connections between math operations and problem contexts (De Corte & Verschaffel, 2006). They can solve a word problem ("Jesse spent $3.45 for bananas, $2.62 for bread, and $3.55 for peanut butter. Can he pay for it all with a $10 bill?") quickly through estimation instead of exact calculation.

Japanese first graders respond to a math problem presented by their teacher. In East Asian countries, classrooms devote more time to exploring math concepts and less to drill and repetition than U.S. classrooms do.

In East Asian countries, students receive a variety of supports for acquiring mathematical knowledge and often excel at math computation and reasoning. Use of the metric system helps Asian children grasp place value. The consistent structure of number words in Asian languages (*ten-two* for 12, *ten-three* for 13) also makes this idea clear (Okamoto, 2015). And because Asian number words are shorter and more quickly pronounced than those in many other languages, they permit more digits to be held in working memory at once, increasing speed of thinking. Furthermore, Chinese parents provide their children with extensive everyday practice in counting and computation—experiences that contribute to the superiority of Chinese over U.S. children's math knowledge, even before they start school (Siegler & Mu, 2008; Zhou et al., 2006). Finally, as we will see later in this chapter, East Asian classrooms devote more time to exploring math concepts and less to drill and repetition than U.S. classrooms do.

⊚ ASK YOURSELF

Connect ■ Explain why gains in executive function are vital for mastery of reading and math in middle childhood.

Apply ■ Lizzie knows that if you have difficulty learning part of a task, you should devote extra attention to that part. But she plays each of her piano pieces from beginning to end instead of practicing the hard parts. Explain why Lizzie does not engage in cognitive self-regulation.

Reflect ■ In your elementary school math education, how much emphasis was placed on computational drill and how much on understanding concepts? How do you think that balance affected your interest and performance in math?

12.3 Individual Differences in Mental Development

12.3a Describe major approaches to defining and measuring intelligence.

12.3b Describe evidence indicating that both heredity and environment contribute to intelligence.

Around age 6, IQ becomes more stable than it was at earlier ages, and it correlates moderately well with academic achievement, typically around .50 to .60. Children with higher IQs are also more likely to attain higher levels of education and enter more cognitively complex, higher paid occupations in adulthood (Deary et al., 2007). Because IQ predicts school performance and educational attainment, it often enters into important educational decisions. Do intelligence tests accurately assess school-age children's ability to profit from academic instruction? Let's look closely at this controversial issue.

12.3.1 Defining and Measuring Intelligence

Virtually all intelligence tests provide an overall score (the IQ), which represents *general intelligence*, or reasoning ability, along with an array of separate scores measuring specific mental abilities. But intelligence is a collection of many capacities, not all of which are included on currently available intelligence tests (Sternberg, 2018b). Test designers use a complicated statistical technique called *factor analysis* to identify the various abilities that intelligence tests measure. It identifies which sets of test items cluster together, meaning that test-takers who do well on one item in the cluster tend to do well on the others. Distinct clusters are called *factors,* each of which represents an ability. Figure 12.5 illustrates typical items included in intelligence tests for children.

Although *group-administered* tests are available that permit large numbers of students to be tested at once, intelligence is most often assessed with *individually administered* tests, which are best suited to identifying highly intelligent children and diagnosing children with learning problems. During an individually administered test, a well-trained examiner not only considers the child's answers but also observes the child's behavior, noting such reactions as attention to and interest in the tasks and wariness of the adult. These observations provide insight into whether the test results accurately reflect the child's abilities. Two individual tests—the Stanford-Binet and the Wechsler—are used especially often.

The contemporary descendent of Alfred Binet's first successful intelligence test is the *Stanford-Binet Intelligence Scales, Fifth Edition,* for individuals from age 2 to adulthood. In addition to general intelligence, it assesses five intellectual factors: general knowledge, quantitative reasoning, visual–spatial processing, working memory, and basic information processing (such as speed of analyzing information). Each factor includes a verbal mode and a nonverbal mode of testing (Roid, 2003; Roid & Pomplun, 2012). The nonverbal mode is useful when assessing individuals with limited English, hearing impairments, or communication disorders. The knowledge and quantitative reasoning factors emphasize culturally loaded, fact-oriented information, such as vocabulary and arithmetic problems. In contrast, the visual–spatial processing, working-memory, and basic information-processing factors are assumed to be less culturally biased because they require little specific information (see the spatial visualization item in Figure 12.5).

The *Wechsler Intelligence Scale for Children (WISC-V)* is the fifth edition of a widely used test for 6- through 16-year-olds. A downward extension of it, the *Wechsler Preschool and Primary Scale of Intelligence–Revised (WPPSI–III),* is appropriate for children 2 years 6 months through 7 years 3 months. The WISC-V measures general intelligence and an array of intellectual factors, five of which are recommended for a comprehensive evaluation of a child's intellectual ability: verbal comprehension, visual–spatial reasoning, fluid reasoning (assessing ability to apply rules in reasoning and to detect conceptual relationships among objects), working memory, and processing speed (Weiss et al., 2015). The WISC-V was designed to downplay culture-dependent information, which is emphasized on only one factor (verbal comprehension). The goal is to provide a test that is as "culture-fair" as possible.

TYPICAL VERBAL ITEMS

Vocabulary — Tell me what *carpet* means.

General Information — What day of the week comes right after Thursday?

Verbal Comprehension — Why do we need police officers?

Similarities — How are a ship and a train alike?

Quantitative Reasoning — If a $60 jacket is 25% off, how much does it cost?

TYPICAL PERCEPTUAL- AND SPATIAL-REASONING ITEMS

Block Design — Make these blocks look just like the picture.

Picture Concepts — Choose one object from each row to make a group of objects that goes together.

Spatial Visualization — Which of the boxes on the right can be made from the pattern on the left?

TYPICAL WORKING-MEMORY ITEMS

Digit Span — Repeat these digits in the same order. Now repeat these digits (a similar series) backward.
2, 6, 4, 7, 1, 8

Letter–Number Sequencing — Repeat these numbers and letters, first giving the numbers, then the letters, each in correct sequence.
8 G 4 B 5 N 2

TYPICAL PROCESSING-SPEED ITEM

Symbol Search — If the shape on the left is the same as any of those on the right, mark YES. If the shape is not the same, mark NO. Work as quickly as you can without making mistakes.

FIGURE 12.5 **Test items like those on commonly used intelligence tests for children.** The verbal items emphasize culturally loaded, fact-oriented information. The perceptual- and spatial-reasoning, working-memory, and processing-speed items emphasize aspects of information processing and are assumed to assess more biologically based skills.

12.3.2 Other Efforts to Define Intelligence

As we have seen, intelligence tests now tap important aspects of information processing. In line with this trend, some researchers have combined the mental-testing approach to defining intelligence with the information-processing approach. These investigators look for relationships between aspects of information processing and children's intelligence test scores. They believe that once we identify the processing skills that separate individuals who test well from those who test poorly, we will know more about how to intervene to improve performance.

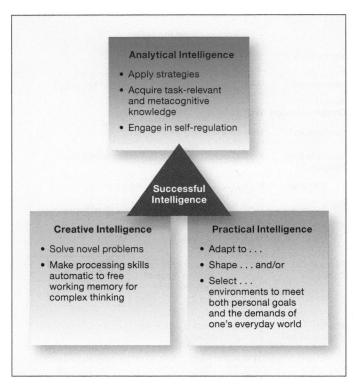

FIGURE 12.6 **Sternberg's triarchic theory of successful intelligence.** People who behave intelligently balance three interrelated intelligences—analytical, creative, and practical—to achieve success in life, defined by their personal goals and the requirements of their cultural communities.

Processing speed, assessed in terms of reaction time on diverse cognitive tasks, is moderately related to IQ (Coyle, 2013; Schubert, Hagemann, & Frischkorn, 2017). Individuals whose nervous systems function more efficiently, permitting them to take in more information and manipulate it quickly, appear to have an edge in intellectual skills. And not surprisingly, executive function strongly predicts general intelligence (Brydges et al., 2012; Schweizer, Moosebrugger, & Goldhammer, 2006). We have seen that the components of executive function are vital for success on a great many cognitive tasks.

Individual differences in intelligence, however, are not entirely due to causes within the child. Throughout this book, we have seen how cultural and situational factors also affect children's thinking. Robert Sternberg has devised a comprehensive theory that regards intelligence as a product of both inner and outer forces.

Sternberg's Triarchic Theory As Figure 12.6 shows, Sternberg's (2008, 2013, 2018) **triarchic theory of successful intelligence** is made up of three broad, interacting intelligences: (1) *analytical intelligence,* or information-processing skills; (2) *creative intelligence,* the capacity to solve novel problems; and (3) *practical intelligence,* application of intellectual skills in everyday situations. Intelligent behavior involves balancing all three intelligences to achieve success in life according to one's personal goals and the requirements of one's cultural community.

Analytical Intelligence *Analytical intelligence* consists of the information-processing components that underlie all intelligent acts: executive function, strategic thinking, knowledge acquisition, and cognitive self-regulation. But on intelligence tests, processing skills are used in only a few of their potential ways, resulting in far too narrow a view of intelligent behavior. As we have seen, children in village societies do not necessarily perform well on measures of "school" knowledge but thrive when processing information in out-of-school situations.

Creative Intelligence In any context, success depends not only on processing familiar information but also on generating useful solutions to new problems. People who are *creative* think more skillfully than others when faced with novelty. Given a new task, they apply their information-processing skills in exceptionally effective ways, rapidly making these skills automatic so that working memory is freed for more complex aspects of the situation. Consequently, they quickly move to high-level performance. Although all of us are capable of some creativity, only a few individuals excel at generating novel solutions.

Practical Intelligence Finally, the application of intelligence is a *practical,* goal-oriented activity aimed at *adapting to, shaping,* or *selecting environments.* Intelligent people skillfully adapt their thinking to fit with both their desires and the demands of their everyday worlds. When they cannot adapt to a situation, they try to *shape,* or change, it to meet their needs. If they cannot shape it, they *select* new contexts that better match their skills, values, or goals. Practical intelligence reminds us that intelligent behavior is never culture-free. Children with certain life histories do well at the behaviors required for success on intelligence tests and adapt easily to the testing conditions and tasks. Others, with different backgrounds, may misinterpret or reject the testing context. Yet these children often display sophisticated abilities in daily life—for example, telling stories, engaging in complex artistic activities, or interacting skillfully with other people.

The triarchic theory emphasizes the complexity of intelligent behavior and the limitations of current intelligence tests in assessing that complexity. For example, out-of-school, practical forms of intelligence are vital for life success and help explain why cultures vary widely in the behaviors they regard as intelligent (Sternberg, 2011). In villages in Kenya, children regarded as intelligent are highly knowledgeable about how to use herbal medicines to treat disease. Among the Yup'ik Eskimo people of central Alaska, intelligent youths are those with expert hunting, gathering, navigating, and fishing skills (Hein, Reich, & Grigorenko, 2015). And U.S. Cambodian, Filipino, Vietnamese, and Mexican immigrant parents, when asked to describe an intelligent first grader, emphasized noncognitive capacities—motivation, self-management, and social skills (Okagaki & Sternberg, 1993).

According to Sternberg, intelligence tests, devised to predict achievement in school, do not capture the intellectual strengths that many children acquire through informal learning experiences in their cultural communities. But systematically measuring those strengths remains challenging. Tests devised to reflect the triarchic theory have not consistently yielded distinct analytical, creative, and practical ability factors (Aljughaiman & Ayoub, 2012; Gubbels et al., 2016). Researchers are not sure whether these findings signify deficiencies in the triarchic theory or in available assessments.

Gardner's Theory of Multiple Intelligences   In yet another view of how information-processing skills underlie intelligent behavior, Howard Gardner's (1983, 1993, 2011) **theory of multiple intelligences** defines intelligence in terms of distinct sets of processing operations that permit individuals to engage in a wide range of culturally valued activities. Dismissing the idea of general intelligence, Gardner proposes at least eight independent intelligences (see Table 12.2).

Gardner believes that each intelligence has a unique neurological basis, a distinct course of development, and different expert, or "end-state," performances. At the same time, he emphasizes that a lengthy process of education is required to transform any raw potential into a mature social role (Gardner, 2011). Cultural values and learning opportunities affect the extent to which a child's intellectual strengths are realized and the way they are expressed.

Gardner's list of abilities has yet to be firmly grounded in research. Neurological evidence for the independence of his abilities is weak. Some exceptionally gifted individuals have abilities that are broad rather than limited to a particular domain (Piirto, 2007). And research with mental tests suggests that several of Gardner's intelligences (linguistic, logico-mathematical, and spatial) have at least some features in common. Nevertheless, Gardner's theory calls attention to several intelligences not tapped by IQ scores and to the importance of assessing children's performance in domains generally regarded as nonacademic, such as music,

TABLE 12.2   Gardner's Multiple Intelligences

INTELLIGENCE	PROCESSING OPERATIONS	END-STATE PERFORMANCE POSSIBILITIES
Linguistic	Sensitivity to the sounds, rhythms, and meaning of words and the functions of language	Poet, journalist
Logico-mathematical	Sensitivity to, and capacity to detect, logical or numerical patterns; ability to handle long chains of logical reasoning	Mathematician
Musical	Ability to produce and appreciate pitch, rhythm (or melody), and aesthetic quality of the forms of musical expressiveness	Instrumentalist, composer
Spatial	Ability to perceive the visual–spatial world accurately, to perform transformations on those perceptions, and to re-create aspects of visual experience in the absence of relevant stimuli	Sculptor, navigator
Bodily-kinesthetic	Ability to use the body skillfully for expressive as well as goal-directed purposes; ability to handle objects skillfully	Dancer, athlete
Naturalist	Ability to recognize and classify all varieties of animals, minerals, and plants	Biologist
Interpersonal	Ability to detect and respond appropriately to the moods, temperaments, motivations, and intentions of others	Therapist, salesperson
Intrapersonal	Ability to discriminate complex inner feelings and to use them to guide one's own behavior; knowledge of one's own strengths, weaknesses, desires, and intelligences	Person with detailed, accurate self-knowledge

Sources: Gardner, 1983, 1993, 2011.

According to Gardner, people are capable of at least eight distinct intelligences. The dance program at their school gives these fourth and fifth graders the opportunity to expand their bodily-kinesthetic intelligence.

movement, and understanding of self and others (Chen & Gardner, 2018).

For example, Gardner's interpersonal and intrapersonal intelligences include a set of skills for accurately perceiving, reasoning about, and regulating emotion that has become known as *emotional intelligence.* Among school-age children and adolescents, measures of emotional intelligence are positively associated with self-esteem, empathy, prosocial behavior, cooperation, leadership skills, and academic performance and negatively associated with internalizing (fear and anxiety) and externalizing (anger and aggression) problems (Brackett, Rivers, & Salovey, 2011; Ferrando et al., 2011). These findings have increased teachers' awareness that providing classroom lessons that coach students in emotional abilities can improve their adjustment.

Review the *core knowledge perspective,* discussed on pages 207–208 in Chapter 6, and compare it with Gardner's view. Gardner also accepts the existence of innately specified, core domains of thought, present at birth or emerging early in life. Then, as children respond to the demands of their culture, they transform those intelligences to fit the activities they are called on to perform. Gardner's multiple intelligences have been helpful in efforts to understand and nurture children's special talents, a topic we will take up at the end of this chapter.

12.3.3 Explaining Individual and Group Differences in IQ

When we compare individuals in terms of academic achievement, years of education, and occupational status, it is clear that certain sectors of the population are advantaged over others. As part of an effort to explain these differences, researchers have compared the IQ scores of ethnic and SES groups. African-American children and adolescents score, on average, 10 to 12 IQ points below European-American children, although the difference has been shrinking over the past several decades (Nisbett, 2009; Nisbett et al., 2012). Hispanic children fall midway between African-American and European-American children, and Asian Americans score slightly higher than their European-American counterparts—by about 3 points (Ceci, Rosenblum, & Kumpf, 1998).

The IQ gap between middle- and low-SES children—about 9 points—accounts for some of the ethnic differences in IQ, but not all (Brooks-Gunn et al., 2003). Of course, IQ varies greatly *within* each ethnic and SES group, and minority top performers are typically indistinguishable from top performers in the European-American majority. Still, these group differences are large enough and of serious enough consequence that they cannot be ignored.

Beginning in the 1970s, the IQ nature–nurture controversy escalated after psychologist Arthur Jensen (1969) claimed that heredity is largely responsible for individual, ethnic, and SES variations in intelligence—a position others asserted as well (Herrnstein & Murray, 1994; Rushton & Jensen, 2006, 2010). These contentions prompted an outpouring of research studies and responses, including ethical challenges reflecting deep concern that the conclusions would fuel social prejudices (Colman, 2016). Let's look closely at some of the important evidence that resulted.

Nature and Nurture   In Chapter 2 we introduced the *heritability estimate.* Recall that heritabilities are obtained from kinship studies, which compare family members. The most powerful evidence on the heritability of IQ involves twin comparisons. The IQ scores of identical twins (who share all their genes) are more similar than those of fraternal twins (who are genetically no more alike than ordinary siblings). On the basis of this and other kinship evidence, researchers estimate that about half the differences in IQ among children can be traced to their genetic makeup.

Recall, however, that heritabilities risk overestimating genetic influences and underestimating environmental influences. Although these measures offer convincing evidence that genes contribute to IQ, disagreement persists over how large that contribution is. As we saw in Chapter 2, the heritability of intelligence is lower in infancy and childhood than at older ages, and it rises with parental education and income—conditions that enable children to realize their genetic potential. Furthermore, heritability estimates do not reveal the complex processes through which genes and experiences influence intelligence as children develop.

As we also noted in Chapter 2, using heritability estimates computed mostly on White twin samples to draw conclusions about the genetic basis of differences between ethnic groups is invalid. Indeed, research using contemporary methods of molecular genetic testing and brain imaging has failed to uncover any relationships among genetic markers, brain anatomy (such as volumes of the frontal and parietal regions of the cerebral cortex), and ethnicity (Butcher et al., 2008; Nisbett et al., 2012; Richardson, 2011).

In this fifth-grade class at an urban elementary school, IQ scores may vary with ethnicity and SES. Research aimed at explaining these differences has generated heated controversy.

Adoption studies shed further light on the origins of the Black–White disparity in IQ. In two investigations, African-American children adopted into economically well-off European-American homes during the first year of life scored high on intelligence tests, attaining mean IQs of 110 and 117 by middle childhood—20 to 30 points higher than the typical scores of children growing up in low-income African-American communities and as high as or higher than the scores of adopted European-American children (Moore, 1986; Scarr & Weinberg, 1983).

These findings are consistent with a wealth of evidence that poverty severely depresses the intelligence of ethnic minority children (Nisbett et al., 2012). Providing additional support for this conclusion, a longitudinal study of a randomly selected sample of nearly 1,000 families from 10 cities across the United States whose children were tested periodically from ages 4 through 15 found that a substantial Black–White gap in IQ appeared in early childhood and persisted into adolescence. A three-step sequence of family conditions accounted for 80 percent of the group difference: (1) greater disadvantage in income, maternal education, and maternal verbal ability and knowledge in Black families, which led to (2) lower birth weight and less effective parenting, reflected in reduced maternal sensitivity and provision of learning materials and more cluttered and crowded home environments, which yielded (3) lower mental-test scores (Cottrell, Newman, & Roisman, 2015). Greater family adversity among the African-American children was already apparent in early childhood.

Dramatic gains in IQ from one generation to the next offer additional evidence that, given stimulating experiences and learning opportunities, members of oppressed groups can move far beyond their current test performance. See the Cultural Influences box on page 454 to learn about the *Flynn effect*.

Cultural Influences   A controversial question raised about ethnic differences in IQ has to do with whether *test bias* contributes to them. If a test samples knowledge and skills that not all groups of children have had an equal chance to learn, or if the testing situation impairs the performance of some groups but not others, the resulting scores will be a biased, or unfair, measure of intelligence.

Some experts reject the idea that intelligence tests are biased, claiming that they are intended to represent success in the common culture. According to this view, because IQ predicts academic achievement equally well for majority and minority children, IQ tests are fair to both groups (Edwards & Oakland, 2006). Others believe that lack of exposure to certain communication styles and knowledge, along with negative stereotypes about the test-taker's ethnic group, can undermine children's performance (McKown, 2013; Sternberg, 2018a). Let's look at the evidence.

Cultural Influences | The Flynn Effect: Massive Generational Gains in IQ

After gathering IQ scores from diverse nations that had either military mental testing or frequent testing of other large, representative samples, James Flynn (1999, 2007) reported a finding so consistent and intriguing that it became known as the **Flynn effect: IQs have increased steadily from one generation to the next.** Evidence for the Flynn effect now exists for more than 30 nations. This dramatic *secular trend* in intelligence test performance holds for industrialized and developing nations, both males and females, and individuals varying in ethnicity and SES (Nisbett et al., 2012; Pietschnig & Voracek, 2015). Gains are greatest on tests of spatial reasoning—tasks often assumed to be "culture-fair" and, therefore, mostly genetically based.

The amount of increase depends on extent of societal modernization (see page 441 in this chapter, to review). Among European and North American countries that modernized by the early twentieth century, IQ gains have been about 3 points per decade. With the attainment of highly favorable economic and social conditions, gains have slowed in most of these countries (Weber, Dekhtyar, & Herlitz, 2017).

Among nations that modernized later, around the mid-twentieth century (such as Argentina),

IQ gains tend to be larger, as much as 5 to 6 points per decade (Flynn & Rossi-Casé, 2011). And nations that began to modernize in the late twentieth century (Caribbean countries, Kenya, Sudan) show even greater increments, especially in spatial reasoning (Khaleefa, Sulman, & Lynn, 2009; Sauce & Matzel, 2018). The degree of societal modernity possible today is far greater than it was a century ago.

Diverse aspects of modernization probably underlie the better reasoning ability of each successive generation. These include improved education, health, and technology (TV, computers, the Internet); more cognitively demanding jobs and leisure activities (reading, chess, video games); a generally more stimulating world; and greater test-taking motivation.

As developing nations continue to advance in IQ, they are projected to catch up with the industrialized world by the end of the twenty-first century (Nisbett et al., 2012). Large, environmentally induced gains in IQ over time present a major challenge to the assumption that ethnic variations in IQ are genetic.

Dramatic generational gains in IQ are related to diverse aspects of societal modernization, such as greater participation by each successive generation in cognitively stimulating leisure activities.

Language and Communication Styles Ethnic minority families often foster unique language skills that do not match the expectations of most classrooms and testing situations. African-American English is a complex, rule-governed dialect used by most African Americans in the United States (Craig & Washington, 2006). Nevertheless, it is often inaccurately viewed as a deficient form of mainstream American English rather than as different from it, and as a low-status dialect associated with poverty.

The majority of African-American children entering school speak African-American English, though they vary greatly in the extent to which they use it. Greater users, who tend to come from low-SES families, quickly learn that the language they bring from home is devalued in school, whereas mainstream American English is respected. Teachers frequently try to "correct" or eliminate their use of African-American English forms, replacing them with mainstream English (Washington & Thomas-Tate, 2009). Because the conventions of their home discourse are distinctly different from those of the language used for learning to read, children who speak mostly African-American English in school generally progress slowly in reading and achieve poorly (Brown et al., 2015).

Many African-American children learn to flexibly shift between African-American English and mainstream English by third grade. But those who continue to speak mostly their African-American dialect through the later grades—the majority of whom live in poverty and therefore have few opportunities outside of school for exposure to mainstream English—fall further behind in reading and in overall

Many African-American children enter school speaking African-American English. Their home discourse differs from mainstream American English, on which their school learning is based.

achievement (Craig, 2015; Craig, Kolenic, & Hensel, 2014). These children have a special need for school programs that facilitate mastery of mainstream English while respecting and accommodating their home language in the classroom.

Research also reveals that ethnic minority parents without extensive education often prefer a *collaborative style of communication* when completing tasks with children. They work together in a coordinated, fluid way, each focused on the same aspect of the problem. This pattern of adult–child engagement has been observed in Native-American, Canadian Inuit, Mexican, and Guatemalan Mayan cultures (López et al., 2012; Rogoff, 2014). With increasing education, parents establish a *hierarchical style of communication,* like that of classrooms and tests. The parent directs each child to carry out an aspect of the task, and children work independently. The sharp discontinuity between home and school communication practices likely contributes to low-SES minority children's lower IQ scores and school performance.

Knowledge Many researchers argue that IQ scores are affected by specific information acquired as part of majority-culture upbringing. In one study, researchers assessed African-American and European-American community college students' familiarity with vocabulary taken from items on an intelligence test. When verbal comprehension, similarities, and analogies test items depended on words and concepts that the European-American students knew better, they scored higher than the African Americans. When the same types of items involved words and concepts that the two groups knew equally well, the two groups did not differ (Fagan & Holland, 2007). Prior knowledge, not reasoning ability, fully explained ethnic differences in performance.

Performance even on nonverbal test items, such as those tapping spatial reasoning, depends on learning opportunities. For example, among children, adolescents, and adults alike, playing video games that require fast responding and mental rotation of visual images increases success on spatial test items (Uttal et al., 2013). Low-income minority children, however, may have less access to games and objects that promote these skills.

Furthermore, the sheer amount of time a child spends in school predicts IQ. In research on large samples of children and adolescents that takes into account both variations in age and completed years of schooling, quantity of schooling exerted a considerably stronger impact on mental-test performance than did advancing age (Cliffordson & Gustafson, 2008; Wang et al., 2016; Winship & Korenman, 1997). In line with these findings, the earlier young people leave school, the greater their loss of IQ points (Ceci, 1999).

At the same time, poverty, oppression, and diminished quality of education can undermine the effects of schooling on intellectual development. For example, in segregated, economically disadvantaged Palestinian towns in Israel and in overcrowded Palestinian refugee camps with entrenched poverty on the West Bank, the impact of schooling on children's mental-test scores is greatly reduced (Jabr & Cahan, 2014a, 2014b). Taken together, these findings indicate that supportive home and community contexts for learning along with opportunities to acquire the knowledge and ways of thinking valued in classrooms have a substantial impact on intelligence test performance.

School-age children become increasingly conscious of ethnic stereotypes, and those from stigmatized groups are especially mindful of them. Fear of being judged on the basis of a negative stereotype may undermine this Hispanic student's performance on a math test.

Stereotypes Imagine trying to succeed at an activity when the prevailing attitude is that members of your group are incompetent. **Stereotype threat**—the fear of being judged on the basis of a negative stereotype—can trigger anxiety that interferes with performance. Mounting evidence confirms that stereotype threat undermines test taking in children and adults (Nadler & Clark, 2011). For example, researchers gave African-American, Hispanic, and European-American 6- to 10-year-olds verbal tasks. Some children were told that the tasks were "not a test." Others were told that they were "a test of how good children are at school problems"—a statement designed to induce stereotype threat in the ethnic minority children. Among children who were aware of ethnic stereotypes (such as "Black people aren't smart"), African Americans and Hispanics performed far worse in the "test" condition than in the "not a test" condition (McKown & Weinstein, 2003). European-American children, in contrast, performed similarly in both conditions.

From third grade on, children become increasingly conscious of ethnic stereotypes, and those from stigmatized groups are especially mindful of them. When confronted with stereotype threat, they well up with anxiety, which reduces mental resources available for doing well on challenging tasks. By early adolescence, many low-SES minority students start to devalue doing well in school, saying it is not important to them (Killen, Rutland, & Ruck, 2011). Self-protective disengagement, sparked by stereotype threat, may be responsible. This weakening of motivation can have serious long-term consequences. Research shows that self-discipline—effort and delay of gratification—predicts changes in school performance, as measured by report card grades, better than IQ does (Duckworth, Quinn, & Tsukayama, 2012).

12.3.4 Reducing Cultural Bias in Testing

Although not all experts agree, many acknowledge that IQ scores can underestimate the intelligence of children from ethnic minority groups. Of special concern is that minority children will be incorrectly labeled as slow learners and assigned to remedial classes, which are far less stimulating than regular classes. To avoid this danger, test scores need to be combined with assessments of children's adaptive behavior—their ability to cope with the demands of their everyday environments. The child who does poorly on an IQ test yet plays a complex game on the playground or figures out how to rewire a broken TV is unlikely to be intellectually deficient.

In addition, flexible testing procedures enhance minority children's performance. In an approach called **dynamic assessment,** an innovation consistent with Vygotsky's zone of proximal development, the adult introduces purposeful teaching into the testing situation to find out what the child can attain with social support (Robinson-Zañartu & Carlson, 2013).

Research shows that children's receptivity to teaching and capacity to transfer what they have learned to novel problems add considerably to the prediction of future performance (Haywood & Lidz, 2007). In one study, first graders diverse in SES and ethnicity participated in dynamic assessment in which they were asked to solve a series of math equations that increased in difficulty, such as $\_\_\_ + 1 = 4$ (easier) and $3 + 6 = 5 + \_\_\_$ (difficult). When a child could not solve an equation, an adult provided increasingly explicit teaching. Beyond static IQ-like measures of children's verbal, math, and reasoning abilities, performance during dynamic assessment strongly predicted end-of-year scores on a test of math story problems, which children usually find highly challenging (Seethaler et al., 2012). Dynamic assessment seemed to evoke reasoning skills and conceptual understandings that children readily transferred to a very different and demanding type of math. Although their initial scores are lower, low-SES ethnic minority children show gains after dynamic assessment that are just as large as those of their cultural-majority agemates (Stevenson, Heiser, & Resing, 2016).

Cultural bias in testing can also be reduced by countering the negative impact of stereotype threat. A variety of brief, school-based interventions are effective. Persuading students that their intelligence depends heavily on effort, not on a stereotype of native endowment, is helpful. Mindfulness training, in which students practice focusing on the present task rather than on distracting thoughts about a negative stereotype, is also effective (Blackwell, Trzesniewski, & Dweck, 2007; Weger et al., 2012). Yet another approach is to encourage minority students to affirm their self-worth by writing a short essay about their most important values (for example, a close friendship or a self-defining skill). This self-affirmation intervention was just as successful in boosting end-of-term grades of poorly performing middle school students as it was for students doing moderately well in school (see Figure 12.7) (Cohen, Garcia, & Master, 2006).

In view of its many problems, should intelligence testing in schools be suspended? Most experts reject this solution. Without testing, important educational decisions would be based only on subjective impressions, perhaps increasing

© LAURA DWIGHT PHOTOGRAPHY

A teacher uses dynamic assessment, introducing purposeful teaching into a testing situation to find out what this third grader can learn with social support.

FIGURE 12.7 **Impact of a self-affirmation intervention on African-American middle school students' end-of-term grade-point average.** In the fall, several hundred students were randomly assigned to either a self-affirmation intervention, in which they wrote brief essays about the personal meaning of their most important values, or a control condition, in which they wrote essays about why their least important values might be meaningful to someone else. African-American students experiencing the self-affirmation condition attained substantially higher end-of-term course grades than did controls; poorly performing and moderately performing students benefitted similarly. European-American students' grades (not shown) were unaffected, indicating that the treatment succeeded by lessening the negative impact of stereotype threat on the African Americans. (Based on Cohen, Garcia, & Master, 2006.)

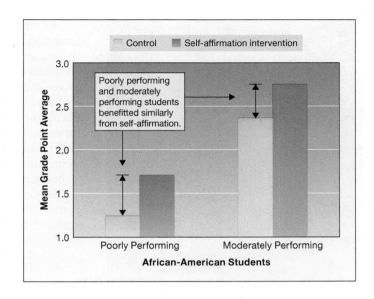

discriminatory placement of minority children. Intelligence tests are useful when interpreted carefully by examiners who are sensitive to cultural influences on test performance. And despite their limitations, IQ scores continue to be valid measures of school learning potential for the majority of Western children.

 ASK YOURSELF

Connect ■ Explain how dynamic assessment is consistent with Vygotsky's zone of proximal development and with scaffolding (see pages 319–320 in Chapter 9).

Apply ■ Josefina, a Hispanic fourth grader, does well on homework assignments. But when her teacher announces, "It's time for a test to see how much you've learned," Josefina usually does poorly. How might stereotype threat explain this inconsistency?

Reflect ■ Do you think that intelligence tests are culturally biased? What observations and evidence influenced your conclusion?

12.4 Language Development

Vocabulary, grammar, and pragmatics continue to develop in middle childhood, though less obviously than at earlier ages. In addition, children's attitude toward language undergoes a fundamental shift. They develop **metalinguistic awareness,** the ability to think about language as a system.

12.4a Describe changes in school-age children's metalinguistic awareness, vocabulary, grammar, and pragmatics.

12.4b Describe bilingual development, the cognitive benefits of bilingualism, and the effectiveness of bilingual education programs.

12.4.1 Vocabulary and Grammar

During the elementary school years, vocabulary increases fourfold, eventually exceeding comprehension of 40,000 words. On average, children learn about 20 new words each day—a rate of growth greater than in early childhood. In addition to the word-learning strategies discussed in Chapter 9, school-age children enlarge their vocabularies by analyzing the structure of complex words. From *happy* and *decide,* they quickly derive the meanings of *happiness* and *decision* (Larsen & Nippold, 2007). They also figure out many more word meanings from context

As at younger ages, children benefit from conversations with more-expert speakers. But because written language contains a far more diverse and complex vocabulary than spoken language, reading contributes enormously to vocabulary growth. Avid readers are exposed to more than 4 million words per year, average readers to 600,000 words. In contrast, children who rarely read encounter only about 50,000 words (Anderson, Wilson, & Fielding, 1988). By second to third grade, reading comprehension and reading habits strongly predict later vocabulary size into high school (Cain & Oakhill, 2011).

A fifth grader encounters new words with complex meanings in a current events article. Stimulating reading experiences contribute greatly to vocabulary growth.

As their knowledge becomes better organized, older school-age children think about and use words more precisely: In addition to the verb *fall,* for example, they also use *topple, tumble,* and *plummet.* Word definitions also illustrate this change. Five- and 6-year-olds offer concrete descriptions referring to functions or appearance—*knife:* "when you're cutting carrots"; *bicycle:* "it's got wheels, a chain, and handlebars." By the end of elementary school, synonyms and explanations of categorical relationships appear—for example, *knife:* "something you could cut with. A saw is like a knife. It could also be a weapon" (Uccelli, Rowe, & Pan, 2017). This advance reflects older children's ability to deal with word meanings on an entirely verbal plane. They can add new words to their vocabulary simply by being given a definition.

School-age children's more reflective and analytical approach to language enables them to appreciate the multiple meanings of words—to recognize, for example, that many words, such as *cool* or *neat,* have psychological as well as physical meanings: "Cool shirt!" or "Neat movie!" This grasp of double meanings permits 8- to 10-year-olds to comprehend subtle metaphors, such as "sharp as a tack" and "spilling the beans" (Nippold, Taylor, & Baker, 1996; Seigneuric et al., 2016). It also leads to a change in children's humor. Riddles and puns that play on different meanings of a key word are common: "Hey, did you take a bath?" "Why, is one missing?"

Mastery of complex grammatical constructions also improves. For example, English-speaking children use the passive voice more frequently, and they more often extend it from an abbreviated form ("It got broken") into full statements ("The glass was broken by Mary") (Tomasello, 2006). Although the passive form is challenging, language input makes a difference. When adults speak a language that emphasizes full passives, such as Inuktitut (spoken by the Inuit people of Arctic Canada), children produce them earlier (Allen & Crago, 1996).

Another grammatical achievement of middle childhood is advanced understanding of infinitive phrases—the difference between "John is eager to please" and "John is easy to please" (Berman, 2007; Chomsky, 1969). Like gains in vocabulary, appreciation of these subtle grammatical distinctions is supported by improved ability to analyze and reflect on language.

LOOK and LISTEN

Record examples of 8- to 10-year-olds' humor, or examine storybooks for humor aimed at second through fourth graders. Does it require a grasp of the multiple meanings of words?

12.4.2 Pragmatics

A more advanced theory of mind—in particular, the capacity for recursive thought—enables school-age children to understand and use increasingly subtle, indirect expressions of meaning (Lee, Torrance, & Olson, 2001). Seven-year-old Lizzie often avoided her daily garbage-disposal chore, so she knew that her mother's comment, "The garbage is beginning to smell," really meant, "Take that garbage out!" Around age 8, children begin to grasp irony and sarcasm (Glenright & Pexman, 2010). After Rena prepared a dish for dinner that Joey didn't like, he quipped sarcastically, "Oh boy, my favorite!" Notice how this remark requires the speaker to consider at least two perspectives simultaneously—in Joey's case, his mother's desire to serve a particular dish despite his objection, expressed through a critical comment with a double meaning.

Furthermore, as a result of improved memory and ability to take the perspective of listeners, children's narratives increase in organization, detail, and expressiveness. A typical 4- or 5-year-old's narrative states what happened: "We went to the lake. We fished and waited. Paul caught a huge catfish!" Six- and 7-year-olds add orienting information (time, place, participants) and connectives ("next," "then," "so," "finally") that lend coherence to the story. Gradually, narratives lengthen into a *classic form* in which events not only build to a high point but resolve: "After Paul reeled in the catfish, Dad cleaned and cooked it. Then we ate it all up!" And evaluative comments rise dramatically, becoming common by age 8 to 9: "The catfish tasted great. Paul was so proud!" (Melzi & Schick, 2017; Ukrainetz et al., 2005).

Because children pick up the narrative styles of significant adults in their lives, their narratives vary widely across cultures. For example, instead of the *topic-focused style* of most

European-American children, who describe an experience from beginning to end, African-American children often use a *topic-associating style* in which they blend several similar experiences. One 9-year-old related having a tooth pulled, then described seeing her sister's tooth pulled, next told how she had removed one of her baby teeth, and concluded, "I'm a pullin-teeth expert … call me, and I'll be over" (McCabe, 1997, p. 164). Like adults in their families and communities, African-American children are more attuned to keeping their listeners interested than to relating a linear sequence of story events. They often embellish their narratives by including fictional elements and many references to characters' motives and intentions (Gorman et al., 2011). As a result, African-American children's narratives are usually longer and more complex than those of European-American children.

In families that regularly eat meals together, children are advanced in language and literacy development. Mealtimes offer many opportunities to relate complex, extended personal stories.

The ability to generate clear oral narratives enhances reading comprehension and prepares children for producing longer, more explicit written narratives. In families who regularly eat meals together, children are advanced in language and literacy development (Snow & Beals, 2006). Mealtimes offer many opportunities to relate personal stories.

12.4.3 Learning Two Languages

Joey and Lizzie speak only one language—English, their native tongue. Yet throughout the world, many children grow up *bilingual,* learning two languages and sometimes more than two. An estimated 23 percent of U.S. 5- to 17-year-olds—more than 12 million children and adolescents—speak a language other than English at home (U.S. Census Bureau, 2019).

Bilingual Development   Children can become bilingual in two ways: Their parents may expose them to both languages at the same time in infancy and early childhood, making them *simultaneous bilinguals*. Alternatively, as in most immigrant families, preschool and school-age children acquire a second language after they already speak the language of their cultural heritage, making them *sequential bilinguals*.

Children who are simultaneous bilinguals separate the language systems early on and attain most language milestones according to a typical timetable (Aguilar-Mediavilla et al., 2017). Although early vocabulary growth in each language tends to be somewhat slower than in their monolingual agemates, the vocabularies of both languages together are similar to or larger in size (Ezeizabarrena & Fernández, 2017; Poulin-Dubois et al., 2013). Preschool simultaneous bilinguals attain normal native ability in the language of their surrounding community and good-to-native ability in the second language, depending on their exposure to it (Serratrice, 2013). In middle childhood, simultaneous bilinguals' use of the most complex grammatical structures may be slightly delayed, but these differences usually diminish and disappear as children are exposed to more language input (Gathercole, 2007).

When preschool and school-age children from immigrant families acquire a second language after they already speak the language of their cultural heritage, the time required to master the second language to the level of native-speaking agemates varies greatly, from 1 to 5 or more years (MacWhinney, 2015; Páez & Hunter, 2015). Influential factors include child motivation, knowledge of the first language (which supports mastery of the second), and quality of communication and of literacy experiences in both languages at home and at school.

Like many bilingual adults, bilingual children sometimes engage in *code switching*—producing an utterance in one language that contains one or more "guest" words from the other—without violating the grammar of either language. Rather than a sign of confusion, code switching is adaptive, reflecting deliberate control of the two languages. Children may engage in code switching because they lack the vocabulary to convey a particular thought in one language, so they use the other. And children who code-switch the most regularly participate in social contexts where code switching is a common practice (Yow, Patrycia, & Flynn, 2016). Bilingual adults frequently code-switch to express cultural identity, and children may follow suit—as when a Korean child speaking English switches to Korean on mentioning her piano teacher, as a sign of respect for authority (Chung, 2006). Opportunities to listen to code switching may facilitate bilingual development. For example, a child accustomed to hearing French sentences with English guest words may rely on sentence-level cues to figure out English word meanings.

Recall from Chapter 6 that, just as with first-language development, a *sensitive period* for second-language development exists. Although mastery must begin sometime in childhood for full development to occur, a precise age cutoff for a decline in second-language learning has not been established (see page 229 in Chapter 6).

Children who become fluent in two languages develop denser gray matter (neurons and connective fibers) and white matter (myelination) in areas of the left cerebral hemisphere devoted to language. And compared to monolinguals, bilinguals show greater activity in these areas and in the prefrontal cortex during linguistic tasks, likely due to the high executive-processing demands of controlling two languages (Costa & Sebastián-Gallés, 2014; Li, Legault, & Litcofsky, 2014). Because both languages are always active, bilingual speakers must continuously decide which one to use in particular social situations and inhibit attention to the other.

This increase in executive processing has diverse cognitive benefits, providing bilinguals with especially efficient executive function skills that can be applied to other tasks (Bialystok, 2015). Bilingual children and adults outperform others on tests of inhibition, sustained and selective attention, flexible thinking, analytical reasoning, concept formation, and false-belief understanding. The higher the degree of bilingualism (balance of proficiency in both languages), the greater the cognitive gains (Bialystok, Craik, & Luk, 2012; Diaz & Farrar, 2018; Thomas-Sunesson, Hakuta, & Bialystok, 2018). Bilingual children are also advanced in certain aspects of metalinguistic awareness, such as detection of errors in grammar, meaning, and conventions of conversation (responding politely, relevantly, and informatively). And children transfer their phonological awareness skills in one language to the other, especially if their two languages share phonological features and letter–sound correspondences, as Spanish and English do (Bialystok, 2013; Siegal, Iozzi, & Surian, 2009). These capacities enhance reading achievement.

Bilingual Education   The advantages of bilingualism provide strong justification for bilingual education programs in schools. In Canada, nearly 20 percent of elementary school students are enrolled in *language immersion programs,* in which English-speaking children typically are taught entirely in French from kindergarten through second grade (Statistics Canada, 2018,). Gradually, English is introduced as a subject in third grade, though French continues to be the main classroom language. This strategy succeeds in developing children who are proficient in both languages and who, by grade 6, achieve as well in reading, writing, and math as their counterparts in the regular English program (Genesee & Jared, 2008; Lyster & Genesee, 2012).

In the United States, some educators believe that time spent communicating in ethnic minority children's native language detracts from English-language achievement, which is crucial for success in the worlds of school and work. Others, committed to developing minority children's native language while fostering mastery of English, note that providing instruction in the native tongue lets minority children know that their heritage is respected. It also prevents inadequate proficiency in both languages. Minority children who gradually lose facility in the first language as a result of being taught only the second end up limited in both languages for a time (McCabe et al., 2013). This circumstance leads to serious academic difficulties and is believed to contribute to the high rates of school failure and dropout among low-SES Hispanic youths, who make up over 70 percent of the U.S. language-minority population.

Many U.S. states have passed laws declaring English to be their official language, creating conditions in which schools have no obligation to teach language minority students in languages other than English. Where bilingual education exists, its goal is to transition minority students to English-only instruction as soon as possible (Wright, 2013). Yet in classrooms where both languages are integrated into the curriculum, minority children are more involved in learning, participate more actively in class discussions, and acquire the second language more easily—gains that predict better academic achievement (Guglielmi, 2008). In contrast, when teachers speak only in a language that children can barely understand, minority children become frustrated, bored, and withdrawn. Under these conditions, U.S. kindergartners with limited English proficiency quickly fall behind their English-proficient counterparts in oral language and reading skills and are likely to struggle academically throughout their school years (Paradis, Genesee, & Crago, 2011). This downward spiral in achievement is greatest in high-poverty schools, where resources to support the needs of language minority children are especially scarce.

The benefits of sustained bilingual education throughout the school years—for language minority and native-English-speaking students alike—have inspired U.S. educators to devise *two-way language immersion programs*. In these classrooms, language-minority students acquiring English and native English-speaking students interested in learning a second language are taught together, with most programs beginning in first grade and running for at least five years, and some extending through twelfth grade (Kim, Hutchinson, & Winsler, 2015). In one approach, called *full immersion,* students mostly learn in the minority language during the first few years and then transition to a setting in which both groups receive half of their educational experiences in English and half in the minority language. In a second approach, called *partial immersion,* students are taught half the time in each language.

In a second-grade two-way language immersion classroom, a bilingual teacher presents a lesson in Spanish. Two-way language immersion programs are increasing rapidly in U.S. public schools. They are especially effective in promoting mastery of both languages and reading achievement.

Two-way immersion programs are growing rapidly in U.S. public schools: More than two thousand exist across the country (Gross, 2016). Programs are especially prevalent in areas where the majority of immigrants share a native language so enough students from the same minority language are available to make up half of classrooms. Consequently, Spanish–English is the most common, followed by Chinese–English, though some large cities offer as many as five minority languages. Evaluations reveal that two-way immersion programs are especially effective in promoting proficiency in both languages and positive attitudes toward school. And academic performance is at least as high in two-way immersion as in English-only classrooms, with immersion students consistently scoring higher in reading achievement (Bialystok, 2018; Lindholm-Leary & Block, 2009; Marian, Shook, & Schroeder, 2013).

So far, two-way immersion is available in only a limited number of languages, leaving immigrant children who speak most of the more than 140 minority languages in the United States without access. Nevertheless, the proliferation of these programs confirms that long-held misconceptions about bilingual education in the United States—for example, that it interferes with immigrant children's progress in learning to speak and read English—have begun to wane. Today, more educators and parents view bilingual education as beneficial for all children and as an asset to American society.

ASK YOURSELF

Connect ■ How can bilingual education promote ethnic minority children's cognitive and academic development?

Apply ■ After soccer practice, 10-year-old Shana remarked, "I'm wiped out!" Megan, her 5-year-old sister, responded, "What did'ya wipe out?" Explain Shana's and Megan's different understandings.

Reflect ■ Considering research on bilingualism, what changes would you make in your own second-language learning, and why?

12.5a Describe the influence of educational philosophies on children's motivation and academic achievement.

12.5b Discuss the role of teacher–student interaction and grouping practices in academic achievement.

12.5c Describe academic benefits of, as well as concerns about, educational media.

12.5d Describe conditions that promote successful placement of children with learning disabilities in regular classrooms.

12.5e Describe the characteristics of gifted children and efforts to meet their educational needs.

12.5f Discuss factors that lead U.S. students to fall behind in academic achievement compared to students in top-achieving nations.

12.5 Children's Learning in School

Evidence cited throughout this chapter indicates that schools are vital forces in children's cognitive development. How do schools exert such a powerful influence? Research looking at schools as complex social systems—educational philosophies, teacher–student relationships, and larger cultural context—provides important insights. As you read about these topics, refer to Applying What We Know on the following page, which summarizes characteristics of high-quality education in elementary school.

12.5.1 Educational Philosophies

Teachers' educational philosophies play a major role in children's learning. Two philosophical approaches have received the most research attention. They differ in what children are taught, the way they are believed to learn, and in how their progress is evaluated.

Traditional versus Constructivist Classrooms In a **traditional classroom,** the teacher is the sole authority for knowledge, rules, and decision making. Students are relatively passive—listening, responding when called on, and completing teacher-assigned tasks. Their progress is evaluated by how well they keep pace with a uniform set of standards for their grade.

A **constructivist classroom,** in contrast, encourages students to *construct* their own knowledge. Although constructivist approaches vary, many are grounded in Piaget's theory, which views children as active agents who reflect on and coordinate their own thoughts rather than absorbing those of others. A glance inside a constructivist classroom reveals richly equipped learning centers, small groups and individuals solving self-chosen problems, and a teacher who guides and supports in response to children's needs. Students are evaluated by considering their progress in relation to their own prior development.

In the 1960s and early 1970s, constructivist classrooms gained in popularity in the United States. Then, as concern arose over the academic progress of children and youths, classrooms returned to traditional instruction—a style that became increasingly pronounced as a result of the 2001 No Child Left Behind Act (NCLBA), followed by its 2015 replacement, the Every Student Succeeds Act (ESSA). ESSA transferred NCLBA's federal control of school academic standards and assessments to the states in an effort to introduce flexibility in approaches to measuring student learning, including evaluations of various types of student work. However, ESSA continues to require students to take annual achievement tests from third through eighth grade and in high school. Consequently, the narrowing of the curricular focus in public schools to preparing students for achievement tests, which resulted from NCLBA, persists (Gewertz, 2018).

Although older elementary school children in traditional classrooms have a slight edge in achievement test scores, constructivist settings are associated with many other benefits—gains in critical thinking, greater social and moral maturity, and more positive attitudes toward school (DeVries, 2001; Rathunde & Csikszentmihalyi, 2005; Walberg, 1986). And as noted in Chapter 9, when teacher-directed instruction is emphasized in preschool and kindergarten, it actually undermines academic motivation and achievement, especially in low-SES children.

The emphasis on knowledge absorption in many kindergarten and primary classrooms has contributed to a trend among parents to delay their child's school entry, especially in higher-SES families and for boys with a birth date close to the cutoff for kindergarten enrollment. Research, however, reveals few long-term academic or social benefits for doing so (Bassok & Reardon, 2013; Dağli & Jones, 2013; Lincove & Painter, 2006). An alternative perspective is that school readiness should be cultivated through classroom experiences that foster children's individual progress.

Recent Philosophical Directions Recent approaches to education, grounded in Vygotsky's sociocultural theory, capitalize on the rich social context of the classroom to spur

APPLYING WHAT WE KNOW

Signs of High-Quality Education in Elementary School

CLASSROOM CHARACTERISTICS	SIGNS OF QUALITY
Physical setting	Space is divided into richly equipped activity centers—for reading, writing, playing math or language games, exploring science, working on construction projects, using computers, and engaging in other academic pursuits. Spaces are used flexibly for individual and small-group activities and whole-class gatherings.
Curriculum	The curriculum helps children both achieve academic standards and make sense of their learning. Subjects are integrated so that children apply knowledge in one area to others. The curriculum is implemented through activities responsive to children's interests, ideas, and everyday lives, including their cultural backgrounds.
Daily activities	Teachers provide challenging activities that include opportunities for small-group and independent work. Groupings vary in size and makeup of children, depending on the activity and on children's learning needs. Teachers encourage cooperative learning and guide children in attaining it.
Interactions between teachers and children	Teachers foster each child's progress and use intellectually engaging strategies, including posing problems, asking thought-provoking questions, discussing ideas, and adding complexity to tasks. They also demonstrate, explain, coach, and assist in other ways, depending on each child's learning needs.
Evaluations of progress	Teachers regularly evaluate children's progress through written observations and work samples, which they use to enhance and individualize teaching. They help children reflect on their work and decide how to improve it. They also seek information and perspectives from parents on how well children are learning and include parents' views in evaluations.
Relationship with parents	Teachers forge partnerships with parents. They hold periodic conferences and encourage parents to visit the classroom anytime, to observe and volunteer.

Source: Copple & Bredekamp, 2009; National Association for the Education of Young Children, 2017.

children's learning. In these **social-constructivist classrooms,** children participate in a wide range of challenging activities with teachers and peers, with whom they jointly construct understandings. As children acquire knowledge and strategies through working together, they become competent, contributing members of their classroom community and advance in cognitive and social development (Bodrova & Leong, 2007; Lourenço, 2012). Vygotsky's emphasis on the social origins of complex mental activities has inspired the following educational themes:

- *Teachers and children as partners in learning.* A classroom rich in both teacher–child and child–child collaboration transfers culturally valued ways of thinking to children.
- *Experience with many types of symbolic communication in meaningful activities.* As children master reading, writing, and mathematics, they become aware of their culture's communication systems, reflect on their own thinking, and bring it under voluntary control. Can you identify research presented earlier in this chapter that supports this theme?
- *Teaching adapted to each child's zone of proximal development.* Assistance that both responds to current understandings and encourages children to take the next step forward helps ensure that each child makes the best progress possible.

Let's look at two examples of a growing number of programs that have translated these ideas into action.

Reciprocal Teaching Originally designed to improve reading comprehension in poorly achieving students, this Vygotsky-inspired teaching method has been extended to other subjects and all schoolchildren (Palincsar & Herrenkohl, 1999). In **reciprocal teaching,** a teacher and a small number of students form a cooperative group and take turns leading dialogues on the content of a text passage. Within the dialogues, group members apply four cognitive strategies: questioning, summarizing, clarifying, and predicting.

The dialogue leader (at first a teacher, later a student) begins by *asking questions* about the content of the text passage. Students offer answers, raise additional questions, and, in case of disagreement, reread the original text. Next, the leader *summarizes* the passage, and students discuss the summary and *clarify* unfamiliar ideas. Finally, the leader encourages students to *predict* upcoming content based on clues in the passage.

Elementary and secondary school students exposed to reciprocal teaching show impressive gains in reading comprehension compared to controls taught in other ways (Okkinga et al., 2018; Schunemann, Spörer, & Brunstein, 2013; Spörer, Brunstein, & Kieschke, 2009). Notice how reciprocal teaching creates a zone of proximal development in which children learn to scaffold one another's progress and assume more responsibility for comprehending text passages. Also, by collaborating with others, children forge group expectations for high-level thinking, more often apply their metacognitive knowledge, and acquire skills vital for learning and success in everyday life.

A teacher and students form a community of learners to plan, plant, and track the growth of a vegetable garden. During this complex, long-term project, all participants—adults as well as children—may become experts who share knowledge, teaching one another.

Communities of Learners Recognizing that collaboration requires a supportive context to be most effective, another Vygotsky-based innovation makes it a schoolwide value. Classrooms become **communities of learners** where teachers guide the overall process of learning but no other distinction is made between adult and child contributors: All participate in joint endeavors and have the authority to define and resolve problems. This approach is based on the assumption that different people have different expertises that can benefit the community and that students, too, may become experts (Sewell, St George, & Cullen, 2013). Classroom activities are often long-term projects addressing complex, real-world problems. In working toward project goals, children and teachers draw on the expertises of one another and of others within and outside the school.

In a rural school in Tanzania, Africa, a researcher knowledgeable about the community-of-learners approach guided teachers in an elementary school in launching several after-school science clubs. The teachers collaborated with 10- to 15-year-old students in investigating how to induce changes in local health, agricultural, and environmental practices. For example, the health club conducted research on the number and type of illnesses that had recently affected their family members; studied the causes, symptoms, treatment, and prevention of serious diseases in their community, such as malaria, HIV/AIDS, and tuberculosis; and shadowed doctors and nurses as they engaged in daily activities at a nearby hospital. Club members shared their findings and experiences with one another and with community representatives, collaborating with them to come up with ways that the knowledge gathered could be used to improve local health practices (Roberts, Brown, & Edwards, 2015). The result was a multifaceted understanding of the topic that would have been too difficult and time-consuming for any learner to acquire alone.

After witnessing student involvement and enthusiasm in the after-school clubs, the Tanzanian teachers, who had previously used traditional teaching strategies, began to infuse community-of-learners collaborative, real-world problem-solving techniques into their classrooms. The community-of-learners approach broadens Vygotsky's concept of the zone of proximal development from a child collaborating with a more expert partner (adult or peer) to multiple, interrelated zones of collaboration.

LOOK and LISTEN

Ask an elementary school teacher to sum up his or her educational philosophy. Is it closest to a traditional, constructivist, or social-constructivist view? Has the teacher encountered any obstacles to implementing that philosophy? Explain.

12.5.2 Teacher–Student Interaction

Elementary and secondary school students describe good teachers as caring, helpful, and stimulating—behaviors associated with gains in motivation, achievement, and positive peer relations (Kiuru et al., 2015; Hughes & Kwok, 2006, 2007; Sabol & Pianta, 2012). But too many U.S. teachers—especially those in schools with many students from low-income families—emphasize repetitive drill over higher-level thinking, such as grappling with ideas and applying knowledge to new situations (Valli, Croninger, & Buese, 2012). This focus on low-level skills becomes increasingly pronounced over the school year as state-mandated achievement testing draws nearer.

Of course, teachers do not interact in the same way with all children. Well-behaved, high-achieving students typically get more support and praise, whereas unruly students have more conflicts with teachers and receive more criticism, which predicts increased unruliness and worsening achievement over time (Henricsson & Rydell, 2004; Rucinski, Brown, & Downer, 2018). Warm, low-conflict teacher–student relationships have an especially strong impact on the academic self-esteem, achievement, and social behavior of low-SES minority students and other children at risk for learning difficulties (Elledge et al., 2016; McCormick, O'Connor, & Horn, 2017; Spilt et al., 2012). But overall, higher-SES students—who tend to be higher-achieving and to have fewer learning and behavior problems—have more sensitive and supportive relationships with teachers (Jerome, Hamre, & Pianta, 2009).

Unfortunately, once teachers' attitudes toward students are established, they can become more extreme than is warranted by children's behavior. Of special concern are **educational self-fulfilling prophecies:** Children may adopt teachers' positive or negative views and start to live up to them. This effect is particularly strong when teachers emphasize competition and publicly compare children, regularly favoring the best students (Weinstein, 2002).

Teacher expectations have a greater impact on low-achieving than high-achieving students (McKown, Gregory, & Weinstein, 2010). When a teacher is critical, high achievers can fall back on their history of success. Low-achieving students' sensitivity to self-fulfilling prophecies can be beneficial when teachers believe in their capacity to learn. But biased teacher judgments are usually slanted in a negative direction. Among students with the same record of school performance, teachers tend to hold lower expectations for those from economically disadvantaged families—circumstances that contribute to declines in their achievement (Ready & Wright, 2011; Spreybroeck et al., 2012; Timmermans, Kuyper, & van der Werf, 2015).

Furthermore, much evidence confirms that academic stereotypes about ethnic minority students have self-fulfilling effects on their behavior (Madon et al., 2011). In one study, African-American and Hispanic elementary school students taught by high-bias teachers (who expected them to do poorly) showed substantially lower end-of-year achievement than their counterparts taught by low-bias teachers (McKown & Weinstein, 2008). Similarly, in a New Zealand study, teachers' negative beliefs about the academic ability of third- to seventh-grade Maori students relative to European-American students predicted nearly a full year's difference in math achievement between the two ethnicities at the end of the school year (Peterson et al., 2016). Recall our discussion of *stereotype threat*. A child in the position of confirming a negative stereotype may respond with especially intense anxiety and reduced motivation, amplifying a negative self-fulfilling prophecy.

12.5.3 Grouping Practices

In many schools, students are assigned to *homogeneous* groups or classes, in which children of similar ability levels are taught together. Homogeneous grouping can be a potent source of self-fulfilling prophecies. Low-group students—who as early as first grade are more likely to be low-SES, minority, and male—get more drill on basic facts and skills, engage in less discussion, and progress at a slower pace. Gradually, they decline in self-esteem and motivation and fall further behind in achievement (Lleras & Rangel, 2009; Worthy, Hungerford-Kresser, & Hampton, 2009).

Unfortunately, widespread SES and ethnic segregation in U.S. schools consigns large numbers of low-SES, minority students to a form of schoolwide, deleterious homogeneous

Fourth graders work together to complete an assignment. Successful cooperative learning (page 466) enhances children's enjoyment of learning and academic achievement.

Social Issues: Education | Magnet Schools: Equal Access to High-Quality Education

Fourth graders at a magnet school in Florida discuss a reading assignment. Because of their rich academic offerings and innovative teaching, magnet schools typically attract students diverse in ethnicity and SES.

Each school-day morning, Emma leaves her affluent suburban neighborhood, riding a school bus to a magnet school in a mostly African-American neighborhood. In her fifth-grade class, she settles into a science project with her friend Zaniya, who lives in the local neighborhood. For the first hour of the day, Emma and Zaniya use a thermometer, ice water, and a stopwatch to determine which of several materials is the best insulator, recording and graphing their data. Throughout the school, which specializes in innovative math and science teaching, students diverse in SES and ethnicity learn side by side.

Despite the 1954 U.S. Supreme Court *Brown v. Board of Education* decision ordering schools to desegregate, school integration began to recede during the 1990s as federal courts canceled their integration orders and returned this authority to states and cities. Since 2000, the racial–ethnic divide in U.S. education has intensified. When minority students from low-SES families attend ethnically mixed schools, most do so with other minorities. Both African-American and Hispanic students are far more likely than European-American students to attend schools where 60 percent or more of the student body lives in poverty (Orfield et al., 2016).

U.S. schools in high-poverty neighborhoods are vastly disadvantaged in funding and therefore in educational opportunities, largely because public education is primarily supported by local property taxes. Federal and state grants-in-aid are not sufficient to close this funding gap between rich and poor districts. Consequently, in segregated neighborhoods, dilapidated school buildings; inexperienced teachers; high teacher turnover rates; outdated, poor-quality educational resources; and school cultures that fail to encourage strong teaching and student motivation are widespread. According to a large-scale study that included millions of public school students, the greater the difference in poverty rates between European-American and African-American students' schools, the larger the achievement gap (Reardon, 2015).

Magnet schools were introduced in the 1970s to promote voluntary desegregation by offering families school choices that would draw students from across neighborhood boundaries. Today, over 3,200 magnets enrolling more than 3.5 million students exist (U.S. Department of Education, 2017a). In addition to the usual curriculum, magnets emphasize a specific area of interest—such as performing arts, math and science, or technology. Families are attracted to magnet schools (hence the name) by their rich academic offerings. Often they are located in economically disadvantaged, minority areas, where they serve the neighborhood student population. Other students, who apply and are typically admitted by lottery, are bussed in—many from well-to-do city and suburban neighborhoods. In another model, all students—including those in the surrounding neighborhood—must apply. In either case, magnet schools are voluntarily desegregated.

The majority of evaluations conducted on magnet schools that use lottery systems for admission indicate that they succeed in enhancing minority student achievement (Pack, 2019; Wang & Herman, 2019). One such study compared Connecticut students enrolled in magnet middle schools with those whose lottery numbers were not drawn and who therefore attended other city schools. Although magnet-school enrollees and nonadmitted applicants were similar in ethnicity, SES, and prior academic achievement, magnet students showed greater gains in reading and math achievement over a two-year period (Bifulco, Cobb, & Bell, 2009). These outcomes were strongest for low-SES, ethnic minority students.

Magnet schools offer a path to SES and ethnic equity in quality of education while also enhancing teaching and learning. They are a promising approach to overcoming the negative forces of SES and ethnic isolation in American schools.

---

grouping. Refer to the Social Issues: Education box above to find out how heterogeneous learning contexts can reduce achievement differences between SES groups and ethnic minority and majority students.

However, small, heterogeneous groups of students working together do not necessarily engage in high-quality discourse that promotes learning, such as elaborating on one another's ideas and engaging in collaborative reasoning. Often their interaction is of lower quality than that of homogeneous groups of above-average students (Murphy et al., 2009; Webb, Nemer, & Chizhik, 1998). For collaboration between heterogeneous peers to succeed, children need extensive training and guidance in **cooperative learning,** in which small groups of classmates work toward common goals—by considering one another's ideas, appropriately challenging one another, providing sufficient explanations to correct misunderstandings, and resolving differences of opinion on the basis of reasons and evidence. When teachers explain, model, and have children role-play how to work together effectively, cooperative learning among heterogeneous peers results in more complex reasoning, greater enjoyment of learning, and achievement gains across a wide range of subjects (Jadallah et al., 2011; Murphy et al., 2017; Slavin, 2015).

Consider an investigation in which teachers taught heterogeneous groups of fourth graders to collaborate in reasoning about controversial issues, such as whether zoos are good places for animals. Over 10 group sessions, the students increasingly engaged in more advanced reasoning by analogy—comparisons that moved beyond surface features ("In a zoo it would be just like being in jail") to higher-order relations ("Pretend this classroom is like a cage. Who would rather be here or recess?"). During discussions, use of analogies "snowballed." When one student introduced an analogy, other students often elaborated on it and contributed new analogies ("'Cause it's like your mom locking you in your room for a week") (Lin et al., 2012). Together, students used analogy as a powerfully persuasive tool, capitalizing on it to introduce new information and perspectives.

12.5.4 Educational Screen Media

Virtually all public schools in industrialized nations have integrated computers into their instructional programs and can access the Internet. And, as noted in Chapter 9, most U.S. children have access to a home computer and one or more mobile devices with an Internet connection, including smartphones and tablets (U.S. Census Bureau, 2018a).

Interactive screen media use is associated with academic progress. Word processing, for example, enables children to write freely, without having to struggle with handwriting. Because they can revise their text's meaning and style and check their spelling, they worry less about making mistakes. As a result, their written products tend to be longer and of higher quality (Clements & Sarama, 2003). And as in early childhood, computer programming projects promote metacognition, reasoning, mathematical and spatial abilities, and creative thinking, and they are common classroom contexts for peer collaboration (Scherer, Siddiq, & Viveros, 2019).

As children get older, they increasingly use interactive media for schoolwork, mostly to search the Web for information and to prepare written assignments—activities linked to improved problem-solving skills and academic achievement (Judge, Puckett, & Bell, 2006; Tran & Subrahmanyam, 2013). The more low-SES middle school students use the Internet for information gathering (either for school or for personal interests), the better their subsequent reading achievement and school grades (Jackson et al., 2011). Perhaps those who use the Web to find information also devote more time to reading, given that many Web pages are heavily text-based. As students work on school projects, social media platforms that offer video chatting and conferencing enable them to collaborate with students in distant locations, which contributes to their engagement and learning (Chassiakos et al., 2016).

Although video game play is increasingly being integrated into classroom teaching because of its rich cognitive benefits, boys are far more likely than girls to be attracted to it. In this classroom, girls are encouraged to play challenging educational games on tablets.

With age, video game play rises dramatically: two-thirds of U.S. 6- to 8-year-olds, and the overwhelming majority of 8- to 18-year-olds, have played at one time or another. Young school-age children, on average, devote 42 minutes per day to gaming, older school-age children and adolescents 80 minutes. Boys are two to three times more likely than girls to be daily players (Rideout, 2015, 2018).

Although video games with violent content are harmful (see Chapter 10), electronic game play is increasingly being integrated into classroom teaching because of its rich cognitive benefits. These include gains in eye-and-hand coordination, visual processing speed, executive function, strategic thinking, spatial reasoning, and problem solving, all of which facilitate children's academic learning. Games emphasizing academic knowledge and skills, such as reading or math, succeed in teaching their intended content (Blumberg et al., 2019). And because adventure games typically involve substantial cognitive challenge—navigating a series of worlds and manipulating variables to overcome obstacles—successful play boosts several of the cognitive abilities just mentioned along with others, including strategic thinking, planning, problem solving, cognitive self-regulation, and (in fantasy role-play games) imagination (Adachi & Willoughby, 2013; Boyan & Sherry, 2011; Valkenburg & Calvert, 2012). Furthermore, playing electronic games collaboratively with peers can promote cooperative skills, which may transfer to other contexts.

Despite unprecedented access to interactive media by today's children, those from low-SES homes remain disadvantaged relative to their higher-SES agemates (as noted in Chapter 9). Furthermore, schools in high-poverty areas are often inadequately equipped with electronic devices and high-speed Internet, and their teachers often lack sufficient training and support to ensure effective classroom use of games and other media tools (Herold, 2017). With respect to gender, boys spend more time with screen media than girls and use them somewhat differently. Boys, as mentioned earlier, play games far more often than girls, and they also devote more time to downloading music, creating Web pages, writing computer programs, and using graphics programs. Girls emphasize information gathering and social communication (Lenhart et al., 2010; Looker & Thiessen, 2003; Rideout, Foehr, & Roberts, 2010). Schools need to ensure that girls and economically disadvantaged students have many opportunities to benefit from the diverse, cognitively enriching aspects of media technology.

Because children find mastering complex game elements highly motivating, designing electronic games to teach academic content is likely to boost achievement for all children. But devoting too much time to screen media—especially playing entertainment video games, even those with nonviolent content—predicts declines in school performance, even after an array of other factors that might explain the association are controlled (Boxer, Groves, & Docherty, 2015; Gnambs et al., 2019; Hofferth, 2010). Like entertainment TV (see Chapter 10), excessive game play detracts from time devoted to homework, reading, and other activities that have vital educational benefits.

© LAURA DWIGHT PHOTOGRAPHY

In this inclusive classroom, extra support from a teaching assistant enables a student with special needs to join his classmates for a small-group writing lesson. When the learning needs of students with disabilities are met, inclusion is beneficial for academic achievement.

12.5.5 Teaching Children with Special Needs

We have seen that effective teachers flexibly adjust their teaching strategies to accommodate students with a wide range of abilities and characteristics. But such adjustments are increasingly challenging at the low and high ends of the ability distribution. How do schools serve children with special learning needs?

Children with Learning Difficulties   U.S. legislation mandates that schools place children who require special supports for learning in the "least restrictive" (as close to normal as possible) environments that meet their educational needs. In **inclusive classrooms,** students with learning difficulties learn alongside typical students in the regular educational setting for part or all of the school day—a practice designed to prepare them for participation in society and to combat prejudices against individuals with disabilities. Largely as the result of parental pressures, an increasing number of students experience *full inclusion*—full-time placement in regular classrooms.

Students with *mild intellectual disability* are sometimes integrated into inclusive classrooms. Typically, their IQs fall between 50 and 70, and they also show problems in adaptive behavior, or skills of everyday living (American Psychiatric Association, 2013). But the largest number of students designated for inclusion—5 to 10 percent of school-age children—have **learning disabilities,** great difficulty with one or more aspects of learning, usually reading. As a result, they do not progress academically at an appropriate rate, even when more intensive instruction is provided in the regular classroom. Often the problems of students with learning disabilities express themselves in other ways—for example, as deficits in processing speed and executive function (Church, 2019; Cornoldi et al., 2014). Their problems cannot be traced to any obvious physical or emotional difficulty or to environmental disadvantage. Instead, deficits in brain functioning are involved (Swanson, Harris, & Graham, 2014). Some learning disabilities run in families, and in certain cases, specific genes have been identified that contribute to the problem (Goldstein, 2011b; Mozzi et al., 2017). In many instances, the cause is unknown.

Although some students benefit academically from inclusion, many do not. Achievement gains depend on both the severity of the disability and the support services available (Downing, 2010). Furthermore, children with disabilities often are rejected by regular-classroom peers. Students with intellectual disability are overwhelmed by the social skills of their classmates; they cannot interact adeptly in a conversation or game. And the processing deficits of some students with learning disabilities lead to problems in social awareness and responsiveness (Nowicki, Brown, & Stepien, 2014).

Does this mean that students with special needs cannot be served in regular classrooms? Not necessarily. Often these children do best when they receive instruction in a resource room for part of the day and in the regular classroom for the remainder (McLeskey & Waldron, 2011). In the resource room, a special education teacher works with students on an individual and small-group basis. Then, with extra support available that fits students' learning needs, they join typically developing classmates for different subjects and amounts of time. Under these conditions, inclusion is beneficial for academic achievement (Tremblay, 2013).

Special steps must be taken to promote positive peer relations in inclusive classrooms. Peer tutoring experiences in which teachers guide typical students in supporting the academic progress of classmates with learning difficulties lead to friendly interaction, improved peer acceptance, and achievement gains (Mastropieri et al., 2013). And when teachers prepare their class for the arrival of a student with special needs, inclusion may foster emotional sensitivity and prosocial behavior among regular classmates.

Gifted Children   In Joey and Lizzie's school, some children were **gifted,** displaying exceptional intellectual strengths. One or two students in every grade have IQ scores above 130, the standard definition of giftedness based on intelligence test performance (Pfeiffer & Yermish, 2014). High-IQ children, as we have seen, have keen memories and an exceptional capacity to solve challenging academic problems. Yet recognition that intelligence tests do not sample the entire range of human cognitive skills, as noted earlier in this chapter, has led to an expanded conception of giftedness.

Creativity and Talent **Creativity** is the ability to produce work that is *original* yet *appropriate*—something that others have not thought of that is useful in some way (Kaufman & Sternberg, 2007). A child with high potential for creativity can be designated as gifted. Tests of creative capacity tap **divergent thinking**—the generation of multiple and unusual possibilities when faced with a task or problem. Divergent thinking contrasts sharply with **convergent thinking,** which involves arriving at a single correct answer and is emphasized on intelligence tests (Guilford, 1985). Consistent with this distinction, correlations between divergent thinking and IQ scores are weak (Guignard & Lubart, 2007; Guignard, Kermarrec, & Tordjman, 2016).

Because highly creative children (like high-IQ children) are often better at some types of tasks than others, a variety of tests of divergent thinking are available (Runco, 1992; Torrance, 1988). A verbal measure might ask children to name uses for common objects (such as a newspaper). A figural measure might ask them to come up with drawings based on a circular motif (see Figure 12.8). A "real-world

As sixth graders rehearse a play they have written, they gain experience in generating original ideas, evaluating those ideas, and choosing the most promising—vital ingredients of creativity.

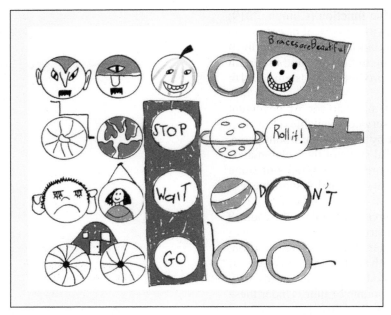

FIGURE 12.8 **Responses of an 8-year-old who scored high on a figural measure of divergent thinking.** This child was asked to make as many pictures as she could from the circles on the page. The titles she gave her drawings, from left to right, are as follows: "Dracula," "one-eyed monster," "pumpkin," "Hula-Hoop," "poster," "wheelchair," "earth," "stop-light," "planet," "movie camera," "sad face," "picture," "beach ball," "the letter O," "car," "glasses." Tests of divergent thinking tap only one of the complex cognitive contributions to creativity. (Reprinted by permission of Laura E. Berk.)

problem" measure requires students to suggest solutions to everyday problems. Responses can be scored for the number of ideas generated and their originality.

Yet critics point out that these measures are poor predictors of creative accomplishment in everyday life because they tap only one of the complex cognitive contributions to creativity (Plucker & Makel, 2010). Also involved are defining new and important problems, evaluating divergent ideas, choosing the most promising, and calling on relevant knowledge to understand and solve problems (Lubart, Georgsdottir, & Besançon, 2009; Plucker, Guo, & Dilley, 2018).

Consider these ingredients, and you will see why people usually demonstrate expertise and creativity in only one or a few related areas. Even individuals designated as gifted by virtue of their high IQ often show uneven ability across academic subjects. Partly for this reason, definitions of giftedness have been extended to include **talent**—outstanding performance in a specific field. Case studies reveal that excellence in such endeavors as creative writing, mathematics, science, music, visual arts, athletics, and leadership has roots in specialized skills that first appear in childhood (Sobotnik, Worrell, & Olszewski-Kubilius, 2016). Highly talented children are biologically prepared to master their domain of interest, and they display a passion for doing so.

But talent must be nurtured. Studies of the backgrounds of talented children and highly accomplished adults often reveal warm, sensitive parents who provide a stimulating home life, are devoted to developing their child's abilities, and provide models of hard work and high achievement. These parents are reasonably demanding but not driving or overambitious (Witte et al., 2015). They arrange for caring teachers while the child is young and for more rigorous master teachers as the child's talent develops.

Compared with their typically developing peers, most gifted children are capable of greater understanding of themselves and others. As a result, they cope especially well with stress and conflict and are usually well adjusted. However, as gifted students move into adolescence, they are more likely than their classmates to experience social isolation, partly because their exceptional abilities and highly driven, independent styles leave them out of step with peers and partly because they enjoy solitude, which is necessary to develop their talents (Pfeiffer & Yermish, 2014). Still, gifted children desire gratifying peer relationships, and some—more often girls than boys—try to become better-liked by hiding their abilities (Neihart & Yeo, 2018).

Finally, whereas many talented youths become experts in their fields and solve problems in new ways, few become highly creative. Rapidly mastering an existing field and thinking flexibly within it require different skills than innovating in that field. Gifted individuals who are restless with the status quo and daring about changing it are rare. And before these individuals become creative masters, they typically spend a decade or more becoming proficient in their field of interest (Simonton, 2018). The world, however, needs both experts and creators.

Educating the Gifted Availability of gifted programs in public schools varies widely across the United States, with fewer than half of states mandating them and only a handful fully funding them. Yet public school programs for the gifted are essential for ensuring equality of educational opportunity (Davidson Institute, 2019; Hughes, 2015). When nurturing children's talents is entirely left to parents, educational enrichment experiences rarely reach those from economically disadvantaged families.

Gifted children thrive in learning environments that permit self-chosen topics for extended projects; encourage critical thinking, complex problem solving, and creativity; and enable interaction with like-minded peers who stimulate one another's learning. Providing opportunities for educational advancement is essential (Little, 2018). Research consistently shows that gifted students who are permitted to move ahead—whether through acceleration to a higher grade or quickening of the pace of learning in particular subjects—far exceed their agemates in academic achievement while at the same time faring well socially (Colangelo & Assouline, 2009). If not sufficiently challenged, gifted students may lose their drive to excel.

Gardner's theory of multiple intelligences has inspired several model programs that provide enrichment to all students in diverse subjects, so any child capable of high-level performance can manifest it. Meaningful activities, each tapping a specific intelligence or set of intelligences, serve as contexts for assessing strengths and weaknesses and, on that basis, teaching new knowledge and original thinking (Hoerr, 2004). For example, linguistic intelligence might be fostered through storytelling or playwriting; spatial intelligence through drawing, sculpting, or media arts; and kinesthetic intelligence through dance or pantomime.

Evidence is still needed on how effectively these programs nurture children's talents and creativity. But they have already succeeded in one way—by highlighting the strengths of some students who previously had been considered unexceptional or even at risk for school failure (Ford, 2012). Consequently, they may be especially useful in identifying talented low-SES, ethnic minority children, whose capacities are particularly likely to be overlooked when giftedness is assessed only with IQ and achievement test scores.

12.5.6 How Well-Educated Are U.S. Children?

Our discussion of schooling has largely focused on how teachers can support the education of children. Yet we have also seen that many factors—both within and outside schools—affect children's learning. Societal values, school resources, quality of teaching, and parental encouragement all play important roles. These multiple influences are especially apparent when schooling is examined in cross-cultural perspective.

In international studies of reading, mathematics, and science achievement, young people in China, South Korea, Japan, and Singapore are consistently top performers. Among Western nations, Canada, Estonia, Finland, the Netherlands, and Switzerland are regularly in the top tier. But U.S. students typically perform at or below the international averages (see Figure 12.9) (Programme for International Student Assessment, 2017).

Why do U.S. students fall behind many other developed nations in academic accomplishments? According to questionnaire responses gathered from parents, students, and teachers to help place

	Country	Average Math Achievement Score
High-Performing Nations	Singapore	571
	China (Hong Kong)	554
	Taiwan	548
	China (Macao)	547
	Japan	536
	South Korea	529
	Switzerland	526
	Estonia	521
	Canada	518
	Netherlands	516
	Finland	514
	Denmark	513
	Belgium	513
	Slovenia	512
	Germany	508
	Poland	505
	Ireland	505
	Norway	504
Intermediate-Performing Nations	Austria	501
	France	499
	New Zealand	497
	Sweden	496
	United Kingdom	496
	Australia	495
	Portugal	495
	Russia	494
	Czech Republic	494
International Average = 492	Italy	491
	Iceland	489
	Spain	489
	Luxembourg	487
	Latvia	483
	Hungary	480
	Slovak Republic	479
	Israel	473
	United States	**470**
Low-Performing Nations	Greece	455
	Romania	442
	Turkey	417
	Mexico	407

FIGURE 12.9 **Average mathematics scores of 15-year-olds by country.** The Programme for International Student Assessment measures achievement of nationally representative samples of 15-year-olds attending public, private, urban, and rural schools in many countries around the world. In recent comparisons of developed nations, the United States performed below the international average in math; in reading and science, its performance was about average. (Adapted from Programme for International Student Assessment, 2017.)

A Finnish teacher passes out materials to her second-grade students. Finland's teachers are highly trained, and their education system—designed to cultivate initiative, problem solving, and creativity in all students—has nearly eliminated SES variations in achievement.

the international comparisons in context, instruction in the United States is less challenging, more focused on absorbing facts, and less focused on high-level reasoning and critical thinking than in other countries. Furthermore, countries with large socioeconomic inequalities (such as the United States) rank lower in achievement, in part because low-SES children tend to experience less favorable family and neighborhood conditions (Condron, 2013). But the United States is also far less equitable than top achieving countries in the quality of education it provides its low-SES and ethnic minority students. U.S. teachers, for example, vary much more in training, salaries, and teaching conditions than teachers in top achieving countries.

Finland is a case in point. In the 1980s, it abandoned a national testing system used to group students by ability and replaced it with curricula, teaching practices, and assessments aimed at cultivating initiative, problem solving, and creativity. Finnish teachers are highly trained: They must complete several years of government-funded graduate-level education (Ripley, 2013). And Finnish education is grounded in equal opportunity for all—a policy that has nearly eliminated SES variations in achievement, despite an influx of immigrant students from low-income families into Finnish schools over the past two decades.

In-depth research on learning environments in East Asian nations, such as Japan, South Korea, and Taiwan, also highlights social forces that foster strong student learning. Among these is cultural valuing of effort. Whereas American parents and teachers tend to regard native ability as the key to academic success, Japanese, Korean, and Taiwanese parents and teachers believe that all children can succeed academically as long as they try hard. East Asian children, influenced by interdependent values, typically view striving to do well in school as a moral obligation—part of their responsibility to family and community (Hau & Ho, 2010). As in Finland, all students in Japan, South Korea, and Taiwan receive the same nationally mandated, high-quality instruction, delivered by teachers who are well-prepared, highly respected in their society, and far better paid than U.S. teachers (Kang & Hong, 2008; U.S. Department of Education, 2018). Academic lessons are particularly well-organized and presented in ways that capture children's attention and encourage high-level thinking (Grow-Maienza, Hahn, & Joo, 2001).

The Finnish and East Asian examples underscore the need for American families, schools, and the larger society to work together to upgrade education. Over the past 15 years, U.S. international rankings in reading, math, and science achievement have declined. And although the U.S. National Assessment of Educational Progress—in which challenging achievement tests are given to nationally representative samples of fourth, eighth, and twelfth graders—has shown slight gains in reading and science scores and moderate gains in math scores since 1990, the increments have not been sufficient to catch up internationally (U.S. Department of Education, 2019).

These disappointing achievement outcomes underscore the need for "a broader, bolder approach" to U.S. education (Weiss & Reville, 2019). Recommended strategies, verified by research, include the following:

- Supporting parents in attaining economic security, creating stimulating home learning environments, monitoring their children's academic progress, and communicating often with teachers
- Investing in high-quality preschool education, so every child arrives at school ready to learn
- Strengthening teacher education
- Providing intellectually challenging, relevant instruction with real-world applications
- Vigorously pursuing school improvements that reduce the large inequities in quality of education between SES and ethnic groups

ASK YOURSELF

Connect ■ Review research on child-rearing styles on pages 392–394 in Chapter 10. What style do gifted children who realize their potential typically experience? Explain.

Apply ■ Sandy wonders why her daughter Mira's teacher often has students work on assignments in small, cooperative groups. Explain the benefits of this approach to Sandy. What must Mira's teacher do to ensure that cooperative learning succeeds?

Reflect ■ What grouping practices were used in your elementary education—homogeneous, heterogeneous, or a combination? What impact do you think those practices had on your motivation and achievement?

SUMMARY

12.1 Piaget's Theory: The Concrete Operational Stage (p. 431)

12.1a Describe advances in thinking and cognitive limitations during the concrete operational stage.

■ In the **concrete operational stage,** children's thought becomes more logical, flexible, and organized. Attainment of conservation requires the capacity for **decentration** and **reversibility.**

■ School-age children are also better at hierarchical classification and **seriation,** including **transitive inference.** Their spatial reasoning improves, as illustrated by their increasingly accurate **cognitive maps.** By the end of middle childhood, they form overall views of large-scale spaces and grasp the meaning of scale and map symbols.

■ Concrete operational children think logically only when dealing with concrete, tangible information, and mastery of concrete operational tasks occurs gradually.

12.1b Discuss follow-up research on concrete operational thought.

■ Specific cultural practices, especially those associated with schooling, promote mastery of certain Piagetian tasks, such as transitive inference problems.

■ Some neo-Piagetian theorists attribute the gradual development of operational thought to expansion of information-processing capacity. Case's theory proposes that gains in working-memory efficiency explain cognitive change within and between Piagetian stages.

12.2 Information Processing (p. 436)

12.2a Describe gains in executive function and memory in middle childhood, along with factors that influence children's progress.

■ Marked improvement in executive function enables school-age children to handle increasingly complex tasks that require integration of working memory, inhibition, and flexible thinking. Heredity and environment combine to influence executive function.

■ Increased speed of thinking supports gains in working-memory capacity. Children with working-memory deficits often experience learning difficulties in school.

■ During middle childhood, attention becomes more sustained, selective, and flexible. Deficits in executive processing and inhibition may underlie symptoms of **attention-deficit hyperactivity disorder (ADHD).**

■ Executive function skills can be improved directly through computer games that provide working memory training, and indirectly through activities such as exercise and mindfulness training.

■ Children become better at planning, particularly when adults turn over responsibility to them and guide and support them as needed.

■ Memory strategies also improve. **Rehearsal** is the first strategy to emerge, followed by **organization** and then **elaboration.** As children gain in processing speed, working-memory capacity, and familiarity with memory strategies, their use of strategies becomes increasingly automatic and effective.

■ Development of the long-term knowledge base facilitates strategic memory processing, as does children's motivation to use what they know.

■ The need for memory strategies is associated with societal modernization and formal schooling.

12.2b Describe the school-age child's theory of mind and capacity to engage in self-regulation.

■ Metacognition improves as school-age children come to view the mind as an active, constructive agent and, consequently, better understand cognitive processes and factors that influence them. Awareness of the role of mental inferences enables mastery of second-order false belief and promotes **recursive thought.**

■ School-age children also become increasingly conscious of how and why mental strategies work and able to discriminate good from bad reasoning.

■ **Cognitive self-regulation,** which develops gradually, predicts academic success. Children benefit from adult instruction in self-regulation, but providing them with opportunities to teach academic content to others is also effective.

12.2c *Describe applications of the information-processing approach to children's learning of reading and mathematics.*

- Skilled reading draws on all aspects of the information-processing system. A combination of whole-language and phonics is most effective for teaching beginning reading. Learning to recognize regularities in the English spelling system strengthens reading comprehension.

- Teaching that combines practice in basic skills with conceptual understanding also is best in mathematics. Students benefit from extensive opportunities to experiment with strategies and reason about number concepts. A vital foundation for mathematical development is the emergence of an increasingly accurate and complete representation of numerical magnitudes in a mental number line.

12.3 Individual Differences in Mental Development (p. 448)

12.3a *Describe major approaches to defining and measuring intelligence.*

- During the school years, IQ becomes more stable and correlates moderately with academic achievement. Most intelligence tests yield an overall score as well as scores for separate intellectual factors.

- Research combining the mental-testing approach with the information-processing approach to defining intelligence reveals a moderate relationship between processing speed and IQ and a strong association between executive function and general intelligence.

- Sternberg's **triarchic theory of successful intelligence** views intelligence as an interaction of analytical intelligence (information-processing skills), creative intelligence (ability to solve novel problems), and practical intelligence (application of intellectual skills in everyday situations).

- Gardner's **theory of multiple intelligences** identifies at least eight mental abilities, each with a distinct biological basis and course of development. It calls attention to several intelligences in nonacademic domains not tapped by IQ scores and to a set of skills that has become known as emotional intelligence.

12.3b *Describe evidence indicating that both heredity and environment contribute to intelligence.*

- Heritability estimates and adoption research reveal that intelligence is a product of both heredity and environment. A wealth of evidence indicates that poverty severely depresses the IQ scores of ethnic minority children. The **Flynn effect,** steady generational gains in IQ in many nations, is closely associated with extent of societal modernization.

- IQ scores are also affected by culturally influenced language and communication styles, acquired knowledge, and sheer amount of time spent in school. **Stereotype threat** can trigger anxiety that impairs test performance. **Dynamic assessment** helps many minority children perform more competently on mental tests.

12.4 Language Development (p. 457)

12.4a *Describe changes in school-age children's metalinguistic awareness, vocabulary, grammar, and pragmatics.*

- **Metalinguistic awareness** contributes to language progress in middle childhood. Vocabulary growth accelerates, and children display a more precise and flexible understanding of word meanings. They also use more complex grammatical constructions and produce more organized, detailed, and expressive narratives.

12.4b *Describe bilingual development, the cognitive benefits of bilingualism, and the effectiveness of bilingual education programs.*

- Children who are simultaneous bilinguals attain most language milestones according to a typical timetable. When preschool and school-age sequential bilinguals acquire their second language, they take from 1 to 5 years to attain the competence of native-speaking agemates.

- Bilingual children have denser gray and white matter in areas of the brain devoted to language and are better at diverse executive function skills and certain aspects of metalinguistic awareness.

- The benefits of sustained bilingual education throughout the school years has led to an increase in two-way language immersion programs in the United States.

12.5 Children's Learning in School (p. 462)

12.5a *Describe the influence of educational philosophies on children's motivation and academic achievement.*

- Older students in **traditional classrooms** have a slight edge in academic achievement over those in **constructivist classrooms,** who gain in academic motivation, critical thinking, and social and moral maturity.

- Vygotsky-inspired **social-constructivist classrooms** use the rich social context of the classroom to promote learning, often employing such methods as **reciprocal teaching** and **communities of learners.** Students benefit from teaching adapted to each child's zone of proximal development and from collaborating with others.

12.5b *Discuss the role of teacher–student interaction and grouping practices in academic achievement.*

- Caring, helpful, and stimulating teaching fosters children's motivation and academic achievement. **Educational self-fulfilling prophecies** have a greater impact on low achievers than high achievers. Teachers who expect ethnic minority students to do poorly have a substantial self-fulfilling impact on their end-of-year academic achievement.

- For collaboration with heterogeneous peers to result in achievement gains, children need extensive training in **cooperative learning.** Ethnically diverse magnet schools are also associated with higher achievement.

12.5c *Describe academic benefits of, as well as concerns about, educational media.*

- Using screen media for schoolwork—including searching for information, preparing assignments, and playing academic and nonviolent adventure games—has cognitive benefits and is linked to improved achievement.

- Low-SES children are disadvantaged in computer and Internet use, and boys spend more time with screen media than girls. Devoting excessive time to entertainment screen media predicts declines in school performance.

12.5d *Describe conditions that promote successful placement of children with learning disabilities in regular classrooms.*

- Students with mild intellectual disability and **learning disabilities** are often placed in **inclusive classrooms** where they learn alongside typical students. Success depends on meeting individual academic needs and promoting positive peer relations.

12.5e *Describe the characteristics of gifted children and efforts to meet their educational needs.*

- **Giftedness** includes high IQ, **creativity,** and **talent.** Tests of creativity that tap **divergent thinking** focus on only one of the ingredients of creativity. Highly talented children generally have warm, sensitive parents who nurture their exceptional abilities.
- Gifted children thrive in learning environments that permit self-chosen topics for extended projects, encourage critical thinking and creativity, and enable interaction with like-minded peers.

12.5f *Discuss factors that lead U.S. students to fall behind in academic achievement compared to students in top-achieving nations.*

- In international studies of achievement, U.S. students typically display average or below-average performance. Compared with education in top-achieving nations, U.S. instruction is less focused on high-level reasoning and critical thinking and less equitable across SES groups.

IMPORTANT TERMS AND CONCEPTS

attention-deficit hyperactivity disorder (ADHD) (p. 437)
cognitive maps (p. 432)
cognitive self-regulation (p. 443)
communities of learners (p. 464)
concrete operational stage (p. 431)
constructivist classroom (p. 462)
convergent thinking (p. 469)
cooperative learning (p. 466)
creativity (p. 469)
decentration (p. 431)

divergent thinking (p. 469)
dynamic assessment (p. 456)
educational self-fulfilling prophecies (p. 465)
elaboration (p. 440)
Flynn effect (p. 454)
gifted (p. 469)
inclusive classrooms (p. 468)
learning disabilities (p. 468)
metalinguistic awareness (p. 457)
organization (p. 440)
reciprocal teaching (p. 463)

recursive thought (p. 443)
rehearsal (p. 440)
reversibility (p. 431)
seriation (p. 432)
social-constructivist classroom (p. 463)
stereotype threat (p. 455)
talent (p. 470)
theory of multiple intelligences (p. 451)
traditional classroom (p. 462)
transitive inference (p. 432)
triarchic theory of successful intelligence (p. 450)

13 | Emotional and Social Development in Middle Childhood

Walking in the Rain
Hennie Brandt, 7 years,
Republic of Namibia

As children reach school age,
empathy increases and friendships become more selective,
developing into mutual
relationships based on trust
and emotional commitment.

*Reprinted with permission from
Children's Museum of the Arts
Permanent Collection, New York, NY*

One afternoon as school dismissed, Joey urgently tapped his best friend Terry on the shoulder. "Gotta talk to you," Joey pleaded. "Everything was going great until I got that word—*porcupine*," Joey went on, referring to the fifth-grade spelling bee that day. "Just my luck! *P-o-r-k,* that's how I spelled it! I can't believe it. Maybe I'm not so good at social studies," Joey confided, "but I *know* I'm one of the best spellers in our class, better than that stuck-up Belinda Brown. I knocked myself out studying those spelling lists. Then *she* got all the easy words. If I *had to* lose, why couldn't it be to a nice person?"

Joey's conversation reflects new emotional and social capacities. By entering the spelling bee, he illustrates a major change of middle childhood: energetic pursuit of meaningful achievement in his culture. As Erik Erikson emphasized, children whose previous experiences have been positive enter middle childhood ready to forge a sense of *industry:* feelings of competence at useful skills and tasks. In cultures everywhere, adults respond to children's improved physical and cognitive capacities by making new demands, and children are ready to benefit from these challenges.

In most of the world, the transition to middle childhood is marked by the beginning of formal schooling. With it comes literacy training, which prepares children for a vast array of specialized careers. In school, children discover their own and others' unique capacities. Notice how the spelling bee induced Joey to size up his own and his classmate's strengths, weaknesses, and personality traits. Schooling also increases opportunities for children to cooperate with agemates, contributing to a growing understanding of the value of division of labor and to an enhanced sense of moral commitment and responsibility. And as time spent with peers rises during the school years, peer relationships become more influential in children's lives. Friendship, for example, means something different to Joey than it did earlier: He counts on his best friend, Terry, for understanding and emotional support.

In this chapter, we take a close look at children's changing views of themselves and others, moral understanding, and peer relationships during middle childhood. Each increases in complexity as children reason more effectively and spend more time in school and with agemates.

Despite changing parent–child relationships, the family remains powerfully influential in middle childhood. Today, family structures are more diverse than ever before. Through Joey's and his younger sister Lizzie's experiences with parental divorce, we will see that family functioning is far more important than family structure in ensuring children's well-being. Finally, we discuss some common emotional problems of middle childhood. ■

13.1 Self-Understanding

In middle childhood, children become able to describe themselves in terms of psychological traits, to compare their own characteristics with those of their peers, and to speculate about the causes of their strengths and weaknesses. These transformations in self-understanding have a major impact on children's self-esteem.

13.1.1 Self-Concept

During the school years, children refine their self-concept, organizing their observations of behaviors and internal states into general dispositions. A major change takes place between ages 8 and 11, as the following self-description by a fourth grader illustrates:

13.1 Describe school-age children's self-concept and self-esteem, and discuss factors that affect their achievement-related attributions.

I'm pretty popular, at least with the girls who I spend time with, but not with the super-popular girls who think they are cooler than everyone else. With my friends, I know what it takes to be liked, so I'm nice to people and helpful and can keep secrets…. Sometimes, if I get in a bad mood I'll say something that can be a little mean and then I'm ashamed of myself. At school, I'm feeling pretty smart in certain subjects like language arts and social studies…. But I'm feeling pretty dumb in math and science, especially when I see how well a lot of the other kids are doing. I now understand that I can be both smart and dumb, you aren't just one or the other. (Harter, 2012, p. 59)

Instead of specific behaviors, this child emphasizes competencies: "smart in certain subjects like language arts and social studies" and "having good English skills." 'She also describes her personality, mentioning both positive and negative traits: "helpful" and "can keep secrets" but sometimes "a little mean." Older school-age children are far less likely than younger children to describe themselves in extreme, all-or-none ways (Harter, 2012).

These evaluative self-descriptions result from school-age children's frequent **social comparisons**—judgments of their appearance, abilities, and behavior in relation to those of others. Notice, in the introduction to this chapter, Joey's observation that he is "one of the best spellers" in his class. Similarly, our fourth grader's self-description mentions feeling "smart" at some subjects but not at others, especially when she sees "how well a lot of the other kids are doing." Whereas 4- to 6-year-olds can compare their own performance to that of a single peer, older children can compare multiple individuals, including themselves (Harter, 2012).

13.1.2 Cognitive, Social, and Cultural Influences on Self-Concept

What factors account for these revisions in self-concept? Cognitive development affects the changing *structure* of the self. School-age children, as we saw in Chapter 12, can better coordinate several aspects of a situation in reasoning about their physical world. Similarly, in the social realm, they combine typical experiences and behaviors into stable psychological dispositions, blend positive and negative characteristics, and compare their own characteristics with those of many peers (Harter, 2012). In middle childhood, children also gain a clearer understanding that traits are linked to specific desires (a "generous" person *wants* to share) and, therefore, are causes of behavior (Yuill & Pearson, 1998).

The changing *content* of self-concept is a product of both cognitive capacities and feedback from others. Sociologist George Herbert Mead (1934) proposed that a well-organized psychological self emerges when children adopt a view of the self that resembles others' attitudes toward the child. Mead's ideas indicate that *perspective-taking skills*—in particular, an improved ability to infer what other people are thinking and to distinguish those viewpoints from one's own—are crucial for developing a self-concept based on personality traits. As we saw in Chapter 12, middle childhood brings the capacity for recursive thought, which enables school-age children to "read" others' messages more accurately and internalize their expectations. As they do so, they form an *ideal self* that they use to evaluate their real self. As we will see, a large discrepancy between the two can greatly undermine self-esteem, leading to sadness, hopelessness, and depression.

Parental support for self-development continues to be vitally important. School-age children with a history of elaborative parent–child conversations about past experiences construct rich, positive narratives about the self and thus have more complex, favorable, and coherent self-concepts (Baddeley & Singer, 2015). Children also look to more people beyond the family for information about themselves as they enter a wider range of settings in school and community. And

As school-age children enter a wider range of settings beyond the family, their self-concepts include frequent reference to social groups. When asked about themselves, these baseball players are likely to mention being a member of a Little League team.

© SYRACUSE NEWSPAPERS/M.GREENLAR/THE IMAGE WORKS

self-descriptions now include reference to social groups: "I'm a Boy Scout and a Prairie City soccer player," said Joey. As children move into adolescence, their sources of self-definition become more selective. Although parents and other adults remain influential, self-concept is increasingly vested in relationships with and feedback from close friends (Oosterwegel & Oppenheimer, 1993; Tarrant, MacKenzie, & Hewitt, 2006).

But recall that the content of self-concept varies from culture to culture. In earlier chapters, we noted that Asian parents stress harmonious interdependence, whereas Western parents emphasize independence and self-assertion. When asked to recall personally significant past experiences (their last birthday, a time their parent scolded them), U.S. school-age children give longer accounts including more personal preferences, interests, skills, and opinions. Chinese children, in contrast, more often refer to social interactions and to others rather than themselves. Similarly, in their self-descriptions, American and European children list more personal attributes ("I'm smart," "I'm good at singing," "I like hockey"); Chinese children, more attributes involving group membership and relationships with others ("I'm in fifth grade," "My friends are crazy about me," "I'm British-born Chinese") (Wang, 2006; Wang, Shao, & Li, 2010). Interestingly, however, in a trend that likely reflects growing valuing of individualistic traits in China's rapidly expanding market economy, Chinese schoolchildren in urban areas have recently increased the mention of personal attributes in their self-descriptions (Dai, Williams, & McGregor, 2016).

13.1.3 Self-Esteem

Recall that most preschoolers have extremely high self-esteem. But as children enter school and receive much more feedback about how well they perform compared with their peers, self-esteem differentiates and also adjusts to a more realistic level.

To study school-age children's self-esteem, researchers ask them to indicate the extent to which statements such as "I'm good at reading" or "I'm usually the one chosen for games" are true of themselves. By age 6 to 7, children in diverse Western cultures have formed at least four broad self-evaluations: academic competence, social competence, physical/athletic competence, and physical appearance. Within these are more refined categories that become increasingly distinct with age (Marsh, 1990; Marsh & Ayotte, 2003; Van den Bergh & De Rycke, 2003). Furthermore, the capacity to view the self in terms of stable dispositions permits school-age children to combine their separate self-evaluations into an overall psychological image of themselves—a global self-esteem (Harter, 2012). As a result, self-esteem takes on the hierarchical structure shown in Figure 13.1 on page 480.

Children attach greater importance to certain self-evaluations than to others. Although individual differences exist, during childhood and adolescence perceived physical appearance correlates more strongly with global self-esteem than does any other self-esteem factor (Baudson, Weber, & Freund, 2016; O'Dea, 2012; von Soest, Wichstrøm, & Kvalem, 2016). Emphasis on appearance—in the media, by parents and peers, and in society—has major implications for young people's overall satisfaction with themselves.

Typically, self-esteem remains high during elementary school but becomes more realistic and nuanced as children evaluate themselves in various areas (Chung et al., 2017; Marsh, Craven, & Debus, 1998). These changes occur as children receive more competence-related feedback, as their performances are increasingly judged in relation to those of others, and as they become cognitively capable of social comparison (Bukowski & Raufelder, 2018).

13.1.4 Influences on Self-Esteem

From middle childhood on, individual differences in self-esteem become increasingly stable (Steiger et al., 2014; Trzesniewski, Donnellan, & Robins, 2003). And positive relationships among self-esteem, valuing of various activities, and success at those activities emerge and strengthen with age. Academic self-esteem predicts how important, useful, and enjoyable children judge school subjects to be, their willingness to try hard, and their achievement (Denissen, Zarrett, & Eccles, 2007; Whitesell et al., 2009; Yeung, 2011). Children with high social

LOOK and LISTEN

Ask several 8- to 11-year-old children to tell you about themselves. Do their self-descriptions include personality traits (both positive and negative), social comparisons, and references to social groups, as is typical in middle childhood?

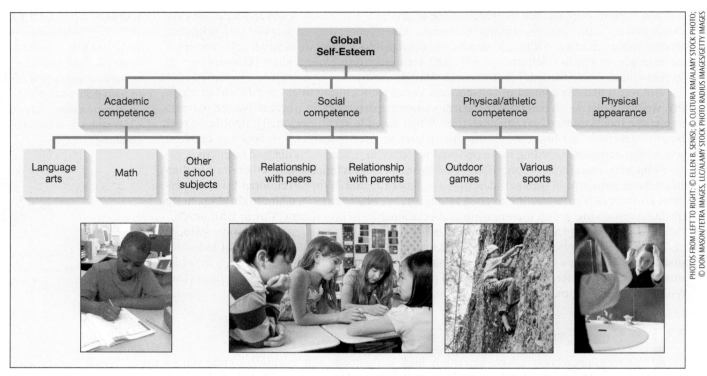

FIGURE 13.1 **Hierarchical structure of self-esteem in the mid-elementary school years.** From their experiences in different settings, children form at least four separate self-esteems: academic competence, social competence, physical/athletic competence, and physical appearance. These differentiate into additional self-evaluations and combine to form a global self-esteem.

self-esteem are consistently better-liked by classmates (Jacobs et al., 2002). And as we saw in Chapter 11, sense of athletic competence is positively associated with investment in and performance at sports.

Furthermore, across age, sex, SES, and ethnic groups, individuals with favorable self-esteem tend to be well-adjusted, sociable, and conscientious. In contrast, a profile of low self-esteem in all areas is linked to anxiety, depression, and increasing antisocial behavior (Kim & Cicchetti, 2006; Robins et al., 2001; Sowislo & Orth, 2013).

Culture, Gender, and Ethnicity Cultural forces profoundly affect self-esteem. An especially strong emphasis on social comparison in school may explain why Chinese and Japanese children, despite their higher academic achievement, score lower than U.S. children in self-esteem—a difference that widens with age (Harter, 2012; Twenge & Crocker, 2002). At the same time, because of cultural valuing of modesty and social harmony, East Asian children rely less on social comparisons to enhance their own self-esteem (Falbo et al., 1997). Rather, they tend to be reserved in positive self-judgments but generous in praise of others.

Gender-stereotyped expectations also affect self-esteem. In one study, the more 5- to 8-year-old girls talked with friends about the way people look, watched TV shows focusing on physical appearance, and perceived their friends as valuing thinness, the greater their dissatisfaction with their physical self and the lower their overall self-esteem a year later (Dohnt & Tiggemann, 2006). And in an investigation of third graders, being overweight was more strongly linked to negative body image for girls than boys (Shriver et al., 2013). By the end of middle childhood, girls feel less confident than boys about their physical appearance and athletic abilities. In academic self-judgments, boys, again, are somewhat advantaged: Whereas girls score higher in language-arts self-esteem, boys tend to have higher math and science self-esteem—even when children of equal skill levels are compared (Jacobs et al., 2002; Kurtz-Costes et al., 2008; Tatangelo & Ricciardelli, 2017). At the same time, girls exceed boys in self-esteem dimensions of close friendship and social acceptance.

Compared with their European-American agemates, African-American children tend to have slightly higher self-esteem, possibly because of warm extended families and a stronger sense of ethnic pride (Gray-Little & Hafdahl, 2000). Consistent with this interpretation, African-American 7- to 10-year-olds randomly assigned to a ten-session, small-group program celebrating Black family life and culture gained in self-esteem relative to agemates assigned to a no-intervention control (Okeke-Adeyanju et al., 2014). But media exposure has the opposite effect: The more TV African-American children watch, the lower their self-esteem—an association that also applies to European-American girls. In contrast, TV viewing predicts higher self-esteem among European-American boys (Martins & Harrison, 2012). Ethnic and gender stereotypes in TV programs may explain these findings.

Finally, in a study of Mexican-American 10- to 16-year-olds living in urban areas in California, academic self-esteem (rather than perceived physical appearance) correlated most strongly with global self-esteem (Harris et al., 2018). Mexican-immigrant parents' pressure on their children to succeed in school as a pathway to a better life may explain this close tie between the youths' perceived academic performance and overall self-worth.

Children learn African drumming skills at a community center during Kwanzaa, a holiday honoring their African heritage. A stronger sense of ethnic pride may contribute to slightly higher self-esteem among African-American children compared with their European-American agemates.

Child-Rearing Practices   School-age children who are securely attached and whose parents use an *authoritative* child-rearing style (see Chapter 10) feel especially good about themselves (Kerns, Brumariu, & Seibert, 2011; Yeung et al., 2016). Warm, positive parenting lets children know that they are accepted as competent and worthwhile. And firm but appropriate expectations, backed up with explanations, help them evaluate their own behavior against reasonable standards. Also, securely attached children are more likely than their insecure counterparts to have learned to take a caring, nonjudgmental attitude toward themselves during times when they struggled or failed—a personal quality called **self-compassion** (Neff & Vonk, 2009; Peter & Gazelle, 2017). Self-compassion protects mental health in the face of threats to self-esteem.

Controlling parents—those who too often help or make decisions for their child—communicate a sense of inadequacy to children. Having parents who are repeatedly disapproving and insulting is also linked to low self-esteem (Atzaba-Poria & Pike, 2015; Wuyts et al., 2015). Children subjected to such parenting need constant reassurance, and many rely heavily on peers to affirm their self-worth—a risk factor for adjustment difficulties, including aggression and antisocial behavior (Donnellan et al., 2005). In contrast, indulgent parenting is associated with unrealistically high self-esteem, which also undermines development. These children—whom researchers label *narcissistic* because they combine an inflated sense of superiority with obsessive worry about what others think of them—are vulnerable to temporary, sharp drops in self-esteem when their overblown self-images are challenged (Lynch et al., 2016; Thomaes et al., 2008, 2013). They tend to lash out at peers who express disapproval and display adjustment problems, including meanness and aggression.

Over the past several decades, parents in Western nations have become increasingly concerned with boosting their children's self-esteem by showering them with praise (Brummelman, Crocker, & Bushman, 2016). Research, however, confirms that children do not benefit from inflated praise ("You're terrific!" "That's fantastic!"). Rather, they may conclude that they are expected to perform fantastically all the time. When children fail to meet this impossibly high standard, they question their self-worth (Brummelman & Thomaes, 2017; Wentzel & Brophy, 2014). Parents more often give inflated praise to children with low self-esteem, in a well-intentioned effort to get them to feel good about themselves. But longitudinal research confirms that inflated praise has the reverse effect: It predicts declines in self-esteem over time. Declining self-esteem, in turn, may induce parents to provide even more inflated praise, yielding a self-sustaining downward spiral in children's evaluations of themselves (Brummelman et al., 2017).

Rather than heaping compliments on children that have no basis in real accomplishment, a better way to foster a positive, secure self-image is to encourage children to strive for worthwhile goals. Over time, a bidirectional relationship between performance and self-worth emerges: Achievement fosters gains in self-esteem, which contributes to further effort and gains in performance.

What can adults do to promote, and to avoid undermining, this mutually supportive relationship between motivation and self-esteem? Answers come from research on the precise content of adults' messages to children in achievement situations.

Achievement-Related Attributions   *Attributions* are our common, everyday explanations for the causes of behavior. Notice how Joey, in talking about the spelling bee at the beginning of this chapter, attributes his disappointing performance to *luck* (Belinda got all the easy words) and his usual success to *ability* (he *knows* he's a better speller than Belinda). Joey also appreciates that *effort* matters: "I knocked myself out studying those spelling lists."

The combination of improved reasoning skills and frequent evaluative feedback permits 10- to 12-year-olds to separate all these variables in explaining performance. Those with favorable academic self-esteem and motivation make **mastery-oriented attributions,** crediting their successes to ability—a characteristic they can improve through trying hard and can count on when faced with new challenges. This **growth mindset about ability**—that it can increase through effort and effective strategies—influences the way mastery-oriented children interpret negative events. They attribute failure to factors that can be changed and controlled, such as insufficient effort or a difficult task that will require greater persistence and struggle to master (Dweck & Molden, 2013). So whether these children succeed or fail, they take an industrious, persistent approach to learning.

In contrast, children who develop **learned helplessness** attribute their failures, not their successes, to ability. When they succeed, they are likely to conclude that external factors, such as luck, are responsible. Unlike their mastery-oriented counterparts, they hold a **fixed mindset about ability**—that it is set in stone and cannot be improved by trying hard (Dweck & Molden, 2013). When a task is difficult, these children feel threatened by the possibility of failure (it means they are "not smart"), experience an anxious loss of control, and give up without really trying.

Children's attributions affect their goals. Mastery-oriented children focus on *learning goals*—seeking information on how best to increase their ability through effort. Hence, their performance improves over time, with students who find schoolwork challenging gaining the most (Burnette et al., 2013). In contrast, learned-helpless children focus on *performance goals*—obtaining positive and avoiding negative evaluations of their fragile sense of ability. Because they fail to connect effort with success, they do not develop the metacognitive and self-regulatory skills necessary for high achievement (see Chapter 12) (Pomerantz & Saxon, 2001). Gradually their ability ceases to predict how well they do.

Influences on Achievement-Related Attributions What accounts for the different attributions of mastery-oriented and learned-helpless children? Surprisingly, parents' mindsets about ability are only weakly related to their children's mindsets. Also, children cannot accurately "read" their parents' mindsets, suggesting parents do not directly pass on these beliefs (Gunderson et al., 2018; Haimovitz & Dweck, 2016, 2017). Rather, parents appear to influence children's mindsets through the feedback they give children in success and failure situations.

When a child succeeds, parents can offer **person praise,** which emphasizes the child's traits ("You're so smart"; "you're very artistic"), or **process praise,** which emphasizes behavior and effort ("you worked really hard"; "you figured it out"). Children—especially those with low self-esteem—respond unfavorably to person praise. They feel more shame following failure if they previously received person praise, less shame if they

When adults offer process praise, children learn that persistence and effective strategies build competence. With remarks such as "You worked really hard on that problem!" this mother fosters a growth mindset about ability and a mastery-oriented approach in her child.

© WILLIAM PERUGINI/ALAMY STOCK PHOTO

previously received process praise or no praise at all (Brummelman, Crocker, & Bushman, 2016). Consistent with a learned-helpless orientation, person praise teaches children that ability is fixed and evident after just one performance, which leads them to question their competence in the face of failure and to retreat from challenges (Pomerantz & Kempner, 2013). In contrast, process praise—consistent with a mastery orientation and growth mindset—teaches children that competence develops through hard work and effective strategies (Pomerantz, Grolnick, & Price, 2013).

The way parents respond to children's failures is just as influential as the way they respond to successes. Parents with a *failure-is-enhancing mindset* see failure as benefitting children's learning and future performance. As a result, they focus on helping children understand how they can use failure experiences to improve. For example, a parent might say, "What did you learn from doing poorly on the test that might help you do better next time?"—communication that promotes a growth mindset in children. In contrast, parents with a *failure-is-debilitating* mindset react to children's failure with doubts about their ability and attempts to comfort them for not having what it takes, as reflected in this response: "It's OK, you can't expect to be good at every subject"—feedback that cultivates a fixed mindset (Haimovitz & Dweck, 2016).

Teachers' messages also affect children's attributions. Teachers who emphasize learning over performance goals tend to have mastery-oriented students. In a study of first and second graders, researchers asked the children's teachers to indicate the extent to which they used learning-oriented practices (emphasizing student understanding and individual progress) and performance-oriented practices (emphasizing grades and other indicators of ability). Learning-oriented teaching predicted a growth mindset about ability in students, whereas performance-oriented teaching predicted a fixed mindset about ability (Park et al., 2016). Furthermore, a survey of 40 middle-school math teachers and over 3,000 of their students revealed that teachers who fostered a growth mindset in students frequently asked them to explain their thinking and praised them for deeper understanding and individual progress (Sun, 2018). In contrast, teachers who promoted a fixed mindset engaged in ability grouping and often publicly complimented high-performing students using person praise, such as ""smart" or "quick" (which implied that others were "not smart" or "slow").

The performance of some children is especially vulnerable to undermining messages from adults. For example, despite their higher achievement, girls more often than boys attribute poor performance to lack of ability. When girls do not do well, teachers and parents tend to fault their ability, reinforcing negative stereotypes (for example, that girls are weak at math) that further erode their interest and performance (Gunderson et al., 2012; Lohbeck, Grube, & Moschner, 2017; Robinson-Cimpian et al., 2014). Similarly, as noted in Chapter 12, low-SES ethnic minority students often receive less favorable teacher feedback, which contributes to declining academic self-esteem and achievement.

Finally, cultural values influence adults' messages to children and, in turn, children's mindsets about ability. Asian parents and teachers are more likely than their American counterparts to view effort as key to success and also as a moral responsibility (Mok, Kennedy, & Moore, 2011; Qu & Pomerantz, 2015). Asians also attend more to failure than to success because failure indicates where corrective action is needed. Americans, in contrast, focus more on success because it enhances self-esteem. Observations of U.S. and Chinese mothers' responses to their fourth and fifth graders' puzzle solutions revealed that the U.S. mothers offered more praise after success, whereas the Chinese mothers more often pointed out the child's inadequate performance. And regardless of success or failure, Chinese mothers made more task-relevant statements aimed at ensuring that children exerted sufficient effort to do well ("You concentrated on it"; "You need to spend more time figuring out this one") (see Figure 13.2). When children continued with the task after mothers left the room, the Chinese children showed greater gains in performance (Ng, Pomerantz, & Lam, 2007).

LOOK and LISTEN

Observe a school-age child working on a challenging homework assignment under the guidance of a parent or other adult. What features of the adult's communication likely foster mastery-oriented attributions? How about learned helplessness? Explain.

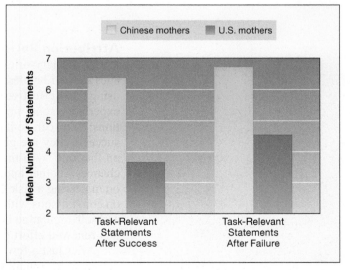

FIGURE 13.2 Chinese and U.S. mothers' task-relevant statements in response to their fourth-grade child's success or failure on puzzle tasks. Observations revealed that regardless of whether their child had just succeeded or failed, Chinese mothers were more likely than U.S. mothers to make task-relevant statements aimed at ensuring that the child exerted high effort. (Based on Ng, Pomerantz, & Lam, 2007.)

APPLYING WHAT WE KNOW

Fostering a Growth Mindset About Ability and a Mastery-Oriented Approach to Learning

CONTEXT	DESCRIPTION
Provision of tasks	Select tasks that are meaningful, responsive to a diversity of student interests, and appropriately matched to current competence so that the child is challenged but not overwhelmed.
Parent and teacher encouragement	Communicate warmth, confidence in the child's abilities, the value of achievement, and the importance of effort, including overcoming obstacles, in success.
	Resist praising children's personal qualities, focusing instead on praising their competent behavior, sustained effort, and successful strategies.
	Model high effort in overcoming failure, including a willingness to try new strategies and to ask for assistance when stuck.
	For teachers: Communicate often with parents, suggesting ways to foster children's effort and progress.
	For parents: Monitor schoolwork; provide scaffolded assistance that promotes knowledge of effective strategies and self-regulation.
Performance evaluations	Make evaluations private; avoid publicizing success or failure through wall posters, stars, privileges for "smart" children, or prizes for "best" performance.
	Emphasize individual progress and self-improvement.
	Provide accurate, constructive feedback to children about their performance.
School environment	Offer small classes, which permit teachers to provide individualized support for mastery.
	Provide for cooperative learning (see page 466 in Chapter 12,) and peer tutoring, in which children assist one another; avoid ability grouping, which makes evaluations of children's progress public.
	Create a growth-mindset atmosphere that sends a clear message that all students can increase their ability through effort and effective strategies.

Sources: Haimovitz & Dweck, 2017; Wentzel & Brophy, 2014.

Attribution Retraining Once learned helplessness has set in, what can be done to replace it with mastery-oriented attributions? An intervention called **attribution retraining** encourages learned-helpless children to believe they can overcome failure by exerting more effort and using more effective strategies. Researchers give children tasks difficult enough that they will experience some failure, followed by repeated feedback that helps them revise their attributions: "You can do it if you try harder. How about taking a different approach?" After children succeed, they are given process praise—"Your new strategy worked. You really tried hard on that one"—so that they attribute their success to both effort and effective strategies, not chance. Another approach is to encourage low-effort children to focus less on grades, more on mastering a task for its own sake, and more on individual performance improvement than on comparisons with classmates (Wentzel & Brophy, 2014). Instruction in effective strategies and self-regulation is also vital, to compensate for development lost in this area and to ensure that renewed effort pays off (Berkeley, Mastropieri, & Scruggs, 2011).

After just a few hours of instruction in attribution retraining, teachers have successfully delivered it to small groups and entire classes, inducing positive changes in students' attributions, motivation, and performance (Chodkiewicz & Boyle, 2014). An even better approach is to prevent learned helplessness, using the techniques summarized in Applying What We Know above.

⟳ ASK YOURSELF

⬛ 13.2 Emotional Development

Greater self-awareness and social sensitivity support advances in emotional competence in middle childhood. Gains take place in experience of self-conscious emotions, emotional understanding, and emotional self-regulation.

13.2 Cite changes in self-conscious emotions, emotional understanding, and emotional self-regulation in middle childhood.

13.2.1 Self-Conscious Emotions

As children integrate social expectations into their self-concepts, self-conscious emotions of pride and guilt become clearly governed by personal responsibility. Unlike preschoolers, school-age children experience pride in a new accomplishment and guilt over a transgression even when no adult is present (Harter, 2012). Also, children no longer report guilt for any mishap, as they did earlier, but only for intentional wrongdoing, such as ignoring responsibilities, cheating, or lying (Ferguson, Stegge, & Damhuis, 1991). These changes reflect the older child's more mature sense of morality, a topic addressed later in this chapter.

When school-age children feel pride or guilt, they connect successes or failures to specific behaviors: "I worked hard on that tough problem, and it paid off" (pride) or "I made a mistake, and now I have to deal with it" (guilt). They tend to feel shame when their violation of a standard is not under their control (Lewis & Ramsay, 2002; Saarni et al., 2006). For example, Lizzie felt ashamed when she dropped a spoonful of spaghetti and had a large spot on her shirt for the rest of the school day. But as children develop a global self-esteem, they may also experience shame after a controllable breach of standards if someone blames them for it by criticizing their personal traits (Muris & Meesters, 2014; Rote & Smetana, 2017). After a parent reprimands a child for poor performance ("Everyone else can do it. Obviously, you don't want to improve!"), the child may hang her head in shame, repeating to herself, "I'm stupid! I'm a terrible kid!"

Pride motivates children to take on further challenges, whereas guilt prompts them to make amends and to strive for self-improvement. But profound feelings of shame (as noted in Chapter 10) are particularly destructive. A shame-induced drop in self-esteem can induce sharp declines in motivation and performance along with withdrawal and depression or intense anger at those who participated in the shame-evoking situation, followed by lashing out with aggression (Mills, 2005; Oedes-Sese et al., 2014). A summary of findings from many studies confirms that children and adolescents who experience guilt after transgressions tend to be well-adjusted—unlikely to react with depression, anger, or aggression. In contrast, those who experience shame are prone to these adjustment problems (Muris & Meesters, 2014).

If this child reacts with guilt to wrongdoing, he is likely to make amends. But adult blame and criticism may cause him to experience intense shame, leading to depression, anger, and a sharp drop in self-esteem.

13.2.2 Emotional Understanding

School-age children's understanding of mental activity means that, unlike preschoolers, they are likely to explain emotion by referring to internal states, such as happy or sad thoughts,

Third graders help prepare meal packages to be sent to Africa to feed children in need. Gains in emotional understanding and perspective taking in middle childhood enable children to respond with empathy to people's general life condition.

rather than to external events (Flavell, Flavell, & Green, 2001). Also, between ages 6 and 12, children become more aware of circumstances likely to spark mixed emotions, each of which may be positive or negative and may differ in intensity, and they increasingly report experiencing more than one emotion at a time (Burkitt, Lowry, & Fotheringham, 2017; Heubeck et al., 2016). For example, recalling the birthday present he received from his grandmother, Joey reflected, "I was very happy I got something but a little sad that I didn't get just what I wanted."

Appreciating mixed emotions helps children realize that people's expressions may not reflect their true feelings (Misailidi, 2006). It also fosters awareness of self-conscious emotions. For example, between ages 6 and 7, children improve sharply in ability to distinguish pride from happiness and surprise (Tracy, Robins, & Lagattuta, 2005). And 8- and 9-year-olds understand that pride combines two sources of happiness—joy in accomplishment and joy that a significant person recognized that accomplishment (Harter, 1999). As well, children of this age refine their grasp of the subtle distinction between guilt and shame (Muris & Meesters, 2014).

Furthermore, older school-age children can reconcile contradictory facial and situational cues in figuring out another's feelings. And they can use information about "what might have happened" to predict how people will feel in a new situation—realizing, for example, that someone will feel a sense of relief when an actual outcome is more favorable than what might have occurred (Guttentag & Ferrell, 2004).

As with self-understanding, gains in emotional understanding are supported by cognitive development and social experiences, especially adults' sensitivity to children's feelings and willingness to discuss emotions. Together, these factors contribute to a rise in empathy as well. As children move closer to adolescence, advances in recursive perspective taking permit an empathic response not just to people's immediate distress but also to their general life condition (Hoffman, 2000). Similar to early childhood, emotional understanding and empathy in middle childhood are linked to favorable social relationships and prosocial behavior (Eisenberg, Spinrad, & Morris, 2013). As Joey and Lizzie imagined how people who are chronically ill or hungry feel and evoked those emotions in themselves, they gave part of their allowance to charity and joined in fundraising projects through school, community center, and scouting.

13.2.3 Emotional Self-Regulation

In Chapter 10, we saw that emotional understanding and effortful control, along with parents' modeling and teaching of emotion-regulation strategies, contribute to young children's ability to manage emotions. These factors continue to play important roles during middle childhood, a period of rapid gains in emotional self-regulation (Zalewski et al., 2011).

By age 10, most children shift adaptively between two general strategies for managing emotion. In **problem-centered coping,** they appraise the situation as changeable, identify the difficulty, and decide what to do about it. If problem solving does not work, they engage in **emotion-centered coping,** which is internal, private, and aimed at controlling distress when little can be done about an outcome (Kliewer, Fearnow, & Miller, 1996; Lazarus & Lazarus, 1994). For example, when faced with an anxiety-provoking test or an angry friend, older school-age children view problem solving and seeking social support as the best strategies. But when outcomes are beyond their control—after receiving a bad grade—they opt for distraction or try to redefine the situation in ways that help them accept it: "Things could be worse. There'll be another test." School-age children's improved ability to appraise situations and reflect on thoughts and feelings means that, compared with preschoolers, they more often use these internal strategies to manage emotion (Brenner & Salovey, 1997).

Cognitive development and a wider range of social experiences permit children to flexibly vary their coping strategies (Zimmer-Gembeck & Skinner, 2011). Furthermore, through interacting with parents, teachers, and peers, school-age children become more knowledgeable about socially approved ways to display negative emotion. With age, they increasingly prefer verbal expression ("Please stop pushing and wait your turn") to crying, sulking, or aggression (Waters & Thompson, 2014). Young school-age children justify these more mature displays of emotion by mentioning avoidance of punishment or disapproval, but by third grade, they begin to emphasize concern for others' feelings. Children with this awareness are rated as especially helpful, cooperative, and socially responsive by teachers and as better-liked by peers (McDowell & Parke, 2000).

When emotional self-regulation has developed well, school-age children acquire a sense of *emotional self-efficacy*— a feeling of being in control of their emotional experience (Thompson & Goodman, 2010). This fosters a favorable self-image and an optimistic outlook, which further help children face emotional challenges.

As at younger ages, school-age children whose parents respond sensitively and helpfully when the child is distressed are emotionally well-regulated—generally upbeat in mood and also empathic and prosocial (Abraham & Kerns, 2013; Vinik, Almas, & Grusec, 2011). When mothers supported their 5-year-olds' emotional development in this way, children demonstrated more effective emotional self-regulation at age 7, which in turn predicted better quality friendships at age 10 (Blair et al., 2014). In contrast, poorly regulated children often experience hostile, dismissive parental reactions to distress (Morris et al., 2007). These children are overwhelmed by negative emotion, a response that interferes with empathy and prosocial behavior.

Finally, culture influences emotional self-regulation. In a striking illustration, researchers studied children in two subcultures—Hindu and Buddhist—in rural Nepal. In response to stories about emotionally charged situations (such as peer aggression or an unjust parental punishment), Hindu children more often said they would feel angry but would try to mask their feelings. Buddhist children, in contrast, interpreted the situation so that they felt "just OK" rather than angry. "Why be angry?" they explained. "The event already happened." Accordingly, Hindu mothers reported that they often teach their children how to control their emotional behavior, whereas Buddhist mothers pointed to the value their religion places on a calm, peaceful disposition (Cole & Tamang, 1998; Cole, Tamang, & Shrestha, 2006). Compared to both Nepalese groups, U.S. children preferred conveying anger verbally in these situations. For example, to an unjust punishment, they answered, "If I say I'm angry, he'll stop hurting me!" (Cole, Bruschi, & Tamang, 2002). Notice how this response fits with the Western emphasis on personal rights and self-expression.

Two boys argue while their friends look on. Through interactions with adults and peers, school-age children acquire socially approved ways to express negative emotions. With age, they increasingly prefer verbal expression to crying, sulking, or aggression.

LOOK and LISTEN

Ask several school-age children how they would manage their emotions in the following situations: (1) a friend is angry with them, and (2) they receive a bad grade on an important test. Do their responses reflect flexible, adaptive coping?

13.3 Moral Development

Recall from Chapter 10 that preschoolers pick up many morally relevant behaviors through modeling and reinforcement. By middle childhood, they have had time to internalize rules for good conduct: "It's good to help others in trouble" or "It's wrong to take something that doesn't belong to you." This change leads children to become considerably more independent and trustworthy.

In Chapter 10, we also saw that children do not just copy their morality from others. As the cognitive-developmental approach emphasizes, they actively think about right and wrong. An expanding social world, the capacity to consider more information when reasoning, and gains in recursive perspective taking lead moral understanding to advance greatly in middle childhood.

13.3 Describe changes in moral understanding during middle childhood, including children's understanding of diversity and inequality.

13.3.1 Moral and Social-Conventional Understanding

During middle childhood, children construct a flexible appreciation of moral rules. They take into account an increasing number of variables—not just actions and their immediate impact, but also the intentions of the actors and the context of their behavior (Killen & Smetana, 2015). For example, between ages 7 and 11, children increasingly say it is acceptable to hit other children in certain situations—in self-defense, to protect someone else from serious bodily injury, or to prevent the other children from hurting themselves (Jambon & Smetana, 2014). Older children focus less on actors' transgressions (hitting) and more on the aim of their actions (trying to prevent harm).

Similarly, by age 7 to 8, children no longer say truth telling is always good and lying is always bad but consider prosocial and antisocial intentions and the context of the behavior. They evaluate certain types of truthfulness very negatively—for example, blunt statements, particularly in public contexts where they are especially likely to have negative social consequences (telling a friend that you don't like her drawing) (Ma et al., 2011).

Although both Chinese and North American schoolchildren consider lying about harmful acts as "very naughty," Chinese children more often rate lying favorably when the intention is modesty, as when a student who has thoughtfully picked up litter from the playground says, "I didn't do it" (Cameron et al., 2012; Lee et al., 2001). Similarly, Chinese children are more likely to favor lying to support the group at the expense of the individual (saying you're sick so, as a poor singer, you won't harm your class's chances of winning a singing competition). In contrast, North American children more often favor lying to support the individual at the expense of the group (asserting that a friend who is a poor speller is actually a good speller because the friend wants to participate in a spelling competition) (Fu et al., 2007, 2016; Lau et al., 2012).

These judgments reflect school-age children's increasingly sophisticated understanding of different reasons for deception. They realize that people may convey inaccurate information because they are biased, trying to be persuasive, concerned about how others will react, or protecting others' welfare. Notice how such perspective taking is *recursive:* Children must consider simultaneously the viewpoints of two or more people—the person who lies and the targets of the lie.

Appreciation of second-order false belief, which depends on recursive thought (see page 442 in Chapter 12), is related to gains in moral judgment in middle childhood. In one study, researchers gave children a morally relevant second-order false-belief task: A child, while helping her teacher clean up, accidently throws out a bag containing a treasured cupcake belonging to a classmate who is out of the room (Fu et al., 2014). School-age children who reasoned accurately about the helper's belief about the bag's contents (trash) and the cupcake owner's belief about the cupcake's location (in a bag in the classroom) assigned less blame to the helper. Using their recursive capacity, these children inferred that *the cupcake owner would understand that the helper thought the bag had trash in it.*

Students follow social convention as they wait their turn at a water cooler. School-age children distinguish social conventions with a clear purpose (making sure everyone gets equal access to the water) from ones with no obvious justification.

As children construct more advanced ideas about justice, they clarify and link moral imperatives and social conventions. School-age children distinguish social conventions with a clear *purpose* (not running in school hallways to prevent injuries) from ones with no obvious justification (not wearing your cap in the classroom) (Buchanan-Barrow & Barrett, 1998; Thornberg et al., 2016). They regard violations of purposeful conventions as closer to moral transgressions.

Furthermore, as with moral rules, older children realize that people's intentions and the context of their actions affect the moral implications of violating a social convention. In one study, 8- to 10-year-olds judged that because of a flag's symbolic value, burning it to express disapproval of a country or to start a cooking fire is worse than burning it accidentally. They also stated that public flag burning is worse than private flag burning because it inflicts emotional harm on others. But they recognized that flag burning is a form of freedom of expression, and most agreed it would be acceptable in a country that treated its citizens unfairly (Helwig & Prencipe, 1999).

In middle childhood, children also realize that people whose *knowledge* differs may not be equally responsible for moral transgressions. Many 7-year-olds would tolerate a teacher who gave more snack to girls than to boys because she thought (incorrectly) that girls need more food. But if her actions reflected an *immoral belief* ("it's all right to be nicer to girls than boys"), almost all children would judge her negatively (Wainryb & Ford, 1998).

13.3.2 Understanding Individual Rights

When children challenge adult authority, they typically do so within the personal domain (Nucci, 2005). As their grasp of moral imperatives and social conventions strengthens, so does their conviction that certain choices, such as hairstyle, friends, and leisure activities, are up to the individual.

Notions of personal choice, in turn, enhance children's moral understanding. As early as age 6, children view freedom of speech and religion as individual rights, even if laws exist that deny those rights (Helwig, 2006; Helwig, Ruck, & Peterson-Badali, 2014). And they regard laws that discriminate against individuals—for example, denying certain people access to medical care or education—as wrong and worthy of violating (Helwig & Jasiobedzka, 2001). In justifying their responses, children appeal to personal privileges and, by the end of middle childhood, to the importance of individual rights for maintaining a fair society.

At the same time, older school-age children place limits on individual choice. Fourth graders faced with conflicting moral and personal concerns—such as whether or not to befriend a classmate of a different race or gender—typically decide in favor of kindness and fairness (Killen et al., 2002). Partly for this reason, prejudice generally declines in middle childhood. High-quality friendships may play an important role in facilitating these moral sensibilities (McDonald et al., 2014). The cooperativeness, responsiveness, and empathic understanding between good friends promotes concern for others' rights and welfare, while also highlighting the circumstances in which some transgressions ought to be forgiven.

New York City schoolchildren participate in the People's Climate March, which advocates for global action to prevent climate change. Children's grasp of personal choice enhances understanding of individual rights, including freedom of speech.

13.3.3 Culture and Moral Understanding

Children and adolescents in diverse cultures use similar criteria to reason about moral, social-conventional, and personal concerns (Nucci, 2005, 2009). For example, Chinese children and youth, whose culture highly values respect for adult authority, nevertheless say that adults have no right to interfere in children's personal matters (Hasebe, Nucci, & Nucci, 2004; Smetana et al., 2017).

Furthermore, U.S. and South Korean children alike claim that a child with no position of authority should be obeyed when she gives a directive that is fair and caring, such as telling others to share candy or to return lost money to its owner. And even in Korean culture, which highly values deference to authority, 7- to 11-year-olds evaluate negatively an adult's order to engage in immoral acts, such as stealing or refusing to share—a response that strengthens with age (Kim, 1998). In sum, children everywhere seem to realize that higher principles, independent of rule and authority, must prevail when people's personal rights and welfare are at stake.

13.3.4 Understanding Diversity and Inequality

By the early school years, children absorb prevailing societal attitudes, associating power and privilege with White people and poverty and inferior status with people of color. They do not necessarily acquire these views directly from parents or friends, whose attitudes may differ from their own (Aboud & Doyle, 1996; Elenbaas & Killen, 2019; Pahlke, Bigler, & Suizzo, 2012). Perhaps White parents are reluctant to discuss their racial and ethnic views with children, and friends also say little. Given limited, direct information from adults and peers, children seem to pick up mainstream beliefs from implicit messages in the media and elsewhere in their environments (Dorn, 2015). Powerful sources include social contexts that present a world sorted into groups, such as racial and ethnic segregation in schools and communities.

In-Group and Out-Group Biases: Development of Prejudice Studies in diverse Western nations confirm that by age 5 to 6, White children generally evaluate their own racial group favorably and other racial groups less favorably or negatively. *In-group favoritism* emerges first; children simply prefer their own group, generalizing from self to similar others (Buttelmann & Böhm, 2014; Dunham, Baron, & Carey, 2011; Nesdale et al., 2004).

The ease with which a trivial group label supplied by an adult can induce in-group favoritism is striking. In one study, European-American 5-year-olds were told that they were members of a group based on T-shirt color. Although no information was provided about group status and the children never met any group members, they still displayed vigorous in-group favoritism (Dunham, Baron, & Carey, 2011). When shown photos of unfamiliar agemates wearing either an in-group or an out-group shirt, the children claimed to like members of their own group better, gave them more resources, and engaged in positively biased recall of group members' behavior.

Out-group prejudice requires a more challenging social comparison between in-group and out-group. But it does not take long for White children to acquire negative attitudes toward ethnic minority out-groups when such attitudes are encouraged by circumstances in their environments. When White Canadian 4- to 7-year-olds living in a White community and attending nearly all-White schools sorted positive and negative adjectives into boxes labeled as belonging to a White child and a Black child, out-group prejudice emerged at age 5 (Corenblum, 2003). Unfortunately, many minority children show a reverse pattern: *out-group favoritism,* in which they assign positive characteristics to the privileged White majority and negative characteristics to their own group (Averhart & Bigler, 1997; Newheiser et al., 2014).

But recall that with age, children pay more attention to inner traits. The capacity to classify the social world in multiple ways enables school-age children to understand that people can be both "the same" and "different"—those who look different need not think, feel, or act differently. Consequently, voicing of negative attitudes toward minorities declines after age 7 or 8 (Aboud, 2008; Raabe & Beelmann, 2011). Around this time, both majority and minority children express *in-group favoritism,* and White children's *prejudice against out-group* members often weakens (Nesdale et al., 2004; Ruble et al., 2004). Most school-age children and adolescents are also quick to verbalize that it is wrong to exclude others from peer-group and learning activities on the basis of skin color—discrimination they evaluate as unfair (Killen et al., 2002).

Fourth graders participate in a nature walk during a school lunch break. Around age 7 or 8, voicing of negative attitudes toward minorities declines, and most children judge exclusion based on skin color to be unfair.

Likewise, children's prejudice against peers affected by poverty declines in middle childhood. For example, in response to hypothetical stories about peer exclusion, 8-year-olds reported more negative moral feelings—such as "sad," accompanied by explanations involving unfairness or other harm to the peer's welfare—if the excluded child was economically disadvantaged than if the child was from another school (but not economically disadvantaged) (Dys et al., 2019).

Yet even in children aware of the injustice of discrimination, prejudice often operates implicitly, without awareness—as it does in many adults (Dunham, Baron, & Banaji, 2006). Consider a study in which U.S. children and adults were shown pictures of computer-generated racially ambiguous faces displaying happy and angry expressions and asked to classify them by race. White participants more often categorized happy faces as White and angry faces as African American or Asian. These implicit biases were evident across all ages tested—as early as 3 or 4. In contrast, African-American participants did not show any racial biases in their responses (Dunham, Chen, & Banaji, 2013). The absence of any in-group favoritism (classifying happy faces as African American) suggests an early emerging, implicit sensitivity to prevailing racial attitudes among African Americans.

These findings raise the question of whether the decline in White children's explicit racial bias during middle childhood is a true decrease, or whether it reflects their growing awareness of widely held standards that deem prejudice to be inappropriate—or both. Around age 10, White children start to avoid talking about race in order to appear unbiased, just as many adults do (Apfelbaum et al., 2008). At least to some degree, then, older school-age children's desire to present themselves in a socially acceptable light may contribute to reduced explicit out-group prejudice, while implicit racial bias persists.

Nevertheless, the extent to which children hold racial and ethnic biases varies depending on the following personal and situational factors:

- *A fixed view of personality traits.* Children who believe personality traits are fixed rather than changeable often judge others as either "good" or "bad." Ignoring motives and circumstances, they readily form prejudices based on limited information. For example, they might infer that "a new child at school who tells a lie to get other kids to like her" is simply a bad person (Levy & Dweck, 1999).
- *Overly high self-esteem.* Children (and adults) with very high self-esteem are more likely to hold racial and ethnic prejudices (Baumeister et al., 2003; Bigler, 2013). These individuals seem to belittle disadvantaged individuals or groups to justify their own extremely favorable self-evaluation.
- *A social world in which people are sorted into groups.* The more adults highlight group distinctions for children and the less interracial contact children experience, the more White children express in-group favoritism and out-group prejudice (Aboud & Brown, 2013).

Reducing Prejudice   Research confirms that an effective way to reduce prejudice is through intergroup contact, in which racially and ethnically different children have equal status, work toward common goals, and become personally acquainted (Tropp & Page-Gould, 2015). Children assigned to cooperative learning groups with peers of diverse backgrounds show low levels of prejudice in their expressions of likability and in their behavior. For example, they form more cross-race friendships (Pettigrew & Tropp, 2006). Sharing thoughts and feelings with close, cross-race friends, in turn, reduces even subtle, unintentional prejudices (Turner, Hewstone, & Voci, 2007). Also, children with higher levels of intergroup contact and more cross-race friendships are more likely to view social exclusion based on race as morally wrong (Killen et al., 2010).

Long-term contact and collaboration among neighborhood, school, and community groups may be the best way to reduce prejudice (Rutland and Killen, 2015). School environments that expose children to broad ethnic and socioeconomic diversity, that teach them to understand and value those differences, that directly address the damage caused by prejudice, and that emphasize moral values of fairness and justice prevent children from forming negative biases and reduce already acquired biases (Beelmann & Heinemann, 2014). Unfortunately, as noted in Chapter 12, segregation is widespread in U.S. schools, which seldom offer exposure to the diversity necessary for countering negative biases. Return to page 466 in Chapter 12 to review efforts of magnet schools to reduce ethnic and socioeconomic segregation.

Furthermore, inducing school-age children to view others' traits as changeable, by discussing with them the many possible influences on those traits, is helpful. The more children believe that people can change their personalities, the more they report liking and perceiving themselves as similar to members of disadvantaged out-groups. Children who believe that human attributes are changeable spend more time volunteering to help people in need—for example, by serving meals to homeless people or reading to poverty-stricken preschoolers (Karafantis & Levy, 2004; Levy et al., 2016). Volunteering may, in turn, promote a view of

© JOEL BERGNER (ARTISTA)

Palestinian and Israeli children and adolescents take a break from mural painting to sing and dance together. Intergroup contact, in which racially and ethnically different children have equal status, work toward common goals, and become personally acquainted, is an effective way to reduce prejudice.

others as changeable by helping children take the perspective of the underprivileged and appreciate the societal conditions that lead to disadvantage, such as restricted educational and job opportunities,

Finally, teaching aimed at increasing the complexity of children's beliefs about racial and economic disadvantage is important. Children as young as age 8 can appreciate inequalities in access to opportunities. And the larger the inequalities they perceive, the more they want to rectify those inequalities by giving more resources—such as material goods or special experiences like a chance to go to an educational summer camp—to those who have suffered deprivation (Chafel & Neitzel, 2005; Elenbaas, 2019; Rizzo & Killen, 2016). Children often explain their desire to take corrective action by referring to broad societal inequalities: "We have houses and clothes and money and get to buy stuff but they don't"; "Kids with little money don't get the same opportunities as those who are rich."

ASK YOURSELF

Connect ■ Cite examples of how older children's capacity to take more information into account enhances their emotional understanding, perspective taking, and moral understanding.

Apply ■ Ten-year-old Marla says her classmate Bernadette will never get good grades because she's lazy. Jane believes that Bernadette tries but can't concentrate because her parents are divorcing. Why is Marla more likely than Jane to develop prejudices?

Reflect ■ Did you attend an integrated elementary school? How might school integration be vital for reducing racial and ethnic prejudice?

13.4 Peer Relations

13.4a Describe changes in peer sociability and friendship in middle childhood.

13.4b Describe categories of peer acceptance and ways to help rejected children.

In middle childhood, the society of peers becomes an increasingly important context for development. Advances in recursive perspective taking permit more sophisticated understanding of self and others, which, in turn, contributes to peer interaction. Compared with preschoolers, school-age children resolve conflicts more effectively, using persuasion and compromise (Mayeux & Cillessen, 2003). Sharing, helping, and other prosocial acts also increase. In line with these changes, aggression declines. But the drop is greatest for physical attacks (Côté et al., 2007). As we will see, verbal and relational aggression continue as children form peer groups.

13.4.1 Peer Groups

By the end of middle childhood, children display a strong desire for group belonging. They form **peer groups,** collectives that generate unique values and standards for behavior and a social structure of leaders and followers. Peer groups organize on the basis of proximity (such as being in the same classroom) and similarity in sex, ethnicity, academic achievement, popularity, and aggression (Rubin et al., 2013). When groups are tracked for 3 to 6 weeks, membership changes very little. When they are followed for a year or longer, substantial change can occur, depending on whether children are reshuffled into different classrooms. For children who remain together, 50 to 70 percent of groups consist mostly of the same children from year to year (Cairns, Xie, & Leung, 1998; Kindermann & Guest, 2018).

The practices of these informal groups lead to a "peer culture" that typically involves a specialized vocabulary, dress code, and place to "hang out." Joey and three other boys formed a club whose "uniform" was T-shirts, jeans, and sneakers. They met at recess on the playground and on Saturdays in the tree house in Joey's backyard. Calling themselves "the pack," the boys devised a secret handshake and chose Joey as their leader. Their activities included improving the clubhouse and playing basketball and video games, and—just as important—keeping unwanted peers and adults out!

As children develop these exclusive associations, the codes of dress and behavior that grow out of them become more broadly influential. Peers who deviate—by "kissing up" to teachers, wearing the wrong clothes, or tattling to get classmates in trouble—are often rebuffed, becoming targets of critical glances and comments. These customs bind peers together, creating a sense of group identity. Within the group, children acquire many social skills—cooperation, leadership, followership, and loyalty to collective goals. Through these experiences, children experiment with and learn about social organizations.

As with other aspects of social reasoning, children evaluate a group's decision to exclude a peer in complex ways. Recall that after age 7 to 8 most children view exclusion on the basis of skin color and economic disadvantage as morally wrong. Similarly, with age children are less likely to endorse excluding someone because of unconventional appearance or behavior. Girls, especially, regard such exclusion as unjust, perhaps because they experience it more often than boys (Killen, Crystal, & Watanabe, 2002). But when a peer threatens group functioning, by acting disruptively or by lacking shared interests or the skills needed to participate in a valued group activity (such as dance or sports), both boys and girls say that exclusion (including gender-based exclusion) is justified—a perspective that strengthens

Peer groups first form in middle childhood. These girls have probably established a social structure of leaders and followers. Their relaxed body language and similar dress suggest a strong sense of group belonging.

with age (Killen et al., 2018; Killen & Stangor, 2001). As these findings reveal, children's moral concerns about the injustice of prejudice coexist with their valuing of group cohesion.

Despite these sophisticated understandings, children do exclude unjustly, often using relationally aggressive tactics. Peer groups—at the instigation of their leaders, who can be skillfully aggressive—frequently oust no longer "respected" children. Some of these castouts, whose own previous hostility toward outsiders reduces their chances of being included elsewhere, turn to other low-status peers with poor social skills (Farmer et al., 2010). Socially anxious children, when ousted, often become increasingly peer-avoidant and thus more isolated (Rubin et al., 2018). In either case, opportunities to acquire socially competent behavior diminish.

School-age children's desire for group belonging can also be satisfied through formal group ties such as scouting, 4-H, and religious youth groups. Adult involvement holds in check the negative behaviors associated with children's informal peer groups. And through working on joint projects and helping in their communities, children gain in social and moral maturity (Vandell et al., 2015).

13.4.2 Friendships

Whereas peer groups provide children with insight into larger social structures, friendships contribute to the development of trust and sensitivity. During the school years, friendship becomes more complex and psychologically based. Consider the following 8-year-old's ideas:

> *Why is Shelly your best friend?* Because she helps me when I'm sad, and she shares. … *What makes Shelly so special?* I've known her longer, I sit next to her and got to know her better. … *How come you like Shelly better than anyone else?* She's done the most for me. She never disagrees, she never eats in front of me, she never walks away when I'm crying, and she helps me on my homework. … *How do you get someone to like you?* … If you're nice to [your friends], they'll be nice to you. (Damon, 1988, pp. 80–81)

As these responses show, friendship has become a mutually agreed-on relationship in which children like each other's personal qualities and respond to one another's needs and desires. And once a friendship forms, *trust* becomes its defining feature. School-age children state that a good friendship is based on acts of kindness, signifying that each person can be counted on to support the other (Hartup & Abecassis, 2004). Consequently, older children regard violations of trust, such as not helping when others need help, breaking promises, and gossiping behind the other's back, as serious breaches of friendship.

School-age children tend to select friends who are similar to themselves in personality and academic achievement. Their friendships are fairly stable: These boys are likely to remain friends for at least a full school year.

Because of these features, school-age children's friendships are more selective. Whereas preschoolers say they have lots of friends, by age 8 or 9 children name only a handful of good friends. Girls, who demand greater closeness than boys, are more exclusive in their friendships. In addition, children tend to select friends similar to themselves in age, sex, race, ethnicity, and SES. Friends also resemble one another in personality (sociability, inattention/hyperactivity, aggression, depression), peer popularity, academic achievement, and prosocial behavior (Rubin et al., 2013). But friendship opportunities offered by children's environments also affect their choices. Children whose parents have cross-race friends form more cross-race friendships (Pahlke, Bigler, & Suizzo, 2012). And as noted earlier, in integrated classrooms with mixed-race collaborative learning groups, students form more cross-race friendships.

Over middle childhood, high-quality friendships remain fairly stable: About 50 to 70 percent endure over a school year, and some last for several years (Berndt, 2004). Gains in friendship support—including compromise, sharing of thoughts and feelings, and prosocial behavior—contribute to this stability (Berndt, 2004; Furman & Rose, 2015). Friendships spanning several situations—such as school, religious institution, and children of parents' friends—are more enduring (Troutman & Fletcher, 2010). Through friendships, children learn the importance of emotional commitment. They come to realize that close relationships can survive disagreements if friends are secure in their liking for each other (Hartup, 2006). Friendship provides an important context in which children learn to tolerate criticism and resolve disputes in ways that meet both partners' needs.

Yet the impact of friendships on children's development depends on the nature of their friends. Children who bring kindness and compassion to their friendships strengthen each other's self-esteem, prosocial tendencies, and psychological adjustment (Bagwell & Bukowski, 2018). But when aggressive children make friends, the relationship is often riddled with hostile interaction and is at risk for breakup, especially when just one member of the pair is aggressive. And within these close ties, children's aggressive tendencies worsen (Henneberger, Coffman, & Gest, 2017; Salmivalli, 2010). Aggressive girls' friendships are high in exchange of private feelings but also full of relational hostility, including jealousy, conflict, and betrayal. Aggressive boys' friendships involve frequent expressions of anger, coercive statements, physical attacks, and enticements to rule breaking (Rubin et al., 2013; Werner & Crick, 2004). These findings indicate that the social problems of aggressive children operate within their closest peer ties. As we will see next, these children often acquire negative reputations in the wider world of peers.

LOOK and LISTEN

Ask an 8- to 11-year-old to tell you what he or she looks for in a best friend. Is *trust* centrally important? Does the child mention personality traits, just as school-age children do in describing themselves (see page 478)?

13.4.3 Peer Acceptance

Peer acceptance refers to likability—the extent to which a child is viewed by a group of agemates, such as classmates, as a worthy social partner. Unlike friendship, likability is not a mutual relationship but a one-sided perspective, involving the group's view of an individual. Nevertheless, better-accepted children tend to be socially competent and, as a result, to have more friends and more positive relationships with them (Mayeux, Houser, & Dyches, 2011).

To assess peer acceptance, researchers usually use self-reports that measure *social preferences*—for example, asking children to identify classmates whom they "like most" or "like least" (Cillessen, 2009). These self-reports yield five general categories of peer acceptance:

- **Popular children,** who get many positive votes (are well-liked)
- **Rejected children,** who get many negative votes (are disliked)
- **Controversial children,** who receive many votes, both positive and negative (are both liked and disliked)
- **Neglected children,** who are seldom mentioned, either positively or negatively
- *Average children,* who receive average numbers of positive and negative votes and account for about one-third of children in a typical elementary school classroom

Another approach assesses *perceived popularity,* children's judgments of whom their classmates admire—"whom everyone wants to be with." Only moderate correspondence exists between the classmates children perceive as popular (believe are admired by many others) and those classified as popular based on peer preferences (receive many "like most" ratings) (McDonald & Asher, 2018).

Peer acceptance is a powerful predictor of both current and later psychological adjustment. Rejected children, especially, are anxious, unhappy, disruptive, and low in self-esteem. Both teachers and parents rate them as having a wide range of emotional and social problems. Peer rejection in middle childhood is also strongly associated with poor school performance, absenteeism, dropping out, substance use, depression, antisocial behavior, and delinquency in adolescence and criminality in adulthood (Ladd, 2005; Rubin et al., 2013).

However, earlier influences—children's personal attributes combined with parenting practices—may largely explain the link between peer acceptance and adjustment. School-age children with peer-relationship problems are more likely to have preexisting, weak emotional self-regulation skills and to have experienced family stress due to low income and insensitive parenting, including coercive discipline (Blair et al., 2014; Trentacosta & Shaw, 2009). Nevertheless, as we will see, rejected children evoke reactions from peers that contribute to their unfavorable development.

Determinants of Peer Acceptance   Why is one child liked while another is rejected? A wealth of research reveals that social behavior plays a powerful role.

Popular Children Socially successful children include those who are well-liked (socially accepted) and those who are admired (high in perceived popularity). **Popular-prosocial children,** who are both socially accepted and admired, combine academic and social competence. They perform well in school, communicate with peers in friendly and cooperative ways, solve social problems constructively, and are more likely than other children to be viewed as leaders (Cillessen & Bellmore, 2004; Mayeux, Houser, & Dyches, 2011).

But other popular children are admired for their socially adept yet belligerent behavior. **Popular-antisocial children** include "tough" boys—athletically skilled but poor students who cause trouble and defy adult authority—and relationally aggressive boys and girls who ignore, exclude, and spread rumors about other children and behave arrogantly and conceitedly but also engage in some prosocial acts (Bowker et al., 2010; Rose, Swenson, & Waller, 2004; Vaillancourt & Hymel, 2006). Despite their aggression and egotism, peers often view these youths as "cool," perhaps because of their athletic abilities and sophisticated but devious social skills.

Although peer admiration gives these children some protection against lasting adjustment difficulties, their antisocial acts require intervention. With age, peers like these high-status, aggressive youths less and less, a trend that is stronger for relationally aggressive girls. The more socially prominent and controlling these girls become, the more they engage in relational aggression (Mayeux, Houser, & Dyches, 2011). Eventually, peers condemn their nasty tactics and reject them.

Peers gather around a popular classmate. Most popular children are prosocial—academically successful, socially sensitive, and cooperative. But some are antisocial, admired for their skill at controlling peer relationships through relational aggression.

Rejected Children Rejected children display a wide range of negative social behaviors. The largest subtype, **rejected-aggressive children,** show high rates of conflict, physical and relational aggression, and hyperactive, inattentive, and impulsive behavior. They are usually deficient in perspective taking, view the social world as threatening, often misinterpret ambiguous behaviors of peers as hostile, and blame others for their social difficulties (Rubin et al., 2013; Troop-Gordon et al., 2018). Compared with popular-antisocial children, they are more extremely antagonistic.

In contrast, **rejected-withdrawn children** are passive and socially awkward. Overwhelmed by social anxiety, they hold negative expectations about interactions with peers and worry about being scorned and attacked. Like their aggressive counterparts, they typically feel like retaliating rather than compromising when conflicts arise, although they less often act on those feelings (Rubin et al., 2013; Troop-Gordon & Asher, 2005).

Rejected children are excluded by peers as early as kindergarten. Rejection, in turn, further impairs biased social information processing, heightening hostility (Lansford et al., 2010). Soon rejected children's classroom participation declines, their feelings of loneliness rise, their academic achievement falters, and they want to avoid school (Buhs, Ladd, & Herald-Brown, 2010; Gooren et al., 2011). Most have few friends, and some have none—a circumstance linked to low self-esteem, mistrust of peers, and severe adjustment difficulties (Ladd et al., 2011; Pedersen et al., 2007).

Both types of rejected children are at risk for peer harassment (Craig et al., 2016). But as the Biology and Environment box on the following page reveals, rejected-aggressive children also act as bullies, and rejected-withdrawn children are especially likely to be victimized.

Controversial and Neglected Children Consistent with the mixed peer opinion they engender, controversial children display a blend of positive and negative social behaviors. They are hostile and disruptive, but they also engage in positive, prosocial acts. Even though some peers dislike them, they have qualities that protect them from exclusion. They have many friends and are happy with their peer relationships (de Bruyn & Cillessen, 2006). But like their popular-antisocial counterparts, they often bully others and engage in calculated relational aggression to sustain their dominance (Putallaz et al., 2007).

Perhaps the most surprising finding on peer acceptance is that neglected children, once thought to be in need of treatment, are usually well-adjusted. Although they engage in low rates of interaction and are considered shy by their classmates, most are just as socially skilled as average children and do not report feeling unhappy about their social life. When they want to, they can break away from their usual, preferred pattern of playing alone, cooperate well with peers and form positive, stable friendships (Ladd & Burgess, 1999; Ladd et al., 2011). Consequently, neglected status (like controversial status) is often temporary. Neglected, socially competent children remind us that an outgoing, gregarious personality style is not the only path to emotional well-being. Nevertheless, a few neglected children are socially anxious and poorly skilled and, thus, at risk for peer rejection.

Helping Rejected Children   A variety of interventions exist to improve the peer relations and psychological adjustment of rejected children. Most involve coaching, modeling, and reinforcing positive social skills, such as how to initiate interaction with a peer, cooperate in play, and respond to another child with friendly emotion and approval. Several of these programs have produced gains in social competence and peer acceptance that are still present from several weeks to a year later (Asher & Rose, 1997; DeRosier, 2007; Holosko, 2015). Combining social-skills training with other treatments increases its effectiveness. Rejected children are often poor students whose low academic self-esteem magnifies their negative interactions with teachers and classmates. Intensive academic tutoring improves both school achievement and social acceptance (O'Neill et al., 1997).

Another approach focuses on training in perspective taking and social problem solving. One eleven-session intervention involved teaching rejected-aggressive children to recognize others' feelings and resolve conflicts constructively within their best friendships, which are typically of low quality (Salvas et al., 2016). Relative to no-intervention controls, participants gained in friendship quality and declined in aggressive behavior.

But many rejected-aggressive children are unaware of their poor social skills and do not take responsibility for their social failures (Lynch et al., 2016; Mrug, Hoza, & Gerdes, 2001). Rejected-withdrawn children, in contrast, are likely to develop a *learned-helpless* approach to peer difficulties—concluding, after repeated rebuffs, that they will never be liked (Wichmann, Coplan, & Daniels, 2004). Both types of rejected children need help attributing their peer difficulties to internal, changeable causes.

As rejected children gain in social skills, teachers must encourage peers to alter their negative opinions. Accepted children often selectively recall rejected children's negative acts while overlooking their positive ones (Mikami, Lerner, & Lun, 2010). Consequently, even in the face of contrary evidence, rejected children's negative reputations tend to persist. Teachers' praise and expressions of liking, along with classroom expectations for social acceptance, can modify peer judgments (De Laet at al., 2014).

LOOK and LISTEN

Contact a nearby elementary school or a school district office to find out what practices are in place to prevent bullying. Inquire about a written anti-bullying policy, and request a copy.

Biology and Environment | Bullies and Their Victims

Follow the activities of aggressive children over a school day, and you will see that they reserve their hostilities for certain peers. A highly destructive form of interaction is **peer victimization,** in which certain children become targets of verbal and physical attacks or other forms of abuse. What sustains these repeated assault–retreat cycles between pairs of children? About 5 to 12 percent of children are bullies, while 8 to 20 percent are repeatedly victimized. Most bullies who engage in face-to-face physical and verbal attacks are boys, but a considerable number of girls bombard vulnerable classmates with verbal and relational hostility (Salmivalli & Peets, 2018).

As bullies move into adolescence, an increasing number attack through electronic means. About 20 to 40 percent of youths have experienced "cyberbullying" through text messages, e-mail, social media sites, or other electronic tools (Kowalski & Limber, 2013). Compared with face-to-face bullying, gender differences in cyberbullying are less pronounced; the indirectness of online aggression may lead girls to prefer it (Menesini & Spiel, 2012). Girls more often use text messages, e-mail, or social media to cyberbully, whereas boys more often distribute embarrassing photos or videos (Menesini, Nicocenti, & Calussi, 2011).

"Traditional" bullying and cyberbullying frequently co-occur: Bullies and victims in one context are frequently involved in the other. But electronic bullying is not always an extension of traditional bullying (Smith et al., 2008). And victims are far less likely to report cyberbullying to parents or adults at school. In many instances, the cyberbully's identity is unknown to the victim and audience.

Many bullies are disliked, or become so, because of their cruelty. But a substantial number are socially prominent, powerful youngsters who are broadly admired for their physical attractiveness, power, or athletic abilities (Vaillancourt et al., 2010). To preserve their high social status, bullies often target already-peer-rejected children, whom classmates are unlikely to defend (Veenstra et al., 2010). This helps explain why peers rarely intervene to help victims, and why about 20 to 30 percent of onlookers encourage bullies, even joining in (Salmivalli & Voeten, 2004). Bullying occurs more often in schools where teachers view it as having few harmful effects and where many students judge engaging in it to be "OK" (Guerra, Williams, & Sadek, 2011; Troop-Gordon, 2015). Indeed, bullies and the peers who assist them typically display social-cognitive deficits, including

overly high self-esteem, pride in their acts, and indifference to harm done to their victims (Hymel et al., 2010).

Depression and other internalizing difficulties increase children's risk of both real-life and cyber victimization (Kochel, Ladd, & Rudolph, 2012; Vaillancourt et al., 2013). Chronic victims tend to be passive when active behavior is expected. Biologically based traits—an inhibited temperament and a frail physical appearance—contribute. But victims also have histories of resistant attachment, overly controlling child rearing, and maternal overprotection—parenting that prompts anxiety, low self-esteem, and dependency, resulting in a fearful demeanor that marks these children and youths as vulnerable (Rubin et al., 2018).

Bullies and the peers who assist them typically display overly high self-esteem, pride in their acts, and indifference to the harm done to their victims. Chronic victims are often easy targets—frail looking, passive, and inhibited.

Other adjustment problems associated with persistent victimization include loneliness, low peer acceptance, poor school performance, disruptive behavior, and school avoidance (Kochel, Ladd, & Rudolph, 2012). And like persistent child abuse, victimization is linked to impaired production of cortisol, suggesting a chronically disrupted physiological response to stress (Vaillancourt, Hymel, & McDougall, 2013).

As instances of traditional bullying and cyberbullying accumulate, victims report substantial interference with daily functioning. Both traditional bullying and cyberbullying are related to declining self-esteem, classroom and school participation, and academic achievement and to rising anxiety, depression, and suicidal thoughts (Ladd, Ettekal, & Kochenderfer-Ladd, 2017; Menesini, Calussi, & Nocentini, 2012; van den Eijnden et al., 2014). Repeated cyberattacks directed at causing widespread damage to the victim's reputation—for example, circulating malicious photos or videos on cell phones or social media sites—magnify these effects.

Aggression and victimization are not polar opposites. One-third to one-half of victims are also aggressive, meting out physical, relational, or cyber hostilities. Bullies usually respond by abusing them again—a cycle that sustains their victim status (Cooley, Fite, & Pederson, 2017). Among rejected children, these bully/victims are the most despised. They often have histories of extremely maladaptive parenting, including child abuse. This combination of highly negative

home and peer experiences places them at severe risk for maladjustment (Lereya, Samara, & Wolke, 2013).

Interventions that change victimized children's negative opinions of themselves and that teach them to respond in nonreinforcing ways to their attackers are helpful. Another way to assist victimized children is to help them acquire the social skills needed to form and maintain a gratifying, supportive friendship (Cuadros & Berger, 2016). When children have a close friend to whom they can turn for help or belong to a clique in which some friends are willing to retaliate on their behalf, bullying episodes typically end quickly (Kendrick, Jutengren, & Stattin, 2012; Zarbatanay et al., 2017). Also, anxious, withdrawn children with friends have fewer adjustment problems than those without friends (Fox & Boulton, 2006).

Although modifying victimized children's behavior can help, the best way to reduce bullying is to change youth environments (including school, sports programs, recreation centers, and neighborhoods), promoting prosocial attitudes and behaviors. Effective approaches include developing school and community codes against both traditional bullying and cyberbullying; teaching child bystanders to intervene; strengthening parental oversight of children and youths' use of cell phones and other screen media; and increasing adult supervision of high-bullying areas in schools, such as hallways, lunchroom, and schoolyard (Fite et al., 2013; Menesini & Salmivalli, 2017).

The U.S. Department of Health and Human Services manages an antibullying website, *www.stopbullying.gov,* that raises awareness of the harmfulness of bullying and provides parents, teachers, and students with information on prevention.

Finally, because rejected children's socially incompetent behaviors often originate in harsh, authoritarian parenting, interventions focusing on the child may not be sufficient (Bierman & Powers, 2009). Without improving the quality of parent–child interaction, rejected children will continue to practice poor interpersonal skills at home and, as a result, may soon return to their old behavior patterns.

13.5 Gender Typing

13.5 Discuss changes in gender-stereotyped beliefs and gender identity during middle childhood.

Children's understanding of gender roles broadens in middle childhood, and their gender identities (views of themselves as relatively masculine or feminine) change as well. We will see how gender stereotypes influence children's attitudes, behaviors, peer relations, and self-perceptions.

13.5.1 Gender-Stereotyped Beliefs

By age 5, gender stereotyping of activities and occupations is well-established. During the school years, knowledge of stereotypes increases in the less obvious areas of personality traits and achievement.

Personality Traits   Research in many cultures reveals that stereotyping of personality traits increases steadily in middle childhood, becoming adultlike around age 11 (Best, 2001; Heyman & Legare, 2004). For example, children typically regard "tough," "aggressive," "rational," and "dominant" as masculine and "gentle," "sympathetic," and "dependent" as feminine.

Children derive these distinctions from observing sex differences in behavior as well as from adult treatment. When helping a child with a task, for example, parents (especially fathers) behave in a more mastery-oriented fashion with sons, setting higher standards, explaining concepts, and pointing out important features of tasks—particularly during gender-typed pursuits, such as science activities (Tenenbaum & Leaper, 2003; Tenenbaum et al., 2005).

Furthermore, elementary school teachers tend to stereotype girls who display "feminine" behavior as diligent and compliant and boys who display "masculine" behavior as lazy and troublesome (Heyder & Kessels, 2015). These perceptions may contribute to boys' reduced academic engagement and lower school grades relative to girls'. At the same time, when teachers are presented with a boy and a girl who are equally successful at math, they tend to see the girl as having to work harder (Robinson-Cimpian et al., 2014). As we saw in our discussion of achievement-related attributions, this downrating of girls' ability negatively affects their performance.

Achievement Areas   Shortly after entering elementary school, school-age children figure out which academic subjects and skill areas are "masculine" and which are "feminine." They often regard reading, spelling, art, and music as more for girls and mathematics, athletics, science, and mechanical skills as more for boys (Cvencek, Meltzoff, & Greenwald, 2011; Eccles, Jacobs, & Harold, 1990). These stereotypes—and the attitudes and behaviors of parents and teachers that promote them—influence children's preferences for and sense of competence at certain subjects and, ultimately, their performance (Muntoni & Retelsdorf, 2018; Plante et al., 2018). As we saw in our discussion of self-esteem, boys tend to feel more competent than girls at math, science, and athletics, whereas girls feel more competent than boys at language arts (see page 480).

An encouraging sign is that some gender-stereotyped beliefs about achievement seem to be changing. In several investigations carried out in Canada, France, and the United States, a majority of elementary and secondary students disagreed that math is a "masculine" subject (Kurtz-Costes et al., 2014; Martinot, Bagès, & Désert, 2012; Plante, Théoret, & Favreau, 2009; Rowley et al., 2007). Furthermore, when Canadian students were given the option of rating math as a "feminine" subject (not offered in previous studies), an impressive number—more girls than boys—viewed it as predominantly feminine. And in a British study, girls viewed

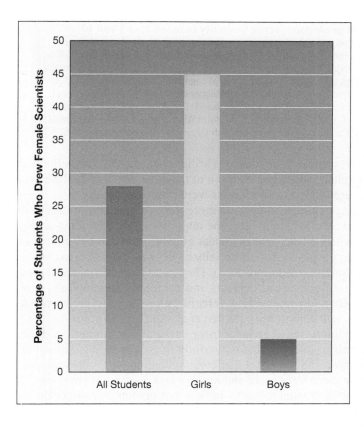

| A girl's drawing of a female scientist.

FIGURE 13.3 **Depiction of scientists as female in U.S. elementary and secondary school students' drawings, 1985–2016.** When more than 70 studies conducted between 1985 and 2016 were examined in which U.S. elementary and secondary school students were asked to draw an image of a scientist, over one-fourth drew female scientists—a dramatic rise over previous decades. Girls, however, did so far more often than boys. (Based on Miller et al., 2018.)

their own gender as having superior math ability, though boys disagreed, believing they were better at math (Nowicki & Lopata, 2017).

Similarly, when researchers examined five decades of studies in which thousands of U.S. elementary and secondary school students were asked to draw an image of a scientist, both girls and boys drew female scientists more often in later decades. In the 1960s and 1970s, less than 1 percent depicted scientists as female, compared with 28 percent between 1985 and 2016—results indicating that the stereotypic view of science as "masculine" has weakened (Miller et al., 2018). Still, as Figure 13.3 shows, girls drew female scientists far more often than boys.

Finally, the overwhelming majority of young people in recent investigations continue to view language arts traditionally—as largely "feminine." And they still perceive girls as doing better in language arts than in math.

Toward Greater Flexibility   Although school-age children are aware of many gender stereotypes, they also develop a more flexible, open-minded view of what males and females *can do,* a trend that continues into adolescence.

In studying gender stereotyping, researchers usually ask children whether or not both genders can display a personality trait or engage in an activity—responses that measure **gender-stereotype flexibility,** or overlap in the characteristics of males and females. In a German study that followed children from age 5 to 10, flexibility increased dramatically from age 7 on regardless of the degree of early gender-stereotype rigidity (see Figure 13.4 on page 500) (Trautner et al., 2005). As they develop the capacity to integrate conflicting social cues, children realize that a person's sex is not a certain predictor of his or her personality traits, activities, and behaviors (Halim & Ruble, 2010). Similarly, by the end of the school years, most children regard gender typing as socially rather than biologically influenced (Taylor, Rhodes, & Gelman, 2009).

Despite this increasing flexibility, many school-age children take a harsh view of certain gender-role violations—boys playing with dolls and wearing girls' clothing, and girls acting noisily and roughly. They are especially intolerant when boys engage in these "cross-gender" acts (Blakemore, 2003). When asked for open-ended descriptions of boys and girls, children most often mention girls' physical appearance ("is pretty," "wears dresses") and boys' activities

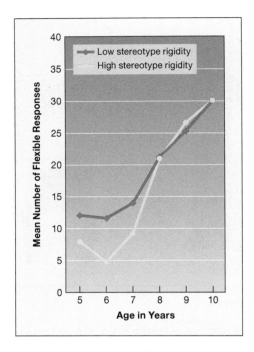

FIGURE 13.4 **Changes in gender-stereotype flexibility between ages 5 and 10.**
German schoolchildren responded annually to a questionnaire assessing the flexibility of their gender-stereotyped beliefs (whether they thought both genders could display a personality trait or engage in an activity). Children differing in degree of gender-stereotype rigidity at age 5 eventually became equally flexible. Findings support the powerful role of cognitive changes in inducing flexibility, since early individual differences in rigidity were not sustained. (From H. M. Trautner et al., 2005, "Rigidity and Flexibility of Gender Stereotypes in Childhood: Developmental or Differential?" *Infant and Child Development, 14,* p. 371. Copyright © 2005 John Wiley & Sons Limited. Reprinted by permission of John Wiley and Sons, Ltd., conveyed through Copyright Clearance Center, Inc.)

and personality traits ("likes trucks," "is rough") (Miller et al., 2009). The salience of these stereotypes helps explain why, when children of the other sex display the behaviors just mentioned, they are likely to experience severe peer disapproval.

Nevertheless, school-age children do extend more flexible gender attitudes to the peer context to some degree. As with ethnicity, the majority regard excluding an agemate from peer group activities on the basis of gender as unfair. But between fourth and seventh grades, more young people—again, especially boys—say it is OK to exclude on the basis of gender than ethnicity (see Figure 13.5). They point to concerns about group functioning related to sex differences in interests and communication styles—boys' preference for active pursuits and commanding, forceful behavior, girls' preference for quiet activities, politeness, and compromise (Killen et al., 2002, p. 56).

In line with these findings, sex-segregated peer associations strengthen during middle childhood and continue to contribute powerfully to gender typing. School-age children come to expect that communication with same-sex peers will be more responsive and involve less discomfort (for example, not knowing what to say)—beliefs that predict gains over time in the number of same-sex friendships children report (Xiao et al., 2019). Teachers and schools might actively arrange for more interaction between boys and girls to broaden the array of relationships children develop and reduce gender-role conformity. Having other-sex friends may contribute, especially, to reduced stereotyping of other-sex peers.

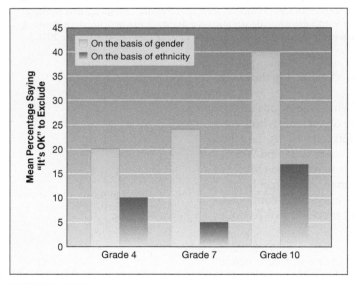

FIGURE 13.5 **Percentage of children and adolescents saying "It's OK" to exclude an agemate from a peer-group activity on the basis of gender and ethnicity.** When asked about excluding an other-sex or other-ethnicity peer from a peer-group activity (a music club in which members trade DVDs), many more young people said that it is OK to do so on the basis of gender than on the basis of ethnicity. Willingness to exclude on the basis of gender increased with age, with many participants justifying their decision by pointing to sex differences in interests and communication styles. (Based on Killen et al., 2002.)

13.5.2 Gender Identity and Behavior

Children who were more strongly gender-typed relative to their agemates in early childhood usually remain so in middle childhood (Golombok et al., 2008). Nevertheless, overall changes do occur, with boys' and girls' gender identities following different paths.

From third to sixth grade, boys tend to strengthen their identification with "masculine" personality traits, whereas girls' identification with "feminine" traits declines. Girls are more likely than boys to describe themselves as having some "other-gender" characteristics. And whereas boys usually stick to "masculine" pursuits, many girls experiment with a wider range of options—from cooking and sewing to sports and science projects—and more often consider traditionally male future work roles, such as firefighter or astronomer. As many as one-third to two-thirds of school-age girls say they are "sort of" or definitely tomboys (Halim, Bryant, & Zucker, 2016).

These changes reflect a mixture of cognitive and social forces. School-age children of both sexes are aware that society attaches greater prestige to "masculine" pursuits. For example, they rate "masculine" occupations as having higher status than "feminine" occupations, and an unfamiliar job as higher in status when portrayed with a male worker than a female worker (Liben, Bigler, & Krogh, 2001; Weisgram, Bigler, & Liben, 2010). Messages from adults and peers are also influential. In Chapter 10, we saw that parents (especially fathers) are especially disapproving when sons, as opposed to daughters, cross gender lines. Similarly, a tomboyish girl can interact with boys without losing the approval of her female peers, but a boy who hangs out with girls is likely to be ridiculed and rejected.

As school-age children make social comparisons and characterize themselves in terms of stable dispositions, their gender identity expands to include the following self-evaluations, which greatly affect psychological adjustment:

- *Gender typicality*—the degree to which the child feels similar to others of the same gender. Although children need not be highly gender typed to view themselves as gender-typical, their psychological well-being depends, to some degree, on feeling that they "fit in" with their same-sex peers.
- *Gender contentedness*—the degree to which the child feels comfortable with his or her gender assignment, which also promotes happiness.
- *Felt pressure to conform to gender roles*—the degree to which the child feels parents and peers disapprove of his or her gender-related traits. Because such pressure reduces the likelihood that children will explore options related to their interests and talents, children who feel strong gender-typed pressure are often distressed.

An 8-year-old launches the rocket she made in her school's Young Astronaut Club. Whereas school-age boys usually stick to "masculine" pursuits, girls experiment with a wider range of options.

In a longitudinal study of third through seventh graders, *gender-typical* and *gender-contented* children gained in self-esteem over the following year. In contrast, children who were *gender-atypical* and *gender-discontented* declined in self-worth. Furthermore, gender-atypical children who reported *intense pressure to conform to gender roles* experienced serious internalizing difficulties—withdrawal, sadness, disappointment, and anxiety (Corby, Hodges, & Perry, 2007; Yunger, Carver, & Perry, 2004). In other research, children who, on gender typicality, expressed an *androgynous* identity—said they felt similar both to peers of the same gender and to peers of the other gender—reported high self-esteem, little felt pressure to conform to gender roles, and few internalizing problems (Pauletti et al., 2017).

Because felt pressure to conform to gender roles predicts maladjustment among gender-atypical children, more experts are advocating interventions that help parents, teachers, and peers become more accepting of children's gender-atypical interests and behaviors and that protect such children from peer harassment (Bigler, 2007; Hill et al., 2010; Smith & Juvonen, 2017). Return to page 390 in Chapter 10, to review related evidence on gender-dysphoric children, who feel profoundly discontented with their birth sex and who strongly identify as the other sex, along with evidence on the best therapeutic approach to help them.

ASK YOURSELF

Connect ■ Describe similarities in development of self-concept, attitudes toward racial and ethnic minorities, and gender-stereotyped beliefs in middle childhood.

Apply ■ What changes in parent–child and teacher–child relationships are likely to help children who are rejected by their peers?

Reflect ■ As a school-age child, did you have classmates you would classify as popular-antisocial? What were they like, and why do you think peers admired them?

13.6 Family Influences

As children move into school, peer, and community contexts, the parent–child relationship changes. At the same time, children's well-being continues to depend on the quality of family interaction. In the following sections, we will see that contemporary diversity in family life—fewer births per family unit, more lesbian and gay parents who are open about their sexual orientation, more never-married parents, and continuing high rates of divorce, remarriage, and maternal employment—have reshaped the family system. As we consider this array of family forms, note how children's well-being, in each instance, depends on the quality of family interaction, which is sustained by supportive ties to kin and community and by favorable public policies.

13.6a Discuss changes in parent–child communication and sibling relationships in middle childhood.

13.6b Explain how children fare in lesbian and gay families and in never-married, single-parent families.

13.6c Cite factors that influence children's adjustment to divorce and blended family arrangements.

13.6d Discuss how maternal employment and life in dual-earner families affect school-age children.

13.6.1 Parent–Child Relationships

In middle childhood, the amount of time children spend with parents declines dramatically. Children's growing independence means that parents must deal with new issues. "I've struggled with how many chores to assign, how much allowance to give, whether their friends are good influences, and what to do about problems at school," Rena remarked. "And then there's the challenge of keeping track of them when they're out—or even when they're home and I'm not there to see what's going on."

Despite these new concerns, child rearing becomes easier for parents who established an authoritative style during the early years. Reasoning is more effective with school-age children because of their greater capacity for logical thinking and their increased respect for parents' expert knowledge. And children of parents who engage in joint decision making when possible are more likely to listen to parents' perspectives in situations where compliance is vital (Russell, Mize, & Bissaker, 2004).

As children demonstrate that they can manage daily activities and responsibilities, effective parents gradually shift control from adult to child—a change associated with favorable academic achievement and high-quality peer relationships (Wang & Fletcher, 2016). Parents do not let go entirely but, rather, engage in **coregulation,** a form of supervision in which they exercise general oversight while letting children take charge of moment-by-moment decision making. Coregulation grows out of a warm, securely attached parent–child relationship based on cooperation, compromise, and mutual respect. Parents must guide and monitor from a distance and effectively communicate expectations when they are with their children. And children must inform parents of their whereabouts, activities, and problems so parents can intervene when necessary (Collins, Madsen, & Susman-Stillman, 2002; Koehn & Kerns, 2018). Coregulation supports and protects children while preparing them for adolescence, when they will make many important decisions themselves.

As at younger ages, mothers spend more time than fathers with school-age children and know more about children's everyday activities, although many fathers are highly involved (Pew Research Center, 2013b). Both parents, however, tend to devote more time to children of their own sex (Lam, McHale, & Crouter, 2012).

Although school-age children often press for greater independence, they know they need their parents' support. A positive parent–child relationship is linked to improved emotional self-regulation in children, reducing the negative impact of stressful events (Brumariu, Kerns, & Seibert, 2012; Hazel et al., 2014). School-age children often turn to parents for affection, advice, affirmation of self-worth, and assistance with everyday problems

13.6.2 Siblings

In addition to parents and friends, siblings continue to be important sources of support. Yet sibling rivalry tends to increase in middle childhood. As children participate in a wider range of activities, parents often compare siblings' traits and accomplishments. The child who gets less parental affection, more disapproval, or fewer material resources is likely to be resentful and show poorer adjustment (McHale, Updegraff, & Whiteman, 2012).

For same-sex siblings who are close in age, parental comparisons become more frequent, resulting in more quarreling and antagonism. This effect is particularly strong when parents are under stress as a result of financial worries, marital conflict, single parenthood, or child negativity (Jenkins, Rasbash, & O'Connor, 2003). Parents whose energies are drained become less careful about being fair. Perhaps because fathers, overall, spend less time with children than mothers, children react especially intensely when fathers prefer one child: Jealousy over attention from fathers predicts sibling conflict (Kolak & Volling, 2011).

To reduce rivalry, siblings often strive to be different from one another (McHale, Updegraff, & Whiteman, 2012). For example, two brothers I know deliberately selected different athletic pursuits and musical instruments. If the older one did especially well at an activity, the younger one did not want to try it. Parents can limit the effects of rivalry by making an effort not to compare children, but some feedback about their competencies is inevitable. As siblings strive to win recognition for their own uniqueness, they shape important aspects of each other's development.

Although conflict tends to rise, many siblings continue to rely on each other for companionship, assistance, emotional support, and resilience in the face of major stressors, such as parental divorce (Conger, Stocker, & McGuire, 2009). Providing parents with training in mediation—how to get siblings to lay down ground rules, clarify their points of disagreement and common ground, and discuss possible solutions—increases siblings' awareness of each other's perspectives, reduces animosity, and enhances siblings' ability to resolve disagreements constructively (Ross & Lazinski, 2014).

When siblings get along well, the older sibling's academic and social competence tends to "rub off on" the younger sibling, fostering more favorable achievement and peer relationships. And both older and younger siblings benefit in empathy and prosocial behavior (Lam, Solmeyer, & McHale, 2012; Padilla-Walker, Harper, & Jensen, 2010). But destructive sibling conflict in middle childhood is associated with negative outcomes, including conflict-ridden peer relationships, anxiety, depressed mood, and later substance use and delinquency, even after other family-relationship factors are controlled (Kim et al., 2007; Ostrov, Crick, & Stauffacher, 2006; Pike & Oliver, 2016). Child conduct problems, in turn, predict worsening of sibling relationship quality over time.

An older brother teaches his sister how to play basketball. Although sibling rivalry tends to increase in middle childhood, siblings also provide each other with emotional support and help with challenging skills.

13.6.3 Only Children

Although sibling relationships bring many benefits, they are not essential for healthy development. Contrary to popular belief, only children are not spoiled, and, in some respects, they are advantaged. U.S. children growing up in one-child and multichild families do not differ in self-rated personality traits (Mottus, Indus, & Allik, 2008). And compared to children with siblings, only children are higher in self-esteem and achievement motivation, do better in school, and attain higher levels of education. One reason may be that only children have somewhat closer relationships with parents, who may exert more pressure for mastery and accomplishment and can invest more time in their child's educational experiences (Falbo, 2012). Furthermore, only children have just as many close, high-quality friends as children with siblings. However, they tend to be less well-accepted in the peer group, perhaps because they have not had opportunities to learn effective conflict-resolution strategies through sibling interaction (Kitzmann, Cohen, & Lockwood, 2002).

Favorable development also characterizes only children in China, where a one-child family policy was strictly enforced in densely populated urban areas for more than three decades, until it was replaced in 2015 by a two-child policy. Compared with agemates who have siblings, Chinese only children are slightly advantaged in cognitive development and academic motivation and achievement. They also report fewer emotional symptoms (such as anxiety, depression, or hostility), perhaps because government disapproval led to tension in families with more than one child (Falbo, 2012; Falbo & Hooper, 2015; Liu et al., 2017). Chinese mothers usually ensure that their children have regular contact with first cousins (who are considered siblings). Perhaps as a result, Chinese only children do not differ from agemates with siblings in social skills and peer acceptance (Hart, Newell, & Olsen, 2003).

13.6.4 Lesbian and Gay Families

According to recent estimates, about 20 to 35 percent of lesbian couples and 5 to 15 percent of gay couples are parents, most through previous heterosexual marriages, some through foster or adoptive parenthood, and a growing number through reproductive technologies (Brewster, Tillman, & Jokinen-Gordon, 2014; Patterson & Farr, 2016). In the past, because of laws assuming that gay men and lesbians could not be adequate parents, those who divorced a heterosexual partner lost custody of their children. Today, child custody and adoption by sexual minority parents is legal in all U.S. states and in many other industrialized nations.

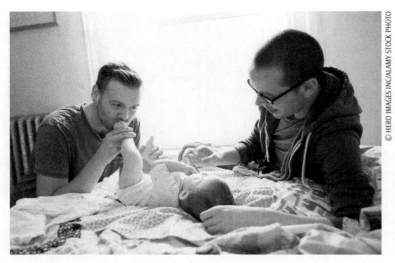

Lesbian and gay parents are as committed to and effective at child rearing as heterosexual parents, and the children of same-sex and other-sex parents develop similarly.

Most research on families headed by same-sex couples is limited to volunteer samples. Findings indicate that lesbian and gay parents are as committed to and effective at child rearing as heterosexual parents and sometimes more so (Bos, 2013). Also, whether born to or adopted by their parents or conceived through donor insemination or surrogacy, children in lesbian and gay families usually do not differ from children of heterosexual parents in peer relations, gender-role behavior, sexual orientation, quality of life, or mental health (Bos & Sandfort, 2010; Goldberg, 2010; Patterson, 2013; Potter, 2012; van Gelderen et al., 2012). And some evidence suggests that children of same-sex parents are better adjusted (Fedewa, Black, & Ahn, 2015; Green et al., 2019).

To surmount the potential bias associated with volunteer samples, some researchers take advantage of large, nationally representative data banks to study lesbian and gay families. Findings indicate that children with same-sex and other-sex parents develop similarly, and that children's adjustment is associated with factors other than parental sexual orientation (Moore & Stambolis-Ruhstorfer, 2013). For example, close parent–child relationships predict better peer relations and a reduction in adolescent delinquency, whereas family transitions (such as parental divorce and remarriage) are related to academic difficulties, regardless of family form (Potter, 2012; Russell & Muraco, 2013).

When extended-family members withhold acceptance, lesbian and gay parents often build "families of choice" through friends, who assume the roles of relatives (Frost, Meyer, & Schwartz, 2016). Usually, however, parents of sexual minorities cannot endure a permanent rift. With time, extended family relationships become more positive and supportive.

A major concern of lesbian and gay parents is that their children will be stigmatized because of their parents' sexual orientation. Peer teasing and harassment are problems for some children of sexual minority parents, but close parent–child relationships, supportive school and neighborhood environments, and connections with other lesbian and gay families protect children from the negative effects of these experiences (Bos, 2013; Patterson, 2017). Overall, children of lesbian and gay parents can be distinguished from other children mainly by issues related to living in discriminatory contexts.

13.6.5　Never-Married Parent Families

Over the past several decades, births to unmarried mothers in industrialized nations have increased dramatically. Today, about 40 percent of U.S. births are to single mothers, more than double the percentage in 1980. Whereas teenage parenthood has declined steadily since 1990, births to single adult women have increased, with a particularly sharp rise during the first decade of the twenty-first century, followed by a period of stability and a recent slight decline (Child Trends, 2018b; Martin et al., 2018).

A growing number of nonmarital births—about 1 in 3—are to cohabiting couples, relationships that are especially common among young adults with low education and income. In addition, more than 12 percent of U.S. children live with a single parent who has never married and does not have a partner. About 90 percent are mothers, 10 percent fathers (Martin et al., 2018; Pew Research Center, 2018d). A far larger share of never-married single parents than cohabiting parents—27 versus 16 percent—live in poverty.

African-American young women are considerably more likely than other same-age women to give birth outside of marriage and less likely to live with the child's father or another partner. Nearly 70 percent of births to African-American mothers are to unmarried women, compared with about one-third to Hispanic and one-fourth to European-American women (Martin et al., 2018). The high African-American rate is mostly due to substantially higher imprisonment and mortality rates (as the result of homicides, chronic diseases, and injuries) among African-American men than men of other ethnicities (Levs, 2015). Largely for these reasons, more than 1 in 6 African-American men have disappeared from daily life and are unavailable to fulfill the roles of father and husband.

African-American fathers who remain in their communities are unfairly stereotyped as prone to desert their children. In fact, they do the opposite: 60 percent live with at least one child, a growing number by cohabiting with the child's mother. Living with children greatly elevates fathers' active participation in child rearing. With respect to parental involvement, African-American residential fathers do as well as or better than residential fathers of other ethnicities (Jones & Mosher, 2013). And as Figure 13.6 illustrates, even when African-American fathers live apart from their children, they are highly involved parents, equaling or exceeding their European-American and Hispanic counterparts.

Never-married African-American parents—especially the large number of mothers rearing children without a partner—tap the extended family, often their own mothers and sometimes male relatives, for help with child rearing (Anderson, 2012). Still, as noted earlier, single parenthood greatly increases financial hardship. Many children in single-mother homes display adjustment problems associated with economic disadvantage (Lamb, 2012; Mather, 2010). Furthermore, children of never-married mothers who lack a father's consistent warmth and involvement show less favorable cognitive development and engage in more antisocial behavior (Sterrett et al., 2015; Waldfogel, Craigie, & Brooks-Gunn, 2010).

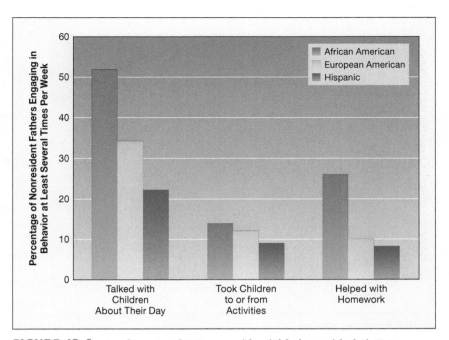

FIGURE 13.6   Involvement of U.S. nonresidential fathers with their 5- to 18-year-old children by ethnicity. A nationally representative sample of over 1,000 nonresidential fathers answered questions about how often they engage in various parenting behaviors with their school-age and adolescent children. African-American fathers' involvement equaled or exceeded that of European-American and Hispanic fathers, as illustrated by the extent to which they talked with children about their day, took children to or from activities, and helped children with homework at least several times per week. African-American nonresident fathers' involvement with infants and preschoolers, including joint play, book reading, and meals (not shown), is similarly high. (Based on Jones & Mosher, 2013.)

But a marital or cohabiting relationship benefits children only when the father is a reliable source of economic and child-rearing support. For example, adolescents who feel close to their nonresident father fare better in school performance and emotional and social adjustment than do adolescents in two-parent homes where a close father tie is lacking (Booth, Scott, & King, 2010). Strengthening coparenting skills, social support, education, and employment opportunities for low-SES parents would greatly enhance the well-being of unmarried parents (both mothers and fathers) and their children.

13.6.6 Divorce

Children's interactions with parents and siblings are affected by other aspects of family life. When Joey was 8 and Lizzie 5, their father, Drake, moved out. During the preceding months, Joey began pushing, hitting, taunting, and calling Lizzie names—fighting that coincided with Rena and her husband's growing marital unhappiness.

Between 1960 and 1985, divorce rates in Western nations rose dramatically before stabilizing in most countries. The United States has experienced a decline in divorces over the past 20 years, largely due to a rise in age at first marriage and a drop in marriage rates. However, this decrease mostly applies to well-educated, financially secure families. As Figure 13.7 on page 506 shows, individuals with less education experience substantially greater marital instability (Lundberg & Pollack, 2015). Because educational and economic disadvantage increases family fragility, divorce rates are higher among low-income ethnic minority couples (Raley, Sweeny, & Wondra, 2015).

Among developed nations, the United States has one of the highest divorce rates. Of the estimated 42 to 45 percent of American marriages that end in divorce, half involve children.

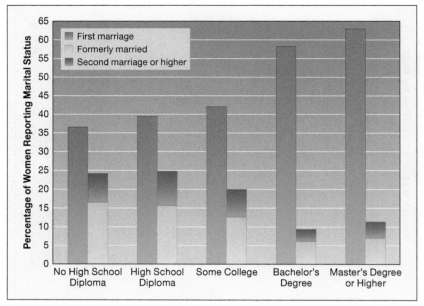

FIGURE 13.7   Current marital status reported by U.S. women varying in level of education. A survey of over 10,000 U.S. women between ages 15 and 44 revealed that increased education is linked to marital stability, whereas limited education is linked to divorce, remarriage, and subsequent divorce. (Based on Lundberg & Pollak, 2015.)

More than one-fourth of U.S. children live in divorced, single-parent households. Although most reside with their mothers, the percentage in father-headed households has increased steadily, to about 17 percent (Grall, 2016).

Children of divorce spend an average of five years in a single-parent home—almost a third of childhood. About 10 percent of U.S. children live with one parent (usually their mother) and a married or cohabiting stepparent (Kreider & Ellis, 2011). Many of these children eventually experience a third major change—the end of their parent's second marriage or cohabiting partnership.

These figures reveal that divorce is a transition that leads to a variety of new living arrangements, accompanied by changes in housing, income, and family roles and responsibilities. Although divorce is stressful for children and increases their risk of adjustment problems, most adjust favorably (Greene et al., 2012; Lamb, 2012). How well children fare depends on many factors: the custodial parent's psychological health, the child's characteristics, and social supports within the family and surrounding community.

Immediate Consequences   "Things were the worst after Drake and I decided to separate," Rena reflected. "We fought over division of our belongings and custody of the children, and the kids suffered. Sobbing, Lizzie told me she was 'sorry she made Daddy go away.' Joey kicked and threw things at home and didn't do his work at school. We had to sell the house; I couldn't afford it alone. And I needed a better-paying job."

Family conflict often rises in newly divorced households as parents try to settle disputes over children and possessions. Once one parent moves out, additional events threaten supportive interactions between parents and children. Mother-headed households typically experience a sharp drop in income. In the United States, nearly 30 percent of divorced mothers with young children live in poverty, and many more are low-income, getting less than the full amount of child support from the absent father or none at all (Grall, 2016). These families often have to move to lower-cost housing, reducing supportive ties to neighbors and friends.

The transition from marriage to divorce typically leads to high maternal stress, depression, and anxiety and to a disorganized family life. Declines in well-being are greatest for mothers of young children (Williams & Dunne-Bryant, 2006). "Meals and bedtimes were at all hours, the house didn't get cleaned, and I stopped taking Joey and Lizzie on weekend outings," said Rena. As children react with distress and anger to their less secure home lives, discipline may become harsh and inconsistent. Over time, contact with noncustodial fathers—and the quality of the father–child relationship—often decreases, particularly when parental conflict is high (Troilo & Coleman, 2012). Fathers who see their children only occasionally are inclined to be permissive and indulgent, making the mother's task of managing the child even more difficult.

The greater children's exposure to parental conflict and inadequate warmth, involvement, and consistent guidance, the poorer children's adjustment (Elam et al., 2016, 2019). About 20 to 25 percent of children in divorced families display severe problems, compared with about 10 percent in nondivorced families (Golombok & Tasker, 2015; Lansford, 2009). At the same time, reactions vary with children's age, temperament, and sex.

Children's Age   Five-year-old Lizzie's fear that she had caused her father to leave home is not unusual. Preschool and young school-age children often blame themselves for a marital breakup and fear that both parents may abandon them (Lansford et al., 2006). Hence, they are more likely to display both anxious, fearful and angry, defiant reactions than older children and adolescents with the cognitive maturity to understand that they are not responsible for their parents' divorce.

Still, many school-age and adolescent youngsters also react strongly, experiencing depressed mood and declining in school performance, becoming unruly, and escaping into undesirable peer activities, such as running away, truancy, substance use, and early sexual activity, particularly when family conflict is high and parental support and supervision are low (Kleinsorge & Covitz, 2012; Sigle-Rushton et al., 2014; Weaver & Scho-field, 2015). Some older children—especially the oldest child in the family—display more mature behavior, willingly taking on extra household tasks, care of younger siblings, and emotional support of a depressed, anxious mother. But if these demands are too great, these children may eventually become resentful and engage in angry, acting-out behavior (Hetherington & Kelly, 2002).

When parents divorce, young children often blame themselves and respond with both fear and anger. This father's soothing words help his daughter understand that she is not responsible for the marital breakup.

Children's Temperament and Sex Exposure to stressful life events and inadequate parenting magnifies the problems of temperamentally difficult children (see Chapter 7). In contrast, easy children are less often targets of parental anger and also cope more effectively with adversity.

These findings help explain sex differences in response to divorce. Girls sometimes respond as Lizzie did, with internalizing reactions such as crying, self-criticism, and withdrawal. More often, children of both sexes show demanding, attention-getting behavior. But in mother-custody families, boys are at slightly greater risk for serious adjustment problems (Amato, 2010). Recall from Chapter 10 that boys are more active and noncompliant—behaviors that increase with exposure to parental conflict and inconsistent discipline. Research reveals that long before the marital breakup, sons of divorcing couples display higher rates of impulsivity, defiance, and aggression—externalizing difficulties that may have been caused by their parents' marital problems while also contributing to them (Shaw, Winslow, & Flanagan, 1999; Strohschein, 2005). As a result, more boys enter the period of turmoil surrounding divorce with reduced capacity to cope with family stress.

Perhaps because their behavior is more unruly, boys of divorcing parents receive less emotional support from mothers, teachers, and peers. And as Joey's behavior toward Lizzie illustrates, the cycles of coercive interaction between distressed children and their divorced mothers soon spread to sibling relationships (Sheehan et al., 2004). After divorce, children who are challenging to rear generally get worse.

Long-Term Consequences   Rena eventually found better-paying work and gained control over the daily operation of the household. After several meetings with a counselor, Rena and Drake realized the harmful impact of their quarreling on Joey and Lizzie. Drake visited regularly and handled Joey's disruptiveness with firmness and consistency. Soon Joey's school performance improved, his behavior problems subsided, and both children seemed calmer and happier.

Most children show improved adjustment by two years after divorce. Yet overall, children and adolescents of divorced parents continue to score slightly lower than children of continuously married parents in academic achievement, self-esteem, social competence, and emotional and behavioral adjustment (Lansford, 2009; Weaver & Schofield, 2015). And divorce is linked to problems with adolescent sexuality and development of intimate ties. Young people who experienced parental divorce—especially more than once—display higher rates of early sexual activity and adolescent parenthood. Some display other difficulties in adulthood—reduced educational attainment, troubled romantic relationships and marriages, and divorce (Amato, 2010). Thus, divorce can have consequences for subsequent generations.

The overriding factor in positive adjustment following divorce is effective parenting—how well the custodial parent handles stress and shields the child from family conflict, and the extent to which each parent uses authoritative child rearing (Lamb, 2012). Parent-training programs can help custodial parents support their children's development. One eleven-session parent-training intervention for mothers of school-age children yielded improved mother–child

Regular contact with both parents and effective coparenting—supporting each other in their child-rearing roles—greatly improves adjustment in children of divorce.

relationships and increased children's coping skills, with effects persisting for six years (Velez et al., 2011).

Where the custodial parent is the mother, regular contact with fathers—especially those who were highly involved in child rearing—is important. The more paternal contact and the warmer the relationship, the less children react with internalizing and externalizing problems (Elam et al., 2016; Poortman, 2018). A few studies report that children's adjustment is slightly better when the father is the custodial parent, perhaps because of fathers' greater economic security (Clarke-Stewart & Hayward, 1996; Guttman & Lazar, 1998; McLanahan, 1999). At the same time, single mothers tend to provide children with more warmth, monitoring, and supervision than fathers (Coles, 2015). In most investigations, children in mother-custody and father-custody homes do not differ in psychological well-being.

Although divorce is painful for children, remaining in an intact but high-conflict family is much worse than making the transition to a low-conflict, single-parent household (Lamb, 2012; Strohschein, 2005). Divorcing parents who manage to set aside their disagreements and engage in effective coparenting, supporting each other in their child-rearing roles, greatly improve their children's chances of growing up competent, stable, and happy.

Divorce Mediation, Joint Custody, and Child Support Awareness that divorce is highly stressful for children and families has led to community-based services aimed at helping them through this difficult time. One such service is **divorce mediation,** a series of meetings between divorcing adults and a trained professional aimed at reducing family conflict, including legal battles over property division and child custody. Mediation increases out-of-court settlements, cooperation and involvement of both parents in child rearing, and parents' and children's feelings of well-being (Douglas, 2006).

Parent education programs, which are widespread, further encourage parents to resolve their disputes. During several sessions, professionals teach parents about the positive impact of constructive conflict resolution and of respectful, cooperative coparenting on children's well-being (Cookston et al., 2006; Pruett et al., 2016). Because of the demonstrated impact of parent education on parental cooperation, courts in many U.S. states may require parents to attend a program.

Joint custody, which grants each parent an equal say in important decisions about the child's upbringing, has become a common outcome of divorce settlements. Children usually reside with one parent and see the other on a fixed schedule, similar to the typical sole-custody arrangement. In other cases, parents share physical custody, and children move between homes. Joint-custody parents usually report little conflict—fortunately so, since the success of the arrangement depends on effective coparenting (Bauserman, 2012). And their children, regardless of living arrangements, tend to be better-adjusted than children in sole-maternal-custody homes (Baude, Pearson, & Drapeau, 2016; Bauserman, 2002).

Finally, many single-parent families depend on child support from the noncustodial parent to relieve financial strain. All U.S. states have procedures for withholding wages from parents who fail to make these payments. Although child support is usually not enough to lift a single-parent family out of poverty, it can ease its burdens substantially. Noncustodial fathers who have generous visitation schedules and see their children often are more likely to pay child support regularly (Amato & Sobolewski, 2004). And increases in paternal contact and in child support over time predict better coparenting relationships (Hofferth, Forry, & Peters, 2010). Applying What We Know on the following page summarizes ways to help children adjust to their parents' divorce.

13.6.7 Blended Families

"If you get married to Wendell and Daddy gets married to Carol," Lizzie wondered aloud to Rena, "then I'll have two sisters and one more brother. And let's see, how many grandmothers and grandfathers? A lot!" exclaimed Lizzie.

APPLYING WHAT WE KNOW

Helping Children Adjust to Their Parents' Divorce

SUGGESTION	EXPLANATION
Shield children from conflict.	Witnessing intense parental conflict is very damaging to children. If one parent insists on expressing hostility, children fare better if the other parent does not respond in kind.
Provide children with as much continuity, familiarity, and predictability as possible.	Children adjust better during the period surrounding divorce when their lives have some stability—for example, the same school, bedroom, babysitter, playmates, and daily schedule.
Explain the divorce and tell children what to expect.	Children may develop fears of abandonment if they are not prepared for their parents' separation. They should be told that their parents will not be living together anymore, which parent will be moving out, and when they will be able to see that parent. If possible, parents should explain the divorce together, providing a reason that each child can understand and assuring children that they are not to blame.
Emphasize the permanence of the divorce.	Fantasies of parents getting back together can prevent children from accepting the reality of their current life. Children should be told that the divorce is final and that they cannot change this fact.
Respond sympathetically to children's feelings.	Children need supportive, understanding responses to their feelings of sadness, fear, and anger. For children to adjust well, their painful emotions must be acknowledged, not denied or avoided.
Engage in authoritative parenting.	Authoritative parenting—providing affection and acceptance, reasonable demands for mature behavior, and consistent, rational discipline—greatly reduces children's risk of maladjustment following divorce.
Promote continuing relationships with both parents.	When parents disentangle their lingering hostility toward the former spouse from the child's need for a continuing relationship with the other parent, children adjust well. Grandparents and other extended-family members can help by not taking sides.

About 60 percent of divorced parents remarry within a few years. Others *cohabit,* or share a sexual relationship and a residence with a partner outside of marriage. Parent, stepparent, and children form a new family structure called a **blended, or reconstituted, family.** For some children, this expanded family network is positive, bringing greater adult attention. But children in blended families usually have more adjustment problems—including internalizing and externalizing symptoms and poor school performance—than children in stable, first-marriage families (Pryor, 2014). Switching to stepparents' new rules and expectations can be stressful, and children often view steprelatives as intruders. How well they adapt is, again, related to the quality of family functioning. This depends on which parent forms a new relationship, the complexity of blended-family relationships, and the child's age and sex. As we will see, older children and girls seem to have the hardest time.

Mother–Stepfather Families Because mothers generally retain custody of children, the most common form of blended family is a mother–stepfather arrangement. Boys tend to adjust quickly, welcoming a stepfather who is warm, who refrains from exerting his authority too quickly, and who offers relief from coercive cycles of mother–son interaction. Mothers' friction with sons also declines as a result of greater economic security, another adult to share household tasks, and an end to loneliness (Visher, Visher, & Pasley, 2003). Stepfathers who marry rather than cohabit are more involved in parenting, perhaps because men who choose to marry a mother with children are more interested in and skilled at child rearing (Hofferth & Anderson, 2003). Girls, however, often have difficulty with their custodial mother's remarriage. Stepfathers disrupt the close ties many girls have established with their mothers, and girls often react with sulky, resistant behavior (Pryor, 2014).

But age affects these findings. Older school-age children and adolescents of both sexes display more irresponsible, acting-out behavior than their peers not in stepfamilies (Hetherington

A girl in a newly formed mother–stepfather family quarrels with her mother. Stepfathers can disrupt the close ties many girls have established with their mothers.

& Stanley-Hagan, 2000; Robertson, 2008). If parents are warmer and more involved with their biological children than with their stepchildren, older children are more likely to notice and challenge unfair treatment. And adolescents often view the new stepparent as a threat to their freedom, especially if they experienced little parental monitoring in the single-parent family. But when teenagers have affectionate, cooperative relationships with their mothers, many develop good relationships with their stepfathers—a circumstance linked to more favorable adolescent well-being (Jensen et al., 2017; Jensen & Lippold, 2018; King, 2009).

Father–Stepmother Families   Remarriage of noncustodial fathers often leads to reduced contact with their biological children, especially when fathers remarry quickly, before they have established postdivorce parent–child routines (Juby et al., 2007). When fathers have custody, children typically react negatively to remarriage. One reason is that children living with fathers often start out with more problems. Perhaps the biological mother could no longer handle the difficult child (usually a boy), so the father and his new partner are faced with a youngster who has behavior problems. In other instances, the father has custody because of a very close relationship with the child, and his remarriage disrupts this bond (Buchanan, Maccoby, & Dornbusch, 1996).

Girls, especially, have a hard time getting along with their stepmothers, either because the remarriage threatens the girl's bond with her father or because she becomes entangled in loyalty conflicts between the two mother figures. But the longer girls live in father–stepmother households, the closer they feel to their stepmothers and the more positive their interaction with them becomes (King, 2007). With time and patience, children of both genders benefit from the support of a second mother figure.

Support for Blended Families   Parenting education and couples counseling can help parents and children adapt to the complexities of blended families. Effective approaches encourage stepparents to move into their new roles gradually by first building a warm, friendly relationship with the child, which enhances feelings of closeness and support and makes more active parenting possible (Ganong et al., 2019; Pryor, 2014). Counselors can offer couples guidance in coparenting to limit loyalty conflicts and provide consistency in child rearing. And tempering parents' unrealistic expectations for children's rapid adjustment—by pointing out that building a unified blended family often takes years—makes it easier for families to endure the transition and succeed.

Unfortunately, the divorce rate for second marriages is even higher than for first marriages. Parents with antisocial tendencies and poor child-rearing skills are particularly likely to have several divorces and remarriages. The more marital transitions children experience, the greater their adjustment difficulties (Amato, 2010). These families usually require prolonged, intensive therapy.

13.6.8 Maternal Employment and Dual-Earner Families

Today, U.S. single and married mothers are in the labor market in nearly equal proportions, and more than three-fourths of those with school-age children are employed (U.S. Bureau of Labor Statistics, 2019). In Chapter 7, we saw that the impact of maternal employment on early development depends on the quality of child care and the continuing parent–child relationship. The same is true in middle childhood.

Maternal Employment and Child Development   When mothers enjoy their work and remain committed to parenting, children develop favorably, displaying higher self-esteem, more positive family and peer relations, less gender-stereotyped beliefs, and better grades in school. Girls, especially, profit from the image of female competence. Regardless of SES, daughters of employed mothers perceive women's roles as involving more freedom of choice and satisfaction and are more achievement- and career-oriented (Hoffman, 2000). Furthermore, stable maternal employment begun in early childhood is linked to higher achievement and fewer behavior problems in elementary school, especially for children of low-income mothers (Lombardi & Coley, 2013, 2014; Lucas-Thompson, Goldberg, & Prause, 2010; Pilkauskas, Brooks-Gunn, & Waldfogel, 2018). Parenting practices and improved financial well-being likely contribute to these benefits. Employed mothers who feel economically more secure are more likely to engage in warmer, more involved parenting.

A small but increasing number of U.S. fathers stay home full-time to care for their children.

In dual-earner households, maternal employment often leads fathers—especially those who believe in the importance of the paternal role and who feel successful at parenting—to take on greater child-rearing responsibilities. A small but increasing number of U.S. fathers (about 2 percent) stay home full-time to care for their children (Pew Research Center, 2018c). Paternal involvement is associated in childhood and adolescence with higher achievement, more mature social behavior, and a flexible view of gender roles; and in adulthood with generally better mental health (Bornstein, 2015; Lamb & Lewis, 2013).

But when employment places heavy demands on parents' schedules or is stressful for other reasons, children are at risk for ineffective parenting. Working many hours, working a nonstandard schedule (such as night or weekend shifts), or experiencing a negative workplace atmosphere is associated with lower quality parenting, fewer joint parent–child activities, poorer cognitive development, and increased behavior problems throughout childhood and adolescence (Johnson et al., 2013; Li et al., 2014; Strazdins et al., 2006, 2013).

Negative consequences are magnified when low-SES mothers spend long days at low-paying, physically exhausting jobs—conditions linked to maternal depression and to harsh, inconsistent discipline (Raver, 2003). In contrast, part-time employment and flexible work schedules are associated with good child adjustment (Buehler & O'Brien, 2011; Youn, Leon, & Lee, 2012). By preventing role overload, these arrangements help parents meet children's needs.

Child Care for School-Age Children   High-quality child care is vital for parents' peace of mind and children's well-being, even during middle childhood. An estimated 7 million 5- to 13-year-olds in the United States are **self-care children,** who regularly look after themselves for some period of time during after-school hours (Child Trends, 2016a). Self-care increases with age and also with SES, perhaps because of the greater safety of higher-income neighborhoods. But when lower-SES parents lack alternatives to self-care, their children spend more hours on their own (Casper & Smith, 2002).

Younger school-age children who spend more hours alone have more adjustment difficulties (Vandell & Posner, 1999). As children become old enough to look after themselves, those who have a history of authoritative child rearing, are monitored by parental phone calls, and have regular after-school chores appear responsible and well-adjusted. In contrast, children left to their own devices are more likely to bend to peer pressures and engage in antisocial behavior (Coley, Morris, & Hernandez, 2004; Vandell et al., 2006).

Before age 8 or 9, most children need supervision because they are not yet competent to handle emergencies. But throughout middle childhood and early adolescence, attending after-school programs with well-trained and supportive staffs, generous

High-quality after-school programs with enrichment activities yield academic and social benefits, especially for low-SES children.

LOOK and LISTEN

In your community, what after-school programs are available, and how plentiful are they in low-income neighborhoods? If possible, visit a program, observing for supportive adult involvement, academic assistance, and enrichment activities.

adult–child ratios, and skill-building activities is linked to better school performance and emotional and social adjustment than unstructured arrangements such as self-care or supervision by a neighbor (Durlak, Weissberg, & Pachan, 2010; Kantaoka & Vandell, 2013). Low-SES children who participate in after-school programs offering academic assistance and enrichment activities (scouting, music and art lessons, clubs) show special benefits. They exceed their self-care counterparts in classroom work habits, academic achievement, and prosocial behavior and display fewer behavior problems (Lauer et al., 2006; Vandell et al., 2006).

Yet after-school programs are in shorter supply and weaker in quality in economically disadvantaged neighborhoods. Programs with inexperienced staff and few constructive activities are not associated with the favorable outcomes just mentioned (Greenberg, 2013; Park & Zhan, 2017). A special need exists for well-planned programs in poverty-stricken areas—ones that provide safe environments, warm relationships with adults, and enjoyable, goal-oriented activities.

ASK YOURSELF

Connect ■ How does each level in Bronfenbrenner's ecological systems theory—microsystem, mesosystem, exosystem, and macrosystem—contribute to effects of parents' employment on children's development?

Apply ■ Steve and Marissa are in the midst of an acrimonious divorce. Their 9-year-old son Dennis has become hostile and defiant. How can Steve and Marissa help Dennis adjust?

Reflect ■ What after-school child-care arrangements did you experience in elementary school? How do you think they influenced your development?

13.7 Some Common Problems of Development

13.7a Cite common fears and anxieties in middle childhood, and discuss their impact on children's adjustment.

13.7b Discuss factors related to child sexual abuse, its consequences for children's development, and its prevention and treatment.

13.7c Cite factors that foster resilience in middle childhood.

We have considered a variety of stressful experiences that place children at risk for future problems. Next, we address two more areas of concern: school-age children's fears and anxieties and the consequences of child sexual abuse. Finally, we sum up factors that help school-age children cope effectively with stress.

13.7.1 Fears and Anxieties

Although fears of the dark, thunder and lightning, and supernatural beings persist into middle childhood, older children's anxieties are also directed toward new concerns. As children begin to understand the realities of the wider world, the possibility of personal harm (being robbed, stabbed, or shot) and media events (war and disasters) often trouble them. Other common worries include academic failure, physical injuries, separation from parents, parents' health, the possibility of dying, and peer rejection (Muris & Field, 2011; Weems & Costa, 2005).

As long as fears are not too intense, most children handle them constructively, using the more sophisticated emotional self-regulation strategies that develop in middle childhood. Consequently, the overall number of fears declines with age, especially for girls, who express more fears than boys throughout childhood and adolescence (Gullone, 2000; Muris & Field, 2011). But about 5 percent of school-age children develop an intense, unmanageable fear called a **phobia.** Although an inhibited temperament increases the risk, children with weak behavioral control and even those who are well-adjusted also acquire phobias (Capriola, Booker, & Ollendick, 2017; Ollendick, King, & Muris, 2002).

Some children with phobias and other anxieties develop *school refusal*—severe apprehension about attending school, often accompanied by physical complaints such as dizziness, nausea, stomachaches, and vomiting (Wimmer, 2013). About one-third of children with school refusal are 5- to 7-year-olds for whom the real fear is maternal separation (Elliott, 1999). Family therapy helps these children, whose difficulty can often be traced to parental overprotection.

Most cases of school refusal appear around age 11 to 13, in children who usually find a particular aspect of school frightening—an overcritical teacher, a school bully, or too much parental pressure to achieve. A change in school environment or parenting practices may be needed. Firm insistence that the child return to school, along with training in how to cope with difficult situations, is also helpful (Kearney, Spear, & Mihalas, 2014).

Severe childhood anxieties may also arise from harsh living conditions. In poverty-stricken, crime-ridden urban neighborhoods and in war-torn areas of the world, many children live in the midst of constant danger, chaos, and deprivation. As the Cultural Influences box on page 514 reveals, they are at risk for long-term emotional distress and behavior problems. Finally, as we saw in our discussion of child abuse in Chapter 10, too often violence and other destructive acts become part of adult–child relationships. During middle childhood, child sexual abuse increases.

13.7.2 Child Sexual Abuse

Until recently, child sexual abuse was considered rare, and adults often dismissed children's claims of abuse. In the 1970s, efforts by professionals and media attention led to recognition of child sexual abuse as a serious and widespread problem. About 57,000 cases in the United States were confirmed in the most recently reported year (U.S. Department of Health and Human Services, 2018a). But this figure greatly underestimates the extent of sexual abuse because most victims either delay disclosure for a long time, tell someone (such as a family member or friend) who takes no further measures, or remain silent (Martin & Silverstone, 2013; Stiller & Hellmann, 2017).

Some children develop school refusal—severe apprehension about attending school. For many younger children, the real fear is maternal separation, often due to parental overprotection.

Characteristics of Abusers and Victims   Globally, an estimated 18 percent of girls and 8 percent of boys are sexually abused during childhood or adolescence (Stoltenborgh et al., 2015). Most cases are reported in middle childhood, but for some victims, abuse begins early in life and continues for many years (Collin-Vézina, Daigneault, & Hébert, 2013).

In the vast majority of cases, the abuser is a male, often a parent or someone the parent knows well—a father, stepfather, live-in boyfriend, uncle, or older brother (Olafson, 2011). If the abuser is a nonrelative, the person is usually someone the child has come to know and trust, such as a teacher, caregiver, clergy member, or family friend (Sullivan et al., 2011). The Internet and smartphones have become avenues through which some perpetrators commit sexual abuse—for example, by exposing children and adolescents to pornography and online sexual advances as a way of "grooming" them for sexual acts offline (Kloess, Beech, & Harkins, 2014). Sadly, a substantial number of abusers are themselves children or adolescents, many of whom are also victims of sexual abuse or other forms of maltreatment (Vizard, 2013).

Abusers make the child comply in a variety of distasteful ways, including deception, bribery, verbal intimidation, and physical force. You may wonder how any adult—especially a parent or close relative—could violate a child sexually. Many offenders deny their own responsibility, blaming the abuse on the willing participation of a seductive youngster. Yet children are not capable of making a deliberate, informed decision to enter into a sexual relationship! Even older children and adolescents are not free to say yes or no. Rather, the responsibility lies with abusers, who tend to have characteristics that predispose them toward sexual exploitation of children. They have great difficulty controlling their impulses and may suffer from psychological disorders, including alcohol and drug abuse. Often, they pick out children who are unlikely to defend themselves or to be believed—those who are physically weak, emotionally deprived, socially isolated, or affected by disabilities (Assink et al., 2019).

Cultural Influences | Impact of Ethnic and Political Violence on Children

Around the world, many children are exposed to armed conflict, terrorism, and other acts of violence stemming from ethnic and political tensions. Some children participate in fighting, either because they are forced or because they want to please adults. Others are kidnapped, assaulted, and tortured. Child bystanders often come under direct fire and may be killed or physically maimed. And many watch in horror as family members, friends, and neighbors are wounded or die. An estimated 250 million children live in conflict-ridden, poor countries. During the past twelve years, wars and civil conflicts have left 31 million homeless and displaced as refugees or voluntary migrants, 6 million physically disabled, and more than 1 million separated from their parents, many for extended time periods or permanently (Masten et al., 2015; UNICEF, 2019).

When war and social crises are temporary, most children can be comforted and do not show long-term emotional difficulties. But chronic danger requires children to make substantial adjustments that can seriously impair their psychological functioning. The greater their exposure to life-threatening experiences, the more likely they are to display symptoms of posttraumatic stress disorder (PTSD)—extreme fear and anxiety, terrifying intrusive memories, depression, irritability, difficulty concentrating, and a pessimistic view of the future. Additional internalizing and externalizing difficulties may emerge, including negative mood, depression, and aggression, especially during times of heightened exposure to violence and atrocities (Eisenberg & Silver, 2011; Khamis, 2019; Miller-Graff & Cummings, 2017) These outcomes seem to be culturally universal, appearing in children in every war zone studied—from Bosnia, Rwanda, and South Sudan to the West Bank, Gaza, Iraq, Afghanistan, Yemen, and Syria.

Parental affection and reassurance are the best protection against lasting problems. When parents offer security, discuss traumatic experiences with children sympathetically, and serve as role models of calm emotional strength, most children can withstand even extreme war-related stressors (Richter, Lye, & Proulx, 2018). Parenting interventions that foster positive child-rearing practices enhance children's well-being (Murphy et al., 2017). But programs must also address parents' wartime stressors, fostering their resilience so they can parent more effectively.

Children separated from their parents are at greatest risk for long-term maladjustment. Without relatives to step in with loving care and guidance, these children must rely on help from the surrounding community. Yet most refugee camps and institutions housing displaced children offer little emotional support (Wessells, 2017).

In recent years, many families fleeing Central American countries riddled with poverty and violence who crossed from Mexico into the United States illegally saw U.S. immigration officials arrest parents along with other adult relatives, take away children, and place them in institutional care. Also, large numbers of older children and adolescents who crossed the U.S. border on their own (often in hopes of reuniting with family members) have been deported, unaccompanied on their return journey by any adult responsible for their care and safety (Sotomayor-Peterson & Montiel-Carabajal, 2014). As their border-crossing attempts and days in shelters increase, these youths report rising loneliness, anxiety, depression, and risky behaviors.

Numerous child welfare and mental health organizations have publicly denounced these U.S. separation and deportation practices. They point to a wealth of evidence confirming that the emotional effects—especially for children and adolescents already suffering from adversity—can last a lifetime (Bouza et al., 2018; Daniel, 2018; MacKenzie, Bosk, & Zeanah, 2017).

Families seeking asylum in the United States line up to be processed by U.S. immigration officials. Many migrant children fleeing poverty and violence in Central American countries have faced separation from their parents and other adult relatives at the southern U.S. border. They are at risk for emotional effects that can last a lifetime.

In addition to keeping families together and supporting positive parenting, education and recreation programs are powerful safeguards of mental health, providing children with consistency in their lives along with teacher and peer supports. Evaluations of school-based interventions in war-torn regions that offer children and adolescents opportunities to express emotions through writing, drawing, and discussion along with relationship-building experiences are highly effective in lessening PTSD symptoms (Peltonen & Punamaki, 2010; Qouta et al., 2012).

When wartime drains families and communities of resources, international organizations must step in and help children. The Children and War Foundation, *www.childrenandwar.org,* offers programs and manuals that train local personnel in how to promote children's adaptive coping. Efforts to preserve children's physical, psychological, and educational well-being may be the best way to stop the transmission of violence to the next generation.

Reported cases of child sexual abuse are linked to poverty, marital instability, resulting weakening of family ties, and other forms of child abuse. Children who live in homes with a constantly changing cast of characters—repeated marriages, separations, and new partners—are especially vulnerable (Murray, Nguyen, & Cohen, 2014). But children in economically advantaged, stable homes are also victims, although their abuse is more likely to escape detection.

Consequences of Sexual Abuse   The adjustment problems of child sexual abuse victims—including anxiety, depression, low self-esteem, mistrust of adults, and anger and hostility—are often severe and can persist for years after the abusive episodes. Younger children frequently react with sleep difficulties, loss of appetite, and generalized fearfulness. Adolescents may run away and show suicidal tendencies, substance abuse, and delinquency. Longitudinal research suggests that rates of obesity and other physical and mental health problems are elevated among survivors of child sexual abuse. At all ages, persistent abuse accompanied by force, violence, or a close relationship to the perpetrator (incest) is especially likely to result in posttraumatic stress disorder (PTSD) and to have lasting effects on mental health. And repeated sexual abuse, like physical abuse, is associated with central nervous system damage (Teicher et al., 2016; van Duin et al., 2018).

Sexually abused children frequently display precocious sexual knowledge and behavior. In adolescence, abused young people often become promiscuous, increasing the risk of teenage pregnancy. As adults, they show elevated arrest rates for sex crimes (mostly against children) and prostitution. Furthermore, women who were sexually abused are likely to choose partners who abuse them and their children. As mothers, they often engage in irresponsible and coercive parenting, including child abuse and neglect (Collin-Vézina, Daigneault, & Hébert, 2013; Krahé & Berger, 2017; Trickett, Noll, & Putnam, 2011). In these ways, the harmful impact of sexual abuse is transmitted to the next generation.

Miami schoolchildren participate in a candlelight vigil sponsored by Amigos for Kids, a nonprofit organization dedicated to preventing child abuse and neglect. Adjustment problems resulting from child abuse, including sexual abuse, are often severe and persistent.

Prevention and Treatment   Treating child sexual abuse is difficult. The reactions of family members—anxiety about harm to the child, anger toward the abuser, and sometimes hostility toward the victim for telling—can increase children's distress. Because sexual abuse typically appears in the midst of other serious family problems, specialized trauma-focused therapy with both children and parents is usually needed (Saunders, 2012). The best way to reduce the suffering of victims is to prevent sexual abuse from continuing. Today, courts are prosecuting abusers more vigorously and taking children's testimony more seriously (see the Social Issues: Health box on page 516).

Education programs that teach school-age children and adolescents to recognize inappropriate sexual advances, use self-protective strategies to repel these approaches, and identify appropriate sources of help reduce the risk of abuse (Morris et al., 2017; Walsh et al., 2018). Yet because of controversies over educating children about sexual abuse, many schools do not offer these interventions. New Zealand is the only country with a national, school-based prevention program targeting sexual abuse available to all elementary and secondary students. In Keeping Ourselves Safe, children and adolescents learn that abusers are rarely strangers. Parent involvement ensures that home and school collaborate in teaching essential knowledge and skills. At the same time, parents learn the importance of creating safe environments and helping their children feel self-confident and secure so they are less likely to be targets of abusers. Evaluations reveal that virtually all New Zealand parents and children support the program and that it has helped many children avoid or report abuse (Sanders, 2006).

13.7.3 Fostering Resilience in Middle Childhood

Throughout middle childhood—and other periods of development—children are confronted with challenging and sometimes threatening situations that require them to cope with psychological stress. In this trio of chapters, we have considered such topics as chronic illness, learning disabilities, achievement expectations, divorce, conflict-ridden living conditions, and sexual abuse. Each taxes children's coping resources, creating serious risks for development.

Social Issues: Health | Children's Eyewitness Testimony

Increasingly, children are being called on to testify in court cases involving child abuse and neglect, child custody, and similar matters. The experience can be difficult and traumatic, requiring children to report on highly stressful events and sometimes to speak against a parent or other relative to whom they feel loyal. In some family disputes, they may fear punishment for telling the truth. In addition, child witnesses face an unfamiliar situation—at the very least an interview in the judge's chambers and at most an open courtroom with judge, jury, spectators, and the possibility of unsympathetic cross-examination. Not surprisingly, these conditions can compromise the accuracy of children's recall.

Age Differences

Previously, children younger than age 5 were rarely asked to testify, and not until age 10 were they assumed fully competent to do so. As a result of societal reactions to rising rates of child abuse and the difficulty of prosecuting perpetrators, legal requirements for child testimony have been relaxed in the United States (Klemfuss & Ceci, 2012). Children as young as age 3 frequently serve as witnesses.

Compared with preschoolers, school-age children provide more detailed narrative accounts of past experiences and are better at accurately inferring others' motives and intentions. Older children are also generally more resistant to misleading questions that attorneys may ask when probing for more information or trying to influence the child's response (Hobbs & Goodman, 2014). Inhibition (ability to suppress impulses and ignore irrelevant information), which improves from early to middle childhood, predicts children's resistance to suggestion (Melinder, Endestad, & Magnussen, 2006).

Nevertheless, when properly questioned, even 3-year-olds can recall recent events accurately (Peterson & Rideout, 1998). And in the face of biased interviewing, adolescents and adults often form elaborate, false memories of events (Ceci et al., 2007).

Suggestibility

Court testimony often involves repeated questioning—a procedure that, by itself, negatively affects children's response consistency and accuracy (Krähenbühl, Blades, & Eiser, 2009). When adults lead witnesses by suggesting incorrect "facts," interrupt their denials, reinforce them for giving desired answers, ask complex and confusing questions, or use a confrontational style, they further increase the likelihood of incorrect reporting by children and adolescents alike (Zajac, O'Neill, & Hayne, 2012).

In one study, 4- to 8-year-olds were asked to recall details about a visitor who had come to their classroom a week earlier. Half the children received a low-pressure interview containing leading questions that implied abuse ("He took your clothes off, didn't he?"). The other half received a high-pressure interview in which an adult told the child that her friends had said "yes" to the leading questions, praised the child for agreeing ("You're doing great"), and, if the child did not agree, repeated the question. Children were far more likely to give false information—even fabricating quite fantastic events—in the high-pressure condition (Finnilä et al., 2003).

By the time children appear in court, weeks, months, or even years have passed since the target events. When a long delay is combined with biased interviewing and with stereotyping of the accused ("He's in jail because he's been bad"), children can easily be misled into giving false information (Quas et al., 2007). The more distinctive, emotional, and personally relevant an event is, the more likely children are to recall it accurately over time. For example, a year later, even when exposed to misleading information, children correctly reported details of an injury that required emergency room treatment (Peterson, Parsons, & Dean, 2004). Children's memories of these experiences remain remarkably intact for as long as five years (Peterson, 2012).

In some sexual abuse cases, anatomically correct dolls or body diagrams are used to prompt children's recall. Although these methods help older children provide more detail, they increase the suggestibility of preschoolers, who may report physical and sexual contact that never happened (Poole & Bruck, 2012). Props may be confusing to very young witnesses because they require dual representation of the doll or drawing as both an object and a symbol—understandings that are still emerging during the preschool years (see page 310 in Chapter 9).

Interventions

Adults must prepare child witnesses so they understand the courtroom process and know what to expect. In some places, "court schools" take children through the setting and give them an opportunity to role-play court activities. Practice interviews—in which children learn to provide the most accurate, detailed information possible and to admit not knowing rather than agreeing or guessing—are helpful for both enhancing children's memory and reducing the stress of testifying (Irvine, Jack, & Zajac, 2016; Nathanson & Saywitz, 2015).

At the same time, legal professionals must use interviewing procedures that increase children's accurate reporting. Unbiased, open-ended questions that prompt children to disclose details—"Tell me what happened" or "You said there was a man; tell me about the man"—reduce suggestibility (Goodman et al., 2014; Steele, 2012). Also, a warm, supportive interview tone fosters accurate recall, perhaps by easing children's anxiety so they feel freer to disagree with an interviewer's false suggestions (Ceci, Bruck, & Battin, 2000).

If children are likely to experience emotional trauma or later punishment (as in a family dispute) for answering questions, courtroom procedures are sometimes adapted to protect them. For example, children can testify over closed-circuit TV so they do not have to face an abuser. When it would be harmful for a child to participate directly, impartial expert witnesses can provide testimony that reports on the child's psychological condition and includes important elements of the child's story.

© BURGER/PHANIE/THE IMAGE WORKS

School-age eyewitnesses are better able than preschoolers to give accurate, detailed descriptions and correctly infer others' motives and intentions. This juvenile court judge can promote accurate recall by using a warm, supportive tone and avoiding leading questions.

APPLYING WHAT WE KNOW

Resources That Foster Resilience in Middle Childhood

TYPE OF RESOURCE	DESCRIPTION
Personal	• Easygoing, sociable temperament • Above-average intelligence • Favorable self-esteem • Persistence in the face of challenge, pleasure in mastery, and a growth mindset about ability • Good emotional self-regulation and flexible coping strategies
Family	• Warm, trusting relationship with at least one parent • Authoritative child-rearing style • Positive discipline, avoidance of coercive tactics • Warm, supportive sibling relationships
School	• Teachers who are warm, helpful, and stimulating; who encourage students to collaborate; and who emphasize effort and self-improvement • Lessons in tolerance and respect and codes against bullying, which promote positive peer relationships and gratifying friendships • Extracurricular activities, including sports and social service pursuits, that strengthen physical, cognitive, and social skills
Community	• High-quality after-school programs that protect children's safety and offer stimulating, skill-building activities • An adult—such as an extended-family member, teacher, or neighbor—who provides warmth and social support and is a positive coping model • Stability of neighborhood residents and services—safe outdoor play areas, community centers, and religious organizations—that relieve parental stress and encourage families and neighbors to share leisure time • Youth groups—scouting, clubs, religious youth groups, and other organized activities—that promote positive peer relationships and prosocial behavior

Note: One or a few resources may be sufficient to foster resilience, since each resource strengthens others.

Nevertheless, only a modest relationship exists between stressful life experiences and psychological disturbance in childhood (Masten, 2014). In our earlier discussions of poverty, troubled family lives, and birth complications, we noted that some children manage to surmount the negative impact of these circumstances. The same is true for school difficulties, family transitions, and child maltreatment. Refer to Applying What We Know above for an overview of factors that promote *resilience*—the capacity to overcome adversity—during middle childhood.

Often just one or a few of these ingredients account for why one child is "stress-resilient" and another is not. Usually, however, personal and environmental factors are interconnected: Each resource favoring resilience strengthens others in a *developmental cascade* (Masten & Cicchetti, 2010). For example, safe, stable neighborhoods with family-friendly community services reduce parents' daily hassles and stress, thereby promoting good parenting (Chen, Howard, & Brooks-Gunn, 2011). In contrast, unfavorable home, school, and neighborhood experiences can also cascade, increasing the chances that children will act in ways that expose them to further hardship. When negative conditions pile up, such as crowded living conditions, neighborhood disorganization, marital discord, and parental insensitivity and abuse, the rate of maladjustment multiplies (Ettekal et al., 2019).

Of great concern are children and adolescents' violent acts. Some forms, such as bullying, gang antisocial conduct, taunting, and other incivilities, have become pervasive in schools

Ten- and eleven-year-olds in a school-based social and emotional learning program take part in a trust exercise. Gains in social competence and supportive relationships are among beneficial outcomes of social and emotional learning that foster resilience.

and communities. Victims of even low-level aggression that persists over time react with elevated anxiety, depressive symptoms, hostility, reduced engagement in school activities, and declines in academic performance (Meyer & Jimerson, 2019).

Several highly effective school-based *social and emotional learning programs* reduce violence (including bullying and gang involvement) and increase academic motivation by fostering social competence and supportive relationships (CASEL, 2013; Sauve & Schonert-Reichl, 2019). Among these is the 4Rs (Reading, Writing, Respect, and Resolution) Program, which provides elementary school students with weekly lessons in emotional and social understanding and skills (Aber et al., 2011). Topics include managing anger, responding with empathy, being assertive, resolving social conflicts, cooperating, appreciating diversity, and identifying and standing up against prejudice and bullying. The program is integrated with language arts: High-quality children's literature, selected for relevance to program themes, complements each lesson. Discussion, writing, and role-playing of the stories deepen students' understanding of conflict, emotions, relationships, and community.

To evaluate the effectiveness of 4Rs, researchers randomly assigned 18 elementary schools in New York City to the program or a control condition. Teachers in 4Rs schools used more supportive instructional techniques—encouraging discussion, making concepts relevant to students' everyday lives, and providing feedback that acknowledges effort. And compared to children in control schools, children who received 4Rs instruction became less depressed and less likely to misinterpret others' acts as hostile. After a second year of intervention, the benefits spread to other related outcomes: Teachers rated 4Rs children as less aggressive, more attentive, and more socially competent compared to children in control schools (Aber et al., 2011). In unsafe neighborhoods, 4Rs transforms schools into places of safety and mutual respect, where learning can occur.

Programs like 4Rs recognize that *resilience* is not a preexisting attribute but rather a capacity that develops, enabling children to use internal and external resources to cope with adversity. Throughout our discussion, we have seen how families, schools, communities, and society as a whole can enhance or undermine the school-age child's developing sense of competence (Masten, 2018; Yule, Houston, & Grych, 2019). Young people whose childhood experiences helped them learn to control impulses, overcome obstacles, strive for self-direction, and respond considerately and sympathetically to others meet the challenges of the next period—adolescence—quite well.

ASK YOURSELF

Connect ■ Explain how factors that promote resilience contribute to children's favorable adjustment following divorce.

Apply ■ Claire told her 6-year-old daughter never to talk to or take candy from strangers. Why is Claire's warning unlikely to protect her daughter from sexual abuse? What preventive actions can Claire take?

Reflect ■ Describe a challenging time during your childhood. What aspects of the experience increased stress? What resources helped you cope with adversity?

SUMMARY

13.1 Self-Understanding (p. 477)

13.1 Describe school-age children's self-concept and self-esteem, and discuss factors that affect their achievement-related attributions.

■ As school-age children gain in perspective-taking skills, their self-concepts increasingly include personality traits, competencies, and **social comparisons.** Self-esteem differentiates further and becomes hierarchically organized and more realistic.

■ Gender stereotypes contribute to sex differences in physical, academic, and social self-esteem. Warm extended families and strong ethnic pride may contribute to the slight self-esteem advantage of African-American over European-American children. Among urban Mexican-American children, global self-esteem (rather than perceived physical appearance) correlates most strongly with academic self-esteem.

■ Authoritative child-rearing is associated with favorable self-esteem, and secure attachment is linked to **self-compassion.** Inflated praise reduces self-esteem rather than raising it.

■ Children with **mastery-oriented attributions** and a **growth mindset about ability** believe ability can be improved through effort and effective strategies. In contrast, children with **learned helplessness** have a **fixed mindset about ability** and attribute success to external factors, such as luck, and failure to low ability, which cannot be modified.

■ **Process praise,** which emphasizes behavior and effort, fosters a growth mindset and mastery orientation, whereas **person praise,** which focuses on the child's traits, is linked to a fixed mindset and learned helplessness. The way parents respond to children's failures—with a failure-is-enhancing mindset or a failure-is-debilitating mindset—is similarly influential.

■ **Attribution retraining** encourages learned-helpless children to believe they can overcome failure by exerting more effort and using effective strategies.

13.2 Emotional Development (p. 485)

13.2 Cite changes in self-conscious emotions, emotional understanding, and emotional self-regulation in middle childhood.

■ Self-conscious emotions of pride and guilt become clearly governed by personal responsibility. Intense shame is particularly destructive, yielding declines in motivation and performance along with withdrawal and depression or intense anger.

■ School-age children develop an appreciation of mixed emotions and recognize that emotional expressions may not reflect people's true feelings. They also reconcile contradictory cues in interpreting another's feelings. Empathy increases and includes sensitivity to people's immediate distress and their general life condition.

■ By age 10, most children can shift adaptively between **problem-centered** and **emotion-centered coping** in regulating emotion. Emotionally well-regulated children develop a sense of emotional self-efficacy and are optimistic, empathic, and prosocial.

© LAURA HARTLEY/ALAMY STOCK PHOTO

13.3 Moral Development (p. 487)

13.3 Describe changes in moral understanding during middle childhood, including children's understanding of diversity and inequality.

■ During middle childhood, children construct a flexible appreciation of moral rules based on intentions and context. Their capacity for recursive thought supports an increasingly sophisticated understanding of the morality of deception and truthfulness. They also clarify and link moral imperatives and social conventions and better understand personal choice and individual rights. Children in diverse cultures use similar criteria to reason about moral, social-conventional, and personal concerns.

■ School-age children absorb prevailing societal attitudes about race, ethnicity, and SES. With age, they pay more attention to inner traits and realize that prejudice violates widely held social standards. Consequently, explicit prejudice typically declines, although prejudice often continues to operate implicitly. Children most likely to hold racial and ethnic biases believe that personality traits are fixed, have overly high self-esteem, and live in a social world that highlights group differences. Long-term, intergroup contact and collaboration may be the best way to reduce prejudice.

13.4 Peer Relations (p. 492)

13.4a Describe changes in peer sociability and friendship in middle childhood.

■ Peer interaction becomes more prosocial, and physical aggression declines. By the end of middle childhood, children strongly desire group belonging and organize into **peer groups.**

■ Friendships develop into mutual relationships based on trust and become more selective. Children tend to choose friends who resemble themselves in age, sex, race, ethnicity, SES, personality, popularity, academic achievement, and prosocial behavior. Girls form closer, more exclusive friendships than boys.

13.4b Describe categories of peer acceptance and ways to help rejected children.

■ Measures of **peer acceptance**—a powerful predictor of psychological adjustment—yield five general categories: **popular children, rejected children, controversial children, neglected children,** and average children.

■ **Popular-prosocial children** are academically and socially competent and more likely than others to be viewed as leaders, while **popular-antisocial children** are aggressive but admired, perhaps for their athletic ability and sophisticated but devious social skills. **Rejected-aggressive children** are especially high in conflict and hostility, and **rejected-withdrawn children** are passive, socially awkward, and frequent targets of **peer victimization.**

■ Coaching in social skills and academic tutoring, and training in perspective taking and social problem solving can help rejected children gain in social competence and peer acceptance. Intervening to improve parent–child interaction is often necessary for lasting change.

13.5 Gender Typing (p. 498)

13.5 Discuss changes in gender-stereotyped beliefs and gender identity during middle childhood.

■ School-age children extend their awareness of gender stereotypes to personality traits and academic subjects, but gender-stereotyped beliefs about achievement in math and science seem to be changing. In addition, **gender-stereotype flexibility** increases during middle childhood. Nevertheless, many children take a harsh view of certain gender-role violations, and sex-segregated peer associations strengthen

■ Boys strengthen their identification with the "masculine" role, whereas girls feel free to experiment with "other-gender" activities. Gender identity includes self-evaluations of gender typicality, contentedness, and felt pressure to conform to gender roles—each of which affects adjustment.

13.6 Family Influences (p. 501)

13.6a *Discuss changes in parent–child communication and sibling relationships in middle childhood.*

■ Despite declines in time spent with parents, **coregulation** allows parents to exercise general oversight of children, who increasingly make their own decisions.

■ Although siblings continue to be sources of mutual support, sibling rivalry tends to increase with greater participation in diverse activities and more frequent parental comparisons. Compared to children with siblings, only children are higher in self-esteem, school performance, and educational attainment.

13.6b *Explain how children fare in lesbian and gay families and in never-married, single-parent families.*

■ Lesbian and gay parents are as committed to and effective at child rearing as heterosexual parents, and their children usually do not differ from the children of heterosexual parents in adjustment and, in some studies, are better adjusted.

■ Never-married parenthood generally increases financial hardship, and children of never-married mothers who lack a father's consistent involvement show less favorable cognitive development and greater antisocial behavior. Parental involvement of African-American fathers, both residential and nonresidential, equals or exceeds that of fathers of other ethnicities.

13.6c *Cite factors that influence children's adjustment to divorce and blended family arrangements.*

■ Although marital breakup is stressful for children, how well they fare depends on parental psychological health, the child's characteristics (age, temperament, and sex), and social supports. Divorce is linked to early sexual activity, adolescent parenthood, and long-term relationship difficulties.

■ The overriding factor in positive adjustment following divorce is effective parenting and both parents continued involvement. **Divorce mediation** and parent education programs can foster parental conflict resolution in the period surrounding divorce. The success of joint custody depends on effective coparenting.

■ In **blended, or reconstituted, families,** girls, older children, and children in father–stepmother families tend to have more adjustment problems. Stepparents can help children adjust by moving into their roles gradually.

13.6d *Discuss how maternal employment and life in dual-earner families affect school-age children.*

■ When employed mothers enjoy their work and remain committed to parenting, their children benefit from higher self-esteem, more positive family and peer relations, less gender-stereotyped beliefs, and better school grades. In dual-earner families, the father's willingness to take on greater child-rearing responsibilities is associated with diverse, positive child outcomes.

■ Authoritative child rearing, parental monitoring, and regular after-school chores lead **self-care children** to be responsible and well-adjusted. Good after-school programs also aid school performance and emotional and social adjustment, especially for low-SES children.

13.7 Some Common Problems of Development (p. 512)

13.7a *Cite common fears and anxieties in middle childhood, and discuss their impact on children's adjustment.*

■ School-age children's fears include personal harm, media events, academic failure, parents' health, and peer rejection. Even well-adjusted children can develop **phobias,** although children with inhibited temperaments are at higher risk. Harsh, dangerous, chaotic, and deprived living conditions like those encountered in war zones or recently by migrant children at the southern U.S. border fleeing poverty and violence in their home countries, can result in long-term emotional stress and behavior problems.

13.7b *Discuss factors related to child sexual abuse, its consequences for children's development, and its prevention and treatment.*

■ Child sexual abuse is generally committed by male family members, more often against girls than against boys. Abusers have characteristics that predispose them toward sexual exploitation of children. Reported cases are associated with poverty and marital instability.

■ Abused children often have severe, persisting adjustment problems. Treatment typically requires specialized trauma-focused therapy with both children and parents. Educational programs that teach children to recognize inappropriate sexual advances and identify sources of help reduce the risk of sexual abuse.

13.7c *Cite factors that foster resilience in middle childhood.*

■ Only a modest relationship exists between stressful life experiences and psychological disturbance in childhood. Children's personal characteristics, a warm family life that includes authoritative parenting, and school and community resources predict resilience. Each resource favoring resilience usually strengthens others, in a developmental cascade.

IMPORTANT TERMS AND CONCEPTS

attribution retraining (p. 484)
blended, or reconstituted, family (p. 509)
controversial children (p. 494)
coregulation (p. 502)
divorce mediation (p. 508)
emotion-centered coping (p. 486)
fixed mindset about ability (p. 482)
gender-stereotype flexibility (p. 499)
growth mindset about ability (p. 482)
learned helplessness (p. 482)

mastery-oriented attributions (p. 482)
neglected children (p. 494)
peer acceptance (p. 494)
peer groups (p. 492)
peer victimization (p. 497)
person praise (p. 482)
phobia (p. 512)
popular-antisocial children (p. 495)
popular children (p. 494)
popular-prosocial children (p. 495)

problem-centered coping (p. 486)
process praise (p. 482)
rejected-aggressive children (p. 495)
rejected children (p. 494)
rejected-withdrawn children (p. 495)
self-care children (p. 511)
self-compassion (p. 481)
social comparisons (p. 478)

Development in
Middle Childhood

© ELIZABETH CREWS/THE IMAGE WORKS

Physical

- Slow gains in height and weight continue. (405)
- Permanent teeth gradually replace primary teeth. (407)
- Prints an increasing number of uppercase, then lowercase, alphabet letters. (422)
- Drawings become more organized and detailed and include some depth cues. (422)
- Games with rules and rough-and-tumble play become common. (423, 425)

Cognitive

- Thought becomes more logical, as shown by the ability to pass Piagetian conservation, class inclusion, and seriation problems. (431–432)

© LAURA DWIGHT PHOTOGRAPHY

- Improves dramatically in speed of information processing. (438)
- Executive function—including working memory, inhibition, flexible shifting of attention, and planning—improves markedly. (436–439)
- Uses memory strategies of rehearsal and then organization. (440)
- Awareness of mental activities, of the impact of psychological factors (such as applying memory strategies) on task performance, and of sources of knowledge (including mental inferences) expands. (440–441)
- Understands second-order false belief; capable of recursive thought. (442–443)
- Uses informal knowledge of number concepts and counting to master more complex mathematical skills. (446–447)

Language

- Vocabulary increases rapidly as children learn about 20 new words each day. (457)
- Word definitions are concrete, referring to functions and appearance. (458)
- Transitions from "learning to read" to "reading to learn." (446)

© IMAGE SOURCE/ALAMY STOCK PHOTO

- Metalinguistic awareness improves. (457)
- Mastery of complex grammatical structures improves. (458)
- Grasps increasingly subtle, indirect expressions of language meaning, including irony and sarcasm. (458)
- Narratives increase in organization, detail, and expressiveness. (458)

Emotional/Social

- Self-concept includes personality traits, competencies, and social comparisons. (478)
- Self-esteem differentiates, is hierarchically organized, and becomes more realistic. (479)
- Self-conscious emotions of pride and guilt are governed by personal responsibility. (485)
- Recognizes that people can experience more than one emotion at a time and that their expressions may not reflect their true feelings. (485–486)

© LAURA DWIGHT PHOTOGRAPHY

- Empathy increases. (486)
- Becomes more independent and trustworthy. (487)
- Constructs a flexible appreciation of moral rules, considering prosocial and antisocial intentions and the context of the behavior. (486)
- Resolves conflicts more effectively; sharing, helping, and other prosocial acts increase. (492)
- Physical aggression declines; verbal and relational aggression continue. (492)

Note: Numbers in parentheses indicate the page or pages on which each milestone is discussed.

Physical

- Adolescent growth spurt begins two years earlier in girls than in boys. (405)
- Executes gross motor skills of running, jumping, throwing, catching, kicking, batting, and dribbling more quickly and with better coordination. (420–421)

- Steady gains in attention and reaction time contribute to improved motor performance. (420–421)
- Ability to represent depth in drawings is clearly evident. (422)
- Dominance hierarchies become more stable, especially among boys. (426)

Cognitive

- Continues to master Piagetian tasks in a step-by-step fashion. (434)
- Spatial reasoning improves; readily draws and reads maps of large-scale spaces and grasps the notion of scale. (432–433)

- Continues to improve in speed of information processing. (438)
- Continues to improve in executive function. (436–440)
- Uses memory strategies of rehearsal and organization more effectively. (440)
- Applies several memory strategies simultaneously; begins to use elaboration. (440)
- General knowledge base (semantic memory) grows larger and becomes better organized. (441)
- Awareness of mental activities, including effective memory strategies and reasoning, becomes more elaborate and refined. (443)
- Cognitive self-regulation improves. (443–444)

Language

- Thinks about and uses words more precisely; word definitions emphasize synonyms and categorical relations. (458)
- Grasps multiple meanings of words, as reflected in comprehension of metaphors and humor. (458)
- Continues to master complex grammatical constructions, such as passive voice and infinitive phrases. (458)

- Narratives lengthen, become more coherent, and include more evaluative comments. (458)

Emotional/Social

- Continues to refine self-concept to include competencies, positive and negative personality traits, and more sophisticated social comparisons. (477–478)
- Distinguishes ability, effort, and external factors (such as luck) in attributions for success and failure. (482)
- Reconciles contradictory facial and situational cues in understanding another's feelings. (486)

- Empathic responding extends to general life conditions. (486)
- Shifts adaptively between problem-centered and emotion-centered strategies in regulating emotion. (486)
- Clarifies and links moral imperatives and social conventions. (488)
- Convictions about matters of personal choice strengthen, and understanding of individual rights expands. (489)
- Explicit outgroup prejudice declines. (490)
- Friendships become more selective and are based on mutual trust. (493–494)
- Peer groups emerge. (492–493)

- Becomes aware of a wider range of gender stereotypes, including personality traits and achievement areas, but has a flexible appreciation of what males and females can do. (498–500)
- Gender identity expands to include self-evaluations of typicality, contentedness, and pressure to conform. (500–501)
- Sibling rivalry tends to increase. (502–503)

Note: Numbers in parentheses indicate the page or pages on which each milestone is discussed.

Glossary

A

academic programs Preschool and kindergarten programs in which teachers structure children's learning, teaching academic skills through formal lessons that often involve repetition and drill. Distinguished from *child-centered programs.* (p. 338)

accommodation In Piaget's theory, that part of adaptation in which new schemes are created and old ones adjusted to produce a better fit with the environment. Distinguished from *assimilation.* (p. 198)

adaptation In Piaget's theory, the process of building schemes through direct interaction with the environment. Consists of two complementary activities: *assimilation* and *accommodation.* (p. 198)

affordances The action possibilities that a situation offers an organism with certain motor capabilities. Discovering affordances plays a major role in perceptual differentiation. (p. 193)

age of viability The age at which the fetus can first survive if born early. Occurs sometime between 22 and 26 weeks. (p. 95)

alcohol-related birth defects (ARBD) A form of fetal alcohol spectrum disorder involving characteristic facial abnormalities and other alcohol-related physical malformations but with typical growth, absence of brain abnormalities, and absence of cognitive and behavioral deficits. Distinguished from *fetal alcohol syndrome (FAS), partial fetal alcohol syndrome (p-FAS),* and *alcohol-related neurodevelopmental disorder (ARDN).* (p. 101)

alcohol-related neurodevelopmental disorder (ARND) A form of fetal alcohol spectrum disorder involving deficient brain growth or profound brain injury and substantial cognitive or behavioral impairment, but with typical physical growth and absence of facial abnormalities. Distinguished from *fetal alcohol syndrome (FAS), partial fetal alcohol syndrome (p-FAS),* and *alcohol-related birth defects (ARBD).* (p. 101)

allele Each of two or more forms of a gene, one inherited from the mother and one from the father, located at the same place on corresponding pairs of chromosomes. (p. 154)

amnion The inner membrane that forms a protective covering around the prenatal organism. (p. 91)

amodal sensory properties Information that overlaps two or more sensory systems, such as rate, rhythm, duration, intensity, and temporal synchrony in visual and auditory input. (p. 191)

amygdala An inner-brain structure that plays a central role in processing of novelty and emotional information. (p. 285)

androgyny The gender identity held by individuals who score high on both traditionally masculine and traditionally feminine personality characteristics. (p. 387)

A-not-B search error The error made by 8- to 12-month-olds who, after reaching several times for an object at one hiding place (A) and then seeing it moved to a second hiding place (B), still search for it in the first hiding place (A). (p. 200)

anoxia Inadequate oxygen supply. (p. 123)

Apgar Scale A rating system on each of five characteristics—heart rate, respiratory effort, reflex irritability, muscle tone, and color—used to assess the newborn baby's physical condition immediately after birth. (p. 120)

applied behavior analysis Observations of behavior and environmental events, followed by systematic changes in those events based on procedures of conditioning and modeling. The goal is to eliminate undesirable behaviors and increase desirable responses. (p. 18)

assimilation That part of adaptation in which the external world is interpreted in terms of current schemes. Distinguished from *accommodation.* (p. 198)

associative play A form of true social interaction in which children engage in separate activities but exchange toys and comment on one another's behavior. Distinguished from *nonsocial activity, parallel play,* and *cooperative play.* (p. 363)

attachment The strong affectionate tie that humans have with special people in their lives, which leads them to experience pleasure and joy when interacting with them and to be comforted by their nearness in times of stress. (p. 256)

Attachment Q-Sort A method of assessing attachment security, suitable for children between 1 and 5 years of age, that yields a score ranging from high to low derived from home observations of a variety of attachment-related behaviors. (p. 259)

attention-deficit hyperactivity disorder (ADHD) A disorder involving inattention, impulsivity, and excessive motor activity, resulting in academic and social problems. (p. 437)

attribution retraining An intervention that encourages learned-helpless children to believe they can overcome failure by exerting more effort and using more effective strategies. (p. 484)

authoritarian child-rearing style A child-rearing style that is low in acceptance and involvement, high in coercive and psychological control, and low in autonomy granting. Distinguished from *authoritative, permissive,* and *uninvolved child-rearing styles.* (p. 393)

authoritative child-rearing style A child-rearing style that is high in acceptance and involvement, adaptive control techniques, and appropriate autonomy granting. Distinguished from *authoritarian, permissive,* and *uninvolved child-rearing styles.* (p. 392)

autobiographical memory Long-lasting representations of personally meaningful one-time events from both the recent and the distant past. (p. 216)

automatic processes Cognitive activities that are so well-learned that they require no space in working memory and, therefore, permit an individual to focus on other information while performing them. (p. 212)

autosomes The 22 matching chromosome pairs in each human cell. (p. 53)

B

babbling Repetition of consonant–vowel combinations in long strings, beginning around 6 months of age. (p. 231)

basic emotions Emotions such as happiness, interest, surprise, fear, anger, sadness, and disgust that are universal in humans and other primates and have a long evolutionary history of promoting survival. (p. 242)

behavioral genetics A field devoted to uncovering the contributions of nature and nurture to the diversity in human traits and abilities. (p. 78)

behaviorism An approach that regards directly observable events—stimuli and responses—as the appropriate focus of study and views the development of behavior as taking place through classical and operant conditioning. (p. 16)

blended, or reconstituted, family A family structure formed through cohabitation or remarriage that includes parent, stepparent, and children. (p. 509)

bonding Parents' feelings of affection and concern for the newborn baby. (p. 145)

brain plasticity The capacity of various parts of the cerebral cortex to take over functions of damaged regions. Declines as hemispheres of the cerebral cortex lateralize. (p. 160)

breech position A position of the baby in the uterus that would cause the buttocks or feet to be delivered first. (p. 125)

C

cardinality The mathematical principle stating that the last number in a counting sequence indicates the quantity of items in the set, and each additional number work is one more than the preceding number. (p. 334)

categorical self Classification of the self according to prominent ways in which people differ, such as by age, sex, physical characteristics, and goodness and badness. Develops between 18 and 30 months. (p. 274)

carrier A heterozygous individual who can pass a recessive trait to his or her children. (p. 55)

central executive In information processing, the conscious, reflective part of the cognitive system that directs the flow of information by deciding what to attend to, coordinating incoming information with information already in the system, and selecting, applying, and monitoring strategies that facilitate memory storage, comprehension, reasoning, and problem solving. (p. 212)

centration In Piaget's theory, the tendency of preoperational children to focus on one aspect of a situation while neglecting other important features. Distinguished from *decentration.* (p. 311)

cephalocaudal trend An organized pattern of physical growth in which the head develops more rapidly than the lower part of the body ("head to tail"). Distinguished from *proximodistal trend*. (p. 155)

cerebellum A structure at the rear and base of the brain that aids in balance and control of body movement. (p. 284)

cerebral cortex The largest, most complex structure of the human brain, containing the greatest number of neurons and synapses, which accounts for the highly developed intelligence of the human species. (p. 158)

cesarean delivery A surgical birth in which the doctor makes an incision in the mother's abdomen and lifts the baby out of the uterus. (p. 125)

child-centered programs Preschool and kindergarten programs in which teachers provide a variety of activities from which children select, and much learning takes place through play. Distinguished from *academic programs*. (p. 337)

child development A field of study devoted to understanding constancy and change from conception through adolescence. (p. 4)

child-rearing styles Combinations of parenting behaviors that occur over a wide range of situations, creating an enduring child-rearing climate. (p. 392)

chorion The outer membrane that forms a protective covering around the prenatal organism. It sends out tiny hairlike villi, from which the placenta begins to develop. (p. 93)

chromosomes Rodlike structures in the cell nucleus that store and transmit genetic information. (p. 51)

chronosystem In ecological systems theory, temporal changes in environments, either externally imposed or arising from within the child, that produce new conditions affecting development. Distinguished from *microsystem, mesosystem, exosystem,* and *macrosystem*. (p. 27)

circular reaction In Piaget's theory, a means of building schemes in which infants try to repeat a chance event caused by their own motor activity. (p. 199)

classical conditioning A form of learning that involves associating a neutral stimulus with a stimulus that leads to a reflexive response. Once the nervous system makes the connection between the two stimuli, the neutral stimulus alone produces the behavior. (p. 173)

clinical interview An interview method in which the researcher uses a flexible, conversational style to probe for the participant's point of view. Distinguished from *structured interview*. (p. 33)

clinical, or case study, method A research method in which the aim is to obtain as complete a picture as possible of one individual's psychological functioning by bringing together a wide range of information, including interviews, observations, and sometimes test scores. (p. 34)

cognitive-developmental theory An approach introduced by Piaget that views children as actively constructing knowledge as they manipulate and explore their world, and in which cognitive development takes place in stages. (p. 18)

cognitive maps Mental representations of spaces, such as classroom, school, or neighborhood. (p. 432)

cognitive self-regulation The process of continuously monitoring progress toward a goal, checking outcomes, and redirecting unsuccessful efforts. (p. 443)

cohort effects The effects of cultural-historical change on the accuracy of longitudinal and cross-sectional research findings. Results based on one cohort—individuals developing in the same time period, who are influenced by particular historical and cultural conditions—may not apply to other cohorts. (p. 41)

communities of learners An educational approach inspired by Vygotsky's theory, in which teachers guide the overall process of learning, but otherwise, no distinction is made between adult and child contributors: All participate in joint endeavors, and students have the authority to define and resolve problems as they work toward project goals, which often address complex real-world issues. (p. 464)

compliance Obedience to requests and commands. (p. 274)

concrete operational stage Piaget's third stage, extending from about 7 to 11 years of age, during which thought becomes logical, flexible, and organized in its application to concrete information, but the capacity for abstract thinking is not yet present. (p. 431)

conditioned response (CR) In classical conditioning, a new response produced by a conditioned stimulus (CS) that is similar to the unconditioned, or reflexive, response (UCR). (p. 172)

conditioned stimulus (CS) In classical conditioning, a neutral stimulus that, through pairing with an unconditioned stimulus (UCS), leads to a new, conditioned response (CR). Distinguished from *unconditioned stimulus*. (p. 172)

confounding variable In an experiment, a variable so closely associated with the independent variable that the researcher cannot tell which one is actually responsible for changes in the dependent variable. (p. 38)

conservation The understanding that certain physical characteristics of objects remain the same, even when their outward appearance changes. (p. 311)

constructivist classroom A classroom grounded in Piaget's view of children as active learners who reflect on and coordinate their own thoughts. Features include richly equipped learning centers, small groups and individuals solving self-chosen problems, a teacher who guides and supports in response to children's needs, and evaluation based on individual students' progress in relation to their own prior development. Distinguished from *traditional classroom* and *social-constructivist classroom*. (p. 462)

contexts Unique combinations of personal and environmental circumstances that can result in different paths of change. (p. 8)

continuous development The view that development is a process of gradually adding more of the same types of skills that were there to begin with. Distinguished from *discontinuous development*. (p. 7)

controversial children Children who receive many votes, both positive and negative, on self-report measures of social preferences, indicating that they are both liked and disliked. Distinguished from *popular, rejected,* and *neglected children*. (p. 494)

convergent thinking The type of thinking emphasized on intelligence tests, which involves arriving at a single correct answer to a problem. Distinguished from *divergent thinking*. (p. 469)

cooing Pleasant vowel-like noises made by infants, beginning around 2 months of age. (p. 231)

cooperative learning Collaboration on a task by a small group of classmates who work toward common goals by considering one another's ideas, appropriately challenging one another, providing sufficient explanations to correct misunderstandings, and resolving differences of opinion on the basis of reasons and evidence. (p. 466)

cooperative play A form of social interaction in which children orient toward a common goal, such as acting out a make-believe theme. Distinguished from *nonsocial activity, parallel play,* and *associative play*. (p. 363)

coparenting The extent to which parents mutually support each other's parenting behaviors. (p. 66)

coregulation A form of supervision in which parents exercise general oversight while permitting children to take charge of moment-by-moment decision making. (p. 502)

core knowledge perspective A perspective that states that infants are born with a set of innate knowledge systems, or core domains of thought, each of which permits a ready grasp of new, related information and therefore supports early, rapid development of certain aspects of cognition. (p. 207)

corpus callosum The large bundle of fibers connecting the two hemispheres of the cerebral cortex. Supports smooth coordination of movements on both sides of the body and integration of many aspects of thinking. (p. 285)

correlational design A research design in which the investigator gathers information on individuals without altering their experiences and then examines relationships between participants' characteristics and their behavior or development. Does not permit inferences about cause and effect. (p. 37)

correlation coefficient A number, ranging from +1.00 to -1.00, that describes the strength and direction of the relationship between two variables. (p. 37)

creativity The ability to produce work that is original yet appropriate—something others have not thought of that is useful in some way. (p. 469)

cross-sectional design A research design in which groups of participants of different ages are studied at the same point in time. Distinguished from *longitudinal design*. (p. 42)

D

decentration In Piaget's theory, the capacity of concrete operational children to focus on several aspects of a problem and relate them. Distinguished from *centration*. (p. 431)

deferred imitation The ability to remember and copy the behavior of models who are not present. (p. 201)

delay of gratification The ability to wait for an appropriate time and place to engage in a tempting act. (p. 274)

deoxyribonucleic acid (DNA) Long, double-stranded molecules that make up chromosomes. (p. 51)

dependent variable In an experiment, the variable the investigator expects to be influenced by the independent variable. Distinguished from *independent variable.* (p. 38)

developmental cognitive neuroscience An area of investigation that brings together researchers from psychology, biology, neuroscience, and medicine to study the relationship between changes in the brain and the developing child's cognitive processing and behavior patterns. (p. 22)

developmental social neuroscience An area of investigation that brings together researchers from psychology, biology, neuroscience, and medicine to study the relationship between changes in the brain and emotional and social development. (p. 22)

developmentally appropriate practice A set of standards, devised by the U.S. National Association for the Education of Young Children, specifying program characteristics that meet young children's developmental and individual needs, based on current research and the consensus of experts. (p. 224)

developmental quotient (DQ) A score on an infant intelligence test, computed in the same manner as an IQ but labeled more conservatively because it does not tap the same dimensions of intelligence measured in older children. (p. 222)

developmental science An interdisciplinary field devoted to the study of all changes humans experience throughout the lifespan. (p. 4)

differentiation theory The view that perceptual development involves the detection of increasingly finer, invariant features of the environment. (p. 192)

difficult child A child whose temperament is characterized by irregular daily routines, slow acceptance of new experiences, and a tendency to react negatively and intensely. Distinguished from *easy child* and *slow-to-warm-up child.* (p. 249)

dilation and effacement of the cervix Widening and thinning of the cervix, as uterine contractions become more frequent and powerful, during the first stage of labor. (p. 119)

discontinuous development A view of development as a process in which new ways of understanding and responding to the world emerge at specific times. Distinguished from *continuous development.* (p. 8)

disorganized/disoriented attachment The attachment pattern reflecting the greatest insecurity, characterizing infants who show confused, contradictory behaviors when reunited with the parent after a separation. Distinguished from *secure, insecure–avoidant,* and *insecure–resistant attachment.* (p. 259)

displaced reference The realization that words can be used to cue mental images of things not physically present. (p. 205)

divergent thinking The type of thinking associated with creativity, which involves generating multiple and unusual possibilities when faced with a task or problem. Distinguished from *convergent thinking.* (p. 469)

divorce mediation A series of meetings between divorcing adults and a trained professional that are aimed at reducing family conflict, including legal battles over property division and child custody. (p. 508)

dominance hierarchy A stable ordering of group members that predicts who will win when conflict arises. (p. 426)

dominant–recessive inheritance A pattern of inheritance in which, under heterozygous conditions, the influence of only one allele is apparent. (p. 55)

dual representation The ability to view a symbolic object as both an object in its own right and a symbol. (p. 310)

dynamic assessment An innovative approach to testing consistent with Vygotsky's zone of proximal development, in which an adult introduces purposeful teaching into the testing situation to find out what the child can attain with social support. (p. 456)

dynamic systems perspective A view that regards the child's mind, body, and physical and social worlds as a dynamic, integrated system. A change in any part of the system leads the child to reorganize his or her behavior so the various components of the system work together again but in a more complex, effective way. (p. 27)

dynamic systems theory of motor development A theory that views new motor skills as reorganizations of previously mastered skills, which lead to more effective ways of exploring and controlling the environment. Each new skill is a joint product of central nervous system development, the body's movement capacities, the goals the child has in mind, and environmental supports for the skill. (p. 179)

E

easy child A child whose temperament is characterized by establishment of regular routines in infancy, general cheerfulness, and easy adaptation to new experiences. Distinguished from *difficult child* and *slow-to-warm-up child.* (p. 249)

ecological systems theory Bronfenbrenner's approach, which views the child as developing within a complex system of relationships affected by multiple levels of the surrounding environment, from immediate settings of family and school to broad cultural values, laws, customs, and resources. (p. 25)

educational self-fulfilling prophecies Teachers' positive or negative views of individual children, who tend to adopt and start to live up to those views. (p. 465)

effortful control The self-regulatory dimension of temperament, involving voluntary suppression of a dominant response in order to plan and execute a more adaptive response. (p. 250)

egocentrism Failure to distinguish the symbolic viewpoints of others from one's own. (p. 311)

elaboration A memory strategy that involves creating a relationship, or shared meaning, between two or more items of information that are not members of the same category. (p. 440)

embryo The prenatal organism from 2 to 8 weeks after conception—the period when the groundwork is laid for all body structures and internal organs. (p. 93)

emergent literacy Children's active efforts to construct literacy knowledge through informal experiences. (p. 333)

emotional self-regulation Strategies for adjusting our emotional state to a comfortable level of intensity so we can accomplish our goals. (p. 247)

emotion-centered coping A strategy for managing emotion that is internal, private, and aimed at controlling distress when little can be done about an outcome. Distinguished from *problem-centered coping.* (p. 486)

empathy The ability to understand another's emotional state and to feel with that person, or respond emotionally in a similar way. (p. 273)

epigenesis Development resulting from ongoing, bidirectional exchanges between heredity and all levels of the environment. (p. 82)

episodic memory Memory for everyday experiences. (p. 326)

ethnography A research method in which an investigator attempts to understand the unique values and social processes of a culture or a distinct social group through participant observation—spending months and sometimes years in the cultural community, gathering field notes. (p. 35)

ethological theory of attachment Bowlby's theory, the most widely accepted view of attachment, which recognizes the infant's emotional tie to the caregiver as an evolved response that promotes survival. (p. 257)

ethology A perspective concerned with the adaptive, or survival, value of behavior and its evolutionary history. (p. 23)

evolutionary developmental psychology A perspective that seeks to understand the adaptive value of species-wide cognitive, emotional, and social competencies as those competencies change with age. (p. 24)

executive function The diverse cognitive operations and strategies that enable us to achieve our goals in cognitively challenging situations. Includes controlling attention by inhibiting impulses and irrelevant actions and by flexibly directing thought and behavior to suit the demands of a task; coordinating information in working memory; and planning. (p. 212)

exosystem In ecological systems theory, social settings that do not contain children but nevertheless affect children's experiences—for example, parents' workplaces, their religious institutions, health and welfare services in the community, and parents' social networks. Distinguished from *microsystem, mesosystem, macrosystem,* and *chronosystem.* (p. 27)

expansions Adult responses that elaborate on children's speech, increasing its complexity. (p. 350)

experience-dependent brain growth Growth and refinement of established brain structures as a result of specific learning experiences that vary widely across individuals and cultures. Distinguished from *experience-expectant brain growth.* (p. 163)

experience-expectant brain growth The young brain's rapidly developing organization, which depends on ordinary experiences—opportunities to explore the environment, interact with people, and hear language and other sounds. Distinguished from *experience-dependent brain growth*. (p. 163)

experimental design A research design in which the investigator randomly assigns participants to two or more treatment conditions and studies the effect that manipulating an independent variable has on a dependent variable. Permits inferences about cause and effect. (p. 38)

F

familism A core Hispanic cultural value that elevates the needs of the family above any concerns of the individual by requiring loyal, cohesive relationships among family members, respect for elders, and mutual emotional and material support. (p. 75)

fast-mapping Children's ability to connect new words with their underlying concepts after only a brief encounter. (p. 345)

fetal alcohol spectrum disorder (FASD) A range of physical, mental, and behavioral outcomes caused by prenatal alcohol exposure, including *fetal alcohol syndrome (FAS), partial fetal alcohol syndrome (p-FAS), alcohol-related neurodevelopmental disorder (ARND),* and *alcohol-related birth defects (ARBD).* (p. 101)

fetal alcohol syndrome (FAS) The most severe form of fetal alcohol spectrum-disorder, involving characteristic facial abnormalities, deficient physical growth, deficient brain growth or profound brain injury, and substantial cognitive and behavioral impairment. Distinguished from *partial fetal alcohol syndrome (p-FAS), alcohol-related neurodevelopmental disorder (ARND),* and *alcohol-related birth defects (ARBD).* (p. 101)

fetal monitors Electronic instruments that track the baby's heart rate during labor. (p. 123)

fetus The prenatal organism from the ninth week to the end of pregnancy—the period during which body structures are completed and rapid growth in size occurs. (p. 94)

fixed mindset about ability The conviction that performance is set in stone and cannot be improved by trying hard. Distinguished from *growth mindset about ability.* (p. 482)

Flynn effect The steady increase in IQ from one generation to the next. (p. 454)

fraternal, or dizygotic, twins Twins resulting from the release and fertilization of two ova. Genetically, they are no more alike than ordinary siblings. Distinguished from *identical, or monozygotic, twins.* (p. 51)

G

gametes Sex cells, or sperm and ova, which contain half as many chromosomes as regular body cells. (p. 53)

gender constancy A full understanding of the biologically based permanence of one's gender, including the realization that sex remains the same over time, even if clothing, hairstyle, and play activities change. (p. 388)

gender identity An image of oneself as relatively masculine or feminine in characteristics. (p. 387)

gender schema theory An information-processing approach to gender typing that explains how environmental pressures and children's cognitions work together to shape gender-role development. (p. 388)

gender-stereotype flexibility The belief that both males and females can display a gender-stereotyped personality trait or activity—that overlap exists in the characteristics of males and females. (p. 499)

gender typing Any association of objects, activities, roles, or traits with one sex or the other in ways that conform to cultural stereotypes. (p. 382)

gene A segment of a DNA molecule that contains instructions for producing various proteins that contribute to the body's growth and functioning. (p. 52)

genetic counseling A communication process designed to help couples assess their chances of giving birth to a baby with a hereditary disorder and choose the best course of action in view of risks and family goals. (p. 60)

gene–environment correlation The view that heredity influences the environments to which individuals are exposed. (p. 80)

gene–environment interaction The view that because of their genetic makeup, individuals differ in their responsiveness to qualities of the environment. (p. 80)

genomic imprinting A pattern of inheritance in which alleles are imprinted, or chemically marked, within the ovum or sperm in such a way that one pair member (either the mother's or the father's) is silenced, leaving the other to be expressed regardless of its makeup. (p. 57)

genotype An individual's genetic makeup. Distinguished from *phenotype.* (p. 51)

germinal period The two-week period from fertilization and formation of the zygote until the tiny mass of cells drifts down and out of the fallopian tube and attaches itself to the wall of the uterus. (p. 91)

gifted Displaying exceptional intellectual strengths, such as high IQ, creativity, or specialized talent. (p. 469)

glial cells Cells that are responsible for myelination of neural fibers, improving the efficiency of message transfer, and that, in certain instances, participate directly in neural communication. (p. 157)

goodness-of-fit model A model that describes how favorable adjustment depends on an effective match, or good fit, between a child's temperament and child-rearing environment. (p. 255)

growth hormone (GH) A pituitary hormone that affects the development of almost all body tissues. (p. 287)

growth mindset about ability The conviction that performance can improve through effort and effective strategies. Distinguished from *fixed mindset about ability.* (p. 482)

guided play An approach to early childhood teaching that integrates child autonomy and playful exploration with adult-guided instruction. (p. 339)

H

habituation A gradual reduction in the strength of a response due to repetitive stimulation. (p. 174)

heritability estimate A measure of the extent to which individual differences in complex traits, such as intelligence or personality, in a specific population are due to genetic factors. (p. 78)

heterozygous Having two different alleles at the same place on a pair of chromosomes. Distinguished from *homozygous.* (p. 54)

hierarchical classification The organization of objects into classes and subclasses on the basis of similarities and differences. (p. 312)

hippocampus An inner-brain structure that plays a vital role in memory and in images of space that help us find our way. (p. 284)

Home Observation for Measurement of the Environment (HOME) A checklist for gathering information about the quality of children's home lives through observation and parental interview. (p. 222)

homozygous Having two identical alleles at the same place on a pair of chromosomes. Distinguished from *heterozygous.* (p. 54)

I

identical, or monozygotic, twins Twins that result when a zygote, during early cell duplication, separates into two clusters of cells that have the same genetic makeup. Distinguished from *fraternal, or dizygotic, twins.* (p. 54)

imitation Learning by copying the behavior of another person. Also known as modeling or observational learning. (p. 176)

implantation Attachment of the blastocyst to the uterine lining, which occurs seven to nine days after fertilization. (p. 91)

inclusive classrooms Classrooms in which students with learning difficulties learn alongside typical students in a regular educational setting for part or all of the school day. (p. 468)

incomplete dominance A pattern of inheritance in which both alleles are expressed in the phenotype, resulting in a combined trait, or one that is intermediate between the two. (p. 56)

independent variable In an experiment, the variable the researcher expects to cause changes in another variable and that the researcher manipulates by randomly assigning participants to treatment conditions. Distinguished from *dependent variable.* (p. 38)

induction A type of discipline in which an adult helps the child notice feelings by pointing out the effects of the child's misbehavior on others. (p. 370)

infantile amnesia The inability of most people to remember events that happened to them before age 3. (p. 216)

infant-directed speech (IDS) A form of communication used by adults to speak to infants and toddlers, consisting of short sentences with high-pitched, exaggerated expression, clear pronunciation, distinct pauses between speech segments, clear gestures to support verbal meaning, and repetition of new words in a variety of contexts. (p. 236)

infant mortality The number of deaths in the first year of life per 1,000 live births. An index used around the world to assess the overall health of a nation's children. (p. 132)

information processing An approach that views the human mind as a symbol-manipulating system through which information flows and that regards cognitive development as a continuous process. (p. 21)

inhibited, or shy, child A child whose temperament is such that he or she reacts negatively to and withdraws from novel stimuli. Distinguished from *uninhibited, or sociable, child.* (p. 251)

insecure–avoidant attachment The attachment pattern characterizing infants who seem unresponsive to the parent when she is present, are usually not distressed by parental separation, and avoid or are slow to greet the parent when she returns. Distinguished from *secure, insecure–resistant,* and *disorganized/disoriented attachment.* (p. 259)

insecure–resistant attachment The attachment pattern characterizing infants who seek closeness to the parent before her departure, are usually distressed when she leaves, and combine clinginess with angry, resistive behavior or with an anxious focus on the parent when she returns. Distinguished from *secure, insecure–avoidant,* and *disorganized/disoriented attachment.* (p. 259)

intelligence quotient (IQ) A score that permits an individual's performance on an intelligence test to be compared to the performances of same-age individuals. (p. 221)

intentional, or goal-directed, behavior A sequence of actions in which schemes are deliberately coordinated to solve simple problems. (p. 200)

intermodal perception Perception that combines information from more than one modality, or sensory system, resulting in an integrated whole. (p. 191)

internal working model A set of expectations, derived from early caregiving experiences, about the availability of attachment figures, their likelihood of providing support during times of stress, and the self's interaction with those figures. Becomes a vital part of personality, serving as a guide for all future close relationships. (p. 258)

intersubjectivity The process by which two participants who begin a task with different understandings arrive at a shared understanding. (p. 320)

irreversibility The inability to mentally go through a series of steps in a problem and then reverse direction, returning to the starting point. Distinguished from *reversibility.* (p. 312)

J

joint attention A state in which the child and caregiver attend to the same object or event and the caregiver labels what the child sees. Contributes greatly to early language development. (p. 232)

K

kinship studies Studies comparing the characteristics of family members to determine the importance of heredity in complex human characteristics. (p. 78)

kwashiorkor A disease caused by an unbalanced diet very low in protein, which usually appears after weaning, between 1 and 3 years of age. Symptoms include an enlarged belly, swollen feet, hair loss, skin rash, and irritable, listless behavior. (p. 170)

L

language acquisition device (LAD) In Chomsky's theory, an innate system containing a universal grammar, or set of rules common to all languages, that enables children, no matter which language they hear, to understand and speak in a rule-oriented fashion as soon as they have learned enough words. (p. 227)

lanugo White, downy hair that covers the entire body of the fetus, helping the vernix stick to the skin. (p. 95)

lateralization Specialization of functions in the two hemispheres of the cerebral cortex. (p. 159)

learned helplessness Attribution of success to external factors such as luck, and failure to low ability, which cannot be improved through effort. Distinguished from *mastery-oriented attributions.* (p. 482)

learning disability Great difficulty with one or more aspects of learning, usually reading, resulting in achievement considerably behind what would be expected on the basis of a child's IQ. (p. 468)

longitudinal design A research design in which participants are studied repeatedly at different ages, and changes are noted as they get older. Distinguished from *cross-sectional design.* (p. 39)

long-term memory store In information processing, the largest storage area in the cognitive system, containing our permanent knowledge base. (p. 212)

M

macrosystem In ecological systems theory, the outermost level of the environment, consisting of cultural values, laws, customs, and resources that influence experiences and interactions at inner levels of the environment. Distinguished from *microsystem, mesosystem, exosystem,* and *chronosystem.* (p. 27)

make-believe play A type of play in which children act out everyday and imaginary activities. (p. 201)

malocclusion A condition in which the upper and lower teeth do not meet properly. (p. 407)

marasmus A disease caused by a diet low in all essential nutrients that usually appears in the first year of life and leads to a wasted condition of the body. (p. 170)

mastery-oriented attributions Attributions that credit success to ability, which can be improved by trying hard, and failure to insufficient effort. Distinguished from *learned helplessness.* (p. 482)

matters of personal choice Concerns that do not violate the rights of others and, therefore, are up to each individual, such as choice of friends, hairstyle, and leisure activities. Distinguished from *moral imperatives* and *social conventions.* (p. 376)

maturation A genetically determined, naturally unfolding course of growth. (p. 13)

meiosis The process of cell division through which gametes are formed and in which the number of chromosomes in each cell is halved. (p. 53)

memory strategies Deliberate mental activities that improve the likelihood of remembering. (p. 326)

mental representation An internal depiction of information that the mind can manipulate. (p. 201)

mesosystem In ecological systems theory, connections between children's microsystems, or immediate settings. Distinguished from *microsystem, exosystem, macrosystem,* and *chronosystem.* (p. 26)

metacognition Thinking about thought; awareness of mental activities. (p. 329)

metalinguistic awareness The ability to think about language as a system. (p. 457)

methylation A biochemical process triggered by certain experiences, in which a set of chemical compounds (called a methyl group) lands on top of a gene and changes its impact, reducing or silencing its expression. (p. 82)

microgenetic design An adaptation of the longitudinal design, in which investigators present children with a novel task and track their mastery over a series of closely spaced sessions to observe how change occurs. (p. 44)

microsystem In ecological systems theory, the innermost level of the environment, consisting of activities and interaction patterns in the child's immediate surroundings. Distinguished from *mesosystem, exosystem, macrosystem,* and *chronosystem.* (p. 26)

mirror neurons Specialized cells in many areas of the cerebral cortex in primates that underlie the ability to imitate by firing identically when a primate hears or sees an action and when it carries out that action on its own. (p. 177)

moral imperatives Rules and expectations that protect people's rights and welfare. Distinguished from *social conventions* and *matters of personal choice.* (p. 376)

mutation A sudden but permanent change in a segment of DNA. (p. 57)

mutual exclusivity bias Early in vocabulary growth, children's assumption that words refer to entirely separate (nonoverlapping) categories. (p. 346)

myelination The coating of neural fibers with myelin, an insulating fatty sheath that improves the efficiency of message transfer. (p. 157)

N

naturalistic observation A research method in which the researcher goes into the natural environment to observe the behavior of interest. Distinguished from *structured observation.* (p. 32)

natural, or prepared, childbirth A group of techniques aimed at reducing pain and medical intervention and making childbirth a rewarding experience. (p. 122)

nature–nurture controversy Debate among theorists about whether genetic or environmental factors are more important influences on development. (p. 9)

neglected children Children who are seldom mentioned, either positively or negatively, on self-report measures of social preferences. Distinguished from *popular, controversial,* and *rejected children.* (p. 494)

Neonatal Behavioral Assessment Scale (NBAS) A test developed to assess a newborn infant's behavior in terms of reflexes, muscle tone, state changes, responsiveness to physical and social stimuli, and other reactions. (p. 143)

neonatal mortality The number of deaths in the first month of life per 1,000 live births. (p. 132)

neural tube During the period of the embryo, the primitive spinal cord that develops from the ectoderm, the top of which swells to form the brain. (p. 94)

neurons Nerve cells that store and transmit information. (p. 155)

neurotransmitters Chemicals released by neurons that cross the synapse to send messages to other neurons. (p. 156)

niche-picking A type of gene–environment correlation in which individuals actively choose environments that complement their heredity. (p. 81)

nocturnal enuresis Bedwetting during the night. (p. 415)

non-rapid-eye-movement (NREM) sleep A regular sleep state in which the body is almost motionless and heart rate, breathing, and brain-wave activity are slow and even. Distinguished from *rapid-eye-movement (REM) sleep.* (p. 137)

nonsocial activity Unoccupied, onlooker behavior and solitary play. Distinguished from *parallel play, associative play,* and *cooperative play.* (p. 363)

normal distribution The bell-shaped distribution that results when individual differences are measured in large samples. Most scores cluster around the mean or average, with progressively fewer falling toward the extremes. (p. 221)

normative approach An approach to development in which measures of behavior are taken on large numbers of individuals, and age-related averages are computed to represent typical development. (p. 14)

O

obesity A greater-than-20-percent increase over healthy weight, based on body mass index (BMI)—a ratio of weight to height associated with body fat. (p. 410)

object permanence The understanding that objects continue to exist when they are out of sight. (p. 200)

operant conditioning A form of learning in which a spontaneous behavior is followed by a stimulus that changes the probability that the behavior will occur again. (p. 173)

ordinality The mathematical principle specifying order relationships (more than and less than) between quantities. (p. 334)

organization In Piaget's theory, the internal rearrangement and linking together of schemes so that they form a strongly interconnected cognitive system. In information processing, a memory strategy that involves grouping related items together to improve recall. (pp. 198, 440)

overextension An early vocabulary error in which a word is applied to a wider collection of objects and events than is appropriate. Distinguished from *underextension.* (p. 233)

overlapping-waves theory A theory of problem solving, which states that when given challenging problems, children try out various strategies and gradually select those that are fastest and most accurate. (p. 328)

overregularization Extension of regular grammatical rules to words that are exceptions. (p. 348)

P

parallel play A limited form of social participation in which a child plays near other children with similar materials but does not interact with them. Distinguished from *nonsocial activity, associative play,* and *cooperative play.* (p. 363)

partial fetal alcohol syndrome (p-FAS) A form of fetal alcohol spectrum disorder involving characteristic facial abnormalities, either deficient physical growth or profound brain injury, and either substantial cognitive or behavioral impairment. Distinguished from *fetal alcohol syndrome (FAS), alcohol-related neurodevelopmental disorder (ARND),* and *alcohol-related birth defects (ARBD).* (p. 101)

peer acceptance Likability, or the extent to which a child is viewed by a group of agemates, such as classmates, as a worthy social partner. (p. 494)

peer groups Collectives of peers who generate unique values and standards for behavior and a social structure of leaders and followers. (p. 492)

peer victimization A destructive form of peer interaction in which particular children become targets of verbal and physical attacks or other forms of abuse. (p. 497)

perceptual narrowing effect Perceptual sensitivity that becomes increasingly attuned with age to information most often encountered. (p. 185)

permissive child-rearing style A child-rearing style that is high in acceptance but either overindulgent or inattentive, low in control, and inappropriately lenient in autonomy granting. Distinguished from *authoritative, authoritarian,* and *uninvolved child-rearing styles.* (p. 393)

person praise Praise from an adult that emphasizes the child's traits, as in "you're so smart" or "you're very artistic." Distinguished from *process praise.* (p. 482)

phenotype An individual's directly observable physical and behavioral characteristics, which are determined by both genetic and environmental factors. Distinguished from *genotype.* (p. 51)

phobia An intense, unmanageable fear. (p. 512)

phonological awareness The ability to reflect on and manipulate the sound structures of spoken language, as indicated by sensitivity to changes in sounds within words, to rhyming, and to incorrect pronunciation. A strong predictor of emergent literacy. (p. 333)

physical aggression A form of aggression that harms others through physical injury to themselves or their property. Distinguished from *verbal aggression* and *relational aggression.* (p. 377)

pincer grasp The well-coordinated grasp that emerges at the end of the first year, involving thumb and index finger opposition. (p. 183)

pituitary gland A gland located at the base of the brain that releases hormones that induce physical growth. (p. 286)

placenta The organ that permits exchange of nutrients and waste products between the bloodstreams of the mother and the embryo, while also preventing the mother's and embryo's blood from mixing directly. (p. 93)

planning Thinking out a sequence of acts ahead of time and allocating attention accordingly to reach a goal. (p. 324)

plasticity Openness of human development to change in response to influential experiences. (p. 9)

polygenic inheritance A pattern of inheritance in which many genes affect the characteristic in question. (p. 58)

popular-antisocial children A subtype of popular children who are admired for their socially adept yet belligerent behavior. Includes "tough" boys who are athletically skilled but poor students who cause trouble and defy adult authority, and relationally aggressive boys and girls. Distinguished from *popular-prosocial children.* (p. 495)

popular children Children who receive many positive votes on self-report measures of social preferences, indicating they are well-liked. Distinguished from *rejected, controversial,* and *neglected children.* (p. 494)

popular-prosocial children A subtype of popular children who are both socially accepted and admired and who combine academic and social competence. Distinguished from *popular-antisocial children.* (p. 495)

pragmatics The practical, social side of language, concerned with how to engage in effective and appropriate communication. (p. 349)

prefrontal cortex The region of the cerebral cortex, lying in front of areas controlling body movement, that is responsible for thought—in particular, for consciousness, inhibition of impulses, integration of information, and use of memory, reasoning, planning, and problem-solving strategies. (p. 159)

prenatal diagnostic methods Medical procedures that permit detection of developmental problems before birth. (p. 62)

preoperational stage Piaget's second stage, extending from about 2 to 7 years of age, in which children undergo an extraordinary increase in representational, or symbolic, activity, although thought is not yet logical. (p. 307)

prereaching The poorly coordinated swipes toward objects of newborn babies. (p. 182)

preterm infants Infants born several weeks or more before their due date. (p. 128)

private speech Self-directed speech that children use to plan and guide their own behavior. (p. 319)

proactive aggression A type of aggression in which children act to fulfill a need or desire—to obtain an object, privilege, space, or social reward, such as adult or peer attention—and unemotionally attack a person to achieve their goal. Also called instrumental aggression. Distinguished from *reactive aggression*. (p. 377)

problem-centered coping A strategy for managing emotion in which the individual appraises the situation as changeable, identifies the difficulty, and decides what to do about it. Distinguished from *emotion-centered coping*. (p. 486)

process praise Praise from an adult that emphasizes the child's behavior and effort, such as "you worked really hard" or "you figured it out." Distinguished from *person praise*. (p. 482)

programmed cell death An aspect of brain growth in which, as synapses form, many surrounding neurons die, making space for these connective structures. (p. 156)

Project Head Start The most extensive U.S. federally funded preschool intervention program, which provides low-SES children with a year or two of preschool education, along with nutritional and health services, and encourages parent involvement in children's learning and development. (p. 339)

prosocial behavior Actions aimed at benefitting others. (p. 362)

protein-coding genes Genes that directly affect the body's characteristics. Distinguished from *regulator genes*. (p. 52)

proximodistal trend An organized pattern of physical growth that proceeds from the center of the body outward. Distinguished from *cephalocaudal trend*. (p. 155)

psychoanalytic perspective An approach to personality development introduced by Freud that assumes children move through a series of stages in which they confront conflicts between biological drives and social expectations. How these conflicts are resolved determines the person's ability to learn, to get along with others, and to cope with anxiety. (p. 14)

psychological control Parental control that attempts to take advantage of children's psychological needs by intruding on and manipulating children's verbal expressions, individuality, and attachments to parents. (p. 393)

psychosexual theory Freud's theory, which emphasizes that how parents manage children's sexual and aggressive drives in the first few years of life is crucial for healthy personality development. (p. 14)

psychosocial theory Erikson's theory, which emphasizes that at each Freudian stage, individuals not only develop a unique personality but also acquire attitudes and skills that help them become active, contributing members of society. (p. 16)

public policies Laws and government programs designed to improve current conditions. (p. 76)

punishment In operant conditioning, removal of a desirable stimulus or presentation of an unpleasant stimulus, either of which decreases the occurrence of a response. (p. 173)

R

random assignment An unbiased procedure for assigning participants to treatment conditions in an experiment, such as drawing numbers out of a hat or flipping a coin. It increases the chances that participants' characteristics will be equally distributed across treatment groups. (p. 38)

rapid-eye-movement (REM) sleep An irregular sleep state in which brainwave activity is similar to that of the waking state. Distinguished from *non-rapid-eye-movement (NREM) sleep*. (p. 137)

reactive aggression An angry, defensive response to provocation or a blocked goal that is intended to hurt another person. Also called hostile aggression. Distinguished from *proactive aggression*. (p. 377)

realistic period The period of vocational development in which older adolescents and young adults focus on a general vocational category and, within it, experiment for a time before settling on a single occupation. Distinguished from *fantasy period* and *tentative period*. (p. 586)

recall The form of memory that involves remembering something not present, by generating a mental image of a past experience. Distinguished from *recognition*. (p. 214)

recasts Adult responses that restructure children's grammatically inaccurate speech into correct form. (p. 350)

reciprocal teaching A teaching method in which a teacher and two to four students form a cooperative group and take turns leading dialogues, creating a zone of proximal development in which children scaffold one another's progress. (p. 463)

recognition The form of memory that involves noticing whether a stimulus is identical or similar to one previously experienced. Distinguished from *recall*. (p. 214)

recovery Following habituation, an increase in responsiveness to a new stimulus. (p. 174)

recursive thought A form of perspective taking that requires the ability to view a situation from at least two perspectives—that is, to reason simultaneously about what two or more people are thinking. (p. 443)

reflex An inborn, automatic response to a particular form of stimulation. (p. 133)

regulator genes Genes that modify the instructions given by protein coding genes, greatly complicating their impact. (p. 52)

rehearsal A memory strategy that involves repeating information to oneself to improve recall. (p. 440)

reinforcer In operant conditioning, a stimulus that increases the occurrence of a response. (p. 173)

rejected-aggressive children A subtype of rejected children who show high rates of conflict, physical and relational aggression, and hyperactive, inattentive, and impulsive behavior. Distinguished from *rejected-withdrawn children*. (p. 495)

rejected children Children who receive many negative votes on self-report measures of social preferences, indicating they are disliked. Distinguished from *popular, controversial,* and *neglected children*. (p. 494)

rejected-withdrawn children A subtype of rejected children who are passive, socially awkward, and overwhelmed by social anxiety. Distinguished from *rejected-aggressive children*. (p. 495)

relational aggression A form of aggression that damages another's peer relationships through social exclusion, malicious gossip, or friendship manipulation. Distinguished from *physical aggression* and *verbal aggression*. (p. 377)

resilience The ability to adapt effectively in the face of threats to development. (p. 10)

reticular formation A structure in the brain stem that maintains alertness and consciousness. (p. 284)

reversibility The capacity to think through a series of steps in a problem and then mentally reverse direction, returning to the starting point. Distinguished from *irreversibility*. (p. 431)

Rh factor incompatibility A condition that arises when the Rh protein is present in the fetus's blood but not in the mother's, causing the mother to build up antibodies to the foreign Rh protein. If these enter the fetus's system, they destroy red blood cells, reducing the oxygen supply to organs and tissues. (p. 109)

rooming in An arrangement in which the newborn baby stays in the mother's hospital room all or most of the time. (p. 145)

rough-and-tumble play A form of peer interaction involving friendly chasing and play-fighting that emerges in the preschool years and peaks in middle childhood. In our evolutionary past, it may have been important for the development of fighting skill. (p. 425)

S

scaffolding Adjusting the support offered during a teaching session to fit the child's current level of performance. As competence increases, the adult gradually and sensitively withdraws support, turning responsibility over to the child. (p. 320)

scale errors Toddlers' attempts to do things that their body size makes impossible, such as trying to put on dolls' clothes, sit in a doll-sized chair, or walk through a door too narrow to pass through. (p. 272)

scheme In Piaget's theory, a specific psychological structure, or organized way of making sense of experience, that changes with age. (p. 198)

scripts General descriptions of what occurs and when it occurs in a particular situation, used to organize, interpret, and predict routine experiences. (p. 326)

secular trends in physical growth Changes in body size from one generation to the next. (p. 407)

secure attachment The attachment pattern characterizing infants who use the parent as a secure base from which to explore and may be distressed by parental separation but actively seek contact and are easily comforted by the parent when she returns. Distinguished from *insecure–avoidant, insecure–resistant,* and *disorganized/disoriented attachment.* (p. 259)

secure base Role of the familiar caregiver as a point from which the infant explores, venturing into the environment and then returning for emotional support. (p. 245)

self-care children Children who regularly look after themselves for some period of time during after-school hours. (p. 511)

self-compassion A personal quality marked by a caring, nonjudgmental attitude toward oneself during times of struggle or failure. (p. 481)

self-concept The set of attributes, abilities, attitudes, and values that an individual believes defines who he or she is. (p. 355)

self-conscious emotions Emotions involving injury to or enhancement of the sense of self, such as guilt, shame, embarrassment, envy, and pride. (p. 246)

self-esteem An aspect of self-concept that involves judgments about one's own worth and the feelings associated with those judgments. (p. 357)

semantic bootstrapping Using semantics, or word meanings, to figure out grammatical rules. (p. 348)

semantic memory Memory for information removed from the context in which it was first learned that has become part of an individual's general knowledge base. Distinguished from *episodic memory.* (p. 326)

sensitive caregiving Caregiving that involves responding promptly, consistently, and appropriately to infants and holding them tenderly and carefully. (p. 262)

sensitive period A time that is biologically optimal for certain capacities to emerge because the individual is especially responsive to environmental influences. (p. 24)

sensorimotor stage Piaget's first stage, spanning the first two years of life, during which infants and toddlers "think" with their eyes, ears, hands, and other sensorimotor equipment. (p. 197)

sensory store In information processing, the part of the cognitive system in which sights and sounds are represented directly and stored briefly before they either decay or are transferred to other mental stores. (p. 211)

separation anxiety Infants' distressed reaction to the departure of their trusted caregiver. (p. 257)

sequential design A research design in which several similar cross-sectional or longitudinal studies (called sequences) are conducted at varying times. (p. 42)

seriation The ability to order items along a quantitative dimension, such as length or weight. (p. 432)

sex chromosomes The twenty-third pair of chromosomes—called XX in females, XY in males—which determines the genetic sex of a newly conceived individual. (p. 53)

shape constancy Perception of an object's shape as the same, despite changes in the shape projected on the retina. (p. 190)

short-term memory store That part of the cognitive system in which attended-to information is retained briefly so that we can actively "work" on it to achieve our goals. (p. 211)

size constancy Perception of an object's size as the same, despite changes in the size of its retinal image. (p. 190)

slow-to-warm-up child A child whose temperament is characterized by inactivity; mild, low-key reactions to environmental stimuli; negative mood; and slow adjustment to new experiences. Distinguished from *easy child* and *difficult child.* (p. 249)

small-for-date infants Infants whose birth weight is below their expected weight considering length of the pregnancy. (p. 128)

social comparisons Judgments of one's own appearance, abilities, and behavior in relation to those of others. (p. 478)

social-constructivist classroom A classroom grounded in Vygotsky's sociocultural theory, in which children participate in a wide range of challenging activities with teachers and peers, with whom they jointly construct understandings. Distinguished from *traditional classroom* and *constructivist classroom.* (p. 463)

social conventions Customs determined by consensus, such as table manners and politeness rituals. Distinguished from *moral imperatives* and *matters of personal choice.* (p. 376)

social learning theory An approach that emphasizes modeling, also known as imitation or observational learning, as a powerful source of development. (p. 17)

social problem solving Generating and applying strategies that prevent or resolve disagreements, resulting in outcomes that are both acceptable to others and beneficial to the self. (p. 367)

social referencing Actively seeking emotional information from a trusted person in an uncertain situation. (p. 246)

social smile The infant's broad grin evoked by the parent's communication, first appearing between 6 and 10 weeks of age. (p. 243)

sociocultural theory Vygotsky's perspective, which focuses on how children acquire the ways of thinking and behaving that make up a community's culture through social interaction, especially cooperative dialogues with more knowledgeable members of society. (p. 24)

sociodramatic play The make-believe play with others that is under way by the end of the second year and that increases rapidly in complexity during early childhood. (p. 308)

socioeconomic status (SES) A measure of an individual's social position and economic well-being that combines three related variables: years of education, the prestige of one's job and the skill it requires, and income. (p. 67)

stage A qualitative change in thinking, feeling, and behaving that characterizes a specific period of development. (p. 8)

standardization The practice of giving an intelligence test to a large, representative sample and using the results as the standard for interpreting individual scores. (p. 221)

states of arousal Degrees of sleep and wakefulness. (p. 136)

statistical learning Detecting frequently occurring patterns in streams of auditory or visual information. (p. 175)

stereotype threat The fear of being judged on the basis of a negative stereotype, which can trigger anxiety that interferes with performance. (p. 455)

stranger anxiety The expression of fear in response to unfamiliar adults, which appears in many infants in the second half of the first year. (p. 245)

Strange Situation A laboratory procedure used to assess the quality of attachment between 1 and 2 years of age by observing the baby's responses to eight short episodes involving brief separations from and reunions with the caregiver in an unfamiliar playroom. (p. 258)

structured interview An interview method in which each participant is asked the same questions in the same way. Distinguished from *clinical interview.* (p. 34)

structured observation A research method in which the investigator sets up a laboratory situation that evokes the behavior of interest so that every participant has an equal opportunity to display the response. Distinguished from *naturalistic observation.* (p. 33)

subculture A group of people with beliefs and customs that differ from those of the larger culture. (p. 74)

sudden infant death syndrome (SIDS) The unexpected death, usually during the night, of an infant younger than 1 year of age that remains unexplained after thorough investigation. (p. 138)

sympathy Feelings of concern or sorrow for another's plight. (p. 362)

synapses The gaps between neurons, across which chemical messages are sent. (p. 155)

synaptic pruning Loss of synapses by seldom-stimulated neurons, a process that returns neurons not needed at the moment to an uncommitted state so they can support future development. (p. 156)

syntactic bootstrapping Figuring out word meanings by observing how words are used in syntax, or the structure of sentences. (p. 346)

T

talent Outstanding performance in a specific field. (p. 470)

telegraphic speech Toddlers' two-word utterances that, like a telegram, focus on high-content words while omitting smaller, less important ones. (p. 234)

temperament Early-appearing, stable individual differences in reactivity (quickness and intensity of emotional arousal, attention, and motor activity) and self-regulation (strategies that modify reactivity). (p. 249)

teratogen Any environmental agent that causes damage during the prenatal period. (p. 97)

theory An orderly, integrated set of statements that describes, explains, and predicts behavior. (p. 7)

theory of multiple intelligences Gardner's theory, which proposes at least eight independent intelligences, defined in terms of distinct sets of processing operations that permit individuals to engage in a wide range of culturally valued activities. (p. 451)

thyroid-stimulating hormone (TSH) A pituitary hormone that stimulates the thyroid gland to release thyroxine, which is necessary for brain development and for growth hormone to have its full impact on body size. (p. 287)

time out A form of mild punishment in which children are removed from the immediate setting until they are ready to act appropriately. (p. 374)

traditional classroom A classroom in which the teacher is the sole authority for knowledge, rules, and decision making and students are relatively passive learners who are evaluated in relation to a uniform set of standards for their grade. Distinguished from *constructivist classroom* and *social-constructivist classroom.* (p. 462)

transition Climax of the first stage of labor, in which the frequency and strength of contractions are at their peak and the cervix opens completely. (p. 119)

transitive inference The ability to seriate, or order items along a quantitative dimension, mentally. (p. 432)

triarchic theory of successful intelligence Sternberg's theory, which identifies three broad, interacting intelligences—analytical, creative, and practical—that must be balanced to achieve success according to one's personal goals and the requirements of one's cultural community. (p. 450)

trimesters Three equal time periods, each lasting three months, into which prenatal development is divided. (p. 94)

U

ulnar grasp The clumsy grasp of the young infant, in which the fingers close against the palm. (p. 183)

umbilical cord The long cord connecting the prenatal organism to the placenta that delivers nutrients and removes waste products. (p. 93)

unconditioned response (UCR) In classical conditioning, a reflexive response that is produced by an unconditioned stimulus (UCS). Distinguished from *conditioned response.* (p. 172)

unconditioned stimulus (UCS) In classical conditioning, a stimulus that leads to a reflexive response. Distinguished from *conditioned stimulus.* (p. 172)

underextension An early vocabulary error in which young children apply a word too narrowly, to a smaller number of objects and events than is appropriate. Distinguished from *overextension.* (p. 233)

uninhibited, or sociable, child A child whose temperament is such that she or he displays positive emotion to and approaches novel stimuli. Distinguished from *inhibited, or shy, child.* (p. 251)

uninvolved child-rearing style A child-rearing style that combines low acceptance and involvement with little control and general indifference to issues of autonomy. Distinguished from *authoritative, authoritarian,* and *permissive child-rearing styles.* (p. 393)

V

verbal aggression A form of aggression that harms others through threats of physical aggression, name-calling, or hostile teasing. Distinguished from *physical* and *relational aggression.* (p. 377)

vernix A white, cheeselike substance that covers the fetus, protecting the skin from chapping due to constant exposure to amniotic fluid. (p. 95)

video deficit effect In toddlers, poorer performance on tasks after watching a video compared to watching a live demonstration. (p. 206)

violation-of-expectation method A method in which researchers show babies an expected event (one that is consistent with reality) and an unexpected event (a variation of the first event that violates reality). Heightened attention to the unexpected event suggests that the infant is "surprised" by a deviation from physical reality and, therefore, is aware of that aspect of the physical world. (p. 201)

visual acuity Fineness of visual discrimination. (p. 143)

W

weight faltering A term applied to infants and young children whose weight (but not height) is substantially below age-related growth norms and who are withdrawn and apathetic. (p. 171)

working memory The number of items that can be briefly held in mind while also engaging in some effort to monitor or manipulate those items—a "mental workspace" that we use to accomplish many activities in daily life. (p. 211)

X

X-linked inheritance A pattern of inheritance in which a recessive gene is carried on the X chromosome, resulting in males being more likely than females to display the recessive trait because the male's sex chromosomes do not match. (p. 56)

Z

zone of proximal development In Vygotsky's theory, a range of tasks too difficult for a child to do alone but that the child can do with the help of more skilled partners. (p. 218)

zygote The newly fertilized cell formed by the union of sperm and ovum at conception. (p. 53)

References

A

Aarhus, L., Tambs, K., Kvestad, E., & Engdahl, B. (2015). Childhood otitis media: A cohort study with 30-year follow-up of hearing (the Hunt Study). *Ear and Hearing, 36,* 302–308.

Abend, O., Kwiatkowski, T., Smith, N. J., Goldwater, S., & Steedman, M. (2017). Bootstrapping language acquisition. *Cognition, 164,* 116–143.

Aber, L., Brown, J. L., Jones, S. M., Berg, J., & Torrente, C. (2011). School-based strategies to prevent violence, trauma, and psychopathology: The challenges of going to scale. *Development and Psychopathology, 23,* 411–421.

Abner, K. S., Gordon, R. A., Kaestner, R., & Korenman, S. (2013). Does child-care quality mediate associations between type of care and development? *Journal of Marriage and Family, 75,* 1203–1217.

Aboud, F. E. (2008). A social-cognitive developmental theory of prejudice. In S. M. Quintana & C. McKown (Eds.), *Handbook of race, racism, and the developing child* (pp. 55–71). Hoboken, NJ: Wiley.

Aboud, F. E., & Brown, C. S. (2013). Positive and negative intergroup contact among children and its effect on attitudes. In G. Hodson & M. Hewstone (Eds.), *Advances in intergroup contact* (pp. 176–199). New York: Psychology Press.

Aboud, F. E., & Doyle, A. (1996). Parental and peer influences on children's racial attitudes. *International Journal of Intercultural Relations, 20,* 371–383.

Abraham, E., Hendler, T., Shapira-Lichter, I., Kanat-Maymon, Y., Zagoory-Sharon, O., & Feldman, R. (2014). Father's brain is sensitive to childcare experiences. *Proceedings of the National Academy of Sciences, 111,* 9792–9797.

Abraham, M. M., & Kerns, K. A. (2013). Positive and negative emotions and coping as mediators of mother–child attachment and peer relationships. *Merrill-Palmer Quarterly, 59,* 399–425.

Achenbach, T. M., Howell C. T., & Aoki, M. F. (1993). Nine-year outcome of the Vermont Intervention Program for low-birthweight infants, *Pediatrics, 91,* 45–55.

Acker, M. M., & O'Leary, S. G. (1996). Inconsistency of mothers' feedback and toddlers' misbehavior and negative affect. *Journal of Abnormal Child Psychology, 24,* 703–714.

Ackerman, J. P., Riggins, T., & Black, M M. (2010). A review of the effects of prenatal cocaine exposure among school-aged children. *Pediatrics, 125,* 554–565.

ACOG (American College of Obstetricians and Gynecologists). (2017). *Vaginal birth after cesarean (VBAC): Resource overview.* Retrieved from www.acog.org/Womens-Health/Vaginal-Birth-After-Cesarean-VBAC

Adachi, P. J. C., & Willoughby, T. (2013). More than just fun and games: The longitudinal relationships between strategic video games, self-reported problem solving skills, and school grades. *Journal of Youth and Adolescence, 42,* 1041–1052.

Adam, E. K., Snell, E. K., & Pendry, P. (2007). Sleep timing and quantity in ecological and family context: A nationally representative time-diary study. *Journal of Family Psychology, 21,* 4–19.

Adamson, L. B., & Frick, J. E. (2003). The still face: A history of a shared experimental paradigm. *Infancy, 4,* 451–473.

Addati, L., Cassirer, N., & Gilchrist, K. (2014). *Maternity and paternity at work: Law and practice across the world.* Geneva, Switzerland: International Labour Organization.

Adelson, S. L. (2012). Practice parameter on gay, lesbian, or bisexual sexual orientation, gender nonconformity, and gender discordance in children and adolescents. *Journal of the American Academy of Child and Adolescent Psychiatry, 51,* 957–974.

Adelstein, S. J. (2014). Radiation risk. In S. T. Treves (Ed.), *Pediatric nuclear medicine and molecular imaging* (pp. 675–682). New York: Springer Science + Business Media.

Adolph, K. E. (2002). Learning to keep balance. In R. V. Kail (Ed.), *Advances in child development and behavior* (Vol. 30, pp. 1–40). Boston: Academic Press.

Adolph, K. E. (2008). Learning to move. *Current Directions in Psychological Science, 17,* 213–218.

Adolph, K. E., Cole, W. G., Komati, M., Garciaguirre, J. S., Badaly, D., Lingeman, J. M., et al. (2012). How do you learn to walk? Thousands of steps and hundreds of falls per day. *Psychological Science, 23,* 1387–1394.

Adolph, K. E., & Franchak, J. M. (2017). The development of motor behavior. *WIREs Cognitive Science, 10,* e1430.

Adolph, K. E., Karasik, L. B., & Tamis-LeMonda, C. S. (2010). Motor skill. In M. H. Bornstein (Ed.), *Handbook of cultural developmental science* (pp. 61–88). New York: Psychology Press.

Adolph, K. E., Kretch, K. S., & LoBue, V. (2014). Fear of heights in infants? *Current Directions in Psychological Science, 23,* 60–66.

Adolph, K. E., & Robinson, S. R. (2013). The road to walking: What learning to walk tells us about development. In P. Zelazo (Ed.), *Oxford handbook of developmental psychology* (pp. 403–443). New York: Oxford University Press.

Adolph, K. E., & Robinson, S. R. (2015). Perceptual development. In L. S. Liben & U. Müller (Eds.), *Handbook of child psychology and developmental science: Vol. 2. Cognitive processes* (7th ed., pp. 113–157). Hoboken, NJ: Wiley.

Adolph, K. E., Tamis-LeMonda, C. S., Ishak, S., Karasik, L. B., & Lobo, S. A. (2008). Locomotor experience and use of social information are posture specific. *Developmental Psychology, 44,* 1705–1714.

Adolph, K. E., Vereijken, B., & Shrout, P. E. (2003). What changes in infant walking and why. *Child Development, 74,* 475–497.

Afifi, T. O., Ford, D., & Gershoff, E. T. (2017). Spanking and adult mental health impairment: The case for the designation of spanking as an adverse childhood experience. *Child Abuse and Neglect, 71,* 24–31.

Aguiar, A., & Baillargeon, R. (2002). Developments in young infants' reasoning about occluded objects. *Cognitive Psychology, 45,* 267–336.

Aguilar-Mediavilla, E., Bul-Legaz, L., López-Penadés, R., & Adrover-Roig, D. (2017). Language development in bilingual Spanish-Catalan children with and without specific language impairment: A longitudinal perspective. In A. A. Benavides & R. G. Schwartz (Eds.), *Language development and disorders in Spanish-speaking children* (pp. 37–62). Cham, Switzerland: Springer International Publishing.

Ahmadlou, M., Gharib, M., Hemmti, S., Vameghi, R., & Sajedi, F. (2013). Disrupted small-world brain network in children with Down syndrome. *Clinical Neurophysiology, 124,* 1755–1764.

Ainsworth, C. (2015). Sex redefined. *Nature, 518,* 288–291.

Ainsworth, M. D. S., Blehar, M. C., Waters, E., & Wall, S. (1978). *Patterns of attachment.* Hillsdale, NJ: Erlbaum.

Aitken, Z., Garrett, C. C., Hewitt, B., Keogh, L., Hocking, J. S., & Kavanagh, A. M. (2015). The maternal health outcomes of paid maternity leave: A systematic review. *Social Science and Medicine, 130,* 32–41.

Akhtar, N., & Montague, L. (1999). Early lexical acquisition: The role of cross-situational learning. *First Language, 19,* 347–358.

Akolekar, R., Beta, J., Picciarelli, G., Ogilive, C., & D'Antonio, F. (2015). Procedure-related risk of miscarriage following amniocentesis and chorionic villus sampling: A systematic review and metaanalysis. *Ultrasound in Obstetrics and Gynecology, 45,* 16–26.

Aksan, N., & Kochanska, G. (2004). Heterogeneity of joy in infancy. *Infancy, 6,* 79–94.

Akutagava-Martins , G. C., Salatino-Liveira, A., Kieling, C. C., Rohde, A., & Hutz, M. H. (2013). Genetics of attention-deficit/hyperactivity disorder: Current findings and future directions. *Expert Review of Neurotherapeutics, 13,* 435–445.

Alarcón-Rubio, D., Sánchez-Medina, J. A., & Prieto-Garcia, J. R. (2014). Executive function and verbal self-regulation in childhood: Developmental linkages between partially internalized private speech and cognitive flexibility. *Early Childhood Research Quarterly, 29,* 95–105.

Alati, R., Al Mamun, A., O'Callaghan, M., Najman, J. M., & Bor, W. (2006). In utero alcohol exposure and prediction of alcohol disorders in early adulthood. *Archives of General Psychiatry, 63,* 1009–1016.

Albers, C. A., & Grieve, A. J. (2007). Test review: Bayley, N. (2006). Bayley Scales of Infant and Toddler Development—Third Edition. San Antonio, TX: Harcourt Assessment. *Journal of Psychoeducational Assessment, 25,* 180–190.

Albert, D., & Steinberg, L. (2011b). Peer influences on adolescent risk behavior. In M. Bardo, D. Fishbein, & R. Milich (Eds.), *Inhibitory control and drug abuse prevention: From research to translation* (pp. 211–226). New York: Springer.

Albert, R. R., Schwade, J. A., & Goldstein, M. H. (2018). The social functions of babbling: Acoustic and contextual characteristics that facilitate maternal responsiveness. *Developmental Science, 21,* e12641.

Alderson-Day, B., & Fernyhough, C. (2015). Inner speech: Development, cognitive functions, phenomenology, and neurobiology. *Psychological Bulletin, 141,* 931–965.

Alexander, J. M., Fabricius, W. V., Fleming, V. M., Zwahr, M., & Brown, S. A. (2003). The development of metacognitive causal explanations. *Learning and Individual Differences, 13,* 227–238.

Alfieri, L., Brooks, P. J., Aldrich, N. J., & Tenenbaum, H. R. (2011). Does discovery-based instruction enhance learning? *Journal of Educational Psychology, 103,* 1–18.

Alibali, M. W., Phillips, K. M. O., & Fischer, A. D. (2009). Learning new problem-solving strategies leads to changes in problem representation. *Cognitive Development, 24,* 89–101.

Aljughaiman, A. M., & Ayoub, A. E. A. (2012). The effect of an enrichment program on developing analytical, creative, and practical abilities of elementary gifted students. *Journal for the Education of the Gifted, 35,* 153–174.

Allan, N. P., Hume, L. E., Allan, D. M., Farrington, A. L., & Lonigan, C. J. (2014). Relations between inhibitory control and the development of academic skills in preschool and kindergarten: A meta-analysis. *Developmental Psychology, 50,* 2368–2379.

Allely, C. S., Gillberg, C., & Wilson, P. (2014). Neurobiological abnormalities in the first few years of life in individuals later diagnosed with autism spectrum disorder: A review of recent data. *Behavioural Neurology.* Retrieved from www.hindawi.com/journals/bn/2014/210780/

Allen, J. W. P., Bennett, D. S., Carmody, D. P., Wang, Y., & Lewis, M. (2014). Adolescent risk-taking as a function of prenatal cocaine exposure and biological sex. *Neurotoxicology and Teratology, 41,* 65–70.

Allen, K. A. (2014). Moderate hypothermia: Is selective head cooling or whole body cooling better? *Advances in Neonatal Care, 14,* 113–118.

Allen, M. L., Nurmosoo, E., & Freeman, N. (2016). Young children show representational flexibility when interpreting drawings. *Cognition, 147,* 21–28.

Allen, S. E. M., & Crago, M. B. (1996). Early passive acquisition in Inukitut. *Journal of Child Language, 23,* 129–156.

Alliance of African Midwives. (2012). *Natural induction of labor.* Retrieved from www.african-midwives.com/2011/natural-induction-of-labour

Alloway, T. P., Bibile, V., & Lau, G. (2013). Computerized working memory training: Can it lead to gains in cognitive skills in students? *Computers in Human Behavior, 29,* 632–638.

Alloway, T. P., Gathercole, S. E., Kirkwood, H., & Elliott, J. (2009). The cognitive and behavioral characteristics of children with low working memory. *Child Development, 80,* 606–621.

Alm, B., Wennergren, G., Mölborg, P., & Lagercrantz, H. (2016). Breastfeeding and dummy use have a protective effect on sudden infant death syndrome. *Acta Paediatrica, 105,* 31–38.

Almas, A. N., Degnan, K. A., Nelson, C. A., & Zeanah, C. H. (2016). IQ at age 12 following a history of institutional care: Findings from the Bucharest Early Intervention Project. *Developmental Psychology, 52,* 1858–1866.

Althaus, N., & Plunkett, K. (2016). Categorization in infancy: Labeling induces a persisting focus on commonalities. *Developmental Science, 19,* 770–780.

Álvarez, M. J., Fernández, D., Gómez-Salgado, J., Rodríguez-González, D., Róson, M., &

Laeña, S. (2017). The effects of massage therapy in hospitalized preterm neonates: A systematic review. *International Journal of Nursing Studies, 69,* 119–136.

Amato, P. R. (2010). Research on divorce: Continuing trends and new developments. *Journal of Marriage and Family, 72,* 650–666.

Amato, P. R., & Fowler, F. (2002). Parenting practices, child adjustment, and family diversity. *Journal of Marriage and the Family, 64,* 703–716.

Amato, P. R., & Sobolewski, J. M. (2004). The effects of divorce on fathers and children: Nonresidential fathers and stepfathers. In M. E. Lamb (Ed.), *The role of the father in child development* (4th ed., pp. 341–367). Hoboken, NJ: Wiley.

American Academy of Pediatrics. (2012). Breastfeeding and the use of human milk. *Pediatrics, 129,* e827–e841.

American Academy of Pediatrics. (2016a). Media and young minds. *Pediatrics, 138,* 5, e20162591.

American Academy of Pediatrics. (2016b). SIDS and other sleep-related infant deaths: Updated 2016 recommendations for a safe infant sleeping environment. *Pediatrics, 138,* e20162938.

American Association of Birth Centers. (2014). *Position statement: Immersion in water during labor and birth.* Retrieved from www.birthcenters.org/webfm_send/145

American Psychiatric Association. (2013). *Diagnostic and statistical manual of mental disorders* (5th ed.). Arlington, VA: Author.

Amit, M. (2010). Vegetarian diets in children and adolescents. *Paediatrics and Child Health, 15,* 303–308.

Amso, D., & Johnson, S. P. (2006). Learning by selection: Visual search and object perception in young infants. *Developmental Psychology, 42,* 1236–1245.

American Psychological Association. (2017). *Ethical principles of psychologists and code of conduct.* Retrieved from www.apa.org/ethics/code

Amsterlaw, J. (2006). Children's beliefs about everyday reasoning. *Child Development, 77,* 443–464.

Anand, K. J., & Campbell-Yeo, M. (2015). Consequences of prenatal opioid use for newborns. *Acta Paediatrica, 104,* 1066–1069.

Anand, V., Downs, S. M., Bauer, N. S., & Carroll, A. E. (2014). Prevalence of infant television viewing and maternal depression symptoms. *Journal of Developmental and Behavioral Pediatrics, 35,* 216–224.

Ananth, C. V., Friedman, A. M., & Gyamfi-Bannerman, C. (2013). Epidemiology of moderate preterm, late preterm and early term delivery. *Clinics in Perinatology, 40,* 601–610.

Andersen, E. (2000). Exploring register knowledge: The value of "controlled improvisation." In L. Menn & N. B. Ratner (Eds.), *Methods for studying language production* (pp. 225–248). Mahwah, NJ: Erlbaum.

Anderson, C. A., & Bushman, B. J. (2018). Media violence and the general aggression model. *Journal of Social Issues, 74,* 386–413.

Anderson, C. A., Bushman, B. J., Donnerstein, E. I., Hummer, T. A., & Warburton, W. (2015). SPSSI research summary on media violence. *Analyses of Social Issues and Public Policy, 15,* 4–19.

Anderson, C. A., Shibuya, A., Ihori, N., Swing, E. L., Bushman, B. J., Sakamoto, A., et al. (2010). Violent video game effects on aggression, empathy, and prosocial behavior

in Eastern and Western countries: A meta-analytic review. *Psychological Bulletin, 136,* 151–173.

Anderson, C. B., Hughes, S. O., & Fuemmeler, B. F. (2009). Parent–child attitude congruence on type and intensity of physical activity: Testing multiple mediators of sedentary behavior in older children. *Health Psychology, 28,* 428–438.

Anderson, C. M. (2012). The diversity, strengths, and challenges of single-parent households. In F. Walsh (Ed.), *Normal family processes: Growing diversity and complexity* (4th ed., pp. 128–148). New York: Guilford.

Anderson, D. M., Huston, A. C., Schmitt, K. L., Linebarger, D. L., & Wright, J. C. (2001). Early childhood television viewing and adolescent behavior. *Monographs of the Society for Research in Child Development, 66*(1, Serial No. 264).

Anderson, D. R., & Subrahmanyam, K. (2017). Digital screen media and cognitive development. *Pediatrics, 140*(Suppl. 2), S57–S61.

Anderson, R. C., Wilson, P. T., & Fielding, L. G. (1988). Growth in reading and how children spend their time outside of school. *Reading Research Quarterly, 23,* 285–303.

Anderson, S., & Leventhal, T. (2014). Exposure to neighborhood affluence and poverty in childhood and adolescence and academic achievement and behavior. *Applied Developmental Science, 18,* 123–138.

Anderson, V., & Beauchamp, M. H. (2013). A theoretical model of developmental social neuroscience. In V. Anderson & M. H. Beauchamp (Eds.), *Developmental social neuroscience and childhood brain insult: Theory and practice* (pp. 3–20). New York: Guilford.

Anderson, V., Spencer-Smith, M., & Wood, A. (2011). Do children really recover better? Neurobehavioural plasticity after early brain insult. *Brain, 134,* 2197–2221.

Anderson, V. A., Spencer-Smith, M. M., Coleman, L., Anderson, P. J., Greenham, M., Jacobs, R., et al. (2014). Predicting neurocognitive and behavioural outcome after early brain insult. *Developmental Medicine & Child Neurology, 56,* 329–336.

Andrews, G., & Halford, G. (2011). Recent advances in relational complexity theory and its application to cognitive development. In P. Barrouillet & V. Gaillard (Eds.), *Cognitive development and working memory* (pp. 47–68). Hove, UK: Psychology Press.

Andrews, G., & Halford, G. S. (2002). A cognitive complexity metric applied to cognitive development. *Cognitive Psychology, 45,* 475–506.

Anisfeld, M. (2005). No compelling evidence to dispute Piaget's timetable of the development of representational imitation in infancy. In S. Hurley & N. Chater (Eds.), *Perspectives on imitation: From neuroscience to social science: Vol. 2. Imitation, human development, and culture* (pp. 107–131). Cambridge, MA: MIT Press.

Ansari, A. (2018). The persistence of preschool effects from early childhood through adolescence. *Journal of Educational Psychology, 110,* 952–973.

Anthonysamy, A., & Zimmer-Gembeck, M. J. (2007). Peer status and behaviors of maltreated children and their classmates in the early years of school. *Child Abuse & Neglect, 31,* 971–991.

Antshel, K. M., Hier, B. O., & Barkley, R. A. (2015). Executive functioning theory and ADHD. In S. Goldstein & J. A. Naglieri (Eds.), *Handbook of executive functioning*

(pp. 107–120). New York: Springer Science + Business Media.

Anzures, G., Quinn, P. C., Pascalis, O., Slater, A. M., Tanaka, J. W., & Lee, K. (2013). Developmental origins of the other-race effect. *Current Directions in Psychological Science, 22,* 173–178.

Apfelbaum, E. P., Pauker, K., Ambady, N., Sommers, S. R., & Norton, M. I. (2008). Learning (not) to talk about race: When older children underperform in social categorization. *Developmental Psychology, 44,* 1513–1518.

Apgar, V. (1953). A proposal for a new method of evaluation in the newborn infant. *Current Research in Anesthesia and Analgesia, 32,* 260–267.

Aram, D., & Levin, I. (2011). Home support of children in the writing process. In S. B. Neuman & D. K. Dickinson (Eds.), *Handbook of early literacy research* (Vol. 3, pp. 189–199). New York: Guilford.

Aram, D., & Levin, I. (2014). Promoting early literacy: The differential effects of parent–child joint writing and joint storybook reading interventions. In R. Chen (Ed.), *Cognitive development: Theories, stages and processes and challenges* (pp. 189–212). Hauppauge, NY: Nova Science.

Arcus, D., & Chambers, P. (2008). Childhood risks associated with adoption. In T. P. Gullotta & G. M. Blau (Eds.), *Family influences on childhood behavior and development* (pp. 117–142). New York: Routledge.

Ardila, A., Bernal, B., & Rosselli, M. (2016). The role of Wernicke's area in language comprehension. *Psychology & Neuroscience, 9,* 340–343.

Arija, V., Esparó, G., Fernández-Ballart, J., Murphy, M. M., Biarnés, E., & Canals, J. (2006). Nutritional status and performance in test of verbal and nonverbal intelligence in 6 year old children. *Intelligence, 34,* 141–149.

Armstrong, K. L., Quinn, R. A., & Dadds, M. R. (1994). The sleep patterns of normal children. *Medical Journal of Australia, 161,* 202–206.

Arnett, J. J. (2015). *Emerging adulthood: The winding road from the late teens through the twenties* (2nd ed.). New York: Oxford University Press.

Arnold, A. P. (2009). The organizational-activational hypothesis as the foundation for a unified theory of sexual differentiation of all mammalian tissues. *Hormones and Behavior, 55,* 570–578.

Arsenio, W. F. (2010). Integrating emotion attributions, morality, and aggression: Research and theoretical foundations. In W. F. Arsenio & E. A. Lemerise (Eds.), *Emotions, aggression, and morality in children: Bridging development and psychopathology* (pp. 75–94). Washington, DC: American Psychological Association.

Artal, R. (2015). The role of exercise in reducing the risks of gestational diabetes mellitus in obese women. *Best Practice & Research, 29,* 123–132.

Artman, L., & Cahan, S. (1993). Schooling and the development of transitive inference. *Developmental Psychology, 29,* 753–759.

Asbjornsen, A. E., Obrzut, J. E., Boliek, C. A., Myking, E., Holmefjord, A., & Reisaeter, S. (2005). Impaired auditory attention skills following middle-ear infections. *Child Neuropsychology, 11,* 121–133.

Asher, S. R., & Rose, A. J. (1997). Promoting children's social-emotional adjustment with peers. In P. Salovey & D. J. Sluyter (Eds.), *Emotional development and emotional intelligence* (pp. 193–195). New York: Basic Books.

Askeland, K. G., Hysing, M., La Greca, A. M., Aar., L. E., Tell, G. S., & Sivertsen, B. (2017). Mental health in internationally adopted adolescents: A meta-analysis. *Psychiatry, 56,* 203–213.

Aslin, R. N. (2017). Statistical learning: A powerful mechanism that operates by mere exposure. *WIREs Cognitive Science, 8,* e1373.

Aslin, R. N., Jusczyk, P. W., & Pisoni, D. B. (1998). Speech and auditory processing during infancy: Constraints on and precursors to language. In D. Kuhn & R. S. Siegler (Eds.), *Handbook of child psychology: Vol. 2. Cognition, perception, and language* (5th ed., pp. 147–198). New York: Wiley.

Aslin, R. N., & Newport, E. L. (2012). Statistical learning: From acquiring specific items to forming general rules. *Psychological Science, 21,* 170–176.

Aspen Institute. (2018). *State of play 2018: Trends and developments.* Retrieved from www.aspenprojectplay.org

Assink, M., van der Put, C. E., Meeuwsen, M. W. C. M., de Jong, N. M., Oort, F. J., Geert, J. J. M., & Hoeve, M. (2019). Risk factors for child sexual abuse victimization: A meta-analytic review. *Psychological Bulletin, 145,* 459–489.

Astington, J. W., & Hughes, C. (2013). Theory of mind: Self-reflection and social understanding. In S. M. Carlson, P. D. Zelazo, & S. Faja (Eds.), *Oxford handbook of developmental psychology: Vol. 2. Self and other* (pp. 398–424). New York: Oxford University Press.

Astington, J. W., & Jenkins, J. M. (1995). Theory of mind development and social understanding. *Cognition and Emotion, 9,* 151–165.

Astington, J. W., Pelletier, J., & Homer, B. (2002). Theory of mind and epistemological development: The relation between children's second-order false belief understanding and their ability to reason about evidence. *New Ideas in Psychology, 20,* 131–144.

Atance, C. M., & Meltzoff, A. N. (2005). My future self: Young children's ability to anticipate and explain future states. *Cognitive Development, 20,* 341–361.

Attanasio, L., & Kozhimannil, K. B. (2015). Patient-reported communication quality and perceived discrimination in maternity care. *Medical Care, 53,* 863–871.

Atzaba-Poria, N., & Pike, A. (2015). Through a cultural lens: Links between maternal and paternal negativity and children's self-esteem. *Journal of Cross Cultural Psychology, 46,* 702–712.

Au, T. K., Sidle, A. L., & Rollins, K. B. (1993). Developing an intuitive understanding of conservation and contamination: Invisible particles as a plausible mechanism. *Developmental Psychology, 29,* 286–299.

Aunola, K., Stattin, H., & Nurmi, J.-E. (2000). Parenting styles and adolescents' achievement strategies. *Journal of Adolescence, 23,* 205–222.

Auster, C. J., & Mansbach, C. S. (2012). The gender marketing of toys: An analysis of color and type of toy on the Disney store website. *Sex Roles, 67,* 375–388.

Averhart, C. J., & Bigler, R. S. (1997). Shades of meaning: Skin tone, racial attitudes, and constructive memory in African-American children. *Journal of Experimental Child Psychology, 67,* 368–388.

Axelin, A., Salantera, S., & Lehtonen, L. (2006). "Facilitated tucking by parents" in pain management of preterm infants—a randomized crossover trial. *Early Human Development, 82,* 241–247.

Ayón, C., Marsiglia, F. A., & Bermudez-Parsai, M. (2010). Latino family mental health: Exploring the role of discrimination and familismo. *Journal of Community Psychology, 38,* 742–756.

Ayoub, C. C., Bartlett, J. D., Chazan-Cohen, R., & Raikes, H. (2014). Early Head Start: Mental health, parenting, and impacts on children. In A. J. Reynolds, A. J. Rolnick, & J. A. Temple (Eds.), *Health and education in early childhood: Predictors, interventions, and policies* (pp. 234–256). New York: Cambridge University Press.

Aznar, A., & Tenenbaum, H. R. (2014). Gender and age differences in parent–child emotion talk. *British Journal of Developmental Psychology, 33,* 148–155.

Azzopardi, D., Strohm, B., Marlow, N., Brocklehurst, P., Deierl, A., Eddama, O., et al. (2016). Effects of hypothermia for perinatal asphyxia on childhood outcomes. *New England Journal of Medicine, 371,* 14 0–149.

B

Bacallao, M. L., & Smokowski, P. R. (2007). The costs of getting ahead: Mexican family system changes after immigration. *Family Relations, 56,* 52–66.

Badanes, L. S., Dmitrieva, J., & Watamura, S. E. (2012). Understanding cortisol reactivity across the day at child care: The potential buffering role of secure attachments to caregivers. *Early Childhood Research Quarterly, 27,* 156–165.

Baddeley, J., & Singer, J. A. (2015). Charting the life story's path: Narrative identity across the life span. In J. D. Clandinin (Ed.), *Handbook of narrative inquiry: Mapping a methodology* (pp. 177–202). Thousand Oaks, CA: Sage.

Badiee, Z., Asghari, M., & Mohammadizadeh, M. (2013). The calming effect of maternal breast milk odor on premature infants. *Pediatrics and Neonatology, 54,* 322–325.

Baer, J. (2002). Is family cohesion a risk or protective factor during adolescent development? *Journal of Marriage and Family, 64,* 668–675.

Baer, J. S., Sampson, P. D., Connor, P. D., & Streissguth, A. P. (2003). A 21-year longitudinal analysis of the effects of prenatal alcohol exposure on young adult drinking. *Archives of General Psychiatry, 60,* 377–386.

Bagwell, C. L., & Bukowski, W. M. (2018). Friendship in childhood and adolescence: Features, effects, and processes. In W. M. Bukowski, B. Laursen, & K. H. Rubin (Eds.), *Handbook of peer interactions, relationships, and groups* (2nd ed., pp. 371–390). New York: Guilford.

Bagwell, C. L., & Coie, J. D. (2004). The best friendships of aggressive boys: Relationship quality, conflict management, and rule-breaking behavior. *Journal of Experimental Child Psychology, 88,* 5–24.

Bahrick, L. E. (2010). Intermodal perception and selective attention to intersensory redundancy: Implications for typical social development and autism. In G. Bremner & T. D. Wachs (Eds.), *Wiley-Blackwell handbook of infant development: Vol. 1* (2nd ed., pp. 120–166). Malden, MA: Blackwell.

Bahrick, L. E., Hernandez-Reif, M., & Flom, R. (2005). The development of infant learning about specific face–voice relations. *Developmental Psychology, 41,* 541–552.

Bahrick, L. E., Hernandez-Reif, M., & Pickens, J. N. (1997). The effect of retrieval cues on visual preferences and memory in infancy: Evidence for a four-phase attention function. *Journal of Experimental Child Psychology, 67,* 1–20.

Bahrick, L. E., & Lickliter, R. (2012). The role of intersensory redundancy in early perceptual, cognitive, and social development. In A. J. Bremner, D. J. Lewkowicz, & C. Spence (Eds.), *Multisensory development* (183–206). Oxford, UK: Oxford University Press.

Bailey, D. H., Zhou, X., Zhang, Y., Cui, J., Fuchs, L. S., Jordan, N. C., et al. (2015). Development of fraction concepts and procedures in U.S. and Chinese children. *Journal of Experimental Child Psychology, 129,* 68–83.

Baillargeon, R., & DeVos, J. (1991). Object permanence in young infants: Further evidence. *Child Development, 62,* 1227–1246.

Baillargeon, R., Li, J., Gertner, Y., & Wu, D. (2011). How do infants reason about physical events? In U. Goswami (Ed.), *Wiley-Blackwell handbook of childhood cognitive development* (2nd ed., pp. 11–48). Chichester, UK: Wiley-Blackwell.

Baillargeon, R., Scott, R. M., & He, Z. (2010). False-belief understanding in infants. *Trends in Cognitive Sciences, 14,* 110–118.

Baillargeon, R. H., Zoccolillo, M., Keenan, K., Côté, S., Pérusse, D., Wu, H.-X., & Boivin, M. (2007). Gender differences in physical aggression: A prospective population-based survey of children before and after 2 years of age. *Developmental Psychology, 43,* 13–26.

Bakermans-Kranenburg, M. J., Steele, H., Zeanah, C. H., Muhamedrahimov, R. J, Vorria, P., & Dobrova-Krol, N. A. (2011). Attachment and emotional development in institutional care: Characteristics and catch up. In R. B. McCall, M. H. van IJzendoorn, F. Juffer, C. J. Groark, & V. K. Groza (Eds), Children without permanent parents: Research, practice, and policy. *Monographs of the Society for Research in Child Development, 76*(4, Serial No. 301), 62–91.

Bakermans-Kranenburg, M. J., & van IJzendoorn, M. H. (2011). Differential susceptibility to rearing environment depending on dopamine-related genes: New evidence and a meta-analysis. *Development and Psychopathology, 23,* 39–52.

Bakermans-Kranenburg, M. J., & van IJzendoorn, M. H. (2015). The hidden efficacy of interventions: Gene× environment experiments from a differential susceptibility perspective. *Annual Review of Psychology, 66,* 381–409.

Bakermans-Kranenburg, M. J., & Van IJzendoorn, M. H. (2016). Attachment, parenting, and genetics. In J. Cassidy & P. R. Shaver (Eds.), *Handbook of attachment: Theory, research, and clinical applications* (3rd ed., pp. 155–179). New York: Guilford.

Bakermans-Kranenburg, M. J., van IJzendoorn, M. H., & Juffer, F. (2003). Less is more: Meta-analyses of sensitivity and attachment interventions in early childhood. *Psychological Bulletin, 129,* 195–215.

Bakermans-Kranenburg, M. J., van IJzendoorn, M. H., Mesman, J., Alink, L. R. A., & Juffer, F. (2008a). Effects of an attachment-based intervention on daily cortisol moderated by dopamine receptor D4: A randomized control trial on 1-to 3-year-olds screened for externalizing behavior. *Development and Psychopathology, 20,* 805–820.

Bakermans-Kranenburg, M. J., van IJzendoorn, M. H., Pijlman, F. T. A., Mesman, J., & Juffer, F. (2008b). Experimental evidence for differential sensitivity: Dopamine D4 receptor polymorphism (DRD4 VNTR) moderates intervention effects on toddlers' externalizing behavior in a randomized control trial. *Developmental Psychology, 44,* 293–300.

Baker-Sennett, J., Matusov, E., & Rogoff, B. (2008). Children's planning of classroom plays with adult or child direction. *Social Development, 17,* 998–1018.

Balaban, M. T., & Waxman, S. R. (1997). Do words facilitate object categorization in 9-month-old infants? *Journal of Experimental Child Psychology, 64,* 3–26.

Balkaya, M., Cheah, S. L., Yu, J., Hart, C. H., & Sun, S. (2018). Maternal encouragement of modest behavior, temperamental shyness, and anxious withdrawal linkages to Chinese American children's social adjustment: A moderated mediation analysis. *Social Development, 27,* 876–890.

Ball, H. L., & Volpe, L. E. (2013). Sudden infant death syndrome (SIDS) risk reduction and infant sleep location—moving the discussion forward. *Social Science and Medicine, 79,* 84–91.

Baltes, P. B., Lindenberger, U., & Staudinger, U. M. (2006). Life span theory in developmental psychology. In R. M. Lerner & W. Damon (Eds.), *Handbook of child psychology: Vol. 1. Theoretical models of human development* (6th ed., pp. 569–664). Hoboken, N. J.: Wiley.

Bamford, C., & Lagattuta, K. H. (2012). Looking on the bright side: Children's knowledge about the benefits of positive versus negative thinking. *Child Development, 83,* 667–682.

Bandura, A. (1977). *Social learning theory.* Englewood Cliffs, NJ: Prentice-Hall.

Bandura, A. (1992). Perceived self-efficacy in cognitive development and functioning. *Educational Psychologist, 28,* 117–118.

Bandura, A. (2001). Social cognitive theory: An agentic perspective. *Annual Review of Psychology, 52,* 1–26.

Bandura, A. (2011). Social cognitive theory. In P. A. M. Van Lange, A. W. Kruglanski, & E. T. Higgins (Eds.), *Handbook of theories of social psychology* (Vol. 1, pp. 349–373). Thousand Oaks, CA: Sage.

Bandura, A. (2016). The power of observational learning through social modeling. In R. J. Sternberg, S. T. Fiske, & D. J. Foss (Eds.), *Scientists making a difference: One hundred eminent behavioral and brain scientists talk about their most important contributions* (pp. 235–239). New York: Cambridge University Press.

Banish, M. T., & Heller, W. (1998). Evolving perspectives on lateralization of function. *Current Directions in Psychological Science, 7,* 1–2.

Banks, M. S. (1980). The development of visual accommodation during early infancy. *Child Development, 51,* 157–173.

Bannard, C., Lieven, E., & Tomasello, M. (2009). Modeling children's early grammatical knowledge. *Proceedings of the National Academy of Sciences, 106,* 17284–17289.

Banse, R., Gawronski, B., Rebetez, C., Gutt, H., & Morton, J. B. (2010). The development of spontaneous gender stereotyping in childhood: Relations to stereotype knowledge and stereotype flexibility. *Developmental Science, 13,* 298–306.

Barber, B. K., & Olsen, J. A. (1997). Socialization in context: Connection, regulation, and autonomy in the family, school, and neighborhood, and with peers. *Journal of Adolescent Research, 12,* 287–315.

Barber, B. K., & Olsen, J. A. (2004). Assessing the transitions to middle and high school. *Journal of Adolescent Research, 19,* 3–30.

Barber, B. K., & Xia, M. (2013). The centrality of control to parenting and its effects. In R. E. Larzelere, A. S. Morris, & A. W. Harrist (Eds.), *Authoritative parenting: Synthesizing nurturance and discipline for optimal child development* (pp. 61–88). Washington, DC: American Psychological Association.

Barbu-Roth, M., Anderson, D. I., Streeter, R. J., Combrouze, M., Park, J., Schultz, B., et al. (2015). Why does infant stepping disappear and can it be stimulated by optic flow? *Child Development, 86,* 441–455.

Barn, R. (2013). "Doing the right thing": Transracial adoption in the USA. *Ethnic and Racial Studies, 36,* 1273–1291.

Barnes, G. M., Hoffman, J. H., Welte, J. W., Farrell, M. P., & Dintcheff, B. A. (2007). Adolescents' time use: Effects on substance use, delinquency and sexual activity. *Journal of Youth and Adolescence, 36,* 697–710.

Barnes, T. N., Wang, F., & O'Brien, K. M. (2017). A meta-analytic review of social problem-solving interventions in preschool settings. *Infant and Child Development, 27,* e2095.

Barnett, W. S. (2011). Effectiveness of early educational intervention. *Science, 333,* 975–978.

Baron-Cohen, S. (2011). What is theory of mind, and is it impaired in ASC? In S. Bolte & J. Hallmayer (Eds.). *Autism spectrum conditions: FAQs on autism, Asperger syndrome, and atypical autism answered by international experts* (pp. 136–138). Cambridge, MA: Hogrefe Publishing.

Baron-Cohen, S., & Belmonte, M. K. (2005). Autism: A window onto the development of the social and the analytic brain. *Annual Review of Neuroscience, 28,* 109–126.

Barr, H. M., Streissguth, A. P., Darby, B. L., & Sampson, P. D. (1990). Prenatal exposure to alcohol, caffeine, tobacco, and aspirin: Effects on fine and gross motor performance in 4-year-old children. *Developmental Psychology, 26,* 339–348.

Barr, R., & Hayne, H. (2003). It's not what you know, it's who you know: Older siblings facilitate imitation during infancy. *International Journal of Early Years Education, 11,* 7–21.

Barr, R., Marrott, H., & Rovee-Collier, C. (2003). The role of sensory preconditioning in memory retrieval by preverbal infants. *Learning and Behavior, 31,* 111–123.

Barr, R., Muentener, P., & Garcia, A. (2007). Age-related changes in deferred imitation from television by 6- to 18-month-olds. *Developmental Science, 10,* 910–921.

Barr, R. G. (2001). "Colic" is something infants do, rather than a condition they "have": A developmental approach to crying phenomena patterns, pacification and (patho)genesis. In R. G. Barr, I. St James-Roberts, & M. R. Keefe (Eds.), *New evidence on unexplained infant crying* (pp. 87–104). St. Louis: Johnson & Johnson Pediatric Institute.

Barr, R. G., Fairbrother, N., Pauwels, J., Green, J., Chen, M., & Brant, R. (2014). Maternal frustration, emotional and behavioural responses to prolonged infant crying. *Infant Behavior and Development, 37,* 652–664.

Barros, R. M., Silver, E. J., & Stein, R. E. K. (2009). School recess and group classroom behavior. *Pediatrics, 123,* 431–436.

Barrouillet, P., & Gaillard, V. (2011a). Advances and issues: Some thoughts about controversial questions. In P. Barrouillet & V. Gaillard (Eds.), *Cognitive development and working memory* (pp. 263–271). Hove, UK: Psychology Press.

Barrouillet, P., & Gaillard, V. (2011b). (Eds.). *Cognitive development and working memory: A dialogue between neo-Piagetian and cognitive approaches*. Hove, UK: Psychology Press.

Barthell, J. E., & Mrozek, J. D. (2013). Neonatal drug withdrawal. *Minnesota Medicine, 96,* 48–50.

Bartholomew, K. S. (2015). Policy options to promote smokefree environments for children and adolescents. Current Problems *in Pediatric and Adolescent Health Care, 45,* 146–181.

Bartick, M., & Smith, L. J. (2014). Speaking out on safe sleep: Evidence-based infant sleep recommendations. *Breastfeeding Medicine, 9,* 417–422.

Bartocci, M., Berggvist, L. L., Lagercrantz, H., & Anand, K. J. (2006). Pain activates cortical areas in the preterm newborn brain. *Pain, 122,* 109–117.

Barton, M. E., & Strosberg, R. (1997). Conversational patterns of two-year-old twins in mother–twin–twin triads. *Journal of Child Language, 24,* 257–269.

Barton, M. E., & Tomasello, M. (1991). Joint attention and conversation in mother–infant–sibling triads. *Child Development, 62,* 517–529.

Bartrip, J., Morton, J., & de Schonen, S. (2001). Responses to mother's face in 3-week to 3-month-old infants. *British Journal of Developmental Psychology, 19,* 219–232.

Bartsch, K., London, K., & Campbell, M. D. (2007). Children's attention to beliefs in interactive persuasion tasks. *Developmental Psychology, 43,* 111–120.

Bartsch, K., & Wellman, H. M. (1995). *Children talk about the mind.* New York: Oxford University Press.

Basavarajappa, B. S., & Subbanna, S. (2016). Epigenetic mechanisms in developmental alcohol-induced neurobehavioral deficits. *Brain Sciences, 6,* 12.

Basinger, B. (2013). Low-income and minority children with asthma. In L. Rubin & J. Merrick (Eds.), *Environmental health disparities with children: Asthma, obesity and food* (pp. 61–72). Hauppauge, NY: Nova Science.

Bassett, D. R., John, D., Conger, S. A., Fitzhugh, E. C., & Coe, D. P. (2015). Trends in physical activity and sedentary behaviors of United States youth. *Journal of Physical Activity & Health, 12,* 1102–1111.

Bassok, D., & Reardon, S. F. (2013). "Academic redshirting" in kindergarten: Prevalence, patterns, and implications. *Educational Evaluation and Policy Analysis, 35,* 283–297.

Bass-Ringdahl, S. M. (2010). The relationship of audibility and the development of canonical babbling in young children with hearing impairment. *Journal of Deaf Studies and Deaf Education, 15,* 287–310.

Bassuk, E. L., DeCandia, C. J., Beach, C. A., & Berman, F. (2014). *America's youngest outcasts: A report card on child homelessness.* Waltham, MA: National Center on Family Homelessness.

Basten, S., & Jiang, Q. (2015). Fertility in China: An uncertain future. *Population Studies, 69,* S97–S105.

Batchelor, J. (2008). "Failure to thrive" revisited. *Child Abuse Review, 17,* 147–159.

Bates, E., & MacWhinney, B. (1987). Competition, variation, and language learning. In B. MacWhinney (Ed.), *Mechanisms of language acquisition* (pp. 157–193). Hillsdale, NJ: Erlbaum.

Bates, E., Marchman, V., Thal, D., Fenson, L., Dale, P., Reznick, J. S., Reilly, J., & Hartung, J. (1994). Developmental and stylistic variation in the composition of early vocabulary. *Journal of Child Language, 21,* 85–123.

Bates, E., Wilson, S. M., Saygin, A. P., Dick, F., Sereno, M. I., Knight, R. T., & Dronkers, N. F. (2003). Voxel-based lesion-symptom mapping. *Nature Neuroscience, 6,* 448–450.

Bates, J. E., Schermerhorn, A. C., & Petersen, I. T. (2012). Temperament and parenting in developmental perspective. In M. Zentner & R. L. Shiner (Eds.), *Handbook of temperament* (pp. 425–441). New York: Guilford.

Bates, J. E., Wachs, T. D., & Emde, R. N. (1994). Toward practical uses for biological concepts. In J. E. Bates & T. D. Wachs (Eds.), *Temperament: Individual differences at the interface of biology and behavior* (pp. 275–306). Washington, DC: American Psychological Association.

Bathelt, J., O'Reilly, H., Clayden, J. D., Cross, J. H., & de Haan, M. (2013). Functional brain network organization of children between 2 and 5 years derived from reconstructed activity of cortical sources of high-density EEG recordings. *NeuroImage, 82,* 595–604.

Baude, A., Pearson, J., & Drapeau, S. (2016). Child adjustment in joint physical custody versus sole custody: A meta-analytic review. *Journal of Divorce and Remarriage, 57,* 338–360.

Baudson, T. G., Weber, K. E., & Freund, P. A. (2016). More than only skin deep: Appearance self-concept predicts most of secondary school students' self-esteem. *Frontiers in Psychology, 7,* Art. No. 1568.

Bauer, P. J. (2006). Event memory. In D. Kuhn & R. Siegler (Eds.), *Handbook of child psychology: Vol. 2. Cognition, perception, and language* (6th ed., pp. 373–425). Hoboken, NJ: Wiley.

Bauer, P. J. (2013). Memory. In S. M. Carlson, P. D. Zelazo, & S. Faja (Eds.), *Oxford handbook of developmental psychology: Vol. 1. Body and mind* (pp. 505–541). New York: Oxford University Press.

Bauer, P. J., Larkina, M., & Deocampo, J. (2011). Early memory development. In U. Goswami (Ed.), *Wiley-Blackwell handbook of childhood cognitive development* (2nd ed., pp. 153–179). Chichester, UK: Wiley-Blackwell.

Bauer, P. J., Wiebe, S. A., Carver, L. J., Lukowski, A. F., Haight, J. C., Waters, J. M., & Nelson, C. A. (2006). Electrophysiological indexes of encoding and behavioral indexes of recall: Examining relations and developmental change late in the first year of life. *Developmental Neuropsychology, 29,* 293–320.

Baumeister, R. F., Campbell, J. D., Krueger, J. I., & Vohs, K. D. (2003). Does high self-esteem cause better performance, interpersonal success, happiness, or healthier lifestyles? *Psychological Science in the Public Interest, 4*(1), 1–44.

Baumgartner, H. A., & Oakes, L. M. (2011). Infants' developing sensitivity to object function: Attention to features and feature correlations. *Journal of Cognition and Development, 12,* 275–298.

Baumrind, D. (1971). Current patterns of parental authority. *Developmental Psychology Monograph, 4* (No. 1, Pt. 2).

Baumrind, D. (2013). Authoritative parenting revisited: History and current status. In R. E. Larzelere, A. S. Morris, & A. W. Harrist (Eds.), *Authoritative parenting: Synthesizing nurturance and discipline for optimal child development* (pp. 11–34). Washington, DC: American Psychological Association.

Baumrind, D., Larzelere, R. E., & Owens, E. B. (2010). Effects of preschool parents' power assertive patterns and practices on adolescent development. *Parenting, 10,* 157–201.

Bauserman, R. (2002). Child adjustment in joint-custody versus sole-custody arrangements: A meta-analytic review. *Journal of Family Psychology, 16,* 91–102.

Bauserman, R. (2012). A meta-analysis of parental satisfaction, adjustment, and conflict in joint custody and sole custody following divorce. *Journal of Divorce & Remarriage, 53,* 464–488.

Baydar, N., & Akcinar, B. (2018). Reciprocal relations between the trajectories of mothers' harsh discipline, responsiveness and aggression in early childhood. *Journal of Abnormal Child Psychology, 45,* 83–97.

Bayley, N. (1969). *Bayley Scales of Infant Development.* New York: Psychological Corporation.

Bayley, N. (1993). *Bayley Scales of Infant Development* (2nd ed.). New York: Psychological Corporation.

Bayley, N. (2005). *Bayley Scales of Infant and Toddler Development* (3rd ed.). (Bayley III). San Antonio, TX: Harcourt Assessment.

Bearak, J., Popinchalk, A., Alkema, L., & Sedgh, G. (2018). Global, regional, and subregional trends in unintended pregnancy and its outcomes from 1990 to 2014: Estimates from a Bayesian hierarchical model. *Lancet, 6,* e380–e389.

Beauchamp, G. K., & Mennella, J. A. (2011). Flavor perception in human infants: Development and functional significance. *Digestion, 83*(Suppl. 1), 1–6.

Bebko, J. M., McMorris, C. A., Metcalfe, A., Ricciuti, C., & Goldstein, G. (2014). Language proficiency and metacognition as predictors of spontaneous rehearsal in children. *Canadian Journal of Experimental Psychology, 68,* 46–58.

Becker, R. E. (2013). Nocturnal enuresis. In S. V. Kothare & A. Ivanenko (Eds.), *Parasomnias: Clinical characteristics and treatment* (pp. 293–301). New York: Springer Science + Media.

Beckett, C., Maughan, B., Rutter, M., Castle, J., Colvert, E., & Groothues, C. (2006). Do the effects of early severe deprivation on cognition persist into early adolescence? Findings from the English and Romanian adoptees study. *Child Development, 77,* 696–711.

Beckham, J. D., Pastula, D. M., Massey, A., & Tyler, K. L. (2016). Zika virus as an emerging global pathogen: Neurological complications of Zika virus. *JAMA Neurology, 73,* 875–879.

Bédard, J., & Chi, M. T. (1992). Expertise. *Current Directions in Psychological Science, 1,* 135–139.

Beelmann, A., & Heinemann, K. S. (2014). Preventing prejudice and improving intergroup attitudes: A meta-analysis of child and adolescent training programs. *Journal of Applied Developmental Psychology, 35,* 10–24.

Behm, I., Zubair, Connolly, G. N., & Alpert, H. R. (2012). Increasing prevalence of smoke-free homes and decreasing rates of sudden infant death syndrome in the United States: An ecological association study. *Tobacco Control, 21,* 6–11.

Behne, T., Liszkowski, U., Carpenter, M., & Tomasello, M. (2012). Twelve-month-olds' comprehension and production of pointing. *British Journal of Developmental Psychology, 30,* 359–375.

Behnke, M., & Smith, V. C. (2013). Prenatal substance abuse: Short- and long-term effects on the exposed fetus. *Pediatrics, 131,* e1009–e1024.

Bélanger, M. J., Atance, C. M., Varghese, A. L., Nguyen, V., & Vendetti, C. (2014). What will I like best when I'm all grown up? Preschoolers' understanding of future preferences. *Child Development, 85,* 2419–2431.

Belcher, D., Lee, A., Solmon, M., & Harrison, L. (2003). The influence of gender-related beliefs and conceptions of ability on women learning the hockey wrist shot. *Research Quarterly for Exercise and Sport, 74,* 183–192.

Bell, E. R., Greenfield, D. B., Bulotsky-Shearer, R. J., & Carter, T. M. (2016). Peer play as a context for identifying profiles of children and examining rates of growth in academic readiness for children enrolled in Head Start. *Journal of Educational Psychology, 108,* 740–745.

Bellagamba, F., Camaioni, L., & Colonnesi, C. (2006). Change in children's understanding of others' intentional actions. *Developmental Science, 9,* 182–188.

Bellagamba, F., Laghi, F., Lonigro, A., & Pace, C. S. (2012). Re-enactment of intended acts from a video presentation by 18- and 24-month-old children. *Cognitive Processes, 13,* 381–386.

Bellinger, D. C., Leviton, A., & Sloman, J. (1990). Antecedents and correlates of improved cognitive performance in children exposed in utero to low levels of lead. *Environmental Health Perspectives, 89,* 5–11.

Belsky, J., & de Haan, M. (2011). Parenting and children's brain development: The end of the beginning. *Journal of Child Psychology and Psychiatry, 52,* 409–428.

Belsky, J., & Fearon, R. M. P. (2002). Early attachment security, subsequent maternal sensitivity, and later child development: Does continuity in development depend on caregiving? *Attachment and Human Development, 4,* 361–387.

Belsky, J., & Fearon, R. M. P. (2008). Precursors of attachment security. In J. Cassidy & P. R. Shaver (Eds.), *Handbook of attachment* (2nd ed., pp. 295–316). New York: Guilford.

Belsky, J., Schlomer, G. L., & Ellis, B. J. (2012). Beyond cumulative risk: Distinguishing harshness and unpredictability as determinants of parenting and early life history strategy. *Developmental Psychology, 48,* 662–673.

Belsky, J., Vandell, D. L., Burchinal, M., Clarke-Stewart, K. A., McCartney, K., & Owen, M. T. (2007). Are there long-term effects of early child care? *Child Development, 78,* 681–701.

Bemmels, H. R., Burt, A., Legrand, L. N., Iacono, W. G., & McGue, M. (2008). The heritability of life events: An adolescent twin and adoption study. *Twin Research and Human Genetics, 11,* 257–265.

Bender, H. L., Allen, J. P., McElhaney, K. B., Antonishak, J., Moore, C. M., Kelly, H. L., & Davis, S. M. (2007). Use of harsh physical discipline and developmental outcomes in adolescence. *Development and Psychopathology, 19,* 227–242.

Benigno, J. P., Byrd, D. L., McNamara, P. H., Berg, W. K., & Farrar, M. J. (2011). Talking through transitions: Microgenetic changes in preschoolers' private speech. *Child Language Teaching and Therapy, 27,* 269–285.

Benner, A. D., Boyle, A., & Sadler, S. (2016). Parental involvement and adolescents' educational success: The roles of prior achievement and socioeconomic status. *Journal of Youth and Adolescence, 45,* 1053–1064.

Benson, J. E., Sabbagh, M. A., Carlson, S. M., & Zelazo, P. D. (2013). Individual differences in executive functioning predict preschoolers' improvement from theory-of-mind training. *Developmental Psychology, 49,* 1615–1627.

Bera, A., Ghosh, J., Singh, A. K., Hazra, A., Mukherjee, S., & Mukherjee, R. (2014). Effect of kangaroo mother care on growth and development of low birthweight babies up to 12 months of age: A controlled clinical trial. *Acta Paediatrica, 103,* 643–650.

Berenbaum, S. A., & Beltz, A. M. (2011). Sexual differentiation in human behavior: Effects of prenatal and pubertal organizational hormones. *Frontiers in Neuroendocrinology, 32,* 183–200.

Bergen, D. (2013). Does pretend play matter? Searching for evidence: Comment on Lillard et al. (2013). *Psychological Bulletin, 139,* 45–48.

Berger, A., Tzur, G., & Posner, M. I. (2006). Infant brains detect arithmetic errors. *Proceedings of the National Academy of Sciences, 103,* 12649–12653.

Berger, L. M., Paxson, C., & Waldfogel, J. (2009). Income and child development. *Children and Youth Services Review, 31,* 978–989.

Berger, S. E. (2010). Locomotor expertise predicts infants' perseverative errors. *Developmental Psychology, 46,* 326–336.

Berger, S. E., & Scher, A. (2017). Naps improve new walkers' locomotor problem solving. *Journal of Experimental Child Psychology, 162,* 292–300.

Berger, S. E., Theuring, C., & Adolph, K. E. (2007). How and when infants learn to climb stairs. *Infant Behavior and Development, 30,* 36–49.

Bergman, A. A., & Connaughton, S. L. (2013). What is patient-centered care really? Voices of Hispanic prenatal patients. *Health Communication, 28,* 789–799.

Bergman, R. (2004). Identity as motivation. In D. K. Lapsley & D. Narvaez (Eds.), *Moral development, self, and identity* (pp. 21–46). Mahwah, NJ: Erlbaum.

Berk, L. E. (2001). Private speech and self-regulation in children with impulse-control difficulties: Implications for research and practice. *Journal of Cognitive Education and Psychology, 2*(1), 1–21.

Berk, L. E. (2006). Looking at kindergarten children. In D. Gullo (Ed.), *K today: Teaching and learning in the kindergarten year* (pp. 11–25). Washington, DC: National Association for the Education of Young Children.

Berk, L. E. (2015). Make-believe play and children's self-regulation. *Speaking about ... Psychology On-Demand Webinars.* Hoboken, NJ: Pearson Education.

Berk, L. E., & Meyers, A. M. (2013). The role of make-believe play in the development of executive function: Status of research and future directions. *American Journal of Play, 6,* 98–110.

Berk, L. E., & Spuhl, S. T. (1995). Maternal interaction, private speech, and task performance in preschool children. *Early Childhood Research Quarterly, 10,* 145–169.

Berkeley, S., Mastropieri, M. A., & Scruggs, T. E. (2011). Reading comprehension strategy instruction and attribution retraining for secondary students with learning and other mild disabilities. *Journal of Learning Disabilities, 44,* 18–31.

Berkowitz, R. L., Roberts, J., & Minkoff, H. (2006). Challenging the strategy of maternal age-based prenatal genetic counseling. *Journal of the American Medical Association, 295,* 1446–1448.

Berlin, L. J., Ipsa, J. M., Fine, M. A., Malone, P. S., Brooks-Gunn, J., Brady-Smith, C., et al. (2009). Correlates and consequences of

spanking and verbal punishment for low-income White, African-American, and Mexican-American toddlers. *Child Development, 80,* 1403–1420.

Berman, R. A. (2007). Developing linguistic knowledge and language use across adolescence. In K. Hirsh-Pasek & R. M. Golinkoff (Eds.), *Action meets word: How children learn verbs* (pp. 347–367). New York: Oxford University Press.

Bernard, J. Y., Armand, M., Peyre, H., Garcia, C., Forhan, A., De Agostini, M., et al. (2017). Breastfeeding, polyunsaturated fatty acid levels in colostrum, and child intelligence quotient at age 5–6 years. *Journal of Pediatrics, 183,* 43–50.

Berndt, T. J. (2004). Children's friendships: Shifts over a half-century in perspectives on their development and effects. *Merrill-Palmer Quarterly, 50,* 206–223.

Bertenthal, B. I., Gredebäck, G., & Boyer, T. W. (2013). Differential contributions of development and learning to infants' knowledge of object continuity and discontinuity. *Child Development, 84,* 413–421.

Bertenthal, B. I., Longo, M. R., & Kenny, S. (2007). Phenomenal permanence and the development of predictive tracking in infancy. *Child Development, 78,* 350–363.

Bertrand, J., & Dang, E. P. (2012). Fetal alcohol spectrum disorders: Review of teratogenicity, diagnosis and treatment issues. In D. Hollar (Ed.), *Handbook of children with special health care needs* (pp. 231–258). New York: Springer Science + Business Media.

Best, D. (2009). From the American Academy of Pediatrics: Technical report—Secondhand and prenatal tobacco smoke exposure. *Pediatrics, 124,* e1017–1044.

Best, D. L. (2001). Gender concepts: Convergence in cross-cultural research and methodologies. *Cross-cultural Research: The Journal of Comparative Social Science, 35,* 23–43.

Bhat, A., Heathcock, J., & Galloway, J. C. (2005). Toy-oriented changes in hand and joint kinematics during the emergence of purposeful reaching. *Infant Behavior and Development, 28,* 445–465.

Bhatt, R. S., Rovee-Collier, C., & Weiner, S. (1994). Developmental changes in the interface between perception and memory retrieval. *Developmental Psychology, 30,* 151–162.

Bhatt, R. S., Wilk, A., Hill, D., & Rovee-Collier, C. (2004). Correlated attributes and categorization in the first half-year of life. *Developmental Psychobiology, 44,* 103–115.

Bialystok, E. (2013). The impact of bilingualism on language and literacy development. In T. K. Bhatia & W. C. Ritchie (Eds.), *Handbook of bilingualism and multilingualism* (pp. 624–648). Chichester, UK: Wiley-Blackwell.

Bialystok, E. (2015). Bilingualism and the development of executive function: The role of attention. *Child Development Perspectives, 9,* 117–121.

Bialystok, E. (2018). Bilingual education for young children: Review of the effects and consequences. *International Journal of Bilingual Education & Bilingualism, 21,* 666–679.

Bialystok, E., Craik, F. I. M., & Luk, G. (2012). Bilingualism: Consequences for mind and brain. *Trends in Cognitive Sciences, 16,* 240–250.

Bialystok, E., & Martin, M. M. (2003). Notation to symbol: Development in children's understanding of print. *Journal of*

Experimental Child Psychology, 86, 223–243.

Bick, J., Dozier, M., Bernard, K., Grasso, D., & Simons, R. (2013). Foster mother–infant bonding: Associations between foster mothers' oxytocin production, electrophysiological brain activity, feelings of commitment, and caregiving quality. *Child Development, 84,* 826–840.

Biederman, J., Fried, R., Petty, C., Mahoney, L., & Faraone, S. V. (2012). An examination of the impact of attention-deficit hyperactivity disorder on IQ: A large controlled family-based analysis. *Canadian Journal of Psychiatry, 57,* 608–616.

Bielawska-Batorowicz, E., & Kossakowska-Petrycka, K. (2006). Depressive mood in men after the birth of their offspring in relation to a partner's depression, social support, fathers' personality and prenatal expectations. *Journal of Reproductive and Infant Psychology, 24,* 21–29.

Bierman, K. L., Domitrovich, C. E., Nix, R. L., Gest, S. D., Welsh, J. A., Greenberg, M. T., et al. (2008). Promoting academic and social-emotional school readiness: The Head Start REDI program. *Child Development, 79,* 1802–1817.

Bierman, K. L., Heinrichs, B. S., Welsh, J. A., Nix, R. L., & Gest, S. D. (2017). Enriching preschool classrooms and home visits with evidence-based programming: Sustained benefits for low-income children. *Journal of Child Psychology and Psychiatry, 58,* 129–137.

Bierman, K. L., Nix, R. L., Heinrichs, B. S., Domitrovich, C. E., Gest, S. D., Welsh, J. A., et al. (2014). Effects of Head Start REDI on children's outcomes 1 year later in different kindergarten contexts. *Child Development, 85,* 140–159.

Bierman, K. L., & Powers, C. J. (2009). Social skills training to improve peer relations. In K. H. Rubin, W. M. Bukowski, & B. Laursen (Eds.), *Handbook of peer interactions, relationships, and groups* (pp. 603–621). New York: Guilford.

Bifulco, R., Cobb, C. D., & Bell, C. (2009). Can interdistrict choice boost student achievement? The case of Connecticut's interdistrict magnet school program. *Educational Evaluation and Policy Analysis, 31,* 323–345.

Bigelow, A. E., & Power, M. (2014). Effects of maternal responsiveness on infant responsiveness and behavior in the still-face task. *Infancy, 19,* 558–584.

Bigler, R. S. (2007, June). Personal communication.

Bigler, R. S. (2013). Understanding and reducing social stereotyping and prejudice among children. In M. Banaji & S. A. Gelman (Eds.), *Navigating the social world: What infants, children, and other species can teach us* (pp. 327–33). New York: Oxford University Press.

Bilir Seyhan, G., Ocak Karabay, S., Arda Tuncdemir, T. B., Greenberg, M. T., & Domitrovich, C. (2019). The effects of Promoting Alternative Thinking Strategies preschool program on teacher–children relationships and children's social competence in Turkey. *International Journal of Psychology, 54,* 61–69.

Bion, R. A. H., Borovsky, A., & Fernald, A. (2013). Fast mapping, slow learning: Disambiguation of novel word–object mappings in relation to vocabulary learning at 18, 24, and 30 months. *Cognition, 126,* 39–53.

Birbeck, D., & Drummond, M. (2015). Research methods and ethics working with young children. In O. N. Saracho (Ed.), *Handbook of research methods in early*

childhood education: Vol. 2. Review of research methodologies (pp. 607–632). Charlotte, NC: IAP Information Age Publishing.

Birch, L. L., & Fisher, J. A. (1995). Appetite and eating behavior in children. *Pediatric Clinics of North America, 42,* 931–953.

Birch, L. L., Fisher, J. O., & Davison, K. K. (2003). Learning to overeat: Maternal use of restrictive feeding practices promotes girls' eating in the absence of hunger. *American Journal of Clinical Nutrition, 78,* 215–220.

Bird, A., & Reese, E. (2006). Emotional reminiscing and the development of an autobiographical self. *Developmental Psychology, 42,* 613–626.

Biringen, Z., Altenhofen, S., Aberle, J., Baker, M., Brosal, A., Bennett, S., et al. (2012). Emotional availability, attachment, and intervention in center-based child care for infants and toddlers. *Development and Psychopathology, 24,* 23–34.

Biringen, Z., Emde, R. N., Campos, J. J., & Appelbaum, M. I. (1995). Affective reorganization in the infant, the mother, and the dyad: The role of upright locomotion and its timing. *Child Development, 66,* 499–514.

Birken, C. S., Parkin, P. C., To, T., & Macarthur, C. (2006). Trends in rates of death from unintentional injury among Canadian children in urban areas: Influence of socioeconomic status. *Canadian Medical Association Journal, 175,* 867–868.

Birney, D. P., & Sternberg, R. J. (2011). The development of cognitive abilities. In M. H. Bornstein & M. E. Lamb (Eds.), *Developmental science: An advanced textbook* (6th ed., pp. 353–388). New York: Psychology Press.

Biro, F. M., & Wien, M. (2010). Childhood obesity and adult morbidities. *American Journal of Clinical Nutrition, 91,* 1499S–1505S.

Bischoff-Köhler, D. (2012). Empathy and self-recognition in phylogenetic and ontogenetic perspective. *Emotion Review, 4,* 40–48.

Bishop, D. V., Holt, G., Whitehouse, A. J., & Groen, M. (2014). No population bias to left-hemisphere language in 4-year-olds with language impairment. *PeerJ, 2,* e507.

Bjorklund, D. F., & Causey, K. B. (2016). *Children's thinking: Cognitive development and individual differences* (6th ed.). Thousand Oaks, CA: Sage.

Bjorklund, D. F., & Causey, K. B. (2018). *Children's thinking: Cognitive development and individual differences* (6th ed.). Thousand Oaks, CA: Sage.

Bjorklund, D. F., & Ellis, B. J. (2014). Children, childhood, and development in evolutionary perspective. *Developmental Review, 34,* 225–264.

Bjorklund, D. F., Schneider, W., Cassel, W. S., & Ashley, E. (1994). Training and extension of a memory strategy: Evidence for utilization deficiencies in high- and low-IQ children. *Child Development, 65,* 951–965.

Bjorklund, D. F., & Sellers, P. D. H. (2014). Memory development in evolutionary perspective. In P. J. Bauer & R. Fivush (Eds.), *Wiley handbook on the development of children's memory* (Vol. 1, pp. 126–156). Chichester, UK: Wiley-Blackwell.

Björkqvist, K. (2018). Gender differences in aggression. *Current Opinion in Psychology, 19,* 39–42.

Black, L. L., Johnson, R., & VanHoose, L. (2015). The relationship between perceived racism/discrimination and health among Black American women: A review of the literature from 2003 to 2013. *Journal of Racial and Ethnic Health Disparities, 2,* 11–20.

Black, M. M. (2005). Failure to thrive. In M. C. Roberts (Ed.), *Handbook of pediatric psychology and psychiatry* (3rd ed., pp. 499–511). New York: Guilford.

Black, R. E. (2017). Patterns of growth in early childhood and infectious disease and nutritional determinants. *Nestle Nutrition Institute Workshop Series, 87,* 63–72.

Black, R. E., Victora, C. G., Walker, S. P., Bhutta, Z. A., Christian, P., de Onis, M. et al. (2013). Maternal and child undernutrition and overweight in low-income and middle-income countries. *Lancet, 382,* 427–451.

Blackwell, C., Moscovis, S., Hall, S., Burns, C., & Scott, R. J. (2015). Exploring the risk factors for sudden infant deaths and their role in inflammatory responses to infection. *Frontiers in Immunology, 6,* 1–8.

Blackwell, L. S., Trzesniewski, K. H., & Dweck, C. S. (2007). Implicit theories of intelligence predict achievement across an adolescent transition: A longitudinal study and an intervention. *Child Development, 78,* 246–263.

Blair, B. L., Perry, N. B., O'Brien, M., Calkins, S. D., Keane, S. P., & Shanahan, L. (2014). The indirect effects of maternal emotion socialization on friendship quality in middle childhood. *Developmental Psychology, 50,* 566–576.

Blair, C. (2010). Stress and the development of self-regulation in context. *Child Development Perspectives, 4,* 181–188.

Blair, C. (2016). Developmental science and executive function. *Current Directions in Psychological Science, 25,* 3–7.

Blair, C., Grander, D. A., Willoughby, M., Mills-Koonce, R., Cox, M., Greenberg, M. T., et al. (2011). Salivary cortisol mediates effects of poverty and parenting on executive functions in early childhood. *Child Development, 82,* 1970–1984.

Blair, C., & Raver, C. C. (2012). Child development in the context of adversity: Experiential canalization of brain and behavior. *American Psychologist, 67,* 309–318.

Blake, J., & Boysson-Bardies, B. de (1992). Patterns in babbling: A cross-linguistic study. *Journal of Child Language, 19,* 51–74.

Blakemore, J. E. O. (2003). Children's beliefs about violating gender norms: Boys shouldn't look like girls, and girls shouldn't act like boys. *Sex Roles, 48,* 411–419.

Blakemore, J. E. O., Berenbaum, S. A., & Liben, L. S. (2009). *Gender development.* New York: Psychology Press.

Blakemore, J. E. O., & Hill, C. A. (2008). The Child Gender Socialization Scale: A measure to compare traditional and feminist parents. *Sex Roles, 58,* 192–207.

Blankenship, S. L., Redcay, E., Dougherty, L. R., & Riggins, T. (2017). Development of hippocampal functional connectivity during childhood. *Human Brain Mapping, 38,* 182–201.

Blankson, A. N., O'Brien, M., Leerkes, E. M., Marcovitch, S., Calkins, S. D., & Weaver, J. M. (2013). Developmental dynamics of emotion and cognition processes in preschoolers. *Child Development, 84,* 346–360.

Blass, E. M., Ganchrow, J. R., & Steiner, J. E. (1984). Classical conditioning in newborn humans 2–48 hours of age. *Infant Behavior and Development, 7,* 223–235.

Bleich, S. N., Vercammen, K. A., Zatz, L. Y., Frelier, J. M., Ebbeling, C. B., & Peeters, A. (2018). Interventions to prevent global childhood overweight and obesity: A systematic review. *Lancet Diabetes & Endocrinology, 6,* 332–346.

Blood-Siegfried, J. (2009). The role of infection and inflammation in sudden infant death syndrome. *Immunopharmacology and Immunotoxicology, 31,* 516–23.

Bloom, P. (1999). The role of semantics in solving the bootstrapping problem. In R. Jackendoff & P. Bloom (Eds.), *Language, logic, and concepts* (pp. 285–309). Cambridge, MA: MIT Press.

Bloom, T., Glass, N., Curry, M. A., Hernandez, R., & Houck, G. (2013). Maternal stress exposures, reactions, and priorities for stress reduction among low-income, urban women. *Journal of Midwifery and Women's Health, 58,* 167–174.

Blumberg, F. C., Deater-Deckard, K., Calvert, S. L., Flynn, R. M., Green, C. S., Arnold, D., & Brooks, P. J. (2019). Digital games as a context for children's cognitive development: Research recommendations and policy considerations. *Social Policy Report of the Society for Research in Child Development, 32*(1).

Bode, M. M., D'Eugenio, D. B., Mettelman, B. B., & Gross, S. J. (2014). Predictive validity of the Bayley, Third Edition, at 2 years for intelligence quotient at 4 years in preterm infants. *Journal of Developmental and Behavioral Pediatrics, 35,* 570–575.

Bodrova, E., & Leong, D. J. (2007). *Tools of the mind: The Vygotskian approach to early childhood education* (2nd ed.). Upper Saddle River, NJ: Merrill Prentice Hall.

Boe, J. L., & Woods, R. J. (2018). Parents' influence on infants' gender-typed toy preferences. *Sex Roles, 79,* 358–373.

Bogin, B. (2001). *The growth of humanity.* New York: Wiley-Liss.

Bogin, B. (2013). Recent advances in growth research: Nutritional, molecular, and endocrine perspectives. In M. W. Gillman, P. D. Gluckman, & R. G. Rosenfeld (Eds.), *Recent advances in growth research: Nutritional, molecular and endocrine perspectives* (Vol. 71, pp. 115–126). Basel, Switzerland: Karger.

Bogin, B., Hermanussen, M., & Scheffler, C. (2018). As tall as my peers: Similarity in body height between migrants and hosts. *Anthropologischer Anzeiger [Journal of Biological and Clinical Anthropology], 74,* 363–374.

Bogin, B., & Varela-Silva, M. (2010). Leg length, body proportion, and health: A review with a note on beauty. International *Journal of Environmental Research and Public Health, 7,* 1047–1075.

Bohannon, J. N., III, & Bonvillian, J. D. (2013). Theoretical approaches to language acquisition. In J. B. Gleason & N. B. Ratner (Eds.), *The development of language* (8th ed., pp. 190–240). Upper Saddle River, NJ: Pearson.

Bohannon, J. N., III, & Stanowicz, L. (1988). The issue of negative evidence: Adult responses to children's language errors. *Developmental Psychology, 24,* 684–689.

Boivin, M., Brendgen, M., Vitaro, F., Dionne, G., Girard, A., Pérusse, D., & Tremblay, R. E. (2013). Strong genetic contribution to peer relationship difficulties at school entry: Findings from a longitudinal twin study. *Child Development, 84,* 1098–1114.

Boivin, M., & Hassan, G. (2015). Ethnic identity and psychological adjustment in transracial adoptees: A review of the literature. *Ethnic and Racial Studies, 38,* 1084–1103.

Bokslag, A., van Weissenbruch, M., Mol, B. W., & de Groot, C. J. (2016). Preeclampsia: Short and long-term consequences for mother and neonate. *Early Human Development, 11,* 47–50.

Boles, R. E., Burdell, A., Johnson, S. L., Gavin, W. J., Davies, P. L., & Bellows, L. L. (2014). Home food and activity assessment. Development and validation of an instrument for diverse families of young children. *Appetite, 80,* 23–27.

Bolin, I. (2006). *Growing up in a culture of respect: Child rearing in highland Peru.* Austin, TX: University of Texas Press.

Bolisetty, S., Bajuk, B., Me, A.-L., Vincent, T., Sutton, L., & Lui, K. (2006). Preterm outcome table (POT): A simple tool to aid counselling parents of very preterm infants. *Australian and New Zealand Journal of Obstetrics and Gynaecology, 46,* 189–192.

Bono, K. E., & Bizri, R. (2014). The role of language and private speech in preschoolers' self-regulation. *Early Child Development and Care, 184,* 658–670.

Bono, M. A., & Stifter, C. A. (2003). Maternal attention-directing strategies and infant focused attention during problem solving. *Infancy, 4,* 235–250.

Book, A. S., Starzyk, K. B., & Quinsey, V. L. (2001). The relationship between testosterone and aggression: A meta-analysis. *Aggression and Violent Behavior, 6,* 579–599.

Booker, J. A., & Dunsmore, J. C. (2017). Affective social competence in adolescence: Current findings and future directions. *Social Development, 26,* 3–20.

Booren, L. M., Downer, J. T., & Vitiello, V. E. (2012). Observations of children's interactions with teachers, peers, and tasks across preschool classroom activity settings. *Early Education and Development, 23,* 517–538.

Booth, A., Scott, M. E., & King, V. (2010). Father residence and adolescent problem behavior: Are youth always better off in two-parent families? *Journal of Family Issues, 31,* 585–605.

Booth, R. D. L., & Happé, F. G. E. (2016). Evidence of reduced global processing in autism spectrum disorder. *Journal of Autism and Developmental Disorders, 46,* ISSN 1573-3472.

Booth-LaForce, C., Groh, A. M., Burchinal, M. R., Roisman, G. I., Owen, M. T., & Cox, M. J. (2014). Caregiving and contextual sources of continuity and change in attachment security from infancy to late adolescence. In C. Booth-LaForce & G. I. Roisman (Eds.), The adult attachment interview: Psychometrics, stability and change from infancy, and developmental origins. *Monographs of the Society for Research in Child Development, 79*(3, Serial No. 314), 67–84.

Borchert, S., Lamm, B., Graf, F., & Knopf, M. (2013). Deferred imitation in 18-month-olds from two cultural contexts: The case of Cameroonian Nso farmer and German-middle class infants. *Infant Behavior and Development, 36,* 717–727.

Borghese, M. M., Tremblay, M. S., Katzmarzyk, P. T., Tudor-Locke, C., Schuna, J. M., Jr., Leduc, G., et al. (2015). Mediating role of television time, diet patterns, physical activity and sleep duration in the association between television in the bedroom and adiposity in 10-year-old children. *International Journal of Behavioral Nutrition and Physical Activity, 12,* Art. No. 60.

Bornstein, M. H. (2015). Children's parents. In M. H. Bornstein & T. Leventhal (Eds.), *Handbook of child psychology and developmental science: Vol. 4. Ecological settings and processes* (7th ed., pp. 55–132). Hoboken, NJ: Wiley.

Bornstein, M. H., & Arterberry, M. E. (1999). Perceptual development. In M. H. Bornstein & M. E. Lamb (Eds.), *Developmental psychology: An advanced textbook* (pp. 231–274). Mahwah, NJ: Erlbaum.

Bornstein, M. H., & Arterberry, M. E. (2003). Recognition, discrimination, and categorization of smiling by 5-month-old infants. *Developmental Science, 6,* 585–599.

Bornstein, M. H., Arterberry, M. E., & Mash, C. (2010). Infant object categorization transcends object–context relations. *Infant Behavior and Development, 33,* 7–15.

Bornstein, M. H., Putnick, D. L., Gartstein, M. A., Hahn, C.-S., Auestad, N., & O'Connor, D. L. (2015). Infant temperament: Stability by age, gender, birth order, term status, and socioeconomic status. *Child Development, 86,* 844–863.

Bornstein, M. H., Vibbert, M., Tal, J., & O'Donnell, K. (1992). Toddler language and play in the second year: Stability, covariation, and influences of parenting. *First Language, 12,* 323–338.

Borst, C. G. (1995). *Catching babies: The professionalization of childbirth, 1870–1920.* Cambridge, MA: Harvard University Press.

Borst, G., Poirel, N., Pineau, A., Cassotti, M., & Houdé, O. (2013). Inhibitory control efficiency in a Piaget-like class-inclusion task in school-age children and adults: A developmental negative priming study. *Developmental Psychology, 49,* 1366–1374.

Bos, H. (2013). Lesbian-mother families formed through donor insemination. In A. E. Goldberg & K. R. Allen (Eds.), *LGBT-parent families: Innovations in research and implications for practice* (pp. 21–37). New York: Springer.

Bos, H., & Sandfort, T. G. M. (2010). Children's gender identity in lesbian and heterosexual two-parent families. *Sex Roles, 62,* 114–126.

Bosseler, A. N., Teinonen, T., Tervaniemi, M., & Huotilainen, M. (2016). Infant-directed speech enhances statistical learning in newborn infants: An ERP study. *PLOS ONE, 11*(9), e0162177.

Bost, K. K., Shin, N., McBride, B. A., Brown, G. L., Vaughn, B. E., & Coppola, G. (2006). Maternal secure base scripts, children's attachment security, and mother–child narrative styles. *Attachment and Human Development, 8,* 241–260.

Bouchard, T. J. (2004). Genetic influence on human psychological traits: A survey. *Current Directions in Psychological Science, 13,* 148–151.

Boucher, O., Bastien, C. H., Saint-Amour, D., Dewailly, E., Ayotte, P., Jacobson, J. L., Jacobson, et al. (2010). Prenatal exposure to methylmercury and PCBs affects distinct stages of information processing: An event-related potential study with Inuit children. *Neurotoxicology, 31,* 373–384.

Boucher, O., Jacobson, S. W., Plusquellec, P., Dewailly, E., Ayotte, P., Forget-Dubois, N., et al. (2012). Prenatal methylmercury, postnatal lead exposure, and evidence of attention deficit/hyperactivity disorder among Inuit children in Arctic Québec. *Environmental Health Perspectives, 120,* 1456–1461.

Boucher, O., Muckle, G., & Bastien, C. H. (2009). Prenatal exposure to polychlorinated biphenyls: A neuropsychologic analysis. *Environmental Health Perspectives, 117,* 7–16.

Bouldin, P. (2006). An investigation of the fantasy predisposition and fantasy style of children with imaginary companions. *Journal of Genetic Psychology, 167,* 17–29.

Bouza, J., Caacho-Thompson, D. E., Carlo, G. C., Franco, X., Coll, C. G., Halgunseth, L. C., et al. (2018). The science is clear:

Separating families has long-term damaging psychological and health consequences for children, families, and communities. *SRCD (Society for Research in Child Development) Statement of the Evidence.* Retrieved from srcd.org/sites/default/files/documents/the_science_is_clear.pdf

Bower, A. A., & Casas, J. F. (2016). What parents do when children are good: Parent reports of strategies for reinforcing early childhood prosocial behaviors. *Journal of Child and Family Studies, 25,* 1310–1324.

Bowers, J. S., & Bowers, P. N. (2017). Beyond phonics: The case for teaching children the logic of the English spelling system. *Educational Psychologist, 52,* 124–141.

Bowker, J. C., Rubin, K. H., Buskirk-Cohen, A., Rose-Krasnor, L., & Both-LaForce, C. (2010). Behavioral changes predicting temporal changes in perceived popular status. *Journal of Applied Developmental Psychology, 31,* 126–133.

Bowlby, J. (1969). *Attachment and loss: Vol. 1. Attachment.* New York: Basic Books.

Bowlby, J. (1980). *Attachment and loss: Vol. 3. Loss.* New York: Basic Books.

Bowman, L. C., Liu, D., Meltzoff, A. N., & Wellman, H. M. (2012). Neural correlates of belief–desire reasoning in 7- and 8-year-old children: An event-related potential study. *Developmental Science, 15,* 618–632.

Boxer, P., Groves, C. L., & Docherty, M. (2015). Video games do indeed influence children and adolescents' aggression, prosocial behavior, and academic performance: A clearer reading of Ferguson (2015). *Perspectives on Psychological Science, 10,* 671–673.

Boyan, A., & Sherry, J. L. (2011). The challenge in creating games for education: Aligning mental models with game models. *Child Development Perspectives, 5,* 82–87.

Boyatzis, C. J. (2000). The artistic evolution of mommy: A longitudinal case study of symbolic and social processes. In C. J. Boyatzis & M. W. Watson (Eds.), *Symbolic and social constraints on the development of children's artistic style* (pp. 5–29). San Francisco: Jossey-Bass.

Boyce, W. T., & Kobor, M. S. (2015). Development and the epigenome: The "synapse" of gene–environment interplay. *Developmental Science, 18,* 1–23.

Boyle, C. A., Boulet, S., Schieve, L. A., Cohen, R. A., Blumberg, S. J., Yeargin-Allsopp, M., et al. (2011). Trends in the prevalence of developmental disabilities in U.S. children, 1997–2008. *Pediatrics, 127,* 1034–1042.

Boysson-Bardies, B. de, & Vihman, M. M. (1991). Adaptation to language: Evidence from babbling and first words in four languages. *Language, 67,* 297–319.

Brackett, M. A., Rivers, S. E., & Salovey, P. (2011). Emotional intelligence: Implications for personal, social, academic, and workplace success. *Social and Personality Compass, 5,* 88–103.

Bradley, R. H. (1994). The HOME Inventory: Review and reflections. In H. W. Reese (Ed.), *Advances in child development and behavior* (Vol. 25, pp. 241–288). San Diego: Academic Press.

Bradley, R. H., & Caldwell, B. M. (1982). The consistency of the home environment and its relation to child development. *International Journal of Behavioral Development, 5,* 445–465.

Bradley, R. H., & Corwyn, R. F. (2003). Age and ethnic variations in family process mediators of SES. In M. H. Bornstein & R. H. Bradley (Eds.), *Socioeconomic status, parenting, and child development* (pp. 161–188). Mahwah, NJ: Erlbaum.

Bradley, R. H., Corwyn, R. F., McAdoo, H. P., & García Coll, C. (2001). The home environments of children in the United States. Part I: Variations by age, ethnicity, and poverty status. *Child Development, 72,* 1844–1867.

Bradley, R. H., McKelvy, L. M., & Whiteside-Mansell, L. (2011). Does the quality of stimulation and support in the home environment moderate the effect of early education programs? *Child Development, 82,* 2110–2122.

Bradley, R. H., Whiteside, L., Mundfrom, D. J., Casey, P. H., Kelleher, K. J.,& Pope, S. K. (1994). Contribution of early intervention and early caregiving experiences to resilience in low-birthweight, premature children living in poverty. *Journal of Clinical Child Psychology, 23,* 425–434.

Brady, K. W., & Goodman, J. C. (2014). The type, but not the amount, of information available influences toddlers' fast mapping and retention of new words. *American Journal of Speech–Language Pathology, 23,* 120–133.

Brady, S. A. (2011). Efficacy of phonics teaching for reading outcomes: Indications from post-NRP research. In S. A. Brady, D. Braze, & C. A. Fowler (Eds.), *Explaining individual differences in reading: Theory and evidence* (pp. 69–96). New York: Psychology Press.

Braine, L. G., Schauble, L., Kugelmass, S., & Winter, A. (1993). Representation of depth by children: Spatial strategies and lateral biases. *Developmental Psychology, 29,* 466–479.

Braine, M. D. S. (1994). Is nativism sufficient? *Journal of Child Language, 21,* 1–23.

Brand, S. R., Schechter, J. C., Hammen, C. L., Brocque, R. L., & Brennan, P. A. (2011). Do adolescent offspring of women with PTSD experience higher levels of chronic and episodic stress? *Journal of Trauma and Stress, 24,* 399–404.

Brannon, E. M., Lutz, D. J., & Cordes, S. (2006). The development of area discrimination and its implications for number representation in infancy. *Developmental Science, 9,* F59–F64.

Brasil, P., Pereira, J. P., Moreira, E., Nogueira, R., Damasceno, L., Mayumi, P. D., et al. (2016). Zika virus infection in pregnant women in Rio de Janeiro. *New England Journal of Medicine, 375,* 2321–2334.

Braswell, G. S. (2006). Sociocultural contexts for the early development of semiotic production. *Psychological Bulletin, 132,* 877–894.

Braswell, G. S., & Callanan, M. A. (2003). Learning to draw recognizable graphic representations during mother–child interactions. *Merrill-Palmer Quarterly, 49,* 471–494.

Braungart-Rieker, J. M., Hill-Soderlund, A. L., & Karrass, J. (2010). Fear and anger reactivity trajectories from 4 to 16 months: The roles of temperament, regulation, and maternal sensitivity. *Developmental Psychology, 46,* 791–804.

Brazelton, T. B., Koslowski, B., & Tronick, E. (1976). Neonatal behavior among urban Zambians and Americans. *Journal of the American Academy of Child Psychiatry, 15,* 97–107.

Brazelton, T. B., & Nugent, J. K. (2011). *Neonatal Behavioral Assessment Scale* (4th ed.). London: Mac Keith Press.

Brazelton, T. B., Nugent, J. K., & Lester, B. M. (1987). Neonatal Behavioral Assessment Scale. In J. D. Osofsky (Ed.), *Handbook of infant development* (2nd ed., pp. 780–817). New York: Wiley.

Breeman, L., Baumann, N., Bartmann, P., Wolke, D., & Warwick, C. (2017). Neonatal predictors of cognitive ability in adults born very preterm: A prospective cohort study. *Developmental Medicine and Child Neurology, 59,* 477–483.

Bremner, J. G., Slater, A. M., & Johnson, S. P. (2015). Perception of object persistence: The origins of object permanence in infancy. *Child Development Perspectives, 9,* 7–13.

Bremner, J. G., Slater, A. M., Mason, U. C., Spring, J., & Johnson, S. P. (2013). Trajectory perception and object continuity: Effects of shape and color change on 4-month-olds' perception of object identity. *Developmental Psychology, 49,* 1021–1026.

Brendgen, M., Boivin, M., Dionne, G., Barker, E. D., Vitaro, F., Girard, A., Tremblay, R., & Pérusse, D. (2011). Gene-environment processes linking aggression, peer victimization, and the teacher–child relationship. *Child Development, 82,* 2021–2036.

Brennan, L. M., Shelleby, E. C., Shaw, D. S., Gardner, F., Dishion, T. J., & Wilson, M. (2013). Indirect effects of the family check-up on school-age academic achievement through improvements in parenting in early childhood. *Journal of Educational Psychology, 105,* 762–773.

Brenner, E., & Salovey, P. (1997). Emotional regulation during childhood: Developmental, interpersonal, and individual considerations. In P. Salovey & D. Sluyter (Eds.), *Emotional literacy and emotional development* (pp. 168–192). New York: Basic Books.

Bretherton, I., Fritz, J., Zahn-Waxler, C., & Ridgeway, D. (1986). Learning to talk about emotions: A functionalist perspective. *Child Development, 57,* 529–548.

Bretherton, I., & Munholland, K. A. (2008). Internal working models in attachment relationships. In J. Cassidy & P. R. Shaver (Eds.), *Handbook of attachment: Theory, research, and clinical applications* (2nd ed., pp. 102–127). New York: Guilford.

Brewster, K. L., Tillman, K. H., & Jokinen-Gordon, H. (2014). Demographic characteristics of lesbian parents in the United States. *Population Research and Policy Review, 33,* 485–502.

Bridges, M., Cohen, S. R., McGuire, L. W., Yamada, H., Fuller, B., Mireles, L., & Scott, L. (2012). Bien Educado: Measuring the social behaviors of Mexican American children. *Early Childhood Research Quarterly, 27,* 555–567.

Bridgett, D. J., Gartstein, M. A., Putnam, S. P., McKay, T., Iddins, R., Robertson, C., et al. (2009). Maternal and contextual influences and the effect of temperament development during infancy on parenting in toddlerhood. *Infant Behavior and Development, 32,* 103–116.

Brisch, K. H., Bechinger, D., Betzler, S., Heineman, H., Kachele, H., Pohlandt, F., et al. (2005). Attachment quality in very low-birthweight premature infants in relation to maternal attachment representations and neurological development. *Parenting: Science and Practice, 5,* 11–32.

Broaders, S., Cook, S. W., Mitchell, Z., & Goldin-Meadow, S. (2007). Making children gesture brings out implicit knowledge and leads to learning. *Journal of Experimental Psychology, General, 136,* 539–550.

Brody, L. R. (1999). *Gender, emotion, and the family.* Cambridge, MA: Harvard University Press.

Brodzinsky, D. M. (2011). Children's understanding of adoption: Developmental and clinical implications. *Professional Psychology: Research and Practice, 42,* 200–207.

Bronfenbrenner, U., & Morris, P. A. (2006). The bioecological model of human development. In R. M. Lerner (Ed.), *Handbook of child psychology: Vol. 1. Theoretical models of human development* (6th ed., pp. 793–828). Hoboken, NJ: Wiley.

Bronson, G. W. (1994). Infants' transitions toward adult-like scanning. *Child Development, 65,* 1243–1261.

Brooker, R. J., Buss, K. A., Lemery-Chalfant, K., Aksan, N., Davidson, R. J., & Goldsmith, H. H. (2013). The development of stranger fear in infancy and toddlerhood: Normative development, individual differences, antecedents, and outcomes. *Developmental Science, 16,* 864–878.

Brooks, K., Xu, X., Chen, W., Zhou, K., Neale, B., & Lowe, N. (2006). The analysis of 51 genes in DSM-IV combined type attention deficit hyperactivity disorder: Association signals in DRD4, DAT1, and 16 other genes. *Molecular Psychiatry, 11,* 935–953.

Brooks, R., & Meltzoff, A. N. (2005). The development of gaze following and its relation to language. *Developmental Science, 8,* 535–543.

Brooks, R., & Meltzoff, A. N. (2008). Infant gaze following and pointing predict accelerated vocabulary growth through two years of age: A longitudinal, growth curve modeling study. *Journal of Child Language, 35,* 207–220.

Brooks, R., & Meltzoff, A. N. (2015). Connecting the dots from infancy to childhood: A longitudinal study connecting gaze following, language, and explicit theory of mind. *Journal of Experimental Child Psychology, 130,* 67–78.

Brooks-Gunn, J., Han, W.-J., & Waldfogel, J. (2010). First-year maternal employment and child development in the first 7 years. *Monographs of the Society for Research in Child Development, 75*(2, Serial No. 296).

Brooks-Gunn, J., Klebanov, P. K., Smith, J., Duncan, G. J., & Lee, K. (2003). The Black–White test score gap in young children. Contributions of test and family characteristics. *Applied Developmental Science, 7,* 239–252.

Brown, A., & Harries, V. (2015). Infant sleep and night feeding patterns during later infancy: Association with breastfeeding frequency, daytime complementary food intake, and infant weight. *Breastfeeding Medicine, 10,* 246–252.

Brown, B. B., Lohr, M. J., & McClenahan, E. L. (1986). Early adolescents' perceptions of peer pressure. *Journal of Early Adolescence, 6,* 139–154.

Brown, C. S., & Bigler, R. S. (2004). Children's perceptions of gender discrimination. *Developmental Psychology, 40,* 714–726.

Brown, C. S., & Stone, E. A. (2018). Environmental and social contributions to children's gender-typed toy play: The role of family, peers, and media. In E. S. Weisgram & L. M. Dinella (Eds.), *Gender typing of children's toys: How early play experiences impact development* (pp. 121–140). New York: American Psychological Association.

Brown, G. L., Mangelsdorf, S. C., Agathen, J. M., & Ho, M.-H. (2008). Young children's psychological selves: Convergence with maternal reports of child personality. *Social Development, 17,* 161–182.

Brown, G. L., Mangelsdorf, S. C., & Neff, C. (2012). Father involvement, paternal sensitivity, and father–child attachment security in the first 3 years. *Journal of Family Psychology, 26,* 421–430.

Brown, G. L., Schoppe-Sullivan, S. J., Mangelsdorf, S. C., & Neff, C. (2010). Observed and reported supportive coparenting as predictors of infant–mother and infant–father attachment security. *Early Child Development and Care, 180,* 121–137.

Brown, J. D., Harris, S. K., Woods, E. R., Buman, M. P., & Cox, J. E. (2012). Longitudinal study of depressive symptoms and social support in adolescent mothers. *Maternal and Child Health Journal, 16,* 894–901.

Brown, K. A., Patel, D. R., & Darmawan, D. (2017). Participation in sports in relation to adolescent growth and development. *Translational Pediatrics, 6,* 150–159.

Brown, M.C., Sibley D. E., Washington, J. A., Rogers, T. T., Edwards, J. R., MacDonald, M. C., & Seidenberg, M. S. (2015). Impact of dialect use on a basic component of learning to read. *Frontiers in Psychology, 6,* Art. No. 196.

Brown, R. W. (1973). *A first language: The early stages.* Cambridge, MA: Harvard University Press.

Browne, J. V., & Talmi, A. (2005). Family-based intervention to enhance infant–parent relationships in the neonatal intensive care unit. *Journal of Pediatric Psychology, 30,* 667–677.

Brownell, C. A., & Kopp, C. B. (2007). Transitions in toddler socioemotional development: Behavior, understanding, relationships. In C. A. Brownell & C. B. Kopp (Eds.), *Socioemotional development in the toddler years: Transitions and transformations* (pp. 1–40). New York: Guilford.

Brownell, C. A., Nichols, S. R., Svetlova, M., Zerwas, S., & Ramani, G. (2010). The head bone's connected to the neck bone: When do toddlers represent their own body topography? *Child Development, 81,* 797–810.

Brownell, C. A., Zerwas, S., & Ramani, G. B. (2007). "So big": The development of body self-awareness in toddlers. *Child Development, 78,* 1426–1440.

Bruderer, A., Danielson, D. K., Kandhadai, P., & Werker, J. F. (2015). Sensorimotor influences on speech perception in infancy. *Proceedings of the National Academy of Sciences, 112,* 13531–13536.

Brugué, M. S., & Burriel, P. (2016). Outlining windows of achievement of intersubjective milestones in typically developing toddlers. *Infant Mental Health Journal, 37,* 356–371.

Brumariu, L. E., Kerns, K. A., & Seibert, A. (2012). Mother–child attachment, emotion regulation, and anxiety symptoms in middle childhood. *Personal Relationships, 19,* 569–585.

Brummelman, E., Crocker, J., & Bushman, B. J. (2016). The praise paradox: When and why praise backfires in children with low self-esteem. *Child Development Perspectives, 10,* 111–115.

Brummelman, E., Nelemans, S. A., Thomaes, S., & Orbio de Castro, B. (2017). When parents' praise inflates, children's self-esteem deflates. *Child Development, 88,* 1799–1809.

Brummelman, E., & Thomaes, S. (2017). How children construct views of themselves: A social-developmental perspective. *Child Development, 88,* 1763–1773.

Bruschweiler-Stern, N. (2004). A multifocal neonatal intervention. In A. J. Sameroff, S. C. McDonough, & K. L. Rosenblum (Eds.), *Treating parent–infant relationship problems* (pp. 188–212). New York: Guilford.

Bruzzese, J., & Fisher, C. B. (2003). Assessing and enhancing the research consent capacity of children and youth. *Applied Developmental Science, 7,* 13–26.

Bryan, A. E., & Dix, T. (2009). Mothers' emotions and behavioral support during interactions with toddlers: The role of child temperament. *Social Development, 18,* 647–670.

Bryant, P., & Nunes, T. (2002). Children's understanding of mathematics. In U. Goswami (Ed.), *Blackwell handbook of childhood cognitive development* (pp. 412–439). Malden, MA: Blackwell.

Brydges, C. R., Reid, C. L., Fox, A. M., & Anderson, M. (2012). A unitary executive function predicts intelligence in children. *Intelligence, 40,* 458–469.

Buchanan, C. M., Maccoby, E. E., & Dornbusch, S. M. (1996). *Adolescents after divorce.* Cambridge, MA: Harvard University Press.

Buchanan-Barrow, E., & Barrett, M. (1998). Children's rule discrimination within the context of the school. *British Journal of Developmental Psychology, 16,* 539–551.

Buchsbaum, D., Dridgers, S., Weisberg, D. S., & Gopnik, A. (2012). The power of possibility: Causal learning, counterfactual reasoning, and pretend play. *Philosophical Transactions of the Royal Society B, 367,* 2202–2212.

Buckingham-Howes, S., Berger, S., Shafer, S., Scaletti, L. A., & Black, M. M. (2013). Systematic review of prenatal cocaine exposure and adolescent development. *Pediatrics, 13,* e1917–e1936.

Budday, S., Steinman, P., & Kuhl, E. (2015). Physical biology of human brain development. *Frontiers in Cellular Neuroscience, 9,* 257.

Buehler, C., & O'Brien, M. (2011). Mothers' part-time employment: Associations with mother and family well-being. *Journal of Family Psychology, 25,* 895–906.

Bugental, D. B., Corpuz, R., & Schwartz, A. (2012). Preventing children's aggression: Outcomes of an early intervention. *Developmental Psychology, 48,* 1443–1449.

Bugental, D. B., & Happaney, K. (2004). Predicting infant maltreatment in low-income families: The interactive effects of maternal attributions and child status at birth. *Developmental Psychology, 40,* 234–243.

Buhrmester, D. (1996). Need fulfillment, interpersonal competence, and the developmental contexts of early adolescent friendship. In W. M. Bukowski, A. F. Newcomb, & W. W. Hartup (Eds.), *The company they keep: Friendship in childhood and adolescence* (p. 168). New York: Cambridge University Press.

Buhrmester, D., & Furman, W. (1990). Perceptions of sibling relationships during middle childhood and adolescence. *Child Development, 61,* 1387–1398.

Buhs, E. S., Ladd, G. W., & Herald-Brown, S. L. (2010). Victimization and exclusion: Links to peer rejection, classroom engagement, and achievement. In S. R. Jimerson, S. M. Swearer, & D. L. Espelage (Eds.), *Handbook of bullying in schools: An international perspective* (pp. 163–172). New York: Routledge.

Bukowski, W. M., & Raufelder, D. (2018). Peers and the self. In W. M. Bukowski, B. Laursen, & K. H. Rubin (Eds.), *Handbook of peer interactions, relationships, and groups* (2nd ed., pp. 141–156). New York: Guilford.

Bulf, H., Johnson, S. P., & Valenza, E. (2011). Visual statistical learning in the newborn infant. *Cognition, 121,* 127–132.

Bullock, M., & Lutkenhaus, P. (1990). Who am I? The development of self-understanding in toddlers. *Merrill-Palmer Quarterly, 36,* 217–238.

Bulotsky-Shearer, R. J., Wen, X., Faria, A.-M., Hahs-Vaughn, D. L., & Korfmacher, J. (2012). National profiles of classroom quality and family involvement: A multilevel examination of proximal influences on Head Start children's school readiness. *Early Childhood Research Quarterly, 27,* 627–639.

Buon, M., Habib, M., & Frey, D. (2017). Moral development: Conflicts and compromises, In J. A. Sommerville & J. Decety (Eds.), *Social cognition: Development across the lifespan* (pp. 129–150). New York: Routledge.

Burchinal, M. (2018). Measuring early care and education quality. *Child Development Perspectives, 12,* 3–9.

Burchinal, M., Kainz, K., & Cai, Y. (2011). How well do our measures of quality predict child outcomes? A meta-analysis and coordinated analysis of data from large-scale studies of early childhood settings. In M. Zeslow (Ed.), *Reasons to take stock and strengthen our measures of quality* (pp. 11–31). Baltimore, MD: Paul H. Brookes.

Burchinal, M., Magnuson, K., Powell, D., & Hong, S. S. (2015). Early child care and education. In M. H. Bornstein & T. Leventhal (Eds.), *Handbook of child psychology and developmental science: Vol. 4. Ecological settings and processes* (7th ed., pp. 223–267). Hoboken, NJ: Wiley.

Bureau, J.-F., Martin, J., Yurkowski, K., Schmiedel, S., Quan, J., Moss, E., et al. (2017). Correlates of child–father and child–mother attachment in the preschool years. *Attachment & Human Development, 19,* 130–150.

Burgos, M., Al-Adeimi, M., & Brown, J. (2017). Protective factors of family life for immigrant youth. *Child and Adolescent Social Work, 34,* 235–245.

Burkitt, E., Lowry, R., & Fotheringham, F. (2016). Children's understanding of mixed emotions in self and other: Verbal reports and visual representations. *Infant and Child Development, 27,* e2076.

Burnette, J. L., O'Boyle, E. H., VanEpps, E. M., Pollack, J. M., & Finkel, E. J. (2013). Mind-sets matter: A meta-analytic review of implicit theories and self-regulation. *Psychological Bulletin, 139,* 655–701.

Burns, C. E. (2000). *Pediatric primary care: A handbook for nurse practitioners.* Philadelphia: Saunders.

Burton, R., Giddy, J., & Stinson, K. (2015). Prevention of mother-to-child transmission in South Africa: An ever-changing landscape. *Obstetric Medicine, 8,* 5–12.

Burts, D. C., Hart, C. H., Charlesworth, R., Fleege, P. O., Mosley, J., & Thomasson, R. H. (1992). Observed activities and stress behaviors of children in developmentally appropriate and inappropriate kindergarten classrooms. *Early Childhood Research Quarterly, 7,* 297–318.

Bush, K. R., & Peterson, G. W. (2008). Family influences on child development. In T. P. Gullotta & G. M. Blau (Eds.), *Handbook of child behavioral issues: Evidence-based approaches to prevention and treatment* (pp. 43–67). New York: Routledge.

Bushman, B. J., Gollwitzer, M., & Cruz, C. (2015). There is broad consensus: Media researchers agree that violent media increase aggression in children, and pediatricians and parents concur. *Psychology of Popular Media Culture, 4,* 200–214.

Bushnell, E. W., & Boudreau, J. P. (1993). Motor development and the mind: The potential role of motor abilities as a determinant of aspects of perceptual development. *Child Development, 64,* 1005–1021.

Bushnell, I. W. R. (2001). Mother's face recognition in newborn infants: Learning and memory. *Infant and Child Development, 10,* 67–74.

Bussey, K. (1992). Lying and truthfulness: Children's definitions, standards, and evaluative reactions. *Child Development, 63,* 129–137.

Buswell, S. D., & Spatz, D. L. (2007). Parent–infant co-sleeping and its relationship to breastfeeding. *Journal of Pediatric Health Care, 21,* 22–28.

Butcher, L. M., Davis, O. S. P., Craig, I. W., & Plomin, R. (2008). Genome-wide quantitative trait locus association scan of general cognitive ability using pooled DNA and 500K single nucleotide polymorphism microarrays. *Genes, Brains and Behavior, 7,* 435–446.

Buttelmann, D., & Böhm, R. (2014). The ontogeny of the motivation that underlies in-group bias. *Psychological Science, 25,* 921–927.

Buttelmann, D., Over, H., Carpenter, M., & Tomasello, M. (2014). Eighteen-month-olds' false beliefs in an unexpected-contents task. *Journal of Experimental Child Psychology, 119,* 120–126.

Butterfill, S. A., & Apperly, I. A. (2013). How to construct a minimal theory of mind. *Mind & Language, 28,* 606–637.

Byrnes, J. P., & Wasik, B. A. (2009). *Language and literacy development: What educators need to know.* New York: Guilford.

C

Cabell, S. Q., Justice, L. M., Logan, J. A. R., & Konold, T. R. (2013). Emergent literacy profiles among prekindergarten children from low-SES backgrounds: Longitudinal considerations. *Early Childhood Research Quarterly, 28,* 608–620.

Cabrera, N. J., Aldoney, D., & Tamis-LeMonda, C. S. (2014). Latino fathers. In N. J. Cabrera & C. S. Tamis-LeMonda (Eds.), *Handbook of father involvement: Multidisciplinary perspectives* (2nd ed., pp. 244–250). New York: Routledge.

Cabrera, N. J., & Bradley, R. H. (2012). Latino fathers and their children. *Child Development Perspectives, 6,* 232–238.

Cabrera, N. J., Fitzgerald, H. E., Bradley, R. H., & Roggman, L. (2007). Modeling the dynamics of paternal influence on children over the life course. *Applied Developmental Science, 11,* 185–189.

Cabrera, N. J., Shannon, J. D., & Tamis-LeMonda, C. (2007). Fathers' influence on their children's cognitive and emotional development: From toddlers to pre-K. *Applied Developmental Science, 11,* 208–213.

Cadima, J., Enrico, M., Ferreira, T., Verschueren, K., Leal, T., & Matos, P. M. (2016). Self-regulation in early childhood: The interplay between family risk, temperament, and teacher interactions. *European Journal of Developmental Psychology, 13,* 341–360.

Cadman, T., Diamond, P. R., & Fearon, P. (2015). Reassessing the validity of the attachment Q-Sort: An updated meta-analysis. *Infant and Child Development, 27,* e2034.

Cai, T., & McPherson, B. (2017). Hearing loss in children with otitis media with effusion:

A systematic review. *International Journal of Audiology, 56,* 65–76.

Cain, K., & Oakhill, J. (2011). Matthew effects in young readers: Reading comprehension and reading experience aid vocabulary development. *Journal of Learning Disabilities, 44,* 431–443.

Cain, M. A., Bornick, P., & Whiteman, V. (2013). The maternal, fetal, and neonatal effects of cocaine exposure in pregnancy. *Clinical Obstetrics and Gynecology, 56,* 124–132.

Cairns, R. B., & Cairns, B. D. (2006). The making of developmental psychology. In R. M. Lerner (Ed.), *Handbook of child psychology: Vol. 1. Theoretical models of human development* (6th ed., pp. 89–165). Hoboken, NJ: Wiley.

Cairns, R. B., Xie, H., & Leung, M.-C. (1998). The popularity of friendship and the neglect of social networks: Toward a new balance. In W. M. Bukowski & A. H. Cillessen (Eds.), *Sociometry then and now: Building on six decades of measuring children's experiences with the peer group* (pp. 25–53). San Francisco: Jossey-Bass.

Calarco, J. M. (2014). Coached for the classroom: Parents' cultural transmission and children's preproduction of educational inequalities. *American Sociological Review, 79,* 1015–1037.

Calderón-Tena, C. O., Knight, G. P., & Carlo, G. (2011). The socialization of prosocial behavioral tendencies among Mexican American adolescents: The role of familism values. *Cultural Diversity & Ethnic Minority Psychology, 17,* 98–106.

Caldwell, B. M., & Bradley, R. H. (1994). Environmental issues in developmental follow-up research. In S. L. Friedman & H. C. Haywood (Eds.), *Developmental follow-up* (pp. 235–256). San Diego: Academic Press.

Calhoun, S. L., Fernandez-Mendoza, J., Vgontzas, A. N., Mayes, S. D., Liao, D., & Bixler, E. O. (2017). Behavioral profiles associated with objective sleep duration in young children with insomnia symptoms. *Journal of Abnormal Child Psychology, 45,* 337–344.

Callaghan, T. C. (1999). Early understanding and production of graphic symbols. *Child Development, 70,* 1314–1324.

Callaghan, T. C., Moll, H., Rakoczy, H., Warneken, F., Lizkowski, U., Behne, T., & Tomasello, M. (2011). Early social cognition in three cultural contexts. *Monographs of the Society for Research in Child Development, 76*(2, Serial No. 299).

Callaghan, T. C., & Rankin, M. P. (2002). Emergence of graphic symbol functioning and the question of domain specificity: A longitudinal training study. *Child Development, 73,* 359–376.

Callanan, M. A., & Siegel, D. R. (2014). Learning conventions and conventionality through conversation. In D. Matthews (Ed.), *Pragmatic development in first language acquisition* (pp. 121–138). Amsterdam, Netherlands: John Benjamins Publishing.

Calvert, S. L. (2015). Children and digital media. In M. H. Bornstein & T. Leventhal (Eds.), *Handbook of cultural developmental science: Vol. 4. Ecological settings and processes* (pp. 299–322). New York: Psychology Press.

Calvert, S. L., Strong, B. L., & Gallagher, L. (2005). Control as an engagement feature for young children's attention to, and learning of, computer content. *American Behavioral Scientist, 48,* 578–589.

Calvigioni, D., Hurd, Y. L., Harkany, T., & Keimpema, E. (2014). Neuronal substrates and functional consequences of prenatal cannabis exposure. *European Child and Adolescent Psychiatry, 23,* 931–941.

Calzada, E. J. (2010). Bringing culture into parent training with Latinos. *Cognitive Behavioral Practice, 17,* 167–175.

Calzada, E. J., Tamis-LeMonda, C. S., & Yoshikawa, H. (2013). Familismo in Mexican and Dominican families from low-income, urban communities. *Journal of Family Issues, 33,* 1–29.

Cameron, C. A., Lau, C., Fu, G., & Lee, K. (2012). Development of children's moral evaluations of modesty and self-promotion in diverse cultural settings. *Journal of Moral Education, 41,* 61–78.

Cameron, C. A., & Lee, K. (1997). The development of children's telephone communication. *Journal of Applied Developmental Psychology, 18,* 55–70.

Cameron, E. E., Sedov, I. D., & Tomfohr-Madsen, L. M. (2016). Prevalence of paternal depression in pregnancy and the postpartum: An updated meta-analysis. *Journal of Affective Disorders, 206,* 189–203.

Cameron, P. A., & Gallup, G. G. (1988). Shadow recognition in human infants. *Infant Behavior and Development, 11,* 465–471.

Campbell, A., Shirley, L., & Candy, J. (2004). A longitudinal study of gender-related cognition and behaviour. *Developmental Science, 7,* 1–9.

Campbell, D., Scott, K. D., Klaus, M. H., & Falk, M. (2007). Female relatives or friends trained as labor doulas: Outcomes at 6 to 8 weeks postpartum. *Birth, 34,* 220–227.

Campbell, D. A., Lake, M. F., Falk, M., & Backstrand, J. R. (2006). A randomized control trial of continuous support in labor by a lay doula. *Journal of Obstetrics and Gynecology and Neonatal Nursing, 35,* 456–464.

Campbell, F. A., Pungello, E. P., Kainz, K., Burchinal, M., Pan, Y., Wasik, B. H., et al. (2012). Adult outcomes as a function of an early childhood educational program: An Abecedarian Project follow-up. *Developmental Psychology, 48,* 1033–1043.

Campbell, F. A., Pungello, E. P., Miller-Johnson, S., Burchinal, M., & Ramey, C. T. (2001). The development of cognitive and academic abilities: Growth curves from an early childhood educational experiment. *Developmental Psychology, 37,* 231–242.

Campbell, F. A., & Ramey, C. T. (2010). Carolina Abecedarian Project. In A. Reynolds, A. J. Rolick, M. M. Englund, & J. A. Temple (Eds.), *Childhood programs and practices in the first decade of life: A human capital integration* (pp. 76–98). New York: Cambridge University Press.

Campbell, F. A., Ramey, C. T., Pungello, E., Sparling, J., & Miller-Johnson, S. (2002). Early childhood education: Young adult outcomes from the Abecedarian Project. *Applied Developmental Science, 6,* 42–57.

Campbell, J. M., Marcinowski, E. C., & Michel, G. F. (2018). The development of neuromotor skills and hand preference during infancy. *Developmental Psychobiology, 60,* 165–175.

Campos, J. J., Anderson, D. I., Barbu-Roth, M. A., Hubbard, E. M., Hertenstein, J. J., & Witherington, D. (2000). Travel broadens the mind. *Infancy, 1,* 149–219.

Campos, J. J., Frankel, C. B., & Camras, L. (2004). On the nature of emotion regulation. *Child Development, 75,* 377–394.

Campos, J. J., Witherington, D., Anderson, D. I., Frankel, C. I., Uchiyama, I., & Barbu-Roth, M. (2008). Rediscovering development in infancy. *Child Development, 79,* 1625–1632.

Camras, L. (2011). Differentiation, dynamical integration and functional emotional development. *Emotion Review, 3,* 138–146.

Camras, L. A. (1992). Expressive development and basic emotions. *Cognition and Emotion, 6,* 267–283.

Camras, L. A., Oster, H., Campos, J. J., & Bakeman, R. (2003). Emotional facial expressions in European-American, Japanese, and Chinese infants. *Annals of the New York Academy of Sciences, 1000,* 1–17.

Camras, L. A., Oster, H., Campos, J. J., Miyake, K., & Bradshaw, D. (1992). Japanese and American infants' responses to arm restraint. *Developmental Psychology, 28,* 578–583.

Camras, L. A., & Shuster, M. M. (2013). Current emotion research in developmental psychology. *Emotion Review, 5,* 321–329.

Camras, L. A., & Shutter, J. M. (2010). Emotional facial expressions in infancy. *Emotion Review, 2,* 120–129.

Canadian Paediatric Society. (2005). Youth and firearms in Canada. *Paediatric Child Health, 10,* 473–477.

Candelaria, M., Teti, D. M., & Black, M. M. (2011). Multi-risk infants: Predicting attachment security from sociodemographic, psychosocial, and health risk among African-American preterm infants. *Journal of Child Psychology and Psychiatry, 52,* 870–877.

Canfield, R., Henderson, C., Cory-Slechta, D., Cox, C., Jusko, T., & Lanphear, B. (2003). Intellectual impairment in children with blood lead concentrations below 10 μg per deciliter. *New England Journal of Medicine, 348,* 1517–1526.

Capirci, O., Contaldo, A., Caselli, M. C., & Volterra, V. (2005). From action to language through gesture. *Gesture, 5,* 155–177.

Capriola, N. N., Booker, J. A., & Ollendick, T. H. (2017). Profiles of temperament among youth with specific phobias: Implications for CBT outcomes. *Journal of Abnormal Child Psychology, 45,* 1449–1459.

Card, N. A., Stucky, B. D., Sawalani, G. M., & Little, T. D. (2008). Direct and indirect aggression during childhood and adolescence: A meta-analytic review of gender differences, intercorrelations, and relations to maladjustment. *Child Development, 79,* 1185–1229.

Cardona Cano, S., Tiemeier, H., Van Hoeken, D., Tharner, A., Jaddoe, V. W., Hofman, A., et al. (2015). Trajectories of picky eating during childhood: A general population study. *International Journal of Eating Disorders, 48,* 570–579.

Carey, F. R., Singh, G. K., Brown, H. S., III, & Wilkinson, A. V. (2015). Educational outcomes associated with childhood obesity in the United States: Cross-sectional results from the 2011–2012 National Survey of Children's Health. *International Journal of Behavioral Nutrition and Physical Activity, 12*(Suppl. 1), S3.

Carey, S. (2009). *The origins of concepts.* Oxford, UK: Oxford University Press.

Carey, S., & Markman, E. M. (1999). Cognitive development. In B. M. Bly & D. E. Rumelhart (Eds.), *Cognitive science* (pp. 201–254). San Diego: Academic Press.

Carlson, S. M., Claxton, L. J., & Moses, L. J. (2015). The relation between executive function and theory of mind is more than skin deep. *Journal of Cognition and Development, 16,* 186–197.

Carlson, S. M., Moses, L. J., & Claxton, S. J. (2004). Individual differences in executive functioning and theory of mind: An investigation of inhibitory control and planning ability. *Journal of Experimental Child Psychology, 87,* 299–319.

Carlson, S. M., & White, R. E. (2013). Executive function, pretend play, and imagination. In R. E. White & S. M. Carlson (Eds.), *Oxford handbook of the development of imagination* (pp. 161–174). New York: Oxford University Press.

Carlson, S. M., White, R. E., & Davis-Unger, A. (2014). Evidence for a relation between executive function and pretense representation in preschool children. *Cognitive Development, 29,* 1–16.

Carlson, S. M., & Zelazo, P. D., & Faja, S. (2013). Executive function. In P. D. Zelazo (Ed.), *Oxford handbook of developmental psychology, Vol. 1: Body and ind* (pp. 706–743). New York: Oxford University Press.

Carlson, V. J., & Harwood, R. L. (2003). Attachment, culture, and the caregiving system: The cultural patterning of everyday experiences among Anglo and Puerto Rican mother–infant pairs. *Infant Mental Health Journal, 24,* 53–73.

Carpenter, R., McGarvey, C., Mitchell, E. A., Tappin, D. M., Vennemann, M. M., Smuk, M., & Carpenter, J. R. (2013). Bed sharing when parents do not smoke: Is there a risk of SIDS? An individual level analysis of five major case-control studies. *British Medical Journal, 3,* e002299.

Carpenter, T. P., Fennema, E., Fuson, K., Hiebert, J., Human, P., & Murray, H. (1999). Learning basic number concepts and skills as problem solving. In E. Fennema & T. A. Romberg (Eds.), *Mathematics classrooms that promote understanding: Studies in mathematical thinking and learning series* (pp. 45–61). Mahwah, NJ: Erlbaum.

Carroll, J. M., & Breadmore, H. L. (2018). Not all phonological awareness deficits are created equal: Evidence from a comparison between children with otitis media and poor readers. *Developmental Science, 21,* 1–12.

Carter, E. B., Temming, L. A., Akin, J., Fowler, S., Macones, G. A., Colditz, G. A., & Tuul, M. G. (2016). Group prenatal care compared with traditional prenatal care: A systematic review and meta-analysis. *Obstetrics and Gynecology, 128,* 551–561.

Casalin, S., Luyten, P., Vliegen, N., & Meurs, P. (2012). The structure and stability of temperament from infancy to toddlerhood: A one-year prospective study. *Infant Behavior and Development, 35,* 94–108.

Casalis, S., & Cole, P. (2009). On the relationship between morphological and phonological awareness: Effects of training in kindergarten and in first-grade reading. *First Language, 29,* 113–142.

Casasola, M., & Park, Y. (2013). Developmental changes in infant spatial categorization: When more is best and when less is enough. *Child Development, 84,* 1004–1019.

Case, A. D., Todd, N. R., & Kral, M. J. (2014). Ethnography in community psychology: Promises and tensions. *American Journal of Community Psychology, 54,* 60–71.

Case, R. (1996). Introduction: Reconceptualizing the nature of children's conceptual structures and their development in middle childhood. In R. Case & Y. Okamoto (Eds.), The role of central conceptual structures in the development of children's thought. *Monographs of the Society for Research in Child Development, 61*(1–2, Serial No. 246), pp. 1–26.

Case, R. (1998). The development of conceptual structures. In D. Kuhn & R. S. Siegler (Eds.), *Handbook of child psychology: Vol. 2. Cognition, perception, and language* (pp. 745–800). New York: Wiley.

Case, R., & Okamoto, Y. (Eds.). (1996). The role of central conceptual structures in the development of children's thought. *Monographs of the Society for Research in Child Development, 61*(1–2, Serial No. 246).

CASEL (Collaborative for Academic, Social, and Emotional Learning). (2013). *CASEL guide: Effective social and emotional learning programs (Preschool and elementary school edition).* Chicago, IL: Author.

Caserta, D., Graziano, A., Lo Monte, G., Bordi, G., & Moscarini, M. (2013). Heavy metals and placental fetal–maternal barrier: A mini-review on the major concerns. *European Review for Medical and Pharmacological Sciences, 17,* 2198–2206.

Casey, B. M. (1986). Individual differences in selective attention among prereaders: A key to mirror-image confusions. *Developmental Psychology, 22,* 824–831.

Casillas, M. (2014). Turn-taking. In D. Matthews (Ed.), *Pragmatic development in first language acquisition* (pp. 53–70). Amsterdam, Netherlands: John Benjamins Publishing.

Casper, L. M., & Smith, K. E. (2002). Dispelling the myths: Self-care, class, and race. *Journal of Family Issues, 23,* 716–727.

Caspi, A., Harrington, H., Milne, B., Amell, J. W., Theodore, R. F., & Moffitt, T. E. (2003). Children's behavioral styles at age 3 are linked to their adult personality traits at age 26. *Journal of Personality, 71,* 495–513.

Caspi, A., Moffitt, T. E., Morgan, J., Rutter, M., Taylor, A., Kim-Cohen, J., & Polo-Tomas, M. (2004). Maternal expressed emotion predicts children's antisocial behavior problems: Using monozygotic-twin differences to identify environmental effects on behavioral development. *Developmental Psychology, 40,* 149–161.

Caspi, A., & Roberts, B. W. (2001). Personality development across the life course: The argument for change and continuity. *Psychological Inquiry, 12,* 49–66.

Caspi, A., & Shiner, L. (2006). Personality development. In N. Eisenberg (Ed.), *Handbook of child psychology: Vol. 3. Social, emotional, and personality development* (6th ed., pp. 300–365). Hoboken, NJ: Wiley.

Cassia, V. M., Turati, C., & Simion, F. (2004). Can a nonspecific bias toward top-heavy patterns explain newborns' face preference? *Psychological Science, 15,* 379–383.

Cassidy, J., & Berlin, L. J. (1994). The insecure/ambivalent pattern of attachment: Theory and research. *Child Development, 65,* 971–991.

Cassidy, J., Jones, J. D., & Shaver, P. R. (2013). Contributions of attachment theory and research: A framework for future research, translation, and policy. *Developmental Psychopathology, 25,* 1415–1434.

Catalano, R., Ahern, J., Bruckner, T., Anderson, E., & Saxton, K. (2009). Gender-specific selection in utero among contemporary human birth cohorts. *Paediatric and Perinatal Epidemiology, 23,* 273–278.

Catalano, R., Zilko, C. E., Saxton, K. B., & Bruckner, T. (2010). Selection in utero: A biological response to mass layoffs. *American Journal of Human Biology, 22,* 396–400.

Catling, C. J., Medley, N., Foureur, M., Ryan, C., Leap, N., & Homer, C. S. (2015). Group versus conventional antenatal care for women. *Cochrane Database of Systematic Reviews, 2,* Art. No. CD007622.

Cavanaugh, D. M., Clemence, K. J., Teale, M. M., Rule, A. C., & Montgomery, S. E. (2017). Kindergarten scores, storytelling, executive function, and motivation improved through literacy-rich guided play. *Early Childhood Education Journal, 45,* 831–843.

Ceci, S. J. (1999). Schooling and intelligence. In S. J. Ceci & W. M. Williams (Eds.), *The nature–nurture debate: The essential readings* (pp. 168–175). Oxford, UK: Blackwell.

Ceci, S. J., Bruck, M., & Battin, D. (2000). The suggestibility of children's testimony. In Bjorklund, D. (Ed), *False-memory creation in children and adults* (pp. 169–201). Mahwah, NJ: Erlbaum.

Ceci, S. J., Kulkofsky, S., Klemfuss, J. Z., Sweeney, C. D., & Bruck, M. (2007). Unwarranted assumptions about children's testimonial accuracy. *Annual Review of Clinical Psychology, 3,* 311–328.

Ceci, S. J., Rosenblum, T. B., & Kumpf, M. (1998). The shrinking gap between high- and low-scoring groups: Current trends and possible causes. In U. Neisser (Ed.), *The rising curve: Long-term gains in IQ and related measures* (pp. 287–302). Washington, DC: American Psychological Association.

Cellini, N. (2017). Memory consolidation in sleep disorders. *Sleep Medicine Reviews, 35,* 101–112.

Centers for Disease Control and Prevention. (2014a). *Children's oral health.* Retrieved from www.cdc.gov/oralhealth/children_adults/child.htm

Centers for Disease Control and Prevention. (2014b). *State indicator report on physical activity: 2014.* Retrieved from www.cdc.gov/physicalactivity/downloads/PA_State_Indicator_Report_2014.pdf

Centers for Disease Control and Prevention. (2015). *One in 10 pregnant women in the United States reports drinking alcohol.* Retrieved from www.cdc.gov/media/releases/2015/p0924-pregnant-alcohol.html

Centers for Disease Control and Prevention. (2016). *Infertility.* Retrieved from www.cdc.gov/nchs/fastats/infertility.htm

Centers for Disease Control and Prevention. (2017a). *Asthma.* Retrieved from www.cdc.gov/nchs/fastats/asthma.htm

Centers for Disease Control and Prevention. (2017b). *Child passenger safety: Get the facts.* Retrieved from www.cdc.gov/motorvehiclesafety/child_passenger_safety/cps-factsheet.html

Centers for Disease Control and Prevention. (2017c). *Combined 7-vaccine series vaccination coverage among children 19–35 months by state, HHS region, and the United States, National Immunization Survey-Child (NIS-Child), 2016.* Retrieved from www.cdc.gov/vaccines/imz-managers/coverage/childvaxview/data-reports/7-series/reports/2016.html

Centers for Disease Control and Prevention. (2017d). *Folic acid.* Retrieved from www.cdc.gov/ncbddd/folicacid/recommendations.html

Centers for Disease Control and Prevention. (2017e). *Health, United States, 2017—data finder.* Retrieved from www.cdc.gov/nchs/hus/contents2017.htm?search=,Child_and_adolescent

Centers for Disease Control and Prevention. (2017f). *Protect the ones you love: Child injuries are preventable.* Retrieved from www.cdc.gov/safechild/index.html

Centers for Disease Control and Prevention. (2017g). *Results from the School Health Policies and Practices Study: 2016.* Retrieved from www.cdc.gov/healthyyouth/data/shpps/pdf/shpps-results_2016.pdf

Centers for Disease Control and Prevention. (2017h). *Sickle cell disease (SCD).* Retrieved from www.cdc.gov/ncbddd/sicklecell/index.html

Centers for Disease Control and Prevention. (2018a). *Breastfeeding report card: United States 2018.* Retrieved from www.cdc.gov/breastfeeding/pdf/2018breastfeedingreportcard.pdf

Centers for Disease Control and Prevention. (2018b). *Cigarette smoking during pregnancy: United States, 2016.* Retrieved from www.cdc.gov/nchs/products/databriefs/db305.htm

Centers for Disease Control and Prevention. (2018c). *Multiple cause of death data, 1999–2017.* Retrieved from wonder.cdc.gov/mcd.html

Centers for Disease Control and Prevention. (2018d). *Obesity and overweight.* Retrieved from www.cdc.gov/nchs/fastats/obesity-overweight.htm

Centers for Disease Control and Prevention. (2018e). *Sudden unexpected infant death and sudden infant death syndrome: Data and statistics.* Retrieved from www.cdc.gov/sids/data.htm

Centers for Disease Control and Prevention. (2018f). *Vital statistics rapid release, quarterly provisional estimates: Age-specific birth rates.* Retrieved from www.cdc.gov/nchs/nvss/vsrr/natality-dashboard.htm#

Centers for Disease Control and Prevention. (2019a). *Children's oral health.* Retrieved from www.cdc.gov/oralhealth/children_adults/child.htm

Centers for Disease Control and Prevention. (2019b). *WISQARS fatal injury reports, national, regional, and state, 1981–2017.* Retrieved from webappa.cdc.gov/sasweb/ncipc/mortrate.html

Cernoch, J. M., & Porter, R. H. (1985). Recognition of maternal axillary odors by infants. *Child Development, 56,* 1593–1598.

Cespedes, E. M., Gillman, M. W., Kleinman, D., Rifas- Shiman, S. L., Redline, S., & Taveras, E. M. (2014). Television viewing, bedroom television, and sleep duration from infancy to mid-childhood. Pediatrics, 133, e1163–1171.

Cetinkaya, M. B., Siano, L. J., & Benadiva, C. (2013). Reproductive outcome of women 43 years and beyond undergoing ART treatment with their own oocytes in two Connecticut university programs. *Journal of Assisted Reproductive Genetics, 30,* 673–678.

Chaddock, L., Erickson, K. I., Prakash, R. S., Kim, J. S., Voss, M. W., Van Patter, M., et al. (2010a). A neuroimaging investigation of the association between aerobic fitness and hippocampal volume and memory performance in preadolescent children. *Brain Research, 1358,* 172–183.

Chaddock, L., Erickson, K. I., Prakash, R. S., VanPatter, M., Voss, M. V., Pontifex, M. B., et al. (2010b). Basal ganglia volume is associated with aerobic fitness in preadolescent children. *Developmental Neuroscience, 32,* 249–256.

Chaddock, L., Erickson, K. I., Prakash, R. S., Voss, M. V., VanPatter, M., Pontifex, M. B., et al. (2012). A functional MRI investigation of the association between childhood aerobic fitness and neurocognitive control. *Biological Psychology, 89,* 260–268.

Chaddock, L., Pontifex, M. B., Hillman, C. H., & Kramer, A. F. (2011). A review of the relation of aerobic fitness and physical activity to brain structure and function in children. *Journal of the International Neuropsychological Society, 17,* 1–11.

Chaddock-Heyman, L., Erickson, K. I., Holtrop, J. L., Voss, M. W., Pontifex, M. B., Raine, L. B., et al. (2014). Aerobic fitness is associated with greater white matter integrity in children. *Frontiers in Human Neuroscience, 8,* 584.

Chaddock-Heyman, L., Erickson, K. I., Voss, M. W., Knecht, A. M., Pontifex, M. B., Castelli, D. M., et al. (2013). The effects of physical activity on functional MRI activation associated with cognitive control in children: A randomized controlled intervention. *Frontiers in Human Neuroscience, 7,* 72.

Chafel, J. A., & Neitzel, C. (2005). Young children's ideas about the nature, causes, justification, and alleviation of poverty. *Early Childhood Research Quarterly, 20,* 433–450.

Chakravorty, S., & Williams, T. N. (2015). Sickle cell disease: A neglected chronic disease of increasing global health importance. *Archives of Disease in Childhood, 100,* 48–53.

Chalabaev, A., Sarrazin, P., & Fontayne, P. (2009). Stereotype endorsement and perceived ability as mediators of the girls' gender orientation–soccer performance relationship. *Psychology of Sport and Exercise, 10,* 297–299.

Chall, J. S. (1983). *Stages of reading development.* New York: McGraw-Hill.

Champaloux, S. W., & Young, D. R. (2015). Childhood chronic health conditions and educational attainment: A social ecological approach. *Journal of Adolescent Health, 56,* 98–105.

Chan, A., Meints, K., Lieven, E., & Tomasello, M. (2010). Young children's comprehension of English SVO word order revisited: Testing the same children in act-out and intermodal preferential looking tasks. *Cognitive Development, 25,* 30–45.

Chan, C. C. Y., Brandone, A. C., & Tardif, T. (2009). Culture, context, or behavioral control? English- and Mandarin-speaking mothers' use of nouns and verbs in joint book reading. *Journal of Cross-Cultural Psychology, 40,* 584–602.

Chan, C. C. Y., Tardif, T., Chen, J., Pulverman, R. B., Zhu, L., & Meng, X. (2011). English- and Chinese-learning infants map novel labels to objects and actions differently. *Developmental Psychology, 47,* 1459–1471.

Chan, S. M. (2010). Aggressive behaviour in early elementary school children: Relations to authoritarian parenting, children's negative emotionality and coping strategies. *Early Child Development and Care, 180,* 1253–1269.

Chandra, A., Copen, C. E., & Stephen, E. H. (2013). *Infertility and impaired fecundity in the United States, 1982–2010: Data from the National Survey of Family Growth.* Hyattsville, MD: Centers for Disease Control and Prevention. Retrieved from www.cdc.gov/nchs/data/nhsr/nhsr067.pdf

Chang, F., Dell, G. S., & Bock, K. (2006). Becoming syntactic. *Psychological Review, 113,* 234–272.

Chapman, R. S. (2006). Children's language learning: An interactionist perspective. In R. Paul (Ed.), *Language disorders from a developmental perspective* (pp. 1–53). Mahwah, NJ: Erlbaum.

Charman, T., Baron-Cohen, S., Swettenham, J., Baird, G., Cox, A., & Drew, A. (2001). Testing joint attention, imitation, and play as infancy precursors to language and theory of mind. *Cognitive Development, 15,* 481–49.

Charney, E. (2017). Genes, behavior, and behavior genetics. *WIREs Cognitive Science, 8,* e1405.

Chase-Lansdale, P. L., Gordon, R., Brooks-Gunn, J., & Klebanov, P. K. (1997).

Neighborhood and family influences on the intellectual and behavioral competence of preschool and early school-age children. In J. Brooks-Gunn, G. Duncan, & J. L. Aber (Eds.), *Neighborhood poverty: Context and consequences for development* (pp. 79–118). New York: Russell Sage Foundation.

Chassiakos, Y. R., Radesky, J., Christakis, D., Moreno, M. A., & Cross, C. (2016). Children and adolescents and digital media. *Pediatrics, 138,* e20162593.

Chauhan, G. S., Shastri, J., & Mohite, P. (2005). Development of gender constancy in preschoolers. *Psychological Studies, 50,* 62–71.

Chawarska, K., Macari, S., & Shic, F. (2013). Decreased spontaneous attention to social scenes in 6-month-old infants later diagnosed with autism spectrum disorders. *Biological Psychiatry, 74,* 195–203.

Cheah, C. S. L., Leung, C. Y. Y., Tahseen, M., & Schultz, D. (2009). Authoritative parenting among immigrant Chinese mothers of preschoolers. *Journal of Family Psychology, 23,* 311–320.

Cheah, C. S. L., & Li, J. (2010). Parenting of young immigrant Chinese children: Challenges facing their social-emotional and intellectual development. In E. L. Grigorenko & R. Takanishi (Eds.), *Immigration, diversity, and education* (pp. 225–241). New York: Routledge.

Chen, E. E., Corriveau, K. H., & Harris, P. L. (2016). Person perception in young children across two cultures. *Journal of Cognition and Development, 17,* 447–467.

Chen, E. S. L., & Rao, N. (2011). Gender socialization in Chinese kindergartens: Teachers' contributions. *Sex Roles, 64,* 103–116.

Chen, J. J., Howard, K. S., & Brooks-Gunn, J. (2011). How do neighborhoods matter across the life span? In K. L. Fingerman, C. A. Berg, J. Smith, & T. C. Antonucci (Eds.), *Handbook of life-span development* (pp. 805–836). New York: Springer.

Chen, J. J., Sun, P., & Yu, Z. (2017). A comparative study on parenting of preschool children between the Chinese in China and Chinese immigrants in the United States. *Journal of Family Issues, 38,* 1267–1287.

Chen, J.-Q., & Gardner, H. (2018). Assessment from the perspective of multiple-intelligences theory: Principles, practices, and values. In D. P. Flanagan & E. M. McDonough (Eds.), *Contemporary intellectual assessment: Theories, tests, and issues* (4th ed., pp. 164–173). New York: Guilford.

Chen, L.-C., Metcalfe, J. S., Jeka, J. J., & Clark, J. E. (2007). Two steps forward and one back: Learning to walk affects infants' sitting posture. *Infant Behavior and Development, 30,* 16–25.

Chen, X. (2010). Shyness-inhibition in childhood and adolescence: A cross-cultural perspective. In K. H. Rubin & R. J. Coplan (Eds.), *The development of shyness and social withdrawal* (pp. 213–235). New York: Guilford.

Chen, X. (2012). Culture, peer interaction, and socioemotional development. *Child Development Perspectives, 6,* 27–34.

Chen, X. (2015). Exploring the implications of social change for human development: Perspectives, issues and future directions. *International Journal of Psychology, 50,* 56–59.

Chen, X., Cen, G., Li, D., & He, Y. (2005). Social functioning and adjustment in Chinese children: The imprint of historical time. *Child Development, 76,* 182–195.

Chen, X., Rubin, K. H., Liu, M., Chen, H., Wang, L., Li, D., et al. (2003). Compliance in Chinese and Canadian toddlers: A cross-cultural study. *International Journal of Behavioral Development, 27,* 428–436.

Chen, X., & Schmidt, L. A. (2015). Temperament and personality. In M. E. Lamb (Ed.), *Handbook of child psychology and developmental science. Vol. 3: Socioemotional processes* (7th ed., pp. 152–200). Hoboken, NJ: Wiley.

Chen, X., Wang, L., & Cao, R. (2011). Shyness-sensitivity and unsociability in rural Chinese children: Relations with social, school, and psychological adjustment. *Child Development, 82,* 1531–1543.

Chen, X., Wang, L., & DeSouza, A. (2006). Temperament, socioemotional functioning, and peer relationships in Chinese and North American children. In X. Chen, D. C. French, & B. H. Schneider (Eds.), *Peer relationships in cultural context* (pp. 123–147). New York: Cambridge University Press.

Chen, Y.-C., Yu, M.-L., Rogan, W., Gladen, B., & Hsu, C.-C. (1994). A 6-year follow-up of behavior and activity disorders in the Taiwan Yu-cheng children. *American Journal of Public Health, 84,* 415–421.

Chen, Y.-J., & Hsu, C.-C. (1994). Effects of prenatal exposure to PCBs on the neurological function of children: A neuropsychological and neurophysiological study. *Developmental Medicine and Child Neurology, 36,* 312–320.

Chess, S., & Thomas, A. (1984). *Origins and evolution of behavior disorders.* New York: Brunner/Mazel.

Chevalier, N. (2015). The development of executive function: Toward more optimal coordination of control with age. *Child Development Perspectives, 9,* 239–244.

Cheyney, M., Bovbjerg, M., Everson, C., Gordon, W., Hannibal, D., & Vedam, S. (2014). Outcomes of care for 16,924 planned home births in the United States: The Midwives Alliance of North America Statistics Project, 2004 to 2009. *Journal of Midwifery and Women's Health, 59,* 17–27.

Child Care Aware. (2017). *Parents and the high cost of child care: 2016 report.* Retrieved from usa.childcareaware.org

Child Trends. (2014a). *Births to unmarried women.* Retrieved from www.childtrends.org/?indicators=births-to-unmarried-women

Child Trends. (2014b). *Charts for Child Trends' family meals indicator.* Retrieved from www.childtrends.org/wp-content/uploads/2016/04/indicator_1460671461.9951.pdf

Child Trends. (2015). *Late or no prenatal care: Indicators on children and youth.* Retrieved from www.childtrends.org/wp-content/uploads/2014/07/25_Prenatal_Care.pdf

Child Trends. (2016a). *Key facts about juvenile incarceration.* Retrieved from www.childtrends.org/indicators/juvenile-detention

Child Trends. (2016b). *Trends in child care.* Retrieved from www.childtrends.org/indicators/child-care

Child Trends. (2018a). *Attitudes toward spanking.* Retrieved from www.childtrends.org/indicators/attitudes-toward-spanking

Child Trends. (2018b). *Births to unmarried women.* Retrieved from www.childtrends.org/indicators/births-to-unmarried-women

Chiong, C., Ree, J., Takeuchi, L., & Erickson, I. (2012). *Print books vs. e-books.* New York: Joan Ganz Cooney Center.

Cho, S., Ryali, S., Geary, D. C., & Menon, V. (2011). How does a child solve 7 + 8? Decoding brain activity patterns associated with counting and retrieval strategies. *Developmental Science, 14,* 989–1001.

Chodkiewicz, A. C., & Boyle, C. (2014). Exploring the contribution of attribution retraining to student perceptions and the learning process. *Educational Psychology in Practice, 30,* 78–87.

Choe, D. E., Olson, S. L., & Sameroff, A. J. (2013). The interplay of externalizing problems and physical discipline and inductive discipline during childhood. *Developmental Psychology, 49,* 2029–2039.

Choi, K., & Kirkorian H. L. (2016). Touch or watch to learn? Toddlers' object retrieval using contingent and noncontingent video. *Psychological Science, 5,* 726–736.

Choi, S., & Gopnik, A. (1995). Early acquisition of verbs in Korean: A cross-linguistic study. *Journal of Child Language, 22,* 497–529.

Chomsky, C. (1969). *The acquisition of syntax in children from five to ten.* Cambridge, MA: MIT Press.

Chomsky, N. (1957). *Syntactic structures.* The Hague: Mouton.

Chong, A., & Mickelson, K. D. (2013). Perceived fairness and relationship satisfaction during the transition to parenthood and the mediating role of spousal support. *Journal of Family Issues, 18,* 1–26.

Chouinard, M. M. (2007). Children's questions: A mechanism for cognitive development. *Monographs of the Society for Research in Child Development, 72*(1, Serial No. 286).

Chouinard, M. M., & Clark, E. V. (2003). Adult reformulations of child errors as negative evidence. *Journal of Child Language, 30,* 637–669.

Christakis, D. A., Garrison, M. M., Herrenkohl, T., Haggerty, K, Rivara, F. P., Zhou, C., & Liekweg, K. (2013). Modifying media content for preschool children: A randomized controlled trial. *Pediatrics, 131,* 431–438.

Christakis, D. A., Zimmerman, F. J., DiGiuseppe, D. L., & McCarty, C. A. (2004). Early television exposure and subsequent attentional problems in children. *Pediatrics, 113,* 708–713.

Christoffersen, M. N. (2012). A study of adopted children, their environment, and development: A systematic review. *Adoption Quarterly, 15,* 220–237.

Chronis-Tuscano, A., Rubin, K., O'Brien, K. A., Coplan, R. J., Thoma, S. R., Dougherty, L. R., et al. (2015). Preliminary evaluation of a multimodal early intervention program for behaviorally inhibited preschoolers. *Journal of Consulting and Clinical Psychology, 83,* 534–540.

Chu, F. W., vanMarle, K., Rouder, J., & Geary, D. C. (2018). Children's early understanding of number predicts their later problem-solving sophistication in addition. *Journal of Experimental Child Psychology, 169,* 73–92.

Chung, H. H. (2006). Code switching as a communicative strategy: A case study of Korean–English bilinguals. *Bilingual Research Journal, 30,* 293–307.

Chung, J. M., Hutteman, R., van Aken, M. A. G., & Denissen, J. J. A. (2017). High, low, and in between: Self-esteem development from middle childhood to young adulthood. *Journal of Research in Personality, 70,* 122–123.

Church, J. A. (2019). Cognitive, intervention, and neuroimaging perspectives on executive function in children with reading disabilities. *New Directions for Child and Adolescent Development, 165,* 25–54.

Church, R. B., & Goldin-Meadow, S. (1986). The mismatch between gesture and speech as an index of transitional knowledge. *Cognition, 23,* 43–71.

Cicchetti, D., & Toth, S. L. (2015). Child maltreatment. In M. E. Lamb (Ed.), *Handbook of child psychology and developmental science: Vol. 3. Socioemotional processes* (7th ed., pp. 513–563). Hoboken, NJ: Wiley.

Cillessen, A. H. N. (2009). Sociometric methods. In K. H. Rubin & W. M. Bukowski (Eds.), *Handbook of peer interactions, relationships, and groups* (pp. 82–99). New York: Guilford.

Cillessen, A. H. N., & Bellmore, A. D. (2004). Social skills and interpersonal perception in early and middle childhood. In P. K. Smith & C. H. Hart (Eds.), *Blackwell handbook of childhood social development* (pp. 355–374). Malden, MA: Blackwell.

Cipriano, E. A., & Stifter, C. A. (2010). Predicting preschool effortful control from toddler temperament and parenting behavior. *Journal of Applied Developmental Psychology, 31,* 221–230.

Ciu, L., Colasante, T., Malti, T., Ribeaud, D., & Eisner, M. P. (2016). Dual trajectories of reactive and proactive aggression from mid-childhood to early adolescence: Relations to sensation seeking, risk taking, and moral reasoning. *Journal of Abnormal Child Psychology, 44,* 663–675.

Clapp, J. F., III, Kim, H., Burciu, B., Schmidt, S., Petry, K., & Lopez, B. (2002). Continuing regular exercise during pregnancy: Effect of exercise volume on fetoplacental growth. *American Journal of Obstetrics and Gynecology, 186,* 142–147.

Clark, E. (2014). Pragmatics in acquisition. *Journal of Child Language, 41,* 105–116.

Clark, E. V. (2007). Young children's uptake of new words in conversation. *Language in Society, 36,* 157–182.

Clark, S. M., Ghulmiyyah, L. M., & Hankins, G. D. (2008). Antenatal antecedents and the impact of obstetric care in the etiology of cerebral palsy. *Clinical Obstetrics and Gynecology, 51,* 775–786.

Clarke-Stewart, K. A. (1998). Historical shifts and underlying themes in ideas about rearing young children in the United States: Where have we been? Where are we going? *Early Development and Parenting, 7,* 101–117.

Clarke-Stewart, K. A., & Hayward, C. (1996). Advantages of father custody and contact for the psychological well-being of school-age children. *Journal of Applied Developmental Psychology, 17,* 239–270.

Clearfield, M. W. (2011). Learning to walk changes infants' social interactions. *Infant Behavior and Development, 34,* 15–25.

Clearfield, M. W., & Westfahl, S. M.-C. (2006). Familiarization in infants' perception of addition problems. *Journal of Cognition and Development, 7,* 27–43.

Cleave, P. L., Becker, S. D., Curran, M. K., Owen Van Horne, A. J., & Fey, M. E. (2015). The efficacy of recasts in language intervention: A systematic review and meta-analysis. *American Journal of Speech–Language Pathology, 24,* 237–255.

Clements, D. H., & Sarama, J. (2003). Young children and technology: What does the research say? *Young Children, 58*(6), 34–40.

Clements, D. H., & Sarama, J. (2012). Learning and teaching early and elementary mathematics. In J. S. Carlson & J. R. Levin (Eds.), *Instructional strategies for improving students' learning* (pp. 205–212). Charlotte, NC: Information Age Publishing.

Clements, D. H., Sarama, J., Spitler, M. E., Lange, A. A., & Wolfe, C. B. (2011). Mathematics learned by young children in an intervention based on learning trajectories: A large-scale cluster randomized trial. *Journal for Research in Mathematics Education, 42*, 127–166.

Cliffordson, C., & Gustafsson, J. E. (2008). Effects of age and schooling on intellectual performance: Estimates obtained from analysis of continuous variation in age and length of schooling. *Intelligence, 36*, 143–152.

Clincy, A. R., & Mills-Koonce, W. R. (2013). Trajectories of intrusive parenting during infancy and toddlerhood as predictors of rural, low-income African American boys' school-related outcomes. *American Journal of Orthopsychiatry, 83*, 194–206.

Coall, D. A., Callan, A. C., Dickins, T. E., & Chisholm, J. S. (2015). Evolution and prenatal development: An evolutionary perspective. In M. E. Lamb (Ed.), *Handbook of child psychology and developmental science: Vol. 3. Socioemotional processes* (7th ed., pp. 57–105). Hoboken, NJ: Wiley.

Cohen, G. L., Garcia, J., & Master, A. (2006). Reducing the racial achievement gap: A social-psychological intervention. *Science, 313*, 1307–1310.

Cohen, L. B. (2010). A bottom-up approach to infant perception and cognition: A summary of evidence and discussion of issues. In S. P. Johnson (Ed.), *Neoconstructivism: The new science of cognitive development* (pp. 335–346). New York: Oxford University Press.

Cohen, L. B., & Brunt, J. (2009). Early word learning and categorization: Methodological issues and recent empirical evidence. In J. Colombo, P. McCardle, & L. Freund (Eds.), *Infant pathways to language: Methods, models, and research disorders* (pp. 245–266). New York: Psychology Press.

Cohen, L. B., & Marks, K. S. (2002). How infants process addition and subtraction events. *Developmental Science, 5*, 186–201.

Cohen-Bendahan, C. C. C., van Doornen, L. J. P., & de Weerth, C. (2014). Young adults' reactions to infant crying. *Infant Behavior and Development, 37*, 33–43.

Cohn, N. (2014). Framing "I can't draw": The influence of cultural frames on the development of drawing. *Culture and Psychology, 20*, 102–117.

Colangelo, N., & Assouline, S. (2009). Acceleration: Meeting the academic and social needs of students. In L. V. Shavinina (Ed.), *International handbook on giftedness* (pp. 1085–1098). Dordrecht, Netherlands: Springer.

Cole, M. (2006). Culture and cognitive development in phylogenetic, historical, and ontogenetic perspective. In D. Kuhn & R. S. Siegler (Eds.), *Handbook of child psychology: Vol. 2. Cognition, perception, and language* (6th ed., pp. 636–685). Hoboken, NJ: Wiley.

Cole, P., Hermon, G., & Yanti, A. (2015). Grammar of binding in the languages of the world: Innate or learned? *Cognition, 141*, 138–160.

Cole, P. M., Armstrong, L. M., & Pemberton, C. K. (2010). The role of language in the development of emotion regulation. In S. D. Calkins & M. A. Bell (Eds.), *Child development at the intersection of emotion and cognition* (pp. 59–77). Washington, DC: American Psychological Association.

Cole, P. M., Bruschi, C. J., & Tamang, B. L. (2002). Cultural differences in children's emotional reactions to difficult situations. *Child Development, 73*, 983–996.

Cole, P. M., LeDonne, E. N., & Tan, P. Z. (2013). A longitudinal examination of maternal emotions in relation to young children's developing self-regulation. *Parenting: Science and Practice, 13*, 113–132.

Cole, P. M., & Tamang, B. L. (1998). Nepali children's ideas about emotional displays in hypothetical challenges. *Developmental Psychology, 34*, 640–648.

Cole, P. M., Tamang, B. L., & Shrestha, S. (2006). Cultural variations in the socialization of young children's anger and shame. *Child Development, 77*, 1237–1251.

Coleman-Jensen, A., Rabitt, M. P., Gregory, C. A., & Singh, A. (2018). *Household food security in the United States in 2017*, ERR-256, U.S. Department of Agriculture, Economic Research Service. Retrieved from www.ers.usda.gov/webdocs/publications/90023/err-256.pdf?v=0

Coles, R. L. (2015). Single-father families: A review of the literature. *Journal of Family Theory & Review, 7*, 144–166.

Coley, R. L., Morris, J. E., & Hernandez, D. (2004). Out-of-school care and problem behavior trajectories among low-income adolescents: Individual, family, and neighborhood characteristics as added risks. *Child Development, 75*, 948–965.

Coley, S. L., Zapata, J. Y., Schwei, R. J., Mihalovic, G. E., Matabele, M. N., Jacobs, E. A., et al. (2018). More than a "number": Perspectives of prenatal care quality from mothers of color and providers. *Women's Health Issues, 28*, 158–164.

Collins, J. W., Rankin, K. M., & David, R. J. (2011). Low birth weight across generations: The effect of economic environment. *Maternal and Child Health Journal, 15*, 438–445.

Collins, W. A., & Hartup, W. W. (2013). History of research in developmental psychology. In P. D. Zelazo (Ed.), *Oxford handbook of developmental psychology* (pp. 13–34). New York: Oxford University Press.

Collins, W. A., Madsen, S. D., & Susman-Stillman, A. (2002). Parenting during middle childhood. In M. H. Bornstein (Ed.), *Handbook of parenting: Vol. 1. Children and parenting* (2nd ed., pp. 73–101). Mahwah, NJ: Erlbaum.

Collin-Vézina, D., Daigneault, I., & Hébert, M. (2013). Lessons learned from child sexual abuse research: Prevalence, outcomes, and preventive strategies. *Child and Adolescent Psychiatry and Mental Health, 7*, 1–9.

Colman, A. M. (2016). Race differences in IQ: Hans Eysenck's contribution to the debate in the light of subsequent research. *Personality and Individual Differences, 103*, 182–189.

Colombo, J., Brez, C. C., & Curtindale, L. M. (2013). Infant perception and cognition. In R. M. Lerner, M. A. Easterbrooks, & J. Mistry (Eds.), *Handbook of psychology: Vol. 6. Developmental psychology* (pp. 61–89). Hoboken, NJ: Wiley.

Colombo, J., Kapa, L., & Curtindale, L. (2011). Varieties of attention in infancy. In L. M. Oakes, C. H. Cashon, M. Casasola, & D. Rakison (Eds.), *Infant perception and cognition* (3–25). New York: Oxford University Press.

Colombo, J., Shaddy, D. J., Richman, W. A., Maikranz, J. M., & Blaga, O. M. (2004). The developmental course of habituation in infancy and preschool outcome. *Infancy, 5*, 1–38.

Common Core. (2019). *English language arts standards. Reading: Foundational skills. Introduction for K–5.* Retrieved from www.corestandards.org/ELA-Literacy/RF/introduction

Conde-Agudelo, A., Belizan, J. M., & Diaz-Rossello, J. (2011). Kangaroo mother care to reduce morbidity and mortality in low birthweight infants. *Cochrane Database of Systematic Reviews, 3*, Art. No. CD002771.

Condron, D. J. (2013). Affluence, inequality, and educational achievement: A structural analysis of 97 jurisdictions, across the globe. *Sociological Spectrum, 33*, 73–97.

Conger, K. J., Stocker, C., & McGuire, S. (2009). Sibling socialization: The effects of stressful life events and experiences. In L. Kramer & K. J. Conger (Eds.), *Siblings as agents of socialization: New directions for child and adolescent development* (No. 126, pp. 44–60). San Francisco: Jossey-Bass.

Conger, R. D., & Donnellan, M. B. (2007). An interactionist perspective on the socioeconomic context of human development. *Annual Review of Psychology, 58*, 175–199.

Conner, D. B., & Cross, D. R. (2003). Longitudinal analysis of the presence, efficacy, and stability of maternal scaffolding during informal problem-solving interactions. *British Journal of Developmental Psychology, 21*, 315–334.

Connor, D. F. (2015). Stimulant and nonstimulant medications for childhood ADHD. In R. A. Barkley (Ed.), *Attention-deficit hyperactivity disorder: A handbook for diagnosis and treatment* (4th ed., pp. 666–685). New York: Guilford.

Conron, K. J., Scott, G., Stowell, G. S., & Landers, S. J. (2012). Transgender health in Massachusetts: Results from a household probability sample of adults. *American Journal of Public Health, 102*, 118–122.

Cooke, J. E., Stuart-Parrigon, K. L., Movahed-Abtahi, M., Koehn, A., & Kerns, K. A. (2016). Children's emotion understanding and mother–child attachment: A meta-analysis. *Emotion, 16*, 1102–1106.

Cookston, J. T., Braver, S. L., Griffin, W. A., De Lusé, S. R., & Miles, J. C. (2006). Effects of the Dads for Life intervention on interparental conflict and coparenting in the two years after divorce. *Family Process, 46*, 123–137.

Cooley, J. L., Fite, P. J., & Pederson, C. A. (2017). Bidirectional associations between peer victimization and functions of aggression in middle childhood: Further evaluation across informants and academic years. *Journal of Abnormal Child Psychology, 45*. Retrieved from doi.org/10.1007/s10802-017-0280-y

Cooper, B. R., & Lanza, S. T. (2014). Who benefits most from Head Start? Latent class moderation to examine differential treatment effects. *Child Development, 85*, 2317–2338.

Cooper, H., Batts, A., Patall, E. A., & Dent, A. L. (2010). Effects of full-day kindergarten on academic achievement and social development. *Review of Educational Research, 80*, 54–70.

Coplan, R. J., & Arbeau, K. A. (2008). The stresses of a "brave new world": Shyness and school adjustment in kindergarten. *Journal of Research in Childhood Education, 22*, 377–389.

Coplan, R. J., Gavinsky-Molina, M. H., Lagace-Seguin, D., & Wichmann, C. (2001). When girls versus boys play alone: Nonsocial play and adjustment in kindergarten. *Developmental Psychology, 37*, 464–474.

Coplan, R. J., Liu J., Ooi, L. L., Chen, X., Li, D., & Ding, X. (2016). A person-oriented analysis of social withdrawal in Chinese children. *Social Development, 25*, 794–811.

Coplan, R. J., & Ooi, L. (2014). The causes and consequences of "playing alone" in childhood. In R. J. Coplan & J. C. Bowker (Eds.), *The handbook of solitude: Psychological perspectives on social isolation, social withdrawal, and being alone* (pp. 111–128). Chichester, UK: Wiley- Blackwell.

Coplan, R. J., Prakash, K., O'Neill, K., & Armer, M. (2004). Do you "want" to play? Distinguishing between conflicted shyness and social disinterest in early childhood. *Developmental Psychology, 40*, 244–258.

Coplan, R. J., Ooi, L. L., & Nocita, G. (2015). When one is company and two is a crowd: Why some children prefer solitude. *Child Development Perspectives, 9*, 133–137.

Copple, C., & Bredekamp, S. (2009). *Developmentally appropriate practice in early childhood programs* (3rd ed.). Washington, DC: National Association for the Education of Young Children.

Corapci, F., Radan, A. E., & Lozoff, B. (2006). Iron deficiency in infancy and mother–child interaction at 5 years. *Journal of Developmental and Behavioral Pediatrics, 27*, 371–378.

Corby, B. C., Hodges, E. V., & Perry, D. G. (2007). Gender identity and adjustment in Black, Hispanic, and White preadolescents. *Developmental Psychology, 26*, 261–266.

Corenblum, B. (2003). What children remember about ingroup and outgroup peers: Effects of stereotypes on children's processing of information about group members. *Journal of Experimental Child Psychology, 86*, 32–66.

Cornoldi, C., Giofr., D., Orsini, A., & Pezzuti, L. (2014). Differences in the intellectual profile of children with intellectual vs. learning disability. *Research in Developmental Disabilities, 35*, 2224–2230.

Cornwell, A. C., & Feigenbaum, P. (2006). Sleep biological rhythms in normal infants and those at high risk for SIDS. *Chronobiology International, 23*, 935–961.

Correa-Chavez, M., Roberts, A. L. D., & Perez, M. M. (2011). Cultural patterns in children's learning through keen observation and participation in their communities. In J. B. Benson (Ed.), *Advances in child development and behavior* (Vol. 40, pp. 209–241). San Diego, CA: Academic Press.

Costa, A., & Sebastián-Gallés, N. (2014). How does the bilingual experience sculpt the brain? *Nature Reviews Neuroscience, 15*, 336–345.

Costacurta, M., Sicuro, L., Di Renzo, L., & Condo, R. (2012). Childhood obesity and skeletal-dental maturity. *European Journal of Paediatric Dentistry, 13*, 128–132.

Cote, L. R., & Bornstein, M. H. (2009). Child and mother play in three U.S. cultural groups: Comparisons and associations. *Journal of Family Psychology, 23*, 355–363.

Côté, S. M., Petitclerc, A., Raynault, M.-F., Falissard, B., Boivin, M., & Tremblay, R. E. (2010). Short- and long-term risk of infections as a function of group child care attendance: An 8-year population-based study. *Archives of Pediatric and Adolescent Medicine, 164*, 1132–1137.

Côté, S. M., Vaillancourt, T., Barker, E. D., Nagin, D., & Tremblay, R. E. (2007). The joint development of physical and indirect aggression: Predictors of continuity and change during childhood. *Development and Psychopathology, 19*, 37–55.

Cottrell, J. M., Newman, D. A., & Roisman, G. I. (2015). Explaining the Black–White gap in cognitive test scores: Toward a theory of adverse impact. *Journal of Applied Psychology, 100*, 1713–1736.

Coubart, A., Izard, V., Spelke, E. S., Marie, J., & Streri, A. (2014). Dissociation between small and large numerosities in newborn infants. *Developmental Science, 17*, 11–22.

Couch, S. C., Glanz, K., Zhou, C., Sallis, J. F., & Saelens, B. E. (2014). Home food environment in relation to children's diet quality and weight status. Journal of the *Academy of Nutrition and Dietetics, 114*, 1569–1579.

Courage, M. L., & Howe, M. L. (2010). To watch or not to watch: Infants and toddlers in a brave new electronic world. *Developmental Review, 30*, 101–115.

Courchesne, E., Mouton, P. R., Calhoun, M. E., Semendeferi, K., Ahrens-Barbeau, C., Hallet, M. J., et al. (2011). Neuron number and size in prefrontal cortex of children with autism. *Journal of the American Medical Association, 306*, 2001–2010.

Cowan, N., & Alloway, T. (2009). Development of working memory in childhood. In M. L. Courage & N. Cowan (Eds.), *Development of memory in infancy and childhood* (pp. 303–342). Hove, UK: Psychology Press.

Cox, B. D. (2013). The past and future of epigenesis in psychology. *New Ideas in Psychology, 31*, 351–354.

Cox, R. G., Zhang, L., Zotti, M. E., & Graham, J. (2011). Prenatal care utilization in Mississippi: Racial disparities and implications for unfavorable birth outcomes. *Maternal and Child Health Journal, 15*, 931–942.

Cox, S. M., Hopkins, J., & Hans, S. L. (2000). Attachment in preterm infants and their mothers: Neonatal risk status and maternal representations. *Infant Mental Health Journal, 21*, 464–480.

Coyle, T. R. (2013). Effects of processing speed on intelligence may be underestimated: Comment on Demetriou et al. (2013). *Intelligence, 41*, 732–734.

Craig, C. M., & Lee, D. N. (1999). Neonatal control of nutritive sucking pressure: Evidence for an intrinsic tau-guide. *Experimental Brain Research, 124*, 371–382.

Craig, H. K. (2015). African American English and its link to reading achievement. In A. Pollatsek & R. Treiman (Eds.), *Oxford handbook of reading* (pp. 431–446). New York: Oxford University Press.

Craig, H. K., Kolenic, G. E., & Hensel, S. L. (2014). African American English-speaking students: A longitudinal examination of style shifting from kindergarten through second grade. *Journal of Speech, Language, and Hearing Research, 57*, 143–157.

Craig, H. K., & Washington, J. A. (2006). *Malik goes to school: Examining the language skills of African American students from preschool–5th grade.* Mahwah, NJ: Erlbaum.

Craig, J. T., Gregus, S. J., Elledge, C., Pastrana, F. A., & Cavell, T. A. (2016). Preliminary investigation of the relation between lunchroom peer acceptance and peer victimization. *Journal of Applied Developmental Psychology, 43*, 101–111.

Craig, L., & Brown, J. E. (2017). Feeling rushed: Gendered time quality, work hours, nonstandard work schedules, and spousal crossover. *Journal of Marriage and Family, 79*, 225–242.

Crair, M. C., Gillespie, D. C., & Stryker, M. P. (1998). The role of visual experience in the development of columns in the cat visual cortex. *Science, 279*, 566–570.

Cramer, S. J. E., Dekker, J., Dankelman, J., Pauws, S. C., Hooper, S. B., & te Pas, A. B. (2018). Effect of tactile stimulation on termination and prevention of apnea of prematurity: A systematic review. *Frontiers in Pediatrics, 6*, 45.

Creasey, G. L., Jarvis, P. A., & Berk, L. E. (1998). Play and social competence. In O. N. Saracho & B. Spodek (Eds.), *Multiple perspectives on play in early childhood education* (pp. 116–143). Albany: State University of New York Press.

Crick, N. R., & Dodge, K. A. (1994). A review and reformulation of social information-processing mechanisms in children's social adjustment. *Psychological Bulletin, 115*, 74–101.

Crick, N. R., Ostrov, J. M., Burr, J. E., Cullerton-Sen, C., Jansen-Yeh, E., & Ralston, P. (2006). A longitudinal study of relational and physical aggression in preschool. *Journal of Applied Developmental Psychology, 27*, 254–268.

Crick, N. R., Ostrov, J. M., & Werner, N. E. (2006). A longitudinal study of relational aggression, physical aggression, and social-psychological adjustment. *Journal of Abnormal Child Psychology, 34*, 131–142.

Crockenberg, S. C., & Leerkes, E. M. (2004). Infant and maternal behaviors regulate infant reactivity to novelty at 6 months. *Developmental Psychology, 40*, 1123–1132.

Cronin, L. D. (2015). Developmental experiences and well-being in sport: The importance of the coaching climates. *Sport Psychologist, 29*, 62–71.

Crookston, B. T., Schott, W., Cueto, S., Dearden, K. A., Engle, P., Georgiadis, A., et al. (2013). Postinfancy growth, schooling, and cognitive achievement: Young lives. *American Journal of Clinical Nutrition, 98*, 1555–1563.

Crosby, B., LeBourgeois, M. K., & Harsh, J. (2005). Racial differences in reported napping and nocturnal sleep in 2- to 8-year-old children. *Pediatrics, 115*, 225–232.

Crosnoe, R., & Benner, A. D. (2015). Children at school. In M. H. Bornstein & T. Leventhal (Eds.), *Handbook of child psychology and developmental science: Vol. 4. Ecological settings and processes* (7th ed., pp. 268–304). Hoboken, NJ: Wiley.

Crouch, J. L., Skowronski, J. J., Milner, J. S., & Harris, B. (2008). Parental responses to infant crying: The influence of child physical abuse risk and hostile priming. *Child Abuse and Neglect, 32*, 702–710.

Csibra, G. (2010). Recognizing communicative intentions in infancy. *Mind and Language, 25*, 141–168.

Cuadros, O., & Berger, C. (2016). The protective role of friendship quality on the wellbeing of adolescents victimized by peers. *Journal of Youth and Adolescence, 45*, 1877–1888.

Cummings, E. M., & Davies, P. T. (2010). *Children, emotional security and marital conflict.* New York: Guilford.

Cummings, E. M., & Miller-Graff, L. E. (2015). Emotional security theory: An emerging theoretical model for youths' psychological and physiological responses across multiple developmental contexts. *Current Directions in Psychological Science, 24*, 208–213.

Curtin, S., & Werker, J. F. (2007). The perceptual foundations of phonological development. In G. Gaskell (Ed.), *Oxford handbook of psycholinguistics* (pp. 579–599). Oxford, UK: Oxford University Press.

Cutas, D., & Smajdor, A. (2015). Postmenopausal motherhood reloaded: Advanced age and in vitro derived gametes. *Hypatia, 30*, 386–402.

Cutuli, J. J., Herbers, J. E., Rinaldi, M., Masten, A. S., & Oberg, C. N. (2010). Asthma and behavior in homeless 4- to 7-year-olds. *Pediatrics, 125*, e145-e151.

Cvencek, D., Meltzoff, A. N., & Greenwald, A. G. (2011). Math–gender stereotypes in elementary school children. *Child Development, 82*, 766–779.

Cyr, C., Euser, E. M., Bakermans-Kranenburg, M. J., & van IJzendoorn, M. H. (2010). Attachment security and disorganization in maltreating and high-risk families: Implications for developmental theory. *Development and Psychopathology, 14*, 843–860.

D

Dabrowska, E. (2015). What exactly is universal grammar, and has anyone seen it? *Frontiers in Psychology, 6*, Art. No. 852.

Dağli, Ü. Y., & Jones, I. (2013). The longitudinal effects of kindergarten enrollment and relative age on children's academic achievement. *Teachers College Record, 115*, 1–40.

Dahl, A., & Chan, S. S. I. (2017). Power assertion in everyday mother–infant interactions. *Infant Behavior and Development, 47*, 58–61.

Dai, Q., Williams, J., & McGregor, E. (2016). Who am I? Self-concept of Scottish-born Chinese children: A comparison with White Scottish, Mainland Chinese, and Hong Kong Chinese children. *Identity, 16*, 239–249.

Dakil, S. R., Cox, M., Lin, H., & Flores, G. (2012). Physical abuse in U.S. children: Risk factors and deficiencies in referrals to support services. *Journal of Aggression, Maltreatment, and Trauma, 21*, 555–569.

Damian, R. I., & Roberts, B. W. (2015). The associations of birth order with personality and intelligence in a representative sample of U.S. high school students. *Journal of Research in Personality, 58*, 96–105.

Damon, W. (1988). *The moral child.* New York: Free Press.

Damon, W., & Hart, D. (1988). *Self-understanding in childhood and adolescence.* New York: Cambridge University Press.

Daniel, E., Madigan, S., & Jenkins, J. (2016). Paternal and maternal warmth and the development of prosociality among preschoolers. *Journal of Family Psychology, 30*, 114–124.

Daniel, J. H. (2018). *Statement of APA (American Psychological Association) president regarding the traumatic effects of separating immigrant families.* Retrieved from www.apa.org/news/press/releases /2018/05/separating-immigrant-families

Daniels, H. (2011). Vygotsky and psychology. In U. Goswami (Ed.), *The Wiley-Blackwell handbook of childhood cognitive development* (2nd ed., pp. 673–696). Malden, MA: Wiley-Blackwell.

Danielson, M. L., Bitsko, R. H., Ghandour, R. M., Kogan, M. D., & Blumberg, S. J. (2018). Prevalence of parent-reported ADHD diagnosis and associated treatment among U.S. children and adolescents, 2016. *Journal of Clinical Child & Adolescent Psychology, 47*, 199–212.

Dannemiller, J. L., & Stephens, B. R. (1988). A critical test of infant pattern preference models. *Child Development, 59*, 210–216.

Danzer, E., & Johnson, M. P. (2014). Fetal surgery for neural tube defects. *Seminars in Fetal and Neonatal Medicine, 19*, 2–8.

Darwin, C. (2003). *The origin of species: 150th anniversary edition.* New York: Signet Classics. (Original work published 1859)

Daskalakis, N., & Yehuda, R. (2014). Site-specific methylation changes in the glucocorticoid receptor exon 1F promoter in relation to life adversity: Systematic review of contributing factors. *Frontiers in Neuroscience, 8*, 369.

Daugherty, A. M., Flinn, R., & Ofen, N. (2017). Hippocampal CA3-dentate gyrus volume uniquely linked to improvement in associative memory from childhood to late adulthood. *Hippocampus, 26*, 220–228.

Daum, M. (2016). Cognitive development during infancy. In B. Hopkins, E. Geangu, & S. Linkenauger (Eds.), *Cambridge encyclopedia of child development* (2nd ed., pp. 277–287). Cambridge, UK: Cambridge University Press.

Davidson Institute. (2019). *Support for gifted programs varies greatly from state to state.* Retrieved from www.davidsongifted.org /Search-Database/entryType/3

Davies, J. (2008). Differential teacher positive and negative interactions with male and female pupils in the primary school setting. *Educational and Child Psychology, 25*, 17–26.

Davies, P. T., & Cichetti, D. (2014). How and why does the 5-HTTLPR gender moderate associations between maternal unresponsiveness and children's disruptive problems? *Child Development, 85*, 484–500.

Davis, E. L., & Buss, K. A. (2012). Moderators of the relation between shyness and behavior with peers: Cortisol dysregulation and maternal emotion socialization. *Social Development, 21*, 801–820.

Davis, E. L., Levine, L. J., Lench, H. C., & Quas, J. A. (2010). Metacognitive emotion regulation: Children's awareness that changing thoughts and goals can alleviate negative emotions. *Emotion, 10*, 498–510.

Davis, K. F., Parker, K. P., & Montgomery, G. L. (2004). Sleep in infants and young children. Part 1: Normal sleep. *Journal of Pediatric Health Care, 18*, 65–71.

Davis, P. E., Meins, E., & Fernyhough, C. (2014). Children with imaginary companions focus on mental characteristics when describing their real-life friends. *Infant and Child Development, 23*, 622–633.

Dawson, C., & Gerken, L. A. (2009). From domain-generality to domain-sensitivity: 4-month-olds learn an abstract repetition rule in music that 7-month-olds do not. *Cognition, 111*, 378–382.

Dayton, C. J., Walsh, T. B., Oh, W., & Volling, B. (2015). Hush now baby: Mothers' and fathers' strategies for soothing their infants and associated parenting outcomes. *Journal of Pediatric Health Care, 29*, 145–155.

Dearing, E., McCartney, K., & Taylor, B. A. (2009). Does higher quality early child care promote low-income children's math and reading achievement in middle childhood? *Child Development, 80*, 1329–1349.

Dearing, E., Wimer, C., Simpkins, S. D., Lund, T., Bouffard, S. M., Caronongan, P., & Kreider, H. (2009). Do neighborhood and home contexts help explain why low-income children miss opportunities to participate in activities outside of school? *Developmental Psychology, 45*, 1545–1562.

Deary, I. J., Strand, S., Smith, P., & Fernandes, C. (2007). Intelligence and educational achievement. *Intelligence, 35*, 13–21.

Deater-Deckard, K., Lansford, J. E., Dodge, K. A., Pettit, G. S., & Bates, J. E. (2003). The development of attitudes about physical punishment: An 8-year longitudinal study. *Journal of Family Psychology, 17*, 351–360.

DeBoer, T., Scott, L. S., & Nelson, C. A. (2007). Methods for acquiring and analyzing infant event-related potentials. In M. de Haan (Ed.), *Infant EEG and event-related potentials* (pp. 5–37). New York: Psychology Press.

de Boisferon, A., Tift, A. H., Minar, N. J., Lewkowicz, D. J. (2017). Selective attention to a talker's mouth in infancy: Role of audiovisual temporal synchrony and linguistic experience. *Developmental Science, 20*, e12381.

Debrabant, J., Gheysen, F., Vingerhoets, G., & Van Waelvelde, H. (2012). Age-related differences in predictive response timing in children: Evidence from regularly relative to irregularly paced reaction time performance. *Human Movement Science, 31,* 801–810.

de Bruyn, E. H., & Cillessen, A. H. N. (2006). Popularity in early adolescence: Prosocial and antisocial subtypes. *Journal of Adolescent Research, 21,* 607–627.

DeCasper, A. J., & Spence, M. J. (1986). Prenatal maternal speech influences newborns' perception of speech sounds. *Infant Behavior and Development, 9,* 133–150.

Declercq, E. R., Sakala, C., Corry, M. P., Applebaum, S., & Herrlich, A. (2014). Major survey findings of Listening to Mothers (SM) III: Pregnancy and Birth. *Journal of Perinatal Education, 23,* 9–16.

de Cock, E. S. A., Henrichs, J., Rijk, C. H. A. M., & van Bakel, H. J. A. (2015). Baby please stop crying: An experimental approach to infant crying, affect, and expected parent self-efficacy. Journal of *Reproductive and Infant Psychology, 33,* 414–425.

De Corte, E., & Verschaffel, L. (2006). Mathematical thinking and learning. In K. A. Renninger & I. E. Sigel (Eds.), *Handbook of child psychology: Vol. 4. Child psychology in practice* (6th ed., pp. 103–152). Hoboken, NJ: Wiley.

de Haan, M. (2015). Neuroscientific methods with children. In P. D. Zelazo (Ed.), *Oxford handbook of developmental psychology: Vol. 1. Body and mind* (pp. 683–712). New York: Oxford University Press.

de Haan, M., & Matheson, A. (2009). The development and neural bases of processing emotion in faces and voices. In M. de Haan & M. R. Gunnar (Eds.), *Handbook of developmental social science* (pp. 107–121). New York: Guilford.

De Hoog, M. L. A., Venekamp, R. P., van der Ent, C. K., Schilder, A., Sanders, E. A. M., Damoiseaux, R. A. M. J., et al. (2014). Impact of early daycare on healthcare resource use related to upper respiratory tract infections during childhood: Prospective WHISTLER cohort study. *BMC Medicine, 12,* 107.

De Laet, S. Doumen, S., Vervoort, E., Colpin, H., Van Leeuwen, K., Goossens, L., & Verschueren, K. (2014). Transactional links between teacher–child relationship quality and perceived versus sociometric popularity: A three-wave longitudinal study. *Child Development, 85,* 1647–1662.

de la Monte, S. M., & Kril, J. J. (2014). Human alcohol related neuropathology. *Acta Neuropathologica, 127,* 71–90.

De Lisi, R., & Gallagher, A. M. (1991). Understanding gender stability and constancy in Argentinean children. *Merrill-Palmer Quarterly, 37,* 483–502.

DeLoache, J. S. (1987). Rapid change in symbolic functioning of very young children. *Science, 238,* 1556–1557.

DeLoache, J. S. (2002). The symbol-mindedness of young children. In W. Hartup & R. A. Weinberg (Eds.), *Minnesota symposia on child psychology* (Vol. 32, pp. 73–101). Mahwah, NJ: Erlbaum.

DeLoache, J. S., Chiong, C., Sherman, K., Islam, N., Vanderborght, M., Troseth, G. L., et al. (2010). Do babies learn from baby media? *Psychological Science, 21,* 1570–1574.

DeLoache, J. S., & Ganea, P. A. (2009). Symbol-based learning in infancy. In A. Woodward & A. Needham (Eds.), *Learning and the infant mind* (pp. 263–285). New York: Oxford University Press.

DeLoache, J. S., LoBue, V., Vanderborght, M., & Chiong, C. (2013). On the validity and robustness of the scale error phenomenon in early childhood. *Infant Behavior and Development, 36,* 63–70.

DeMarie, D., & Lopez, L. M. (2014). Memory in schools. In P. J. Bauer & R. Fivush (Eds.), *Wiley handbook on the development of children's memory* (Vol. 2, pp. 836–864). Malden, MA: Wiley-Blackwell.

DeMarie, D., Miller, P. H., Ferron, J., & Cunningham, W. R. (2004). Path analysis tests of theoretical models of children's memory performance. *Journal of Cognition and Development, 5,* 461–492.

Denham, S. (1998). *Emotional development in young children.* New York: Guilford.

Denham, S., Warren, H., von Salisch, M., Benga, O., Chin, J., & Geangu, E. (2011). Emotions and social development in childhood. In P. K. Smith & C. H. Hart (Eds.), *Wiley-Blackwell handbook of childhood social development* (2nd ed., pp. 413–433). Chichester, UK: Wiley-Blackwell.

Denham, S. A., Bassett, H. H., Way, E. E., Mincic, M., Zinsser, K., & Graling, K. B. (2012). Preschoolers' emotion knowledge: Self-regulatory foundations and predictions of early school success. *Cognition and Emotion, 26,* 667–679.

Denissen, J. J. A., Zarrett, N. R., & Eccles, J. S. (2007). I like to do it, I'm able, and I know I am: Longitudinal couplings between domain-specific achievement, self-concept, and interest. *Child Development, 78,* 430–447.

Dennis, M., Spiegler, B. J., Simic, N., Sinopoli, K. J., Wilkinson, A., Yeates, K. O., et al. (2014). Functional plasticity in childhood brain disorders: When, what, how, and whom to assess. *Neuropsychological Review, 24,* 389–408.

Dennis, T. A., & Kelemen, D. A. (2009). Preschool children's views on emotion regulation: Functional associations and implications for social–emotional adjustment. *International Journal of Behavioral Development, 33,* 243–252.

Denno, D. M., & Paul, S. L. (2017). Child health and survival in a changing world. *Pediatric Clinics of North America, 64,* 735–754.

de Onis, M. (2017). Child growth and development. In S. de Pee, D. Taren, & M. Bloem (Eds.), *Nutrition and health in a developing world* (pp. 119–141). New York: Springer Science + Business Media.

Deprest, J. A., Devlieger, R., Srisupundit, K., Beck, V., Sandaite, I., Rusconi, S., et al. (2010). Fetal surgery is a clinical reality. *Seminars in Fetal & Neonatal Medicine, 15,* 58–67.

DeRosier, M. E. (2007). Peer-rejected and bullied children: A safe schools initiative for elementary school students. In J. E. Zins, M. J. Elias, & C. A. Maher (Eds.), *Bullying, victimization, and peer harassment* (pp. 257–276). New York: Haworth.

de Rosnay, M., Copper, P. J., Tsigaras, N., & Murray, L. (2006). Transmission of social anxiety from mother to infant: An experimental study using a social referencing paradigm. *Behavior Research and Therapy, 44,* 1165–1175.

de Rosnay, M., & Hughes, C. (2006). Conversation and theory of mind: Do children talk their way to socio-cognitive understanding? *British Journal of Developmental Psychology, 24,* 7–37.

DeSisto, C. L., Kim, S. Y., & Sharma, A. J. (2014). Prevalence estimates of gestational diabetes mellitus in the United States, Pregnancy Risk Assessment Monitoring System (PRAMS), 2007–2010. *Preventing Chronic Disease, 11,* 130415.

Dessens, A. B., Slijper, F. M. E., & Drop, S. L. S. (2005). Gender dysphoria and gender change in chromosomal females with congenital adrenal hyperplasia. *Archives of Sexual Behavior, 34,* 389–397.

de Villiers, J. G., & de Villiers, P. A. (2014). The role of language in theory of mind development. *Topics in Language Disorders, 34,* 313–328.

Devine, R. T., Bignardi, G., & Hughes, C. (2016). Executive function mediates the relations between parental behaviors and children's early academic ability. *Frontiers in Psychology, 7,* Art. No. 1902.

Devine, R. T., & Hughes, C. (2018). Family correlates of false belief understanding in early childhood: A meta-analysis. *Child Development, 89,* 12682.

Devine, R. T., White, N., Ensor, R., & Hughes, C. (2016). Theory of mind in middle childhood: Longitudinal associations with executive function and social competence. *Developmental Psychology, 52,* 758–771.

DeVries, R. (2001). Constructivist education in preschool and elementary school: The sociomoral atmosphere as the first educational goal. In S. L. Golbeck (Ed.), *Psychological perspectives on early childhood education* (pp. 153–180). Mahwah, NJ: Erlbaum.

de Waal, F. B. M. (2001). *Tree of origin.* Cambridge, MA: Harvard University Press.

de Weerth, C., & St James-Roberts, I. (2017). Prolonged infant crying and colic. In B. Hopkins, E. Geangu, & S. Linkenauger (Eds.), *Cambridge encyclopedia of child development* (pp. 717–722). New York: Cambridge University Press.

Deynoot-Schaub, M. J. G., & Riksen-Walraven, J. M. (2006a). Peer contacts of 15-month-olds in childcare: Links with child temperament, parent–child interaction and quality of childcare. *Social Development 15,* 709–729.

Deynoot-Schaub, M. J. G., & Riksen-Walraven, J. M. (2006b). Peer interaction in child care centres at 15 and 23 months: Stability and links with children's socioemotional adjustment. *Infant Behavior and Development, 29,* 276–288.

Diamond, A. (2004). Normal development of prefrontal cortex from birth to young adulthood: Cognitive functions, anatomy, and biochemistry. In D. T. Stuss & R. T. Knight (Eds.), *Principles of frontal lobe function* (p. 474). New York: Oxford University Press.

Diamond, A., Cruttenden, L., & Neiderman, D. (1994). AB with multiple wells: 1. Why are multiple wells sometimes easier than two wells? 2. Memory or memory + inhibition. *Developmental Psychology, 30,* 192–205.

Diamond, G., Senecky, Y., Reichman, H., Inbar, D., & Chodick, G. (2015). Parental perception of developmental vulnerability after inter-country adoption: A 10-year follow-up study: Longitudinal study after inter-country adoption. *International Journal of Disabilities and Human Development, 14,* 75–80.

Diaz, A., & Bell, M. A. (2012). Frontal EEG asymmetry and fear reactivity in different contexts at 10 months. *Developmental Psychobiology, 54,* 536–545.

Diaz, V., & Farrar, M. J. (2018). Do bilingual and monolingual preschoolers acquire false belief understanding similarly? The role of executive functioning and language. *First Language, 38,* 382–398.

Dickinson, D. K., Golinkoff, R. M., & Hirsh-Pasek, K. (2010). Speaking out for language: Why language is central to reading development. *Educational Researcher, 39,* 305–310.

Dickinson, D. K., & McCabe, A. (2001). Bringing it all together: The multiple origins, skills, and environmental supports of early literacy. *Learning Disabilities Research and Practice, 16,* 186–202.

Dick-Read, G. (1959). *Childbirth without fear.* New York: Harper & Brothers.

Dickson, D. J., Richmond, A. D., Brendgen, M., Vitaro, F., Laursen, B., Dionne, G., & Boivin, M. (2015). Aggression can be contagious: Longitudinal associations between proactive aggression and reactive aggression among young twins. *Aggressive Behavior, 41,* 455–466.

DiDonato, M. D., & Berenbaum, S. A. (2011). The benefits and drawbacks of gender typing: How different dimensions are related to psychological adjustment. *Archives of Sexual Behavior, 40,* 457–463.

Diepstra, H., Trehub, S. E., Eriks-Brophy, A., van Lieshout, P. H. H. M. (2017). Imitation of non-speech oral gestures by 8-month-old infants. *Language and Speech, 60,* 154–166.

DiLalla, L. F., Bersted, K., & John, S. G. (2015). Evidence of reactive gene-environment correlation in preschoolers' prosocial play with unfamiliar peers. *Developmental Psychology, 51,* 1464–1475.

Dinella, L. M., & Weisgram, E. (2018). Gender-typing of children's toys: Causes, consequences, and correlates. *Sex Roles, 79,* 253–259.

Di Pasquale, R., & Celsi, L. (2017). Stigmatization of overweight and obese peers among children. *Frontiers in Psychology, 8,* Art. No. 524.

DiPietro, J. A., Bornstein, M. H., Costigan, K. A., Pressman, E. K., Hahn, C.-S., & Painter, K. (2002). What does fetal movement predict about behavior during the first two years of life? *Developmental Psychobiology, 40,* 358–371.

DiPietro, J. A., Costigan, K. A., & Voegtline, K. M. (2015). Studies in fetal behavior: Revisited, renewed, and reimagined. *Monographs of the Society for Research in Child Development, 80*(3, Serial No. 318).

DiPietro, J. A., Hodgson, D. M., Costigan, K. A., & Hilton, S. C. (1996). Fetal neurobehavioral development. *Child Development, 67,* 2553–2567.

DiPietro, J. A., Novak, M. F. S. X., Costigan, K. A., Atella, L. D., & Reusing, S. P. (2006). Maternal psychological distress during pregnancy in relation to child development at age two. *Child Development, 77,* 573–587.

Dirks, M. A., Persram, R., Recchia, H. A., & Howe, N. (2015). Sibling relationships as sources of risk and resilience in the development and maintenance of internalizing and externalizing problems during childhood and adolescence. *Clinical Psychology Review, 42,* 145–155.

Dishion, T. J., Shaw, D., Connell, A., Gardner, F., Weaver, C., & Wilson, M. (2008). The family checkup with high-risk indigent families: Preventing problem behavior by increasing parents' positive behavior support in early childhood. *Child Development, 79,* 1395–1414.

Dittmar, M., Abbot-Smith, K., Lieven, E., & Tomasello, M. (2014). Familiar verbs are not always easier than novel verbs: How German preschool children comprehend active and passive sentences. *Cognitive Science, 38,* 128–151.

Dix, T., Stewart, A. D., Gershoff, E. T., & Day, W. H. (2007). Autonomy and children's reactions to being controlled: Evidence that both compliance and defiance may be positive markers in early development. *Child Development, 78,* 1204–1221.

Doan, S. N., Tardif, T., Miller, A., Olson, S., Kessler, D., Felt, B., & Wang, L. (2017). Consequences of 'tiger' parenting: A cross-cultural study of maternal psychological control and children's cortisol stress response. *Developmental Science, 20,* e12404.

Dodd, V. L. (2005). Implications of kangaroo care for growth and development in preterm infants. *JOGNN, 34,* 218–232.

Dodge, K. A., Coie, J. D., & Lynam, D. (2006). Aggression and antisocial behavior in youth. In N. Eisenberg (Ed.), *Handbook of child psychology: Vol. 3. Social, emotional, and personality development* (6th ed., pp. 719–788). Hoboken, NJ: Wiley.

Dodge, K. A., & Haskins, R. (2015). Children and government. In M. H. Bornstein & T. Leventhal (Eds.), *Handbook of child psychology and developmental science: Vol. 4. Ecological settings and processes* (7th ed., pp. 654–703). Hoboken, NJ: Wiley.

Dodge, K. A., McLoyd, V. C., & Lansford, J. E. (2006). The cultural context of physically disciplining children. In V. C. McLoyd, N. E. Hill, & K. A. Dodge (Eds.), *African-American family life: Ecological and cultural diversity* (pp. 245–263). New York: Guilford.

Dodge, K. A., Pettit, G. S., McClaskey, C. L., & Brown, M. M. (1986). Social competence in children. *Monographs of the Society for Research in Child Development, 51*(2, Serial No. 213).

Dohnt, H., & Tiggemann, M. (2006). The contribution of peer and media influences to the development of body satisfaction and self-esteem in young girls: A prospective study. *Developmental Psychology, 42,* 929–936.

Dombroski, J., & Newman, R. S. (2014). Toddlers' ability to map the meaning of new words in multi-talker environments. *Journal of the Acoustical Society of America, 115,* 2964–2973.

Domitrovich, C. E., Cortes, R. C., & Greenberg, M. T. (2007). Improving young children's social and emotional competence: A randomized trial of the preschool "PATHS" curriculum. *Journal of Primary Prevention, 28,* 67–91.

Domitrovich, C. E., Gest, S. D., Gill, S., Bierman, K. L., Welsh, J. A., & Jones, D. (2009). Fostering high-quality teaching with an enriched curriculum and professional development support: The Head Start REDI program. *American Educational Research Journal, 46,* 567–597.

Don, B. P., & Mickelson, K. D. (2014). Relationship satisfaction trajectories across the transition to parenthood among low-risk parents. *Journal of Marriage and Family, 76,* 677–692.

Dondi, M., Simion, F., & Caltran, G. (1999). Can newborns discriminate between their own cry and the cry of another newborn infant? *Developmental Psychology, 35,* 418–426.

Donnellan, M. B., Trzesniewski, K. H., Robins, R. W., Moffitt, T. E., & Caspi, A. (2005). Low self-esteem is related to aggression, antisocial behavior, and delinquency. *Psychological Science, 16,* 328–335.

Donnelly, J. E., Greene, J. L., Gibson, C. A., Smith, B. K., Washburn, R. A., Sullivan, D. K., DuBose, K., et al. (2009). Physical activity across the curriculum (PAAC): A randomized controlled trial to promote physical activity and diminish overweight and obesity in elementary school children. *Preventive Medicine, 49,* 336–341.

Donnelly, J. E., Hillman, C. H., Castelli, D., Etnier, J. L., Lee, S., Tomporowski, P., et al.

(2016). Physical activity, fitness, cognitive function, and academic achievement. *Medicine and Science in Sports and Exercise, 48,* 1197–1222.

Dorn, B. (2015). Pre- and post-welfare reform media portrayals of poverty in the United States: The continuing importance of race and ethnicity. *Politics & Policy, 43,* 142–162.

Dorris, M. (1989). *The broken cord.* New York: Harper & Row.

Dorwie, F. M., & Pacquiao, D. F. (2014). Practices of traditional birth attendants in Sierra Leone and perceptions by mothers and health professionals familiar with their care. *Journal of Transcultural Nursing, 25,* 33–41.

Doss, B. D., Cicila, L. N., Hsueh, A. C., Morrison, K. R., & Carhart, K. (2014). A randomized controlled trial of brief coparenting and relationship interventions during the transition to parenthood. *Journal of Family Psychology, 28,* 483–494.

Doss, B. D., Rhoades, G. K., Stanley, S. M., & Markman, H. J. (2009). The effect of the transition to parenthood on relationship quality: An 8-year prospective study. *Journal of Personality and Social Psychology, 96,* 601–619.

Douglas, E. M. (2006). *Mending broken families: Social policies for divorced families.* Lanham, MD: Rowman & Littlefield.

Dowker, A. (2003). Younger children's estimates for addition: The zone of partial knowledge and understanding. In A. J. Baroody & A. Dowker (Eds.), *The development of arithmetic concepts and skills: Constructing adaptive expertise* (pp. 243–265). Mahwah, NJ: Erlbaum.

Downes, K. L., Shenassa, E. D., & Grantz, K. L. (2017). Neonatal outcomes associated with placental abruption. *American Journal of Epidemiology, 186,* 1319–1328.

Downing, J. E. (2010). *Academic instruction for students with moderate and severe intellectual disabilities.* Thousand Oaks, CA: Corwin.

Doyle, C., & Cicchetti, D. (2017). From the cradle to the grave: The effect of adverse caregiving environments on attachment relationships throughout the lifespan. *Clinical Psychology, 24,* 203–217.

Drake, K., Belsky, J., & Fearon, R. M. P. (2014). From early attachment to engagement with learning in school: The role of self-regulation and persistence. *Developmental Psychology, 50,* 1350–1361.

Driver, J., Tabares, A., Shapiro, A. F., & Gottman, J. M. (2012). Couple interaction in happy and unhappy marriages: Gottman Laboratory studies. In F. Walsh (Ed.), *Normal family processes: Growing diversity and complexity* (pp. 57–77). New York: Guilford.

Druet, C., Stettler, N., Sharp, S., Simmons, R. K., Cooper, C., Smith, G. D., et al. (2012). Prediction of childhood obesity by infancy weight gain: An individual-level meta-analysis. *Paediatric and Perinatal Epidemiology, 26,* 19–26.

Drummond, J. D. K., Hammond, S. I., Satlof-Bedrick, E., Waugh, W. E., & Brownell, C. A. (2017). Helping the one you hurt: Toddlers' rudimentary guilt, shame, and prosocial behavior after harming another. *Child Development, 88,* 1382–1397.

Dubois, L., Kyvik, K. O., Girard, M., Tatone-Tokuda, F., Pérusse, D., Hjelmborg, J., et al. (2012). Genetic and environmental contributions to weight, height, and BMI from birth to 19 years of age: An international study of over 12,000 twin pairs. *PLOS ONE, 7*(2), e30153.

Duckworth, A. L., Quinn, P. D., & Tsukayama, E. (2012). What No Child Left Behind leaves behind: The roles of IQ and self-control in predicting standardized achievement test scores and report card grades. *Journal of Educational Psychology, 104,* 439–451.

Dudani, A., Macpherson, A., & Tamim, H. (2010). Childhood behavior problems and unintentional injury: A longitudinal, population-based study. *Journal of Developmental and Behavioral Pediatrics, 31,* 276–285.

Dueker, G. L., Modi, A., & Needham, A. (2003). 4.5-month-old infants' learning, retention and use of object boundary information. *Infant Behavior and Development, 26,* 588–605.

Duncan, G. J., Dowsett, C. J., Claessens, A., Magnuson, K., Huston, A. C., Klebanov, P., et al. (2007). School readiness and later achievement. *Developmental Psychology, 43,* 1428–1446.

Duncan, G. J., & Magnuson, K. A. (2003). Off with Hollingshead: Socioeconomic resources, parenting, and child development. In M. H. Bornstein & R. H. Bradley (Eds.), *Socioeconomic status, parenting, and child development* (pp. 83–106). Mahwah, NJ: Erlbaum.

Duncan, G. J., Magnuson, K., Kalil, A., & Ziol-Guest, K. (2012). The importance of early childhood poverty. *Social Indicators Research, 108,* 87–98.

Duncan, G. J., Magnuson, K. A., & Votruba-Drzal, E. (2015). Children and socioeconomic status. In M. H. Bornstein & T. Leventhal (Eds.), *Handbook of child psychology and developmental science: Vol. 4. Ecological settings and processes* (7th ed., pp. 534–573). Hoboken, NJ: Wiley.

Duncan, S. C., Strycker, L. A., & Chaumeton, N. R. (2015). Sports participation and positive correlates in African American, Latino, & White girls. *Applied Developmental Science, 19,* 206–216.

Dundek, L. H. (2006) Establishment of a Somali doula program at a large metropolitan hospital. *Journal of Perinatal and Neonatal Nursing, 20,* 128–137.

Dunham, Y., Baron, A. S., & Banaji, M. R. (2006). From American city to Japanese village: A cross-cultural investigation of implicit race attitudes. *Child Development, 77,* 1129–1520.

Dunham, Y., Baron, A. S., & Carey, S. (2011). Consequences of "minimal" group affiliations in children. *Child Development, 82,* 793–811.

Dunham, Y., Chen, E. E., & Banaji, M. R. (2013). Two signatures of implicit intergroup attitudes: Developmental invariance and early enculturation. *Psychological Science, 24,* 860–868.

Dunkel-Schetter, C. (2011). Psychological science on pregnancy: Stress processes, biopsychosocial models, and emerging research issues. *Annual Review of Psychology, 62,* 531–558.

Dunkel-Shetter, C., & Lobel, M. (2012). Pregnancy and birth: A multilevel analysis of stress and birth weight. In T. A. Revenson, A. Baum, & J. Singer (Eds.), *Handbook of Health Psychology* (2nd ed., pp. 431–463). London: Psychology Press.

Dunn, J. (1989). Siblings and the development of social understanding in early childhood. In P. G. Zukow (Ed.), *Sibling interaction across cultures* (pp. 106–116). New York: Springer-Verlag.

Dunn, J. (1994). Temperament, siblings, and the development of relationships. In W. B. Carey & S. C. McDevitt (Eds.),

Prevention and early intervention (pp. 50–58). New York: Brunner/Mazel.

Dunn, J. (2004). Sibling relationships. In P. K. Smith & C. H. Hart (Eds.), *Handbook of childhood social development* (pp. 223–237). Malden, MA: Blackwell.

Dunn, J. (2005). Moral development in early childhood and social interaction in the family. In M. Killen & J. G. Smetana (Eds.), *Handbook of moral development* (pp. 331–350). Mahwah, NJ: Erlbaum.

Dunn, J. (2014). Sibling relationships across the lifespan. In D. Hindle & S. Sherwin-White (Eds.), *Sibling matters: A psychoanalytic, developmental, and systemic approach* (pp. 151–168). London, UK: Karnac Books.

Dunn, J., Cutting, A. L., & Demetriou, H. (2000). Moral sensibility, understanding others, and children's friendship interactions in the preschool period. *British Journal of Developmental Psychology, 18,* 159–177.

Dunn, J. R., Schaefer-McDaniel, N. J., & Ramsay, J. T. (2010). Neighborhood chaos and children's development: Questions and contradictions. In G. W. Evans & T. D. Wachs (Eds.), *Chaos and its influence on children's development: An ecological perspective* (pp. 173–189). Washington, DC: American Psychological Association.

Dunn, K., & Bremner, J. G. (2017). Investigating looking and social looking measures as an index of infant violation of expectation. *Developmental Science, 20,* e12452.

Dupierrix, E., de Boisferon, A. H., Méary, D., Lee, K., Quinn, P. C., Di Giorgio, E., et al. (2014). Preference for human eyes in human infants. *Journal of Experimental Child Psychology, 123,* 138–146.

Durbin, D. R., & Hoffman, B. D. (2018). Child passenger safety. *Pediatrics, 142,* e20182460.

duRivage, N., Keyes, K., Leray, E., Pez, O., Bilfoi, A., Ko., C., et al. (2015). Parental use of corporal punishment in Europe: Intersection between public health and policy. *PLOS ONE, 10*(2), e0118059.

Durkin, M. S., Laraque, D., Lubman, I., & Barlow, B. (1999). Epidemiology and prevention of traffic injuries to urban children and adolescents. *Pediatrics, 103,* e74.

Durlak, J. A., Weissberg, R. P., & Pachan, M. (2010). A meta-analysis of after-school programs that seek to promote personal and social skills in children and adolescents. *American Journal of Community Psychology, 45,* 294–309.

Durrant, J. E., Plateau, D. P., Ateah, C., Stewart-Tufescu, A., Jones, A., Ly, G., et al. (2014). Preventing punitive violence: Preliminary data on the Positive Discipline in Everyday Parenting (PDEP) Program. *Canadian Journal of Community Mental Health, 33,* 109–125.

Durwood, L., McLaughlin, K. A., & Olson, K. R. (2017). Mental health and self-worth in socially transitioned transgender youth. *Journal of the American Academy of Child and Adolescent Psychiatry, 56,* 116–123.

Duszak, R. S. (2009). Congenital rubella syndrome—major review. *Optometry, 80,* 36–43.

Dweck, C. S., & Molden, D. C. (2013). Self-theories: Their impact on competence motivation and acquisition. In A. J. Elliott & C. J. Dweck (Eds.), *Handbook of confidence and motivation* (pp. 122–140). New York: Guilford.

Dys, S. P., Peplak, J., Colasante, T., & Malti, T. (2019). Children's sympathy and sensitivity to excluding economically disadvantaged peers. *Developmental Psychology, 55,* 482–487.

Dyson, M. W., Olino, T. M., Durbin, C. E., Goldsmith, H. H., Bufferd, S. J., Miller, A. R., & Klein, D. N. (2015). The structural and rank-order stability of temperament in young children based on a laboratory-observational measure. *Psychological Assessment, 27,* 1388–1401.

E

Ebeling, K. S., & Gelman, S. A. (1994). Children's use of context in interpreting "big" and "little." *Child Development, 65,* 1178–1192.

Eccles, J. S., Jacobs, J., & Harold, R. D. (1990). Gender-role stereotypes, expectancy effects, and parents' role in the socialization of gender differences in self-perceptions and skill acquisition. *Journal of Social Issues, 46,* 183–201.

Eckerman, C. O., & Peterman, K. (2001). Peers and infant social/communicative development. In G. Bremner & A. Fogel (Eds.), *Blackwell handbook of infant development* (pp. 326–350). Malden, MA: Blackwell.

Edelson, L. R., Mokdad, C., & Martin, N. (2016). Prompts to novel and familiar fruits and vegetables in families with 1–3 year-old children: Relationships with food acceptance and intake. *Appetite, 99,* 138–148.

Edelstein, R. S., Chopik, W. J., Saxbe, D. E., Wardecker, B. M., Moors, A. C., & LaBelle, O. P. (2017). Prospective and dyadic associations between expectant parents' prenatal hormone changes and postpartum parenting outcomes. *Developmental Psychobiology, 59,* 77–90.

Eder, R. A., & Mangelsdorf, S. C. (1997). The emotional basis of early personality development: Implications for the emergent self-concept. In R. Hogan, J. Johnson, & S. Briggs (Eds.), *Handbook of personality psychology* (pp. 209–240). San Diego, CA: Academic Press.

Edwards, O. W., & Oakland, T. D. (2006). Factorial invariance of Woodcock-Johnson III scores for African Americans and Caucasian Americans. *Journal of Psychoeducational Assessment, 24,* 358–366.

Edwards-Leeper, L., Leibowitz, S., & Sanggnjanavanich, V. F. (2016). Affirmative practice with transgender and gender nonconforming youth: Expanding the model. *Psychology of Sexual Orientation and Gender Diversity, 3,* 165–172.

Egeland, B., Jacobvitz, D., & Sroufe, L. A. (1988). Breaking the cycle of abuse. *Child Development, 59,* 1080–1088.

Ehri, L. C., & Roberts, T. (2006). The roots of learning to read and write: Acquisition of letters and phonemic awareness. In D. K. Dickinson & S. B. Neuman (Eds.), *Handbook of early literacy research* (Vol. 2, pp. 113–131). New York: Guilford.

Eichstedt, J. A., Serbin, L. A., Poulin-Dubois, D., & Sen, M. G. (2002). Of bears and men: Infants' knowledge of conventional and metaphorical gender stereotypes. *Infant Behavior and Development, 25,* 296–310.

Eilertsen, E. M., Gjerde, L. C., Kendler, K. S., Røysamb, E., Aggen, S. H., Gustavson, K., et al. (2019). Development of ADHD symptoms in preschool children: Genetic and environmental contributions. *Development and Psychopathology, 31,* 1299–1305.

Eisbach, A. O. (2004). Children's developing awareness of diversity in people's trains of thought. *Child Development, 75,* 1694–1707.

Eisenberg, N. (2003). Prosocial behavior, empathy, and sympathy. In M. H. Bornstein & L. Davidson (Eds.), *Well-being: Positive development across the life course* (pp. 253–265). Mahwah, NJ: Erlbaum.

Eisenberg, N. (2010). Empathy-related responding: Links with self-regulation, moral judgment, and moral behavior. In M. Mikulincer & P. R. Shaver (Eds.), *Prosocial motives, emotions, and behavior: The better angels of our nature* (pp. 129–148). Washington, DC: American Psychological Association.

Eisenberg, N., Eggum, N. D., & Edwards, A. (2010). Empathy-related responding and moral development. In W. F. Arsenio & E. A. Lemerise (Eds.), *Emotions, aggression, and morality in children: Bridging development and psychopathology* (pp. 115–135). Washington, DC: American Psychological Association.

Eisenberg, N., Hofer, C., Sulik, M. J., & Spinrad, T. I. (2014). Self-regulation, effortful control, and their socioemotional correlates. In J. J. Gross (Ed.), *Handbook of emotion regulation* (pp. 157–172). New York: Guilford.

Eisenberg, N., & Silver, R. C. (2011). Growing up in the shadow of terrorism. *American Psychologist, 66,* 468–481.

Eisenberg, N., Smith, C. L., & Spinrad, T. L. (2011). Effortful control: Relations with emotion regulation, adjustment, and socialization in childhood. In K. D. Vohs & R. F. Baumeister (Eds.), *Handbook of self-regulation: Research, theory, and applications,* (2nd ed., pp. 263–283). New York: Guilford.

Eisenberg, N., Spinrad, T. L., & Knafo-Noam, A. (2015). Prosocial development. In M. E. Lamb (Ed.), *Handbook of child psychology and developmental science: Vol. 3. Socioemotional processes* (7th ed., pp. 610–656). Hoboken, NJ: Wiley.

Eisenberg, N., Spinrad, T. L., & Morris, A. S. (2013). Prosocial development. In P. D. Zelazo (Ed.), *Oxford handbook of developmental psychology, Vol. 2: Self and other* (pp. 300–325). New York: Oxford University Press.

Eisner, M. P., & Malti, T. (2015). Aggressive and violent behavior. In M. E. Lamb (Ed.), *Handbook of child psychology and developmental science: Vol. 3. Socioemotional processes* (7th ed., pp. 794–841). Hoboken, NJ: Wiley.

Eivers, A. R., Brendgen, M., Vitaro, F., & Borge, A. I. H. (2012). Concurrent and longitudinal links between children's and their friends' antisocial and prosocial behavior in preschool. *Early Childhood Research Quarterly, 27,* 137–146.

Ekas, N. V., Lickenbrock, D. M., & Braungart-Rieker, J. M. (2013). Developmental trajectories of emotion regulation across infancy: Do age and the social partner influence temporal patterns? *Infancy, 18,* 729–754.

Ekéus, C., Högberg, U., & Norman, M. (2014). Vacuum assisted birth and risk for cerebral complications in term newborn infants: A population-based cohort study. *BMC Pregnancy and Childbirth, 14,* 36.

Ekman, P., & Friesen, W. (1972). Constants across culture in the face and emotion. *Journal of Personality and Social Psychology, 17,* 124–129.

Ekman, P., & Matsumoto, D. (2011). Reading faces: The universality of emotional expression. In M. A. Gernsbacher, R. W. Pew, L. M. Hough, & J. R. Pomerantz (Eds.), *Psychology and the real world: Essays illustrating fundamental contributions to society* (pp. 140–146). New York: Worth.

Elam, K. K., Sandler, I., Wolchik, S., & Tein, J.-Y. (2016). Non-residential father–child involvement, interparental conflict and mental health of children following divorce: A person-focused approach. *Journal of Youth and Adolescence, 45,* 581–593.

Elam, K. K., Sandler, I., Wolchik, S. A., & Rogers, A. (2019). Latent profiles of post-divorce parenting time, conflict, and quality: Children's adjustment associations. *Journal of Family Psychology, 33,* 499–510.

Elder, G. H., Jr., Shanahan, M. J., & Jennings, J. A. (2015). Human development in time and place. In M. H. Bornstein & T. Leventhal (Eds.), *Handbook of child psychology: Vol. 4. Ecological settings and processes* (pp. 6–54). Hoboken, NJ: Wiley.

Elenbaas, L. (2019). Perceptions of economic inequality are related to children's judgments about access to opportunities. *Developmental Psychology, 55,* 471–481.

Elenbaas, L., & Killen, M. (2016). Age-related changes in children's associations of economic resources and race. *Frontiers in Psychology, 7,* Art. No. 884.

Elias, C. L., & Berk, L. E. (2002). Self-regulation in young children: Is there a role for sociodramatic play? *Early Childhood Research Quarterly, 17,* 1–17.

Elicker, J., Englund, M., & Sroufe, L. A. (1992). Predicting peer competence and peer relationships in childhood from early parent–child relationships. In R. D. Parke & G. W. Ladd (Eds.), *Family–peer relationships: Modes of linkage* (pp. 77–106). Hillsdale, NJ: Erlbaum.

Elk Grove Unified School District. (2018). *Time of Remembrance: Reiko Nagumo.* Retrieved from blogs.egusd.net/tor /interviews/world-war-ii/reiko-nagumo/

Elks, C. E., den Hoed, M., Zhao, J. H., Sharp, S. J., Wareham, N. J., Loo, R. J., & Ong, K. K. (2012). Variability in the heritability of body mass index: A systematic review and meta-regression. *Frontiers in Endocrinology, 3,* 29.

Elledge, L. C., Elledge, A. R., Newgent, R. A., & Cavell, T. A. (2016). Social risk and peer victimization in elementary school: The protective role of teacher–student relationships. *Journal of Abnormal Child Psychology, 44,* 691–703.

Elliott, J. G. (1999). School refusal: Issues of conceptualization, assessment, and treatment. *Journal of Child Psychology and Psychiatry and Allied Disciplines, 40,* 1001–1012.

Elliott, L. (2018). SES disparities in early math abilities: The contributions of parents' math cognitions, practices to support math, and math talk. *Developmental Review, 49,* 1–15.

Ellis, A. E., & Oakes, L. M. (2006). Infants flexibly use different dimensions to categorize objects. *Developmental Psychology, 42,* 1000–1011.

Ellis, R. R., & Simmons, T. (2014). *Coresident grandparents and their grandchildren: 2012.* Washington, DC: U.S. Census Bureau. Retrieved from www.census.gov /content/dam/Census/library/publications /2014/demo/p20-576.pdf

Else-Quest, N. M. (2012). Gender differences in temperament. In M. Zentner & R. L. Shiner (Eds.), *Handbook of temperament* (pp. 479–496). New York: Guilford.

Else-Quest, N. M., Hyde, J. S., Goldsmith, H. H., & Van Hulle, C. A. (2006). Gender differences in temperament: A meta-analysis. *Psychological Bulletin, 132,* 33–72.

El-Sheikh, M., Bub, K. L.,Kelly, R. J., & Buckhalt, J. A. (2013). Children's sleep and adjustment: A residualized change analysis. *Developmental Psychology, 49,* 1591–1601.

El-Sheikh, M., Kelly, R. J., Buckhalt, J. A., & Hinnant, B. (2010). Children's sleep and adjustment over time: The role of socioeconomic context. *Child Development, 81,* 870–883.

Endendijk, J. J., Groeneveld, M G., van Berkel, S. R., Hallers-Haalboom, E. T., Mesman, J., & Bakermans-Kranenburg, M. J. (2013). Gender stereotypes in the family context: Mothers, fathers, and siblings. *Sex Roles, 68,* 577–590.

Endendijk, J. J., Groeneveld, M. G., van der Pol, L., van Berkel, S. R., Hallers-Haalboom, E. T., Bekermans-Kranenburg, M. J., & Mesman, J. (2017). Gender differences in child aggression: Relations with gender-differentiated parenting and parents' gender-role stereotypes. *Child Development, 88,* 299–316.

Endendijk, J. J., Groeneveld, M. G., van der Pol, L. D., van Berkel, S. R., Hallers-Haalboom, E. T., Mesman, J., & Bakermans-Kranenburg, M. J. (2014). Boys don't play with dolls: Mothers' and fathers' gender talk during picture book reading. *Parenting: Science and Practice, 14,* 141–161.

Ennemoser, M., & Schneider, W. (2007). Relations of television viewing and reading: Findings from a 4-year longitudinal study. *Journal of Educational Psychology, 99,* 349–368.

Enoch, M.-A., Steer, C. D., Newman, T. K., Gibson, N., & Goldman, D. (2010). Early life stress, MAOA, and gene–environment interactions predict behavioral disinhibition in children. *Genes, Brain, and Behavior, 9,* 65–74.

Epstein, L. H., & Anzman-Frasca, S. (2017). The promise of early childhood self-regulation for obesity prevention. *Pediatrics, 139,* e20170389.

Epstein, L. H., Roemmich, J. N., & Raynor, H. A. (2001). Behavioral therapy in the treatment of pediatric obesity. *Pediatric Clinics of North America, 48,* 981–983.

Erickson, J. D., Patterson, J. M., Wall, M., & Neumark-Sztainer, D. (2005). Risk behaviors and emotional well-being in youth with chronic health conditions. *Children's Health Care, 34,* 181–192.

Erikson, E. H. (1950). *Childhood and society.* New York: Norton.

Erikson, E. H. (1968). *Identity, youth, and crisis.* New York: Norton.

Espy, K. A., Fang, H., Johnson, C., Stopp, C., & Wiebe, S. A. (2011). Prenatal tobacco exposure: Developmental outcomes in the neonatal period. *Developmental Psychology, 47,* 153–156.

Espy, K. A., Molfese, V. J., & DiLalla, L. F. (2001). Effects of environmental measures on intelligence in young children: Growth curve modeling of longitudinal data. *Merrill-Palmer Quarterly, 47,* 42–73.

Esseily, R., Rat-Rischer, L., O'Regan, K., & Fagard, J. (2013). Understanding the experimenter's intention improves 16-month-olds' observational learning of the use of a novel tool. *Cognitive Development, 28,* 1–9.

Ettekal, I., Eiden, R. D., Nickerson, A. B., Molnar, D. S., & Schuetze, P. (2019). Developmental cascades to children's conduct problems: The role of prenatal substance use, economic adversity, maternal depression and sensitivity, and children's conscience. *Development and Psychopathology, 31,* 1–19.

Evanoo, G. (2007). Infant crying: A clinical conundrum. *Journal of Pediatric Health Care, 21,* 333–338.

Evans, G. W., Fuller-Rowell, T. E., & Doan, S. N. (2012). Childhood cumulative risk and obesity: The mediating role of self-regulatory ability. *Pediatrics, 129,* e68–e73.

Evans, G. W., Gonnella, C., Marcynyszn, L. A. Gentile, L., & Slapekar, N. (2005). The role of chaos in poverty and children's socioemotional adjustment. *Psychological Science, 16,* 560–565.

Evans, G. W., Li, D., & Sepanski Whipple, S. (2013). Cumulative risk and child development. *Psychological Bulletin, 139,* 1342–1396.

Evans, G. W., & Schamberg, M. A. (2009). Childhood poverty, chronic stress, and adult working memory. *Proceedings of the National Academy of Sciences, 106,* 6545–6549.

Evans, N., & Levinson, S. C. (2009). The myth of language universals: Language diversity and its importance for cognitive science. *Behavioral and Brain Sciences, 32,* 429–492.

Eyler, L. T., Pierce, K., & Courchesne, E. (2012). A failure of left temporal cortex to specialize for language is an early emerging and fundamental property of autism. *Brain, 135,* 949–960.

Ezeizabarrena, M.-J., & Fernández, I. G. (2017). Language delay and amount of exposure to the language: Two (un)related phenomena in early Spanish–Basque bilingualism. In A. A. Benavides & R. G. Schwartz (Eds.), *Language development and disorders in Spanish-speaking children* (pp. 147–166). Cham, Switzerland: Springer International Publishing.

Ezkurdia, I., Juan, D., Rodriguez, J. M., Frankish, A., Diekhans, M., Harrow, J., et al. (2014). Multiple evidence strands suggest that there may be as few as 19,000 human protein-coding genes. *Human Molecular Genetics, 23,* 5866–5878.

F

Faas, A. E., March, S. M., Moya, P. R., & Molina, J. C. (2015). Alcohol odor elicits appetitive facial expressions in human neonates prenatally exposed to the drug. *Physiology & Behavior, 148,* 78–86.

Fabes, R. A., Eisenberg, N., Hanish, L. D., & Spinrad, T. L. (2001). Preschoolers' spontaneous emotion vocabulary: Relations to likability. *Early Education and Development, 12,* 11–27.

Fabes, R. A., Eisenberg, N., McCormick, S. E., & Wilson, M. S. (1988). Preschoolers' attributions of the situational determinants of others' naturally occurring emotions. *Developmental Psychology, 24,* 376–385.

Fabes, R. A., Martin, C. L., & Hanish, L. D. (2003). Young children's play qualities in same-, other-, and mixed-sex peer groups. *Child Development, 74,* 921–932.

Fagan, J. F., III, & Holland, C. R. (2007). Racial equality in intelligence: Predictions from a theory of intelligence as processing. *Intelligence, 35,* 319–334.

Fagan, J. F., III, Holland, C. R., & Wheeler, K. (2007). The prediction, from infancy, of adult IQ and achievement. *Intelligence, 35,* 225–231.

Fagan, J. F., III. (1973). Infants' delayed recognition memory and forgetting. *Journal of Experimental Child Psychology, 16,* 424–450.

Fagan, M. K. (2015). Why repetition? Repetitive babbling, auditory feedback, and cochlear implantation. *Journal of Experimental Child Psychology, 137,* 125–136.

Fagard, J., Florean, C., Peetkovic, M., Rat-Fischer, L., Fattori, P., & O'Regan, J. K. (2015). When do infants understand that they can obtain a desired part of a composite object by grasping another part? *Infant Behavior and Development, 41,* 169–178.

Fagard, J., & Pezé, A. (1997). Age changes in interlimb coupling and the development of bimanual coordination. *Journal of Motor Behavior, 29,* 199–208.

Fagard, J., Rat-Rischer, L., Esseily, R., Somogyi, E., & O'Regan, J. K. (2016). What does it take for an infant to learn how to use a tool by observation? *Frontiers in Psychology, 7,* Art. No. 267.

Fagard, J., Rat-Fischer, L., & O'Regan, J. K. (2014). The emergence of use of a rake-like tool: A longitudinal study in human infants. *Frontiers in Psychology, 5,* Art. No. 491.

Fagard, J., Spelke, E., & von Hofsten, C. (2009). Reaching and grasping a moving object in 6-, 8-, and 10-month-old infants: Laterality and performance. *Infant Behavior and Development, 32,* 137–146.

Fagen, J., Ohr, P., & Boller, K. (2016). Carolyn Rovee-Collier's legacy to applied psychology, intervention, and public policy. *Developmental Psychobiology, 58,* 918–922.

Fagot, B. I. (1985). Changes in thinking about early sex role development. *Developmental Review, 5,* 83–98.

Fagot, B. I., & Hagan, R. I. (1991). Observations of parent reactions to sex-stereotyped behaviors: Age and sex effects. *Child Development, 62,* 617–628.

Fair, J., Flom, R., Jones, J., & Martin, J. (2012). Perceptual learning: 12 month olds' discrimination of monkey faces. *Child Development, 83,* 1996–2006.

Falbo, T. (2012). Only children: An updated review. *Journal of Individual Psychology, 68,* 38–49.

Falbo, T., & Hooper, S. Y. (2015). China's only children and psychopathology: A quantitative synthesis. *American Journal of Orthopsychiatry, 85,* 259–274.

Falbo, T., Poston, D. L., Jr., Triscari, R. S., & Zhang, X. (1997). Self-enhancing illusions among Chinese schoolchildren. *Journal of Cross-Cultural Psychology, 28,* 172–191.

Fantz, R. L. (1961, May). The origin of form perception. *Scientific American, 204*(5), 66–72.

Farmer, T. W., Irvin, M. J., Leung, M.-C., Hall, C. M., Hutchins, B. C., & McDonough, E. (2010). Social preference, social prominence, and group membership in late elementary school: Homophilic concentration and peer affiliation configurations. *Social Psychology of Education, 13,* 271–293.

Farroni, T., Csibra, G., Simion, F., & Johnson, M. H. (2002). Eye contact detection in humans from birth. *Proceedings of the National Academy of Sciences, 99,* 9602–9605.

Farroni, T., Massaccesi, S., Menon, E., & Johnson, M. H. (2007). Direct gaze modulates face recognition in young infants. *Cognition, 102,* 396–404.

Farver, J. M., & Branstetter, W. H. (1994). Preschoolers' prosocial responses to their peers' distress. *Developmental Psychology, 30,* 334–341.

Fassbender, I., Teubert, M., & Lohaus, A. (2016). The development of preferences for own-race versus other-race faces in 3-, 6- and 9-month-old Caucasian infants. *European Journal of Developmental Psychology, 13,* 152–165.

Fast, A. A., & Olson, K. R. (2018). Gender development in transgender preschool children. *Child Development, 89,* 620–637.

Fattal, I., Friedmann, N., & Fattal-Valevski, A. (2011). The crucial role of thiamine in the development of syntax and lexical retrieval: A study of infantile thiamine deficiency. *Brain, 134,* 1720–1739.

Fattal-Valevski, A., Azouri-Fattal, I., Greenstien, Y. J., Fuindy, M., Blau, A., & Zelnik, N. (2009). Delayed language development due to infantile thiamine deficiency. *Developmental Medicine and Child Neurology, 51,* 629–634.

Fay-Stammbach, T., Hawes, D. J., & Meredith, P. (2014). Parenting influences on executive function in early childhood: A review. *Child Development Perspectives, 8,* 258–264.

Fedewa, A. L., Black, W. W., & Ahn, S. (2015). Children and adolescents with same-gender parents: A meta-analytic approach in assessing outcomes. *Journal of GLBT Family Studies, 11,* 1–34.

Feeney, B. C., & Monin, J. K. (2016). Divorce through the lens of attachment theory. In J. Cassidy & P. R. Shaver (Eds.), *Handbook of attachment: Theory, research, and clinical applications* (3rd ed., pp. 941–965). New York: Guilford.

Feeney, B. C., & Woodhouse, S. S. (2016). Caregiving. In J. Cassidy & P. R. Shaver (Eds.), *Handbook of attachment: Theory, research, and clinical applications* (3rd ed., pp. 827–851). New York: Guilford.

Feldman, R. (2003). Infant–mother and infant–father synchrony: The coregulation of positive arousal. *Infant Mental Health Journal, 24,* 1–23.

Feldman, R. (2006). From biological rhythms to social rhythms: Physiological precursors of mother–infant synchrony. *Developmental Psychology, 42,* 175–188.

Feldman, R. (2007a). Maternal–infant contact and child development: Insights from the kangaroo intervention. In L. L'Abate (Ed.), *Low-cost approaches to promote physical and mental health: Theory, research, and practice* (pp. 323–351). New York: Springer.

Feldman, R. (2007b). Maternal versus child risk and the development of parent–child and family relationships in five high-risk populations. *Development and Psychopathology, 19,* 293–312.

Feldman, R. (2014). Synchrony and the neurobiological basis of social affiliation. In M. Mikulincer & P. R. Shaver (Eds.), *Mechanisms of social connection: From brain to group* (pp. 145–166). Washington, DC: American Psychological Association.

Feldman, R., Eidelman, A. I., & Rotenberg, N. (2004). Parenting stress, infant emotion regulation, maternal sensitivity, and the cognitive development of triplets: A model for parent and child influences in a unique ecology. *Child Development, 75,* 1774–1791.

Feldman, R., & Klein, P. S. (2003). Toddlers' self-regulated compliance to mothers, caregivers, and fathers: Implications for theories of socialization. *Developmental Psychology, 39,* 680–692.

Feldman, R., Rosenthal, Z., & Eidelman, A. (2014). Maternal–preterm skin-to-skin contact enhances child physiologic organization and cognitive control across the first 10 years of life. *Biological Psychiatry, 75,* 56–64.

Feldman, R., Sussman, A. L., & Zigler, E. (2004). Parental leave and work adaptation at the transition to parenthood: Individual, marital, and social correlates. *Journal of Applied Developmental Psychology, 25,* 459–479.

Feliciano, C., & Lanuza, Y, R. (2015). The immigrant advantage in adolescent educational expectations. *International Migration Review, 50,* 758–792.

Feng, X., & Hooper, E. G. (2017). From compliance to self-regulation. Development during early childhood. *Social Development, 26,* 981–995.

Ferguson, T. J., Stegge, H., & Damhuis, I. (1991). Children's understanding of guilt and shame. *Child Development, 62,* 827–839.

Fergusson, D. M., Boden, J. M., Horwood, J., Miller, A. L., & Kennedy, M. A. (2011). MAOA, abuse exposure, and antisocial behavior: 30-year longitudinal study. *British Journal of Psychiatry, 198,* 457–463.

Fernald, A., & Marchman, V. A. (2012). Individual differences in lexical processing at 18 months predict vocabulary growth in typically developing and late-talking toddlers. *Child Development, 82,* 203–222.

Fernald, A., Marchman, V. A., & Weisleder, A. (2013). SES differences in language processing skill and vocabulary are evident at 18 months. *Developmental Science, 16,* 234–248.

Fernald, A., & Morikawa, H. (1993). Common themes and cultural variations in Japanese and American mothers' speech to infants. *Child Development, 64,* 637–656.

Fernald, A., Taeschner, T., Dunn, J., Papousek, M, Boysson-Bardies, B., & Fukui, I. (1989). A cross-language study of prosodic modifications in mothers' and fathers' speech to preverbal infants. *Journal of Child Language, 16,* 477–502.

Fernald, L. C., Grantham-McGregor, S. M., Manandhar, D. S., & Costello, A. (2003). Salivary cortisol and heart rate in stunted and nonstunted Nepalese school children. *European Journal of Clinical Nutrition, 57,* 1458–1465.

Fernandes, M., Stein, A., Srinivasan, K., Menezes, G., & Ramchandani, P. J. (2015). Foetal exposure to maternal depression predicts cortisol responses in infants: Findings from rural South India. *Child: Care, Health and Development, 41,* 677–686.

Fernandez-Rio, J., Cecchini, J. A., Ménde-Gimenez, A., Mendez-Alonso, D., & Prieto, J. A. (2017). Self-regulation, cooperative learning, and academic self-efficacy: Interactions to prevent school failure. *Frontiers in Psychology, 8,* Art. No. 22.

Fernyhough, C. (2016). *The voices within: The history and science of how we talk to ourselves.* New York: Basic Books.

Fernyhough, C., & Fradley, E. (2005). Private speech on an executive task: Relations with task difficulty and task performance. *Cognitive Development, 20,* 103–120.

Ferrando, M., Prieto, M. D., Almeida, L. S., Ferándiz, C., Bermejo, R., López-Pina, J. A., et al. (2011). Trait emotional intelligence and academic performance: Controlling for the effects of IQ, personality, and self-concept. *Journal of Psychoeducational Assessment, 29,* 150–159.

Ferrari, P. F., & Coudé, G. (2011). Mirror neurons and imitation from a developmental and evolutionary perspective. In A. Vilain, C. Abry, J.-L. Schwartz, & J. Vauclair (Eds.), *Primate communication and human language* (pp. 121–138). Amsterdam, Netherlands: John Benjamins.

Ferrari, P. F., Tramacere, A., Simpson, E. A., & Iriki, A. (2013). Mirror neurons through the lens of epigenetics. *Trends in Cognitive Sciences, 17,* 450–457.

Ferrari, P. F., Visalberghi E., Paukner A., Fogassi L., Ruggiero A., Suomi, S. (2006). Neonatal imitation in rhesus macaques. *PLOS Biology, 4,* e302.

Ferry, A. L., Hespos, S. J., & Waxman, S. R. (2010). Categorization in 3- and 4-month-old infants: An advantage of words over tones. *Child Development, 81,* 472–479.

Field, T. (2011). Prenatal depression effects on early development: A review. *Infant Behavior and Development, 34*, 1–14.

Field, T., Hernandez-Reif, M., & Freedman, J. (2004). Stimulation programs for preterm infants. *Social Policy Report of the Society for Research in Child Development, 18*(1).

Fiese, B. H., & Bost, K. K. (2016). Family ecologies and child risk for obesity: Focus on regulatory processes. *Family Relations, 65*, 94–107.

Fiese, B. H., Foley, K. P., & Spagnola, M. (2006). Routine and ritual elements in family mealtimes: Contexts for child well-being and family identity. *New Directions for Child and Adolescent Development, 111*, 67–90.

Fiese, B. H., & Schwartz, M. (2008). Reclaiming the family table: Mealtimes and child health and well-being. *Social Policy Report of the Society for Research in Child Development, 22*(4), 3–18.

Fiese, B. H., & Winter, M. A. (2010). The dynamics of family chaos and its relation to children's socioemotional well-being. In G. W. Evans & T. D. Wachs (Eds.), *Chaos and its influence on children's development: An ecological perspective* (pp. 49–66). Washington, DC: American Psychological Association.

Fifer, W. P., Byrd, D. L., Kaku, M., Eigsti, I. M., Isler, J. R., Grose-Fifer, J., et al. (2010). Newborn infants learn during sleep. *Proceedings of the National Academy of Sciences, 107*, 10320–10323.

Figueiredo, B., Dias, C. C., Pinto, T. M., & Field, T. (2016). Infant sleep–wake behaviors at two weeks, three and six months. *Infant Behavior and Development, 44*, 169–178.

Figueiredo, B., Pinto, T. M., Pacheco, A., & Field, T. (2017). Fetal heart rate variability mediates prenatal depression effects on neonatal neurobehavioral maturity. *Biological Psychology, 123*, 294–301.

Filipi, A. (2014). Conversation analysis and pragmatic development. In D. Matthews (Ed.), *Pragmatic development in first language acquisition* (pp. 71–86). Amsterdam, Netherlands: John Benjamins Publishing.

Findlay, L. C., & Coplan, R. J. (2008). Come out and play: Shyness in childhood and the benefits of organized sports participation. *Canadian Journal of Behavioural Science, 40*, 153–161.

Finnilä, K., Mahlberga, N., Santtilia, P., & Niemib, P. (2003). Validity of a test of children's suggestibility for predicting responses to two interview situations differing in degree of suggestiveness. *Journal of Experimental Child Psychology, 85*, 32–49.

Fiori, S., & Guzzetta, A. (2015). Plasticity following early-life brain injury: Insights from quantitative MRI. *Seminars in Perinatology, 39*, 141–146.

Fisch, S. M. (2015). Learning from educational television. In D. Lemish (Ed.), *Routledge international handbook of children, adolescents and media* (pp. 403–409). New York: Routledge.

Fischer, K. W., & Bidell, T. (1991). Constraining nativisit inferences about cognitive capacities. In S. Carey & R. Gelman (Eds.), *The epigenesis of mind: Essays on biology and cognition* (pp. 199–235). Hillsdale, NJ: Erlbaum.

Fischer, K. W., & Bidell, T. R. (2006). Dynamic development of action and thought. In R. M. Lerner (Ed.), *Handbook of child psychology: Vol. 1. Theoretical models of human development* (6th ed., pp. 313–399). Hoboken, NJ: Wiley.

Fischman, M. G., Moore, J. B., & Steele, K. H. (1992). Children's one-hand catching as a function of age, gender, and ball location. *Research Quarterly for Exercise and Sport, 63*, 349–355.

Fiser, J., & Aslin, R. N. (2002). Statistical learning of new virtual feature combinations by infants. *Proceedings of the National Academy of Sciences, 99*, 15822–15826.

Fish, M. (2004). Attachment in infancy and preschool in low socioeconomic status rural Appalachian children: Stability and change and relations to preschool and kindergarten competence. *Development and Psychopathology, 16*, 293–312.

Fisher, C. B., Hoagwood, K., Boyce, C., Duster, T., Frank, D. A., & Grisso, T. (2002). Research ethics for mental health science involving ethnic minority children and youths. *American Psychologist, 57*, 1024–1040.

Fisher, K. R., Hirsh-Pasek, K., Newcombe, N. S., & Golinkoff, R. M. (2013). Taking shape: Supporting preschoolers' acquisition of geometric knowledge through guided play. *Child Development, 84*, 1872–1878.

Fite, P. J., Stauffacher, K., Ostrov, J. M., & Colder, C. R. (2008). Replication and extension of Little et al.'s (2003) forms and functions of aggression measure. *International Journal of Behavioral Development, 32*, 238–242.

Fite, P. J., Williford, A., Cooley, J. L., DePaolis, K., Rubens, S. L., & Vernberg, E. M. (2013). Patterns of victimization locations in elementary school children: Effects of grade level and gender. *Child and Youth Care Forum, 42*, 585–597.

Fivush, R. (2011). The development of autobiographical memory. *Annual Review of Psychology, 62*, 559–582.

Fivush, R., & Haden, C. A. (2005). Parent–child reminiscing and the construction of a subjective self. In B. D. Homer & C. S. Tamis-LeMonda (Eds.), *The development of social cognition and communication* (pp. 315–336). Mahwah, NJ: Erlbaum.

Fivush, R., & Wang, Q. (2005). Emotion talk in mother–child conversations of the shared past: The effects of culture, gender, and event valence. *Journal of Cognition and Development, 6*, 489–506.

Fivush, R., & Zaman, W. (2014). Gender, subjective perspective, and autobiographical consciousness. In P. J. Bauer & R. Fivush (Eds.), *Wiley handbook on the development of children's memory* (pp. 586–604). Hoboken, NJ: Wiley-Blackwell.

Flak, A. L., Su, S., Bertrand, J., Denny, C. H., Kesmodel, U. S., & Cogswell, M. E. (2014). The association of mild, moderate, and binge prenatal alcohol exposure and child neuropsychological outcomes: A meta-analysis. *Alcoholism: Clinical and Experimental Research, 38*, 214–226.

Flavell, J. H., Flavell, E. R., & Green, F. L. (2001). Development of children's understanding of connections between thinking and feeling. *Psychological Science, 12*, 430–432.

Flavell, J. H., Green, F. L., & Flavell, E. R. (1995). Young children's knowledge about thinking. *Monographs of the Society for Research in Child Development, 60*(1, Serial No. 243).

Flavell, J. H., Green, F. L., & Flavell, E. R. (2000). Development of children's awareness of their own thoughts. *Journal of Cognition and Development, 1*, 97–112.

Fletcher, R., St George, J., & Freeman, E. (2013). Rough and tumble play quality: Theoretical foundations for a new measure of father–child interaction. *Early Child Development and Care, 183*, 746–759.

Floccia, C., Christophe, A., & Bertoncini, J. (1997). High-amplitude sucking and newborns: The quest for underlying mechanisms. *Journal of Experimental Child Psychology, 64*, 175–198.

Flom, R. (2013). Intersensory perception of faces and voices in infants. In P. Belin, S. Campanella, & T. Ethofer (Eds.), *Integrating face and voice in person perception* (pp. 71–93). New York: Springer.

Flom, R., & Bahrick, L. E. (2007). The development of infant discrimination of affect in multimodal and unimodal stimulation: The role of intersensory redundancy. *Developmental Psychology, 43*, 238–252.

Flom, R., & Bahrick, L. E. (2010). The effects of intersensory redundancy on attention and memory: Infants' long-term memory for orientation in audiovisual events. *Developmental Psychology, 46*, 428–436.

Flom, R., & Pick, A. D. (2003). Verbal encouragement and joint attention in 18-month-old infants. *Infant Behavior and Development, 26*, 121–134.

Flynn, E., & Siegler, R. (2007). Measuring change: Current trends and future directions in microgenetic research. *Infant and Child Development, 16*, 135–149.

Flynn, J. R. (1999). Searching for justice: The discovery of IQ gains over time. *American Psychologist, 54*, 5–20.

Flynn, J. R. (2007). *What is intelligence? Beyond the Flynn effect.* New York: Cambridge University Press.

Flynn, J. R., & Rossi-Casé, L. (2011). Modern women match men on Raven's Progressive Matrices. *Personality and Individual Differences, 50*, 799–803.

Fomon, S. J., & Nelson, S. E. (2002). Body composition of the male and female reference infants. *Annual Review of Nutrition, 22*, 1–17.

Fonnesbeck, C. J., McPheeters, M. L., Krishnaswami, S., Lindegren, M. L., & Reimschisel, T. (2013). Estimating the probability of IQ impairment from blood phenylalanine for phenylketonuria patients: A hierarchical meta-analysis. *Journal of Inherited Metabolic Disease, 36*, 757–766.

Forcada-Guex, M., Pierrehumbert, B., Borghini, A., Moessinger, A., & Muller-Nix, C. (2006). Early dyadic patterns of mother–infant interactions and outcomes of prematurity at 18 months. *Pediatrics, 118*, e107–114.

Ford, D. Y. (2012). Gifted and talented education: History, issues, and recommendations. In K. R. Harris, S. Graham, T. Urdan, S. Graham, J. M. Royer, & M. Zeidner (Eds.), *APA educational psychology handbook: Vol. 2. Individual differences and cultural contextual factors* (pp. 83–110). Washington, DC: American Psychological Association.

Ford, N. D., Patel, S. A., & Narayan, V. (2017). Obesity in low- and middle-income countries: Burden, drivers, and emerging challenges. *Annual Review of Public Health, 38*, 145–164.

Forman, D. R., Aksan, N., & Kochanska, G. (2004). Toddlers' responsive imitation predicts preschool-age conscience. *Psychological Science, 15*, 699–704.

Forsyth, R. (2014). Would you rather have your brain injury at five or twenty-five? *Developmental Medicine & Child Neurology, 56*, 297.

Foster, W. A., & Miller, M. (2007). Development of the literacy achievement gap: A longitudinal study of kindergarten through third grade. *Language, Speech, and Hearing Services in Schools, 38*, 173–181.

Fox, C. L., & Boulton, M. J. (2006). Friendship as a moderator of the relationship between social skills problems and peer victimization. *Aggressive Behavior, 32*, 110–121.

Fox, N. A., Henderson, H. A., Pérez-Edgar, K., & White, L. K. (2008). The biology of temperament: An integrative approach. In C. A. Nelson & M. Luciana (Eds.), *Handbook of developmental cognitive neuroscience* (2nd ed., pp. 839–853). Cambridge, MA: MIT Press.

Foy, J. G., & Mann, V. (2003). Home literacy environment and phonological awareness in preschool children: Differential effects for rhyme and phoneme awareness. *Applied Psycholinguistics, 24*, 59–88.

Fraiberg, S. (1971). *Insights from the blind.* New York: Basic Books.

Franchak, J. M., & Adolph, K. E. (2012). What infants know and what they do: Perceiving possibilities for walking through openings. *Developmental Psychology, 48*, 1254–1261.

Frank, M. C., Amso, D., & Johnson, S. P. (2014). Visual search and attention to faces during early infancy. *Journal of Experimental Child Psychology, 118*, 13–26.

Frank, M. C., Vul, E., & Johnson, S. P. (2011). Development of infants' attention to faces during the first year. *Cognition, 110*, 160–170.

Frankel, L. A., Umemura, T., Jacobvitz, D., & Hazen, N. (2015). Marital conflict and parental responses to infant negative emotions: Relations with toddler emotional regulation. *Infant Behavior and Development, 40*, 73–83.

Frankford, D. M., Bennington, L. K., & Ryan, J. G. (2015). Womb outsourcing: Commercial surrogacy in India. *American Journal of Maternal/Child Nursing, 40*, 284–290.

Fredricks, J. A., & Eccles, J. S. (2002). Children's competence and value beliefs from childhood through adolescence: Growth trajectories in two male-sex-typed domains. *Developmental Psychology, 38*, 519–533.

Freeman, H., & Newland, L. A. (2010). New directions in father attachment. *Early Child Development and Care, 180*, 1–8.

Frejka, T., Sobotka, T., Hoem, J. M., & Toulemon, L. (2008). Childbearing trends and policies in Europe. *Demographic Research, 19*, 5–14.

Freud, S. (1973). *An outline of psychoanalysis.* London: Hogarth. (Original work published 1938)

Friedlmeier, W., Corapci, F., & Cole, P. M. (2011). Socialization of emotions in cross-cultural perspective. *Social and Personality Psychology Compass, 5*, 410–427.

Friedman-Krauss, A. H., Barnett, W. S., Wieienfeld, G. G., Kasmin, R., DiCrecchio, N., & Horowitz, M. (2018). *The state of preschool: 2017.* New Brunswick, NJ: National Institute for Early Education Research, Rutgers University. Retrieved from http://nieer.org/wp-content/uploads/2019/02/State-of-Preschool-2017-Full-2-13-19_reduced.pdf

Friedman, S. L., Scholnick, E. K., Bender, R. H., Vandergrift, N., Spieker, S., Hirsh-Pasek, et al. (2014). Planning in middle childhood: Early predictors and later outcomes. *Child Development, 85*, 1446–1460.

Friedmann, N., & Haddad-Hanna, M. (2014). The comprehension of sentences derived by syntactic movement in Palestinian Arabic-speaking children with hearing impairment. *Applied Psycholinguistics, 35*, 473–513.

Friedmann, N., & Rusou, D. (2015). Critical period for first language: The crucial role of language input during the first year of life. *Current Opinion in Neurobiology, 35,* 27–34.

Friedmann, N., & Szterman, R. (2011). The comprehension and production of Wh-questions in deaf and hard-of-hearing children. *Journal of Deaf Studies and Deaf Education, 16,* 212–235.

Fries, A. B. W., & Pollak, S. D. (2004). Emotion understanding in postinstitutionalized Eastern European children. *Development and Psychopathology, 16,* 355–369.

Fries, A. B. W., Ziegler, T. E., Kurian, J. R., Jacoris, S., & Pollak, S. D. (2005). Early experience in humans is associated with changes in neuropeptides critical for regulating social behavior. *Proceedings of the National Academy of Sciences, 102,* 17237–17240.

Frontline. (2012). *Poor kids.* Retrieved from https://www.pbs.org/wgbh/frontline/film/poor-kids/

Frost, D. M., Meyer, I. H., & Schwartz, S. (2016). Social support networks among diverse sexual minority populations. *American Journal of Orthopsychiatry, 86,* 91–102.

Frota, S., Butler, J., Correia, S., Severino, C., Vicente, S., & Vigário, M. (2016). Infant communicative development assessed with the European Portuguese MacArthur–Bates Communicative Development Inventories short forms. *First Language, 36,* 525–545.

Fry, D. P. (2014). Environment of evolutionary adaptedness, rough-and-tumble play, and the selection of restraint in human aggression. In D. Narvaez, K. Valentino, A. Fuentes, J. J. McKenna, & P. Gray (Eds.), *Ancestral landscapes in human evolution: Culture, childrearing and social wellbeing* (pp. 169–188). New York: Oxford University Press.

Fu, G., Luo, Y. C., Heyman, G. D., Wang, B., Cameron, C. A., & Lee, K. (2016). Moral evaluations of lying for one's own group. *Infant and Child Development, 25,* 355–370.

Fu, G., Xiao, W. S., Killen, M., & Lee, K. (2014). Moral judgment and its relation to second-order theory of mind. *Developmental Psychology, 50,* 2085–2092.

Fu, G., Xu, F., Cameron, C. A., Heyman, G., & Lee, K. (2007). Cross-cultural differences in children's choices, categorizations, and evaluations of truths and lies. *Developmental Psychology, 43,* 278–293.

Fuchs, L. S., Malone, A. S., Schumacher, R. F., Namkung, J., Hamlett, C. L., Jordan, N. C., et al. (2016). Supported self-explaining during fraction intervention. *Journal of Educational Psychology, 108,* 493–508.

Fudvoye, J., & Parent, A. S. (2017). Secular trends in growth. *Annals of Endocrinology, 78,* 88–91.

Fuertes, M., Faria, A., Beeghly, M., & Lopes-dos-Santos, P. (2016). The effects of parental sensitivity and involvement in caregiving on mother–infant and father–infant attachment in a Portuguese sample. *Journal of Family Psychology, 30,* 147–156.

Fuligni, A. J. (2004). The adaptation and acculturation of children from immigrant families. In U. P. Gielen & J. Roopnarine (Eds.), *Childhood and adolescence: Cross-cultural perspectives* (pp. 297–318). Westport, CT: Praeger.

Fuligni, A. S., Han, W.-J., & Brooks-Gunn, J. (2004). The Infant–Toddler HOME in the 2nd and 3rd years of life. *Parenting: Science and Practice, 4,* 139–159.

Fuller-Thomson, E., & Minkler, M. (2005). Native American grandparents raising grandchildren: Findings from the Census 2000 Supplementary Survey and implications for social work practice. *Social Work, 50,* 131–139.

Fuller-Thomson, E., & Minkler, M. (2007). Mexican American grandparents raising grandchildren: Findings from the Census 2000 American Community Survey. *Families in Society, 88,* 567–574.

Furman, W., & Rose, A. J. (2015). Friendships, romantic relationships, and peer relationships. In M. E. Lamb (Ed.), *Handbook of child psychology and developmental science: Vol. 3. Socioemotional processes* (7th ed., pp. 932–974). Hoboken, NJ: Wiley.

Fushiki, S. (2013). Radiation hazards in children—lessons from Chernobyl, Three Mile Island and Fukushima. *Brain & Development, 35,* 220–227.

Fuson, K. C., & Burghard, B. H. (2003). Multidigit addition and subtraction methods invented in small groups and teacher support of problem solving and reflection. In A. J. Baroody & A. Dowker (Eds.), *The development of arithmetic concepts and skills* (pp. 267–304). Mahwah, NJ: Erlbaum.

G

Gabard-Durnam, L. J., Flannery, J., Goff, B., Gee, D. G., Humphreys, K. L., Telzer, E., et al. (2014). The development of human amygdala functional connectivity at rest from 4 to 23 years: A cross-sectional study. *NeuroImage, 95,* 193–207.

Galbally, M., Lewis, J., van IJzendoorn, M., & Permezel, M. (2011). The role of oxytocin in mother–infant relations: A systematic review of human studies. *Harvard Review of Psychiatry, 19,* 1–14.

Galland, B. C., Taylor, B. J., Elder, D. E., & Herbison, P. (2012). Normal sleep patterns in infants and children: A systematic review. *Sleep Medicine Reviews, 16,* 213–222.

Galler, J. R., Bryce, C. P., Waber, D. P., Hock, R. S., Harrison, R., Eaglesfield, G. D., et al. (2012). Infant malnutrition predicts conduct problems in adolescents. *Nutritional Neuroscience, 15,* 186–192.

Galloway, J. C., & Thelen, E. (2004). Feet first. Object exploration in young infants. *Infant Behavior and Development, 27,* 107–112.

Gallup. (2013). *Desire for children still norm in U.S.* Retrieved from www.gallup.com/poll/164618/desire-children-norm.aspx

Gamble, W. C., & Modrey-Mandell, K. (2008). Family relations and the adjustment of young children of Mexican descent: Do family cultural values moderate these associations? *Social Development, 17,* 358–379.

Ganea, P. A., Allen, M. L., Butler, L., Carey, S., & DeLoache, J. S. (2009). Toddlers' referential understanding of pictures. *Journal of Experimental Child Psychology, 104,* 283–295.

Ganea, P. A., Ma, L., & DeLoache, J. S. (2011). Young children's learning and transfer of biological information from picture books to real animals. *Child Development, 82,* 1421–1433.

Ganea, P. A., Shutts, K., Spelke, E., & DeLoache, J. S. (2007). Thinking of things unseen: Infants' use of language to update object representations. *Psychological Science, 8,* 734–739.

Ganger, J., & Brent, M. R. (2004). Reexamining the vocabulary spurt. *Developmental Psychology, 40,* 621–632.

Ganong, L., Jensen, T., Sanner, C., Russell, L., & Coleman, M. (2019). Stepfathers' affinity-seeking with stepchildren, stepfather–stepchild relationship quality, marital quality, and stepfamily cohesion among stepfathers and mothers. *Journal of Family Psychology, 33,* 521-531.

Garasky, S., Stewart, S. D., Gundersen, C., Lohman, B., & Eisenmann, J. C. (2009). Family stressors and child obesity. *Social Science Research, 38,* 755–766.

Garcia, A. J., Koschnitzky, J. E., & Ramirez, J. M. (2013). The physiological determinants of sudden infant death syndrome. *Respiratory Physiology and Neurobiology, 189,* 288–300.

Garcia, D. J., Janis, R., & Flom, R. (2015). Children's recognition of pride. *Journal of Experimental Child Psychology, 137,* 85–98.

Garcia, M. M., Shaw, D. S., Winslow, E. B., & Yaggi, K. E. (2000). Destructive sibling conflict and the development of conduct problems in young boys. *Developmental Psychology, 36,* 44–53.

Garde, J. B., Suryavanshi, R. K., Jawale, B. A., Deshmukh, V., Dadhe, D. P., & Suryavanshi, M. K. (2014). An epidemiological study to know the prevalence of deleterious oral habits among 6 to 12 year old children. *Journal of International Oral Health, 6,* 39–43.

Gardner, H. (1980). *Artful scribbles: The significance of children's drawing* (p. 64). New York: Basic Books.

Gardner, H. (1983). *Frames of mind: The theory of multiple intelligences.* New York: Basic Books.

Gardner, H. (1993). *Multiple intelligences: The theory in practice.* New York: Basic Books.

Gardner, H. (2011). The theory of multiple intelligences. In M. A. Gernsbacher, R. W. Pew, L. M. Hough, & J. R. Pomerantz (Eds.), *Psychology and the real world: Essays illustrating fundamental contributions to society* (pp. 122–130). New York: Worth.

Gardner, L. A., Magee, C. A., & Vella, S. A. (2017). Enjoyment and behavioral intention predict organized youth sport participation and dropout. *Journal of Physical Activity and Health, 14,* 861–865.

Gardner, M., & Sandberg, D. E. (2011). Growth hormone treatment for short stature: A review of psychosocial assumptions and empirical evidence. *Pediatric Endocrinology Reviews, 9,* 579–588.

Gardner-Neblett, N., & Iruka, I. U. (2015). Oral narrative skills: Explaining the language-emergent literacy link by race/ethnicity and SES. *Developmental Psychology, 7,* 889–904.

Garner, P. W. (2003). Child and family correlates of toddlers' emotional and behavioral responses to a mishap. *Infant Mental Health Journal, 24,* 580–596.

Garte, R. R. (2015). Intersubjectivity as a measure of social competence among children attending Head Start: Assessing the measure's validity and relation to context. *International Journal of Early Childhood, 47,* 189–207.

Gartstein, M. A., Gonzalez, C., Carranza, J. A., Ahadi, S. A., Ye, R., Rothbart, M. K., & Yang, S. W. (2006). Studying cross-cultural differences in the development of infant temperament: People's Republic of China, the United States of America, and Spain. *Child Psychiatry and Human Development, 37,* 145–161.

Gartstein, M. A., Slobodskaya, H. R., & Kinsht, I. A. (2003). Cross-cultural differences in temperament in the first year of life: United States of America (U.S.) and Russia. *International Journal of Behavioral Development, 27,* 316–328.

Gartstein, M. A., Slobodskaya, H. R., Zylicz, P. O., Gosztyla, D., & Nakagawa, A. (2010). A cross-cultural evaluation of temperament: Japan, USA, Poland and Russia. *International Journal of Psychology and Psychological Therapy, 10,* 55–75.

Gaskill, R. L., & Perry, B. D. (2012). Child sexual abuse, traumatic experiences, and their impact on the developing brain. In P. Goodyear-Brown (Ed.), *Handbook of child sexual abuse: Identification, assessment, and treatment* (pp. 29–47). Hoboken, NJ: Wiley.

Gaskins, S. (1999). Children's daily lives in a Mayan village: A case study of culturally constructed roles and activities. In R. Göncü (Ed.), *Children's engagement in the world: Sociocultural perspectives* (pp. 25–61). Cambridge, UK: Cambridge University Press.

Gaskins, S. (2013). Pretend play as culturally constructed activity. In M. Taylor (Ed.), *Oxford handbook on the development of the imagination* (pp. 224–251). Oxford, UK: Oxford University Press.

Gaskins, S. (2014). Children's play as cultural activity. In L. Brooker, M. Blaise, & S. Edwards (Eds.), *Sage handbook of play and learning in early childhood* (pp. 31–42). London: Sage.

Gaskins, S. (2015). Childhood practices across cultures: Play and household work. In L. A. Jensen (Ed.), *Oxford handbook of human development and culture* (pp. 185–197). New York: Oxford University Press.

Gaskins, S., Haight, W., & Lancy, D. F. (2007). The cultural construction of play. In A. Göncü & S. Gaskins (Eds.), *Play and development: Evolutionary, sociocultural, and functional perspectives* (pp. 179–202). Mahwah, NJ: Erlbaum.

Gathercole, S. E., & Alloway, T. P. (2008). Working memory and classroom learning. In S. K. Thurman & C. A. Fiorello (Eds.), *Applied cognitive research in K–3 classrooms* (pp. 17–40). New York: Routledge/ Taylor & Francis Group.

Gathercole, V. C. M. (2007). Miami and North Wales, so far and yet so near: Constructivist account of morpho-syntactic development in bilingual children. *International Journal of Bilingual Education and Bilingualism, 10,* 224–247.

Gathercole, V. C. M., Sebastián, E., & Soto, P. (1999). The early acquisition of Spanish verbal morphology: Across-the-board or piecemeal knowledge? *International Journal of Bilingualism, 3,* 133–182.

Gauvain, M., & Munroe, R. L. (2009). Contributions of societal modernity to cognitive development: A comparison of four cultures. *Child Development, 80,* 1628–1642.

Geangu, E., Benga, O., Stahl, D., & Striano, T. (2010). Contagious crying beyond the first days of life. *Infant Behavior and Development, 33,* 279–288.

Geary, D. C., & VanMarle, K. (2016). Young children's core symbolic and nonsymbolic quantitative knowledge in the prediction of later mathematics achievement. *Developmental Psychology, 52,* 2130–2144.

Geary, D. C., & vanMarle, K. (2018). Growth of symbolic number knowledge accelerates after children understand cardinality. *Cognition, 177,* 69–78.

Geary, D. C., vanMarle, K., Chu, F., Rouder, J., Hoard, M. K., & Nugent, L. (2018). Early conceptual understanding of cardinality predicts superior school-entry number system knowledge. *Psychological Science, 29,* 191–205.

Geerts, C. C., Bots, M. L., van der Ent, C. K., Grobbee, D. E., & Uiterwaal, C. S. (2012).

Parental smoking and vascular damage in their 5-year-old children. *Pediatrics, 129,* 45–54.

Gelman, R. (1972). Logical capacity of very young children: Number invariance rules. *Child Development, 43,* 75–90.

Gelman, R., & Shatz, M. (1978). Appropriate speech adjustments: The operation of conversational constraints on talk to two-year-olds. In M. Lewis & L. A. Rosenblum (Eds.), *Interaction, conversation, and the development of language* (pp. 27–61). New York: Wiley.

Gelman, S. A. (2003). *The essential child.* New York: Oxford University Press.

Gelman, S. A., & Kalish, C. W. (2006). Conceptual development. In D. Kuhn & R. Siegler (Eds.), *Handbook of child psychology: Vol. 2. Cognition, perception, and language* (6th ed., 687–733). New York: Wiley.

Gelman, S. A., Taylor, M. G., & Nguyen, S. P. (2004). Mother–child conversations about gender. *Monographs of the Society for Research in Child Development, 69*(1, Serial No. 275).

Genc, S., Smith, R. E., Malpas, C. B., Anderson, V., Nicholson, J. M., Efron, D., et al. (2018). Development of white matter fibre density and morphology over childhood: A longitudinal fixel-based analysis. *NeuroImage, 183,* 666–676.

Gendler, M. N., Witherington, D. C., & Edwards, A. (2008). The development of affect specificity in infants' use of emotion cues. *Infancy, 13,* 456–468.

Genesee, F., & Jared, D. (2008). Literacy development in early French immersion programs. *Canadian Psychology, 49,* 140–147.

Gentile, D. A., Li, D., Khoo, A., Prot, S., & Anderson, C. A. (2014). Mediators and moderators of long-term effects of violent video games on aggressive behavior. *JAMA Pediatrics, 168,* 450–457.

Gergely, G., & Watson, J. (1999). Early socio-emotional development: Contingency perception and the social-biofeedback model. In P. Rochat (Ed.), *Early social cognition: Understanding others in the first months of life* (pp. 101–136). Mahwah, NJ: Erlbaum.

Gernhardt, A., Rübeling, H., & Keller, H. (2014). Self and family conceptions of Turkish migrant, native German, and native Turkish children: A comparison of children's drawings. *International Journal of Intercultural Relations, 40,* 154–166.

Gershoff, E. T., & Grogan-Kaylor, A. (2016). Spanking and child outcomes: Old controversies and new meta-analyses. *Journal of Family Psychology, 30,* 453–469.

Gershoff, E. T., Grogan-Kaylor, A., Lansford, J. E., Chang, L., Zelli, A., Deater-Deckard, K., et al. (2010). Parent discipline practices in an international sample: Associations with child behaviors and moderation by perceived normativeness. *Child Development, 81,* 487–502.

Gershoff, E. T., Lansford, J. E., Sexton, H. R., Davis-Kean, P., & Sameroff, A. J. (2012). Longitudinal links between spanking and children's externalizing behaviors in a national sample of White, Black, Hispanic, and Asian American families. *Child Development, 83,* 838–843.

Gerson, S., & Woodward, A. L. (2010). Building intentional action knowledge with one's hands. In S. P. Johnson (Ed.), *Neoconstructivism: The new science of cognitive development* (pp. 295–313). New York: Oxford University Press.

Gesell, A. (1933). Maturation and patterning of behavior. In C. Murchison (Ed.),

A handbook of child psychology. Worcester, MA: Clark University Press.

Geurten, M., Catale, C., & Meulemans, T. (2015). When children's knowledge of memory improves children's performance in memory. *Applied Cognitive Psychology, 29,* 244–252.

Gewertz, C. (2018, April 3). ESSA offers testing flexibility. So why aren't states using it? *Education Week, 37*(25), 21–22.

Ghosh, J. K. C., Heck, J. E., Cockburn, M., Su, J., Jerrett, M., & Ritz, B. (2013). Prenatal exposure to traffic-related air pollution and risk of early childhood cancers. *American Journal of Epidemiology, 178,* 1233–1239.

Gibbs, J. C. (2019). *Moral development and reality* (4th ed.). New York: Oxford University Press.

Gibson, E. J. (1970). The development of perception as an adaptive process. *American Scientist, 58,* 98–107.

Gibson, E. J. (2003). The world is so full of a number of things: On specification and perceptual learning. *Ecological Psychology, 15,* 283–287.

Gibson, E. J., & Walk, R. D. (1960). The "visual cliff." *Scientific American, 202,* 64–71.

Gibson, J. J. (1979). *The ecological approach to visual perception.* Boston: Houghton Mifflin.

Giedd, J. N., Lalonde, F. M., Celano, M. J., White, S. L., Wallace, G. L., Lee, N. R., et al. (2009). Anatomical brain magnetic resonance imaging of typically developing children and adolescents. *Journal of the American Academy of Child and Adolescent Psychiatry, 48,* 465–470.

Giles, A., & Rovee-Collier, C. (2011). Infant long-term memory for associations formed during mere exposure. *Infant Behavior and Development, 34,* 327–338.

Giles, J. W., & Heyman, G. D. (2005). Young children's beliefs about the relationship between gender and aggressive behavior. *Child Development, 76,* 107–121.

Giles-Sims, J., Straus, M. A., & Sugarman, D. B. (1995). Child, maternal, and family characteristics associated with spanking. *Family Relations, 44,* 170–176.

Gill, S. V., Adolph, K. E., & Vereijken, B. (2009). Change in action: How infants learn to walk down slopes. *Developmental Science, 12,* 888–902.

Gillon, G. T. (2018). *Phonological awareness: From research to practice* (2nd ed.). New York: Guilford.

Gilmore, J. H., Shi, F., Woolson, S. L., Knickmeyer, R. C., Short, S. J., Lin, W., et al. (2012). Longitudinal development of cortical and subcortical gray matter from birth to 2 years. *Cerebral Cortex, 22,* 2478–2485.

Ginsburg, H. P., Lee, J. S., & Boyd, J. S. (2008). Mathematics education for young children: What it is and how to promote it. *Social Policy Report of the Society for Research in Child Development, 12*(1).

Glass, R. I., & Stoll, B. J. (2018). Oral rehydration therapy for diarrheal diseases: A 50-year perspective. *JAMA, 320,* 865–866.

Gleason, J. B. (2013). The development of language: An overview and a preview. In J. B. Gleason & N. B. Ratner (Eds.), *The development of language* (8th ed., pp. 1–29). Upper Saddle River, NJ: Pearson.

Gleason, T. R. (2013). Imaginary relationships. In M. Taylor (Ed.), *Oxford handbook of the development of imagination* (pp. 251–271). New York: Oxford University Press.

Gleason, T. R. (2017). The psychological significance of play with imaginary companions in early childhood. *Learning and Behavior, 45,* 432–440.

Gleason, T. R., Sebanc, A. M., & Hartup, W. W. (2000). Imaginary companions of preschool children. *Developmental Psychology, 36,* 419–428.

Gleitman, L. R., Cassidy, K., Nappa, R., Papfragou, A., & Trueswell, J. C. (2005). Hard words. *Language Learning and Development, 1,* 23–64.

Glenright, M., & Pexman, P. M. (2010). Development of children's ability to distinguish sarcasm and verbal irony. *Journal of Child Language, 37,* 429–451.

Global Burden of Disease Injury Collaborators. (2018). Global mortality from firearms, 1990–2016. *Journal of the American Medical Association, 320,* 792–814.

Glover, V., Ahmed-Salim, Y., & Capron, L. (2016). Maternal anxiety, depression, and stress during pregnancy: Effects on the fetus and the child and underlying mechanisms. In N. Reissland & B. S. Kisilevsky (Eds.), *Fetal development* (pp. 213–227). New York: Springer.

Gluckman, P. D., Sizonenko, S. V., & Bassett, N. S. (1999). The transition from fetus to neonate—an endocrine perspective. *Acta Paediatrica Supplement, 88*(428), 7–11.

Gnambs, T., Stasielowicz, L., Wolter, I., & Appel, M. (2019). Do computer games jeopardize educational outcomes? A prospective study on gaming times and academic achievement. *Psychology of Popular Media and Culture, 8.* Retrieved from psycnet.apa.org/search/results?id =87b61b29-6020-caeb-7769-0fa59bfe76bc

Gnepp, J. (1983). Children's social sensitivity: Inferring emotions from conflicting cues. *Developmental Psychology, 19,* 805–814.

Gnoth, C., Maxrath, B., Skonieczny, T., Friol, K., Godehardt, E., & Tigges, J. (2011). Final ART success rates: A 10 years survey. *Human Reproduction, 26,* 2239–2246.

Goble, P. Martin, C. L., Hanish, L. D., & Fabes, R. A. (2012). Children's gender-typed activity choices across preschool social contexts. *Sex Roles, 67,* 435–451.

Goeke-Morey, M. C., Papp, L. M., & Cummings, E. M. (2013). Changes in marital conflict and youths' responses across childhood and adolescence: A test of sensitization. *Development and Psychopathology, 25,* 241–251.

Gogate, L., & Hollich, G. (2016). Early verb–action and noun–object mapping across sensory modalities: A neuro-developmental view. *Developmental Neuropsychology, 41,* 293–307.

Gogate, L. J., & Bahrick, L. E. (2001). Intersensory redundancy and 7-month-old infants' memory for arbitrary syllable–object relations. *Infancy, 2,* 219–231.

Goh, Y. I., & Koren, G. (2008). Folic acid in pregnancy and fetal outcomes. *Journal of Obstetrics and Gynaecology, 28,* 3–13.

Goldberg, A. E. (2010). *Lesbian and gay parents and their children: Research on the family life cycle.* Washington, DC: American Psychological Association.

Goldberg, A. E., & Garcia, R. L. (2016). Gender-typed behavior over time in children with lesbian, gay, and heterosexual parents. *Journal of Family Psychology, 30,* 854–865.

Goldberg, A. E., Kashy, D. A., & Smith, J. Z. (2012). Gender-typed play behavior in early childhood: Adopted children with lesbian, gay, and heterosexual parents. *Sex Roles, 67,* 503–513.

Golden, J. C., & Jacoby, J. W. (2018). Playing princess: Preschool girls' interpretations of gender stereotypes in Disney princess media. *Sex Roles, 79,* 299–313.

Goldin-Meadow, S. (2015). From action to abstraction: Gesture as a mechanism of

change. *Developmental Review, 38,* 167–184.

Goldin-Meadow, S., Cook, S. W., & Mitchell, Z. A. (2009). Gesturing gives children new ideas about math. *Psychological Science, 20,* 267–272.

Goldschmidt, L., Richardson, G. A., Cornelius, M. D., & Day, N. L. (2004). Prenatal marijuana and alcohol exposure and academic achievement at age 10. *Neurotoxicology and Teratology, 26,* 521–532.

Goldstein, S. (2011a). Attention-deficit/ hyperactivity disorder. In S. Goldstein & C. R. Reynolds (Eds.), *Handbook of neurodevelopmental and genetic disorders in children* (2nd ed., pp. 131–150). New York: Guilford.

Goldstein, S. (2011b). Learning disabilities in childhood. In S. Goldstein, J. A. Naglieri, & M. DeVries (Eds.), *Learning and attention disorders in adolescence and adulthood: Assessment and treatment* (2nd ed., pp. 31–58). Hoboken, NJ: Wiley.

Goldstein, T. R., & Woolley, J. (2016). Ho! Ho! Who? Parent promotion of belief in and live encounters with Santa Claus. *Cognitive Development, 39,* 113–127.

Golinkoff, R. M., & Hirsh-Pasek, K. (2006). Baby wordsmith: From associationist to social sophisticate. *Current Directions in Psychological Science, 15,* 30–33.

Golinkoff, R. M., & Hirsh-Pasek, K. (2008). How toddlers begin to learn verbs. *Trends in Cognitive Sciences, 12,* 397–403.

Golinkoff, R. M., Hoff, E., Rowe, M. L., Tamis-LeMonda, C. S., & Hirsh-Pasek, K. (2019). Language matters: Denying the existence of the 30-million-word gap has serious consequences. *Child Development, 90,* 985–992.

Golomb, C. (2004). *The child's creation of a pictorial world* (2nd ed.). Mahwah, NJ: Erlbaum.

Golombok, S., Blake, L., Casey, P., Roman, G., & Jadva, V. (2013). Children born through reproductive donation: A longitudinal study of psychological adjustment. *Journal of Child Psychology and Psychiatry, 54,* 653–660.

Golombok, S., Readings, J., Blake, L., Casey, P., Mellish, L., Marks, A., & Jadva, V. (2011). Children conceived by gamete donation: Psychological adjustment and mother–child relationships at age 7. *Journal of Family Psychology, 25,* 230–239.

Golombok, S., Rust, J., Zervoulis, K., Croudace, T., Golding, J., & Hines, M. (2008). Developmental trajectories of sex-typed behavior in boys and girls: A longitudinal general population study of children aged 2.5–8 years. *Child Development, 79,* 1583–1593.

Golombok, S., & Tasker, F. (2015). Socioemotional development in changing families. In M. E. Lamb (Ed.), *Handbook of child psychology and developmental science: Vol. 3. Socioemotional processes* (7th ed., pp. 419–463). Hoboken, NJ: Wiley.

Gomez-Perez, E., & Ostrosky-Solis, F. (2006). Attention and memory evaluation across the life span: Heterogeneous effects of age and education. *Journal of Clinical and Experimental Neuropsychology, 28,* 477–494.

Gonzales, N. A., Coxe, S., Roosa, M. W., White, R. M. B., Knight, G. P., Zeiders, K. H., & Saenz, D. (2010). Economic hardship, neighborhood context, and parenting: Prospective effects on Mexican-American adolescents' mental health. *American Journal of Community Psychology, 47,* 98–113.

Gonzalez, A.-L., & Wolters, C. A. (2006). The relation between perceived parenting practices and achievement motivation in mathematics. *Journal of Research in Childhood Education, 21*, 203–217.

González-Rivera, M., & Bauermeister, J. A. (2007). Children's attitudes toward people with AIDS in Puerto Rico: Exploring stigma through drawings and stories. *Qualitative Health Research, 17*, 250–263.

Goodman, A., Schorge, J., & Greene, M. F. (2011). The long-term effects of in utero exposures—the DES story. *New England Journal of Medicine, 364*, 2083–2084.

Goodman, G. S., Ogle, C. M., McWilliams, K., Narr, R. K., & Paz-Alonso, P. M. (2014). Memory development in the forensic context. In P. J. Bauer & R. Fivush (Eds.), *Wiley handbook on the development of children's memory* (pp. 921–941). Hoboken, NJ: Wiley.

Goodman, J., Dale, P., & Li, P. (2008). Does frequency count? Parental input and the acquisition of vocabulary. *Journal of Child Language, 35*, 515–531.

Goodman, J. H., Prager, J., Goldstein, R., & Freeman, M. (2015). Perinatal dyadic psychotherapy for postpartum depression: A randomized controlled pilot trial. *Archives of Women's Mental Health, 18*, 493–506.

Goodman, S. H., Rouse, M. H., Long, Q., Shuang, J., & Brand, S. R. (2011). Deconstructing antenatal depression: What is it that matters for neonatal behavioral functioning? *Infant Mental Health Journal, 32*, 339–361.

Goodvin, R., Meyer, S., Thompson, R. A., & Hayes, R. (2008). Self-understanding in early childhood: Associations with child attachment security and maternal negative affect. *Attachment and Human Development, 10*, 433–450.

Goodvin, R., & Romdall, L. (2013). Associations of mother–child reminiscing about negative past events, coping, and self-concept in early childhood. *Infant and Child Development, 22*, 383–400.

Goodwin, A. P., & Ahn, S. (2010). A meta-analysis of morphological interventions: Effects on literacy achievement of children with literacy difficulties. *Annals of Dyslexia, 60*, 183–208.

Goodwin, A. P., & Ahn, S. (2013). A meta-analysis of morphological interventions in English: Effects on literacy outcomes for school-age children. *Scientific Studies of Reading, 17*, 257–285.

Gooren, E. M. J. C., Pol, A. C., Stegge, H., Terwogt, M. M., & Koot, H. M. (2011). The development of conduct problems and depressive symptoms in early elementary school children: The role of peer rejection. *Journal of Clinical Child and Adolescent Psychology, 40*, 245–253.

Gopnik, A., & Nazzi, T. (2003). Words, kinds, and causal powers: A theory theory perspective on early naming and categorization. In D. H. Rakison & L. M. Oakes (Eds.), *Early category and concept development* (pp. 303–329). New York: Oxford University Press.

Gopnik, A., & Tenenbaum, J. B. (2007). Bayesian networks, Bayesian learning and cognitive development. *Developmental Science, 10*, 281–287.

Gordon, I., Zagoory-Sharon, O., Leckman, J. F., & Feldman, R. (2010). Oxytocin and the development of parenting in humans. *Biological Psychiatry, 68*, 377–382.

Gorman, B. K., Fiestas, C. E., Peña, E. D., & Clark, M. R. (2011). Creative and stylistic devices employed by children during a storybook narrative task: A cross-cultural study. *Language, Speech, and Hearing Services in Schools, 42*, 167–181.

Gormley, W. T., Jr., & Phillips, D. (2009). *The effects of pre-K on child development: Lessons from Oklahoma.* Washington, DC: National Summit on Early Childhood Education, Georgetown University.

Goswami, U. (1996). Analogical reasoning and cognitive development. In H. Reese (Ed.), *Advances in child development and behavior* (Vol. 26, pp. 91–138). New York: Academic Press.

Gottlieb, G. (1998). Normally occurring environmental and behavioral influences on gene activity: From central dogma to probabilistic epigenesis. *Psychological Review, 105*, 792–802.

Gottlieb, G. (2007). Probabilistic epigenesis. *Developmental Science, 10*, 1–11.

Gottlieb, G., Wahlsten, D., & Lickliter, R. (2006). The significance of biology for human development: A developmental psychobiological systems of view. In R. M. Lerner (Ed.), *Handbook of child psychology: Vol. 1. Theoretical models of human development* (6th ed., pp. 210–257). Hoboken, NJ: Wiley.

Gottman, J. M., Gottman, J. S., & Shapiro, A. (2010). A new couples approach to interventions for the transition to parenthood. In M. S. Schulz, M. K. Pruett, P. K. Kerig, & R. D. Parke (Eds.), *Strengthening couple relationships for optimal child development* (pp. 165–179). Washington, DC: American Psychological Association.

Goyal, M. S., Iannotti, L. L., & Raichle, M. E. (2018). Brain nutrition: A life span approach. *Annual Review of Nutrition, 38*, 381–399.

Graber, J. A., Nichols, T., Lynne, S. D., Brooks-Gunn, J., & Botwin, G. J. (2006). A longitudinal examination of family, friend, and media influences on competent versus problem behaviors among urban minority youth. *Applied Developmental Science, 10*, 75–85.

Graber, J. A., Seeley, J. R., Brooks-Gunn, J., & Lewinsohn, P. M. (2004). Is pubertal timing associated with psychopathology in young adulthood? *Journal of the American Academy of Child and Adolescent Psychiatry, 43*, 718–726.

Graham, S., & Perin, D. (2007). A meta-analysis of writing instruction for adolescent students. *Journal of Educational Psychology, 99*, 445–476.

Graham-Bermann, S. A., & Howell, K. H. (2011). Child maltreatment in the context of intimate partner violence. In J. E. B. Myers (Ed.), *Child maltreatment* (3rd ed., pp. 167–180). Thousand Oaks, CA: Sage.

Gralinski, J. H., & Kopp, C. B. (1993). Everyday rules for behavior: Mothers' requests to young children. *Developmental Psychology, 29*, 573–584.

Grall, T. (2016). Custodial mothers and fathers and their child support: 2013. *Current Population Reports*, P60–255. Retrieved from www.census.gov/content/dam/Census /library/publications/2016/demo/P60-255 .pdf

Granic, I., Hollenstein, T., Dishion, T. J., & Patterson, G. R. (2003). Longitudinal analysis of flexibility and reorganization in early adolescence: A dynamic systems study of family interactions. *Developmental Psychology, 39*, 606–617.

Granier-Deferre, C., Bassereau, S., Ribeiro, A., Jacquet, A. Y., & Lecanuet, J.-P. (2003). *Cardiac "orienting" response in fetuses and babies following in utero melody-learning.* Paper presented at the 11th European Conference on Developmental Psychology, Milan, Italy.

Grant, K. B., & Ray, J. A. (2010). *Home, school, and community collaboration: Culturally responsive family involvement.* Thousand Oaks, CA: Sage Publications.

Grant, S. L., Mizzi, T., & Anglim, J. (2016). 'Fat, four-eyed and female' 30 years later: A replication of Harris, Harris, and Bochner's (1982) early study of obesity stereotypes. *Australian Journal of Psychology, 68*, 290–300.

Gratier, M., & Devouche, E. (2011). Imitation and repetition of prosodic contour in vocal interaction at 3 months. *Developmental Psychology, 47*, 67–76.

Gray, K. A., Day, N. L., Leech, S., & Richardson, G. A. (2005). Prenatal marijuana exposure: Effect on child depressive symptoms at ten years of age. *Neurotoxicology and Teratology, 27*, 439–448.

Gray, M. R., & Steinberg, L. (1999). Unpacking authoritative parenting: Reassessing a multidimensional construct. *Journal of Marriage and the Family, 61*, 574–587.

Gray-Little, B., & Hafdahl, A. R. (2000). Factors influencing racial comparisons of self-esteem: A quantitative review. *Psychological Bulletin, 126*, 26–54.

Grech, V. (2014). The effect of warfare on the secular trends in sex ratios at birth in Israel, Egypt, and Kuwait over the past 60 years. *Libyan Journal of Medicine, 9*, 23448.

Green, B. L., Tarte, J. M., Harrison, P. M., Nygren, M., & Sanders, M. B. (2014). Results from a randomized trial of the Healthy Families Oregon accredited statewide program: Early program impacts on parenting. *Children and Youth Services Review, 44*, 288–298.

Green, G. E., Irwin, J. R., & Gustafson, G. E. (2000). Acoustic cry analysis, neonatal status and long-term developmental outcomes. In R. G. Barr, B. Hopkins, & J. A. Green (Eds.), *Crying as a sign, a symptom, and a signal* (pp. 137–156). Cambridge, UK: Cambridge University Press.

Green, R.-J., Rubio, R. J., Rothblum, E. D., Bergman, K., & Katuzny, K. E. (2019). Gay fathers by surrogacy: Prejudice, parenting, and well-being of female and male children. *Psychology of Sexual Orientation and Gender Diversity, 6*, 269–283.

Greenberg, J. P. (2013). Determinants of after-school programming for school-age immigrant children. *Children and Schools, 35*, 101–111.

Greendorfer, S. L., Lewko, J. H., & Rosengren, K. S. (1996). Family and gender-based socialization of children and adolescents. In F. L. Smoll & R. E. Smith (Eds.), *Children and youth in sport: A biopsychological perspective* (pp. 89–111). Dubuque, IA: Brown & Benchmark.

Greene, S. M., Anderson, E. R., Forgatch, M. S., DeGarmo, D. S., & Hetherington, E. M. (2012). Risk and resilience after divorce. In F. Walsh (Ed.), *Normal family processes: Growing diversity and complexity* (4th ed., pp. 102–127). New York: Guilford.

Greenfield, P. M. (1992, June). *Notes and references for developmental psychology.* Conference on Making Basic Texts in Psychology More Culture-Inclusive and Culture-Sensitive, Western Washington University, Bellingham, WA.

Greenfield, P. M. (2004). *Weaving generations together: Evolving creativity in the Maya of Chiapas.* Santa Fe, NM: School of American Research.

Greenough, W. T., & Black, J. E. (1992). Induction of brain structure by experience: Substrates for cognitive development. In M. Gunnar & C. A. Nelson (Eds.), *Minnesota symposia on child psychology* (pp. 155–200). Hillsdale, NJ: Erlbaum.

Greer, T., & Lockman, J. J. (1998). Using writing instruments: Invariances in young children and adults. *Child Development, 69*, 888–902.

Gregory, A., & Weinstein, R. S. (2004). Connection and regulation at home and in school: Predicting growth in achievement for adolescents. *Journal of Adolescent Research, 19*, 405–427.

Gregory, R., Cheng, H., Rupp, H. A., Sengelaub, D. R., & Helman, J. R. (2015). Oxytocin increases VTA activation to infant and sexual stimuli in nulliparous and postpartum women. *Hormones and Behavior, 69*, 82–88.

Grewen, K., Burchinal, M., Vachet, C., Gouttard, S., Gilmore, J. H., Lin, W., et al. (2014). Prenatal cocaine effects on brain structure in early infancy. *Neuroimage, 101*, 114–123.

Griffin, D. K., Fishel, S., Gordon, T., Yaron, Y., Grifo, J., Hourvitz, A., et al. (2017). Continuing to deliver: The evidence for pre-implantation genetic screening. *British Medical Journal, 356*, j752.

Grigoriadis, S., VonderPorten, E. H., Mamisashvili, L., Eady, A., Tomlinson, G., Dennis, C. L., et al. (2013). The effect of prenatal antidepressant exposure on neonatal adaptation: A systematic review and meta-analysis. *Journal of Clinical Psychiatry, 74*, e309–e320.

Grogan-Kaylor, A., Ma, J., & Graham-Bermann, S. A. (2018). The case against physical punishment. *Current Opinion in Psychology, 19*, 22–27.

Groh, A. M., Fearon, R. M. P., Bakermans-Kranenburg, M. J., Van IJzendoorn, M. H., Steele, R. D., & Roisman, G. I. (2014). The significance of attachment security for children's social competence with peers: A meta-analytic study. *Attachment and Human Development, 16*, 103–136.

Groh, A. M., Narayan, A. J., Bakermans-Kranenberg, M. J., Roisman, G. I., Vaughn, B. E., Fearon, R. M. P., & van IJzendoorn, M. H. (2017). Attachment and temperament in the early life course: A meta-analytic review. *Child Development, 88*, 770–795.

Gross, N. (2016, August 3). *Dual-language programs on the rise across the U.S.* Education Writers Association Blog: Latino Ed Beat. Retrieved from www.ewa.org /blog-latino-ed-beat/dual-language -programs-rise-across-us

Grossmann, K., Grossmann, K. E., Kindler, H., & Zimmermann, P. (2008). A wider view of attachment and exploration: The influence of mothers and fathers on the development of psychological security from infancy to young adulthood. In J. Cassidy & P. R. Shaver (Eds.), *Handbook of attachment: Theory, research, and clinical applications* (2nd ed., pp. 880–905). New York: Guilford.

Grossmann, K., Grossmann, K. E., Spangler, G., Suess, G., & Unzner, L. (1985). Maternal sensitivity and newborns' orientation responses as related to quality of attachment in Northern Germany. In I. Bretherton & E. Waters (Eds.), Growing points of attachment theory and research. *Monographs of the Society for Research in Child Development, 50*(1–2, Serial No. 209).

Grossmann, T., Striano, T., & Friederici, A. D. (2007). Developmental changes in infants' processing of happy and angry facial expressions: A neurobehavioral study. *Brain and Cognition, 64,* 30–41.

Grossniklaus, H. E., Nickerson, J. M., Edelhauser, H. F., Bergman, L. A. M. K., & Berglin, L. (2013). Anatomic alterations in aging and age-related diseases of the eye. *Investigative Ophthalmology and Visual Science, 54,* 23–27.

Grow-Maienza, J., Hahn, D.-D., & Joo, C.-A. (2001). Mathematics instruction in Korean primary schools: Structures, processes, and a linguistic analysis of questioning. *Journal of Educational Psychology, 93,* 363–376.

Gruendel, J., & Aber, J. L. (2007). Bridging the gap between research and child policy change: The role of strategic communications in policy advocacy. In J. L. Aber, S. J. Bishop-Josef, S. M. Jones, K. T. McLearn, & D. A. Phillips (Eds.), *Child development and social policy: Knowledge for action* (pp. 43–58). Washington, DC: American Psychological Association.

Grünebaum, A., McCullough, L. B., Brent, R. L., Arabin, B., Levene, M. I., & Chervenak, F. A. (2015). Perinatal risks of planned home births in the United States. *American Journal of Obstetrics and Gynecology, 212*(350), e1–6.

Grusec, J. E. (2006). The development of moral behavior and conscience from a socialization perspective. In M. Killen & J. Smetana (Eds.), *Handbook of moral development* (pp. 243–265). Philadelphia: Erlbaum.

Grusec, J. E., Danyliuk, T., Kil, H., & O'Neill, D. (2017). Perspectives on parent discipline and child outcomes. *International Journal of Behavioral Development, 41,* 465–471.

Grzyb, B. J., Cangelosi, A., Cattani, A., & Floccia, C. (2017). Decreased attention to object size information in scale errors performers. *Infant Behavior and Development, 47,* 72–82.

Guadalupe, T., Willems, R. M., Zwiers, M., Vasquez, A. A., Hoogman, M., Hagoort, P., et al. (2014). Differences in cerebral cortical anatomy of left- and right-handers. *Frontiers in Psychology, 5,* Art. No. 261.

Gubbels, J., Segers, E., Keuning, J., & Verhoeven, L. (2016). The Aurora-a Battery as an assessment of triarchic intellectual abilities in upper primary grades. *Gifted Child Quarterly, 60,* 226–238.

Guedes, M., Pereira, M., Pires, R., Carvalho, P., & Canavarro, M. C. (2015). Childbearing motivations scale: Construction of a new measure and its preliminary psychometric properties. *Journal of Child and Family Studies, 24,* 180–194.

Guellaï, B., Streri, A., Chopin, A., & Rider, D. (2016). Newborns' sensitivity to the visual aspects of infant-directed speech: Evidence from point-line displays of talking faces. *Journal of Experimental Psychology: Human Perception and Performance, 42,* 1275–1281.

Guerra, N. G., Williams, K. R., & Sadek, S. (2011). Understanding bullying and victimization during childhood and adolescence: A mixed methods study. *Child Development, 82,* 295–310.

Guest, A. M. (2013). Cultures of play during middle childhood: Interpretive perspectives from two distinct marginalized communities. *Sport, Education and Society, 18,* 167–183.

Guggenheim, J. A., St Pourcain, B., McMahon, G., Timpson, N. J., Evans, D. M., & Williams, C. (2015). Assumption-free estimation of the genetic contribution to refractive error across childhood. *Molecular Vision, 21,* 621–632.

Guglielmi, R. S. (2008). Native language proficiency, English literacy, academic achievement, and occupational attainment in limited-English-proficient students: A latent growth modeling perspective. *Journal of Educational Psychology, 100,* 322–342.

Guignard, J.-H., Kermarrec, S., & Tordjman, S. (2016). Relationships between intelligence and creativity in gifted and non-gifted children. *Learning and Individual Differences, 52,* 209–215.

Guignard, J.-H., & Lubart, T. I. (2007). A comparative study of convergent and divergent thinking in intellectually gifted children. *Gifted and Talented International, 22*(1), 9–15.

Guilford, J. P. (1985). The structure-of-intellect model. In B. B. Wolman (Ed.), *Handbook of intelligence* (pp. 225–266). New York: Wiley.

Guimond, F. A., Brendgen, M., Forget-Dubois, N., Dionne, G., Vitaro, F., Tremblay, R. E., & Boivin, M. (2012). Associations of mother's and father's parenting practices with children's observed social reticence in a competitive situation: A monozygotic twin difference study. *Journal of Abnormal Child Psychology, 40,* 391–402.

Gullone, E. (2000). The development of normal fear: A century of research. *Clinical Psychology Review, 20,* 429–451.

Gunderson, E. A., Ramirez, G., Levine, S. C., & Beilock, S. L. (2012). The role of parents and teachers in the development of gender-related math attitudes. *Sex Roles, 66,* 153–166.

Gunderson, E. A., Sorhagen, N. S., Gripshover, S. J., Dweck, C. S., Goldin-Meadow, S., & Levine, S. C. (2018). Parent praise to toddlers predicts fourth grade academic achievement via children's incremental mindsets. *Developmental Psychology, 54,* 397–409.

Günes, P. M. (2015). The role of maternal education in child health: Evidence from a compulsory schooling law. *Economics of Education Review, 47,* 1–16.

Gunnar, M. R., & Cheatham, C. L. (2003). Brain and behavior interfaces: Stress and the developing brain. *Infant Mental Health Journal, 24,* 195–211.

Gunnar, M. R., & de Haan, M. (2009). Methods in social neuroscience: Issues in studying development. In M. de Haan & M. R. Gunnar (Eds.), *Handbook of developmental social neuroscience* (pp. 13–37). New York: Guilford.

Gunnar, M. R., Doom, J. R., & Esposito, E. A. (2015). Psychoneuroendocrinology of stress: Normative development and individual differences. In M. E. Lamb (Eds.), *Handbook of child psychology and developmental science: Vol. 3. Socioemotional processes* (pp. 106–151). Hoboken, NJ: Wiley.

Gunnar, M. R., Kryzer, E., Van Ryzin, M. J., & Phillips, D. A. (2011). The import of the cortisol rise in child care differs as a function of behavioral inhibition. *Developmental Psychology, 47,* 792–803.

Gunnar, M. R., Morison, S. J., Chisholm, K., & Schuder, M. (2001). Salivary cortisol levels in children adopted from Romanian orphanages. *Development and Psychopathology, 13,* 611–628.

Gunnar, M. R., & Quevedo, K. (2007). The neurobiology of stress and development. *Annual Review of Psychology, 58,* 145–173.

Guo, G., & VanWey, L.K. (1999). Sibship size and intellectual development: Is the relationship causal? *American Sociological Review, 64,* 169–187.

Gupta, J. K., Hofmeyr, G. J., & Shehmar, M. (2012). Position in the second stage of labour for women without epidural anaesthesia. *Cochrane Database of Systematic Reviews, 5,* Art. No. CD002006.

Guralnick, M. J. (2012). Preventive interventions for preterm children: Effectiveness and developmental mechanisms. *Journal of Developmental and Behavioral Pediatrics, 33,* 352–364.

Gurrola, M., Ayón, C., & Moya Salas, L. (2016). Mexican adolescents' education and hopes in an anti-immigrant environment: The perspectives of first- and second-generation youth and parents. *Journal of Family Issues, 37,* 494–519.

Gustafson, G. E., Green, J. A., & Cleland, J. W. (1994). Robustness of individual identity in the cries of human infants. *Developmental Psychobiology, 27,* 1–9.

Guterman, N. B., Lee, S. J., Taylor, C. A., & Rathouz, P. J. (2009). Parental perceptions of neighborhood processes, stress, personal control, and risk for physical child abuse and neglect. *Child Abuse and Neglect, 33,* 897–906.

Gutierrez-Galve, L., Stein, A., Hanington, L., Heron, J., & Ramchandani, P. (2015). Paternal depression in the postnatal period and child development: *Mediators and moderators. Pediatrics, 135,* e339–347.

Guttentag, C. L., Landry, S. H., Williams, J. M., Baggett, K. M., Noria, C. W., Borkowski, J. G., et al. (2014). "My baby & me": Effects of an early comprehensive parenting intervention on at-risk mothers and their children. *Developmental Psychology, 50,* 1482–1496.

Guttentag, R., & Ferrell, J. (2004). Reality compared with its alternatives: Age differences in judgments of regret and relief. *Developmental Psychology, 40,* 764–775.

Guttman, J., & Lazar, A. (1998). Mother's or father's custody: Does it matter for social adjustment? *Educational Psychology: An International Journal of Experimental Educational Psychology, 18,* 225–234.

Guyer, C., Huber, R., Fontijn, J., Bucher, H. U., Nicolai, H., Werner, H., et al. (2015). Very preterm infants show earlier emergence of 24-hour sleep-wake rhythms compared to term infants. *Early Human Development, 91,* 37–42.

Guzzo, K. B. (2014). Trends in cohabitation outcomes: Compositional changes and engagement among never-married young adults. *Journal of Marriage and Family, 76,* 826–842.

Gweon, H., Dodell-Feder, D., Bedney, M., & Saxe, R. (2012). Theory of mind performance in children correlates with functional specialization of a brain region for thinking about thoughts. *Child Development, 83,* 1853–1868.

Gwiazda, J., & Birch, E. E. (2001). Perceptual development: Vision. In E. B. Goldstein (Ed.), *Blackwell handbook of perception* (pp. 636–668). Oxford, UK: Blackwell.

H

Hackman, D. A., Gallop, R., Evans, G. W., & Farah, M. J. (2015). Socioeconomic status and executive function: Developmental trajectories and mediation. *Developmental Science, 18,* 686–702.

Hadd, A. R., & Rodgers, J. L. (2017). Intelligence, income, and education as potential influences on a child's home environment: A (maternal) sibling comparison design. *Developmental Psychology, 53,* 1286–1299.

Hafner, J. W., Kok, S. J., Wang, H., Wren, D. L., Aitken, M. E., Med, B. K., et al. (2017). Child passenger restraint system misuse in rural versus urban children: A multisite case-control study. *Pediatric Emergency Care, 33,* 663–669.

Haimovitz, K., & Dweck, C. S. (2016). Parents' views of failure predict children's fixed and growth intelligence mind-sets. *Psychological Science, 27,* 859–869.

Haimovitz, K., & Dweck, C. S. (2017). The origins of children's growth and fixed mindsets: New research and a new proposal. *Child Development, 88,* 1849–1859.

Hainline, L. (1998). The development of basic visual abilities. In A. Slater (Ed.), *Perceptual development: Visual, auditory, and speech perception in infancy* (pp. 37–44). Hove, UK: Psychology Press.

Hair, N. L., Hanson, J. L., Wolfe, B. L., & Pollak, S. D. (2015). Association of child poverty, brain development, and academic achievement. *JAMA Pediatrics, 169,* 822–829.

Hakim, F., Kheirandish-Gozal, L., & Gozal, D. (2015). Obesity and altered sleep: A pathway to metabolic derangements in children? *Seminars in Pediatric Neurology, 22,* 77–85.

Hakuta, K., Bialystok, E., & Wiley, E. (2003). Critical evidence: A test of the critical period hypothesis for second-language acquisition. *Psychological Science, 14,* 31–38.

Halford, G. S., & Andrews, G. (2011). Information-processing models of cognitive development. In U. Goswami (Ed.), *Wiley-Blackwell handbook of childhood cognitive development* (2nd ed., pp. 697–722). Hoboken, NJ: Wiley-Blackwell.

Halim, M. L., & Ruble, D. (2010). Gender identity and stereotyping in early and middle childhood. In J. C. Chrisler & D. R. McCreary (Eds.), *Handbook of gender research in psychology* (pp. 495–525). New York: Springer.

Halim, M. L., Ruble, D. N., & Tamis-LeMonda, C. S. (2013). Four-year-olds' beliefs about how others regard males and females. *British Journal of Developmental Psychology, 2013,* 128–135.

Halim, M. L., Ruble, D. N., Tamis-LeMonda, C. S., Zosuls, K. M., Lurye, L. E., & Greulich, F. K. (2014). Pink frilly dresses and the avoidance of all things "girly": Children's appearance rigidity and cognitive theories of gender development. *Developmental Psychology, 50,* 1091–1101.

Halim, M. L., Zosuls, K. M., Ruble, D. N., Tamis-LeMonda, C. S., Baeg, S., Walsh, A., & Moy, K. H. (2016). Children's dynamic gender identities across development and the influence of cognition, context, and culture. In C. S. Tamis-LeMonda & L. Balter (Eds.), *Child psychology: A handbook of contemporary issues* (3rd ed., pp. 193–218). New York: Psychology Press.

Halim, M. L. D. (2016). Princesses and superheroes: Social-cognitive influences on early gender rigidity. *Child Development Perspectives, 10,* 155–160.

Halim, M. L. D., Bryant, D., & Zucker, K. J. (2016). Early gender development in children and links with mental and physical health. In K. J. Zucker (Ed.), *Health promotion for children and adolescents* (pp. 191–213). New York: Springer Science + Business Media.

Hall, G. S. (1904). *Adolescence.* New York: Appleton-Century-Crofts.

Halldorsdottir, T., & Binder, E. B. (2017). Gene x environment interactions: From molecular mechanisms to behavior. *Annual Review of Psychology, 68,* 215–241.

Halpern, D. F. (2012). *Sex differences in cognitive abilities* (4th ed.). New York: Psychology Press.

Hamby, S., Roberts, L. T., Taylor, E., Hagler, M., & Kaczkowski, W. (2017). Families, poly-victimization, & resilience portfolios: Understanding risk, vulnerability, & protection across the span of childhood. In D. M. Teti (Ed.), *Parenting and family processes in child maltreatment and intervention* (pp. 3–22). New York; Springer Science+Media.

Hami, J., Shojae, F., Vafaee-Nezhad, S., Lotfi, N., Kheradmand, H., & Haghir, H. (2015). Some experimental and clinical aspects of the effects of the maternal diabetes on developing hippocampus. *World Journal of Diabetes, 15,* 412–422.

Hamlin, J. K. (2013). Moral judgment and action in preverbal infants and toddlers: Evidence for an innate moral core. *Current Directions in Psychological Science, 22,* 186–193.

Hamlin, J. K., & Wynn, K. (2011). Young infants prefer prosocial to antisocial others. *Cognitive Development, 26,* 30–39.

Hammond, S. I., Müller, U., Carpendale, J. I. M., Bibok, M. B., & Lieberman-Finestone, D. (2012). The effects of parental scaffolding on preschoolers' executive function. *Developmental Psychology, 48,* 271–281.

Hammons, A. J., & Fiese, B. H. (2011). Is frequency of shared family meals related to the nutritional health of children and adolescents? *Pediatrics, 127,* e1565–1574.

Hampton, T. (2014). Studies probe links between childhood asthma and obesity. *Journal of the American Medical Association, 311,* 1718–1719.

Hanawalt, B. A. (1993). *Growing up in medieval London: The experience of childhood in history.* New York: Oxford University Press.

Hanawalt, B. A. (2003). The child in the Middle Ages and the Renaissance. In W. Koops & M. Zuckerman (Eds.), *Beyond the century of childhood: Cultural history and developmental psychology.* Philadelphia: University of Pennsylvania Press.

Hanioka, T., Ojima, M., Tanaka, K., & Yamamoto, M. (2011). Does secondhand smoke affect the development of dental caries in children? A systematic review. *International Journal of Environmental Research and Public Health, 8,* 1503–1509.

Hanish, L. D., Sallquist, J., DiDonato, M., Fabes, R. A., & Martin, C. L. (2012). Aggression by whom—aggression toward whom: Behavioral predictors of same- and other-gender aggression in early childhood. *Developmental Psychology, 48,* 1450–1462.

Hanna-Attisha, M., LaChance, J., Sadler, R. C., & Schnepp, A. C. (2016). Elevated blood lead levels in children associated with the Flint drinking water crisis: A spatial analysis of risk and public health response. *American Journal of Public Health, 106,* 283–290.

Hannon, E. E., & Johnson, S. P. (2004). Infants use meter to categorize rhythms and melodies: Implications for musical structure learning. *Cognitive Psychology, 50,* 354–377.

Hannon, E. E., & Trehub, S. E. (2005a). Metrical categories in infancy and adulthood. *Psychological Science, 16,* 48–55.

Hannon, E. E., & Trehub, S. E. (2005b). Tuning in to musical rhythms: Infants learn more readily than adults. *Proceedings of the National Academy of Sciences, 102,* 12639–12643.

Hans, S. L., & Jeremy, R. J. (2001). Postneonatal mental and motor development of infants exposed in utero to opiate drugs. *Infant Mental Health Journal, 22,* 300–315.

Hansen, A. R., Duncan, D. T., Tarasenko, Y. N., Yan, F., & Zhang, J. (2014).

Generational shift in parental perceptions of overweight among school-aged children. *Pediatrics, 134,* 481–488.

Hansen, M. B., & Markman, E. M. (2009). Children's use of mutual exclusivity to learn labels for parts of objects. *Developmental Psychology, 45,* 592–596.

Hanson, J. L., Hair, N., Shen, D. G., Shi, F., Gilmore, J. H., Wolfe, B. L., et al. (2013). Family poverty affects the rate of human infant brain growth. *PLOS ONE, 10*(12), e0146434.

Hao, L., & Woo, H. S. (2012). Distinct trajectories in the transition to adulthood: Are children of immigrants advantaged? *Child Development, 83,* 1623–1639.

Hao, M., Liu, Y., Shu, H., Xing, A., Jiang, Y., & Li, P. (2015). Developmental changes in the early child lexicon in Mandarin Chinese. *Journal of Child Language 42,* 505–537.

Harlow, H. F., & Zimmerman, R. (1959). Affectional responses in the infant monkey. *Science, 130,* 421–432.

Harris, M. A., Wetzel, E., Robins, R. W., Donnellan, M. B., & Trzesniewski, K. H. (2018). The development of global and domain self-esteem from ages 10 to 16 for Mexican-origin youth. *International Journal of Behavioral Development, 42,* 4–16.

Harrison, S., Rowlinson, M., & Hill, A. J. (2016). 'No fat friend of mine': Young children's responses to overweight and disability. *Body Image, 18,* 65–73.

Hart, B. (2004). What toddlers talk about. *First Language, 24,* 91–106.

Hart, B., & Risley, T. R. (1995). *Meaningful differences in the everyday experience of young American children.* Baltimore: Paul H. Brookes.

Hart, C. H., Burts, D. C., Durland, M. A., Charlesworth, R., DeWolf, M., & Fleege, P. O. (1998). Stress behaviors and activity type participation of preschoolers in more and less developmentally appropriate classrooms: SES and sex differences. *Journal of Research in Childhood Education, 12,* 176–196.

Hart, C. H., Newell, L. D., & Olsen, S. F. (2003). Parenting skills and social–communicative competence in childhood. In J. O. Greene & B. R. Burleson (Eds.), *Handbook of communication and social interaction skills* (pp. 753–797). Mahwah, NJ: Erlbaum.

Harter, S. (1999). *The construction of self: A developmental perspective.* New York: Guilford.

Harter, S. (2012). *The construction of the self: Developmental and sociocultural foundations* (2nd ed.). New York: Guilford.

Hartley, D., Blumenthal, T., Carrillo, M., DiPaolo, G., Esralew, L., Gardiner, K., et al. (2015). Down syndrome and Alzheimer's disease: Common pathways, common goals. *Alzheimer's and Dementia, 11,* 700–709.

Hartmann, T., Möller, I., & Krause, C. (2015). Factors underlying male and female use of violent video games. *New Media and Society, 17,* 1761–1776.

Hartshorn, K. (2003). Reinstatement maintains a memory in human infants for 1½ years. *Developmental Psychobiology, 42,* 269–282.

Hartshorn, K., Rovee-Collier, C., Gerhardstein, P., Bhatt, R. S., Klein, P. J., Aaron, F., Wondoloski, T. L., & Wurtzel, N. (1998a). Developmental changes in the specificity of memory over the first year of life. *Developmental Psychobiology, 33,* 61–78.

Hartshorn, K., Rovee-Collier, C., Gerhardstein, P., Bhatt, R. S., Wondoloski, T. L., Klein, P., Gilch, J., Wurtzel, N., & Campos-

deCarvalho, M. (1998b). The ontogeny of long-term memory over the first year-and-a-half of life. *Developmental Psychobiology, 32,* 69–89.

Hartup, W. W. (2006). Relationships in early and middle childhood. In A. L. Vangelisti & D. Perlman (Eds.), *Cambridge handbook of personal relationships* (pp. 177–190). New York: Cambridge University Press.

Hartup, W. W., & Abecassis, M. (2004). Friends and enemies. In P. K. Smith & C. H. Hart (Eds.), *Blackwell handbook of childhood social development* (pp. 285–306). Malden, MA: Blackwell.

Hasebe, Y., Nucci, L., & Nucci, M. S. (2004). Parental control of the personal domain and adolescent symptoms of psychopathology: A cross-national study in the United States and Japan. *Child Development, 75,* 815–828.

Hau, K.-T., & Ho, I. T. (2010). Chinese students' motivation and achievement. In M. H. Bond (Ed.), *Oxford handbook of Chinese psychology* (pp. 187–204). New York: Oxford University Press.

Hauck, T. S., Lau, C., Foa, L. L., Kurkyak, P., & Tu, K. (2017). ADHD treatment in primary care: Demographic rfactor, medication trends, and treatment predictors. *Canadian Journal of Psychiatry, 62,* 393–402.

Hauf, P., Aschersleben, G., & Prinz, W. (2007). Baby do–baby see! How action production influences action perception in infants. *Cognitive Development, 22,* 16–32.

Hausmann, L. R., Hannon, M. J., Kresevic, D. M., Hanusa, B. H., Kwoh, C. K., & Ibrahim, S. A. (2011). Impact of perceived discrimination in healthcare on patient–provider communication. *Medical Care, 49,* 626–633.

Hauspie, R., & Roelants, M. (2012). Adolescent growth. In N. Cameron & R. Bogin (Eds.), *Human growth and development* (2nd ed., pp. 57–79). London: Elsevier.

Havstad, S. L., Johnson, D. D., Zoratti, E. M., Ezell, J. M., Woodcroft, K., Ownby, D. R., et al. (2012). Tobacco smoke exposure and allergic sensitization in children: A propensity score analysis. *Respirology, 17,* 1068–1072.

Hawsawi, A. M., Bryant, L. O., & Goodfellow, L. T. (2015). Association between exposure to secondhand smoke during pregnancy and low birthweight: A narrative review. *Respiratory Care, 60,* 135–140.

Hay, D. (2017). The early development of human aggression. *Child Development Perspectives, 11,* 102–106.

Hayatbakhsh, M. R., Flenady, V. J., Gibbons, K. S., Kingsbury, A. M., Hurrion, E., Mamun, A. A., & Najman, J. M. (2012). Birth outcomes associated with cannabis use before and during pregnancy. *Pediatric Research, 71,* 215–219.

Hayne, H. (2004). Infant memory development: Implications for childhood amnesia. *Developmental Review, 24,* 33–73.

Hayne, H., & Gross, J. (2015). 24-month-olds use conceptual similarity to solve new problems after a delay. *International Journal of Behavioral Development, 39,* 339–345.

Hayne, H., Herbert, J., & Simcock, G. (2003). Imitation from television by 24- and 30-month-olds. *Developmental Science, 6,* 254–261.

Hayne, H., Rovee-Collier, C., & Perris, E. E. (1987). Categorization and memory retrieval by three-month-olds. *Child Development, 58,* 750–767.

Hayslip, B., Blumenthal, H., & Garner, A. (2014). Health and grandparent–grandchild

well-being: One-year longitudinal findings for custodial grandfamilies. *Journal of Aging and Health, 26,* 559–582.

Haywood, H. C., & Lidz, C. (2007). *Dynamic assessment in practice.* New York: Cambridge University Press.

Haywood, K., & Getchell, N. (2014). *Life span motor development* (6th ed.). Champaign, IL: Human Kinetics.

Hazel, N. A., Oppenheimer, C. W., Young, J. R., & Technow, J. R. (2014). Parent relationship quality buffers against the effect of peer stressors on depressive symptoms from middle childhood to adolescence. *Developmental Psychology, 50,* 2115–2123.

Hazen, N. L., McFarland, L., Jacobvitz, D., & Boyd-Soisson, E. (2010). Fathers' frightening behaviours and sensitivity with infants: Relations with fathers' attachment representations, father–infant attachment, and children's later outcomes. *Early Child Development and Care, 180,* 51–69.

Healthy Families America. (2011). *Healthy Families America FAQ.* Retrieved from https://www.healthyfamiliesamerica.org /about/

Healy, S. J., Murray, L., Cooper, P. J., Hughes, C., & Halligan, S. J. (2015). A longitudinal investigation of maternal influences on the development of child hostile attributions and aggression. *Journal of Clinical Child and Adolescent Psychology, 44,* 80–92.

Hein, S., Reich, J., & Grigorenko, E. (2015). Cultural manifestation of intelligence in formal and informal learning environments during childhood. In L. A. Jensen (Ed.), *Oxford handbook of human development and culture* (pp. 214–229). New York: Oxford University Press.

Heinrich-Weltzien, R., Zorn, C., Monse, B., & Kromeyer-Hauschild, K. (2013). Relationship between malnutrition and the number of permanent teeth in Filipino 10- to 13-year-olds. *BioMed Research International, 2013,* Art. No. 205950.

Hellemans, K. G., Sliwowska, J. H., Verma, P., & Weinberg, J. (2010). Prenatal alcohol exposure: Fetal programming and later life vulnerability to stress, expression and anxiety disorders. *Neuroscience and Biobehavioral Reviews, 34,* 791–807.

Helwig, C. C. (2006). Rights, civil liberties, and democracy across cultures. In M. Killen & J. G. Smetana (Eds.), *Handbook of moral development* (pp. 185–210). Philadelphia: Erlbaum.

Helwig, C. C., & Jasiobedzka, U. (2001). The relation between law and morality: Children's reasoning about socially beneficial and unjust laws. *Child Development, 72,* 1382–1393.

Helwig, C. C., & Prencipe, A. (1999). Children's judgments of flags and flag-burning. *Child Development, 70,* 132–143.

Helwig, C. C., Ruck, M. D., & Peterson-Badali, M. (2014). Rights, civil liberties, and democracy. In C. C. Helwig, M. D. Ruck, & M. Peterson-Badali (Eds.), *Handbook of moral development* (2nd ed., pp. 46–69). New York: Psychology Press.

Helwig, C. C., & Turiel, E. (2004). Children's social and moral reasoning. In P. K. Smith & C. H. Hart (Eds.), *Blackwell handbook of childhood social development* (pp. 476–490). Malden, MA: Blackwell.

Helwig, C. C., Zelazo, P. D., & Wilson, M. (2001). Children's judgments of psychological harm in normal and canonical situations. *Child Development, 72,* 66–81.

Henbest, V., & Apel, K. (2017). Effective word reading instruction: What does the evidence tell us? *Communication Disorders Quarterly, 39,* 303–311.

Henderlong, J., & Lepper, M. R. (2002). The effects of praise on children's intrinsic motivation: A review and synthesis. *Psychological Bulletin, 128,* 774–795.

Henderson, A. M. E., & Woodward, A. L. (2012). Nine-month-old infants generalize object labels, but not object preferences, across individuals. *Developmental Science, 15,* 641–652.

Henderson, T. L., & Bailey, S. J. (2015). Grandparents rearing grandchildren: A culturally variant perspective. In S. Browning & K. Pasley (Eds.), *Contemporary families: Translating research into practice* (pp. 230–247). New York: Routledge.

Henneberger, A. K., Coffman, D. L., & Gest, S. D. (2017). The effect of having aggressive friends on aggressive behavior in childhood: Using propensity scores to strengthen causal inference. *Social Development, 26,* 295–309.

Henning, A., Spinath, F. M., & Aschersleben, G. (2011). The link between preschoolers' executive function and theory of mind and the role of epistemic states. *Journal of Experimental Psychology, 108,* 513–531.

Henricsson, L., & Rydell, A.-M. (2004). Elementary school children with behavior problems: Teacher–child relations and self-perception. A prospective study. *Merrill-Palmer Quarterly, 50,* 111–138.

Hepach, R., Kante, N., & Tomasello, M. (2017). Toddlers help a peer. *Child Development, 88,* 1642–1652.

Hepach, R., Vaish, A., & Tomasello, M. (2013). Young children sympathize less in response to unjustified emotional distress. *Developmental Psychology, 49,* 1132–1138.

Hepper, P. (2015). Behavior during the prenatal period: Adaptive for development and survival. *Child Development Perspectives, 9,* 38–43.

Hepper, P. G., Dornan, J., & Lynch, C. (2012). Sex differences in fetal habituation. *Developmental Science, 15,* 373–383.

Herbert, J., Gross, J., & Hayne, H. (2007). Crawling is associated with more flexible memory retrieval by 9-month-old infants. *Developmental Science, 10,* 183–189.

Herbert, M., Kalleas, D., Cooney, D., Lamb, M., & Lister, L. (2015). Meiosis and maternal aging: Insights from aneuploid oocytes and trisomy births. *Cold Spring Harbor Perspectives in Biology, 7,* a017970

Hernandez, D. J., Denton, N. A., & Blanchard, V. L. (2011). Children in the United States of America: A statistical portrait by race-ethnicity, immigrant origins, and language. *Annals of the American Academy of Political and Social Science, 633,* 102–127.

Herold, B. (2017, June 12). Poor students face digital divide in how teachers learn to use tech. *Education Week.* Retrieved from www.edweek.org/ew/articles/2017/06/14/poor-students-face-digital-divide-in-teacher-technology-training.html

Heron, T. E., Hewar, W. L., & Cooper, J. O. (2013). *Applied behavior analysis.* Upper Saddle River, NJ: Pearson.

Heron-Delaney, M., Anzures, G., Herbert, J. S., Quinn, P. C., Slater, A. M., Tanaka, J. W., et al. (2011). Perceptual training prevents the emergence of the other race effect during infancy. *PLOS ONE, 6,* 231–255.

Herrnstein, R. J., & Murray, C. (1994). *The bell curve.* New York: Free Press.

Hespos, S. J., Ferry, A. L., Cannistraci, C. J., Gore, J., & Park, S. (2010). Using optical imaging to investigate functional cortical activity in human infants. In A. W. Roe (Ed.), *Imaging the brain with optical methods* (pp. 159–176). New York: Springer Science + Business Media.

Hesse, E., & Main, M. (2006). Frightening, threatening, and dissociative parental behavior in low-risk samples: Description, discussion, and interpretations. *Development and Psychopathology, 18,* 309–343.

Hetherington, E. M., & Kelly, J. (2002). *For better or for worse: Divorce reconsidered.* New York: Norton.

Hetherington, E. M., & Stanley-Hagan, M. (2000). Diversity among stepfamilies. In D. H. Demo, K. R. Allen, & M. A. Fine (Eds.), *Handbook of family diversity* (pp. 173–196). New York: Oxford University Press.

Heubeck, B. G., Butcher, P. R., Thorneywork, K., & Wood, J. (2016). Loving and angry? Happy and sad? Understanding and reporting of mixed emotions in mother–child relationships by 6- to 12-year-olds. *British Journal of Psychology, 34,* 245–260.

Hewlett, B. S. (1992). Husband–wife reciprocity and the father–infant relationship among Aka pygmies. In B. S. Hewlett (Ed.), *Father–child relations: Cultural and biosocial contexts* (pp. 153–176). New York: Aldine De Gruyter.

Heyder, A., & Kessels, U. (2015). Do teachers equate male and masculine with lower academic engagement? How students' gender enactment triggers gender stereotypes at school. *Social Psychology of Education, 18,* 467–485.

Heyman, G. D., & Legare, C. H. (2004). Children's beliefs about gender differences in the academic and social domains. *Sex Roles, 50,* 227–239.

Heywood, C. (2013). *A history of childhood: Children and childhood in the West from medieval to modern times.* Oxford, UK: Polity.

Hicken, B. L., Smith, D., Luptak, M., & Hill, R. D. (2014). Health and aging in rural America. In J. Warren & K. B. Smalley (Eds.), *Rural public health: Best practices and preventive models* (pp. 241–254). New York: Springer.

Hickling, A. K., & Wellman, H. M. (2001). The emergence of children's causal explanations and theories: Evidence from everyday conversation. *Developmental Psychology, 37,* 668–683.

Hicks, J. H., & Goedereis, E. A. (2009). The importance of context and the gain-loss dynamic for understanding grandparent caregivers. In K. Shifren (Ed.), *How caregiving affects development: Psychological implications for child, adolescent, and adult caregivers* (pp. 169–190). Washington, DC: American Psychological Association.

Hiffler, L., Rakotoambinina, B., Lafferty, N., & Garcia, D. M. (2016). Thiamine deficiency in tropical pediatrics: New insights into a neglected but vital metabolic challenge. *Frontiers in Nutrition, 3,* 16.

Hilbert, D. D., & Eis, S. D. (2014). Early intervention for emergent literacy development in a collaborative community pre-kindergarten. *Early Childhood Education Journal, 42,* 105–113.

Hildreth, K., & Rovee-Collier, C. (2002). Forgetting functions of reactivated memories over the first year of life. *Developmental Psychobiology, 41,* 277–288.

Hill, A. L., Degnan, K. A., Calkins, S. D., & Keane, S. P. (2006). Profiles of externalizing behavior problems for boys and girls across preschool: The roles of emotion regulation and inattention. *Developmental Psychology, 42,* 913–928.

Hill, D. B., Menvielle, E., Sica, K. M., & Johnson, A. (2010). An affirmative intervention for families with gender variant children: Parental ratings of child mental health and gender. *Journal of Sex and Marital Therapy, 36,* 6–23.

Hill, J. L., Brooks-Gunn, J., & Waldfogel, J. (2003). Sustained effects of high participation in an early intervention for low-birth-weight premature infants. *Developmental Psychology, 39,* 730–744.

Hilliard, L. J., & Liben, L. S. (2010). Differing levels of gender salience in preschool classrooms: Effects on children's gender attitudes and intergroup bias. *Child Development, 81,* 1787–1798.

Hindle, D., & Sherwin-White, S. (2014). Siblings in middle childhood. In D. Hindle & S. Sherwin-White (Eds.), *Sibling matters: A psychoanalytic, developmental, and systemic approach* (pp. 151–168). London, UK: Karnac Books.

Hines, M. (2015). Gendered development. In M. E. Lamb (Ed.), *Handbook of child psychology and developmental science: Vol. 3. Socioemotional processes* (7th ed., pp. 842–887). Hoboken, NJ: Wiley.

Hines, M., & Davis, J. (2018). Sex hormones and children's gender-typed toy play. In E. S. Weisgram & L. M. Dinella (Eds.), *Gender typing of children's toys: How early play experiences impact development* (pp. 97–120). Washington, DC: American Psychological Association.

Hoang, D. H., Pagnier, A., Guichardet, K., Dubois-Teklali, F., Schiff, I., Lyard, G., et al. (2014). Cognitive disorders in pediatric medulloblastoma: What neuroimaging has to offer. *Journal of Neurosurgery, 14,* 136–144.

Hobbs, S. D., & Goodman, G. S. (2014). Child witnesses in the legal system: Improving child interviews and understanding juror decisions. *Behavioral Sciences & the Law, 32,* 681–685.

Hodel, A. S., Hunt, R. H., Cowell, R. A., Van Den Heuvel, S. E., Gunnar, M. R., & Thomas, K. M. (2015). Duration of early adversity and structural brain development in post-institutionalized adolescents. *NeuroImage, 105,* 112–119.

Hodges, J., & Tizard, B. (1989). Social and family relationships of ex-institutional adolescents. *Journal of Child Psychology and Psychiatry, 30,* 77–97.

Hodnett, E. D., Gates, S., Hofmeyr, G. J., & Sakala, C. (2012). Continuous support for women during childbirth. *Cochrane Database of Systematic Reviews, 7,* Art. No. CD003766.

Hoehn, T., Hansmann, G., Bührer, C., Simbruner, G., Gunn, A. J., Yager, J., et al. (2008). Therapeutic hypothermia in neonates: Review of current clinical data, ILCOR recommendations and suggestions for implementation in neonatal intensive care units. *Resuscitation, 78,* 7–12.

Hoekstra, C., Willemsen, G., van Beijsterveldt, C. E., Lambalk, C. B., Montgomery, G. W., & Boomsma, D. I. (2010). Body composition, smoking, and spontaneous dizygotic twinning. *Fertility and Sterility, 93,* 885–893.

Hoekstra, C., Zhao, Z. Z., Lambalk, C. B., Willemsen, G., Martin, N. G., Boomsma, D. I., & Montgomery, G. W. (2008). Dizygotic twinning. *Human Reproduction Update, 14,* 37–47.

Hoerr, T. (2004). How MI informs teaching at New City School. *Teachers College Record, 106,* 40–48.

Hoff, E. (2006). How social contexts support and shape language development. *Developmental Review, 26,* 55–88.

Hoff, E. (2013). Interpreting the early language trajectories of children from low-SES and language minority homes: Implications for closing achievement gaps. *Developmental Psychology, 49,* 4–14.

Hoff, E., Laursen, B., & Tardif, T. (2002). Socioeconomic status and parenting. In M. H. Bornstein (Ed.), *Handbook of parenting: Vol. 2. Biology and ecology of parenting* (pp. 231–252). Mahwah, NJ: Erlbaum.

Hofferth, S. L. (2003). Race/ethnic differences in father involvement in two-parent families: Culture, context, or economy? *Journal of Family Issues, 24,* 185–216.

Hofferth, S. L. (2010). Home media and children's achievement and behavior. *Child Development, 81,* 1598–1610.

Hofferth, S. L., & Anderson, K. G. (2003). Are all dads equal? Biology versus marriage as a basis for paternal investment. *Journal of Marriage and the Family, 65,* 213–232.

Hofferth, S. L., Forry, N. D., & Peters, H. E. (2010). Child support, father–child contact, and preteens' involvement with nonresidential fathers: Racial/ethnic differences. *Journal of Family Economic Issues, 31,* 14–32.

Hoffman, L. W. (2000). Maternal employment: Effects of social context. In R. D. Taylor & M. C. Wang (Eds.), *Resilience across contexts: Family, work, culture, and community* (pp. 147–176). Mahwah, NJ: Erlbaum.

Hoffner, C., & Badzinski, D. M. (1989). Children's integration of facial and situational cues to emotion. *Child Development, 60,* 411–422.

Holden, G. W., Williamson, P. A., & Holland, G. W. O. (2014). Eavesdropping on the family: A pilot investigation of corporal punishment in the home. *Journal of Family Psychology, 28,* 401–406.

Holditch-Davis, D., Belyea, M., & Edwards, L. J. (2005). Prediction of 3-year developmental outcomes from sleep development over the preterm period. *Infant Behavior and Development, 79,* 49–58.

Hollich, G. J., Hirsh-Pasek, K., & Golinkoff, R. M. (2000). Breaking the language barrier: An emergentist coalition model for the origins of word learning. *Monographs of the Society for Research in Child Development, 65*(3, Serial No. 262).

Höllwarth, M. E. (2013). Prevention of unintentional injuries: A global role for pediatricians. *Pediatrics, 132,* 4–7.

Holmes, J., Gathercole, S. E., & Dunning, D. L. (2010). Poor working memory: Impact and interventions. In P. Bauer (Ed.), *Advances in child development and behavior* (Vol. 39, pp. 1–43). London: Academic Press.

Holosko, M. J. (2015). The empirical base for the implementation of social skills training with maltreated children. In J. S. Wodarski, M. J. Holosko, & M. D. Feit (Eds.), *Evidence-informed assessment and practice in child welfare* (pp. 261–278). Cham, Switzerland: International Publishing.

Homan, G. J. (2016). Failure to thrive: A practical guide. *American Family Physician, 94,* 295–299.

Hong, D. S., Hoeft, F., Marzelli, M. J., Lepage, J.-F., Roeltgen, D., Ross, J., et al. (2014). Influence of the X-chromosome on neuroanatomy: Evidence from Turner and Klinefelter syndromes. *Journal of Neuroscience, 34,* 3509–3516.

Hood, M., Conlon, E., & Andrews, G. (2008). Preschool home literacy practices and children's literacy development: A longitudinal analysis. *Journal of Educational Psychology, 100,* 252–271.

Hoogenhout, M., & Malcolm-Smith, S. (2017). Theory of mind predicts severity level in autism. *Autism, 21,* 242–252.

Hopf, L., Quraan, M. A., Cheung, M. J., Taylor, M. J., Ryan, J. D., & Moses, S. N. (2013). Hippocampal lateralization and memory in children. *Journal of the International Neuropsychological Society, 19,* 1042–1052.

Hopkins, B., & Westra, T. (1988). Maternal handling and motor development: An intracultural study. *Genetic, Social and General Psychology Monographs, 14,* 377–420.

Horne, R. S. C. (2017). Sleep disorders in newborns and infants. In S. Nevsimalov & O. Bruni (Eds.), *Sleep disorders in children* (pp. 129–153). Cham, Switzerland: Springer International.

Horner, T. M. (1980). Two methods of studying stranger reactivity in infants: A review. *Journal of Child Psychology and Psychiatry, 21,* 203–219.

Horta, B. L., Loret de Mola, C., & Victoria, C. G. (2015). Breastfeeding and intelligence: A systematic review and meta-analysis. *Acta Paediatrica, 104,* 14–19.

Houlihan, J., Kropp. T. Wiles, R., Gray, S., & Campbell, C. (2005). *Body burden: The pollution in newborns.* Washington, DC: Environmental Working Group.

Houston-Price, C., Owen, L. H., Kennedy, O. B., & Hill, C. (2019). Parents' experiences of introducing toddlers to fruits and vegetables through repeated exposure, with and without prior visual familiarization to foods: Evidence from daily diaries. *Food Quality and Preference, 71,* 291–300.

Houts, R. M., Barnett-Walker, K. C., Paley, B., & Cox, M. J. (2008). Patterns of couple interaction during the transition to parenthood. *Personal Relationships, 15,* 103–122.

Hovdenak, N., & Haram, K. (2012). Influence of mineral and vitamin supplements on pregnancy outcome. *European Journal of Obstetrics & Gynecology and Reproductive Biology, 164,* 127–132.

Howe, M. L. (2014). The co-emergence of self and autobiographical memory: An adaptive view of early memory. In P. J. Bauer & R. Fivush (Eds.), *Wiley handbook on the development of children's memory* (pp. 545–567). Hoboken, NJ: Wiley-Blackwell.

Howe, M. L. (2015). Memory development. In L. S. Liben & U. Müller (Eds.), *Handbook of child psychology and developmental science: Vol. 2. Cognitive processes* (7th ed., pp. 203–249). Hoboken, NJ: Wiley.

Howe, N., Aquan-Assee, J., & Bukowski, W. M. (2001). Predicting sibling relations over time: Synchrony between maternal management styles and sibling relationship quality. *Merrill-Palmer Quarterly, 47,* 121–141.

Howell, K. K., Coles, C. D., & Kable, J. A. (2008). The medical and developmental consequences of prenatal drug exposure. In J. Brick (Ed.), *Handbook of the medical consequences of alcohol and drug abuse* (2nd ed., pp. 219–249). New York: Haworth Press.

Howell, S. R., & Becker, S. (2013). Grammar from the lexicon: Evidence from neural network simulations of language acquisition. In D. Bittner & N. Ruhlig (Eds.), *Lexical bootstrapping: The role of lexis and semantics in child language* (pp. 245–264). Berlin: Walter de Gruyter.

Howes, C. (2016). Children and child care: A theory of relationships within cultural communities. In E. Sanders & A. W. Guerra (Eds.), *The culture of child care* (pp. 3–24). New York: Oxford University Press.

Hoyme, H. E., Kalberg, W. O., Elliott, A. J., Blankenship, J., Buckley, D., Marais, A.-S., et al. (2016). Updated clinical guidelines for diagnosing fetal alcohol spectrum disorders. *Pediatrics, 138,* e20154256.

Hsu, A. S., Chater, N., & Vitányi, P. (2013). Language learning from positive evidence, reconsidered: A simplicity-based approach. *Topics in Cognitive Science, 5,* 35–55.

Hsu, H.-C., & Iyer, S. N. (2016). Early gesture, early vocabulary, and risk of language impairment in preschoolers. *Research in Developmental Disabilities, 57,* 201–210.

Huang, B. H. (2014). The effects of age on second language grammar and speech production. *Journal of Psycholinguistic Research, 43,* 397–420.

Huang, C.-C. (2006). Child support enforcement and father involvement for children in never-married mother families. *Fathering, 4,* 97–111.

Huang, H., Coleman, S., Bridge, J. A., Yonkers, K., & Katon, W. (2014). A meta-analysis of the relationship between antidepressant use in pregnancy and the risk of preterm birth and low birth weight. *General Hospital Psychiatry, 36,* 13–18.

Huang, Y., Hauck, F. R. F., Signore, C., Yu, A., Raju, T. N. K., Huang, T. T.-K., et al. (2013). Influence of bedsharing activity on breastfeeding duration among U.S. mothers. *JAMA Pediatrics, 167,* 1038–1044.

Hubbs-Tait, L., Nation, J. R., Krebs, N. F., & Bellinger, D. C. (2005). Neurotoxicants, micronutrients, and social environments: Individual and combined effects on children's development. *Psychological Science in the Public Interest, 6,* 57–121.

Hudson, J. A., Fivush, R., & Kuebli, J. (1992). Scripts and episodes: The development of event memory. *Applied Cognitive Psychology, 6,* 483–505.

Hudson, J. A., & Mayhew, E. M. Y. (2009). The development of memory for recurring events. In M. L. Courage & N. Cowan (Eds.), *The development of memory in infancy and childhood* (pp. 69–91). Hove, UK: Psychology Press.

Huebner, C. E., & Payne, K. (2010). Home support for emergent literacy: Follow-up of a community-based implementation of dialogic reading. *Journal of Applied Developmental Psychology, 31,* 195–201.

Huerta, M. del C., Adema, W., Baxter, J., Han, W.-J., Lausten, M., Lee, R., & Waldfogel, J. (2013). Fathers' leave, fathers' involvement and child development: Are they related? Evidence from four OECD countries. *OECD Social, Employment and Migration Working Papers,* No. 140, OECD Publishing, Paris. Retrieved from www.oecd-ilibrary.org/social-issues-migration-health/fathers-leave-fathers-involvement-and-child-development_5k4dlw9w6czq-en

Huesmann, L. R., Moise-Titus, J., Podolski, C., & Eron, L. D. (2003). Longitudinal relations between children's exposure to TV violence and their aggressive and violent behavior in young adulthood: 1977–1992. *Developmental Psychology, 39,* 201–221.

Hughes, C. (2015). Great gifted education. In W. W. Murawski & K. L. Scott (Eds.), *What really works in elementary education* (pp. 234–252). Thousand Oakes, CA: Corwin Press.

Hughes, C., & Dunn, J. (1998). Understanding mind and emotion: Longitudinal associations with mental-state talk between young friends. *Developmental Psychology, 34,* 1026–1037.

Hughes, C., & Ensor, R. (2010). Do early social cognition and executive function predict individual differences in preschoolers' prosocial and antisocial behavior? In B. W. Sokol, U. Müller, J. I. M. Carpendale, A. R. Young, & G. Iarocci (Eds.), *Social interaction and the development of social understanding and executive functions* (pp. 418–441). New York: Oxford University Press.

Hughes, C., Ensor, R., & Marks, A. (2010). Individual differences in false belief understanding are stable from 3 to 6 years of age and predict children's mental state talk with school friends. *Journal of Experimental Child Psychology, 108,* 96–112.

Hughes, C., Marks, A., Ensor, R., & Lecce, S. (2010). A longitudinal study of conflict and inner state talk in children's conversations with mothers and younger siblings. *Social Development, 19,* 822–837.

Hughes, J. N., & Kwok, O. (2006). Classroom engagement mediates the effect of teacher–student support on elementary students' peer acceptance. *Journal of School Psychology, 43,* 465–480.

Hughes, J. N., & Kwok, O. (2007). Influence of student–teacher and parent–teacher relationships on lower achieving readers' engagement and achievement in the primary grades. *Journal of Educational Psychology, 99,* 39–51.

Hullegie, S., Bruijning-Verhagen, P., Uiterwaal, C. S. P. M., van der Ent, C. K., Smit, H. A., & de Hoog, M. L. A. (2016). First-year daycare and incidence of acutegastroenteritis. *Pediatrics, 137,* e20153356.

Humphrey, T. (1978). Function of the nervous system during prenatal life. In U. Stave (Ed.), *Perinatal physiology* (pp. 651–683). New York: Plenum.

Hunnius, S., & Geuze, R. H. (2004a). Developmental changes in visual scanning of dynamic faces and abstract stimuli in infants: A longitudinal study. *Infancy, 6,* 231–255.

Hunnius, S., & Geuze, R. H. (2004b). Gaze shifting in infancy: A longitudinal study using dynamic faces and abstract stimuli. *Infant Behavior and Development, 27,* 397–416.

Hunt, C. E., & Hauck, F. R. (2006). Sudden infant death syndrome. *Canadian Medical Association Journal, 174,* 1861–1869.

Huntsinger, C., Jose, P. E., Krieg, D. B., & Luo, Z. (2011). Cultural differences in Chinese American and European American children's drawing skills over time. *Early Childhood Research Quarterly, 26,* 134–145.

Hursti, U.-K. (1999). Factors influencing children's food choice. *Annals of Medicine, 31,* 26–32.

Huston, A. C., Bobbitt, K. C., & Bentley, A. (2015). Time spent in child care: How and why does it affect social development? *Developmental Psychology, 51,* 621–634.

Huttenlocher, J., Waterfall, H., Veasilyeva, M., Vevea J., & Hedges, L. (2010). Sources of variability in children's language growth. *Cognitive Psychology, 61,* 343–365.

Huttenlocher, P. R. (2002). *Neural plasticity: The effects of environment on the development of the cerebral cortex.* Cambridge, MA: Harvard University Press.

Huyck, M. H. (1996). Continuities and discontinuities in gender identity in midlife. In V. L. Bengtson (Ed.), *Adulthood and aging* (pp. 98–121). New York: Springer-Verlag.

Hyde, J. S. (2014). Gender similarities and differences. *Annual Review of Psychology, 65,* 373–398.

Hymel, S., Schonert-Reichl, K. A., Bonanno, R. A., Vaillancourt, T., & Henderson, N. R. (2010). Bullying and morality: Understanding how good kids can behave badly. In S. Jimerson, S. M. Swearer, & D. L. Espelage (Eds.), *Handbook of bullying in schools: An international perspective* (pp. 101–118). New York: Routledge.

I

Ibanez, G., Bernard, J. Y., Rondet, C., Peyre, H., Forhan, A., Kaminski, M., & Saurel-Cubizolles, M.-J. (2015). Effects of antenatal maternal depression and anxiety on children's early cognitive development: A prospective cohort study. *PLOS ONE, 10*(8), e0135849.

Ilioi, E., Blake, L., Jadva, V., Roman, G., & Golombok, S. (2017). The role of age of disclosure of biological origins in the psychological well-being of adolescents conceived by reproductive donation: A longitudinal study from age 1 to 14. *Journal of Child Psychology and Psychiatry, 58,* 315–324.

Imai, M., & Haryu, E. (2004). The nature of word-learning biases and their roles for lexical development: From a cross-linguistic perspective. In D. G. Hall & S. R. Waxman (Eds.), *Weaving a lexicon* (pp. 411–444). Cambridge, MA: MIT Press.

Imai, M., Li, L., Haryu, E., Okada, H., Hirsh-Pasek, K., Golinkoff, R. M., & Shigematsu, J. (2008). Novel noun and verb learning in Chinese-, English-, and Japanese-speaking children. *Child Development, 79,* 979–1000.

Ingoldsby, E. M., Shelleby, E., Lane, T., & Shaw, D. S. (2012). Extrafamilial contexts and children's conduct problems. In V. Maholmes & R. B. King (Eds.), *Oxford handbook of poverty and child development* (pp. 404–422). New York: Oxford University Press.

Insana, S. P., & Montgomery-Downs, H. E. (2012). Sleep and sleepiness among first-time postpartum parents: A field- and laboratory-based multimethod assessment. *Developmental Psychobiology, 55,* 361–372.

Insel, T. R. (2014). Brain somatic mutations: The dark matter of psychiatric genetics? *Molecular Psychiatry, 19,* 156–158.

Irvine, B., Jack, F., & Zajac, R. (2016). Preparing children for cross-examination: Do the practice questions matter? *Psychology, Crime & Law, 22,* 858–878.

Ishida, M., & Moore, G. E. (2013). The role of imprinted genes in humans. *Molecular Aspects of Medicine, 34,* 826–840.

Ishihara, K., Warita, K., Tanida, T., Sugawara, T., Kitagawa, H., & Hoshi, N. (2007). Does paternal exposure to 2,3,7, 8-tetrachlorodibenzo-p-dioxin (TCDD) affect the sex ratio of offspring? *Journal of Veterinary Medical Science, 69,* 347–352.

Ishii-Kuntz, M. (2013). Work environment and Japanese fathers' involvement in child care. *Journal of Family Issues, 34,* 252–271.

Izard, C. E., King, P. A., Trentacosta, C. J., Laurenceau, J. P., Morgan, J. K, Krauthamer-Ewing, E. S., & Finlon, K. J. (2008). Accelerating the development of emotion competence in Head Start children. *Development and Psychopathology, 20,* 369–397.

Izard, V., Sann, C., Spelke, E. S., & Streri, A. (2009). Newborn infants perceive abstract numbers. *Proceedings of the National Academy of Sciences, 106,* 10382–10385.

J

Jabès, A., & Nelson, C. A. (2014). Neuroscience and child well-being. In A. Ben-Arieh, F. Casas, I. Frønes, & J. E. Korbin (Eds.), *Handbook of child well-being: Vol. 1* (pp. 219–247) Dordrecht, Germany: Springer Reference.

Jabr, D., & Cahan, S. (2014a). Between-context variability of the effect of schooling on cognitive development: Evidence from the Middle East. *School Effectiveness and School Improvement, 25*, 1–26.

Jabr, D., & Cahan, S. (2014b). Schooling effects on cognitive development in a difficult environment: The case of refugee camps in the West Bank. *International Studies in Sociology of Education, 24*, 165–188.

Jack, F., Simcock, G., & Hayne, G. (2012). Magic memories: Young children's verbal recall after a 6-year delay. *Child Development, 83*, 159–172.

Jackson, L. A., von Eye, A., Witt, E. A., Zhao, Y., & Fitzgerald, H. E. (2011). A longitudinal study of the effects of Internet use and videogame playing on academic performance and the roles of gender, race and income in these relationships. *Computers in Human Behavior, 27*, 228–239.

Jacobs, J. E., Lanza, S., Osgood, D. W., Eccles, J. S., & Wigfield, A. (2002). Changes in children's self-competence and values: Gender and domain differences across grades one through twelve. *Child Development, 73*, 509–527.

Jadallah, M., Anderson, R. C., Nguyen-Jahiel, K., Miller, B. W., Kim, I.-H., Kuo, L.-J., et al. (2011). Influence of a teacher's scaffolding moves during child-led small-group discussions. *American Educational Research Journal, 48*, 194–230.

Jadva, V., Casey, P., & Golombok, S. (2012). Surrogacy families 10 years on: Relationship with the surrogate, decisions over disclosure and children's understanding of their surrogacy origins. *Human Reproduction, 27*, 3008–3014.

Jaffe, M., Gullone, E., & Hughes, E. K. (2010). The roles of temperamental dispositions and perceived parenting behaviours in the use of two emotion regulation strategies in late childhood. *Journal of Applied Developmental Psychology, 31*, 47–59.

Jaffee, S. R., Bowes, L., Ouellet-Morin, I., Fisher, H. L., Moffitt, T. E., Merrick, M. T., & Arseneault, L. (2013). Safe, stable, nurturing relationships break the intergenerational cycle of abuse: A prospective nationally representative cohort of children in the United Kingdom. *Journal of Adolescent Health, 53*, S4–S10.

Jaffee, S. R., & Christian, C. W. (2014). The biological embedding of child abuse and neglect: Implications for policy and practice. *Social Policy Report of the Society for Research in Child Development, 28*(1).

Jahja, R., Huijbregts, S. C. J., de Sonneville, L. M. J., van der Meere, J. J., & van Spronsen, F. J. (2014). Neurocognitive evidence for revision of treatment targets and guidelines for phenylketonuria. *Journal of Pediatrics, 164*, 895–899.

Jambon, M., & Smetana, J. G. (2014). Moral complexity in middle childhood: Children's evaluations of necessary harm. *Developmental Psychology, 50*, 22–33.

Jambon, M., & Smetana, J. G. (2018). Individual differences in prototypical moral and conventional judgments and children's proactive and reactive aggression. *Child Development, 89*, 1343–1359.

Jang, A. S., Jun, Y. J., & Park, M. K. (2016). Effects of air pollutants on upper airway disease. *Current Opinion in Allergy and Clinical Immunology, 16*, 13–17.

Jansen, J., de Weerth, C., & Riksen-Walraven, J. M. (2008). Breastfeeding and the mother–infant relationship. *Developmental Review, 28*, 503–521.

Jansen, P. W., Roza, S. J., Jaddoe, V. W. V., Mackenbach, J. D., Raat, H., Hofman, A.,

et al. (2012). Children's eating behavior, feeding practices of parents and weight problems in early childhood: Results from the population-based Generation R Study. *International Journal of Behavioral Nutrition and Physical Activity, 9*, 130–138.

Janssens, J. M. A. M., & Deković, M. (1997). Child rearing, prosocial moral reasoning, and prosocial behavior. *International Journal of Behavioral Development, 20*, 509–527.

Jaudes, P. K., & Mackey-Bilaver, L. (2008). Do chronic conditions increase young children's risk of being maltreated? *Child Abuse and Neglect, 32*, 671–681.

Jedrychowski, W., Perera, F. P., Jankowski, J., Mrozek-Budzyn, D., Mroz, E., Flak, E., et al. (2009). Very low prenatal exposure to lead and mental development of children in infancy and early childhood. *Neuroepidemiology, 32*, 270–278.

Jelenkovic, A., Sund, R., Hur, Y. M., Yokoyama, Y., Hjelmborg, J. V., Möller, S., et al. (2016). Genetic and environmental influences on height from infancy to early adulthood: An individual-based pooled analysis from 45 twin cohorts. *Scientific Reports, 6*, 28496.

Jenkins, J. M., Rasbash, J., & O'Connor, T. G. (2003). The role of the shared family context in differential parenting. *Developmental Psychology, 39*, 99–113.

Jenni, O. G., & Carskadon, M. A. (2012). Sleep behavior and sleep regulation from infancy through adolescence: Normative aspects. *Sleep Medicine Clinics, 7*, 529–538.

Jennifer, D., & Cowie, H. (2009). Engaging children and young people actively in research. In K. Bryan (Ed.), *Communication in healthcare* (pp. 135–163). New York: Peter Lang.

Jensen, A. R. (1969). How much can we boost IQ and scholastic achievement? *Harvard Educational Review, 39*, 1–123.

Jensen, A. R. (2001). Spearman's hypothesis. In J. M. Collis & S. Messick (Eds.), *Intelligence and personality: Bridging the gap in theory and measurement* (pp. 3–24). Mahwah, NJ: Erlbaum.

Jensen, T. M., & Lippold, M. A. (2018). Patterns of stepfamily relationship quality and adolescents' short-term and long-term adjustment. *Journal of Family Psychology, 32*, 1130–1141.

Jensen, T. M., Lippold, M. A., Mills-Koonce, R., & Fosco, G. M. (2017). Stepfamily relationship quality and children's internalizing and externalizing problems. *Family Process, 56*, 12284.

Jerome, E. M., Hamre, B. K., & Pianta, R. C. (2009). Teacher–child relationships from kindergarten to sixth grade: Early childhood predictors of teacher-perceived conflict and closeness. *Social Development, 18*, 915–945.

Ji, C. Y., & Chen, T. J. (2008). Secular changes in stature and body mass index for Chinese youth in sixteen major cities, 1950s–2005. *American Journal of Human Biology, 20*, 530–537.

Jia, P., Xue, H., Zhang, J., & Wang, Y. (2017). Time trend and demographic and geographic disparities in childhood obesity prevalence in China–evidence from twenty years of longitudinal data. *International Journal of Environmental Research and Public Health, 14*, 369.

Jiang, Q., Li, Y., & Sánchez-Barricarte, J. J. (2016). Fertility intention, son preference, and second childbirth: Survey findings from Shaanxi Province of China. *Social Indicators Research, 125*, 935–953.

Jiang, X., & Nardelli, J. (2016). Cellular and molecular introduction to brain development. *Neurobiology of Disease, 92*, 3–17.

Jin, M. K., Jacobvitz, D., Hazen, N., & Jung, S. H. (2012). Maternal sensitivity and infant attachment security in Korea: Cross-cultural validation of the Strange Situation. *Attachment & Human Development, 14*, 33–44.

Jing, M., & Li, H. (2015). Effect of partner's gender on early pretend play: A preliminary study of Singapore Chinese preschoolers. *Early Child Development and Care, 185*, 1216–1237.

Jipson, J. L., & Gelman, S. A. (2007). Robots and rodents: Children's inferences about living and nonliving kinds. *Child Development, 78*, 1675–1688.

Joanisse, M. F., & McClelland, J. L. (2015). Connectionist perspectives on language learning, representation and processing. *WIREs Cognitive Science, 6*, 235–247.

Joh, A. S., & Adolph, K. E. (2006). Learning from falling. *Child Development, 77*, 89–102.

Johansson, M., Forssman, L., & Bohlin, G. (2014). Individual differences in 10-month-olds' performance on the A-not-B task. *Development and Aging, 55*, 130–135.

Johnson, A. D., Ryan, R. M., & Brooks-Gunn, J. (2012). Child-care subsidies: Do they impact the quality of care children experience? *Child Development, 83*, 1444–1461.

Johnson, C., & Mindell, J. A. (2011). Family-based interventions for sleep problems of infants. In M. El-Sheikh (Ed.), *Sleep and development: Familial and socio-cultural considerations* (pp. 375–402). New York: Oxford University Press.

Johnson, E. K., & Seidl, A. (2008). Clause segmentation by 6-month-old infants: A crosslinguistic perspective. *Infancy, 13*, 440–455.

Johnson, J. G., Cohen, P., Smailes, E. M., Kasen, S., & Brook, J. S. (2002). Television viewing and aggressive behavior during adolescence and adulthood. *Science, 295*, 2468–2471.

Johnson, M. H. (2001). The development and neural basis of face recognition: Comment and speculation. *Infant and Child Development, 10*, 31–33.

Johnson, M. H., & de Haan, M. (2015). *Developmental cognitive neuroscience: An introduction* (4th ed.). Chichester, UK: Wiley-Blackwell.

Johnson, R. C., & Schoeni, R. F. (2011). Early-life origins of adult disease: National longitudinal population-based study of the United States. *American Journal of Public Health, 101*, 2317–2324.

Johnson, S., Li, J., Kendall, G., Strazdins, L., & Jacoby, P. (2013). Mothers' and fathers' work hours, child gender, and behavior in middle childhood. *Journal of Marriage and Family, 75*, 56–74.

Johnson, S. B., Riis, J. L., & Noble, K. G. (2016). State of the art review: Poverty and the developing brain. *Pediatrics, 137*, e20153075.

Johnson, S. C., Dweck, C. S., & Chen, F. S. (2007). Evidence for infants' internal working models of attachment. *Psychological Science, 18*, 501–502.

Johnson, S. C., Dweck, C., Chen, F. S., Stern, H. L., Ok, S.-J., & Barth, M. (2010). At the intersection of social and cognitive development: Internal working models of attachment in infancy. *Cognitive Science, 34*, 807–825.

Johnson, S. L. (2000). Improving preschoolers' self-regulation of energy intake. *Pediatrics, 106*, 1429–1435.

Johnson, S. P. (2011). A constructivist view of object perception in infancy. In L. M. Oakes, C. H. Cashon, M. Casasola, & D. Rakison (Eds.), *Infant perception and cognition* (pp. 51–68). New York: Oxford University Press.

Johnson, S. P., Bremner, J. G., Slater, A., Mason, U., Foster, K., & Cheshire, A. (2003). Infants' perception of object trajectories. *Child Development, 74*, 94–108.

Johnson, S. P., Fernandes, K. J., Frank, M. C., Kirkham, N. Z., Marcus, G. F., et al. (2009). Abstract rule learning for visual sequences in 8- and 11-month-olds. *Infancy, 14*, 2–18.

Johnson, S. P., & Hannon, E. E. (2015). Perceptual development. In L. S. Liben & U. Müller (Eds.), *Handbook of child psychology and developmental science: Vol. 2. Cognitive processes* (7th ed., pp. 63–112). Hoboken, NJ: Wiley.

Johnson, S. P., & Shuwairi, S. M. (2009). Learning and memory facilitate predictive tracking in 4-month-olds. *Journal of Experimental Child Psychology, 102*, 122–130.

Johnson, S. P., Slemmer, J. A., & Amso, D. (2004). Where infants look determines how they see: Eye movements and object perception performance in 3-month-olds. *Infancy, 6*, 185–201.

Johnston, M. V., Nishimura, A., Harum, K., Pekar, J., & Blue, M. E. (2001). Sculpting the developing brain. *Advances in Pediatrics, 48*, 1–38.

Joinson, C., Sullivan, S., von Gontard, A., & Heron, J. (2016). Early childhood psychological factors and risk for bedwetting at school age in a UK cohort. *European Child and Adolescent Psychiatry, 25*, 519–528.

Jokhi, R. P., & Whitby, E. H. (2011). Magnetic resonance imaging of the fetus. *Developmental Medicine and Child Neurology, 53*, 18–28.

Jones, A., Charles, P., & Benson, K. (2013). A model for supporting at-risk couples during the transition to parenthood. *Families in Society, 94*, 166–173.

Jones, D. J., & Lindahl, K. M. (2011). Coparenting in extended kinship systems: African American, Hispanic, Asian heritage, and Native American families. In J. P. McHale & K. M. Lindahl (Eds.), *Coparenting* (pp. 61–79). Washington, DC: American Psychological Association.

Jones, J., & Mosher, W. D. (2013). *Fathers' involvement with their children: United States, 2006–2010. National Health Statistics Reports, No. 71*. Hyattsville, MD: National Center for Health Statistics.

Jones, J., & Placek, P. (2017). *Adoption by the numbers*. Washington, DC: National Council for Adoption. Retrieved from www.adoptioncouncil.org/files/large/249e5e967173624

Jones, S. (2009). The development of imitation in infancy. *Philosophical Transactions of the Royal Society B, 364*, 2325–2335.

Jones, S. (2017). Can newborn infants imitate? *WIREs Cognitive Science, 8*, e1410.

Jordan, B. (1993). *Birth in four cultures*. Prospect Heights, IL: Waveland.

Jose, A., O'Leary, D., & Moyer, A. (2010). Does premarital cohabitation predict subsequent marital stability and marital quality? A meta-analysis. *Journal of Marriage and Family, 72*, 105–116.

Joshi, M. S., Maclean, M., & Stevens, C. (2018). Accident frequency and unrealistic optimism: Children's assessment of risk. *Accident Analysis and Prevention, 111*, 142–146.

Josselyn, S. A., & Frankland, P. W. (2012). Infantile amnesia: A neurogenic hypothesis. *Learning and Memory, 19,* 423–433.

Juby, H., Billette, J.-M., Laplante, B., & Le Bourdais, C. (2007). Nonresident fathers and children: Parents' new unions and frequency of contact. *Journal of Family Issues, 28,* 1220–1245.

Judge, S., Puckett, K., & Bell, S. M. (2006). Closing the digital divide: Update from the Early Childhood Longitudinal Study. *Journal of Educational Research, 100,* 52–60.

Juffer, F., & van IJzendoorn, M. H. (2012). Review of meta-analytical studies on the physical, emotional, and cognitive outcomes of intercountry adoptees. In J. L. Gibbons & K. S. Rotabi (Eds.), *Intercountry adoption: Policies, practices, and outcomes* (pp. 175–186). Burlington, VT: Ashgate Publishing.

Jukic, A. M., Evenson, K. R., Daniels, J. L., Herring, A. H., Wilcox, A. J., Harmann, K. E., et al. (2012). A prospective study of the association between vigorous physical activity during pregnancy and length of gestation and birthweight. *Maternal and Child Health Journal, 16,* 1031–1044.

Junge, C., Kooijman, V., Hagoort, P., & Cutler, A. (2012). Rapid recognition at 10 months as a predictor of language development. *Developmental Science, 15,* 463–473.

Jürgensen, M., Hiort, O., Holterhus, P.-M., & Thyen, U. (2007). Gender role behavior in children with XY karyotype and disorders of sex development. *Hormones and Behavior, 51,* 443–453.

Jusczyk, P. W. (2002). Some critical developments in acquiring native language sound organization. *Annals of Otology, Rhinology and Laryngology, 189,* 11–15.

Jusczyk, P. W., & Krumhansl, C. L. (1993). Pitch and rhythmic patterns affecting infants' sensitivity to musical phrase structure. *Journal of Experimental Psychology: Human Perception and Performance, 19,* 627–640.

Jusczyk, P. W., & Luce, P. A. (2002). Speech perception. In H. Pashler & S. Yantis (Eds.), *Steven's handbook of experimental psychology: Vol. 1. Sensation and perception* (3rd ed., pp. 493–536). New York: Wiley.

Justice, E. M. (1986). Developmental changes in judgments of relative strategy effectiveness. *British Journal of Developmental Psychology, 4,* 75–81.

Justice, L. M., Jiang, H., & Strasser, K. (2018). Linguistic environment of preschool classrooms: What dimensions support children's language growth? *Early Childhood Research Quarterly, 42,* 79–92.

Jutras-Aswad, D., DiNieri, J. A., Harkany, T., & Hurd, Y. L. (2009). Neurobiological consequences of maternal cannabis on human fetal development and its neuropsychiatric outcome. *European Archives of Psychiatry and Clinical Neuroscience, 259,* 395–412.

K

Kaar, J. L., Shapiro, A. L. B., Fell, D. M., & Johnson, S. L. (2016). Parental feeding practices, food neophobia, and child food preferences: What combination of factors results in children eating a variety of foods? *Food Quality and Preference, 50,* 57–64.

Kabali, H. K., Irigoyen, M. M., Nunez-Davis, R., Budacki, J. G., Mohanty, S. H., Leister, K. P., & Bonner, Jr., R. L. (2015). Exposure and use of mobile media devices by young children. *Pediatrics, 136,* 1044–1050.

Kagan, J. (2003). Behavioral inhibition as a temperamental category. In R. J. Davidson, K. R. Scherer, & H. H. Goldsmith (Eds.), *Handbook of affective sciences* (pp. 320–331). New York: Oxford University Press.

Kagan, J. (2010). Emotions and temperament. In M. H. Bornstein (Ed.), *Handbook of cultural developmental science* (pp, 175–194). New York: Psychology Press.

Kagan, J. (2013a). Contextualizing experience. *Developmental Review, 33,* 273–278.

Kagan, J. (2013b). Equal time for psychological and biological contributions to human variation. *Review of General Psychology, 17,* 351–357.

Kagan, J. (2013c). *The human spark: The science of human development.* New York: Basic Books.

Kagan, J. (2013d). Temperamental contributions to inhibited and uninhibited profiles. In P. D. Zelazo (Ed.), *The Oxford handbook of developmental psychology* (pp. 142–164). New York: Oxford University Press.

Kagan, J., Snidman, N., Kahn, V., & Towsley, S. (2007). The preservation of two infant temperaments into adolescence. *Monographs of the Society for Research in Child Development, 72*(2, Serial No. 287).

Kahn, U. R., Sengoelge, M., Zia, N., Razzak, J. A., Hasselberg, M., & Laflamme, L. (2015). Country level economic disparities in child injury mortality. *Archives of Disease in Childhood, 100,* s29–s33.

Kail, R. V. (2003). Information processing and memory. In M. H. Bornstein, L. Davidson, C. L. M. Keyes, K. A. Moore, and the Center for Child Well-Being (Eds.), *Well-being: Positive development across the life course* (pp. 269–280). Mahwah, NJ: Erlbaum.

Kail, R. V., & Ferrer, E. F. (2007). Processing speed in childhood and adolescence: Longitudinal models for examining developmental change. *Child Development, 78,* 1760–1770.

Kail, R. V., McBride-Chang, C., Ferrer, E., Cho, J.-R., & Shu, H. (2013). Cultural differences in the development of processing speed. *Developmental Science, 16,* 476–483.

Kaiser Family Foundation. (2015). *How will the uninsured fare under the Affordable Care Act?* Retrieved from www.kff.org/health-reform/fact-sheet/how-will-the-uninsured-fare-under-the-affordable-care-act

Kaiser Family Foundation. (2017). *Where are states today? Medicaid and CHIP eligibility levels for children, pregnant women, and adults.* Retrieved from www.kff.org/medicaid/fact-sheet/where-are-states-today-medicaid-and-chip

Kakihara, F., Tilton-Weaver, L., Kerr, M., & Stattin, H. (2010). The relationship of parental control to youth adjustment: Do youths' feelings about their parents play a role? *Journal of Youth and Adolescence, 39,* 1442–1456.

Kaldy, Z., Guillory, S. B., & Blaser, E. (2016). Delayed match retrieval: A novel anticipation-based visual working memory paradigm. *Developmental Science, 19,* 892–900.

Kaminsky, Z., Petronis, A., Wang, S.-C., Levine, B., Ghaffar, O., Floden, D., et al. (2007). Epigenetics of personality traits: An illustrative study of identical twins discordant for risk-taking behavior. *Twin Research and Human Genetics, 11,* 1–11.

Kampmann, U., Madsen, L. R., Skajaa, G. O., Iversen, D. S., Moeller, N., & Ovesen, P. (2015). Gestational diabetes: A clinical update. *World Journal of Diabetes, 6,* 1065–1072.

Kanazawa, S. (2012). Intelligence, birth order, and family size. *Personality and Social Psychology Bulletin, 38,* 1157–1164.

Kang, N. H., & Hong, M. (2008). Achieving excellence in teacher workforce and equity in learning opportunities in South Korea. *Educational Researcher, 37,* 200–207.

Kann, L., McManus, T., Harris, W. A., Shanklin, S. L., Flint, K. H., Queen, B., et al. (2018). Youth risk behavior surveillance—United States, 2017. *Morbidity and Mortality Weekly Report, 67*(8), 1–114. Retrieved from www.cdc.gov/mmwr/volumes/67/ss/ss6708a1.htm

Kantaoka, S., & Vandell, D. L. (2013). Quality of afterschool activities and relative change in adolescent functioning over two years. *Applied Developmental Science, 17,* 123–134.

Kanters, M. A., Bocarro, J. N., Edwards, M., Casper, J., & Floyd, M. F. (2013). School sport participation under two school sport policies: Comparisons by race/ethnicity, gender, and socioeconomic status. *Annals of Behavioral Medicine 45*(Suppl. 1), S113–S121.

Karafantis, D. M., & Levy, S. R. (2004). The role of children's lay theories about the malleability of human attributes in beliefs about and volunteering for disadvantaged groups. *Child Development, 75,* 236–250.

Karasik, L. B., Adolph, K., Tamis-LeMonda, C. S., & Zuckerman (2012). Carry on: Spontaneous object carrying in 13-month-old crawling and walking infants. *Developmental Psychology, 48,* 389–397.

Karasik, L. B., Tamis-LeMonda, C. S., & Adolph, K. E. (2011). Transition from crawling to walking and infants' actions with objects and people. *Child Development, 82,* 1199–1209.

Karasik, L. B., Tamis-LeMonda, C. S., Adolph, K. E., & Dimitroupoulou, K. A. (2008). How mothers encourage and discourage infants' motor actions. *Infancy, 13,* 366–392.

Karevold, E., Ystrom, E., Coplan, R. J., Sanson, A. V., & Mathiesen, K. S. (2012). A prospective longitudinal study of shyness from infancy to adolescence: Stability, age-related changes, and prediction of socio-emotional functioning. *Journal of Abnormal Child Psychology, 40,* 1167–1177.

Karkhaneh, M., Rowe, B. H., Saunders, L. D., Voaklander, D. C., & Hagel, B. E. (2013). Trends in head injuries associated with mandatory bicycle helmet legislation targeting children and adolescents. *Accident Analysis and Prevention, 59,* 206–212.

Karra, M., Subramanian, S. V., & Fink, G. (2017). Height in healthy children in low- and middle-income countries: An assessment. *American Journal of Clinical Nutrition, 105,* 121–126.

Karrass, J., & Braungart-Rieker, J. M. (2005). Effects of shared parent–infant book reading on early language acquisition. *Applied Developmental Psychology, 26,* 133–148.

Kärtner, J., Holodynski, M., & Wörmann, V. (2013). Parental ethnotheories, social practice and the culture-specific development of social smiling in infants. *Mind, Culture, and Activity, 20,* 79–95.

Kärtner, J., Keller, H., Chaudhary, N., & Yovsi, R. D. (2012). The development of mirror self-recognition in different sociocultural contexts. *Monographs of the Society for Research in Child Development, 77*(4, Serial No. 305).

Kastens, K. A., & Liben, L. S. (2007). Eliciting self-explanations improves children's performance on a field-based map skills task. *Cognition and Instruction, 25,* 45–74.

Kataoka, S., & Vandell, D. L. (2013). Quality of afterschool activities and relative change in adolescent functioning over two years. *Applied Developmental Science, 17,* 123–134.

Katz, J., Lee, A. C. C., Lawn, J. E., Cousens, S., Blencowe, H., Ezzati, M., et al. (2013). Mortality risk in preterm and small-for-gestational-age infants in low-income and middle-income countries: A pooled country analysis. *Lancet, 382,* 417–425.

Katzmarzyk, P. T., & Leonard, W. R. (1998). Climatic influences on human body size and proportions: Ecological adaptations and secular trends. *American Journal of Physical Anthropology, 106,* 483–503.

Katz-Wise, S. L., Priess, H. A., & Hyde, J. S. (2010). Gender-role attitudes and behavior across the transition to parenthood. *Developmental Psychology, 46,* 18–28.

Kaufman, J. C., & Sternberg, R. J. (2007, July/August). Resource review: Creativity. *Change, 39,* 55–58.

Kaufmann, K. B., Büning, H., Galy, A., Schambach, A., & Grez, M. (2013). Gene therapy on the move. *EMBO Molecular Medicine, 5,* 1642–1661.

Kavanaugh, R. D. (2006). Pretend play. In B. Spodek & O. N. Saracho (Eds.), *Handbook of research on the education of young children* (2nd ed., pp. 269–278). Mahwah, NJ: Erlbaum.

Kavšek, M. (2004). Predicting later IQ from infant visual habituation and dishabituation: A meta-analysis. *Journal of Applied Developmental Psychology, 25,* 369–393.

Kavšek, M. (2009). The perception of subjective contours and neon color spreading figures in young infants. *Attention, Perception, & Psychophysics, 71*(2), 412–420.

Kavšek, M. (2013). The onset of sensitivity to horizontal disparity in infancy: A short-term longitudinal study. *Infant Behavior and Development, 36,* 329–343.

Kavšek, M., & Bornstein, M. H. (2010). Visual habituation and dishabituation in preterm infants: A review and meta-analysis. *Research in Developmental Disabilities, 31,* 951–975.

Kavšek, M., & Braun, S. K. (2016). Binocular vision in infancy: Responsiveness to uncrossed horizontal disparity. *Infant Behavior and Development, 44,* 219–226.

Kavšek, M., Yonas, A., & Granrud, C. E. (2012). Infants' sensitivity to pictorial depth cues: A review and meta-analysis. *Infant Behavior and Development, 35,* 109–128.

Kayed, N. S., & Van der Meer, A. L. (2009). A longitudinal study of prospective control in catching by full-term and preterm infants. *Experimental Brain Research, 194,* 245–258.

Kearney, C. A., Spear, M., & Mihalas, S. (2014). School refusal behavior. In L. Grossman & S. Walfish (Eds.), *Translating psychological research into practice* (pp. 83–88). New York: Springer.

Keating-Lefler, R., Hudson, D. B., Campbell-Grossman, C., Fleck, M. O., & Westfall, J. (2004). Needs, concerns, and social support of single, low-income mothers. *Issues in Mental Health Nursing, 25,* 381–401.

Keefe, M. R., Barbosa, G. A., Froese-Fretz, A., Kotzer, A. M., & Lobo, M. (2005). An intervention program for families with irritable infants. *American Journal of Maternal/Child Nursing, 30,* 230–236.

Keen, R. (2011). The development of problem solving in young children: A critical cognitive skill. *Annual Review of Psychology, 62,* 1–24.

Keller, H., Bard, K., Morelli, G., Chaudhary, N., Vicedo, M., Rosabal-Coto, M., et al. (2018). The myth of universal sensitive responsiveness: Comment on Mesman et al. (2017). *Child Development, 89,* 1921–1928.

Keller, H., Borke, Y. J., Kärtner, J., Jensen, H., & Papaligoura, Z. (2004). Developmental consequences of early parenting experiences: Self-recognition and self-regulation in three cultural communities. *Child Development, 75,* 1745–1760.

Keller, H., & Chaudhary, N. (2017). Is the mother essential for attachment? Models of care in different cultures. In H. Keller & K. A. Bard (Eds.), *Contextualizing attachment: The cultural nature of attachment* (pp. 109–137). Cambridge, MA: MIT Press.

Keller, H., & Otto, H. (2009). The cultural socialization of emotion regulation during infancy. *Journal of Cross-Cultural Psychology, 40,* 996–1011.

Keller, S. S., Crow, T., Foundas, A., Amunts, K., & Roberts, N. (2009). Broca's area: Nomenclature, anatomy, typology and symmetry. *Brain and Language, 109,* 29–48.

Kelley, S. A., Brownell, C. A., & Campbell, S. B. (2000). Mastery motivation and self-evaluative affect in toddlers: Longitudinal relations with maternal behavior. *Child Development, 71,* 1061–1071.

Kellman, P. J., & Arterberry, M. E. (2006). Infant visual perception. In D. Kuhn & R. Siegler (Eds.), *Handbook of child psychology: Vol. 2. Cognition, perception, and language* (6th ed., pp. 109–160). Hoboken, NJ: Wiley.

Kellou, N., Sandalinas, F., Copin, N., & Simon, C. (2014). Prevention of unhealthy weight in children by promoting physical activity using a socio-ecological approach: What can we learn from intervention studies? *Diabetes & Metabolism, 40,* 258–271.

Kelly, D. J., Liu, S., Ge, L., Quinn, P. C., Slater, A. M., Lee, K., et al. (2007). Cross-race preferences for same-race faces extend beyond the African versus Caucasian contrast in 3-month-old infants. *Infancy, 11,* 87–95.

Kelly, D. J., Quinn, P. C., Slater, A. M., Lee, K., Ge, L., & Pascalis, O. (2009). The other-race effect develops during infancy: Evidence of perceptual narrowing. *Psychological Science, 18,* 1084–1089.

Kelly, R., & Hammond, S. (2011). The relationship between symbolic play and executive function in young children. *Australasian Journal of Early Childhood, 36*(2), 21–27.

Kempe, C. H., Silverman, B. F., Steele, P. W., Droegemueller, P. W., & Silver, H. K. (1962). The battered-child syndrome. *Journal of the American Medical Association, 181,* 17–24.

Kendrick, D., Barlow, J., Hampshire, A., Stewart-Brown, S., & Polnay, L. (2008). Parenting interventions and the prevention of unintentional injuries in childhood: Systematic review and meta-analysis. *Child: Care, Health and Development, 34,* 682–695.

Kendrick, K., Jutengren, G., & Stattin, H. (2012). The protective role of supportive friends against bullying perpetration and victimization. *Journal of Adolescence, 35,* 1069–1080.

Kennedy, B. C., Wallin, D. J., Tran, P. V., & Georgieff, M. K. (2016). Long-term brain and behavioral consequences of early-life iron deficiency. In N. Reissland & B. S. Kisilevsky (Eds.), *Fetal development* (pp. 295–316). New York: Springer.

Keren, M., Feldman, R., Namdari-Weinbaum, I., Spitzer, S., & Tyano, S. (2005). Relations between parents' interactive style in dyadic and triadic play and toddlers' symbolic capacity. *American Journal of Orthopsychiatry, 75,* 599–607.

Keresztes, A., Bender, A. R., Bodammer, N. C., Lindenberger, U., Shing, Y. L., & Werkle-Bergner, M. (2017). Hippocampal maturity promotes memory distinctiveness in childhood and adolescence. *Proceedings of the National Academy of Sciences, 114,* 9212–9217.

Kerns, K. A., Brumariu, L. E., & Seibert, A. (2011). Multi-method assessment of mother–child attachment: Links to parenting and child depressive symptoms in middle childhood. *Attachment and Human Development, 13,* 315–333.

Kerstis, B., Aarts, C., Tillman, C., Persson, H., Engström, G., Edlund, B., et al. (2016). Association between parental depressive symptoms and impaired bonding with the infant. *Archives of Women's Mental Health, 19,* 87–94.

Keven, N., & Akins, K. A. (2017, September). Neonatal imitation in context: Sensory-motor development in the perinatal period. *Behavioral and Brain Sciences, 40,* 1–107.

Khaleefa, O., Sulman, A., & Lynn, R. (2009). An increase of intelligence in Sudan, 1987–2007. *Journal of Biosocial Science, 41,* 279–283.

Khaleque, A., & Rohner, R. P. (2002). Perceived parental acceptance–rejection and psychological adjustment: A meta-analysis of cross cultural and intracultural studies. *Journal of Marriage and Family, 64,* 54–64.

Khaleque, A., & Rohner, R. P. (2012). Pancultural associations between perceived parental acceptance and psychological adjustment of children and adults: A meta-analytic review of worldwide research. *Journal of Cross-Cultural Psychology, 43,* 784–800.

Khamis, V. (2019). Post-traumatic stress disorder and emotion dysregulation among Syrian refugee children and adolescents resettled in Lebanon and Jordan. *Child Abuse and Neglect, 89,* 29–39.

Kidd, C., Piantadosi, S. T., & Aslin, R. N. (2012). The Goldilocks effect: Human infants allocate attention to visual sequences that are neither too simple nor too complex. *PLOS ONE, 7*(5), e36399.

Kiel, E. J., Premo, J. E., & Buss, K. A. (2016). Maternal encouragement to approach novelty: A curvilinear relation to change in anxiety for inhibited toddlers. *Journal of Abnormal Child Psychology, 44,* 433–444.

Kieras, J. E., Tobin, R. M., Graziano, W. G., & Rothbart, M. K. (2005). You can't always get what you want: Effortful control and children's responses to undesirable gifts. *Psychological Science, 16,* 391–396.

Killen, M., Crystal, D., & Watanabe, H. (2002). The individual and the group: Japanese and American children's evaluations of peer exclusion, tolerance of difference, and prescriptions for conformity. *Child Development, 73,* 1788–1802.

Killen, M., & Dahl, A. (2018). Moral judgment: Reflective, interactive, spontaneous, challenging, and always evolving. In K. Gray & J. Graham (Eds.), *Atlas of moral psychology* (pp. 20–30). New York: Guilford.

Killen, M., Kelly, M. C., Richardson, C., Crystal, D., & Ruck, M. (2010). European American children's and adolescents' evaluations of interracial exclusion. *Group Processes and Intergroup Relations, 13,* 283–300.

Killen, M., Lee-Kim, J., McGlothlin, H., & Stangor, C. (2002). How children and adolescents evaluate gender and racial exclusion. *Monographs of the Society for Research in Child Development, 67*(4, Serial No. 271).

Killen, M., Margie, N. G., & Sinno, S. (2006). Morality in the context of intergroup relationships. In M. Killen & J. G. Smetana (Eds.), *Handbook of moral development* (pp. 155–183). Mahwah, NJ: Erlbaum.

Killen, M., Mulvey, K. L., Richardson, C., Jampol, N., & Woodward, A. (2011). The accidental transgressor: Morally relevant theory of mind. *Cognition, 119,* 197–215.

Killen, M., Rutland, A., Rizzo, M. T., & McGuire, L. (2018). Intergroup exclusion, moral judgments, and social cognition. In W. M. Bukowski, B. Laursen, & K. H. Rubin (Eds.), *Handbook of peer interactions, relationships, and groups* (2nd ed., pp. 470–487). New York: Guilford.

Killen, M., Rutland, A., & Ruck, M. (2011). Promoting equity, tolerance, and justice in childhood. *Social Policy Report of the Society for Research in Child Development, 25*(4).

Killen, M., & Smetana, J. G. (2015). Origins and development of morality. In M. Killen & J. G. Smetana (Eds.), *Handbook of child psychology and developmental science: Vol. 3. Socioemotional processes* (7th ed., pp. 701–749). Hoboken, NJ: Wiley.

Killen, M., & Stangor, M. (2001). Children's social reasoning about inclusion and exclusion in gender and race peer group contexts. *Child Development, 72,* 174–186.

Kilmer, R. P., Cook, J. R., Crusto, C., Strater, K. P., & Haber, M. G. (2012). Understanding the ecology and development of children and families experiencing homelessness: Implications for practice, supportive services, and policy. *American Journal of Orthopsychiatry, 82,* 389–401.

Kim, B.-R., Chow, S.-M., Bray, B., & Teti, D. M. (2017). Trajectories of mothers' emotional availability: Relations with infant temperament in predicting attachment security. *Attachment & Human Development, 19,* 38–57.

Kim, G., Walden, T. A., & Knieps, L. J. (2010). Impact and characteristics of positive and fearful emotional messages during infant social referencing. *Infant Behavior and Development, 33,* 189–195.

Kim, H. Y., Schwartz, K., Cappella, E., & Seidman, E. (2014). Navigating middle grades: Role of social contexts in middle grade school climate. *American Journal of Community Psychology, 54,* 28–45.

Kim, J., & Cicchetti, D. (2006). Longitudinal trajectories of self-system processes and depressive symptoms among maltreated and nonmaltreated children. *Child Development, 77,* 624–639.

Kim, J. M. (1998). Korean children's concepts of adult and peer authority and moral reasoning. *Developmental Psychology, 34,* 947–955.

Kim, J.-Y., McHale, S. M., Crouter, A. C., & Osgood, D. W. (2007). Longitudinal linkages between sibling relationships and adjustment from middle childhood through adolescence. *Developmental Psychology, 43,* 960–973.

Kim, S., & Kochanska, G. (2012). Child temperament moderates effects of parent–child mutuality on self-regulation: A relationship-based path for emotionally negative infants. *Child Development, 83,* 1275–1289.

Kim S., & Kochanska, G. (2015). Mothers' power assertion; children's negative, adversarial orientation; and future behavior problems in low-income families: Early maternal responsiveness as a moderator of the developmental cascade. *Journal of Family Psychology, 29,* 1–9.

Kim, S., Kochanska, G., Boldt, L. J., Nordling, J. K., & O'Bleness, J. J. (2014). Developmental trajectory from early responses to transgressions to future antisocial behavior: Evidence for the role of the parent-child relationship from two longitudinal studies. *Development and Psychopathology, 26,* 93–103.

Kim, Y., Calzada, E. J., Barajas-Gonzales, R. G., Huang, D.-Y., Brotman, L. M., Castro, A., & Pichardo, C. (2018). The role of authoritative and authoritarian parenting in the early academic achievement of Latino students. *Journal of Educational Psychology, 110,* 119–132.

Kim, Y. K., Hutchison, L. A., & Winsler, A. (2015). Bilingual education in the United States: An historical overview and examination of two-way immersion. *Educational Review, 67,* 236–252.

Kimhi, Y., Shoam-Kugelmas, D., Agam Ben-Artzi, G., Ben-Moshe, I., & Bauminger-Zviely, N. (2014). Theory of mind and executive function in preschoolers with typical development versus intellectually able preschoolers with autism spectrum disorder. *Journal of Autism and Developmental Disorders, 44,* 2341–2354.

Kindermann, T. A., & Guest, S. D. (2018). The peer group: Linking conceptualizations, theories, and methods. In W. M. Bukowski, B. Laursen, & K. H. Rubin (Eds.), *Handbook of peer interactions, relationships, and groups* (2nd ed., pp. 84–105). New York: Guilford.

King, A. C., & Bjorklund, D. F. (2010). Evolutionary developmental psychology. *Psicothema, 22,* 22–27.

King, V. (2007). When children have two mothers: Relationships with nonresident mothers, stepmothers, and fathers. *Journal of Marriage and Family, 69,* 1178–1193.

King, V. (2009). Stepfamily formation: Implications for adolescent ties to mothers, nonresident fathers, and stepfathers. *Journal of Marriage and Family, 71,* 954–968.

Kinnunen, M.-L., Pietilainen, K., & Rissanen, A. (2006). Body size and overweight from birth to adulthood. In L. Pulkkinen & J. Kaprio (Eds.), *Socioemotional development and health from adolescence to adulthood* (pp. 95–107). New York: Cambridge University Press.

Kinsella, M. T., & Monk, C. (2009). Impact of maternal stress, depression and anxiety on fetal neurobehavioral development. *Clinical Obstetrics and Gynecology, 52,* 425–440.

Kirkham, N. Z., Cruess, L., & Diamond, A. (2003). Helping children apply their knowledge to their behavior on a dimension-switching task. *Developmental Science, 6,* 449–476.

Kirkorian, H. L. (2018). When and how do interactive digital media help children connect what they see on and off the screen? *Child Development Perspectives, 12,* 210–214.

Kirkorian, H. L., & Choi, K. (2017). Associations between toddlers' naturalistic media experience and observed learning from screens. *Infancy, 22,* 271–277.

Kirkorian, H. L., Choi, K., & Pempek, T. A. (2016). Toddlers' word learning from contingent and noncontingent video on touch screens. *Child Development, 87,* 405–413.

Kisilevsky, B. S. (2016). Fetal auditory processing: Implications for language development? In G. H. A. Visser & E. J. H. Mulder (Eds.), *Fetal development* (pp. 133–152). New York: Springer.

Kisilevsky, B. S., & Hains, S. M. J. (2011). Onset and maturation of fetal heart rate response to the mother's voice over late gestation. *Developmental Science, 14,* 214–223.

Kisilevsky, B. S., Hains, S. M. J., Brown, C. A., Lee, C. T., Cowperthwaite, B., & Stutzman, S. S. (2009). Fetal sensitivity to properties of maternal speech and language. *Infant Behavior and Development, 32,* 59–71.

Kisilevsky, B. S., Hains, S. M. J., Lee, K., Muir, D. W., Xu, F., Fu, G., Zhao, Z. Y., & Yang, R. L. (1998). The still-face effect in Chinese and Canadian 3- to 6-month-old infants. *Developmental Psychology, 34,* 629–639.

Kit, B. K., Ogden, C. L., & Flegal, K. M. (2014). Epidemiology of obesity. In W. Ahrens & I. Pigeot (Eds.), *Handbook of Epidemiology* (2nd ed., pp. 2229–2262). New York: Springer Science + Business Media.

Kitsantas, P., & Gaffney, K. F. (2010). Racial/ethnic disparities in infant mortality. *Journal of Perinatal Medicine, 38,* 87–94.

Kitzman, H. J., Olds, D. L., Cole, R. E., Hanks, C. A., Anson, E. A., Arcoleo, K. J., et al. (2010). Enduring effects of prenatal and infancy home visiting by nurses on children: Follow-up of a randomized trial among children at age 12 years. *Archives of Pediatric and Adolescent Medicine, 164,* 412–418.

Kitzmann, K. M., Cohen, R., & Lockwood, R. L. (2002). Are only children missing out? Comparison of the peer-related social competence of only children and siblings. *Journal of Social and Personal Relationships, 19,* 299–316.

Kiuru, N, Aunola, K., Lerkkanen, M. K., Pakarinen, E., Poskiparta, E., Ahonen, T., et al. (2015). Positive teacher and peer relations combine to predict primary school students' academic skill development. *Developmental Psychology, 51,* 434–446.

Kjønniksen, L., Anderssen, N., & Wold, B. (2009). Organized youth sport as a predictor of physical activity in adulthood. *Scandinavian Journal of Medicine and Science in Sports, 19,* 646–654.

Kjønniksen, L., Torsheim, T., & Wold, B. (2008). Tracking of leisure-time physical activity during adolescence and young adulthood: A 10-year longitudinal study. *International Journal of Behavioral Nutrition and Physical Activity, 5,* 69.

Klahr, D., Matlen, B., & Jirout, J. (2013). Children as scientific thinkers. In G. J. Feist & M. E. Gorman (Eds.), *Handbook of the psychology of science* (pp. 223–247). New York: Springer.

Klebanov, P. K., Brooks-Gunn, J., McCarton, C., & McCormick, M. C. (1998). The contribution of neighborhood and family income to developmental test scores over the first three years of life. *Child Development, 69,* 1420–1436.

Kleinsorge, C., & Covitz, L. M. (2012). Impact of divorce on children: Developmental considerations. *Pediatrics in Review, 33,* 147–155.

Klemfuss, J. Z., & Ceci, S. J. (2012). Legal and psychological perspectives on children's competence to testify in court. *Developmental Review, 32,* 81–204.

Klemmensen, A.K., Tabor, A., Østerdal, M. L., Knudsen, V.K., Halldorsson, T. I., Mikkelsen, T. B., et al. (2009). Intake of vitamin C and E in pregnancy and risk of pre-eclampsia: Prospective study among 57,346 women. *BJOG, 116,* 964–974.

Kliegman, R. M., Stanton, B. F., St. Geme, J. W., & Schor, N. (Eds.). (2015). *Nelson textbook of pediatrics* (20th ed.). Philadelphia: Saunders.

Kliewer, W., Fearnow, M. D., & Miller, P. A. (1996). Coping socialization in middle childhood: Tests of maternal and paternal influences. *Child Development, 67,* 2339–2357.

Kloep, M., Hendry, L. B., Taylor, R., & Stuart-Hamilton, I. (2016). *Development from adolescence to early adulthood: A dynamic systemic approach to transitions and transformations.* London: Psychology Press.

Kloess, J. A., Beech, A. R., & Harkins, L. (2014). Online child sexual exploitation: Prevalence, process, and offender characteristics. *Trauma, Violence, & Abuse, 15,* 126–139.

Kloss, O., Eskin, N. A. M., & Suh, M. (2018). Thiamin deficiency on fetal brain development with and without prenatal alcohol exposure. *Biochemistry and Cell Biology, 96,* 169–177.

Knafo, A., & Plomin, R. (2006). Parental discipline and affection and children's prosocial behavior: Genetic and environmental links. *Journal of Personality and Social Psychology, 90,* 147–164.

Knafo, A., Zahn-Waxler, C., Davidov, M., Hulle, C. V., Robinson, J. L., & Rhee, S. H. (2009). Empathy in early childhood: Genetic, environmental, and affective contributions. In O. Vilarroya, S. Altran, A. Navarro, K. Ochsner, & A. Tobena (Eds.), *Values, empathy, and fairness across social barriers* (pp. 103–114). New York: New York Academy of Sciences.

Knafo-Noam, A., Uzefovsky, F., Israel, S., Davidov, M., & Zahn-Waxler, C. (2015). The prosocial personality and its facets: Genetic and environmental architecture of mother-reported behavior of 7-year-old twins. *Frontiers in Psychology, 6,* Art. No. 112.

Knight, C. J., Berrow, S. R., & Harwood, C. G. (2017). Parenting in sport. *Current Opinion in Psychology, 16,* 93–97.

Knobloch, H., & Pasamanick, B. (Eds.). (1974). *Gesell and Amatruda's Developmental Diagnosis.* Hagerstown, MD: Harper & Row.

Knopf, M., Kraus, U., & Kressley-Mba, R. A. (2006). Relational information processing of novel unrelated actions by infants. *Infant Behavior and Development, 29,* 44–53.

Knudsen, B., Fischer, M., & Aschersleben, G. (2015). The development of Arabic digit knowledge in 4- to 7-year-old children. *Journal of Numerical Cognition, 1,* 21–37.

Knudsen, E. I. (2004). Sensitive periods in the development of the brain and behavior. *Journal of Cognitive Neuroscience, 16,* 1412–1425.

Kobayashi, T., Hiraki, K., & Hasegawa, T. (2005). Auditory-visual intermodal matching of small numerosities in 6-month-old infants. *Developmental Science, 8,* 409–419.

Kochanska, G. (1991). Socialization and temperament in the development of guilt and conscience. *Child Development, 62,* 1379–1392.

Kochanska, G., & Aksan, N. (2006). Children's conscience and self-regulation. *Journal of Personality, 74,* 1587–1617.

Kochanska, G., Aksan, N., & Carlson, J. J. (2005). Temperament, relationships, and young children's receptive cooperation with their parents. *Developmental Psychology, 41,* 648–660.

Kochanska, G., Aksan, N., Prisco, T. R., & Adams, E. E. (2008). Mother–child and father–child mutually responsive orientation in the first 2 years and children's outcomes at preschool age: Mechanisms of influence. *Child Development, 79,* 30–44.

Kochanska, G., Boldt, L. J., Kim, S., Yoon, J. E., & Philibert, R. A. (2015). Developmental interplay between children's biobehavioral risk and the parenting environment from toddler to school age: Prediction of socialization outcomes in preadolescence. *Development and Psychopathology, 27,* 775–790.

Kochanska, G., Gross, J. N., Lin, M.-H., & Nichols, K. E. (2002). Guilt in young children: Development, determinants, and relations with broader system standards. *Child Development, 73,* 461–482.

Kochanska, G., & Kim, S. (2014). A complex interplay among the parent–child relationship, effortful control, and internalized rule-compatible conduct in young children: Evidence from two studies. *Developmental Psychology, 50,* 8–21.

Kochanska, G., Kim, S., Barry, R. A., & Philibert, R. A. (2011). Children's genotypes interact with maternal responsive care in predicting children's competence: Diathesis-stress or differential susceptibility? *Development and Psychopathology, 23,* 605–616.

Kochanska, G., & Knaack, A. (2003). Effortful control as a personality characteristic of young children: Antecedents, correlates, and consequences. *Journal of Personality, 71,* 1087–1112.

Kochanska, G., Murray, K. T., & Harlan, E. T. (2000). Effortful control in early childhood: Continuity and change, antecedents, and implications for social development. *Developmental Psychology, 36,* 220–232.

Kochel, K. P., Ladd, G. W., & Rudolph, K. D. (2012). Longitudinal associations among youth depressive symptoms, peer victimization, and low peer acceptance: An interpersonal process perspective. *Child Development, 83,* 637–650.

Koehn, A. J., & Kerns, K. A. (2018). Parent–child attachment: Meta-analysis of associations with parenting behaviors in middle childhood and adolescence. *Attachment & Human Development, 20,* 378–405.

Kohen, D. E., Leventhal, T., Dahinten, V. S., & McIntosh, C. N. (2008). Neighborhood disadvantage: Pathways of effects for young children. *Child Development, 79,* 156–169.

Kohlberg, L. (1966). A cognitive-developmental analysis of children's sex-role concepts and attitudes. In E. E. Maccoby (Ed.), *The development of sex differences* (pp. 82–173). Stanford, CA: Stanford University Press.

Kolak, A. M., & Volling, B. L. (2011). Sibling jealousy in early childhood: Longitudinal links to sibling relationship quality. *Infant and Child Development, 20,* 213–226.

Kolak, A. M., & Volling, B. L. (2013). Coparenting moderates the association between firstborn children's temperament and problem behavior across the transition to siblinghood. *Journal of Family Psychology, 27,* 355–364.

Koletzko, B., Beyer, J., Brands, B., Demmelmair, H., Grote, V., Haile, G., et al. (2013). Early influences of nutrition on postnatal growth. *Nestlé Nutrition Institute Workshop Series, 71,* 11–27.

Kolling, T., Óturai, G., & Knopf, M. (2014). Is selective attention the basis for selective imitation in infants? An eye-tracking study of deferred imitation with 12-month-olds. *Journal of Experimental Child Psychology, 124,* 18–35.

Kollmann, M., Haeusler, M., Haas, J., Csapo, B., Lang, U., & Klaritsch, P. (2013). Procedure-related complications after genetic amniocentesis and chorionic villus sampling. *Ultraschall in der Medizen, 34,* 345–348.

Kollmeyer, M., Schultes, M.-T., Schober, B., Hodosi, T., & Spiel, C. (2018). Parents' judgments about the desirability of toys for their children: Associations with gender role attitudes, gender-typing of toys, and demographics. *Sex Roles, 79,* 329–341.

Konner, M. (2010). *The evolution of childhood: Relationships, emotion, mind.* Cambridge, MA: Harvard University Press.

Konner, M. J. (1977). Infancy among the Kalahari Desert San. In P. H. Leiderman, S. R. Tulkin, & A. Rosenfield (Eds.), *Culture and infancy: Variations in the human experience* (pp. 287–328). New York: Academic Press.

Konrad, C., Herbert, J. S., Schneider, S., & Seehagen, S. (2016a). The relationship between prior night's sleep and measures of infant imitation. *Developmental Psychobiology, 58,* 450–461.

Konrad, C., Seehagen, S., Schneider, S., & Herbert, J. S. (2016b). Naps promote flexible memory retrieval in 12-month-old infants. *Developmental Psychobiology, 58,* 866–874.

Kontos, A. P., Elbin, R. J., Fazio-Sumrock, V. C., Burkhart, S., Swindell, H., Maroon, J., et al. (2013). Incidence of sports-related concussion among youth football players aged 8–12 years. *Journal of Pediatrics, 163,* 717–720.

Kooijman, V., Hagoort, P., & Cutler, A. (2009). Prosodic structure in early word segmentation: ERP evidence from Dutch ten-month-olds. *Infancy, 14,* 591–612.

Kopas, M. L. (2014). A review of evidence-based practices for management of the second stage of labor. *Journal of Midwifery & Women's Health, 59,* 264–276.

Kopp, C. B., & Neufeld, S. J. (2003). Emotional development during infancy. In R. Davidson, K. R. Scherer, & H. H. Goldsmith (Eds.), *Handbook of affective sciences* (pp. 347–374). Oxford, UK: Oxford University Press.

Korotchikova, I., Stevenson, N. J., Livingstone, V., Ryan, C. A., & Boylan, G. B. (2016). Sleep–wake cycle of the healthy term newborn infant in the immediate postnatal period. *Clinical Neurophysiology, 127,* 2095–2101.

Koss, K. J., Hostinar, C. E., Donzella, B., & Gunnar, M. R. (2014). Social deprivation and the HPA axis in early deprivation. *Psychoneuroendocrinology, 50,* 1–13.

Kotecha, S. J., Gallacher, D. J., & Kotecha, S. (2016). The respiratory consequences of early-term birth and delivery by caesarean sections. *Paediatric Respiratory Reviews, 19,* 49–55.

Kouklari, E.-C., Thompson, T., Monks, C. P., & Tsermentseli, S. (2017). Hot and cool executive function and its relation to theory of mind in children with and without autism spectrum disorder. *Journal of Cognition and Development, 18,* 399–418.

Kowalski, R. M., & Limber, S. P. (2013). Psychological, physical, and academic correlates of cyberbullying and traditional bullying. *Journal of Adolescent Health, 53,* S13–S20.

Kozer, E., Costei, A. M., Boskovic, R., Nulman, I., Nikfar, S., & Koren, G. (2003). Effects of aspirin consumption during pregnancy on pregnancy outcomes: Meta-analysis. *Birth Defects Research: Part B, Developmental and Reproductive Toxicology, 68,* 70–84.

Kozulin, A. (Ed.). (2003). *Vygotsky's educational theory in cultural context.* Cambridge, UK: Cambridge University Press.

Krahé, B. (2016). Violent media effects on aggression: A commentary from a cross-cultural perspective. *Analyses of Social Issues and Public Policy, 16,* 439–442.

Krahé, B., & Berger, A. (2017). Gendered pathways from child sexual abuse to sexual aggression victimization and perpetration in adolescence and young adulthood. *Child Abuse & Neglect, 63,* 261–272.

Krähenbühl, S., Blades, M., & Eiser, C. (2009). The effect of repeated questioning on children's accuracy and consistency in eyewitness testimony. *Legal and Criminological Psychology, 14,* 263–278.

Kral, T. V. E., & Faith, M. S. (2009). Influences on child eating and weight development from a behavioral genetics perspective. *Journal of Pediatric Psychology, 34,* 596–605.

Kranjac, A. W., Kimbro, R. T., Denney, J. T., & Osiecki, K. M. (2017). Comprehensive neighborhood portraits and child asthma. *Maternal Child and Health Journal, 21,* 1552–1562.

Krcmar, M., & Cingel, D. P. (2014). Parent–child joint reading in traditional and electronic formats. *Media Psychology, 17,* 262–281.

Krcmar, M., Grela, B., & Lin, K. (2007). Can toddlers learn vocabulary from television? An experimental approach. *Media Psychology, 10,* 41–63.

Kreider, R. M., & Ellis, R. (2011). Living arrangements of children: 2009. *Current Population Reports,* P70–126. Retrieved from www.census.gov/prod/2011pubs/p70-126.pdf

Kreppner, J., Kumsta, R., Rutter, M., Beckett, C., Castle, J., Stevens, S., et al. (2010). Developmental course of deprivation-specific psychological patterns: Early manifestations, persistence to age 15, and clinical features. *Monographs of the Society for Research in Child Development, 75*(1, Serial No. 295), 79–101.

Kreppner, J., Rutter, M., Beckett, C., Castle, J., Colvert, E., Groothues, C., et al. (2007). Normality and impairment following profound early institutional deprivation: A longitudinal follow-up into early adolescence. *Developmental Psychology, 43,* 931–946.

Kretch, K. S., & Adolph, K. E. (2013a). Cliff or step? Posture-specific learning at the edge of a drop-off. *Child Development, 84,* 226–240.

Kretch, K. S., & Adolph, K. E. (2013b). No bridge too high: Infants decide whether to cross based on the probability of falling not the severity of the potential fall. *Developmental Science, 16,* 336–351.

Kretch, K. S., Franchak, J. M., & Adolph, K. E. (2014). Crawling and walking infants see the world differently. *Child Development, 85,* 1503–1518.

Kuczynski, L., & Lollis, S. (2002). Four foundations for a dynamic model of parenting. In J. R. M. Gerris (Ed.), *Dynamics of parenting.* Hillsdale, NJ: Erlbaum.

Kuhl, P. K., Ramirez, R. R., Bosseler, A., Lin, J. L., & Imada, T. (2014). Infants' brain responses to speech suggest analysis by synthesis. *Proceedings of the National Academy of Sciences, 111,* 11238–11245.

Kuhl, P. K., Tsao, F.-M., & Liu, H.-M. (2003). Foreign-language experience in infancy: Effects of short-term exposure and social interaction on phonetic learning. *Proceedings of the National Academy of Sciences, 100,* 9096–9101.

Kuhn, D. (1995). Microgenetic study of change: What has it told us? *Psychological Science, 6,* 133–139.

Kulkarni, A. D., Jamieson, D. J., Jones, H. W., Jr., Kissin, D. M., Gallo, M. F., Macaluso, M., et al. (2013). Fertility treatments and multiple births in the United States. *New England Journal of Medicine, 369,* 2218–2225.

Kumar, M., Chandra, S., Ijaz, Z., & Senthilselvan, A. (2014). Epidural analgesia in labour and neonatal respiratory distress: A case-control study. *Archives of Disease in Childhood—Fetal and Neonatal Edition, 99,* F116–F119.

Kunnen, S. (Ed.). (2012). *A dynamic systems approach to adolescent development.* London: Routledge.

Kuo, P. X., Volling, B. L., & Gonzales, R. (2018). Gender role beliefs, work–family conflict, and father involvement after the birth of a second child. *Psychology of Men & Masculinity, 19,* 243–256.

Kuppens, S., & Ceulemans, E. (2018). Parenting styles: A closer look at a well-known concept. *Journal of Child and Family Studies, 28,* 168–181.

Kuppens, S., Laurent, L., Heyvaert, M., & Onghena, P. (2013). Associations between parental control and relational aggression in children and adolescents: A multilevel and sequential meta-analysis. *Developmental Psychology, 49,* 1697–1712.

Kurdziel, L., Duclos, K., & Spencer, R. M. C. (2013). Sleep spindles in midday naps enhance learning in preschool children. *Proceedings of the National Academy of Sciences, 110,* 17267–17271.

Kurian, M. A., Gissen, P., Smith, M., Heales, S. J. R., & Clayton, P. T. (2011). The monoamine neurotransmitter disorders: An expanding range of neurological syndromes. *Lancet Neurology, 10,* 721–733.

Kurtz-Costes, B., Copping, K. E., Rowley, S. J., & Kinlaw, C. R. (2014). Gender and age differences in awareness and endorsement of gender stereotypes. *European Journal of Psychology and Education, 29,* 603–618.

Kurtz-Costes, B., Rowley, S. J., Harris-Britt, A., & Woods, T. A. (2008). Gender stereotypes about mathematics and science and self-perceptions of ability in late childhood and early adolescence. *Merrill-Palmer Quarterly, 54,* 386–409.

Kwon, M.-K., Luck, S. J., & Oakes, L. M. (2014). Visual short-term memory for complex objects in 6- and 8-month-old infants. *Child Development, 85,* 564–577.

L

Ladd, G. W. (2005). *Children's peer relationships and social competence: A century of progress.* New Haven, CT: Yale University Press.

Ladd, G. W., Birch, S. H., & Buhs, E. S. (1999). Children's social and scholastic lives in kindergarten: Related spheres of influence? *Child Development, 70,* 1373–1400.

Ladd, G. W., & Burgess, K. B. (1999). Charting the relationship trajectories of aggressive, withdrawn, and aggressive/withdrawn children during early grade school. *Child Development, 70,* 910–929.

Ladd, G. W., Kochenderfer-Ladd, B., Eggum, N. D., Kochel, K. P., & McConnell, E. M. (2011). Characterizing and comparing the friendships of anxious-solitary and unsociable preadolescents. *Child Development, 82,* 1434–1453.

Ladd, G. W., LeSieur, K., & Profilet, S. M. (1993). Direct parental influences on young children's peer relations. In S. Duck (Ed.), *Learning about relationships* (Vol. 2, pp. 152–183). London: Sage.

Lagattuta, K. H. (2014). Linking past, present, and future: Children's ability to connect mental states and emotions across time. *Child Development Perspectives, 8,* 90–95.

Lagattuta, K. H., & Thompson, R. A. (2007). The development of self-conscious emotions: Cognitive processes and social influences. In J. L. Tracy, R. W. Robins, & J. P. Tangney (Eds.). *The self-conscious emotions: Theory and research* (pp. 91–113). New York: Guilford.

Laible, D. (2007). Attachment with parents and peers in late adolescence: Links with emotional competence and social behavior. *Personality and Individual Differences, 43,* 1185–1197.

Laible, D. (2011). Does it matter if preschool children and mothers discuss positive vs. negative events during reminiscing? Links with mother-reported attachment, family emotional climate, and socioemotional development. *Social Development, 20,* 394–411.

Laible, D., & Song, J. (2006). Constructing emotional and relational understanding: The role of affect and mother–child discourse. *Merrill-Palmer Quarterly, 52,* 44–69.

Laible, D., & Thompson, R. A. (2002). Mother–child conflict in the toddler years: Lessons in emotion, morality, and relationships. *Child Development, 73,* 1187–1203.

Lalonde, C. E., & Chandler, M. J. (1995). False-belief understanding goes to school: On the social-emotional consequences of coming early or late to a first theory of mind. *Cognition and Emotion, 9,* 167–185.

Lam, C. B., McHale, S. M., & Crouter, A. C. (2012). Parent–child shared time from middle childhood to late adolescence: Developmental course and adjustment correlates. *Child Development, 83,* 2089–2103.

Lam, C. B., Solmeyer, A. R., & McHale, S. M. (2012). Sibling relationships and empathy across the transition to adolescence. *Journal of Youth and Adolescence, 41,* 1657–1670.

Lam, H. S., Kwok, K. M., Chan, P. H., So, H. K., Li, A. M., Ng, P. C., et al. (2013). Long term neurocognitive impact of low dose prenatal methylmercury exposure in Hong Kong. *Environment International, 54,* 59–64.

Lam, J. (2015). Picky eating in children. *Frontiers in Pediatrics, 3,* 41.

Lamaze, F. (1958). *Painless childbirth.* London: Burke.

Lamb, M. E. (2012). Mothers, fathers, families, and circumstances: Factors affecting children's adjustment. *Applied Developmental Science, 16,* 98–111.

Lamb, M. E., & Lewis, C. (2013). Father–child relationships. In N. J. Cabrera & C. S. Tamis-LeMonda (Eds.), *Handbook of father involvement* (2nd ed., pp. 119–134). New York: Routledge.

Lamb, M. E., Thompson, R. A., Gardner, W., Charnov, E. L., & Connell, J. P. (1985). Infant–mother attachment: The origins and developmental significance of individual differences in the Strange Situation: Its study and biological interpretation. *Behavioral and Brain Sciences, 7,* 127–147.

Lamkaddem, M., van der Straten, A., Essink-Bot, M. L., van Eijsden, M., & Vrijkotte, T. (2014). Etnische verschillen in het gebruik van kraamzorg [Ethnic differences in uptake of professional maternity care assistance]. *Nederlands Tijdschrift voor Geneeskunde, 158*(A7718).

Lamm, B., Keller, H., Teiser, J., Gudi, H., Yovsi, R. D., Freitag, C., et al. (2017). Waiting for the second treat: Developing culture-specific modes of self-regulation. *Child Development, 88,* 12847.

Lamminmaki, A., Hines, M., Kuiri-Hanninen, T., Kilpelainen, L., Dunkel, L., & Sankilampi, U. (2012). Testosterone measured in infancy predicts subsequent sex-typed behavior in boys and girls. *Hormones and Behavior, 61,* 611–616.

Lampl, M. (1993). Evidence of saltatory growth in infancy. *American Journal of Human Biology, 5,* 641–652.

Lampl, M., & Johnson, M. L. (2011). Infant growth in length follows prolonged sleep and increased naps. *Sleep, 34,* 641–650.

Lancy, D. F. (2014). *The anthropology of childhood.* Cambridge, UK: Cambridge University Press.

Lane, J. D., Wellman, H. N., Olson, S. L., Labounty, J., & Kerr, D. C. R. (2010). Theory of mind and emotion understanding predict moral development in early childhood. *British Journal of Developmental Psychology, 28,* 871–889.

Lang, I. A., Llewellyn, D. J., Langa, K. M., Wallace, R. B., Huppert, F. A., & Melzer, D. (2008). Neighborhood deprivation, individual socioeconomic status, and cognitive function in older people: Analyses from the English Longitudinal Study of Ageing. *Journal of the American Geriatric Society, 56,* 191–198.

Lange, S., Probst, C., Gmel, G., Rehm, J., Burd, L., & Popova, S. (2017). Global prevalence of fetal alcohol spectrum disorder among children and youth: A systematic review and meta-analysis. *JAMA Pediatrics, 171,* 948–956.

Langley, H. A., Coffman, J. L., & Ornstein, P. A. (2017). The socialization of children's memory: Linking maternal conversational style to the development of children's autobiographical and deliberate memory skills. *Journal of Cognition and Development, 18,* 63–86.

Lanphear, B., Hornung, R., Khoury, J., Yolton, K., Baghurst, P., Bellinger, D., et al. (2005). Low-level environmental lead exposure and children's intellectual function: An international pooled analysis. *Environmental Health Perspectives, 113,* 894–899.

Lansford, J. E. (2009). Parental divorce and children's adjustment. *Perspectives on Psychological Science, 4,* 140–152.

Lansford, J. E., Criss, M. M., Dodge, K. A., Shaw, D. S., Pettit, G. S., & Bates, J. E. (2009). Trajectories of physical discipline: Early childhood antecedents and developmental outcomes. *Child Development, 80,* 1385–1402.

Lansford, J. E., Criss, M. M., Laird, R. D., Shaw, D. S., Pettit, G. S., Bates, J. E., & Dodge, K. A. (2011). Reciprocal relations between parents' physical discipline and children's externalizing behavior during middle childhood and adolescence. *Development and Psychopathology, 23,* 225–238.

Lansford, J. E., Malone, P. S., Castellino, D. R., Dodge, K. A., Pettit, G., & Bates, J. E. (2006). Trajectories of internalizing, externalizing, and grades for children who have and have not experienced their parents' divorce or separation. *Journal of Family Psychology, 20,* 292–301.

Lansford, J. E., Malone, P. S., Dodge, K. A., Pettit, G. S., & Bates, J. E. (2010). Developmental cascades of peer rejection, social information processing biases, and aggression during middle childhood. *Development and Psychopathology, 22,* 593–602.

Lansford, J. E., Wagner, L. B., Bates, J. E., Dodge, K. A., & Pettit, G. S. (2012). Parental reasoning, denying privileges, yelling, and spanking: Ethnic differences and associations with child externalizing behavior. *Parenting: Science and Practice, 12*, 42–56.

Laranjo, J., Bernier, A., Meins, E., & Carlson, S. M. (2010). Early manifestations of children's theory of mind: The roles of maternal mind-mindedness and infant security of attachment. *Infancy, 15*, 300–323.

Larsen, J. A., & Nippold, M. A. (2007). Morphological analysis in school-age children: Dynamic assessment of a word learning strategy. *Language, Speech, and Hearing Services in Schools, 38*, 201–212.

Larzelere, R. E., Cox, R. B., Jr., & Mandara, J. (2013). Responding to misbehavior in young children: How authoritative parents enhance reasoning with firm control. In R. E. Larzelere, A. S. Morris, & A. W. Harrist (Eds.), *Authoritative parenting: Synthesizing nurturance and discipline for optimal child development* (pp. 89–111). Washington, DC: American Psychological Association.

Larzelere, R. E., Schneider, W. N., Larson, D. B., & Pike, P. L. (1996). The effects of discipline responses in delaying toddler misbehavior recurrences. *Child and Family Behavior Therapy, 18*, 35–7.

Lashley, F. R. (2007). *Essentials of clinical genetics in nursing practice.* New York: Springer.

Laski, E. V., & Siegler, R. S. (2014). Learning from number board games: You learn what you encode. *Developmental Psychology, 50*, 853–864.

Latendresse, G., & Ruiz, R. J. (2011). Maternal corticotropin-releasing hormone and the use of selective serotonin reuptake inhibitors independently predict the occurrence of preterm birth. *Journal of Midwifery and Women's Health, 56*, 118–126.

Lau, Y. L., Cameron, C. A., Chieh, K. M., O'Leary, J., Fu, G., & Lee, K. (2012). Cultural differences in moral justifications enhance understanding of Chinese and Canadian children's moral decisions. *Journal of Cross-Cultural Psychology, 44*, 461–477.

Lauer, J. E., Udelson, H. B., Jeon, S. O., & Lourenco, S. F. (2015). An early sex difference in the relation between mental rotation and object preference. *Frontiers in Psychology, 6*, 558.

Lauer, P. A., Akiba, M., Wilkerson, S. B., Apthorp, H. S., Snow, D., & Martin-Glenn, M. (2006). Out-of-school time programs: A meta-analysis of effects for at-risk students. *Review of Educational Research, 76*, 275–313.

Laufer, B. I., Chater-Diehl, E. J., Kapalanga, J., & Singh, S. M. (2017). Long-term alterations to DNA methylation as a biomarker of prenatal alcohol exposure: From mouse models to human children with fetal alcohol spectrum disorders. *Alcohol, 60*, 67–75.

Lauricella, A. R., Gola, A. A. H., & Calvert, S. L. (2011). Toddlers' learning from socially meaningful video characters. *Media Psychology, 14*, 216–232.

Laursen, B., & Adams, B. (2018). Conflict between peers. In W. M. Bukowski B. Laursen & K. H. Rubin (Eds.), *Handbook of peer interaction, relationships, and groups* (pp. 265–283). New York: Guilford.

Lavelli, M., & Fogel, A. (2005). Developmental changes in the relationship between the infant's attention and emotion during early face-to-face communication: The 2-month transition. *Developmental Psychology, 41*, 265–280.

Lavelli, M., & Fogel, A. (2013). Interdyad differences in early mother–infant face-to-face communication: Real-time dynamics and developmental pathways. *Developmental Psychology, 49*, 2257–2271.

Lavigne, É., Bélair, M. A., Do, M. T., Stieb, D. M., Hystad, P., van Donkelaar, A., et al. (2017). Maternal exposure to ambient air pollution and risk of early childhood cancers: A population-based study in Ontario, *Canada. Environment International, 100*, 139–147.

Law, E. C., Sideridis, G. D., Prock, L. A., & Sheridan, M. A. (2014). Attention-deficit/ hyperactivity disorder in young children: Predictors of diagnostic stability. *Pediatrics, 133*, 659–667.

Lawson, G. M., & Farah, M. (2017). Executive function as a mediator between SES and academic achievement throughout childhood. *International Journal of Behavioral Development, 41*, 94–104.

Lawson, G. M., Hook, C. J., Hackman, D. A., & Farah, M. J. (2016). Socioeconomic status and the development of executive function: Behavioral and neuroscience approaches. In J. A. Griffin, P. McCardle, & L. S. Freund (Eds.), *Executive function in preschool-age children: Integrating measurement, neurodevelopment, and translational research* (pp. 259–278). Washington, DC: American Psychological Association.

Lazar, I., & Darlington, R. (1982). Lasting effects of early education: A report from the Consortium for Longitudinal Studies. *Monographs of the Society for Research in Child Development, 47*(2–3, Serial No. 195).

Lazarus, R. S., & Lazarus, B. N. (1994). *Passion and reason.* New York: Oxford University Press.

Leaper, C. (1994). Exploring the correlates and consequences of gender segregation: Social relationships in childhood, adolescence, and adulthood. In C. Leaper (Ed.), *New directions for child development* (No. 65, pp. 67–86). San Francisco: Jossey-Bass.

Leaper, C. (2000). Gender, affiliation, assertion, and the interactive context of parent—child play. *Developmental Psychology, 36*, 381–393.

Leaper, C. (2013). Gender development during childhood. In P. D. Zelazo (Ed.), *Oxford handbook of developmental psychology, Vol. 2: Self and other* (pp. 326–377). New York: Oxford University Press.

Leaper, C., Anderson, K. J., & Sanders, P. (1998). Moderators of gender effects on parents' talk to their children: A meta-analysis. *Developmental Psychology, 34*, 3–27.

Leaper, C., Tenenbaum, H. R., & Shaffer, T. G. (1999). Communication patterns of African-American girls and boys from low-income, urban backgrounds. *Child Development, 70*, 1489–1503.

Learmonth, A. E., Lamberth, R., & Rovee-Collier, C. (2004). Generalization of deferred imitation during the first year of life. *Journal of Experimental Child Psychology, 88*, 297–318.

Leavell, A. S., Tamis-LeMonda, C. S., Ruble, D. N., Zosuls, K. M., & Cabrera, N. J. (2011). African American, White, and Latino fathers' activities with their sons and daughters in early childhood. *Sex Roles, 66*, 53–65.

Lebel, C., & Beaulieu, C. (2011). Longitudinal development of human brain wiring continues from childhood into adulthood. *Journal of Neuroscience, 31*, 10937–10947.

Le Bouc, Y. (2017). Have we finally solved the enigma of the small size of Pygmies? *Annals of Endocrinology, 78*, 83–87.

Lecanuet, J.-P., Granier-Deferre, C., & DeCasper, A. (2005). Are we expecting too much from prenatal sensory experiences? In B. Hopkins & S. P. Johnson (Eds.), *Prenatal development of postnatal functions* (pp. 31–49). Westport, CT: Praeger.

Lecanuet, J.-P., Granier-Deferre, C., Jacquet, A.-Y., Capponi, I., & Ledru, L. (1993). Prenatal discrimination of a male and female voice uttering the same sentence. *Early Development and Parenting, 2*, 217–228.

LeCroy, C. W., & Krysik, J. (2011). Randomized trial of the Healthy Families Arizona home visiting program. *Children and Youth Services Review, 33*, 1761–1766.

LeCuyer, E., & Houck, G. M. (2006). Maternal limit-setting in toddlerhood: Socialization strategies for the development of self-regulation. *Infant Mental Health Journal, 27*, 344–370.

LeCuyer, E. A., Christensen, J. J., Kearney, M. H., & Kitzman, H. J. (2011). African American mothers' self-described discipline strategies with young children. *Issues in Comprehensive Pediatric Nursing, 34*, 144–162.

Lee, C.-Y. S., & Doherty, W. J. (2007). Marital satisfaction and father involvement during the transition to parenthood. *Fathering, 5*, 75–96.

Lee, E. A., Torrance, N., & Olson, D. R. (2001). Young children and the say/mean distinction: Verbatim and paraphrase recognition in narrative and nursery rhyme contexts. *Journal of Child Language, 28*, 531–543.

Lee, E. H., Zhou, Q., Eisenberg, N., & Wang, Y. (2012). Bidirectional relations between temperament and parenting styles in Chinese children. *International Journal of Behavioral Development, 37*, 57–67.

Lee, G. Y., & Kisilevsky, B. S. (2013). Fetuses respond to father's voice but prefer mother's voice after birth. *Developmental Psychobiology, 56*, 1–11.

Lee, H. Y., & Hans, S. L. (2015). Prenatal depression and young low-income mothers' perception of their children from pregnancy through early childhood. *Infant Behavior and Development, 40*, 183–192.

Lee, K. (2011). Impacts of the duration of Head Start enrollment on children's academic outcomes: Moderation effects of family risk factors and earlier outcomes. *Journal of Community Psychology, 39*, 495–507.

Lee, K., Xu, F., Fu, G., Cameron, C. A., & Chen, S. (2001). Taiwan and Mainland Chinese and Canadian children's categorization and evaluation of lie- and truth-telling: A modesty effect. *British Journal of Developmental Psychology, 19*, 525–542.

Lee, K. W. K., Richmond, R., Hu, P., French, L., Shin, J., Bourdon, C., et al. (2015). Prenatal exposure to maternal cigarette smoking and DNA methylation: Epigenome-wide association in a discovery sample of adolescence and replication in an independent cohort at birth through 17 years of age. *Environmental Health Perspectives, 123*, 193–199.

Lee, S. J., Ralston, H. J., Partridge, J. C., & Rosen, M. A. (2005). Fetal pain: A systematic multidisciplinary review of the evidence. *Journal of the American Medical Association, 294*, 947–954.

Lee, Y. (2013). Adolescent motherhood and capital: Interaction effects of race/ethnicity on harsh parenting. *Journal of Community Psychology, 41*, 102–116.

Leeman, J., Crandell, J. L., Lee, A., Bai, J., Sandelowski, M., & Knaff, K. (2016). Daily functioning and the well-being of children with chronic conditions: A meta-analysis. *Research in Nursing & Health, 39*, 229–243.

Leerkes, E. M. (2010). Predictors of maternal sensitivity to infant distress. *Parenting: Science and Practice, 10*, 219–239.

Leet, T., & Flick, L. (2003). Effect of exercise on birth weight. *Clinical Obstetrics and Gynecology, 46*, 423–431.

Lefkovics, E., Baji, I., & Rigó, J. (2014). Impact of maternal depression on pregnancies and on early attachment. *Infant Mental Health Journal, 35*, 354–365.

Legare, C. H., & Gelman, S. A. (2008). Bewitchment, biology, or both: The co-existence of natural and supernatural explanatory frameworks across development. *Cognitive Science, 32*, 607–642.

Legare, C. H., Zhu, L., & Wellman, H. (2013). Examining biological explanations in Chinese preschool children: A cross-cultural comparison. *Journal of Cognition and Culture, 13*, 67–93.

Lehman, M., & Hasselhorn, M. (2012). Rehearsal dynamics in elementary school children. *Journal of Experimental Child Psychology, 111*, 552–560.

Lehman, P. J., & Carl, R. L. (2017). Growing pains: When to be concerned. *Sports Health, 9*, 132–138.

Lehnung, M., Leplow, B., Ekroll, V., Herzog, A., Mehdorn, M., & Ferstl, R. (2003). The role of locomotion in the acquisition and transfer of spatial knowledge in children. *Scandinavian Journal of Psychology, 44*, 79–86.

Lehr, V. T., Zeskind, P. S., Ofenstein, J. P., Cepeda, E., Warrier, I., & Aranda, J. V. (2007). Neonatal facial coding system scores and spectral characteristics of infant crying during newborn circumcision. *Clinical Journal of Pain, 23*, 417–424.

Leibowitz, S., & de Vries, A. L. C. (2016). Gender dysphoria in adolescence. *International Review of Psychiatry, 28*, 21–35.

Leijten, P., Gardner, F., Landau, S., Harris, V., Mann, J., Hutchings, J., et al. (2018). Research review. Harnessing the power of individual participant data in a meta-analysis of the benefits and harms of the Incredible Years parenting program. *Journal of Child Psychology and Psychiatry, 59*, 99–109.

Lejeune, F., Marcus, L., Berne-Audeoud, F., Streri, A., Debillon, T., & Gentaz, E. (2012). Intermanual transfer of shapes in preterm human infants from 33 to 34 + 6 weeks postconceptional age. *Child Development, 83*, 794–800.

LeMare, L., & Audet, K. (2014). Behavior problems in post-institutionalized Romanian adoptees: Explanatory parameters in the adoptive home. *Merrill-Palmer Quarterly, 60*, 245–273.

Lemay, M. (2015, February 26). A letter to my son Jacob on his 5th birthday. Retrieved from www.boston.com/culture/parenting /2015/02/26/a-letter-to-my-son-jacob-on -his-5th-birthday

Lemche, E., Lennertz, I., Orthmann, C., Ari, A., Grote, K., Hafker, J., & Klann-Delius, G. (2003). Emotion-regulatory process in evoked play narratives: Their relation with mental representations and family interactions. *Praxis der Kinderpsychologie und Kinderpsychiatrie, 52*, 156–171.

Lemola, S. (2015). Long-term outcomes of very preterm birth: Mechanisms and interventions. *European Psychologist, 20*, 128–137.

Lenhart, A., Purcell, K., Smith, A., & Zickuhr, K. (2010). *Social media & mobile Internet* use among teens and young adults. Washington, DC: Pew Research Center.

Lereya, S. T., Samara, M., & Wolke, D. (2013). Parenting behavior and the risk of becoming a victim and a bully/victim: A meta-analysis study. *Child Abuse and Neglect, 37,* 1091–1108.

Lerner, R. M. (2015). Preface. In W. F. Overton & P. C. Molenar (Eds.), *Handbook of child psychology and developmental science: Vol. 1. Theory and method* (pp. xv–xxi). Hoboken, NJ: Wiley.

Lerner, R. M., Agans, J. P., DeSouza, L. M., & Hershberg, R. M. (2014). Developmental science in 2025: A predictive review. *Research in Human Development, 11,* 255–272.

Lernout, T., Theeten, H., Hens, N., Braeckman, T., Roelants, M., Hoppenbrouwers, K., & Van Damme, P. (2013). Timeliness of infant vaccination and factors related with delay in Flanders, Belgium. *Vaccine, 32,* 284–289.

Leslie, A. M. (2004). Who's for learning? *Developmental Science, 7,* 417–419.

Lett, D. (1997). *L'enfant des miracles: Enfance et société au Moyen Age (XIIe–XIIIe siecle).* Paris: Aubier.

Levendosky, A. A., Bogat, G. A., Huth-Bocks, A. C., Rosenblum, K., & von Eye, A. (2011). The effect of domestic violence on the stability of attachment from infancy to preschool. *Journal of Clinical Child and Adolescent Psychology, 40,* 398–410.

Leventakou, V., Roumeliotaki, T., Sarri, K., Koutra, K., Kampouri, M., Kyriklaki, A., et al. (2016). Dietary patterns in early childhood and child cognitive and psychomotor development: The Rhea mother–child cohort study in Crete. *British Journal of Nutrition, 115,* 1431–1437.

Leventhal, T., & Brooks-Gunn, J. (2003). Children and youth in neighborhood contexts. *Current Directions in Psychological Science, 12,* 27–31.

Leventhal, T., & Dupéré, V. (2011). Moving to opportunity: Does long-term exposure to "low-poverty" neighborhoods make a difference for adolescents? *Social Science and Medicine, 73,* 737–743.

Leventhal, T., Dupéré, V., & Shuey, E. A. (2015). Children in neighborhoods. In M. H. Bornstein & T. Leventhal (Eds.), *Handbook of child psychology: Vol. 4. Ecological settings and processes* (7th ed., pp. 493–533). Hoboken, NJ: Wiley.

Levin, I., & Bus, A. G. (2003). How is emergent writing based on drawing? Analyses of children's products and their sorting by children and mothers. *Developmental Psychology, 39,* 891–905.

LeVine, R. A., Dixon, S., LeVine, S., Richman, A., Leiderman, P. H., Keefer, C. H., & Brazelton, T. B. (1994). *Child care and culture: Lessons from Africa.* New York: Cambridge University Press.

LeVine, R. A., LeVine, S., Schnell-Anzola, B., Rowe, M. L., & Dexter, E. (2012). *Literacy and mothering: How women's schooling changes the lives of the world's children.* New York: Oxford University Press.

Levs, J. (2015) *All in: How our work-first culture fails dads, families, and businesses—and how we can fix it together.* New York: HarperOne.

Levy, S. R., & Dweck, C. S. (1999). The impact of children's static vs. dynamic conceptions of people on stereotype information. *Child Development, 70,* 1163–1180.

Levy, S. R., Lytle, A., Shin, J. E., & Hughes, J. M. (2016). Understanding and reducing racial and ethnic prejudice among children and adolescents. In T. D. Nelson (Ed.), *Handbook of prejudice, stereotyping, and discrimination* (2nd ed., pp. 455–483). New York: Psychology Press.

Lewis, M. (1995). Embarrassment: The emotion of self-exposure and evaluation. In J. P. Tangney & K. W. Fischer (Eds.), *Self-conscious emotions* (pp. 198–218). New York: Guilford.

Lewis, M. (1998). Emotional competence and development. In D. Pushkar, W. M. Bukowski, A. E. Schwartzman, E. M. Stack, & D. R. White (Eds.), *Improving competence across the lifespan* (pp. 27–36). New York: Plenum.

Lewis, M. (2014). *The rise of consciousness and the development of emotional life.* New York: Guilford.

Lewis, M. (2017). Selfhood. In B. Hopkins, E. Geangu, & S. Linkenauger (Eds.), *Cambridge encyclopedia of child development* (2nd ed., pp. 487–491). New York: Cambridge University Press.

Lewis, M., & Brooks-Gunn, J. (1979). *Social cognition and the acquisition of self.* New York: Plenum.

Lewis, M., & Ramsay, D. (2002). Cortisol response to embarrassment and shame. *Child Development, 73,* 1034–1045.

Lewis, M., & Ramsay, D. (2004). Development of self-recognition, personal pronoun use, and pretend play during the 2nd year. *Child Development, 75,* 1821–1831.

Lewis, M., Ramsay, D. S., & Kawakami, K. (1993). Differences between Japanese infants and Caucasian American infants in behavioral and cortisol response to inoculation. *Child Development, 64,* 1722–1731.

Lewis, M., Sullivan, M. W., & Kim, H. M.-S. (2015). Infant approach and withdrawal in response to a goal blockage: Its antecedent causes and its effect on toddler persistence. *Developmental Psychology, 51,* 1553–1563.

Lew-Williams, C., Pelucchi, B., & Saffran, J. R. (2011). Isolated words enhance statistical language learning in infancy. *Developmental Science, 14,* 1323–1329.

Li, J., Johnson, S. E., Han, W., Andrews, S., Kendall, G., Strazdins, L. & Dockery, A. (2014). Parents' nonstandard work schedules and child well-being: A critical review of the literature. *Journal of Primary Prevention, 35,* 53–73.

Li, P., Legault, J., & Litcofsky, K. A. (2014). Neuroplasticity as a function of second language learning: Anatomical changes in the human brain. *Cortex, 58,* 301–324.

Li, W., Farkas, G., Duncan, G. J., Burchinal, M. R., & Vandell, D. L. (2013). Timing of high-quality child care and cognitive, language, and preacademic development. *Developmental Psychology, 49,* 1440–1451.

Li, X. Q., Zhu, P., Myatt, L., & Sun, K. (2014). Roles of glucocorticoids in human parturition: A controversial fact? *Placenta, 35,* 291–296.

Liben, L. S. (2006). Education for spatial thinking. In K. A. Renninger & I. E. Sigel (Eds.), *Handbook of child psychology: Vol. 4. Child psychology in practice* (6th ed., pp. 197–247). Hoboken, NJ: Wiley.

Liben, L. S. (2009). The road to understanding maps. *Current Directions in Psychological Science, 18,* 310–315.

Liben, L. S., & Bigler, R. S. (2002). The developmental course of gender differentiation: Conceptualizing, measuring, and evaluating constructs and pathways. *Monographs of the Society for Research in Child Development, 67*(2, Serial No. 269).

Liben, L. S., Bigler, R. S., & Krogh, H. R. (2001). Pink and blue collar jobs: Children's judgments of job status and job aspirations in relation to sex of worker. *Journal of Experimental Child Psychology, 79,* 346–363.

Liben, L. S., & Downs, R. M. (1993). Understanding person–space–map relations: Cartographic and developmental perspectives. *Developmental Psychology, 29,* 739–752.

Liben, L. S., Myers, L. J., Christensen, A. E., & Bower, C. A. (2013). Environmental-scale map use in middle childhood: Links to spatial skills, strategies, and gender. *Child Development, 84,* 2047–2063.

Lickliter, R., & Honeycutt, H. (2013). A developmental evolutionary framework for psychology. *Review of General Psychology, 17,* 184–189.

Lidstone, J. S. M., Meins, E., & Fernyhough, C. (2010). The roles of private speech and inner speech in planning during middle childhood: Evidence from a dual task paradigm. *Journal of Experimental Child Psychology, 107,* 438–451.

Lidz, J. (2007). The abstract nature of syntactic representations. In E. Hoff & M. Shatz (Eds.), *Blackwell handbook of language development* (pp. 277–303). Malden, MA: Blackwell.

Lidz, J., Gleitman, H., & Gleitman, L. (2004). Kidz in the 'hood: Syntactic bootstrapping and the mental lexicon. In D. G. Hall & S. R. Waxman (Eds.), *Weaving a lexicon* (pp. 603–636). Cambridge, MA: MIT Press.

Liew, J., Eisenberg, N., Spinrad, T. L., Eggum, N. D., Haugen, R. G., Kupfer, A., et al. (2010). Physiological regulation and fearfulness as predictors of young children's empathy-related reactions. *Social Development, 20,* 111–134.

Li-Grining, C. P. (2007). Effortful control among low-income preschoolers in three cities: Stability, change, and individual differences. *Developmental Psychology, 43,* 208–221.

Lillard, A. S. (2008). *Montessori: The science behind the practice.* New York: Oxford University Press.

Lillard, A. S., Heise, M. J., Richey, E. M., Tong, X., Hart, A., & Bray, P. M. (2017). Montessori preschool elevates and equalizes child outcomes: A longitudinal study. *Frontiers in Psychology, 8,* Art. No. 1783.

Lillard, A. S., Lerner, M. D., Hopkins, E. J., Dore, R. A., Smith, E. D., & Palmquist, C. M. (2013). The impact of pretend play on children's development: A review of the evidence. *Psychological Bulletin, 139,* 1–34.

Lillard, A. S., Nishida, T., Massaro, D., Vaish, A., Ma, L., & McRoberts, G. (2007). Signs of pretense across age and scenario. *Infancy, 11,* 130.

Lillard, A. S., & Peterson, J. (2011). The immediate impact of different types of television on young children's executive function. *Pediatrics, 128,* 644–649.

Lin, L. Y., Cherng, R. J., Chen, Y. J., & Yang, H. N. (2015). Effects of television exposure on developmental skills among young children. *Infant Behavior and Development, 38,* 20–26.

Lin, T.-J., Anderson, R. C., Hummel, J. E., Jadallah, M., Miller, B. W., Nguyen-Jahiel, K., et al. (2012). Children's use of analogy during collaborative reasoning. *Child Development, 83,* 1429–1443.

Lincove, J. A., & Painter, G. (2006). Does the age that children start kindergarten matter? Evidence of long-term educational and social outcomes. *Educational Evaluation and Policy Analysis, 28,* 153–179.

Lind, J. N., Li, R., Perrine, C. G., & Shieve, L. A. (2014). Breastfeeding and later psychosocial development of children at 6 years of age. *Pediatrics, 134,* S36–S41.

Lindholm-Leary, K., & Block, N. (2009). Achievement in predominantly low SES/Hispanic dual language schools. *International Journal of Bilingual Education and Bilingualism, 13,* 43–60.

Lindsey, E. W. (2017). Mutual positive emotion with peers, emotion knowledge, and preschoolers' peer acceptance. *Social Development, 26,* 349–366.

Lindsey, E. W., & Colwell, M. J. (2013). Pretend and physical play: Links to preschoolers' affective social competence. *Merrill-Palmer Quarterly, 59,* 330–360.

Lindsey, E. W., & Mize, J. (2000). Parent–child physical and pretense play: Links to children's social competence. *Merrill-Palmer Quarterly, 46,* 565–591.

Linebarger, D. L., & Piotrowski, J. T. (2010). Structure and strategies in children's educational television: The roles of program type and learning strategies in children's learning. *Child Development, 81,* 1582–1597.

Lingwood, J., Blades, M., Farran, E. K., & Courbois, Y. (2015). The development of wayfinding abilities in children: Learning routes with and without landmarks. *Journal of Environmental Psychology, 41,* 74–80.

Linver, M. R., Martin, A., & Brooks-Gunn, J. (2004). Measuring infants' home environment: The IT-HOME for infants between birth and 12 months in four national data sets. *Parenting: Science and Practice, 4,* 115–137.

Lionetti, F., Pastore, M., & Barone, L. (2015). Attachment in institutionalized children: A review and meta-analysis. *Child Abuse and Neglect, 42,* 135–145.

Lippolis, R., & De Angelis, M. (2016). Proteomics and human diseases. *Journal of Proteomics & Bioinformatics, 9,* 63–74.

Lipton, J. S., & Spelke, E. S. (2003). Origins of number sense: Large-number discrimination in human infants. *Psychological Science, 14,* 396–401.

Liszkowski, U., Carpenter, M., & Tomasello, M. (2007). Pointing out new news, old news, and absent referents at 12 months of age. *Developmental Science, 10,* F1–F7.

Litovsky, R. Y., & Ashmead, D. H. (1997). Development of binaural and spatial hearing in infants and children. In R. H. Gilkey & T. R. Anderson (Eds.), *Binaural and spatial hearing in real and virtual environments* (pp. 571–592). Mahwah, NJ: Erlbaum.

Little, C. A. (2018). Teaching strategies to support the education of gifted learners. In S. I. Pfeiffer (Ed.), *APA handbook of giftedness and talent* (pp. 371–386). Washington, DC: American Psychological Association.

Liu, J., Chen, X., Coplan, R. J., Ding, X., Zarbatany, L., & Ellis, W. (2015). Shyness and unsociability and their relations with adjustment in Chinese and Canadian children. *Journal of Cross-Cultural Psychology, 46,* 371–386.

Liu, J., Chen, X., Zhou, Y., Li, D., Fu, R., & Coplan, R. J. (2017). Relations of shyness-sensitivity and unsociability with adjustment in middle childhood and early adolescence in suburban Chinese children. *International Journal of Behavioral Development, 41,* 681–687.

Liu, L., & Kager, R. (2015). Understanding phonological acquisition through phonetic perception: The influence of exposure and acoustic salience. *Phonological Studies, 18,* 51–58.

Liu, L., & Kager, R. (2016). Perception of a native vowel contrast by Dutch monolingual and bilingual infants: A bilingual perceptual lead. *International Journal of Bilingualism, 20,* 335–345.

Liu, J., Raine, A., Venables, P. H., Dalais, C., & Mednick, S. A. (2003). Malnutrition at age 3 years and lower cognitive ability at age 11 years. *Archives of Paediatric and Adolescent Medicine, 157,* 593–600.

Liu, N., Chen, Y., Yang, X., & Hu, Y. (2017). Do demographic characteristics make differences? Demographic characteristics as moderators in the associations between only child status and cognitive/noncognitive outcomes in China. *Frontiers in Psychology, 8,* Art. No. 423.

Liu, S., Xiao, N. G., Quinn, P. C., Zhu, D., Ge, L., Pascalis, O., & Lee, K. (2015). Asian infants show preference for own-race but not other-race female faces: The role of infant caregiving arrangements. *Frontiers in Psychology, 6,* Art. No. 593.

Lleras, C., & Rangel, C. (2009). Ability grouping practices in elementary school and African American/Hispanic achievement. *American Journal of Education, 115,* 279–304.

Llewellyn, C., & Wardle, J. (2015). Behavioral susceptibility to obesity: Gene–environment interplay in the development of weight. *Physiology & Behavior, 152,* 494–501.

Lloyd, M. E., Doydum, A. O., & Newcombe, N. S. (2009). Memory binding in early childhood: Evidence for a retrieval deficit. *Child Development, 80,* 1321–1328.

Loche, S., Carta, L., Ibba, A., & Guzzetti, C. (2014). Growth hormone treatment in non-growth hormone-deficient children. *Annals of Pediatric Endocrinology & Metabolism, 19,* 1–7.

Loehlin, J. C., & Martin, N. G. (2001). Age changes in personality traits and their heritabilities during the adult years: Evidence from Australian twin registry samples. *Personality and Individual Differences, 30,* 1147–1160.

Loganovskaja, T. K., & Loganovsky, K. N. (1999). EEG, cognitive and psychopathological abnormalities in children irradiated in utero. *International Journal of Psychophysiology, 34,* 213–224.

Loganovsky, K. N., Loganovskaja, T. K., Nechayev, S. Y., Antipchuk, Y. Y., & Bomko, M. A. (2008). Disrupted development of the dominant hemisphere following prenatal irradiation. *Journal of Neuropsychiatry and Clinical Neurosciences, 20,* 274–291.

Lohbeck, A., Grube, D., & Moschner, B. (2017). Academic self-concept and causal attributions for success and failure amongst elementary school children. *International Journal of Early Years Education, 25,* 190–203.

Loman, M. M., & Gunnar, M. R. (2010). Early experience and the development of stress reactivity and regulation in children. *Neuroscience and Biobehavioral Reviews, 34,* 867–876.

Lombardi, C. M., Casey, B. M., Thomson, D., & Nguyen, H. N. (2017). Maternal support of young children's planning and spatial concept learning as predictors of later math (and reading) achievement. *Early Childhood Research Quarterly, 41,* 114–125.

Lombardi, C. M., & Coley, R. L. (2013). Low-income mothers' employment experiences: Prospective links with young children's development. *Family Relations, 62,* 514–528.

Lombardi, C. M., & Coley, R. L. (2014). Early maternal employment and children's school readiness in contemporary families. *Developmental Psychology, 50,* 2071–2084.

Longstaffe, S., Moffatt, M. E., & Whalen, J. C. (2000). Behavioral and self-concept changes after six months of enuresis treatment: A randomized, controlled trial. *Pediatrics, 105,* 935–940.

Lonigan, C. J. (2015). Literacy development. In L. S. Liben & U. Müller (Eds.), *Handbook of child psychology and developmental science: Vol. 2. Cognitive processes* (7th ed., pp. 763–805). Hoboken, NJ: Wiley.

Lonigan, C. J., Purpura, D. J., Wilson, S. B., Walker, J., & Clancy-Menchetti, J. (2013). Evaluating the components of an emergent literacy intervention for preschool children at risk for reading difficulties. *Journal of Experimental Child Psychology, 114,* 111–130.

Looker, D., & Thiessen, V. (2003). *The digital divide in Canadian schools: Factors affecting student access to and use of information technology.* Ottawa: Statistics Canada, Catalogue no. 81-597-X. Retrieved from citeseerx.ist.psu.edu/viewdoc /download?doi=10.1.1.112.2301&rep =rep1&type=pdf

López, A. Nafaji, B., Rogoff, B., & Mejía-Arauz, R. (2012). Collaboration and helpfulness as cultural practices. In J. Valsiner (Ed.), *Handbook of cultural psychology* (pp. 869–884). New York: Oxford University Press.

Lopez, N. V., Schembre, S., Belcher, B. R., O'Connor, S., Maher, J. P., Arbel, R., et al. (2018). Parenting styles, food-related parenting practices, and children's healthy eating: A mediation analysis to examine relationships between parenting and child diet. *Appetite, 128,* 205–213.

Lopomo, A., Burgio, E., & Migliore, L. (2016). Epigenetics of obesity. *Progress in Molecular Biology and Translational Science, 140,* 151–184.

Lopresti, A. L., & Drummond, P. D. (2013). Obesity and psychiatric disorders: Commonalities in dysregulated biological pathways and their implications for treatment. *Progress in Neuro-Psychopharmacology & Biological Psychiatry, 45,* 92–99.

Lora, K. R., Sisson, S. B., DeGrace, B. W., & Morris, A. S. (2014). Frequency of family meals and 6–11-year-old children's social behaviors. *Journal of Family Psychology, 28,* 577–582.

Lorber, M. F., & Egeland, B. (2011). Parenting and infant difficulty: Testing a mutual exacerbation hypothesis to predict early onset conduct problems. *Child Development, 82,* 2006–2020.

Lorenz, K. Z. (1952). *King Solomon's ring.* New York: Crowell.

Louie, V. (2001). Parents' aspirations and investment: The role of social class in the educational experiences of 1.5- and second-generation Chinese Americans. *Harvard Educational Review, 71,* 438–474.

Louis, J., Cannard, C., Bastuji, H., & Challamel, M.-J. (1997). Sleep ontogenesis revisited: A longitudinal 24-hour home polygraphic study on 15 normal infants during the first two years of life. *Sleep, 20,* 323–333.

Lourenço, O. (2003). Making sense of Turiel's dispute with Kohlberg: The case of the child's moral competence. *New Ideas in Psychology, 21,* 43–68.

Lourenço, O. (2012). Piaget and Vygotsky: Many resemblances, and a crucial difference. *New Ideas in Psychology, 30,* 281–295.

Lourenço, O. M. (2016). Developmental stages, Piagetian stages in particular: A critical review. *New Ideas in Psychology, 40,* 123–137.

Love, J. M., Chazan-Cohen, R., & Raikes, H. (2007). Forty years of research knowledge and use: From Head Start to Early Head Start and beyond. In J. L. Aber, S. J. Bishop-Josef, S. M. Jones, K. T. McLearn, & D. Phillips (Eds.), *Child development and social policy: Knowledge for action* (pp. 79–95). Washington, DC: American Psychological Association.

Love, J. M., Kisker, E. E., Ross, C., Raikes, H., Constantine, J., Boller, K., & Brooks-Gunn, J. (2005). The effectiveness of early Head Start for 3-year-old children and their parents: Lessons for policy and programs. *Developmental Psychology, 41,* 885–901.

Low, M., Farrell, A., Biggs, B., & Pasricha, S. (2013). Effects of daily iron supplementation in primary-school-aged children: Systematic review and meta-analysis of randomized controlled trials. *Canadian Medical Association Journal, 185,* E791–E802.

Low, S. M., & Stocker, C. (2012). Family functioning and children's adjustment: Associations among parents' depressed mood, marital hostility, parent–child hostility, and children's adjustment. *Journal of Family Psychology, 19,* 394–403.

Lowis, G. W., & McCaffery, P. G. (2004). Sociological factors affecting the medicalization of midwifery. In E. van Teijlingen, G. Lowis, P. McCaffery, & M. Porter (Eds.), *Midwifery and the medicalization of childbirth: Comparative perspectives* (pp. 5–41). New York: Nova Science.

Lozada, M., & Carro, N. (2016). Embodied action improves cognition in children: Evidence from a study based on Piagetian conservation tasks. *Frontiers in Psychology, 7,* Art. No. 393.

Lubart, T. I., Georgsdottir, A., & Besançon, M. (2009). The nature of creative giftedness and talent. In T. Balchin, B. Hymer, & D. J. Matthews (Eds.), *The Routledge international companion to gifted education* (pp. 42–49). New York: Routledge.

Luby, J., Belden, A., Sullivan, J., Hayen, R., McCadney, A., & Spitznagel, E. (2009). Shame and guilt in preschool depression: Evidence for elevations in self-conscious emotions in depression as early as age 3. *Journal of Child Psychology and Psychiatry, 50,* 1156–1166.

Luby, J. L., Belden, A. C., Whalen, D., Harms, M. P., & Barch, D. M. (2016). Breastfeeding and childhood IQ: The mediating role of gray matter volume. *Journal of the American Academy of Child and Adolescent Psychiatry, 55,* 367–375.

Lucassen, N., Tharner, A., Van IJzendoorn, M. H., Bakermans-Kranenburg, M. J., Volling, B. L., Verhulst, F. C., et al. (2011). The association between paternal sensitivity and infant–father attachment security: A meta-analysis of three decades of research. *Journal of Family Psychology, 25,* 986–992.

Lucas-Thompson, R. G., & Clarke-Stewart, K. A. (2007). Forecasting friendship: How marital quality, maternal mood, and attachment security are linked to children's peer relationships. *Journal of Applied Developmental Psychology, 28,* 499–514.

Lucas-Thompson, R. G., Goldberg, W. A., & Prause, J. (2010). Maternal work early in the lives of children and its distal associations with achievement and behavior problems: A meta-analysis. *Psychological Bulletin, 136,* 915–942.

Luche, C. D., Floccia, C., Granjon, L., & Nazzi, T. (2017). Infants' first words are not phonetically specified: Own name recognition in British English-learning 5-month-olds. *Infancy, 22,* 362–388.

Luecken, L. J., Lin, B., Coburn, S. S., MacKinnon, D. P., Gonzales, N. A., & Crnic, K. A. (2013). Prenatal stress, partner support, and infant cortisol reactivity in low-income Mexican American families. *Psychoneuroendocrinology, 38,* 3092–3101.

Luhmann, M., Hofmann, W., Eid, M., & Lucas, R. E. (2012). Subjective well-being and adaptation to life events: A meta-analysis. *Journal of Personality and Social Psychology, 102,* 592–615.

Luijk, M. P. C. M., Tharner, A., van IJzendoorn, M. H., Bakermans-Kranenburg, M. J., Jaddoe, W. V., & Hofman, A. (2011). The association between parenting and attachment is moderated by a polymorphism in the mineralocorticoid receptor gene: Evidence for differential susceptibility. *Biological Psychology, 88,* 37–40.

Lukowski, A. F., Koss, M., Burden, M. J., Jonides, J., Nelson, C. A., Kaciroti, N., et al. (2010). Iron deficiency in infancy and neurocognitive functioning at 19 years: Evidence of long-term deficits in executive function and recognition memory. *Nutritional Neuroscience, 13,* 54–70.

Lukowski, A., Wiebe, S. A., & Bauer, P. J. (2009). Going beyond the specifics: Generalization of single actions, but not temporal order, at 9 months. *Infant Behavior and Development, 32,* 331–335.

Lundberg, S., & Pollak, R. A. (2015). The evolving role of marriage: 1950–2010. *Future of Children, 25,* 29–50.

Luo, L., Ma, X., Zhao, W., Xu, L., Becker, B., & Kendrick, K. M. (2015). Neural systems and hormones mediating attraction to infant and child faces. *Frontiers in Psychology, 6,* Art. No. 970.

Lussier, A. A., Islam, S. A., & Kobor, M. S. (2018). Epigenetics and genetics of development. In R. Gibb & B. Kolb (Eds.), *Neurobiology of brain and behavioral development* (pp. 153–210). San Diego, CA: Elsevier.

Lussier, A. A., Morin, A. M., Macisaac, J. L., Salmon, J., Weinberg, J., Reynolds, J. N., et al. (2018). DNA methylation as a predictor of fetal alcohol spectrum disorder. *Clinical Epigenetics, 10,* 5.

Lussier, P., Corrado, R., & Tzoumakis, S. (2012). Gender differences in physical aggression and associated developmental correlates in a sample of Canadian preschoolers. *Behavioral Sciences and the Law, 30,* 643–671.

Lustig, C., & Lin, Z. (2016). Memory: Behavior and neural basis. In K. W. Schaie & S. L. Willis (Eds.), *Handbook of the psychology of aging* (8th ed., pp. 147–163). Waltham, MA: Elsevier.

Luthar, S. S., & Barkin, S. H. (2012). Are affluent youth truly "at risk"? Vulnerability and resilience across diverse samples. *Development and Psychopathology, 24,* 429–449.

Luthar, S. S., Barkin, S., & Crossman, E. J. (2013). "I can, therefore I must": Fragility in the upper-middle classes. *Development and Psychopathology, 25,* 1529–1549.

Luthar, S. S., Crossman, E. J., & Small, P. J. (2015). Resilience and adversity. In M. E. Lamb & R. M. Lerner (Eds.), *Handbook of child psychology and developmental science: Vol. 3. Socioemotional processes* (pp. 247–286). Hoboken, NJ: Wiley.

Luthar, S. S., & Latendresse, S. J. (2005). Children of the affluent: Challenges to well-being. *Current Directions in Psychological Science, 14,* 49–53.

Lynch, R. J., Kistner, J. A., Stephens, H. F., & David-Ferdon, C. (2016). Positively biased self-perceptions of peer acceptance and subtypes of aggression in children. *Aggressive Behavior, 42,* 82–96.

Lyon, T. D., & Flavell, J. H. (1994). Young children's understanding of "remember" and "forget." *Child Development, 65,* 1357–1371.

Lyster, R., & Genesee, F. (2012). Immersion education. In Carol A. Chapelle (Ed.), *Encyclopedia of Applied Linguistics* (pp. 2608–2614). Hoboken, NJ: Wiley.

Lytton, H., & Gallagher, L. (2002). Parenting twins and the genetics of parenting. In M. H. Bornstein (Ed.), *Handbook of parenting: Vol. 1. Children and parenting* (pp. 227–253). Mahwah, NJ: Erlbaum.

M

Ma, F., Xu, F., Heyman, G. D., & Lee, K. (2011). Chinese children's evaluations of white lies: Weighing the consequences for recipients. *Journal of Experimental Child Psychology, 108,* 308–321.

Ma, W., Golinkoff, R. M., Hirsh-Pasek, K., McDonough, C., & Tardif, T. (2009). Imagine that! Imageability predicts the age of acquisition of verbs in Chinese children. *Journal of Child Language, 36,* 405–423.

Ma, W., Golinkoff, R. M., Houston, D., & Hirsh-Pasek, K. (2011). Word learning in infant- and adult-directed speech. *Language Learning and Development, 7,* 209–225.

Maas, F. K. (2008). Children's understanding of promising, lying, and false belief. *Journal of General Psychology, 13,* 301–321.

Maccarrone, M., Guzmán, M., Mackie, K., Dherty, P., & Harkany, T. (2014). Programming of neural cells by (endo) cannabinoids: From physiological rules to emerging therapies. *Nature Reviews Neuroscience, 15,* 786–801.

Maccoby, E. E. (1998). *The two sexes: Growing up apart, coming together.* Cambridge, MA: Belknap/Harvard University Press.

Maccoby, E. E. (2002). Gender and group process: A developmental perspective. *Current Directions in Psychological Science, 11,* 54–58.

Macdonald, J. A., Beauchamp, M. H., Crigan, J. A., & Anderson, P. J. (2014). Age-related differences in inhibitory control in the early school years. *Child Neuropsychology, 20,* 509–526.

MacDorman, M. F., & Gregory, E. C. W. (2015). Fetal and perinatal mortality: United States, 2013. *National Vital Statistics Reports, 64*(8). Retrieved from www.cdc.gov/nchs/data/nvsr/nvsr64/nvsr64_08.pdf

MacKenzie, M. J., Bosk, E., & Zeanah, C. H. (2017). Separating families at the border—consequences for children's health and well-being. *New England Journal of Medicine, 376,* 2314–2315.

MacKenzie, M. J., Nicklas, E., Waldfogel, J., & Brooks-Gunn, J. (2013). Spanking and child development across the first decade of life. *Pediatrics, 132,* e1118–1125.

Mackey, K., Arnold, M. L., & Pratt, M. W. (2001). Adolescents' stories of decision making in more and less authoritative families: Representing the voices of parents in narrative. *Journal of Adolescent Research, 16,* 243–268.

Mackie, S., Show, P., Lenroot, R., Pierson, R., Greenstein, D. K., & Nugent, T. F., III. (2007). Cerebellar development and clinical outcome in attention deficit hyperactivity disorder. *American Journal of Psychiatry, 164,* 647–655.

MacWhinney, B. (2005). Language development. In M. H. Bornstein & M. E. Lamb (Eds.), *Developmental science: An advanced textbook* (5th ed., pp. 359–387). Mahwah, NJ: Erlbaum.

MacWhinney, B. (2015). Language development. In L. S. Liben & U. Müller (Eds.), *Handbook of child psychology and developmental science: Vol. 2. Cognitive processes* (7th ed., pp. 296–338). Hoboken, NJ: Wiley.

Macy, M. L., Butchart, A. T., Singer, D C., Gebremariam, A., Clark, S. J., & Davis, M. M. (2015). Looking back on rear-facing car seats: Surveying U.S. parents in 2011 and 2013. *Academic Pediatrics, 15,* 526–533.

Madigan, S., Bakermans-Kranenburg, M. J., van IJzendoorn, M. H., Moran, G., Pederson, D. R., & Benoit, D. (2006). Unresolved states of mind, anomalous parental behavior, and disorganized attachment: A review and meta-analysis of a transmission gap. *Attachment and Human Development, 8,* 89–111.

Madole, K. L., Oakes, L. M., & Rakison, D. H. (2011). Information-processing approaches to infants' developing representation of dynamic features. In L. M. Oakes, C. H. Cashon, M. Casasola, & D. Rakison (Eds.), *Infant perception and cognition* (153–178). New York: Oxford University Press.

Madon, S., Willard, J., Guyll, M., & Scherr, K. C. (2011). Self-fulfilling prophecies: Mechanisms, power, and links to social problems. *Social and Personality Psychology Compass, 5/8,* 578–590.

Maglione, M. A., Das, L., Raaen, L., Smith, A., Chari, R., Newberry, S., et al. (2014). Safety of vaccines used for routine immunization of U.S. children: A systematic review. *Pediatrics, 134,* 325–337.

Maguire, D., Taylor, S., Armstrong, K., Shaffer-Hudkins, E., Germain, A. M., Brooks, S. S., & Cline, G. J. (2016). Long-term outcomes of infants with neonatal abstinence syndrome. *Neonatal Network, 35,* 277–286.

Main, M., & Goldwyn, R. (1998). *Adult attachment classification system.* London: University College.

Main, M., & Solomon, J. (1990). Procedures for identifying infants as disorganized/disoriented during the Ainsworth Strange Situation. In M. Greenberg, D. Cicchetti, & M. Cummings (Eds.), *Attachment in the preschool years: Theory, research, and intervention* (pp. 121–160). Chicago: University of Chicago Press.

Majdandĉzić, M., & van den Boom, D. C. (2007). Multimethod longitudinal assessment of temperament in early childhood. *Journal of Personality, 75,* 121–167.

Majnemer, A., & Barr, R. G. (2005). Influence of supine sleep positioning on early motor milestone acquisition. *Developmental Medicine and Child Neurology, 47,* 370–376.

Malatesta, C. Z., Grigoryev, P., Lamb, C., Albin, M., & Culver, C. (1986). Emotion socialization and expressive development in preterm and full-term infants. *Child Development, 57,* 316–330.

Malina, R. M., & Bouchard, C. (1991). *Growth, maturation, and physical activity.* Champaign, IL: Human Kinetics.

Mandal, C., Halder, D., Jung, K. H., & Chai, Y. G. (2017). Gestational alcohol exposure altered DNA methylation status in the developing fetus. *International Journal of Molecular Sciences, 18*(7), 1386.

Mandara, J., Varner, F., Greene, N., & Richman, S. (2009). Intergenerational family predictors of the Black–White achievement gap. *Journal of Educational Psychology, 101,* 867–878.

Mandler, J. M. (2004). Thought before language. *Trends in Cognitive Sciences, 8,* 508–513.

Mandler, J. M., & McDonough, L. (1996). Drinking and driving don't mix: Inductive generalization in infancy. *Cognition, 59,* 307–335.

Mangelsdorf, S. C., Schoppe, S. J., & Buur, H. (2000). The meaning of parental reports: A contextual approach to the study of temperament and behavior problems. In V. J. Molfese & D. L. Molfese (Eds.), *Temperament and personality across the life span* (pp. 121–140). Mahwah, NJ: Erlbaum.

Maratsos, M. (2000). More overregularizations after all: New data and discussion on Marcus, Pinker, Ullman, Hollander, Rosen, & Xu. *Journal of Child Language, 27,* 183–212.

Marcon, R. A. (1999). Positive relationships between parent–school involvement and public school inner-city preschoolers' development and academic performance. *School Psychology Review, 28,* 395–412.

Marcovitch, S., O'Brien, M., Calkins, S. D., Leerkes, E. M., Weaver, J. M., & Levine, D. W. (2015). A longitudinal assessment of the relation between executive function and theory of mind at 3, 4, and 5 years. *Cognitive Development, 33,* 40–55.

Marcus, G. F., Fernandes, K. J., & Johnson, S. P. (2012). The role of association in early word learning. *Frontiers in Developmental Psychology, 3,* 283.

Mares, M.-L., & Pan, Z. (2013). Effects of Sesame Street: A meta-analysis of children's learning in 15 countries. *Journal of Applied Developmental Psychology, 34,* 140–151.

Marey-Sarwan, I., Keller, H., & Otto, H. (2016). Stay close to me: Stranger anxiety and maternal beliefs about children's socio-emotional development among Bedouins in the unrecognized villages in the Naqab. *Journal of Cross-Cultural Psychology, 47,* 319–332.

Marian, V., Shook, A., & Schroeder, S. R. (2013). Bilingual two-way immersion programs benefit academic achievement. *Bilingual Research Journal, 36,* 167–186.

Marin, M. M., Rapisardi, G., & Tani, F. (2015). Two-day-old newborn infants recognize their mother by her axillary odour. *Acta Paediatrica, 104,* 237–240.

Markant, J. C., & Thomas, K. M. (2013). Postnatal brain development. In P. D. Zelazo (Ed.), *Oxford handbook of developmental psychology: Vol. 1. Body and mind* (pp. 129–163). New York: Oxford University Press.

Markman, E. M. (1992). Constraints on word learning: Speculations about their nature, origins, and domain specificity. In M. R. Gunnar & M. P. Maratsos (Eds.), *Minnesota Symposia on Child Psychology* (Vol. 25, pp. 59–101). Hillsdale, NJ: Erlbaum.

Markunas, C. A., Xu, Z., Harlid, S., Wade, P. A., Lie, R. T., Taylor, J. A., & Wilcox, A. J. (2014). Identification of DNA methylation changes in newborns related to maternal smoking during pregnancy. *Environmental Health Perspectives, 10,* 1147–1153.

Marlier, L., & Schaal, B. (2005). Human newborns prefer human milk: Conspecific milk odor is attractive without postnatal exposure. *Child Development, 76,* 155–168.

Marom, T., Tan, A., Wilkinson, G. S., Pierson, K. S., Freeman, J. L., & Chonmaitree, T. (2014). Trends in otitis media-related health care utilization in the United States, 2001–2011. *JAMA Pediatrics, 168,* 68–75.

Marsee, M. A., & Frick, P. J. (2010). Callous-unemotional traits and aggression in youth. In W. F. Arsenio & E. A. Lemerise (Eds.), *Emotions, aggression, and morality in children: Bridging development and psychopathology* (pp. 137–156). Washington, DC: American Psychological Association.

Marsh, H. W. (1990). The structure of academic self-concept: The Marsh/Shavelson model. *Journal of Educational Psychology, 82,* 623–636.

Marsh, H. W., & Ayotte, V. (2003). Do multiple dimensions of self-concept become more differentiated with age? The differential distinctiveness hypothesis. *Journal of Educational Psychology, 95,* 687–706.

Marsh, H. W., Craven, R., & Debus, R. (1998). Structure, stability, and development of young children's self-concepts: A multicohort–multioccasion study. *Child Development, 69,* 1030–1053.

Marsh, H. W., Ellis, L. A., & Craven, R. G. (2002). How do preschool children feel about themselves? Unraveling measurement and multidimensional self-concept structure. *Developmental Psychology, 38,* 376–393.

Marsh, H. W., Gerlach, E., Trautwein, U., Lüdtke, O., & Brettschneider, W.-D. (2007). Longitudinal study of preadolescent sport self-concept and performance: Reciprocal effects and causal ordering. *Child Development, 78,* 1640–1656.

Marsh, H. W., & Kleitman, S. (2005). Consequences of employment during high school: Character building, subversion of academic goals, or a threshold? *American Educational Research Journal, 42,* 331–369.

Marshall, P. J., & Meltzoff, A. N. (2014). Neural mirroring mechanisms and imitation in human infants. *Philosophical Transactions of the Royal Society B, 369,* 20130620.

Marshall-Baker, A., Lickliter, R., & Cooper, R. P. (1998). Prolonged exposure to a visual pattern may promote behavioral organization in preterm infants. *Journal of Perinatal and Neonatal Nursing, 12,* 50–62.

Martin, A., Onishi, K. H., & Vouloumanos, A. (2012). Understanding the abstract role of speech in communication at 12 months. *Cognition, 123,* 50–60.

Martin, A., Razza, R. A., & Brooks-Gunn, J. (2012). Specifying the links between household chaos and preschool children's development. *Early Child Development and Care, 182,* 1247–1263.

Martin, C. L., Andrews, N. C. Z., England, D. E., Zosuls, K., & Ruble, D. N. (2017). A dual identity approach for conceptualizing and measuring children's gender identity. *Child Development, 88,* 167–182.

Martin, C. L., Cook, R. E., & Andrews, N. C. Z. (2017). Reviving androgyny: A modern day perspective on flexibility of gender identity and behavior. *Sex Roles, 76,* 592–603.

Martin, C. L., & Fabes, R. A. (2001). The stability and consequences of young children's same-sex peer interactions. *Developmental Psychology, 37,* 431–446.

Martin, C. L., Fabes, R. A., Hanish, L., Leonard, S., & Dinella, L. M. (2011). Experienced and expected similarity to same-gender peers: Moving toward a comprehensive model of gender segregation. *Sex Roles, 65,* 421–434.

Martin, C. L., & Halverson, C. F. (1987). The role of cognition in sex role acquisition. In D. B. Carter (Ed.), *Current conceptions of sex roles and sex typing: Theory and research* (pp. 123–137). New York: Praeger.

Martin, C. L., Kornienko, O., Schaefer, D. R., Hanish, L. D., Fabes, R. A., & Goble, P. (2013). The role of sex of peers and gender-typed activities in young children's peer affiliative networks: A longitudinal analysis of selection and influence. *Child Development, 84,* 921–937.

Martin, C. L., & Ruble, D. (2004). Children's search for gender cues: Cognitive perspectives on gender development. *Current Directions in Psychological Science, 13,* 67–70.

Martin, C. L., Ruble, D. N., & Szkrybalo, J. (2002). Cognitive theories of early gender development. *Psychological Bulletin, 128,* 903–933.

Martin, E. K., & Silverstone, P. H. (2013). How much child sexual abuse is "below the surface," and how can we help adults identify it early? *Frontiers in Psychiatry, 4,* 1–10.

Martin, J. A., Hamilton, B. E., Osterman, J. K., Driscoll, A. K., & Mathews, T. J. (2017). *Births: Final data for 2015. National Vital Statistics Reports, 66*(1). Retrieved from www.cdc.gov/nchs/data/nvsr/nvsr66/nvsr66_01.pdf

Martin, J. A., Hamilton, B. E., Osterman, M. J. K., Driscoll, A. K., & Drake, P. (2018). Births: Final data for 2017. *National Vital Statistics Reports, 67*(8). Retrieved from www.cdc.gov/nchs/data/nvsr/nvsr67/nvsr67_08-508.pdf

Martin, K., Bremner, A., Salmon, J., Rosenberg, M., & Giles-Corti, B. (2012). School and individual-level characteristics are associated with children's moderate to vigorous-intensity physical activity during school recess. *Australian and New Zealand Journal of Public Health, 36,* 469–477.

Martinez-Frias, M. L., Bermejo, E., Rodríguez-Pinilla, E., & Frías, J. L. (2004). Risk for congenital anomalies associated with different sporadic and daily doses of alcohol consumption during pregnancy: A case-control study. *Birth Defects Research, Part A, Clinical and Molecular Teratology, 70,* 194–200.

Martinot, D., Bagès, C., & Désert, M. (2012). French children's awareness of gender stereotypes about mathematics and reading: When girls improve their reputation in math. *Sex Roles, 66,* 210–219.

Martins, N., & Harrison, K. (2012). Racial and gender differences in the relationship between children's television use and self-esteem: A longitudinal panel study. *Communication Research, 39,* 338–357.

Martlew, M., & Connolly, K. J. (1996). Human figure drawings by schooled and unschooled children in Papua New Guinea. *Child Development, 67,* 2743–2762.

Marzolf, D. P., & DeLoache, J. S. (1994). Transfer in young children's understanding of spatial representations. *Child Development, 65,* 1–15.

Masataka, N. (1996). Perception of motherese in a signed language by 6-month-old deaf infants. *Developmental Psychology, 32,* 874–879.

Mascaro, J. S., Rentscher, K. E., Hackett, P. D., Mehl, M. R., & Rilling, J. K. (2017). Child gender influences paternal behavior, language, and brain function. *Behavioral Neuroscience, 13,* 262–273.

Mascolo, M. F., & Fischer, K. W. (2007). The codevelopment of self and sociomoral emotions during the toddler years. In C. A. Brownell & C. B. Kopp (Eds.), *Socioemotional development in the toddler years: Transitions and transformations* (pp. 66–99). New York: Guilford.

Mascolo, M. F., & Fischer, K. W. (2015). Dynamic development of thinking, feeling, and acting. In W. F. Overton & P. C. M. Molenar (Eds.), *Handbook of child psychology and developmental science:*

Vol. 1. Theory and method (7th ed., pp. 113–161). Hoboken, NJ: Wiley.

Mash, C., & Bornstein, M., H. (2012). 5-month-olds' categorization of novel objects: Task and measure dependence. *Infancy, 17,* 179–197.

Masten, A. S. (2013). Risk and resilience in development. In P. D. Zelazo (Ed.), *Oxford handbook of developmental psychology: Vol. 2. Self and other* (pp. 579–607). New York: Oxford University Press.

Masten, A. S. (2014). Global perspectives on resilience in children and youth. *Child Development, 85,* 6–20.

Masten, A. S. (2016). Resilience in developing systems: The promise of integrated approaches. *European Journal of Developmental Psychology, 13,* 297–312.

Masten, A. S. (2018). Resilience theory and research on children and families: Past, present, and future. *Journal of Family Theory & Review, 10,* 12–31.

Masten, A. S., & Cicchetti, D. (2010). Developmental cascades. *Development and Psychopathology, 22,* 491–495.

Masten, A. S., Narayan, A. J., Silverman, W. K., & Osofsky, J. D. (2015). Children in war and disaster. In M. H. Bornstein & T. Leventhal (Eds.), *Handbook of child psychology and developmental science: Vol. 4. Ecological settings and processes* (7th ed., pp. 704– 745). Hoboken, NJ: Wiley.

Mastropieri, D., & Turkewitz, G. (1999). Prenatal experience and neonatal responsiveness to vocal expressions of emotion. *Developmental Psychobiology, 35,* 204–214.

Mastropieri, M. A., Scruggs, T. E., Guckert, M., Thompson, C. C., & Weiss, M. P. (2013). Inclusion and learning disabilities: Will the past be prologue? In J. P. Bakken, F. E. Oblakor, & A. Rotatori (Eds.), *Advances in special education* (Vol. 25, pp. 1–17). Bingley, UK: Emerald Group Publishing.

Masur, E. F., Flynn, V., & Olson, J. (2015). The presence of background television during young children's play in American homes. *Journal of Children and Media, 9,* 349–367.

Masur, E. F., Flynn, V., & Olson, J. (2016). Infants' background television exposure during play: Negative associations to vocabulary acquisition. *First Language, 36,* 109–123.

Masur, E. F., & Rodemaker, J. E. (1999). Mothers' and infants' spontaneous vocal, verbal, and action imitation during the second year. *Merrill-Palmer Quarterly, 45,* 392–412.

Mather, M. (2010, May). *U.S. children in single-mother families* (PRB Data Brief). Washington, DC: Population Reference Bureau.

Mathewson, K. J., Chow, C. H. T., Dobson, K. G., Pope, E. I., Schmidt, L. A., & Van Lieshout, R. J. (2017). Mental health of extremely low birth weight survivors: A systematic review and meta-analysis. *Psychological Bulletin, 143,* 347–383.

Matthews, H. (2014, January 14). A billion dollar boost for child care and early learning. CLASP: *Policy Solutions That Work for Low-Income People.* Retrieved from https://www.clasp.org/blog/billion-dollar-boost-child-care-and-early-learning

Mattson, S. N., Crocker, N., & Nguyen, T. T. (2012). Fetal alcohol spectrum disorders: Neuropsychological and behavioral features. *Neuropsychological Review, 21,* 81–101.

Maurer, D., & Lewis, T. (2013). Human visual plasticity: Lessons from children treated for congenital cataracts. In J. K. E. Steeves &

L. R. Harris (Eds.), *Plasticity in sensory systems* (pp. 75–93). New York: Cambridge University Press.

Mayberry, R. I. (2010). Early language acquisition and adult language ability: What sign language reveals about the critical period for language. In M. Marshark & P. E. Spencer (Eds.), *Oxford handbook of deaf studies, language, and education* (Vol. 2, pp. 281–291). New York: Oxford University Press.

Mayeux, L., & Cillessen, A. H. N. (2003). Development of social problem solving in early childhood: Stability, change, and associations with social competence. *Journal of Genetic Psychology, 164,* 153–173.

Mayeux, L., Houser, J. J., & Dyches, K. D. (2011). Social acceptance and popularity: Two distinct forms of peer status. In A. H. N. Cillessen, D. Schwartz, & L. Mayeux (Eds.), *Popularity in the peer system* (pp. 79–102). New York: Guilford.

Maynard, A. E. (2002). Cultural teaching: The development of teaching skills in Maya sibling interactions. *Child Development, 73,* 969–982.

Maynard, A. E., & Greenfield, P. M. (2003). Implicit cognitive development in cultural tools and children: Lessons from Maya Mexico. *Cognitive Development, 18,* 489–510.

Mazoyer, B., Zago, L., Jobard, G., Crivello, F., Joliot, M., Perchey, G., et al. (2014). Gaussian mixture modeling of hemispheric lateralization for language in a large sample of healthy individuals balanced for handedness. *PLOS ONE, 9*(6), e101165.

Mazul, M. C., Salm Ward, T. C., & Ngui, E. M. J. (2017). Anatomy of good prenatal care: Perspectives of low income African-American women on barriers and facilitators to prenatal care. *Journal of Racial and Ethnic Health Disparities, 4,* 79–86.

Mazumdar, M., Bellinger, D. C., Gregas, M., Abanilla, K., Bacic, J., & Needleman, H. L. (2011). Low-level environmental lead exposure in childhood and adult intellectual function: A follow-up study. *Environmental Health, 10,* 24.

Mbarek, H., Steinberg, S., Nyholt, D. R., Gordon, S. D., Miller, M. B., McRae, A. F., et al. (2016). Identification of common genetic variants influencing spontaneous dizygotic twinning and female fertility. *American Journal of Human Genetics, 98,* 898–908.

McAlister, A. R., & Peterson, C. C. (2013). Siblings, theory of mind, and executive functioning in children aged 3–6 years: New longitudinal evidence. *Child Development, 84,* 1442–1458.

McBride-Chang, C., Tardif, T., Cho, J. R., Shu, H. U. A., Fletcher, P., Stokes, S. F., et al. (2008). What's in a word? Morphological awareness and vocabulary knowledge in three languages. *Applied Psycholinguistics, 29,* 437–462.

McCabe, A. (1997). Developmental and cross-cultural aspects of children's narration. In M. Bamberg (Ed.), *Narrative development: Six approaches* (pp. 137–174). Mahwah, NJ: Erlbaum.

McCabe, A., Tamis-LeMonda, C. S., Bornstein, M. H., Cates, C. B., Golinkoff, R., Guerra, A. W., et al. (2013). Multilingual children: Beyond myths and toward best practices. *Society for Research in Child Development Social Policy Report of the Society for Research in Child Development, 27*(4).

McCartney, K., Dearing, E., Taylor, B., & Bub, K. (2007). Quality child care supports the

achievement of low-income children: Direct and indirect pathways through caregiving and the home environment. *Journal of Applied Developmental Psychology, 28,* 411–426.

McCarton, C. (1998). Behavioral outcomes in low birth weight infants. *Pediatrics, 102,* 1293–1297.

McCarty, M. E., & Ashmead, D. H. (1999). Visual control of reaching and grasping in infants. *Developmental Psychology, 35,* 620–631.

McCarty, M. E., & Keen, R. (2005). Facilitating problem-solving performance among 9- and 12-month-old infants. *Journal of Cognition and Development, 6,* 209–228.

McClure, E. R., Chentsova-Dutton, Y. E., Barr, R. F., Holochwost, S. J., & Parrott, W. G. (2015). "FaceTime doesn't count": Video chat as an exception to media restrictions for infants and toddlers. *International Journal of Child–Computer Interaction, 6,* 1–6.

McColgan, K. L., & McCormack, T. (2008). Searching and planning: Young children's reasoning about past and future event sequences. *Child Development, 79,* 1477–1479.

McCormack, S. E., Cousminer, D. L., Chesi, A., Mitchell, J. A., Roy, S. M., Kalkwarf, H. J., et al. (2017). Association between linear growth and bone accrual in a diverse cohort of children and adolescents. *JAMA Pediatrics, 171*(9), e171769.

McCormack, T., & Atance, C. M. (2011). Planning in young children: A review and synthesis. *Developmental Review, 31,* 1–31.

McCormick, M. C., Brooks-Gunn, J., Buka, S. L., Goldman, J., Yu, J., Salganik, M., Scott, D. T., et al. (2006). Early intervention in low birth weight premature infants: Results at 18 years of age for the Infant Health and Development Program. *Pediatrics, 117,* 771–780.

McCormick, M. P., O'Connor, E. E., & Horn, E. P. (2017). Can teacher–child relationships alter the effects of early socioeconomic status on achievement in middle childhood? *Journal of School Psychology, 64,* 76–92.

McCune, L. (1993). The development of play as the development of consciousness. In M. H. Bornstein & A. O'Reilly (Eds.), *New directions for child development* (No. 59, pp. 67–79). San Francisco: Jossey-Bass.

McDonald, K. L., & Asher, S. R. (2018). Peer acceptance, peer rejection, and popularity: Social-cognitive and behavioral perspectives. In W. M. Bukowski, B. Laursen, & K. H. Rubin (Eds.), *Handbook of peer interactions, relationships, and groups* (pp. 429–446). New York: Guilford.

McDonald, K. L., Malti, T., Killen, M., & Rubin, K. (2014). Best friends' discussion of social dilemmas. *Journal of Youth and Adolescence, 43,* 233–244.

McDonough, C., Song, L., Hirsh-Pasek, K., & Golinkoff, R. M. (2011). An image is worth a thousand words: Why nouns tend to dominate verbs in early word learning. *Developmental Science, 14,* 181–189.

McDonough, L. (1999). Early declarative memory for location. *British Journal of Developmental Psychology, 17,* 381–402.

McDowell, D. J., & Parke, R. D. (2000). Differential knowledge of display rules for positive and negative emotions: Influences from parents, influences on peers. *Social Development, 9,* 415–432.

McElwain, N. L., & Booth-LaForce, C. (2006). Maternal sensitivity to infant distress and nondistress as predictors of infant–mother attachment security. *Journal of Family Psychology, 20,* 247–255.

McFarland-Piazza, L., Hazen, N., Jacobvitz, D., & Boyd-Soisson, E. (2012). The development of father–child attachment: Associations between adult attachment representations, recollections of childhood experiences and caregiving. *Early Child Development and Care, 182,* 701–721.

McGee, L. M., & Richgels, D. J. (2004). *Literacy's beginnings: Supporting young readers and writers* (4th ed.). Boston: Allyn and Bacon.

McGee, L. M., & Richgels, D. J. (2012). *Literacy's beginnings: Supporting young readers and writers* (6th ed.). Boston: Allyn and Bacon.

McGillion, M., Herbert, J. S., Pine, J., Vihman, M., dePaolis, R., Keren-Portnoy, T., & Matthews, D. (2017). What paves the way to conventional language? The predictive value of babble, pointing, and socioeconomic status. *Child Development, 88,* 156–166.

McGonigle-Chalmers, M., Slater, H., & Smith, A. (2014). Rethinking private speech in preschoolers: The effects of social presence. *Developmental Psychology, 50,* 829–836.

McGrath, S. K., & Kennell, J. H. (2008). A randomized controlled trial of continuous labor support for middle-class couples: Effect on cesarean delivery rates. *Birth: Issues in Perinatal Care, 35,* 9–97.

McHale, S. M., Updegraff, K. A., Helms-Erikson, H., & Crouter, A. C. (2001). Sibling influences on gender development in middle childhood and early adolescence: A longitudinal study. *Developmental Psychology, 37,* 115–125.

McHale, S. M., Updegraff, K. A., & Whiteman, S. D. (2012). Sibling relationships and influences in childhood and adolescence. *Journal of Marriage and Family, 74,* 913–930.

McIntyre, S., Blair, E., Badawi, N., Keogh, J., & Nelson, K. B. (2013). Antecedents of cerebral palsy and perinatal death in term and late preterm singletons. *Obstetrics and Gynecology, 122,* 869–877.

McKee, C., Long, L., Southward, L. H., Walker, B., & McCown, J. (2016). The role of parental misconception of child's body weight in childhood obesity. *Journal of Pediatric Nursing, 31,* 196–203.

McKenna, J. J. (2002, September/October). Breastfeeding and bedsharing: Still useful (and important) after all these years. *Mothering, 114,* 28–37.

McKenna, J. J., & McDade, T. (2005). Why babies should never sleep alone: A review of the co-sleeping controversy in relation to SIDS, bedsharing, and breastfeeding. *Paediatric Respiratory Reviews, 6,* 134–152.

McKenna, J. J., & Volpe, L. E. (2007). Sleeping with baby: An Internet-based sampling of parental experiences, choices, perceptions, and interpretations in a Western industrialized context. *Infant and Child Development, 16,* 359–385.

McKeown, M. G., & Beck, I. L. (2009). The role of metacognition in understanding and supporting reading comprehension. In D. J. Hacker, J. Dunlosky, & A. C. Graesser (Eds.), *Handbook of metacognition in education* (pp. 7–25). New York: Routledge.

McKown, C. (2013). Social equity theory and racial-ethnic achievement gaps. *Child Development, 84,* 1120–1136.

McKown, C., Gregory, A., & Weinstein, R. S. (2010). Expectations, stereotypes, and self-fulfilling prophecies in classroom and school life. In J. L. Meece & J. S. Eccles (Eds.), *Handbook of research on schools, schooling and human development* (pp. 256–274). New York: Routledge.

McKown, C., & Weinstein, R. S. (2003). The development and consequences of stereotype consciousness in middle childhood. *Child Development, 74,* 498–515.

McKown, C., & Weinstein, R. S. (2008). Teacher expectations, classroom context, and the achievement gap. *Journal of School Psychology, 46,* 235–261.

McKusick-Nathans Institute of Genetic Medicine. (2018). *Online Mendelian inheritance in man: An online catalog of human genes and genetic disorders.* Retrieved from www.omim.org

McLanahan, S. (1999). Father absence and the welfare of children. In E. M. Hetherington (Ed.), *Coping with divorce, single parenting, and remarriage: A risk and resiliency perspective* (pp. 117–145). Mahwah, NJ: Erlbaum.

McLaughlin, K. A., Fox, N. A., Zeanah, C. H., & Nelson, C. A. (2011). Adverse rearing environments and neural development in children: The development of frontal electroencephalogram asymmetry. *Biological Psychiatry, 70,* 1008–1015.

McLaughlin, K. A., Sheridan, M. A., & Nelson, C. A. (2017). Neglect as a violation of species-expectant experience: Neurodevelopmental consequences. *Biological Psychiatry, 82,* 462–471.

McLaughlin, K. A., Sheridan, M. A., Tibu, F., Fox, N. A., Zeanah, C. H., & Nelson, C. H., III. (2015). Causal effects of the early caregiving environment on development of stress response systems in children. *Proceedings of the National Academy of Sciences, 112,* 5637–5642.

McLaughlin, K. A., Sheridan, M. A., Winter, W., Fox, N. A., Zeanah, C. H., Nelson, C. H., III, et al. (2014). Widespread reductions in cortical thickness following severe early-life deprivation: A neurodevelopmental pathway to attention-deficit hyperactivity disorder. *Biological Psychiatry, 76,* 629–638.

McLeskey, J., & Waldron, N. L. (2011). Educational programs for elementary students with learning disabilities: Can they be both effective and inclusive? *Learning Disabilities: Research and Practice, 26,* 48–57.

McLoyd, V. C., Aikens, N. L., & Burton, L. M. (2006). Childhood poverty, policy, and practice. In K. A. Renninger & I. E. Sigel (Eds.), *Handbook of child psychology: Vol. 4. Child psychology in practice* (6th ed., pp. 700–778). Hoboken, NJ: Wiley.

McLoyd, V. C., Kaplan, R., Hardaway, C. R., & Wood, D. (2007). Does endorsement of physical discipline matter? Assessing moderating influences on the maternal and child psychological correlates of physical discipline in African-American families. *Journal of Family Psychology, 21,* 165–175.

McMillan, B. T. M., & Saffran, J. R. (2016). Learning in complex environments: The effects of background speech on early word learning. *Child Development, 87,* 1841–1855.

McNeil, D. G., Jr. (2014, March 5). Early treatment is found to clear H.I.V. in a 2nd baby. *New York Times,* p. A1.

Mead, G. H. (1934). *Mind, self, and society.* Chicago: University of Chicago Press.

Meece, D. & Mize, J. (2011). Preschoolers' cognitive representations of peer relationships: Family origins and behavioural correlates. *Early Childhood Development and Care, 181,* 63–72.

Meehan, C. L., & Hawks, S. (2014a). Cooperative breeding and attachment among Aka foragers. In N. Quinn & J. Mageo (Eds.), *Attachment reconsidered: Cultural perspectives on a Western theory* (pp. 85–113). New York: Palgrave.

Meehan, C. L., & Hawks, S. (2014b). Maternal and allomaternal responsiveness: The significance of cooperative caregiving in attachment theory. In H. Otto & H. Keller (Eds.), *Different faces of attachment* (pp. 113–140). New York: Cambridge University Press.

Mehta, C. M., & Strough, J. (2009). Sex segregation in friendships and normative contexts across the life span. *Developmental Review, 29,* 201–220.

Mei, J. (1994). The Northern Chinese custom of rearing babies in sandbags: Implications for motor and intellectual development. In J. H. A. van Rossum & J. I. Laszlo (Eds.), *Motor development: Aspects of normal and delayed development* (pp. 41–48). Amsterdam, Netherlands: VU Uitgeverij.

Meins, E., Fernyhough, C., Wainwright, R., Clark-Carter, D., Gupta, M. D., Fradley, E., & Tucker, M. (2003). Pathways to understanding mind: Construct validity and predictive validity of maternal mind-mindedness. *Child Development, 74,* 1194–1211.

Melby, J. N., Conger, R. D., Fang, S., Wichrama, K. A. S., & Conger, K. J. (2008). Adolescent family experiences and educational attainment during early adulthood. *Developmental Psychology, 44,* 1519–1536.

Melby-Lervag, M., & Hulme, C. (2010). Serial and free recall in children can be improved by training: Evidence for the importance of phonological and semantic representations in immediate memory tasks. *Psychological Science, 21,* 1694–1700.

Melinder, A., Endestad, T., & Magnussen, S. (2006). Relations between episodic memory, suggestibility, theory of mind, and cognitive inhibition in the preschool child. *Scandinavian Journal of Psychology, 47,* 485–495.

Mellon, M. W., & Houts, A. C. (2018). Behavioral treatment for enuresis and encopresis. In J. R. Weisz & A. E. Kazden (Eds.), *Evidence-based psychotherapies for children and adolescents* (3rd ed., pp. 325–341). New York: Guilford.

Meltzoff, A. (2017). Elements of a comprehensive theory of infant imitation. *Behavioral and Brain Sciences, 40,* e396.

Meltzoff, A. N., & Kuhl, P. K. (1994). Faces and speech: Intermodal processing of biologically relevant signals in infants and adults. In D. J. Lewkowicz & R. Lickliter (Eds.), *The development of intersensory perception: Comparative perspectives* (pp. 335–369). Hillsdale, NJ: Erlbaum.

Meltzoff, A. N., & Moore, M. K. (1977). Imitation of facial and manual gestures by human neonates. *Science, 198,* 75–78.

Meltzoff, A. N., & Moore, M. K. (1994). Imitation, memory, and the representation of persons. *Infant Behavior and Development, 17,* 83–99.

Meltzoff, A. N., & Williamson, R. A. (2010). The importance of imitation for theories of social-cognitive development. In J. G. Bremner & T. D. Wachs (Eds.), *Wiley-Blackwell handbook of infant development* (2nd ed., pp. 345–364). Oxford, UK: Wiley.

Meltzoff, A. N., & Williamson, R. A. (2013). Imitation: Social, cognitive, and theoretical perspectives. In P. D. Zelazo (Ed.), *Oxford handbook of developmental psychology: Vol. 1. Body and mind* (pp. 651–682). New York: Oxford University Press.

Melzer, D. K., & Palermo, C. O. (2016). Mommy, you are the princess and I am the queen: How preschool children's initiation and language use during pretend play relate to complexity. *Infant and Child Development, 25,* 221–230.

Melzi, G., & Schick, A. R. (2013). Language and literacy in the school years. In J. B. Gleason & N. B. Ratner (Eds.), *Development of language* (8th ed., pp. 329–365). Upper Saddle River, NJ: Pearson.

Melzi, G., & Schick, A. R. (2017). Language and literacy in the school years. In J. B. Gleason (Ed.), *Development of language* (9th ed., pp. 257–284). Hoboken, NJ: Pearson.

Memo, L., Gnoato, E., Caminiti, S., Pichini, S., & Tarani, L. (2013). Fetal alcohol spectrum disorders and fetal alcohol syndrome: The state of the art and new diagnostic tools. *Early Human Development, 89S1,* S40–S43.

Mendez, M., Durtschi, J., Neppl, T. K., & Stith, S. M. (2016). Corporal punishment and externalizing behaviors in toddlers: The moderating role of positive and harsh parenting. *Journal of Family Psychology, 30,* 887–895.

Menesini, E., Calussi, P., & Nocentini, A. (2012). Cyberbullying and traditional bullying: Unique, additive, and synergistic effects on psychological health symptoms. In Q. Li, D. Cross, & P. K. Smith (Eds.), *Cyberbullying in the global playground* (pp. 245–265). Malden, MA: Wiley-Blackwell.

Menesini, E., Nicocenti, A., & Calussi, P. (2011). The measurement of cyberbullying: Dimensional structure and relative item severity and discrimination. *Cyberspychology and Behavior, 14,* 267–274.

Menesini, E., & Salmivalli, C. (2017). Bullying in the schools: The state of knowledge and effective interventions. *Psychology, Health & Medicine, 22,* 240–253.

Menesini, E., & Spiel, C. (2012). Introduction: Cyberbullying: Development, consequences, risk and protective factors. *European Journal of Developmental Psychology, 9,* 163–167.

Mennella, J. A., & Beauchamp, G. K. (1998). Early flavor experiences: Research update. *Nutrition Reviews, 56,* 205–211.

Ment, L. R., Vohr, B., Allan, W., Katz, K. H., Schneider, K. C., Westerveld, M., Cuncan, C. C., & Makuch, R. W. (2003). Change in cognitive function over time in very low-birth-weight infants. *Journal of the American Medical Association, 289,* 705–711.

Menting, A. T. A., Orobio de Castro, B., & Matthys, W. (2013). Effectiveness of the Incredible Years parent training to modify disruptive and prosocial child behavior: A meta-analytic review. *Clinical Psychology Review, 33,* 901–913.

Meredith, N. V. (1978). *Human body growth in the first ten years of life.* Columbia, SC: State Printing.

Mermelshtine, R. (2017). Parent–child learning interactions: A review of the literature on scaffolding. *British Journal of Educational Psychology, 87,* 241–254.

Merrick, J. (2016). Unintentional injuries in childhood and years of potential life lost. *International Journal of Child and Adolescent Health, 9,* 277–278.

Merz, E. C., Harlé, K. M., Noble, K. G., & McCall, R. B. (2016). Executive function in previously institutionalized children. *Child Development Perspectives, 10,* 105–110.

Merz, E. C., McDonough, L., Huang, Y. L., Werner, E., & Monk, C. (2017). The mobile conjugate reinforcement paradigm in a lab setting. *Developmental Psychobiology, 59,* 668–672.

Mesman, J., van IJzendoorn, M. H., & Bakermans-Kranenburg, M. J. (2009). The many faces of the still-face paradigm: A review and meta-analysis. *Developmental Review, 29,* 120–162.

Mesman, J., van IJzendoorn, M. H., & Sagi-Schwartz, A. (2016). Cross-cultural patterns of attachment: Universal and contextual dimensions. In J. Cassidy & P. R. Shaver (Eds.), *Handbook of attachment: Theory, research, and clinical applications* (3rd ed., pp. 852–877). New York: Guilford.

Messinger, D. S., & Fogel, A. (2007). The interactive development of social smiling. In R. Kail (Ed.), *Advances in child development and behavior* (Vol. 35, pp. 327–366). Oxford, UK: Elsevier.

Meyer, M. J., & Jimerson, S. R. (2019). The importance of school safety and violence prevention. In M. J. Meyer & S. R. Jimerson (Eds.), *School safety and violence prevention: Science, practice, policy* (pp. 3–16). Washington, DC: American Psychological Association.

Meyer, R. (2009). Infant feeding in the first year. 1: Feeding practices in the first six months of life. *Journal of Family Health Care, 19,* 13–16.

Meyer, S., Raikes, H. A., Virmani, E. A., Waters, S., & Thompson, R. A. (2014). Parent emotion representations and the socialization of emotion regulation in the family. *International Journal of Behavioral Development, 38,* 164–173.

Meyers, A. B., & Berk, L. E. (2014). Make-believe play and self-regulation. In L. Brooker, M. Blaise, & S. Edwards (Eds.), *Sage handbook of play and learning in early childhood* (pp. 43–55). London: Sage.

Micalizzi, L., Wang, M., & Saudino, K. J. (2017). Difficult temperament and negative parenting in early childhood: A genetically informed cross-lagged analysis. *Developmental Science, 20,* e12355.

Michalik, N. M., Eisenberg, N., Spinrad, T. L., Ladd, B., Thompson, M., & Valiente, C. (2007). Longitudinal relations among parental emotional expressivity and sympathy and prosocial behavior in adolescence. *Social Development, 16,* 286–309.

Michel, G. F., Babik, I., Sheu, C.-F., & Campbell, J. M. (2014). Latent classes in the developmental trajectories of infant handedness. *Developmental Psychology, 50,* 349–359.

Michiels, D., Grietens, H., Onghena, P., & Kuppens, S. (2010). Perceptions of maternal and paternal attachment security in middle childhood: Links with positive parental affection and psychological adjustment. *Early Child Development and Care, 180,* 211–225.

Migration Policy Institute. (2015). *Children in U.S. immigrant families.* www.migrationpolicy.org/programs/data-hub/charts/children-immigrant-families

Mikami, A. Y., Lerner, M. D., & Lun, J. (2010). Social context influences on children's rejection by their peers. *Child Development Perspectives, 4,* 123–130.

Mikkila, V., Rasanen, L., Raitakari, O. T., Pietinen, P., & Viikari, J. (2005). Consistent dietary patterns identified from childhood to adulthood: The Cardiovascular Risk in Young Finns Study. *British Journal of Nutrition, 93,* 923–931.

Milan, S., Snow, S., & Belay, S. (2007). The context of preschool children's sleep: Racial/ethnic differences in sleep locations, routines, and concerns. *Journal of Family Psychology, 21,* 20–28.

Miles, G., & Siega-Riz, M. (2017). Trends in food and beverage consumption among infants and toddlers: 2005–2012. *Pediatrics, 139,* e20163290.

Mileva-Seitz, V. R., Bakermans-Kranenburg, M. J., Battaini, C., & Luijk, M. P. C. M. (2017). Parent–child bed-sharing: The good, the bad, and the burden of evidence. *Sleep Medicine Reviews, 32,* 4–27.

Milevsky, A., Schlechter, M., Netter, S., & Keehn, D. (2007). Maternal and paternal parenting styles in adolescents: Associations with self-esteem, depression, and life satisfaction. *Journal of Child and Family Studies, 16,* 39–47.

Miller, D. I., Nolla, K. M., Eagly, A. H., & Uttal, D. H. (2018). The development of children's gender-science stereotypes: A meta-analysis of 5 decades of U.S. draw-a-scientist studies. *Child Development, 89,* 1943–1955.

Miller, G. E., Chen, E., Fok, A. K., Walker, H., Lim, A., Hiholls, E. F., et al. (2009). Low early-life social class leaves a biological residue manifested by decreased glucocorticoid and increased proinflammatory signaling. *Proceedings of the National Academy of Sciences, 106,* 14716–14721.

Miller, L. E., Grabell, A., Thomas, A., Bermann, E., & Graham-Bermann, S. A. (2012). The associations between community violence, television violence, parent–child aggression, and aggression in sibling relationships of a sample of preschoolers. *Psychology of Violence, 2,* 165–178.

Miller, P. (2016). *Theories of developmental psychology* (6th ed.). New York: Worth.

Miller, P. J. (2014). Entries into meaning: Socialization via narrative in the early years. In M. J. Gelfand, C.-Y. Chiu, & Y.-Y. Hong (Eds.), *Advances in culture and psychology* (Vol. 4, pp. 124–176). New York: Oxford University Press.

Miller, P. J., Fung, H., Lin, S., Chen, E. C., & Boldt, B. R. (2012). How socialization happens on the ground: Narrative practices as alternate socializing pathways in Taiwanese and European-American families. *Monographs of the Society for Research in Child Development, 77*(1, Serial No. 302).

Miller, P. J., Fung, H., & Mintz, J. (1996). Self-construction through narrative practices: A Chinese and American comparison of early socialization. *Ethos, 24,* 1–44.

Miller, P. J., Wang, S., Sandel, T., & Cho, G. E. (2002). Self-esteem as folk theory: A comparison of European American and Taiwanese mothers' beliefs. *Parenting: Science and Practice, 2,* 209–239.

Miller, P. J., Wiley, A. R., Fung, H., & Liang, C.-H. (1997). Personal storytelling as a medium of socialization in Chinese and American families. *Child Development, 68,* 557–568.

Miller, S. A. (2009). Children's understanding of second-order mental states. *Psychological Bulletin, 135,* 749–773.

Miller, S. A. (2013). Effects of deception on children's understanding of second-order false belief. *Infant and Child Development, 22,* 422–429.

Miller, S. A., Hardin, C. A., & Montgomery, D. E. (2003). Young children's understanding of the conditions for knowledge acquisition. *Journal of Cognition and Development, 4,* 325–356.

Miller, T. R. (2015). Projected outcomes of Nurse–Family Partnership home visitation during 1996–2013, USA. *Prevention Science, 16,* 765–777.

Miller-Graff, L. E., & Cummings, E. M. (2017). The Israeli–Palestinian conflict: Effects on youth adjustment, available interventions, and future research directions. *Developmental Review, 43,* 1–47.

Miller-Graff, L. E., Cummings, E. M., & Bergman, K. N. (2016). Effects of a brief psychoeducational intervention for family conflict: Constructive conflict, emotional insecurity and child adjustment. *Journal of Abnormal Child Psychology, 44,* 1399–1410.

Mills, D., & Conboy, B. T. (2005). Do changes in brain organization reflect shifts in symbolic functioning? In L. Namy (Ed.), *Symbol use and symbolic representation* (pp. 123–153). Mahwah, NJ: Erlbaum.

Mills, D., Plunkett, K., Prat, C., & Schafer, G. (2005). Watching the infant brain learn words: Effects of language and experience. *Cognitive Development, 20,* 19–31.

Mills, M., Rindfuss, R. R., McDonald, P., & te Velde, E. (2011). Why do people postpone parenthood? Reasons and social policy incentives. *Human Reproduction Update, 17,* 848–860.

Mills, R. S. L. (2005). Taking stock of the developmental literature on shame. *Developmental Review, 25,* 26–63.

Mills, R. S. L., & Grusec, J. E. (1989). Cognitive, affective, and behavioral consequences of praising altruism. *Merrill-Palmer Quarterly, 35,* 299–326.

Min, J., Chiu, D. T., & Wang, T. (2013). Variation in the heritability of body mass index based on diverse twin studies: A systematic review. *Obesity Review, 14,* 871–882.

Mindell, J. A., Li, A. M., Sadeh, A., Kwon, R., & Goh, D. Y. T. (2015). Bedtime routines for young children: A dose-dependent association with sleep outcomes. *Sleep, 38,* 717–722.

Mindell, J. A., Sadeh, A., Kwon, R., & Goh, D. Y T. (2013). Cross-cultural differences in the sleep of preschool children. *Sleep Medicine, 14,* 1283–1289.

Mireault, G. C., Crockenberg, S. C., Heilman, K., Sparrow, J. E., Cousineau, K., & Rainville, B. (2017). Social, cognitive, and physiological aspects of humour perception from 4 to 8 months: Two longitudinal studies. *British Journal of Developmental Psychology, 36,* 98–109.

Mireault, G. C., Crockenberg, S. C., Sparrow, J. E., Cousineau, K., Pettinato, C., & Woodard, K. (2015). Laughing matters: Infant humor in the context of parental affect. *Journal of Experimental Child Psychology, 136,* 30–41.

Mireault, G. C., Crockenberg, S. C., Sparrow, J. E., Pettinato, C. A., Woodard, K. C., & Malzac, K. (2014). Social looking, social referencing and humor perception in 6- and 12-month-olds. *Infant Behavior and Development, 37,* 536–545.

Misailidi, P. (2006). Young children's display rule knowledge: Understanding the distinction between apparent and real emotions and the motives underlying the use of display rules. *Social Behavior and Personality, 34,* 1285–1296.

Mischel, W., & Liebert, R. M. (1966). Effects of discrepancies between observed and imposed reward criteria on their acquisition and transmission. *Journal of Personality and Social Psychology, 3,* 45–53.

Mistry, J., & Dutta, R. (2015). Human development and culture. In W. F. Overton & P. C. Molenar (Eds.), *Handbook of child psychology and developmental science: Vol. 1. Theory and method* (pp. 369–406). Hoboken, NJ: Wiley.

Mistry, R. S., Biesanz, J. C., Chien, N., Howes, C., & Benner, A. D. (2008). Socioeconomic status, parental investments, and the cognitive and behavioral outcomes of low-income children from immigrant and native households. *Early Childhood Research Quarterly, 23,* 193–212.

Miyamoto, S., Romano, P. S., Putnam-Hornstein, E., Thurston, H., Dharmar, M., & Joseph, J. G. (2017). Risk factors for fatal and non-fatal child maltreatment in families previously investigated by CPS: A case-control study. *Child Abuse and Neglect, 63,* 222–232.

Mize, J., & Pettit, G. S. (2010). The mother–child playgroup as socialisation context: A short-term longitudinal study of mother–child–peer relationship dynamics. *Early Child Development and Care, 180,* 1271–1284.

Mok, M. M. C., Kennedy, K. J., & Moore, P. J. (2011). Academic attribution of secondary students: Gender, year level and achievement level. *Educational Psychology, 31,* 87–104.

Mokomane, M., Kasvosve, I., de Melo, E., Pernica, J. M., & Goldfarb, D. M. (2018). The global problem of child diarrhoeal diseases: Emerging strategies in prevention and management. *Therapeutic Advances in Infectious Diseases, 5,* 29–43.

Molina, M., Sann, C., Morgane, D., Touré, Y., Guillois, B., & Jouen, F. (2015). Active touch in late-preterm and early-term neonates. *Developmental Psychobiology, 57,* 322–335.

Moll, H., & Meltzoff, A. N. (2011). How does it look? Level 2 perspective-taking at 36 months of age. *Child Development, 82,* 661–673.

Moll, H., & Tomasello, M. (2006). Level I perspective-taking at 24 months of age. *British Journal of Developmental Psychology, 24,* 603–613.

Moll, K., Ramus, F., Bartling, J., Bruder, J., Kunze, S., Neuhoff, N., et al. (2014). Cognitive mechanisms underlying reading and spelling development in five European orthographies. *Learning and Instruction, 29,* 65–77.

Moller, K., Hwang, C. P., & Wickberg, B. (2008). Couple relationship and transition to parenthood: Does workload at home matter? *Journal of Reproductive and Infant Psychology, 26,* 57–68.

Molloy, C. S., Wilson-Ching, M., Anderson, V. A., Roberts, G., Anderson, P. J., Doyle, L. W., et al. (2013). Visual processing in adolescents born extremely low birth weight and/or extremely preterm. *Pediatrics, 132,* e704–e712.

Molnar, D. S., Levitt, A., Eiden, R. D., & Schuetze, P. (2014). Prenatal cocaine exposure and trajectories of externalizing behavior problems in early childhood: Examining the role of maternal negative affect. *Development and Psychopathology, 26,* 515–528.

Mondloch, C. J., Lewis, T., Budreau, D. R., Maurer, D., Dannemillier, J. L., Stephens, B. R., & Kleiner-Gathercoal, K. A. (1999). Face perception during early infancy. *Psychological Science, 10,* 419–422.

Monk, C., Georgieff, M., Xu, D., Hao, X., Bansal, R., Gustafsson, H., et al. (2016). Maternal prenatal iron status and tissue organization in the neonatal brain. *Pediatric Research, 79,* 482–488.

Monk, C., Georgieff, M. K., & Osterholm, E. A. (2013). Research review: Maternal prenatal distress and poor nutrition—mutually influencing risk factors affecting infant neurocognitive development. *Journal of Child Psychology and Psychiatry, 54,* 115–130.

Monk, C. S., Weng, S.-J., Wiggins, J. L., Kurapati, N., Louro, H. M. C., Carrasco, M., et al. (2010). Neural circuitry of emotional face processing in autism spectrum disorders. *Journal of Psychiatry and Neuroscience, 35,* 105–114.

Montague, D. P. F., & Walker-Andrews, A. S. (2001). Peekaboo: A new look at infants' perception of emotion expressions. *Developmental Psychology, 37,* 826–838.

Montgomery, D. E., & Koeltzow, T. E. (2010). A review of the day–night task: The Stroop paradigm and interference control in young children. *Developmental Review, 30,* 308–330.

Montirosso, R., Casini, E., Provenzi, L., Putnam, S. P., Morandi, F., Fedeli, C., et al. (2015). A categorical approach to infants' individual differences during the still-face paradigm. *Infant Behavior and Development, 38,* 67–76.

Moody, A., Justice, L. M., & Cabell, S. Q. (2010). Electronic versus traditional storybooks: Relative influence on preschool children's engagement and communication. *Journal of Early Childhood Literacy, 10,* 294–313.

Moon, C., Cooper, R. P., & Fifer, W. P. (1993). Two-day-old infants prefer their native language. *Infant Behavior and Development, 16,* 495–500.

Moore, C., Mealiea, J., Garon, N., & Povinelli, D. (2007). The development of body self-awareness. *Infancy, 11,* 157–174.

Moore, E. G. J. (1986). Family socialization and the IQ test performance of traditionally and transracially adopted Black children. *Developmental Psychology, 22,* 317–326.

Moore, K. L., Persaud, T. V. N., & Torchia, M. G. (2016). *Before we are born: Essentials of embryology and birth defects* (9th ed.). Philadelphia: Elsevier.

Moore, M., & Mindell, J. A. (2012). Sleep-related problems in childhood. In C. M. Morin & C. A. Espie (Eds.), *Oxford handbook of sleep and sleep disorders* (pp. 729–745). New York: Oxford University Press.

Moore, M. K., & Meltzoff, A. N. (1999). New findings on object permanence: A developmental difference between two types of occlusion. *British Journal of Developmental Psychology, 17,* 563–584.

Moore, M. K., & Meltzoff, A. N. (2004). Object permanence after a 24-hr delay and leaving the locale of disappearance: The role of memory, space, and identity. *Developmental Psychology, 40,* 606–620.

Moore, M. K., & Meltzoff, A. N. (2008). Factors affecting infants' manual search for occluded objects and the genesis of object permanence. *Infant Behavior and Development, 31,* 168–180.

Moore, M. R., & Stambolis-Ruhstorfer, M. (2013). LGBT sexuality and families at the start of the twenty-first century. *Annual Review of Sociology, 39,* 491–507.

Moran, G. F., & Vinovskis, M. A. (1986). The great care of godly parents: Early childhood in Puritan New England. *Monographs of the Society for Research in Child Development, 50*(4–5, Serial No. 211).

Morawska, A., & Sanders, M. (2011). Parental use of time out revisited: A useful or harmful parenting strategy? *Journal of Child and Family Studies, 20,* 1–8.

Morelli, G. (2015). The evolution of attachment theory and cultures of human attachment in infancy and early childhood. In L. A. Jensen (Ed.), *Oxford handbook of human development and culture: An interdisciplinary perspective* (pp. 149–164). New York: Oxford University Press.

Morelli, G. A., Chaudhary, N., Gottlieb, A., Keller, H., Murray, M., Quinn, N., et al.

(2017). Taking culture seriously: Developing a pluralistic theory of attachments. In H. Keller & K. A. Bard (Eds.), *Contextualizing attachment: The cultural nature of attachment* (pp. 139–169). Cambridge, MA: MIT Press.

Morelli, G. A., Rogoff, B., & Angelillo, C. (2003). Cultural variation in young children's access to work or involvement in specialized child-focused activities. *International Journal of Behavioral Development, 27,* 264–274.

Morelli, G. A., Rogoff, B., Oppenheim, D., & Goldsmith, D. (1992). Cultural variation in infants' sleeping arrangements: Questions of independence. *Developmental Psychology, 28,* 604–613.

Moreno, A. J., Klute, M. M., & Robinson, J. L. (2008). Relational and individual resources as predictors of empathy in early childhood. *Social Development, 17,* 613–637.

Morra, S., & Panesi, S. (2017). From scribbling to drawing: The role of working memory. *Cognitive Development, 43,* 142–158.

Morrill, M. I., Hines, D. A., Mahmood, S., & Córdova, J. V. (2010). Pathways between marriage and parenting for wives and husbands: The role of coparenting. *Family Process, 49,* 59–73.

Morris, A., Gabert-Quillen, C., & Delahanty, D. (2012). The association between parent PTSD/depression symptoms and child PTSD symptoms: A meta-analysis. *Journal of Pediatric Psychology, 37,* 1076–1088.

Morris, A. S., Silk, J. S., Morris, M. D. S., & Steinberg, L. (2011). The influence of mother–child emotion regulation strategies on children's expression of anger and sadness. *Developmental Psychology, 47,* 213–225.

Morris, A. S., Silk, J. S., Steinberg, L., Myers, S. S., & Robinson, L. R. (2007). The role of the family context in the development of emotion regulation. *Social Development, 16,* 362–388.

Morris, M. C., Douros, C. D., Janecek, K., Freeman, R., Mielock, A., & Garber, J. (2017). Community-level moderators of a school-based childhood sexual assault prevention program. *Child Abuse & Neglect, 63,* 295–306.

Morrissey, T., Dunifon, R. E., & Kalil, A. (2011). Maternal employment, work schedules, and children's body mass index. *Child Development, 82,* 66–81.

Morrissey, T. W. (2013). Multiple child care arrangements and common communicable illnesses in children aged 3 to 54 months. *Maternal and Child Health Journal, 17,* 1175–1184.

Morrongiello, B. A., Fenwick, K. D., & Chance, G. (1998). Crossmodal learning in newborn infants: Inferences about properties of auditory-visual events. *Infant Behavior and Development, 21,* 543–554.

Morrongiello, B. A., Kane, A., & Zdzieborski, D. (2011). "I think he is in his room playing a video game": Parental supervision of young elementary-school children at home. *Journal of Pediatric Psychology, 36,* 708–717.

Morrongiello, B. A., & Kiriakou, S. (2004). Mothers' home-safety practices for preventing six types of childhood injuries: What do they do, and why? *Journal of Pediatric Psychology, 29,* 285–297.

Morrongiello, B. A., McArthur, B. A., & Spence, J. R. (2016). Understanding gender differences in childhood injuries: Examining longitudinal relations between parental reactions and boys' versus girls' injury-risk behaviors. *Health Psychology, 35,* 523–530.

Morrongiello, B. A., Ondejko, L., & Littlejohn, A. (2004). Understanding toddlers' in-home injuries: I. Context, correlates, and determinants. *Journal of Pediatric Psychology, 29,* 415–431.

Morrongiello, B. A., Widdifield, R., Munroe, K., & Zdzieborski, D. (2014). Parents teaching young children home safety rules: Implications for childhood injury risk. *Journal of Applied Developmental Psychology, 35,* 254–261.

Mosby, L., Rawls, A. W., Meehan, A. J., Mays, E., & Pettinari, C. J. (1999). Troubles in interracial talk about discipline: An examination of African American child rearing narratives. *Journal of Comparative Family Studies, 30,* 489–521.

Moshman, D. (2003). Developmental change in adulthood. In J. Demick & C. Andreoletti (Eds.), *Handbook of adult development* (pp. 43–61). New York: Plenum.

Moss, E., Cyr, C., Bureau, J.-F., Tarabulsy, G. M., & Dubois-Comtois, K. (2005). Stability of attachment during the preschool period. *Developmental Psychology, 41,* 773–783.

Moss, E., Smolla, N., Guerra, I., Mazzarello, T., Chayer, D., & Berthiaume, C. (2006). Attachment and self-reported internalizing and externalizing behavior problems in a school period. *Canadian Journal of Behavioural Science, 38,* 142–157.

Mossey, P. A., Little, J., Munger, R. G., Dixon, M. J., & Shaw, W. C. (2009). Cleft lip and palate. *Lancet, 374,* 1773–1785.

Mottus, R., Indus, K., & Allik, J. (2008). Accuracy of only children stereotype. *Journal of Research in Personality, 42,* 1047–1052.

Mottweiler, C. M., & Taylor, M. (2014). Elaborated role play and creativity in preschool age children. *Psychology of Aesthetics, Creativity, and the Arts, 8,* 277–286.

Mozzi, A., Riva, V., Foni, D., Sironi, M., Marino, C., Molteni, M., et al. (2017). A common genetic variant in FOXP2 is associated with language-based learning (dis)abilities: Evidence from two Italian independent samples. *American Journal of Medical Genetics B: Neuropsychiatric Genetics, 174,* 578–586.

Mrug, S., Hoza, B., & Gerdes, A. C. (2001). Children with attention-deficit/hyperactivity disorder: Peer relationships and peer-oriented interventions. In D. W. Nangle & C. A. Erdley (Eds.), *The role of friendship in psychological adjustment* (pp. 51–77). San Francisco: Jossey-Bass.

Mu, Q., & Fehring, R. J. (2014). Efficacy of achieving pregnancy with fertility-focused intercourse. *American Journal of Maternal Child Nursing, 39,* 35–40.

Mueller, B. R., & Bale, T. L. (2008). Sex-specific programming of offspring emotionality after stress early in pregnancy. *Journal of Neuroscience, 28,* 9055–9065.

Muenssinger, J., Matuz, T., Schleger, F., Kiefer-Schmidt, I., Goelz, R. Wacker-Gussmann, A., et al. (2013). Auditory habituation in the fetus and neonate: An fMEG study. *Developmental Science, 16,* 287–295.

Muis, K. R., Psaradellis, C., Chevrier, M., Di Leo, I., & Lajoie, S. P. (2015). Learning by preparing to teach: Fostering self-regulatory processes and achievement during complex mathematics problem solving. *Journal of Educational Psychology, 108,* 474–492.

Müller, O., & Krawinkel, M. (2005). Malnutrition and health in developing countries. *Canadian Medical Association Journal, 173,* 279–286.

Müller, U., & Kerns, K. (2015). The development of executive function. In L. S. Liben & U. Müller (Eds.), *Handbook of child psychology and developmental science: Vol. 2. Cognitive processes* (7th ed., pp. 571–623). Hoboken, NJ: Wiley.

Müller, U., Liebermann-Finestone, D. P., Carpendale, J. I. M., Hammond, S. I., & Bibok, M. B. (2012). Knowing minds, controlling actions: The developmental relations between theory of mind and executive function from 2 to 4 years of age. *Journal of Experimental Child Psychology, 111,* 331–348.

Mullett-Hume, E., Anshel, D., Guevara, V., & Cloitre, M. (2008). Cumulative trauma and posttraumatic stress disorder among children exposed to the 9/11 World Trade Center attack. *American Journal of Orthopsychiatry, 78,* 103–108.

Mullins, E., Lees, C., & Brocklehurst, P. (2017). Is continuous electronic fetal monitoring useful for all women in labour? *British Medical Journal, 359,* j5423.

Mumme, D. L., Bushnell, E. W., DiCorcia, J. A., & Lariviere, L. A. (2007). Infants' use of gaze cues to interpret others' actions and emotional reactions. In R. Flom, K. Lee, & D. Muir (Eds.), *Gaze-following: Its development and significance* (pp. 143–170). Mahwah, NJ: Erlbaum.

Muntoni, F., & Retelsdorf, J. (2018). Gender-specific teacher expectations in reading: The role of teachers' gender stereotypes. *Contemporary Educational Psychology, 54,* 212–220.

Munzer, T. G., Miller, A. L., Peterson, K. E., Brophy-Herb, H. E., Horodynski, M. A., Contreras, D., et al. (2018). Media exposure in low-income preschool-aged children is associated with multiple measures of self-regulatory behavior. *Journal of Developmental and Behavioral Pediatrics, 39,* 303–309.

Muraca, G. M., Sabr, Y., Lisonkova, S., Skoll, A., Brant, R., Cundiff, G. W., & Joseph, K. S. (2017). Perinatal and maternal morbidity and mortality after attempted operative vaginal delivery at midpelvic station. *Canadian Medical Association Journal, 189,* E764.

Murawski, N. J., Moore, E. M., Thomas, J. D., & Riley, E. P. (2015). Advances in diagnosis and treatment of fetal alcohol spectrum disorders: From animal models to human studies. *Alcohol Research, 37,* 97–108.

Muret-Wagstaff, S., & Moore, S. G. (1989). The Hmong in America: Infant behavior and rearing practices. In J. K. Nugent, B. M. Lester, & T. B. Brazelton (Eds.), *Biology, culture, and development* (Vol. 1, pp. 319–339). Norwood, NJ: Ablex.

Muris, P., & Field, A. P. (2011). The "normal" development of fear. In W. K. Silverman, & A. P. Field (Eds.), *Anxiety disorders in children and adolescents* (2nd ed., pp. 76–89). Cambridge, UK: Cambridge University Press.

Muris, P., & Meesters, C. (2014). Small or big in the eyes of the other: On the developmental psychopathology of self-conscious emotions as shame, guilt, and pride. *Clinical Child and Family Psychology Review, 17,* 19–40.

Murphy, J. B. (2013). Access to in vitro fertilization deserves increased regulation in the United States. *Journal of Sex and Marital Therapy, 39,* 85–92.

Murphy, P. K., Greene, J. A., Firetto, C. M., Li, M., Lobczowski, N. G., Duke, R. F., et al. (2017). Exploring the influence of homogeneous versus heterogeneous grouping on students' text-based discussions and comprehension. *Contemporary Educational Psychology, 51,* 336–355.

Murphy, P. K., Wilkinson, I. A. G., Soter, A. O., Hennessey, M. N., & Alexander, J. F. (2009). Examining the effects of classroom discussion on students' high-level comprehension of text: A meta-analysis. *Journal of Educational Psychology, 101,* 740–764.

Murphy, T. H., & Corbett, D. (2009). Plasticity during recovery: From synapse to behaviour. *Nature Reviews Neuroscience, 10,* 861–872.

Murphy, T. P., & Laible, D. J. (2013). The influence of attachment security on preschool children's empathic concern. *International Journal of Behavioral Development, 37,* 436–440.

Murray, L. K., Nguyen, A., & Cohen, J. A. (2014). Child sexual abuse. *Pediatric Clinics of North America, 23,* 321–337.

Murray, L., Tran, T., Thang, V. V., Cass, L., & Fisher, J. (2018). How do caregivers understand and respond to unsettled infant behaviour in Vietnam? A qualitative study. *Child: Care, Health and Development, 44,* 62–70.

Mussen, P. H., & Eisenberg-Berg, N. (1977). *Roots of caring, sharing, and helping.* San Francisco: Freeman.

Myant, K. A., & Williams, J. M. (2005). Children's concepts of health and illness: Understanding of contagious illnesses, noncontagious illnesses and injuries. *Journal of Health Psychology, 10,* 805–819.

Myers, L. J., LeWitt, R. B., Gallo, R. E., & Maselli, N. M. (2017). Baby FaceTime: Can toddlers learn from online video chat? *Developmental Science, 20,* e12430.

Myers, L. J., & Liben, L. S. (2008). The role of intentionality and iconicity in children's developing comprehension and production of cartographic symbols. *Child Development, 79,* 668–684.

Myowa-Yamakoshi, M., Tomonaga, M., Tanaka, M., & Matsuzawa, T. (2004). Imitation in neonatal chimpanzees *(Pan troglodytes). Developmental Science, 7,* 437–442.

N

Nadel, J., Prepin, K., & Okanda, M. (2005). Experiencing contingency and agency: First step toward self-understanding in making a mind? *Interaction Studies, 6,* 447–462.

Nader, P. R., O'Brien, M., Houts, R., Bradley, R., Belsky, J., Crosnoe, R., et al. (2006). Identifying risk for obesity in early childhood. *Pediatrics, 118,* e594–e601.

Nadler, J. T., & Clark, M. H. (2011). Stereotype threat: A meta-analysis comparing African Americans to Hispanic Americans. *Journal of Applied Social Psychology, 9,* 139–142.

Nærde, A., Ogden, T., Janson, H., & Zachrisson, H. D. (2014). Normative development of physical aggression from 8 to 26 months. *Developmental Psychology, 6,* 1710–1720.

Nagy, E., Pal, A., & Orvos, H. (2014). Learning to imitate individual finger movements by the human neonate. *Developmental Science, 17,* 841–857.

Naigles, L. R., & Swenson, L. D. (2007). Syntactic supports for word learning. In E. Hoff & M. Shatz (Eds.), *Blackwell handbook of language development* (pp. 212–231). Malden, MA: Blackwell.

Nan, C., Piek, J., Warner, C., Mellers, D., Krone, R. E., Barrett, T., & Zeegers, M. P. (2013). Trajectories and predictors of developmental skills in healthy twins up to 24 months of age. *Infant Behavior and Development, 36,* 670–678.

Nánez, J., Sr., & Yonas, A. (1994). Effects of luminance and texture motion on infant defensive reactions to optical collision. *Infant Behavior and Development, 17,* 165–174.

Nanri, H., Shirasawa, T., Ochiai, H., Nomoto, S., Hoshino, H., & Kokaze, A. (2017). Rapid weight gain during infancy and early childhood is related to higher anthropometric measurements in preadolescence. *Child: Care, Health, and Development, 43,* 435–440.

Narr, K. L., Woods, R. P., Lin, J., Kim, J., Phillips, O. R., Del'Homme, M., et al. (2009). Widespread cortical thinning is a robust anatomical marker for attention-deficit/hyperactivity disorder. *Journal of the American Academy of Child and Adolescent Psychiatry, 48,* 1014–1022.

Nash, K., Stevens, S., Clairman, H., & Rovet, J. (2018). Preliminary findings that a targeted intervention leads to altered brain function in children with fetal alcohol spectrum disorder. *Brain Sciences, 8,* 8010007.

Nash, K., Stevens, S., Greenbaum, R., Weiner, J, Koren, G., & Rovet, J. (2015). Improving executive functioning in children with fetal alcohol spectrum disorders. *Child Neuropsychology, 21,* 191–209.

Nassr, A. A., Erfani, H., Fisher, J. E., Ogunleye, O. K., Espinosa, J., Belfort, M. A., et al. (2018). Fetal interventional procedures and surgeries: A practical approach. *Journal of Perinatal Medicine, 46,* 701–715.

Nathanson, R., & Saywitz, K. J. (2015). Preparing children for court: Effects of a model court education program on children's anticipatory anxiety. *Behavioral Sciences and the Law, 33,* 459–475.

National Association for the Education of Young Children. (2017). *DAP in the early primary grades.* Retrieved from www.naeyc.org/dap/primary

National Child Traumatic Stress Network. (2009). *Sexual development and behavior in children: Information for parents and caregivers.* Retrieved from www.nctsn.org/sites/default/files/resources//sexual_development_and_behavior_in_children.pdf

National Coalition for the Homeless. (2012). *Education of homeless children and youth.* Retrieved from www.nationalhomeless.org/factsheets/education.html

National Institutes of Health. (2018a). *Safe to sleep.* Retrieved from www1.nichd.nih.gov/sts/Pages/default.aspx

National Institutes of Health. (2018b). *What was the Human Genome Project and why has it been important?* Retrieved from ghr.nlm.nih.gov/primer/hgp/description

National Survey of Children's Health. (2016). *Data Resource Center for Child and Adolescent Health.* Retrieved from www.childhealthdata.org/learn-about-the-nsch/topics_questions/2016-nsch-guide-to-topics-and-questions

Natsuaki, M. N., Shaw, D. S., Neiderhiser, J. M., Ganiban, J. M., Harold, G. T., Reiss, D., et al. (2014). Raised by depressed parents: Is it an environmental risk? *Clinical Child and Family Psychology Review, 17,* 357–367.

Nauta, J., van Mechelen, W., Otten, R. H. J., & Verhagen, E. A. L. M. (2014). A systematic review on the effectiveness of school and community-based injury prevention programmes on risk behaviour and injury risk in 8–12 year old children. *Journal of Science and Medicine in Sport, 17,* 165–172.

Nazareth, A., Weisberg, S. M., Margulis K., & Newcombe, N. S. (2018). Charting the development of cognitive mapping. *Journal of Experimental Child Psychology, 170,* 86–106.

NCD-RisC (Non-Communicable Disease Risk Factor Collaboration). (2017). Worldwide trends in body-mass index, underweight, overweight, and obesity from 1975 to 2016: A pooled analysis of 2,416 population-based measurement studies in 128.9 million children, adolescents, and adults. *Lancet, 390,* 2627–2642.

Ncube, C. N., Enquobahrie, D. A., Burke, J. G., Ye, F., Marx, J., & Albert, S. M. (2017). Transgenerational transmission of preterm birth risk: The role of race and generational socio-economic neighborhood context. *Maternal and Child Health Journal, 21,* 1616–1626.

Needham, A. (2001). Object recognition in 4.5-month-old infants. *Journal of Experimental Child Psychology, 78,* 3–24.

Needleman, H. L., MacFarland, C., Ness, R. B., Reinberg, S., & Tobin, M. J. (2002). Bone lead levels in adjudicated delinquents: A case control study. *Neurotoxicology and Teratology, 24,* 711–717.

Neff, K. D., & Vonk, R. (2009). Self-compassion versus global self-esteem: Two different ways of relating to oneself. *Journal of Personality, 77,* 23–50.

Neihart, M., & Yeo, L. S. (2018). Psychological issues unique to the gifted student. In S. I. Pfeiffer, E. Shaunessy-Dedrick, & M. Foley-Nicpon (Eds.), *APA handbook of giftedness and talent* (pp. 497–510). Washington, DC: American Psychological Association.

Neitzel, C., & Stright, A. D. (2003). Mothers' scaffolding of children's problem solving: Establishing a foundation of academic self-regulatory competence. *Journal of Family Psychology, 17,* 147–159.

Nelson, A. M. (2012). A comprehensive review of evidence and current recommendations related to pacifier use. *Journal of Pediatric Nursing, 27,* 690–699.

Nelson, C. A., & Bosquet, M. (2000). Neurobiology of fetal and infant development: Implications for infant mental health. In C. H. Zeanah, Jr. (Ed.), *Handbook of infant mental health* (2nd ed., pp. 37–59). New York: Guilford.

Nelson, C. A., Fox, N. A., & Zeanah, C. H. (2014). *Romania's abandoned children: Deprivation, brain development, and the struggle for recovery.* Cambridge, MA: Harvard University Press.

Nelson, D. A., Robinson, C. C., & Hart, C. H. (2005). Relational and physical aggression of preschool-age children: Peer status linkages across informants. *Early Education and Development, 16,* 115–139.

Nelson, D. A., Yang, C., Coyne, S. M., Olsen, J. A., & Hart, C. H. (2013). Parental psychological control dimensions: Connections with Russian preschoolers' physical and relational aggression. *Journal of Applied Developmental Psychology, 34,* 1–8.

Nelson, J. M., James, T. D., Chevalier, N., Clark, C. A. C., & Espy, K. A. (2016). Structure, measurement, and development of preschool executive function. In J. A. Griffin, P. McCardle & L. S. Freund (Eds.), *Executive function in preschool-age children* (pp. 65–89). Washington, DC: American Psychological Association.

Nelson, K. (1973). Structure and strategy in learning to talk. *Monographs of the Society for Research in Child Development, 38*(1–2, Serial No. 149).

Nelson, K. (2003). Narrative and the emergence of a consciousness of self. In G. D. Fireman & T. E. McVay, Jr. (Eds.), *Narrative and consciousness: Literature,* psychology, and the brain (pp. 17–36). London: Oxford University Press.

Nepomnyaschy, L., & Donnelly, L. (2015). Father involvement and childhood injuries. *Journal of Marriage and Family, 77,* 628–646.

Nesdale, D., Durkin, K., Maas, A., & Griffiths, J. (2004). Group status, outgroup ethnicity, and children's ethnic attitudes. *Applied Developmental Psychology, 25,* 237–251.

Neugebauer, R., Fisher, P. W., Turner, J. B., Yamabe, S., Sarsfield, J. A., & Stehling-Ariza, T. (2009). Post-traumatic stress reactions among Rwandan children and adolescents in the early aftermath of genocide. *International Journal of Epidemiology, 38,* 1033–1045.

Neuman, S. B. (2003). From rhetoric to reality: The case for high-quality compensatory prekindergarten programs. *Phi Delta Kappan, 85*(4), 286–291.

Neuman, S. B. (2006). The knowledge gap: Implications for early education. In D. K. Dickinson & S. B. Neuman (Eds.), *Handbook of early literacy research* (Vol. 2, pp. 29–40). New York: Guilford.

Neumann, M. M., & Neumann, D. L. (2017). The use of touch-screen tablets at home and pre-school to foster emergent literacy. *Journal of Early Childhood Literacy, 17,* 203–220.

Neville, H. J., & Bavelier, D. (2002). Human brain plasticity: Evidence from sensory deprivation and altered language experience. In M. A. Hofman, G. J. Boer, A. J. G. D. Holtmaat, E. J. W. van Someren, J. Berhaagen, & D. F. Swaab (Eds.), *Plasticity in the adult brain: From genes to neurotherapy* (pp. 177–188). Amsterdam: Elsevier Science.

Neville, H. J., & Bruer, J. T. (2001). Language processing: How experience affects brain organization. In D. B. Bailey, Jr., J. T. Bruer, F. J. Symons, & J. W. Lichtman (Eds.), *Critical thinking about critical periods* (pp. 151–172). Baltimore: Paul H. Brookes.

Nevin, R. (2006). Understanding international crime trends: The legacy of preschool lead exposure. *Environmental Research, 104,* 315–316.

Newheiser, A., Dunham, Y., Merrill, A., Hoosain, L., & Olson, K. R. (2014). Preference for high status predicts implicit outgroup bias among children from low-status groups. *Developmental Psychology, 50,* 1081–1090.

Newhook, J. T., Pyne, J., Winters, K., Feder, S., Holmes, C., Tosh, J., et al. (2018). A critical commentary on follow-up studies and "desistance" theories about transgender and gender-nonconforming children. *International Journal of Transgenderism, 19,* 212–224.

Newnham, C. A., Milgrom, J., & Skouteris, H. (2009). Effectiveness of a modified mother–infant transaction program on outcomes for preterm infants from 3 to 24 months of age. *Infant Behavior and Development, 32,* 17–26.

Newson, J., & Newson, E. (1975). Intersubjectivity and the transmission of culture: On the social origins of symbolic functioning. *Bulletin of the British Psychological Society, 28,* 437–446.

Newton, E. K., Laible, D., Carlo, G., Steele, J. S., & McGinley, M. (2014). Do sensitive parents foster kind children, or vice versa? Bidirectional influences between children's prosocial behavior and parental sensitivity. *Developmental Psychology, 50,* 1808–1816.

Newton, S., Braithwaite, D., & Akinyemiju, T. F. (2017). Socio-economic status over the life course and obesity: Systematic review and meta-analysis. *PLOS ONE, 12*(5), e0177151.

Ng, F. F., Pomerantz, E. M., & Deng, C. (2014). Why are Chinese mothers more controlling than American mothers?: "My child is my report card." *Child Development, 85,* 355–369.

Ng, F. F., Pomerantz, E. M., & Lam, S. (2007). European-American and Chinese parents' responses to children's success and failure: Implications for children's responses. *Developmental Psychology, 43,* 1239–1255.

NICHD (National Institute of Child Health and Human Development) Early Child Care Research Network. (1997). The effects of infant child care on infant–mother attachment security: Results of the NICHD Study of Early Child Care. *Child Development, 68,* 860–879.

NICHD (National Institute of Child Health and Human Development) Early Child Care Research Network. (1998). Relations between family predictors and child outcomes: Are they weaker for children in child care? *Developmental Psychology, 34,* 1119–1128.

NICHD (National Institute of Child Health and Human Development) Early Child Care Research Network. (1999). Child care and mother–child interaction in the first 3 years of life. *Developmental Psychology, 35,* 1399–1413.

NICHD (National Institute of Child Health and Human Development) Early Child Care Research Network. (2000a). Characteristics and quality of child care for toddlers and preschoolers. *Applied Developmental Science, 4,* 116–135.

NICHD (National Institute of Child Health and Human Development) Early Child Care Research Network. (2000b). The relation of child care to cognitive and language development. *Child Development, 71,* 960–980.

NICHD (National Institute of Child Health and Human Development) Early Child Care Research Network. (2001). Before Head Start: Income and ethnicity, family characteristics, child care experiences, and child development. *Early Education and Development, 12,* 545–575.

NICHD (National Institute of Child Health and Human Development) Early Child Care Research Network. (2002). The interaction of child care and family risk in relation to child development at 24 and 36 months. *Applied Developmental Science, 6,* 144–156.

NICHD (National Institute of Child Health and Human Development) Early Child Care Research Network. (2003a). Does amount of time spent in child care predict socioemotional adjustment during the transition to kindergarten? *Child Development, 74,* 976–1005.

NICHD (National Institute of Child Health and Human Development) Early Child Care Research Network. (2003b). Does quality of child care affect child outcomes at age 4½? *Developmental Psychology, 39,* 451–469.

NICHD (National Institute of Child Health and Human Development) Early Child Care Research Network. (2004). Type of child care and children's development at 54 months. *Early Childhood Research Quarterly, 19,* 203–230.

NICHD (National Institute of Child Health and Human Development) Early Child Care Research Network. (2006). Child-care effect sizes for the NICHD Study of Early Child Care and Youth Development. *American Psychologist, 61,* 99–116.

Nicholls, A. L., & Kennedy, J. M. (1992). Drawing development: From similarity of features to direction. *Child Development, 63,* 227–241.

Nichols, K. E., Fox, N., & Mundy, P. (2005). Joint attention, self-recognition, and neurocognitive function in toddlers. *Infancy, 7,* 35–51.

Nicolaou, E., Quach, J., Lum, J., Roberts, G., Spencer-Smith, M., Gathercole, S., et al. (2017). Changes in verbal and visuospatial working memory from grade 1 to grade 3 of primary school: Population longitudinal study. *Child: Care, Health, and Development, 44,* 392–400.

Nicolopoulou, A., & Ilgaz, H. (2013). What do we know about pretend play and narrative development? A response to Lillard, Lerner, Hopkins, Dore, Smith, and Palmquist on "The impact of pretend play on children's development: A review of the evidence." *American Journal of Play, 6,* 55–81.

Nielsen, M. (2012). Imitation, pretend play, and childhood: Essential elements in the evolution of human culture? *Journal of Comparative Psychology, 126,* 170–181.

Nielsen, M., & Christie, T. (2008). Adult modeling facilitates young children's generation of novel pretend acts. *Infant and Child Development, 17,* 151–162.

Nielsen, N. M., Hansen, A. V., Simonsen, J., & Hviid, A. (2011). Prenatal stress and risk of infectious diseases in offspring. *American Journal of Epidemiology, 173,* 990–997.

Nikulina, V., & Widom, C. S. (2013). Child maltreatment and executive functioning in middle adulthood: A prospective examination. *Neuropsychology, 27,* 417–427.

Nikulina, V., Widom, C. S., & Czaja, S. (2011). The role of childhood neglect and childhood poverty in predicting academic achievement and crime in adulthood. *American Journal of Community Psychology, 48,* 309–321.

Nippold, M. A., Taylor, C. L., & Baker, J. M. (1996). Idiom understanding in Australian youth: A cross-cultural comparison. *Journal of Speech and Hearing Research, 39,* 442–447.

Nisbett, R. E. (2009). *Intelligence and how to get it.* New York: Norton.

Nisbett, R. E., Aronson, J., Blair, C., Dickens, W., Flynn, J., Halpern, D. F., et al. (2012). Intelligence: New findings and theoretical developments. *American Psychologist, 67,* 130–159.

Nishitani, S., Miyamura, T., Tagawa, M., Sumi, M., Takase, R., Doi, H., Moriuchi, H., & Shinohara, K. (2009). The calming effect of a maternal breast milk odor on the human newborn infant. *Neuroscience Research, 63,* 66–71.

Nix, R. L., Bierman, K. L., Heinrichs, B. S., Gest, S. D., Welsh, J. A., & Domitrovich, C. E. (2016). The randomized controlled trial of Head Start REDI: Sustained effects on developmental trajectories of social–emotional functioning. *Journal of Consulting and Clinical Psychology, 84,* 310–322.

Noble, K. G., Engelhardt, L. E., Brito, N. H., Mack, L. J., Nail, E. J., Angal, J., et al. (2015a). Socioeconomic disparities in neurocognitive development in the first two years of life. *Developmental Psychobiology, 57,* 535–551.

Noble, K. G., Fifer, W. P., Rauh, V. A., Nomura, Y., & Andrews, H. F. (2012). Academic achievement varies with gestational age among children born at term. *Pediatrics, 130,* e257–e264.

Noble, K. G., Houston, S. M., Brito, N. H., Bartsch, H., Kan, E., Kuperman, J. M., et al. (2015b). Family income, parental education and brain structure in children and adolescents. *Nature Neuroscience, 18,* 773–778.

Nomaguchi, K., & Milkie, M. A. (2016). Sociological perspectives on parenting stress: How social structure and culture shape parental strain and the well-being of parents and children. In K. Deater-Deckard & R. Panneton (Eds.), *Parental stress and early child development: Adaptive and maladaptive outcomes* (pp. 47–73). Cham, Switzerland: Springer International.

Noonan, C. W., Kathman, S. J., Sarasua, S. M., & White, M. C. (2003). Influence of environmental zinc on the association between environmental and biological measures of lead in children. *Journal of Exposure Analysis and Environmental Epidemiology, 13,* 318–323.

Noordstar, J. J., van der Net, J., Jak, S., Helders, P. J. M., & Jongmans, M. J. (2016). Global self-esteem, perceived athletic competence, and physical activity in children: A longitudinal cohort study. *Psychology of Sport and Exercise, 22,* 83–90.

Northstone, K., & Emmett, P. M. (2008). Are dietary patterns stable throughout early and mid-childhood? A birth cohort study. *British Journal of Nutrition, 100,* 1060–1076.

Northstone, K., Joinson, C., Emmett, P., Ness, A., & Paus, T. (2012). Are dietary patterns in childhood associated with IQ at 8 years of age? A population-based cohort study. *Journal of Epidemiological Community Health, 66,* 624–628.

Noterdaeme, M., Mildenberger, K., Minow, F., & Amorosa, H. (2002). Evaluation of neuromotor deficits in children with autism and children with a specific speech and language disorder. *European Child and Adolescent Psychiatry, 11,* 219–225.

Nowicki, E. A., Brown, J., & Stepien, M. (2014). Children's thoughts on the social exclusion of peers with intellectual or learning disabilities. *Journal of Intellectual Disability Research, 58,* 346–357.

Nowicki, E. A., & Lopata, J. (2017). Children's implicit and explicit gender stereotypes about mathematics and reading ability. *Social Psychology of Education, 20,* 329–345.

Nucci, L. (2005). Culture, context, and the psychological sources of human rights concepts. In W. Edelstein & G. Nunner-Winkler (Eds.), *Morality in context* (pp. 365–394). Amsterdam: Elsevier.

Nucci, L. (2009). *Nice is not enough: Facilitating moral development.* Upper Saddle River, NJ: Prentice Hall.

Nucci, L. P., & Gingo, M. (2011). The development of moral reasoning. In U. Goswami (Ed.), *The Wiley-Blackwell handbook of childhood cognitive development* (2nd ed., pp. 420–444). Hoboken, NJ: Wiley.

O

Oakes, L. M., Ross-Sheehy, S., & Luck, S. J. (2007). The development of visual short-term memory in infancy. In L. M. Oakes & P. J. Bauer (Eds.), *Short- and long-term memory in infancy and early childhood* (pp. 75–102). New York: Oxford University Press.

Obeidat, H. M., & Shuriquie, M. A. (2015). Effect of breast-feeding and maternal holding in relieving painful responses in full-term neonates: A randomized clinical trial. *Journal of Perinatal and Neonatal Nursing, 29,* 248–254.

Oberecker, R., & Friederici, A. D. (2006). Syntactic event-related potential components in 24-month-olds' sentence comprehension. *NeuroReport, 17,* 1017–1021.

Obradović, J., Yousafzai, A. K., Finch, J. E., & Rasheed, M. A. (2016). Maternal scaffolding and home stimulation: Key mediators of early intervention on children's cognitive development. *Developmental Psychology, 52,* 1409–1421.

O'Brien, K. M., Franco, M. G., & Dunn, M. G. (2014). Women of color in the workplace: Supports, barriers, and interventions. In M. L. Miville & A. D. Ferguson (Eds.), *Handbook of race–ethnicity and gender in psychology* (pp. 247–270). New York: Springer Science + Business Media.

O'Brien, M., Weaver, J. M., Nelson, J. A., Calkins, S. D., Leerkes, E. M., & Marcovitch, S. (2011). Longitudinal associations between children's understanding of emotions and theory of mind. *Cognition and Emotion, 25,* 1074–1086.

O'Connor, T. G., Marvin, R. S., Rutter, M., Olrich, J. T., Britner, P. A., & the English and Romanian Adoptees Study Team. (2003). Child–parent attachment following early institutional deprivation. *Development and Psychopathology, 15,* 19–38.

O'Connor, T. G., Rutter, M., Beckett, C., Keaveney, L., Dreppner, J. M., & the English and Romanian Adoptees Study Team. (2000). The effects of global severe privation on cognitive competence: Extension and longitudinal follow-up. *Child Development, 71,* 376–390.

O'Dea, J. A. (2012). Body image and self-esteem. In T. F. Cash (Ed.), *Encyclopedia of body image and human appearance* (pp. 141–147). London: Elsevier.

O'Donnell, K. J., & Meaney, M. J. (2016). Fetal origins of mental health: The developmental origins of health and disease hypothesis. *American Journal of Psychiatry, 174,* 319–327.

OECD (Organisation for Economic Cooperation and Development). (2017a). *Education at a glance 2017: OECD indicators.* Retrieved from http://www.oecd.org/education/education-at-a-glance-19991487.htm

OECD (Organisation for Economic Cooperation and Development). (2017b). *Obesity update 2017.* Retrieved from www.oecd.org/health/obesity-update.htm

OECD (Organisation for Economic Cooperation and Development). (2017c). *OECD Health statistics 2017.* Retrieved from www.oecd.org/els/health-systems/health-data.htm

OECD (Organisation for Economic Cooperation and Development). (2018). *Poverty rate (indicator).* Retrieved from data.oecd.org/inequality/poverty-rate.htm

Oedes-Sese, G. V., Matthews, T. A., & Lewis, M. (2014). Shame and pride and their effects on student achievement. In R. Pekrun & L. Linnenbrink-Garcia (Eds.), *International handbook of emotions in education* (pp. 246–264). New York: Routledge.

Office of Head Start. (2018). *Head Start Program facts: Fiscal year 2017.* https://eclkc.ohs.acf.hhs.gov/sites/default/files/pdf/hs-program-fact-sheet-2017_0.pdf

Oftinger, A.-L., & Camos, V. (2018). Developmental improvement in strategies to maintain verbal information in working memory. *International Journal of Behavioral Development, 42,* 182–191.

Ogden, C. L., Carroll, M. D., Kit, B. K., & Flegal, K. M. (2014). Prevalence of childhood and adult obesity. *Journal of the American Medical Association, 311,* 806–814.

Ogden, C. L., Carroll, M. D., Lawman, H. G., Frayar, C. D., Kruszon-Moran, D., Kit, B. K., & Flegal, K. M. (2016). Trends in obesity prevalence among children and adolescents in the United States, 1988–1994 through 2013–2014. *JAMA, 315,* 2292–2299.

Ohgi, S., Arisawa, K., Takahashi, T., Kusumoto, T., Goto, Y., Akiyama, T., & Saito, H. (2003a). Neonatal behavioral assessment scale as a predictor of later developmental disabilities of low-birth-weight and/or premature infants. *Brain and Development, 25,* 313–321.

Ohgi, S., Takahashi, T., Nugent, J. K., Arisawa, K., & Akiyama, T. (2003b). Neonatal behavioral characteristics and later behavioral problems. *Clinical Pediatrics, 42,* 679–686.

Okagaki, L., & Sternberg, R. J. (1993). Parental beliefs and children's school performance. *Child Development, 64,* 36–56.

Okami, P., Weisner, T., & Olmstead, R. (2002). Outcome correlates of parent–child bedsharing: An eighteen-year longitudinal study. *Developmental and Behavioral Pediatrics, 23,* 244–253.

Okamoto, Y. (2015). Mathematics learning in the USA and Japan. In R. C. Kadosh & A. Dowker (Eds.), *Oxford handbook of numerical cognition* (pp. 415–429). New York: Oxford University Press.

Okeke-Adeyanju, N., Taylor, L., Craig, A. B., Smith, R. E., Thomas, A., Boyle, A. E., et al. (2014). Celebrating the strengths of Black youth: Increasing self-esteem and implications for prevention. *Journal of Primary Prevention, 35,* 357–369.

Okkinga, M., van Steensel, R., van Gelderen, A. J. S., & Sleegers, P. J. C. (2018). Effects of reciprocal teaching on reading comprehension of low-achieving adolescents: The importance of specific teacher skills. *Journal of Research in Reading, 41,* 20–41.

Olafson, E. (2011). Child sexual abuse: Demography, impact, and interventions. *Journal of Child and Adolescent Trauma, 4,* 8–21.

Olds, D. L., Eckenrode, J., Henderson, C., Kitzman, H., Cole, R., Luckey, D., et al. (2009). Preventing child abuse and neglect with home visiting by nurses. In K. A. Dodge & D. L. Coleman (Eds.), *Preventing child maltreatment* (pp. 29–54). New York: Guilford.

Olds, D. L., Kitzman, H., Cole, R., Robinson, J., Sidora, K., Luckey, D. W., et al. (2004). Effects of nurse home-visiting on maternal life course and child development: Age 6 follow-up results of a randomized trial. *Pediatrics, 114,* 1550–1559.

Olds, D. L., Kitzman, H., Hanks, C., Cole, R., Anson, E., Sidora-Arcoleo, K., et al. (2007). Effects of nurse home visiting on maternal and child functioning: Age-9 follow-up of a randomized trial. *Pediatrics, 120,* e832–e845.

Olds, D. L., Robinson, J., O'Brien, R., Luckey, D. W., Pettitt, L. M., Henderson, C. R., Jr., et al. (2002). Home visiting by paraprofessionals and by nurses: A randomized, controlled trial. *Pediatrics, 110,* 486–496.

Olineck, K. M., & Poulin-Dubois, D. (2009). Infants' understanding of intention from 10 to 14 months: Interrelations among violation of expectancy and imitation tasks. *Infant Behavior and Development, 32,* 404–415.

Olino, T. M., Durbin, C. E., Klein, D. N., Hayden, E. P., & Dyson, M. W. (2013). Gender differences in young children's temperamental traits: Comparisons across observational and parent-report methods. *Journal of Personality, 81,* 119–129.

Ollendick, T. H., King, N. J., & Muris, P. (2002). Fears and phobias in children: Phenomenology, epidemiology, and aetiology. *Child and Adolescent Mental Health, 7,* 98–106.

Oller, D. K. (2000). *The emergence of the speech capacity.* Mahwah, NJ: Erlbaum.

Olson, K. R. (2016). Prepubescent transgender children: What we do and do not know. *Journal of the American Academy of Child and Adolescent Psychiatry, 55,* 155–156.

Olson, K. R., Key, A. C., & Eaton, N. R. (2015). Gender cognition in transgender children. *Psychological Science, 26,* 467–474.

Olson, S. L., Lopez-Duran, N., Lunkenheimer, E. S., Chang, H., & Sameroff, A. J. (2011). Individual differences in the development of early peer aggression: Integrating contributions of self-regulation, theory of mind, and parenting. *Development and Psychopathology, 23,* 253–266.

O'Neil, R., Welsh, M., Parke, R. D., Wang, S., & Strand, C. (1997). A longitudinal assessment of the academic correlates of early peer acceptance and rejection. *Journal of Clinical Child Psychology, 26,* 290–303.

O'Neill, M., Bard, K. A., Kinnell, M., & Fluck, M. (2005). Maternal gestures with 20-month-old infants in two contexts. *Developmental Science, 8,* 352–359.

Ontai, L. L., & Thompson, R. A. (2008). Attachment, parent–child discourse and theory-of-mind development. *Social Development, 17,* 47–60.

Ooki, S. (2014). An overview of human handedness in twins. *Frontiers in Psychology, 5,* Art. No. 10.

Oosterwegel, A., & Openheimer, L. (1993). *The self-system: Developmental changes between and within self-concepts.* Hillsdale, NJ: Erlbaum.

Ophoff, D., Slaats, M. A., Boudewyns, A., Glazemakers, I., Van Hoorenbeeck, K., & Verhulst, S. L. (2018). Sleep disorders during childhood: A practical review. *European Journal of Pediatrics, 177,* 641–648.

Orbio de Castro, B., Veerman, J. W., Koops, W., Bosch, J. D., & Monshouwer, H. J. (2002). Hostile attribution of intent and aggressive behavior: A meta-analysis. *Child Development, 73,* 916–934.

Ordonana, J. R., Caspi, A., & Moffitt, T. E. (2008). Unintentional injuries in a twin study of preschool children: Environmental, not genetic, risk factors. *Journal of Pediatric Psychology, 33,* 185–194.

O'Reilly, J., & Peterson, C. C. (2014). Theory of mind at home: Linking authoritative and authoritarian parenting styles to children's social understanding. *Early Child Development and Care, 184,* 1934–1947.

Orfield, G., Ee, J., Frankenberg, E., & Siegel-Hawley, G. (2016, May 16). *Brown at 62: School segregation by race, poverty and state.* Los Angeles: UCLA Civil Rights Project. Retrieved from https://escholarship.org/uc/item/5ds6k0rd

Oshima-Takane, Y., & Robbins, M. (2003). Linguistic environment of secondborn children. *First Language, 23,* 21–40.

Osina, M. A., Saylor, M. M., & Ganea, P. A. (2017). Out of reach, out of mind? Comprehension of references to hidden inaccessible objects. *Child Development, 88,* 1572–1580.

Ostad, S. A. (2015). Private speech use in arithmetical calculation: Relationship with phonological memory skills in children with and without mathematical difficulties. *Annals of Dyslexia, 65,* 103–119.

Osterholm, E. A., Hostinar, C. E., & Gunnar, M. R. (2012). Alterations in stress responses of the hypothalamic-pituitary-adrenal axis in small for gestational age infants. *Psychoneuroendocrinology, 37,* 1719–1725.

Ostrov, J. M., Crick, N. R., & Stauffacher, K. (2006). Relational aggression in sibling and peer relationships during early childhood. *Journal of Applied Developmental Psychology, 27,* 241–253.

Ostrov, J. M., Gentile, D. A., & Mullins, A. D. (2013). Evaluating the effect of educational media exposure on aggression in early childhood. *Journal of Applied Developmental Psychology, 34,* 38–44.

Otsuka, Y., Nakato, E., Kanazawa, S., Yamaguchi, M. K., Watanabe, S., & Kakigi, R. (2007). Neural activation to upright and inverted faces in infants measured by near infrared spectroscopy. *NeuroImage, 34,* 399–406.

Otter, M., Schrander-Stempel, C. T. R. M., Didden, R., & Curfs, L. M. G. (2013). The psychiatric phenotype in triple X syndrome: New hypotheses illustrated in two cases. *Developmental Neurorehabilitation, 15,* 233–238.

Otto, H., & Keller, H. (2015). A good child is a calm child: Mothers' social status, maternal conceptions of proper demeanor, and stranger anxiety in one-year-old Cameroonian Nso children. *Psychological Topics, 1,* 1–25.

Ovalle, W., Pomerantz, W. J., Anderson, B. L., & Gittelman, M. A. (2016). Severe unintentional injuries sustained by Ohio children: Is there urban/rural variation? *Journal of Trauma and Acute Care Surgery, 81,* S14–S19.

Overton, W. F., & Molenaar, P. C. M. (2015). Concepts, theory, and method in developmental science: A view of the issues. In W. F. Overton & P. C. Molenar (Eds.), *Handbook of child psychology and developmental science: Vol. 1. Theory and method* (pp. 1–8). Hoboken, NJ: Wiley.

Owen, C. G., Whincup, P. H., Kaye, S. J., Martin, R. M., Smith, G. D., Cook, D. G., et al. (2008). Does initial breastfeeding lead to lower blood cholesterol in adult life? A quantitative review of the evidence. *American Journal of Clinical Nutrition, 88,* 305–314.

Owens, E. B., Cardoos, S. L., & Hinshaw, S. P. (2015). Developmental progression and gender differences among individuals with ADHD. In R. A. Barkley (Ed.), *Attention-deficit hyperactivity disorder: A handbook for diagnosis and treatment* (pp. 223–255). New York: Guilford Press.

Oyserman, D., Bybee, D., Mowbray, C., & Hart-Johnson, T. (2005). When mothers have serious mental health problems: Parenting as a proximal mediator. *Journal of Adolescence, 28,* 443–463.

Özçaliskan, S. (2005). On learning to draw the distinction between physical and metaphorical motion: Is metaphor an early emerging cognitive and linguistic capacity? *Journal of Child Language, 32,* 291–318.

P

Pack, G. (2019). The case for magnet schools. In R. A. Fox & N. K. Buchanan (Eds.), *Wiley handbook of school choice* (pp. 180–193). Malden, MA: Wiley Blackwell.

Padilla-Walker, L. M., Harper, J. M., & Jensen, A. C. (2010). Self-regulation as mediators between parenting and adolescents' prosocial behaviors. *Journal of Research on Adolescence, 22,* 400–408.

Páez, M., & Hunter, C. (2015). Bilingualism and language learning for immigrant-origin children and youth. In C. Suárez-Orozco, M. Abo-Zena, & A. K. Marks (Eds.), *Transitions: The development of children of immigrants* (pp. 165–183). New York: New York University Press.

Pahlke, E., Bigler, R. S., & Suizzo, M.-A. (2012). Relations between colorblind socialization and children's racial bias: Evidence from European American mothers and their preschool children. *Child Development, 83,* 1164–1179.

Palacios, J., & Brodzinsky, D. M. (2010). Adoption research: Trends, topics, outcomes. *International Journal of Behavioral Development, 34,* 270–284.

Palkovitz, R., Fagan, J., & Hull, J. (2013). Coparenting and children's well-being. In N. Cabrera and C. S. LeMonda (Eds.), *Handbook of father involvement: Multidisciplinary perspectives* (2nd ed., pp. 202– 219). New York: Routledge.

Palincsar, A. S., & Herrenkohl, L. R. (1999). Designing collaborative contexts: Lessons from three research programs. In A. M. O'Donnell & A. King (Eds.), *Cognitive perspectives on peer learning. The Rutgers Invitational Symposium on Education Series* (pp. 151–177). Mahwah, NJ: Erlbaum.

Pan, H. W. (1994). Children's play in Taiwan. In J. L. Roopnarine, J. E. Johnson, & F. H. Hooper (Eds.), *Children's play in diverse cultures* (pp. 31–50). Albany: SUNY Press.

Pappas, A., & Korzeniewski, S. J. (2016). Long-term cognitive outcomes of birth asphyxia and the contribution of identified perinatal asphyxia to cerebral palsy. *Clinics in Perinataology, 43,* 559–572.

Parade, S. H., Dickstein, S., Schiller, M., Hayden, L., & Seifer, R. (2015). Stability of child behavioral style in the first 30 months of life: Single timepoint and aggregated measures. *International Journal of Behavioral Development, 39,* 121–129.

Paradis, J., Genesee, F., & Crago, M. B. (2011). *Dual language development and disorders: A handbook on bilingualism and learning* (2nd ed.). Baltimore, MD: Brookes.

Parameswaran, G. (2003). Experimenter instructions as a mediator in the effects of culture on mapping one's neighborhood. *Journal of Environmental Psychology, 23,* 409–417.

Parent, J., Sanders, W., & Forehand, R. (2016). Youth screen time and behavioral health problems: The role of sleep duration and disturbances. *Journal of Developmental and Behavioral Pediatrics, 37,* 277–284.

Pariera, K. L. (2016). Barriers and prompts to parent–child sexual communication. *Journal of Family Communication, 16,* 277–283.

Parish-Morris, J., Golinkoff, R. M., & Hirsh-Pasek, K. (2013). From coo to code: A brief story of language development. In P. D. Zelazo (Ed.), *Oxford handbook of developmental psychology: Vol. 1. Body and mind* (pp. 867–908). New York: Oxford University Press.

Parish-Morris, J., Pruden, S., Ma, W., Hirsh-Pasek, K., & Golinkoff, R. M. (2010). A world of relations: Relational words. In B. Malt & P. Wolf (Eds.), *Words and the mind: How words capture human experience* (pp. 219–242). New York: Oxford University Press.

Park, D., Gunderson, E. A., Tsukayama, E., Levine, S. C., & Beilock, S. L. (2016). Young children's motivational frameworks and math achievement: Relation to teacher-reported instructional practices, but not teacher theory of intelligence. *Journal of Educational Psychology, 108,* 300–313.

Park, H., & Lau, A. S. (2016). Socioeconomic status and parenting priorities: Child independence and obedience around the world. *Journal of Marriage and Family, 78*, 43–59.

Park, H., & Zhan, M. (2017). The impact of after-school childcare arrangements on the developmental outcomes of low-income children. *Children and Youth Services Review, 73*, 230–241.

Parke, R. D. (2002). Fathers and families. In M. H. Bornstein (Ed.), *Handbook of parenting: Vol. 3* (2nd ed., pp. 27–73). Mahwah, NJ: Erlbaum.

Parke, R. D., Simpkins, S. D., McDowell, D. J., Kim, M., Killian, C., Dennis, J., Flyr, M. L., Wild, M., & Rah, Y. (2004). Relative contributions of families and peers to children's social development. In P. K. Smith & C. H. Hart (Eds.), *Blackwell handbook of childhood social development* (pp. 156–177). Malden, MA: Blackwell.

Parker, J. G., Low, C. M., Walker, A. R., & Gamm, B. K. (2005). Friendship jealousy in young adolescents: Individual differences and links to sex, self-esteem, aggression, and social adjustment. *Developmental Psychology, 41*, 235–250.

Parker, P. D., Schoon, I., Tsai, Y.-M., Nagy, G., Trautwein, U., & Eccles, J. (2012). Achievement, agency, gender, and socioeconomic background as predictors of postschool choices: A multicontext study. *Developmental Psychology, 48*, 1629–1642.

Parten, M. (1932). Social participation among preschool children. *Journal of Abnormal and Social Psychology, 27*, 243–269.

Pascalis, O., de Haan, M., & Nelson, C. A. (1998). Long-term recognition memory for faces assessed by visual paired comparison in 3- and 6-month-old infants. *Journal of Experimental Psychology: Learning, Memory, and Cognition, 24*, 249–260.

Pascalis, O., de Haan, M., & Nelson, C. A. (2002). Is face processing species-specific during the first year of life? *Science, 296*, 1321–1323.

Paschall, K. W., & Mastergeorge, A. M. (2018). A longitudinal, person-centered analysis of Early Head Start mothers' parenting. *Infant Mental Health Journal, 39*, 70–84.

Patel, S., Gaylord, S., & Fagen, J. (2013). Generalization of deferred imitation in 6-, 9-, and 12-month-old infants using visual and auditory contexts. *Infant Behavior and Development, 36*, 25–31.

Pathman, T., Larkina, M., Burch, M. M., & Bauer, P. J. (2013). Young children's memory for the times of personal past events. *Journal of Cognition and Development, 14*, 120–140.

Patrick, K. E., Millet, G., & Mindell, J. A. (2016). Sleep differences by race in preschool children: The roles of parenting behaviors and socioeconomic status. *Behavioral Sleep Medicine, 14*, 467–479.

Patterson, C. J. (2013). Children of lesbian and gay parents: Psychology, law, and policy. *Psychology of Sexual Orientation and Gender Diversity, 1*(S), 27–34.

Patterson, C. J. (2017). Parents' sexual orientation and children's development. *Child Development Perspectives, 11*, 45–49.

Patterson, C. J., & Farr, R. H. (2016). Children of lesbian and gay parents: Reflections on the research–policy interface. In K. Durkin & H., R. Schaffer (Eds.), *Wiley handbook of developmental psychology in practice: Implementation and impact* (pp. 121–142). Chichester, UK: Wiley Blackwell.

Patterson, G. R., & Fisher, P. A. (2002). Recent developments in our understanding of parenting: Bidirectional effects, causal models, and the search for parsimony. In M. H. Bornstein (Ed.), *Handbook of

parenting* (Vol. 5, pp. 59–88). Mahwah, NJ: Erlbaum.

Patton, G. C., Coffey, C., Carlin, J. B., Sawyer, S. M., Williams, J., Olsson, C. A., et al. (2011). Overweight and obesity between adolescence and young adulthood: A 10-year prospective cohort study. *Journal of Adolescent Health, 48*, 275–280.

Paukner, A., Ferrari, P. F., & Suomi, S. J. (2011). Delayed imitation of lipsmacking gestures by infant rhesus macaques (*Macaca mulatta*). *PLOS ONE, 6*(12), e28848.

Paukner, A., Simpson, E. A., Ferrari, P. F., Mrozek, T., & Suomi, S. J. (2014). Neonatal imitation predicts how infants engage with faces. *Developmental Science, 17*, 833–840.

Pauletti, R. E., Menon, M., Cooper, P. J., & Aults, C. D. (2017). Psychological androgyny and children's mental health: A new look with new measures. *Sex Roles, 76*, 705–718.

Paulson, J. F., & Bazemore, S. D. (2010). Prenatal and postpartum depression in fathers and its association with maternal depression: A meta-analysis. *JAMA, 303*, 1961–1969.

PBS (Public Broadcasting System). (2018). *We'll meet again. Children of World War II: Reiko Nagumo.* Retrieved from www.pbs.org/meet-again/episodes/children-wwii

Pedersen, S., Vitaro, F., Barker, E. D., & Anne, I. H. (2007). The timing of middle-childhood peer rejection and friendship: Linking early behavior to early adolescent adjustment. *Child Development, 78*, 1037–1051.

Peirano, P., Algarin, C., & Uauy, R. (2003). Sleep–wake states and their regulatory mechanisms throughout early human development. *Journal of Pediatrics, 143*, S70–S79.

Pelham, W. E. (2016). Treatment sequencing for childhood ADHD: A multiple-randomization study of adaptive medication and behavioral interventions. *Journal of Clinical Child & Adolescent Psychology, 43*, 396–415.

Pellegrini, A. D. (2003). Perceptions and functions of play and real fighting in early adolescence. *Child Development, 74*, 1522–1533.

Pellegrini, A. D. (2004). Rough-and-tumble play from childhood through adolescence: Development and possible functions. In P. K. Smith & C. H. Hart (Eds.), *Blackwell handbook of childhood social development* (pp. 438–453). Malden, MA: Blackwell.

Pellegrini, A. D., Huberty, P. D., & Jones, I. (1995). The effects of recess timing on children's playground and classroom behaviors. *American Educational Research Journal, 32*, 845–864.

Pellegrini, A. D., Kato, K., Blatchford, P., & Baines, E. (2002). A short-term longitudinal study of children's playground games across the first year of school: Implications for social competence and adjustment to school. *American Educational Research Journal, 39*, 991–1015.

Peltonen, K., & Punamaki, R.-L. (2010). Preventive interventions among children exposed to trauma of armed conflict: A literature review. *Aggressive Behavior, 36*, 95–116.

Pennington, B. F. (2015). Atypical cognitive development. In L. S. Liben & U. Müller (Eds.), *Handbook of child psychology and developmental science: Vol. 2. Cognitive processes* (7th ed., pp. 995–1042). Hoboken, NJ: Wiley.

Pennisi, E. (2012). ENCODE Project writes eulogy for junk DNA. *Science, 337*, 1160–1161.

Peralta de Mendoza, O. A., & Salsa, A. M. (2003). Instruction in early comprehension and use of a symbol–referent relation. *Cognitive Development, 18*, 269–284.

Perego, G., Caputi, M., & Ogliari, A. (2016). Neurobiological correlates of psychosocial deprivation in children: A systematic review of neuroscientific contributions. *Child and Youth Care Forum, 45*, 329–352.

Peres, K. G., Cascaes, A. M., Nascimento, G. G., & Victora, C. G. (2015). Effect of breastfeeding on malocclusions: A systematic review and meta-analysis. *Acta Paediatrica, 104*, 54–61.

Perez, J. D., Rubinstein, N. D., & Dulac, C. (2016). New perspectives on genomic imprinting, an essential and multifaceted mode of epigenetic control in the developing and adult brain. *Annual Review of Neuroscience, 39*, 347–384.

Pérez-Pereira, M., Fernández, P., Resches, M., & Gómez-Taibo, M. L. (2016). Does temperament influence language development? Evidence from preterm and full-term children. *Infant Behavior and Development, 42*, 11–21.

Perlmutter, M. (1984). Continuities and discontinuities in early human memory: Paradigms, processes, and performances. In R. V. Kail, Jr., & N. R. Spear (Eds.), *Comparative perspectives on the development of memory* (pp. 253–287). Hillsdale, NJ: Erlbaum.

Perone, S., Madole, K. L., Ross-Sheehy, S., Carey, M., & Oakes, L. M. (2008). The relation between infants' activity with objects and attention to object appearance. *Developmental Psychology, 44*, 1242–1248.

Perroud, N., Rutembesa, E., Paoloni-Giacobino, A., Mutabaruka, J., Mutesa, L., Stenz, L., et al. (2014). The Tutsi genocide and transgenerational transmission of maternal stress: Epigenetics and biology of the HPA axis. *World Journal of Biological Psychiatry, 15*, 334–345.

Perry, L. K., Axelsson, E. L., & Horst, J. S. (2016). Learning what to remember: Vocabulary knowledge and children's memory for object names and features. *Infant and Child Development, 25*, 247–258.

Pesonen, A.-K., Räikkönen, K., Heinonen, K., & Komsi, N. (2008). A transactional model of temperamental development: Evidence of a relationship between child temperament and maternal stress over five years. *Social Development, 17*, 326–340.

Peter, C. J., Fischer, L. K., Kundakovic, M., Garg, P., Jakovcevski, M., Dincer, A., et al. (2016). DNA methylation signatures of early childhood malnutrition associated with impairments in attention and cognition. *Biological Psychiatry, 80*, 765–774.

Peter, D., & Gazelle, H. (2017). Anxious solitude and self-compassion and self-criticism trajectories in early adolescence: Attachment security as a moderator. *Child Development, 88*, 1834–1848.

Peters, R. D. (2005). A community-based approach to promoting resilience in young children, their families, and their neighborhoods. In R. D. Peters, B. Leadbeater, & R. J. McMahon (Eds.), *Resilience in children, families, and communities: Linking context to practice and policy* (pp. 157–176). New York: Kluwer Academic.

Peters, R. D., Bradshaw, A. J., Petrunka, K., Nelson, G., Herry, Y., Craig, W. M., et al. (2010). The Better Beginnings, Better Futures Project: Findings from grade 3 to grade 9. *Monographs of the Society for Research in Child Development, 75* (3, Serial No. 297).

Peters, R. D., Petrunka, K., & Arnold, R. (2003). The Better Beginnings, Better Futures Project: A universal, comprehensive, community-based prevention approach for primary school children and their families. *Journal of Clinical Child and Adolescent Psychology, 32*, 215–227.

Peterson, C. (2012). Children's autobiographical memories across the years: Forensic implications of childhood amnesia and eyewitness memory for stressful events. *Developmental Review, 32*, 287–306.

Peterson, C., Parsons, T., & Dean, M. (2004). Providing misleading and reinstatement information a year after it happened: Effects on long-term memory. *Memory, 12*, 1–13.

Peterson, C., & Rideout, R. (1998). Memory for medical emergencies experienced by 1- and 2-year-olds. *Developmental Psychology, 34*, 1059–1072.

Peterson, C., Warren, K. L., & Short, M. M. (2011). Infantile amnesia across the years: A 2-year follow-up of children's earliest memories. *Child Development, 82*, 1092–1105.

Peterson, E. R., Rubie-Davies, C., Osborne, D., & Sibley, C. (2016). Teachers' explicit expectations and implicit prejudiced attitudes to educational achievement: Relations with student achievement and the ethnic achievement gap. *Learning and Instruction, 42*, 123–140.

Petitto, L. A., Holowka, S., Sergio, L. E., Levy, B., & Ostry, D. J. (2004). Baby hands that move to the rhythm of language: Hearing babies acquiring sign languages babble silently on the hands. *Cognition, 93*, 43–73.

Petitto, L. A., Holowka, S., Sergio, L. E., & Ostry, D. (2001). Language rhythms in babies' hand movements. *Nature, 413*, 35–36.

Petitto, L. A., & Marentette, P. F. (1991). Babbling in the manual mode: Evidence for the ontogeny of language. *Science, 251*, 1493–1496.

Petrill, S. A., & Deater-Deckard, K. (2004). The heritability of general cognitive ability: A within-family adoption design. *Intelligence, 32*, 403–409.

Pettigrew, T. F., & Tropp, L. R. (2006). A meta-analytic test of intergroup contact theory. *Journal of Personality and Social Psychology, 90*, 751–783.

Pettit, G. S., Brown, E. G., Mize, J., & Lindsey, E. (1998). Mothers' and fathers' socializing behaviors in three contexts: Links with children's peer competence. *Merrill-Palmer Quarterly, 44*, 173–193.

Pew Research Center. (2013a). *Among 38 nations, U.S. is the outlier when it comes to paid parental leave.* Retrieved from www.pewresearch.org/fact-tank/2013/12/12/mong-38-nations-u-s-is-the-holdout-when-it-comes-to-offering-paid-parental-leave

Pew Research Center. (2013b). *Modern parenthood: Roles of moms and dads converge as they balance work and family.* Retrieved from www.pewsocialtrends.org/2013/03/14/modern-parenthood-roles-of-moms-and-dads-converge-as-they-balance-work-and-family/

Pew Research Center. (2015). *For most highly educated women, motherhood doesn't start until the 30s.* Retrieved from www.pewresearch.org/fact-tank/2015/01/15/for-most-highly-educated-women-motherhood-doesnt-start-until-the-30s

Pew Research Center. (2018a). *7 facts about American dads.* Retrieved from www.pewresearch.org/fact-tank/2018/06/13/fathers-day-facts

Pew Research Center. (2018b). *7 facts about U.S. moms.* Retrieved from www.

pewresearch.org/fact-tank/2018/05/10/facts-about-u-s-mothers

Pew Research Center. (2018c). *Stay-at-home moms and dads account for about one-in-five U.S. parents.* Retrieved from www.pewresearch.org/fact-tank/2018/09/24/stay-at-home-moms-and-dads-account-for-about-one-in-five-u-s-parents

Pew Research Center. (2018d). *The changing profile of unmarried parents: A growing share are living with a partner.* Retrieved from www.pewsocialtrends.org/2018/04/25/the-changing-profile-of-unmarried-parents

Pew Research Center. (2018e). *They're waiting longer, but U.S. women today more likely to have children than a decade ago.* Retrieved from www.pewsocialtrends.org/2018/01/18/theyre-waiting-longer-but-u-s-women-today-more-likely-to-have-children-than-a-decade-ago

Pezzella, F. S., Thornberry, T. P., & Smith, C. A. (2016). Race socialization and parenting styles: Links to delinquency for African American and White adolescents. *Youth Violence and Juvenile Justice, 14,* 448–467.

Pfäffle, R., Land, C., Schönau, E., Holterhus, P.-M., Ross, J. L., Piras de Oliveira, C., et al. (2018). Growth hormone treatment for short stature in the USA, Germany and France: 15 years of surveillance in the Genetics and Neuroendocrinology of Short-Stature Study (GeNeSIS). *Hormone Research in Paediatrics, 90,* 169–180.

Pfeiffer, S. I., & Yermish, A. (2014). Gifted children. In L. Grossman & S. Walfish (Eds.), *Translating psychological research into practice* (pp. 57–64). New York: Springer.

Philbrook, L. E., & Teti, D. M. (2016). Bidirectional associations between bedtime parenting and infant sleep: Parenting quality, parenting practices, and their interaction. *Journal of Family Psychology, 30,* 431–441.

Phillips, D. A., & Lowenstein, A. E. (2011). Early care, education, and child development. *Annual Review of Psychology, 62,* 483–500.

Phillips, D., Gormley, W., & Anderson, S. (2016). The effects of Tulsa's CAP Head Start program on middle-school academic outcomes and progress. *Developmental Psychology, 52,* 1247–1261.

Piaget, J. (1926). *The language and thought of the child.* New York: Harcourt, Brace & World. (Original work published 1923)

Piaget, J. (1930). *The child's conception of the world.* New York: Harcourt, Brace, & World. (Original work published 1926)

Piaget, J. (1951). *Play, dreams, and imitation in childhood.* New York: Norton. (Original work published 1945)

Piaget, J. (1952). *The origins of intelligence in children.* New York: International Universities Press. (Original work published 1936)

Piaget, J. (1971). *Biology and knowledge.* Chicago: University of Chicago Press.

Piasta, S. B., Groom, L. J., Kahn, K. S., Skibbe, L. E., & Bowles, R. P. (2018). Young children's narrative skill: Concurrent and predictive associations with emergent literacy and early word reading skills. *Reading and Writing, 31,* 1479–1498.

Pickens, J., Field, T., & Nawrocki, T. (2001). Frontal EEG asymmetry in response to emotional vignettes in preschool age children. *International Journal of Behavioral Development, 25,* 105–112.

Pierroutsakos, S. L., & Troseth, G. L. (2003). Video verite: Infants' manual investigation of objects on video. *Infant Behavior and Development, 26,* 183–199.

Pierson, L. (1996). Hazards of noise exposure on fetal hearing. *Seminars in Perinatology, 20,* 21–29.

Pietschnig, J., & Voracek, M. (2015). One century of global IQ gains: A formal meta-analysis of the Flynn effect (1909–2013). *Perspectives on Psychological Science, 10,* 282–306.

Piirto, J. (2007). *Talented children and adults* (3rd ed.). Waco, TX: Prufrock Press.

Pike, A., & Oliver, B. R. (2016). Child behavior and sibling relationship quality: A cross-lagged analysis. *Journal of Family Psychology, 31,* 250–255.

Pilkauskas, N. V., Brooks-Gunn, J., & Waldfogel, J. (2018). Maternal employment stability in early childhood: Links with child behavior and cognitive skills. *Developmental Psychology, 54,* 410–427.

Pine, J. M. (1995). Variation in vocabulary development as a function of birth order. *Child Development, 66,* 272–281.

Ping, R. M., & Goldin-Meadow, S. (2008). Hands in the air: Using ungrounded iconic gestures to teach children conservation of quantity. *Developmental Psychology, 44,* 1277–1287.

Pinker, S. (1999). *Words and rules: The ingredients of language.* New York: Basic Books.

Pinkerton, R., Ori., R. B., Lima, A. A., Rogawski, E. T., Ori., M. O., Patrick, P. D., et al. (2016). Early childhood diarrhea predicts cognitive delays in later childhood independently of malnutrition. *American Journal of Tropical Medicine and Hygiene, 95,* 1004–1010.

Pinquart, M. (2017). Associations of parenting dimensions and styles with externalizing problems of children and adolescents: An updated meta-analysis. *Developmental Psychology, 53,* 873–932.

Pinquart, M., Feuner, C., & Ahnert, L. (2013). Meta-analytic evidence for stability in attachments from infancy to early adulthood. *Attachment & Human Development, 15,* 189–218.

Pipp, S., Easterbrooks, M. A., & Brown, S. R. (1993). Attachment status and complexity of infants' self- and other-knowledge when tested with mother and father. *Social Development, 2,* 1–14.

Pipp, S., Easterbrooks, M. A., & Harmon, R. J. (1992). The relation between attachment and knowledge of self and mother in one-year-old infants to three-year-old infants. *Child Development, 63,* 738–750.

Piquero, A. R., Jennings, W. G., Diamond, B., Farrington, D. P., Tremblay, R. E., Welsh, B. C., & Gonzales, J. M. (2016). A meta-analysis update on the effects of early family/parent training programs on antisocial behavior and delinquency. *Journal of Experimental Criminality, 12,* 229–248.

Planalp, E. M., & Braungart-Rieker, J. M. (2015). Trajectories of regulatory behaviors in early infancy: Determinants of infant self-distraction and self-comforting. *Infancy, 20,* 129–159.

Plante, I., O'Keefe, P. A., Aronson, J., Fréchette-Simard, C., & Goulet, M. (2018). The interest gap: How gender stereotype endorsement about abilities predicts differences in academic interests. *Social Psychology of Education, 22,* 227–245.

Plante, I., Théoret, M., & Favreau, O. E. (2009). Student gender stereotypes: Contrasting the perceived maleness and femaleness of mathematics and language. *Educational Psychology, 29,* 385–405.

Platt, M. P. W. (2014). Neonatology and obstetric anaesthesia. *Archives of Disease in Childhood—Fetal and Neonatal Edition, 99,* F98.

Pleck, J. H. (2012). Integrating father involvement in parenting research. *Parenting: Science and Practice, 12,* 243–253.

Plomin, R., DeFries, J. C., & Knopik, V. S. (2013). *Behavioral genetics* (6th ed.). New York: Worth.

Plomin, R., & Deary, I. J. (2015). Genetics and intelligence differences: Five special findings. *Molecular Psychiatry, 20,* 98–108.

Plomin, R., DeFries, J. C., Knopik, V. S., & Neiderhiser, J. M. (2016). Top 10 replicated findings from behavioral genetics. *Psychological Science, 11,* 3–23.

Plomin, R., & Spinath, F. M. (2004). Intelligence: Genetics, genes, and genomics. *Journal of Personality and Social Psychology, 86,* 112–129.

Plotka, R., & Busch-Rossnagel, N. A. (2018). The role of length of maternity leave in supporting mother–child interactions and attachment security among American mothers and their infants. *International Journal of Child Care and Education Policy, 12,* 2.

Plucker, J. A., Guo, J., & Dilley, A. (2018). Research-guided programs and strategies for nurturing creativity. In S. I Pfeiffer, E. Shaunessy-Dedrick, & M. Foley-Nicpon (Eds.), *APA handbook of giftedness and talent* (pp. 387–397). Washington, DC: American Psychological Association.

Plucker, J. A., & Makel, M. C. (2010). Assessment of creativity. In J. C. Kaufman & R. J. Sternberg (Eds.), *Cambridge handbook of creativity* (pp. 48–73). New York: Cambridge University Press.

Pluess, M., & Belsky, J. (2011). Prenatal programming of postnatal plasticity? *Development and Psychopathology, 23,* 29–38.

Poehlmann, J., Schwichtenberg, A. J. M., Shlafer, R. J., Hahn, E., Bianchi, J.-P., & Warner, R. (2011). Emerging self-regulation in toddlers born preterm or low birth weight: Differential susceptibility to parenting. *Developmental and Psychopathology, 23,* 177–193.

Polakowski L. L., Akinbami, L. J., & Mendola, P. (2009). Prenatal smoking cessation and the risk of delivering preterm and small-for-gestational-age newborns. *Obstetrics and Gynecology, 114,* 318–325.

Polanska, K., Jurewicz, J., & Hanke, W. (2013). Review of current evidence on the impact of pesticides, polychlorinated biphenyls, and selected metals on attention deficit/hyperactivity disorder in children. *International Journal of Occupational Medicine and Environmental Health, 26,* 16–38.

Polderman, T. J., Benyamin, B., De Leeuw, C. A., Sullivan, P. F., Van Bochoven, A., Visscher, P. M., & Possthuma, D. (2015). Meta-analysis of the heritability of human traits based on fifty years of twin studies. *Nature Genetics, 47,* 702–709.

Polderman, T. J. C., de Geus, J. C., Hoekstra, R. A., Bartels, M., van Leeuwen, M., Verhulst, F. C., et al. (2009). Attention problems, inhibitory control, and intelligence index overlapping genetic factors: A study in 9-, 12-, and 18-year-old twins. *Neuropsychology, 23,* 381–391.

Pomerantz, E. M., Grolnick, W. S., & Price, C. E. (2013). The role of parents in how children approach achievement: A dynamic process perspective. In A. J. Elliott & C. J. Dweck (Eds.), *Handbook of confidence and motivation* (pp. 259–278). New York: Guilford.

Pomerantz, E. M., & Kempner, S. G. (2013). Mothers' daily person and process praise: Implications for children's theory of intelligence and motivation. *Developmental Psychology, 13,* 2040–2046.

Pomerantz, E. M., & Saxon, J. L. (2001). Conceptions of ability as stable and self-evaluative processes: A longitudinal examination. *Child Development, 72,* 152–173.

Pong, S., & Landale, N. S. (2012). Academic achievement of legal immigrants' children: The roles of parents' pre- and postmigration characteristics in origin-group differences. *Child Development, 83,* 1543–1559.

Poole, D. A., & Bruck, M. (2012). Divining testimony? The impact of interviewing props on children's reports of touching. *Developmental Review, 32,* 165–180.

Poole, K. L., Van Lieshout, R. J., & Schmidt, L. A. (2017). Exploring relations between shyness and social anxiety disorder: The role of sociability. *Personality and Individual Differences, 110,* 55–59.

Poortman, A.-R. (2018). Post-divorce parent–child contact and child well-being: The importance of predivorce parental involvement. *Journal of Marriage and Family, 80,* 671–683.

Poplinger, M., Talwar, V., & Crossman, A. (2011). Predictors of children's prosocial lie-telling: Motivation, socialization variables, and moral understanding. *Journal of Experimental Child Psychology, 110,* 373–392.

Popova, S., Lange, S., Probst, C., Gmel, G., & Rehm, J. (2018). Global prevalence of alcohol use and binge drinking during pregnancy, and fetal alcohol spectrum disorder. *Biochemistry and Cell Biology, 96,* 237–240.

Portes, A., & Rumbaut, R. G. (2005), Introduction: The second generation and the Children of Immigrants Longitudinal Study. *Ethnic and Racial Studies, 28,* 983–999.

Posid, T., & Cordes, S. (2018). How high can you count? Probing the limits of children's counting. *Developmental Psychology, 54,* 875–889.

Posner, M. I., & Rothbart, M. K. (2007). Temperament and learning. In M. I. Posner & M. K. Rothbart (Eds.), *Educating the human brain* (pp. 121–146). Washington, DC: American Psychological Association.

Posner, M. I., Rothbart, M. K., Sheese, B. E., & Voelker, P. (2012). Control networks and neuromodulators of early development. *Developmental Psychology, 48,* 827–835

Potter, D. (2012). Same-sex parent families and children's academic achievement. *Journal of Marriage and Family, 74*, 556–571.

Poulin, F., & Denault, A.-S. (2012). Other-sex friendships as a mediator between parental monitoring and substance use in girls and boys. *Journal of Youth and Adolescence, 41,* 1488–1501.

Poulin-Dubois, D., Bialystok, E., Blaye, A., Polonia, A., & Yott, J. (2013). Lexical access and vocabulary development in very young bilinguals. *International Journal of Bilingualism, 17,* 57–70.

Pouscoulous, N. (2014). "The elevator's buttocks": Metaphorical abilities in children. In M. A. Callanan & D. R. Siegel (Eds.), *Pragmatic development in first language acquisition* (pp. 239–260). Amsterdam, Netherlands: John Benjamins Publishing.

Povinelli, D. J. (2001). The self: Elevated in consciousness and extended in time. In C. Moore & K. Lemmon (Eds.), *The self in time: Developmental perspectives* (pp. 75–95). Mahwah, NJ: Erlbaum.

Prado, E. L., & Dewey, K. G. (2014). Nutrition and brain development in early life. *Nutrition Reviews, 72,* 267–284.

Preissler, M. A., & Bloom, P. (2008). Two-year-olds use artist intention to understand drawings. *Cognition, 106,* 512–518.

Principe, G. F. (2011). *Your brain on childhood: The unexpected side effects of classrooms, ballparks, family rooms, and the minivan.* Amherst, NY: Prometheus Books.

Principi, N., Baggi, E., & Esposito, S. (2012). Prevention of acute otitis media using currently available vaccines. *Future of Microbiology, 7,* 457–465.

Proffitt, D. R., & Bertenthal, B. I. (1990). Converging operations revisited: Assessing what infants perceive using discrimination measures. *Perception and Psychophysics, 47,* 1–11.

Programme for International Student Assessment. (2017). *PISA data explorer: 2015 results.* Retrieved from www.oecd.org/pisa/data

Proietti, E., Röösli, M., Frey, U., & Latzin, P. (2013). Air pollution during pregnancy and neonatal outcome: A review. *Journal of Aerosol Medicine and Pulmonary Drug Delivery, 26,* 9–23.

Proulx, M., & Poulin, F. (2013). Stability and change in kindergartners' friendships: Examination of links with social functioning. *Social Development, 22,* 111–125.

Provenzi, L., Borgotti, R., Menozzi, G., & Montirosso, R. (2015). Mother–infant dyadic reparation and individual differences in vagal tone affect 4-month-old infants' social stress regulation. *Journal of Experimental Child Psychology, 140,* 158–170.

Provenzi, L., Giusti, L., & Montirosso, R. (2016). Do infants exhibit significant cortisol reactivity to the face-to-face still-face paradigm? A narrative review and meta-analysis. *Developmental Review, 42,* 34–55.

Pruden, S. M., Hirsh-Pasek, K., Golinkoff, R. M., & Hennon, E. A. (2006). The birth of words: Ten-month-olds learn words through perceptual salience. *Child Development, 77,* 266–280.

Pruett, M. K., Cowan, C. P., Cowan, P. A., Pradham, L., Robins, S., & Pruett, K. D. (2016). Supporting father involvement in the context of separation and divorce. In L. Drozd, M. Saini, & N. Olesen (Eds.), *Parenting plan evaluations: Applied research for the family court* (2nd ed., pp. 85–117). New York: Oxford University Press.

Pryor, J. (2014). *Stepfamilies: A global perspective on research, policy, and practice.* New York: Routledge.

Pugliese, C. E., Anthony, L. G., Strang, J. F., Dudley, K., Wallace, G. L., Naiman, D. Q., et al. (2016). Longitudinal examination of adaptive behavior in autism spectrum disorders: Influence of executive function. *Journal of Autism and Developmental Disorders, 13,* 467–477.

Puglisi, M. L., Hulme, C., Hamilton, L. G., & Snowling, M. J. (2017). The home literacy environment is a correlate, but perhaps not a cause, of variations in children's language and literacy development. *Scientific Studies of Reading, 21,* 498–514.

Puhl, R. M., & Latner, J. D. (2007). Stigma, obesity, and the health of the nation's children. *Psychological Bulletin, 133,* 557–580.

Pujol, J., Soriano-Mas, C., Ortiz, H., Sebastián-Gallés, N., Losilla, J. M., & Deus, J. (2006). Myelination of language-related areas in the developing brain. *Neurology, 66,* 339–343.

Puma, M., Bell, S., Cook, R., Heid, C., Broene, P., Jenkins, F., et al. (2012). *Third grade follow-up to the Head Start Impact Study final report.* OPRE Report #2012-45b. Washington, DC: U.S. Department of Health and Human Services.

Punamaki, R. L. (2006). Ante- and perinatal factors and child characteristics predicting parenting experience among formerly infertile couples during the child's first year: A controlled study. *Journal of Family Psychology, 20,* 670–679.

Purcell-Gates, V. (1996). Stories, coupons, and the TV guide: Relationships between home literacy experiences and emergent literacy knowledge. *Reading Research Quarterly, 31,* 406–428.

Putallaz, M., Grimes, C. L., Foster, K. J., Kupersmidt, J. B., Coie, J. D., & Dearing, K. (2007). Overt and relational aggression and victimization: Multiple perspectives within the school setting. *Journal of School Psychology, 45,* 523–547.

Q

Qi, Z., & Ding, S. (2016). Obesity-associated sympathetic overactivity in children and adolescents: The role of catecholamine resistance in lipid metabolism. *Journal of Pediatric Endocrinology & Metabolism, 29,* 113–125.

Qin, L., and Pomerantz, E. M. (2013). Reciprocal pathways between American and Chinese early adolescents' sense of responsibility and disclosure to parents. *Child Development, 84,* 1887–1895.

Qin, S., Cho, S., Chen, T., Rosenberg-Lee, M., Geary, D. C., & Menon, V. (2014). Hippocampal-neocortical functional reorganization underlies children's cognitive development. *Nature Neuroscience, 17,* 1263–1269.

Qouta, S. R., Palosaari, E., Diab, M., & Punamäki, R.-L. (2012). Intervention effectiveness among war-affected children: A cluster randomized controlled trial on improving mental health. *Journal of Traumatic Stress, 25,* 288–298.

Qu, Y., & Pomerantz, E. M. (2015). Divergent school trajectories in early adolescence in the United States and China: An examination of underlying mechanisms. *Journal of Youth and Adolescence, 44,* 2095–2109.

Quas, J. A., Malloy, L. C., Melinder, A., Goodman, G. S., & D'Mello, M. (2007). Developmental differences in the effects of repeated interviews and interviewer bias on young children's event memory and false reports. *Developmental Psychology, 43,* 823–837.

Quinn, P. C. (2008). In defense of core competencies, quantitative change, and continuity. *Child Development, 79,* 1633–1638.

Quinn, P. C., Kelly, D. J., Lee, K., Pascalis, O., & Slater, A. (2008). Preference for attractive faces extends beyond conspecifics. *Developmental Science, 11,* 76–83.

R

Raabe, T., & Beelmann, A. (2011). Development of ethnic, racial, and national prejudice in childhood and adolescence: A multinational meta-analysis of age differences. *Child Development, 82,* 1715–1737.

Raby, K. L., Steele, R. D., Carlson, E. A., & Sroufe, L. (2015). Continuities and changes in infant attachment patterns across two generations. *Attachment & Human Development, 17,* 414–428.

Racanello, A., & McCabe, P. C. (2010). Role of otitis media in hearing loss and language deficits. In P. C. McCabe & S. R. Shaw (Eds.), *Pediatric disorders* (pp. 22–31). Washington, DC: Corwin Press

Racz, S. J., McMahon, R. J. , & Luthar, S. S. (2011). Risky behavior in affluent youth: Examining the co-occurrence and consequences of multiple problem behaviors. *Journal of Child and Family Studies, 20,* 120–128.

Radesky, J. S., Kistin, C., Eisenberg, S., Gross, J., Block, G., Zuckerman, B., et al. (2016). Parent perspectives on their mobile technology use: The excitement and exhaustion of parenting while connected. *Journal of Developmental and Behavioral Pediatrics, 37,* 694–701.

Radesky, J. S., Kistin, C. J., Zuckerman, B., Nitzberg, K., Gross, J., Kaplan-Sanoff, M., et al. (2014). Patterns of mobile device use by caregivers and children during meals in fast food restaurants. *Pediatrics, 133,* e843–e849.

Raikes, H. A., Robinson, J. L., Bradley, R. H., Raikes, H. H., & Ayoub, C. C. (2007). Developmental trends in self-regulation among low-income toddlers. *Social Development, 16,* 128–149.

Raikes, H. H., Chazan-Cohen, R., Love, J. M., & Brooks-Gunn, J. (2010). Early Head Start impacts at age 3 and a description of the age 5 follow-up study. In A. J. Reynolds, A. J. Rolnick, M. M. Englund, & J. Temple (Eds.), *Childhood programs and practices in the first decade of life: A human capital integration* (pp. 99–118). New York: Cambridge University Press.

Rajhans, P., Jessen, S., Missana, M., & Grossmann, T. (2016). Putting the face in context: Body expressions impact facial emotion processing in human infants. *Developmental Cognitive Neuroscience, 19,* 115–121.

Rakison, D. H. (2005). Developing knowledge of objects' motion properties in infancy. *Cognition, 96,* 183–214.

Rakison, D. H. (2010). Perceptual categorization and concepts. In J. G. Bremner & T. D. Wachs (Eds.), *Wiley-Blackwell handbook of infant development* (2nd ed., pp. 243–270). Oxford, UK: Wiley.

Rakison, D. H., & Lawson, C. A. (2013). Categorization. In P. D. Zelazo (Ed.), *Oxford handbook of developmental psychology: Vol. 1. Body and mind* (pp. 591–627). New York: Oxford University Press.

Rakoczy, H., Tomasello, M., & Striano, T. (2004). Young children know that trying is not pretending: A test of the "behaving-as-if" construal of children's early concept of pretense. *Developmental Psychology, 40,* 388–399.

Rakoczy, H., Tomasello, M., & Striano, T. (2005). How children turn objects into symbols: A cultural learning account. In L. Namy (Ed.), *Symbol use and symbol representation* (pp. 67–97). New York: Erlbaum.

Raley, R. K., Sweeney, M. M., & Wondra, D. (2015). The growing racial and ethnic divide in U.S. marriage patterns. *Future of Children, 25,* 89–105.

Ramachandrappa, A., & Jain, L. (2008). Elective cesarean section: Its impact on neonatal respiratory outcome. *Clinics in Perinatology, 35,* 373–393.

Raman, L., & Gelman, S. A. (2004). A cross-cultural developmental analysis of children's and adults' understanding of illness in South Asia (India) and the United States. *Journal of Cognition and Culture, 4,* 293–317.

Ramchandani, P. G., Stein, A., O'Connor, T. G., Heron, J., Murray, L., & Evans, J. (2008). Depression in men in the postnatal period and later child psychopathology: A population cohort study. *Journal of the American Academy of Child and Adolescent Psychiatry, 47,* 390–398.

Ramey, C. T., Ramey, S. L., & Lanzi, R. G. (2006). Children's health and education. In K. A. Renninger & I. E. Sigel (Eds.), *Handbook of child psychology: Vol. 4. Child psychology in practice* (6th ed., pp. 864–892). Hoboken, NJ: Wiley.

Ramírez, N. F., Ramírez, R. R., Clarke, M., Taulu, S., & Kuhl, P. K. (2017). Speech discrimination in 11-month-old bilingual and monolingual infants: A magnetoencephalography study. *Developmental Science, 20,* e12427.

Ramírez-Esparza, N., García-Sierra, A., & Kuhl, P. K. (2014). Look who's talking: Speech style and social context in language input to infants are linked to concurrent and future speech development. *Developmental Science, 17,* 880–891.

Ramírez-Esparza, N., Kuhl, P. K., & García-Sierra, A. (2017). The impact of early social interactions on later language development in Spanish–English bilingual infants. *Child Development, 88,* 1216–1234.

Ramos, M. C., Guerin, D. W., Gottfried, A. W., Bathurst, K., & Oliver, P. H. (2005). Family conflict and children's behavior problems: The moderating role of child temperament. *Structural Equation Modeling, 12,* 278–298.

Ramsey-Rennels, J. L., & Langlois, J. H. (2006). Differential processing of female and male faces. *Current Directions in Psychological Science, 15,* 59–62.

Ramus, F. (2002). Language discrimination by newborns: Teasing apart phonotactic, rhythmic, and intonational cues. *Annual Review of Language Acquisition, 2,* 85–115.

Ranke, M. B., & Wit, J. M. (2018). Growth hormone—past, present and future. *Nature Reviews Endocrinology, 14,* 285–300.

Ransburg, N., Reiser, M., Munzert, J., & Jovanovic, B. (2017). Concurrent anticipation of two object dimensions during grasping in 10-month-old infants: A quantitative analysis. *Infant Behavior and Development, 48,* 164–174.

Rasmus, S., Allen, J., & Ford, T. (2014). "Where I have to learn the ways how to live:" Youth resilience in a Yup'ik village in Alaska. *Transcultural Psychiatry,* 51, 735–756.

Rasmussen, C., Ho, E., & Bisanz, J. (2003). Use of the mathematical principle of inversion in young children. *Journal of Experimental Child Psychology, 85,* 89–102.

Rat-Fischer, L., O'Regan, J. K., & Fagard, J. (2012). The emergence of tool use during the second year of life. Journal of *Experimental Child Psychology, 113,* 440–446.

Rathunde, K., & Csikszentmihalyi, M. (2005). The social context of middle school: Teachers, friends, and activities in Montessori and traditional school environments. *Elementary School Journal, 106,* 59–79.

Raver, C. C. (2003). Does work pay psychologically as well as economically? The role of employment in predicting depressive symptoms and parenting among low-income families. *Child Development, 74,* 1720–1736.

Ray, E., & Heyes, C. (2011). Imitation in infancy: The wealth of the stimulus. *Developmental Science, 14,* 92–105.

Rayfield, S., & Plugge, E. (2017). Systematic review and meta-analysis of the association between maternal smoking in pregnancy and childhood overweight and obesity.

Journal of Epidemiology and Community Health, 71, 162–173.

Rayner, K., Pollatsek, A., & Starr, M. S. (2003). Reading. In A. F. Healy & R. W. Proctor (Eds.), *Handbook of psychology: Experimental psychology* (Vol. 4, pp. 549–574). New York: Wiley.

Raz, S., Piercy, J. C., Heitzer, A. M., Peters, B. N., Newman, J. B, DeBastos, A. K., et al. (2016). Neuropsychological functioning in preterm-born twins and singletons at preschool age. Journal of the International *Neuropsychological Society, 22,* 865–877.

Re, L., & Birkhoff, J. M. (2015). The 47, XYY syndrome, 50 years of certainties and doubts: A systematic review. *Aggression and Violent Behavior, 22,* 9–17.

Ready, D. D., & Wright, D. L. (2011). Accuracy and inaccuracy in teachers' perceptions of young children's cognitive abilities: The role of child background and classroom context. *American Educational Research Journal, 48,* 335–360.

Reardon, S. F. (2015). *School segregation and racial academic achievement gaps* (CEPA Working Paper No. 15-12). Stanford, CA: Stanford Center for Education Policy Analysis. Retrieved from cepa.stanford.edu /wp15-12

Reed, C. E., & Fenton, S. E. (2013). Exposure to diethylstilbestrol during sensitive life stages: A legacy of heritable health effects. *Birth Defects Research. Part C, Embryo Today: Reviews, 99,* 134–146.

Reed, R. K. (2005). *Birthing fathers.* New Brunswick, NJ: Rutgers University Press.

Reese, E. (2002). A model of the origins of autobiographical memory. In J. W. Fagen & H. Hayne (Eds.), *Progress in infancy research* (Vol. 2, pp. 215–260). Mahwah, NJ: Erlbaum.

Reese, E., & Newcombe, R. (2007). Training mothers in elaborative reminiscing enhances children's autobiographical memory and narrative. *Child Development, 78,* 1153–1170.

Reich, S. M., Yau, J. C., & Warschauer, M. (2016). Tablet-based ebooks for young children: What does the research say? *Journal of Developmental and Behavioral Pediatrics, 37,* 585–591.

Reiss, D. (2003). Child effects on family systems: Behavioral genetic strategies. In A. C. Crouter & A. Booth (Eds.), *Children's influence on family dynamics* (pp. 3–36). Mahwah, NJ: Erlbaum.

Rennie, J., & Rosenbloom, L. (2011). How long have we got to get the baby out? A review of the effects of acute and profound intrapartum hypoxia and ischaemia. *Obstetrician & Gyaenecologist, 13,* 169–174.

Rentner, T. L., Dixon, L. D., & Lengel, L. (2012). Critiquing fetal alcohol syndrome health communication campaigns targeted to American Indians. *Journal of Health Communication, 17,* 6–21.

Repacholi, B. M., & Gopnik, A. (1997). Early reasoning about desires: Evidence from 14- and 18-month-olds. *Developmental Psychology, 33,* 12–21.

Resnick, I., Jordan, N. C., Hansen, N., Rajan, V., Rodrigues, J., Siegler, R. S., & Fuchs, R. S. (2016). Developmental growth trajectories in understanding of fraction magnitude from fourth through sixth grade. *Developmental Psychology, 52,* 746–757.

Resnick, M., & Silverman, B. (2005). *Some reflections on designing construction kits for kids.* Proceedings of the Conference on Interaction Design and Children, Boulder, CO.

Reuben, A., Caspi, A., Belsky, D. W., Broadbent, J., Harrington, H., Sugden, K.,

& Houts, R. M. (2017). Association of childhood blood lead levels with cognitive function and socioeconomic status at age 38 years and with IQ change and socioeconomic mobility between childhood and adulthood. *JAMA, 317,* 1244–1251.

Reynolds, R. M. (2013). Programming effects of glucocorticoids. *Clinical Obstetrics and Gynecology, 56,* 602–609.

Rhoades, B. L., Greenberg, M. T., & Domitrovich, C. E. (2009). The contribution of inhibitory control to preschoolers' social-emotional competence. *Journal of Applied Developmental Psychology, 30,* 310–320.

Ribner, A., Fitzpatrick, C., & Blair, C. (2017). Family socioeconomic status moderates associations between television viewing and school readiness skills. *Journal of Developmental and Behavioral Pediatrics, 38,* 233–239.

Richardson, G. A., Goldschmidt, L., Larkby, C., & Day, N. L. (2015). Effects of prenatal cocaine exposure on adolescent development. *Neurotoxicology and Teratology, 49,* 41–48.

Richardson, H. L., Walker, A. M., & Horne, R. S. C. (2008) Sleep position alters arousal processes maximally at the high-risk age for sudden infant death syndrome. *Journal of Sleep Research, 17,* 450–457.

Richardson, K., & Norgate, S. H. (2006). A critical analysis of IQ studies of adopted children. *Human Development, 49,* 339–350.

Richardson, K. A., Hester, A., & McLemore, G. L. (2016). Prenatal cannabis exposure—the "first hit" to the endocannabinoid system. *Neurotoxicology and Teratology, 58,* 5–14.

Richardson, S. S. (2011). Race and IQ in the postgenomic era: The microcephaly case. *BioSocieties, 6,* 420–446.

Richter, L. M., Lye, S. J., & Proulx, K. (2018). Nurturing care for young children under conditions of fragility and conflict. *New Directions for Child and Adolescent Development, 159,* 13–26.

Rideout, V. (2013). *Zero to eight: Children's media use in America 2013.* San Francisco: Common Sense Media. Retrieved from www.commonsensemedia.org/research /zero-to-eight-childrens-media-use-in -america-2013

Rideout, V. (2015). *The Common Sense census: Media use by tweens and teens.* San Francisco: Common Sense Media.

Rideout, V. (2018). *The Common Sense census: Media use by kids age zero to eight.* San Francisco: Common Sense Media.

Rideout, V., & Hamel, E. (2006). *The media family: Electronic media in the lives of infants, toddlers, preschoolers and their parents.* Menlo Park, CA: Henry J. Kaiser Family Foundation.

Rideout, V. J., Foehr, U. G., & Roberts, D. F. (2010). *Generation M²: Media in the lives of 8- to 18-year-olds.* Menlo Park, CA: Henry J. Kaiser Family Foundation.

Rieffe, C., Terwogt, M. M., & Cowan, R. (2005). Children's understanding of mental states as causes of emotions. *Infant and Child Development, 14,* 259–272.

Riggins, T., Cheatham, C., Stark, E., & Bauer, P. J. (2013). Elicited imitation performance at 20 months predicts memory abilities in school age children. *Journal of Cognition and Development, 14,* 593–606.

Riggs, K. J., Jolley, R. P., & Simpson, A. (2013). The role of inhibitory control in the development of human figure drawing in young children. *Journal of Experimental Child Psychology, 114,* 537–542.

Rijlaarsdam, J., Stevens, G. W. J. M., van der Ende, J., Arends, L. R., Hofman, A., Jaddoe, V. W. V., et al. (2012). A brief observational

instrument for the assessment of infant home environment: Development and psychometric testing. *International Journal of Methods in Psychiatric Research, 21,* 195–204.

Rindermann, H., & Ceci, S. J. (2008). *Education policy and country outcomes in international cognitive competence studies.* Graz, Austria: Institute of Psychology, Karl-Franzens-University Graz.

Ripley, A. (2013). *The smartest kids in the world: And how they got that way.* New York: Simon and Schuster.

Ripple, C. H., & Zigler, E. (2003). Research, policy, and the federal role in prevention initiatives for children. *American Psychologist, 58,* 482–490.

Ris, M. D., Dietrich, K. N., Succop, P. A., Berger, O. G., & Bornschein, R. L. (2004). Early exposure to lead and neuropsychological outcome in adolescence. *Journal of the International Neuropsychological Society, 10,* 261–270.

Ristic, J., & Enns, J. T. (2015). Attentional development. In L. S. Liben & U. Müller (Eds.), *Handbook of child psychology and developmental science: Vol. 2. Cognitive processes* (pp. 158–202). Hoboken, NJ: Wiley.

Ristori, J., & Steensma, T. D. (2016). Gender dysphoria in childhood. *International Review of Psychiatry, 28,* 13–20.

Rittig, N., Hagstroem, S., Mahler, B., Kamperis, K., Siggaard, C., Mikkelsen, M. M., et al. (2014). Outcome of a standardized approach to childhood urinary symptoms—long-term follow-up of 720 patients. *Neurourology and Urodynamics, 33,* 475–481.

Rittle-Johnson, B., Schneider, M., & Star, J. R. (2015). Not a one-way street: Bidirectional relations between procedural and conceptual knowledge of mathematics. *Educational Psychology Review, 27,* 587–597.

Ritz, B., Oiu, J., Lee, P. C., Lurmann, F., Penfold, B., Erin Weiss, R., et al. (2014). Prenatal air pollution exposure and ultrasound measures of fetal growth in Los Angeles, California. *Environmental Research, 130,* 7–13.

Rivkees, S. A. (2003). Developing circadian rhythmicity in infants. *Pediatrics, 112,* 373–381.

Rizzo, M. T., & Killen, M. (2016). Children's understanding of equity in the context of inequality. *British Journal of Developmental Psychology, 34,* 569–581.

Roben, C. K. P., Bass, A. J., Moore, G. A., Murray-Kolb, L., Tan, P. Z., Gilmore, R. O., et al. (2012). Let me go: The influences of crawling experience and temperament on the development of anger expression. *Infancy, 17,* 558–577.

Roberts, B. W., & DelVecchio, W. F. (2000). The rank-order consistency of personality traits from childhood to old age: A quantitative review of longitudinal studies. *Psychological Bulletin, 126,* 3–25.

Roberts, D. M., Brown, A. M. B., & Edwards, L. (2015). Participatory action research in two primary schools in a rural Tanzanian village: An exploration of factors to cultivate changes in teaching and learning. *Educational Action Research, 23,* 366–382.

Roberts, J. E., Burchinal, M. R., & Durham, M. (1999). Parents' report of vocabulary and grammatical development of American preschoolers: Child and environment associations. *Child Development, 70,* 92–106.

Robertson, J. (2008). Stepfathers in families. In J. Pryor (Ed.), *International handbook of stepfamilies: Policy and practice in legal,*

research, and clinical environments (pp. 125–150). Hoboken, NJ: Wiley.

Robin, D. J., Berthier, N. E., & Clifton, R. K. (1996). Infants' predictive reaching for moving objects in the dark. *Developmental Psychology, 32,* 824–835.

Robins, R. W., Tracy, J. L., Trzesniewski, K., Potter, J., & Gosling, S. D. (2001). Personality correlates of self-esteem. *Journal of Research in Personality, 35,* 463–482.

Robinson, C. C., Anderson, G. T., Porter, C. L., Hart, C. H., & Wouden-Miller, M. (2003). Sequential transition patterns of preschoolers' social interactions during child-initiated play: Is parallel-aware play a bidirectional bridge to other play states? *Early Childhood Research Quarterly, 18,* 3–21.

Robinson, G. E. (2015). Controversies about the use of antidepressants in pregnancy. *Journal of Nervous and Mental Disease, 203,* 159–163.

Robinson, T. N., Banda, J. A., Hale, L., Lu, A. S., Fleming-Milici, F., Calvert, S. L., & Wartella, E. (2017). Screen media exposure and obesity in children and adolescents. *Pediatrics, 140* (S2), e20161758.

Robinson-Cimpian, J. P., Lubienski, S. T., Ganley, C. M., & Copur-Gencturk, Y. (2014). Teachers' perceptions of students' mathematics proficiency may exacerbate early gender gaps in achievement. *Developmental Psychology, 50,* 1262–1281.

Robinson-Zañartu, C., & Carlson, J. (2013). Dynamic assessment. In K. F. Geisinger (Ed.), *APA handbook of testing and assessment in psychology: Vol. 3. Testing and assessment in school psychology and education* (pp. 149–168). Washington, DC: American Psychological Association.

Rochat, P. (1989). Object manipulation and exploration in 2- to 5-month-old infants. *Developmental Psychology, 25,* 871–884.

Rochat, P. (1998). Self-perception and action in infancy. *Experimental Brain Research, 123,* 102–109.

Rochat, P. (2013). Self-conceptualizing in development. In P. Zelazo (Ed.), *Oxford handbook of developmental psychology* (Vol. 2, pp. 378–397). New York: Oxford University Press.

Rochat, P. (2015). Layers of awareness in development. *Developmental Review, 38,* 122–145.

Rochat, P., & Hespos, S. J. (1997). Differential rooting responses by neonates: Evidence for an early sense of self. *Early Development and Parenting, 6,* 105–112.

Rochat, P., & Striano, T. (2002). Who's in the mirror? Self–other discrimination in specular images by four- and nine-month-old infants. *Child Development, 73,* 35–46.

Roche, K. M., Ensminger, M. E., & Cherlin, A. J. (2007). Variations in parenting and adolescent outcomes among African American and Latino families living in low-income, urban areas. *Journal of Family Issues, 28,* 882–909.

Rodgers, J. L., Cleveland, H. H., van den Oord, E., & Rowe, D. C. (2000). Resolving the debate over birth order, family size, and intelligence. *American Psychologist, 55,* 599–612.

Rodriguez, E. M., Dunn, M. J., & Compas, B. E. (2012). Cancer-related sources of stress for children with cancer and their parents. *Journal of Pediatric Psychology, 37,* 185–197.

Roelfsema, N. M., Hop, W. C., Boito, S. M., & Wladimiroff, J. W. (2004). Three-dimensional sonographic measurement of normal fetal brain volume during the second half of pregnancy. *American Journal of Obstetrics and Gynecology, 190,* 275–280.

Rogoff, B. (2003). *The cultural nature of human development.* New York: Oxford University Press.

Rogoff, B. (2014). Learning by observing and pitching in to family and community endeavors: An orientation. *Human Development, 57,* 69–81.

Rogoff, B., Correa-Chavez, M., & Silva, K.G. (2011). Cultural variation in children's attention and learning. In M. A. Gernsbacher, R. W. Pew, L. M. Hough, & J. R. Pomerantz (Eds.), *Psychology and the real world: Essays illustrating fundamental contributions to society* (pp. 154–163). New York: Worth.

Rogoff, B., & Waddell, K. J. (1982). Memory for information organized in a scene by children from two cultures. *Child Development, 53,* 1224–1228.

Rohner, R. P., & Veneziano, R. A. (2001). The importance of father love: History and contemporary evidence. *Review of General Psychology, 5,* 382–405.

Roid, G. (2003). *The Stanford-Binet Intelligence Scales, Fifth Edition, interpretive manual.* Itasca, IL: Riverside Publishing.

Roid, G. H., & Pomplun, M. (2012). The Stanford-Binet Intelligence Scales, Fifth Edition. In D. P. Flanagan & P. L. Harrison (Eds.), *Contemporary intellectual assessment: Theories, tests and issues* (pp. 249–268). New York: Guilford.

Roisman, G. I., & Fraley, R. C. (2008). Behavior-genetic study of parenting quality, infant-attachment security, and their covariation in a nationally representative sample. *Developmental Psychology, 44,* 831–839.

Roizen, N. J. (2013). Down syndrome. In M. L. Matshaw, N. J. Roizen, & G. R. Lotrecchiano (Eds.), *Children with disabilities* (pp. 307–318). Baltimore: Paul H. Brookes.

Romano, A. M., & Lothian, J. A. (2008). Promoting, protecting, and supporting normal birth: A look at the evidence. *Journal of Obstetric, Gynecologic, and Neonatal Nursing, 37,* 94–104.

Romano, E., Babchishin, L., Pagani, L. S., & Kohen, D. (2010). School readiness and later achievement: Replication and extension using a nationwide Canadian survey. *Developmental Psychology, 46,* 995–1007.

Roman-Rodriguez, C. F., Toussaint, T., Sherlock, D. J., Fogel, J., & Hsu, C.-D. (2014). Preemptive penile ring block with sucrose analgesia reduces pain response to neonatal circumcision. *Urology, 83,* 893–898.

Romeo, R. R., Leonard, J. A., Robinson, S. T., West, M. R., Mackey, A. P., Rowe, M. L., & Gabrieli, J. D. E. (2018). Beyond the 30-million-word gap: Children's conversational exposure is associated with language-related brain function. *Psychological Science, 29,* 700–710.

Ronald, A., & Hoekstra, R. (2014). Progress in understanding the causes of autism spectrum disorders and autistic traits: Twin studies from 1977 to the present day. In S. H. Rhee & A. Ronald (Eds.), *Advances in Behavior Genetics* (Vol. 2, pp. 33–65). New York: Springer.

Ronfani, L., Brumatti, L. V., Mariuz, M., Tognin, V., Bin, M., Ferluga, V., et al. (2015). The complex interaction between home environment, socioeconomic status, maternal IQ and early child neurocognitive development: A multivariate analysis of data collected in a newborn cohort study. *PLOS ONE, 10*(5), e0127052.

Roopnarine, J. L. (2016). Family socialization practices and childhood development in Caribbean cultural communities. In J. L. Roopnarine & D. Chadee (Eds.), *Caribbean psychology: Indigenous contributions to a global discipline* (pp. 71–96). Washington, DC: American Psychological Association.

Roopnarine, J. L., Hossain, Z., Gill, P., & Brophy, H. (1994). Play in the East Indian context. In J. L. Roopnarine, J. E. Johnson, & F. H. Hooper (Eds.), *Children's play in diverse cultures* (pp. 9–30). Albany: SUNY Press.

Roopnarine, J. L., Krishnakumar, A., Metindogan, A., & Evans, M. (2006). Links between parenting styles, parent–child academic interaction, parent–school interaction, and early academic skills and social behaviors in young children of English-speaking Caribbean immigrants. *Early Childhood Research Quarterly, 21,* 238–252.

Roozen, S., Peters, G.-J. Y., Kok, G., Townend, D., Nijuis, J., & Curfs, L. (2016). Worldwide prevalence of fetal alcohol spectrum disorders: A systematic literature review including meta-analyses. *Alcoholism: Clinical and Experimental Review, 40,* 18–32.

Rosander, K., & von Hofsten, C. (2004). Infants' emerging ability to represent occluded object motion. *Cognition, 91,* 1–22.

Rosander, K., & von Hofsten, C. (2011). Predictive gaze shifts elicited during observed and performed action in 10-month-old infants and adults. *Neuropsychologia, 49,* 2911–2917.

Rose, A. J., Swenson, L. P., & Waller, E. M. (2004). Overt and relational aggression and perceived popularity: Developmental differences in concurrent and prospective relations. *Developmental Psychology, 40,* 378–387.

Rose, S. A., Jankowski, J. J., & Senior, G. J. (1997). Infants' recognition of contour-deleted figures. *Journal of Experimental Psychology: Human Perception and Performance, 23,* 1206–1216.

Roseberry, S., Hirsh-Pasek, K., Parish-Morris, J., & Golinkoff, R. M. (2009). Live action: Can young children learn verbs from video? *Child Development, 80,* 1360–1375.

Rosen, A. B., & Rozin, P. (1993). Now you see it, now you don't: The preschool child's conception of invisible particles in the context of dissolving. *Developmental Psychology, 29,* 300–311.

Rosen, C. S., & Cohen, M. (2010). Subgroups of New York City children at high risk of PTSD after the September 11 attacks: A signal detection analysis. *Psychiatric Services, 61,* 64–69.

Roseth, C. J., Pellegrini, A. D., Bohn, C. M., van Ryzin, M., & Vance, N. (2007). Preschoolers' aggression, affiliation, and social dominance relationships: An observational, longitudinal study. *Journal of School Psychology, 45,* 479–497.

Roskos, K. A., & Christie, J. F. (2013). Gaining ground in understanding the play–literacy relationship. *American Journal of Play, 6,* 82–97.

Ross, A. J., Mallett, C. J., & Parkes, J. F. (2015). The influence of parent sport behaviours on children's development: Youth coach and administrator perspectives. *International Journal of Sports Science and Coaching, 10,* 605–621.

Ross, H., Friedman, O., & Field, A. (2015). Toddlers assert and acknowledge ownership rights. *Social Development, 24,* 341–356.

Ross, H. S., & Lazinski, M. J. (2014). Parent mediation empowers sibling conflict resolution. *Early Education and Development, 25,* 259–275.

Ross, J. L., Roeltgen, D. P., Kushner, H., Zinn, A. R., Reiss, A., Bardsley, M. Z., et al. (2012). Behavioral and social phenotypes in boys with 47, XYY syndrome or 47, XXY Klinefelter syndrome. *Pediatrics, 129,* 769–778.

Ross, M. G., & Desai, M. (2017). Developmental origins of adult health and disease. In S. G. Gabbe, J. R. Niebyl, J. L. Simpson, M. B. Landon, H. L. Galan, E. R. M. Jauniaux, & D. A. Discoll (Eds.), *Obstetrics: Normal and problem pregnancies* (7th ed., pp. 83–98). Philadelphia, PA: Saunders.

Ross, N., Medin, D. L., Coley, J. D., & Atran, S. (2003). Cultural and experiential differences in the development of folkbiological induction. *Cognitive Development, 18,* 25–47.

Rossi, B. V. (2014). Donor insemination. In J. M. Goldfarb (Ed.), *Third-party reproduction* (pp. 133–142). New York: Springer.

Roszel, E. L. (2015). Central nervous system deficits in fetal alcohol spectrum disorder. *Nurse Practitioner, 40,* 24–33.

Rote, W. M., & Smetana, J. G. (2017). Situational and structural variation in youth perceptions of maternal guilt induction. *Developmental Psychology, 53,* 1940–1953.

Rothbart, M. K. (2011). *Becoming who we are: Temperament and personality in development.* New York: Guilford.

Rothbart, M. K. (2015). The role of temperament in conceptualizations of mental disorder. In B. Probst (Ed.), *Critical thinking in clinical assessment and diagnosis* (pp. 133–149). Cham, Switzerland: Springer International Publishing.

Rothbart, M. K., Ahadi, S. A., & Evans, D. E. (2000). Temperament and personality: Origins and outcome. *Journal of Personality and Social Psychology, 78,* 122–135.

Rothbart, M. K., & Bates, J. E. (2006). Temperament. In N. Eisenberg (Ed.), *Handbook of child psychology: Vol. 3. Social, emotional, and personality development* (6th ed., pp. 99–166). Hoboken, NJ: Wiley.

Rothbart, M. K., Sheese, B. F., & Posner, M. I. (2014). Temperament and emotion regulation. In J. J. Gross (Ed.), *Handbook of emotion regulation* (pp. 305–320). New York: Guilford.

Rothbaum, F., Morelli, G., & Rusk, N. (2011). Attachment, learning, and coping: The interplay of cultural similarities and differences. In M. J. Gelfand, C.-Y. Chiu, & Y.-Y. Horng (Eds.), *Advances in culture and psychology* (pp. 153–215). Oxford, UK: Oxford University Press.

Rotheram-Fuller, E. J., Tomlinson, M., Scheffler, A., Weichle, T. W., Rezvan, P. H., Comulada, W. S., & Rotheram-Borus, M. J. (2018). Maternal patterns of antenatal and postnatal depressed mood and the impact on child health at 3-years postpartum. *Journal of Consulting and Clinical Psychology, 86,* 218–230.

Rouselle, L., Palmers, E., & Noël, M.-P. (2004). Magnitude comparison in preschoolers: What counts? Influence of perceptual variables. *Journal of Experimental Child Psychology, 87,* 57–84.

Rousseau, P. V., Matton, F., Lecuyer, R., & Lahaye, W. (2017). The Moro reaction: More than a reflex, a ritualized behavior of nonverbal communication. *Infant Behavior and Development, 46,* 169–177.

Rovee-Collier, C. (1999). The development of infant memory. *Current Directions in Psychological Science, 8,* 80–85.

Rovee-Collier, C., & Barr, R. (2001). Infant learning and memory. In G. Bremner & A. Fogel (Eds.), *Blackwell handbook of infant development* (pp. 139–168). Oxford, UK: Blackwell.

Rovee-Collier, C., & Bhatt, R. S. (1993). Evidence of long-term memory in infancy. *Annals of Child Development, 9,* 1–45.

Rovee-Collier, C., & Cuevas, K. (2009). Multiple memory systems are unnecessary to account for infant memory development: An ecological model. *Developmental Psychology, 45,* 160–174.

Rowe, M. L. (2008). Child-directed speech: Relation to socioeconomic status, knowledge of child development and child vocabulary skill. *Journal of Child Language, 35,* 185–205.

Rowe, M. L. (2012). A longitudinal investigation of the role of quantity and quality of child-directed speech in vocabulary development. *Child Development, 83,* 1762–1774.

Rowe, M. L., & Goldin-Meadow, S. (2009). Early gesture selectively predicts later language learning. *Developmental Science, 12,* 182–187.

Rowe, M. L., Raudenbush, S. W., & Goldin-Meadow, S. (2012). The pace of vocabulary growth helps predict later vocabulary skill. *Child Development, 83,* 508–525.

Rowe, R., Maughan, B., & Goodman, R. (2004). Childhood psychiatric disorder and unintentional injury: Findings from a national cohort study. *Journal of Pediatric Psychology, 29,* 119–130.

Rowland, C. F. (2007). Explaining errors in children's questions. *Cognition, 104,* 106–134.

Rowland, C. F., & Pine, J. M. (2000). Subject-auxiliary inversion errors and wh-question acquisition: "What children do know?" *Journal of Child Language, 27,* 157–181.

Rowley, S. J., Kurtz-Costes, B., Mistry, R., & Feagans, L. (2007). Social status as a predictor of race and gender stereotypes in late childhood and early adolescence. *Social Development, 16,* 150–168.

Ruba, A. L., Johnson, K. M., Harris, L. T., & Wilbourn, M. P. (2017). Developmental changes in infants' categorization of anger and disgust facial expressions. *Developmental Psychology, 53,* 1826–1832.

Rübeling, H. (2014). "Zeichnen und malen im kinderlltag: Angebote und einstellungen [Drawing and painting in children's everyday life: Offers and attitudes]." In A. Gernhardt, R. Balakrishnon, & H. Drexler (Eds.), *Kinder zechnen ihre Wlt—Entwicklung und kultur* [Children draw their world—Development and culture], pp. 41–45. Berlin, Germany: das netz.

Rubens, D., & Sarnat, H. B. (2013). Sudden infant death syndrome: An update and new perspectives of etiology. *Handbook of Clinical Neurology, 112,* 867–874.

Rubin, C., Maisonet, M., Kieszak, S., Monteilh, C., Holmes A., Flanders, D., et al. (2009). Timing of maturation and predictors of menarche in girls enrolled in a contemporary British cohort. *Paediatric and Perinatal Epidemiology, 23,* 492–504.

Rubin, K. H., Begle, A. S., & McDonald, K. L. (2012). Peer relations and social competence in childhood. In V. Anderson & M. H. Beauchamp (Eds.), *Developmental social neuroscience and childhood brain insult: Theory and practice* (pp. 23–44). New York: Guilford.

Rubin, K. H., Bowker, J. C., Barstead, M. G., & Coplan, R. J. (2018). Avoiding and withdrawing from the peer group. In W. M. Bukowski, B. Laursen, & K. H. Rubin (Eds.), *Handbook of peer interactions, relationships, and groups* (2nd ed., pp. 322–346). New York: Guilford.

Rubin, K. H., Bowker, J. C., McDonald, K. L., & Menzer, M. (2013). Peer relationships in childhood. In P. D. Zelazo (Ed.), *Oxford handbook of developmental psychology, Vol. 2: Self and other* (pp. 242–275). New York: Oxford University Press.

Rubin, K. H., Bukowski, W. M., & Parker, J. G. (2006). Peer interactions, relationships, and groups. In N. Eisenberg (Ed.), *Handbook of child psychology: Vol. 3. Social, emotional, and personality development* (6th ed., pp. 571–645). Hoboken, NJ: Wiley.

Rubin, K. H., Burgess, K. B., & Hastings, P. D. (2002). Stability and social-behavioral consequences of toddlers' inhibited temperament and parenting behaviors. *Child Development, 73,* 483–495.

Rubin, K. H., Coplan, R., Chen, X., Bowker, J., & McDonald, K. L. (2011). Peer relationships in childhood. In M. E. Lamb & M. H. Bornstein (Eds.), *Social and personality development: An advanced textbook* (pp. 309–360). New York: Psychology Press.

Rubin, K. H., Coplan, R. J., & Bowker, J. C. (2009). Social withdrawal in childhood. *Annual Review of Psychology, 60,* 141–171.

Rubin, K. H., Fein, G. G., & Vandenberg, B. (1983). Play. In E. M. Hetherington (Ed.), *Handbook of child psychology: Vol. 4. Socialization, personality, and social development* (4th ed., pp. 693–744). New York: Wiley.

Rubin, K. H., Watson, K. S., & Jambor, T. W. (1978). Free-play behaviors in preschool and kindergarten children. *Child Development, 49,* 539–536.

Ruble, D. N., Alvarez, J., Bachman, M., Cameron, J., Fuligni, A., Garcia Coll, C. T., & Rhee, E. (2004). The development of a sense of "we": The emergence and implications of children's collective identity. In M. Bennett & F. Sani (Eds.), *The development of the social self* (pp. 29–76). Hove, UK: Psychology Press.

Ruble, D. N., Martin, C. L., & Berenbaum, S. A. (2006). Gender development. In N. Eisenberg (Ed.), *Handbook of child psychology: Vol. 3. Social, emotional, and personality development* (6th ed., pp. 858–932). Hoboken, NJ: Wiley.

Ruble, D. N., Taylor, L. J., Cyphers, L., Greulich, F. K., Lurye, L. E., & Shrout, P. E. (2007). The role of gender constancy in early gender development. *Child Development, 78,* 1121–1136.

Rucinski, C. L., Brown, J. L., & Downer, J. T. (2018). Teacher–child relationships, classroom climate, and children's social–emotional and academic development. *Journal of Educational Psychology, 110,* 992–1004.

Ruck, M. D., Keating, D. P., Saewyc, E. M., Earls, F., & Ben-Arieh, A. (2014). The United Nations Convention on the Rights of the Child: Its relevance for adolescents. *Journal of Research on Adolescence, 26,* 16–29.

Rudnicka, A., Kapetanakis, V. V., Wathem, A. K., Logan, N. S., Gilmartin, B., Whincup, P. H., et al. (2016). Global variations and time trends in the prevalence of childhood myopia, a systematic review and quantitative meta-analysis: Implications for aetiology and early prevention. *British Journal of Ophthalmology, 100,* 882–890.

Rudy, D., Carlo, G., Lambert, M. C., & Awong, T. (2014). Undergraduates' perceptions of parental relationship-oriented guilt induction versus harsh psychological control: Does cultural group status moderate their associations with self-esteem? *Journal of Cross-Cultural Psychology, 45,* 905–920.

Rueter, M. A., Connor, J. J., Pasch, L., Anderson, K. N., Scheib, J. E., Koerner, A. F., & Damario, M. (2016). Sharing information with children conceived using in vitro fertilization: The effect of parents' privacy orientation. *Journal of Reproductive and Infant Psychology, 34,* 90–102.

Ruff, C. (2002). Variation in human body size and shape. *Annual Review of Anthropology, 31,* 211–232.

Ruffman, T. (2014). To belief or not belief: Children's theory of mind. *Developmental Review, 34,* 265–293.

Ruffman, T., & Langman, L. (2002). Infants' reaching in a multi-well A not B task. *Infant Behavior and Development, 25,* 237–246.

Ruffman, T., Slade, L., Devitt, K., & Crowe, E. (2006). What mothers say and what they do: The relation between parenting, theory of mind, language, and conflict/cooperation. *British Journal of Developmental Psychology, 24,* 105–124.

Ruiz, R. J., Dwivedi, A. K., Mallawaarachichi, I., Bacazar, H. G., Stowe, R. P., Ayers, K. S., & Pickler, R. (2015). Psychological, cultural and neuroendocrine profiles of risk for preterm birth. *BMC Pregnancy and Childbirth, 15,* 204.

Runco, M. A. (1992). Children's divergent thinking and creative ideation. *Developmental Review, 12,* 233–264.

Rushton, J. P. (2012). No narrowing in mean Black–White IQ differences—Predicted by heritable g. *American Psychologist, 67,* 500–501.

Rushton, J. P., & Jensen, A. R. (2006). The totality of available evidence shows the race IQ gap still remains. *Psychological Science, 17,* 921–922.

Rushton, J. P., & Jensen, A. R. (2010). The rise and fall of the Flynn effect as a reason to expect a narrowing of the Black–White IQ gap. *Intelligence, 38,* 213–219.

Russell, A. (2014). Parent–child relationships and influences. In P. K. Smith & C. H. Hart (Eds.), *Wiley-Blackwell handbook of childhood social development* (2nd ed., pp. 337–355). Malden, MA: Wiley-Blackwell.

Russell, A., Mize, J., & Bissaker, K. (2004). Parent–child relationships. In P. K. Smith & C. H. Hart (Eds.), *Blackwell handbook of childhood social development* (pp. 204–222). Malden, MA: Blackwell.

Russell, S. T., & Muraco, J. A. (2013). Representative data sets to study LGBT-parent families. In A. E. Goldberg & K. R. Allen (Eds.), *LGBT-parent families: Innovations in research and implications for practice* (pp. 343–356). New York: Springer.

Russo, A., Semeraro, F., Romano, M. R., Mastropasqua, R., Dell'Omo, R., & Costagliola, C. (2014). Myopia onset and progression: Can it be prevented? *International Ophthalmology, 34,* 693–705.

Rust, J., Golombok, S., Hines, M., Johnston, K., Golding, J., & the ALSPAC Study Team. (2000). The role of brothers and sisters in the gender development of preschool children. *Journal of Experimental Child Psychology, 77,* 292–303.

Ruthsatz, J., & Urbach, J. B. (2012). Child prodigy: A novel cognitive profile places elevated general intelligence, exceptional working memory and attention to detail at the root of prodigiousness. *Intelligence, 40,* 419–426.

Rutland, A., & Killen, M. (2015). A developmental science approach to reducing prejudice and social exclusion: Intergroup processes, social-cognitive development, and moral reasoning. *Social Issues and Policy Review, 9,* 121–154.

Rutter, M. (2011). Biological and experiential influences on psychological development. In D. P. Keating (Ed.), *Nature and nurture in early child development* (pp. 7–44). New York: Cambridge University Press.

Rutter, M., & the English and Romanian Adoptees Study Team. (1998). Developmental catch-up, and deficit, following adoption after severe global early privation. *Journal of Child Psychology and Psychiatry, 39,* 465–476.

Rutter, M., O'Connor, T. G., & the English and Romanian Adoptees Study Team. (2004). Are there biological programming effects for psychological development? Findings from a study of Romanian adoptees. *Developmental Psychology, 40,* 81–94.

Rutter, M., Sonuga-Barke, E. J., Beckett, C., Castle, J., Kreppner, J., Kumsta, R., et al. (2010). Deprivation-specific psychological patterns: Effects of institutional deprivation. *Monographs of the Society for Research in Child Development, 75*(1, Serial No. 295).

Ryan, R. M., & Deci, E. L. (2017). *Self-determination theory: Basic psychological needs in motivation, development, and wellness.* New York: Guilford.

Ryding, M., Konradsson, K., Kalm, O., & Prellner, K. (2002). Auditory consequences of recurrent acute purulent otitis media. *Annals of Otology, Rhinology, and Laryngology, 111* (3, Pt. 1), 261–266.

S

Saarni, C., Campos, J. J., Camras, L. A., & Witherington, D. (2006). Emotional development: Action, communication, and understanding. In N. Eisenberg (Ed.), *Handbook of child psychology: Vol. 3. Social, emotional, and personality development* (6th ed., pp. 226–299). Hoboken, NJ: Wiley.

Sabo, D. and Veliz, P. (2011). *Progress without equity: The provision of high school athletic opportunity in the United States, by gender 1993–94 through 2005–06.* East Meadow, NY: Women's Sports Foundation.

Sabol, T. J., & Pianta, R. C. (2012). Recent trends in research on teacher–child relationships. *Attachment and Human Development, 14,* 213–231.

Sadler, T. W. (2014). *Langman's medical embryology* (13th ed.). Baltimore, MD: Lippincott Williams & Wilkins.

Safar, K., & Moulson, M. C. (2017). Facial expressions of emotion in infancy: A replication and extension. *Developmental Psychology, 59,* 507–514.

Safe Kids Worldwide. (2015). *Overview of childhood injury morbidity and mortality in the U.S.: Fact sheet 2015.* Retrieved from www.safekids.org/sites/default/files /documents/skw_overview_fact_sheet _november_2014.pdf

Saffran, J. R. (2017). Learning is not a four-letter word. In D. Cicchetti & M R. Gunnar (Eds.), *Minnesota Symposia on Child Psychology* (Vol. 35, pp. 159–188). Hoboken, NJ: Wiley.

Saffran, J. R., Aslin, R. N., & Newport, E. L. (1996). Statistical learning by 8-month-old infants. *Science, 27,* 1926–1928.

Saffran, J. R., & Thiessen, E. D. (2003). Pattern induction by infant language learners. *Developmental Psychology, 39,* 484–494.

Saffran, J. R., Werker, J. F., & Werner, L. A. (2006). The infant's auditory world: Hearing, speech, and the beginnings of language. In D. Kuhn & R. Siegler (Eds.), *Handbook of child psychology: Vol. 2. Cognition, perception, and language* (6th ed., pp. 58–108). Hoboken, NJ: Wiley.

Sale, A., Berardi, N., & Maffei, L. (2009). Enrich the environment to empower the brain. *Trends in Neurosciences, 32,* 233–239.

Salihu, H. M., Shumpert, M. N., Slay, M., Kirby, R. S., & Alexander, G. R. (2003). Childbearing beyond maternal age 50 and fetal outcomes in the United States. *Obstetrics and Gynecology, 102,* 1006–1014.

Salley, B. J., & Dixon, W. E., Jr. (2007). Temperamental and joint attentional predictors of language development. *Merrill-Palmer Quarterly, 53,* 131–154.

Salmivalli, C. (2010). Bullying and the peer group: A review. *Aggression and Violent Behavior, 15,* 112–120.

Salmivalli, C., & Peets, K. (2018). Bullying and victimization. In W. M. Bukowski, B. Laursen, & K. H. Rubin (Eds.), *Handbook of peer interactions, relationships, and groups* (2nd ed., pp. 322–346). New York: Guilford.

Salmivalli, C., & Voeten, M. (2004). Connections between attitudes, group norms, and behaviour in bullying situations. *International Journal of Behavioral Development, 28,* 246–258.

Salmon, D. A., Dudley, M. Z., Glanz, J. M., & Omer, S. B. (2015). Vaccine hesitancy: Causes, consequences, and a call to action. *American Journal of Preventive Medicine, 49,* S391–S398.

Salomo, D., & Liszkowski, U. (2013). Sociocultural settings influence the emergence of prelinguistic deictic gestures. *Child Development, 84,* 1296–1307.

Salomonis, N. (2014). Systems-level perspective of sudden infant death syndrome. *Pediatric Research, 76,* 220–229.

Salvas, M.-C., Vitaro, F., Brendgen, M., & Cantin, S. (2016). Prospective links between friendship and early physical aggression: Preliminary evidence supporting the role of friendship quality through a dyadic intervention. *Merrill-Palmer Quarterly, 62,* 285–305.

Sampaio, R. C., & Truwit, C. L. (2001). Myelination in the developing human brain. In C. A. Nelson & M. Luciana (Eds.), *Handbook of developmental cognitive neuroscience* (pp. 35–44). Cambridge, MA: MIT Press.

Samuelson, L., & McMurray, B. (2017). What does it take to learn a word? *WIREs Cognitive Science, 8,* e1421.

Sánchez, B., Colón, Y., & Esparza, P. (2005). The role of sense of school belonging and gender in academic adjustment of Latino adolescents. *Journal of Youth and Adolescence, 34,* 619–628.

Sánchez, B., Esparza, P., Colón, Y., & Davis, K. E. (2010). Tryin' to make it during the transition from high school: The role of family obligation attitudes and economic context for Latino emerging adults. *Journal of Adolescent Research, 25,* 858–884.

Sanders, O. (2006). *Evaluating the Keeping Ourselves Safe Programme.* Wellington, NZ: Youth Education Service, New Zealand Police.

Sandman, C. A., Glynn, L. M., & Davis, E. P. (2016). Neurobehavioral consequences of fetal exposure to gestational stress. In N. Reissland & B. S. Kisilevsky (Eds.), *Fetal development* (pp. 229–265). New York: Springer.

San Juan, V., & Astington, J. W. (2012). Bridging the gap between implicit and explicit understanding: How language development promotes the processing and representation of false belief. *British*

Journal of Developmental Psychology, 30, 105–122.

Sann, C., & Streri, A. (2007). Perception of object shape and texture in human newborns: Evidence from cross-modal transfer tasks. *Developmental Science, 10,* 399–410.

Sann, C., & Streri, A. (2008). The limits of newborn's grasping to detect texture in a cross-modal transfer task. *Infant Behavior and Development, 31,* 523–531.

Sansavini, A., Bertoncini, J., & Giovanelli, G. (1997). Newborns discriminate the rhythm of multisyllabic stressed words. *Developmental Psychology, 33,* 3–11.

Saracho, O. N. (2014). Theory of mind: Understanding young children's pretense and mental states. *Early Child Development and Care, 184,* 1281–1294.

Sarici, H., Telli, O., Ozgur, B. C., Demirbas, A., Ozgur, S., & Karagoz, M. A. (2016). Prevalence of nocturnal enuresis and its influence on quality of life in school-aged children. *Journal of Pediatric Urology, 12,* 159.e1–6.

Sarnecka, B. W., & Wright, C. E. (2013). The idea of an exact number: Children's understanding of cardinality and equinumerosity. *Cognitive Science, 37,* 1493–1506.

Sasser, T. R., Bierman, K. L., Heinrichs, B., & Nix, R. L. (2017). Preschool intervention can promote sustained growth in the executive-function skills of children exhibiting early deficits. *Psychological Science, 28,* 1719–1730.

Sauce, B., & Matzel, L. D. (2018). The paradox of intelligence: Heritability and malleability coexist in hidden gene–environment interplay. *Psychological Bulletin, 144,* 26–47.

Saucier, J. F., Sylvestre, R., Doucet, H., Lambert, J., Frappier, J. Y., Charbonneau, L., & Malus, M. (2002). Cultural identity and adaptation to adolescence in Montreal. In F. J. C. Azima & N. Grizenko (Eds.), *Immigrant and refugee children and their families: Clinical, research, and training issues* (pp. 133–154). Madison, WI: International Universities Press.

Saudino, K. J. (2003). Parent ratings of infant temperament: Lessons from twin studies. *Infant Behavior and Development, 26,* 100–107.

Saudino, K. J., & Micalizzi, L. (2015). Emerging trends in behavioral genetic studies of child temperament. *Child Development Perspectives, 9,* 144–148.

Saudino, K. J., & Plomin, R. (1997). Cognitive and temperamental mediators of genetic contributions to the home environment during infancy. *Merrill-Palmer Quarterly, 43,* 1–23.

Saunders, B. E. (2012). Determining best practice for treating sexually victimized children. In P. Goodyear-Brown (Ed.), *Handbook of child sexual abuse: Identification, assessment, and treatment* (pp. 173–198). Hoboken, NJ: Wiley.

Sauve, J. A., & Schonert-Reichl, K. A. (2019). Creating caring classroom and school communities: Lessons learned from social and emotional learning programs and practices. In J. A. Fredricks, A. L. Reschly, & S. L. Christenson (Eds.), *Handbook of student engagement interventions* (pp. 279–295). San Diego, CA: Academic Press.

Saxe, G. B. (1988, August–September). Candy selling and math learning. *Educational Researcher, 17*(6), 14–21.

Saxton, M., Backley, P., & Gallaway, C. (2005). Negative input for grammatical errors: Effects after a lag of 12 weeks. *Journal of Child Language, 32,* 643–672.

Saygin, A. P., Leech, R., & Dick, F. (2010). Nonverbal auditory agnosia with lesion to Wernicke's area. *Neuropsychologia, 48,* 107–113.

Saylor, M. M., Ganea, P. A., & Vázquez, M. D. (2011). What's mine is mine: Twelve-month-olds use possessive pronouns to identify referents. *Developmental Science, 14,* 859–864.

Saylor, M. M., & Troseth, G. L. (2006). Preschoolers use information about speakers' desires to learn new words. *Cognitive Development, 21,* 214–231.

Scarr, S., & McCartney, K. (1983). How people make their own environments: A theory of genotype–environment effects. *Child Development, 54,* 424–435.

Scarr, S., & Weinberg, R. A. (1983). The Minnesota adoption studies: Genetic differences and malleability. *Child Development, 54,* 260–267.

Schaal, B., Marlier, L., & Soussignan, R. (2000). Human foetuses learn odours from their pregnant mother's diet. *Chemical Senses, 25,* 729–737.

Schaal, S., Dusingizemungu, J.-P., Jacob, N., & Elbert, T. (2011). Rates of trauma spectrum disorders and risks of post-traumatic stress disorder in a sample of orphaned and widowed genocide survivors. *European Journal of Psychotraumatology, 2.* Retrieved from www.ncbi.nlm.nih.gov/pmc/articles/PMC3402134

Scher, A., Epstein, R., & Tirosh, E. (2004). Stability and changes in sleep regulation: A longitudinal study from 3 months to 3 years. *International Journal of Behavioral Development, 28,* 268–274.

Scher, A., Tirosh, E., Jaffe, M., Rubin, L., Sadeh, A., & Lavie, P. (1995). Sleep patterns of infants and young children in Israel. *International Journal of Behavioral Development, 18,* 701–711.

Scherer, R., Siddiq, F., & Viveros, B. S. (2019). The cognitive benefits of learning computer programming: A meta-analysis of transfer effects. *Journal of Educational Psychology, 111,* 764–792.

Scherrer, J. L. (2012). The United Nations Convention on the Rights of the Child as policy and strategy for social work action in child welfare in the United States. *Social Work, 57,* 11–22.

Schlagmüller, M., & Schneider, W. (2002). The development of organizational strategies in children: Evidence from a microgenetic longitudinal study. *Journal of Experimental Child Psychology, 81,* 298–319.

Schleepen, T. M. J., & Jonkman, L. M. (2014). A longitudinal study of semantic grouping strategy use in 6–11-year-old children: Investigating developmental phases, the role of working memory, and strategy transfer. *Journal of Genetic Psychology, 175,* 451–471.

Schmidt, A. T., Waldow, K. J., Grove, W. M., Salinas, J. A., & Georgieff, M. K. (2007). Dissociating the long-term effects of fetal/neonatal iron deficiency on three types of learning in the rat. *Behavioral Neuroscience, 121,* 475–482.

Schmidt, L. A., Fox, N. A., Schulkin, J., & Gold, P. W. (1999). Behavioral and psychophysiological correlates of self-presentation in temperamentally shy children. *Developmental Psychobiology, 30,* 127–140.

Schmidt, L. A., Tang, A., Day, K. L., Lahat, A., Boyle, M. H., Saigal, S., & Van Lieshout, R. J. (2017). Personality development within a generational context: Life course outcomes of shy children. *Child Psychiatry and Human Development, 48,* 632–641.

Schmitz, S., Fulker, D. W., Plomin, R., Zahn-Waxler, C., Emde, R. N., & DeFries, J. C. (1999). Temperament and problem behaviour during early childhood. *International Journal of Behavioral Development, 23,* 333–355.

Schneider, W. (1986). The role of conceptual knowledge and metamemory in the development of organizational processes in memory. *Journal of Experimental Child Psychology, 42,* 218–236.

Schneider, W. (2002). Memory development in childhood. In U. Goswami (Ed.), *Blackwell handbook of childhood cognitive development* (pp. 236–256). Malden, MA: Blackwell.

Schneider, W., & Bjorklund, D. F. (1992). Expertise, aptitude, and strategic remembering. *Child Development, 63,* 461–473.

Schneider, W., & Bjorklund, D. F. (1998). Memory. In D. Kuhn & R. S. Siegler (Eds.), *Handbook of child psychology: Vol. 2. Cognition, perception, and language* (5th ed., pp. 467–521). New York: Wiley.

Schneider, W., & Ornstein, P. A. (2015). The development of children's memory. *Child Development Perspectives, 9,* 190–195.

Schneider, W., & Pressley, M. (1997). *Memory development between two and twenty* (2nd ed.). Mahwah, NJ: Erlbaum.

Schoenmaker, C., Juffer, F., van IJzendoorn, M. H., van den Dries, L., Linting, M., van der Voort, A., & Bakermans-Kranenburg, M. J. (2015). Cognitive and health-related outcomes after exposure to early malnutrition: The Leiden longitudinal study of international adoptees. *Children and Youth Services Review, 48,* 80–86.

Schonberg, R. L. (2012). Birth defects and prenatal diagnosis. In M. L. Batshaw, N. J. Roizen, & G. R. Lotrecchiano (Eds.), *Children with disabilities* (7th ed., pp. 47–60). Baltimore: Paul H. Brookes.

Schöner, G., & Thelen, E. (2006). Using dynamic field theory to rethink infant habituation. *Psychological Review, 113,* 273–299.

Schonert-Reichl, K. A., & Lawlor, M. S. (2010). The effects of a mindfulness-based education program on pre- and early adolescents' well-being and social and emotional competence. *Mindfulness, 1,* 137–151.

Schonert-Reichl, K. A., Oberle, E., Lawlor, M. S., Abbott, D., Thomson, K., Oberlander, T. F., et al. (2015). Enhancing cognitive and social-emotional development through a simple-to-administer mindfulness-based school program for elementary school children: A randomized controlled trial. *Developmental Psychology, 51,* 52–66.

Schoon, I., Jones, E., Cheng, H., Maughan, B. (2012). Family hardship, family instability, and cognitive development. *Journal of Epidemiology and Community Health, 66,* 716–722.

Schoppe-Sullivan, S. J., Brown, G. L., Cannon, E. A., Mangelsdorf, S. C., & Sokolowski, M. S. (2008). Maternal gatekeeping, coparenting quality, and fathering behavior in families with infants. *Journal of Family Psychology, 22,* 389–398.

Schoppe-Sullivan, S. J., Mangelsdorf, S. C., Brown, G. L., & Sokolowski, M. S. (2007). Goodness-of-fit in family context: Infant temperament, marital quality, and early coparenting behavior. *Infant Behavior and Development, 30,* 82–96.

Schott, J. M., & Rossor, M. N. (2003). The grasp and other primitive reflexes. *Journal of Neurological and Neurosurgical Psychiatry, 74,* 558–560.

Schroeder, R. D., Bulanda, R. E., Giordano, P. C., & Cernkovich, S. A. (2010). Parenting and adult criminality: An examination of direct and indirect effects by race. *Journal of Adolescent Research, 25,* 64–98.

Schubert, A.-L., Hagemann, D., & Frischkorn, G. T. (2017). Is general intelligence little more than the speed of higher-order processing? *Journal of Experimental Psychology: General, 146,* 1498–1512.

Schulz, L. O., & Chaudhari, L. S. (2015). High-risk populations: The Pimas of Arizona and Mexico. *Current Obesity Report, 4,* 92–98.

Schulz, M. S., Cowan, C. P., & Cowan, P. A. (2006). Promoting healthy beginnings: A randomized controlled trial of a preventive intervention to preserve marital quality during the transition to parenthood. *Journal of Consulting and Clinical Psychology, 74,* 20–31.

Schulze, C., Grassmann, S., & Tomasello, M. (2013). 3-year-old children make relevant inferences in indirect verbal communication. *Child Development, 84,* 2079–2093.

Schultz, T. R. (2011). Computational modeling of infant concept learning: The developmental shift from features to correlations. In L. M. Oakes, C. H. Cashon, M. Casasola, & D. Rakison (Eds.), *Infant perception and cognition* (125–152). New York: Oxford University Press.

Schunemann, N., Sporer, N., & Brunstein, J. C. (2013). Integrating self-regulation in whole-class reciprocal teaching: A moderator–mediator analysis of incremental effects on fifth graders' reading comprehension. *Contemporary Educational Psychology, 38,* 289–305.

Schunk, D. H., & Zimmerman, B. J. (2013). Self-regulation and learning. In W. M. Reynolds, G. E. Miller, & I. B. Weiner (Eds.), *Handbook of psychology: Vol. 7. Educational psychology* (pp. 45–68). Hoboken, NJ: Wiley.

Schutte, A. R., & DeGirolamo, G. J. (2017). Dynamical systems approaches. In B. Hopkins, E. Geangu, & S. Linkenauger (Eds.), *Cambridge encyclopedia of child development* (2nd ed., pp. 60–70). Cambridge, UK: Cambridge University Press.

Schwanenflugel, P. J., Henderson, R. L., & Fabricius, W. V. (1998). Developing organization of mental verbs and theory of mind in middle childhood: Evidence from extensions. *Developmental Psychology, 34,* 512–524.

Schwartz, C. E., Kunwar, P. S., Greve, D. N., Kagan, J., Snidman, N. C., & Bloch, R. B. (2012). A phenotype of early infancy predicts reactivity of the amygdala in male adults. *Molecular Psychiatry, 17,* 1042–1050.

Schwarz, N. (2008). Self-reports: How the questions shape the answers. In R. H. Fazio & R. E. Petty (Eds.), *Attitudes: Their structure, function, and consequences* (pp. 49–67). New York: Psychology Press.

Schwarzer, G., Freitag, C., & Schum, N. (2013). How crawling and manual object exploration are related to the mental rotation abilities of 9-month-old infants. *Frontiers in Psychology, 4,* Art. No. 97.

Schwebel, D. C., & Brezausek, C. M. (2007). Father transitions in the household and young children's injury risk. *Psychology of Men and Masculinity, 8,* 173–184.

Schwebel, D. C., & Gaines, J. (2007). Pediatric unintentional injury: Behavioral risk factors and implications for prevention. *Journal of Developmental and Behavioral Pediatrics, 28,* 245–254.

Schwebel, D. C., Roth, D. L., Elliott, M. N., Chien, A. T., Mrug, S., Shipp, E., et al. (2012). Marital conflict and fifth-graders' risk for injury. *Accident Analysis and Prevention, 47,* 30–35.

Schwebel, D. C., Roth, D. L., Elliott, M. N., Windle, M., Grunbaum, J. A., Low, B., et al. (2011). The association of activity level, parent mental distress, and parental involvement and monitoring with unintentional injury risk in fifth graders. *Accident Analysis and Prevention, 43,* 848–852.

Schweinhart, L. J. (2010). The challenge of the High/Scope Perry Preschool study. In A. J. Reynolds, A. J. Rolnick, M. M. Englund, & J. Temple (Eds.), *Childhood programs and practices in the first decade of life: A human capital integration* (pp. 199–213). New York: Cambridge University Press.

Schweinhart, L. J., Montie, J., Xiang, Z., Barnett, W. S., Belfield, C. R., & Nores, M. (2005). *Lifetime effects: The High/Scope Perry Preschool Study through age 40.* Ypsilanti, MI: High/Scope Press.

Schweizer, K., Moosbrugger, H., & Goldhammer, F. (2006). The structure of the relationship between attention and intelligence. *Intelligence, 33,* 589–611.

Schwenck, C., Bjorklund, D. F., & Schneider, W. (2007). Factors influencing the incidence of utilization deficiencies and other patterns of recall/strategy-use relations in a strategic memory task. *Child Development, 22,* 197–212.

Schwier, C., van Maanen, C., Carpenter, M., & Tomasello, M. (2006). Rational imitation in 12-month-old infants. *Infancy, 10,* 303–311.

Schwilling, D., Vogeser, M., Kirchhoff, F., Schwaiblmair, F., Boulesteix, A.-L., Schulze, A., et al. (2014). Live music reduces stress levels in very low-birthweight infants. *Acta Paediatrica, 104,* 360–367.

Scott, R. M., & Fisher, C. (2012). 2.5-year-olds use cross-situational consistency to learn verbs under referential uncertainty. *Cognition, 122,* 163–180.

Scrimgeour, M. B., Davis, E. L., & Buss, K. A. (2016). You get what you get and you don't throw a fit!: Emotion socialization and child physiology jointly predict early prosocial development. *Developmental Psychology, 52,* 102–116.

Seburg, E. M., Olson-Bullis, B. A., Bredeson, D. M., Hayes, M. G., & Sherwood, N. E. (2015). A review of primary care-based childhood obesity prevention and treatment interventions. *Current Obesity Report, 4,* 157–173.

Sechi, G., Sechi, E., Fois, C., & Kumar, N. (2016). Advances in clinical determinants and neurological manifestations of B vitamin deficiency in adults. *Nutrition Reviews, 74,* 281–300.

Sedgh, G., Finer, L. B., Bankole, A., Eilers, M. A., & Singh, S. (2015). Adolescent pregnancy, birth, and abortion rates across countries: Levels and recent trends. *Journal of Adolescent Health, 56,* 223–230.

Seethaler, P. M., Fuchs, L. S., Fuchs, D., & Compton, D. L. (2012). Predicting first graders' development of calculation versus word-problem performance: The role of dynamic assessment. *Journal of Educational Psychology, 104,* 224–234.

Seibert, A., & Kerns, K. (2015). Early mother–child attachment: Longitudinal prediction to the quality of peer relationships in middle childhood. *International Journal of Behavioral Development, 39,* 130–138.

Seibert, A. C., & Kerns, K. A. (2009). Attachment figures in middle childhood. *International Journal of Behavioral Development, 33,* 347–355.

Seidl, A., Hollich, G., & Jusczyk, P. (2003). Early understanding of subject and object wh-questions. *Infancy, 4,* 423–436.

Seigneuric, A., Megherbi, H., Bueno, S., & Lebahar, J. (2016). Children's comprehension skill and the understanding of nominal metaphors. *Journal of Experimental Child Psychology, 150,* 346–363.

Sekido, R., & Lovell-Badge, R. (2009). Sex determination and SRY: Down to a wink and a nudge? *Trends in Genetics, 25,* 19–29.

Semega, J. L., Fontenot, K. R., & Kollar, M. A. (2017). *Income and poverty in the United States: 2016.* U.S. Census Bureau, Current Population Reports, P60–259. Washington, DC: U.S. Government Printing Office.

Senechal, M., & LeFevre, J. (2002). Parental involvement in the development of children's reading skill: A five-year longitudinal study. *Child Development, 73,* 445–460.

Sengpiel, V., Elind, E., Bacelis, J., Nilsson, S., Grove, J., Myhre, R., et al. (2013). Maternal caffeine intake during pregnancy is associated with birth weight but not with gestational length: Results from a large prospective observational cohort study. *BMC Medicine, 11,* 42.

Senju, A., Csibra, G., & Johnson, M. H. (2008). Understanding the referential nature of looking: Infants' preference for object-directed gaze. *Cognition, 108,* 303–319.

Senn, T. E., Espy, K. A., & Kaufmann, P. M. (2004). Using path analysis to understand executive function organization in preschool children. *Developmental Neuropsychology, 26,* 445–464.

Serratrice, L. (2013). The bilingual child. In T. K. Bhatia & W. C. Ritchie (Eds.), *Handbook of bilingualism and multilingualism* (pp. 87–108). Chichester, UK: Wiley-Blackwell.

Sesame Workshop. (2018). *Where we work: All locations.* Retrieved from www.sesameworkshop.org/where-we-work

Sette, S., Spinrad, T. L., & Baumgartner, E. (2017). The relations of preschool children's emotion knowledge and socially appropriate behaviors to peer likability. International *Journal of Behavioral Development, 41,* 532–541.

Sevigny, P. R., & Loutzenhiser, L. (2010). Predictors of parenting self-efficacy in mothers and fathers of toddlers. *Child: Care, Health and Development, 36,* 179–189.

Sewell, A., St George, A., & Cullen, J. (2013). The distinctive features of joint participation in a community of learners. *Teaching and Teacher Education, 31,* 46–55.

Shafer, R. J., Raby, K. L., Lawler, J. M., Hesemeyer, P. S., & Roisman, G. I. (2015). Longitudinal associations between adult attachment states of mind and parenting quality. *Attachment & Human Development, 17,* 83–95.

Shahaeian, A., Peterson, C. C., Slaughter, V., & Wellman, H. M. (2011). Culture and the sequence of steps in theory of mind development. *Developmental Psychology, 47,* 1239–1247.

Shai, D., & Meins, E. (2018). Parental embodied mentalizing and its relation to mind-mindedness, sensitivity, and attachment security. *Infancy, 23,* 857–872.

Shanahan, T., & Lonigan, C. L. (2010). The National Early Literacy Panel: A summary of the process and the report. *Educational Researcher, 39,* 279–285.

Sharp, K. L., Williams, A. J., Rhyner, K. T., & Hardi, S. S. (2013). The clinical interview. In K. F. Geisinger, B. A. Bracken, J. F. Carlson, J. C. Hansen, N. R. Kuncel, S. P. Reise, et al. (Eds.), *APA handbook of testing and assessment in psychology* (Vol. 2, pp. 103–117). Washington, DC: American Psychological Association.

Shaul, S., & Schwartz, M. (2014). The role of executive functions in school readiness among preschool-age children. *Reading and Writing, 27,* 749–768.

Shaw, D., Sitnick, S., Brennan L., Choe, D. E., Dishion, T. J., Wilson, M. N., & Gardner, F. (2016). The long-term effectiveness of the Family Check-Up on school-age children's conduct problems: Moderation by neighborhood deprivation. *Development and Psychopathology, 28,* 1471–1486.

Shaw, D. S., Hyde, L. W., & Brennan, L. M. (2012). Early predictors of boys' antisocial trajectories. *Development and Psychopathology, 24,* 871–888.

Shaw, D. S., Lacourse, E., & Nagin, D. S. (2005). Developmental trajectories of conduct problems and hyperactivity from ages 2 to 10. *Journal of Child Psychology and Psychiatry, 46,* 931–942.

Shaw, D. S., Winslow, E. B., & Flanagan, C. (1999). A prospective study of the effects of marital status and family relations on young children's adjustment among African-American and European-American families. *Child Development, 70,* 742–755.

Shaw, P., Brierley, B., & David, A. S. (2005). A critical period for the impact of amygdala damage on the emotional enhancement of memory? *Neurology, 65,* 326–328.

Shaw, P., Eckstrand, K., Sharp, W., Blumenthal, J., Lerch, J. P., & Greenstein, D. (2007). Attention-deficit/hyperactivity disorder is characterized by a delay in cortical maturation. *Proceedings of the National Academy of Sciences, 104,* 19649–19654.

Shearer, R. J. B., McWayne, C. M., Mendez, J. L., & Manz, P. H. (2016). Preschool peer play interactions, a developmental context for ALL children: Rethinking issues of equity and opportunity. In K. E. Sanders & A. W. Guerra (Eds.), *The culture of child care: Attachment, peers, and quality in diverse communities* (pp. 179–202). New York: Oxford University Press.

Sheehan, G., Darlington, Y., Noller, P., & Feeney, J. (2004). Children's perceptions of their sibling relationships during parental separation and divorce. *Journal of Divorce and Remarriage, 41,* 69–94.

Shields, B., Wacogne, I., & Wright, C. M. (2012). Weight faltering and failure to thrive in infancy and early childhood. *British Medical Journal, 345,* e5931.

Shimizu, M., Park, H., & Greenfield, P. M. (2014). Infant sleeping arrangements and cultural values among contemporary Japanese mothers. *Frontiers in Psychology, 5,* Art. No. 718.

Shin, N., Kim, M., Goetz, S., & Vaughn, B. E. (2014). Dyadic analyses of preschool-aged children's friendships: Convergence and differences between friendship classifications from peer sociometric data and teacher reports. *Social Development, 23,* 178–195.

Shiner, R. L. (2015). The development of temperament and personality traits in childhood and adolescence. In M. Mikulincer & P. R. Shaver (Eds.), *APA handbook of personality and social psychology: Vol. 4. Personality and individual differences* (pp. 85–105). Washington, DC: American Psychological Association.

Shirley, K., Rutfield, R., Hall, N., Fedor, N., McCaughey, V. K., & Zajac, K. (2015). Combinations of obesity prevention strategies in U.S. elementary schools: A critical review. *Journal of Primary Prevention, 36,* 1–20.

Shisler, S., Eiden, R. D., Molnar, D. S., Schuetze, P., Huestis, M., & Hornish, G. (2017). Smoking in pregnancy and fetal growth: The case for more intensive assessment. *Nicotine and Tobacco Research, 19,* 525–531.

Shonkoff, J. P., & Garner, A. S. (2012). The lifelong effects of early childhood adversity and toxic stress. *Pediatrics, 129,* e232–e246.

Shope, T. R. (2014). Infectious diseases in early education and child care programs. *Pediatrics in Review, 35,* 182–193.

Shriver, L. H., Harrist, A. W., Page, M., Hubbs-Tait, L., Moulton, M., & Topham, G. (2013). Differences in body esteem by weight status, gender, and physical activity among young elementary school-aged children. *Body Image, 10,* 78–84.

Shtulman, A., & Yoo R. I. (2015). Children's understanding of physical possibility constrains their belief in Santa Claus. *Cognitive Development, 34,* 51–62.

Siberry, G. K. (2015). Preventing and managing HIV infection in infants, children, and adolescents in the United States. *Pediatrics in Review, 35,* 268–286.

Sidebotham, P., Heron, J., & the ALSPAC Study Team. (2003). Child maltreatment in the "children of the nineties": The role of the child. *Child Abuse and Neglect, 27,* 337–352.

Siegal, M., Iozzi, L., & Surian, L. (2009). Bilingualism and conversational understanding in young children. *Cognition, 110,* 115–122.

Siega-Riz, A. M., Deming, D. M., Reidy, K. C., Fox, M. K., Condon, E., & Briefel, R. R. (2010). Food consumption patterns of infants and toddlers: Where are we now? *Journal of the American Dietetic Association, 110,* S38–S51.

Siegler, R. S. (1996). *Emerging minds: The process of change in children's thinking.* New York: Oxford University Press.

Siegler, R. S. (2006). Microgenetic analyses of learning. In D. Kuhn & R. Siegler (Eds.), *Handbook of child psychology: Vol. 2. Cognition, perception, and language* (6th ed., pp. 464–510). Hoboken, NJ: Wiley.

Siegler, R. S. (2009). Improving preschoolers' number sense using information-processing theory. In O. A. Barbarin & B. H. Wasik (Eds.), *Handbook of child development and early education: Research to practice* (pp. 429–454). New York: Guilford.

Siegler, R. S. (2016). Magnitude knowledge: The common core of numerical development. *Developmental Science, 19,* 341–361.

Siegler, R. S., & Braithwaite, D. W. (2017). Numerical development. *Annual Review of Psychology, 68,* 187–213.

Siegler, R. S., Duncan, G. J., Davis-Kean, P. E., Duckworth, K., Claessens, A., Engel, M., et al. (2012). Early predictors of high school mathematics achievement. *Psychological Science, 23,* 691–697.

Siegler, R. S., & Mu, Y. (2008). Chinese children excel on novel mathematics problems even before elementary school. *Psychological Science, 19,* 759–763.

Siegler, R. S., & Svetina, M. (2006). What leads children to adopt new strategies? A microgenetic/cross-sectional study of class inclusion. *Child Development, 77,* 997–1015.

Sigle-Rushton, W., Lyngstad, T. H., Andersen, P. L., & Kravdal, Ø. (2014). Proceed with caution? Parents' union dissolution and children's educational achievement. *Journal of Marriage and Family, 76,* 161–174.

Sigurdsson, S., Eythorsson, E., Hrafnkelsson, B., Erlensdóttir, H., Kristinsson, K. G., & Haraldsson, Á. (2018). Reduction in all-cause acute otitis media in children <3 years of age in primary care following vaccination with 10-valent pneumococcal haemophilus influenzae protein-D conjugate vaccine: A whole-population study. *Clinical Infectious Diseases, 67*, 1213–1219.

Silbereis, J. C., Pochareddy, S., Zhu, Y., Li, M., & Sestan, N. (2016). The cellular and molecular landscapes of the developing human central nervous system. *Neuron, 89*, 248–268.

Silk, J. S., Sessa, F. M., Morris, A. S., Steinberg, L., & Avenevoli, S. (2004). Neighborhood cohesion as a buffer against hostile maternal parenting. *Journal of Family Psychology, 18*, 135–146.

Silk, T. J., & Wood, A. G. (2011). Lessons about neurodevelopment from anatomical magnetic resonance imaging. *Journal of Developmental and Behavioral Pediatrics, 32*, 158–168.

Silverman, I., Choi, J., & Peters, M. (2007). The hunter-gatherer theory of sex differences in spatial abilities. *Archives of Sexual Behavior, 36*, 261–268.

Simcock, G., Garrity, K., & Barr, R. (2011). The effect of narrative cues on infants' imitation from television and picture books. *Child Development, 82*, 1607–1619.

Simcock, G., & Hayne, H. (2003). Age-related changes in verbal and nonverbal memory during early childhood. *Developmental Psychology, 39*, 805–814.

Simion, F., Cassia, V. M., Turati, C., & Valenza, E. (2001). The origins of face perception: Specific versus nonspecific mechanisms. *Infant and Child Development, 10*, 59–65.

Simmonds, M., Llewellyn, A., Owen, C. G., & Woolacott, N. (2016). Predicting adult obesity from childhood obesity: A systematic review and meta-analysis. *Obesity Reviews, 17*, 95–107.

Simons, H. (2014). Case study research: In-depth understanding in context. In P. Leavy (Ed.) *Oxford handbook of qualitative research* (pp. 455–470). New York: Oxford University Press.

Simonton, D. K. (2018). From giftedness to eminence: Developmental landmarks across the lifespan. In S. I Pfeiffer, E. Shaunessy-Dedrick, & M. Foley-Nicpon (Eds.), *APA handbook of giftedness and talent* (pp. 273–285). Washington, DC: American Psychological Association.

Simpson, E. A., Murray, L., Paukner, A., & Ferrari, P. F. (2014). The mirror neuron system as revealed through neonatal imitation: Presence from birth, predictive power, and evidence of plasticity. *Philosophical Transactions B, 369*, 20130289.

Simpson, E. A., Varga, K., Frick, J. E., & Fragaszy, D. (2011). Infants experience perceptual narrowing for nonprimate faces. *Infancy, 16*, 318–328.

Singer, L. T., Minnes, S., Min, M. O., Lewis, B. A., & Short, E. J. (2015). Prenatal cocaine exposure and child outcomes: A conference report based on a prospective study from Cleveland. *Human Psychopharmacology, 30*, 285–289.

Singleton, J. L., & Newport, E. L. (2004). When learners surpass their models: The acquisition of American Sign Language from inconsistent input. *Cognitive Psychology, 49*, 370–407.

Sirois, S., & Jackson, I. (2007). Social cognition in infancy: A critical review of research on higher-order abilities. *European Journal of Developmental Psychology, 4*, 46–64.

Sirois, S., & Jackson, I. R. (2012). Pupil dilation and object permanence in infants. *Infancy, 17*, 61–78.

Slagt, M., Dubas, J. S., Deković, M., & van Aken, A. G. (2016). Differences in sensitivity to parenting depending on child temperament: A meta-analysis. *Psychological Bulletin, 142*, 1068–1110.

Slater, A., & Johnson, S. P. (1999). Visual sensory and perceptual abilities of the newborn: Beyond the blooming, buzzing confusion. In A. Slater & S. P. Johnson (Eds.), *The development of sensory, motor and cognitive capacities in early infancy* (pp. 121–141). Hove, UK: Sussex Press.

Slater, A., Quinn, P. C., Kelly, D. J., Lee, K., Longmore, C. A., McDonald, P. R., & Pascalis, O. (2011). The shaping of the face space in early infancy: Becoming a native face processor. *Child Development Perspectives, 4*, 205–211.

Slater, A., Riddell, P., Quinn, P. C., Pascalis, O., Lee, K., & Kelly, D. J. (2010). Visual perception. In J. G. Bremner & T. D. Wachs (Eds.), *Wiley-Blackwell handbook of infant development: Vol. 1. Basic research* (2nd ed., pp. 40–80). Chichester, UK: Wiley-Blackwell.

Sloane, S., Baillargeon, R., & Premack, D. (2012). Do infants have a sense of fairness? *Psychological Science, 23*, 196–204.

Slobodskaya, H. R., Gartstein, M. A., Nakagawa, A., & Putnam, S. P. (2013). Early temperament in Japan, the United States, and Russia: Do cross-cultural differences decrease with age? *Journal of Cross-Cultural Psychology, 44*, 438–460.

Slonims, V., & McConachie, H. (2006). Analysis of mother–infant interaction in infants with Down syndrome and typically developing infants. *American Journal of Mental Retardation, 111*, 273–289.

Sloutsky, V. (2015). Conceptual development. In L. S. Liben & U. Müller (Eds.), *Handbook of child psychology and developmental science: Vol. 2. Cognitive processes* (7th ed., pp. 469–518). Hoboken, NJ: Wiley.

Small, M. (1998). *Our babies, ourselves.* New York: Anchor.

Smarius, L. J. C. A., Striedeer, T. G. A., Loomans, E. M., Doreleijers, T. A. H., Vrijkotte, T. G. M., & Gemke, R. J. (2017). Excessive infant crying doubles the risk of mood and behavioral problems at age 5: Evidence for mediation by maternal characteristics. *European Child and Adolescent Psychiatry, 26*, 293–302.

Smetana, J. G. (2006). Social-cognitive domain theory: Consistencies and variations in children's moral and social judgments. In M. Killen & J. G. Smetana (Eds.), *Handbook of moral development* (pp. 119–154). Mahwah, NJ: Erlbaum.

Smetana, J. G., Ball, C., Yau, J., & Wong, M. (2017). Effect of type of maternal control on American and Chinese children's evaluations of personal domain events. *Social Development, 26*, 146–164.

Smetana, J. G., Rote, W. M., Jambon, M., Tasopoulos-Chan, M., Villalobos, M., & Comer, J. (2012). Developmental changes and individual differences in young children's moral judgments. *Child Development, 83*, 683–696.

Smit, D. J. A., Boersma, M., Schnack, H. G., Micheloyannis, S., Doomsma, D. I., Pol, H. E. H., et al. (2012). The brain matures with stronger functional connectivity and decreased randomness of its network. *PLOS ONE, 7*(5), e36896.

Smith, B. H., & Shapiro, C. J. (2015). Combined treatments for ADHD. In R. A. Barkley (Ed.), *Attention-deficit hyperactivity disorder: A handbook for diagnosis and treatment* (4th ed., pp. 686–704). New York: Guilford.

Smith, C. L., Calkins, S. D., Keane, S. P., Anastopoulos, A. D., & Shelton, T. L. (2004). Predicting stability and change in toddler behavior problems: Contributions of maternal behavior and child gender. *Developmental Psychology, 40*, 29–42.

Smith, D. S., & Juvonen, J. (2017). Do I fit in? Psychosocial ramifications of low gender typicality in early adolescence. *Journal of Adolescence, 60*, 161–170.

Smith, G. C. (2016). Grandparents raising grandchildren. In S. Whitbourne (Ed.), *Encyclopedia of adulthood and aging* (Vol. 2, pp. 581–586). Malden, MA: Wiley Blackwell.

Smith, J. P., & Forrester, R. (2013). Who pays for the health benefits of exclusive breastfeeding? An analysis of maternal time costs. *Journal of Human Lactation, 29*, 547–555.

Smith, L. A., Geller, N. L., Kellams, A. L., Colson, E. R., Rybin, D. V., Heeren, T., & Corwin, M. J. (2016). Infant sleep location and breastfeeding practices in the United States, 2011–2014. *Academic Pediatrics, 16*, 540–549.

Smith, L. B., Jones, S. S., Landau, B., Gershkoff-Stowe, L., & Samuelson, L. (2002). Object name learning provides on-the-job training for attention. *Psychological Science, 13*, 13–19.

Smith, P. K., Mahdavi, J., Carvalho, M., Fisher, S., Russell, S., & Tippett, N. (2008). Cyberbullying: Its nature and impact in secondary school pupils. *Journal of Child Psychology and Psychiatry, 49*, 376–385.

Smits, J., & Monden, C. (2011). Twinning across the developing world. *PLOS ONE, 6*(9), e25239.

Smyke, A. T., Zeanah, C. H., Fox, N. A., Nelson, C. A., & Guthrie, D. (2010). Placement in foster care enhances quality of attachment among young institutionalized children. *Child Development, 81*, 212–223.

Snell, E. K., Adam, E. K., & Duncan, G. J. (2007). Sleep and the body mass index and overweight status of children and adolescents. *Child Development, 78*, 309–323.

Snow, C. E., & Beals, D. E. (2006). Mealtime talk that supports literacy development. In R. W. Larson, A. R. Wiley, & K. R. Branscomb (Eds.), *Family mealtime as a context of development and socialization* (pp. 51–66). San Francisco: Jossey-Bass.

Sobel, D. M. (2006). How fantasy benefits young children's understanding of pretense. *Developmental Science, 9*, 63–75.

Sobotnik, R. F., Worrell, F. C., & Olszewski-Kubilius, P. (2016). The psychological science of talent development. In M. Neihart, S. Pfeiffer, & T. L. Cross (Eds.), *The social and emotional development of gifted children: What do we know?* (pp. 145–157). Waco, TX: Prufrock Press.

Society of Health and Physical Educators. (2009a). *Active start: A statement of physical activity guidelines for children from birth to age 5.* Reston, VA: Author.

Society of Health and Physical Educators. (2009b). *Policy and environment in physical education.* Retrieved from www.shapeamerica.org/publication/son/resources/teachingtools/teachertoolbox/policyandenvironment.aspx

Society of Health and Physical Educators. (2016). *Shape of the nation: Status of physical education in the USA.* Retrieved from www.shapeamerica.org/advocacyson/2016/upload/Shape-of-the-Nation-2016-2016_web.pdf

Soderstrom, M. (2008). Early perception–late comprehension of grammar? The case of verbal –s: A response to de Villiers & Johnson (2007). *Journal of Child Language, 35*, 671–676.

Soderstrom, M., Seidl, A., Nelson, D. G. K., & Jusczyk, P. W. (2003). The prosodic bootstrapping of phrases: Evidence from prelinguistic infants. *Journal of Memory and Language, 49*, 249–267.

Soh, D. W., Skocic, J., Nash, K., Stevens, S., Turner, G. R., & Rovet, J. (2015). Self-regulation therapy increases frontal gray matter in children with fetal alcohol spectrum disorder: Evaluation by voxel-based morphometry. *Human Neuroscience, 9*, 108.

Solomon, J., & George, C. (2011). The disorganized attachment-caregiving system. In J. Solomon & C. George (Eds.), *Disorganized attachment and caregiving* (pp. 3–24). New York: Guilford.

Sommerville, J. A., Schmidt, M. F. H., Yun, J. E., & Burns, M. (2013). The development of fairness expectations and prosocial behavior in the second year of life. *Infancy, 18*, 40–66.

Soos, I., Biddle, S. J. H., Ling, J., Hamar, P., Sandor, I., Boros-Balint, I., et al. (2014). Physical activity, sedentary behaviour, use of electronic media, and snacking among youth: An international study. *Kinesiology, 46*, 155–163.

Sorkhabi, N., & Mandara, J. (2013). Are the effects of Baumrind's parenting styles culturally specific or culturally equivalent? In R. E. Larzelere, A. S. Morris, & A. W. Harrist (Eds.), *Authoritative parenting: Synthesizing nurturance and discipline for optimal child development* (pp. 113–135). Washington, DC: American Psychological Association.

Soska, K. C., & Adolph, K. E. (2014). Postural position constrains multimodal object exploration in infants. *Infancy, 19*, 138–161.

Soska, K. C., Adolph, K. E., & Johnson, S. P. (2010). Systems in development: Motor skill acquisition facilitates three-dimensional object completion. *Developmental Psychology, 46*, 129–138.

Sotomayor-Peterson, M., & Montiel-Carbajal, M. (2014). Psychological and family well-being of unaccompanied Mexican child migrants sent back from the U.S. border region of Sonora-Arizona. *Hispanic Journal of Behavioral Sciences, 36*, 111–123.

Sowislo, J. F., & Orth, U. (2013). Does low self-esteem predict depression and anxiety? A meta-analysis of longitudinal studies. *Psychological Bulletin, 139*, 213–240.

Spangler, G., Johann, M., Ronai, Z., & Zimmermann, P. (2009). Genetic and environmental influence on attachment disorganization. *Journal of Child Psychology and Psychiatry, 50*, 952–961.

Spelke, E. S. (2016). Core knowledge and conceptual change: A perspective on social cognition. In D. Barner & A. S. Baron (Eds.), *Core knowledge and conceptual change* (pp. 279–300). New York: Oxford University Press.

Spelke, E. S., & Kinzler, K. D. (2013). Core knowledge. In S. M. Downes & E. Machery (Eds.), *Arguing about human nature: Contemporary debates* (pp. 107–116). New York: Routledge.

Spelke, E. S., Phillips, A., & Woodward, A. L. (1995). Infants' knowledge of object motion and human action. In D. Sperber, D. Premack, & A. J. Premack (Eds.), *Causal cognition: A multidisciplinary debate* (pp. 44–78). New York: Oxford University Press.

Spence, M. J., & DeCasper, A. J. (1987). Prenatal experience with low-frequency

maternal voice sounds influences neonatal perception of maternal voice samples. *Infant Behavior and Development, 10,* 133–142.
Spencer, J. P., Perone, S., & Buss, A. T. (2011). Twenty years and going strong: A dynamic systems revolution in motor and cognitive development. *Child Development Perspectives, 5,* 260–266.
Spere, K. A., Schmidt, L. A., Theall-Honey, L. A., & Martin-Chang, S. (2004). Expressive and receptive language skills of temperamentally shy preschoolers. *Infant and Child Development, 13,* 123–133.
Spilt, J., Hughes, J. N., Wu, J.-Y., & Kwok, O.-M. (2012). Dynamics of teacher–student relationships: Stability and change across elementary school and the influence on children's academic success. *Child Development, 83,* 1180–1195.
Spinner, L., Cameron, L., & Calogero, R. (2018). Peer toy play as a gateway to children's gender flexibility: The effect of (counter)stereotypic portrayals of peers in children's magazines. *Sex Roles, 79,* 314–328.
Spitzmueller, C., Wang, Z., Zhang, J., Thomas, C. L., Fisher, G., Matthews, R. A., & Strathearn, L. (2016). Got milk? Workplace factors related to breastfeeding among working mothers. *Journal of Organizational Behavior, 37,* 692–718.
Spivey, L. A., & Edwards-Leeper, L. (2019). Future directions in affirmative psychological interventions with transgender children and adolescents. *Journal of Clinical Child and Adolescent Psychology, 48,* 343–356.
Spock, B., & Needlman, R. (2011). *Dr. Spock's baby and child care* (9th ed.). New York: Gallery Books.
Spoelstra, M. N., Mari, A., Mendel, M., Senga, E., van Rheenen, P., van Dijk, T. H., et al. (2012). Kwashiorkor and marasmus are both associated with impaired glucose clearance related to pancreatic β-cell dysfunction. *Metabolism: Clinical and Experimental, 61,* 1224–1230.
Sporer, N., Brunstein, J. C., & Kieschke, U. (2009). Improving students' reading comprehension skills: Effects of strategy instruction and reciprocal teaching. *Learning and Instruction, 19,* 272–286.
Spreybroeck, S., Kuppens, S., Van Damme, J., Van Petegem, P., Lamote, C., et al. (2012). The role of teachers' expectations in the association between children's SES and performance in kindergarten: A moderated mediation analysis. *PLOS ONE, 7*(4), e34502.
SRCD (Society for Research in Child Development). (2007). *SRCD ethical standards for research with children.* www.srcd.org/about-us/ethical-standards-research
SRCD (Society for Research in Child Development) Equity and Justice Committee. (2018). *Mission.* Retrieved from http://equityandjustice.srcd.org/mission/
Sroufe, L. A. (2016). The place of attachment in development. In J. Cassidy & P. R. Shaver (Eds.), *Handbook of attachment: Theory, research, and clinical applications* (3rd ed., pp. 997–1011). New York: Guilford.
Sroufe, L. A. (2002). From infant attachment to promotion of adolescent autonomy: Prospective, longitudinal data on the role of parents in development. In J. G. Borkowski & S. L. Ramey (Eds.), *Parenting and the child's world* (pp. 187–202). Mahwah, NJ: Erlbaum.
Sroufe, L. A., Coffino, B., & Carlson, E. A. (2010). Conceptualizing the role of early experience: Lessons from the Minnesota Longitudinal Study. *Developmental Review, 30,* 36–51.
Sroufe, L. A., Egeland, B., Carlson, E., & Collins, W. (2005). *Minnesota Study of Risk and Adaptation from birth to maturity: The development of the person.* New York: Guilford.
St George, J., Fletcher, R., & Palazzi, K. (2017). Comparing fathers' physical and toy play and links to child behaviour: An exploratory study. *Infant and Child Development, 26,* e1958.
St James-Roberts, I. (2007). Infant crying and sleeping: Helping parents to prevent and manage problems. *Sleep Medicine Clinics, 2,* 363–375.
St James-Roberts, I. (2012). *The origins, prevention and treatment of infant crying and sleep problems.* London: Routledge.
St James-Roberts, I., Roberts, M., Hovish, K., & Owen, C. (2015). Video evidence that London infants can resettle themselves back to sleep after waking in the night, as well as sleep for long periods, by 3 months of age. *Journal of Developmental and Behavioral Pediatrics, 36,* 324–329.
Stanzione, C., & Schick, B. (2014). Environmental language factors in theory of mind development: Evidence from children who are deaf/hard-of-hearing or who have specific language impairment. *Topics in Language Disorders, 34,* 296–312.
Stark, R., & Gibb, R. (2018). Hormones and development. In R. Gibb & B. Kolb (Eds.), *The neurobiology of brain and behavioral development* (pp. 391–412). San Diego, CA: Elsevier.
Statistics Canada. (2018). *Elementary–secondary education survey for Canada, the provinces and territories, 2016/2017.* Retrieved from www150.statcan.gc.ca/t1/tbl1/en/tv.action?pid=3710000701
Stattin, H., & Skoog, T. (2016). Pubertal timing and its developmental significance for mental health and adjustment. In M. Friedman (Ed.), *Encyclopedia of mental health* (2nd ed., pp. 386–397). San Diego, CA: Academic Press.
Steele, H., & Steele, M. (2014). Attachment disorders: Theory, research, and treatment considerations. In M. Lewis & K. D. Rudolph (Eds.), *Handbook of developmental psychopathology* (3rd ed., pp. 357–370). New York: Springer Science + Business Media.
Steele, L. C. (2012). The forensic interview: A challenging intervention. In P. Goodyear-Brown (Ed.), *Handbook of child sexual abuse: Identification, assessment, and treatment* (pp. 99–119). Hoboken, NJ: Wiley.
Steensma, T. D., & Cohen-Kettenis, P. T. (2015). More than two developmental pathways in children with gender dysphoria? *Journal of the American Academy of Child and Adolescent Psychiatry, 54,* 147.
Steiger, A. E., Allemand, M., Robins, R. W., & Fend, H. A. (2014). Low and decreasing self-esteem during adolescence predicts adult depression two decades later. *Journal of Personality and Social Psychology, 106,* 325–338.
Stein, G. L., Cupito, A. M., Mendez, J. L., Prandoni, J., Huq, N., & Westerberg, D. (2014). Familism through a developmental lens. *Journal of Latina/o Psychology, 2,* 224–250.
Stein, G. L., Gonzalez, L. M., Cuipito, A. M., Kiang, L., & Supple, A. J. (2015). The protective role of familism in the lives of Latino adolescents. *Journal of Family Issues, 36,* 1255–1273.
Stein, G. L., & Polo, A. J. (2014). Parent–child cultural value gaps and depressive symptoms among Mexican American youth. *Journal of Child and Family Studies, 23,* 189–199.
Steinberg, L., Blatt-Eisengart, I., & Cauffman, E. (2006). Patterns of competence and adjustment among adolescents from authoritative, authoritarian, indulgent, and neglectful homes: A replication in a sample of serious juvenile offenders. *Journal of Research on Adolescence, 16,* 47–58.
Steinberg, L., & Silk, J. S. (2002). Parenting adolescents. In M. H. Bornstein (Ed.), *Handbook of parenting: Vol. 1. Children and parenting* (pp. 103–134). Mahwah, NJ: Erlbaum.
Steiner, J. E. (1979). Human facial expression in response to taste and smell stimulation. In H. W. Reese & L. P. Lipsitt (Eds.), *Advances in child development and behavior* (Vol. 13, pp. 257–295). New York: Academic Press.
Steiner, J. E., Glaser, D., Hawilo, M. E., & Berridge, D. C. (2001). Comparative expression of hedonic impact: Affective reactions to taste by human infants and other primates. *Neuroscience and Biobehavioral Reviews, 25,* 53–74.
Stenberg, G. (2017). Does contingency in adults' responding influence 12-month-old infants' social referencing? *Infant Behavior and Development, 49,* 9–20.
Stensland, S., Thoresen, S., Wentzel-Larsen, T., & Dyb, G. (2015). Interpersonal violence and overweight in adolescents: The HUNT study. *Scandinavian Journal of Public Health, 43,* 18–26.
Sternberg, R. J. (2008). The triarchic theory of successful intelligence. In N. Salkind (Ed.), *Encyclopedia of educational psychology* (Vol. 2, pp. 988–994). Thousand Oaks, CA: Sage.
Sternberg, R. J. (2011). The theory of successful intelligence. In R. J. Sternberg & S. B. Kaufman (2011). *Cambridge handbook of intelligence* (pp. 504–527). New York: Cambridge University Press.
Sternberg, R. J. (2013). Contemporary theories of intelligence. In W. M. Reynolds & G. E. Miller (Eds.), *Handbook of psychology: Vol. 7. Educational psychology* (2nd ed., pp. 23–44). Hoboken, NJ: Wiley.
Sternberg, R. J. (2018a). Theories of intelligence. In S. I. Pfeiffer, E. Shaunessy-Dedrick, & M. Foley-Nicpon (Eds.), *APA handbook of giftedness and talent* (pp. 145–161). Washington, DC: American Psychological Association.
Sternberg, R. J. (2018b). The triarchic theory of successful intelligence. In D. P. Flanagan & E. M. McDonough (Eds.), *Contemporary intellectual assessment: Theories, tests, and issues* (4th ed., pp. 174–194). New York: Guilford.
Sternberg, R. J., & Jarvin, L. (2003). Alfred Binet's contributions as a paradigm for impact in psychology. In R. J. Sternberg (Ed.), *The anatomy of impact: What makes the great works of psychology great* (pp. 89–107). Washington, DC: American Psychological Association.
Sterrett, E. M., Kincaid, C., Ness, E., Gonzalez, M., McKee, L. G., & Jones, D. J. (2015). Youth functioning in the coparenting context: A mixed methods study of African American single mother families. *Journal of Child and Family Studies, 24,* 455–469.
Stevenson, C. E., Heiser, W. J., & Resing, W. C. M. (2016). Dynamic testing: Assessing cognitive potential of children with culturally diverse backgrounds. *Learning and Individual Differences, 47,* 27–36.
Stevenson, R., & Pollitt, C. (1987). The acquisition of temporal terms. *Journal of Child Language, 14,* 533–545.
Stewart, P. W., Lonky, E., Reihman, J., Pagano, J., Gump, B. B., & Darvill, T. (2008). The relationship between prenatal PCB exposure and intelligence (IQ). *Environmental Health Perspectives, 116,* 1416–1422.
St George, J. M., Wroe, J. K., & Cashin, M. E. (2018). The concept and measurement of fathers' stimulating play: A review. *Attachment & Human Development, 20,* 634–658.
Stiles, J. (2012). The effects of injury to dynamic neural networks in the mature and developing brain. *Developmental Psychobiology, 54,* 343–349.
Stiles, J., Brown, T. T., Haist, F., & Jernigan, T. L. (2015). Brain and cognitive development. In L. S. Liben & U. Müller (Eds.), *Handbook of child psychology and developmental science: Vol. 2. Cognitive processes* (7th ed., pp. 9–62). Hoboken, NJ: Wiley.
Stiles, J., Nass, R. D., Levine, S. C., Moses, P., & Reilly, J. S. (2009). Perinatal stroke: Effects and outcomes. In K. O. Yeates, M. D. Ris, H. G. Taylor, & B. Pennington (Eds.), *Pediatric neuropsychology: Research, theory and practice* (2nd ed., pp. 181–210). New York: Guilford.
Stiles, J., Reilly, J. S., & Levine, S. C. (2012). *Neural plasticity and cognitive development.* New York: Oxford University Press.
Stiles, J., Stern, C., Appelbaum, M., & Nass, R. (2008). Effects of early focal brain injury on memory for visuospatial patterns: Selective deficits of global–local processing. *Neuropsychology, 22,* 61–73.
Stiller, A., & Hellman, D. F. (2017). In the aftermath of disclosing child sexual abuse: Consequences, needs, and wishes. *Journal of Sexual Aggression, 23,* 251–265.
Stipek, D. (2004). Teaching practices in kindergarten and first grade: Different strokes for different folks. *Early Childhood Research Quarterly, 19,* 548–568.
Stipek, D. (2011). Classroom practices and children's motivation to learn. In E. Zigler, W. S. Gilliam, & W. S. Barnett (Eds.), *The pre-K debates: Current controversies and issues* (pp. 98–103). Baltimore, MD: Paul H. Brookes.
Stipek, D., Franke, M., Clements, D., Farran, D., & Coburn, C. (2017). PK–3: What does it mean for instruction? *Social Policy Report of the Society for Research in Child Development, 30*(2).
Stipek, D. J., Feiler, R., Daniels, D., & Milburn, S. (1995). Effects of different instructional approaches on young children's achievement and motivation. *Child Development, 66,* 209–223.
Stipek, D. J., Gralinski, J. H., & Kopp, C. B. (1990). Self-concept development in the toddler years. *Developmental Psychology, 26,* 972–977.
St James-Roberts, I., Roberts, M., Hovish, K., & Owen, C. (2015). Video evidence that London infants can resettle themselves back to sleep after waking in the night, as well as sleep for long periods, by 3 months of age. *Journal of Developmental and Behavioral Pediatrics, 36,* 324–329.
St James-Roberts, I., Roberts, M., Hovish, K., & Owen, C. (2017). Video evidence that parenting methods predict which infants develop long night-time sleep periods by three months of age. *Primary Health Care Research and Development, 18,* 212–226.
Stoltenborgh, M., Bakermans-Kranenburg, Alink, L. R. A., & van IJzendoorn, M. H. (2015). The prevalence of child

maltreatment across the globe: Review of a series of meta-analyses. *Child Abuse Review, 24,* 37–50.

Stoner, R., Chow, M. L., Boyle, M. P., Sunkin, S. M., Mouton, P. R., Roy, S., et al. (2014). Patches of disorganization in the neocortex of children with autism. *New England Journal of Medicine, 370,* 1209–1219.

Stoodley, C. J. (2016). The cerebellum and neurodevelopmental disorders. *Cerebellum, 15,* 34–37.

Storch, S. A., & Whitehurst, G. J. (2001). The role of family and home in the literacy development of children from low-income backgrounds. In P. R. Britto & J. Brooks-Gunn (Eds.), *The role of family literacy environments in promoting young children's emerging literacy skills (New directions for child and adolescent development,* No. 92, pp. 53–71). San Francisco: Jossey-Bass.

Storey, A. E., & Ziegler, T. E. (2016). Primate paternal care: Interactions between biology and social experience. *Hormones and Behavior, 77,* 260–271.

Strang, T. M., & Piasta, S. B. (2016). Socioeconomic differences in code-focused emergent literacy skills. *Reading and Writing, 29,* 1337–1362.

Strazdins, L., Clements, M. S., Korda, R. J., Broom, D. H., & D'Souza, R. M. (2006). Unsociable work? Nonstandard work schedules, family relationships, and children's well-being. *Journal of Marriage and the Family, 68,* 394–410.

Strazdins, L., O'Brien, L. V., Lucas, N., & Roders, B. (2013). Combining work and family: Rewards or risks for children's mental health? *Social Science and Medicine, 87,* 99–107.

Streit, C., Carlo, G., Ispa, J. M., & Palermo, F. (2017). Negative emotionality and discipline as long-term predictors of behavioral outcomes in African American and European American children. *Developmental Psychology, 53,* 1013–1026.

Streri, A. (2005). Touching for knowing in infancy: The development of manual abilities in very young infants. *European Journal of Developmental Psychology, 2,* 325–343.

Stretesky, P., & Lynch, M. (2004). The relationship between lead and crime. *Journal of Health and Social Behavior, 45,* 214–229.

Striano, T., & Rochat, P. (2000). Emergence of selective social referencing in infancy. *Infancy, 1,* 253–264.

Stright, A. D., Herr, M. Y., & Neitzel, C. (2009). Maternal scaffolding of children's problem solving and children's adjustment in kindergarten: Hmong families in the United States. *Journal of Educational Psychology, 101,* 207–218.

Stright, A. D., Neitzel, C., Sears, K. G., & Hoke-Sinex, L. (2002). Instruction begins in the home: Relations between parental instruction and children's self-regulation in the classroom. *Journal of Educational Psychology, 93,* 456–466.

Strohschein, L. (2005). Parental divorce and child mental health trajectories. *Journal of Marriage and Family, 67,* 1286–1300.

Stronach, E. P., Toth, S. L., Rogosch, F., Oshri, A., Manle, J. T., & Cicchetti, D. (2011). Child maltreatment, attachment security and internal representations of mother and mother–child relationships. *Child Maltreatment, 16,* 137–154.

Stroud, C. B., Meyers, K. M., Wilson, S., & Durbin, C. (2015). Marital quality spillover and young children's adjustment: Evidence for dyadic and triadic parenting as mechanisms. *Journal of Clinical Child and Adolescent Psychology, 44,* 800–813.

Stryer, B. K., Tofler, I. R., & Lapchick, R. (1998). A developmental overview of child and youth sports in society. *Child and Adolescent Psychiatric Clinics of North America, 7,* 697–719.

Stulp, G., & Barrett, L. (2016). Evolutionary perspectives on human height variation. *Biological Reviews, 91,* 206–234.

Sturge-Apple, M. L., Davies, P. T., Cicchetti, D., Hentges, R., & Coe, J. L. (2017). Family instability and children's effortful control in the context of poverty: Sometimes a bird in the hand is worth two in the bush. *Development and Psychopathology, 29,* 685–696.

Sturge-Apple, M. L., Davies, P. T., Winter, M. A., Cummings, E. M., & Schermerhorn, A. (2008). Interparental conflict and children's school adjustment: The explanatory role of children's internal representations of interparental and parent–child relationships. *Developmental Psychology, 44,* 1678–1690.

Su, D., Toure, D., Do, K., & Ramos, A. K. (2019). Assessing racial and ethnic differences in attitudes toward the use of physical discipline in parenting: A mixed-methods approach. *Journal of Social Service Research, 45,* 455–465.

Suárez-Orozco, C., Abo-Zena, M. M., & Marks, A. K. (2015). Unique and shared experiences of immigrant origin children and youth. In C. Suárez-Orozco, M. M. Abo-Zena, & A. K. Marks (Eds.), *Transitions: The development of children of immigrants* (pp. 1–26). New York: New York University Press.

Suárez-Orozco, C., Pimental, A., & Martin, M. (2009). The significance of relationships: Academic engagement and achievement among newcomer immigrant youth. *Teachers College Record, 111,* 712–749.

Subica, A. W., Agarwal, N., Sullivan, J. G., & Link, B. G. (2017). Obesity and associated health disparities among understudied multiracial, Pacific Islander, and American Indian adults. *Obesity, 25,* 2128–2136.

Subrahmanyam, K., Gelman, R., & Lafosse, A. (2002). Animate and other separably moveable things. In G. Humphreys (Ed.), *Category-specificity in brain and mind* (pp. 341–371). London: Psychology Press.

Substance Abuse and Mental Health Services Administration. (2016). *Results from the 2015 National Survey on Drug Use and Health: Summary of national findings.* Rockville, MD: Author. Retrieved from www.samhsa.gov/data/sites/default/files /NSDUH-FFR1-2015/NSDUH-FFR1-2015 /NSDUH-FFR1-2015.pdf

Suddendorf, T., Simcock, G., & Nielsen, M. (2007). Visual self-recognition in mirrors and live videos: Evidence for a developmental asynchrony. *Cognitive Development, 22,* 185–196.

Sudmant, P. H., Mallick, S., Nelson, B. J., Hormozdian, F., Krumm, N., Huddleston, J., et al. (2015). Global diversity, population stratification, and selection of human copy-number variation. *Science, 349,* 1174–1181.

Sullivan, J., Beech, A. R., Craig, L. A., & Gannon, T. A. (2011). Comparing intra-familial and extra-familial child sexual abusers with professionals who have sexually abused children with whom they work. *International Journal of Offender Therapy and Comparative Criminology, 55,* 56–74.

Sullivan, M. W., & Lewis, M. (2003). Contextual determinants of anger and other negative expressions in young infants. *Developmental Psychology, 39,* 693–705.

Sullivan, P. F., Daly, M. J., & O'Donovan, M. (2012). Genetic architectures of psychiatric disorders: The emerging picture and its implications. *Nature Reviews Genetics, 13,* 537–551.

Sun, J. T., An, M., Yan, X. B., Li, G. H., & Wang, D. B. (2018). Prevalence and related factors for myopia in school-aged children in Qingdao. *Journal of Ophthalmology,* Art. No. 9781987.

Sun, K. L. (2018). The role of mathematics teaching in fostering student growth mindset. *Journal of Research in Mathematics Education, 49,* 330–355.

Sunderam, S., Kissin, D. M., Crawford, S. B., Folger, S. G., Jamieson, D. J., Warner, L., et al. (2015). Assisted reproductive technology surveillance—United States, 2012. *Morbidity and Mortality Weekly Report, 64*(SS06), 1–29. Retrieved from www.cdc .gov/mmwr/preview/mmwrhtml/ss6406a1 .htm

Super, C. M. (1981). Behavioral development in infancy. In R. H. Monroe, R. L. Monroe, & B. B. Whiting (Eds.), *Handbook of cross-cultural human development* (pp. 181–270). New York: Garland.

Super, C. M., & Harkness, S. (2009). The developmental niche of the newborn in rural Kenya. In J. K. Nugent, B. J. Petrauskas, & T. B. Brazelton (Eds.), *The newborn as a person: Enabling healthy development worldwide* (pp. 85–97). Hoboken, NJ: Wiley.

Super, C. M., & Harkness, S. (2010). Culture and infancy. In J. G. Bremner & T. D. Wachs (Eds.), *Wiley-Blackwell handbook of infant development: Vol. 1. Basic research* (2nd ed., pp. 623–649). Chichester, UK: Wiley-Blackwell.

Super, C. M., Harkness, S., van Tijen, N., van der Vlugt, E., Fintelman, M., & Dijkstra, J. (1996). The three R's of Dutch childrearing and the socialization of infant arousal. In S. Harkness & C. M. Super (Eds.), *Parents' cultural belief systems* (pp. 447–466). New York:

Supple, A. J., & Small, S. A. (2006). The influence of parental support, knowledge, and authoritative parenting on Hmong and European American adolescent development. *Journal of Family Issues, 27,* 1214–1232.

Swanson, H. L., Harris, K. R., & Graham, S. (2014). Overview of foundations, causes, instruction, and methodology in the field of learning disabilities. In H. L. Swanson, K. R. Harris, & S. Graham (Eds.), *Handbook of learning disabilities* (pp. 3–14). New York: Guilford Press.

Swenson, C. C., & Logan, S. L. (2017). Children as victims: Preventing and reporting child maltreatment and abuse. In P. M. Kleespies (Ed.), *Oxford handbook of behavioral emergencies and crises* (pp. 73–84). New York: Oxford University Press.

Swinson, J., & Harrop, A. (2009). Teacher talk directed to boys and girls and its relationship to their behaviour. *Educational Studies, 35,* 515–524.

Szterman, R., & Friedmann, N. (2014). Relative clause reading in hearing impairment: Different profiles of syntactic impairment. *Frontiers in Psychology, 5,* Art. No. 1229.

T

Taga, G., Asakawa, K., Maki, A., Konishi, Y., & Koisumi, H. (2003). Brain imaging in awake infants by near-infrared optical topography. *Proceedings of the National Academy of Sciences, 100,* 10723.

Tager-Flusberg, H. (2014). Autism spectrum disorder: Developmental approaches from infancy through early childhood. In M. Lewis & K. D. Rudolph (Eds.), *Handbook of developmental psychopathology* (pp. 651–664). New York: Springer.

Takahashi, K. (1990). Are the key assumptions of the "Strange Situation" procedure universal? A view from Japanese research. *Human Development, 33,* 23–30.

Tamis-LeMonda, C. S., & McFadden, K. E. (2010). The United States of America. In M. H. Bornstein & T. Leventhal (Eds.), *Handbook of cultural developmental science: Vol. 4. Ecological settings and processes* (pp. 299–322). New York: Psychology Press.

Tamm, L., Nakonezny, P. A., & Hughes, C. W. (2014). An open trial of metacognitive executive function training for young children with ADHD. *Journal of Attention Disorders, 18,* 551–559.

Tamnes, C. K., Bos, G. N., van de Kamp, F., & Peters, S. (2018). Longitudinal development of hippocampal subregions from childhood to adulthood. *Developmental Cognitive Neuroscience, 30,* 212–222.

Tanaka-Arakawa, M. M., Matsui, M., Tanaka, C., Uematsu, A., Uda, S., Miura, K., et al. (2015). Developmental changes in the corpus callosum from infancy to early adulthood: A structural magnetic resonance imaging study. *PLOS ONE, 10*(7), e0133090.

Tanner, J. M., Healy, M., & Cameron, N. (2001). *Assessment of skeletal maturity and prediction of adult height* (3rd ed.). Philadelphia: Saunders.

Tao, S. (2018). Girls' education is improving, but not for all girls—how can we accelerate change? *UNICEF Think Piece Series: Gender and Equity.* UNICEF Eastern and Southern Africa Regional Office, Nairobi. Retrieved from blogs.unicef.org/blog/girls -education-improving-not-all

Taras, V., Sarala, R., Muchinsky, P., Kemmelmeier, M., Singelis, T. M., Avsec, A., et al. (2014). Opposite ends of the same stick? Multi-method test of the dimensionality of individualism and collectivism. *Journal of Cross-Cultural Psychology, 45,* 213–245.

Tardif, T. (2006). But are they really verbs? Chinese words for action. In K. Hirsh-Pasek & R. M. Golinkoff (Eds.), *Action meets word: How children learn verbs* (pp. 477–498). New York: Oxford University Press.

Tardif, T., Fletcher, P., Liang, W., Zhang, Z., Kaciroti, N., & Marchman, V. A. (2008). Baby's first 10 words. *Developmental Psychology, 44,* 929–938.

Tarrant, M., MacKenzie, L., & Hewitt, L. A. (2006). Friendship group identification, multidimensional self-concept, and experience of developmental tasks in adolescence. *Journal of Adolescence, 29,* 627–640.

Tarullo, A. R., Balsam, P. D., & Fifer, W. P. (2011). Sleep and infant learning. *Infant and Child Development, 20,* 35–46.

Tarullo, A. R., & Gunnar, M. R. (2006). Child maltreatment and the developing HPA axis. *Hormones and Behavior, 50,* 632–639.

Tarullo, A. R., Isler, J. R., Condon, C., Violaris, K., Balsam, P. D., & Fifer, W. P. (2015). Neonatal eyelid conditioning during sleep. *Developmental Psychobiology, 58,* 875–882.

Tatangelo, G. L., & Ricciardelli, L. A. (2017). Children's body image and social comparisons with peers and the media. *Journal of Health Psychology, 22,* 776–787.

Taumoepeau, M., & Ruffman, T. (2006). Mother and infant talk about mental states relates to desire language and emotion understanding. *Child Development, 77,* 465–481.

Taylor, C. A., Manganello, J. A., Lee, S. J., & Rice, J. C. (2010). Mothers' spanking of 3-year-old children and subsequent risk of children's aggressive behavior. *Pediatrics, 125*, e1057–e1065.

Taylor, C., Schorr, L. B., Wilkins, N., & Smith, L. S. (2018). Systemic approach for injury and violence prevention: What we can learn from the Harlem Children's Zone and Promise Neighborhoods. *Injury Prevention, 24*, 132–137.

Taylor, M., Carlson, S. M., Maring, B. L., Gerow, L., & Charley, C. M. (2004). The characteristics and correlates of fantasy in school-age children: Imaginary companions, impersonation, and social understanding. *Developmental Psychology, 40*, 1173–1187.

Taylor, M., Esbensen, B. M., & Bennett, R. T. (1994). Children's understanding of knowledge acquisition: The tendency for children to report that they have always known what they have just learned. *Child Development, 65*, 1581–1604.

Taylor, M. C., & Hall, J. A. (1982). Psychological androgyny: Theories, methods, and conclusions. *Psychological Bulletin, 92*, 347–366.

Taylor, M. G., Rhodes, M., & Gelman, S. A. (2009). Boys will be boys; cows will be cows: Children's essentialist reasoning about gender categories and animal species. *Child Development, 80*, 461–481.

Taylor, Z. E., Eisenberg, N., Spinrad, T. L., Eggum, N. D., & Sulik, M. J. (2013). The relations of ego-resiliency and emotion socialization to the development of empathy and prosocial behavior across early childhood. *Emotion, 15*, 822–831.

Team Up for Youth. (2014). *The perils of poverty: The health crisis facing our low-income girls . . . and the power of sports to help.* Retrieved from www.afterschoolnetwork.org/sites/main/files/file-attachments/perils_poverty.pdf

Tecwyn, E. C., Thorpe, S. K. S., & Chappell, J. (2014). Development of planning in 4- to 10-year-old children: Reducing inhibitory demands does not improve performance. *Journal of Experimental Child Psychology, 125*, 85–101.

Tehranifar, P., Wu, H.-C., McDonald, J. A., Jasmine, F., Santella, R. M., Gurvich, I., et al. (2018). Maternal cigarette smoking during pregnancy and offspring DNA methylation in midlife. *Epigenetics, 13*, 129–134.

Teicher, M. H., Samson, J. A., Anderson, C. M., & Ohashi, K. (2016). The effects of childhood maltreatment on brain structure, function and connectivity. *Nature Reviews Neuroscience, 17*, 652–666.

Teinonen, T., Fellman, V., Näätänen, R., Alku, P., & Huotilainen, M. (2009). Statistical language learning in neonates revealed by event-related brain potentials. *BMC Neuroscience, 10*, 21.

Temple, C. M., & Shephard, E. E. (2012). Exceptional lexical skills but executive language deficits in school starters and young adults with Turner syndrome: Implications for X chromosome effects on brain function. *Brain and Language, 120*, 345–359.

Temple, J. L., Giacomelli, A. M., Roemmich, J. N., & Epstein, L. H. (2007). Overweight children habituate slower than nonoverweight children to food. *Physiology and Behavior, 9*, 250–254.

Tenenbaum, H. R., Hill, D., Joseph, N., & Roche, E. (2010). "It's a boy because he's painting a picture": Age differences in children's conventional and unconventional gender schemas. *British Journal of Psychology, 101*, 137–154.

Tenenbaum, H. R., & Leaper, C. (2002). Are parents' gender schemas related to their children's gender-related cognitions?

A meta-analysis. *Developmental Psychology, 38*, 615–630.

Tenenbaum, H. R., & Leaper, C. (2003). Parent–child conversations about science: The socialization of gender inequities? *Developmental Psychology, 39*, 34–57.

Tenenbaum, H. R., Snow, C. E., Roach, K. A., & Kurland, B. (2005). Talking and reading science: Longitudinal data on sex differences in mother–child conversations in low-income families. *Journal of Applied Developmental Psychology, 26*, 1–19.

ten Tusscher, G. W., & Koppe, J. G. (2004). Perinatal dioxin exposure and later effects—A review. *Chemosphere, 54*, 1329–1336.

Terni, B., López-Murcia, F. J., & Llobet, A. (2017). Role of neuron-glia interactions in developmental synapse elimination. *Brain Research Bulletin, 129*, 74–81.

Teti, D. M., Saken, J. W., Kucera, E., & Corns, K. M. (1996). And baby makes four: Predictors of attachment security among preschool-age firstborns during the transition to siblinghood. *Child Development, 67*, 579–596.

Thakur, G. A., Sengupta, S. M., Grizenko, N., Schmitz, N., Pagé, V., & Joober, R. (2013). Maternal smoking during pregnancy and ADHD: A comprehensive clinical and neurocognitive characterization. *Nicotine & Tobacco Research, 15*, 149–157.

Thatcher, R. W., Walker, R. A., & Giudice, S. (1987). Human cerebral hemispheres develop at different rates and ages. *Science, 236*, 1110–1113.

Thelen, E., & Adolph, K. E. (1992). Arnold Gesell: The paradox of nature and nurture. *Developmental Psychology, 28*, 368–380.

Thelen, E., & Corbetta, D. (2002). Microdevelopment and dynamic systems: Applications to infant motor development. In N. Granott & J. Parziale (Eds.), *Microdevelopment: Transition processes in development and learning* (pp. 59–79). New York: Cambridge University Press.

Thelen, E., Fisher, D. M., & Ridley-Johnson, R. (1984). The relationship between physical growth and a newborn reflex. *Infant Behavior and Development, 7*, 479–493.

Thelen, E., Schöner, G., Scheier, C., & Smith, L. B. (2001). The dynamics of embodiment: A field theory of infant perseverative reaching. *Behavioral and Brain Sciences, 24*, 1–34.

Thelen, E., & Smith, L. B. (1998). Dynamic systems theories. In R. M. Lerner (Ed.), *Handbook of child psychology: Vol. 1. Theoretical models of human development* (5th ed., pp. 563–634). New York: Wiley.

Thelen, E., & Smith, L. B. (2006). Dynamic systems theories. In R. M. Lerner (Ed.), *Handbook of child psychology: Vol. 1. Theoretical models of human development* (6th ed., pp. 258–312). Hoboken, NJ: Wiley.

Thibodeau, R. B., Gilpin, A. T., Brown, M. M., & Meyer, B. A. (2016). The effects of fantastical pretend-play on the development of executive functions: An intervention study. *Journal of Experimental Child Psychology, 145*, 120–138.

Thiessen, E. D., Girard, S., & Erickson, L. C. (2016). Statistical learning and the critical period: How a continuous learning mechanism can give rise to discontinuous learning. *WIREs Cognitive Science, 7*, 276–288.

Thiessen, E. D., Kronstein, A. T., & Hufnagle, D. G. (2012). The extraction and integration framework: A two-process account of statistical learning. *Psychological Bulletin, 139*, 792–814.

Thiessen, E. D. & Saffran, J. R. (2003). When cues collide. Use of stress and statistical cues to word boundaries by 7- to 9-month-old infants. *Developmental Psychology, 39*, 709–716.

Thiessen, E. D., & Saffran, J. R. (2007). Learning to learn: Infants' acquisition of stress-based strategies for word segmentation. *Language Learning and Development, 3*, 75–102.

Thomaes, S., Brummelman, E., Reijntjes, A., & Bushman, B. J. (2013). When Narcissus was a boy: Origins, nature, and consequences of childhood narcissism. *Child Development Perspectives, 7*, 22–26.

Thomaes, S., Stegge, H., Bushman, B. J., & Olthof, T. (2008). Trumping shame by blasts of noise: Narcissism, self-esteem, shame, and aggression in young adolescents. *Child Development, 79*, 1792–1801.

Thomas, A., & Chess, S. (1977). *Temperament and development.* New York: Brunner/Mazel.

Thomas, K. A., & Tessler, R. C. (2007). Bicultural socialization among adoptive families: Where there is a will, there is a way. *Journal of Family Issues, 28*, 1189–1219.

Thomas, S. R., O'Brien, K. A., Clarke, T. L., Liu, Y., & Chronis-Tuscano, A. (2015). Maternal depression history moderates parenting responses to compliant and noncompliant behaviors of children with ADHD. *Journal of Abnormal Child Psychology, 43*, 1257–1269.

Thomason, M. E., Brown, J. A., Dassanayake, M. T., Shastri, R., Marusak, H. A., Hernandez-Andrade, E., et al. (2014). Intrinsic functional brain architecture derived from graph theoretical analysis in the human fetus. *PLOS ONE, 9*(5), e94423.

Thomas-Sunesson, F., Hakuta, K., & Bialystok, E. (2018). Degree of bilingualism modifies executive control in Hispanic children in the USA. *International Journal of Bilingual Education and Bilingualism, 21*, 197–206.

Thompson, A., Hollis, C., & Richards, D. (2003). Authoritarian parenting attitudes as a risk for conduct problems: Results of a British national cohort study. *European Child and Adolescent Psychiatry, 12*, 84–91.

Thompson, A. A., Walters, M. C., Kwiatkowski, J., Rasko, J. E. J., Ribeil, J.-A., Hongeng, S., et al. (2018). Gene therapy in patients with transfusion-dependent ß-thalassemia. *New England Journal of Medicine, 378*, 1479–1493.

Thompson, J. A., & Sonnenschein, S. (2015). Full-day kindergarten and children's later reading: The role of early word reading. *Journal of Applied Developmental Psychology, 42*, 58–70.

Thompson, J. M., Waldie, K. E., Wall, C. R., Murphy, R., & Mitchell, E. A. (2014). Associations between acetaminophen use during pregnancy and ADHD symptoms measured at ages 7 and 11 years. *PLOS ONE, 9*(9), e108210.

Thompson, P. M., Giedd, J. N., Woods, R. P., MacDonald, D., Evans, A. C., & Toga, A. W. (2000). Growth patterns in the developing brain detected by using continuum mechanical tensor maps. *Nature, 404*, 190–192.

Thompson, R. A. (2006). The development of the person: Social understanding, relationships, conscience, self. In N. Eisenberg (Ed.), *Handbook of child psychology: Vol. 3. Social, emotional, and personality development* (6th ed., pp. 24–98). Hoboken, NJ: Wiley.

Thompson, R. A. (2013). Attachment theory and research: Précis and prospect. In P. D. Zelazo (Ed.), *Oxford handbook of developmental psychology: Vol. 2. Self and*

other (pp. 191–216). New York: Oxford University Press.

Thompson, R. A. (2014). Conscience development in early childhood. In M. Killen & J. G. Smetana (Eds.), *Handbook of moral development* (2nd ed., pp. 73–92). New York: Psychology Press.

Thompson, R. A. (2015). Relationships, regulation, and early development. In M. E. Lamb (Ed.), *Handbook of child psychology and developmental science: Vol. 3. Socioemotional processes* (7th ed., pp. 201–246). Hoboken, NJ: Wiley.

Thompson, R. A. (2016). Early attachment and later development: Reframing the questions. In J. Cassidy & P. R. Shaver (Eds.), *Handbook of attachment: Theory, research, and clinical applications* (3rd ed., pp. 330–348). New York: Guilford.

Thompson, R. A., & Goodman, M. (2010). Development of emotion regulation: More than meets the eye. In A. M. Kring & D. M. Sloan (Eds.), *Emotion regulation and psychopathology: A transdiagnostic approach to etiology and treatment* (pp. 38–58). New York: Guilford.

Thompson, R. A., & Goodvin, R. (2007). Taming the tempest in the teapot. In C. A. Brownell & C. B. Kopp (Eds.), *Socioemotional development in the toddler years: Transitions and transformations* (pp. 320–341). New York: Guilford.

Thompson, R. A., Meyer, S., & McGinley, M. (2006). Understanding values in relationships: The development of conscience. In M. Killen & J. G. Smetana (Eds.), *Handbook of moral development* (pp. 267–298). Mahwah, NJ: Erlbaum.

Thompson, R. A., & Nelson, C. A. (2001). Developmental science and the media. *American Psychologist, 56*, 5–15.

Thompson, R. A., Winer, A. C., & Goodvin, R. (2011). The individual child: Temperament, emotion, self, and personality. In M. H. Bornstein & M. E. Lamb (Eds.), *Developmental science: An advanced textbook* (6th ed., pp. 427–468). Hoboken, NJ: Taylor & Francis.

Thornberg, R., Thornberg, U. B., Alamaa, R., & Daud, N. (2016). Children's conceptions of bullying and repeated conventional transgressions: Moral, conventional, structuring, and personal-choice making. *Educational Psychology, 36*, 95–111.

Thorne, B. (1993). *Gender play: Girls and boys in school.* New Brunswick, NJ: Rutgers University Press.

Thornton, S. (1999). Creating conditions for cognitive change: The interaction between task structures and specific strategies. *Child Development, 70*, 588–603.

Tien, A. (2013). Bootstrapping and the acquisition of Mandarin Chinese: A natural semantic metalanguage perspective. In D. Bittner & N. Ruhlig (Eds.), *Lexical bootstrapping: The role of lexis and semantics in child language* (pp. 39–72). Berlin: Walter de Gruyter.

Tienari, P., Wahlberg, K. E., & Wynne, L. C. (2006). Finnish adoption study of schizophrenia: Implications for family interventions. *Families, Systems, and Health, 24*, 442–451.

Tienari, P., Wynne, L. C., Laksy, K., Moring, J., Nieminen, P., Sorri, A., et al. (2003). Genetic boundaries of the schizophrenia spectrum: Evidence from the Finnish adoptive family study of schizophrenia. *The American Journal of Psychiatry, 160*, 1587–1594.

Tikotzky, L., Sharabany, R., Hirsch, I., & Sadeh, A. (2010). "Ghosts in the Nursery": Infant sleep and sleep-related cognitions of parents raised under communal sleeping arrangements. *Infant Mental Health Journal, 31,* 312–334.

Timmermans, A. C., Kuyper, H., & van der Werf, G. (2015). Accurate, inaccurate, or biased teacher expectations: Do Dutch teachers differ in their expectations at the end of primary education? *British Journal of Educational Psychology, 85,* 459–478.

Tincoff, R., & Jusczyk, P. W. (1999). Some beginnings of word comprehension in 6-month-olds. *Psychological Science, 10,* 172–175.

Tinsley, B. J. (2003). *How children learn to be healthy.* Cambridge, UK: Cambridge University Press.

Tishkoff, S. A., & Kidd, K. K. (2004). Implications of biogeography of human populations for "race" and medicine. *Nature Genetics, 36* (11s): S21–7.

Tizard, B., & Rees, J. (1975). The effect of early institutional rearing on the behaviour problems and affectional relationships of four-year-old children. *Journal of Child Psychology and Psychiatry, 16,* 61–73.

Todd, B. K., Fischer, R. A., Di Costa, S., Roestorf, A., Harbour, K., Hardiman, P., & Barry, J. A. (2017). Sex differences in children's toy preferences: A systematic review, meta-regression, and meta analysis. *Infant and Child Development, 27,* e2054.

Tomalski, P., Moore, D. G., Ribeiro, H., Axelsson, E. L., Murphy, E., Karmiloff-Smith, A., et al. (2013). Socioeconomic status and functional brain development—Associations in early infancy. *Developmental Science, 16,* 676–687.

Tomasello, M. (2000). Do young children have adult syntactic competence? *Cognition, 74,* 209–253.

Tomasello, M. (2003). *Constructing a language: A usage-based theory of language acquisition.* Cambridge, MA: Harvard University Press.

Tomasello, M. (2006). Acquiring linguistic constructions. In D. Kuhn & R. Siegler (Eds.), *Handbook of child psychology: Vol. 2: Cognition, perception, and language* (6th ed., pp. 255–298). Hoboken, NJ: Wiley.

Tomasello, M. (2011). Language development. In U. Goswami (Ed.), *Wiley-Blackwell handbook of childhood cognitive development* (2nd ed., pp. 239–257). Malden, MA: Wiley-Blackwell.

Tomasello, M., & Akhtar, N. (1995). Two-year-olds use pragmatic cues to differentiate reference to objects and actions. *Cognitive Development, 10,* 201–224.

Tomasello, M., Akhtar, N., Dodson, K., & Rekau, L. (1997). Differential productivity in young children's use of nouns and verbs. *Journal of Child Language, 24,* 373–387.

Tomasello, M., & Brandt, S. (2009). Flexibility in the semantics and syntax of children's early verb use. *Monographs of the Society for Research in Child Development, 74*(2, Serial No. 293), 113–126.

Tomasello, M., Call, J., & Hare, B. (2003). Chimpanzees understand psychological states—the question is which ones and to what extent. *Trends in Cognitive Sciences, 7,* 153–156.

Tomasello, M., Carpenter, M., & Liszkowski, U. (2007). A new look at infant pointing. *Child Development, 78,* 705–722.

Tomasello, M., & Gonzales-Cabrera, I. (2017). The role of ontogeny in the evolution of human cooperation. *Human Nature, 28,* 274–288.

Tomyr, L., Ouimet, C., & Ugnat, A. (2012). A review of findings from the Canadian Incidence Study of reported child abuse and neglect (CIS). *Canadian Journal of Public Health, 103,* 103–112.

Tong, S., Baghurst, P., Vimpani, G., & McMichael, A. (2007). Socioeconomic position, maternal IQ, home environment, and cognitive development. *Journal of Pediatrics, 151,* 284–288.

Tong, S., McMichael, A. J., & Baghurst, P. A. (2000). Interactions between environmental lead exposure and sociodemographic factors on cognitive development. *Archives of Environmental Health, 55,* 330–335.

Toomela, A. (1999). Drawing development: Stages in the representation of a cube and a cylinder. *Child Development, 70,* 1141–1150.

Toomela, A. (2002). Drawing as a verbally mediated activity: A study of relationships between verbal, motor, visuospatial skills and drawing in children. *International Journal of Behavioral Development, 26,* 234–247.

Törnell, S., Ekéus, C., Hultin, M., Håkansson, J., Thunberg, J., & Högberg, U. (2015). Low Apgar score, neonatal encephalopathy and epidural analgesia during labour: A Swedish registry study. *Anaesthesiologica Scandinavica, 59,* 486–495.

Toro, J. M., & Trobalon, J. B. (2005). Statistical computations over a speech stream in a rodent. *Perception and Psychophysics, 67,* 867–875.

Torquati, J. C., Raikes, H. H., Huddleston-Casas, C. A., Bovaird, J. A., & Harris, B. A. (2011). Family income, parent education, and perceived constraints as predictors of observed program quality and parent rated program quality. *Early Childhood Research Quality, 26,* 453–464.

Torrance, E. P. (1988). The nature of creativity as manifest in its testing. In R. J. Sternberg (Ed.), *The nature of creativity: Contemporary psychological perspectives* (pp. 43–75). New York: Cambridge University Press.

Tottenham, N. (2012). Human amygdala development in the absence of species-expected caregiving. *Developmental Psychobiology, 54,* 598–611.

Tottenham, N., Hare, T. A., & Casey, B. J. (2009). A developmental perspective on human amygdala function. In P. J. Whalen & E. A. Phelps (Eds.), *The human amygdala* (pp. 107–117). New York: Guilford.

Townsend, D. A., & Rovee-Collier, C. (2007). *The transitivity of 6-month-olds' preconditioned memories in deferred imitation.* Paper presented at the annual meeting of the Eastern Psychological Association, Philadelphia.

Tracy, J. L., Robins, R. W., & Lagattuta, K. H. (2005). Can children recognize pride? *Emotion, 5,* 251–257.

Tran, P., & Subrahmanyam, K. (2013). Evidence-based guidelines for informal use of computers by children to promote the development of academic, cognitive and social skills. *Ergonomics, 56,* 1349–1362.

Träuble, B., & Pauen, S. (2011). Cause or effect: What matters? How 12-month-old infants learn to categorize artifacts. *British Journal of Developmental Psychology, 29,* 357–374.

Trautner, H. M., Ruble, D. N., Cyphers, L., Kirsten, B., Behrendt, R., & Hartman, P. (2005). Rigidity and flexibility of gender stereotypes in childhood: Developmental or differential? *Infant and Child Development, 14,* 365–381.

Trehub, S. E. (2001). Musical predispositions in infancy. *Annals of the New York Academy of Sciences, 930,* 1–16.

Trehub, S. E. (2016). Infant musicality. In S. Hallam, I. Cross, & M. Thaut (Eds.), *Oxford handbook of music psychology* (2nd ed., pp.

386–397). Oxford, UK: Oxford University Press.

Tremblay, P. (2013). Comparative outcomes of two instructional models for students with learning disabilities: Inclusion with co-teaching and solo-taught special education. *Journal of Research in Special Educational Needs, 13,* 251–258.

Tremblay, R. E. (2000). The development of aggressive behavior during childhood: What have we learned in the past century? *International Journal of Behavioral Development, 24,* 129–141.

Tremblay, R. E. (2015). Developmental origins of chronic physical aggression. An international perspective on using singletons, twins and epigenetics. *European Journal of Criminology, 12,* 551–561.

Trentacosta, C. J., Criss, M. M., Shaw, D. S., Lacourse, E., Hyde, L. W., & Dishion, T. J. (2011). Antecedents and outcomes of joint trajectories of mother–son conflict and warmth during middle childhood and adolescence. *Child Development, 82,* 1676–1690.

Trentacosta, C. J., & Shaw, D. S. (2009). Emotional self-regulation, peer rejection, and antisocial behavior: Developmental associations from early childhood to early adolescence. *Journal of Applied Developmental Psychology, 30,* 356–365.

Triandis, H. C., & Gelfand, M. J. (2012). A theory of individualism and collectivism. In P. A. M. Van Lange, A. W. Kruglanski, & E. T. Higgins (Eds.), *Handbook of theories of social psychology* (Vol. 2, pp. 498–520). Thousand Oaks, CA: Sage.

Trickett, P. K., Noll, J. G., & Putnam, F. W. (2011). The impact of sexual abuse on female development: Lessons from a multigenerational, longitudinal research study. *Development and Psychopathology, 23,* 453–476.

Troilo, J., & Coleman, M. (2012). Full-time, part-time full-time, and part-time fathers: Father identities following divorce. *Family Relations, 61,* 601–614.

Troller-Renfree, S., Zeanah, C. H., Nelson, C. A., & Fox, N. A. (2018). Neural and cognitive factors influencing the emergence of psychopathology: Insights from the Bucharest Early Intervention Project. *Child Development Perspectives, 12,* 28–33.

Tronick, E., & Lester, B. M. (2013). Grandchild of the NBAS: The NICU Network Neurobehavioral Scale (NNNS): A review of the research using the NNNS. *Journal of Child and Adolescent Psychiatric Nursing, 26,* 193–203.

Tronick, E. Z., Thomas, R. B., & Daltabuit, M. (1994). The Quechua manta pouch: A caretaking practice for buffering the Peruvian infant against the multiple stressors of high altitude. *Child Development, 65,* 1005–1013.

Trønnes, H., Wilcox, A. J., Lie, R. T., Markestad, T., & Moster, D. (2014). Risk of cerebral palsy in relation to pregnancy disorders and preterm birth: A national cohort study. *Developmental Medicine and Child Neurology, 56,* 779–785.

Troop-Gordon, W. (2015). The role of the classroom teacher in the lives of children victimized by peers. *Child Development Perspectives, 9,* 55–60.

Troop-Gordon, W., & Asher, S. R. (2005). Modifications in children's goals when encountering obstacles to conflict resolution. *Child Development, 76,* 568–582.

Troop-Gordon, W., Gordon, R. D., Vogel-Ciernia, L., Lee, E. E., & Visconti, K. J. (2018). Visual attention to dynamic scenes

of ambiguous provocation and children's aggressive behavior. *Journal of Clinical Child & Adolescent Psychology, 47,* 925–940.

Tropp, L. R., & Page-Gould, E. (2015). Contact between groups. In M. Mikulincer & P. R. Shaver (Eds.), *APA handbook of personality and social psychology: Vol. 2. Group processes* (pp. 535–560). Washington, DC: American Psychological Association.

Troseth, G. L. (2003). Getting a clear picture: Young children's understanding of a televised image. *Developmental Science, 6,* 247–253.

Troseth, G. L., Saylor, M. M., & Archer, A. H. (2006). Young children's use of video as a source of socially relevant information. *Child Development, 77,* 786–799.

Troutman, D. R., & Fletcher, A. C. (2010). Context and companionship in children's short-term versus long-term friendships. *Journal of Social and Personal Relationships, 27,* 1060–1074.

Trzesniewski, K. H., Donnellan, M. B., & Robins, R. W. (2003). Stability of self-esteem across the life span. *Journal of Personality and Social Psychology, 84,* 205–220.

Tsai, L.-Y., Chen, Y.-L., Tsou, K.-I., & Mu, S.-C. (2015). The impact of small-for-gestational-age on neonatal outcome among very-low-birth-weight infants. *Pediatrics and Neonatology, 56,* 101–107.

Tsang, C. D., & Conrad, N. J. (2010). Does the message matter? The effect of song type on infants' pitch preferences for lullabies and playsongs. *Infant Behavior and Development, 33,* 96–100.

Tseng, V., Easton, J. Q., & Supplee, L. H. (2017). Research–practice partnerships: Building two-way streets of engagement. *Social Policy Report of the Society for Research in Child Development, 30*(4).

Tsoi, M.-F., Cheung, C.-L., & Cheung, T. T. (2016). Continual decrease in blood lead level in Americans: United States National Health Nutrition and Examination Survey 1999–2014. *American Journal of Medicine, 129,* 1213–1218.

Tuchfarber, B. S., Zins, J. E., & Jason, L. A. (1997). Prevention and control of injuries. In R. Weissberg, T. P. Gullotta, R. L. Hampton, B. A. Ryan, & G. R. Adams (Eds.), *Enhancing children's wellness* (pp. 250–277). Thousand Oaks, CA: Sage.

Turati, C., Cassia, V. M., Simion, F., & Leo, I. (2006). Newborns' face recognition: Role of inner and outer facial features. *Child Development, 77,* 297–311.

Turati, C., & Quadrelli, E. (2017). Face perception and recognition. In B. Hopkins, E. Geangu & Linkenauger (Eds.), *Cambridge encyclopedia of child development* (pp. 304–309). New York: Cambridge University Press.

Turkheimer, E., Pettersson, E., & Horn, E. E. (2014). A phenotypic null hypothesis for the genetics of personality. *Annual Review of Psychology, 65,* 515–540.

Turner, P. J., & Gervai, J. (1995). A multidimensional study of gender typing in preschool children and their parents: Personality, attitudes, preferences, behavior, and cultural differences. *Developmental Psychology, 31,* 759–772.

Turner, R. N., Hewstone, M., & Voci, A. (2007). Reducing explicit and implicit outgroup prejudice via direct and extended contact: The mediating role of self-disclosure and intergroup anxiety. *Journal of Personality and Social Psychology, 93,* 369–388.

Tustin, K., & Hayne, H. (2010). Defining the boundary: Age-related changes in childhood amnesia. *Developmental Psychology, 46,* 1046–1061.

Twenge, J. M., & Crocker, J. (2002). Race and self-esteem: Meta-analyses comparing Whites, Blacks, Hispanics, Asians, and American Indians and comment on Gray-Little and Hafdahl (2000). *Psychological Bulletin, 128,* 371–408.

Tyano, S., Keren, M., Herrman, H., & Cox, J. (2010). *Parenthood and mental health.* Oxford, UK: Wiley-Blackwell.

Tyler, C. P., Paneth, N., Allred, E. N., Hirtz, D., Kuban, K., McElrath, T., et al. (2012). Brain damage in preterm newborns and maternal medication: The ELGAN Study. *American Journal of Obstetrics and Gynecology, 207*(192), e1–9.

U

Uccelli, P., Rowe, M. L., & Pan, B. A. (2017). Semantic development: Learning the meanings of words. In J. B. Gleason & N. B. Ratner (Eds.), *Development of language* (9th ed., pp. 77–103). Hoboken, NJ: Pearson.

Ukrainetz, T. A., Justice, L. M., Kaderavek, J. N., Eisenberg, S. L., Gillam, R., & Harm, H. M. (2005). The development of expressive elaboration in fictional narratives. *Journal of Speech, Language, and Hearing Research, 48,* 1363–1377.

Ulber, J., Hamann, K., & Tomasello, M. (2015). How 18- and 24-month-old peers divide resources among themselves. *Journal of Experimental Child Psychology, 140,* 228–244.

Underwood, M. K. (2003). *Social aggression in girls.* New York: Guilford.

UNESCO (United Nations Educational, Scientific and Cultural Organization). (2018, February). *One in five children, adolescents and youth is out of school.* Fact Sheet No. 48. Retrieved from uis.unesco.org/sites/default/files/documents/fs48-one-five-children-adolescents-youth-out-school-2018-en.pdf

UNICEF (United Nations Children's Fund). (2017a). *From the first hour of life: Making the case for infant and young child breastfeeding everywhere.* Retrieved from data.unicef.org/resources/first-hour-life-new-report-breastfeeding-practices

UNICEF (United Nations Children's Fund). (2017b). *Levels and trends in child mortality: Report 2017.* New York: Author.

UNICEF (United Nations Children's Fund). (2017c). *The State of the World's Children 2017 Statistical Tables.* Retrieved from data.unicef.org/resources/state-worlds-children-2017-statistical-tables

UNICEF (United Nations Children's Fund). (2018). *Levels and trends in child malnutrition: Key findings of the 2018 edition of the Joint Child Malnutrition Estimates.* Retrieved from data.unicef.org/wp-content/uploads/2018/05/JME-2018-brochure-.pdf

UNICEF (United Nations Children's Emergency Fund). (2019). *Children in war and conflict.* Retrieved from www.unicefusa.org/mission/emergencies/conflict

United Nations. (2017). *World population prospects: Key findings & advance tables.* Retrieved from esa.un.org/unpd/wpp/Publications/Files/WPP2017_KeyFindings.pdf

Updegraff, K. A., McHale, S. M., Whiteman, S. D., Thayer, S. M., & Delgado, M. Y. (2005). Adolescent sibling relationships in Mexican American families: Exploring the role of familism. *Journal of Family Psychology, 19,* 512–522.

Updegraff, K. A., Umaña-Taylor, A. J., McHale, S. M., Wheeler, L. A., & Perez-Brena, N. J. (2012). Mexican-origin youth's cultural orientations and adjustment: Changes from early to late adolescence. *Child Development, 83,* 1655–1677.

U.S. Bureau of Labor Statistics. (2019). *Employment characteristics of families—2018.* Retrieved from www.bls.gov/news.release/famee.nr0.htm

U.S. Census Bureau. (2016). Children with grandparents by presence of parents, sex, and selected characteristics. In *Current Population Survey, 2016 Annual Social and Economic Supplement.* Retrieved from www.census.gov/data/tables/2016/demo/families/cps-2016.html

U.S. Census Bureau. (2017a). *American Community Survey (ACS): 2016 data release.* Retrieved from www.census.gov/programs-surveys/acs

U.S. Census Bureau. (2017b). *Fertility of women in the United States: 2016.* Retrieved from www.census.gov/topics/health/fertility/data/tables.html

U.S. Census Bureau. (2018a). *Computer and Internet use in the United States: 2016.* American Community Survey Reports, ACS–39. www.census.gov/content/dam/Census/library/publications/2018/acs/ACS-39.pdf

U.S. Census Bureau. (2018b). *International data base.* Retrieved from www.census.gov/data-tools/demo/idb/informationGateway.php

U.S. Census Bureau. (2019). *American Community Survey (ACS): 2019 data release.* Retrieved from www.census.gov/programs-surveys/acs/news/data-releases.html?#

U.S. Department of Agriculture. (2017). *Expenditures on children by families, 2015.* Miscellaneous Publication No. 1528-2015. Retrieved from https://fns-prod.azureedge.net/sites/default/files/crc2015_March2017.pdf

U.S. Department of Agriculture. (2018). *About WIC.* Retrieved from www.fns.usda.gov/wic/about-wic

U.S. Department of Education. (2017a). *Common Core of data. Public elementary/secondary school universe survey data, 2015–2016.* Retrieved from nces.ed.gov/pubsearch/pubsinfo.asp?pubid=2018052

U.S. Department of Education. (2017b). *Digest of education statistics: 2016.* Retrieved from nces.ed.gov/pubs2017/2017094.pdf

U.S. Department of Education. (2018). *Digest of education statistics: 2017.* Retrieved from nces.ed.gov/programs/digest/d17

U.S. Department of Education. (2019). *The Nation's Report Card: How did U.S. students perform on the most recent assessments?* Retrieved from www.nationsreportcard.gov

U.S. Department of Health and Human Services. (2006). *Research to practice: Preliminary findings from the Early Head Start Prekindergarten Follow-Up, Early Head Start Research and Evaluation Project.* Washington, DC: Author.

U.S. Department of Health and Human Services. (2010). *Head Start Impact Study: Final report.* Washington, DC: U.S Government Printing Office.

U.S. Department of Health and Human Services. (2014a). *Breastfeeding: A fact sheet from the Office on Women's Health.* Retrieved from www.womenshealth.gov/files/documents/fact-sheet-breastfeeding.pdf

U.S. Department of Health and Human Services. (2014b). *The role of program quality in determining Head Start's impact on child development.* OPRE Report #2014-10. Retrieved from www.acf.hhs.gov/sites/default/files/opre/hs_quality_report_4_28_14_final.pdf

U.S. Department of Health and Human Services. (2017). *What causes Down syndrome?* Retrieved from www.nichd.nih.gov/health/topics/down/conditioninfo/causes

U.S. Department of Health and Human Services. (2018a). *Child maltreatment 2016.* Retrieved from www.acf.hhs.gov/sites/default/files/cb/cm2016.pdf

U.S. Department of Health and Human Services. (2018b). *Health, United States, 2017 with special feature on mortality.* Retrieved from www.cdc.gov/nchs/data/hus/hus17.pdf

U.S. Department of Health and Human Services. (2019). *Child maltreatment 2017.* Retrieved from www.acf.hhs.gov/sites/default/files/cb/cm2017.pdf

Uttal, D. H., Meadow, N. G., Tipton, E., Hand, L. L., Alden, A. R., Warren, C., & Newcombe, N. S. (2013). The malleability of spatial skills: A meta-analysis of training studies. *Psychological Bulletin, 139,* 352–402.

V

Vaever, M. S., Krogh, M. T., Smith-Nielsen, J., Christensen, T. T., & Tharner, A. (2015). Infants of depressed mothers show reduced gaze activity during mother–infant interaction at 4 months. *Infancy, 20,* 445–454.

Vaillancourt, T., Brittain, H. L., McDougall, P., & Duku, E. (2013). Longitudinal links between childhood peer victimization, internalizing and externalizing problems, and academic functioning: Developmental cascades. *Journal of Abnormal Child Psychology, 41,* 1203–1215.

Vaillancourt, T., & Hymel, S. (2006). Aggression and social status: The moderating roles of sex and peer-valued characteristics. *Aggressive Behavior, 32,* 396–408.

Vaillancourt, T., Hymel, S., & McDougall, P. (2013). The biological underpinnings of peer victimization: Understanding why and how the effects of bullying can last a lifetime. *Theory into Practice, 52,* 241–248.

Vaillancourt, T., McDougall, P., Hymel, S., & Sunderani, S. (2010). Respect or fear? The relationship between power and bullying behavior. In S. R. Jimerson, S. M. Swearer, & D. L. Espelage (Eds.), *Handbook of bullying in schools: An international perspective* (pp. 211–222). New York: Routledge.

Vaillant-Molina, M., Bahrick, L. E., & Flom, R. (2013). Young infants match facial and vocal emotional expressions of other infants. *Infancy, 18,* E97–111.

Vaish, A., Missana, M., & Tomasello, M. (2011). Three-year-old children intervene in third-party moral transgressions. *British Journal of Developmental Psychology, 29,* 124–130.

Vaish, A., & Striano, T. (2004). Is visual reference necessary? Contributions of facial versus vocal cues in 12-month-olds' social referencing behavior. *Developmental Science, 7,* 261–269.

Vakil, E., Blachstein, H., Sheinman, M., & Greenstein, Y. (2009). Developmental changes in attention tests norms: Implications for the structure of attention. *Child Neuropsychology, 15,* 21–39.

Valentino, K., Nuttall, A. K., Comas, M., McDonell, C. G., Piper, B., Thomas, T., et al. (2014). Mother–child reminiscing and autobiographical memory specificity among preschool-age children. *Developmental Psychology, 50,* 1197–1207.

Valenza, E., & Bulf, H. (2011). Early development of object unity: Evidence for perceptual completion in newborns. *Developmental Science, 14,* 799–808.

Valiente, C., Eisenberg, N., Fabes, R. A., Shepard, S. A., Cumberland, A., & Losoya, S. H. (2004). Prediction of children's empathy-related responding from their effortful control and parents' expressivity. *Developmental Psychology, 40,* 911–926.

Valiente, C., Lemery-Chalfant, K., & Swanson, J. (2010). Prediction of kindergartners' academic achievement from their effortful control and emotionality: Evidence for direct and moderated relations. *Journal of Educational Psychology, 102,* 550–560.

Valkenburg, P. M., & Calvert, S. L. (2012). Media and the child's developing imagination. In D. G. Singer & J. L. Singer (Eds.), *Handbook of children and the media* (pp.157–170). Thousand Oaks, CA: Sage.

Valli, L., Croninger, R. G., & Buese, D. (2012). Studying high-quality teaching in a highly charged policy environment. *Teachers College Record, 114*(4), 1–33.

Van Beijsterveldt, C. E. M., Overbeek, L. I. H., Rozendaal, L., McMaster, M. T. B., Glasner, T. J., Bartels, M., et al. (2016). Chorionicity and heritability estimates from twin studies: The prenatal environment of twins and their resemblance across a large number of traits. *Behavioral Genetics, 46,* 304–314.

Vandell, D. L., Belsky, J., Burchinal, M., Steinberg, L., Vandergrift, N., & the NICHD Early Child Care Research Network. (2010). Do effects of early child care extend to age 15 years? Results from the NICHD Study of Early Child Care and Youth Development. *Child Development, 81,* 737–756.

Vandell, D. L., Larson, R. W., Mahoney, J. L., & Watts, T. W. (2015). Children's organized activities. In M. H. Bornstein & T. Leventhal (Eds.), *Handbook of child psychology and developmental science: Vol. 4. Ecological settings and processes* (6th ed., pp. 305–344). Hoboken, NJ: Wiley.

Vandell, D. L., & Mueller, E. C. (1995). Peer play and friendships during the first two years. In H. C. Foot, A. J. Chapman, & J. R. Smith (Eds.), *Friendship and social relations in children* (pp. 181–208). New Brunswick, NJ: Transaction.

Vandell, D. L., & Posner, J. K. (1999). Conceptualization and measurement of children's after-school environments. In S. L. Friedman & T. D. Wachs (Eds.), *Measuring environment across the life span* (pp. 167–196). Washington, DC: American Psychological Association.

Vandell, D. L., Reisner, E. R., & Pierce, K. M. (2007). *Outcomes linked to high-quality after-school programs: Longitudinal findings from the Study of Promising After-School Programs.* Retrieved from www.purdue.edu/hhs/hdfs/fii/wp-content/uploads/2015/07/s_iafis04c04.pdf

Vandell, D. L., Reisner, E. R., Pierce, K. M., Brown, B. B., Lee, D., Bolt, D., & Pechman, E. M. (2006). *The study of promising after-school programs: Examination of longer term outcomes after two years of program experiences.* Madison, WI: University of Wisconsin. Retrieved from www.researchgate.net/publication/237570724_The_Study_of_Promising_After-School_Programs_Examination_of_Longer_Term_Outcomes_After_Two_Years_of_Program_Experiences

van den Akker, A. L. Deković, M., Prinzie, P., & Asscher, J. J. (2010). Toddlers' temperament profiles: Stability and relations to negative and positive parenting. *Journal of Abnormal Child Psychology, 38,* 485–495.

Van den Bergh, B. R. H., & De Rycke, L. (2003). Measuring the multidimensional self-concept and global self-worth of 6- to 8-year-olds. *Journal of Genetic Psychology, 164,* 201–225.

van den Dries, L., Juffer, F., van IJzendoorn, M. H., & Bakermans-Kranenburg, M. J. (2009). Fostering security? A meta-analysis of attachment in adopted children. *Children and Youth Services Review, 31,* 410–421.

van den Eijnden, R., Vermulst, A., van Rooij, A. J., Scholte, R., & van de Mheen, D. (2014). The bidirectional relationships between online victimization and psychosocial problems in adolescents: A comparison with real-life victimization. *Journal of Youth and Adolescence, 43,* 790–802.

Vanderbilt, K. E., Liu, D., & Heyman, G. D. (2011). The development of distrust. *Child Development, 82,* 1372–1380.

Vanderlaan, J., Hall, P. J., & Lewitt, M. (2018). Neonatal outcomes with water birth: A systematic review and meta-analysis. *Midwifery, 59,* 27–38.

van der Meer, A. L. (1997). Keeping the arm in the limelight: Advanced visual control of arm movements in neonates. *European Journal of Paediatric Neurology, 4,* 103–108.

van de Vijver, F. J. R. (2011). Bias and real difference in cross-cultural differences: Neither friends nor foes. In F. J. R. van de Vijver, A. Chasiotis, & H. F. Byrnes (Eds.), *Fundamental questions in cross-cultural psychology* (pp. 235–258). Cambridge, UK: Cambridge University Press.

Van Duin, E. M., Verlinden, E., Vrolijk-Bosschaart, T. F., Diehle, J., & Verhoeff, A. P. (2018). *European Journal of Psychotraumatology, 9,* 1503524.

van Geel, M., & Vedder, P. (2011). The role of family obligations and school adjustment in explaining the immigrant paradox. *Journal of Youth and Adolescence, 40,* 187–196.

van Gelderen, L., Bos, H. M. W., Gartrell, N., Hermanns, J., & Perrin, E. C. (2012). Quality of life of adolescents raised from birth by lesbian mothers: The U.S. National Longitudinal Family Study. *Journal of Developmental and Behavioral Pediatrics, 33,* 17–23.

van Grieken, A., Renders, C. M., Wijtzes, A. I., Hirasing, R. A., & Raat, H. (2013). Overweight, obesity and underweight is associated with adverse psychosocial and physical health outcomes among 7-year-old children: The "Be Active, Eat Right" Study. *PLOS ONE, 8*(6), e67383.

Van Hulle, C. A., Goldsmith, H. H., & Lemery, K. S. (2004). Genetic, environmental, and gender effects on individual differences in toddler expressive language. *Journal of Speech, Language, and Hearing Research, 47,* 904–912.

van IJzendoorn, M. H., & Bakermans-Kranenburg, M. J. (2006). DRD4 7-repeat polymorphism moderates the association between maternal unresolved loss or trauma and infant disorganization. *Attachment and Human Development, 8,* 291–307.

van IJzendoorn, M. H., & Bakermans-Kranenburg, M. J. (2015). Genetic differential susceptibility on trial: Meta-analytic support from randomized controlled experiments. *Development and Psychopathology, 27,* 151–162.

van IJzendoorn, M. H., Bakermans-Kranenburg, M. J., & Ebstein, R. P. (2011).

Methylation matters in child development: Toward developmental behavioral epigenetics. *Child Development Perspectives, 5,* 305–310.

van IJzendoorn, M. H., Belsky, J., & Bakermans-Kranenburg, M. J. (2012). Serotonin transporter genotype 5-HTTLPR as a marker of differential susceptibility: A meta-analysis of child and adolescent gene-by-environment studies. *Translational Psychiatry, 2,* e147.

van IJzendoorn, M. H., & Kroonenberg, P. M. (1988). Cross-cultural patterns of attachment: A meta-analysis of the Strange Situation. *Child Development, 59,* 147–156.

van IJzendoorn, M. H., & Sagi-Schwartz, A. (2008). Cross-cultural patterns of attachment: Universal and contextual dimensions. In J. Cassidy & P. R. Shaver (Eds.), *Handbook of attachment* (2nd ed., pp. 880–905). New York: Guilford.

van IJzendoorn, M. H., Vereijken, C. M. J. L., Bakermans-Kranenburg, M. J., & Riksen-Walraven, J. M. (2004). Assessing attachment security with the Attachment Q Sort: Meta-analytic evidence for the validity of the Observer AQS. *Child Development, 75,* 1188–1213.

VanMarle, K., & Wynn, K. (2006). Six-month-old infants use analog magnitudes to represent duration. *Developmental Science, 9,* 41–49.

Vannuccini, S., Bocchi, C., Severi, F. M., Challis, J. R., & Petraglia, F. (2016). Endocrinology of human parturition. *Annales De 'endocrinologie [Annals of Endocrinology], 77,* 105–113.

van Schijndel, T. J. P., Visser, I., van Bers, B. M. C. W., & Raijmakers, M. E. J. (2015). Preschoolers perform more informative experiments after observing theory-violating evidence. *Journal of Experimental Child Psychology, 131,* 104–119.

Varnhagen, C. (2007). Children and the Internet. In J. Gackenbach (Ed.), *Psychology and the Internet* (2nd ed., pp. 37–54). Amsterdam: Elsevier.

Vasconcelos, M. M. A., East, P., Blanco, E., Lukacz, E. S., Caballero, G., Lozoff, B., & Gahagan, S. (2017). Early behavioral risks of childhood and adolescent daytime urinary incontinence and nocturnal enuresis. *Journal of Developmental and Behavioral Pediatrics, 38,* 736–742.

Vaughn, B. E., Bost, K. K., & van IJzendoorn, M. H. (2008). Attachment and temperament. In J. Cassidy & P. R. Shaver (Eds.), *Handbook of attachment: Theory, research, and clinical applications* (2nd ed., pp. 192–216). New York: Guilford.

Vaughn, B. E., Kopp, C. B., & Krakow, J. B. (1984). The emergence and consolidation of self-control from eighteen to thirty months of age: Normative trends and individual differences. *Child Development, 55,* 990–1004.

Vedova, A. M. (2014). Maternal psychological state and infant's temperament at three months. *Journal of Reproductive and Infant Psychology, 32,* 520–534.

Veenstra, R., Lindenberg, S., Munniksma, A., & Dijkstra, J. K. (2010). The complex relation between bullying, victimization, acceptance, and rejection: Giving special attention to status, affection, and sex differences. *Child Development, 81,* 480–486.

Velez, C. E., Wolchik, S. A., Tien, J., & Sandler, I. (2011). Protecting children from the consequences of divorce: A longitudinal study of the effects of parenting on children's coping processes. *Child Development, 82,* 244–257.

Venables, P. H., & Raine, A. (2016). Impact of malnutrition on intelligence at 3 and 11 years of age: The mediating role of temperament. *Developmental Psychology, 52,* 205–220.

Venekamp, R. P., Mick, P., Schilder, A. G., & Nunez, D. A. (2018). Grommets (ventilation tubes) for recurrent acute otitis media in children. *Cochrane Database of Systematic Reviews, 5,* CD012017.

Venezia, M., Messinger, D. S., Thorp, D., & Mundy, P. (2004). The development of anticipatory smiling. *Infancy, 6,* 397–406.

Veneziano, R. A. (2003). The importance of paternal warmth. *Cross-Cultural Research, 37,* 265–281.

Ventola, C. L. (2016). Immunization in the United States: Recommendations, barriers, and measures to improve compliance. *Pharmacy and Therapeutics, 41,* 426–436.

Verdu, P. (2016). African pygmies. *Current Biology,* R12–R14.

Verhage, M. L., Schuengel, C., Fearon, R. M. P., Oosterman, M., Bakermans-Dranenburg, M. J., & van IJzendoorn, M. H. (2016). Narrowing the transmission gap: A synthesis of three decades of research on intergenerational transmission of attachment. *Psychological Bulletin, 142,* 337–366.

Verissimo, M., & Salvaterra, F. (2006). Maternal secure-base scripts and children's attachment security in an adopted sample. *Attachment and Human Development, 8,* 261–273.

Vernon-Feagans, L., & Cox, M. (2013). The Family Life Project: An epidemiological and developmental study of young children living in poor rural families. *Monographs of the Society for Research in Child Development, 78*(5, Serial No. 310).

Vernon-Feagans, L., Hurley, M. M., Yont, K. M., Wamboldt, P. M., & Kolak, A. (2007). Quality of childcare and otitis media: Relationship to children's language during naturalistic interactions at 18, 24, and 36 months. *Journal of Applied Developmental Psychology, 28,* 115–133.

Verreet, T., Verslegers, M., Quintens, R., Baatout, S., & Benotmane, M. A. (2016). Current evidence for developmental, structural, and functional brain defects following prenatal radiation exposure. *Neural Plasticity,* Art. No. 1243527.

Vespa, J. (2017). The changing economics and demographics of young adulthood: 1975–2016. *Current Population Reports,* No. P20–579. Retrieved from www.census.gov/library/publications/2017/demo/p20-579.html

Vicedo, M. (2017). Putting attachment in its place: Disciplinary and cultural contexts. *European Journal of Developmental Psychology, 14,* 684–699.

Viddal, K. R., Berg-Nielsen, T. S., Wan, M. W., Green, J., Hygen, B. W., Wichstrøm, L., et al. (2015). Secure attachment promotes the development of effortful control in boys. *Attachment & Human Development, 17,* 319–335.

Vieites, V., & Reeb-Sutherland, B. C. (2017). Individual differences in non-clinical maternal depression impact infant affect and behavior during the still-face paradigm across the first year. *Infant Behavior and Development, 47,* 13–21.

Vinden, P. G. (1996). Jun'n Quechua children's understanding of mind. *Child Development, 67,* 1707–1716.

Vinden, P. G. (2002). Understanding minds and evidence for belief: A study of Mofu children in Cameroon. *International Journal of Behavioral Development, 26,* 445–452.

Vinik, J., Almas, A., & Grusec, J. (2011). Mothers' knowledge of what distresses and what comforts their children predicts children's coping, empathy, and prosocial behavior. *Parenting: Science and Practice, 11,* 56–71.

Virant-Klun, I. (2015). Postnatal oogenesis in humans: A review of recent findings. *Stem Cells and Cloning: Advances and Applications, 8,* 49–60.

Visher, E. B., Visher, J. S., & Pasley, K. (2003). Remarriage families and stepparenting. In F. Walsh (Ed.), *Normal family processes: Growing diversity and complexity* (pp. 153–175). New York: Guilford.

Vissers, L. E. L. M., Gilissen, C., & Veltman, J. A. (2016). Genetic studies in intellectual disability and related disorders. *Nature Reviews: Genetics, 17,* 9–18.

Vistad, I., Cvancarova, M., Hustad, B. L., & Henriksen, T. (2013). Vaginal breech delivery: Results of a prospective registration study. *BMC Pregnancy and Children, 13,* 153.

Vitaro, F., Boivin, M., Brendgen, M., Girard, A., & Dionner, G. (2012). Social experiences in kindergarten and academic achievement in grade 1: A monozygotic twin difference study. *Journal of Educational Psychology, 2,* 366–380.

Vitaro, F., & Brendgen, M. (2012). Subtypes of aggressive behaviors: Etiologies, development, and consequences. In T. Bliesner, A. Beelmann, & M. Stemmler (Eds.), *Antisocial behavior and crime: Contributions of developmental and evaluation research to prevention and intervention* (pp. 17–38). Cambridge, MA: Hogrefe.

Vitrup, B., & Holden, G. W. (2010). Children's assessments of corporal punishment and other disciplinary practices: The role of age, race, SES, and exposure to spanking. *Journal of Applied Developmental Psychology, 31,* 211–220.

Vizard, E. (2013). Practitioner review: The victims and juvenile perpetrators of child sexual abuse—assessment and intervention. *The Journal of Child Psychology and Psychiatry, 54,* 503–515.

Vlach, H. A. (2016). How we categorize objects is related to how we remember them: The shape bias as a memory bias. *Journal of Experimental Child Psychology, 152,* 12–30.

Vlahovicova, K., Melende-Torres, G. J., Leijten, P., Knerr, W., & Gardner, F. (2017). Parenting programs for the prevention of child physical abuse recurrence: A systematic review and meta-analysis. *Clinical Child and Family Review, 20,* 351–365.

Voegtline, K. M., Costigan, K. A., Pater, H. A., & DiPietro, J. A. (2013). Near-term fetal response to maternal spoken voice. *Infant Behavior and Development, 36,* 526–533.

Vogel, C. A., Xue, Y., Maiduddin, E. M., Carlson, B. L., & Kisker, E. E. (2010). *Early Head Start children in grade 5: Long-term follow-up of the Early Head Start Research and Evaluation Study sample* (OPRE Report No. 2011-8). Washington, DC: U.S. Department of Health and Human Services.

Volling, B. L. (2001). Early attachment relationships as predictors of preschool children's emotion regulation with a distressed sibling. *Early Education and Development, 12,* 185–207.

Volling, B. L. (2012). Family transitions following the birth of a sibling: An empirical review of changes in the firstborn's adjustment. *Psychological Bulletin, 138,* 497–528.

Volling, B. L., & Belsky, J. (1992). Contribution of mother–child and father–child relationships to the quality of sibling interaction: A longitudinal study. *Child Development, 63,* 1209–1222.

Volling, B. L., Gonzalez, R., Oh, W., Song, J. H., Yu, T., Rosenberg, L., et al. (2017). Developmental trajectories of children's adjustment across the transition to siblinghood: Pre-birth predictors and sibling outcomes at one year. *Monographs of the Society for Research in Child Development, 82*(3, Serial No. 326).

Volling, B. L., Mahoney, A., & Rauer, A. J. (2009). Sanctification of parenting, moral socialization, and young children's conscience development. *Psychology of Religion and Spirituality, 1,* 53–68.

Vondra, J. I., Shaw, D. S., & Kevenides, M. C. (1995). Predicting infant attachment classification from multiple, contemporaneous measures of maternal care. *Infant Behavior and Development, 18,* 415–425.

von Gontard, A., Heron, J., & Joinson, C. (2011). Family history of nocturnal enuresis and urinary incontinence: Results from a large epidemiological study. *Journal of Urology, 185,* 2303–2306.

von Hofsten, C. (1993). Prospective control: A basic aspect of action development. *Human Development, 36,* 253–270.

von Hofsten, C. (2004). An action perspective on motor development. *Trends in Cognitive Sciences, 8,* 266–272.

von Hofsten, C., & Rosander, K. (1998). The establishment of gaze control in early infancy. In S. Simion & G. Butterworth (Eds.), *The development of sensory, motor and cognitive capacities in early infancy* (pp. 49–66). Hove, UK: Psychology Press.

Von Salisch, M., Haenel, M., & Denham, S. A. (2015). Self-regulation, language skills, and emotion knowledge in young children from northern Germany. *Early Education and Development, 26,* 792–806.

von Soest, T., Wichstrøm, L., & Kvalem, I. L. (2016). The development of global and domain-specific self-esteem from age 13 to 31. *Journal of Personality and Social Psychology, 110,* 592–608.

Vouloumanos, A. (2010). Three-month-olds prefer speech to other naturally occurring signals. *Language Learning and Development, 6,* 241–257.

Vranekovic, J., Bozovic, I. B., Grubic, Z., Wagner, J., Pavlinic, D., Dahoun, S., et al. (2012). Down syndrome: Parental origin, recombination, and maternal age. *Genetic Testing and Molecular Biomarkers, 16,* 70–73.

Vukasović, T., & Bratko, D. (2015). Heritability of personality: A meta-analysis of behavior genetic studies. *Psychological Bulletin, 141,* 769–785.

Vuoksimaa, E., Koskenvuo, M., Rose, R. J., & Kaprio, J. (2009). Origins of handedness: A nationwide study of 30,1671 adults. *Neuropsychologia, 47,* 1294–1301.

Vygotsky, L. S. (1978). *Mind in society: The development of higher psychological processes.* Cambridge, MA: Harvard University Press. (Original works published 1930, 1933, and 1935)

Vygotsky, L. S. (1987). Thinking and speech. In R. W. Rieber, A. S. Carton (Eds.), & N. Minick (Trans.), *The collected works of L. S. Vygotsky: Vol. 1. Problems of general psychology* (pp. 37–285). New York: Plenum. (Original work published 1934)

W

Waber, D. P., Bryce, C. P., Girard, J. M., Zichlin, M., Fitzmaurice, G. M., & Galler, J. R. (2014). Impaired IQ and academic skills in adults who experienced moderate to severe infantile malnutrition: A 40-year study. *Nutritional Neuroscience, 17,* 58–64.

Wadell, P. M., Hagerman, R. J., & Hessl, D. R. (2013). Fragile X syndrome: Psychiatric manifestations, assessment and emerging therapies. *Current Psychiatry Reviews, 9,* 53–58.

Wadsworth, M. E., Rindlaub, L., Hurwich-Reiss, E., Rienks, S., Bianco, H., & Markman, H. J. (2013). A longitudinal examination of the adaptation to poverty-related stress model: Predicting child and adolescent adjustment over time. *Journal of Clinical Child and Adolescent Psychology, 42,* 713–725.

Wagenaar, K., van Wessenbruch, M. M., van Leeuwen, F. E., Cohen-Kettenis, P. T., Delemarre-van de Waal, H. A., Schats, R., et al. (2011). Self-reported behavioral and socioemotional functioning of 11- to 18-year-old adolescents conceived by in vitro fertilization. *Fertility and Sterility, 95,* 611–616.

Wagnsson, S., Lindwall, M., & Gustafsson, H. (2014). Participation in organized sport and self-esteem across adolescence: The mediating role of perceived sport competence. *Journal of Sport & Exercise Psychology, 36,* 584–594.

Wainryb, C., & Ford, S. (1998). Young children's evaluations of acts based on beliefs different from their own. *Merrill-Palmer Quarterly, 44,* 484–503.

Wakefield, E. M., Congdon, E., Novack, M., Goldin-Meadow, S., & James, K. H. (2014). *Understanding the neural effects of learning with gesture: Does gesture help learners because it is grounded in action?* Paper presented at the annual meeting of the International Society of Gesture Studies, San Diego, CA.

Wakefield, E. M., & James, K. H. (2015). Effects of learning with gesture on children's understanding of a new language concept. *Developmental Psychology, 51,* 1105–1114.

Walberg, H. J. (1986). Synthesis of research on teaching. In M. C. Wittrock (Ed.), *Handbook of research on teaching* (3rd ed., pp. 214–229). New York: Macmillan.

Walden, T., Kim, G., McCoy, C., & Karrass, J. (2007). Do you believe in magic? Infants' social looking during violations of expectations. *Developmental Science, 10,* 654–663.

Waldfogel, J., Craigie, T.-A., & Brooks-Gunn, J. (2010). Fragile families and child wellbeing. *Future of Children, 20,* 87–112.

Waldfogel, J., & Zhai, F. (2008). Effects of public preschool expenditures on the test scores of fourth graders: Evidence from TIMMS. *Educational Research and Evaluation, 14,* 9–28.

Waldorf, K. M. A., & McAdams, R. M. (2013). Influence of infection during pregnancy on fetal development. *Reproduction, 146,* R151–R162.

Walfisch, A., Sermer, C., Cressman, A., & Koren, G. (2013). Breast milk and cognitive development—the role of confounders: A systematic review. *British Medical Journal, 3,* e003259.

Walker, C. (2014). *Early Head Start participants, programs, families and staff in 2013.* Retrieved from www.clasp.org /resources-and-publications/publication-1 /HSpreschool-PIR-2013-Fact-Sheet.pdf

Walker, C. M., Walker, L. B., & Ganea, P. A. (2013). The role of symbol-based experience in early learning and transfer from pictures: Evidence from Tanzania. *Developmental Psychology, 49,* 1315–1324.

Walker, O. L., Degnan, K. A., Fox, N. A., & Henderson, H. A. (2013). Social problem solving in early childhood: Developmental change and the influence of shyness. *Journal of Applied Developmental Psychology, 34,* 185–193.

Walker, O. L., & Henderson, H. A. (2012). Temperament and social problem solving competence in preschool: Influences on academic skills in early elementary school. *Social Development, 21,* 761–779.

Walker, S. M. (2013). Biological and neurodevelopmental implications of neonatal pain. *Clinics in Perinatology, 40,* 471–491.

Wallace, C. E., & Russ, S. W. (2015). Pretend play, divergent thinking, and math achievement in girls: A longitudinal study. *Psychology of Aesthetics, Creativity, and the Arts, 9,* 296–305.

Walsh, K., Zwi, K., Woolfenden, S., & Shlonsky, A. (2018). School-based education programs for the prevention of child sexual abuse: A Cochrane systematic review and meta-analysis. *Research on Social Work Practice, 28,* 33–55.

Walton, G. E., Armstrong, E. S., & Bower, T. G. R. (1998). Newborns learn to identify a face in eight-tenths of a second? *Developmental Science, 1,* 79–84.

Wang, D., & Fletcher, A. C. (2016). Parenting style and peer trust in relation to school adjustment in middle childhood. *Journal of Child and Family Studies, 25,* 988–998.

Wang, J., & Herman, J. (2019). Magnet schools: History, description, and effects. In R. A. Fox & N. K. Buchanan (Eds.), *Wiley handbook of school choice* (pp. 158–179). Malden, MA: Wiley Blackwell.

Wang, M. (2016). Iron deficiency and other types of anemia in infants and children. *American Family Physician, 15,* 270–278.

Wang, M.-T., & Kenny, S. (2014). Parental physical punishment and adolescent adjustment: Bidirectionality and the moderation effects of child ethnicity and parental warmth. *Journal of Abnormal Child Psychology, 42,* 717–730.

Wang, M.-T., & Sheikh-Khalil, S. (2014). Does parental involvement matter for student achievement and mental health in high school? *Child Development, 85,* 610–625.

Wang, Q. (2004). The emergence of cultural self-constructs: Autobiographical memory and self-description in European American and Chinese children. *Developmental Psychology, 40,* 3–15.

Wang, Q. (2006). Relations of maternal style and child self-concept to autobiographical memories in Chinese, Chinese immigrant, and European American 3-year-olds. *Child Development, 77,* 1794–1809.

Wang, Q. (2008). Emotion knowledge and autobiographical memory across the preschool years: A cross-cultural longitudinal investigation. *Cognition, 108,* 117–135.

Wang, Q., Doan, S. N., & Song, Q. (2010). Talking about internal states in mother–child reminiscing influences children's self-representations: A cross-cultural study. *Cognitive Development, 25,* 380–393.

Wang, Q., Shao, Y., & Li, Y. J. (2010). "My way or mom's way?" The bilingual and bicultural self in Hong Kong Chinese children and adolescents. *Child Development, 81,* 555–567.

Wang, S., Baillargeon, R., & Paterson, S. (2005). Detecting continuity violations in infancy: A new account and new evidence from covering and tube effects. *Cognition, 95,* 129–173.

Wang, T., Ren, X., Schweizer, K., & Xu, F. (2016). Schooling effects on intelligence development: Evidence based on national samples from urban and rural China. *Educational Psychology, 36,* 831–844.

Wang, Z., & Deater-Deckard, K. (2013). Resilience in gene–environment transactions. In S. Goldstein & R. B. Brooks (Eds.), *Handbook of resilience in children* (2nd ed., pp. 57–72). New York: Springer Science + Business Media.

Ward, T. C. S. (2015). Reasons for mother–infant bedsharing: A systematic narrative synthesis of the literature and implications for future research. *Maternal and Child Health Journal, 19,* 675–690.

Warneken, F., & Tomasello, M. (2009). Varieties of altruism in children and chimpanzees. *Trends in Cognitive Sciences, 13,* 397.

Warneken, F., & Tomasello, M. (2013). Parental presence and encouragement do not influence helping in young children. *Infancy, 18,* 345–368.

Warnock, F., & Sandrin, D. (2004). Comprehensive description of newborn distress behavior in response to acute pain (newborn male circumcision). *Pain, 107,* 242–255.

Warren, A. R., & Tate, C. S. (1992). Egocentrism in children's telephone conversations. In R. M. Diaz & L. E. Berk (Eds.), *Private speech: From social interaction to self-regulation* (pp. 245–264). Hillsdale, NJ: Erlbaum.

Warreyn, P., Roeyers, H., & De Groote, I. (2005). Early social communicative behaviours of preschoolers with autism spectrum disorder during interaction with their mothers. *Autism, 9,* 342–361.

Washington, J. A., & Thomas-Tate, S. (2009). How research informs cultural-linguistic differences in the classroom: The bi-dialectal African American child. In S. Rosenfield & V. Berninger (Eds.), *Implementing evidence-based academic interventions in school settings* (pp. 147–164). New York: Oxford University Press.

Washington, T., Gleeson, J. P., & Rulison, K. L. (2013). Competence and African American children in informal kinship care: The role of family. *Children and Youth Services Review, 35,* 1305–1312.

Wasik, B. A., & Bond, M. A. (2001). Beyond the pages of a book: Interactive book reading and language development in preschool classrooms. *Journal of Educational Psychology, 93,* 243–250.

Wasik, B. A., Hindman, A. H., & Snell, E. K. (2016). Book reading and vocabulary development: A systematic review. *Early Childhood Research Quarterly, 37,* 39–57.

Wasserman, E. A., & Rovee-Collier, C. (2001). Pick the flowers and mind your As and 2s! Categorization by pigeons and infants. In M. E. Carroll & J. B. Overmier (Eds.), *Animal research and human health: Advancing human welfare through behavioral science* (pp. 263–279). Washington, DC: American Psychological Association.

Wassner, A. J. (2017). Pediatric hypothyroidism: Diagnosis and treatment. *Pediatric Drugs, 19,* 291–301.

Watamura, S. E., Phillips, D., Morrissey, T. W., McCartney, K., & Bub, K. (2011). Double jeopardy: Poorer social–emotional outcomes for children in the NICHD SECCYD experiencing home and child-care environments that confer risk. *Child Development, 82,* 48–65.

Waters, E., Merrick, S., Treboux, D., Crowell, J., & Albersheim, L. (2000). Attachment security in infancy and early adulthood: A twenty-year longitudinal study. *Child Development, 71*, 684–689.

Waters, E., Vaughn, B. E., Posada, G., & Kondo-Ikemura, K. (Eds.). (1995). Caregiving, cultural, and cognitive perspectives on secure-base behavior and working models: New growing points of attachment theory and research. *Monographs of the Society for Research in Child Development, 60*(2–3, Serial No. 244).

Waters, S. F., & Thompson, R. A. (2014). Children's perceptions of the effectiveness of strategies for regulating anger and sadness. *International Journal of Behavioral Development, 38*, 174–181.

Watrin, J. P., & Darwich, R. (2012). On behaviorism in the cognitive revolution: Myth and reactions. *Review of General Psychology, 16*, 269–282.

Watson, J. B., & Raynor, R. (1920). Conditioned emotional reactions. *Journal of Experimental Psychology, 3*, 1–14.

Waugh, W. E., & Brownell, C. A. (2015). Development of body-part vocabulary in toddlers in relation to self-understanding. *Early Child Development and Care, 185*, 1166–1179.

Waxman, S. R., & Lidz, J. L. (2006). Early word learning. In D. Kuhn & R. Siegler (Eds.), *Handbook of child psychology: Vol. 2. Cognition, perception, and language* (6th ed., pp. 464–510). Hoboken, NJ: Wiley.

Waxman, S. R., & Senghas, A. (1992). Relations among word meanings in early lexical development. *Developmental Psychology, 28*, 862–873.

Weaver, J. M., & Schofield, T. J. (2015). Mediation and moderation of divorce effects on children's behavior problems. *Journal of Family Psychology, 29*, 39–48.

Webb, A. R., Heller, H. T., Benson, C. sB., & Lahav, A. (2015). Mother's voice and heartbeat sounds elicit auditory plasticity in the human brain before full gestation. *Proceedings of the National Academy of Sciences, 112*, 3152–3157.

Webb, N. M., Nemer, K. M., & Chizhik, A. W. (1998). Equity issues in collaborative group assessment: Group composition and performance. *American Educational Research Journal, 35*, 607–651.

Weber, C., Hahne, A., Friedrich, M., & Friederici, A. (2004). Discrimination of word stress in early infant perception: Electrophysiological evidence. *Cognitive Brain Research, 18*, 149–161.

Weber, D., Dekhtyar, S., & Herlitz, A. (2017). The Flynn effect in Europe—effects of sex and region. *Intelligence, 60*, 39–45.

Webster-Stratton, C., & Reid, M. J. (2010). The Incredible Years Parents, Teachers, and Children Training Series: A multifaceted treatment approach for young children with conduct disorders. In J. R. Weisz & A. E. Kazdin (Eds.), *Evidence-based psychotherapies for children and adolescents* (2nd ed., pp. 194–210). New York: Guilford.

Webster-Stratton, C., Rinaldi, J., & Reid, J. M. (2011). Long-term outcomes of Incredible Years parenting program: Predictors of adolescent adjustment. *Child and Adolescent Mental Health, 16*, 38–46.

Wechsler, D. (2012). *Wechsler preschool and primary scale of intelligence* (4th ed) (WPPSI–IV). Upper Saddle River, NJ: Pearson.

Weech-Maldonado, R., Hall, A., Bryant, T., Jenkins, K. A., & Elliott, M. N. (2012). The relationship between perceived discrimination and patient experiences with health care. *Medical Care, 50*, S62–S68.

Weems, C. F., & Costa, N. M. (2005). Developmental differences in the expression of childhood anxiety symptoms and fears. *Journal of the American Academy of Child and Adolescent Psychiatry, 44*, 656–663.

Weger, U. W., Hooper, N., Meier, B. P., & Hopthrow, T. (2012). Mindful maths: Reducing the impact of stereotype threat through a mindfulness exercise. *Consciousness and Cognition, 21*, 471–475.

Weiland, C., & Yoshikawa, H. (2013). Impacts of a prekindergarten program on children's mathematics, language, literacy, executive function, and emotional skills. *Child Development, 84*, 2112–2130.

Weinfield, N. S., Sroufe, L. A., & Egeland, B. (2000). Attachment from infancy to early adulthood in a high-risk sample: Continuity, discontinuity, and their correlates. *Child Development, 71*, 695–702.

Weinfield, N. S., Whaley, G. J. L., & Egeland, B. (2004). Continuity, discontinuity, and coherence in attachment from infancy to late adolescence: Sequelae of organization and disorganization. *Attachment and Human Development, 6*, 73–97.

Weinstein, R. S. (2002). *Reaching higher: The power of expectations in schooling.* Cambridge, MA: Harvard University Press.

Weinstock, M. (2008). The long-term behavioural consequences of prenatal stress. *Neuroscience and Biobehavioral Reviews, 32*, 1073–1086.

Weisberg, D. S., Hirsh-Pasek, K., Golinkoff, R. M., Kittredge, A. K., & Klahr, D. (2016). Guided play: Principles and practices. *Current Directions in Psychological Science, 25*, 177–182.

Weisberg, D. S., Zosh, J. M., Hirsh-Pasek, K., & Golinkoff, R. M. (2013). Talking it up: Play, language development, and the role of adult support. *American Journal of Play, 6*, 39–54.

Weisgram, E. S., Bigler, R. S., & Liben, L. S. (2010). Gender, values, and occupational interests among children, adolescents, and adults. *Child Development, 81*, 778–796.

Weisgram, E. S., & Bruun, S. T. (2018). Predictors of gender-typed toy purchases by prospective parents and mothers: The roles of childhood experiences and gender attitudes. *Sex Roles, 79*, 342–357.

Weisgram, E. S., Fulcher, M., & Dinella, L. M. (2014). Pink gives girls permission: Exploring the roles of explicit gender labels and gender-typed colors on preschool children's toy preferences. *Journal of Applied Developmental Psychology, 35*, 401–409.

Weisleder, A., & Fernald, A. (2013). Talking to children matters: Early language experience strengthens processing and builds vocabulary. *Psychological Science, 24*, 2143–2152.

Weisman, O., Magori-Cohen, R., Louzoun, Y., Eidelman, A. I., & Feldman, R. (2011). Sleep–wake transitions in premature neonates predict early development. *Pediatrics, 128*, 706–714.

Weiss, E., & Reville, P. (2019). *Broader, bolder, better: How schools and communities help students overcome the disadvantages of poverty.* Cambridge, MA: Harvard Education Press.

Weiss, L., Saklofske, D., Holdnack, J., & Prifitera, A. (2015). *WISC-V assessment and interpretation.* San Diego, CA: Academic Press.

Weller, E. B., Kloos, A. L., & Weller, R. A. (2006). Mood disorders. M. K. Dulcan & J. M. Wiener (Eds.), *Essentials of child and adolescent psychiatry* (pp. 267–320).

Washington, DC: American Psychiatric Association.

Wellman, H. M. (2011). Developing a theory of mind. In U. Goswami (Ed.), *Wiley-Blackwell handbook of childhood cognitive development* (2nd ed., pp. 258–284). Malden, MA: Wiley-Blackwell.

Wellman, H. M. (2012). Theory of mind: Better methods, clearer findings, more development. European *Journal of Developmental Psychology, 9*, 313–330.

Wellman, H. M., Fang, F., Liu, D., Zhu, L., & Liu, G. (2006). Scaling of theory-of-mind understandings in Chinese children. *Psychological Science, 17*, 1075–1081.

Wellman, H. M., Lopez-Duran, S., LaBounty, J., & Hamilton, B. (2008). Infant attention to intentional action predicts preschool theory of mind. *Developmental Psychology, 44*, 618–623.

Wen, A., Weyant, R. J., McNeil, D. W., Crout, R. J., Neiswanger, K., Marazita, M. L., & Foxman, B. (2017). Bayesian analysis of the association between family-level factors and siblings' dental caries. *JDR Clinical & Translational Research, 2*, 278–286.

Wender, P. H., & Tomb, D. A. (2017). *ADHD: A guide to understanding symptoms, causes, diagnosis, treatment, and changes over time in children, adolescents, and adults* (5th ed.). New York: Oxford University Press.

Wentworth, N., Benson, J. B., & Haith, M. M. (2000). The development of infants' reaches for stationary and moving targets. *Child Development, 71*, 576–601.

Wentzel, K. R., & Brophy, J. E. (2014). *Motivating students to learn.* Hoboken, NJ: Taylor & Francis.

Werner, E. E. (2001). *Journeys from childhood to midlife: Risk, resilience, and recovery.* Ithaca, NY: Cornell University Press.

Werner, E. E. (2005). Resilience and recovery: Findings from the Kauai Longitudinal Study. *Research, Policy, and Practice in Children's Mental Health, 19*(1), 11–14.

Werner, E. E. (2013). What can we learn about resilience from large-scale longitudinal studies? In S. Goldstein & R. Brooks (Eds.), *Handbook of resilience in children* (2nd ed., pp. 87–102). New York: Springer Science + Business Media.

Werner, E. E., & Smith, R. S. (1982). *Vulnerable but invincible: A study of resilient children.* New York: McGraw-Hill.

Werner, E. E., & Smith, R. S. (1992). *Overcoming the odds: High risk children from birth to adulthood.* Ithaca, NY: Cornell University Press.

Werner, N. E., & Crick, N. R. (2004). Maladaptive peer relationships and the development of relational and physical aggression during middle childhood. *Social Development, 13*, 495–514.

Wessells, M. G. (2017). Children and armed conflict: Interventions for supporting war-affected children. *Peace and Conflict: Journal of Peace Psychology, 23*, 4–13.

Westermann, G., Sirois, S., Shultz, T. R., & Mareschal, D. (2006). Modeling developmental cognitive neuroscience. *Trends in Cognitive Sciences, 10*, 227–232.

Whaley, S. E., Koleilat, M., Whaley, M., Gomez, J., Meehan, K., & Saluja, K. (2012). Impact of policy changes on infant feeding decisions among low-income women participating in the Special Supplemental Nutrition Program for Women, Infants, and Children. *American Journal of Public Health, 102*, 2269–2273.

Wheatley, R. R., Kelley, M. A., Peacock, N., & Delgado, J. (2008). Women's narratives on quality prenatal care: A multicultural perspective. *Qualitative Health Research, 18*, 1586–1598.

Whipple, E. E. (2006). Child abuse and neglect: Consequences of physical, sexual, and emotional abuse of children. In H. E. Fitzgerald, B. M. Lester, & B. Zuckerman (Eds.), *The crisis in youth mental health: Vol 1. Childhood disorders* (pp. 205–229). Westport, CT: Praeger.

Whipple, N., Bernier, A., & Mageau, G. A. (2011). Broadening the study of infant security of attachment: Maternal autonomy-support in the context of infant exploration. *Social Development, 20*, 17–32.

Whitehurst, G. J., & Lonigan, C. J. (1998). Child development and emergent literacy. *Child Development, 69*, 848–872.

Whitesell, N. R., Mitchell, C. M., Spicer, P., and the Voices of Indian Teens Project Team. (2009). A longitudinal study of self-esteem, cultural identity, and academic success among American Indian adolescents. *Cultural Diversity and Ethnic Minority Psychology, 15*, 38–50.

Wichman, A. L., Rodgers, J. L., & MacCallum, R. C. (2007). Birth order has no effect on intelligence: A reply and extension of previous findings. *Personality and Social Psychology Bulletin, 33*, 1195–1200.

Wichmann, C., Coplan, R. J., & Daniels, T. (2004). The social cognitions of socially withdrawn children. *Social Development, 13*, 377–392.

Widen, S. C. (2013). Children's interpretation of facial expressions: The long path from valence-based to specific discrete categories. *Emotion Review, 5*, 72–77.

Widen, S. C., & Russell, J. A. (2011). In building a script for an emotion do preschoolers add its cause before its behavior consequence? *Social Development, 20*, 471–485.

Wiebe, S. A., Fang, H., Johnson, C., James, K. E., & Espy, K. A. (2014). Determining the impact of prenatal tobacco exposure on self-regulation at 6 months. *Developmental Psychology, 50*, 1746–1756.

Wilcox, T., & Woods, R. (2009). Experience primes infants to individuate objects. In A. Woodward & A. Needham (Eds.), *Learning and the infant mind* (pp. 117–143). New York: Oxford University Press.

Willatts, P. (1999). Development of means–end behavior in young infants: Pulling a support to retrieve a distant object. *Developmental Psychology, 35*, 651–667.

Williams, G. R. (2008). Neurodevelopmental and neurophysiological actions of thyroid hormone. *Journal of Neuroendocrinology, 20*, 784–794.

Williams, J. L., & Corbetta, D. (2016). Assessing the impact of movement consequences on the development of early reaching in infancy. *Frontiers in Psychology, 7*, Art. No. 587.

Williams, K., & Dunne-Bryant, A. (2006). Divorce and adult psychological well-being: Clarifying the role of gender and age. *Journal of Marriage and Family, 68*, 1178–1196.

Williams, M. S., & Shellenberger, S. (1996). *"How does your engine run?" A leader's guide to The Alert Program for Self-Regulation.* Albuquerque, NM: TherapyWorks, Inc.

Williams, S. T., Mastergeorge, A. M., & Ontai, L. L. (2010). Caregiver involvement in infant peer interactions: Scaffolding in a social context. *Early Childhood Research Quarterly, 25*, 251–266.

Wilson-Ching, M., Molloy, C. S., Anderson, V. A., Burnett, A., Roberts, G., Cheong, J. L., et al. (2013). Attention difficulties in a contemporary geographic cohort of adolescents born extremely preterm/ extremely low birth weight. *Journal of the International Neuropsychological Society, 19,* 1097–1108.

Wimmer, M. B. (2013). *Evidence-based practices for school refusal and truancy.* Bethesda, MD: NASP.

Winkler, I., Háden, G. P., Ladinig, O., Sziller, I., & Honing, H. (2009). Newborn infants detect the beat in music. *Proceedings of the National Academy of Sciences, 106,* 2468–2471.

Winner, E. (1986, August). Where pelicans kiss seals. *Psychology Today, 20*(8), 25–35.

Winship, C., & Korenman, S. (1997). Does staying in school make you smarter? The effect of education on IQ in The Bell Curve. In B. Devlin, S. E. Fienberg, D. P. Resnick, & K. Roeder (Eds.), *Intelligence, genes, & success: Scientists respond to The Bell Curve* (pp. 215–234). New York: Springer-Verlag.

Winsler, A., Abar, B., Feder, M. A., Rubio, D. A., & Schunn, C. D. (2007). Private speech and executive functioning among high functioning children with autism spectrum disorders. *Journal of Autism and Developmental Disorders, 37,* 1617–1635.

Witherington, D. C. (2005). The development of prospective grasping control between 5 and 7 months: A longitudinal study. *Infancy, 7,* 143–161.

Witherington, D. C., Campos, J. J., Harriger, J. A., Bryan, C., & Margett, T. E. (2010). Emotion and its development in infancy. In G. Bremner & T. D. Wachs (Eds.), *Wiley-Blackwell handbook of infant development: Vol. 1. Basic research* (2nd ed., pp. 568–591). Hoboken, NJ: Wiley-Blackwell.

Witte, A. L., Kiewra, K. A., Kasson, S. C., & Perry, K. R. (2015). Parenting talent: A qualitative investigation of the roles parents play in talent development. *Roeper Review, 37,* 84–96.

Wojcik, E. H., & Saffran, J. R. (2015). Toddlers encode similarities among novel words from meaningful sentences. *Cognition, 138,* 10–20.

Wolf, A. W., Jimenez, E., & Lozoff, B. (2003). Effects of iron therapy on infant blood lead levels. *Journal of Pediatrics, 143,* 789–795.

Wolfe, D. A. (2005). *Child abuse* (2nd ed.) Thousand Oaks, CA: Sage.

Wolff, P. H. (1966). The causes, controls and organization of behavior in the neonate. *Psychological Issues, 5*(1, Serial No. 17).

Wong, K. (2014). The 1 percent difference. *Scientific American, 311*(3),100.

Wood, J. N., Kouider, S., & Carey, S. (2009). Acquisition of singular-plural morphology. *Developmental Psychology, 45,* 202–206.

Wood, R. M. (2009). Changes in cry acoustics and distress ratings while the infant is crying. *Infant and Child Development, 18,* 163–177.

Woods, A. M., Graber, K. C., Daum, D. M., & Gentry, C. (2015). Young school children's recess physical activity: Movement patterns and preferences. *Journal of Teaching in Physical Education, 34,* 496–516.

Woodward, A. (2009). Infants' grasp of others' intentions. *Current Directions in Psychological Science, 18,* 53–57.

Woolley, J. D. (1997). Thinking about fantasy: Are children fundamentally different thinkers and believers from adults? *Child Development, 68,* 991–1011.

Woolley, J. D. (2000). The development of beliefs about direct mental–physical causality in imagination, magic, and religion. In K. S. Rosengren, C. N. Johnson, & P. L. Harris (Eds.), *Imagining the impossible* (pp. 99–129). New York: Cambridge University Press.

Woolley, J. D., Browne, C. A., & Boerger, E. A. (2006). Constraints on children's judgments of magical causality. *Journal of Cognition and Development, 7,* 253–277.

Woolley, J. D., & Cornelius, C. A. (2013). Beliefs in magical beings and cultural myths. In M. Taylor (Ed.), *Oxford handbook of the development of imagination* (pp. 61–74). New York: Oxford University Press.

Woolley, J. D., Cornelius, C. A., & Lacy, W. (2011). Developmental changes in the use of supernatural explanations for unusual events. *Journal of Cognition and Culture, 11,* 311–337.

Woolley, J. D., & Cox, V. (2007). Development of beliefs about storybook reality. *Developmental Science, 10,* 681–693.

World Bank. (2018a). *Adolescent fertility rate (births per 1,000 women ages 15–19).* Retrieved from data.worldbank.org /indicator/SP.ADO.TFRT?year_high _desc=false

World Bank. (2018b). *Fertility rate, total (births per woman).* Retrieved from data.worldbank.org/indicator/SP.DYN .TFRT.IN?

World Health Organization. (2017a). *HIV/ AIDS: Data and statistics.* Retrieved from www.who.int/hiv/data/en

World Health Organization. (2017b). *Immunization, vaccines, and biologicals: Data, statistics and graphics.* Retrieved from www.who.int/immunization /monitoring_surveillance/data/en

World Health Organization. (2017c). *Rubella: Fact sheet No 367.* Retrieved from www. who.int/mediacentre/factsheets/fs367/en/

World Health Organization. (2017d). *The World Health Organization's infant feeding recommendation.* Retrieved from www. who.int/nutrition/topics/infantfeeding _recommendation/en

World Health Organization. (2018). *Diarrhoeal disease.* Retrieved from http://www.who. int/news-room/fact-sheets/detail/diarrhoeal -disease

Wörmann, V., Holodynski, M., Kärtner, J., & Keller, H. (2012). A cross-cultural comparison of the development of the social smile: A longitudinal study of maternal and infant imitation in 6- and 12-week-old infants. *Infant Behavior and Development, 35,* 335–347.

Wörmann, V., Holodynski, M., Kartner, J., & Keller, H. (2014). The emergence of social smiling: The interplay of maternal and infant imitation during the first three months in cross-cultural comparison. *Journal of Cross-Cultural Psychology, 45,* 339–361.

Worthman, C. M. (2011). Developmental cultural ecology of sleep. In M. El-Sheikh (Ed.), *Sleep and development: Familial and socio-cultural considerations* (pp. 167–194). New York: Oxford University Press.

Worthy, J., Hungerford-Kresser, H., & Hampton, A. (2009). Tracking and ability grouping. In L. Christenbury, R. Bomer, & P. Smargorinsky (Eds.), *Handbook of adolescent literacy research* (pp. 220–235). New York: Guilford.

Worton, S. K., Caplan, R., Nelson, G., Pancer, S. M., Loomis, C., Peters, R. D., & Hayward, K. (2014). Better Beginnings, Better Futures: Theory, research, and knowledge transfer of a community-based initiative for children and families. *Psychosocial Intervention, 23,* 135–143.

Woythaler, M., McCormick, M. C., Mao, W.-Y., & Smith, V. C. (2015). Late preterm infants and neurodevelopmental outcomes at kindergarten. *Pediatrics, 136,* 424–431.

Wright, B. C. (2006). On the emergence of the discriminative mode for transitive inference. *European Journal of Cognitive Psychology, 18,* 776–800.

Wright, B. C., Robertson, S., & Hadfield, L. (2011). Transitivity for height versus speed: To what extent do the under-7s really have a transitive capacity? *Thinking and Reasoning, 17,* 57–81.

Wright, B. C., & Smailes, J. (2015). Factors and processes in children's transitive inference deductions. *Journal of Cognitive Psychology, 27,* 967–978.

Wright, J. P., Dietrich, K., Ris, M., Hornung, R., Wessel, S., Lanphear, B., et al. (2008). Association of prenatal and childhood blood lead concentrations with criminal arrests in early adulthood. *PLOS Medicine, 5*(5), e101.

Wright, M. O., & Masten, A. S. (2015). Pathways to resilience in context. In L. C. Theron, M. Ungar, & L. Liebenberg (Eds.), *Youth resilience and culture: Commonalities and complexities* (pp. 3–22). New York: Springer Science + Business Media.

Wright, W. E. (2013). Bilingual education. In T. K. Bhatia & W. C. Ritchie (Eds.), *Handbook of bilingualism and multilingualism* (pp. 598–623). Chichester, UK: Wiley-Blackwell.

Wrotniak, B. H., Epstein, L. H., Raluch, R. A., & Roemmich, J. N. (2004). Parent weight change as a predictor of child weight change in family-based behavioral obesity treatment. *Archives of Pediatric and Adolescent Medicine, 158,* 342–347.

Wu, L.-T., Woody, G. E., Yang, C., Pan, J.-J., & Blazer, D. G. (2011). Racial/ethnic variations in substance-related disorders among adolescents in the United States. *Archives of General Psychiatry, 68,* 1176–1185.

Wulczyn, F. (2009). Epidemiological perspectives on maltreatment prevention. *Future of Children, 19,* 39–66.

Wuyts, D., Vansteenkiste, M., Soenens, B., & Assor, A. (2015). An examination of the dynamics involved in parental child-invested contingent self-esteem. *Parenting: Science and Practice, 15,* 55–74.

Wyman, E., Rakoczy, H., & Tomasello, M. (2009). Normativity and context in young children's pretend play. *Cognitive Development, 24,* 146–155.

Wynn, K. (1992). Addition and subtraction by human infants. *Nature, 358,* 749–750.

Wynn, K., & Bloom, P. (2014). The moral baby. In M. Killen & J. G. Smetana (Eds.), *Handbook of moral development* (2nd ed., pp. 435–453). New York: Psychology Press.

Wynn, K., Bloom, P., & Chiang, W.-C. (2002). Enumeration of collective entities by 5-month-old infants. *Cognition, 83,* B55–B62.

X

Xiao, S. X., Cook, R. E., Martin, C. L., Nielson, M. G., & Field, R. D. (2019). Will they listen to me? An examination of in-group gender bias in children's communication beliefs. *Sex Roles, 80,* 172–185.

Xu, F., Han, Y., Sabbagh, M. A., Wang, T., Ren, X., & Li, C. (2013). Developmental differences in the structure of executive function in middle childhood and adolescence. *PLOS ONE, 8*(10), e77770.

Xu, F., Spelke, E., & Goddard, S. (2005). Number sense in human infants. *Developmental Science, 8,* 88–101.

Y

Yadav, S., & Chakraborty, P. (2017). Children aged two to four are able to scribble and draw using a smartphone app. *Acta Paediatrica, 106,* 991–994.

Yang, B., Ren, B. X., & Tang, F. R. (2017). Prenatal irradiation-induced brain neuropathology and cognitive impairment. *Brain & Development, 39,* 10–22.

Yang, C.-K., & Hahn, H.-M. (2002). Cosleeping in young Korean children. *Developmental and Behavioral Pediatrics, 23,* 151–157.

Yanovski, J. A. (2015). Pediatric obesity. An introduction. *Appetite, 93,* 3–12.

Yarrow, M. R., Scott, P. M., & Waxler, C. Z. (1973). Learning concern for others. *Developmental Psychology, 8,* 240–260.

Yavorsky, J. E., Dush, C. M. K., & Schoppe-Sullivan, S. J. (2015). The production of inequality: The gender division of labor across the transition to parenthood. *Journal of Marriage and Family, 77,* 662–679.

Yeung, A. S. (2011). Student self-concept and effort: Gender and grade differences. *Educational Psychology, 31,* 749–772.

Yeung, J. W. K., Cheung, C.-K., Kwok, S. Y. C. L., & Leung, J. T. Y. (2016). Socialization effects of authoritative parenting and its discrepancy on children. *Journal of Child and Family Studies, 25,* 1980–1990.

Yeung, S. P., & Wong, W. I. (2018). Gender labels on gender-neutral colors: Do they affect children's color preferences and play performance? *Sex Roles, 79,* 260–272.

Yirmiya, N., Erel, O., Shaked, M., & Solomonica-Levi, D. (1998). Meta-analyses comparing theory of mind abilities of individuals with autism, individuals with mental retardation, and normally developing individuals. *Psychological Bulletin, 124,* 283–307.

Yogman, M., Garner, A., Hutchinson, J., Hirsh-Pasek, K., & Golinkoff, R. M. (2018). The power of play: A pediatric role in enhancing development in young children. *Pediatrics, 142,* e20182058.

Yong, M. H., & Ruffman, T. (2014). Emotional contagion: Dogs and humans show a similar physiological response to human infant crying. *Behavioural Processes, 108,* 155–165.

Yook, J.-H., Han, J.-Y., Choi, J.-S., Ahn, H.-K., Lee, S.-W., Kim, M.-Y., et al. (2012). Pregnancy outcomes and factors associated with voluntary pregnancy termination in women who had been treated for acne with isotretinoin. *Clinical Toxicology, 50,* 896–901.

Yoshida, H., & Smith, L. B. (2003). Known and novel noun extensions: Attention at two levels of abstraction. *Child Development, 74,* 564–577.

Yoshikawa, H., Aber, J. L., & Beardslee, W. R. (2012). The effects of poverty on the mental, emotional, and behavioral health of children and youth: Implications for prevention. *American Psychologist, 67,* 272–284.

Yoshikawa, H., Weiland, C., Brooks-Gunn, J., Burchinal, M. R., Espinosa, L. M., Gormley, W. T., et al. (2013). *Investing in our future: The evidence base on preschool education.* Ann Arbor, MI: Society for Research in Child Development. Retrieved from fcd-us.org/resources/evidence-base -preschool

Youn, M. J., Leon, J., & Lee, K. J. (2012). The influence of maternal employment on children's learning growth and the role of parental involvement. *Early Child Development and Care, 182,* 1227–1246.

Young, S. E., Friedman, N. P., Miyake, A., Willcutt, E. G., Corley, R. P., Haberstick, B. C., et al. (2009). Behavioral disinhibition: Liability for externalizing spectrum disorders and its genetic and environmental relation to response inhibition across adolescence. *Journal of Abnormal Psychology, 118,* 117–130.

Yousafzai, A. K., Rasheed, M. A., Rizvi, A., Armstrong, R., & Bhutta, Z. A. (2014). Effect of integrated responsive stimulation and nutrition interventions in the Lady Health Worker programme in Pakistan on child development, growth, and health outcomes: A cluster-randomised factorial effectiveness trial. *Lancet, 384,* 1282–1293.

Yousafzai, A. K., Yakoob, M. Y., & Bhutta, Z. A. (2013). Nutrition-based approaches to early childhood development. In P. R. Britto, P. L. Engle, & C. M. Super (Eds.), *Handbook of early childhood development research and its impact on global policy* (pp. 202–226). New York: Oxford University Press.

Yow, W. Q., Patrycia, F., & Flynn, S. (2016). Code-switching in childhood. In E. Nicoladis & S. Montanari (Eds.), *Bilingualism across the lifespan: Factors moderating language proficiency* (pp. 81–100). Washington, DC: American Psychological Association.

Yu, C., Suanda, S. H., & Smith, L. B. (2019). Infant sustained attention but not joint attention to objects at 9 months predicts vocabulary at 12 and 15 months. *Developmental Science, 22,* e12735.

Yu, R. (2002). On the reform of elementary school education in China. *Educational Exploration, 129,* 56–57.

Yu, Y., & Kushnir, T. (2016). When what's inside counts: Sequence of demonstrated actions affects preschoolers' categorization by nonobvious properties. *Developmental Psychology, 52,* 400–410.

Yucel, M., & Vaish, A. (2018). Young children tattle to enforce moral norms. *Social Development, 27,* 924–936.

Yuill, N., & Pearson, A. (1998). The developmental bases for trait attribution: Children's understanding of traits as causal mechanisms based on desire. *Developmental Psychology, 34,* 574–586.

Yule, K., Houston, J., & Grych, J. (2019). Resilience in children exposed to violence: A meta-analysis of protective factors across ecological contexts. *Clinical Child and Family Psychological Review, 22,* 406–431

Yunger, J. L., Carver, P. R., & Perry, D. G. (2004). Does gender identity influence children's psychological well-being? *Developmental Psychology, 40,* 572–582.

Z

Zachrisson, H. D., Dearing, E., Lekhal, R., & Toppelberg, C. O. (2013). Little evidence that time in child care causes externalizing problems during early childhood in Norway. *Child Development, 84,* 1152–1170.

Zack, E., & Barr, R. (2016). The role of interactional quality in learning from touch screens during infancy: Context matters. *Frontiers in Psychology, 7,* Art. No. 1264.

Zajac, R., O'Neill, S., & Hayne, H. (2012). Disorder in the courtroom? Child witnesses under cross-examination. *Developmental Review, 32,* 181–204.

Zalewski, M., Lengua, L. J., Wilson, A. C., Trancik, A., & Bazinet, A. (2011). Emotion regulation profiles, temperament, and adjustment problems in preadolescents. *Child Development, 82,* 951–966.

Zarbatanay, L., Tremblay, P. F., Ellis, W. E., Chen, X., Kinal, M., & Boyko, L. (2017). Peer clique participation of victimized children: Characteristics and implications for victimization over a school year. *Merrill-Palmer Quarterly, 63,* 485–513.

Zaslow, M. J., Weinfield, N. S., Gallagher, M., Hair, E. C., Ogawa, J. R., Egeland, B., Tabors, P. O., & De Temple, J. M. (2006). Longitudinal prediction of child outcomes from differing measures of parenting in a low-income sample. *Developmental Psychology, 42,* 27–37.

Zeegers, M. A. J., Colonnesi, C., Stams, G. J. M., & Meins, E. (2017). Mind matters: A meta-analysis on parental mentalization and sensitivity as predictors of infant–parent attachment. *Psychological Bulletin, 143,* 1245–1272.

Zelazo, N. A., Zelazo, P. R., Cohen, K. M., & Zelazo, P. D. (1993). Specificity of practice effects on elementary neuromotor patterns. *Developmental Psychology, 29,* 686–691.

Zelazo, P. D., Anderson, J. E., Richler, J., Wallner-Allen, K., Beaumont, J. L., & Weintraub, S. (2013). NIH toolbox cognition battery (CB): Measuring executive function and attention. In P. D. Zelazo & P. J. Bauer (Eds.), National Institutes of Health Toolbox Cognition Battery (NIH Toolbox CB): Validation for children between 3 and 15 years. *Monographs of the Society for Research in Child Development, 78*(4, Serial No. 309), 16–33.

Zelazo, P. D., & Carlson, S. M. (2012). Hot and cool executive function in childhood and adolescence: Development and plasticity. *Child Development Perspectives, 6,* 354–360.

Zelazo, P. D., & Lyons, K. E. (2012). The potential benefits of mindfulness training in early childhood: A developmental social cognitive neuroscience perspective. *Child Development Perspectives, 6,* 154–160.

Zemp, M., Nussbeck, F. W., Cummings, E. M., & Bodenmann, G. (2017). The spillover of child-rearing stress into parents' relationship mediated by couple communication. *Family Relations, 66,* 317–330.

Zhang, W., Wei, X., Ji, L., Chen, L., & Deater-Deckard, K. (2017). Reconsidering parenting in Chinese culture: Subtypes, stability, and change of maternal parenting style during early adolescence. *Journal of Youth and Adolescence, 46,* 1117–1136.

Zhao, Y., & Castellanos, F. X. (2016). Discovery science strategies in studies of the pathophysiology of child and adolescent psychiatric disorders: Promises and limitations. *Journal of Child Psychology and Psychiatry, 57,* 421–439.

Zhou, X., Huang, J., Wang, Z., Wang, B., Zhao, Z., Yang, L., & Zheng-zheng, Y. (2006). Parent–child interaction and children's number learning. *Early Child Development and Care, 176,* 763–775.

Ziemer, C. J., Plumert, J. M., & Pick, A. D. (2012). To grasp or not to grasp: Infants' actions toward objects and pictures. *Infancy, 17,* 479–497.

Zimmer-Gembeck, M. J., & Skinner, E. A. (2011). The development of coping across childhood and adolescence: An integrative review and critique of research. *International Journal of Behavioral Development, 35,* 1–17.

Zimmerman, B. J., & Labuhn, A. S. (2012). Self-regulation of learning: Process approaches to personal development. In K. R. Harris, S. Graham, T. Urdan, C. B. McCormick, G. M. Sinatra, & J. Sweller (Eds.), *APA educational psychology handbook: Vol. 1. Theories, constructs, and critical issues* (pp. 399–425). Washington, DC: American Psychological Association.

Zimmerman, F. J., & Christakis, D. A. (2005). Children's television viewing and cognitive outcomes. *Archives of Pediatrics and Adolescent Medicine, 159,* 619–625.

Zimmerman, F. J., Christakis, D. A., & Meltzoff, A. N. (2007). Television and DVD/video viewing in children younger than 2 years. *Archives of Pediatrics and Adolescent Medicine, 161,* 473–479.

Zimmermann, L. K., & Stansbury, K. (2004). The influence of emotion regulation, level of shyness, and habituation on the neuroendocrine response of three-year-old children. *Psychoneuroendocrinology, 29,* 973–982.

Zitzmann, M. (2013). Effects of age on male fertility. *Best Practice & Research Clinical Endocrinology and Metabolism, 27,* 617–628.

Ziv, Y. (2013). Social information processing patterns, social skills, and school readiness in preschool children. *Journal of Experimental Child Psychology, 114,* 306–320.

Zmyj, N., & Buttelmann, D. (2014). An integrative model of rational imitation in infancy. *Infant Behavior and Development, 37,* 21–28.

Zoëga, H., Rothman, K. J., Huybrechts, K. F., Olafsson, O., Baldursson, G., Almarsdottir, A. B., et al. (2012). A population-based study of stimulant drug treatment of ADHD and academic progress in children. *Pediatrics, 130,* e53–e62.

Zoghbi, H. Y., & Beaudet, A. L. (2016). Epigenetics and human disease. *Cold Spring Harbor Perspectives in Biology, 8*(2), a019497.

Zolotor, A. J., & Puzia, M. E. (2010). Bans against corporal punishment: A systematic review of the laws, changes in attitudes and behaviours. *Child Abuse Review, 19,* 229–247.

Zolotor, A. J., Theodore, A. D., Runyan, D. K., Chang, J. J., & Laskey, A. L. (2011). Corporal punishment and physical abuse: Population-based trends for three-to-11-year-old children in the United States. *Child Abuse Review, 20,* 57–66.

Zosuls, K. M., Ruble, D. N., Tamis-LeMonda, C. S., Shrout, P. E., Bornstein, M. H., & Greulich, F. K. (2009). The acquisition of gender labels in infancy: Implications for gender-typed play. *Developmental Psychology, 45,* 688–701.

Zucker, K. J., & Lawrence, A. A. (2009). Epidemiology of gender identity disorder: Recommendations for the Standards of Care of the World Professional Association for Transgender Health. *International Journal of Transgenderism, 11,* 8–18.

Zukow-Goldring, P. (2002). Sibling caregiving. In M. H. Bornstein (Ed.), *Handbook of parenting: Vol. 3* (2nd ed., pp. 253–286). Hillsdale, NJ: Erlbaum.

Zukowski, A. (2013). Putting words together. In J. B. Gleason & N. B. Ratner (Eds.), *The development of language* (pp. 120–162). Upper Saddle River, NJ: Pearson.

Zur, O., & Gelman, R. (2004). Young children can add and subtract by predicting and checking. *Early Childhood Research Quarterly, 19,* 121–137.

Subject Index

Figures and tables are indicated by f *and* t *following page numbers.*

A

Abortion
sex-selective, 56
spontaneous. *See* Miscarriage
Abuse
of child. *See* Child maltreatment
of partner, 397
sexual. *See* Sexual abuse
of substances. *See* Substance use and abuse
Academic achievement
in attention-deficit hyperactivity disorder, 437
attributions related to, 482–484
and bilingual education, 460–461
of bullying victims, 497
child-rearing styles affecting, 393
cognitive self-regulation affecting, 444
cultural influences on, 471f, 471–472
divorce of parents affecting, 507
early intervention programs affecting, 340–341
early literacy skills affecting, 333, 334
and educational philosophies, 462
in familism, 75
family beliefs on, 36
family mealtimes affecting, 69f
gender stereotypes on, 498–499
of immigrant youths, 36
in inclusive classrooms, 468–469
intelligence quotient as predictor of, 14, 337, 448, 453
international comparisons of, 471f, 471–472
lead exposure affecting, 167
in magnet schools, 466
of maltreatment victims, 397, 398
in mindfulness training, 439
neighborhood influences on, 72
of only children, 503
and planning skills, 325, 440
poverty affecting, 71, 73–74, 286, 436, 466
preschool programs affecting, 338
recess time affecting, 427
of rejected children, 495, 496
self-affirmation intervention affecting, 456, 457f
and self-esteem, 479, 480, 481
and self-fulfilling prophecies, 465
siblings affecting, 503
socioeconomic status affecting, 68, 73–74, 286, 436, 465, 466, 472
teacher–student interaction affecting, 465
working memory capacity affecting, 438
Academic learning, 462–472. *See also* Education
Academic programs in preschool and kindergarten, 338
Acceptance
in child rearing, 392, 392t, 393
in peer relations. *See* Peer acceptance
Accidental injuries. *See* Injuries, unintentional
Accommodation in cognitive development, 198, 311
Achievement
ability and effort in, 482
academic. *See* Academic achievement

attributions related to, 482–484
and fixed mindset about ability, 482, 483
gender stereotypes on, 483, 498–499
and growth mindset about ability, 482, 483, 484
and learned helplessness, 482, 483
person and process types of praise in, 482–483
self-conscious emotions in, 485
and self-esteem, 482–484
Acquired immune deficiency syndrome
in middle childhood, 416
in pregnancy, 105t, 106
Activity level
prenatal nicotine exposure affecting, 100, 101
and temperament, 249, 250, 250t, 251
Adaptation
of baby to labor and delivery, 119
coping strategies in. *See* Coping strategies
Darwin on, 13
ethology of, 23–24
evolutionary developmental psychology on, 24
to family changes, 66
and habituation, 96
of immigrant youths, 36
Piaget on, 18, 198
and practical intelligence, 450
and resilience, 10
Adjustment
affluence affecting, 68–69, 69f
attachment security affecting, 267, 271
in blended families, 509, 510
of bullying victims, 497
child care affecting, 266
child-rearing styles affecting, 394, 481
divorce of parents affecting, 506, 507, 508, 509
early intervention programs affecting, 340, 341
effortful control affecting, 247, 250
in familism, 75
family mealtimes affecting, 69, 69f
and fears in middle childhood, 512
and friendships, 366
and gender identity, 387, 501
grandparent primary caregivers affecting, 267
of immigrant youths, 36
in lesbian and gay families, 504
maltreatment in childhood affecting, 397, 515
maternal employment affecting, 511, 512
to parenthood, 145–149, 148f
and peer acceptance, 495, 496
of self-care children, 511
and self-conscious emotions, 361, 485
of sexual abuse victims, 515
and shyness, 255–256
in single-parent families, 505
sleep affecting, 287
and sleeping arrangements in infancy, 165
temperament affecting, 249, 254
of transgender children, 390
violence affecting, 514

Adolescence (11 to 18 years old)
in adoption, 64
aggression in, 380
attachment in, 260
autonomy in, 66, 75
in blended families, 509–510
brain development in, 285
bullying in, 497
catch-up growth in, 167
cognitive development in, 19t, 20
conflicts with parents in, 66
definition of, 6
divorce of parents affecting, 507
in dual-earner families, 511
exposure to ethnic and political violence in, 514
in familism, 75
family in, 75
fetal alcohol exposure affecting, 102, 103
formal operational stage in, 19t, 20, 435
gender dysphoria in, 390
genital stage of psychosexual development in, 15t
health issues in, 416
hippocampus in, 285
identity *versus* role confusion in, 15t
of immigrant youths, 36
inhibition in, 252
injuries in, 417, 417f
in lesbian and gay families, 504
memory in, 285
neighborhood influences in, 72–73
obesity in, 411, 413, 414
parent relationships in, 66. *See also* Parent–adolescent relationships
physical punishment in, 374
play in, 426
poverty rate in, 286
pregnancy and parenthood in. *See* Adolescent pregnancy and parenthood
puberty in, 6, 408, 413
sequential study of, 43
sexual abuse during, 513
of sexual abuse victims, 515
sleep in, 288
temperament in, 254
Adolescent pregnancy and parenthood, 504
health care in, 111f
international differences in, 76t
Nurse–Family Partnership in, 110
prenatal development in, 110
of sexual abuse victims, 515
single-mother families in, 148
Adoption, 64
adolescence in, 64
affection toward infant in, 145
age at time of, 64, 162, 162f
attachment security in, 163, 261–262
deprivation prior to, 64, 162–163
and environmental influences on gene expression, 81
and gene–environment correlation, 81
heritability research in, 78–79
intelligence and IQ research in, 453
international, 64
by lesbian and gay couples, 503–504
schizophrenia research in, 79, 81
in surrogate motherhood, 61
Adrenal androgens, 408

Adulthood
emerging, 6
obesity risk in, 169–170
psychosocial stages in, 15t
Advance-planning tasks, 439, 439f
Affect, positive, and temperament, 250t
Affluence, 68–69
family mealtimes in, 69, 69f
Affordable Care Act, 76, 133, 292
Affordances, discovery of, 192–193
Afghanistan, war-related violence in, 514
Africa. *See also specific countries.*
body size of children in, 406
breastfeeding and bottle-feeding in, 168
child-organized games in, 424
communities-of-learners approach to education in, 464
neonatal behavioral assessment in, 143–144
symbolic understanding of pictures in, 205–206
African Americans
academic achievement of, 457f, 465, 466
asthma of, 416
body size of, 155
child-rearing beliefs and practices of, 374, 395
communication style of, 454–455
cosleeping of parents and children, 165, 288
culturally sensitive health care for, 112
discipline and punishment of children, 374, 395
extended families of, 74, 505
food insecurity of, 171
grandparents as caregivers of, 267
home environment and IQ of, 453, 454–455
intelligence and IQ of, 79, 337, 452, 453, 454–455
low-birth-weight infants of, 127–128
narrative style of, 459
in never-married parent families, 504–505
overweight and obese, 411
prenatal health care of, 111f, 112
quality of educational opportunities for, 466
self-affirmation intervention on, 457f
self-esteem of, 481
sensitivity to racial attitudes among, 491
sickle cell anemia of, 55–56
in single-parent families, 504–505
skeletal age of, 155
sleep during early childhood, 287, 288
stereotype threat affecting, 455–456, 465
vocabulary development affecting intelligence testing of, 455
After-school programs, 72, 73, 511–512
Age
in adolescence, 6. *See also* Adolescence
of adopted children, 64, 162, 162f
in brain injury, 160, 161
of children in blended families, 509–510
during divorce of parents, 506–507
in early childhood, 6. *See also* Early childhood
in emerging adulthood, 6
in eyewitness testimony of children, 516
of fetal viability, 95, 127

Name Index

Italic "*n*" following page numbers indicates source note accompanying an illustration, figure, or table.